AUGUSTIN BEA

the cardinal of unity

by
Stjepan Schmidt, S. J.

Translated from the Italian by
Leslie Wearne

New City Press

Sponsored by a group of North American Cardinals and Bishops

to
Johannes Cardinal Willebrands
who, together with Cardinal Bea,
built up the Secretariat for Christian Unity
and took up and developed Cardinal Bea's legacy

Published in the United States by New City Press
86 Mayflower Avenue, New Rochelle, New York 10801
©1992 New City Press, New York

Translated by Leslie Wearne from the original Italian edition
Agostino Bea—il cardinale dell'unità
©1987 Città Nuova, Rome, Italy
English translation personally checked and approved by the author.

Library of Congress Cataloging-in-Publication Data:

Schmidt, Stjepan, 1914-
    [Agostino Bea--il cardinale dell'unità.   English]
    Augustin Bea, the cardinal of unity / Stjepan Schmidt ; translated
by Leslie Wearne.

    Translation of Agostino Bea--il cardinale dell'unità.
    ISBN 1-56548-016-3 : $49.00
    1. Bea, Augustin, 1881-1968. 2. Cardinals--Biography.
3. Biblical scholars--Biography. 4. Ecumenists--Biography.
I. Title.
BX4705.B2585S3613   1992
282'.092--dc20
[B]   92-17612

Printed in the United States of America

TABLE OF CONTENTS

Part One — General Preparation (1881–1949)

His Birthplace and Family Home — 25; Junior High School — 31; The "Ecumenical Atmosphere" of Constance — 33; "I'm Going to Be a Jesuit" — 36; High School Graduation at Another School — 38; Theology Student — 39; Religious Vocation: Struggle and Victory — 42

The Novitiate — 47; The Decisive Influence of a Man of God — 50; The Path to the Priesthood — 52; Special Studies: A Fragmented Curriculum — 60; Tertianship — 63

Superior of a "War Residence" (August 1914—January 1917) — 65; Professor of Sacred Scripture and Prefect of Studies (February 1917–Summer 1921) — 69; Provincial Superior (1921-1924) — 73; Rome: In Charge of the Training of Future Teachers of Philosophy and Theology — 79; An Important Interlude (October 1928—June 1930) — 84

1. Director of the Institute — 91;
    Specific Events during the Papacy of Pius XI — 94
    Specific Events during the Papacy of Pius XII — 101
    Extension of the Premises of the Institute — 109
2. Professor and Scholar — 112;
    a. Teacher — 113
    b. Scholar and Writer — 116
    Was Bea a Conservative? — 119
3. A Priest and Apostle at the Service of Christ and Thus of the Church and of Souls — 123;
    a. Completion of the Picture of Bea's Commitments and Activities — 123
    b. The Spirit, the Underlying Motivations and the Ultimate Aim of Bea's Activity — 125

Part Two — More Immediate Preparation (1949–1958)

Bea's Work as Teacher and Scholar — 134; Bea's Work at the Holy Office — 138; Work for Liturgical Reform — 145; Apostolic Visitator — 148; Active Participation in the Life of the Society of Jesus — 149; Various Kinds of Vacation — 150; Health — 153; "The Symptoms of Old Age" — 155; A Cardinal's Hat in View — 158; A Painful Personal Process Lasting Ten Years — 158

Part Four — The Last Three Years of the Cardinal's Life

FOREWORD

I met Augustin Bea for the first time in 1951 at the Pontifical Biblical Institute, where he had been rector for many years and was still working as a lecturer. I had gone to talk to him about a new ecumenical initiative, for I felt the time was ripe for the creation of a Catholic Conference for Ecumenical Questions, to give theologians of various nationalities, particularly Europeans, an opportunity to meet one another for joint examination of the problems of divisions between Christians in the perspective of the ecumenical movement, which had the aim of restoring full communion among all those who believe in Christ, the Son of God, and have been baptized in the name of the Father, the Son and the Holy Spirit.

Father Bea welcomed me with the courteous benevolence that was his most striking character trait, and immediately showed deep understanding of the whole matter I had come to discuss, and also great interest in the initiative I wanted to promote.

He gave me his encouragement, and indeed asked me to come back to see him and keep him abreast of how the undertaking was proceeding. I did not forget his invitation, but returned year after year in order to talk about the Catholic Conference, which was organizing regular meetings attended by about sixty theologians. Although my visits would sometimes coincide with one of his rest periods, Father Bea used to insist on seeing me, and showed great interest in the work of the Catholic Conference for Ecumenical Questions. In the period up to 1960, the conference organized ten meetings at which the main subjects of contemporary ecumenical interest were studied. In practice the conference continued its work up to the eve of the Council. As will be recalled, 1959 was the year that Pope John XXIII announced an Ecumenical Council of the Church and then set up the *Secretariatus ad christianorum unitatem fovendam*, which he chose Cardinal Augustin Bea to head, and which had the task of ensuring that the ecumenical insights arising from the thinking of this great pope was integrated into the preparatory work for the Council.

Once Augustin Bea had been appointed President of the Secretariat for Christian Unity, he asked the Holy Father if I could be assigned to assist him, and I was therefore nominated Secretary of the Secretariat. I still remember something that Cardinal Bea said right at the start of our collaboration: "I certainly won't mind if you happen to make a mistake, but I would mind very much if you didn't work or if you did nothing to produce practical results."

This was the start of a relationship that was based in our everyday life, and was built up day after day during the preparations for the Council, in the years of the Council itself, and then in the years that we were allowed together after the close of the Council and until his death in 1968. He headed the secretariat with conviction and with a sureness that sprang from the knowledge that he was working to implement the plan drawn up by the Council.

Nineteen years after Cardinal Bea's death, Father Stjepan Schmidt, S.J., his faithful private secretary, is publishing a biography of the man known as "the cardinal of unity." I am sincerely grateful to Father Schmidt for his painstaking, skillful work, which restores the personality and work of the first President of the

9

Secretariat for Christian Unity to us as a three-dimensional whole. Writing a biography of Augustin Bea means writing a part of our history and going over a period that was crucial for the Church as it received fresh life with the breath of the Second Vatican Council. And remembering always means making the person we are recalling present again in our midst.

If I am not mistaken, the expression used as the title of the biography, *The Cardinal of Unity*, was used for the first time by the publication *Informations Catholiques Internationales* in order to stress the fact that unity was Augustin Bea's special mission. Other people have expressed the same idea by calling him "the ambassador of unity." However, there was another aspect to his activity, constituted by his work for the unity of the whole human family, and one chapter of the biography is entitled "One Human Family Freely United in Truth, Justice and Love" and gives extensive coverage to this facet of his work. I have already had an opportunity—in the context of the *International Augustin Bea Prize*, which was established after his death—to explain how this dimension of his activity went hand in hand with the other, complementing it, so to speak.

After he became President of the Secretariat for Christian Unity, Augustin Bea used to look back over his long life, which had been so rich in events and changes, seeing it in a new perspective and saying: "In God's plan, my whole life has been a preparation for this mission. I could not do what I have to do today if I had not held such a variety of positions and responsibilities." And it is precisely on the basis of this autobiographical observation that the author views the cardinal's whole prior life as a prelude to his task as President of the Secretariat for Christian Unity, entitling the first two parts of the work "General Preparation (1881-1949)" and "More Immediate Preparation (1949-1958)" (in other words, the ten years prior to his creation as cardinal and his nomination as president of the secretariat).

Despite the fact that the maximum attention in the biography was purposely dedicated to his work as cardinal, it also provides considerable hitherto unknown details about the other periods of his life, on the basis of his statements or autobiographical writings, as well as his voluminous correspondence for the years 1949-1958. When reading these pages, it is not difficult to see the importance for the future president of the secretariat of the years of high school spent in places that were confessionally mixed, or the years of higher education in the three public and therefore pluralistic universities of Freiburg im Breisgau, Innsbruck and Berlin. Then came the equally important years of university teaching and research work on an international level in the sphere of biblical studies. In these decades Bea was entrusted with various leadership tasks at the heart of the Catholic Church and in close contact with the highest ecclesiastical authorities. In this connection the chapters of the biography that describe his relations with Pope Pius XII and give the background to the Bea of ecumenism are particularly significant.

The long years that Bea devoted to exegetical studies were the solid basis on which his contributions to the Council would be based, both for the drafting of the Dogmatic Constitution on Divine Revelation *Dei verbum*, and the Declaration on the Relation of the Church to Non-Christian Religions *Nostra aetate*, particularly the section on the relation of the Church to the Jewish people. The biography recalls the preparation of these contributions—particularly those concerning the liturgy—in the chapters entitled "The Liturgist" and "The Theologian."

The biography then moves on to a more specific consideration of *the years of the Council*. I must admit that I was very curious to read these chapters, for they describe events and experiences that I had shared, and I wondered what method the author of the biography would adopt in order to provide a rounded portrait of the cardinal's multi-faceted personality and activity. I also wondered whether the biography would really be able to conjure up all the excitement of those years, and whether it would meet the still more difficult challenge of giving a full idea of their importance and grandeur to any reader who had not been personally involved.

In this connection, I am happy to say that Father Schmidt has made intelligent use of all the material that could throw light on the events of those years and on the man who played one of the leading roles. Apart from the many weighty volumes of official documents from the Council, the author has drawn widely on the private collection of papers that Cardinal Bea left to the Southern German Province of the Society of Jesus (his original province). Father Schmidt was also able to consult the vast mass of the cardinal's writings, including lectures, statements and interviews. In order to give an idea of the sheer volume of this material, we have only to recall that when Augustin Bea was made cardinal he had published 130 works, and that by the time he died the number had risen to over 400. (A list of his publications is given in an appendix to the biography.)

Father Schmidt did not stop here, however, but also patiently collected memories and first-hand reports from all those who had known Father or Cardinal Bea. Lastly, the biography also had the benefit of the personal memories of the author himself, who was the cardinal's private secretary and shared his life for quarter of a century. Although he had the honor of enjoying the cardinal's friendship and was also his very close, though self-effacing, assistant, he has not allowed his account to degenerate into a simple book of reminiscence.

Apart from the great wealth of the material itself, we would note the lively manner in which the author presents not only events, but also the thinking of his subject. It would be fair to say that Bea's voice is the only one we hear. The descriptions of events are neither dry nor impersonal, because it is the cardinal himself who conjures them up for us through his comments and appraisals.

In the closing chapter entitled "Some Elements for a Portrait," the author introduces us to the inner secret of the personality of this man—a secret that has roots in the Constitutions that St. Ignatius wrote for the Society of Jesus and that is the underlying thread and unifying force holding the whole fabric of his life together: the conviction of being nothing but an "instrument" in all things and all events—an intelligent and free instrument, yes, but always an instrument in the hand of God and Christ, the Lord of the Church. The biography ends with a reflection that I want to quote in full: "In the light of the spirituality of being an instrument in God's hand, the many elements of our portrait come together and are knitted into one complex but integrated whole."

Referring back to the title of this biography, we can thus say that Augustin Bea was "the cardinal of unity" also, and indeed firstly, because he was deeply united within himself. The fact that he saw himself simply as an instrument to lead people to God and God to people gave his personality an inner harmony, orienting it to deep union with God in Christ. It is here that we must look for the secret of the incredible effectiveness of his witness and of his action in support of unity in the broadest sense of the word.

In his introduction to the biography, Father Schmidt expresses his gratitude to his religious superiors, especially the Father General of the Society of Jesus, Pedro Arrupe, and Father Arrupe's successor, Peter-Hans Kolvenbach, for entrusting him with the task of producing this work. I should like to express similar gratitude to Father Schmidt. Writing the life of Augustin Bea also means relating part of the history of the Secretariat for Christian Unity, as well as highlighting Bea's very fundamental contribution to the implementation of the conciliar thought of Pope John XXIII, particularly two of its basic thrusts: the quest for the unity of all Christians in order to fulfill the high-priestly prayer of Jesus prior to his death and glorification, and the concern to establish dialogue with the Jewish people. I think that many people will share my gratitude.

I very much hope that this book receives as wide a readership as it deserves, and not only in its original Italian, but also in the various translations that are now being made.

Cardinal Johannes Willebrands

INTRODUCTION

Does Cardinal Bea need any preliminary presentation? Certainly not for the generation that lived through the Council. However, a quarter of a century—in other words the space of a whole generation—has passed since then. So let us start by saying that he was a German Jesuit born in 1881. He was an exegete, but above all he was Rector of the Pontifical Biblical Institute in Rome for nineteen years. There were two particularly important facts connected with this period of his life: Pius XII's encyclical *Divino afflante Spiritu* on biblical studies (1943), which has rightly been called the *magna carta* of Catholic biblical studies, and a new Latin translation of the Psalms, which Pope Pius XII had entrusted to a group of professors from the Pontifical Biblical Institute under the direction of its rector, Father Bea, and which helped foster reform of the sacred liturgy. A last fact to be borne in mind is that for thirteen years Father Bea was Pius XII's confessor and respected advisor.

A completely new and decisive period began when this Jesuit was "discovered" by Pope John XXIII, who made him a cardinal and, a few months later, appointed him first President of the Secretariat for Christian Unity. Right from the time of the first announcement of the Council, the pope emphasized its ecumenical dimension, and it would be left to the Secretariat for Christian Unity to find ways and means of making this a reality through the presence of growing numbers of official observers at the Council as representatives of Christian World Communions. The secretariat would also draft some fundamental documents concerning the most burning—and often thorny—problems of the day, and steer them through the Council; in this way it would deal with ecumenism, religious freedom, and attitudes to non-Christian religions, particularly Judaism.

At the close of the Council, the secretariat became a department of central Church government. Now that the Catholic Church had officially entered the modern ecumenical movement, contacts with the whole gamut of Christian World Communions had to be developed, and it was also important to make sure that conciliar decisions on ecumenism were integrated into the life of the Catholic Church on all levels. In the last three years of Cardinal Bea's life, dialogue was thus opened up with the Anglican Communion, the World Lutheran Federation, the World Methodist Council and the World Council of Churches. As regards ecumenism within the Catholic Church itself, the first world meeting of delegates from the ecumenical commissions of the various conferences of bishops was organized in 1967, and a first part of the *Ecumenical Directory* was promulgated— a document that would encourage and regulate the ecumenical activity of Catholics.

In conclusion, we would say that while the Council was in its planning stages, Cardinal Bea had expressed the hope that it would bring about a general mobilization on all levels in the Catholic Church "in favor of ecumenism," and in the Decree on Ecumenism the Council did in fact proclaim just such a general mobilization when it solemnly declared: "The concern for restoring unity involves the whole Church, faithful and clergy alike. It extends to everyone, according to the talent of each, whether it be exercised in daily Christian living or in theological and historical studies" (no. 5).

1. We are obviously dealing with fairly recent events, and this can naturally raise the question of whether a scientific biography of our subject is yet possible, and more particularly what sources we have at our disposition for such a work. The following is a general overview of these sources:

(a) as concerns the cardinal's life as a whole:

a rich collection of notes from spiritual exercises, retreats, etc., stretching from 1902 to 1968;

a large collection of evidence which the author of the present work has collected from people who lived with Father and then Cardinal Bea at various periods in his life, or who at least came into frequent contact with him; these people were careful to indicate whether their evidence could be used during their lifetimes or not, and the author has obviously respected their wishes;

(b) as concerns the time before he was made cardinal:

the manuscripts of lectures given in over forty years of academic teaching (1917-1959);

for the years 1949-1959 we also have a rich collection of correspondence— over three thousand letters in all;

publications produced in forty years of academic activity, a full list of which (nos 1 to 126) is given in an appendix;

(c) as concerns the period as cardinal:

above all we have the vast and very fundamental collection of official documents concerning the preparation and proceedings of the Second Vatican Council (39 folio-sized volumes; further information will be found under "Abbreviations" below);

we also have the cardinal's own publications from this period (over three hundred in number, listed in Appendix 1 to the present work);

it is true that we have none of the cardinal's correspondence or other writings that were in any way official, for in accordance with the rules of the Holy See, all this material has been placed in the secret Vatican archives, and as current regulations stand it will not be made available for about sixty years; even so, this gap is in large part compensated for by the fact that we do have what can be called the cardinal's private files, which contain a rich collection of notes, drafts, and other documents that the author of the present biography was able to gather in his position as private secretary and close assistant to Cardinal Bea during the whole of this last period; Bea left this material to the Jesuit Province of Southern Germany (Munich) to which he belonged; although it will also remain restricted for several decades, the present author has been allowed to consult it with a view to producing this biography.

2. In all modesty, the author also believes that the lack of access to official documents is to a large extent counterbalanced by the fact that he was in close personal contact with the subject for close to a quarter of a century. From 1944 until Bea's death in 1968 the author lived with him, first at the Pontifical Biblical Institute, and then at the Brazilian College, where Bea went to live after being made

cardinal. From 1944 to 1947 he studied under him at the Biblical Institute, and then spent almost ten years producing his dissertation in biblical sciences under his direction, during which time Bea also started honoring him with his friendship. Then during the years as cardinal, from 1959 to 1968, in accordance with the dispositions of his religious superiors, he was his private secretary and thus worked in close collaboration with him. Although the author can therefore claim to be an eye-witness, so to speak, this does not mean that he intends writing from memory; he writes in scientific terms on the basis of the various sources, trying to strike a fruitful balance between his own memories and maximum objectivity; his own experience and memories help him to understand and interpret the sources, although these are always carefully checked. This strictly scientific method also means that the subject has been allowed to speak for himself wherever possible.

3. The use of the sources is a straightforward matter for the most part, and the only explanation needed concerns two categories: correspondence from 1949 to 1959, and unofficial material concerning Bea's activity as cardinal. In both cases, the relatively recent date of the events and the fact that some of the people involved are still alive obviously means that we have to respect certain limits. However, in order to ensure that this study is as historically accurate as possible, we have tried to footnote our assertions as much as possible, and we therefore adopted a method that is sometimes used in similar cases, referring simply to the file number of the document on which we are basing ourselves, without giving the nature of the document or the name of the person involved; all this material is very well catalogued, so that when the files are eventually opened it will be easy to identify the documents concerned.

The author set some limits of his own on the use of notes from spiritual exercises, retreats, etc. He himself published those dating from the period 1959 to 1968 (accounting for a little over fifteen percent of all this material) in the volume *Augustin Cardinal Bea: Spiritual Profile. Notes from the Cardinal's Diary.* Along with the actual text and relative explanatory notes, the author gave a summary intended as a sort of spiritual portrait of this famous retreatant, so that the volume thus represents a fairly complete illustration of the cardinal's spiritual life. We have therefore preferred not to lengthen our biography with such extracts, making only occasional use of these notes, although as an exception to this rule, at the end of the period 1881 to 1958 we shall devote one chapter to a spiritual portrait of our subject on the eve of his being made cardinal.

4. We would refer briefly to the *structure* of the work in order to give a more precise idea of the author's intentions. When Bea, at the age of almost eighty, became President of the Secretariat for Christian Unity, he said: "The whole of my far from brief life has been a preparation for this task." Taking his cue from these words, in the first part of the biography the author describes the first seventy years, viewing this period as basic general preparation, while in the second part he describes the ten years immediately prior to nomination as cardinal (1949-1959), viewing this as more specific or immediate preparation. The third part is concerned with the Council, encompassing its planning stages and the actual event. The fourth and last part describes the post-conciliar development of ecumenism and gives an

overall view of the cardinal's activities during the last three years of his life. This division immediately points up the different degrees of importance of the various periods, and these differences are also reflected in the amount of detailed attention given to the individual periods in this biography, as we shall now explain.

When his superiors entrusted the author with the task of writing this biography in the 1970s, he was working full-time at the Secretariat for Christian Unity, which of course meant that he was unable to work in the archives in order to find out more about the periods of the subject's life with which he was not personally acquainted (always supposing that such material was accessible and not reserved). The question was how to proceed. The choice basically lay between (a) postponing the undertaking until he had the time to devote himself to such research in the archives, with all the risks inherent in such a delay, and (b) giving as complete a picture as was at present possible of the period with which he was not personally familiar, while devoting himself mostly to describing the events he had witnessed at first-hand. The second alternative seemed decidedly preferable, particularly since the period when he was himself present was undoubtedly the most important and central one in the subject's life.

The author thus established a scale for the amount of detailed attention given to the different periods of the subject's life. Although he does feel that he has also offered a considerable contribution as concerns knowledge of the earliest, more general groundwork (1881-1949), it must be admitted that this section is less detailed than the others. A great effort was, however, made over details of the next ten years (those immediately prior to being made cardinal), while the last period—his time as cardinal—was investigated in the light of all the sources now available and accessible.

5. If we wanted to describe the content of this book in a few words, we could use the formula "life, thought, and action," which effectively expresses what the author has sought to offer, in other words not only the life and activity of his subject, but also the thought—which does in a sense occupy pride of place. As can be seen from the list of his publications, the cardinal devoted a good deal of care to commenting and explaining events, especially those in the ecumenical field, so that if we tend to give a vast number of quotations from the cardinal's writings, the aim is not that of producing an anthology of his publications, but rather that of using his thoughts to provide further information on events, in other words trying to see them through our subject's eyes.

6. Lastly, the author was fully aware that apart from being illustrated and summarized, the cardinal's thinking also needs to be examined within the framework of earlier and contemporary ecumenical publications, just as his thinking on the unity of the human family must be compared with other publications of the same kind. In this way it would become possible to establish affinities and borrowings, and thus its originality or lack of such. However, the author did not feel called upon to perform this task. The vast bulk of the cardinal's publications is so great and the task of summarizing his thinking already in itself so enormous, that it did not leave the author any space for further considerations. The task of comparing the cardinal's thought with that of the ecumenical sphere, and more generally with human thought, is left to further scholarship.

7. In this connection, however, we must point out and explain the cuts made in this abridged edition of the biography. The author started with the consideration that there are four of the cardinal's works which would permit him to make cuts: as concerns ecumenism, this applies to the works *The Unity of Christians* and *Ecumenism in Focus*; as concerns relations with the Jewish people, to the cardinal's commentary *The Church and the Jewish People* on the Council document *Nostra aetate*; and lastly, the book *The Unity in Freedom* gives an ample treatment of the subject of the unity of the human family. Our cuts are thus for the most part concerned with Chapters 5, 7, 8 and 10 of Part Three, and Chapters 1 and 2 of Part Four. Similarly, the bibliography of the cardinal's works and also that of works *on* the cardinal have been kept as brief as possible.

8. The English translation has been made from the Italian typescript of an abridged version. The text contained a number of citations that were originally written in German and have not been published—except, of course, in the German edition of the present biography (*Augustin Bea, Kardinal der Einheit*; Graz, 1989); the English translation of such citations has been made on the basis of the originals, but apart from a few exceptions, no reference is made to the German edition of the biography in order not to increase the volume of the footnotes unnecessarily.

* * *

In conclusion, I should like to thank my religious superiors who gave me this task: Most Rev. Pedro Arrupe, Father General of the Society of Jesus, and his successor Peter-Hans Kolvenbach, who confirmed the assignment.

I offer my thanks to Miss Corinna De Martini for her faithful and painstaking assistance in preparing the original Italian manuscript.

I wish to thank very sincerely Ms. Leslie Wearne, the translator of this biography, for her intelligent, accurate and dedicated work.

I am also very grateful to New City Press, the U.S. publishing house responsible for this English-language edition, for their courage in undertaking publication of such a long and demanding work.

Above all, I wish to offer my gratitude to the Giver of every good thing (cf. James 1:17) for having provided his support in the long years during which this study was being prepared. May he bless its future progress and grant that through this humble work the activity of the first President of the Secretariat for Christian Unity may continue to help the church pursue the great aim "that all may be one" (John 17:21).

ABBREVIATIONS

1. Sources

Arch   refers exclusively to the private archives, or files, which the cardinal left to his original Jesuit province, the Provincia Germaniae Superioris (with headquarters in Munich); reference is thus not being made either to the Secret Vatican Archives, where the official part of his legacy is deposited, or to the files of the Pontifical Council for Promoting Christian Unity.

P   letters of the cardinal's private secretary.

N   (sometimes with the addition of a lower-case letter): Father Bea's letters, as found in the aforementioned files (Arch).

L   papers concerning the Council—both preparation and actual proceedings.

R   manuscripts of the cardinal's talks and interviews, again from the aforementioned files (Arch).

Ra   complete material regarding the various journeys, talks, etc., again from the same files.

Rb   material concerning the cardinal's books, again from the same files.
Similarly, other material from these files, which covers various spheres of the cardinal's activity, is indicated with an upper-case letter (sometimes together with a lower-case one). Sometimes the subject-matter gives an idea of the nature of the material; however, as with the authors of letters, discretion normally forbids any further indication of their nature.

ArchWit   evidence collected from witnesses who knew Father, later Cardinal, Bea, also found in the same files.

Dates   a small notebook entitled *Daten aus meinem Leben* (= *The Dates of My Life*), a detailed *curriculum vitae* in which the subject noted down the main events in his life as these occurred.

Biblio.   (with the addition of a number) the list of the cardinal's publications, found in an appendix at the end of the biography.

2. Abbreviated Titles of the Cardinal's Works

Chiesa-Ebrei = *La Chiesa e il popolo ebraico*.
> English translation: *Church-Jews* = *The Church and the Jewish People*. Cf. Biblio. 172

Der Mensch Bea = *Der Mensch Bea. Augzeichnungen des Kardinals*.
> English translation: *Spiritual Profile* = *Augustin Cardinal Bea: Spiritual Profile. Notes from the Cardinal's Diary*. Cf. Biblio. 191a.

Ecumenismo = *Ecumenismo nel Concilio*.
> English translation: *Ecumenism* = *Ecumenism in Focus*. Cf. Biblio. 190

Friede = *Friede zwischen Christen*.
> English translation: *Peace* = *Peace among Christians*. Cf. Biblio. 174

Il cammino = *Il cammino all'unione dopo il Concilio*.
> English translation: *The Way* = *The Way to Unity after the Council*. Cf. Biblio. 173.

La Chiesa e l'umanità.
> English translation: *The Church and Mankind*. Cf. Biblio. 175.

La Parola di Dio = *La Parola di Dio e l'umanità*.
> English translation: *The Word of God* = *The Word of God and Mankind*. Cf. Biblio. 189.

La storicità dei Vangeli.
> English translation: *Synoptic Gospels* = *The Study of the Synoptic Gospels.* Cf. Biblio. 171.

L'unione dei cristiani.
> English translation: *The Unity of Christians.* Cf. Biblio. 169.

Servire = *Servire: Un' idea-forza del Concilio.*
> English translation: *We who serve* = *We who serve. A Basic Council Theme and Its Biblical Foundations.* Cf. Biblio. 191.

Unity in Freedom = *Unity in Freedom. Reflections on the Human Family.* Cf. Biblio. 170.

Note: articles by the cardinal are cited simply according to their numbers in our bibliography. For example, Biblio. 126 = "La scienza biblica da Leone XIII a Pio XII," *Divinitas*, IV (1959), 322-341.

3. Works Frequently Cited

BM   *Augustin Kardinal Bea. Wegbereiter der Einheit*, ed. Maria Buchmüller (Augsburg, 1971)

Caprile   *Il Concilio Vaticano Secondo*, ed. G. Caprile (Rome, n.d.):
> vol. I, "Annunzio e preparazione" (= "Announcement and preparation") (parts I-II);
> vol. II, "Primo periodo" (= "First period");
> vol. III, "Secondo periodo" (= "Second period");
> vol. IV, "Terzo periodo" (= "Third period");
> vol. V, "Quarto periodo" (= "Fourth period").
> (References are simply made to the author's name, volume and page.)

JI   E.M. Jung-Inglessis, *Augustin Bea, Kardinal der Einheit* (Recklinghausen 1962)

LB   Bernard Leeming, *Agostino Cardinal Bea* (Notre Dame, Ind., 1964)

Simposio   *Simposio Card. Agostino Bea (16-19 Dic. 1981)* (Rome 1983)

Bea-Preis   *Augustin Bea-Preis. Einheit der Menschheit in Freiheit*, ed. S. Schmidt (Lugano, n.d.)
> English edition: Bea Prize = Augustine Bea Prize, Unity of Mankind in Freedom, ed. S. Schmidt (Lugano, n.d.)

All biblical citations are taken from the Revised Standard Version, Catholic Edition

All translations of the documents of the Second Vatican Council are taken from Austin Flannery (gen. ed.), *Vatican Council II: The Conciliar and Post Conciliar Documents* (rev. ed.: Collegeville, Minn., 1984)

4. The Second Vatican Council: Terminology and Abbreviations

Ante-preparatory phase: from the 1959 announcement until mid-1960

Preparatory phase: from November 1960 to Summer 1962

(Note: the various commissions and certain secretariats were involved in this phase, and the documents they prepared were examined by the Central Preparatory Commission.)

"Period" is the official term used to indicate the four sessions into which the plenary meetings of Vatican II were divided: the first from 11 October to 7 December 1962, the second from 29 September to 4 December 1963, the third from 14 September to 21 November 1964, and the fourth from 14 September to 7 December 1965.

"Inter-session" is an unofficial term used for want of a better expression to indicate the intervals between the various periods.

GC   General Congregation. This indicates one of the *non*-public plenary meetings of the Council, as opposed to the public sessions which were dedicated to the opening and closing of the periods and the promulgation of documents. The General Congregations were numbered progressively, continuing through all four periods (there were 168 in all), and the same applies to the public sessions (10 in all).

"Schema" indicates the first draft of a document drawn up by a commission or a secretariat. In much simplified terms, it can be said that the schema had to pass through the following stages: after a first general discussion, there was a vote to accept it as the basis of a future Council document; this was followed by a detailed chapter-by-chapter discussion; the schema was then redrafted in the light of all these discussions, and the individual parts and also the whole document were submitted to the vote; this was followed by an examination of further amendments, the results of which were again voted on; an overall vote was taken on the resulting text, within the framework of a General Congregation, and for the sake of convenience we shall refer to this vote as "the first reading"; this was followed by a last, formal vote in public session, which we shall call "the second reading."

"Observer-delegates" (or simply "observers") were representatives at the Council of the various churches, ecclesial communities or Christian World Communions.

AD	*Acta et Documenta.* This is the collection of documents that came from the ante-preparatory phase (Series I) and the preparatory phase (Series II). Series II is divided into two parts, the first of which contains the Acts of the Central Preparatory Pontifical Commission, while the second contains draft documents drawn up by commissions and secretariats. (Note: with a few exceptions, our study is not concerned with the Acts of the ante-preparatory phase.) The following are the full Latin titles of the collection in question:
AD	*Acta et Documenta Concilio Ecumenico Vaticano II Apparando,* Series II, vol. II = *Acta Pontificiae Commissionis Centralis Praeparatoriae* [or "Proceedings of the Central Preparatory Commission"] (Vatican City, 1965-1968); this volume is divided into four parts, corresponding to the various sessions of the aforementioned Central Commission; we cite simply the volume and the relevant part, e.g. II/III.
AD	*Acta et Documenta Concilio Ecumenico Vaticano II Apparando,* Series II, vol. III = *Acta Commissionum Secretariatuum Praeparatoriorum Concilii Vaticani II,* Parts I-II (Vatican City, 1969); these contain the drafts from the various commissions and secretariats; we cite simply the volume and the relevant part.
Schemata	*Schemata Constitutionum et Decretorum de quibus disceptabitur in Concilii sessionibus,* 4 series (corresponding in fact to the 4 volumes); these contain the schemata or drafts as *amended* by the two *sub*commissions of the Central Commission and sent to the Council; we cite the series and page.
AS	*Acta Synodalia Sacrosancti Concilii Oecumenici Vaticani II* (Vatican City); one volume is devoted to each period, divided into a certain number of parts; thus *AS* II/V indicates Part V of the Acts of the second period.
CDD	*Sacrosanctum Concilium Vaticanum Secundum: Constitutiones, Decreta, Declarationes,* ed. and annotated General Secretariat (Vatican City, 1966); this is the official collection of the documents promulgated by the Council.

5. Abbreviations of Council Documents

AA	*Apostolicam actuositatem,* Decree on the Apostolate of the Laity
AG	*Ad gentes divinitus,* Decree on the Church's Missionary Activity
CD	*Christus Dominus,* Decree on the Pastoral Office of Bishops in the Church
DH	*Dignitatis humanae,* Declaration on Religious Liberty
DV	*Dei verbum,* Dogmatic Constitution on Divine Revelation

GE	*Gravissimum educationis*, Declaration on Christian Education
GS	*Gaudium et spes*, Pastoral Constitution on the Church in the Modern World
IM	*Inter mirifica*, Decree on the Means of Social Communication
LG	*Lumen gentium*, Dogmatic Constitution on the Church
NA	*Nostra aetate*, Declaration on the Church's Relations with Non-Christian Religions
OE	*Orientalium ecclesiarum*, Decree on the Catholic Oriental Churches
OT	*Optatam totius*, Decree on the Training of Priests
PC	*Perfectae caritatis*, Decree on the Up-to-date Renewal of Religious Life
PO	*Presbyterorum ordinis*, Decree on the Life and Ministry of Priests
SC	*Sacrosanctum concilium*, Constitution on the Sacred Liturgy
UR	*Unitatis redintegratio*, Decree on Ecumenism

6. Publications Frequently Cited

AAS	*Acta Apostolicae Sedis* (Vatican City)
CC	*La Civiltà Cattolica* (Rome)
EncCatt	*Enciclopedia Cattolica* (Vatican City)
EB	*Enchiridion Biblicum*, Documenta ecclesiastica Sacram Scripturam spectantia (3rd ed.: Naples/Rome, 1956)
IS	*Information Service*, English bulletin of the Secretariat for Christian Unity
SI	*Service d'Information*, the same bulletin in French
LThK	*Lexikon für Theologie und Kirche* (2nd ed.: Freiburg im Breisgau, 1957-1968)
OD	*Concilium Vaticanum Secundum, Observateurs Délégués et Hôtes du Secretariat pour l'unité des chrétiens au Deuxième Concile Oecuménique du Vatican* (Vatican City, 1965); official list of observer-delegates and guests at the Council
TAG	*Tomos Agapis* (Vatican-Phanar, 1958-1970; Rome-Istanbul, 1971); public statements and correspondence between the Holy See and the Ecumenical Patriarchate; these are official Latin, Greek or French texts, but in the case of the Latin and Greek ones, French translations are always given as well.
THS	*Toward the Healing of Schism* (New York, 1987); English translation of *TAG*
OssRom	*L'Osservatore Romano*, Italian-language Vatican daily newspaper, with weekly English edition

7. Note

In accounts of episodes from the cardinal's life, words in quotes convey the gist and not the actual words, unless the contrary is specifically stated. This does not, however, apply to extracts from letters and suchlike, when quotes indicate that we are giving a precise textual quotation.

"ct" indicates that an already existing translation has been corrected to render it more faithful to the original.

Part One

GENERAL PREPARATION
(1881--1949)

In May 1956, on the occasion of Augustin Bea's seventy-fifth birthday, the well-known Swiss ecumenist, Otto Karrer, who had been a friend of the future cardinal since their early twenties, wrote an article in his honor in the publication Christlicher Sonntag. When he sent a copy to Bea together with his good wishes, Bea wrote back thanking him and saying: "Of course I must say, looking back, that God has led me by quite different paths from those I imagined and made of me something I never even dreamed." And with his typical realism and modesty he added: "I hope at least that I have not been too ham-fisted and that I shall not be so in the future, in the position in which the Lord has placed me. In this spirit I accept your good wishes with warmest thanks." [1]

In this first part of our work, we want to follow Bea along these "paths" that were so different and varied, up to the time he was nominated confessor to Pius XII, and then move beyond this, continuing on to the end of his time as Rector of the Pontifical Biblical Institute in Rome. We shall draw on the various sources indicated in the introduction, especially Bea's autobiographical writings and his letters, which provide such a wealth of information between them that this part can to a considerable extent take on an almost autobiographical character.

---

1. N 1956/79, German original in O. Karrer, Streiflichter. Aus Briefen an mich 1933-1975 (Frankfurt/Stuttgart, 1976), pp. 44-45.

CHAPTER 1

FAMILY, EDUCATION, PRIESTLY AND RELIGIOUS VOCATION

(1881–1902)

As can be seen from the title, we shall be moving fast, for this chapter covers about twenty years of our subject's life, introducing us first of all to his family, and allowing us to see the influence it has on the young Augustin's life and the development of his character. It is a considerable sacrifice when his parents allow him to go away to school, where they support him with much difficulty. The boy's orientation toward the priesthood, envisaged as being lived out as a diocesan priest, develops fairly early on in his home environment. His secondary and high school education bring him into contact with various circles, each of which helps mould his character and mind. After a certain amount of searching, it is during this period that the boy takes the unexpected decision to live the priesthood in a religious order—the Society of Jesus. Some years of enforced waiting follow, but after a vigorous struggle he overcomes his father's objections, and at the age of twenty-one goes abroad to enter the novitiate (for the order has been expelled from Bismarck's Germany).

His Birthplace and Family Home

Augustin Bea was born at Riedböhringen, a small village in the Baar region, a plateau about 2,500 feet above sea-level situated on the borders of the Black Forest, some six miles from the source of the Danube. Its "Alemann" population has the reputation of being people with clear ideas and broad views, calm and reflective in their work, and capable of waiting patiently for the harvest of their fields.[1] Bea's view of his fellow citizens can be seen clearly in the expression he sometimes uses in his letters to excuse his outspoken language: "I have a great deal of Alemann blood, and that's why I speak out so frankly."[2] Normally, however, the pastoral context of his letters means that he tends to describe his people more in a moral and religious perspective, saying that they are a strangely harsh, reserved type of people, who do not like being ordered around.[3] Although the region is known as "cold Baar" on account of its climate, Bea feels that this is also true from the religious viewpoint, not least because of the liberalizing

---

1. Cf. BM, pp. 24-25. For historical information, cf. "Riedböhringen in der Baar," in M. Buchmüller, F. Buchmüller and G. Walser, "Kurienkardinal Augustin Bea aus Riedböhringen, Landkreis Donaueschingen," in *Ekkhart-Jahrbuch 1977 der "Badischen Heimat,"* 69-77.

2. N 1955/105; 1956/25, 57, 110; 1957/168.

3. Cf. N 1956/51; 1955/105; 1953/148; 1955/113.

influence of one of the last bishops of what was the diocese of Constance, J.H. Wessenberg,[4] although Bea hurries to add that despite this it does possess rich religious resources.[5]

A 1952 episode provides an illustration of his opinion. The parish where he was born wanted to mark the fortieth anniversary of his ordination to the priesthood with a solemn celebration. At the last minute, when all the preparations had been made, Bea felt forced to cancel his journey, mostly because of his health. The faithful parish priest, Hermann Hahn, tried to make up for this so far as possible, traveling personally to Rome to bring Bea the various gifts, including a copy of the crucifix he used to pray before in an old shrine in Riedböhringen. The cardinal greatly appreciated the gift, and hung it above his prie-dieu, writing his fellow citizens a long message of thanks, in which he said: "I should like to send each one of you a similar copy of the holy cross as a sign of my gratitude so that it might accompany and protect each of you along your life's path. However, I imagine it is not necessary, for I suppose that, following the noble old tradition of our forebears, the cross still hangs in the place of honor in the holy corner in every house, so that the Savior can take every member of the family under his protection and bless him from his cross."[6]

Cardinal Bea was born on 28 May 1881 to Karl Bea of Riedböhringen and his wife Maria (née Merk), who came from the village of Gutmadingen, about seven miles away. In an autobiographical notebook entitled *The Dates of My Life* he notes that "it was the Saturday after Ascension," adding that he was baptized the following day in the parish church of St. Genesius.[7] His parents had been married at a relatively late age, on 5 April 1880, when his father was already thirty-three and his mother twenty-six.[8] The boy was named after his paternal grandfather Augustin, and he was to remain an only child. His father was a carpenter, who also had a small field of his own which he farmed.

When we come to describe his parents, we are lucky enough to have fairly detailed information written down by their son a few years before his death. A first significant pointer is the fact that, in accordance with the wishes of their famous son, they are buried together with him in the parish church of Riedböhringen. In 1965, the religious and civil authorities of his hometown had expressed the wish of its citizens for the honor of receiving his mortal remains, and he was pleased to agree, with the sole condition that he be buried together with his parents. It was then about fifty years since the death of his parents, and in the normal course of things their graves were due to be eliminated. The cardinal's condition was accepted, so that the parents now rest together with their illustrious son in the parish church. In July 1967 the cardinal attended their

---

4. Cf. N 1956/51. On the complex and controversial figure of J.H. Wessenberg (1774-1860), who was vicar general of the diocese of Constance for a long period, cf. *LThK*, X, 1063-1064.

5. Cf. N 1953/148; 1952/70. Cf. "Das Christentum und die kirchlichen Verhältnisse in der Baar," in Buchmüller, Buchmüller and Walser, "Kurienkardinal," 60-69.

6. 1952/141.

7. Cf. *Dates*.

8. Cf. BM, p. 38.

reburial, preaching a homily that represents the most beautiful monument to his parents, and is a source of precious information for us on his parents and on his own childhood. We shall thus base ourselves mainly on this homily.

He told his fellow townsmen why he wanted to be buried with his parents, saying with deep gratitude: "The Second Vatican Council says that 'the parental home is so to speak the first church, a kind of domestic church, in which God's praise is proclaimed and God's word is preached.' I can say all this was true of my home, offering deep thanks to God, and also to my dear parents, my first mentors and educators. I learned to pray at my mother's knee, and to this day I remember the series of Our Fathers we prayed together for the souls in purgatory, to the Guardian Angel, to the Most Blessed Virgin, for our parents and relatives, and so on. It was not only a question of encouragement to pray, but also a practice of prayer day in, day out, with prayers before meals, morning prayers and evening prayers. It was here, at my mother's side, that I learned to pray."

"And at my father's side," Bea then emphasized, "I was introduced into the church. I was barely three when my father took me up into the gallery of the church. . . . From there I could look down onto the altar . . . and I saw the priest elevating the sacred host and giving the holy blessing with the monstrance, and in my child's mind I told myself that it must be really wonderful to be a priest and be able to bless like that. And this idea soon found expression as I built my own little altar at home in a corner of the living room. My mother used to help look after this little altar and gradually extended it. Every year she used to go to the shrine of Our Lady at Einsiedeln at least once—in those days people went on foot—and when she came back, she'd bring a gift with her for her small son—a little statue of Our Lady, the divine Savior, St. Peter, St. Louis or the Guardian Angel, for instance, and then she'd show me how to set everything up nicely."[9]

The upbringing Bea received from his parents was, as he at once points out, by no means permissive: "I had to be obedient and 'good.' And the rod was not spared. On one occasion, when I was seven years old, I was sitting in the first or second of the children's pews in the front of the church . . . and my father saw me from the gallery, whispering with my neighbor. When I came home, he was waiting with the cane behind the front door, to show his young son that he wasn't to chat in church. As you can see, his son didn't forget the lesson."[10]

He then gratefully recalled the sacrifice his parents made in order to let him study, and how they "took leave of their only child in tears, yet made the sacrifice in order to fulfill God's will. In this way they laid the foundations of my future career."[11] We should remember that these sacrifices also entailed a considerable material element because of the family's very modest financial circumstances, as can be seen from the fact that later on the city hall issued him a certificate of penury so that he could enter the archbishop's seminary for theological studies.[12]

---

9. R 1967/20, pp. 2-3; cf. also BM, pp. 287ff.

10. *Ibid.*

11. *Ibid.*

12. Cf. BM, pp. 46-47.

In 1966 when Augustin Bea opened the elementary school in Riedböhringen that bears his name, he had this to say: "I know very well from the experience of my late father and mother that it is not easy to bear the cost of educating a boy or a girl. And when the means are slender, as was the case in my family, the sacrifice is naturally all the greater."[13]

As Bea said, this was followed by another still heavier sacrifice for his parents: "Later came the even harder sacrifice of giving up all hope that I would support them in their old age, when they granted their permission for me to enter a religious order—and of all orders that of the Jesuits, which was at that time banned in Germany. Even on her death-bed, my mother told me several times that she had never regretted this sacrifice and that she thanked the Lord God that she had given her consent."[14] His account closed with the words: "As you can see, . . . I truly have reason to thank the Lord God for giving me parents who were so steeped in their holy faith and zealous in the fulfillment of their religious duties, and who made all the sacrifices needed in order to let their only child fulfill his vocation and become what the Lord God planned for him."[15]

Apart from this information provided by Bea himself, we have various other details that help give a fuller picture of his parents and also of his own childhood, some of which can be taken chronologically, while others are of a more general nature.

Most of these details concern *his mother Maria*, whom he always remembered very vividly despite the passing of the years. When he was over seventy, he still remembered that his mother had been baptized the day of the definition of the Immaculate Conception of the Blessed Virgin Mary (8 December 1854) and that she celebrated her "saint's day" on the feast of the Immaculate Conception.[16] He also remembered her sensitive nature and how she used to worry; for instance, she did not want her small son to go sleighing on the snow-covered hill above their home because she felt it was too dangerous, and it was even worse for her when the child used to clamber up the scaffolding his carpenter father would put up when building the local wooden houses. "What a worry children are," his mother would moan, although she only had one.

While these were fairly normal mother's worries, there was one trait that she passed on to her son. If his father did not come home when expected, his mother could not rest until he did, and Bea used to show the same kind of anxiety when he was a superior, up to the very last years of his life; for example if his confreres did not come back on time from some trip, he would be so worried that he would be incapable of either working or resting.

We have already mentioned the shrine of the Holy Cross which used to exist in Riedböhringen, and when Bea was a boy there was still a small chapel dedicated to it not far from his home. Recalling this, Bea wrote: "As a child I often went with my dear mother to the 'Holy Cross' and prayed there in the tiny chapel that had

---

13. R 1966/18, p. 3.
14. *Ibid.*
15. *Ibid.*
16. Cf. N 1954/53; Nb 1953/359.

been preserved as the last reminder of the former pilgrimage church."[17] We also mentioned his mother's pilgrimages to the shrine of Our Lady at Einsiedeln. In 1954 Bea urged his relatives to "dare" make a pilgrimage to Rome, pointing out that such a venture would be almost as easy as those people used to make to Einsiedeln when he was a boy, "except that our dear mothers used to do it mostly on foot! And the old people said that on such pilgrimages one should put raw peas in one's shoes"[18] as a penance. His mother went even more often to the shrine of Our Lady of Sorrows in the Benedictine Monastery of Beuron, which was much closer, and if Bea wrote in his 1960 retreat notes that he had been particularly devoted to Our Lady of Sorrows since childhood, the source of this certainly lies in these pilgrimages his mother used to make.[19]

We would add one last detail. When Bea made his will, he left his executor a large-grained rosary as a sign of special affection and devotion, for it had belonged to his mother, from whom he had taken it after sitting with her during her last hours and then kept with him until the end of his own life as a very dear keepsake.

As concerns *his father*, Bea observed in the above-mentioned talk that the "school" of his childhood home provided not only his religious upbringing, but also the fundamental elements of human knowledge. "My father taught me to read and write, even before I went to elementary school, and he also taught me the basics of arithmetic. He was a carpenter, and I learned to draw and sketch from him—all, as I have already said, before I went to elementary school when I was nearly seven."[20] We can imagine the father sitting down with the bright young boy, especially in the long winter evenings, explaining things to him and guiding his hand, while the mother took care of various household tasks in another part of the small living room. In later life Bea was often responsible for building houses and schools, as we shall see, and he had undoubtedly received a basic grounding for this, however modest, in his childhood home.

When someone asked the cardinal later on how he managed to do so much, he answered with a smile: "I do one thing after another." Similarly in a letter to members of his family he explained: "Despite all my work, I do not get ruffled but simply do one thing after another, as my father did when he had repairs to carry out."[21]

On several occasions Bea referred to the following principle as learned from

17. N 1952/141.

18. N 1954/50; 1955/80.

19. Cf. Med. 1960/VII/4; *Spiritual Profile*, p. 61. Cf. also the 1945 retreat: "Mary accompanied me as Mother, precisely as Our Lady of Sorrows, from the earliest years of my childhood onward in my daily prayers, in my pilgrimages to Neudingen and Beuron, etc." (Med. VIII/2, ms; cf. also the 1952 retreat, Med. VIII/1, ms.). In the pilgrimage church of Beuron, the Virgin Mary is venerated as Our Lady of Sorrows, which is not the case at Einsiedeln. However, with regard to Einsiedeln we should note that the annual celebration of the "consecration of the chapel by the angels" is held on the feast of the Seven Sorrows in September. This of course soon led people—especially the masses—to link this shrine with our Lady of Sorrows. (Information supplied by Father Engelbert Giersbach, O.S.B., procurator of Einsiedeln Monastery in Rome.)

20. R 1967/20; BM, p. 289.

21. Nb 1964/330.

his father: "If people give you something, go ahead and accept it, because either they are sincere and it is therefore all right to accept, or they are not sincere and in that case they deserve to be punished for their lack of sincerity."

Now we can give a few facts about *Augustin's childhood*. In 1957 he wrote to a family that was living in what had been his maternal grandmother's home in Gutmadingen, telling them that he "often visited that house as a small boy and as a student,"[22] and recalling that during one of these visits there was the funeral of some relative. He wanted to go and ring the bell, but his grandmother felt it would be dangerous and therefore made him join the cortège together with the grown-ups. Although the small boy obeyed, he was so upset that after the funeral he told his grandmother that he wanted to go home, and thus he returned to Riedböhringen earlier than planned.

His tidiness was always exemplary, and he himself indicated the source of this trait, recalling a charming detail from the wise upbringing he received from his grandmother. She once bought him a small plate at a local fair with the motto: "Keep things tidy and love order, for it saves you time and effort."[23]

When the small boy first went to elementary school after Easter 1888, he had already received a good grounding from his father, and Bea later remembered two particular episodes from this period. One day the teacher told the pupils to make up sentences, and Augustin's was: "The *Auer* is hanging on the wall." In German the word for "peasant" is *Bauer*, which in Bea's local dialect becomes *Buur*, and knowing this the boy thought he must change *Uhr* (clock) into *Auer*. When the teacher asked him what an *Auer* was, the small boy pointed to the clock. The teacher explained that it was an *Uhr* and not an *Auer*, but the boy wanted to know why it was, "if we say *Buur* and in literary language it's *Bauer*." The teacher's only answer was: "I don't know why, but that's what it is."

I do not know if the following question belongs to this or a slightly earlier period: "How do people know the names of the stars if they've never been there?"

Bea also remembered how a girl in the same class at elementary school told his mother that Augustin had been kept in as punishment. His mother wanted to know why. "Because he passed someone the answer." As we can see, children are obviously the same the world over. And it was certainly not the worst of crimes.

The boy's inclinations started showing themselves during this period, and it was particularly his mother who recognized them. In 1959 Bea wrote about this to his friend Fridolin Amann: "My late mother noted early on that Augustin did not like working on the land, but that he would rather do something in the house, or read or study. She was quite right. And this has remained the case throughout my life. I was certainly more drawn to becoming a school-teacher than a farmer."[24]

Apart from the little altars he used to build, the inclination to teach also

22. Nb 1957/220.

23. When he was nearing seventy-five, Bea wrote to his family: "Both my grandmothers lived to over eighty and set me a good example. It looks as if I'm going to follow it. On the other hand, I never knew either of my grandfathers" (Nb 1955/54; cf. 1957/314; 1958/243).

24. Nc 1959/44; R 1966/18.

appeared fairly early, although in a strange, childish way. Bea told me: "I used to line up some pumpkins on a bench, pick up a cane, and school would begin. Naturally these pupils were sometimes inattentive or slow, and then the cane would come into use."

When the boy was eleven, a serious threat arose, which looked likely to put an end to everything, for Augustin contracted tuberculosis. His mother took him to a doctor, who examined him and then sent him out of the room. However, the boy realized it was something serious and left the door ajar so that he heard the doctor telling his mother: "I'm sorry, Mrs. Bea. Give him whatever he wants to eat. The boy can't live more than three months."[25] When Bea described this episode, he added: "Three years later I met the same doctor again and told him who I was: 'It's me, doctor, I'm that boy. As you see, I'm still here.' 'Very pleased to see you,' was the embarrassed reply." In one of the letters already cited, Bea gently observed: "As we see, doctors can sometimes make mistakes," adding, "but this episode did teach me that we must not sin against our own health."[26] I do not know if this experience was responsible, but on several occasions I heard him say: "If I hadn't become a priest, I'd have been a doctor."

In the previously quoted speech in his hometown at the opening of the elementary school that bears his name, Bea gratefully remembered his parish priest Thaddäus Hierholzer and his teacher Leopold Herzog, who noticed the boy's talents and encouraged his parents to let him continue with his education.[27] The priest made a considerable personal contribution, and in the *curriculum vitae* composed in 1900 prior to entering the archdiocesan seminary, Bea noted: "From Christmas 1892 to Fall 1893, the parish priest gave me lessons in the basic elements of the Latin language."[28] This excellent preparation enabled him to start junior high school with better prospects.

On 9 April 1893, a few months before he entered junior high school, he received first communion in the parish church, although he would not receive the sacrament of confirmation until 9 May 1896, three years later. When Bea noted this in *Dates*, he added: "This too [like his birth] on a Saturday."

Junior High School

In fall 1961 the cardinal visited the school he attended for the four years of junior high school, describing his first day there in an informal conversation: "Eight days ago it was sixty-seven years since I first crossed the threshold of the Lender Institute of Instruction and Education as a poor, timid farmer's son who had received private tuition from his parish priest. I was very much struck by the inscription I saw over the doorway: *Initium sapientiae timor Domini* [Fear

25. Nb 1959/390; Nc 1961/67; BM, p. 254.

26. Nb 1959/390.

27. Cf. R 1966/18, p. 2.

28. BM, p. 43.

of the Lord is the beginning of wisdom], and my heart was beating fast. . . . My respected parish priest had prepared me for the second grade, but for some unknown reason—maybe simply an oversight—they tested me for the third grade, asking questions about things I neither knew nor could have hoped to know. Yet the result of this examination was: 'Accepted for the third class for a trial period until Christmas.' And that was the beginning of my scientific career. Thanks be to God, the little farmer's son survived the trial period, although not so brilliantly, for his Christmas report card bore the overall mark of 'Pass'. . . . The little boy had mustered his courage and set to work—and succeeded."[29]

We would add a few comments here. The school bore the name of its founder, the priest Franz Xaver Lender (1830-1913), who had built it in his parish of Sasbach in 1875. Although it was not a seminary as such, it must be said that a large proportion of the clergy of the Baden region received their early education there.[30] In the aforementioned talk Bea did in fact say: "At my time the institute was more or less set up so as to produce as many priests as possible."[31] As far as later years were concerned, a boyhood friend, the priest Fridolin Amann, who was head master of the school for many years, wrote to the cardinal in 1962 as follows: "Even during the Hitler years this school produced more priests than all the other schools in the archdiocese put together."[32]

Augustin's departure from Riedböhringen took place on about 10 September 1893, and he referred to it in a number of his letters. Thus in 1956 he wrote to a female cousin: "It was in these days, sixty-three years ago, that I set out for school in Sasbach. I was twelve years old, and I left together with Franz Honold, who became ambassador in Berlin later in life and who died ten years ago."[33]

In 1956 Bea also wrote to his friend Father Amann about the speech he was to give at the liturgical and pastoral congress shortly to be held in Assisi: "But now I have finished it, and all I have to do is read it. . . . If I had not had so much experience, I would be daunted by the prospect of addressing a dozen cardinals and several hundred bishops, but . . . one gets used to anything. And this is the timid little lad of those Sasbach years . . . !"[34]

The records contain all the school report cards from Sasbach—three for every year. In view of the misunderstanding over his entrance examination, it is not surprising that the boy needed a little time to catch up with his companions who had begun the year with the benefit of the usual coaching. We shall not give the individual marks in evaluating his progress (a choice we shall explain later), but rather his position in class, which was also given in the report cards. After a bare three months, in December 1893, Augustin was already fourteenth out of forty-five students, in the following March he was fourth, and in December 1894

---

29. *Sasbacher* (1962), p. 21.
30. Cf. *LThK*, VI, 943.
31. *Sasbacher* (1962), p. 23.
32. Nc 1962/85.
33. Nb 1956/238.
34. Nc 1956/26.

he was second out of fifty—and this latter report card also bore the remark "Conduct: exemplary." At the end of the school year 1894-1895 he was top of a class of forty-six and again had an excellent mark for conduct. He kept the same position the following year, winning first prize for school work and a special prize for conduct.

However, if we look at the individual marks on his report cards, it is surprising that for at least half the subjects this boy who was top of his class did not receive the maximum mark (or "1") but only "2." This may be why Bea left the school after four years, at the end of the fifth grade (in 1897). In the above-mentioned talk he had this to say: "If you asked me why I did it, I would have to admit frankly that I do not know. . . . Maybe I was dissatisfied with something or other."[35] In light of the fact that he was top of his class, the theory Buchmüller puts forward in her biography—that Bea found the teachers too severe[36]—seems probable. However, it must be added that Bea always felt deep gratitude to the school, as he wrote to the head master in 1956: "I owe a great debt of gratitude to your school: the religious and moral principles I learned there have accompanied me throughout my life."[37]

We should lastly observe that the problem of poverty was a constant factor in Bea's education throughout these years. In his speech at the opening of the Augustin Bea School in 1966, apart from expressing his gratitude to his parents, he also thanked his fellow townsmen as follows: "My success in my studies owed a great deal to the financial support of my fellow citizens and the families I knew. When I said goodbye to my relatives and acquaintances at the end of my vacations, they always opened their purses, and I could usually return to school with enough to get by for the next nine months."[38]

The "Ecumenical Atmosphere" of Constance

In the course of his talk at the school in Sasbach, after mentioning his reasons for leaving the Lender Institute, he observed that the decision was in any case providential because it led him into "an ecumenical atmosphere." Here we can immediately give a vivid illustration related by Bea himself: "When my nomination as cardinal was announced in November 1959, one of the first telegrams of congratulation came from Günther Dehn, Professor Emeritus of Evangelical Theology at Berlin University, who was my fellow student in 1897 at Constance High School (on the lake of the same name)—or rather, if I may say so, my 'competitor' for the position of top of the class. Various Christian confessions and religious faiths were represented in the class, but we got on well together, and that was when I began to learn how you can remain faithful to your own

---

35. *Sasbacher*, p. 22.
36. BM, p. 40.
37. N 1956/49; *Sasbacher*, p. 22.
38. R 1966/18, p. 3.

faith while offering those of other confessions not so much a cold respect, but true esteem and indeed sincere love. I came from a town with an exclusively Catholic population, and this was my first school of practical ecumenism."[39]

In 1962 Bea's fellow student Dehn published his memoirs and sent a copy to Bea.[40] He speaks at some length about the city of Constance and his studies there, and also mentions Bea (on p. 39), providing some interesting information on the history of the city and the atmosphere there at that time. He recalls that the school was founded by the Jesuits in 1604 and that it originally bore the name of the great medieval mystic Blessed Heinrich Seuse, a Dominican. In Bea's time the general population still referred to it by that name, and it was still housed in the building that had previously been the Jesuit school.

Bea lived in a diocesan dormitory house called Konradi House while attending school in Constance. Dehn writes: "There were between six and eight students from Konradi House in every class. We always rather looked down on them. They were poorly dressed and we thought they did not wash enough. . . . However, this did not prevent us from thoroughly exploiting them. The authorities at Konradi House insisted that they be very conscientious over their homework, so we made them give us their translations during recreation . . . or else we copied their language and math homework. . . . " Dehn concludes: "Later I was sorry I had not been friendlier toward them."[41]

Dehn also observes: "I often asked myself in later years whether those boys [from Konradi House] were aware of the difference between what our teachers told us—which had a humanistic orientation, although in no way that of what is called Christian humanism—and what they learned in their house."[42] I think that Bea did to some extent realize. Thus in 1956 when he wrote to his friend Fridolin Amann as follows about the Jesuit Father R. Lombardi's Better World Movement, he was probably also thinking of his studies in Constance: "It cannot be denied that we are in a period of 'spiritual' revival that we would have considered impossible in the rationalistic atmosphere of our youth."[43] On the other hand, Bea did not mention other aspects touched on by Dehn in any of his letters, and never even mentioned them in our own conversations.

The teachers were also confessionally mixed. For example, Bea's homeroom teacher, Dr. W. Martens, the history professor, was an Evangelical, while his wife was a practicing Catholic. Moreover, his children were also brought up as Catholics, a very unusual situation at that time for the family of a government employee who belonged to the Evangelical faith. In a letter many years later Bea observed that this fact had certainly not helped the professor's career.[44] More than fifty years later Bea wrote to one of the professor's daughters as follows: "I owe a great deal to your father both as teacher and as a man of

39. R 1967/19, p. 1; cf. also *Sasbacher*, p. 22.
40. Günther Dehn, *Die alte Zeit—Die vorigen Jahre* (2nd ed.: Munich, 1964).
41. *Ibid.*, pp. 38-39.
42. *Ibid.*, p. 39.
43. Nc 1956/26.
44. Cf. Nc 1955/18.

character."[45] Martens had communicated something of the love of history that was to remain with Bea throughout his life. Bea used to enjoy relating the following episode in connection with this teacher. When he entered Constance High School, Bea was given a supplementary history examination by the professor. The examiner asked the date of a certain event, and when the applicant gave his answer the examiner said he was wrong. However, the applicant persisted: "Maybe you have a different text book, sir, but the one we used in Sasbach gave this date." The teacher lost some of his sureness and accepted the reply. As we can see, Bea was no longer the shy little farmer's boy of Sasbach days.

Bea's fellow students also included Wendelin Rauch, who was Archbishop of Freiburg-im-Breisgau from 1948 to 1954, and Fridolin Amann, whom we shall have frequent occasion to meet again.[46] Bea's class also included Frederik, son of the then head master of the school, the Latin and German scholar, Dr. E. Böckel. The boy unfortunately had considerable difficulty with his father's subjects, so that the latter often found himself in the embarrassing position of trying desperately to drag the right answer from his son. Even in 1953 Bea still recalled the teacher's constant refrain: "But Frederik, you *must* know!"[47] The whole class naturally took advantage of the situation, knowing that the teacher could not punish Frederik's companions when *they* found themselves in a similar position.

Bea almost immediately started receiving excellent marks at this school too, and at the beginning of December, after a bare three months, his report card ended with the observation: "We can commend him most warmly as one of our most capable and hard-working students." From the end of April onward Bea was top of a class of twenty-four, and he eventually received the end-of-year prize. As in the case of the Sasbach report cards, however, we should note that this did not mean that he received the highest marks possible ("1" or "very good") in every subject, so that we find a "2" (= "good") in German, math and singing, while gymnastics was marked "2+" ("almost very good").

Apparently his fellow students also recognized Bea's supremacy, at least if we are to credit the much later words of one of them, Eugen Demoll, an Evangelical who chose a military career and reached the rank of Lieutenant-General. In 1953 he had "rediscovered" Bea with the help of Günther Dehn, and referring to Bea's "dizzying rise to the heights of the Vatican" he wrote to him as follows: "I think all your companions in the sixth form could already have foretold this for you."[48]

This is also the year that we first find Bea applying for and receiving a grant of two hundred marks, which the Council of the Grand-Duchy granted for educational purposes with the income of the Joachim Lutz Foundation. Thus we

45. N 1954/48; this positive opinion is shared by Dehn, *Die alte Zeit*, pp. 37-38.
46. Cf. Bea's autobiographical account in E. Schmidt, "Vom Schüler zum Lehrer," *St. Konradsblatt*, 44/1960, no. 13 of 27/3/1960, p. 303.
47. Cf. N 1953/21.
48. Cf. N 1953/55; also N 1953/21.

can see that financial problems were always with him. It was probably at this time that he also started to improve his situation by giving private lessons to younger students.

"I'm Going to Be a Jesuit"

Although his stay in Constance lasted only one year, before going on to the next period we must discuss an important decision he made in 1898: the choice of a religious vocation in the Society of Jesus. We cannot be sure whether the decision was made during his time in Constance, or if it came later during his summer vacation, or at the beginning of the new school year. We have very precise information on the fact itself and on certain details, but other details are unknown.

We shall first of all see the basic information given by the two chief figures, Bea and Fridolin Amann. Thanking his friend for his good wishes on his fiftieth anniversary in religious life, Bea wrote: "It was when I was on retreat in Feldkirch [in Austria] in 1898 that I decided to become a Jesuit."[49] In his letter Amann had written: "That morning hour when we were still absorbed by the effects of the retreat and told each other of our decision to become Jesuits etched itself extraordinarily deeply in my memory and has come back to me again and again in the course of the years."[50] A few years later Amann wrote Bea a letter that provides us with clearer information on the respective roles of the two men: "I recall very clearly that you surprised me after the first retreat in Feldkirch with your decisive declaration, 'I'm going to be a Jesuit.' The statement sounded so determined and persuasive that I at once replied: 'Me too.' "[51] Maybe this precise division of roles goes some way to explaining the fact that Amann was prevented from implementing his own decision—as he would often recall.[52]

Bea's decision did not occur out of the blue, as an entertaining episode in the summer of 1960 goes to show. After taking part in the International Eucharistic Congress in Munich, Bea, who was already a cardinal, made a solemn visit to his "dear Beuron," where he was welcomed at the entrance by Archabbot Benedikt Reetz, O.S.B., who began his greetings as follows: "I've heard that the young Augustin Bea often visited Beuron Abbey and that to start with he wanted to be a Benedictine, but that he found he did not have one of the qualities needed for such a vocation: a talent for singing. Later, he heard an abbot primate singing in Rome and observed: 'That's what I could have done!' " We would add that the reference is to Abbot von Stotzingen of the famous Einsiedeln Abbey. As is usually the case, the anecdote contains some truth. In the first place, it is a fact that Bea often made the pilgrimage to Beuron. In 1952 he wrote to his Benedictine friend Father

---

49. Nc 1952/3.
50. Nc 1952/2.
51. Nc 1960/57; cf. Nc 1959/51.
52. Cf. Nc 1952/2; Nc 1960/57.

Athanasius Miller, who was then Secretary of the Pontifical Biblical Commission and was staying at Beuron Abbey: "How I wish I could be in the beautiful monastery of Beuron today! When I was a student I so often prayed there, and—I may as well say it, although it may sound strange coming from a Jesuit—I left a part of my heart there. During your stay in Beuron, remember me once at the altar of Our Lady and tell her that I am the boy who came to her so often fifty or sixty years ago."[53] When speaking of his appointment as a member of the Pontifical Commission for the Reform of the Liturgy in the days of Pius XII, Bea said that it was at Beuron that he learned to love the liturgy.[54]

The background to the decision also includes a pilgrimage Bea and his friend Amann made to the marian shrine at Einsiedeln, which Bea mentioned when writing to Amann in 1951: "I still recall that pleasant (though not always devout) pilgrimage we made to Einsiedeln together, I think it was fifty-three years ago."[55] In explanation of the phrase "not always devout," Amann himself told me that at a certain point the two pilgrims were sitting outside the monastery and Amann said to his friend: "But what are we doing here? Didn't we come to pray?"

While Bea considered the Benedictine Order to start with, later on he thought about the Capuchins, for he was attracted by their missions to the people. However, the victory eventually went to the Society of Jesus, with the final push coming from his reading of the magazine published by the German Jesuits, *Stimmen der Zeit*.[56] The source of Bea's specific vocation is thus to be found in the work of the pen, in other words in study and writing.[57]

Four years would then pass between his decision and its implementation, and at this point we must wonder *how his parents felt* about their son's choice. We find an answer in a letter their son wrote them a number of years later, in January 1902, in the decisive period for the implementation of his vocation: "You know it is not the first time I have had to come to you with this thought. You gave me a negative reply on the previous occasion, and it was probably better in those circumstances."[58] If we remember Bea's statement that his mother never stood in the way of his religious vocation,[59] we can conclude that the negative reply

53. N 1952/161; cf. also Na 1959/455 ("Since childhood I have had links with the Benedictine Order through names such as Maria Einsiedeln and Beuron").

54. Cf. Nc 1955/19.

55. Nc 1951/1.

56. JI, p. 10, explains that in the years 1863-1873 the student house of the German Jesuits was located in what is today the Benedictine Abbey of Maria Laach. The house also held the offices of a magazine published by the German Jesuits, which thus bore the name *Stimmen aus Maria Laach*, although after the magazine moved to other offices, the name was changed to the present *Stimmen der Zeit* (or "Voices of the Time").

57. The details of the complicated story of Bea's religious vocation come partly from my own memories, but also from the evidence given by Father Max Zerwick, S.J., who worked with Bea at the Pontifical Biblical Institute in Rome for twelve years; this is found in *An unsere Freunde* (review of the southern German province of the Society of Jesus, with headquarters in Munich), 1960/2, p. 23; cf. also JI, p. 10.

58. Letter of 20 January 1902 which for certain reasons does not yet have a file number.

59. Cf. p. 28 above.

probably came mostly from his father, although a letter from Bea to his friend Amann indicates that his other relatives were also involved to some extent: "It was in 1898 . . . that I decided to become a Jesuit. However, it was only some years later that I could implement my decision, after the difficulties created by one of my uncles were eliminated with his death."[60]

High School Graduation at Another School

After barely a year, Bea was forced to change schools again. While he had left Sasbach of his own accord, outside circumstances forced him to leave Constance, for Konradi House was to be refurbished or restructured. If I remember correctly, I think that it was to be totally restored, which would of course have taken longer. Bea wrote about this break half a century later to his previously mentioned friend E. Demoll: "I have never been able to forget Constance. The year I spent there made the town and also the school very dear to me, and I felt more at home there than I did later on in Rastatt"[61]—the city where he continued his education and where he was given a place in a similar recently opened diocesan institution, whose boarders attended the public high school of the grand-duchy.

The atmosphere at the new school was similar to that of Constance, and was seen particularly in the way that Catholic authors were treated in literature classes. Bea recalled that when there was a free choice of subject the Catholic students would purposely choose the great Catholic writers and bravely defend this choice in the face of any criticism from their teachers.

We do not have much detailed information on this period, except for his report card, as for the two previous periods, and also his high school diploma. It is not surprising that after the change of school, his first report cards were less outstanding than the final one from Constance. At the end of the first semester in December 1898, apart from two subjects in which he received "good to very good" (German language and geography), the rest of the subjects were only marked "good" (or "2"), except for singing and gymnastics which received even lower marks, although we do not have his position in comparison with the other members of his class. However, the new student soon began to improve, and at the end of the school year he was given a "very good" in seven subjects and a "good" in only four, and his high school diploma in summer 1900 ended with the overall mark of "very good."

It is surprising that Bea never obtained "very good" in religion but only "good to very good," and he himself laid the responsibility for this roundly at the teacher's door: "He insisted that we learn and repeat his lessons by heart, and I was incapable of doing this, just as I still am today."[62]

---

60. Nc 1952/3.

61. N 1953/21.

62. N 1951/29; this was his normal way of explaining the matter. Dr. A. Grosskinsky, head master

He also received a "good" in two other subjects, gymnastics and singing, and in connection with the latter in a 1951 letter to a school-friend who had sent him a musical composition by his father, he wrote: "I found your late father's composition very interesting, but you must not ask me for any opinion. Despite their efforts, my teachers at Rastatt, and before that at Sasbach and Constance, were unable to awaken this muse within me."[63]

For this year too the files also contain papers concerning a study grant: on 18 April 1899, the treasury of the princely house of Fürstenberg informed the student Bea that "this year too" (1899/1900) the prince was so gracious as to grant him the sum of one hundred and fifty marks from the Elizabethan Foundation, which would be paid in two installments. The document ends with the observation: "The aforementioned sum must be returned if you later of your own free will decide to abandon your theology studies."

After graduation, the rector of the dormitory house, Dr. C. Holl, gave the student a note of recommendation to the ordinariate of the Archdiocese of Freiburg, which contained the following words: "Bea is a very talented and equally hard-working student. . . . Alongside these qualities, he has a balanced, calm, firm character so that one can rely on him in every respect. . . . I believe that Bea will be able to become an excellent priest one day."[64] The reference is all the more valuable in that it was the fruit of three years of observation, for Dr. Holl had been in charge of Konradi House in Constance for the year when our young subject was studying there, and when that institute was closed, he too moved to Restatt, again as rector.[65]

Theology Student

In the Buchmüller biography we find a reproduction of Bea's application for admission to the seminary of the Archdiocese of Freiburg. It is in Bea's own handwriting and was sent to the ordinariate of the archdiocese on 3 September 1900. At the foot of the page on the left, someone else has added—obviously after November 1959—*"Kurienkardinal"* (or "cardinal of the curia").[66] We would make a passing observation on the handwriting of the application: when it is compared with that of various later samples of Bea's writing, even those from his very last years, we can see how the writing he would retain until the end of his life was already basically formed at this young age.[67]

---

of Rastatt High School in 1961, gives the following variation: after visiting the grave of this teacher, the cardinal said that the reason was "that even then the student Bea dared uphold his own unusual ideas" (ArchWit).

63. N 1951/29.

64. W. Reinhard, "Kardinal Augustin Bea," *Der Christliche Sonntag.*

65. Cf. *Dates*, p. 2; JI, p. 10.

66. BM, p. 42.

67. This acute and accurate observation is made by A.M. Renner in *ibid.*, p. 54; for reproductions, see pp. 41-43, comparing with pp. 139, 167.

The reader may feel that if Bea wanted to be a Jesuit, this was surely the right moment to start moving in that direction, and I believe that the young man was of the same opinion. However, his father had once again insisted that his son should do one or two years of theology first, and Augustin had bowed to his father's wishes.

In the request, the applicant says that "on account of limited financial resources" he was forced to ask for a reduction in the cost of board and lodging. His circumstances are confirmed with a notably meticulous "certificate of penury" issued by Riedböhringen City Hall and signed by three different officials.[68] A last paper bears the parish priest's testimonial on the candidate's vocation,[69] a document in which Augustin is described as a young man with "magnificent talents," "tireless diligence" and "exemplary moral and religious behavior," so that he enjoys "corresponding respect and a very good reputation" in the whole town.

Bea was accepted, and found a number of his old friends from Sasbach among the forty-eight students.[70] When thinking back to his life in the college, he particularly remembered the "reviser," Father J. Schofer, who helped the budding theologians in their studies and whom he spoke of in a 1955 letter to his friend Amann as follows: "I now find the practical commonsense that the reviser Schofer passed on to us most useful in my work at the Holy Office."[71] Bea also particularly enjoyed remembering the small college chapel, where "I prayed and sang when I was a student," and which witnessed "quite a number of my struggles and worries over my vocation to the Society of Jesus."[72]

Among his teachers he was always pleased to remember Professor G. Hoberg, who was his professor for Old Testament exegesis.[73] Bea was Hoberg's favorite student, and the latter would have liked to make him his successor. In 1957 Bea wrote: "Hoberg would have liked to keep me in Freiburg, but my path led in another direction, in order to reach the same goal."[74] When Bea left to enter the Society of Jesus in spring 1902 and went to say goodbye, the professor asked in rallying tones: "But why the Jesuits? You can become a professor of exegesis here with us too." Bea replied: "That's not why I'm going to the Jesuits."

Another teacher whom Bea was always happy to talk about was Professor Xaver Kraus, an archeologist and art historian, who instilled in him a love for archeology, a subject Bea would be much involved with in later years.[75] At the end of the first semester, Bea and his class had an oral examination from Kraus

---

68. Cf. *ibid.*, pp. 46-47.
69. Cf. *ibid.*, pp. 44-45.
70. Cf. Nr 1959/26; N 1954/86.
71. Nc 1955/19; Joseph Schofer (1866/1930) played important roles in various different spheres, including that of the Catholic "Center Party"; cf. *LThK*, IX, 444.
72. N 1952/70; Nb 1953/96.
73. Gottfried Hoberg (1857/1924); cf. *LThK 1*, V, 397; among other things, he was at one time a consultant to the Pontifical Biblical Commission in Rome.
74. N 1957/44; cf. also *Sasbacher*, p. 24; Schmidt, "Vom Schüler zum Lehrer," p. 303.
75. Father Xaver Kraus (1840/1901); on this scholar, cf. *LThK*, VI, 596.

on the first ten centuries of church history. During the examination one of the students mentioned Dante's name, and Kraus, who also had an excellent knowledge of Dante, immediately asked if any of the students had read Dante. Bea, who had studied Italian and read a little Dante, said that *he* had. "Which is the best edition?" asked the professor, and when the student said he did not know, the professor told him that it was the Scartazzini edition and asked him to take it from the shelf and to read and translate a verse. After Bea had done so, the professor ended with an exhortation: "Always keep your love for the beautiful Italian tongue," and then turned to the next student: "Who were the victims of Septimius Severus' persecution?" *Our* student obviously expected to be asked some question on the history of the church in its first ten centuries, but it never came. A few days later he received a certificate (which is now found in the files), stating that he had passed the examination in church history with the mark "excellent, or better than excellent." It should be pointed out that "excellent" ("1") was the highest mark, but that the professor was apparently so satisfied that, good linguist that he was, he coined a new mark for this particular student.

Bea also recalled that when this same professor spoke about St. Francis of Assisi he described his humility with an imaginative phrase that was particularly apt in ecclesiastical circles: "Francis of Assisi had no ambition to show a flash of purple under his collar." Bea also said that it was common knowledge that Kraus was no admirer of the Jesuits, preferring St. Philip Neri, so that when they came to St. Ignatius of Loyola in his lessons, the professor would say: "We should now talk about Iñigo of Loyola, but you can find all you need to know about him in my book, so let's move on to Philip Neri."[76]

The certificates with Bea's marks for both semesters of the academic year 1900-1901 are found in the files: for the first semester he received "excellent" ("1") in all subjects, except for apologetics ("almost excellent"), while in the second he received "excellent" in every subject without exception and his diligence was praised.

As regards the respect Bea enjoyed among his fellow students,[77] we have words written by one of them, W. Rauch, when the latter was Archbishop of Freiburg.[78] It is found in a letter offering good wishes for Bea's fiftieth anniversary of religious life, and the personality of the writer and the tone of the letter rule out any suspicion that these were empty compliments—or, worse, syco-

---

76. Kraus died the year of that memorable examination. In 1957, his diaries started to appear in print, edited by H. Schiel. In April 1961, however, Fridolin Amann told his friend, now cardinal, the upsetting news that the Holy Office had asked the editor of the diaries to withdraw them quietly from circulation. For Amann this step was all the more painful because when he was head master of the Sasbach school the editor was "one of his most faithful students" (cf. Nc 1961/70). At this time Bea was not a member of the Holy Office, and I do not know whether he did anything to avoid the harm that this measure of the Holy Office could cause. However, I do know from private conversations that Bea felt that the diaries in question could be damaging to their author's reputation.

77. Various names of Bea's companions are found in KBL, p. 303.

78. Wendelin Rauch (1885-1954); cf. *LThK*, VIII, 1011.

phantic flattery. Apart from anything else, the letter ends by recalling the thought of the decisive moment of death. After thanking Bea for what he had personally meant to him, the archbishop broadened his perspective and expressed his gratitude for the good example that Bea, "continuing the influence you had on us young students," had given with his entry into the religious order and with his conduct in religious life. "I can still see you today, pacing very earnestly through our study room with measured steps; your face and your steps were in themselves teaching and admonition for us. In many ways we followed this example, even though we were not always explicitly conscious of the fact. And surely influence that does not need to become explicitly conscious, but that attracts through its inner force alone, is the best kind."[79]

In *The Dates of My Life* Bea notes that on 8 December 1900 he was received into the marian congregation of theology students, a fact he recalled with particular joy and fondness. He would also relate how at the beginning of the next academic year, the members of the marian group made an effort to help the new arrivals and also to win new members for their congregation.

Religious Vocation: Struggle and Victory

In his 1947 retreat notes, Father Bea wrote as follows while meditating on the calling of the apostles: "The Savior prepared my vocation over a long period too: from the first little altar at home to the 'Follow me' in Tisis in 1898 and Freiburg in 1902."[80] Augustin found important help during this long preparation in a young priest named Peter Huber, who was assistant priest at Riedböhringen, and Bea used to mention him repeatedly in his correspondence fifty years later. Thus in 1952, while the celebrations to mark the fortieth anniversary of his ordination to the priesthood were being organized, he wrote to the parish priest of Riedböhringen: "I should be very happy if Father Huber could participate. At the time that my entry into the Society of Jesus was being discussed, he was a faithful support and help to me."[81] We can imagine the kind of priest he was from a letter he wrote in 1952, at the age of seventy-eight, saying that he was happy to have worked for over fifty years in a Catholic country parish.[82] At about the same time, Bea expressed his joy at "rediscovering" him after so many years, and added: "It is so long ago that you as a young priest and I as a theology student went for walks together. . . . Yet I have not forgotten that time, nor have I forgotten what you did for me then with your help and advice. I think that God has a special reward in store for you for that."[83]

In January 1902 there came new incentive to be done with delays. In the precious little notebook entitled *The Dates of My Life*, Bea noted: "1902, 3-6 January: retreat preached by Father Kollmann, S.J. Decision to enter the

---

79. N 1952/71.
80. Med. IV/4 (ms.).
81. N 1952/106.
82. Cf. N 1952/150.
83. N 1951/47.

Society." In order to eliminate a maybe obvious suspicion, we would at once add that in a letter dated 7 February 1902 Bea stated that he had indeed discussed the subject with the retreat director, but that the latter "said neither yes nor no" and did not try to influence him in any way.

In the very personal part of Bea's files there is an envelope marked "Choice of vocation and entry" (into the Society of Jesus), which contains letters referring to the steps taken in contacting the superiors of the order he had chosen. However, the most precious items of all are the correspondence on the subject with his parents. His parents' letters, but particularly Bea's, are real gems, and it would be extremely interesting to publish the complete correspondence one day, for it allows us to follow very closely the series of events and vicissitudes. Despite the considerable speed with which everything took place, there were quite a number of crises and painful surprises. About three weeks passed between the first announcement to his parents of the decision he had made during the retreat and their definitive consent. We shall try to present the sequence of events, giving a brief summary of the various letters.

As the only son of poor parents, wanting to join an order that had been banned from Germany for about thirty years, Bea was well aware of the major obstacles standing in the way of his vocation. He admitted to himself the enormous suffering he would cause his parents when he announced this choice to them and asked their consent. Two weeks passed between the retreat and the letter to his parents, two weeks that must have been filled with anxious reflection on his part as to how he was to tell them the painful news. The outcome was a letter dated 20 January, which covers twelve small but tightly-packed pages. Bea listed all the difficulties connected with the vocation he had chosen: the general difficulties of living according to the three religious vows, and the more particular difficulties of life in the Society of Jesus, especially as regards the vow of obedience. There was also the question of his entering the most hated and persecuted of orders, which would mean that he would have to live in exile. He added that the purpose of listing the various difficulties in this way was to show what serious and detailed consideration he had given to his choice and the problems entailed, and also said that this list of difficulties had been hidden in his desk for two years. Well then, he asked, why did he accept all this? His reply: "Simply in order to follow what I believe is the Lord's will for me."

As concerned his filial duties and his responsibility for his parents' future, he first of all exhorted them to trust in God's fatherly providence, but also revealed a considerable grasp of practical reality, quoting figures to show that his parents could live without his support, and wound up with the following assurance: "And if the very worst should occur, I know from a reliable source that the order itself would contribute to your keep."

In order to illustrate the religious motives that guided his reflection and his choice, he enclosed a copy he had made of the letter that St. John Berchmans had sent to his own parents explaining his choice of the religious life. Bea added: "I ratify this letter word for word."

He assured his parents that he had written the letter with a trembling hand,

and concluded by asking them to talk things over with their parish priest, who was worthy of all their trust, and above all to pray a great deal.

The reply was not long in coming and seemed a fairly positive start. His father replied on 23 January: "Having asked the advice of the parish priest, we are not opposed to your intentions. However, we give our consent without great joy, and indeed with deep sorrow; we must bow before God's will." Nevertheless, he then begged his son to consider the matter again, since it involved a difficult vocation and meant taking on heavy duties for the whole of his life. For her part, his mother added: "I too went to see the parish priest about this matter, and he gave me strength; before going to see him I went to church, for God is the best counselor."

Bea replied the next day, thanking his parents for their consent, saying that they had "pronounced a word I have been awaiting for years," and adding that his joy was mixed with bitterness since he knew how much the word must have cost them.

In the meantime his parents had written to the faithful assistant parish priest Peter Huber to tell him of their son's decision. Father Huber replied on 31 January, encouraging them to accept the Lord's will fully.

After receiving his parents' positive reply, young Bea set about things in a way that showed that he already possessed the energy that we shall find later on in his life. He wrote first to the novice master of the order, Father J.B. Müller, to obtain information and advice (the letter has not survived), and Müller replied on 2 February, telling him not to get upset over difficulties with his parents and giving him information on the practical possibilities of entering the order. It was probably on the basis of this letter that Bea wrote to the relevant provincial superior of the order on 4 February, asking to have the examination or interview with four members of the order (required as a condition for admission) on 11 February in Switzerland.

On the same day, 4 February, Bea joyfully wrote to tell his parents that the novice master at Feldkirch had said he should be able to enter the novitiate immediately after the Easter vacation. He also quoted a lengthy passage from Father Müller's letter, recognizing the great sacrifice asked of his parents, but saying that it would be a source of divine blessings for them and would gain them an eternal reward.

This letter unleashed the storm. When his parents gave their consent, they probably imagined that the decision would be implemented in the more distant future, whereas events seemed to be occurring with great rapidity. Until now it had always been Bea's father who replied while his mother simply added a postscript at the end, but this time his mother wrote on her own on 6 February,[84] telling him that his father was in deepest depression and desolation in his suffering and sorrow, and saying that his heart "weighed a ton." She feared his father would fall ill, as his strength was waning by the hour. The whole matter could not even be mentioned to him, and although he was not withdrawing his consent, he was in a state close to collapse. The letter finishes with the words: "My child, have pity."

---

84. The letter is dated 6 January, but someone else has written "February" above the date, and indeed 6 January was not possible if the storm mentioned in the letter had already broken out, since their son had not told them about his fresh decision until 20 January.

Her son replied the following day with a letter of eight tightly-packed pages. "I received the letter in which you beg me to abandon my intentions. . . . First of all I went to our Savior in the tabernacle and begged him for comfort and help." He agreed that the whole matter was so serious and important that it required further reflection, and this, he wrote, was also the purpose of the interview or examination he was to have with four representatives of the order. "I shall explain the whole situation to them as clearly and frankly as possible, and shall give them your letters to read. . . . However, first of all I shall pray very earnestly and have others pray too, and you too must pray that everything will be done according to God's will."

The letter continues by stating that the idea of the order was not suggested to him by others. Only a few people had been told and *they* had tried to dissuade him. The parish priest of Riedböhringen, Father Geisser, who knew of his intentions, had advised him to wait until the end of his studies.

In a clear, energetic style remarkable in a young man of twenty-one, Bea addressed his father directly, writing: "My dear Father, you gave me your consent. *I return it to you,* for it was hasty and unconsidered. . . . Until you can make the sacrifice fully and totally, I cannot say that I have my parents' agreement, and thus I cannot be received into the order. . . . I have only one weapon now . . . : *prayer.*" He said that he was sure that God, who sees into all hearts, "will certainly not want your hearts to break with anxiety, but will . . . strengthen and console your hearts and spirits to such an extent that you will be able to make even the greatest sacrifice with ease. . . . You must not reply at once, saying that you give me your permission *anew.* No! Give the question serious, mature reflection; seek advice once again from your parish priest or from those of neighboring parishes. . . . Then tell me all your reasons, without exception. . . . In the meantime, *no anxiety or worry, but only trust in God and prayer.*"

In point of fact, the storm passed faster than could have been foreseen. His father wrote back on 10 February saying that he had twice been to seek the advice of the parish priest of Stockingen, who had given him such comfort and illumination that he was now able to send his son "a few words of consolation. . . . In accordance with God's wise decision I do not wish to stand in the way of your intention. . . . It is God's will, and I cannot oppose it. . . . It is in God alone that we find our salvation." In her postscript his mother employed similar expressions to convey her acceptance of God's will, and remarked: "You can thank the Almighty every day that in the crucial hour he led Father back onto the right path. . . . "

Bea wrote a letter of gratitude on 13 February: "When I read your letter, my joy was complete. The vocation examination went well, so far as I could judge, and now the last barrier has fallen that could still have hindered my entry. Nonetheless, a drop of bitterness did fall into the cup of joy: the thought of how heavy the sacrifice must have lain on your hearts."

The next day, his father confirmed that his consent was irrevocable, and in her postscript his mother showed her sensitivity when she told him: "You can look forward to your vacation, for no one will have any angry words for you."

We felt it was important to give ample coverage of this interesting episode, since it reveals a number of things. It shows his parents' characters, and particularly their deep religious sense. On the other hand, their son's struggle reveals many facets of his character, but especially the high degree of human and spiritual maturity he had reached.

After his parents' consent, Bea still needed his archbishop's permission, for when he entered the theological college—and with a reduction in the fees—he had started on the path to becoming a priest in the service of the archdiocese. In a 1957 letter thanking the then Archbishop of Freiburg, W. Rauch, for his good wishes on his fiftieth anniversary of religious life, Bea wrote: "When Father Freidhoff, the principal [of the college], asked your predecessor, Archbishop Thomas, to allow me to go to the Jesuits, the Archbishop replied: 'Very well, let us allow him to go. However, I hope that for every priest who joins a religious order God will send me three hard-working secular priests.' "[85] Bea added: "I do not know whether the three actually came. But in any case, I have always remained in close contact with the archdiocese. . . . Entering the order also meant leaving the archdiocese, and that was indeed a sacrifice. I owed it a great deal and would have been glad to have paid off my debt of gratitude with my work. However, I believed I had to follow God's call. . . . "[86]

From a letter of 23 February to his parents we learn that he still had a series of examinations to take, so that he would not reach home until 3 or 4 March. In the same letter he told them that the provincial superior had said he could enter the novitiate on 7 April, "the Monday following the first Sunday after Easter." He concluded: "I shall therefore be able to stay even longer than four weeks, and I hope that with God's help everything will go well."

During his vacation the provincial's assistant wrote to him on 7 March to say that his entry had been postponed for two days, adding: "May this be a day of great joy for you." In reply to a letter he had written to Father J.B. Müller (it will be recalled that he was novice master at Feldkirch), the latter wrote to him on 3 April, adding above all words of religious comfort for his parents and asking him to tell them that he was more than glad to be at their disposition if they ever wished to ask him for information or anything else. "Through their son's entry, they too are now in closer relation with us."

Father E. Thill, who was to become his novice master, wrote to him in similar terms on 1 April, and also told him that he had no objection to Bea's entering on 8 April, as was his wish.

---

85. N 1952/71.
86. *Ibid.*

CHAPTER 2

A LONG, EXACTING SPIRITUAL AND INTELLECTUAL FORMATION

(1902–1914)

Ever since St. Ignatius of Loyola founded the Society of Jesus, its members have been obliged to undergo a long period of testing and formation. In contrast with almost all the other regular orders of the time, the novitiate was given for two whole years, during which the candidate was to receive his religious and spiritual formation. This was also the first step for Augustin. After this period, members who were to become priests did three years of philosophical studies and four years of theology, although these seven years would be broken by a few years of teaching in a boys' school. Bea did his three years of philosophy normally, and then spent about three years as a teacher of Latin, Greek and various other subjects at Sittard School in Holland. His theological studies were shortened by a year in view of the two years he had already done at the Freiburg theological faculty before entering the order. The spiritual formation imparted during the novitiate, and also of course cultivated throughout his studies, was completed in very typical style at the end of his studies with another extended period of further training lasting about ten months.

Yet all this was not enough. Those whom the order intended entrusting with teaching in boys' schools, or in the student houses created for its young members, then received further training for this work with more specialized studies. Thus Bea was first sent to Innsbruck University to study the classics, although these studies were interrupted after the first semester. A few years later he was sent to Berlin University to study ancient oriental languages for the same purpose, since it was planned that he should teach holy scripture in the order's theologate. However, these studies were also broken off after one semester. Over a period of twelve years the young man therefore received the complete religious and intellectual training usual in the order, whereas his specialized studies and training had barely begun.

The Novitiate

We are able to follow Bea's farewell to his parents, which was so painful for them, from a pencil-written letter their son wrote on 7 April in the train he took from Donaueschingen to Freiburg (he excuses the bad handwriting caused by the jolting of the train[1]): "The painful hour of departure is now behind us, and,

---

1. Cf. p. 3r. Bea wrote on sheets torn from a notebook, and since the sheet and not the sides are

47

trusting in God, we must look serenely to the future" (p. 1v). Most of the letter is concerned with comforting his parents, and we repeatedly find such words as: "Weep no more, . . . rather, give thanks to the Lord for showing such great grace both to you and to me" (pp. 2r, 2v); "Let us seek comfort by looking up to heaven and to our Mother, Our Lady of Sorrows" (p. 3v). This latter theme is also found in the above-mentioned letter from Father J.B. Müller.

He wrote that he would probably spend the night in Heidelberg (p. 3r), after which his journey continued to Cologne. He recalled this stop sixty years later, for in the manuscript of the public talk he gave in Cologne in March 1964 at the close of "Brotherhood Week," we find the following addition in his own handwriting: "I have always loved Cologne, which has been important to me ever since I first set foot there in spring 1902."[2] En route, he also found time to make a pilgrimage to the famous shrine of Our Lady at Kevelaer, near the Dutch border, before finally reaching the novitiate, which at that time was at Blijenbeek in Holland.[3]

In all orders and religious congregations, the novitiate serves the purpose of introducing the candidate to the various aspects of life in the relative community. In the case of the Jesuits, the novitiate lasts two years, preceded by a brief introduction given in the course of a "candidature" lasting a few weeks. The candidate is still dressed in ordinary lay clothes during this initial period and does not receive the religious habit until he has completed it. Bea's candidature lasted from 9 to 27 April, as he notes in *Dates*, which is particularly detailed during this period. Thus he received the habit on the feast of St. Peter Canisius, Doctor of the Church, who is known as "the second apostle of Germany."

Apart from the progressive explanation of the spirit of the order and its constitutions and rules, the accent during the novitiate is placed on a series of "experiments" or trials. One of these is the "pilgrimage," which is a journey of variable length undertaken by the novices in groups of two or three, on foot and without money, during which they must beg for their board and lodging, so that the trip entails some sacrifice and humiliation; the purpose is to test the spiritual progress made by the novice. Another of these experiments could be to help in a hospital for a month without pay. However, the most important of these experiments is the "Great Retreat," which is the Spiritual Exercises of St. Ignatius in their complete form and lasts about one month. Bea made it a little over seven months after his entry, starting on 24 November and finishing on Christmas Eve. Remaining within the limits fixed for this biography, we shall not go into the details of the young novice's spiritual development. Moreover, there is a further reason for following this line here, in the fact that the young Bea's spiritual development did not draw its deepest inspiration from these exercises but, as we shall see below, from other sources.

numbered, we indicate the number of the sheet, adding "r" (= *recto* or front) or "v" (= *verso* or back).

2. R 1964/13, p. 1.

3. Bea's German passport is found in the files. It was issued on 3 April 1902 for his journey to Holland and was valid until 1 October 1904.

We shall, however, explain at once why this retreat, which is normally decisive for the spiritual life of a novice, did not have this effect on Bea. The reason lay with the novice master, whose character and style were one of the major difficulties the novice encountered. Half a century later—and thus surely after enough time had elapsed—Bea wrote about him to Father L. Esch, who had been in the novitiate with him: "It would seem that we, the last survivors of Blijenbeek, were a pretty hardy generation, despite our good novice master Thill, who gave me plenty to put up with during the novitiate."[4] Father Esch, who was the famous apostle of the Catholic organization "New Germany" between the two world wars, replied: "The good novice master Thill gave the others plenty to put up with too."[5] In Bea's case, the novice master's manner and behavior had a more specific source in his concern that the young man might be proud of his two years at a German university. And Bea did in fact explain his novice master's behavior as follows: "Of course I already had my high school diploma and had even studied at a German university."[6] We should note that, since the order had its own student houses, it very seldom sent members to study in public universities. This concern meant that the novice master tried to give the novice practice in humility, although in such a way that the intelligent novice soon caught on and took care to behave in such a way that the exercise lost a great deal of its point and thus its efficacity.

An example of the severity practiced at that time can be seen in the fact that when Bea's parents asked to have a photograph of their son in his Jesuit habit, it was necessary to go as far as the provincial superior for permission to have the photograph taken.[7] Obviously, the danger of vanity had to be taken into account!

The following episode shows that the novice master's suspicions on Bea's possible temptation to pride did have some foundation, albeit slight. Meetings were periodically held in the novitiate at which the novice master would ask all the novices to state the defects they had observed in one or other of their companions. When it was Bea's turn, one of the novices said: "Carissimus [the title given to novices] is sometimes ironic." The novice master then said to Bea: "Carissime, it would be better to be irenic."[8]

During the second year of his novitiate, "on 22 May, Friday in the novena of Pentecost," as Bea noted, there was a fire in the novitiate that destroyed the dormitories. After the Jesuits had been expelled from Germany, the novitiate had been lodged in the castle of Count Hoensbroech, with the dormitories arranged in wooden cabins. Bea was amused to describe the novices' behavior

---

4. N 1952/90.

5. *Ibid.*

6. *Ibid.*

7. Probably the photograph published in BM, p. 60.

8. Who could have foreseen that half a century later the word "irenicism" together with the expression "false irenicism" would play such an important role in ecumenism, and thus in Bea's life? First the well-known *Instruction of the Holy Office on the Ecumenical Movement* (1949) (to which Bea had contributed as consultant), and then the conciliar *Decree on Ecumenism* (no. 11) both warned against "false irenicism." For the instruction, cf. *AAS*, XLII (1950), 142-147.

during this crisis. The fire took place in the early afternoon when the novices were all together in the living room, occupied in spiritual reading. When someone opened the door and shouted: "Our dormitories are burning!" the head of the novices, L. Esch, replied in Latin, the novices' official language: "Nos habemus lectionem *De Imitatione Christi*."[9] None of the novices moved until the Jesuit who was assistant to the novice master arrived, shouting: "What are you doing? Go and help put out the fire!" Only after this intervention on the part of authority did the novices move, but by then it was too late and there was nothing to be done. After this incident, a new solution was sought, and a few months later the novitiate was transferred to the town of Exaeten.

Shortly after the fire, Bea had to pass the second test: together with a novice called Jungbluth he made the "pilgrimage" on foot. The journey lasted about three weeks, and we read in *Dates* that they visited the towns of "Telgte, Münster, etc." It is interesting to note that about two months later *Dates* also gives the precise date of Pope Pius X's election and coronation.

The Decisive Influence of a Man of God

His spiritual exercises for this second year as a novice (3 to 12 September) were preached by Father W. Eberschweiler. Although he was still a novice, Bea left the community of the novitiate immediately after these exercises and moved to the juniorate, which was for young religious who had already received a certain formation and might have taken their first vows. They devoted themselves above all to the study of homiletics and the classical languages they would need in their future studies. The move was particularly important for Bea since in the new community he found the above-mentioned Father Eberschweiler as spiritual director, which had a decisive influence on the whole future orientation of his spiritual life. In a letter written over fifty years later, Bea spoke of the "rather brusque manner" of the novice master, comparing it with Eberschweiler's "kindness, charity and supernatural spirit."[10]

Bea wrote about this man of God and his meeting with him in a letter to Father L. Esch: "But I still remember well the relief I felt when I first spoke with the good Father Eberschweiler."[11] He explained the reason for this reaction in a letter from the same period written to Father P. Krumscheid, S.J., vice-postulator of the cause for Father Eberschweiler's beatification: "I had Father Eberschweiler as my spiritual father from 1903 to 1904 during my juniorate in Exaeten, and he left an indelible impression on me. After the rather brusque manner of our novice master Father J.E. Thill, his kindness, charity and supernatural spirit struck me even during my first conversation with him. At that time—i.e. over fifty years ago—we *juniores* already considered him a saint, and there was talk of his visions and levitation. This was all spoken of very seriously

---

9. "We have the reading of *The Imitation of Christ*."

10. N 1951/78.

11. N 1952/90.

and with great veneration for him. His love for 'the Father' was proverbial. Of course, we young fellows did not always grasp his elevated spirituality; yet we were deeply impressed by the knowledge that it was a 'reality' for him, 'facts' as he often said."[12]

The references to spirituality would appear to be the most important elements in these observations. Naturally, holiness and its more exceptional symptoms made an impression, but we should point out that Bea spoke of his kindness and charity, of his lively faith in supernatural realities, and of his love for the heavenly Father—all traits of Father Eberschweiler's spiritual character as seen in his biography.[13] These features were certainly new at that time and in those circles, which tended to be dominated by the so-called "school" of Father M. Meschler, S.J.,[14] who emphasized the ascetical life and the practice of the virtues, whereas Eberschweiler's life was very deeply rooted in the theology and spirituality of the New Testament, particularly St. Paul.[15] It took time for this new spirit to become established, especially since Father Eberschweiler had great difficulty in expressing himself and getting others to understand his thought, a fact that caused him great suffering. This explains Bea's remark to the effect that the young men did not always understand Father Eberschweiler's "elevated spirituality." Later on, the biblical movement would also considerably help the development of this type of spirituality.[16]

On the basis of the above, as well as a large number of private conversations with Bea, I think it is fair to say that Father Eberschweiler's spiritual direction and the two courses of exercises that Bea made under his direction (see below) were decisive for Bea's spiritual orientation.

In the light of all this, it is easy to understand why, fifty years later, Bea did not hesitate to advise people in need to invoke the intercession of Father Eberschweiler. In 1956, he wrote to a cousin of his who was suffering from major problems with her health: "I enclose a small picture of our Father Eberschweiler, who died in the odor of sanctity and whose cause for beatification has already been presented. Numerous prayers (hundreds!) have been answered. . . . The venerable Servant of God has already helped many people, so why should he not help the cousin of his former spiritual child too?!"[17] Later

---

12. N 1951/78.

13. W. Eberschweiler (1837-1921); cf. *LThK*, III, 633, with an ample bibliography.

14. M. Meschler (1830-1912); cf. *EncCatt*, VIII, 751-752, and *LThK*, VII, 316, which lists his main works, which have been republished many times.

15. Cf. the article on Eberschweiler in *Dictionnaire de Spiritualité ascétique et mystique*, IV, 31-32. We would not wish our comparison of Eberschweiler's spirituality with that of Meschler to be misunderstood, for we certainly do not undervalue the vast work and influence of Meschler and his school. We simply wish to highlight the positive aspects and special originality of the gifts the Lord had given to Father Eberschweiler.

16. The article cited in the previous note gives a summary of the special spirituality of this priest, noting in particular that he was maybe the only person who spoke so clearly of joy at this time (1870-1880), and that as early as 1863 he formulated the intention of serving the Lord in joy (*ibid.*, p. 31). Bea was probably also very sensitive to this specific aspect of his spiritual director's spirituality.

17. N 1956/153.

on, Bea accepted the role of *cardinal ponens* (or proposer of the cause) in the cause for the beatification of his former spiritual director.

A little over two years after his entry, on "17 April, the second Sunday after Easter" as we read in *Dates*, Bea made his "first vows," as they are called in the order. These are the three religious vows of poverty, chastity and obedience, and although juridically speaking they are "simple" rather than "solemn" vows, they do nevertheless signify perpetual consecration to the Lord on the part of the religious.

Next came four more months of classical and homiletic studies, and in August Bea made his eight-day annual retreat, which was also preached by Father Eberschweiler. A few days later, on 14 August, he received minor orders from Bishop Drehmanns of Roermond in Holland.[18]

This period ended with two and a half weeks in the Lippspringe Sanatorium, a phenomenon we shall meet with several times during Bea's youth. The reason was obviously not some simple cold, but a resurgence of the lung complaint he had had in his childhood and which was to cause him further problems on a number of occasions.

The Path to the Priesthood

About two and a half years after his entry, Bea began what was then the normal course of formation in the Society of Jesus: philosophy studies, then a few years of practical teaching work in one of the order's schools, and finally theological studies, with ordination to the priesthood and a special final examination covering both philosophy and theology. For some Jesuits—as was the case for Bea—various other specialized studies are incorporated into this framework, but we shall speak of these later.

1. *Philosophy studies* covered a period of three years (1904-1907) and were done in the order's student house in the little town of Valkenburg near Maastricht in Holland. The sources do not give us much information concerning this period, and even *Dates* tells us very little. The latter notebook says that Bea arrived there on 18 September, gives the dates of the yearly exercises, together with the name of the director, and notes various changes in the hierarchy of the house and the religious province. Thus we learn in connection with the last point that Bea's former novice master, Father J.E. Thill, was made provincial superior on 1 January 1907. Finally, we read that Bea was "beadle" during the academic year 1906-1907; in other words, he was in charge of good order and of maintaining contacts with superiors.

It is surprising to find that the usual information does not include anything concerning problems with his health during this period, although he in fact suffered from a tubercular relapse and had to stay in the above-mentioned Lippspringe Sanatorium for a fairly long period (over a month). In a letter that Bea wrote to a

---

18. According to liturgical usage at that time, these were the orders of ostiary, lector, exorcist and acolyte.

relative in 1959, he mentioned the sickness he had suffered and survived in his infancy, and added: " . . . and I have survived two further tubercular attacks."[19] Now one of these occurred in 1913, as we shall see below, but it is difficult to ascertain the date of the other. I clearly remember that Bea told me several times that during his philosophy studies he was admitted to the Lippspringe Sanatorium for a fairly long period—so long, indeed, that he felt called on to complain to his superior that he was wasting time unnecessarily, to which he received the brusque reply: "That's none of your business. Stay there until further orders."

2. Having passed his philosophy examination, Bea went to *St. Louis High School at Sittard* near Maastricht in Holland at the beginning of July 1907. The task entrusted to him was not that of "prefect of discipline," but that of teacher. As he himself recalled later, he taught Latin, Greek, German and math.[20] In *Dates* he noted that during the first year he was home-room teacher for the fourth grade, and during the following two years (1908/1909 and 1909/1910) for the fifth grade.[21] His apparent promotion from the fourth to the fifth grade was in fact due to the need to resolve a problematic situation. The fifth grade was a very rowdy class, and the father who had been in charge for the previous year had been unable to keep order, so that the boys did as they pleased. It goes to show the value Bea's superiors placed on his firmness of character that they entrusted him with such a difficult class. Bea related how he started that year with a succinct announcement that went somewhat as follows: "I know you, and you know me. I shall be the kind of teacher you want: it depends entirely on you and your behavior. And now let's start translating our text" (I do not remember what the text in question was). After a short time, one of the ringleaders started acting up. Bea reacted coldly, observing: "Apparently you want to be the first to be sent to the vice-rector" (which at that time and in that school meant several resounding blows on the palms of both hands). The boy paid no attention to the warning, and did therefore become the first to experience the young teacher's severity. When he returned to the room with bright red marks on his palms, he tried to put a brave smile on it, but the class got the message, and from then on there were no further problems with discipline.

Another example involved a boy from an aristocratic family whom Bea reproved for his laziness, asking him how he would manage later in life if he learned nothing now. The boy replied: "I'm the chief heir of a noble family." To which Bea at once rejoined: "So that gives you the right to stay ignorant!"

Although these two examples may be interesting, taken alone they could give us a distorted picture of *Bea as teacher*, and in any case they are certainly not able to give us a full enough view. However, this is made up for by some surprising personal notes from Bea. There is a folder bearing the title *Interna* (Latin for "personal matters") in the files. It contains a few yellowed pages

---

19. Nb 1956/390.

20. Cf. Nc 1958/33.

21. As regards the titles of the various grades, it should be noted that the system in use at that school (and generally in Germany at the time) was different from the American and British systems. Suffice it to say that high school or secondary education lasted nine years.

headed "Daily schedule for a good religious" and is dated 1908. However, the author also noted the years when he revised the text: 1909, 1911 and 1912. Apart from a whole series of resolutions for the spiritual and religious life, it gives a list of principles to be followed in teaching. I think it is worth quoting the section concerning this latter point:

"At school I shall not be a tyrant, but a teacher who follows Jesus' patient, mild example. I shall keep meticulously to good order and demand the same from the pupils. I shall examine them thoroughly and carefully check everything I have given them to learn. However, I shall not be short-tempered or impatient; when I have to reprimand them I shall not use offensive language; I shall not be hasty in punishing, but shall punish in such a way that they understand that I am moved by charity and am doing it for their own good. I shall not speak of the faults and defects of my pupils during recreation, and shall do so on other occasions only if there is a valid reason. I shall prepare my lessons with the greatest care, leaving aside every other occupation. ([Note in the margin:] I shall strive to use the best teaching method and to be fully conversant with the subject to be taught.) In all things I shall show that I seek nothing other than the temporal well-being and the eternal salvation of the pupils. I shall never speak of them harshly and angrily, nor as though I felt teaching was a burden. Rather, I shall speak of them calmly and with due respect."

Obviously these "rules" must be understood and assessed in the context of the country and the people among which they had their origin, as well as the situation for which they were written and the teaching methods prevalent at the time. A few remarks will suffice here. At that time, the era of human rights was still far in the future, and no one had so much as dreamed of "children's rights." As concerns teaching methods, people used to say—half jokingly, but half seriously—that a teacher's task was that of making his pupils suffer.

We have no means of knowing to what extent these "rules" reflect their author's awareness of possible dangers innate in his own character and to what extent they constitute a positive reaction to events and forms of behavior observed around him, but both aspects are most probably reflected in these pages. In any case, the "schedule" speaks well of its author.

We also have the words of one of Bea's students, written fifty years after having Bea as his teacher: "For us boys, Father Bea was always one of the most outstanding priests, and one to whom we were most attached, although he was basically strict. . . . So we boys always thought that Father Bea . . . would become a major figure." [22]

We do not know how many hours a week Bea taught, but the degree to which teaching absorbed his energies is revealed in something he wrote later on which is also interesting for other reasons as well. In 1958, when writing to his friend Amann to tell him about his article "Biblical Modernism according to the Encyclical *Pascendi*"[23] which was about to appear in print, he remarked: "The

22. Letter of K. Lucas, Na 17/427.
23. Cf. Biblio. 120.

whole modernist question touched me very little at the time. From 1907 to 1910 I was in Sittard, teaching Latin, Greek, German and mathematics (!), and therefore had no time to spare for theological questions of this kind."[24]

His *health* gave him some difficulties during this period too, for he had to have his appendix removed in March 1910 at the end of his third year of teaching. The operation was performed in a hospital in Aachen; it is interesting that Bea also noted the name of the surgeon in *Dates*.[25] Two weeks later he left the hospital, and a few days later went to Innsbruck University to study classical philology. We shall give further details of these studies in due course.

3. At the beginning of September we find Bea back in the Valkenburg student house, where he was to begin his *theology studies*. These studies normally lasted four years, but since Bea had already done three semesters of theology at Freiburg University, this was reduced to two and a half years. Apart from this, the information given in *Dates* is meager for this period too. Certain details of life in the religious community are noted, along with the date of the examination for the first part of moral theology and of a public debate on the sacrament of confirmation, in which Bea apparently played a leading role. On 30 April 1911 Bea received the sub-diaconate, and the next day was ordained deacon by the same Bishop Drehmanns of Roermond who had given him his minor orders.[26]

As had happened during his philosophy studies, for the academic year 1911-1912 Bea was again beadle—this time, of course, for the community of theology students. We have several authenticated details of his time in office which reveal both his shrewdness and his courage. The beadle's task also included that of defending "rights" that the students had acquired by custom and tradition, as well as that of obtaining the occasional legitimate minor relief for his companions.

The first incident of interest is linked to the weather in Holland, and particularly in the region where the student house was situated, which is known for its long, dreary periods of cloud and fog. After one such period, a fine day at last arrived, and Bea thought it reasonable to ask the rector of the college for an afternoon's walk as a special favor. The rector refused for reasons that tell us something about his personality: "No, otherwise you'll note it in the diary, and next year your successor will come and ask for it again on the basis of 'custom and tradition.' " Surprised and a little irritated, Bea retorted: "Father Rector, if you go on this way, you can't be surprised if the students are fed up." "Are the students disgruntled?" asked the rector calmly: "Sit down, and tell me why." Bea leapt at the opportunity and gave a detailed account of all the students' complaints, lasting three-quarters of an hour. Having listened very calmly, the rector concluded: "Thank you for telling me all this. In fact, you should have told me long ago. But for the walk the answer's still no." And Bea replied: "I didn't expect anything else."

After his ordination to the diaconate, Bea was occasionally sent out to act as deacon in church services elsewhere, especially during Lent and the Easter season,

24. Nc 1958/33.
25. Cf. also Nb 1952/38.
26. The original certificates are found in the files.

and on these occasions the vice-beadle stood in for him. At that time, the students of the order normally had to use Latin in any correspondence with their confreres, whether students or priests. However, on major feast-days they were allowed to use German for a few days. During Bea's absence the vice-beadle therefore went to see the rector, saying that according to tradition they could write their letters in German for the two weeks after Easter. The rector's reply was that it was too long and that one week was quite enough. All the poor vice-beadle's reasoning was to no avail, until his last attempt: "But, Father, the students will say that the vice-beadle is incapable of obtaining even what we have always had." Since it was a question of assuring respect for authority, albeit only that of a vice-beadle, the rector gave way. When Bea learned of the incident, he thought hard over how to manage for the next occasion, the feast of Pentecost. Finally he went to the rector and said: "Father, until now we've always been allowed to write letters in German for one week following Pentecost. I think four days would be enough." "Yes," replied the rector, "you're right, four days are quite enough."

Toward the end of the academic year the rector was to be changed. Although these changes were arranged in great secrecy at that time, the beadle had realized what was in the air from various signs, and he startled the minister (the rector's chief assistant) by asking "When is the rector going to change?" Caught by surprise, the minister was unable to deny the matter. A few days later, when the old rector asked the minister whether the house was aware of the forthcoming change, he was told: "The others know nothing. Just the beadle, and I've no idea how." The rector, who was normally a calm man, banged his fist on the table, exclaiming: "He has no right to know that!" After the new rector had taken over, the ex-rector asked Bea: "Now you can tell me frankly. How did you find out?" The beadle replied: "Father, when you're organizing a change of this kind, you shouldn't start taking the books off the shelves bit by bit, or it's obvious you're planning to move out."

Of course these episodes have to be seen and evaluated in the context of the country and the time in which they occurred. Their interest for us lies in the fact that they reveal the intelligence, ability and energy of the young Bea.

4. When we come to the major event of his *priestly ordination, Dates* becomes much richer and more detailed. We shall quote the relevant extracts and then add a few observations.

"16-24 August 1912. Spiritual exercises in preparation for my ordination to the priesthood. The day before [ordination], confession: I am confident I have thus cleansed all that is past." Some clarifying remarks follow (based on opinions current in moral theology) concerning the "intention" and other points related to celebration of mass. The text then continues: "25 August. I have been ordained priest by Archbishop Jürgens of Bombay. Thanks be to God and the Blessed Virgin Mary."[27]

"26 August. First holy mass, at the altar of the rosary, in honor of the Most

---

27. In letter N 1952/132 Bea gives a list of the twenty-seven Jesuits ordained together with him; cf. also N 1952/162.

Sacred Heart of Jesus. Assistant: Father Wilhelm Richter. Servers: Brothers Karrer and Strasser."[28]

"31 August. At home for the first time in ten years. Father is sick."

"1 September. Owing to the circumstances, a kind of second first mass at home. Father must stay at home; I brought him holy communion."[29]

Our *comments* concern the circumstances of this first mass at home. Father Steppe was parish priest of Riedböhringen at the time, and we have details about him both from his assistant priest, Father P. Huber, and from Bea himself, both of whom call him "a guileless soul" and "a golden soul."[30] Father Huber tells us that it was he who built the new church, or, more precisely, doubled the length of the existing building, in this way erecting an eternal memorial to himself. Bea adds: "He was a holy priest, to whom I owe a great deal. He took care of my parents with much kindness and love when they were left alone, and attended both of them at their deaths."[31]

In 1952, Bea was told an amusing story by an elderly Salvatorian missionary in the United States. The event in question took place the very year of Bea's first mass. When the priest heard of the celebrations for the fortieth anniversary of Bea's ordination to the priesthood, he wrote to him as follows: "In 1912 I was begging in Baden as bursar for our missions. . . . Father Steppe had been a good friend of mine since we were in high school together. I cannot remember whether the event I want to tell you happened in Riedböhringen or Hausen im Tal. I climbed up into the pulpit, but the good parish priest did not warn me that the four Evangelists were standing in niches around the pulpit, and, what is more, that the niches stuck out a little toward the pulpit. I became a little lively in my sermon and my knee struck one of the niches and, horror of horrors, St. Luke crashed to the floor with a great noise, breaking his nose in the process. I went trembling to the presbytery, and my good friend Steppe had no harsh words for me, although he did say that I must have misquoted scripture and that was why St. Luke made a dash for it."[32] Bea replied: "The event . . . took place in my home village [Riedböhringen]. People still remember the shock St. Luke's 'fall' gave them." Exegete that he was, he concluded: "But if he were to have fallen at every wrong quotation, he would have been falling all the time."[33]

There is another interesting episode involving the good parish priest and Bea, and the day of the latter's first mass. At this time, of course, the Jesuits were

---

28. It was customary in the order for what was truly the very first mass to be said in the religious house or community, and only later could the newly ordained priest go to his hometown for the "first mass," whether solemn or not. Brother Karrer was the future noted ecumenist, O. Karrer. ("Brother" was the title given to young student religious before they became priests.) Karrer left the order later, but remained on good terms and in frequent correspondence with Father Bea.

29. Cf. also R 1967/20, p. 1, where, in 1967, Bea stated: "My father was sick, but from his window he could see the procession that came to take me for my first mass."

30. Cf. N 1952/150.

31. N 1952/201.

32. Letter of Father Marcellino Moltz, S.D.S., of 27 July 1952, N 1952/201.

33. N 1952/201.

banned from Germany, and in preparation for the great day the parish priest, maybe with excessive prudence, asked the civil authorities whether a Jesuit might at least celebrate his first mass there. The reply was worthy of Solomon: "Yes, but the sermon may not be preached by another Jesuit." When Bea was informed, his decision was equally solomonic: "Then I shall preach it myself." And so he did. The authorities later reproved the parish priest for allowing the newly ordained priest to preach the homily at his first mass. His reply (decided on with Bea?) was as follows: "You said that *another* Jesuit could not preach the sermon. And no other Jesuit did, for it was preached by the celebrant himself." Bea referred to this incident in 1955 in a letter expressing his thanks to the ambassador of the Federal Republic of Germany for the award of the "Grand Cross of Merit," and allowing himself the liberty of observing how times had changed: "When I celebrated my first solemn high mass in my home village in 1912, no other Jesuit was permitted to preach the sermon, since that would clearly have endangered the security of the empire. And today the President of the Federal Republic is awarding the Grand Cross of Merit to a Jesuit!"[34]

On 12 September, Bea noted in *Dates*: "I took leave of my home: very painful for my parents." Then, with a beginner's zeal, he recorded the priestly ministries he had performed in various places between 13 September and 6 October, with the number of homilies, confessions, etc.

5. Less than three months after his first mass in his own country, with a son's affection Bea recorded details in *Dates* concerning the *last days of his beloved father*. They are brief sentences that strike like the knell of a tolling bell.

"13 October. Dr. Frey informed me that Father is suffering from cancer of the esophagus."

"12 November. Called home by telegraph. Father is dying. I find him still in fairly good shape."

"Monday, 18 November. My good father died this night at 11:30 after intense suffering."

"21 November. Burial (Thursday), Feast of the Presentation of the Blessed Virgin Mary."[35]

"25 November. I took leave of my mother."

6. According to the practice then followed in the order, Bea had been ordained at the end of his penultimate year of theology studies, so that he now had to return to the student house to complete his course. This period was devoted above all to preparing for the *final examination*, which covered all the essential points of both philosophy and theology.

The examination Bea took on 26 April 1913 lasted the normal two hours. The candidate was not given the result immediately, but only in the context of

---

34. N 1955/94. We learn from the correspondence between Fathers Huber and Bea that in 1950, despite the fact that he was eighty years old, the worthy Father Steppe braved the journey to Rome for Holy Year. He bore the strain very well, but soon after this he started to weaken rapidly, and died in May 1952; cf. N 1952/150.

35. We would note in passing that Cardinal Bea's funeral in his hometown also fell on 21 November, the Feast of the Presentation of the Virgin in the Temple, and on a Thursday.

the so-called "tertianship" which we shall discuss below, and even then the actual marks were not given to the student, who was simply told whether or not he had passed, while the marks were kept in the files of the religious province. When Bea was made provincial superior of the order for southern Germany in 1921, he found the following note by one of his predecessors in the files: "I have lost Bea's marks, but I know he sat an excellent examination."

We find confirmation that the results were excellent in a detail that to some extent echoes Bea's behavior during the entrance examination for the school in Constance, as described in our previous chapter. One of the four members of the examining board raised an objection based on a text from St. Paul, without indicating the precise reference. The candidate respectfully asked where the text in question was to be found. The examiner did not know, and after unsuccessfully consulting one of his colleagues on the board, he told the candidate: "I don't know the exact reference, but Paul certainly says this." And the candidate replied: "As far as I recall, this statement occurs in such and such a context, and in that case the meaning is this. I cannot say any more. As you know, a text must be interpreted in light of its context. I'll be able to give you a more precise answer when you let me have a precise reference." The ill-advised examiner tried another such objection without a reference, but to his great chagrin he met with a similar reply.

However, let us go back a few weeks to recount an episode that throws light on several aspects of Bea's development. On 6 April—that is, about three weeks prior to the great examination and in the midst of his last-minute studying—we find Bea as a speaker at a public meeting concerning the question of the Jesuits' being banned from Germany. In his memoirs, Henrich Köhler, a well-known German statesman, speaks of the Catholics' public battle to have the so-called "Jesuit law" repealed: "Along with Father Bea of the Society of Jesus, . . . Father Padberg and others, I travelled from place to place, from town to town, in order to stir up the people against the incomprehensible restraint imposed by the imperial government in Berlin."[36] I was at first surprised and then skeptical on reading this. Bea had never made the slightest reference to such journeys, nor could I imagine where this tour could be fitted into his *curriculum vitae*. However, I subsequently found a small package labelled "publications before 1921" and containing a newspaper cutting giving details about just such a meeting of Catholics, which had taken place in Bühl on 6 April 1913.[37] The speakers at this meeting were, in their order of speaking, "the Jesuit Father Bea" and "Herr Oberrevisor Köhler, Karlsruhe." This report shows us a new facet of our subject: Bea as a public speaker, indeed as a successful public speaker. We are therefore justified in giving a few extracts in order to provide a clearer picture.

The speaker began by saying how his visit to places he had once been familiar with had saddened him "since he had to recall that it was no longer his country

36. H. Köhler, *Lebenserinnerungen des Politikers und Staatsmannes 1878-1949*, ed. Franz Zilken (Stuttgart, 1964), p. 70.

37. Cf. *Acher- und Bühler Bote*, LXXX (8 April 1913).

because he was a Jesuit. Anyone who had occasion to spend a long time abroad would be able to appreciate what one's homeland must mean to one. Thus there must be something bad about the Jesuits, if they are so mercilessly kept out of their homeland." This led him to his main point: "Since the law would not permit him to speak of religious questions, he wished to speak about the Jesuit order and its nature. . . . Catholics had a right to hear a Jesuit, but the Jesuits had been banned from the country for forty years. . . . Truth and love were the lodestar of what he had to say."

This was followed by a reference to what happened during voting on abolition of the Jesuit law by the imperial parliament, in which he said that Catholics "find it offensive in the highest degree that, at the last moment, a pamphlet on the alleged misdoings of the Jesuits was presented to the members of parliament on the day they were to vote concerning the abolition of the Jesuit law, although the pamphlet has already frequently been shown to be nothing but lies and calumnies."

It had also been stated that abolition of the Jesuit law would lead to Germany's being overrun by Jesuits. After observing that there would be at the most 120 or 130 priests, he added: " . . . and, according to them, these priests would shatter the foundations of the mighty German Empire! So we must say: 'We Germans fear God and 120 Jesuits.' "

The report closed with the words: "With this, the Reverend Father concluded his one-and-a-half-hour, magnificent, rigorously logical address, which was followed almost breathlessly by the crowd, and interminable, tempestuous applause then announced its agreement with the speaker and gave loud expression to the great joy Catholics would have in welcoming the good fathers back among us."[38]

Special Studies: A Fragmented Curriculum

Apart from the philosophical and theological training received by all members of the order who are to perform a priestly apostolate, some members also have to continue with specialized studies in order to qualify, for example, as teachers of various subjects in the schools and student houses of the order. In Bea's case, we have very full information, not only from *Dates*, but also from various later statements of Bea himself. We receive a picture of a somewhat surprising, not to say strange, curriculum.

At the beginning of his philosophical studies he was asked to devote himself to ethnological studies at the same time, so that he would then be able to assist

---

38. *Ibid.* Another special circumstance should be noted. As we saw above, on 26 April, in other words three weeks after this meeting, Bea took the big final examination in philosophy and theology. The fact that during his preparation for such an examination he saw no difficulty in undertaking the trip from Holland to southern Germany, together with the long talk he had to give, is a very clear indication of the extent to which he had mastered the extensive material for these finals, and also of his self-confidence.

one of his professors, V. Cathrein, who was making a study of the religions of primitive peoples.[39] However, this plan must have been dropped, since we hear no more about it.

At Sittard School he had apparently taught Latin, Greek and German with such success that it was decided to have him study these subjects to a more advanced level so that he could teach them at Stella Matutina College in Feldkirch.[40] After his period of teaching in Sittard was over and he had recovered from his appendectomy, he therefore started studying philology, Greek and Latin at Innsbruck University on 13 April.[41] However, after a few months he was forced to break off because the Superior General of the order had decreed that throughout the order specialized studies of his type were not to be done until theological studies had been completed.[42]

There was a new change in orientation in the course of this theological studies, when the prefect of studies decided that there was no sense in Bea's studying philology: "You'll never be a professor at Feldkirch."[43] The idea was to make him a professor of theology. However, at the end of his theological studies, it was decided that he should eventually teach sacred scripture, and he was therefore sent to Berlin University, where he began studying oriental languages on 28 April 1913.[44] *Dates* tells us that these studies lasted until the beginning of August, and also adds: "Continuation of my studies was made impossible by the decision [of his superiors] to have me make my tertianship" (which we shall discuss in due course). Here again, a decree from higher up had intervened, for it had been decided that there should not be any extended interval between the end of theological studies and tertianship. Bea had tried to make his provincial superior see what a pity it would be to break off studies that he had only just begun, but his superior, a Swiss, answered in his characteristically picturesque style: "You're right; but if I don't send you to do your tertianship, Father General will box my ears left and right."

A little later, *Dates* says that during his tertianship it was suggested that Bea should go to the Pontifical Biblical Institute that Pope Pius X had recently founded in Rome, in order to continue his training for teaching sacred scripture. However, the plan came to nought because of the problem of Bea's health.

---

39. Cf. R 1967/19, p. 5. On V. Cathrein (1845-1931), cf. *EncCatt*, III, 1163, and *LThK*, II, 980.

40. Cf. *Sasbacher*, p. 23.

41. Cf. R 1967/19, p. 10. JI, p. 13, mentions a number of Bea's teachers.

42. Cf. *Sasbacher*, p. 24.

43. Cf. *ibid.*

44. In Berlin Bea met up with his companion from Riedböhringen and Sasbach days, Franz Honold (cf. N 1953/5). Later on he would recall a number of his lecturers in an autobiographical article: "I feel deep veneration in remembering a number of my professors of oriental sciences in Berlin, all of them non-Catholics. They were true celebrities, each in his own field: Eduard Meyer, historian of the ancient East; Hermann Strack, specialist in the Hebrew language; Jakob Barth, in the Semitic languages; and Joseph Marquart, in other eastern languages" (R 1967/19, pp. 2-3). Contacts with the latter were to grow closer—especially through his disciple, Giuseppe Messina, S.J., who was later Professor of Persian at the Pontifical Biblical Institute—and the same institute would in due course acquire Marquart's vast library *en bloc*, so that it is now found in the great library of the institute (cf. N 1956/151).

During his tertianship he had a troublesome attack of pleurisy which lasted about three weeks. When a doctor was consulted to find out whether it was a good idea to send him to study in Rome, the man asked to see an X-ray, and then gave it as his opinion that Bea would never be able to bear the Roman climate. The plan was therefore dropped.[45]

We may wonder over the reasons for the breaks and uncertainties in this tortuous path, which could hardly have been pleasant in human terms either. It has quite rightly been pointed out that, apart from the changing requirements of the work situation in any province of the order, in our case the large number of changes also sprang from the fact that Bea had such a wealth of qualities and gifts that he would have been capable of performing a wide range of jobs.[46]

It is also very interesting to consider Bea's own comments when he described these events.[47] As we have seen from the beginning, for example, he would emphasize the idea that the very fact of having been so to speak sent from pillar to post had in fact given him a useful training for his difficult ecumenical mission. In his autobiographical essay, "Paths to Ecumenism," Bea was anxious to eliminate any possible misunderstanding: "Why have I referred to these facts? Certainly not to deny the authority which, in my order as in the church at large, guided me as I obeyed it. Nor do I intend to criticize my superiors who ruled me in this way. Superiors, of course, are not always free to do what they would like, and are dependent on many changeable circumstances. I have described these ups and downs rather to illustrate how experience has taught me a healthy realism—taught me to see clearly men's limits and the inadequacy of their work."[48] Then, broadening his perspective, he observed: "It seems to me that the slightly tortuous path into which obedience has directed my life . . . is an image of the path of mankind through history. Certainly the path of humanity, seen merely through human eyes, is as tortuous as could be, full of failures and grave misadventures. It is nonetheless certain that it is guided, in a manner secret and unseen yet real and effective, toward the realization of God's plan with and for mankind."[49]

---

45. In this connection there is a certain ambiguity in our sources. R 1967/19, p. 10, dates the X-ray and the doctor's diagnosis to 1913, and thus probably prior to the journey to Berlin, whereas *Dates* dates the pleurisy and the plan of studying in Rome to 1914. Since *Dates* was more or less contemporary with the events, we have taken this as more reliable than Bea's other statements, which date from 1967.

46. Cf. also J. Willebrands in his funeral oration in 1968, cited in BM, p. 311.

47. We shall omit certain comments that concern more specific points, as for example when Bea observed that maybe the new Latin translation of the Psalms (produced between 1941 and 1945 by the Pontifical Biblical Institute) would not have become what it in fact did if the then rector of the institute had not studied classical philology in his youth (cf. *Sasbacher*, p. 24). W. Zerwick in turn observes that Bea's somewhat unconventional training, with its variety of experiences, was useful to him, for example, in his position as religious superior of young students of the order (*ibid.*, p. 22).

48. Biblio. 363, p. 20.

49. *Ibid.*, p. 22.

Tertianship

The general formation of a Jesuit ends with what is called the "tertianship," so that apart from the two years of testing and formation in the novitiate, a third year is added at the end of philosophy and theology studies. Although there are certain variations, it is similar to the novitiate in that it entails further study of the constitutions and rules of the order, a more practical pastoral training, and above all the "great exercises," in other words the full exercises of St. Ignatius, which last one month.

Basically, the only information we have on this period is found in *Dates*, which is unusually rich and detailed here, so that we shall simply quote the relevant passages and then offer our comments.

Bea started his tertianship on 14 September 1913 in the house at Exaeten where he had done the second part of his novitiate. The details open with the following observation: "Once again I'm 'beadle,' despite all my efforts to avoid this." In place of the novice master, there is an "instructor" for the tertianship, and in our case the instructor was the same man who had been Bea's novice master, J.E. Thill. It is easy to see that this fact caused difficulties for Bea similar to those he had in the novitiate.

On 15 October the "great exercises" began, and within this context Bea notes on 20 October: "I made my account of conscience to Father Instructor for the period of the scholasticate [the period of studies]. I think things are clear now, and so is what I have to do. Thanks be to God."

Two days later we find a note on the confession that is made in the first week of the exercises: "Today is the last day of the first week of the exercises,[50] and I must close the accounts of all my past life; I have made a general confession for the whole period following the novitiate. I now commend everything to God's mercy, and shall not think of it again. In the hour of my death, may he judge me benevolently for this time and its sins. After confession I prayed to the Lord, asking that if he ever saw that I was going to commit a serious sin, he would make me die on the spot instead. I commended myself individually to each of the saints of our Society, asking them to intercede for me so that I might become like them. Now bless the Lord all you servants of the Lord."[51]

The last note concerning the great exercises is dated 17 November: "Today the great retreat ends. It was a time of great interior suffering and difficulty for me. However, I confidently hope that precisely for this reason it was maybe a period rich in blessings and graces for me, and also for others. Thanks be to God and the Blessed Virgin Mary."

Like various other periods, this one was also marked by *health problems*, so that *Dates* immediately goes on to say: "Soon after the great retreat I was struck

---

50. The "great retreat" is divided into four "weeks" which are of different lengths, but differ most of all in their specific aims. The first, which our text is talking about, is devoted to purification and thus to meditation on the creation and on sin and its consequences—which is why it also entails confession.

51. Psalm 133:1.

down by a long attack of pleurisy. Although it was not dangerous, I was bedridden from 12 December until the beginning of January." However, the after-effects lasted considerably longer, so that he added: "I was not able to go out for apostolic work until March."[52] As we have seen, these health problems also interfered with plans to have him continue his studies in order to be able to teach sacred scripture. All plans were, however, effectively frustrated by the outbreak of the First World War on 2 August 1914, and in connection with this latter point *Dates* continues: "In the middle of our tertianship, on 29 June, came the news of the assassination of the heir to the Austrian throne, and this cast the shadow of war over the world from now on." His tertianship ended with the eight-day spiritual exercises (which were once again given by Father J.E. Thill): "On 15 July I leave peaceful Exaeten and say farewell to my twenty-nine tertianship companions who will be scattered to the four corners of the earth."

---

52. Cf. also Nb 345, which says that the sickness lasted two months; cf. also Nb 37.

CHAPTER 3

PROFESSOR OF SACRED SCRIPTURE, PROVINCIAL SUPERIOR, AND THE CALL TO ROME

(1914–1930)

At the point we have now reached, it would seem that the young religious should now begin the work toward which his last specialized studies have oriented him, in other words teaching sacred scripture. However, any such plans went astray in the emergency that arose with the First World War, so that he became superior of a religious house in a Germany in which the order was still banned. Only toward the end of the war was he finally able to devote himself to biblical teaching, although the series of changes that were to mark the next ten years of his life began very soon after this. First of all, for three years he was provincial superior of South Germany, a religious province that had only just been founded and where he had to start from scratch in many spheres. As soon as the really essential things had been done, he was called to Rome, where once again he was given the task of dealing with a new project—that of setting up a specialized international study house for future teachers of philosophy and theology for the whole order. Apart from this, he was to give the course of special introduction to the Old Testament at the Pontifical Biblical Institute. After a bare four years, the student house, which was now firmly established, was entrusted to other hands, while Bea increased his activity at the Biblical Institute. He was also given a new task of great responsibility, although it would last only six months—that of "visitator" to the mission at Hiroshima in Japan which had been entrusted to the order. This task entailed a general review of the whole project, but especially of the planned reconstruction of the Catholic University, which had been destroyed by the 1923 earthquake. It can thus be seen that our subject's first sixteen years of activity were marked not only by frequent changes but also by the assumption of increasingly weighty and broad-ranging responsibilities.

Superior of a "War Residence" (August 1914—January 1917)

The day he finished his year of tertianship, Bea observed in *Dates*: "I am to go to Valkenburg, but it is not yet sure that I shall be teaching exegesis. I am to stay provisionally at Valkenburg." On 2 August we find: "War breaks out," followed by: "Due to a special disposition of Providence I am sent to Aachen. To start with I live with the 'Brothers' in Richardstrasse, then I rent a house at 27 Jakobstrasse, until, at my suggestion, the new Provincial, Father Kösters, buys the house at 7 Schildstrasse. I am the first superior; at the same time I am head of the Marian Congregation for Professional People which was founded by our Fathers in 1867; I take care of our members' dealings with the military authorities."

Let us try to gain a fuller view of what was involved. By good fortune I have been able to gather evidence from a number of members who either lived with Bea during this period or were at least close enough to observe events and in particular the task in question.

We would first of all clear up one point that will certainly puzzle more than one reader, in other words, how this religious house could exist and operate in Germany despite the laws banning Jesuits from the German Empire. It must be admitted that things were not easy. Someone reported its existence to the authorities, and there was an official investigation. The order's position was that it was not a residence in the legal sense, but a "post" or "station" at the service of members of the order who were performing military service. The civil authorities refused to accept this argument, but said that given the circumstances, it could be tolerated until the end of the war. In 1917 the law against the Jesuits was repealed, after which there were no more problems.[1]

The problem sprang from the special situation of the order vis-à-vis Germany. The Jesuits were exiled but remained German citizens, and thus liable for military conscription. The files contain the certificate rejecting Bea for military service, but informing him that he had to report regularly to the military authorities. Someone who remembers those days told us that in September 1914 the students who had already received the order of the subdiaconate had been ordered to report for a military check-up. Then in the spring of 1915, all the students from Valkenburg were drafted and assigned to the medical corps.[2] There were also a certain number of priests who worked as army chaplains. Obviously some kind of reference point was needed inside Germany in order to negotiate with the military authorities. It was also necessary to have someone there to act as immediate superior for members who were serving in the armed forces in the country in various capacities, especially since communications with Holland were very difficult. There was also a third factor, for the novice master at Exaeten took advantage of the short distance between there and Aachen and sent the novices to Aachen to serve in the army hospital as an "experiment" for the novitiate; and this meant that the Aachen house was needed as a place for these novices to live during the test.

We shall here give some basic details of certain special features of the organization of the German medical corps at that time. On the basis of regulations passed in 1899, it included a number of orders of chivalry, including the Rhine-Westphalia Association of the Knights of Malta, which had been founded in 1859. In line with the provisions contained in the aforesaid regulations, this association made agreements with various religious orders and congregations according to which it would use their members in the service organized by the

1. Cf. JI, p. 15; LB, p. 13.
2. Cf. J. Schmitz, S.J., ArchWit.

association. It was obviously preferable from many points of view for religious to perform their military medical service in this organization rather than in that of the army, and this meant that in the course of the First World War the association was able to establish as many as fourteen thousand hospital beds.[3]

The files contain some important documents that give information on this matter and also to some extent on exactly how things went in practice. After Bea was made cardinal, the Grand Master of the Sovereign Order of Malta was deliberating awarding him the Grand Cross of Balì of Order and Devotion, and in this connection the Rhine Association sent him photocopies of the documents and other papers found in its files concerning his contacts with it during this period.

We can thus examine this aspect of the activities of the superior of the Aachen residence. The above-mentioned documentation includes a long letter from Bea to the president of the association, dated 11 August, in other words just a few days after he had taken over his post. The letter is a mine of information and shows how Bea set about his task with energy and foresight. He starts by expressing his appreciation of a first result: the enrollment of fifteen members of the order in the association's service.[4] He then says that he realizes the problem caused by the fact that his confreres have not received the necessary training, adding that a training course has therefore been started at the Valkenburg student house. Further, with a view to future planning, he asks how many people the association envisages being able to accept during the war, adding that the order would very soon be in a position to offer it seventy or eighty people. Apparently about seventy people in all were in fact taken on in due course.[5]

Let us now return to our residence in order to see what work and life were like there. One of the people who lived there as a novice gives us details of the timetable and the working conditions of the novices, and also describes how these affected the work-load of the superior of the house. Mass at 5:15 a.m., then "at the double" to the hospital. The work was exhausting and continued without a break from their arrival until they left at ten in the evening. Aachen was in fact the first German post inside the frontier, and the military trains tried to unload the most seriously wounded and desperate cases there, so that the hospital was always full to overflowing. "Father Bea insisted that the novices stop work on the dot of ten in the evening. He waited up for us personally and did not go to bed until we were back. He would accept no excuse. If we had done well, he would talk with us for a while, partly also to give us a chance to warm ourselves a little, since his room was the only one in the house that could be heated, apart from the kitchen."[6] The writer also describes the extreme poverty of the furnishings of the rooms: "A rickety chair and a bed; no electric

---

3. Cf. the publication for the first centenary of the association, *Festschrift zur Hundertjahrfeier der Genossenschaft Rheinisch-Westfälischer Malteser-Devotionsritter (1859-1959)*, p. 56.

4. There were ten priests, four students, one lay brother.

5. The files also contain a group photograph showing sixty-three people.

6. Cf. the account of H. Koffler, S.J., "Statio X," pp. 3-4, ArchWit.

light, no heater, no curtains at the windows, no table. If you wanted to draw up your 'points' for meditation [for the following day], you had to sit on the floor, pull the chair between your legs, and try to read by the light of a stub of candle."[7] Another witness says that the furnishings of the superior's room were the simplest imaginable.[8]

Another witness who worked very closely with Bea for about eighteen months describes the superior's work, saying that he was always busy until late at night and never even took time off for a walk; moreover, he did not manage to finish his breviary until the evening. Apart from dealing with the military authorities and the Maltese Association, there was a great deal of correspondence. And any Jesuits on leave from the army used to spend a few days at the Aachen house. There were also many visitors from Valkenburg and from the city itself. Bea used to keep visits from outsiders as short as possible, but since the superior was the only priest in the house, everything tended to fall on his shoulders.[9] As Bea himself notes, during the spring and summer of 1916 he also had to replace the provincial superior's secretary, who was sick.[10]

Since this was the first time Bea was a religious superior, it is interesting to hear how he was judged from this point of view. One person who was under his rule at this time says briefly: "Father Bea made a helpful, friendly impression on me."[11] The man who worked most closely with Bea for eighteen months describes him as follows: "As a superior, Father Bea was strict, and demanded punctuality and obedience. We had to be conscientious in observing the period of morning meditation and also that of the mid-day examination and evening litany." He adds: "He was kind and patient with the members of the house. . . . He was very hospitable in welcoming visiting members . . . and was always willing to place himself at their disposal."[12]

Let us close with an *overall look* at this period. First we have the evidence of two witnesses, both of them positive. One says that it was Bea's merit that the young students were assigned to the medical corps instead of being enlisted in the active services,[13] while the other says in more general terms: "Bea performed his task with shrewdness and success."[14] The president of the association also wrote to Bea in 1916 when the latter was about to give up his position: "If everything else in the voluntary medical service had worked as things did with the Jesuits, many things would have been resolved much more easily and smoothly."[15] The positive judgment is also backed up by the large

---

7. *Ibid.*
8. Cf. H. Huber, S.J., ArchWit.
9. Cf. *ibid.*
10. Cf. *Dates.*
11. J. Hoffe, S.J., ArchWit.
12. H. Huber, S.J., ArchWit. H. Koffler, S.J., was the only one who found Bea rigid and overly strict at this time. In fact, throughout his life Bea himself was aware of the danger inherent in his character of being formal and cold (*steif*); cf. *Der Mensch Bea*, p. 34.
13. Cf. K. Wehner, S.J., ArchWit.
14. O. von Nell-Breuning, S.J., ArchWit.
15. Letter of 31 December 1916.

number of decorations that the association awarded toward the end of the war to members of the order who had worked with it: seven gold medals, one of which went to Bea, and twenty-seven silver ones.[16] Bea himself obviously does not talk of success or failure, but simply observes: "It was a difficult job, given my tender age, but also very instructive."[17]

Professor of Sacred Scripture and Prefect of Studies (February 1917–Summer 1921)

We find the following entry in *Dates*: "On 24 January 1917 Father Hugo Amann is appointed to succeed me. I am transferred to Valkenburg to teach Old Testament exegesis. I begin lectures in mid-February."

Bea also enjoyed describing an episode connected with the beginning of these lectures. Obviously the new professor also wanted to prepare his lectures in advance, so far as he could. However, as can be imagined, border controls were very thorough, especially on the Dutch side, and there was also the problem of language, for how could the customs officials check Latin texts? Bea decided to write the outline for his first lesson on a postcard and mail it to himself.

In *Dates* Bea gives details of the various subjects dealt with in his lectures: twice the question of the Pentateuch (the first five books of the Old Testament), eight special lectures specifically on the prophets, the inspiration of sacred scripture, the revelation of the Old Testament, the prophets of the post-exilic period, and the poetic writings.

In a letter written to the father general of the order some years later, Bea explained *the method* he followed in teaching sacred scripture during these years: "It was my principle . . . not to hide any major modern-day difficulty from the students, but at the same time to offer a solution that was based on a conscientious examination of every aspect of the problem and was as faithful as possible to the tradition and magisterium of the church."[18] In 1952 one of his students from those days wrote to him, still recalling his lectures of introduction to the Old Testament and his clear presentation of the major lines of the Old Testament.[19] In about 1960, another student also recalled the lectures on the prophets, saying that they were very useful for preaching.

Although he may have been a beginner at teaching sacred scripture and therefore needed time to prepare a certain reserve of lectures, he very soon found that he was gradually being entrusted with other tasks as well, all of them relatively demanding. In spring 1918 he was appointed director of a famous Latin commentary on sacred scripture, the *Cursus Scripturae Sacrae*, founded in 1880 by three Jesuits, R. Cornely, J. Knabenbauer and F. von Hummelauer.[20]

---

16. There is a full list and the dates of the awards in the files.
17. Cf. *Dates*.
18. Letter of 2 May 1924.
19. Cf. N 1952/64.
20. R. Cornely (1830-1908); cf. *EncCatt*, IV, 570; *LThK*, III, 59. J. Knabenbauer (1839-1911); cf.

The fact that the job was given to a man who had only just started on his teaching career shows the great respect Bea already enjoyed in the order. He would continue with the task of teaching in one form or another for several decades.

In April 1919 he received another job entailing great responsibility: that of Prefect of Studies for the whole order, which thus encompassed both philosophy and theology students. According to the system then in force in the schools of the order, this task covered both the complex planning of studies and courses, and also the duty of supervising the studies of the individual students. The task was all the more demanding since at that time there were no deans for the individual faculties. And in our case it was made considerably more difficult by the conditions of the immediate post-war period. A large number of young students who had been forced to break off their studies when they were drafted were now returning after three or four years, and a solution had to be found for each individual case; it should also be remembered that these war veterans had to be helped to return to a type of academic work that would have been hard enough for many of them even in normal times. It is worth noting that the evidence we can gather on this aspect of Bea's work is almost all positive: "He was prudent and ready to meet one half-way"[21]; "he was kind, well-disposed, understanding"[22]; "he was unusually understanding and broad-minded for those days, especially in comparison with other teachers; today we would say he was 'human' "[23]; "he welcomed me with a warmth and simplicity that I would never have expected from a professor"[24]; "I shall never be able to forget my meeting with you in Valkenburg, when you showed such warm personal interest in a student thirsty for learning, pointing me along the road to knowledge."[25] The words of a last witness are particularly telling: "[Bea] strengthened my fidelity to the church and her teaching with words and example."[26]

Let us add some specific examples to illustrate the above statements. In his memoirs, the renowned, unshakable opponent of Nazism, Friedrich Mucker-mann, S.J., describes how Bea helped him in this period. While he was studying he was already taking part in various meetings, etc., and was therefore worried

EncCatt, VII, 721; *LThK*, VI, 355. F. von Hummelauer (1842-1914); cf. *EncCatt*, VI, 1508-1509; *LThK*, V, 535. Later on, the premises of the commentary were moved to Rome—a move that was criticized in Germany. It must be admitted in all honesty that after the move the collection did not increase to any appreciable degree, although we would not like to express an opinion as to whether this was a result of the move or of other circumstances.

21. H. Schröder, S.J., ArchWit.
22. K. Pauli, S.J., ArchWit.
23. H. Seelen, S.J., ArchWit.
24. H. Deitmer, S.J., ArchWit.
25. L. Born, S.J., Na 1959/69.
26. F.M. Sladeczek, S.J., ArchWit. After hearing the foregoing opinions, it is difficult to accept the general judgment of another witness, who also usually tends to be fairly critical, and who says "that Bea was not particularly well liked by the students, because he was somewhat dry and official in his manner" (H. Koffler, S.J., ArchWit). We should, however, note that the same witness also says that the activity of the Prefect of Studies was for the most part judged positively, in that he was able to identify with the person he was talking to, appreciating his particular interests and encouraging his talents.

that his rector might forbid such activities, considering them detrimental to his studies. He therefore explained the situation to the Prefect of Studies, who assured him that he would certainly stand up for him where his superiors were concerned. And the Prefect of Studies did in fact dissolve the superior's doubts and objections, so that the latter let him go ahead.[27]

Bea himself related the following example on more than one occasion. Some students came to him, complaining that they were gaining nothing from certain philosophy lectures and asking that they be allowed to study on their own instead of listening to the lectures. Bea's reply was brief and to the point: "I'm concerned that you should learn philosophy; the study method is of no interest to me."

In 1959 another student from those days wrote as follows: "As Prefect of Studies you were very kind to me. I had expressed my wish to read the New Testament in Greek, and when I went back to my room, I found that a thoughtful hand had placed Zorell's dictionary on my desk. In September 1921 you offered to let me drop a certain subject . . . although I had not even asked."[28]

The well-known Swiss ecumenist, O. Karrer, who was a student at Valkenburg in those days, remembers him as follows: "He was an unusually noble man, a priest and religious who was generous in the spirit of charity and service to others. He was then [and until 1921] teaching the Old Testament. He was a man of spirit, character, deep piety, and kindness. He used to say that the best form of intelligence is an openness inspired by love."[29]

Apart from the teaching and other jobs, Bea also managed to publish a few articles, at least in the first part of this period. We shall note in passing that he had written his very first article in 1911, when he was a theology student. It was a reflection on a study by Adolf Harnack on the Acts of the Apostles and the Synoptic Gospels, and was entitled, interestingly enough, "Are We Returning to Tradition?"[30] Now, however, the death of the famous Protestant exegete J. Wellhausen[31] gave Bea an opportunity to produce two articles attempting an overall evaluation of the research of this scholar and in particular of his theory regarding the sources of the Pentateuch.[32] The first article described the ingenious system built up by Wellhausen and recognized its merits, while the second contained a critical evaluation. There was a space of about one month between the appearance of the two articles; and a short time after the first appeared, Bea received a warning from the Roman authorities of the order, saying that he should not praise a non-Catholic author in this way. Bea's brief response was that they should wait for the second article.[33]

---

27. Cf. Friedrich Muckermann, *Im Kampf Zwischen zwei Epochen*, ed. and intro. Nikolaus Junk (Mainz, 1973), p. 195.
28. W. Hofer, S.J., Na 1959/309.
29. BM, p. 157.
30. Cf. Biblio. 13.
31. J. Wellhausen (1844-1918); cf. *EncCatt*, XII, 1665-1666; *LThK*, X, 1020-1021.
32. Cf. Biblio. 14, 15.
33. As concerns this episode, cf. the autobiographical article R 1967/19, p. 4. We would also in passing mention the article on the subject of "Antisemitism, the Theory of Race, and the Old Testament" (cf. Biblio. 16), which described the already considerable number of phenomena

Bea's *solemn religious profession* took place in this period. As we said when speaking of the vows he made at the end of the novitiate, in the Society of Jesus the candidate is subjected to a long trial period before the order binds him to itself definitively with religious vows, which are "solemn" in the juridical sense too. Apart from the years devoted to study, the trial lasts for about ten years, and in Bea's case solemn religious profession took place after almost seventeen years. After preparing himself through eight days of spiritual exercises, Bea made this profession on 15 August 1918 in the chapel of the Valkenburg studentate. Apart from the three normal religious vows, there was also the fourth one of absolute obedience to any task the pope might choose to give him. There were also other simple (i.e. non-solemn) vows, one of which bound the religious to protect the strictness of the constitutions of the order with regard to religious poverty, while the other bound him to refuse any ecclesiastical honor he might be offered, unless it was imposed by the Holy Father under pain of sin.

Some months prior to profession, Bea suffered a great sorrow with the last sickness and *death of his mother*. He had always felt closer to his mother than his father, and the bond had become even stronger after his father's death. He was an only child, and after his mother's death he must have felt truly orphaned. The shock of the loss can be seen from the unusual wealth of details found in *Dates*. First he notes that his mother had been sick with influenza and pleurisy for some time. I believe that at this point her son had tried to obtain an allowance of white bread for her, in view of her state of health, but that the permit came through when it was too late. On 20 January the son received a telegram calling him home, and Bea notes: "I have the consolation of spending another three weeks at my mother's side in her last illness." Next we find: "On 9 February, at 1:05 in the afternoon, a Saturday, my beloved mother dies." "My father and my mother have forsaken me, but the Lord has taken me in."[34] "On a Saturday she gave me life, and on a Saturday she left me."

After noting the funeral, which was attended by many people, Bea adds these observations and reflections: "During her last sickness, my mother twice assured me that she had never regretted giving her permission for me to enter the Society of Jesus. It was the greatest sacrifice of her life. May she rest in peace. She was the model of a truly Christian, deeply religious, strong wife and mother. She often put me in mind of the mother of my patron saint, Augustine."[35]

If we take a look back over Bea's path until this point, we can see that it had apparently become the rule for him to suffer *health problems* in every period.

---

connected with the birth of racism and explained the Catholic position on the question. Nobody can be surprised that we do not yet find all the nuanced attitudes of the Second Vatican Council in the young professor's attitude toward the Jewish people.

34. Cf. Psalm 26:10 (in the Vulgate): *Pater et mater dereliquerunt me; Dominus autem assumpsit me.* The author is referring to his religious vocation, with which the Lord welcomed him "into his house."

35. It may seem surprising that in 1919 Bea notes in *Dates* the marriage of his cousin Rosa Bea (daughter of one of his uncles), but we find the explanation in the observation that follows the entry: "She had tended my mother so faithfully in her last sickness," for Augustin was always deeply touched by anything concerning his mother.

The number of heavy commitments, added of course to the hardships and privations inevitable in the immediate post-war period, as well as his grief over the loss of his mother, had now reduced his defenses, and in particular weakened his heart. Bea spoke to me about this on various occasions. *Dates* makes no reference to it, but he did mention it in a 1953 letter to a member of his family, who had heart problems and to whom he wrote to offer some comfort: "I myself have had a weak heart for thirty-five years now, but in spite of this I have lived to old age. If you work calmly, even a weak heart can hold out for a long time."[36] As a result of his condition, Bea had to suspend his activity for some weeks.

Provincial Superior (1921-1924)

Despite the expulsion of the order from Bismarck's Germany, it did nothing but grow after the law was passed: while at the moment of expulsion in 1872 there were 755 members in Germany, when the relative law was repealed in 1917 the number had doubled.[37] However, it must be said that when the law of proscription was abolished, not all these members returned to work inside the country. After they had been forbidden to work in their own country, the German Jesuits had scattered throughout the vast world of the missions, either taking over responsibility for certain already existing missionary territories or creating new ones, so that they were now working in the United States (the Buffalo mission), southern Brazil, and India (the Bombay-Poona mission),[38] although the missionaries were expelled from the latter during the First World War because of their nationality.

Even so, the number of members who returned to Germany, together with the extension of the field of the apostolate, meant that immediately after the return it was felt necessary to divide the vast territory of the province, at least for administrative purposes. A "vice-provincial superior" was therefore appointed for the houses situated in southern Germany, but after four years of further growth, the time seemed ripe to set about a total division, creating one province for the south and another for the north. Father Bea, barely forty, was appointed superior of the new southern province.[39]

What was the situation Bea found when he took up his position? When he was made cardinal in 1960, he described it as follows in a message of greeting broadcast by the Bavarian radio: "It was a time when there were many things

---

36. Nb 1953/178.
37. The official list (called the "catalogue") gives 755 members for the year of expulsion (1872), and 1207 members for the year of return (1917), although the 347 German Jesuits working in various missions of the order (apart from the two missions of southern Brazil and Bombay-Poona in India, which were then entrusted to the German Jesuits) must be added to the latter figure.
38. For the previous history of the order in Germany, see BM, p. 58.
39. The official name of the province was taken from the old Roman name of "Germania Superior," while the northern province was called "Germania Inferior." These names seem to be based above all on geographical features, inasmuch as the mountainous south is higher than the north.

to build or rebuild in the field of work entrusted to me."[40] The order had returned to Germany after an absence of almost half a century. The war was only just over, and although the results were not as great as the terrible destruction caused by the Second World War, there were still the general conditions created by the country's defeat, with all its economic and social consequences. Thus the Jesuits returned to a Germany that had undergone some profound changes, and apart from the task of organizing a new religious province, they had to create types of work that were in many ways new in order to meet the new situation. Bea was faced with a far from easy task.

We shall draw mainly on two sources in order to describe the work of the new provincial: Bea's memories as given in the aforementioned 1960 radio message, and the description of Bea's activity as provincial by the archivist of the southern German province, H. Grünewald, which was published in M. Buchmüller's work.[41] Obviously a number of projects had already been set up in the territory in the first four years after the return from exile, including the writers' house, which published the magazine *Stimmen der Zeit*, and a residence for pastoral work in Munich; the parish of St. Kunigunda in Nuremberg was also in its very early days, as was a retreat house near Munich.

After visiting all the existing houses in order to gain a personal overview of the situation and of what was needed, Bea set to work, trying on the one hand to respond to the offers or requests of the church authorities, and on the other to meet the needs that seemed most important and most pressing. Thus the offer of the church authorities for the Jesuits to take up pastoral work again in the huge, old baroque church of the order in Munich, St. Michael, was accepted. The church authorities also entrusted them with the important job of guiding the male marian congregation in Munich, a task that Bea handed to Father Rupert Mayer, who was thus to become the great apostle of Munich.[42] On its own initiative the order then assumed responsibility for pastoral work on the university campuses and among professional people in the three cities of Munich, Karlsruhe and Heidelberg. It also devoted considerable attention to the care of priests and to fostering priestly vocations. It worked to develop the parish of Nuremberg which we mentioned above, and the retreat house on Lake Starnberg near Munich was rebuilt. It should also be observed that Bea had no hesitation over closing houses or dropping ministries that seemed less important in comparison with more pressing and useful things.[43]

Formation of the younger generation of the order was a major concern with the new provincial. In 1922 there were 125 novices in the two novitiates in Germany, so that it was clear that the Valkenburg student house would soon be insufficient. After some searching, Bea managed to purchase a piece of land just outside Munich and to build a large philosophy study house. When he was called to Rome

---

40. R 1960/28, p. 2.

41. Cf. BM, pp. 64-66.

42. Father Rupert Mayer (1876-1945); cf. *LThK*, VII, 214. He was beatified by Pope John Paul II in 1987. As cardinal, Bea was official relator in the cause for beatification.

43. Cf. H. Grünewald, in BM, p. 66.

in September 1924 to take over another job, the house was already half-built, so that it was able to open its doors in 1925. However, since the problem of space for philosophy students presented itself prior to that date, the college opened in temporary quarters in the large novice house at Tisis (Vorarlberg), with Bea again personally opening the new academic year on 15 September 1924. Since the sister province of Austria was in similar difficulties, Bea willingly agreed to accept a good number of Austrian philosophy students at his college.

When the two provinces were created, the southern German one was also entrusted with the mission in southern Brazil. Bea wanted to visit this mission in person, but his three years at the head of the province did not allow him time to make such a journey—especially since in the course of this already short period he was busy for three months (8 September—8 December 1923) at a long general congregation (the name used for the order's general chapter), which had the main task of bringing the constitutions of the order into line with the new Code of Canon Law promulgated by Pope Benedict XV. It is, however, interesting that Bea did attempt to introduce an important innovation in the sphere of the Brazilian mission. The mission received its new recruits mostly from among German migrants, so that the language used was German, which obviously constituted an obstacle to expansion prospects for the order. Bea wrote to the superior of the mission asking that the use of Portuguese be introduced, even if only gradually: "Otherwise you will never have native vocations from the country." We are, however, forced to add that it would be a considerable number of years before this suggestion was put into practice.

This episode was relatively unusual for those times, and it leads to a general question as to Bea's *style of governing* and dealing with his confreres. We have the evidence of a good number of contemporaries who belonged to the province Bea headed and who thus spoke from personal experience.[44] "He was fatherly, kindly and a patient listener"[45]; "he had a straightforward manner and did not give himself airs; he was openly benevolent"[46]; "he was friendly, caring, ready to help, and unassuming in dealings with the young members"[47]; "he was very simple and kindhearted, and understood the concerns of ordinary folk; there was something radiant about him that moulded me interiorly"[48]; "he gave me the impression of a good Jesuit, a man of faith, superior intelligence and great prudence."[49]

This combination of prudence and skill is illustrated by an episode that Bea himself enjoyed recounting. A little while before his nomination as provincial was announced, rumors, or at least conjectures, began to circulate. At this point, one of his colleagues who had previously been his professor came to ask him "in confidence" whether the rumors were true. Bea was a little embarrassed, but

---

44. It should be noted that with one exception, these witnesses are none of them the same as those mentioned in previous chapters.
45. Hermann Riederer, S.J., ArchWit.
46. Josef Barmettler, S.J., ArchWit. Leo Kohler, S.J., still recalled in 1952 how Provincial Bea had welcomed and encouraged him; cf. the letter attached to N 1952/132.
47. Simon Schaible, S.J., ArchWit.
48. F.X. Spohn, S.J., ArchWit.
49. Walter Brugger, S.J., ArchWit; similarly Karl Thuer, S.J., ArchWit.

also anxious to preserve secrecy, and although he already had the decree of nomination in his pocket, he answered: "There was a risk, but it has passed." After this apparently negative answer, the other man felt authorized to deny the rumors. Some weeks later, the same man was on vacation in the aforementioned retreat house on Lake Starnberg, when Bea arrived. He asked in surprise why he was there. "Tomorrow I'll be announced as provincial," answered Bea with a smile. "But you told me you wouldn't be!" "No, I didn't say that: I said that the danger had passed, because I already had the decree in my pocket. After a child falls down a well there's no longer any danger that he'll fall. . . . "[50]

Various aspects of his thought and of his style of government can also be seen from a number of authenticated episodes. A first one concerns the teaching methods then used at Stella Matutina High School, which the order had opened at Feldkirch in Austria, very close to the German border, after it was expelled from Germany. Until that time, it had been the rule for the pupils, whatever their age, to go out for walks two by two in a line. The new provincial suggested that the older pupils should be shown greater trust and therefore given a certain amount of freedom, so as to help develop their characters and prepare them for the independence they would need later on when they went to college. There were obviously difficulties: "What if they go into a bar?" people objected. To which the provincial replied: "And what if they go to bars after they're at college?" The answer was: "We won't be responsible then." "But your educational methods will be," observed the provincial. A few days later one of the teachers was weighed down with the pupils' homework when he bumped into the provincial's secretary and remarked: "Look! This boy's been cheating again. . . . And Father Provincial wants us to trust them."

The provincial's realism was as striking as his openness. Once he had a long discussion with his advisors over various candidates for a position as rector, for unfortunately all the candidates had some defect. The provincial finally said: "Let's find someone who can do the job fairly well and not as badly as the others." In this way they found someone who eventually performed the job very well when it came to it.

Another episode shows that Bea was not afraid of frank speaking. He asked Father F. Hayler, a typical Bavarian, what he would say if he were appointed as one of his counselors.[51] "You'd have to be ready to hear the truth from me," was

50. In view of the unanimously positive opinions of those subject to Bea's government, we can ignore the negative views voiced by H. Koffler, S.J. (ArchWit), a member of the northern province who has already been quoted a number of times. These criticisms seem to be clearly influenced by the difficulties involved in the division of possessions and personnel between the two provinces. The process was in fact so fraught with difficulties that the two provincial superiors were called to Rome, where they negotiated from 10 to 21 December 1921 under the supervision of the Father General, in accordance with the basic principles laid down, as usual, by the supreme government of the order. The agreements reached by the two "negotiators" were ratified by the Father General as they appeared. All these circumstances represent sufficient guarantee of the way Bea himself acted in this matter.

51. According to the custom of the order, the provincial superior has three official counselors who are appointed by the Father General.

the answer. "That's what I want," replied the provincial, and the deal was struck. The provincial then entrusted the same Father Hayler with the task of supervising building and restoration work throughout the province, including work on the aforementioned philosophy study house, and in this position he rendered the whole province very valuable service. He also became provincial superior for a while in the 1930s.

We know of one particularly telling example of how Bea could combine prudent reflection with the practice of obedience. It was decided that a member should obtain specialized qualifications in order to teach experimental and philosophical psychology. Bea took advantage of a good opportunity and talked it over personally with the Father General, Wlodimir Ledóchowski, suggesting that the candidate should be sent to Vienna University, where there was a very good specialist in experimental psychology. The general, however, said that the candidate should be sent to the Pontifical Gregorian University in Rome. When the provincial objected that the latter offered no course in experimental psychology, the general refused to change his mind. Bea obeyed, but asked the man in question to give him a list at the end of the year, reporting the subjects and numbers of courses he had taken. This list showed that the Gregorian University did not in fact have any relevant courses. The provincial sent the information to the general, observing that given the situation there was obviously no point in having the man waste time at that university. Therefore, he concluded, unless he heard to the contrary, he would recall the man and send him to Vienna University. He expected to receive a reproof, but the Superior General's answer was as follows: "You are right in what you say about the Gregorian University, and you are therefore free to act as you propose." The episode would later have an aftermath connected with Bea's call to Rome, as we shall see.[52]

To end this section, let us try to give an overview and (so far as is possible on the basis of the limited material at our disposal) a *general evaluation* of Bea's rule. He himself in fact offers some initial help in this task. After the decision to call him to Rome in 1924, he wrote to the Father General, warning that the provincial counselors would probably try to have the decision reversed, claiming that it was vital that he continue at the head of the province. Bea went on to say that he could refute the lines of reasoning they might adopt. This led him on to a description of the point reached in the construction of the new province: the major problems concerning development of the province and its relations with neighboring prov-

---

52. In the course of his term in office, the provincial also had to deal with a case that was particularly painful for him, when the future great ecumenist, O. Karrer, then a young priest, suddenly left the order, and in his first confused state also the church. The provincial suffered all the more over this since Karrer came from the same Black Forest area as himself and had served at his first mass, while Bea had in turn assisted at Karrer's first mass (cf. Karrer's evidence in BM, p. 157). By good fortune, and thanks to the very close interest and concern of the regional superior of the order, things were sorted out, and Father Bea arranged for Karrer to be received into the diocese of Chur (cf. *ibid.*). On this case, cf. Josef Wicki, "Dokumente zur Glaubens- und Berufskrise von Otto Karrer, 1922-1924," *Archivum Hist. Soc. Iesu*, LI (1982), 285-299. Ever after this, Karrer remained in trusting and close correspondence with Father, and later Cardinal, Bea.

inces had been solved; building work on the college for philosophy students was going well; and any property questions would be sufficiently clarified in the course of the next summer. Bea thus concluded: "What the province needs now is a calm, smooth development, and this can maybe be better assured by the kind of man who is envisaged as my successor than by me."[53]

This summing up on Bea's part should not be misunderstood as expressing satisfaction with what he had done. Far from it. In the last letter that he wrote to the Father General as provincial, he referred to "my youth and inexperience," thanking the general for the patience and indulgence he had shown him, and asking forgiveness for "the mistakes, blunders and omissions." He then added: "I sincerely beg you, Father, to give me a penance for all this."[54] Similarly, in his letter of farewell to the province, he thanked his fellow Jesuits for their charity and patience, and asked them to forgive "mistakes and blunders."[55]

A French Jesuit who would spend a month in the province four years later says that Bea was much respected, but that there were still echoes of the sacrifices connected with the building of the college for philosophy students: the residence communities had had to suffer privations, even at table, in order to help pay off the debts.[56] If we want to gain a better understanding of the situation, we should remember the special and unforeseeable financial difficulties that arose in Germany while the college was being built. This was the period of so-called "stabilization" of the German mark, which was accompanied by incredible inflation. On more than one occasion, Bea described how he came back in December 1923 from the general congregation held in Rome, and found that his tram ticket from the station to the house cost as much as the whole return journey to Rome. In these circumstances, he was forced to scale down the plans for the college—and indeed the original plan was never completed. However, this decision only reduced the difficulties, but did not eliminate them.

Let us close with the overall judgment of Bea's term in office given by his successor in his first letter to the members of the province. The new provincial thanked Bea for the "indefatigable labor and care" with which he had developed the province, "fostering its prosperity so successfully, despite the difficulties of the times," and also for the "charity and goodness we all found in him."[57]

The general's assistant for the provinces of Germany in turn expressed himself in complete agreement with this acknowledgment.[58] Even while bearing in mind the type of language normally used in such circumstances, there still seem to be sufficient elements for an overall positive judgment on Bea's work as provincial superior, and indeed the authors of the two letters were not exuberant Mediterranean-type characters, but cool northern people (the German assistant, for instance, was Dutch).

---

53. Letter of 2 May 1924.
54. Letter of 10 September 1924.
55. Letter of 21 September 1924.
56. Georges Jarlot, S.J., ArchWit.
57. This is a letter from Theobald Fritz, S.J., a copy of which is found in the archives.
58. The relative letter of R. van Oppenraaij, S.J., is found in the archives.

Rome: In Charge of the Training of Future Teachers of Philosophy and Theology

In a previous chapter we saw the considerable uncertainty that reigned during Bea's formation as to what specific permanent task would be entrusted to him for the future. It would appear that the same kind of thing continued even now that he had started working. Thus the job in the Aachen residence was followed by the appointment as professor of sacred scripture combined with that of Prefect of Studies, and after some years this was broken off and he was called on to head the new province of southern Germany. Then after a bare three years, once the essential aspects had been taken care of, he had to leave this position in order to set about another pioneering task in Rome—that of organizing the specialized training of those members of the order who would be called on to teach philosophy and theology in the student houses of the order.

We have detailed information on this last move, since we possess the relative correspondence between Bea and the general. If we want to understand the situation, we must remember that all this was before Pius XI's 1931 apostolic constitution *Deus scientiarum Dominus*, which laid down rules for all advanced ecclesiastical studies throughout the church.[59] In the order, ecclesiastical studies still basically fell under the regulations found in the ancient *Ratio studiorum* of Father General R. Acquaviva, dating back to the end of the sixteenth century. These regulations were in force until 1773, the year that the order was dissolved by Pope Clement XIV, but were then adapted by Father General G.F. Roothaan in 1832, especially with regard to ecclesiastical studies.[60] At the time with which we are concerned, people were obviously aware that a revision was needed, and the problem had been under consideration for some time. The 1923 general congregation—in which Bea had also taken part, as we have seen, in his position as provincial of the southern German province—had been particularly concerned with this subject,[61] and it was on this occasion that Father General spoke to Bea about it, mentioning the possibility of calling him to Rome in this connection.[62] Less than two months later, the general told him that he had now taken a definitive decision to do so, and as soon as Bea's three-year term as provincial was over he was to come to Rome to undertake the task of setting up the "Biennium"—the college that would offer young members of the order the possibility of special studies and research to prepare them to teach philosophy and theology.[63] We do not have Bea's reply, but from correspondence with the provincial of the Rome province of the order, which was in charge of the

---

59. On this constitution, cf. *EncCatt*, IV, 1500, and Biblio. 4.

60. Cf. *EncCatt*, X, 543-546.

61. Cf. the official publication *Statuta Congregationis Generalis XXVII* (Rome, 1924), no. 97, especially para. 4.

62. Cf. Bea's letter to Cardinal Franz Ehrle, S.J., of 25 July 1924. On this cardinal (1845-1934), cf. *LThK*, III, 719, and, more generally, *EncCatt*, V, 185-187.

63. Letter of the general dated 13 February 1924.

university institutes of Rome (as would also be the case for the "Biennium"), we can conclude that the general's letter received a positive reply.[64]

There is an interesting and authenticated detail that explains to some extent why the general thought of *Bea* for this task. When Bea was already installed in his new job, someone was talking with Ledóchowski and asked where Father Bea was and what he was doing. The general's reply was that he had called him to Rome as superior of the Biennium. Then, referring back to the case of the student whom Bea as provincial had wanted to have specialize in experimental psychology, he added: "He knew how to criticize when he was provincial. Let's see if he will be able to improve things now."

Two months later, Bea's commitments in Rome grew. Father General told him that a professor of special introduction to the Old Testament was needed at the Pontifical Biblical Institute and asked him if he could take over this job as well.[65] Ten days later Bea answered that it did not seem too difficult to him, since he had already given the whole special introduction to the Old Testament not once, but twice, while he was teaching at Valkenburg.[66] This task would not, he said, prevent him from fulfilling the plan to teach biblical theology at the Pontifical Gregorian University, which the general had been talking of from the moment he called him to Rome. Indeed, he had already studied the whole of the theology of the Old Testament, and with due preparation he would be able to teach the part concerning the New Testament too.[67]

Although the call to Rome could be seen as an honor inasmuch as it was a mark of his superiors' trust, it did involve a whole series of difficulties and sacrifices. We hardly need mention the need to leave his own country and a religious province that was still in its infancy and was only just starting to find its feet. Apart from this, his new tasks involved a fair number of unknown factors, which will gradually come to light as we examine the correspondence: there was the problem of meeting the needs and taking account of the leanings of students from every part of the world and from very different backgrounds[68]; there was also the question of the extent of Bea's task and formative influence, in other words whether it was solely a matter of supervising the students and their research, or also of organizing courses and thus influencing the choice of their teachers.[69] Moreover, there was the problem of ensuring the existence of at least a small library of the works and publications essential for both his teaching assignments.[70]

He also had to learn a new language. At that time there was a rule in the order that members had to learn the language of the place where they were living,

---

64. Bea to the provincial superior of the Rome province of the society, Father G. Filograssi, S.J., dated 16 March 1924, and Filograssi's reply dated 21 March 1924.

65. Cf. letter of 21 April 1924.

66. The *special* introduction (as opposed to the *general* introduction to sacred scripture) deals with questions of authorship, date of composition, and the authenticity, etc., of the individual books of the Old Testament.

67. Cf. letter of 2 May 1924.

68. Cf. letter to Father G. Filograssi of 24 March 1924.

69. Cf. the already cited letter to Cardinal F. Ehrle of 25 July 1924.

70. Cf. the already cited letter to the general of 2 May 1924.

unless one's own could be more useful there, and Italian was the language in everyday use in the Roman institutes. The following episode is interesting in this connection. Although Father General had a perfect command of the German language and usually spoke it with Bea, on the occasion of his first visit to the Biennium he unexpectedly began to speak Italian. After a short time, he observed: "I simply wanted to be sure that you had learned the local language," and then continued the conversation in German. Bea had in fact already studied Italian when he was younger, as we saw in the episode involving his teacher of church history, F.X. Kraus, but he was certainly far from being able to speak it with any ease.

It is significant that despite all these unknown factors and difficulties, Bea should have written to the general: "As for myself, I want nothing except that the will of God be done; I do not mind whether my field of work is in Rome or elsewhere; I leave this unreservedly up to you, Father."[71]

Bea arrived in Rome a little early in order to take part in a conference of "cosmologists" (specialists in the branch of scholastic philosophy concerned with the philosophy of the cosmos). As early as May, he had written to Father General as follows: "In view of the fact that I shall also be responsible for future philosophy teachers, a congress such as this would certainly be very helpful so that I can learn about present teaching and the relative debates, and also get to know the specialists in this field. The part of my task involving future philosophy teachers will undoubtedly be more difficult, because I am less familiar with this field."[72]

In October Bea was appointed religious superior of the Biennium, which was named "Blessed Robert Bellarmine House." From the very beginning, the new superior had to deal with an unusual difficulty. The Biennium students were to live in the building adjoining the Gesù Church, which had been the general curia of the order from the sixteenth century onward. At the time of the unification of Italy and the fall of the Papal States, the building had been confiscated by the authorities of the new nation. The Lateran Treaty of 1929 between state and church was being worked out in the years with which we are concerned here, so that parts of the old curia of the order were being returned. Bea would often describe how this took place only slowly and piecemeal, so that they were only able to give the young students rooms as each of them arrived. The chapel of the community was to be the beautiful baroque one that had belonged to the Marian Congregation of Noblemen, but when it was finally returned they found it stacked high with paper, having been used as an office.

The correspondence we have already cited indicates how Bea saw the field of work and the tasks awaiting him. Before this period he had of course realized the great importance of the Roman institutes (the Pontifical Gregorian University and the Pontifical Biblical Institute), but he had come to understand it better at the recent general congregation.[73] Bea felt that the aim of the Biennium was

---

71. *Ibid.*

72. *Ibid.*

73. Cf. the already cited letter to Cardinal F. Ehrle of 25 July 1924, and also that to the general's

that of acting as "a seed-bed for capable and enthusiastic teachers."[74] This meant that it was a very difficult task: "The task I am to take up is an important one, with heavy responsibilities, because it is basically concerned with the future of the scientific work of the whole Society of Jesus."[75] Even so he set to work, "trusting in the prayers that so many of my confreres had promised in those days."[76]

As regards the organization of studies, he soon realized that the main difficulty for the Biennium was that of obtaining good teachers who would truly place themselves at the service of the young members in order to guide them in their research, dissertations, and so on.[77] The problem was that the professors at the Gregorian University were already so loaded down with work, and particularly with dissertations from the large number of students, that they simply could not take on any more.

Bea therefore did not mince words in telling Father General that if they were not able to provide their students with the necessary guides and supervisors for their research, there was no point in asking the provinces to send them their future teachers in order to have them trained at the Biennium. Father General's response is worth noting, for once he had heard Bea out he replied: "All right. Go and visit our student houses, give me a list of good teachers, and I'll have them come to Rome." In the vacation after his first academic year in Rome, Bea therefore visited the student houses of various European countries, after which the Biennium had five or six internationally known professors at its exclusive disposition.[78] When Bea talked about this later on, he would observe, maybe a little wryly: "After I left my job as head of the Biennium in 1928, people found it convenient to use these professors for teaching at the Gregorian University, so that the Biennium tended to lose its advantages."

Various people have spoken of *Bea's style as superior*. One witness said that when he visited him "he complained about how exhausting it was talking with the Biennium students, because he wanted to speak to each of them in their own language."[79] One of the first students, J.E. Janot, wrote in 1959 that even thirty-five years later he still remembered the "fatherly welcome" the superior had given him and the two members who arrived at the same time, Fathers Salet and Vignon.[80] One of the descriptions we have is particularly detailed: "The day after my arrival, he personally took me to deal with the various official details [to the police, because the speaker was not Italian, for enrollment, etc.]. There were about thirty of us Biennium students, ten for philosophy and twenty for

Germanic assistant of 7 September 1924.

74. Cf. letter to Cardinal F. Ehrle of 25 July 1924.

75. Letter to the general of 10 September 1924.

76. The already cited letter to the Germanic assistant of 7 September 1924.

77. The already quoted provincial superior Father G. Filograssi, who had previously taught exegesis at the Pontifical Gregorian University, had foreseen this from the outset; cf. letter of 29 March 1924 to Bea.

78. The names are found in LB, p. 16.

79. Cf. A. Skrinjar, S.J., ArchWit.

80. Cf. Na 1959/334.

theology. Bea insisted on religious discipline, the visit during meditation and examinations of conscience,[81] and in the evening we had to be back in the house by the time the evening Angelus bell rang, as was normal at that time. Relations with Father Bea were easy: it was simple to understand his explanations of things as concerns both religious life and studies. Bea presided over community recreation,[82] and he would give it life with his warmth and friendliness."[83] A member who spent a bare two months in the house tells how Bea used to take a walk with him "almost every afternoon" immediately after lunch, when, as the Romans say, the only people who go out are "dogs and Germans"; the expedition always had some specific destination—some interesting ancient site or monument, for example the Forum, the Palatine, the Catacombs of St. Sebastian or St. Agnes, St. Clement's Church, or the Ostia archeological excavations.[84]

Alongside his activity as superior of the Biennium, he also gave university lectures at the Pontifical Biblical Institute, and the correspondence shows that Bea saw this too as a "difficult and delicate" task, and considered the assignment "a mark of the trust that Father General had in him."[85] Father General himself confirmed this point of view when he pointed out that after Pius XI's recent *motu proprio* it was a mark "of the very greatest trust."[86] In the document in question the pope had decreed that in future nobody could teach sacred scripture in seminaries who had not first attended the relative courses and obtained the necessary academic qualifications, either at the Pontifical Biblical Commission or at the Pontifical Biblical Institute.[87] The general emphasized the great responsibility this placed on those who taught at the Biblical Institute.[88]

In the four years with which we are concerned here, Bea gave lectures on the following subjects at the Biblical Institute: special introduction to the minor prophets, critical and literary questions concerning respectively the Pentateuch, the Books of Samuel, Chronicles and the major prophets.

As regards biblical theology of the New Testament, which he taught at the Pontifical Gregorian University, we do not find the precise subjects noted until the third year (1926-1927): Christology in the Gospel of St. John, with the addition of seminars on the dogmatic themes of the Letters to the Ephesians and Colossians; the next year the subject was the Holy Spirit in the New Testament, with seminars on the messianic prophecies.

Here we shall give some first-hand *opinions on Bea as teacher.* "We liked

---

81. At that time the ancient practice of the order was still in force according to which, during the time devoted to these religious practices (which each person performed in his own room), a person entrusted with this task by the superior used to visit the rooms in order to check up on their performance.

82. This was also one of the customs of certain provinces.

83. G. Jarlot, S.J., ArchWit.

84. H. Koffler, S.J., ArchWit.

85. Letter to the general of 2 May 1924.

86. Letter of the general of 21 May 1924.

87. Cf. Bea's article for the twenty-fifth anniversary of the Biblical Institute, Biblio. 3, p. 23.

88. Letter of the general of 21 May 1924.

him because of the clear, systematic way he explained things."[89] "His lectures held one's attention," and he gave a clear explanation of the problems and the weak points of the arguments in favor of the two-source theory. In explaining the different modes of expression, he took account of the literary genre, which was in turn partly determined by content (stories, for example, or laws), and he gave suggestions as to further research and the attempt to solve the most difficult problems.[90] He said once: "We are neither liberals nor conservatives, we are simply looking for the truth."[91] On another occasion he said that the disciple must go beyond what he has learned from his teacher, but when he has done so he must gratefully acknowledge that he has based his work on that of his teacher and of the teachers who went before him.[92]

* * *

Toward the end of this period, Bea had some new problems with his health, which led to another of his interesting experiences with doctors. He had stomach pains and therefore went to seek advice. After examining his X-rays, the doctor diagnosed an ulcer and said that he needed surgery. When Father General was told, he said that Bea should wait for the summer vacation and obtain a second opinion in Germany. Bea therefore went to see the famous Munich surgeon, Professor Lebsche, who told him to eat the various foods that would be expected to cause problems for his stomach. After each of these experiments, he had an X-ray taken. Then, when he had examined all the X-rays, he told the patient: "Look, your so-called ulcer appears in different parts of the stomach according to what you've eaten. So it's simply a reaction of the walls of your stomach to food that you find hard to digest. I'll make you a list of food to avoid, and you'll be fine." And he turned out to be quite right. In 1953 Bea wrote to a relative: "I've been on a diet for twenty-five years now."[93] And there was never any further talk of surgery for the rest of his life.

An Important Interlude (October 1928—June 1930)

In 1957 Bea wrote as follows to a fellow Jesuit who was coming to the end of his term as provincial superior: "I have always been relieved of my jobs in order to be given even greater responsibilities."[94] When Bea was relieved of his

---

89. J. Ledit, S.J., ArchWit.
90. Cf. J. Schildenberger, O.S.B., ArchWit.
91. Cf. A. Skrinjar, S.J., ArchWit.
92. Cf. J. Schildenberger, O.S.B., ArchWit.
93. Nb 1953/93; cf. also Nc 1956/25.
94. N 1957/1.

position as superior of the Biennium in October 1928, the greater responsibilities involved a considerable increase in his teaching at the Pontifical Biblical Institute. This new period was thus marked by very intense teaching activity, but above all by the special job of "visitator" to the Catholic University of Tokyo and the whole Hiroshima mission.

Let us first take a look at *the teaching activity*. The immediate reason was that the Biblical Institute needed a replacement for a lecturer in Old Testament exegesis and they thought that Bea could do this job as well. In fact we find the following entry in *Dates*: "I move completely to the Biblical Institute: apart from the special introduction to the Old Testament, I also take Old Testament exegesis for the second year, as well as methodology and the course on the inspiration of sacred scripture."

The burden he was expected to shoulder was all the heavier if we bear in mind that until the academic year 1930-1931 Bea also continued to teach biblical theology at the Pontifical Gregorian University, which meant three lectures per week for one semester.[95] Apart from these lectures, Bea also gave the Biblical Institute, for example in the academic year 1928-1929, seven hours weekly in the first semester and four in the second,[96] and it should be noted that these were university-level, or rather post-graduate level, lectures.

It may be interesting to give the main subjects Bea dealt with in his lectures in this period. The core was made up of lectures on the exegesis of Exodus in the first year (two hours per week throughout the year) and the Books of Ezra and Nehemiah in the second (here again, two hours per week throughout the year). In both years there were also the course on the inspiration and hermeneutics of sacred scripture (two hours per week for one semester), the history of Old Testament times (one semester in 1928-1929) and seminars on exegetical questions concerning the Book of Genesis in the first year, and on the comparative study of the laws of Deuteronomy and those of Exodus and Leviticus in the second.

Apart from his teaching activity, there was a considerable amount of *writing*. In November 1928 his study of the question of the Pentateuch appeared[97] as part of the series of manuals for the use of theology students that the institute had been publishing for some time on the different branches of biblical science. Then at the end of the period, in June 1930, Bea also published a hundred-page study on "historical and dogmatic questions" concerning the inspiration and hermeneutics of sacred scripture[98]; although this second volume was printed, however, it was produced "for private use" by students. Both publications show that after he came to Rome Bea returned in earnest to the scientific work that had been interrupted by his term as provincial, and also how seriously he worked in Rome despite the commitments entailed by his position as superior of the Biennium.

In the spring of 1929 he was entrusted with another important responsibility

---

95. Cf. the *Liber Annuus* of the university for the year in question.

96. Cf. the *Acta Pontificii Instituti Biblici* for the year in question.

97. Cf. *Dates*; also Biblio. 1.

98. Cf. *Dates*; also Biblio. 2.

when he was called to become a member of the pontifical commission which Pius XI instructed to arrange the reform of higher ecclesiastical studies.[99]

The work of the commission resulted in Pius XI's constitution *Deus scientiarum Dominus*, which remained in force until the recent post-conciliar reforms, which in turn resulted in John Paul II's apostolic constitution *Sapientia Christiana*.[100] Having helped draft the important document of Pius XI, Bea did all he could to make sure that it was known and understood, and in particular that its contribution to biblical science was recognized.[101]

The great event of this period, however, was Bea's mission as *"visitator" to the Catholic University of Tokyo and the Hiroshima Mission* (June-October 1929). We have a detailed account from the Jesuit Father Paul Pfister, who was a missionary in Japan for several decades and was superior of the Japanese vice-province of the order for several years starting in 1949. He was thus in a position to provide first-hand information on the basis both of personal knowledge and of perusal of the relative documents.

Let us first consider the *background*. At the request of St. Pius X, the order had created a Catholic university in Tokyo and undertaken its running. In 1923, one of the earthquakes so sadly frequent in Japan destroyed the main building. Temporary arrangements were made, but they obviously could not continue indefinitely. The problem was to find the necessary funds for building work, apart from which the university was expected to deposit a large sum in order to obtain State recognition. The northern German province, which was directly responsible for the university, was going through a very difficult period because of inflation, which had wiped out even the capital that the German bishops had gathered for the university before the war. It was this desperate situation that gave rise to the idea of selling the land in the city center on which the university had been built and using the money to purchase a less expensive plot on the outskirts, while using what was left over to pay for building work. The plan had been approved by the superiors of the order, and indeed the land on the outskirts had already been bought. Even so, a good number of Jesuits told Father General Ledochowski that the plan to move the university would seriously prejudice future development. In this situation, the general made Bea visitor, entrusting him with the task of visiting the Hiroshima mission, and more particularly examining the question of the university.[102]

This assignment obviously indicated great trust, but it also entailed considerable responsibility. Bea had of course already had several years' experience of government, but here he was faced with a country and situation that were

99. Cf. *Dates*.

100. Cf. *AAS*, LXXI (1979), 469-520.

101. Cf. Biblio. 21, 20; see also Bea's article published in 1941 to mark the tenth anniversary of the same constitution, Biblio. 44.

102. In church language a "visitator" is a kind of special inspector sent by church authorities to examine special or particularly difficult situations on the spot, and then report back to his superiors, or sometimes resolve the problems himself. In the Society of Jesus a visitator is the plenipotentiary envoy of the superior general and has full authority even over the major superior of the territory involved.

completely new to him. It is therefore not difficult to understand the slight anxiety that led him to ask Father General: "But, Father, what is *your* opinion on the question of the university?" "I have no opinion. You go and see, and decide," was the general's brief reply.

For some reason that is not known to us, Bea decided to make the outward journey via Russia, Siberia and Korea. Foreseeing difficulties over the transit visa for Russia and Siberia, he took advantage of a journey to Berlin to have the apostolic nuncio, Eugenio Pacelli, ask the Russian embassy whether there was any hope of obtaining such a visa. The answer was in the affirmative, although since Bea was resident in Rome, the visa application would have to be made to the Soviet embassy in Italy. However, when Bea went to the latter he received a categorical refusal. "What do you mean? I checked with the apostolic nunciature in Berlin," objected Bea, "and they told me there was no problem." "Are you in contact with the apostolic nunciature in Berlin?" he was asked. "Yes," answered Bea. "Wait a moment then." And after a short wait, the clerk came back with the necessary approval.

At the end of a long, wearying journey—the Trans-Siberian Railroad traveled at about twenty-five miles per hour in those days—the visitator finally reached his destination, having visited Seoul on the way.

Bea immediately set to work, discussing the question of the university with its founder and rector, Father H. Hoffmann, studying the situation, and inspecting the sites in question. Having grasped the vital elements, he had a full-dress meeting of the community called. He himself described this meeting as follows: "I opened the discussion by pointing out that we had to distinguish between two orders of question: (1) the question of which locations would allow the best possible development of the university, and thus whether to retain the present site or move to the outskirts; and (2) the financial problem." As regards the first question, everybody agreed that it was far better for the university to remain in its present location. When objections were raised to this solution on the basis of the financial problem, the visitator asked them to hold to the distinction between the two questions. Everybody finally recognized that it would be best to retain the old location. Bea summed up the situation as follows: "So we're all agreed that it's best not to move the university. We shall have to give up the idea of relocation as a solution to the economic problem, and find some other way of solving it." In order to preclude any second thoughts, Bea cabled Father General the same day: "All agreed best university stay center city." This was the story as Bea told it.

We would now add two accounts from people exceptionally well-placed to speak about the positive outcome of his mission. One is the previously mentioned Father Pfister,[103] and the other is Father B. Bitter, S.J., who helped organize the journey and for several decades was treasurer of the Hiroshima mission, which then became the Japanese vice-province. Both emphasize the

---

103. P. Pfister speaks of this not only in his statement (ArchWit), but also in a letter to Father Bea, N 1952/50.

credit the visitator deserves for keeping the magnificent downtown position for the Catholic university.[104] Bitter's account is particularly telling because as treasurer of the mission for several decades it was he who had to bear the burden of the debt contracted to build the university, as we shall see below.[105]

Pfister says that Bea must also be credited with having speeded up construction work. Indeed, the visitator—who had acquired considerable experience some years before in building the college for philosophy students belonging to the southern German province—personally drew up the basic plan for the new university. Although the university had about two hundred students at that time, the visitator's plan envisaged a university for one thousand two hundred.[106] In later correspondence, Bea emphasized how startled the other fathers were,[107] raising objections such as: "We'll never have so many students; on the contrary, it's important to stay small." The visitator did not let them frighten him, but simply observed: "When you've gone beyond that number, you can go on building over here on the other side. You can build enough room for two thousand four hundred students." As we shall see, the future proved him totally right.

Father Pfister also refers briefly to what Bea did as visitator to the apostolic vicariate in Hiroshima, saying that he had full discussions with Apostolic Vicar J. Ross, S.J., and with the missionaries in charge of the various missionary posts, examining the major problems of the missionary apostolate and the main difficulties of the times, and encouraging them all to persevere with faith and trust in preaching the gospel and building up the church in Japan.

He came home by sea, via Hongkong, Singapore, Ceylon, etc. It throws an interesting and significant sidelight on Bea's personality that he kept a kind of short diary during this part of his journey, which is now found in the archives. It takes up thirty-three pages of a pocket note-book, beginning on 9 October and ending on 21 November, and is full of interesting information about places and people he visited and met, etc.

Bea always retained a great love for the church in Japan and a deep understanding of its problems. He himself spoke of this in later correspondence: "I have never forgotten the few months I spent in Tokyo and at the Hiroshima Mission; I shall remember the vice-province with joy and interest as long as I live"[108]; "I have Japan deep in my heart."[109]

---

104. ArchWit.
105. In 1959, when it was announced that Bea had been made a cardinal, the then provincial and future father general, Father P. Arrupe, wrote to Bea saying that the announcement had been received in Japan with great joy: "It can never be forgotten that we have you to thank for the fact that the university is still in the center of the city today" (Na 1959/24).
106. In N 1955/94 Bea speaks of a plan for seven to nine hundred students. Pfister on the other hand speaks of twelve hundred, and I personally heard this latter figure from Bea on several occasions.
107. Cf. N 1955/94.
108. N 1952/50.
109. N 1951-112. Someone who works in the archives of the general curia of the order has kindly told me that there is a huge mass of papers under the heading "Japonia 1004," including a typed

With the assistance of Pfister's account, we can add a few words on the fruits of Bea's visit and the successive development of the university. The new building went up according to Bea's plans and was ready three years later in 1932. The English province of the order had helped them obtain a large loan from an English bank, and after they had been paying off the interest for about twenty years, they were finally able to clear the whole debt in the 1950s.[110] Bea also provided help for the actual building work, suggesting that those in charge of the northern German province should send the lay brother, Ignazius Groppe, S.J., to Japan, since he was an architect and could therefore provide very valuable assistance.

The new building would survive the heavy bombing of 1945, although not without a certain amount of damage. During the war the university also managed to purchase further tracts of land adjoining the university, and later on other buildings were put up here. The number of students gradually rose to nine thousand. "Thus, with the Lord's help, the hopes Bea expressed during his visit were fulfilled," concluded Father Pfister. For his part, Bea wrote to Pfister in 1953 as follows: "If I compare what I saw in Tokyo and the mission in 1929 with the present state of affairs, it almost seems like a miracle."[111]

---

110. I received these details from Father Pfister in a letter of 21 June 1977 (ArchWit).
111. N 1952/50.

CHAPTER 4

RECTOR OF THE PONTIFICAL BIBLICAL INSTITUTE

(1930–1949)

After his return from Japan Bea was able to enjoy a relatively calm year of work, although he did have a large number of lessons at both the Biblical Institute and the Gregorian University. And he really did need a little peace and quiet. It was barely a year since he had taken over exegesis of the Old Testament at the Biblical Institute, as well as the special introduction.

However, this peace did not last long, for on 6 July 1930 he was nominated rector of the institute, as the position was then called. Until then the task had been shared between two fathers: the Spaniard A. Fernandez, S.J., was head of the institute, in other words of the teaching and scientific work, while the American J.G. O'Rourke, S.J., was religious superior of the community of professors (although this always included a certain number of young members of the order who were specializing in biblical studies). However, Bea was immediately entrusted with both jobs.

In order to give an initial idea of Bea's new task, we should explain that the Biblical Institute was a specialized university institute founded by Pope Saint Pius X in 1909. In the address given in the presence of Pope John XXIII on the fiftieth anniversary of the institute in February 1960, Bea described the intentions of the founder, saying that he "wanted to stem the disorientation that was rampant in the church at that time, especially because of discussions and difficulties in the biblical sphere. The institute was to be in Rome, where it would be under the eye of the supreme pontiffs and would work according to their instructions; it was to be a center for biblical studies provided with the best biblical scholars and all suitable or necessary scientific instruments, and was to be capable of training teachers who were well versed in biblical subjects for the theological schools of the Catholic world."[1]

The fact that such an institute was entrusted wholly to Bea is an indication of the trust he already enjoyed both with the head of his own order and with the Roman Congregation for Seminaries and Institutes of Study, which was officially responsible for nominating the rector of the institute. At the time Bea certainly never imagined that he would have to bear this responsibility for nineteen long years.

This period is of great—indeed, fundamental—importance to our biography, for the breadth and weighty nature of the tasks performed for almost twenty years provide a measure of his remarkably varied talents, his qualities and his energy. By its very nature, the job meant that he moved deep into the Roman world and particularly the offices of the Holy See, so that he was even in lively and not infrequent contact with the popes of those years. On the other hand, the

---

1. *Biblica*, XLI (1960), 9-10.

very international atmosphere provided by the teaching and student bodies of the institute meant that he had to learn to work with people from a wide variety of cultural, mental and linguistic backgrounds, a feature that was even truer of the scientific work carried out by the institute in various publications, as we shall see. Added to this were the many contacts at international meetings, and interconfessional contacts would also be established very soon and would gradually grow.

In order to make the wealth of material at our disposition as clear as possible, we shall present it under three main headings: (1) director of the institute[2]; (2) teacher and scholar; and (3) priest and apostle at the service of the church.

1. Director of the Institute

We shall start by presenting what we can describe as Bea's *ordinary activity* as head of the institute, after which we shall discuss the *special events* that were so abundant in the exceptionally long period of nineteen years during which Bea held this twofold responsibility.

In considering Bea's tasks and activity as Director of the Pontifical Biblical Institute, we must remember what was said about the aims of the institute as intended by its saintly founder Pope Pius X: training teachers of sacred scripture and furthering Catholic biblical knowledge. These aims are pursued in practical terms with specialized university-level teaching and scientific work.[3]

In order to understand the complexity of the task entrusted to the institute, we must bear in mind that interpreters of sacred scripture must look for the meaning that each author intended to express when speaking or writing in specific historical circumstances that depended on his times and culture. Study of sacred scripture thus inevitably entails study of the so-called orientalistic sciences, in other words the branches of knowledge that concern the ancient Near East: the languages and civilizations of the countries (ancient Mesopotamia, Egypt, Arabia, Phoenicia and Asia Minor) that constituted the special environment in which Israel lived in the different periods of its history and in which the Bible was born. In his encyclical *Divino afflante Spiritu*, Pius XII said that anyone who wants to interpret sacred scripture adequately "must, as it were, go back wholly in spirit to those remote centuries of the East, and with the aid of history, archeology, ethnology and other sciences, accurately determine what genres of writing, so to speak, the authors of that ancient period would be likely

---

2. The usual title is "rector" of the institute, but for the sake of clarity and in order to remain closer to the Italian, we have preferred to speak of the "director" of the institute.

3. In several of his publications, Bea himself explained the aims and activity of the institute, first of all in the Latin work published to mark the twenty-fifth anniversary of the institute (Biblio. 3), then in 1947 in the Supplement to the *Dictionnaire de la Bible* (Biblio. 65), and lastly in 1951 in the *Enciclopedia Cattolica* (Biblio. 88).

to use, and in fact did use."[4] This means that it is particularly important to study various types of writing from those periods.

To be more precise, this involves study of the languages in which the various books of the Old and New Testaments were written — Hebrew, Aramaic and Greek. After this come the "auxiliary subjects" (or "related studies") of history, geography and archeology. Lastly there is the study of thirteen languages of the ancient Near East, all but three of which fall under one of four main headings: Semitic, Assyriological, Egyptological and Sanskrit-Iranian.[5]

Having described the vast field covered by the institute, we must now give some further details of the two types of work that the institute performs, in other words, training teachers of sacred scripture for theological faculties and seminaries through specialized university-level teaching, and study and research.

We would cite two sets of statistics in order to give some idea of the extent of the influence exercised by the institute with the training of teachers of sacred scripture for the whole Catholic world. For its first twenty-five years (until 1934) Bea gave the following figures: the institute had had about nine hundred students; of these, the members of diocesan clergy came from two hundred and fifty different dioceses, while the religious came from sixty orders or congregations.[6] The second set of figures dates from 1959 and refers to the first fifty years: the institute had had about two thousand five hundred students in all, coming from sixty-five countries, with diocesan priests from 484 different dioceses and religious from 117 orders or congregations.[7] Ex-students included ten cardinals and forty-eight archbishops or bishops. We would add that after 1959 the number of students grew by leaps and bounds, so that while there were about one hundred and eighty students per year in the late 1950s, the number rose to over three hundred during the next ten years.

One further figure goes to show the complexity and the very high level of the studies in question. It was not until 1928 that the Holy See granted the institute the right to bestow a degree in sacred scripture. Even so, in the first five years (until 1934) only four were given,[8] while no more than eighty were given in the thirty years between 1930 and 1960.[9]

Similarly, we shall give only a few brief details regarding the second type of work—that of *study and scientific research*. In the strictly biblical field the

---

4. Pius XII, *Divino afflante Spiritu* (1943), English translation N.C.W.C. (Boston, n.d.), p. 20 (ct).

5. For those who may be interested, they are as follows. Semitic section: Arabic, Aramaic, Syriac, Ethiopic. Assyriological section: Sumerian and Akkadian. Egyptological section: Egyptian and Coptic. Sanskrit-Iranian section: Sanskrit and Iranian. Apart from these sections, there are also Armenian, Georgian and Hittite.

6. Cf. Biblio. 3, pp. 46, 48. The figure is certainly not large, but it should be borne in mind that we are not dealing with "mass production" here, inasmuch as the chairs of sacred scripture in the Catholic Church are limited in number, and at that time there were even fewer. Development of an awareness of the need for special studies in this area took time.

7. Cf. S. Schmidt, "Cinquant'anni del Pontificio Istituto Biblico," *CC*, 1960/I, 618.

8. Cf. Biblio. 3, p. 49.

9. Cf. Schmidt, "Cinquant'anni," p. 618.

institute produces a scholarly review and a more popular review.[10] There are also three scientific series of exegetical studies of documentary value.[11] The institute also acts as publisher for all these publications.

Bea considerably broadened and enriched the field of *studies of the ancient East*. Until that time various studies had been published, especially by the famous orientalist Anton Deimel,[12] but there were no regular publications. Bea must be credited with the initiative for having a similar special faculty of orientalistic studies set up within the institute in 1932, with the right to grant a license (or diploma) and then a degree. This acted as a spur to this type of study and considerably improved the quality of such work. It is noteworthy that the initiative should have come not from a specialist in orientalistic studies, but from a biblicist and exegete. The institute was thus able to make a place for itself in the sphere of orientalistic research and could act as host to the International Congress of Orientalists in 1935. Bea also started the review *Orientalia*, together with the corresponding series of fuller studies entitled *Analecta Orientalia*.

We would lastly recall two important *instruments* for all this work. Obviously an institute of this kind cannot operate without an adequate library; and in the essay Bea published for the twenty-fifth anniversary of the institute, he said that at that time its library contained about one hundred thousand volumes, a remarkable number for an institute that had been in existence for so short a time.

The other instrument was the branch established by the institute in the heart of the Holy Land, in Jerusalem. Although the saintly founder of the institute had expressed hopes for such an extension, these could not be fulfilled until 1927.[13] This house offered hospitality to students who wanted to obtain first-hand knowledge of Palestine and the neighboring biblical countries, and it had the particularly demanding task of organizing study trips, mostly for the institute's students, through the biblical countries of Asia Minor, Lebanon and Syria, Palestine and Egypt; such journeys lasted about one month.[14] From the beginning Bea showed a lively interest in this branch, visiting it for the first time only a few months after his appointment (October 1930). The house would play a particularly important part in a project that contributed a great deal to gaining the institute the respect of the scientific world — the archeological excavations carried out in the Jordan Valley. We shall say more about this initiative in due course.

All we have just said as introduction to the institute and its activity in the twofold field of the Bible and the orientalistic sciences, teaching and research, was of course Bea's regular field of activity as director. It is not difficult to imagine the amount of contacts and discussions, reflection, decisions and

10. The scholarly review *Biblica* was founded in 1921, and the more popular review *Verbum Domini* only slightly later, although the latter ceased publication for various reasons in 1969.
11. Exegetical studies and studies on biblical theology and the history of exegesis are collected in *Analecta Biblica*, those that help explain the Bible with orientalistic material in *Biblica et Orientalia*, while *Documenta Biblica et Ecclesiastica* publishes studies of more documentary value.
12. Cf. *LThK*, III, 195.
13. Cf. Biblio. 3, pp. 67-68.
14. Cf. *ibid.*, p. 70.

responsibilities entailed. Even so, it must also be added that Bea did not confine himself to directing things, but took a broad hand in the actual work as both teacher and scholar. Apart from this, from the outset he personally assumed the position of chief editor of the scholarly review *Biblica*, continuing in this post throughout his whole period as director.

Specific Events during the Papacy of Pius XI

(a) One of the first of Bea's more striking initiatives concerned the organization of the *Italian Biblical Week* for professors of sacred scripture in Italy. We have a detailed first-hand report on this from Mgr. G. Scattolòn, who was in correspondence with Bea for many years and was later for a long time Secretary of the Italian Biblical Association, which was more or less born from that initiative.[15] He says that as early as 1925 Father Alberto Vaccari had been asked to hold summer courses for teachers of sacred scripture in Italy, and although Vaccari would have liked to organize such courses, this was never possible, due to a lack of sufficient understanding on the part of those in charge of the institute at that time. As soon as Bea was nominated rector, he gave his vice-rector, the same Father Vaccari, his encouragement, and that very year it was possible to hold the first "Italian Biblical Week." The initiative received strong encouragement from Pope Pius XI, who had in the past taught Hebrew in a seminary for six years[16] and thus had a clear understanding of the importance and necessity of the project. He regularly granted audiences to those attending the courses, and it was he who decided that the week should be held every year (and indeed it was not easy to obtain permission to cancel it when large-scale difficulties arose in the years 1935 and 1938).[17] The pope's interest was so keen that in 1937 he asked that the two main lectures be given in his presence at Castel Gandolfo. These were Bea's lecture on "Prehistory and the Interpretation of Genesis" and Vaccari's on "The Mosaic Question and Philology."[18]

In order to take the various threads of our material in order, we would immediately mention the interest and support Bea continued to give to this project, repeatedly taking part in the "weeks" with lectures on major subjects.[19] After attending them for a number of years, it was he who suggested, together with Father Silverio Zedda, S.J., that teachers of sacred scripture in Italy should form an association.[20] With Bea's active support, the suggestion was put into operation during the 1948 Italian Biblical Week, when the "Italian Biblical Association" was constituted; this association was one of the very first in Italy to unite various categories of teachers of the sacred sciences.

---

15. ArchWit. Cf. also the article the cardinal wrote in 1968 for the twentieth anniversary of the Italian Biblical Association, Biblio. 440.

16. Cf. Biblio. 32, p. 122.

17. Cf. *ibid.*, p. 129.

18. Cf. *ibid.*, p. 130. The main points of Bea's lecture were published in Biblio. 27.

19. In 1948 on the anthropological problem in Genesis 1-2 (cf. Biblio. 10); in the years 1950 and 1952 on the Dead Sea Scrolls (cf. Biblio. 77, 92).

20. Cf. G. Scattolòn, ArchWit.

(b) Although very modest, Bea's contribution was still interesting in connection with the special *jubilee year* that Pius XI decided should be held to mark the *nineteenth centenary of the Redemption*. Just before Christmas 1932, the Rector of the Biblical Institute had a private audience with Pius XI in order to give him the good wishes of the institute and to offer him copies of its main publications of that year. The pope surprised him by asking: "When did Our Lord die?" "Your Holiness knows that I'm an Old Testament specialist," answered Bea, smiling a little. "I know, but this is still something you should know," replied the pope. Fortunately Bea did in fact know, and he explained that from the point of view of the chronology of the New Testament only two hypotheses were possible: either the year 30 or the year 33. "All right," said the pope, "write me an opinion on the question," and then went on: "So many pointless jubilees are held, but the nineteenth centenary of the Redemption is something really worth celebrating. I've thought for a long time about what could be done, and I've requested prayers from various monasteries, asking the Lord to grant me light. This morning after holy mass I had the idea of an extraordinary jubilee. Nobody knows yet. I've only asked the Director of Vatican Radio to keep the station on stand-by." "Holy Father," asked Bea, "when would you like to have the opinion? For the end of the year?" "Yes," said the pope, "toward then."

However, Bea was already familiar with the pope's energetic ways, and as soon as he got back to the house he asked Father Urban Holzmeister, S.J., the specialist in New Testament chronology, to prepare the opinion. He himself had almost finished translating it into Italian when he received a telephone call from the pope's privy chamberlain, Mgr. Carlo Confalonieri, a future cardinal: "Father, His Holiness is waiting for something from you." "Yes: tell the pope he will have it at eleven thirty," was the ready answer. There is a photocopy of the paper in question in the archives, and it is dated 23 December 1932. In his speech to the Sacred College the next day, the pope announced his intention of proclaiming an extraordinary jubilee for the nineteenth centenary of the Redemption.

This jubilee was celebrated in 1933 with widespread participation on the part of Christians.

(c) In 1934 the *institute celebrated its twenty-fifth year of existence*, and this was marked by an "academy" held in the presence of the Holy Father. Pius XI had sent the rector of the institute a handwritten letter of congratulations on the occasion,[21] and although this can be seen in part as a routine gesture, it was not in the normal run of things that apart from noting the progress and achievements of the institute, the pope should go into further detail, emphasizing the number of students who had passed through the institute and the constant growth of its library and of publications by its professors, etc.

(d) We have already noted Bea's special interest in the work of the *Jerusalem branch of the institute*. After his first visit (in 1930), he made another in 1934,

---

21. Reproduced in BM, pp. 78-79.

and indeed on this latter occasion he stayed in the Middle East from July to October, joining the students on a long study trip. The diary Bea kept on this trip is now found in the archives, and it contains a great many details about the journey, with the departure on 19 July, the times of trains to Brindisi, and notes on things to see in Bari and Brindisi. Then come his visits to Athens (for which he had even drawn up his own plan of the Acropolis), Corinth, Nicea, etc. These are followed by some notes on his travels in Palestine, Lebanon and Syria, then notes on the journey from Jerusalem to the Negeb, Sinai, Elat, Aqaba and Jordan, then back to Jerusalem, ending up with the return to Italy by sea. These travel notes are often accompanied by sketches or descriptions of places, digs, etc., and there are also details of the sickness of various travel companions and similar observations.

Bea visited Jerusalem a third time, from 17 December 1936 to 11 January 1937, although the diary of this third journey stops on 26 December.

(e) One of the important matters dealt with in this last visit to Jerusalem was the *archeological excavations at Teleilat Ghassul* in the lower Jordan Valley. The dig was directed by those in charge of the Jerusalem center and did a great deal to increase the standing of the institute in the world of biblical and orientalistic studies. Excavations had been started in 1929, after various benefactors—including Pope Pius XI himself, who made contributions on two occasions[22]—had made sufficient funds available. Father Alexis Mellon, S.J., director of the Jerusalem center, was in charge, and the beginning was marked by one of those incidents that are not infrequent in this type of work. One of the local workers—obviously an "expert" in his own way—had falsified an inscription in order to ensure a good bonus, and this misled those in charge into thinking that they had found the remains of Sodom and Gomorrah. The director was delighted, and sent a telegram to the rector in Rome. However, two or three days later he unfortunately had to retract.

The incident of the presumed discovery of Sodom and Gomorrah even had echoes in an audience with Pius XI, who was well-known for his lively interest in every kind of research, particularly in the historical and archeological fields.[23] (In his article on the pope's attitude to biblical studies, Bea says that when the pope was offered somewhat voluminous publications on the eve of the major feasts, he used to say: "We'll leave it for now: we can't look at them when so many children are waiting for us. We shall allow ourselves the pleasure of looking at them at our leisure in a few days' time when there are no audiences."[24] It was the same interest that led the pope to help with the expenses of the excavations in question on repeated occasions, as we have already said.) When Bea now entered the antechamber for the audience in question, the pope's privy chamberlain was a little surprised: "Father, the audience will be fairly short because at twelve His Holiness is receiving the Roman nobility for their new year's wishes." "That's all right," said Bea. In the course of their conversation,

---

22. Cf. Biblio. 32, p. 125.

23. Cf. *ibid.*

24. Cf. *ibid.*, p. 124.

the pope asked for news of the dig in question, and was especially keen to learn more about rumors that they had discovered nothing less than the remains of Sodom and Gomorrah. Bea explained that the story had originated with a worker's fraud, as often happens with work of this kind. Pius XI then remarked: "All right, but these cities must be *somewhere*." Bea had to explain that according to a number of scholars they were now under water somewhere in the Dead Sea. The pope was so interested in the discussion that the audience went on for forty minutes. We can imagine the looks Bea received from the assembled nobles when he emerged, and what they must have thought of someone for whom the pope dared keep such important people as themselves waiting.

Much later, in the aforementioned address given before Pope John XXIII, Bea gave the following evaluation of the dig: "It was very rich in valuable results and brought to light a culture that had been completely unknown until then, dating from roughly 3500 to 3200 B.C., and today commonly referred to as 'Ghasulian.' There are two splendidly illustrated volumes giving the results of this important research, which was interrupted by the last world war and the struggles between the Arabs and Israel. However, it has now been possible to resume it, and apparently it promises some valuable contributions to knowledge of the prehistory and history of the region chosen by God as the cradle of his chosen people."[25]

(f) It is interesting that it was Pius XI who opened the door to the *first ecumenical contacts* for Bea and for the institute. Two respected German Evangelical scholars, Johannes Hempel and Paul Volz, were organizing the first international congress of Old Testament exegetes, to be held in Göttingen in 1935, and for the first time in history the Pontifical Biblical Institute was invited to such a meeting. It was an unusual situation, and the prefect of the relative Roman congregation, Cardinal Gaetano Bisleti, was uncertain how to proceed. Bea then asked if he would object if he, as rector, laid the case before the pope. Once he had received permission, Bea went and explained the situation to Pius XI, and he himself described the result in the autobiographical article we have already quoted several times, saying that Pius XI, "who had been a librarian by profession for most of his life, first at the Ambrosiana in Milan and later at the Vatican Library, had in fact had a great deal of experience of contacts with scholars of every kind. He therefore replied, as decidedly and vigorously as usual: 'Why not accept? Go ahead, and take some good professors with you who will be able to answer questions.' It was a very courageous decision for those times, and was to prove remarkably fruitful. Indeed, the delegation from the institute was so well received at the meeting that its leader, the rector of the institute, was invited to chair its closing session."[26]

The participation of the delegation from the institute and of Catholic exegetes in general was a great success. The rector of the institute was asked to give the first lecture, which concerned the Teleilat Ghassul excavations.[27] Bea closes his

---

25. Biblio. 129, p. 14; cf. also Biblio. 3, pp. 76-77.
26. R 1967/19, pp. 2-3.
27. In the archives we have concordant statements from Professor Josef Ziegler of Würzburg and

account by saying: "Frequent contacts with non-Catholic scholars from every part of the world thus began, contacts that would increase still further after 1935 when the institute acted as host in Rome to the International Congress on the Ancient East."[28]

(g) It was in roughly the same period that a *certain trend in interpreting sacred scripture* began to appear in Italy which could have constituted a serious danger for the institute itself. A multi-volume commentary on sacred scripture had appeared in 1935 under the title, *La Sacra Scrittura, Psicologia, commento, meditazione*,[29] written by the priest Dolindo Ruotolo, under the pseudonym of Dain Cohenel. The work attacked the study and scientific interpretation of sacred scripture, saying that they were based "on rationalistic and modernistic foundations."[30] In the wake of this work, various booklets signed by bishops appeared in defense of Cohenel's commentary and method. The campaign and the attacks continued for a number of years and were still going on, as we shall see, even after the papacy of Pius XI.

I know from Father Bea that some of these publications were even sent to Pius XI, who said: "Look at this stuff they're sending me," and threw them away. However, the pontiff did not stop at mere words, but acted decisively in defense of authentic scientific work and of the Biblical Institute in particular. To this end he twice presided in person over the discussion of dissertations at the biblical faculty of the institute,[31] on both occasions speaking out strongly in favor of the authentic scientific study of sacred scripture. The first time was in May 1938 when he presided over the discussion of the thesis of a Salesian priest, Giorgio Castellino, on the subject *Le lamentazioni e gli inni in Babilonia e Israele*,[32] and on this occasion the pope expressed both regret that those in charge too often undervalue academic degrees and the biblical sciences, and also the desire that each diocese should have at least one priest holding an academic qualification in biblical sciences.[33]

Barely six months later—and only a few months prior to his death—the pope repeated the gesture, presiding over the discussion of the thesis of the Norbertine priest, Benjamin Wambacq, entitled *L'épithète divin. Yahweh Sebaoth*.[34] In his article on Pius XI and biblical studies, to which we have already referred a number of times, Bea explained the reason for the pope's presence, quoting the expressions used by the pontiff himself on that occasion. The pope wanted to be sure that none of those in charge of studies in Rome or those doing such

---

Father J. Schildenberger, O.S.B., of Beuron; cf. also *L'unione dei cristiani*, p. 89 (*The Unity of Christians*, pp. 94-95).

28. R 1967/19, p. 3; cf. also *The Unity of Christians*, p. 95. It should be noted that the Congress of Orientalists took place in 1935 and not in 1938.

29. Or "Sacred Scripture: Psychology, commentary and meditation."

30. For Dolindo Ruotolo (1882-1970), cf. Dolindo Ruotolo, *Fui chiamato Dolindo che significa dolore. Pagine di autobiografia* (Naples, 1972).

31. Cf. Biblio. 32, p. 128.

32. Or "Lamentations and Hymns in Babylon and Israel."

33. Cf. *ibid.*

34. Or The Divine Atribute: "Lord of Hosts."

studies should be left in ignorance of his views and wishes in this connection, and that no one should have reason to misrepresent them or discount them. For this reason he wanted the occasion to have the widest possible coverage, so that, while the previous discussion had taken place at Castel Gandolfo, this time he wanted it to take place in the Great Hall of Blessings and explicitly asked that as many students as possible should attend.[35] At the end of this second discussion, the pope referred back to his words on the other occasion, saying ". . . that, from the height of that place, he had already on another occasion declared how much he cared about the Biblical Institute, and even more so those biblical studies that are cultivated there with such diligence and zeal, and to such praise."[36]

In order not to break the thread of our narrative, we shall immediately continue with an account of developments in this connection during the papacy of Pius XII, for despite the solemn warnings of Pius XI, the opponents had not laid down their arms, but were in fact hoping that Pius XII would enable them to obtain the victory that had so far eluded them. They boasted that many cardinals and bishops had approved their views, and even cited names. A letter from Bea dated 21 March 1940 tells us about their machinations: "You yourself have already guessed the true value of 'the authoritative approval of so many cardinals and bishops.' One cardinal told me: 'We receive a heap of books each week, and it would be physically impossible to read them all. For the sake of good manners, one sends a word of thanks and encouragement, but certainly without any intention of recommending the work in question.' And he was very indignant that his words had been twisted in this way. Another cardinal told me that he had sent a simple note of thanks, together with the price of the book. And there his name was among those who 'highly commend' the work. Cardinal Ehrle wrote a personal note, expressing thanks for the book and saying that he had sent it on to the Biblical Institute—and he too appears among those approving it."[37]

The Biblical Institute itself was drawn directly into the affair, since the name of its vice-rector, Father Alberto Vaccari, was mentioned a number of times in one of the pamphlets. Despite these references, "the institute had received neither the first nor the second pamphlet of the two bishops, nor indeed the actual work of Cohenel or other writings supporting his views. Only after a long lapse of time did Father Vaccari himself receive the two pamphlets," observes Bea again.[38] Father Vaccari wanted to reply with an article, but the fact that the other side cited the support of so many cardinals and bishops was somewhat intimidating. The letter we have been quoting from tells us that he appealed to the

35. Cf. *ibid.* The main points of this speech by the pope are found in Luigi Gonzaga da Fonseca, "Pius XI, Pontifex Maximus de studiorum Biblicorum momento et necessitate," *Verbum Domini*, XVIII (1939), 187-190; cf. also *Biblica*, XIX (1938), 356ff; *Acta Pontificii Instituti Biblici*, IV, 132.

36. *Biblica*, XX (1939), 116; cf. also *Acta Pontificii Instituti Biblici*, IV, 177-178. (At that time, the indirect form was often used in such addresses.)

37. Letter to G. Scattolòn of 21 March 1940 (ArchWit).

38. *Ibid.*

Sacred Congregation of the Holy Office, which imposed silence on both sides until it had reached its decision.

The rector of the institute did not stand by passively either. "As concerns the institute," wrote Bea in the same letter, "against which the booklet appeared to be making serious accusations, I addressed Mgr. Sanna, Bishop of Gravina, officially, asking him to state whether the insinuation of 'teaching on a rationalistic and modernistic basis' was directed against the institute, and if so to submit proof to the Sacred Congregation for Seminaries. A few days later I received a formal reply stating that these accusations were not directed against the 'venerable Pontifical Biblical Institute.' I of course passed this declaration on to the Sacred Congregation for Seminaries, the Cardinal Prefect of which is ready to take energetic steps if the propaganda against Father Vaccari continues in the seminaries."[39]

Although the pamphlets in question were capable of damaging the good name of the institute with certain local authorities, the central ones were quite another matter. In this connection Bea wrote in the same letter: "We know that we have the highest authorities of the Roman Curia on our side and that they strongly disapproved of the conduct of the two signatories of the pamphlet."[40] However, the approach adopted—that of "dragging even cardinals and bishops into the debate—is an embarrassment also to the Roman authorities, although the respect due to the hierarchy means that they must proceed in a very delicate manner. This is why the whole matter moves forward so slowly."[41] Even so, in November 1940, the Sacred Congregation of the Holy Office placed Cohenel's commentary on the index of forbidden books.[42]

Despite this reverse, they had the courage to try their luck again on 24 May 1941, presenting Pius XII with a statement with a title that summarizes all the attacks and could be translated in English as: "A very serious danger for the church and for souls. The critical-scientific system in the study and interpretation of sacred scripture, its grievous perversion and its aberrations." They also had the bad taste to distribute "faithful copies" throughout Italy, bearing the words "Valid as original manuscript. Fully reserved to conscience."[43]

On the pope's instructions, the Pontifical Biblical Commission then stepped in, above all in order to avoid any harmful effects that such writings might have on the training of future priests as regards biblical studies. The commission decided to send a long letter "to the Archbishops and Bishops of Italy" in which it clearly defined the authentic method of studying sacred scripture. The letter describes the views contained in the statement sent to the pope as follows: "The philological, historical, archeological, etc., examinations of the Bible are noth-

---

39. *Ibid.*
40. *Ibid.*
41. *Ibid.*
42. Cf. *AAS*, XXXII (1940), 553. The author immediately expressed his obedience in a public letter; cf. Ruotolo, *Fui chiamato Dolindo*, pp. 487-488.
43. Cf. *AAS*, XXXIII (1941), 465; also S. Lyonnet, "Le Cardinal Bea et le développment des études bibliques," *Rivista Biblica* (1969), 371-392; cf. pp. 378-379.

ing but rationalism, naturalism, modernism, skepticism, atheism, etc., and in order to understand the Bible the spirit must be given free rein."[44] The letter then deals with the literal meaning of sacred scripture, the use of the Vulgate, textual criticism, study of oriental languages and the auxiliary sciences—all points that would later be found, along with others, in the encyclical *Divino afflante Spiritu*.[45] The document also explicitly takes up the defense of the Biblical Institute, saying that since it was founded by St. Pius X its work "has not ceased to develop under the eyes of the Supreme Pontiffs along lines so consistent as not to require proof."[46]

Specific Events during the Papacy of Pius XII

(a) A New Latin Translation of the Psalms

In the years after the Second World War, there was a story current at the Biblical Institute that had a certain air of credibility and that described an exchange said to have taken place between Father Bea and Pius XI, in which Bea suggested the correction of the Latin Psalter used in the Roman Breviary in order to make it more faithful to the original texts. "It's difficult," was the pope's reply. Bea did not drop the subject, but went on to explain that the possibilities ranged from a simple correction to a totally new translation. The pope repeated more clearly that there were many obstacles. Bea still persisted, but at this point the pope cut him off: "It's impossible. Do you have other things to talk about?"[47]

At the beginning of the papacy of Pius XII, on 19 January 1941, the director of the institute received formal instructions to produce a new Latin translation of the psalms with the help of experts from the institute.[48] What led to such an apparently sudden decision? Bea told me that in his first audience with Pius XII (I do not know the date), he mentioned this project among the various possibilities for action, but that he never heard anything more about it. M. Zerwick thinks that the decision came from a suggestion made by Father Bea. However, we have very explicit evidence to the contrary. First of all, there is that of Cardinal D. Tardini, who says that one of the three plans that Pius XII told him of "a short time after his election" was "the new translation of the psalms, so that the clergy could better understand and appreciate the beauties of the daily liturgical

44. *AAS*, XXXIII (1941), 465-472.
45. On the significance of this letter for the drafting of the encyclical, see Lyonnet, "Le Cardinal Bea," pp. 378-381.
46. A full commentary on the various points in the letter are found in the book of A. Vaccari, *Lo studio della S. Scrittura. Lettera della Pont. Comm. Biblica con introduzione e commenti* (Rome, 1943); cf. also Bea's short note on this letter, Biblio. 50.
47. The basic truth of this account is supported by M. Zerwick, in BM, p. 77. However, the account given by H. Bacht, "Kardinal Bea: Wegbereiter der Einheit," *Catholica* (Paderborn), XXXV (1981), 181, is not so exact. It is interesting to note that even St. Pius X had considered a new Latin translation of the psalter; cf. Bea's note, "S. Pius X et nova versio Latina Psalterii," *Biblica*, XXXVI (1955), 561.
48. For details see the relative article by Bea, published in booklet form as *La nuova traduzione latina del Salterio. Origine e spirito* (Rome, 1945) (Biblio. 7), p. 3.

prayer."[49] Added to this is the unambiguous evidence of Pius XII's private secretary, Father Leiber, S.J.,[50] and lastly that of Father Bea himself.[51] Thus the pope's decision came as a complete surprise to the rector. *Dates* simply notes that on 19 January 1941, the relative commission was formed, made up of six professors from the institute who were particularly qualified for the various aspects of the work: textual criticism, philology, ancient translations, and exegesis.

The criteria for the translation were set by the pope himself, as can be seen in his *motu proprio* of 24 March 1945, *In cotidianis precibus*, which authorized publication of the new translation and its use in the breviary. The instructions were that the translation "should faithfully interpret the original texts and bear in mind, so far as possible, the venerable Vulgate and the other ancient versions, weighing up their various lessons along the lines of sound criticism."[52]

It is easy to see that respecting all these criteria and ensuring their harmonization required considerable commitment and work. In the already quoted article in which Bea describes the practical work of the commission, he says that they had to discuss the various drafts "in plenary sessions, then reformulate and amend them on the basis of the observations made during the discussion, and then discuss them again, until after three, four and sometimes five discussions they seemed to conform to the instructions received and to the purpose for which this new translation was intended."[53]

The commission met regularly on Wednesday evenings, since there were no lessons on Thursdays and the professors were therefore freer. It is worth noting that even within the community of the institute, they managed to keep the strictest secrecy right up to the end.

Finally, in the month of August 1944, "after three and a half years of work, the manuscript of the new translation could be submitted to the Supreme Pontiff, who had shown a lively interest in the progress of the discussions and their results throughout the time of preparation."[54] Bea immediately goes on to say that on 8 September the Holy Father instructed that both the text itself and also its liturgical edition, with the psalms divided up according to the psalter in the breviary, should be sent for printing.[55]

When Bea submitted the manuscript of the new translation to the pope, he explicitly stated that he would be quite happy if the work were examined by other experts, but the pope answered: "You are experts. Why should we need any others?"[56]

---

49. Cf. D. Tardini, *Pio XII* (Vatican City, 1960), p. 76; the other two points of the plan were the definition of the Assumption and the excavations under St. Peter's.

50. Cf. R. Leiber, "Pius XII," *Stimmen der Zeit*, LXXXV/163 (1958-1959), 81-100, cf. p. 91.

51. Cf. BM, p. 77. We should therefore correct H. Bacht's statement ("Kardinal Bea," p. 181) attributing the whole responsibility to Father Bea.

52. Biblio. 7, p. 4.

53. *Ibid.*

54. *Ibid.*

55. Cf. *ibid.*

56. This detail, which I heard directly from Bea himself, is borne out by another highly qualified

Bea personally supervised the publication of the new translation, giving every psalm a title and also a short introduction that indicated its aim, literary genre and structure, and adding brief notes or comments, as well as the critical apparatus. This is why the *Liber Psalmorum* has been included in the bibliography of his works (no. 6). The first printing of the *Liber Psalmorum*, which ran to eight thousand copies, was sold out in less than five months,[57] prior even to the appearance of the liturgical edition, and this goes to show how keenly people had been waiting for a new translation. It is also undeniable that among other things the work also gave the Pontifical Biblical Institute considerable publicity, so that the number of students went up from less than 140 prior to the Second World War to about 180 after the war.

This whole story gives rise to a series of questions. The first of these concerns the choice of the *classical language* for the new translation and the resulting move away from the "Christian Latin" of the Vulgate.[58] The work received more criticism on this point than on any other. For his part, Bea tenaciously spoke out in defense of the choice.[59] We should note in the first place that the *motu proprio* said nothing about the *type of Latin* to be used. Bea's study indicates that the translators were basically aiming at classical Latin, although within certain limits,[60] and I can say with certainty that this choice was the result of a precise decision of the pope himself. Although it was in keeping with his well-known love for the classical writers, it was dictated above all by a pastoral line of reasoning: if, as was explicitly stated in the *motu proprio*, the aim was that of offering priests a psalter that was comprehensible to them, it had to be offered in the language that they had studied at school. Father Bea himself told me that he would personally have preferred to remain closer to the Vulgate, but that he had accepted the pope's decision in the spirit of obedience.[61] This same spirit

---

witness, Max Zerwick, S.J., who had at that time been Bea's close colleague at the institute for more than ten years (cf. BM, p. 78). The following statement by S. Lyonnet is therefore frankly surprising: "Many people are undoubtedly unaware that there was a version of this translation [of the psalms] in a Latin that was strikingly close to that of the Vulgate—he showed it to me—and that Pius XII had it rewritten in a more classical Latin" ("Le Cardinal Bea," p. 373). How are we to reconcile this "rewriting" with the two explicit statements given above, and above all how could such a rewrite have been produced in the short time mentioned above between submission of the manuscript and its approval? Maybe the two versions Lyonnet speaks of were simply two samples produced purely as illustrations of the pope's intentions.

57. Letter to G. Scattolòn of 20 July 1945 (ArchWit).

58. In the study *Il nuovo Salterio* (Biblio. 8) Bea speaks at greater length about the type of language chosen: it was clear that "a classical Ciceronian type of Latin was out of the question" (p. 109); in view of the practical purpose of the translation—the prayer of priests with the obligation of praying the breviary—"apart from strictly Christian expressions, a type of Latin closer to that of the classics" was chosen, closer, in other words, to that "of the authors of the first century B.C. and the first two centuries A.D." (p. 113), which was the Latin that future priests would have learned at school (*ibid.*).

59. Cf. *ibid.*, pp. 102-152, esp. pp. 113-114.

60. Cf. *ibid.*, pp. 20-28.

61. This is also borne out by the well-known liturgical expert, Aimé Martimort. In a conversation that took place after the death of Pope Pius XII but before Bea was made cardinal, Father Bea spoke about the psalter, explaining that he had acted "only out of obedience; he himself would

was also why he then energetically defended the choice of the classical language.

The work on the psalms had *a sequel* some years later. *Dates* notes that in May 1949 the sessions of the commission that had translated the psalms were resumed in order to produce a similar translation of the passages from the Old Testament that were to be used in the Roman Breviary. In this case too the work was of course undertaken on the specific request of Pope Pius XII. The sessions were suspended when Bea became cardinal, and he later placed the fruit of this work—that is, the translations prepared over a period of almost ten years—at the disposition of the Commission for the Neo-Vulgate, which we shall discuss later.

It was within the context of this work that the idea began to arise that something of a similar kind should be done for the New Testament, at least for the passages to be read in the breviary, although a new translation was not envisaged in this case, but simple *a correction of the Vulgate*. Rules for this were drawn up and approved by Pope Pius XII, and these would in fact form the starting point for the revision of the whole Vulgate after the Council.

As we know, the Council took certain decisions concerning the psalter, and more specifically the *Piiano* translation,[62] saying: "The task of reviewing the psalter, already happily begun, is to be finished as soon as possible. It shall take into account the style of Christian Latin, the liturgical use of the psalms—including the singing of the psalms—and the entire tradition of the Latin Church."[63] The essential element in this instruction was the return to the psalter of the Vulgate, and the work was carried out in the first years after the Council, as we shall see in due course. This leads us to wonder *what is now left of the work of Pius XII* which began with the new translation of the psalms. In view of the fact that the Council decided on a return to the "Christian Latin" of the Vulgate for the psalms, it might seem that nothing at all has remained, but this is far from being the case. Pius XII's work provided the basic impulse that led to the later revision not only of the psalter but of the entire Vulgate. His central idea has itself remained, in other words, the need for the Latin translation to correspond to the original texts. John Oesterreicher has rightly said that here Pius XII gave a practical demonstration of the primacy that the original texts of sacred scripture have over translation, and in particular over the venerable Vulgate itself.[64] And we would add that he did so two years before he presented this principle in the encyclical *Divino afflante Spiritu*. Furthermore, the revision of the *whole* Vulgate was basically carried out according to the principles that Pius XII had approved for the revision of the New Testament, as we shall see in due course. It can therefore be claimed that the revision of the Vulgate is

---

have tended to be more in favor of a simple revision of the Vulgate, but Pius XII was anxious to have a psalter in Ciceronian Latin" (ArchWit, p. 6). For the New Testament, on the other hand, Pius XII himself preferred a simple revision of the Vulgate (*ibid.*).

62. So called because it was ordered by *Pius* XII.

63. *SC*, no. 91.

64. Cf. *Simposio*, p. 35.

basically a fruit of the principle underlying the decision to undertake the *Piiano* translation, even if its specific approach to the psalter was not retained. The *Piiano* translation was also extremely helpful in the work of revising the psalter after the Council, and we would add that one of the most notable qualities of the *Piiano* translation, its intelligibility, was also handed on in large measure to the psalter in the Neo-Vulgate.

(b) Bea's Contribution to the Encyclical Divino afflante Spiritu

One of the great merits of the papacy of Pius XII in the doctrinal field was that of having recognized and acted on the great solicitations that were born and grew up partly between the two wars, and more especially immediately after the First World War, concerning sacred scripture, ecclesiology and liturgy. As regards sacred scripture, in 1943 he published the encyclical *Divino afflante Spiritu*, which has rightly been called the *magna carta* of modern biblical studies, with *Mystici Corporis* on the church appearing at almost the same time, and *Mediator Dei* on the liturgy four years later.

As we have already noted, the encyclical on sacred scripture was preceded by the letter of the Pontifical Biblical Commission that dealt with trends of the Dain Cohenel type and with a whole series of subjects that would then be taken up again by *Divino afflante Spiritu*—obviously in this case with the authority and depth that are the hallmarks of an encyclical.

Let us take a closer look at *the content and importance* of this encyclical, as the cardinal saw these after some time had passed, on the twenty-fifth anniversary of its promulgation, in 1968. He spoke about it on the Bavarian radio on this occasion, explaining the importance of the document as follows: "It briefly set forth the results of fifty years of Catholic biblical study, taking them as the basis for further work. In these fifty years study of sacred scripture had received major new assistance from the results obtained in various secular fields of study, particularly archeology—and here I am thinking of the large amount of excavation undertaken in the Middle East and of the discoveries it led to in the fields of literature, history, linguistics and ethnology. On the basis of these results, the encyclical outlines the task that they have set for biblical science and also establishes a wide-ranging program for the purpose: study of original texts (as opposed to translations), with the help of the results of linguistic research; and a detailed, searching explanation of the individual books and biblical texts in the light of the cultures of the ancient East."[65]

Let us now consider *the influence* that the encyclical had on Catholic biblical studies, once again as this was viewed by the cardinal, who spoke of it in a retrospective conversation on the history of the Italian Biblical Association. After noting that "the path from the first beginnings to the foundation of the Italian Biblical Association was not easy," he went on to observe: "It reflected and felt the effects of the fraught situation of contemporary Catholic biblical science itself, which would only find itself fully with the encyclical *Divino afflante Spiritu* and set courageously and energetically to work to implement

---

65. Quoted in BM, p. 266.

the grandiose and far-seeing program outlined by that papal document. This slow process of maturation, and particularly the encyclical itself, highlighted— as is even clearer today—the objectives that the Italian Biblical Association was to serve."[66]

When the encyclical appeared, we students at the Biblical Institute were surprised by the similarity between certain points of teaching in the encyclical and Bea's aforementioned manual on the inspiration of sacred scripture (1930), so that we joked that some things that had not previously been placed in quotes in Bea's book would have to be from now on as citations from the encyclical. In considering how much truth there was in this observation, let us say at once that we are not talking of some exclusive contribution on Bea's part, and that we do not intend minimizing other contributions. We would also note the limitations imposed on the present research by the fact that the question obviously cannot be treated in depth except on the basis of all the papers concerning the drafting of the encyclical, which will not be possible until this material is made available for consultation.

What can we say while awaiting such fuller study? We have *two first-hand accounts*. The first is that of Father R. Gagnebet, O.P., a professor at the Pontifical University of St. Thomas Aquinas in Rome, who writes that before meeting Father Bea, "I had heard much praise of him from two of my professors who had known him well. The first was the famous theologian Garrigou-La-grange, his colleague at the Holy Office as consultor; these two spirits, who were so different from one another, were able to understand and respect one another. The second was Father G. Vosté, Secretary of the Biblical Commission, who had worked closely with Father Bea and who met with him almost every week to discuss biblical questions. I am not absolutely certain, but I have reason to believe that these two [Vosté and Bea] were the main writers of *Divino afflante Spiritu* and of the famous letter to Cardinal Suhard."[67]

Father G. Duncker, O.P., who was also consultor to the Pontifical Biblical Commission for many years and a friend of Father Bea, is still more explicit: "It is a public secret . . . that *Divino afflante Spiritu* was written by the Biblical Commission; and the lion's share of this work must undoubtedly be attributed to Father Bea, the right hand of the then secretary of the commission, our Father Vosté, who always had the greatest trust in him."[68]

There is also one particular point in the encyclical to which Father Bea apparently made an *especially large contribution*, in other words, the teaching on *literary genres*, which was something very new, and indeed one of the points where the encyclical so to speak "rehabilitated" approaches that had been seen as dangerous or as taboo in the wake of various "unfortunate incidents." Why was this so? Such research had been pioneered by the great Dominican exegete Father M.J. Lagrange in the years 1895-1897,[69] and later (1904) by Father F. de

---

66. Quoted in ms. R 1968/15, pp. 6-7; cf. Biblio. 440.

67. ArchWit. We shall discuss the letter to Cardinal Suhard below.

68. G. Duncker, "Ricordando il Cardinale Agostino Bea," *Angelicum*, LIX (1982), 47.

69. Father Lagrange's thought in this connection has been clearly set forth and compared with that

Hummelauer, S.J., author among other things of eight weighty volumes of exegesis of the various historical books of the Old Testament, which were published in the series entitled Cursus Scripturae Sacrae. The relative booklet by de Hummelauer had been placed on the index.[70] Father Lagrange was not treated as severely as this, but the Consistorial Congregation (today the Congregation for Bishops) had banned a number of his works from use in seminaries.[71]

It is against this background that we must consider the question of who made the largest contribution toward ensuring that this subject was treated in the encyclical *Divino afflante Spiritu*, and, moreover, treated as positively as it in fact was. So far as I know, only two authors have addressed this question. In his study on Bea's contribution to the biblical sciences—a work we have already cited a number of times—Stanislas Lyonnet, S.J., emphasizes the credit that should be given to Father Lagrange in connection with the question of literary genres, also pointing out that the President and the Secretary of the Biblical Commission, Cardinal E. Tisserant and Father G. Vosté, O.P., had both studied under Father Lagrange.[72] As regards Bea, Lyonnet sees his contribution above all in the agreement between his work and the encyclical on *the path to be followed* in order to identify literary genres. As he did in his teaching and in his management of the institute, Bea had always emphasized the importance of the auxiliary sciences, and similarly the encyclical emphasizes the study of oriental literature in order to identify the literary genres current among those ancient peoples.[73]

About twenty years prior to Lyonnet's work, E. Galbiati had studied the question in an article that set up two lines of comparison: between the theory of literary genres of Father Lagrange and that of the encyclical on the one hand, and between the relative teaching of Bea on this subject and that of the encyclical on the other.[74] Although he recognizes the credit that must undeniably go to Lagrange as the first to raise and discuss the question, the author reaches the conclusion that "the line of thinking of the encyclical coincides with that of Lagrange on only a few points. Sometimes it is decidedly different, and on certain points it follows a parallel line but on another level."[75]

On the other hand when he comes to compare the encyclical and the teaching

---

of the encyclical *Divino afflante Spiritu* by Enrico Galbiati in his article "I generi letterari secondo il P. Lagrange e la 'Divino Afflante Spiritu,' " *La Scuola Cattolica*, LXXV (1947), 178-186 and 282-292.

70. For an evaluation of the theory, see the biographical article published by Bea in the Supplement to the *Dictionnaire de la Bible* (Biblio. 47). We shall return to this below.

71. Cf. Galbiati, "I generi letterari," p. 185, note 14.

72. Cf. Lyonnet, "Le Cardinal Bea," p. 377.

73. Cf. *ibid.*, p. 381. We must in all honesty, however, add Lyonnet's observation that in his lessons Bea upheld opinions that at least in principle would have led to interpretations that were more nuanced, if not divergent. Lyonnet goes on to say that Bea's students were not at all surprised to find these same principles stated in the encyclical *Divino afflante Spiritu* (cf. *ibid.*, p. 377).

74. Cf. Galbiati, "I generi letterari."

75. *Ibid.*, p. 291.

set forth by Bea in his study on the inspiration of sacred scripture and biblical hermeneutics, Galbiati notes that *Bea's influence is clear even in the wording*, and he in fact places the relative paragraphs of the encyclical[76] side by side with the text in which Bea speaks of literary genres. The following elements that are expressed in the encyclical are thus found in Bea's work: (i) the assertion of the existence of distinct "literary genres," inasmuch as the ancient writers and the eastern peoples did not follow the same norms as those followed by recent authors in our western culture in their ways of expressing themselves and writing; (ii) the assertion of the great importance and precise significance of study of these literary genres for exegesis; the aim of studying the literary genres used by the sacred authors is not that of weakening or actually denying the historical value of the texts, but rather that of gaining a deeper understanding of what the sacred author wanted to say.[77]

Another two important elements found in the encyclical are also found in a biographical article on Father de Hummelauer, which Bea published two years prior to the appearance of the encyclical, and in which he evaluates this author's theory of literary genres and makes the following observations: the author states his theory of literary genres *a priori*, whereas in order to establish it he would have needed more detailed examination of the relative Old Testament texts, closer study of the Catholic tradition, in particular as concerns illumination of the intellects of the sacred authors on the part of the Spirit who is the inspirer of the sacred books, and lastly more adequate study of the characteristic features of the historiography of ancient peoples.[78] We thus find Bea stating, as the encyclical would later do: (i) that the literary genres must not be established *a priori*, in other words in an abstract manner, but rather on the basis of study of ancient eastern literature; and (ii) the need for more serious study of the characteristic features of ancient historiography.[79] All this indicates that Bea's contribution (so far as we are today able to demonstrate) was not confined, as Lyonnet thought, to the generic contribution of having asserted the importance of the auxiliary sciences, but was much more specific, and even extended to the actual wording used in the encyclical.

However, we should maybe add another *element of a psychological nature*. As was said above, the ill favor met with by the first attempts to face the question of literary genres meant that the subject came to be seen as dangerous and best avoided, so that slow careful groundwork was needed before it could be rehabilitated. I believe Bea was referring to this when he told me privately that he was convinced that the subject and doctrine of literary genres would not have been found in the encyclical *Divino afflante Spiritu* if he had not slowly prepared the way. Bea in fact had the necessary courage, prudence and prestige to face the problem right from the first edition of his book on the inspiration of sacred

---

76. As concerns the encyclical, this refers in particular to the text found on pp. 20-21 of the English translation.

77. As concerns Bea, this refers to *De Sacrae Scripturae inspiratione* (2nd ed.) (Biblio. 2), p. 111.

78. Cf. Biblio. 47, p. 146.

79. Cf. *Divino afflante Spiritu*, p. 20.

scripture (1930). The slow preparation had thus begun thirteen years prior to the encyclical.[80]

I think that Bea also exercised a similar influence as concerns the way in which the encyclical explains *the nature of the inspiration* of the sacred books. In his manual on inspiration, Bea had in fact notably revived St. Thomas' teaching on "prophecy" and thus the idea that the inspired author was used by the Holy Spirit as an intelligent and free "instrument,"[81] so that in full possession of his own faculties and capacities he would write down, as true author, all the things—and only those things—that the Spirit desired should be written. The encyclical underwrote this teaching in full.[82]

The great importance of Bea's twofold contribution to the encyclical can also be seen from the fact that the Council included both points—the teaching on inspiration and that on literary genres—in the Constitution on Divine Revelation.[83]

Extension of the Premises of the Institute

In an audience with Pius XI, Father Bea had tried to explain that the present quarters of the institute had slowly become too small; for example, he said, there would soon be no further space in the library—to which Pius XI, an ex-librarian, had replied: "Then don't put useless things in it." Unintimidated, Bea persisted: "We don't have enough rooms for the professors, and the lecture halls are small and dark." "I know, but I have no money," was the pope's prompt reply.

The truth, however, is that the pope had been considering the matter for some time, and Bea himself bore this out in the already cited address he gave in the presence of Pope John XXIII: "We know from reliable sources that Pius XI, who realized the insecure situation of the institute, had already generously made provisions when discussing the Lateran Treaties, reserving to the Holy See the building situated behind the Church of the Twelve Apostles, which is only separated from the old premises of the institute by the narrow Via del Vaccaro."[84] Being a good administrator, however, and thinking that the Biblical Institute did not need it immediately, the pope had handed it to the Italian government for fifteen years. The latter had used it to house the headquarters of the Roman army corps. However, in these fifteen years, the increase in the tasks of the institute and in its activities and needs meant that the building assigned to it by St. Pius X had gradually become more and more cramped, because of the greater number of professors and students. Considering only the number of students, we would simply recall what we said above: while the largest number

---

80. Christian Pesch, S.J., was to some extent a forerunner of Bea here; cf. Galbiati, "I generi letterari," p. 288. We do not mean what we say to be taken as minimizing the elements emphasized by Lyonnet; above all, the fraternal collaboration between Bea and one of Father Lagrange's students, Father Vosté, was providential.

81. Cf. Biblio. 2, pp. 7-10, 40-71.

82. Cf. *Divino afflante Spiritu*, pp. 19-20.

83. Cf. *DV*, nos. 11-12.

84. Biblio. 129, p. 15.

of students before the Second World War was 140, in the post-war period the average rose to 180.[85]

When the situation was brought to Pius XII's attention in 1944 with a question about the above-mentioned building, the pope, who had been Pius XI's Secretary of State and was therefore familiar with the matter, immediately said: "Of course! That building has been intended for the institute right from the start." Apart from this, the pope said he would personally take care of the considerable costs of the far from easy renovation work, which took about three years.[86] While the work was under way, he showed repeated interest in its progress, asking, "They're not doing anything unnecessary, are they?"

Bea, for his part, could once more contribute his experience as "builder." Moreover, when most of the community moved to the new building in mid-1949, major alterations were made to quite a number of rooms in the old building, in order to create new space for classrooms, the library, etc. As can be seen, Father Bea played an important role in this whole matter too, although it does seem an over-statement to call him the "second founder" of the institute on this basis, as some people have tried to do. If this title should go to anyone, Pius XII would seem the right person.[87]

* * *

As we have said, Bea was not only director of the institute but also superior of the religious community, and both positions automatically lead one to wonder *what he was like as a person, and how he seemed in his dealings with other people.*

In the first place, people often emphasize his diligence or hard-working character, and he has been described as "a man of work."[88] If we consider all the various fields of activity we have tried to describe, it is easy to see that it must have taken an uncommon amount of energy to remain well in control of them all. However, apart from all this activity, there was also that of "professor and scholar," as we shall see in the following section.

A second quality that is often emphasized is his *talent for organization*,[89] and people have even sometimes tended to see this as his main contribution to the institute during his time at its head, maybe comparing it with his contribution to research and other aspects. I think that what we shall be saying in the rest of the present chapter will show clearly enough that this is an unjustified and superficial over-simplification.

---

85. Cf. Schmidt, "Cinquant'anni," p. 621.

86. Cf. Bea's address, *Biblica*, XLI (1960), 15.

87. On Pius XII's work, cf. Biblio. 109, pp. 74-75; the day of the solemn canonization of the founder of the institute, St. Pius X, the pope issued handwritten instructions that the two buildings—the old one and the new one—should be assigned as premises for the institute (cf. *AAS*, XLVI [1954], 399-400).

88. L. Semkowski, S.J., who lived with Bea for twenty years; also J.N. Zoré, S.J., who worked with Bea on various tasks within the Society of Jesus (ArchWit).

89. L. Semkowski, S.J. (ArchWit).

First-hand witnesses stress the fact that he was calm and objective in business dealings,[90] with a capacity for moderate, secure judgment,[91] a great sense of balance and much prudence.[92]

The qualities we have listed thus far—diligence, organizational talent and also a kind of shrewd prudence—could also put us in mind of an excellent manager. We are still left with the whole question of how he treated other people and how he behaved in his dealings with them, and in this regard too we have some very clear reports. These often stress his "calm welcoming quality,"[93] and his friendliness and kindness in dealing with others.[94] "He was kindly and almost always smiling."[95] He knew how to listen,[96] he was understanding,[97] he was an inspired advisor and counselor,[98] he was welcoming and paternally encouraging,[99] and he was always ready to help people and render service.[100] Father N. de Boynes, S.J., Assistant General, Vicar General and finally Delegate of Father General J.B. Janssens for the inter-provincial houses, spoke of Father Bea as superior of the community as follows: "He is an ideal superior; he never raises his voice; he rarely interferes; the community just has to watch him in order for everything to proceed in perfect order."[101]

It cannot be automatically expected that the superior of a religious community who is also a working man will place himself broadly at the disposition of his confreres. Bea, however, organized things as follows: he would set aside two hours in the early morning—a time that his companions jokingly called "the

90. J. Kahmann, CSsR; Karl Wehner, S.J.; J.N. Zoré, S.J. (ArchWit).

91. J.N. Zoré, S.J. (ArchWit).

92. E. Porta, S.J.; L. Semkowski, S.J. (ArchWit).

93. P. Dezza, S.J., who was Rector of the Pontifical Gregorian University for ten years during Bea's time as Rector of the Biblical Institute and was in close contact with Bea.

94. Among his ex-students (ArchWit): Cardinal Franz König, Bishop A. Piazza, and Fathers J. Kahmann, CSsR, F. Laconi, S.D.B., and S. Zedda, S.J., as well as Father E. Porta, S.J., who was for many years provincial superior of the Roman province of the society.

95. His fellow Jesuit and ex-student, the Dutchman Leo Rood, who also observes that he sometimes had the impression that when dealing with guests of a certain rank Bea indulged in flattery (ArchWit).

96. The already cited Bishop A. Piazza, and, among Bea's fellow Jesuits and students, the American John Collins and the already cited S. Zedda (ArchWit).

97. Among the already cited witnesses (ArchWit): Cardinal F. König, and Fathers P. Dezza, S.J., and F. Laconi, S.D.B.

98. His student and fellow Jesuit, the Englishman Charles Hughes (ArchWit).

99. Bishop A. Piazza (ArchWit).

100. Fathers E. Porta, S.J. and P. Dezza, S.J., and, among his students and fellow Jesuits, S. Zedda and L. Rood (ArchWit). The only exception is his ex-student Benjamin Wambacq, O.Praem. (ArchWit), who would work closely with Bea later on as Secretary of the Pontifical Biblical Commission: he mentions, "to tell the truth," difficulties with Bea while he was working on his degree thesis. We shall discuss this in our next section (on Bea as professor).

101. Cf. E. des Places, S.J. (ArchWit). R. North, S.J. (ArchWit) observes on the one hand that Father Bea was "probably the best superior" he ever had (p. 2), but on the other hand that he had considerable reservations over the way in which he guided the work of the commission at the institute that prepared a new translation of the passages of the Old Testament used in the breviary (p. 3). I have received no similar observations from other members of the commission, and one cannot base a judgment on the opinion of a single witness.

holy hour"—for his own work, especially the preparation of lessons, but for the rest of the day he was always available. He had a personal principle that seemed paradoxical: "I always have time and I never have time," which he would explain by saying that he always had time for the things that needed it, but never had time to waste.

A particular aspect of this readiness to help others was his sense of *hospitality*, which is praised by many witnesses: "He offered me hospitality every time I visited Rome"[102]; "in order to give me the possibility of working in the library of the institute, he told me that while he was rector I could stay in the institute free of charge during the summer months."[103] We also find a very pleasant detail in connection with the generous help given, as we have seen, to the Italian Biblical Weeks: until those taking part in the meetings became too numerous, these courses used to end with a meal offered by the rector, at which the participants would eat together with the professors of the institute.[104]

One person stresses a special type of assistance that Bea was always ready to offer those for whom he was responsible, saying that when necessary he did not hesitate to take up the cudgels in their defense.[105] We saw one example of a number of such cases, when he energetically defended the vice-rector of the institute, Father Alberto Vaccari, against the attacks of certain circles in connection with the Dain Cohenel case.

This way of dealing with others was not purely pragmatic, but was based on a deep respect—and indeed an authentic love—for other people. One day a student who was a religious complained that his various other commitments meant that he had not had time to work on his thesis, and Bea told him: "You may not have had time to devote yourself properly to your studies during these past years, but the human contacts you've had with so many different types of people are worth not just one, but many theses." When this same religious was then nominated provincial inspector, and observed that now he would have to give up all hope of ever completing his thesis, Bea's answer was: "The best thesis is that of doing the will of God."[106] We shall consider the religious aspect reflected in these last two reports more fully in the final section of the present chapter (3).

2. Professor and Scholar

Apart from the duties involved in managing the institute as scientific institution and religious community, we must also consider Bea's work as teacher and scholar, both fields that had their own importance: apart from anything else,

102. Father Bruno Bitter, S.J., whom we have already met in the present chapter on the occasion of Bea's journey to Japan (ArchWit).
103. The Slovenian ex-student, Father Albin Skrinjar, S.J. (ArchWit).
104. Mgr. G. Scattolòn (ArchWit).
105. E. Lamalle, S.J. (ArchWit).
106. Both details are drawn from the observations of F. Laconi, S.D.B. (ArchWit).

in the teaching field his duty of solidarity with the other professors meant that he had to bear his part of the burden, while the scientific authority of the rector and indirectly of the institute itself depended in good measure on his activity as scholar and writer.

a. Teacher

We should first of all consider some figures. Taking account of lessons, seminars, etc., from the very earliest years Bea had an average of four lessons per week, except in certain exceptional situations, although they were often distributed unevenly between the first and second semesters.[107] We should note that these were university-level lectures, not "institutional" courses as ordinary courses of philosophical and theological training would have been; they were specialized courses in which the material varies considerably. Thus in our case too, apart from the course on the inspiration and hermeneutics of sacred scripture and the methodology of biblical research, which were given each year, the material varied a great deal, obviously within the limits of the chair in question. When Bea became rector he kept the two main spheres that he had held previously: *special introduction* to the Old Testament, and the *exegesis of the historical books* of the Old Testament.[108] However, a great variety was possible even within this framework.

(i) If we arrange the lessons given in his nineteen years as rector (1930-1949) *according to subject*, we obtain the following picture of his lessons. In the field of *special introduction* to the various books of the Old Testament: Pentateuch (three times), Deuteronomy (once), Isaiah (twice), Daniel (four times). *Exegesis*: Genesis 1-11 (four times), Exodus (five times), Joshua (three times), Nehemiah (twice), Isaiah (once), Song of Solomon (once), Job (once), Ecclesiastes (once). *Seminars*: Genesis (six times), Exodus (three times), 1 Kings (once), Nehemiah (twice), Ecclesiasticus (Sirach) (once), Amos (once), the encyclical *Divino afflante Spiritu* (once). Added to this were certain *auxiliary disciplines*: history of Old Testament times (once), archeology (five times), geography (three times). Lastly, there were some *special courses*: excavations in Palestine (twice), topography of the city of Jerusalem (four times). The situation became particularly difficult after the outbreak of war, when a number of professors had to leave Rome and there was no way of replacing them, so that Bea took on a considerable part of their teaching load too.

(ii) We have various sources of information on *how he prepared his lessons, his teaching method, etc.* As concerns preparation, Bea wrote about his own

---

107. Information taken from the official year book *Acta Pontificii Instituti Biblici*.

108. For the year 1938-1939 the Scottish American Robert Dyson, S.J., came to the institute and taught both the special introduction and exegesis of the Old Testament. However, he then had to leave Rome because of the war, so that from 1940-1941 Bea had to take on these two subjects again. Moreover, from 1939-1940 professors in other subjects became unavailable, and Bea had to take over archeology and then also biblical geography. From 1945-1946, due to internal requirements of the institute, Bea would also teach certain other prophetic or didactic books of the Old Testament.

approach when giving some practical advice to an ex-student of the institute: "I myself prepare each lecture I give for one or two hours, even after forty years of teaching! However, something is added to our store of scientific and teaching knowledge each year, and after giving the whole course it becomes easier the second time."[109] As concerns these "one or two hours" of immediate preparation, the whole community at the institute knew that after breakfast and until ten-thirty Bea wanted absolutely no interruptions, for this was the time set aside for his personal work, and in particular for preparation of his lessons. In this way his lessons grew steadily richer as he continued teaching. Bea wrote as follows to an ex-student from Sittard High School: "Generally speaking, all of us find that we really start to learn once we leave our school desks. I can personally say that I learned almost everything I now teach after I had finished my studies, and that I am still learning." And here Bea quotes the motto of the well-known scholar Cardinal Giovanni Mercati, Librarian of the Holy Roman Church: "Paratus semper doceri."[110]

Bea adopted this motto, commenting on it as follows in his autobiographical article of 1967: "The desire for a continual intellectual renewal is needed. In this sense I have more than once told my students, 'What I teach you, I have learned in my activity as professor.' I have told them, too, that I had always learned much from them. They, indeed, with their questions and difficulties, press— even force—the teacher to clarify and give greater precision to his thinking."[111] This explains what Bea meant when he told me more than once that he always been lucky enough to have to deal with young people, for such contacts had kept him young. Naturally the young people were also instinctively won over by this attitude, and all the more so since it was combined with another element, which Bea expressed once as follows: "I don't try to convince people, for that is the task of the truth."[112]

It is also interesting to see the *method Bea used for class-notes*, and also recommended to students for their future teaching. He would say that it is best not to give the complete text of the lessons, because they lose much of their interest if you do. All that is needed is a good outline with bibliography and other similar indications that students would find difficult to take down during the lesson itself.[113] Bea also made considerable use of the blackboard both for the outline of his lessons and for illustrations in archeology lessons, etc. In this connection it is interesting to note his observation to someone starting to teach when he himself was still provincial superior: "The lesson was good, but remember that the teacher's effectiveness is in direct proportion to the consumption of chalk."[114]

---

109. N 1958/159.
110. N 1954/183 ("Always ready to learn"). Giovanni Mercati (1866-1957), a great scholar in the field of the history of theology, etc.
111. Biblio. 363, p. 16.
112. Cf. the Swiss Jesuit Emmanuel Höfer (ArchWit).
113. Cf. also JI, p. 20, and BM, p. 82.
114. This teacher was Max Zerwick, S.J.; cf. BM, p. 82.

(iii) Bea's approach to *examining students* is particularly interesting. Referring to the type of professor who tries to surprise those taking examinations with what they have not studied, Bea said: "I am not interested in what a candidate does not know but in what he does know."[115] He would try to discover this, beginning with an easy question, partly to put the candidate at his ease, and then moving on to increasingly difficult questions if the candidate answered well. Then if the candidate became confused, he would go back to an easy question in order to reassure him, and so on. If Bea knew he was dealing with a fairly weak candidate, he never moved on to the difficult questions, so that such candidates were sometimes surprised by their low marks, saying that they had answered all the questions, but forgetting to take into account the level of the questions. On the other hand, if he knew he was dealing with a very capable candidate, he moved to difficult questions almost at once, so that the candidate was examined "with a view to a mark of ten."[116] Obviously, as Bea himself said, this manner of giving examinations made it an exhausting job. He used to find it particularly difficult to examine students who tended to learn everything by heart—a tendency he felt was especially prevalent in members of a certain religious order. In such cases, reference to a given subject was enough to set off a sort of disk, and the professor would have a hard time interrupting the flow in order to discover exactly how much the candidate had really understood.

(iv) There is unanimous agreement on Bea's far from ordinary *teaching gifts*: he was "an ideal teacher,"[117] "a magnificent and versatile teacher"[118]; "he was clear, easy to follow; . . . it was a joy to follow him; . . . I esteemed him more than any of the other professors"[119]; "he was an incomparable lecturer: conscientiously prepared for every lesson, very clear and full in his presentation, knowledgable and open to all opinions."[120] His concern to adapt his approach for weaker and slower students was another facet of these teaching gifts,[121] and when explaining the need for such adaptation, he used to say somewhat paradoxically that teachers can never underestimate the capacity of their students to understand their lectures.[122]

Although he was personally very methodical, he used to warn people that you should never stick mechanically and blindly to advice on method. In this connection he wrote very realistically to a priest who had known him for a number of years: "The method I have described is an ideal, and you can never completely attain an ideal, and certainly not at the first attempt. . . . The method is more an

---

115. Biblio. 363, p. 16.
116. In the Roman ecclesiastical universities the marks went from 1 to 10, so that the top mark possible was 10, equaling "first-class honors" or "summa cum laude."
117. His ex-student, Bishop Telesforo G. Cioli, O.Carm. (ArchWit).
118. Father F. Laconi, S.D.B. (ArchWit).
119. Leo Rood, S.J. (ArchWit).
120. Bishop A. Piazza (ArchWit); cf. also J. Mejia, "El Cardenal Bea," *Confraternidad Judeo-Cristiana de la Republica Argentina* (November-December 1958), p. 2.
121. Father J. Kahmann, CSsR (ArchWit).
122. Bea would use the German phrase, obviously jokingly: "Man kann sich die Schüler nie dumm genug vorstellen" ("You can never plumb the depths of the lack of intelligence of students").

orientation than a system to be followed at all costs."[123] He was just as realistic over the fruits of a lecture, however good the method used: "And as regards incompetent or lazy students, they will always be with us! Even the students at our institute do not all show the same keenness and interest. The teacher has to aim his lessons at a reasonable average of students, and accept that some of them will always lag behind, because of either a lack of ability or a lack of interest."[124]

Three people with personal experience have spoken about Bea's approach to *directing degree dissertations*. The first says: "He gave me a precious bibliography. . . . When my work was ready, not everybody was willing to accept it, but Father Bea demonstrated that we have the right to carry out research along new paths, and he supported me, judging that my research had not been lacking in results, whether few or many, that were worthy of note."[125] The second says that Bea "went to the considerable trouble of examining the various parts [of my dissertation] as they were completed, and giving me suggestions for improvements. I mention this detail because I know that he was extremely busy at the time, and sometimes you could even see this. . . . He would concentrate on the material under discussion without giving any sign of impatience or haste."[126] Although the third person has much praise for Bea's lectures, he feels duty-bound to report his totally negative experience with Bea as director of his thesis: "He gave me no instructions or orientations for my research, indeed not even the slightest bibliographical suggestion. . . . When I found myself faced with difficulties and explained them to him, he invariably replied, 'You must continue your research,' but without indicating how."[127] For our aims it is enough to note the facts; it seems unnecessary to look for further explanations.

b. Scholar and Writer

As he told me more than once, Bea was the first to recognize that the many onerous commitments involved in heading the institute and the school meant that he could not devote himself to further demanding research and study. On the other hand, he also realized the importance of publications for the scientific prestige of the rector and thus indirectly of the institute itself, and he therefore tried to "be present" at least with a few articles and reviews.

(i) We begin with a simple description of Bea's literary output during his time as rector, including book reviews—which are not listed in our bibliography or included in the official year book giving the "acts" of the institute.[128] The

123. Letter to Mgr. G. Scattolòn of 8 November 1942 (ArchWit).
124. N 1958/159.
125. E. Galbiati, "writer" at the Ambrosiana (ArchWit).
126. J. Kahmann, CSsR (ArchWit).
127. The witness is Father B. Wambacq, O.Praem., who would later be Secretary of the Pontifical Biblical Commission and as such would work closely with Bea (ArchWit).
128. It was apparently Bea who introduced the system of including the publications of the professors in the already cited official year book. These listings began to appear right at the start of his time as rector, in the issue of 1 November 1930. As regards reviews, which are not given in our bibliography, a list drawn up by Bea himself is found in the archives and covers the years 1925 to 1944.

importance we therefore attribute to such reviews may at first sight seem surprising, inasmuch as they often tend to be routine or superficial work. However, this was not the case with Bea, who always held—and particularly in his lectures on the methodology of study and biblical research—that a review must represent a contribution to the progress of knowledge. He himself always followed this principle, and I know of several cases in which authors he had reviewed expressed their appreciation of his observations.

In the first place, let us take a look at the figures for his output *in chronological order*. In the first years (1930-1934) only a very few articles and reviews appeared,[129] due in part to the inevitable difficulties at the start of such a demanding job, and in part to the fact that during this period Bea was preparing the second, expanded editions of his manual on the Pentateuch (which appeared in 1933) and that on the inspiration of sacred scripture (which appeared in 1934).[130] The number of reviews and then also the number of articles rose considerably after 1935.[131] This is all the more striking when we consider that in 1939 the chair in biblical archeology was left vacant, so that Bea had to take on this subject as well and immediately set about preparing the relative class-notes.[132] Despite the fact that the time-consuming work on the new Latin translation of the psalms began in 1941, even in the following years we still find a considerable number of articles and reviews.[133] Later on the reviews stopped almost completely, and the number of articles also fell; as we have seen, this was the period when Bea was preparing the new Latin translation of the psalter for publication, which appeared under the title *Liber Psalmorum*.[134] Almost immediately after this, Bea set himself the task of explaining "the origin and spirit of the new translation." Since the work received criticism as well as approval, Bea produced a book on the question, explaining the whole matter in depth.[135] The enormous positive echo the translation aroused throughout the world, especially among the clergy, provided him with confirmation—if he needed it—of the great importance that the initiative had for the life and prayer of the church. The translation of his book on the psalter into five European languages[136] was obviously the source of further work for the author. Thus only a few articles appeared in these years, whereas the number suddenly rose again starting in 1949.[137]

(ii) We shall also give some details on the *content* of the studies, which were concerned primarily with his specific teaching fields of biblical introduction and

---

129. For books and articles, cf. Biblio. 2, 3, 19-24; there were also six reviews.
130. The study on the Pentateuch grew by 60 pages, and that on inspiration by 50 (cf. Biblio. 1 and 2).
131. In the period 1935-1940 there were 23 articles and 28 reviews.
132. Cf. Biblio. 4 and 5; and for the speed with which Bea produced his first class-notes on archeology, cf. JI, p. 20, and BM, p. 81.
133. In the period 1941-1943 there were 14 articles and 10 reviews.
134. Cf. Biblio. 6.
135. Cf. Biblio. 59a and 8.
136. Cf. Biblio. 8.
137. In the period 1945-1949 there were 14 articles.

exegesis. Thus we have three reviews concerned with questions of general
introduction to sacred scripture, seven with questions of general introduction to
the Old Testament or special introduction to various books of the Old Testament,
seven with exegesis of various books of the Old Testament, and eight with studies
of biblical theology. It should be noted that the authors of the works reviewed
include some of the foremost and most highly respected non-Catholics.[138] Thus a
certain kind of ecumenical dialogue had begun even then, if only in seed-form.
However, it undoubtedly made a major contribution to laying the groundwork for
the future explicit dialogue mentioned above, and thus for Bea's future mission.

So far as the *auxiliary biblical sciences* are concerned, his contributions in
the field of *archeology* are particularly numerous—indeed, in this case there are
more articles than reviews.[139] It should be noted that such publications started
some years before circumstances led Bea to take over the relative chair, so that
we can reasonably conclude that he had a particular inclination toward this type
of study. However, it was not simply a case of personal sympathy for the subject,
however legitimate, for Bea told me more than once: "I set about indicating new
discoveries and their importance for the Old Testament, because other people,
whose field really included the subject, were not doing so." In other words,
partly because he was rector of the institute, Bea felt in a way responsible for
progress in Catholic exegesis and did all he could to make sure that it took note
of new discoveries as such, but above all of the importance they had for
understanding and interpreting the word of God. Hence we have first and
foremost the articles in which the discoveries are explicitly placed in relation to
the Old Testament.[140] The same sense of responsibility meant that Bea always
bore in mind the training of future priests in the field of sacred scripture, which
would be the purpose of his reviews of various text books or teaching manuals.[141]

(iii) One special feature of Bea's approach was his concern to make sure that
people knew and understood *papal documents*, and not only those concerned
exclusively with biblical matters, but also more general ones that did, however,
also affect the study of sacred scripture in various ways. In practical terms this
referred to Pius XI's constitution *Deus scientiarum Dominus* on the reform of
ecclesiastical studies,[142] the encyclical *Divino afflante Spiritu*,[143] and later the
famous letter of the Pontifical Biblical Commission to Cardinal Suhard on the
question of the Pentateuch and primordial history.[144] Max Zerwick rightly
observes that after helping draft these documents, Bea was especially well

---

138. To mention a few: Johannes Hempel, Martin Buber, O. Eissfeldt, A. Alt, W. Rudolph, and M.
    Noth.
139. There were 21 articles as against a mere 5 reviews.
140. Cf. Biblio. 30, 37, 32; cf. also M. Zerwick in BM, p. 72.
141. Thus we have the reviews of Lusseau-Colomb's manual, Robert-Tricot's *Initiation biblique*,
    and T.W. Manson's *A Companion to the Bible*, etc.
142. Cf. Biblio. 20, 44.
143. Cf. Biblio. 53, 54. There was also the short commentary on the letter of the Pontifical Biblical
    Commission to the Archbishops and Bishops of Italy which we spoke of above; *Biblica*, XXIII
    (1942), 106-108.
144. Cf. Biblio. 67; we shall speak further about this study below.

qualified to interpret them and also felt partly responsible for seeing that they were effectively and adequately implemented.[145]

(iv) There is a last category, which could be called *historical-biographical*. It covers the above-cited article on the good services of Pius XI to biblical studies,[146] the portrait of Father de Hummelauer,[147] and lastly a series of obituaries, which were sometimes accompanied by the bibliography of the deceased.[148] Most of these obituaries were written about Bea's fellow Jesuits, but the list also includes members of other religious orders or congregations.[149] B. Leeming rightly sees this as an illustration of Bea's characteristic interest in individuals and his wish to recognize and point out their merits.[150] Most of the obituaries appeared in *Biblica*, of which Bea was editor,[151] and it is worth noting that although he could have entrusted the task to some of the other professors he chose to write them himself.

* * *

Was Bea a Conservative?

People have often described Bea as a conservative,[152] while others, although fewer, say that he held to tradition but was open.[153] Obviously we cannot confine ourselves to such generalizations, but must face the question more precisely and if possible in concrete terms.

So let us hear some first-hand views. The first is that of the Dominican Father G. Duncker, professor of Old Testament exegesis at the Pontifical University of St. Thomas Aquinas. As a member of the Pontifical Biblical Commission and also as a "qualifier" for the Holy Office, he was in frequent contact with Father Bea in a variety of connections, including a number of more delicate matters. He observes that in his writings Bea "can be seen as a learned man with a vast cultural background, completely *au fait* with the literature around the Bible, moderate and prudent in his judgments, somewhat, it must be admitted, conservative in orientation, although open to the various new theories and ideologies.

---

145. Cf. BM, p. 75.
146. Cf. Biblio 32. This would later be followed by similar studies on St. Pius X (Biblio. 90, 105) and Pius XII (Biblio. 109).
147. Cf. Biblio 47.
148. Cf. Biblio. 19, 30a, 36, 43, 48, 59, 59b, 60.
149. Especially the members of the Dominican Order M.J. Lagrange (Biblio. 30a), V. Scheil (Biblio. 48) and B. Allo (Biblio. 59b).
150. Cf. LB, p. 10.
151. The well-known Jewish scholar, Professor Shemaryahu Talmon, describes an episode from the beginning of his relations with the editor of *Biblica*. After helping him to clarify certain points in his article, Bea published it and said that he was ready not only to publish other contributions from Jewish or Israeli scholars, but also to publish articles written in Hebrew. Talmon observes that he would find it difficult to name any other journal of the importance and repute of *Biblica* that at that time, or even today, would have taken a similar attitude; cf. *Simposio*, p. 104.
152. Thus Lyonnet, "Le Cardinal Bea," pp. 376-377; also R. North, S.J. (ArchWit, p. 2) and B. Kipper, S.J. (ArchWit).
153. Thus L. Semkowski, S.J. (ArchWit). Other similar opinions will be seen shortly.

He always told his students about these, trying in his own way to sift the wheat from the chaff."[154] However, Duncker goes further: "Father Bea grew visibly in his understanding and interpretation of sacred scripture. . . . This is a point that I greatly admired in Bea the biblicist: his honesty in admitting that certain things that he had once been convinced of, and had defended and propagated in all sincerity, could no longer be upheld because other arguments had become more convincing and forceful. As a biblicist Father Bea went through a true evolution."[155] In support of this statement, Duncker refers to Bea's influence on the encyclical *Divino afflante Spiritu*.[156]

The other account is given by Father M. Zerwick, S.J., who was Father Bea's close collaborator during his time as rector. He gives the following analysis of the latter's publications, saying that his bibliography "shows the rector of the Biblical Institute to be a man of broad interests, as it were a watchman on guard. If something new and promising appeared in the field of biblical and related studies, Bea received it with lively interest, keeping abreast of developments, informing the public with talks and articles, and, when appropriate, pointing out the link between such new things and the Catholic interpretation of sacred scripture."[157] Elsewhere the same witness gives the following practical and psychological description of Father Bea's attitude: "He managed to combine two opposite tendencies harmoniously within himself: on the one hand a pronounced inclination for conservative opinions, which was the fruit of his temperament and training, and was then reinforced by a sense of responsibility developed during his long years in positions of leadership; and, on the other hand, a clear perception that rigorous and indefatigable scientific work . . . is indispensable if it is to prove fruitful. This insight was based on the deep-seated conviction that the truth is one and indivisible, which of itself rules out the possibility of any real opposition between the tested results of the profane sciences and the witness of sacred scripture."[158]

Concluding his analysis of Bea's publications, Zerwick quotes the words Bea used to describe "the spirit" found in the many biblical documents of Pope Pius XII: "a spirit of deep faith and veneration for the written word of God, a watchful and prudent spirit, careful to preserve the Catholic interpretation of these sacred books whole and unblemished, a spirit of healthy and sober modernity that neglects nothing that could contribute to a better understanding of the sacred texts, a spirit of apostolic zeal that seeks to carry their teaching into the hearts of all the faithful and into all the branches of human life."[159] And Zerwick

---

154. Duncker, "Ricordando il Cardinale Agostino Bea," p. 46.

155. *Ibid.*, pp. 46-47. R. North, S.J. (ArchWit) challenges anyone to find places in Father Bea's writings where he has retracted anything. I have not made any research of this type. However, it may also be a question of teaching method. We shall see below that in the case of the letter to Cardinal Suhard, Father Bea felt it was best not to repeal (and thus retract) the "responses" of the Pontifical Biblical Commission, but to offer a new interpretation of the various underlying problems.

156. Cf. Duncker, "Ricordando il Cardinale Agostino Bea," p. 47.

157. BM, p. 72.

158. *Ibid.*, p. 18.

comments: "This is the spirit of Pius XII and consequently also *the spirit that Father Bea worked to serve*, out of elective affinity and fidelity."[160]

We would add some *observations of Father Bea himself*, which bring some new elements to light. In his retreat notes from 1948, the second to last year of his term as rector, he speaks at length of his work at the Biblical Institute and lists as constant features a sense of balance that steers clear of exaggeration, and very serious scientific work: "May the apostolate of science, which means holding to the correct central line and encouraging all valid initiatives, enable the institute to maintain its high level and make constant progress."[161]

Let us now take a closer look at *one of the main reasons* why Bea was considered a conservative: his study on the Pentateuch. Father Duncker describes the following episode in this connection: "I remember very well how he told me one day when he was already a cardinal, 'It's such a pity and so unjust that I should now be quoted on the basis of a book I wrote thirty years ago, just as if nothing had changed in the meantime! Were I to write the book now, it would turn out very differently.' He was talking about his book on the Pentateuch, which was of a fairly conservative cast."[162] In a 1958 letter, Bea himself explains what his intentions were in 1928 when he compiled the book, saying that he "had tried to stir the positions in the Catholic camp that had remained stationary on that problem, drawing attention to various elements that should be taken into account in accordance with the state of the science at that time."[163] In those years the situation was different from that later created with the encyclical *Divino afflante Spiritu*, so that it was necessary to move gradually and prudently in this fairly delicate area.

Along similar lines, Bea several times pointed out to me how the abstract, forced way in which his fellow Jesuit Franz de Hummelauer had approached the problem of literary genres had aroused a strong backlash, which had tended to block research in this field for decades instead of fostering it. And *prudence was all the more vital* after Bea had become not only a professor but rector of the Pontifical Biblical Institute, which had to work according to the orders and, so to speak, under the eyes of the supreme pontiffs. Any false or merely rash step could now have much more serious consequences than it would if committed by a research scholar who was working simply as an individual. In the article on Pius XI and biblical studies from which we have already quoted, Bea highlights not only the pontiff's interest and love for research, but also his concern over the purity of doctrine. Indeed, in one of his speeches the pope had commended precisely these two points to the members of the Biblical Institute.[164] It was thus the clear will of the church and the pope.

Apart from his prudence, Father Bea also worked, as he did over the question

---

159. Quoting from Biblio. 124, p. 11.
160. BM, p. 83.
161. Ms. Med. 1948/IV/3.
162. Duncker, "Ricordando il Cardinale Agostino Bea," p. 46. Cf. the reports that speak of this study on the Pentateuch: Lyonnet, "Le Cardinal Bea," p. 377; R. Noth S.J., ArchWit, p. 2 (Pentateuch and Isaiah II); B. Kipper, S.J., ArchWit (Pentateuch).
163. N 1958/55.
164. Cf. Biblio. 32, p. 124.

of literary genres, *to prepare the ground for further progress.* A number of Bea's ex-students agree in saying that his teaching very often contained elements of new solutions in seed-form.[165]

An extremely significant example is the story of the *letter* that the Pontifical Biblical Commission addressed *to Cardinal E.C. Suhard,* Archbishop of Paris, in 1948, for according to the evidence of Father Duncker, "Father Bea played a major role, together with Father Vosté," in drawing up this document.[166] The letter dealt with the question of the authorship of the Pentateuch and "primordial history," that is the first eleven chapters of Genesis.[167] The events leading up to this letter make it clear that with this document the church itself provided us with an example of the prudent teaching methods we have discussed. The document was occasioned by the request addressed to the Holy See to abolish the "responses" that the Biblical Commission had published on the problem in question at the time of St. Pius X.[168] We have Father Bea's explicit statement on this.[169] Now in 1977 Father Duncker told me that Pius XII had been favorably inclined toward granting the request and abolishing the "responses," but that Father Bea had managed to persuade him that this was not a wise step, because if he did people could claim that any other instructions of the Pontifical Biblical Commission had only temporary validity. It was therefore better to offer a new interpretation of the problems in question.[170] It might be added that simple abolition would have left the faithful without any positive orientation in this very delicate area. Thus the Holy See preferred the positive path of providing a deeper explanation of the elements of the problem and indicating the direction in which a solution should be sought.

Father Bea therefore contributed to some very real progress in this delicate field too. And after the magisterium had thus opened the way for further research, Bea saw no difficulty in publishing a commentary on the letter in question, a commentary that has been defined as "courageous" for various reasons.[171]

His contribution to this letter shows that he was fully aware of the advances made by science and of the need for a revision of his manual on the Pentateuch. In the 1950s he repeatedly spoke to me about plans for a new, updated edition, but his growing number of commitments in various departments of the Roman curia prevented him from carrying them out. And he was the first to suffer the consequences. His commentary on the letter to Cardinal Suhard shows the direction such a revision would have taken, had it been possible to prepare it.

---

165. Cf. Lyonnet, "Le Cardinal Bea," p. 377; E. Galbiati, ArchWit.
166. Cf. Duncker, "Ricordando il Cardinale Agostino Bea," p. 47.
167. The text of the letter is found in *AAS,* XL (1948), 45-48.
168. For the responses, cf. *ASS,* XXXIX (1906), 377-378, and *AAS,* I (1909), 567-569.
169. Cf. Biblio. 80, p. 13: the Pontifical Biblical Commission "was asked to rescind the two decrees that deal with the mosaicity of the Pentateuch and the historicity of the first three chapters of Genesis." Similarly, see Biblio. 109, p. 76.
170. Father G. Duncker told me this on 18 November 1977.
171. Cf. Lyonnet, "Le Cardinal Bea," p. 383.

3. A Priest and Apostle at the Service of Christ and Thus of the Church and of Souls

On 28 May 1941, Bea made the following entry in *Dates*: "Sixtieth birthday (great celebrations on the part of my country and the German College). I celebrated holy mass in thanksgiving for all the good things received during these years." Then he added this reflection: "Let us hasten toward eternal joy, while using time diligently."[172]

In this reflection the main accent is naturally on the orientation toward the eternal destination, but this is also the source of a very strong accent on "exploiting time diligently," inasmuch as speeding toward the eternal shores is expressed in this life by the exploitation of time with the aim of working for the Lord and his kingdom. And this was truly Bea's most characteristic feature, which meant that his activity extended even beyond the many commitments we have described. The aim of this last section is therefore in the first place to complete our picture of Bea's activities, and in the second to illustrate the spirit that inspired him in all his fields of activity. Such multiple activity undoubtedly has value in itself, but we cannot see its true nature and depth unless we manage to discern its underlying motivations and the immediate and ultimate aims to which it is addressed.

a. Completion of the Picture of Bea's Commitments and Activities

First of all this involves various special jobs that were entrusted to him from time to time by the superior general of his order, and then his preaching commitments (spiritual exercises, exhortations to religious communities, and things of a similar kind).

(i) Special tasks in the service of the order. The Father General of the Society of Jesus at that time, Father Wlódimir Ledóchowski,[173] had a certain reputation as a centralizer, and people sometimes complained about his interference in the running of the houses in Rome. When Bea was nominated Rector of the Biblical Institute, he was maybe referring to this reputation when he asked him: "Father General, when I've got to the point that I don't know what to do, can I come to you?"—meaning that he would come only when the matter was outside his competence and capacities as rector. Father General replied: "But you can always come to me, you're always welcome." Upon which Bea said: "All right, but I'm thinking that you are General and I am Rector of the Biblical Institute." When Bea related this exchange, he observed that Father General understood and never interfered in things that came under the rector's responsibility.

It would be a mistake, however, to see this episode as indicating that relations between the rector and the general were marked by diffidence, or even by

---

172. The author alters and slightly shortens a thought found in the ancient collect for the feast of St. Stanislas Kostka, "Tempus instanter redimentes ad gaudia aeterna festinemus."

173. W. Ledóchowski (1866-1942), 26th Father General of the Society of Jesus; for details, see *EncCatt*, VII, 1017-1018.

distance. On the contrary, I believe Ledóchowski had great trust in Bea. Bea himself told me so in confidence on more than one occasion, and it was more than borne out by those special missions that are called "assignments as visitator" in the Society of Jesus, like the time when Bea was visitator for the Hiroshima mission and the Catholic University of Tokyo.[174] The few facts noted in *Dates* for this period do, however, include these tasks, their scope and their duration. They involved visits to various colleges for philosophy or theology training, and were specifically concerned with these studies. Bea was visitator to Posillipo College in Naples, to the College of St. Ignatius in Valkenburg, then immediately after this to Maastricht College in Holland, and later to Innsbruck College.[175] We would note in particular the last three, which took place in the course of a single year and took up two and a half months in all. In 1941, Bea was given the task of "visiting" the Canisianum College in Innsbruck, which had at that time sought refuge at Sitten in Switzerland.[176] Lastly there was the long visitation to the German College in Rome, which lasted over four months.[177]

The details of these visitations are still restricted, and for our purposes we would simply note the added labor and responsibility they entailed. A glance at the dates is enough to indicate that these tasks entailed lengthy periods away from Rome and thus a break in Bea's work at the Biblical Institute, which he then had to catch up on once he got back. However, the tasks themselves meant above all long, exhausting conversations with all the components of the colleges in question, decisions to be taken, and lastly the compilation of reports for Father General.

However, we have not yet come to the end of the list of such extra tasks. In 1938, from 12 March to 9 May, a general congregation of the order was held in Rome (like the one Bea attended in 1923 as provincial of the southern German province). Bea was elected a delegate by the province of southern Germany, to which he still juridically belonged. Apart from the necessary preparation, this meant two months of wearying sessions and hard work. The congregation was expected to deal, among other things, with the question of education in the order, especially training in philosophy and theology. Both because of the fact that he had been a member of the pontifical commission that drew up the guidelines for the reform of ecclesiastical studies throughout the church, as we saw above, and also because of the experience he had acquired in the above-mentioned visitations to various colleges, Bea was very much involved in the various stages of work: prior to the congregation he helped prepare the relative studies and drafts, and after it he was appointed to the special commission responsible for working out the new curriculum of philosophical and theological studies. The work of the commission began after the close of the congregation and went on until June

174. Cf. our previous chapter.
175. Posillipo, 2-6 February 1932; Valkenburg, 6 April to 13 May 1936; Maastricht, 14-18 May 1936; Innsbruck, 29 September—26 October 1936.
176. 25 March—8 April 1941.
177. 28 November 1948—March 1949.

of the following year (1939). One of the other members of the commission gave Bea this testimonial: "His judgment was moderate and sure, he was objective in discussions. . . . We worked really well and harmoniously together. . . . In 'polishing' certain instructions, Father Bea was somewhat 'diplomatic,' as some of his friends told me."[178] The same person observes more generally, in reference to Bea's special responsibilities: "He had rendered Father General Ledóchowski quite a large number of services, and the latter therefore had great trust in him. Anything Father Bea sent him was approved in advance."[179]

(ii) Preaching retreats and similar activities. As if all the tasks described so far were not enough, so far as possible Bea also gave courses of spiritual exercises, particularly to young Jesuit students and religious sisters, and exhortations to religious communities and to Roman colleges for future priests, etc. The archives contain many notes for his courses of spiritual exercises, and we have a number of first-hand reports. A younger Jesuit wrote to him in 1952 saying that throughout his philosophy studies (1933) Bea had given them the spiritual exercises and thus laid the foundations for what he later gave him as visitator and counselor.[180] Another person says: "In 1940 Father Bea directed . . . our sisters' retreat. . . . We could feel that he was a true religious. . . . He preached not only with his words, but with the whole of his person. . . . His behavior was simple and worthy of a religious, serious, but also kindly, irradiating inner peace and balance."[181] A religious sister remembers four courses of exercises: "We were particularly struck by the depth of his religious life, his fidelity to his religious vows in the spirit of the rule of his order, and his fidelity to the church. Everything about him was modest, simple and open."[182] The same sister adds that his advice was of great help to her community.

Apart from sacrificing his valuable time, Bea was also ready to accept considerable physical effort in order to undertake this kind of commitment. In the course of the last year of the Second World War, he gave regular exhortations to a community of English sisters on Via Nomentana, and since public transport was not running at that time, he had no hesitation over walking—a forty-five minute journey each way.

b. The Spirit, the Underlying Motivations and the Ultimate Aim of Bea's Activity

We should not take what has been said about Bea's special priestly and apostolic activities as meaning that he exercised his zeal as priest and apostle solely in this particular kind of ministry, which in any case was obviously fairly limited in view of all his other duties. However, we can say that in everything he did—as rector, teacher and scholar, and in the tasks performed in the service

---

178. Father Giovanni Zoré, S.J., who lived at the general curia for a long time and was therefore in a position to know how things stood (ArchWit).
179. *Ibid.*
180. Cf. N 1952/59.
181. Sister Norbertine Deppe of the Sisters of Christian Charity (ArchWit).
182. Sister Maria Verona of the Sisters of Our Lady (ArchWit).

of his own order and the Holy See—Bea acted consciously as priest and apostle, letting himself be guided by a deep religious and supernatural spirit.

(i) Let us first take a look at his *teaching* in this perspective. His many students at the Pontifical Biblical Institute will certainly remember the way he explained the method of biblical teaching to future priests, stressing that it was not enough simply to deal with one or another text in exegesis schools, but that all the texts essential for the history of salvation must be explained. We can therefore say that the teachings of the encyclical *Divino afflante Spiritu* (1943) and the later instruction of the Pontifical Biblical Commission (1950)[183] on the need for exegesis schools to act as a spur to religious life, offering nourishment for the spiritual life and material for preaching, would reflect his lectures on the methodology of teaching sacred scripture.

In this perspective it is interesting to see how Bea presented the objectives that were in the final analysis behind Pius XI's moves to foster biblical studies. He used to say that the pope was not concerned simply with the advance of biblical studies, but first and foremost bore in mind the ultimate and highest aim of every science, which is the apostolic one.[184] He also said that anyone who knew Pius XI realized that all his concern over biblical studies was to be seen in function of the higher aim of the glory of God and the salvation of souls; the pope was certainly inspired and stimulated by an innate love of learning, but the good of the church was a stronger and more effective inspiration than any merely natural inclination.[185] Bea also described the attitudes of St. Pius X and Pius XII toward biblical studies in similar terms.[186]

(ii) However, this was also true in a *general* way of his whole life and all his activity. We have some first-hand reports in this connection; though few in number, they are precise and come from very reliable sources. A fellow Jesuit who lived with Bea for twenty years says: "I knew nothing of his interior life; I can only say that I never found anything to object to in his religious spirit and piety."[187] A layman who was in frequent contact with Bea over a period of thirty years speaks of his veneration for Bea, "that priestly soul, simple as a child, humble as a saint."[188] "He was marked by the supernatural spirit in everything he did," says another Jesuit.[189] A former student, who later became a bishop,

---

183. Found respectively in *AAS*, XXXV (1943), 297-326, and *AAS*, XLII (1950), 495-505.

184. Cf. the article already cited a number of times, Biblio. 32, p. 123.

185. Cf. *ibid.*, p. 130.

186. For St. Pius X, cf. Biblio. 90, 105; for Pius XII, cf. Biblio. 109, 124; cf. also 126, and the evidence of M. Zerwick, S.J., in BM, p. 83.

187. The already extensively quoted Father L. Semkowski, S.J. (ArchWit).

188. Giovanni Sabetti (ArchWit). M. Zerwick, S.J. (ArchWit) describes the following episode: "It was on the day that Father Janssens was elected General [September 1946]. At eleven in the morning I met Father Rector . . . who said to me: 'Still no news from the curia [about the election]?! I now almost believe I'm the one. . . .' The tone reveals everything here, and I can state that he was *not* joking. I went on my way, amazed at such self-confidence." In this connection, I would comment that I remember Father Bea telling me on a number of occasions that humility does not lie in ignoring or denying the gifts received from the Lord, but in attributing them to God alone.

189. G. Zoré, S.J. (ArchWit).

writes that Bea enjoyed "great prestige with everybody," derived "above all from his clearly supernatural cast," and that he "could discern opinions quickly and surely, which was the fruit of authentic wisdom, flowing from a finely honed and ever watchful *sensus fidei*."[190] Another person who had frequent dealings with Bea for twenty years and who was, as he says, honored by his friendship, sums up his very detailed account by saying that in the years spent with Bea "with love for study of the word of God one learned to grow in the knowledge and love of Christ, the church and its visible head. . . . [Bea] was a great teacher, but above all a great religious."[191]

(iii) The *notes* he made during his various *spiritual exercises* in this period show very clearly that it was this spirit that guided Bea in all his activities, and we shall quote a few indicative examples taken almost at random. "I must submit the serious, demanding everyday work I perform in positions of great responsibility to the idea of the glory of God."[192] "Everything I do, even the smallest things, is work for God and for his church."[193] "I must use my authority, my influence in the most varied circles within the church . . . for the glory of God, for the greater good of the church, . . . and for souls."[194] "I must be a servant of God through and through in everything, for everyone and for everything . . .; in this way I shall become an apostle for others."[195] When meditating on the mission Christ gave the apostles to go out into the whole world to preach the gospel (Mark 16:15), Bea made the original observation: "Although I do not go out into the world, priests from all over the world come to us, so that we can carry out our teaching mission in a very special way in their regard, and they can then truly carry the teaching they have received out into the whole world."[196]

(iv) This underlying attitude was also the source of Bea's *fidelity to the tradition and magisterium of the church*, an essential feature of all his activity that is often overshadowed, if not totally forgotten. We have already seen that as early as 1924 Bea wrote to the Father General of the order, describing his line of conduct in teaching as follows: on the one hand not to keep students from knowing about major difficulties placed in the way of sacred scripture in modern exegesis, but on the other hand to seek a solution, conscientiously weighing up all the elements of the problem in absolute fidelity to tradition and the magisterium.[197] When he became professor and then rector of the Biblical Institute, his reasons of deep conviction were reinforced by those of fidelity to the specific mission the popes had entrusted to the institute. Anyone who attended Father Bea's courses on sacred scripture and is familiar with his writings will undoubtedly agree that this fidelity and obedience to the church was a keynote of both. For example, the course on the methodology of teaching sacred scripture that

190. Bishop A. Piazza, ex-student of the institute, Bishop of Albenga-Imperia, Italy (ArchWit).
191. F. Laconi, S.D.B., in his letter of 4 September 1974 (ArchWit).
192. Ms. Med. 1933/I/1.
193. Med. 1934/IV/3.
194. Med. 1945/I/1.
195. Med. 1945/I/2.
196. Med. 1934/VIII/3.
197. Letter of 2 May 1924.

he gave at the institute for many, many years was interwoven with elements taken from the various documents that the magisterium of the church has devoted to this subject from the time of Leo XIII onward. He approached all the other subjects he taught or wrote about in the same way, naturally insofar as the authority of the church had specifically spoken or insofar as there existed at least orientations as to the path to be followed.

However, we are not talking about some passive obedience, but about an active attitude, which was capable of intellectual initiative. We have seen how he devoted long years of patient labor to the difficult subject of literary genres, thus laying the groundwork for further developments in the teaching of the church. In this way he was already practicing in advance the call that the Council would later address to exegetes in its Constitution on Divine Revelation: "It is the task of exegetes to work . . . toward a better understanding and explanation of the meaning of sacred scripture in order that their research may help the church to form a firmer judgment."[198] After the church had spoken out on a given point, Father Bea was then concerned to introduce and explain the relative document to the general public.[199]

* * *

When Pope John XXIII spoke to the members of the Pontifical Biblical Institute on its fiftieth anniversary, he said: "Your work is thus supremely priestly and must be inspired by that zeal that is concerned solely with souls, their needs and the dangers threatening them. . . . In this light it is easy to understand the fundamental requirement of absolute fidelity to the sacred deposit of faith and the magisterium of the church."[200] I think that this is the best definition of the spirit that guided Bea in his activity as rector, professor and scholar: in everything he did he was basically a priest and apostle, in the service of Christ and thus of the church and souls.

---

198. *DV*, no. 12.
199. I therefore do not think N. Lohfink is justified in his presentation of Father Bea's contribution, for he repeatedly speaks of the "liberation" of Catholic biblical science performed by the encyclical *Divino afflante Spiritu* (cf. *Hinwendung*, pp. 57, 64-65, etc.). Seen in their context, such expressions would seem to imply liberation from the theological norm of interpretation of sacred scripture, which is the tradition and magisterium of the church, whereas the encyclical fully affirms this norm (cf. English translation, p. 16), as the Council would later do (cf. *DV*, no. 12).
200. Cf. *Biblica*, XLI (1960), 6.

PART TWO

MORE IMMEDIATE PREPARATION
(1949--1958)

At the beginning of July 1949, when Bea was relieved of his position as Rector of the Pontifical Biblical Institute in Rome, a post he had held for exactly nineteen years, any outsider could have seen this as the first step toward retirement. Although Bea did retain his position as confessor to Pope Pius XII and had some months previously been nominated as a consultor to the very important Vatican department of the Holy Office, both jobs entailed the maximum discretion, so that those not involved could easily have had the impression that although they were certainly positions of considerable prestige, they did not entail the kind of responsibility that could exercise any great influence in the life of the church. This also explains why the work Bea performed after his appointment as first President of the Secretariat for Christian Unity should have caused such surprise and constituted the "revelation" of a new and different Bea for the public at large.

Historians, however, will see things from a different viewpoint. If they compare the period with which we are now concerned with Bea's great mission as cardinal, they must consider the role the period 1949 to 1958 played as concerns the future activity of Cardinal Bea and reflect on whether the various tasks and activities of that period maybe laid the groundwork for his future mission, and if they did, to what extent?

As concerns the chronological bounds of this period, we should note that it ends with the death of Pope Pius XII in October 1958. Although the majority of Bea's commitments did in fact continue after this event, it had a very deep effect on his life, bringing an end to that regular contact with the Vicar of Christ that had in various ways played a determining role in Bea's life and activity since 1945. The twelve months or so that passed before he was made cardinal are therefore more a kind of intermezzo than anything else, and we shall treat them as such.

It is easy to see the importance of the following chapters for an overall understanding of the cardinal's personality and work. In a certain sense they are also more important than those in the third part of our study, which is devoted to the actual period as cardinal: although Bea as cardinal and his work do obviously still require a great deal of further analysis, they have already been the subject of various studies, whereas the ten years immediately prior to them have remained almost totally unknown. Even the authors who do speak of the time prior to his being made cardinal refer not so much to our period as to his time as Rector of the Biblical Institute.

If we bear in mind this fundamental importance of the ten years we are about to examine, it is easy to appreciate how fortunate we are in possessing for this precise period those thousands of letters we spoke of in the introduction to the book. This correspondence has already provided us with a great deal of information on Bea's life in previous periods, but it will provide much more on the subjects we shall be considering in this second part. The letters hardly ever speak specifically of their author's past, and the various references of this kind are more reflections made in passing, while the real object of the letters is current life and activity with their relative problems. This correspondence, together with Bea's own publications, will thus be our main source and will lend depth and color to the information drawn from other sources. Apart from what the present author has already published on the background and preparation for Bea's ecumenical work,[1] none of this material has been published before, since the relative sources are not accessible to the public and will not be for some considerable time.

In order to introduce this important period, we shall first give a general picture of the "outside events" that form the context of the various specific matters we shall speak about in the remainder of this part of our study. Such matters will be chosen mainly with a view to the third part of our study, which means that we shall be considering how far the various aspects of Bea's work and activity as cardinal can be discerned here in this preparatory period, if only in less conspicuous and explicit terms.

---

1. Cf. the present author's "Il Cardinale Bea: sua preparazione alla missione ecumenica," Archivum Hist. Pont., XVI (1978), 313-316.

CHAPTER 1

EVER BROADER RESPONSIBILITIES

In the first months of 1949, Cardinal Giuseppe Pizzardo, Prefect of the Sacred Congregation for Seminaries and Institutes of Study (which corresponds to what is now called the Congregation for Catholic Education), had to discuss the nomination of Bea's successor as Rector of the Biblical Institute with Pope Pius XII. While the pope, to whom Bea had explained his reasons for stepping down, was of a mind to accept the resignation, Cardinal Pizzardo was not at all happy about it. He had great trust in Bea and would have liked the institute to remain in his hands. Wanting to put an end to the cardinal's persistence, Pius XII produced the joke: "Your Eminence, if I don't let him go, he'll refuse me absolution!" This line (and we can guarantee that the story is true) was all the more significant in that the pope almost never joked about holy matters.

We can thus wonder about the reasons for the change—and also why that particular moment was chosen—if Bea still enjoyed such trust among his highest ecclesiastical superiors. A few days before he stepped down as rector, Bea wrote as follows to the superior of the Jesuit province of southern Germany: "After my appointment in the spring as consultor to the Holy Office (a job that takes a great deal of time and entails a number of obligations) it was no longer possible to continue [as rector] and I myself asked the Holy Father not to stand in the way of this change. Things have finally worked out, and I can return to 'private life.' "[1]

Apart from the reason Bea gives here, I think we must add another factor that considerably hastened his decision. As we saw in the previous chapter, for months he had been very much taken up with the job of "visitator" to the Pontifical German College in Rome (from November 1948 to March 1949). This venerable institution, which owed its existence to the personal initiative of St. Ignatius of Loyola, was now in its fourth century of life and was suffering from a fair number of problems—partly also as a result of the recent war. During Bea's long period of residence in Rome, he had forged considerable links with the college, and this meant that he worked with a particular will, dedicating a great deal of his time to the task. The visitation was drawing to a close, when he was nominated consultor to the Holy Office on 5 March 1949. This was the proverbial last straw in Bea's situation. He told me that for months he had been oppressed by the feeling—fairly unusual in a man of his fiber, who had successfully taken charge of so many different situations in the course of his life—that he was no longer capable of taking care of all his duties, particularly those as rector.

It also seemed a good moment for a change, because the building work on the new premises of the institute was almost complete. (In May 1949, on the

---

1. Nn 1 (1949); cf. Nc 1 (1951).

fortieth anniversary of the foundation of the institute, the new chapel could be blessed and the community itself could move to the new premises.[2]) There were still repairs and conversion work to be carried out on the old premises in order to create new lecture halls, but the plans had already been approved and everything was ready for work to begin.

The aim of the present chapter is that of offering a general picture of Bea's life and activity, his progressive involvement in ever broader and more important tasks, and the various ups and downs entailed. The chapter will therefore provide the general context, so that it can act as a frame of reference for the following chapters, which will describe specific aspects of Bea's varied activities. However, we shall try together to discover the underlying significance of all this, and see the direction in which the barque of Bea's life was bound.

Bea's Work as Teacher and Scholar

Despite his heavy commitments at the Holy Office, in the euphoric feeling of liberation from his nineteen years' responsibility as rector, Bea had high hopes of finding time to devote himself to his personal work[3] and publishing something of the wealth of material he had gathered and prepared in his many years of study and teaching.[4] Such was also the intention of the Father General, who strongly encouraged Bea in this direction, saying that he was ready to help by freeing him of his less important responsibilities. In 1951 Bea was thus able to step down as editor of the review *Biblica*, a position he had held for over twenty years. Apart from this, the general was able to persuade the heads of the Holy Office to free Bea from consultation on more juridical affairs, for example the marriage cases reserved to this department.[5] We shall now see how things really worked out!

In the first place, Bea continued with his activity as teacher and scholar, although on a somewhat decreasing scale. As regards his work as scholar, moreover, he suffered increasingly from outside influences, so that more than one of his letters mentions regretfully that he was writing, and thus publishing, on subjects that others had asked him to write on rather than matters he had himself chosen.

1. His *teaching* activity is very quickly taken care of. The syllabus of the Biblical Institute shows that throughout this period he retained his favorite course on the inspiration and interpretation of sacred scripture (two hours a week, always in the first semester) and the two courses on methodology: that of study of sacred scripture, and that of the method of teaching it. For nine years, in other words so long as church regulations on age-limits for teachers permitted,

---

2. Cf. Ng 1 (1949).

3. Cf. N 1949/12.

4. Cf. Nn 1 (1949).

5. These involved applications for the dissolution of ratified but non-consummated marriages, and applications on the basis of the so-called "pauline privilege" (cf. 1 Cor. 7:15) and "petrine privilege."

he also continued with a free course on exegesis of the didactic books of the Old Testament, alternating the following: Job (four times), Song of Solomon (three times), Ecclesiastes (twice). It should also be noted that in the same period he published new Latin translations of Ecclesiastes (1950) and the Song of Solomon (1953).[6]

Still within the framework of his official activity at the institute, we should note his work on *a new Latin translation of the Old Testament readings* used in the Roman breviary. In the previous chapter we mentioned the task entrusted to the institute in this connection in May 1949. Bea was entrusted with the position of president of the commission, as he had been for the psalter, and he retained the position on the express wish of the Holy Father even when he was no longer rector of the institute. As had been the case for the psalter, the commission held weekly meetings, usually on Wednesday evening.

2. Bea's work as *scholar* was closely linked with that of lecturer and bore strong marks of coming from a man whose position means that he is more and more often expected to give public talks. Such lectures are then published, together with other writings that are also often written on outside request, and form a special type of literary production. Obviously this observation is simply meant to indicate the type of work involved, without in any way belittling its intrinsic value.

First of all there were some purely scientific studies in which Bea was working in his own specific field. Thus we have the following: a critical survey of some recent works on biblical introduction; the concept of the encyclical *Divino afflante Spiritu* that the authors of the sacred books are to be seen as "instruments" of the Holy Spirit[7]; progress in interpretation of sacred scripture; Mary in the protogospel (Gen. 3:15); the idea of peace in the Old Testament; and lastly the question of two types of exegesis, one drawing its inspiration first and foremost from the science of religions and the other mainly from theology.[8] Many publications carried articles by Bea concerning the Hebrew scrolls that were discovered in the area of the Dead Sea in 1947 and the following years.[9] We should also mention a series of articles in the Italian *Enciclopedia cattolica* on subjects connected with biblical studies and biblical archeology.[10] Similarly there were various entries of a bibliographical or other nature in the Supplement to the French *Dictionnaire de la Bible*.[11]

The definition of the *bodily assumption of Mary into heaven* as declared by Pius XII gave rise to a series of articles on scriptural and ecumenical subjects: sacred scripture as the ultimate foundation for the dogma of the assumption; the importance of the bull of definition of the immaculate conception, *Ineffabilis Deus*, for biblical hermeneutics; the definition of the assumption and Protestants.[12]

---

6. Cf. Biblio. 9 and 11.
7. We discussed this in our previous chapter.
8. Cf. respectively Biblio. 84, 86, 89, 93, 97, 125.
9. Cf. Biblio. 75, 77, 92, 96.
10. Cf. Biblio. 71, 72, 74, 77a, 79.
11. Cf. Biblio. 85, 88.
12. Cf. Biblio. 82, 104, 99.

As he did in various of these studies, Bea also set about the task of interpreting other important papal documents in various articles. Thus we have two studies on the well-known encyclical *Humani generis* of Pius XII, one giving a general explanation and the other discussing its bearing on biblical studies.[13] The studies published for the fiftieth anniversary of the encyclical *Pascendi* on modernism are of a similar nature, one of them studying the way in which the encyclical presents biblical modernism, while the other considers the significance of the encyclical for biblical studies.[14]

These latter studies bring us into the field of the *history of biblical science.* Bea first of all sketched out its main features from Leo XIII to Pius XII. He devoted a series of articles to the contribution of recent popes to biblical science: St. Pius X[15] and Pius XII.[16] In this context, we should also note the studies published to mark the tenth anniversary of the "Piiano Psalter."[17]

The union between his work as exegete and his work in the liturgical field led to the 1956 talk he gave in Assisi to the First Pastoral Liturgical Congress, which was then published as an article under the title "The Pastoral Value of the Word of God."[18] On the other hand, the inaugural speech to the Roman Pontifical Theological Academy[19] moves out of the strictly biblical sector, ranging over the vast field of the whole of theology.

We have already observed that in a good number of cases his publications were the texts of public lectures. This is the case in eleven of the articles mentioned.[20]

3. Bea's production as scholar is thus far from negligible. Not only does the relative bibliography hold about fifty entries, but in these works the author covers a vast range of subjects. However, the description of this pastoral activity can easily be misleading, giving the impression that their author could be and was indeed satisfied with them, whereas the truth was quite otherwise.

As we saw above, when Bea was freed of his responsibilities as rector, he hoped that he would now have time to follow up certain projects that he had been nurturing for long years. However, he very soon realized that there were considerable difficulties in the way of such hopes. As early as 1951 he was writing: "I really have more to do now than when I was rector."[21] His letters reveal an enforced, progressive *separation from biblical studies, which was particularly painful* to him, for such work had been his ideal since he was a young man and had been his chosen occupation for many years—so far as he was able to devote himself to it, and we have evidence, as we shall soon see,

---

13. Cf. Biblio. 83, 80.
14. Cf. Biblio. 120, 123.
15. Cf. Biblio. 90, 105.
16. Cf. Biblio. 109, 124.
17. Cf. Biblio. 100, 112.
18. Cf. Biblio. 111, which also gives the various translations.
19. Cf. Biblio. 114; see also 113.
20. Cf. Biblio. 77, 89, 91-92, 97-99, 105, 111, 123. In another seven cases the articles were written following special requests from the journals in question.
21. N 1951/18.

that he was in fact able to devote less than ten percent of his time to it. Even so, in this period he often quoted a saying of his fatherly patron, Cardinal Franz Ehrle: "I still have enough work for another ten years." Then after a few years had passed, there was always work for another ten years.[22] Thus Bea often wrote, for example: "I have been studying and collecting large amounts of material for many years, and I feel that I could now produce something useful."[23] There were *two specific projects* involved here: a new edition (the third) of his study on the inspiration and interpretation of sacred scripture, and a second edition of his work on transformism, which dealt with the theory of evolution in its application to humankind and in particular to the origin of our bodies.[24] The first subject was especially dear to him. Having taught it for a quarter of a century, he would have liked to round things off by publishing a new and much enlarged—maybe so much as tripled—edition of his study on the subject.[25] However, toward the end of each academic year he regularly noted that his work-load had been so heavy that year that he had been able to do very little of his personal work, although he would comfort himself with the hope that things would maybe go better next year.

We must thus wonder about *the rest of Bea's work*, in other words, about the activities that commanded his attention so imperiously and took up almost all his time. The precious items Bea bequeathed us include two notebooks containing a register of his correspondence for the ten years now under consideration. Although there are a few gaps,[26] these books contain a little under three thousand five hundred entries. If we supplement the explicit notes in the register with our knowledge of the recipients and the various circumstances, we can divide the correspondence into seven main categories, indicating a fairly exact number of letters for each: biblical science and Pontifical Biblical Institute, 260, as well as 34 concerning the work of the Pontifical Biblical Commission; the Holy Office, 185; the Schönstatt movement,[27] and his relations with the Society of Catholic Apostleship (the Pallottine Fathers), 170; the liturgy and liturgical reform, 158; ecumenism, 149; relations with his own order, 103; his work as apostolic visitator to the Poor Sisters of St. Francis of Assisi in Aachen (1956-1959), 95; various letters concerning the Holy Father, 54; the preparation and publication of a liturgical adaptation of the Little Office of the Blessed Virgin, 54.

We would add *two observations*. First of all, biblical science and related matters accounted for a mere 7.5% of all the correspondence. We should also note that the proportion concerning the Holy Office is more than doubled if we

---

22. Cf. N 1951/44; 1952/150.
23. N 1952/83.
24. For the former project, see N 1951/11; 1952/192; 1953/185. For the latter (cf. Biblio. 10), see N 1953/185; 1954/114, 116. In this connection, see our chapter "Rector of the Pontifical Biblical Institute."
25. Cf. N 1949/30. The letter Ng 1955/45 says that the new edition could reach three times the size of the previous one.
26. The following are missing: the whole of 1950; three months of 1951; almost four months of 1952; four and a half months of 1954. About two years in all are thus missing.
27. Cf. in this connection *LThK*, IX, 457-458.

remember that it was his work in this Vatican department that involved Bea both in questions connected with the Schönstatt movement and in ecumenism. As regards the latter, we would point out that at that time the Holy Office was in fact the only Vatican department with authority in the sphere of contacts with brethren in other churches and ecclesial communities.

Bea's Work at the Holy Office

1. Even of itself, the full title of the department known as the Holy Office said a great deal: "Supreme Sacred Congregation of the Holy Office." It was a congregation—or what we would tend to call an assembly in more modern usage—of a certain number of cardinals, which acted as the "heart" of this central organ of church government and played a decisive role in it. The work material for this assembly was prepared not only by the relative office, but more particularly by a group of between twelve and eighteen counselors ("consultors" in the language of the Roman curia). The opinions of these consultors, and above all those of the cardinals, were then submitted in the last instance for the decision of the Holy Father. And this was no mere formality. The congregation had no authority to take any decision because at that time, unlike the majority of Vatican congregations, the head of the department (the "prefect") was not a cardinal, but the pope himself, while the most senior of the member cardinals only had the title of "secretary."

What were the subjects with which the Holy Office was concerned? In other words, which was the particular sphere of its authority? It may be helpful to recall that it was the successor of the congregation that prior to the reform carried out by Pope St. Pius X was called the Sacred Universal Roman Inquisition and had been given its form by Paul III in 1542.[28] It is therefore immediately clear that it is not to be confused with the courts of the medieval Inquisition. Its doctrinal sphere of competence concerned faith and morals, and the validity of the sacraments. The congregation was essentially a court to judge offenses that directly or indirectly concerned these areas, for example membership in a masonic body or other society condemned by the church. In the same context, the congregation was also entrusted with the examination and banning of books that offended against faith or morals, which meant placing them on the "index," and it could also grant permission to read books that had been banned in this way.[29] The congregation was also responsible for preparing the dissolution of ratified but non-consummated marriages, as well as dissolutions in virtue of the so-called "pauline privilege" and "petrine privilege."[30] The question of "mixed marriages," in other words marriages between Catholics and other Christians or non-Christians, also came under its ruling, as did questions concerning the

---

28. Cf. *LThK*, V, 1345.

29. Cf. *EncCatt*, IV, 313-315. It is indicative of the open mentality of St. Pius X that from the time he founded the Biblical Institute of Rome he granted its rector a general faculty to allow its students to read banned books when their studies required this.

30. On these privileges, cf. *EncCatt*, X, 49-55.

practice of the eucharistic fast of priests. It also had some competence regarding the liturgical language of the holy mass, inasmuch as this concerned a sacrament.

We can grasp the huge breadth of its tasks better still if we bear in mind the distinction between its normal work on the subjects listed above and its various types of special work, among which we should mention the assistance the department provided as concerned the papal magisterium. The vast number of documents—encyclicals and various speeches—published by Pius XII during his time as pope allows us to obtain some idea of the huge amount of work that this entailed for the Holy Office. We are not saying that the Holy Office "supervised" the pope, merely that when dealing with such delicate matters it was obviously a matter of elementary prudence for the pope to consult the people who were his foremost assistants in governing the church. And we should not imagine that it was always a question of mere consultation. The more important and solemn the document in question, the greater must be the caution in proceeding. We shall in due course discuss some of these important documents, but for now we shall mention only one example: the definition of the assumption of the Blessed Virgin Mary into heaven (1950), which was preceded by over ten years of study by a special commission, presided over by Bishop (later Cardinal) Alfredo Ottaviani and made up of fifteen theologians specializing in various branches of the theological sciences, Bea among them.

But what do we really know about the work of this congregation? Such work of course always came under the strictest and almost proverbial "secrecy of the Holy Office." Certainly the major part of these matters remain confidential and will be so for a long time to come; and this applies both to those that did not end with a conclusive document or decision that was made public, and naturally also to the discussions and proceedings even in cases of published decisions. Everything concerning the assistance provided by the department in the drafting of papal documents, etc., is also secret. However, in the period with which we are concerned there were also a certain number of decisions or documents that were published. We have found the following in the official publication *Acta Apostolicae Sedis*: an instruction on sacred art[31]; another on situation ethics[32]; and one that gives a more detailed explanation of the principles laid down by Pius XII on the eucharistic fast.[33] In the same period the section concerned with the index of prohibited books was also particularly active, and we in fact find twenty-two cases of books placed on the index. We would add that it would seem reasonable to assume that the Holy Office exercised a very considerable influence on the drafting of the encyclical *Humani generis*.[34] People openly said so at the time, and it is certainly more than probable.

31. Cf. *AAS*, XLIV (1952), 542-546.
32. Cf. *AAS*, XLVIII (1956), 144-145; on the same subject, see *LThK*, IX, 804-806.
33. Cf. apostolic constitution *Christus Dominus* of 6 January 1953, in *AAS*, XLV (1953), 15-24; the instruction of the Holy Office of the same date, in *ibid.*, 47-51.
34. Cf. *AAS*, XLII (1950), 561-578. As we have already said, we are concerned here with an overall picture and general presentation of the relative events. We are therefore not entering into discussions of content, and still less of Bea's attitude in this connection. Such considerations will form the subject-matter of a later chapter.

2. Moving on to *Bea's work at the Holy Office*, I would note at the outset that on more than one occasion I heard him praise the thoroughness of the method and work of the Holy Office, which was in his opinion better than that of any of the other congregations. The following is a short description of the approach followed.

The permanent office prepared the relative documentation, which was then handed to the consultors, who met with the strictest regularity every Monday morning for a meeting that sometimes lasted as long as three or four hours. At these meetings, the various individuals first stated their views, after which the chairman of the meeting (who bore the title of "assessor") summed up these opinions. A vote was taken, and the written opinions of the consultors and the result of the vote were then submitted to the cardinals, who discussed the same subject ten days later at one of *their* meetings, which were held with equally strict regularity on Wednesday mornings. The "assessor" then took the results of the meetings of both consultors and cardinals to the pope for a definitive decision. One last point: in one of the later meetings of the consultors, they were informed of the decisions taken by the pope, an element that was obviously of great help in providing future orientation.

The thoroughness of the whole approach to the work also meant that the consultors were allowed the *maximum freedom* in expressing their opinions. Bea mentioned this to me more than once. In a statement preserved in our archives, Cardinal Ottaviani said that the following phrase was current among both cardinals and consultors at the Holy Office: "Here we are at the Holy Office we can say anything we want, without fear of offending others or running the risk of condemnation."[35]

As regards the actual meetings of the consultors of the Holy Office, Bea spoke to me several times about the experience that he described as follows in the autobiographical article from which we have already quoted a number of times: "Even when I have very carefully studied and worked through the agenda, I have always realized afresh that the other members put their finger on things that escaped me, and in this way made their indispensable contribution which I then had to recognize and accept in all honesty."[36]

Apart from good sense, such an admission also indicates a good dose of modesty. In fact, in the above-cited statement Cardinal Ottaviani speaks about Bea in the following terms: "He was so good and so humble that he did not mind taking on even the more humble jobs, for example translations that he was asked to make because with his good knowledge of German he could translate certain documents with a reliability not only as to language, but also as to doctrine."[37]

In this connection we have a detailed statement from Mario Castellano, O.P., who was at that time "First Companion to the Commissary of the Holy Office": "I remember well that he sat on my left, always arriving very punctually and with his homework carefully done on all the subjects to be discussed (and there were always a large number). He expressed his opinion clearly and concisely. . . . He

35. ArchWit.

36. Biblio. 363, p. 18.

37. ArchWit.

was a humble man, Pope Pius XII's personal advisor. He kept to his place, like someone who has a service to perform, and his calm, measured words were valuable because of the principles on which they were based and not because of the prestige of the speaker. He never made even the slightest reference to his closeness to Pius XII and the trust the Holy See had in him."[38]

Naturally his work was not only involved with "humble jobs." His collaboration was, on the contrary, much appreciated and he enjoyed a great deal of trust. "He was highly respected in this work," says Cardinal Ottaviani. "Indeed, so much so that he was, so to speak, promoted to the position of a cardinal-member."[39] For his part, Bea told me: "Ottaviani would never dream of taking any action concerning Germany without consulting me." The tangible proof of this respect was seen in the plan for a council, which was drawn up between 1948 and 1951 on the instructions of Pius XII by a commission presided over by Cardinal Ottaviani. Bea was to be secretary of the subcommission on sacred scripture, and as such, maybe also a member of the special preparatory commission.[40]

What proportion of Bea's overall activities were concerned with his work at the Holy Office? From the beginning he noted that it took up *"the major part" of his time.*[41] Three years later, we read that his work at the Holy Office was on its own sufficient to take up "half one man's energies."[42] Another three years later the situation was unchanged, with such work taking up two and sometimes three days per week.[43] And as if all the homework and study for the meetings were not enough, they were supplemented with a prior discussion of the subjects scheduled for each meeting with two fellow Jesuits who were professors at the Gregorian University and were also consultors: Father F. Hürth, a moral theologian, and Father J. Creusen, a canon law expert. The purpose of these discussions was obviously not that of agreeing on some common line—the three of them were too different and too conscientious for such a thing—but simply in order to fill out their own study by taking into account viewpoints different from their own. We would add that the meetings of the consultors continued beyond the academic year: one year Bea notes that the last such meeting was to take place on 20 July, but that another would then be added on the 24th and another on the 27th of the month.[44] Here again the individuals attended with the strictest regularity, and only in very exceptional cases were they excused.[45]

Bea was obviously not new to such work, for he had been a member of the previously mentioned commission that had worked for ten years on the definition of the assumption of Mary into heaven. He also told his friend Amann that the appreciation of the practicalities of life that he had learned from J. Schofer,

---

38. ArchWit.

39. ArchWit.

40. Cf. Caprile, I, 1, p. 19.

41. Cf. N 1949/12; 1949/30.

42. Cf. Nn 11 (1952).

43. Cf. N 1955/194.

44. Cf. N 1953/76; see also N 1954/99; after the meeting on 26 July, Bea brought "two large packages of papers" back to the house.

45. Cf. Nn 3 (1949).

the "reviser" for theological students during his studies in Freiburg, was useful in this work.[46]

As if all this were not enough, he had no hesitation over taking on "mercy cases." Bishop Igino Cardinale, who was at that time an official at the Secretariat of State, speaks of this in a statement in our files, saying that he was struck by Father Bea's "readiness" to take on similar cases: "I am talking in particular about cases under examination at the old Holy Office, where the approach was based more on juridical considerations at that time, than on those of another order. His usual expression was that he would try to get such cases 'out of the freezer.' He did not allow the legalistic aspects of such questions to intimidate him; his attention was full of comprehension and compassion, although he only gave this aspect the importance that it might deserve in application to individual cases. I think that it was his deep biblical knowledge that gave him such an understanding view of human affairs."[47]

Apart from all the work connected with the weekly meetings, there was also his *"homework,"* which entailed giving written reports or "opinions" on various subjects and books. The register of his letters indicates the following figures for written opinions produced in the various years: in some years there are barely one or two[48]; in others the figure grows[49]; but there are a few in which the figure reaches or even exceeds ten.[50] The overall figure is sixty-seven. However, we should add the fact that Bea personally typed both the opinions for the meetings and the written opinions mentioned here. He could in theory have obtained assistance, for example that of a lay brother, who would have had to take an oath at the Holy Office and could then have copied the texts. I personally tried several times to persuade Bea to do this, but he always rejected the idea. Apart from other considerations, I think that the main reason was the delicate nature of the material involved, for he did not want to make the brother in question read things that might sometimes have disturbed him. Not that he doubted the brother's maturity, but the material was often of a kind that even priests are not accustomed to hearing. (It should be recalled, as we said above, that the Holy Office was a court dealing with the defense of faith and morals, and thus with errors against the faith and with certain offenses against morality.)

3. Apart from all this work, there were also other activities *indirectly* connected with that of the Holy Office and concerned with the Schönstatt movement on the one hand and ecumenism on the other. This was partly because Bea's conscientiousness meant that he made sure he kept abreast of matters that could at some future moment come to concern his work at the Holy Office, and partly because those who were in some way involved, or at least interested, in the relative questions turned to him for advice and also to provide him with information, etc.

46. Cf. Nc 19 (1959).
47. ArchWit.
48. For the years 1951 and 1952, one; for 1954, four; for 1959, five.
49. Six opinions each for the years 1957 and 1958.
50. For the year 1953, ten; for 1955, eighteen; for 1956, sixteen.

The Schönstatt movement is "an apostolic movement that has the aim of spreading, defending and strengthening the Christian life," seeking to carry the thought of the apostolate out to the wider levels of the faithful, and also helping other organizations in the apostolic education of their members. The movement developed within the framework of the apostolic work of the Society of Catholic Apostleship (the Pallottine fathers). Apart from the Apostolic Alliance and the League which were linked to the Pallottine fathers, there were also certain affiliated groups that had their own distinct organization: the secular institutes of the Sisters of Mary (2450 members in 1960), the Schönstatt Women (480 members), and lastly the Schönstatt Priests (600 members).[51] This is obviously not the place to go into a detailed description either of the movement or of its relations with the Holy Office, or again of the problematic relations between the movement and the Society of Catholic Apostleship. It will suffice to note in a general way that the Holy Office stepped in a number of times concerning the movement, and above all that the register of Bea's letters contains over 170 entries referring in some way to the movement, and that they become particularly frequent from 1953 onward. Bea's letters on this matter obviously say nothing about the work of the Holy Office, which was as always confidential, but they do provide an indication of Bea's general attitude and also of the basis for this attitude. Bea was concerned: (a) that so much precious energy should not be lost to the apostolate; (b) that diocesan priests in the movement should always remain closely united with their own bishops, in keeping with the thought of St. Ignatius Martyr, whose famous letters speak of the union between a bishop and his clergy; and (c) that the disputing parties should be brought to the negotiating table so that the problem should not be a burden to the Holy See but be resolved by those on a lower level according to the principle of subsidiarity.[52] It is not difficult to see that Bea was here anticipating the great principles enunciated by Vatican II.

The other field into which Bea was increasingly drawn by his work at the Holy Office was that of *ecumenism*. We have already recalled that at that time the Holy Office was the only Vatican department with authority concerning relations between the Catholic Church and other Christians. We can add the fact that the famous "instruction" of the Holy Office on the ecumenical movement—which represented the basic reference point for all Catholic ecumenical work until the conciliar decree on ecumenism was promulgated—appeared right at the beginning of Bea's work in this department.[53] If, as we have seen, Bea's work at the Holy Office meant that he became increasingly involved in matters connected with German Catholicism, this obviously included the various aspects of ecumenical work, at least in Germany. This was certainly particularly providential as preparation for his future mission, although we may be justified

---

51. Cf. the relative article of H.M. Köster in *LThK*, IX, 457-458.
52. Cf. Nk 11 (1956).
53. Cf. *AAS*, XLII (1950), 142-147.

in wondering about the *type* of ecumenism that was born in this specific context. Be that as it may, it is clear that this particular activity meant a considerable increase in Bea's already heavy work-load.

4. Lastly we should note Bea's *special position and his heavy responsibilities.*

His position. With his appointment as consultor to the Holy Office, he entered what could at that time be called the heart of the Roman curia. In those days the Holy Office with good reason and in full awareness of its significance bore the title of "Supreme Sacred Congregation of the Holy Office." However, apart from the heavy work-load involved, Bea found that his presence in these circles had another far from pleasant facet, which he illustrated by putting the following words in the mouths of those in charge of the curia: "You have to be careful with Bea, you know, because he sees the pope every week."

His responsibilities. It must in fact be observed that his appointment as consultor to the Holy Office was closely connected with his position as the pope's confessor. As we have seen, the pope had first met Bea when the former was nuncio in Munich and the latter was provincial superior of the southern German Jesuit province. Then, from the time that he chose him as his own confessor, the pope took to asking his advice more and more often. He wanted to be able to discuss with Bea the serious problems that were submitted to him by the Holy Office, and therefore wanted him to be fully involved as consultor so that he would be fully conversant with these matters, both through personal study and through participation in the regular weekly meetings of that department. Bea was thus doubly duty-bound to study the questions in maximum depth, first for the meetings at the Holy Office, and then in order to be able to advise the pope if asked. In 1955, he referred to this position when writing confidentially to the Jesuit superior of southern Germany: "The longer I spend at the Holy Office, . . . the greater my responsibility becomes, because the pope gives my suggestions and the relative motivations very careful consideration."[54]

His special responsibility referred particularly to *Germany.* (Someone close to these matters told me that here Bea had succeeded the Verbite Father J. Grendel.[55]) As a result Bea often spent his vacations in Germany, which meant laying aside his own inclinations and preferences, because apart from the exhausting journey it also entailed a considerable number of visits and meetings with various people. He wrote that it was also in the interests of the Holy Office that he should spend his vacations in Germany.[56] The reason for the increased volume of his correspondence is also to be sought in this connection: "Since I have been at the Holy Office my correspondence has not stopped growing."[57] And it was not only his correspondence that grew, but also the number of visits he received, particularly those of German bishops. Thus he noted: "A lot of bishops are now making *ad limina* visits, and this also takes up a great deal of my time."[58]

---

54. Ng 45 (1955).

55. Cf. N 1958/110.

56. Cf. Nn 3 (1949).

57. Ng 45 (1955).

58. Ni 55 (1958).

One last feature of this work was the fact that it was *for the most part hidden*, not only from the general public, but from everybody except a restricted circle of initiates. Referring to the relatively small number of his own publications, Bea observed that what he was then writing for the congregations could not be published,[59] and that the greater part of his work was of such a nature that it did not see the light of day, at least not under his own name; at least, he added, this saved him from any temptation to pride,[60] and he went on to say that what he was then writing would be discovered in the archives of the Roman curia by some historian after a number of centuries—"if people are still writing history by then."[61]

Work for Liturgical Reform

"The two main congregations for which I act as consultor—the Holy Office and the Congregation of Rites—give me more than enough to do, so that during the academic year it is very hard to find time for my own work," wrote Bea.[62] Thus we see Bea himself putting his work at the Sacred Congregation of Rites (as the department responsible for the liturgy was then called) alongside that for the Holy Office. When he was appointed consultor to this department on 12 August 1950, quite a number of people wondered what an exegete could be expected to contribute in this field, and they tried to explain his appointment by linking it with his work on the new Latin psalter. However, this did not seem really convincing. And indeed there was a much deeper reason: for three years Bea had been a member of the "commission of eight" for the reform of the liturgy, which had begun its work "in the catacombs" as the then secretary of the commission, Bishop Annibale Bugnini, put it.[63]

This still leaves us with the *question* of why precisely Bea was included in this type of work; and this doubt does not of course spring from the saying then current in clerical circles, especially among the religious clergy, that the Jesuits "don't sing and don't understand the rubrics."[64] As regards this saying, Bea believed that he could bear personal witness to the contrary, saying that the Schott Missal (the popular edition of the missal first produced in 1876 at Beuron Abbey, which allowed the faithful to follow the liturgy more attentively) "was my trusty companion from my early youth."[65] Elsewhere he said: "I have always been interested in the liturgy and I have studied it and its history."[66] Until Bea

59. Cf. N 1953/184.
60. Cf. N 1952/1.
61. Cf. N 1952/210.
62. N 1955/94.
63. Cf. the Latin newsletter of the Council for Implementation of Liturgical Reform, *Notitiae*, IV (1968), 360.
64. The saying was usually given in "kitchen Latin" as "Non cantant, non rubricant."
65. Ny 58 (1956).
66. Nr 13 (1966); cf. N 1955/194.

was able to reveal the secret of his participation in the work of the commission of eight, he used to explain his appointment with the fact that an exegete was needed for liturgical reform.[67] Bea could at this point refer to the reform without betraying any secret, inasmuch as the renewed Easter vigil had been published in 1951, although only in optional form. In 1955, however, the reform of the whole Holy Week was published in official form.

I heard about this from Bea at the time, and I think that I can reveal the facts today. Bea himself had apparently presented the pope with a reasoned statement in which he explained that in view of the scientific studies of the last decades, the necessary data now existed for a reform of the sacred liturgy. The pope found the suggestion valid and he therefore sent it on to Cardinal Clemente Micara, who was then prefect of the Congregation of Rites. This led the cardinal to pay a personal visit to the Pontifical Biblical Institute for a discussion with Father Bea over what could be done. Thus, although Bea was not a "professional liturgist," he played a part in the start of the modern liturgical reform. Obviously we cannot state that there were no other factors of a similar kind involved, and we therefore do not mean to claim that Bea played any exclusive role.[68]

As regards the work itself, Bea was the first to admit that he needed to study the matter in greater depth.[69] The aforementioned witness, A. Bugnini, who was in a position to know the facts, said that Bea did his homework for the meetings very conscientiously.[70] Bugnini also publicly paid him the following tribute: "Study, love and scrupulous preparation provided Father Bea with an uncommon level of knowledge and understanding of the liturgy, and, more surprisingly, of its pastoral aspects. His contribution to the work of the commission of eight was therefore very appreciable."[71]

We can therefore understand the position that Bugnini described Bea as enjoying in the commission of eight: "Everybody eventually came to wait for and welcome his contributions, in which he would make observations that were always pertinent, firmly based and very prudent, and suggest orientations in which various people often thought they could recognize or at least glimpse the thought of the Holy Father Pius XII, to whom he was one of the few to have frequent access."[72] In his written statement Bugnini does, however, note that Bea never so much as hinted that he might be interpreting the pope's thought.[73]

67. Cf. N 1955/194; Nc 19 (1955).
68. A Martimort (ArchWit, p. 14) reports Father F. Antonelli, O.F.M.'s opinion—or rather conviction—that it was the report he presented to Pius XII in 1946 or 1947 that provided the decisive spur for the creation of the reform commission. Martimort also mentions (p. 15) the petition of the French and German bishops for a reform of the Easter vigil. However, the commission had started work in 1947 and the reform appeared in 1951.
69. Cf. N 1955/194.
70. Statement preserved in the archives.
71. Bugnini, in *Notitiae*, p. 361. In the statement found in the archives, J. Jungmann says that Bea's liturgical knowledge "was not above average," whereas his understanding of the pastoral effects of the liturgy definitely was.
72. Bugnini, in *Notitiae*, p. 361.
73. ArchWit.

We find a further indication of the respect he enjoyed in the following note that Father Ferdinando Antonelli wrote to him when he was sick in 1957: "In agreement with His Eminence the Prefect, we did not hold our meeting last Tuesday, because we wanted to wait until you could be present."[74]

Bea's contribution to the liturgy was not, however, confined to his work with the commission. It is true that he often refused invitations to take part in meetings of specialists.[75] In connection with the meeting held in Montserrat in 1957, he wrote: "I am not going, because I know I do not have the necessary scientific knowledge."[76] He modestly and realistically felt that he was invited less for his knowledge than for his position.[77] Even so, he gave his help whenever and wherever he could. Quite a number of liturgists saw him as "a friend and counselor," as the well-known German liturgist Johannes Wagner put it.[78] On the basis of his letters, we can maybe extend this statement, saying that he provided stimulation and encouragement, advised people on the path to be followed and the correct door at which to knock, revised the drafts of petitions, and helped people to make their way through the maze of red tape, arranging for letters to reach the Holy Father "by some certain means," etc.[79]

The name and authority Bea had gained in the liturgical world were seen at the *First International Pastoral-Liturgical Congress*, the "backbone" of which, as Bugnini put it, was made up, alongside a lecture from Father Joseph Jungmann, S.J., of one from Bea on "The Pastoral Value of the Word of God in the Liturgy."[80] In this lecture Bea adopted a suggestion on the "two tables," which Cardinal Lercaro had made at the Lugano meeting three years previously. According to *The Imitation of Christ*, two tables are found in the treasury of the church: the word of God and the eucharist.[81] Bea explained that St. Pius X had proposed the table of the eucharist more broadly to the faithful, but that the table of the word of God was still waiting for similar treatment.

The same Joseph Jungmann records a significant detail from this meeting. At one point a certain amount of tension had developed between the Cardinal Prefect of the Congregation of Rites, His Eminence Gaetano Cicognani, a strenuous defender of Latin in the liturgy, and succesive speakers; the situation had deteriorated to the point that the audience was strongly applauding any references to possible reforms in this area. Jungmann says that Johannes Wagner told him that at the last moment Bea omitted all the phrases in his own speech

---

74. N 1957/284; cf. N 1958/236.
75. Cf. for example Ni 53 (1958); Np 10 (1957); N 1957/320; 1958/156, 176.
76. N 1957/320.
77. Cf. Np 10 (1957): "People do like to have a 'name.' "
78. Cf. BM, p. 208.
79. These statements could be backed up with quite a number of specific quotations, but this would take us too far afield.
80. Cf. Bugnini's statement as found in the archives.
81. Cf. *The Imitation of Christ*, IV, 11, 4. This is the account J. Wagner gives in BM, pp. 208-209. The comparison between eucharist and word of God was of course taken up and adopted by the conciliar Constitution on Divine Revelation, in the section dealing with the word of God in the life of the church (no. 21).

that could have provoked applause and therefore further aggravated the tension.[82] I personally remember Bea telling me about the relative passages, for example in Father Jungmann's speech, and saying that they had made him uneasy. He knew too well from experience that in such cases increasing the tension can harm one's cause and that the only way of overcoming difficulties of this kind was through a calm, gradual labor of persuasion.

We can thus see that Bea gave liturgical reform his effective support from its very beginnings. In the years 1947-1950 the commission had drawn up "a whole plan of reform of the calendar, missal, breviary, pontifical, ritual and martyrology."[83] This had given rise first to the publication of an optional renewed liturgy of the Easter Vigil in 1951, then to the reform of the whole of Holy Week in 1955, and finally to a "general decree" on the simplification of the rubrics.[84] On the other hand, with the constitution *Christus Dominus*, Pius XII had not only reformed the eucharistic fast, but had given the church the great gift of evening mass. Today we are obviously accustomed to this, and after the great reforms that the Second Vatican Council brought about in the area of the liturgy it is very difficult to realize what this step really meant at the time. In 1951 Bea wrote: "The great reform is far off; I shall not see it," and, referring to the renewal of the liturgy of the Easter vigil, he said that it represented "a pretty daring step."[85] He also told me that he had once spoken to Pius XII about the joy with which the various countries had welcomed the new discipline of the eucharistic fast, and particularly the evening mass, as well as the fruits that these changes were bearing, and that the pope had observed: "But it took courage."

Apostolic Visitator

As if all the work we have seen until now were not enough, in 1956 Bea was entrusted with the position of apostolic visitator to the Congregation of the Poor Sisters of St. Francis, which was founded by Blessed Franziska Chervier and had its mother house at Aachen at that time.[86] The congregation had spread well in the United States, and it was now facing the problems of the necessary adaptation to local situations—apart from the natural difficulties in comprehension between two such distant countries. Since Bea's commitments in Rome as well as his age meant that he could not go in person, he appointed personal representatives, although this only partially alleviated the burden. The details of the visitation are obviously kept secret, but for our purposes it is enough to note that in the three years that this task took, it brought Bea a little under one hundred extra letters, many of them in English. The apostolic visitation did not,

---

82. Cf. Jungmann's statement as found in the archives.

83. Bugnini, in *Notitiae*, p. 361.

84. Cf. *LThK*, VII, 1278.

85. N 1951/11.

86. Cf. *LThK*, IV, 280; IX, 394.

however, manage to prevent the two parties to the dispute from parting company some years later.

Active Participation in the Life of the Society of Jesus

It is not usual to see a man so burdened with work finding the time and energy to play an active part in the life of his order, including his own religious province. However, such involvement is reflected in a hundred or so letters to various people.

The central and most onerous point, as in some previous years, was his *participation in the general congregation* of the order, to which he was elected as representative of the southern German province. The general congregation was held in the fall of 1957 and lasted about ten weeks. Apart from preliminary preparation, for Bea this meant six, and sometimes more, hours of meetings a day for two and a half months; there were sixty-seven sessions in all, without counting consultations with individuals.[87] The congregation was held at the general curia in Rome, so that Bea had the work of the congregation added to various of his usual commitments, while those that were incompatible (for example, his lessons at the Biblical Institute) had to be made up later on, when his backlog had to be fitted in with all his current work.

At the general congregation, Bea concerned himself particularly with the question of modernizing the central government of the order, and also with lightening the heavy load of responsibilities borne by the Father General.[88] He was also concerned with the matter of liturgical life in the order, particularly in the formation of young members.[89] Lastly, he devoted special attention to the apostolate of the press.[90]

Apart from the general congregation, he also paid a great deal of attention to the good of the order, worrying, for example, that its members should conform to its constitutions and observe fidelity to the teaching of the church with loyal prudence.[91] He warmly recommended greater communication and cooperation between the various reviews published by the order and also between the Roman university institutes.[92] On the wishes of the Father General he took part in the drawing up of regulations on the care of liturgical life in the order, especially in the formation of young members.[93]

Bea's participation in the life of *his own religious province* was particularly keen. We therefore find him asking to be kept regularly up to date on events.[94]

---

87. Cf. Nb 21 (1957).
88. Cf. Np 5 (1957); see also Nt 13 (1957); N 1957/15.
89. Cf. Np 7 (1957).
90. Cf. Nw 48 (1957); see also Np 3 (1957).
91. Cf. Nq 41, 43 (1954); Nt 11 (1950).
92. Cf. Nw 48 (1957); Nq 9 (1951).
93. Cf. Nh 17 (1959).
94. Cf. Ng 18 (1952).

He also assured the provincial superior that there was never a day on which he did not recall the superior and the province in his prayers.[95] Since he himself had once been provincial superior, he took the liberty of sending the new superior certain suggestions; thus he recommended a very careful selection of candidates,[96] and also stressed the need for the province—and hence the order in general—to avoid wasting its energies on many activities that could be performed by others, but to make sure it had truly first-class men who could exercise a decisive influence on the development of society.[97]

In short, his heavy responsibilities in the service of the Holy See had in no way weakened his relations with his own order, nor the lively sense of family, and thus of solidarity, that was seen in spiritual union and effective collaboration in working for its good on the universal and local levels.

Various Kinds of Vacation

It is a little unusual to devote a section specifically to vacations, and if it were simply a question of rest there would be no reason to discuss the matter. However, in our case there were a certain number of problems connected with vacations, and these provide a significant illustration of the kind of life and activity that Bea was leading.

The first problem was that of finding and assuring the necessary time. To start with, there was the uncertainty over when his commitments in Rome, and especially those with the pope, would allow him to leave, and for how long; and this applied particularly in cases involving journeys back to his own country. Bea described his situation as that of being bound to Rome with many chains.[98] The letters speaking of vacation plans are full of conditions: "If there are no unexpected changes concerning the Holy Father's departure for Castel Gandolfo, I think I can leave . . . "; "it also depends on whether the Holy Father grants me two weeks' or three weeks' leave . . . "; "as far as I can see, I think I can do this. . . ."[99] More than once he in fact had to change all his plans, altering dates, appointments, and so on, almost at the last moment.[100]

As regards the vacations themselves, we must remember, as we said above, that since his work at the Holy Office involved him closely in the problems of the German Catholic world, he felt it was important to obtain direct experience of the situation in that country from time to time, and he therefore used the short periods of leave the pope granted him for this purpose. This of course meant that the relative meetings and the visits he made and received did not tend to entail pleasant holiday-time conversations: they may have represented a certain change from the rest of the year, but it was not always a restful one.

95. Cf. Ng 23 (1952).
96. Cf. Np 3 (1957).
97. Cf. Ng 4 (1951).
98. Cf. for example N 1952/108.
99. Cf. N 1953/62, 68.
100. Cf. for example N 1954/99, 114.

A third factor that also involved Bea in a certain number of commitments and a whole series of visits was his *relations with his hometown and region*. And here we must start with some remarks on the revival and development of these contacts.

There is first of all the surprising fact that after the death of his mother in 1918 Bea never returned home for as many as thirty-two years. This can partly be explained by the fact that he was an only son and that his only close relatives were two cousins, the daughters of his father's brother, one of whom, Rosa Bea, had cared for his mother so lovingly during her last sickness. In a 1948 letter Bea mentions that he had made plans to visit Germany several times but that they had always fallen through.[101] Things are explained more fully in an article by one of the main figures in the story, the parish priest of Riedböhringen, Hermann Hahn,[102] who had issued a first invitation in 1939, in response to which Bea had planned a visit for 1940, although he was forced to abandon the idea because of difficulties connected with the war. It was Bea who took up contacts again in 1949, and the visit took place in 1950. It was a great event for the clergy and population of the region. The president of the State of Baden even honored the celebrations with his presence—a fact in striking contrast with the 1912 prohibition on having "another Jesuit" preach the homily at Bea's first mass.

The visit marked a strong renewal in relations with Bea's whole vast, if more distant, family, with three other visits following in the ten years we are considering here.[103] These visits also gave birth to a steady stream of correspondence. In the period between 1950 and 1959 there were no fewer than 470 letters addressed to his various relatives. Bea took a close interest in all their doings, sharing in their joys and sorrows, and did what he could to help them, especially in spiritual terms, showing a rare sensitivity and pastoral ability.[104]

All this now aggravated the *problem* of Bea's vacations. He was anxious that such visits should have a truly pastoral character,[105] and he therefore accepted various priestly tasks. Apart from these, there would be a long exchange with the clergy of the region, and a meeting with the people at which Bea talked about Rome and events there. There were also a fair number of visits to or from members of his family. All of this explains why his relatives' suggestion that he could rest at Riedböhringen met with the realistic retort: "How could I rest if I stayed with you, when I have often found that I still had the whole breviary to recite in the evening because I had not had time during the day?"[106] Bea was so aware of all the pressures that inevitably accompanied his visits home that he sometimes insisted that they should be made incognito, or at least remain secret until the last moment.[107] After vacations when such plans were successful, he would say that he had managed to get a good rest.[108]

---

101. Cf. Ni 1 (1948).
102. Cf. BM, pp. 272, 275.
103. In the years 1953, 1954 and 1957.
104. The relative letters bear the code Nb, and have also provided us with many biographical details.
105. Cf. N 1952/70; 1954/24.
106. Cf. Nb 351 (1958).
107. Cf. N 1953/59.
108. Cf. N 1953/102; Nb 49 (1953).

There were, however, other summers when the vast number of his commitments throughout the year meant that he felt the strong need for a real rest. In the ten years now under consideration, journeys to Germany therefore alternated with a *rest near Rome*, at the Holy Shepherd Villa in Gallicano, belonging to the German-Hungarian College.

It is therefore easy to see that "rest" was a fairly relative term, especially in vacations entailing a journey back to Germany. The following are a few examples. In 1954 Bea had planned to leave on 15 August, traveling via Munich to the Jesuit Novice House at Neuhausen near Stuttgart, where he was to enjoy about a week's rest. From 23 to 30 August he was to visit Riedböhringen, after which he was to return to Rome, again via Munich. However, for a number of reasons his departure had to be postponed until 22 August, and in order to honor his commitments in his hometown, Bea took the Innsbruck route, traveling directly to Riedböhringen, where the following tasks were awaiting him: a homily, a solemn high mass, and one or two talks or discussions. On 31 August he went to Neuhausen, on 5 September to Munich, and on 10 September he was back in Rome again.[109]

The other example is from 1957, when his plans envisaged arrival in Freiburg im Breisgau on 29 July, with two days dedicated to seeing various people, and a visit to Riedböhringen from 1 to 8 August, where, among other things, he was to bless a nephew's marriage and preach at the first mass of a Dominican who was a distant relative. This was to be followed by a few days' rest at the Neuhausen novitiate, a visit to his friend Amann in Constance, and his return to Rome via Innsbruck on 16 August.[110]

On one occasion his sense of self-preservation led him simply to cancel the planned visit almost at the last moment. This happened in 1952, and we have already referred briefly to this episode in a previous chapter. The above-mentioned parish priest of Riedböhringen, H. Hahn, wanted to organize a special celebration to mark the fortieth anniversary of Bea's ordination, and the latter had accepted, assuming that it would be a purely local and fairly restricted celebration. However, he then learned that Father Hahn had had it announced in the diocesan newspaper, and that the item had then been taken up by a Catholic news agency and thus become generally known in Germany and Austria.[111] It had already been announced that the universities of Freiburg im Breisgau and Vienna, both of which had bestowed honorary degrees on Bea shortly before, were to take part. At this point Bea stopped everything, telling them that the state of his health made it impossible for him to attend.[112] He sent a long message to the people, to make up in a way for the sermon he would have preached on that occasion.[113]

Bea later confirmed that a quiet rest at home had done him a great deal of

109. Cf. N 1954/99, comparing with N 1954/114.
110. Cf. N 1957/165, 166.
111. Cf. Nb 355 (1953).
112. Cf. N 1952/113.
113. Cf. N 1952/141.

good.[114] This experience encouraged him to seek this kind of rest on other occasions, and to warn his town and family about it in advance. This happened particularly when he felt tired, either because he had been sick during the previous year or because he had been too over-burdened with work.[115] In these cases he sought refuge at Holy Shepherd Villa for two weeks' holiday, which was often immediately followed by the eight days of spiritual exercises.[116] However, Bea often took advantage of his vacations to catch up on his correspondence,[117] so that we not infrequently find letters dated during this or similar periods of vacation.

Health

Having seen the enormous work-load Bea carried, and also the small amount of rest he allowed himself, it is natural to wonder how he bore up under such constant calls on his strength, and thus about the state of his health. And the question is all the more logical if we remember that in many periods of his life, if not all, his health was fairly indifferent, and that even the periods of rest he allowed himself were decidedly limited in time and quality.

His letters do of course repeatedly speak in *very brave* or even triumphant tones: "I am working as I did twenty years ago"[118] or "as if I were fifty years old."[119] In 1956 he wrote to his friend Amann: "As concerns my mental powers, I have not observed any signs of old age, and physically there is nothing to worry about."[120] He liked to quote the words of Pius XI: "We've lived a long time, but we're still young."[121] Elsewhere he added: "Maybe it's really my strong interest in current questions that keeps me young and fresh."[122]

However, other letters provide a glimpse behind this façade, or at least show us the other side of the coin. It is in itself revealing that he should, for example, have observed with satisfaction: "I have survived the winter well, although it was the harshest I remember in my thirty-two years in Rome: it snowed as many as eight times."[123] Or again: "I have not taken even a single day off for sickness during the whole academic year."[124] Such emphasis on these details indicates that they were unusual and that things did not usually go so well. If we take a chronological look at his medical record we find a whole series of incidents, some of them disturbingly serious. He was having heart problems in February 1951,[125] and a few months later, at the beginning of August, his heart was giving

---

114. Cf. Nb 354 (1952).
115. Cf. for example Nb 68, 381 (1958).
116. Cf. Nb 367 (1955).
117. Cf. Nb 115 (1956).
118. N 1955/55.
119. N 1952/90; Nb 55 (1954).
120. Nc 25 (1956)
121. Nc 36 91956); Nn 12 (1952).
122. Nk 8 (1956).
123. Nb 55 (1955); cf. Nb 58, 370 (1956).
124. Nb 59 (1956); cf. Nb 154, 372 (1956).
125. Cf. N 1951/44.

even greater cause for concern, so that his physician considered his condition fairly serious.[126] In the first months of 1952 he had a long drawn-out bout of influenza with a persistent high temperature.[127] In the spring of 1953 he asked the superior of the southern German Jesuit province if he could be dispensed from taking part in the provincial congregation, giving the following reason for the request: "Two weeks ago, the doctor again told me I must avoid all physical strain because of the state of my heart."[128] In April 1954 he wrote: "The winter was a severe trial for me, and I have not yet recovered."[129] If the years 1955 and 1956 passed without incident, he would pay all the more dearly in the following years. In the fall of 1957 he took part, as we have seen, in the general congregation of the order. All those attending were vaccinated against Asian flu, and although the vaccine apparently protected Bea throughout the meeting, he returned home with a heavy cold, which developed into a serious attack of influenza, with a successive relapse.[130]

How are we to reconcile the portrait given here of a man with such indifferent health with the fact that he was able to deal with the vast range of commitments and heavy work-load we have seen? I think that the first factor was, as he said, his lively interest in current problems, together with his strong personal sense of duty. Another factor was the considerable joy he found in his work, so that he wrote: "My ideal would be to work until the Lord calls me without warning."[131] This overall attitude gave rise to a clear-sighted "strategy" in the use of his strength, so that with careful discipline he was able to derive the maximum yield from his limited energies. "I must be careful," he wrote, "not to expect my heart and stomach to do more than they are able."[132] He was therefore careful to keep to his diet, and was also aware that he had to avoid subjecting his body to any strain that could tax it excessively.[133] Thus he could say: "I have had a bad heart for thirty-five years, but I have reached old age. Even with a weak heart, if you work calmly you can keep going for a long time."[134] However, no strategy could prevent energies that were so over-extended from failing every now and then. At such times he had to bring the same will-power and common sense into play, under the watchful supervision and assistance of his doctor, in order to recover his strength so that he could continue on his way.

---

126. Cf. N 1952/113; 1951/44; Nb 347 (1951); 351 (1952).
127. Cf. Ni 13 (1952).
128. Ng 25 (1953).
129. Nr 33 (1954).
130. Cf. Nb 113 (1957); Np 10 (1957); Nb 9, 23, 379, 381 (1958).
131. N 1952/90.
132. Nb 41 (1952).
133. Cf. Nb 107 (1956): "The stay in Assisi [for the pastoral-liturgical congress] tired me a great deal because of constantly having to go up and down the steep streets." Sending his acceptance of an invitation to take part in the 1952 International Eucharistic Congress in Barcelona, with a talk on the idea of peace in the Old Testament, he requested in advance that he should be excused from taking part in any celebrations and receptions, and that he should be allowed to leave on the first plane after he had given his talk.
134. Nb 178 (1953).

"The Symptoms of Old Age"

"When you think about it, jubilees, honorary degrees and such things are symptoms of old age and give us cause for reflection," wrote Bea to the superior of the southern German Jesuit province, who had sent him good wishes for his fiftieth anniversary of religious life.[135] It was a phrase he often used in similar contexts. If we consider such events here, we obviously do not intend using them as items in some kind of eulogy, but rather because these special occasions often throw light on certain aspects of a man's character that we might otherwise not notice. If, as we have seen, Bea felt that he was still "young," we may wonder about his attitude to such symptoms of advancing age.

We would note in the first place that his letters contain very few references to his two honorary degrees in theology, one from the theological faculty of the University of Freiburg im Breisgau, and the other from the University of Vienna. At Christmas 1949, the Dean of the *Freiburg Faculty*, Johannes Vincke, sent Bea a letter telling him that "in consideration of the rich fruits of research and theological doctrine," the faculty of Bea's "native region" had "nominated him with unanimous esteem honorary doctor of theology." The writer also enclosed the relative diploma.[136] A few days later, Bea sent a letter of appreciation, recalling a number of his professors, and expressing the hope that he might become worthy of such an honor through work in the field of theology—so far as other commitments in the service of the church permitted.[137]

The conferral of the degree on the part of the *Theological Faculty of Vienna University* in 1951, on the other hand, involved Bea in giving a solemn lecture on the history of exegesis from the beginning of the present century onward.[138] The reception of this honor thus entailed a considerable effort for him, and strangely enough it is mostly this aspect that we find in his letters: "The Viennese doctor's hat," he wrote, "has upset my whole schedule. Just before Christmas I had to set to work on a scholarly lecture for the celebrations [of conferral], then hurry off to Vienna, where there was a terrible rush, as I got there on Wednesday morning, and had to leave again on Friday morning. The celebration took place on Thursday, with everything that went with it. I came home tired out, and it has taken me a good while to recover. I suffered the after-effects throughout the spring."[139]

These two degrees put me in mind of an episode that took place some years later. Bea had gone to the United States in order to receive an honorary degree from a local Catholic university, and a very eminent cardinal asked him why he

---

135. Nn 11b (1952).

136. Cf. Nr 1 (1949).

137. Cf. *ibid.* The correspondence contains no other reference to this honorary degree. If I remember correctly, Bea wondered several times about this way of doing things, without any kind of celebration. Maybe the reason is to be sought in post-war conditions in Germany.

138. The material from this lecture was then used in the article listed as no. 95 in our bibliography.

139. Nb 141 (1951). Bea was so exhausted that he changed his original plan to visit Munich in the summer; cf. Nb 346 (1951).

had come. Bea explained, obviously thinking in European terms and assuming that honorary degrees always had the significance attributed them in Europe. He then added that it was already his third, to which the cardinal responded with a slight smile: "I have forty-three."

In 1952 Bea was nominated an honorary member of the important international and interconfessional biblical association, *The Society for Old Testament Studies*. Although ninety percent of the members belonged to various non-Catholic confessions, the president of the association that year was the English biblical scholar and Catholic priest, M.T. Barton, and the members had also happily accepted the suggestion of holding its meeting in Rome at the Pontifical Biblical Institute. The event was also important from the ecumenical point of view. Bea used his good offices to arrange for the participants to be received in audience by Pope Pius XII, although he thought it wise to make sure that the pope realized that the majority of those attending the meeting were not Catholics. To which Pius XII answered imperturbably: "It does not matter. People of every faith come here."

A significant indication of the ecumenical situation at that time is found in Bea's observation: "How many things have become possible today! The *Osservatore Romano* published the text of the Holy Father's speech, together with the list of those attending the audience."[140] One of the Catholic participants who was familiar with the general psychology of the other members wrote: ". . . the audience . . . gave all our members the chance of seeing and speaking with our Holy Father, and was certainly a great event in their lives. I believe it succeeded in fully exorcising the evil spirit of prejudice and ill-will nourished by so many centuries of the Protestant nightmare."[141]

In 1954, the president of the Federal Republic of West Germany decorated Bea with the *Grand Cross of Merit*. In this connection, the recipient observed wryly that it was not the heaviest of the crosses he had to bear.[142] Joking apart, he pointed out the change in attitudes from those of the "cultural struggle" of his youth, when the Society of Jesus was considered a danger to the German Empire and banned from the country.[143] Then, broadening his gaze far beyond his own personal situation, he wrote: "The decoration—which many people deserve as much as I do—gave me particular pleasure because it shows that today the work of the clergy and of Germans abroad is understood and appreciated as a contribution to the good of our people and country. In the difficult days of Nazism and the war we were in fact able to do a great deal for the reputation of the German people."[144] We shall mention in passing one last honor: in 1957 Bea's hometown granted him honorary citizenship, a fact that appears barely once in his correspondence.[145]

---

140. Nq 17 (1952).
141. Nv 11 (1952).
142. Cf. Nb 55 (1955).
143. Cf. Nb 94 (1955).
144. Nz 43 (1954).
145. Cf. N 1957/202.

On 8 April 1952, Bea celebrated his "golden anniversary" of *fifty years in religious life*. Today other Jesuits are almost automatically informed of this and similar jubilees in the annual lists of members of the various provinces. In his modesty, Bea did everything he could to prevent the news from leaking out,[146] although this modesty was not totally disinterested, for he wanted to avoid being snowed under with all the letters it would provoke, all of which would need answering. The most prestigious greetings came from Pope Pius XII in a telegram written in classical Latin and bearing the pope's personal signature, a particularly rare occurrence at that time. Bea copied the telegram into his notebook, *The Dates of My Life*: the pope congratulated Bea for what he had accomplished in the field of knowledge and piety, and imparted his apostolic blessing, with good wishes for him and his work.[147]

Despite all his attempts to prevent the news from getting out, Bea found that the anniversary still brought him many letters from all over the world and also a number of personal visits.[148] However, it must be said that he much appreciated these expressions of good wishes. Thus he wrote: "They make me realize that we belong to a great society [that of Jesus], made up of many dear brothers; this is maybe the strongest impression I have gained from this anniversary."[149] As regarded himself personally, he repeatedly quoted Paul's words: "By the grace of God, I am what I am" (1 Cor. 15:10). One example will suffice: "You are right: if I have one duty it is that of thanking the Lord for these fifty years, full of work but also of countless great graces and divine favors. In these days I am feeling more than ever: 'Gratia Dei sum id quod sum.' When I entered the novitiate as a poor candidate fifty years ago, I did not (and could not) have any idea of what the Lord had in store."[150]

He made the following reflections in a letter to his close friend Amann: "Fifty years have passed—and what years they have been! If I could have foreseen everything, it would have been hard to find the courage to accept it in advance. . . . In any case, I have had not so much as one unhappy hour in the order; on the contrary, I can do nothing but thank the Lord for all he has given me."[151]

---

146. Cf. N 1954/48, 113.

147. The Latin text of the telegram as found in *Dates* is as follows: "Tibi quinquagesimum religiosae vitae annum absolventi gratulationibus nostris pie docteque a te gesta honestamus atque Apostolicam Benedictionem peramanter impertimus quae tibi inceptisque tuis novum caelestis gratiae afflatum auxiliumque conciliet." It is the second to last note Bea made in *Dates*; the last would be that of his consecration as bishop on 19 April 1962, when he had already been a cardinal for two years.

148. Cf. N 1952/48b.

149. Nn 11b (1952).

150. N 1952/45; this letter was addressed to Father John O'Rourke, S.J., Bea's predecessor as Rector of the Biblical Institute. Cf. also N 1952/71, 155; Nn 11b (1952).

151. Nc 3 (1952).

A Cardinal's Hat in View

In the years prior to the second and last consistory for the creation of cardinals by Pope Pius XII (held in January 1953), Bea's letters repeatedly referred to rumors about the possibility that he would be made cardinal. In 1951 he wrote to the dear friend of his youth, Chaplain Huber: "In my hometown they expect me to be made cardinal and prefect of the Sacred Congregation of Rites, but certainly nothing will come of it."[152] In June 1953, Bea himself spoke in veiled terms of a "danger" that had apparently passed.[153] However, starting at Christmas 1952, probably after the list of future cardinals had already been published, he became much more positive: "If you have been waiting," he wrote to a young friend, "for the creation of a certain cardinal deacon, you'll have to wait a good deal longer. I am sure that it will not happen."[154] And again: "Do not look for my name in the list of future cardinals; during my last years I should like to work in peace and tranquillity for God and his church."[155]

We may ask how Bea could be so sure, and what had really happened. I think I can now reveal what I heard from an absolutely unimpeachable source. Pius XII was apparently tending toward the idea of creating Bea cardinal. I do not know how, but the Father General of the Society of Jesus learned about this, and in line with the precise instructions contained in the constitutions of the order he tried to talk the pope out of the idea. "In fact," Pius XII was to say, "he brought me such convincing arguments that I laid the plan aside." It seems clear from the various circumstances that Bea must have been told what was happening, which is what gave him the certainty seen in the letters quoted above.[156]

A Painful Personal Process Lasting Ten Years

At the end of this chapter we shall try to *summarize* not so much the varied aspects of Bea's activity as the main lines and underlying tendencies these reveal.

The first fact to be noted is the very concentrated activity that was such a heavy burden to him: "I'm weighed down by so much work."[157] The same thought is expressed in a hunting metaphor: "I'm being hounded by a pack of dogs."[158] We also find: "Every day I'm harnessed to more than one cart, so that I am unable to pull any of them very much further forward"[159]; "and then each

---

152. N 1951/47.
153. Cf. Ng 30 (1953).
154. Ni 20 (1952).
155. Nb 261 (1952).
156. R. Kaiser, *Inside the Council. The Story of Vatican II* (London, 1963), p. 36, is thus incorrect when he says that Bea "declined" the hat.
157. N 1957/22.
158. N 1956/151.
159. N 1954/190.

of the people who give me tasks to do thinks that he is the only one for whom I have anything to do"[160]; "luckily Father General leaves me in peace whenever possible, because he knows I have my hands full with work for the Holy See"[161]; "I often have so much to do that I have no idea where to begin"[162]; "people press in on me from every side, so that I often have to refuse, in order to be able to perform at least my strict duty."[163]

The second fact was the unavoidable progressive *separation from biblical studies*, which we mentioned at the end of our description of his work as scholar. We often find letters expressing regret over this state of affairs: "Unfortunately, I find no time for scientific work."[164] The thought of scientific work "is receding considerably into the background"[165] and "will soon be reduced to zero."[166] "I have had to eliminate many things that I had included in my schedule"[167]; "I have gradually moved away from the areas that were my special fields of study."[168] Every now and then he returned to his two pet projects—a reworking of his studies on inspiration and transformism—hoping to complete them the following year.[169] He used to set to work with a will during his summer vacations; for example in July 1955, after all the crushing work of the academic year, he worked away at the new edition of his book on inspiration, telling people happily that he had finished the historical section.[170] As regards the transformism project, on the other hand, in 1956 he observed with a touch of sadness: "Maybe I shall never publish it."[171] And in fact neither of the projects was ever completed.

How did he react to this unavoidable process of separation? Sometimes he would try to console himself with the thought: "Of course we have to step aside in favor of the younger troops."[172] And he did sometimes almost savor the joy of having led the way, as he observed the arrival of these younger troops and saw them continuing further along the same path.[173] At first he felt that his work in the Vatican congregations meant that he had abandoned his beautiful academic work in order to move to administrative tasks, but he comforted himself with the thought that this was just another way of serving the church,[174] or else reflected: "I have to do everything except what I want. Never mind: we must do what the Lord wants."[175] Comparing his present work with his scholarly

---

160. N 1958/215.
161. N 1958/225.
162. N 1953/159.
163. N 1952/108.
164. N 1952/83; 1953/184; 1956/148; 1958/110, 107, 221, 269.
165. N 1952/57.
166. N 1955/194.
167. N 1952/1.
168. N 1956/204; cf. also N 1953/54.
169. Cf. N 1953/185.
170. Cf. N 1953/93.
171. N 1956/50.
172. N 1952/83. Cf. 1955/180; 1952/45.
173. Cf. N 1958/215.
174. Cf. N 1949/30; 1958/126.
175. N 1953/67.

work, he observed: "Most of what I do is of such a nature that it never sees the light of day, at least not under my name. However, this of course has its good side too, for I am delivered from the temptation to pride in my literary production!"[176] "Basically, I am doing what the Lord wants."[177] And he wrote to his friend Amann, saying: "When you come down to it, I am doing this too [his work] for the glory of God and the good of the church."[178]

However, he gradually came to realize the utility, depth and breadth of his tasks: "I am one of the few Germans who hold a position of such standing in the Roman curia, and I am much in demand simply on account of my relations with the Holy Father."[179] Sometimes he spoke with a sober sense of realism: "I am called to deal more and more with thousands of other things, which somebody has to do and where I can do a certain amount of good and prevent various things that would be less good."[180] He asked for a fellow Jesuit's prayers because, he wrote, "I have gradually become involved in difficult and important work, so that I have great need of the light of the Holy Spirit."[181] Then he became more explicit: "I am devoting myself wholeheartedly to tasks that have a close bearing on the life of the church."[182] On one occasion he went so far as to write: "I shall soon have to say that I am occupied in caring for the church in all its aspects,[183] particularly the suffering church and people in distress. This is a fine activity; there are other people who can do exegesis."[184]

* * *

In the ten years examined in this chapter we have thus seen Bea live through a painful personal process, and one that was all the more painful inasmuch as he saw it simply as a *sacrifice* accepted in the service of the church, whereas in the light of his future mission we can say with hindsight that the Lord was using this painful process to mould his mind and bring him gradually out of the relatively restricted field of the work he had been engaged in until then, and above all was using his relations with the pope to help him to share increasingly closely in concern for the whole church.

The words with which the Letter to the Hebrews describes the course of Abraham's life are maybe applicable here: "By faith Abraham obeyed when he was called to go out to a place which he was to receive as an inheritance; and he went out, not knowing where he was to go" (11:8). Bea too had set out in the eighth decade of his life on a path that was almost totally new, without knowing where it was to lead him in accordance with God's plans. Extending the

176. N 1952/1.
177. N 1952/206.
178. Nc 16 (1955).
179. N 1958/111b.
180. N 1958/222.
181. N 1957/82.
182. N 1955/180.
183. Cf. 2 Cor. 11:28 ("anxiety for all the churches").
184. N 1955/180.

comparison with Abraham, God had shown Bea a new land—the very broad interests of the universal church—but not the promised land, in other words, the great mission for which he was preparing him. Looked at in human terms, it seemed more than anything as if he was to use his last remaining strength for God and the church. Bea accepted the new direction of his life through faith and in obedience to the authority of the church. And he did so with the strength that came to him from his first vocation, his religious vocation to the Society of Jesus, the spirit of which is distinguished by the two key concepts of glory of God and service of the church.

CHAPTER 2

FATHER BEA AND PIUS XII

When Bea was nominated President of the Secretariat for Christian Unity in 1960, the then President of the Reformed Church of France explained his reservations about this appointment not only with the fact that Bea was a Jesuit, but also with the fact that he had been a trusted advisor of the "conservative" Pope Pius XII.[1] Nor do I believe that he was alone in this opinion. In any case, it shows how necessary it is to study his relations with Pius XII, so far as is possible, if we are to understand Bea. And it seems all the more important if we bear in mind the surprising fact that Bea then became a trusted advisor of Pope John XXIII, for more than one person will certainly have wondered how the same man could have enjoyed the trust of two such different pontiffs. The first clues can be found by studying relations between Bea and Pius XII.

It therefore seems a real stroke of luck that we possess a wealth of material for such a study, all of it hitherto unpublished, in other words over 130 letters in which Bea speaks of Pius XII in various connections, sometimes at considerable length. He also sometimes mentions him in the notes from his spiritual exercises.

It is hardly necessary to point out that in the letters in question Bea does not speak as the pope's confessor, just as he does not touch on anything concerning sacramental confession. He was in fact so strict on this point that he always refused to give evidence in the cause for the beatification of Pius XII in order to avoid even the appearance of speaking of matters concerning the secrecy of the confessional. However, as we shall see, he did have many other kinds of contact with the pope, and these enabled him to know him and speak about him with some authority.

Our introduction to the subject-matter of this chapter also makes it clear that we do not intend to study the personality of Pius XII. Certainly the correspondence will provide much interesting information that could be used by his biographers. However, this is not our aim here, for our interest is Bea's view of the pope and his attitudes toward him. In other words, we shall be looking at the reflected light that Bea's observations about the pope throw on his own personality and attitudes.

The aim dictates *the method* to be followed, for we shall not be concerned with checking Bea's remarks and statements against other sources or biographies of Pius XII. On the one hand, Bea himself was an extremely well-placed witness, and on the other, our main interest is the light that his evidence throws on himself, and not the historical accuracy of this evidence. We shall sometimes, however, make an exception by comparing the information provided by our correspondence with the evidence of four highly reliable witnesses whom we

---

1. Cf. Pierre Bourguet, "Opinions sur le Concile," *La Revue Réformée*, XII (1961), 48.

can list in the chronological order of their writings. The first is Robert Leiber, S.J., who was Eugenio Pacelli's private secretary for almost forty years, from the time he was nuncio in Berlin until his death.[2] The second is Cardinal Domenico Tardini, who was the pope's close assistant during the whole of his time as pope, and was in fact Pro-Secretary of State during the last four years.[3] The third is Cardinal Mario Nasalli Rocca, who was head chamberlain to Pius XII.[4] The last witness is Sister Pascalina Lehnert of the Congregation of the Teaching Sisters of the Holy Cross, who was housekeeper to Eugenio Pacelli for about forty years, starting from his time as nuncio, then after he became cardinal and finally when he was Pope Pius XII.[5]

We begin with the story of *Bea's appointment* to this important position, a story that throws light on a number of aspects of Pius XII's character. While he was secretary of state, his confessor was the Italian Jesuit, Father A. Garagnani (1881-1944), director of the Higher Institute of Religious Education at the Pontifical Gregorian University. When he became pope, he changed confessors for certain practical reasons, which Bea himself explained as follows. When Pius XI was pope, it was discovered on several occasions that important papers had been removed, and had reached unauthorized hands. The explanation lay in the fact that the pope often worked in what was called the private library, to which a fair number of people had access for one reason or another. Pius XII decided on two lines of conduct: not to work in the private library, and to limit access to his private rooms as much as possible. And since he had three German nuns to keep house for him, he decided to call on a German-speaking priest who could act as confessor both for the sisters and himself. He therefore chose Father F. van Laak, S.J., who was professor of dogmatic theology at the Gregorian University. When van Laak died in December 1941, the pope called on Father A. Merk, S.J., professor of New Testament exegesis at the Biblical Institute. At the beginning of 1945, however, Father Merk fell seriously ill, dying at the beginning of April. Toward the end of March, when Father Merk's condition

2. Robert Leiber (1887/1967) studied history at Berlin University, because his superiors had assigned him the task of continuing L. von Pastor's monumental work *History of the Popes*. This was where Nuncio Pacelli met him and asked his religious superiors if he could have him as his assistant. Leiber then followed Pacelli to Rome, where he was appointed professor of history at the faculty of church history of the Pontifical Gregorian University. With reference to this change in assignments, his fellow Jesuits joked that Father Leiber would make history rather than writing it. On Leiber, cf. the study of his fellow Jesuit and colleague at the Gregorian University, Burkhart Schneider, "Uno storico della Chiesa," *OssRom* (8 April 1967), p. 3. Cf. R. Leiber, "Pius XII," *Stimmen der Zeit*, LXXXIV/59/163 (1958), 81-100; we shall cite this article simply with the name of its author.
3. Cf. Cardinal Domenico Tardini, *Pio XII* (Vatican City, 1960); we shall cite this book simply with the name of its author. On Tardini, cf. Giulio Nicolini, *Il Cardinale Domenico Tardini* (Padua, 1980); cf. also various articles in the supplement to the *OssRom* of 28 February 1988; the first-hand report-cum-study by Cardinal Agostino Casaroli, "Nella Segreteria di Stato a servizio di tre Papi," *OssRom* (2 March 1988), p. 5, is particularly interesting.
4. Cf. Cardinal Mario Nasalli Rocca, *Accanto ai Papi* (Vatican City, 1976); we shall cite this book simply with the name of its author.
5. Cf. Sister M. Pascalina Lehnert, *Ich durfte ihm dienen: Erinnerungen an Papst Pius XII* (3rd ed.: Würzburg, 1983); we shall cite this book simply with the name of its author.

was deteriorating and hope of a recovery was ebbing, the pope called on Father Bea to succeed him, observing, "I hope that this one lasts," a phrase that Bea took as an expression of the pope's wish that Bea should be his last confessor.[6]

We know from Bea himself that he had first met Pius XII when Bea was provincial superior of the Jesuit province of southern Germany, which had its headquarters in Munich, where Pacelli was apostolic nuncio. Bea also said: "Even then he often sought my advice on the interpretation of various texts of sacred scripture. The same thing continued after he had returned to Rome in 1929 and become Secretary of State."[7] It is interesting that despite this long acquaintance the pope should have chosen him as confessor only after two other choices had failed.

Confessor and Advisor

1. What were Bea's *tasks and duties* in this position? In the first place, obviously those of hearing confessions, both those of the sisters and those of the pope. Apart from exceptional cases, a car therefore collected Bea every Saturday shortly before five in the afternoon and drove him to the Vatican. I know that he prepared very conscientiously for this appointment, partly by going over the liturgy of the following day in order to draw inspiration for a more effective exhortation for his penitents.

The sisters' confessions and also that of the pope took place with the greatest simplicity in the confessional. The sisters would naturally step aside for the pope, allowing him to choose his own moment. The only clue the confessor had as to whether the next penitent was the pope or a sister was the color of their dress.[8] When Bea finished confessing the last sister, the pope had therefore often already made his thanksgiving, and in these cases he would fairly regularly invite Bea into his study for about twenty minutes of conversation, which could sometimes stretch to as much as half an hour—a fact that said a great deal, for the pope was extremely frugal in the use of his time.

2. Bea often said that Pius XI had told his confessor, a certain Father Alisiardi: "Father, remember that you are confessor and nothing else."[9] In our case the confessor had not been given any such instruction. Although Bea had known the pope for a long time, however, he himself observed the greatest discretion: "In relations with the Holy Father I must keep within the bounds of my office and not meddle in matters that lie beyond its field."[10] He wrote as follows to

---

6. Cf. Nr 13 (1956).

7. Biblio. 363, p. 17; cf. also the memoirs published in BM, p. 268.

8. Without revealing that he himself was the pope's confessor, in 1950 Bea wrote as follows in an effort to correct something that had been published: "Like any pope, Pius XII has specific times set aside in order to see his confessor, and he does not need to receive 'comfort and encouragement' from him 'fairly often'; such remarks are completely at odds with the pope's character" (N 1950/7b).

9. *Ibid.*

10. N 1957/250; cf. Nm 3 (1955), p. 4.

another Jesuit, who had asked him to obtain a personal favor from the pope: "For the sake of the Holy Father himself, I must steer clear of anything that is not connected with my position, and above all I must avoid laying personal wishes such as this before him, if their fulfillment is not of exceptional interest to the church. I know for certain that the Holy Father much appreciates my discretion in this matter."[11] Discretion over matters of church government was even more vital. Referring both to his own position and to that of Father Leiber, the pope's private secretary, Bea wrote: "Neither of us has the right to involve himself if he is not expressly asked to do so."[12]

In the reply quoted above, it is important to note that Bea says that he must avoid putting forward anything that is not "of exceptional interest to the church," for when one or both of these conditions was met, he did not hesitate to step beyond the restricted bounds of his position. It is, for example, interesting and very significant that Bea often presented the Holy Father with gifts of books and other works on behalf either of the author or the publisher. Obviously he did this because it was clearly in the interests of the church that authors of such books or their relative publishers should receive encouragement. However, a large part of the reason was also to be found in the pope's great interest in books. At that time I heard well-informed people quote Pius XII as saying that he could waste time in two ways: one was when he took up Cicero's *Orations*, which he greatly loved and admired, and the other was when he went into the library and began to look through the books.[13] D. Tardini says that the reason the pope often delayed his departure for his vacation at Castel Gandolfo in the summer was the need to choose and gather together the books he wanted to take with him: "And there were a large number, because his thirst for work and his care in checking facts meant that he always needed a great number of books." When Tardini asked him why he did not leave the stifling heat of Rome, he received the reply: "What can I do, Monsignor? I have so many books to take with me, and I still haven't finished making my selection."[14]

There were a particularly large number of cases when Bea presented the pope with publications of the German Catholic publishing house Herder of Freiburg im Breisgau, for example the great dictionary *Der Grosse Herder* and the dictionary on the science of education *Lexikon der Pädagogik*.[15] On this occasion Bea told the publishers that the pope had taken the work to Castel Gandolfo with him and that he was using it a great deal.[16] On another occasion, after the publishers had offered a similar work, Bea wrote back asking them to send it at once because the pope wanted to take it to Castel Gandolfo with him.[17] On yet

---

11. N 1957/249.
12. Nm 3 (3955), p. 4; cf. Nr 18 (1958).
13. As regards Cicero, this story is confirmed by Leiber, p. 82.
14. Cf. Tardini, p. 134, note 23; cf. also Lehnert, pp. 79-81, with many details about the pope's library.
15. See the many letters dealing with the presentation of various works: Nz 24, 26, 31, 33, 37, 40, 42, 43, 48, 59, 70, 73.
16. Cf. Nz 59 (1956).
17. Cf. Nz 31 (1953); compare with Nz 33 (1953).

another occasion Bea told the same publishers that the pope had shown great interest and expressed his pleasure that they had undertaken publication of new editions of the two well-known encyclopedic dictionaries *Lexikon für Theologie und Kirche* and *Staatslexikon*.[18]

Such works were always submitted to the pope with a note from Bea explaining their content and value. After the book had been submitted to the pope, Bea used to inform the author or publisher, saying that the pope was having a letter of thanks sent through the Secretariat of State, for except in a few cases when he preferred to send his thanks through Bea, the pope made sure that those concerned received a formal letter of thanks and commendation.

3. The due discretion that Bea observed on his part obviously did not prevent the pope from turning to him increasingly often for advice, as we have seen in the previous chapter in connection with Bea's work at the Holy Office. In view of the pope's very sensitive nature, Bea's reserve may in fact have made it easier for the pope to ask for his advice. As concerns the character of Pius XII, Tardini observes perspicaciously: "In particularly difficult moments, his sharp intelligence with its grasp of detail sometimes meant that he could see all the possible solutions quickly and clearly. The pros and cons, the advantages and disadvantages, of each one were immediately clear to him, with the relative favorable and unfavorable consequences. He would therefore sometimes be uncertain and hesitant, almost as if he were unsure of himself."[19] Nasalli Rocca relates that on two occasions the pope asked him to request the advice of "that authentic servant of God, Father Cappello," in regard to his own personal problems. When he objected, "But the pope can decide however he chooses in such cases," he received the reply, "I decide for others, but not for myself."[20] Obviously if the pope turned to him for advice, Bea put himself wholly at his disposal, and indeed tried to anticipate such cases and prepare himself for them. Thus, for example, when the nomination of the bishop of a major German diocese was under consideration, Bea sought information, giving the following reason for his request: "I may possibly receive a request for an opinion from the competent authority. I could of course say, 'I don't know anything about it,' but I could then be told, 'Why don't you find out?' " And Bea wound up: "In my position, it is not pleasant to find yourself in such situations."[21]

Obviously Bea's discretion in this connection was such that he hardly ever mentions the details of this activity either in his letters or elsewhere. However, when he says that his position as "intermediary" between the pope and other people entailed a volume of correspondence that would alone be almost enough to keep one man busy,[22] we can gain some idea of Bea's involvement in this

---

18. Cf. Nz 59 (1956); the first is the great 11-volume dictionary on theology and the church, *LThK* (later on expanded with 3 volumes of commentary on the documents of the Second Vatican Council), and the second is a 6-volume juridical-sociological encyclopedia on the State and its attributions.

19. Tardini, p. 70; see also Leiber, p. 84.

20. Nasalli Rocca, p. 60.

21. N 1958/111b.

22. Cf. Ni 56 (1958).

area. We should also remember that one of the reasons for his appointment as consultor at the Holy Office was precisely so that the pope could discuss the various questions with him.

In the previous chapter we saw how much Bea's position as confessor curtailed his freedom of movement, so that even his vacations completely depended on when the pope granted him time off and for how long. He in fact wrote several times in the context of the pope's various sicknesses and relative periods of convalescence (which we shall come to shortly): "Until the pope has fully recovered, I cannot be away from Rome for any length of time."[23] When he was invited to give talks or attend meetings outside Rome, Bea also used to excuse himself by saying that he could not leave Rome for many days, both because of his Monday appointment at the Holy Office, and also because of his Saturday one "in the Vatican."

4. Apart from the actual commitments and the restrictions on his freedom of movement involved by his position, there was also the *psychological burden* of anxiety that the pope's strength might give way under the excessive weight of the work-load he took on himself. Especially after 1953 and the first serious sickness that the pope suffered in January of that year, Bea's letters repeatedly expressed concern that the pope was working too hard and exceeding his strength. Bea certainly admired the huge amount of work that the pope performed at his desk, in his speeches and in governing the church, describing it as "almost incredible," and considering it "a miracle" that a man of seventy-seven could hold out so well.[24] His admiration did not, however, cloud his sober realism, so that his letters continually expressed concern that the pope was exhausting himself.[25] Bea's worries were obviously not unjustified, as can be seen from the fact given by Tardini that at the end of the year the pope "had lost so much weight that he weighed a bare 125 pounds," although he was just over six feet tall.[26] He would therefore certainly not have had too much strength. Then two years later came the particularly heavy work connected with the Holy Year celebrations, and in January 1953 the first serious crisis in his health.

Bea tried to curb such zeal for activity: "All of us who are close to the pope have to keep asking him not to wear himself out."[27] Bea tried in particular to persuade the pope to give fewer of his major speeches.[28]

Another type of activity that Bea felt tired the pope out a great deal was what were known as the "special audiences"[29] (audiences for small groups) and also what were known as the "hand-kissing audiences," to which a considerable

23. N 1955/50. Cf. Nb 55 (1955); 366 (1955).

24. Cf. N 1953/173; 1953/19.

25. Cf. N 1953/19; 1955/50; 1956/22.

26. Cf. Tardini, p. 39; I remember that at that time there was a story in Rome that an ordinary working woman who saw him at a general audience exclaimed: "Poor thing, how thin he is!" Nasalli Rocca notes, without referring to any particular period in the pope's life: "Pius XII weighed 128 pounds" (p. 76).

27. N 1958/73; cf. N 1956/45.

28. Cf. N 1954/114.

29. Cf. N 1953/47.

number of people were admitted, and which therefore entailed prior study of the relative information and then rapid adaptation to constantly changing people and situations. Bea observed that the audiences were certainly an apostolate, but that it was more important that the pope should husband his strength for his duties of governing the church.[30] If Bea tried to restrain the pope's zeal and activity in this way, the advice was obviously given within the framework of friendship and not as confessor. And the result? Bea's answer shows respect but is frank: "The pope refuses to discuss the subject,"[31] and "He does not spare himself, because his sense of duty is too strong to allow this."[32] In 1953 Bea noted: "We have so many pilgrims that it is almost a permanent Holy Year, and the pope would like to be everything to everybody."[33] The pope's attitude in this connection was undoubtedly partly a result of his very high concept of the papacy.[34]

Paradoxically, Bea observes that this lively activity did not slacken off in any way at Castel Gandolfo, where the situation in fact worsened in a certain sense. In 1952, for example, the pope was sick, with a temperature and a racing pulse, but refused to rest, holding his audiences exactly as normal so that outsiders had no idea that anything was wrong.[35] In 1955 Bea wrote: "Experience shows that the vacation period and the summer months are more dangerous for the pope, for his work increases because of the audiences and speeches he gives."[36] In his last years the pope would therefore almost have exhausted his resources by the end of his stay at Castel Gandolfo.[37]

Anxiety was particularly great in the context of the three serious health crises the pope suffered in January 1953, January 1954 and December 1954. During the third of these sicknesses, Bea said that it had cost him a great deal of time and caused much concern and anxiety.[38] During the successive periods of convalescence, Bea's letters often mention the pope's health, with phrases such as: "He's better, but still too weak to start giving audiences yet," "it will be a long convalescence," "he has survived the winter well," etc.[39] We also find: "He came through the ceremonies for the two canonizations very well" and similarly "the celebrations for his eightieth birthday."[40] Sometimes Bea would wind up with the wish: "Let us hope that he does not go back to giving so many audiences."[41] In the background there was always the fear of a dangerous

---

30. Cf. N 1954/104; cf. Lehnert, p. 110, where we read that the pope would come back from such audiences perspiring and exhausted.
31. N 1956/22.
32. N 1955/143.
33. Ng 30 (1953).
34. Cf. Nasalli Rocca, p. 59.
35. Cf. N 1953/125.
36. N 1955/50.
37. Cf. Nb 366 (1955).
38. Cf. N 1954/211, 213; 1959/229.
39. Cf. for example N 1953/17; 1958/19.
40. N 1954/77, 82.
41. N 1954/104.

relapse. A few months after the serious sickness of December 1954, Bea therefore wrote: "The pope is better, but he is starting to work too hard again, so we have to fear a relapse; the more attacks he suffers, the greater the danger that they will lead to complete collapse one day."[42]

As we can see, Bea's discretion certainly did not indicate any coldness; since he had been called to work so closely with the pope, he felt personally concerned in anything connected with his life and activity. Bearing in mind the actual work involved and also the psychological burden of worry, it is easy to understand that it was no empty phrase when he wrote in 1958, a short time after the pope's death: "I am glad to have been freed from the position of confessor to the pope, which is a far from enviable one."[43]

Pius XII Seen through Bea's Eyes

Bea's worries and fears over the pope's health were all the greater in proportion to his respect, indeed admiration, for the pope, and thus to his conviction of the great importance of the pope's life and work for the church and for humanity. This leads us to a more detailed examination of *how Bea saw Pius XII* and his personality, and we have a considerable amount of clues and information in this connection.

1. We can start by giving a few of Bea's phrases that can be seen as a kind of spiritual portrait of Pius XII. In 1955 he wrote a long letter attempting to refute a series of criticisms of the pope that were being voiced in certain quarters at that time, and he concluded by saying: "Anyone who knows Pius XII well can never feel sufficient admiration for his selflessness, conscientiousness, diligence, spirit of faith, and dedication to his exalted office."[44]

(a) Let us start with his *diligence*. Tardini mentions the pope's fear, "which I would call more of a scruple, of losing so much as a single minute of his time, denying himself the rest he did need and giving up even those moments of recreation that are so helpful in recouping one's forces. Even the daily walk of one hour prescribed by his doctors was used for reading."[45]

His attitude to music is very interesting in this connection. When Leiber discusses the pope's early education, he notes that he played the violin very well and had a great feeling and love for music in general.[46] Nasalli Rocca says that he particularly liked the music of German composers. However, we find Bea writing that the pope was very strict with himself over listening to music and only allowed himself to do so if it was immediately connected with an apostolic interest: "I myself have seen how at a performance he would leave after a few minutes, with the excuse that there was important work waiting for him. . . . And

42. N 1955/50; cf. Ng 44 (1955).
43. N 1958/305.
44. Nm 3 (1956), p. 5.
45. Tardini, p. 52.
46. Cf. Leiber, p. 82.

he did not permit himself to play the violin except when he was suffering from great mental and physical exhaustion."[47] Nasalli Rocca gives an example in which the pope saw music as being linked with "an apostolic interest," saying that one day the pope told him: "When I am preparing my speeches I need music, and then I feel that something of those sounds and that singing is transmitted to me." Then, obviously referring to certain types of music that he preferred, he added: "You see, Monsignor, when I listen to music, I feel I am praying; when such pieces come to an end, I have the impression that I am coming out of a meditation."[48]

(b) Earlier on we described Bea's concern over the fact that the pope worked too hard and pushed himself beyond his own resources. This concern did not prevent Bea from respecting and indeed admiring the pope's total dedication to his duties, which meant that he would not dream of sparing himself. And it seems that when Bea called the pope his "model" in certain letters,[49] he was thinking of this particular quality. Bea was very well aware of the huge burden that the pope bore, as yet another episode goes to show: during Pius XII's last sickness I said to Bea, maybe a little naïvely, that we could still always pray for the pope and maybe ask for a miracle. Bea looked at me and surprised me with his response: "Knowing the burden this man has to carry, I would not dare ask for such a grace."

Such extreme dedication on the part of the pope came from his very strong sense of the duties imposed by his high office. It is interesting in this connection to note that Bea once told me that Pius XII had said that in the present state of the papacy, the pope could not be sick for long and thus unable to carry out his duties. In the context of this view he had studied the theological problem of whether a pope could resign from his position, and he had reached the conclusion that he could. He therefore said: "If I were to suffer from a long sickness that prevented me from exercising my office, I should resign." The accuracy of this information is fully borne out by Domenico Tardini, who writes: "Pius XII told me more than once in December 1954 that if he were not to get better, he would resign as pope. 'I am staying at my post,' he said, 'solely because the doctors have assured me that I shall make a full recovery.' "[50]

However, such a resignation proved unnecessary because, in the words used by both Leiber and Bea, the pope was called away "in the midst of his work."[51] And Bea adds, "just as the pope himself would have wished."[52] Tardini says that the pope had in a way foreseen this. Speaking of the pope's last days, he writes: "Three years earlier he had told someone close to him: 'I shall die suddenly. But I have asked the Lord to give me one day to prepare myself.' On the morning

47. N 1958/265; cf. also Lehnert, p. 85.

48. Nasalli Rocca, p. 72.

49. Cf. Nc 25 (1956); N 1953/173. This is also borne out by Höfer, "Das geistliche Profil des Kardinals Bea," p. 57.

50. Tardini, p. 168, note 84. Leiber too (p. 81) explicitly states that the pope firmly intended retiring if he became incapable of exercising his office. Cf. also Lehnert, p. 161.

51. N 1958/249, 253, 255, 263, 265, 268.

52. Ibid.

of that 7th October [1958], he told the same person: 'This is my day.' "[53]
According to Bea, however, the call also had what we might call a natural basis,
so that he wrote about the cause of the pope's death as follows: "The pope's
body was, as I had often observed, completely worn out, and in the last months
of his life only his strength of will kept him going when he appeared in public."[54]

2. A major feature in Bea's picture of Pius XII was his *magisterium* and the
body of doctrine to which he gave birth and which ranges over the vast gamut
of problems raised by the culture and society of his times.

(a) After the death of Pius XII, Bea compared him with his successor John
XXIII, observing that the latter dedicated less "attention to doctrinal questions
than his great predecessor, who was of course unique in this respect."[55] As early
as 1955 Bea wrote: "Today many new questions are arising to which only the
church can give a reply, and here Pius XII leads the way with his example."[56]
Later on, in an interview on the eve of the Council, when he was already cardinal,
Bea would develop his thought in this connection, starting by saying that Pius
XII was "clearly a man of an entirely different stamp" from John XXIII "and
perhaps fundamentally a lonely man in his greatness and in his keen personal
austerity and life." He went on to say: "It should perhaps be added that it will
be many years, if not centuries, before the immense work of this pope and his
enduring influence on the church and even on the history of humanity can be
properly evaluated." Then he moved on to an evaluation of the magisterium of
Pius XII: "In the midst of a terrible and catastrophic war and during the period
of reconstruction which followed it, his help was solicited from all sides as was
no other man's. All classes and professions asked him for guidance or words of
encouragement. And it was during all this that uninterruptedly he sowed the
seed, almost unbelievably abundant, that is to be found in the twenty-two
volumes of his speeches and radio messages. . . . It can even be said, in a certain
sense, that the teaching spread by Pius XII has become the spiritual air that we
constantly breathe without even being aware of it. In this sense Pius XII and his
work remain fundamental also for the Council, especially on account of its
breadth which takes into account every single one of the problems of humanity
today and seeks to solve them in the light of the gospel as it is preserved and
taught by the church, and thereby to reconquer modern man to the faith, to the
church, to Christ and to God."[57]

When John XXIII first became pope, Father Bea spoke repeatedly about Pius
XII as "doctor of the church." Thus he wrote that although John XXIII had no
wish to anticipate the judgment of the church, he counted Pius XII among the
blessed and praised him as a doctor of the church. "And I think that he is right."[58]

---

53. Tardini, p. 54.
54. N 1958/342.
55. Nm 72 (1959).
56. N 1955/187.
57. *The Unity of Christians*, pp. 206-207. Later on Pope Paul VI was to describe Pius XII's teaching
    work as a "vast and fruitful preparation for the doctrinal and pastoral words of Vatican II which
    followed" (cf. *Insegnamenti di Paolo VI*, XIII [1975], 216).
58. N 1959/6; Bea was probably referring among other things to the speech given on 3 November

And again: "Pius XII remains a doctor of the church for the future too, even if officially he has not (or not yet) been declared such."[59]

However, it was not simply a question of a vast body of teaching, which was moreover carefully relevant to contemporary circumstances, but also of the extreme attention given to the formulation of doctrine.[60] In the context of the definition of the assumption of the blessed Virgin into heaven, Bea told me: "No one who was not personally involved can have any idea of how much work and how many precautions a step of this kind entails."

In his teaching, the pope was very careful to respect the freedom of individuals and the gifts of the Spirit that each person has received, and also the laws of the theological sciences. Writing to a non-Catholic brother, Bea observed that when the pope spoke of St. Louis Marie Grignion de Montfort's "perfect devotion" to the Virgin, he was not imposing it on anyone, but leaving the faithful full freedom in the matter, so long as their piety moved within the framework of Catholic teaching and healthy devotion.[61] Bea wrote to someone else that the pope would certainly not extend the feast of the co-redemptrix to the whole church, because the relative doctrine had not yet been sufficiently clarified and still needed to mature within the church.[62] In both cases, the pope's attitude seems all the more significant if we bear in mind his great personal devotion to Our Lady.

(b) We must, however, admit that the *forms* of the pope's teaching, and in particular the number of his speeches and the vast range of subjects dealt with, were the object of criticism, especially in the last years of his papacy, for some people felt that he talked too much and about far too many subjects. Bea answered the first part of the objection by saying that the pope gave a great many speeches simply because people asked him to do so, and it was difficult to refuse one group after agreeing to another's request; we could therefore say that the speeches were almost wrung from the pope. However, Bea went on to say that there was a deeper reason, for the pope saw this activity as an apostolate that only he could exercise.[63] The groups that requested such audiences contained people who had never in their lives heard either a Catholic priest or the viewpoint of the church on their own branch of study or field of activity; and experience showed that these people went away from such audiences inwardly enriched and with an orientation for their own life and work. The subject of such speeches could obviously not be purely and simply of a religious and spiritual nature, for these people wanted to hear something about their own problems and interests. It was a unique apostolate, and entailed enormous sacrifices of time and energy on the pope's part.[64]

1958 on taking possession of the Lateran Cathedral; cf. *Discorsi, messaggi, colloqui del S. Padre Giovanni XXIII*, I, 39.

59. N 1959/11.

60. Cf. Ns 1 (1948). Cf. also Leiber, p. 86, who says that his doctrinal formulations were of a crystal clarity and that he had an almost physical repugnance for anything that obscured the truth.

61. Cf. N 1958/223.

62. Cf. N 1953/60; also Leiber, p. 86.

63. Cf. also Leiber, p. 94.

64. Cf. Nm 3 (1955), p. 3.

This last observation brings us to the answer to the second part of the criticism, in other words that the pope talked about far too many subjects. Here Bea pointed out that the pope spoke about difficult problems that were raised by contemporary life and had the most serious implications; and if he did not do so, he would be accused of not being up-to-date and of lacking in contemporary relevance.[65] For his part, Tardini says that basically such criticism sprang from a mistaken notion that the pope wanted to show how knowledgeable he was in all these fields. Tardini answers this accusation by saying that the pope was too intelligent to indulge in such illusions. "The statements and observations of a cultural and scientific nature—often confined to a few bare references—were like a runway for a flight toward the spiritual heights of his apostolic ministry."[66] In other words, the pope wanted to show that he understood as much as was necessary of his listeners' particular field in order to be able to give them the orientations of a religious and moral nature that they asked of him.

People also sometimes criticized the fact that all the speeches were published in the *Osservatore Romano*. Bea answered by saying that there might certainly be a case to be made here, but that we must remember on the one hand that those involved were keen to see the speeches published and circulated, and on the other that they would always be published in one way or another—with the risk of errors and omissions. In order to avoid this, it was thought preferable to publish them officially, accepting the risk that some people could find this excessive.[67]

(c) "The pope is the first to suffer from the 'excessive number' of his speeches," Bea again said. It is of course true that Pius XII had a certain inclination for speeches and homilies, as the following episode indicates. In 1929 Bea visited him in Berlin shortly before he left his position as nuncio to become secretary of state. Bea allowed himself to observe: "Your Excellency, they're saying in Rome that you're packing your bags." Pacelli's response was: "They've said so many times, and it was never true, but this time it is. I'd have liked a diocese, because my ideal is to preach, confirm, etc. But the Holy Father wants me to go back to Rome, and I have to obey."[68] However, this personal inclination did not mean that his speeches, especially their preparation, were not "a heavy burden" for him.[69] Some people might doubt this, on the basis of the widely held belief that the speeches of important people are in fact written by their assistants, while the speaker simply has to read them — after, in the best of views, maybe making the odd alteration. Not only does Bea rule out such a thing in the case of Pius XII, but he provides us with detailed information on how the pope prepared his speeches.

---

65. Cf. N 1957/168.
66. Tardini, pp. 58-59.
67. Cf. Nm 3 (1955), p. 3.
68. Memoirs in BM, p. 268. Nasalli Rocca, p. 66, quotes the pope as telling him: " . . . from the day I was made bishop, as nuncio, I immediately began to long for a diocese, especially a small one." Pius XII's housekeeper also said the same thing in her memoirs; cf. Lehnert, p. 42.
69. Cf. Nm 3 (1955), p. 3.

In connection with a major speech that Pius XII gave to the general congregation of the Society of Jesus in 1957,[70] a fellow Jesuit wrote to Bea saying that the speech had lost a great deal of its value because it had been prepared by the Father General. Bea replied that the pope was obviously free to ask anyone he chose to draft a speech for him.[71] However, it should be borne in mind that it was not his habit simply to take a draft of this type and read it. He himself gave it a thorough reworking, checking the references,[72] correcting what seemed less valid, and not being satisfied until he himself felt that all the points were clear. Whatever he said in a speech was therefore his own work and the expression of his authority as pope.[73]

Considering this method of preparing speeches, it is easy to understand why Tardini says that the speeches "were the joy of their hearers, the cross of their author," and goes on to say: "He used to remember that Pius XI had said to him: 'Speaking almost every day on so many subjects is a very heavy burden.' "[74] "His speeches [were] often the product of sleepless nights," says Nasalli Rocca.[75] Elsewhere Tardini recalls that the pope had confided to "those closest to him what a terrible amount of work his many speeches meant for him. However, in the last months of his life this remark took on the tones of a lament."[76]

Apart from the pope's conscientiousness, which we have already mentioned, the underlying reason for such meticulous preparation was his sharp awareness of the duties that his high office imposed on him. In his concern over the pope's health, Bea once tried to persuade him that he did not always need to receive pilgrims with a long speech, but that a few words of greeting and encouragement would be enough, to which Pius XII answered: "Yes, but it's still the pope speaking." Similarly Tardini says that Pius XII used to say that the pope always had to "speak as pope."[77]

3. A series of Bea's observations concern Pius XII in his *governing role*.

(a) One of his prime qualities in this field was linked to his conscientiousness and was his concern to make sure that he had the *fullest information possible*. "You must realize," writes Bea, "that the pope does not obtain his information from news-cuttings [as crowned heads did at that time], but has about half a dozen

70. Cf. *AAS*, IL (1957), 806-812.
71. In the family circle of the religious houses where the pope's various assistants lived, their names were known. Thus it was known that Father R. Leiber, S.J., had been Cardinal Pacelli's private secretary and now acted as secretary to Pius XII; Father W. Hentrich, S.J., took care of the pope's private library; Father H. Lennerz, S.J., provided opinions on questions of dogmatic theology; Father F. Hürth, S.J., on those of moral theology and canon law; and Father G. Gundlach, S.J., on those of the social sciences. We should probably add the names of certain members of the House of Writers of *La Civiltà Cattolica* and some members of the general curia, etc. Cf. the present author's "Il Cardinale Bea: sua preparazione," p. 333.
72. Leiber, p. 85, who speaks of the pope as checking citations, as does Tardini, pp. 61-62.
73. Cf. N 1957/279.
74. Tardini, p. 56.
75. Nasalli Rocca, p. 56.
76. Tardini, p. 64.
77. Cf. *ibid.*, p. 59.

newspapers of various leanings brought in from the news-stands each day."[78] Nasalli Rocca says that while he was head chamberlain, he himself usually brought these papers to the pope.[79] It is true that a "survey of the international press" was started in 1948 for the offices of the Roman curia. This internal service provided summaries of articles of any importance, but it must be noted that the pope was not satisfied with summaries. "It was not unusual," writes Tardini, "for the pope to tell me: 'That summary is very well done. I have read all the documents concerned and I can see that nothing has been left out.' "[80] This was made easier by the fact that according to Tardini he "read extraordinarily fast and with so much attention that he immediately grasped the most salient points."[81]

(b) He was equally conscientious in *weighing up* things and suggestions. "He makes a very careful examination," writes Bea, "of everything that is submitted to him. I know this from long experience gained as counselor to four Roman congregations. Many people would be amazed if they realized exactly how well informed the pope is and how prudently he reflects on things. One is often struck by the thought that the Spirit of God is at work here."[82]

In assessing suggestions and other things, his long experience meant that the pope tended to show a sober prudence, so that he could seem almost pessimistic. When discussing an instruction of the Pontifical Biblical Commission on the teaching of sacred scripture in seminaries, the pope asked Bea if he thought it would bear any fruit. Wanting to be prudent, Bea answered: "Maybe fifty percent, Holy Father." "Sometimes I have to be satisfied with twenty percent," observed the pope.

In the same context, Father Bea's correspondence contains some very interesting information on how Pius XII used to approach the nomination of bishops. In the first place, the Holy Father used to concern himself very personally in these matters.[83] "It is widely known that the Holy Father attaches much importance to the nomination of a bishop, even an auxiliary one . . . and that he insists on being kept personally informed on all aspects." In connection with the nomination of a particular auxiliary bishop, "he himself told me that someone had objected that the candidate chosen would be wasted in a position as auxiliary; now he [the pope] does not see it like this; we are dealing with the case of a bishop, and for this purpose the best is good enough."[84] On another occasion Bea wrote: "The Holy Father is concerned that even auxiliary bishops should be good theologians, so that they are not only capable of confirming, . . . but also of bringing their own influence to bear in the cathedral chapter in favor of sound doctrine and morality."[85]

(c) As concerned *his capacity to take decisions* independently of any outside influence, Eugenio Pacelli had various character traits that did not help him here.

---

78. Nm 3 (1955), p. 5.
79. Cf. Nasalli Rocca, p. 77.
80. Tardini, p. 135, note 25.
81. *Ibid.*, pp. 50-51.
82. Nm 3 (1955), p. 2.
83. Cf. N 1954/224.
84. N 1955/78.
85. Nr 10 (1955).

We have already seen Tardini's observation that a first source of difficulty was "his sharp intelligence with its grasp of detail" which meant that "he could see all the possible solutions quickly and clearly."[86] In addition, he was "by natural temperament mild and somewhat timid. He was not born with a fighter's disposition."[87] This was linked, as we shall see, with a sensitivity toward others. This combination of factors explains, in Bea's view, why there were so few consistories.[88] J. Höfer, whom we have already cited, describes an episode that he heard from Bea himself and that is very illuminating here. In a certain situation Bea felt it was his duty to suggest a certain line of action to the pope, although he realized that the latter would find it difficult to accept the idea. The result was that for two weeks the pope suffered from uncertainty and was unable to take any decision. Bea concluded: "On that occasion I understood the pope and his way of acting, and I have been careful never to try anything of the same kind again."[89]

Despite these difficulties innate in his character, the pope was extremely careful to take decisions *only according to his own conscience* and independently of outside influences. Tardini mentions a highly significant example in this connection, saying that after the death of the secretary of state Cardinal Maglione, the pope did not want to appoint a successor, and that "this decision was maybe due in part to the fact that his mildness of character meant that he could tend to be a little over-influenced by others."[90] This desire for independence, so that he could follow his own conscience alone, led the pope to take courageous and even audacious decisions, so that in some cases Pius XII, unlike his predecessors Benedict XV and Pius XI, even altered decisions unanimously adopted by the cardinals of some Roman congregations, as Tardini again notes.[91]

Pacelli had in fact worked on himself so well that he could be sure that nothing would interfere with his determination to follow the promptings of *his own conscience* alone.[92] When people objected that Pius XII was too dependent on his various advisors, both official and unofficial, Bea could therefore answer:

---

86. Tardini, p. 70. "He did not find it easy to take decisions," says Bea in BM, p. 268.

87. Tardini, p. 69.

88. Cf. BM, p. 268.

89. Höfer, "Das gesitliche Profil des Kardinals Bea," p. 57. H. H. Harms, "Anwalt der Einheit. Kurienkardinal Augustin Bea," *Sonntagsblatt* (Hanover), XIX/22 (29 May 1966), describes a conversation between the pope and Father Bea. The pope had said that he was like the father of the prodigal son, always ready to welcome back children who return to the Catholic Church. To which Bea apparently observed: "Holy Father, in the parable the father ran out to greet his son." I have never heard about this episode from other sources, and in the light of what we have just seen, I would doubt its authenticity.

90. Tardini, p. 79.

91. *Ibid.*, p. 154.

92. Tardini relates a revealing fact in this connection, saying that the pope was "a little nervous of receiving high church dignitaries and priests . . . in the fear of not being able to turn down the numerous and insistent requests of every kind that they would make" (p. 72; in the same context, see also pp. 71-72 for a detailed explanation of this fear). In this connection Sister Pascalina gives the opinion of a religious whom the pope quite often consulted: "It's best not to be friends with the Holy Father if you have ambitions" (Lehnert, p. 151).

"I had a great many dealings with the 'authoritarian' Pius XI, and I would much sooner have tried to make him change an opinion or plan than I would the Pius XII who was gentle in manner, but very firm in practice—and I think that I knew him."[93] Elsewhere he also observes: "It was much easier to obtain something from Pius XI than from Pius XII. The latter was always kind and polite, but the moment he realized that someone was trying to influence him he would become withdrawn."[94]

(d) The aforementioned gentleness of character went hand-in-hand with a *sensitive concern for others*. Tardini observes that the pope's difficulties over nominations, and in particular over the creation of cardinals, sprang "from the fear of placing other people in difficult positions, and also a little from the desire to satisfy other people's aspirations."[95]

Nasalli Rocca says that he once found the pope sitting in a corner of his office at Castel Gandolfo, while the furniture had been moved back, out of the way of puddles of water that had obviously come in during the night. When Nasalli Rocca expressed his surprise, Pius XII simply observed: "It was past midnight when it started. I didn't want to disturb anyone, so I tried to deal with it myself."[96]

On one occasion Bea was also the object of a gracious gesture of sensitive concern on the pope's part. In one of their usual Saturday evening conversations after the sisters had finished their confessions, talk turned, so far as I recall, to the question of a certain concordat. Now, when he was nuncio in Germany the pope had negotiated three concordats,[97] and according to Bea he was convinced of the value of this kind of relation between church and state. His confessor was less certain, and this fact came out in the present discussion. Bea felt that it was his duty to express his opinion frankly and give his reasons. The pope's sensitive nature meant that after lively discussions of this kind (as also if his duty had meant that he had had to disappoint or upset someone toward the end of the day), a sleepless night could follow,[98] as happened on the occasion in question. The next day the pope was worried that his confessor had been similarly afflicted, and he sent him two bottles of good wine in consolation. The confessor had, however, slept well.

(e) We shall add a word on the pope's *humility*. In connection with the publicity that had unfortunately, and to the distress of the pope himself, been given to the vision of Christ that he received during his serious sickness in December 1954 (and we shall speak of this in due course), people in certain lay

---

93. Nm 51 (1958). "If anyone tried to give him reasons against a decision he had taken, this could cause him a sleepless night," Bea recalls in BM, p. 268. Cf. also Cardinal G. Siri's interview in L. Brunelli and T. Ricci, "Papa Pacelli visto da vicino," *30 Giorni*, VI/3 (1988), 47-51: "Once the decision had been taken, he carried it out without much hesitation," despite the fact that he was "extremely timid" (p. 48).
94. Nm 3 (1955), p. 4.
95. Tardini, p. 74.
96. Nasalli Rocca, p. 58.
97. Cf. Leiber, p. 95.
98. Lehnert, p. 87, says that the pope suffered greatly from insomnia, and if something upset him or he received a piece of bad news this could cause a sleepless night.

intellectual circles in Europe criticized the pope for allowing such publicity and thus encouraging "a cult of his own personality." When a correspondent told Father Bea about this, the latter replied: "In the case of Pius XII (whom I think I know to some extent) there is no question of a personality cult (in private contacts he is the most modest of men) but rather of a 'father' who likes to give his children pleasure. If these 'children' exploit him financially, this does not even occur to him in his modesty."[99]

In this context, when referring in his letters to the celebrations for the pope's eightieth birthday, Bea repeatedly states: "The pope was against having any celebration at all, but he had to give in to insistent pressure from those around him. For him the celebration was nothing but an additional burden."[100]

In connection with the pope's humility, Bea more than once told me about the following authentic episode dating from the time of the German occupation of Rome. German military personnel were strictly forbidden to attend papal audiences, but since the police could not hope to keep all of them under surveillance, they used to concentrate the attention on officers. One day, two policeman patroling the colonnade of St. Peter's Square noticed some officers entering for an audience. In order to avoid a public scene, they did not intercept them, but waited for the guilty parties to emerge again. The Swiss Guards, however, had noticed all this and warned the appropriate people, so that the officers were allowed to leave by another entrance. After a long wait, the police realized that they had been tricked, and in their annoyance they themselves asked to be received in audience the next day. When they were in the presence of the pope, who was greeting the participants individually, they had the effrontery to ask him how may exits the Vatican had. The pope, who had been informed of the previous day's events, answered: "So many, my son, that we can get the better of even the shrewdest of people!"

(f) After the amazing, not to say miraculous, development of ecumenism under the inspiration of John XXIII and the Council, it may surprise some people if we speak of the *ecumenical attitudes of Pius XII*. However, Bea often stressed these. In a letter to a representative of the World Council of Churches, he said that Pius XII had genuine confidence in other Christians and was sympathetic toward efforts to foster the authentic unity of Christians.[101] In this connection he could also have recalled the instruction on the ecumenical movement that had been published under the papacy of Pius XII as early as 1949. After the pope's death Bea wrote that this loss represented a serious blow for ecumenism, and expressed the hope that his successor would have the same interest in ecumenism.[102] When he was already cardinal, Bea would speak about the same

---

99. Nm 2 (1955).
100. N 1956/40. Cf. Nc 21 (1956); Ni 39 (1956). Lehnert, p. 77, stresses that Pius XII was extremely simple in his everyday life, and that even during his sickness "he was not concerned for himself," but was "undemanding, modest" (p. 161).
101. Cf. N 1957/76. Leiber notes (p. 94) that the many audiences granted to international congresses struck the non-Catholics from every country and continent more even than the Catholics. For such visitors the experience represented a practical preparation for ecumenism.
102. Cf. N 1958/260, 242.

subject on the eve of the Council, saying: "For instance, in his encyclical on the church as the mystical body of Christ, Pius XII expressed such tender love for our separated brethren as may surprise us, coming from such a jurist. In addition, it is well known how often he expressed a desire for closer cooperation of all Christians in fields not directly concerned with faith, as for example in social and relief activities, in working for peace, and so on."[103]

If we bear in mind all the various elements that went to make up Bea's picture of Pius XII and his standing in the church and the world, it is easy for us to understand that in 1954 he should have expressed the opinion that in the present world situation a man like Pius XII was almost indispensable for the church and the world.[104] And also that one year later he should have written that it would be difficult to find a successor for Pius XII who could represent the authority of the papacy as credibly.[105] Thus also at the end of 1958 Bea felt that Pius XII's death constituted "an irreparable loss" for the church[106] and that the events and expressions of sentiment attending his funeral bore eloquent testimony to the importance of Pius XII for the church and for the whole of humankind.[107]

December 1954: The Sickness, and the Vision of the Lord Christ

Bea's view of Pius XII is seen particularly clearly in connection with the events of December 1954 and the vision of Christ that the pope had when he was so seriously sick. Bea spoke about it because of various criticisms leveled against the pope in this connection, and it is therefore inevitable that his statements should have a defensive air. Bea does say, however, that for him it was simply a question of "bearing witness to the truth."[108] We have therefore preferred to leave these events in their natural context and treat them here, rather than including them in our previous summary. Bea's words do not lose any of their value and still reveal his relative attitudes in various ways.

1. In order to understand Bea's statements, we must remember the *varied* and often divergent *reactions* that were seen in different quarters when news of the pope's vision leaked out. Some people, even in the *non*-Catholic press, saw it as an event of primary religious importance.[109] On the other hand, one of Bea's correspondents told him that the news of the vision had caused disgust and dismay among the faithful, especially in intellectual circles.[110] The publicity given to the fact gave the impression that the pope, or at least certain groups

---

103. *The Unity of Christians*, p. 182. Cf. also Nm 13 (1956), p. 3; Leiber, p. 86.
104. Cf. N 1954/226.
105. Cf. N 1955/143.
106. Cf. N 1958/260.
107. Cf. N 1958/259.
108. Nm 3 (1955). Compare also with the positive witness of Cardinal G. Siri in the interview with Brunelli and Ricci, "Papa Pacelli visto da vicino," p. 50.
109. The respected Hamburg newspaper *Die Welt* carried the news on its front page on 10 December 1955, attributing great importance to this "event in the sphere of the spirit"; cf. Nm 13 (1956).
110. Cf. N 1956/13, pp. 2-3.

around him, were hungry for visions and miracles, as if faith in his position and office were founded on such things.

This is why Bea now stepped in, and in a fairly full and energetic manner, despite the discretion he normally maintained in such circumstances. Major theological and pastoral issues were at stake; and above all the figure of the pope was at the center of the question, with certain criticisms unjustly making him appear in a somewhat sinister light.

2. Bea speaks of the subject in *three long documents*: two letters, one from December 1955 and the other from January 1956, and a long statement completely dedicated to questions connected with the vision.[111] Let us give some idea of the historical background to these documents. The second of the two letters deserves special mention because it led to unexpected developments. The noted Swiss ecumenist and theologian, Otto Karrer, who was an old friend of Bea, had told him about the criticisms that had been made of the fact that news of the vision had been made public, and also about the pastoral concern that he himself felt in this connection. Bea answered with a letter of five tightly packed pages, trying to clarify the question point by point, and was very surprised a little later when the main points of this letter appeared in the form of an article in the Swiss Jesuit review *Orientierung*, for Karrer had published them as "information received from a Roman theologian close to the pope."[112] Bea wrote to Karrer, thanking him for the copy of the issue in question, and adding: "I really should be angry with you for not asking my permission, for in something planned for publication I would not have written with the frank language we Alemanns[113] usually use." He thanked him, even so, for having covered the relative reflections with his own signature.[114] We should immediately point out that our main interest is in Bea's thinking, so that we shall refer not to the text of the article, but to that of the original letter.

The third document was completely dedicated to questions connected with the vision, and we shall for now simply say that its aim was that of providing material for an interview, in which Bea was not, however, to figure at all. This must suffice as introduction to the document; the time is not in fact ripe to give information on the further developments in this connection, particularly since they make no difference to the content of the document, for Bea never changed or corrected the text.

Bea approaches the subject by stressing at the outset that a Catholic's very conception of faith means that he or she is used to dealing with similar events by submitting them to a *critical examination*. Such an examination naturally presumes accurate knowledge of all the facts and circumstances, and no genuinely objective examination is possible if this is lacking.[115] Even in this case, however, there is still the general principle that when such mystical phenomena

---

111. Cf. Nm 3 (1955); N 1956/13; Nm 13 (1956).
112. Cf. *Orientierung*, XX/2 (1956), 13-15.
113. Cf. p. 25 above.
114. Cf. N 1956/25.
115. Cf. Nm 13 (1956), p. 1.

appear in someone with a deeply religious and sober cast of spirit who is capable of evaluating them, we must approach the interior life of such a man with deep respect.[116] This respect will obviously be all the greater if the man in question is the vicar of Christ.[117]

3. Here we should note that Bea does not mention the source from which he received news of the vision. Before entering into Bea's critical examination of the phenomenon, we shall therefore quote the account of the vision given by an exceptional witness, Cardinal Domenico Tardini, so that this can provide the background to Bea's reflections.

The first element of the *pope's situation* was his sickness: "He was suffering indescribably. Those hiccups! He was simply one single, unbroken, tearing spasm—a convulsive shudder that constantly racked his throat, his chest, his whole body. He could neither drink nor eat nor sleep.

"Despite all this, in the midst of these spasms, his mind was, as always, enlightened and enlightening. His serenity was imperturbable, and his piety edifying.

"He kept the book of the exercises of St. Ignatius permanently on his bed, very often in his hands, and he took delight—and also gave his visitors delight—in repeating, with much devotion, the beautiful prayer: 'Anima Christi, sanctifica me.' "[118]

Then there is the *vision itself*, which Tardini describes as follows: "He [the pope] said to me: 'I'm telling you: other people might think that they're a sick man's hallucinations. Yesterday morning I clearly heard a voice (*clearly*, I say!),' and the pope touched his right ear, 'that said: "Now a vision is coming." But nothing in fact came. This morning, while I was at holy mass, I saw the Lord for a moment. It was just a moment, but I saw him clearly.' "[119] The pope spoke about this again two days later, and Tardini describes this too: "He spread his arms as he does when he gives his blessing, looked up to heaven, and said: 'Voca me!' Then he added: 'I thought the Lord was calling me back, but here I still am!' . . . He took up the little book of the exercises of St. Ignatius again, and said: 'Here is my comfort.' "[120]

4. Now we can move on to Bea's explanations. As concerns the actual fact of the vision, he states: "It is certain that the Holy Father had the vision and that he is convinced that it was *not* an illusion."[121] However, it was not simply a case of some subjective certainty on the pope's part. Bea is convinced that in this case we have all the human guarantees we can ask for in order to accept the authenticity

---

116. Cf. N 1956/13, p. 4.

117. Cf. *ibid.*; Nm 3 (1955), p. 2.

118. Tardini, pp. 93-94.

119. *Ibid.*, pp. 95-96.

120. *Ibid.*, p. 96. Sister Pascalina's account is very low-key. The only time that Pius XII made any reference in this connection was when he said (in Italian!): "Our Lord has been in the place where you are now" (Lehnert, p. 159). The sister adds: "The pope said nothing else to me about these events."

121. Nm 3 (1955), p. 1; cf. also the above-cited account of Tardini, where the pope explicitly rules out any possibility of "a sick man's hallucinations."

of the event: the person who had the vision is the most qualified of men in terms of knowledge (including psychological learning), experience, and the very great conscientiousness that everybody admits he has—not to mention the position he holds. If such a man says that Christ has appeared to him, we have all the human guarantees possible as to the truth of the fact. Naturally, the pope's evaluation of his mystical experience is merely a human judgment, for the charism of infallibility does not come into it. Therefore, the belief we place in his claims in this regard is not the same as the act of faith with which we accept the gospel and the doctrine of the church, but is a purely human trust, of the sort placed in a man capable of knowing the truth and sincere in bearing witness to it.[122] The vision therefore has no connection with dogma and the doctrine of the faith.[123]

The vision was accompanied by another factor that Bea considered to be of fundamental importance: in other words, the fact that the pope *came through the very dangerous crisis* that could have cost him his life. Bea repeatedly says that he is convinced that this process was not due to natural forces,[124] and on other occasions he speaks explicitly of a "miracle."[125] A more careful examination of the relative texts, however, allows us to specify that Bea did *not* mean that it was a miracle in the sense of a *complete cure*, but simply a recovery from a very critical condition when this was least to be expected in human terms. In one of his letters about the event, Bea explicitly says that he is referring to the unexpected recovery from the crisis.[126]

The decisive text is as follows: "I was able to observe the pope very closely both prior to his sickness and during it, and I think that I am in a better position than most to permit myself a judgment. Well, I am personally convinced that his recovery was a miracle, whatever the doctors say. And anyone who sees him today [in 1956] and saw him two or three years ago, can only confirm that this miracle is still continuing."[127]

Bea also offers us an explanation of the *spiritual fruit* of the vision for the pope, if we examine it in context: "The pope's health had been very poor for some time, so that he could fulfill his heavy commitments only by stretching his energies to their limits. With the addition of the serious sickness that brought him to the threshold of the grave, it is understandable that he should have prayed: 'O Lord, ask me to come to you.' "[128]

---

122. Cf. Nm 13 (1956), p. 2.
123. Cf. N 1956/13; Nm 3 (1955), p. 1; Nm 13 (1956), p. 4.
124. Cf. N 1955/188; 1956/19; Ni 38 (1955).
125. Cf. N 1956/54, 59, 115; Nb 369 (1955); Nc 11 (1954). This is all the more significant in that elsewhere Bea appears somewhat diffident about claims as to "miracles" performed by the pope; cf. Nm 3 (1955). Cf. also in this connection Nc 11 (1954), where Bea refers to the pope's recovery after his sickness of January 1954, saying: "We could almost speak of a miracle."
126. Cf. N 1956/19.
127. N 1956/13, p. 3. Sister Pascalina agrees fully: "The fact is that Pius XII's state of health is now making enormous progress" (Lehnert, p. 160).
128. Nm 13 (1956), p. 5; judging from the expressions used by the pope two days after the vision, it would seem probable that he was referring here to the previous verse of the prayer "Anima Christi": "In the hour of death, call me."

There is still the question of *why such publicity* was given to the matter if it was something that concerned the pope personally. Bea answers that strictly speaking no one gave it any publicity, but rather that someone who knew about it was led into an indiscretion by some journalists,[129] and that the media then took up the story. The pope was very distressed by the leak. The next question is that of why the pope did not deny the story, if the leak had taken place against his wishes. Because, replies Bea, he would have been acting against his conscience: if he was convinced that he had had the vision, he could not say that the story was untrue, and he could not even remain silent, because that would be interpreted as a denial.[130] Moreover, denying or concealing it would have been like ingratitude toward God.[131] Simply and without ceremony, he therefore publicly recognized what he saw as a gift of God.[132] In other words, we must see his confirmation of the truth of the news as a consequence of "the nobility of character and the deep religious spirit of Pius XII."[133]

5. Lastly, Bea refers to the various reactions that the news of the vision gave rise to among the faithful, setting forth some reflections on *the pastoral aspects* of the matter. With reference to the dismay that one correspondent said the news had caused among intellectuals, Bea answers that he has also received the exact opposite reaction from members of the faithful, for whom the news has meant joy and encouragement. He adds that Catholics know that their faith is not based on the pope's vision, but that even so they are neither ashamed of supernatural events nor surprised at them, knowing how such phenomena have flourished throughout the history of the church; on the other hand, certain intellectuals today do not know how to deal with them, and thus try to explain them with the help of psychology or parapsychology. The church knows that they are part of its life, like the miracles and prophecies promised by Christ himself.[134] It should also be borne in mind that such events can revive the joy in believing. In the present case, Christian people have probably instinctively seen the vision as God's confirmation of the pope's activity in favor of the church and the whole world. Here Bea recalls St. Paul's teaching that such free gifts are given to individuals for the utility and edification of the church (cf. 1 Cor. 12:7; 14:12).[135] Naturally, even before the vision became publicly known, it had already been given to the pope for the good of the church. However, when it became public there was the additional benefit of encouragement and comfort for the faithful,

---

129. Cf. Nm 3 (1955), pp. 1-2; N 1956/13, p. 2.

130. Cf. N 1956/13, p. 2.

131. Cf. Nm 13 (1956), p. 4.

132. N 1956/13, p. 2.

133. Cf. Nm 13 (1955), p. 4. In the same context Bea denies any connection between the leak and suggestions that the vision was made public in order to lay the groundwork for the pope's future beatification. In fact, anyone familiar with canon law knows that for beatification only miracles that took place after the death of the relative servant of God are counted; cf. Nm 13 (1956), p. 4.

134. Cf. N 1956/13, pp. 2-3.

135. Cf. Nm 13 (1956), pp. 3, 6.

because God had intervened so strikingly to help the pope, and thus the church.[136]

Did Pius XII Die "in the Odor of Sanctity"?

We shall now briefly consider Bea's opinion on this question, mainly for the sake of historical completeness, in view of the fact that he speaks of it fairly often. Here he acts (especially *during the pope's life*) as a witness recounting the relative facts, although it is sometimes clear that he is in agreement as to their interpretation. We would state at the outset that he was far from credulous in this matter. In 1955 he writes that people are saying that the pope has healed a boy who was born blind, but that this is pure invention, and nobody in the Vatican knows anything about it. He adds that there have been cases where someone has obtained a grace after receiving the pope's blessing, and people have immediately said it was a miracle. They may be right, he adds, but it is impossible to prove, and it would be better not to talk about it at all.[137] Despite this prudence, Bea himself writes in the same year: "Many people put great store in the pope's blessing and prayers."[138] He even describes the specific case of the foundress of a major contemporary lay movement, who was in a very serious condition after a traffic accident. People asked for the Holy Father's blessing for her. Since the Holy See had not yet given its opinion on the movement in question, Pius XII answered: "Of course, but it must be clearly understood that the blessing is not to be taken as approval of the movement." And he gave his blessing. The woman "started recovering almost at once, and is now convalescing."[139] When someone told the pope about this, he simply answered: "If the saints have done such things, why should the vicar of Christ not do them too?"

After the pope's death, however, statements of this kind become more frequent and more explicit in Bea's letters. A bishop wrote to him saying that he was more inclined to pray *to* the pope than *for* him, and Bea answers that the same thing happens to him too.[140]

We can see that these are not simply emotional statements if we look at the portrait of Pius XII that Bea gave a year later, when he was already a cardinal: "Pius XII was not a martyr in the usual sense of the term. Even so, he was a martyr:

---

136. At that time there was also talk of Pius XII's apparently having seen the sun spinning, in other words the phenomenon with which the last great appearance of the blessed Virgin at Fatima ended on 13 October 1917. A certain cardinal was responsible for publicly making this particular leak. With reference to this vision, Bea notes briefly that the fact that the account is incorrect on truly essential points goes to show that the pope was not responsible for the publicity in this case either. Pius XII chose not to correct the account in order not to add fuel to the fire. Cf. Nm 3 (1955), p. 4; Nasalli Rocca, p. 60.

137. Cf. Nm 3 (1955), pp. 4-5.

138. Ni 38 (1955).

139. N 1957/317.

140. Cf. N 1958/254. Cf. also N1 63, where Bea writes, three weeks after the pope's death, that he has today said holy mass for the pope, but that he does not think he has any need of this.

a martyr to his duty, to his love for the church, to his love for souls. The instruments of his martyrdom were his daily sacrifices. He moved among the splendors of the Vatican, with its great halls and its art treasures, without paying them any attention, poor in spirit—as is expressed in his last will and testament, which is of admirable grandeur—walking along the hard path of duty, work and suffering until the time came when he was no longer able to raise his trembling hand to bless."[141]

This explains why Father Bea repeatedly encourages people to turn to the dead pontiff for help. He tells a relative with health problems to make a novena to Pius XII who, he says, has already answered many prayers and worked miracles.[142] Similarly he writes to another relative, enclosing "a relic" (a picture with a scrap of cloth from the pope's robe) and adding: "Tell him you are a relative of the one who was his confessor." He also says: "Recently Pope John XXIII has publicly said that he is certain that Pius XII will be canonized, although not immediately."[143] Only a short while after the pope's death he writes: "Trustworthy people say that Pius XII's help is being invoked and that people are receiving graces. Prayers are being made for him to be raised to the honor of the altars." Bea concludes with the hope: "May the Lord grant that these prayers be soon answered."[144]

He becomes even more active when he can assume that people are already favorably disposed, so that he writes to a German bishop as follows: "At this moment there is a large-scale movement afoot to obtain the Holy Father's permission for the introduction of the cause for beatification. The three German cardinals have also taken a hand in this matter. . . . For my part, I have suggested that consideration should be given to the possibility that all the German bishops as a group should make a move in this direction. . . . Holy pictures have already been distributed throughout the world—over three million. . . . There is probably no further need for proof of the fact that Pius XII died in the odor of sanctity. The cases of answered prayers—which are now being counted in their thousands and are coming in from every part of the world—speak clearly in support of this view. I have heard from reliable sources that there have been several miracles of the first order. . . . There is therefore more than enough material for the introduction of the cause for beatification."[145] In another letter the writer therefore asks someone to suggest a petition for beatification from Cardinal A. Stepinac, Archbishop of Zagreb, and also from the Society of Jesus.[146]

---

141. R 1959/60, 8, p. 5.
142. Cf. Nb 161 (1959).
143. Nb 247 (1959).
144. N 1958/325. We would note in passing that R. Leiber disagreed on this point (cf. N 1959/131); he does not mention it in his article, but he repeatedly expressed this view to various people, and maybe even in some interviews; it would not appear necessary to investigate the reasons for this attitude. Nasalli Rocca, on the other hand, tends to share Bea's opinion (cf. p. 80). Tardini does not mention it, although there is one quite significant fact that gives an indication of his opinion: on his own initiative, he composed a prayer for the beatification of Pius XII; cf. the account of Sister Pascalina Lehnert in *Pius XII. In Memoriam* (Rome, 1984), p. 415.
145. N 1959/79.
146. Cf. N 1959/79a.

* * *

In conclusion to this chapter we would consider the question of *the spirit* in which Bea fulfilled his office in the service of the pope. In the course of the chapter we have repeatedly seen that when Bea spoke of the deep respect owed to the pope, he appealed to the fact that he is "Christ's vicar on earth."[147] This comes out particularly clearly in Bea's correspondence about the speech that Pius XII gave to the members of the general congregation of the Society of Jesus in 1957. As we saw, certain Jesuits told Bea of their reservations and criticisms. Bea's answer is all the firmer inasmuch as, according to the constitutions of the order and in virtue of a special vow made by those members who solemnly profess the "four vows," the pope is in a very special and strict sense the highest superior of the order.[148] Bea therefore says that the speech is "the expression of the will of the pope, to whom we have promised obedience with our vows."[149] Consequently the general congregation cannot do other than obey what the pope has asked.[150] Neither Father General nor the general congregation itself, he says, accepts the distinction that some people are seeking to make here between the pope's wishes and orders.[151]

It is clear that such statements are an expression not simply of a theoretical principle but also of the deeply held attitude of Bea himself. Even so, it is particularly interesting, as an exception to our general rule, to examine this attitude of his in the light of that genuine source in which Bea reveals his inner self before the Lord alone, in other words the notes from his spiritual retreats.[152]

Since Bea tends to mention actual facts of any sort fairly seldom, he rarely mentions the pope and his service to him. However, the few cases in which he does so are very explicit and revealing. In his 1954 retreat he speaks of the various appearances of the Risen One and of the sending out of the apostles to the whole world, observing: "The little church of the upper room gave birth to the present world-wide church." Then he refers to the pope's general audiences, adding: "All peoples and races come to Peter's successor, the Roman Pontiff."[153]

In 1946, while meditating on the Savior's walking on the lake by night, he makes this reflection: "The Savior is close with his help; he is particularly close to the successor of St. Peter; he takes him by the hand and leads him safely through the billows; this has been clearly shown in recent days." Bea finds this thought a source of confidence for the church and for himself with this reflection: "I am close to the successor of Peter and I am the object of the Savior's prayer and concern."[154]

---

147. Cf. Nm 3 (1955), p. 2; 13 (1956), p. 6; N 1956/13, p. 4; N 1957/16, 168.
148. Cf. N 1957/249. On the Jesuits, see *EncCatt*, IV, 82.
149. N 1957/279.
150. Cf. N 1957/249.
151. Cf. Nr 15 (1958).
152. I say "as an exception to our general rule," since from the beginning we have systematically chosen not to include the vast material represented by the notes from his spiritual retreats among the main sources for our study. However, this obviously does not rule out brief references to this material on certain occasions.
153. 1954/VIII/3.
154. 1946/VI/2.

The most explicit—and in a certain sense the most original—evidence is found in a meditation from the 1955 retreat. The object of the meditation is the appearance of the Risen One to the apostles and the threefold question addressed to Peter: "Simon, son of John, do you love me more than these?" (John 21:15). Bea writes: "At the Sea of Tiberias the Lord shows me the foundation, the underlying attitude for all my work in the immediate service of Christ's vicar on earth: in my case too it must be love—love for him, the first Shepherd, and love for the souls for whom I labor. And the closer my task is to that of Christ's vicar, the more this question applies to me: 'Do you love me *more than these*?' This is the spirit in which I must perform all I do for the doctrine and life of the church. . . . All my activity must therefore be based on this supernatural view and draw its inspiration from it."[155]

Bea also draws the relevant consequences of this deep conception of faith. In the last-mentioned retreat, he adopts the principle "Love means obedience."[156] In the context in question, Bea applies it to love for God, but another meditation from the same retreat shows that Bea also sees one of the consequences of love for the "first Shepherd" as being the requirement of obedience to his vicar on earth, the pope. Thus, speaking of the specific obedience of religious, he writes: "My obedience is not referred so much to a single superior: in my present position, strictly speaking, in everything I must be constantly alert to the slightest indication and must always show myself to be happy and willing in this."[157]

If Bea bases himself on love for the first Shepherd as regards his service to the vicar of Christ, we are justified in taking a reflection that Bea makes concerning his way of serving Christ and applying it to this service: "I must remember that I have to perform everything I do as the friend of the Lord. Indeed, the Lord told his apostles: 'No longer do I call you servants, . . . but friends' (John 15:15). I must therefore wholeheartedly embrace the Lord's interests; I am not some clerk who is satisfied to put in his daily hours, but a friend who looks after his friend's interests and wants to please him. If I see my apostolate in this way, it will be a source of joy for me and will also be fruitful."[158]

In the final analysis, this attitude of "taking to heart" the Savior's interests, and thus also those of his vicar on earth, provides the explanation of Bea's behavior toward Pius XII in all its breadth. It was why he was not only always attentive to the slightest nod—which could basically also apply in the case of a clerk—but also went further, undertaking the task of defending the pope against misunderstandings and criticisms. This heartfelt commitment was also the source of Bea's concern over the pope's overwork, health, and so on. Although they were not in fact said with explicit reference to the pope's service, it also

155. 1955/VIII/3.
156. Cf. 1955/VIII/4.
157. 1955/IV/3.
158. 1955/V/2.

explains Bea's words: "The most beautiful thing would be if I could die working for the Lord."[159] And these: "My remaining years must be like a candle that is consumed as it burns on the altar."[160]

159. 1949/II/4.
160. 1949/III/2.

CHAPTER 3

THE THEOLOGIAN

In January 1957 the work of the "resurrected" Roman Pontifical Theological Academy had its solemn inauguration. The academy had been founded in 1718 by Clement XI, and after a long period of abeyance it had been decided to give it a new lease on life.[1] Bea was asked to give the opening address, and he began with these words: "I should have preferred—and I tried, as was my duty—to refuse the honor of speaking in the name of the Most Reverend Academicians at this solemn moment, since there are many illustrious members among you who are called theologians much more justly than I, who have cultivated only one corner of the great theological field as my own special area. However, I was almost forced by higher authority, and therefore resigned myself and set to work." This said, the speaker then explained his aim, saying that he would not confine himself to his own corner of the great theological field, "but, drawing on the experiences of a fairly long life involving the variety of activities to which Divine Providence has been pleased to call me, I thought I would take a general look at the task contemporary theologians are called on to perform in the specific circumstances of our times."[2]

A little earlier, Bea had been admitted to membership of the academy. In other words, other people saw him as a "theologian" in the broad sense of the word, in which study of sacred scripture is also a supremely theological task. He himself considered himself a theologian, too, so that he did not hesitate to suggest a vast and demanding plan of work to the illustrious academy—as we shall see in the course of the present chapter. We shall hence be speaking of Bea as theologian in this broad sense.

Our introduction does not, however, mean that our main purpose is that of setting forth the plan of work proposed by Bea in that inaugural speech. We shall of course be drawing on it, but our purpose is the much broader one of describing if possible the full, real-life figure of Bea as theologian in all its aspects, on the basis of our various sources, and particularly his publications.

It is not difficult to see that this chapter will bring us to the more specific preparation that Bea received for his future mission, for it will describe the theological grounding that allowed him to exercise such a deep influence at the Council. It is, moreover, clear that his work as first President of the Secretariat for Christian Unity also rested to a large extent on this basis.[3]

---

1. Cf. *OssRom* (23 January 1957), pp. 1-2. On the academy, see also *EncCatt*, I, 167.
2. Biblio. 114, p. 31.
3. For this chapter, apart from our usual source (Bea's correspondence), we also have a major new source in the numerous publications, which we shall now discuss.

A Reference Point: The Word of God, Preserved and Interpreted by the Church

Our starting point is *the question of biblical hermeneutics*, in other words the method of interpreting sacred scripture. Bea had been concerned with this matter for several decades, from the time of the first edition of his study *De Scripturae Sacrae inspiratione. Quaestiones historicae et dogmaticae*.[4] Even in the period with which we are now concerned, however, he published a number of studies on the question, first and foremost the various articles describing the history of Catholic biblical science,[5] then the study of Catholic biblical hermeneutics in the light of the bull *Ineffabilis Deus* with which Pius IX defined the immaculate conception as a dogma of the Catholic faith,[6] and lastly the article on advances in the interpretation of sacred scripture.[7]

Then in his correspondence we find repeated reference to the idea that we cannot expect to prove everything from scripture alone, while leaving tradition aside.[8] He refers to this point particularly when speaking of mariology, saying that it is impossible to do mariology with exegesis of the bare words of sacred scripture alone.[9] In his article on the Blessed Virgin in the protogospel he takes the specific example of interpretation of Genesis 3:15 and shows the difference in results according to whether the aforementioned correct method is applied or not.[10] In 1953 he examined the situation of biblical science at the time, observing that in Protestant exegesis the positive sciences prevailed and there was an absence of the "Catholic principles" of exegesis, which then has serious consequences in the field of mariology.[11] We must now consider precisely what these principles are.

(a) In order to understand these principles we must refer back to Catholic doctrine on the divine inspiration of sacred scripture. Referring to the relative doctrine found in the encyclicals *Providentissimus Deus* of Leo XIII and *Divino afflante Spiritu* of Pius XII, the Council states in this connection: "To compose the sacred books, God chose certain men who, all the while he employed them in this task, made full use of their powers and faculties so that, though he acted in them and by them, it was as true authors that they consigned to writing whatever he wanted written, and no more."[12]

On the same basis the Council immediately draws the conclusion: "Since, therefore, all that the inspired authors, or sacred writers, affirm should be

---

4. Or "Historical and Dogmatic Questions on the Inspiration of Sacred Scripture." The first edition was in 1930; cf. Biblio. 2.
5. Cf. Biblio. 109, 90, 124, 126.
6. Cf. Biblio. 104.
7. Cf. Biblio. 89.
8. Cf. N 1955/24; 1954/117.
9. Cf. N 1953/64.
10. Cf. Biblio. 93. In Nw 18 (1953), Bea explicitly stresses that this was his intention in composing the article in question.
11. Cf. N 1953/162.
12. *DV*, 11.

regarded as affirmed by the Holy Spirit, we must acknowledge that the books of scripture, firmly, faithfully and without error, teach that truth which God, for the sake of our salvation, wished to see confided to the sacred scriptures."[13]

We are therefore dealing with a work that is both human word or work *and* word of God, and the rules for interpreting sacred scripture flow from this fact. Insofar as it is the word of a human author who was writing in a specific period and had his own individual character, etc., in order to understand it the interpreter must "go back wholly in spirit to those remote centuries of the East and, with the aid of history, archeology, ethnology and other sciences, accurately determine" the meaning of the ancient writer.[14] However, we must also bear in mind that it is divine work and word; and here one of the principles of *Catholic ecclesiology* comes into play, in other words that commentators must bear in mind that it is "a divinely inspired text, the care and interpretation of which have been confided to the church by God himself."[15] It follows that we must take into account all the various forms in which the aforesaid interpretation that the church gives to the written word of God is manifested. Hence the same encyclical goes on to say that we must take into account "explanations and declarations of the teaching authority of the church, as likewise the interpretations given by the holy fathers, and even 'the analogy of faith.' "[16]

(b) This norm, observes Bea, is "fundamental for the whole of Catholic biblical science and distinguishes it clearly from the Protestant approach to the interpretation of sacred scripture."[17] It is no surprise that this norm is not always respected and followed. Thus the encyclical *Humani generis* found it necessary to reprove those who "in their interpretation of scripture . . . will not take into account the harmony of revealed truths with one another, nor pay any attention to the tradition of the church. They will make of holy scripture, as scholars interpret it each after his own human fashion, a balance by which they can assay the teaching of the fathers and of the church, when they ought to be interpreting holy scripture according to the mind of the church, since the church, by our Lord Christ's own appointment, is authorized to guard and to interpret the whole deposit of divine revelation."[18]

Bea considers these words of the encyclical in greater depth, explaining that the attitude described "has been censured and condemned by the church from earliest times. St. Leo the Great (541) was already insisting that it is not licit to think of the divine scriptures otherwise than as the blessed apostles and our fathers learned and taught."[19] Moreover, the Council of Trent formally stated: "[Let] no one, relying on his own prudence, twist holy scripture . . . according

13. *Ibid.*
14. Cf. *Divino afflante Spiritu*, English translation, p. 20. Cf. Bea's commentary on the encyclical (Biblio. 53), p. 217.
15. *Divino afflante Spiritu*, English translation, p. 16.
16. *Ibid.*. See also *DV*, 12.
17. Commentary on *Humani generis* (Biblio. 80), pp. 420-421.
18. Pius XII, *Humani generis*, translation by Mgr. Ronald A. Knox (London, 1959), p. 13; cf. Biblio. 80, p. 420.
19. Biblio. 80, p. 420.

to his own mind, contrary to the meaning that holy mother church has held and holds—since it belongs to her to judge the true meaning and interpretation of holy scripture—and [let] no one dare to interpret the scripture in a way contrary to the unanimous consensus of the fathers."[20]

As can be seen, apart from the general rules that apply to interpretation of all human documents, particularly historical ones, Catholic hermeneutics also entails specifically *theological elements and criteria*, inasmuch as sacred scripture is the word of God, the preservation and interpretation of which God himself has entrusted to the church. And these theological elements are common to all the theological sciences. Citing the encyclical *Humani generis*, Bea then recalls that "a theologian must constantly be having recourse to the fountains of divine revelation. It is for him to show how and where the teaching given by the living voice of the church is contained in scripture and in our sacred tradition, 'be it explicitly, or implicitly.' "[21] And he confirms this with the significant observation from the same encyclical: " . . . the study of these hallowed sources gives the sacred sciences a kind of perpetual youth; avoid the labor of probing deeper and deeper yet into the sacred deposit, and your speculations—experience shows it—grow barren."[22]

Bea goes on to observe that the way of doing exegesis that is censured by *Humani generis* wanted to be independent of any outside constraint, and claimed to be free and exclusively scientific.[23] Bea answers this by saying that Catholic exegesis cannot be "independent" in this sense: "It is and must be a theological discipline that receives its laws and norms, as all theology does, from the teaching authority of the church. It would be an error in principle and also supremely damaging to try to follow the example of the Protestants on this point, for one would thus be denying the Catholic principle of tradition, which distinguishes Catholics from non-Catholics, and always will."[24] He then adds: "Nor should it be feared that a sincerely and genuinely Catholic exegesis is not 'scientific.' . . . Theology itself, to which all Catholic exegesis belongs, is a true science that starts from objective and absolutely certain principles, deals with a body of data of the same kind, adopts a method in keeping with these data, and sets forth the results of its investigation in a system devised for the purpose."[25]

(c) In his study of Protestant reactions to the definition of the dogma of the bodily assumption of the Blessed Virgin Mary into heaven, Bea considers the above-mentioned ecclesiological principle in greater depth. In the light of the bull of definition, *Munificentissimus Deus*, he states that the teaching authority of the church not only guards and preserves the deposit of faith, but *develops it with an ever deeper understanding*: "The Catholic Church recognizes a legitimate *pro-*

20. *Ibid.* The English translation of the decree of the Council of Trent on sacred books is taken from J. Neuner and J. Dupuis (eds.), *The Christian Faith* (Bangalore, 1978), p. 71.
21. Inaugural speech (Biblio. 114), p. 40; for the text of *Humani generis*, see English translation, pp. 11-12.
22. *Ibid.*; English translation, p. 12.
23. Cf. *ibid.*, English translation, p. 9.
24. Biblio. 80, pp. 421-422.
25. *Ibid.*, p. 422.

gress in dogma, and knows that revealed truths are 'preserved for ever pure and whole' and are 'handed on without contamination, without addition and without reduction' by the living magisterium of the church, not through purely human agency, but with the assistance of the Spirit of truth. The universal church cannot therefore err when considering a religious truth as revealed by God, and this applies no less in the twentieth century than it did in the second or the twelfth."[26] This principle operates in the definition of the assumption in the following way: "In the twentieth century the Catholic bishops almost unanimously declared that they and the flock entrusted to them hold 'that the bodily assumption of the Most Blessed Virgin can be proposed and defined as a dogma of faith.' When the supreme pontiff solemnly defined the dogma of the bodily assumption of the Blessed Virgin Mary, he was therefore simply confirming the faith of the universal church with his supreme infallible judgment. Thus it is not true that he was breaking away from the obedience of the apostles of Jesus Christ, as has been said, but by proclaiming the dogma he was faithful to the order that Christ gave to St. Peter and his successors: 'Feed my sheep' (John 21:17)."[27]

The precise and full meaning of the term "tradition" can be clearly seen from the foregoing: it does not mean simply "tradition" or "traditions" as historical fact, but "the Tradition" as *ecclesial fact*, in other words as evidence of the proclamation and interpretation of the deposit of faith on the part of the successors of the apostles, who are the authentic masters to whom Christ entrusted this task and to whom he grants a special kind of assistance of the Holy Spirit so that they can perform it. Bea studies the concept of "Tradition" in the bull *Ineffabilis Deus*, and reaches the conclusion that "Tradition" in the dogmatic sense of the word is not simply what can be historically ascertained from past ages: "Tradition is also found in the living magisterium of the present church, resting on correct foundations."[28] And just as the Holy Spirit guided the church in apostolic times and then in successive ages, so it guides it in present times and guarantees its fidelity to the deposit received from the apostles and handed on from generation to generation until today.[29]

Active Fidelity to the Church and Its Magisterium

The principles explained so far were not simply academic convictions so far as Bea was concerned. He drew all the relative consequences and committed himself to working with the church and its teaching authority.

---

26. Biblio. 99, p. 90; the words in quotes are taken from the bull *Munificentissimus Deus*.

27. *Ibid.* Bea's reference to the function of the *sensus fidei* of the people should be noted ("they and the flock"). The function of the *sensus fidei* in the definition is also stressed in N 1958/223. We shall speak further in due course about progress "with an ever deeper understanding" of revelation.

28. Cf. Biblio. 104, p. 17; we have given a translation of the original Latin, which is, if the truth be told, a little obscure: ". . . sed eam [Traditionem] inveniri etiam in Magisterio vivo Ecclesiae praesentis *debitis fundamentis innixo*" (emphasis ours).

29. Cf. N 1956/56.

This can be seen throughout his correspondence. He stresses that the first duty of the church is that of protecting the purity of the proclamation of the faith. The statement that the word of Christ should "strengthen your brethren" (Luke 22:32) still applies today.[30] If this is the duty of the church in general, it follows that the supreme magisterium, as the highest authority, has the right and the duty to safeguard this same purity.[31] In the face of certain tendencies found in a more unenlightened kind of ecumenism, he states (just as he will do when he becomes president of the secretariat) that we must clearly show people that the Catholic Church will not allow itself to be reformed "as concerns the essential points of dogma."[32] He gives the following rule to a teacher worried over certain new trends in exegesis and theology: "Hold to the old, firm doctrine and also take account of new results that rest on solid arguments."[33] In virtue both of this great personal fidelity and of his love for his own order, he undertakes to ensure that the same fidelity is also practiced within the latter, a resolution that is all the stronger in view of the fact that the constitutions of the order are particularly exacting on this point, for reasons of pastoral effectiveness.[34]

Bea becomes even firmer and more energetic when dealing with *distortions that have wide repercussions* for the purity of the faith. In such cases he does not hesitate to use fairly strong language. The encyclical *Pascendi* on modernism, he says, saved the church "from a danger that involved the foundations of the Catholic faith." St. Pius X cut "the infected members" out from the body of the church when they tried to impose their views under the pretext of doing good; it may have been painful, but "no surgery is easy."[35] At the beginning of the inaugural address to the Roman Pontifical Theological Academy, Bea gives an overview of the doctrinal situation, starting with the elements that represent threats; thus he lists philosophical systems such as existentialism, evolutionism and immanentism.[36] It should, however, be observed that there is no question here of unmotivated statements, imaginary dangers or some kind of witch-hunt. For example, as regards biblical modernism, Bea offers a very thorough analysis on the basis of the writings of Loisy as well as those of other authors of that time.[37]

Fidelity to the doctrine of the church and its magisterium is seen especially in two specific fields: in his comments on the documents of the magisterium, and in the way he speaks of the work of the Holy Office in his letters. We would add that in both fields his fidelity to the church is in no way excessive or fanatical, but extremely calm and balanced.

---

30. Cf. N 1956/110.
31. Cf. *ibid.*.
32. Cf. Nm 47 (1958).
33. N 1958/163.
34. Cf. Nw 38 (1954); Nz 11 (1950); Nq 43 (1954); 47 (1954); cf. the Constitutions of the Society of Jesus, Part IV, Chap. 5, no. 4.
35. "L'enciclica 'Pascendi' e gli studi biblici," *Biblica*, XXXIX (1958) (Biblio. 123), 131, 133, 138.
36. Cf. Biblio. 114, pp. 33, 38.
37. Cf. "Il Modernismo Biblico secondo l'enciclica 'Pascendi,' " *Divinitas*, II (1958) (Biblio. 120), 14-24; Biblio. 123, pp. 124-133.

1. As was the case with his time as Rector of the Biblical Institute, in the present period we again find quite a number of *commentaries on papal documents*, and we have already mentioned one or two of these above. We would now add two commentaries on the encyclical *Humani generis* which are very revealing both because of the sensitive nature of the subject-matter and also because of the method Bea follows, taking great care over frankly pointing out the deviations censured by the encyclical, while stressing the *positive and encouraging aspects* of the document.

(a) The encyclical *Humani generis* of Pius XII was concerned above all with what was known as "new theology"[38] and its applications to the various branches of the theological sciences. Although making due distinctions and recognizing nuances, the encyclical's main aim was that of pointing out deviations and errors. This fairly negative character was felt particularly strongly at that time, coming as it did after other encyclicals of the same pope which had on the contrary been very positive: *Mystici corporis* on the church as mystical body (1943), *Divino afflante Spiritu* on biblical studies (1943), and *Mediator Dei* on the liturgy (1947). An encyclical does not of its nature refer specifically to individual scholars, but rather to theories or systems of thinking, and this was also true of *Humani generis*. Indirectly, however, when it came to drawing its conclusions on the administrative level, it had painful consequences for a number of scholars. Referring to his own order, Bea speaks of the "deep impression" that the encyclical made on it, and says that someone with a good knowledge of the history of the order described that moment as "the darkest hour" in the whole history of the order as far as theological and philosophical studies were concerned.[39] It is very instructive to see how Bea acted in this situation.

Despite the delicacy of the situation, Bea certainly did not hold back in order to avoid compromising himself or making enemies in certain circles. He told me that he felt it was important that he should personally write an article for the philosophical and theological review of the German Jesuits in order to make sure that the document was presented in a fair, balanced manner. Similarly, in another study he explained its importance for biblical studies.[40]

(b) Let us consider the latter article first. Bea begins by observing: "Sacred scripture is not the main subject-matter of the encyclical." A bare seven years earlier, in fact, the pope "had already spoken about biblical studies in the encyclical *Divino afflante Spiritu*. Even so, perhaps to some extent because the encyclical had been published in the middle of the war, those seven years had shown that its teaching had not filtered through to all sectors."[41] The questions considered by *Humani generis* therefore include "not a few connected with the

38. The encyclical does not itself use this expression; Pius XII had first used it some years earlier in a speech to the general congregation of the Society of Jesus; cf. Biblio. 80, p. 36. Despite this fact, we shall use the expression for the sake of convenience.
39. Cf. N 1951/62.
40. Cf. Biblio. 83 and 80 respectively.
41. Biblio. 80, p. 417.

doctrine on inspiration and biblical inerrancy, problems of sacred hermeneutics, and exegesis of certain important biblical texts."[42] However, precisely because *Humani generis* was preceded by *Divino afflante Spiritu*—as well as *Providentissimus Deus* of Leo XIII, which has justly been called the magna carta of biblical studies—the task of explaining it was not particularly difficult. Moreover, since both the previous encyclicals, especially *Divino afflante Spiritu*, had expressed their teaching for the most part in positive terms, all one had to do was refer back to that teaching in order to make sure that any commentary on the relative part of *Humani generis* did not remain purely negative.

(c) The task of presenting and explaining the encyclical *Humani generis* as a whole was a more complicated and delicate matter. However, Bea frankly sets forth all its views on the new opinions and trends that it said had the effect of divesting of its meaning the terminology that had been established through the centuries and replacing it with the terminology in use prior to the doctrinal clarifications of the great Councils, for example the language of sacred scripture or the fathers of the church. This, it said, tended to undermine the intangible immutability of dogmas, and the root of such approaches was "false irenicism" and "dogmatic relativism." Bea unhesitatingly accepts the judgment of the encyclical that these opinions and trends could prove fatal to the purity of Catholic doctrine.[43] The most dangerous root of the doctrinal tendencies condemned in *Humani generis* is the attempt to dilute the teaching of the church by reinterpreting it in such a way as to obtain a formulation in which Catholics have common ground with non-Catholics. This may lead to unity, "but a unity in common ruin."[44] It should be noted that all his statements on the tendencies spoken of in *Humani generis* are based on a careful analysis of the encyclical in the light of previous discussions of the problems it considers.[45]

However, it is revealing that Bea also strives to point out the undeniable *positive contributions* of the encyclical—not in order to comfort those who felt attacked by it, but because of his concern to provide an objective and balanced view of the document. There was an obvious danger that the painful impression created by the warnings about deviations might close the eyes of certain readers to the positive elements that were undeniably present.[46] Thus Bea notes that the

---

42. *Ibid.*

43. Cf. Biblio. 83, pp. 36, 38, 41-42. For further details on the concepts of "irenicism" and "dogmatic relativism," see *EncCatt*, X, 684ff; "Irenismus," *LThK*, V, 749-750; "Relativismus," *LThK*, VIII, 1159ff.

44. Cf. Biblio. 83, pp. 40-41, 39.

45. Cf. *ibid.*, p. 37, note 4. Bea notes at this point that he will refrain from making repeated references to the bibliography in the course of his article, since the journal in which it is appearing has already informed him that it will be publishing specialized articles on the individual questions involved.

46. We would note in passing that similar observations could be made in connection with the article "L'enciclica 'Pascendi' e gli studi biblici" (Biblio. 123). While Bea confines himself to a retrospective, purely historical view in the article "Il modernismo biblico secondo l'enciclica 'Pascendi' " (Biblio. 120), in "L'enciclica 'Pascendi' e gli studi biblici" he proceeds differently: after noting the serious dangers of modernism as it is presented in the encyclical in question, he goes on to stress the positive contributions of St. Pius X to Catholic biblical science,

encyclical certainly does not intend "fettering scientific research,"[47] and repeatedly stresses that the encyclical is emphatically in favor of progress.[48] In particular, the terminology used to express the doctrine of the faith can obviously be improved. He also notes that the encyclical strongly recommends "a return to the sources" of the fathers of the church, because this will lead to a rejuvenation of theology.[49]

2. Let us now consider Bea's views on the *activity of the Holy Office.*[50] It is surprising how much information we find in his letters, although he never broke the proverbial grave-like silence on any more specific matters.[51] The presence of this information in his correspondence springs from the fact that he felt he had a duty to clarify people's ideas on the activity of the Holy Office and also to defend its work.

(a) In the first place it should be borne in mind, observes Bea, that the Holy Office is *not* concerned with *private opinions* so long as these do not constitute a danger for others or for the community as a whole. "Important people have better things to do than bother about all the private opinions there may be."[52] On the other hand, the church will always uphold its right and duty to inform its members of writings that it considers dangerous for them, whether through the index or some other means.[53] Bea writes to an old school-friend describing the kind of work he does at the Holy Office, observing that the Holy Office is basically a court, and then adding that, being an ecclesiastical court, it is a little different from a civil one: in every case it considers it has to bear in mind not only the legal aspect but also the pastoral aspect, allowing the latter to play a certain part in decisions, although never in such a way as to offend justice.[54] Here we can immediately see that the underlying reason for these measures—measures that are certainly not very pleasant for those affected—is the responsibility of the magisterium of the church for its members, particularly those who have least grounding to meet such threats; in other words, such measures are based on the principle that the "supreme law" of the church is the salvation of souls. Bea is so sure of the excellence of this cause that he spontaneously undertakes to defend it,[55] and to inform the general public about various specific measures of this kind.[56]

It should be added that the Holy Office acts according to the principle of

particularly with the foundation of the Biblical Institute in Rome. In connection with this latter study, cf. also Nc 33 (1958). This positive contribution is more fully described in the study "Il beato Pio X, gli studi biblici e l'Istituto Biblico" (Biblio. 90).

47. Biblio. 83, p. 38.
48. Cf. *ibid.*, pp. 36, 40. 48.
49. Cf. *ibid.*, p. 44. Cf. *EB*, no. 598; Biblio. 93, p. 10; Biblio. 82, p. 86; Biblio. 89, p. 103.
50. We have already spoken of his work at the Holy Office. Here we are concerned with seeing how he explains and evaluates its activity.
51. Cf. Ns 7 (1950).
52. N 1957/245; cf. Nm 53 (1958).
53. Cf. N 1957/193.
54. Cf. N 1951/29.
55. Cf. N 1955/110; 1955/155; Nm 54 (1958).
56. Cf. for example Nw 24 (1953).

subsidiarity, in other words only when and where the action of those who are primarily and immediately responsible—i.e. the local authority, the diocesan bishop—is no longer sufficient. The latter is the first person who must keep watch, specifically by censoring books, in order to ban anything that can be dangerous for the faith of his flock,[57] and it is thus much better if things work at this level and the Holy Office does not have to step in.[58] The same principle that primary responsibility lies with the local authority also means that when the Holy Office does intervene, it must do so in consultation with that authority; and Bea told me more than once that he had often pointed this out in his work at the Holy Office. In reference to the case of the action of the Holy Office with regard to the Schönstatt Movement,[59] he writes that it would not be right to deal with it without consulting the competent local authorities.[60]

(b) In the light of the foregoing, it is easy to see why Bea says that he is no friend of accusations and the outlawing of books by putting them on the *index of forbidden books*.[61] As we know, the index as such was abolished after the Council, and control is now exercised in other ways. Here, however, we are referring to the situation at that time. In one case when someone has called for the intervention of the authorities, he says that the matter can be clarified by theologians, through discussion and further study, which will be more productive.[62] We find letters in which he explicitly *discourages* correspondents from laying accusations on the Holy Office.[63] He also points out that we cannot assume that every report or complaint made to the Holy Office will come to anything, for the decision is often one of non-intervention.[64] As concerns the number of cases of books placed on the index, he challenges a correspondent to take a publisher's catalogue and calculate the percentage of works affected. "It is a minute number," he says, adding: "We are all too aware here that such measures can certainly not eliminate every truly dangerous work."[65] Elsewhere he stresses the fact that in the atmosphere of those days, placing a work on the index could be counter-productive and act more as an advertisement in its favor.[66]

Bea is also perfectly well aware that the institution of the index needs to be *reformed*: "We are all convinced that in our present times the question of the index requires revision." He adds, however: "In matters of this kind, where the salvation of souls is at stake, Rome is not in the habit of acting hastily; the question calls for careful examination, and must be studied with the assistance of experienced parties."[67]

---

57. Cf. Nm 56 (1958).
58. Cf. N 1955/110; 1958/223.
59. Cf. p. 137 above.
60. Cf. N 1957/251.
61. Cf. N 1955/110.
62. Cf. N 1958/21; 1955/68.
63. Cf. N 1957/292; Nm 44 (1958).
64. Cf. N 1956/13, 110.
65. N 1955/110.
66. Cf. N 1955/68; 1959/98; Nw 29 (1953); Nm 85 (1959).
67. N 1957/193. Part of the original of this letter is found in O. Karrer, *Streiflichter. Aus Briefen*

Conservation and Progress

It is not difficult to see that the Catholic principles explained thus far are not only complex, but also, especially since the Reformation of the sixteenth century, the subject of bitter argument; this means that they are always in danger of being misinterpreted. To start with a first misapprehension, the concept of "tradition" immediately puts people in mind of a "conservative" mentality that is opposed to progress. We shall now consider Bea's views on this point.

Studying progress in interpretation of sacred scripture, Bea has no difficulty in admitting that the nature of Catholic exegesis "is fairly conservative," although he immediately adds that it too "must take the scientific and spiritual situation into account."[68] It is this contact with real life that gives rise to *progress* in our understanding of the word of God, says Bea, and then goes on to explain that this understanding "on our part depends on many factors, some natural and others supernatural. In the first place there is the ability of the exegete himself, which in the last analysis comes from God, the 'Father of lights' (James 1:17). Then there is the whole intellectual, cultural, spiritual and even material environment, which has an influence on the exegete's thinking. There are also the various needs of the church, major theological controversies, heresies, and dangerous trends in exegesis itself. Apart from all this, there is the special light God gives to the actual exegete."[69]

In another context Bea gives a fuller explanation of the influence that comes from the intellectual, cultural and spiritual environment, following Pius XII in saying that it is necessary to "take advantage of everything offered by modern science in order to obtain an ever more perfect knowledge of the meaning and import of the word of God."[70]

However, it is obviously not only a case of development and progress in understanding of the word of God through the work of *exegetes*. There is the more general fact of the growth in understanding of the word of God within the church as a whole. For example, in his study of Protestant reactions to the definition of the bodily assumption of Mary into heaven, Bea states that "the Catholic Church recognizes *a legitimate progress in dogma*" and has proclaimed the relative dogma "not in order to place obstacles in the way of efforts to reach unity, but in faithful obedience to an internal law of its doctrinal development, under the inspiration and guidance of the Holy Spirit."[71]

The *factors* on which this development depends are largely the same as those Bea listed above as factors in progress in interpretation of sacred scripture. As

---

an mich 1933-1945 (Frankfurt/Stuttgart, 1976), p. 55. The connection between the index and the salvation of souls is also made in N 1957/168; a correspondent had suggested that a certain procedure could be followed before the Holy Office stepped in, but Bea did not agree (cf. N 1956/13; N 1956/155.

68. Biblio. 89, p. 99.
69. *Ibid.*, pp. 85-86.
70. "Pio XII e gli studi biblici" (Biblio. 109), p. 79; cf. also p. 67.
71. Biblio. 99, pp. 90, 92.

we know, Vatican II also speaks of the progress of the church in understanding the word of God, listing its essential and spiritual factors: "the contemplation and study of believers, . . . the intimate sense of spiritual realities which they experience, . . . and the preaching of those who have received . . . the sure charism of truth."[72] Bea adds factors that we can describe as external or environmental, describing elsewhere the function of these, stating that "outside circumstances are not a determining element, but merely an *occasion*" of such progress in theology, in other words "an impulse given to theological work, which will then find the solution to difficulties in the revealed truth itself, as the whole history of Catholic dogma clearly shows."[73]

Such progress in the understanding of divine revelation is in turn illustrated by the fact that in the history of salvation we find that revelation itself takes place in a progressive manner, gradually being filled out according to God's plan to bring humanity to fuller knowledge. Bea can hence observe that with improvements in the method of exegesis it has become possible to see "the different phases [of doctrine] in the New Testament, both in the gospels and in the teaching of the apostles, in other words, the development, progress or 'evolution' (in the positive sense of the word) of divine revelation." Thus biblical theology has arisen "as the *systematic* presentation of the origin, development and gradual perfecting of the various religious doctrines in the successive phases of revelation. . . . And this is maybe the greatest and most important progress that exegesis has made in the course of the centuries."[74] This progress of divine revelation in the history of salvation is in a way reflected in the fact that "as the centuries go by, the church is always advancing toward the plenitude of divine truth, until eventually the words of God are fulfilled in her."[75]

I think that more than one reader will be surprised to find this view expressed in Pius XII's encyclical *Humani generis*, which has often been judged as uncompromisingly conservative. In his detailed commentary on the encyclical Bea quotes the following passage in this connection: "God is Truth itself; he it is who has created, and who directs the human intellect. He does not mean it to be contrasting, each day that passes, some new point of view with one it has already solidly acquired. He means it to eliminate any error that may have entered into its calculations, and then to build up new truth on the foundation of the old; that is the order of nature's own architecture, and it is from nature that we derive our knowledge of truth." And the pope adds: "It is not for the Christian, be he theologian or philosopher, to give every latest fantasy of the day a thoughtless and hasty welcome. He will weigh it carefully, and with a just balance."[76] After close examination of the position of the encyclical in the philosophical field, Bea can therefore state: "The encyclical thus combines a

---

72. *DV*, 8.
73. Inaugural address (Biblio. 114), pp. 37-38.
74. Biblio. 89, p. 102; cf. also Biblio. 95, p. 101.
75. *DV*, 8.
76. "Die Enzyklika 'Humani Generis' " (Biblio. 83), p. 40, quoting *Humani generis*; English translation of *Humani generis*, p. 15.

healthy conservatism with the search for organic, scientifically-based progress."[77] And the encyclical can rightly address the following call to teachers in the academic field: "With all their powers, in a generous spirit of rivalry, let them enlarge the bounds of the sciences they teach. . . . Let them devote careful study to any new problems which our modern culture, and the progressive spirit of the age, may raise."[78]

No less than faithful preservation of the deposit of faith, progress is thus a law and requirement inherent in the nature and life of the church. This deep understanding of the law of progress leads Bea to demand that we avoid returning again and again to fresh speculation on certain age-old problems, however important, but that we devote ourselves above all "to tasks we are set today by the great problems of our times and by the present needs of the church."[79] Thus, having assumed a commitment to a healthy preservation in the sense of fidelity to its own identity, even Pius XII can state "that with regard to science and modern technology, it [the church] does not take up a position of opposition, but acts more as a counterweight or a balancing factor."[80] And Bea adds that in this "the Holy Father himself set the most splendid example in his speeches, allocutions and radio messages, considering all the questions raised by modern life, on the basis of the doctrine of the church."[81]

As can be seen, the two concepts of conservation and progress do not apply only to theology, but to any serious intellectual work that wishes to produce lasting fruit. In ancient times the Latin tag *nova et vetera* was coined for this method. Bea describes the plan of work for the Roman Pontifical Theological Academy, explaining it in the following terms: "The problems that arise today are not always completely new, but are often new aspects of old truths which have assumed special importance in our present circumstances. Precisely because of this fact, we obviously cannot simply repeat old solutions; our response must take into account the specific present-day situation and the problems that are now arising. However, it is equally clear that we cannot simply disregard work already done in past centuries and strike out along totally new paths. We must harmoniously combine *nova* and *vetera* in a carefully considered and prudent *synthesis*."[82] In the same context Bea refers to one of Pius XII's speeches to show that this is a general law of human life. Partly summarizing and partly quoting from the speech in question, Bea writes: "We must 'combine the dynamic force of reform with the static quality of traditions'; alongside 'dynamic evolution by means of personal and free action,' there must always be 'a certain basis of tradition and staticity in order to safeguard certainty,' not only in ordinary life, but also in scientific work, and for special reasons in theological work."[83]

77. Biblio. 83, p. 49.
78. *Humani generis*, English translation, p. 24; cf. Biblio. 80, p. 40.
79. Biblio. 114, p. 42.
80. *Ibid.*, p. 45, citing *AAS*, LXVII (1955), 681.
81. *Ibid.*
82. *Ibid.*, p. 38; cf. also Biblio. 95, p. 100.
83. Biblio. 114, p. 38, note 8j, referring to the 1956 Christmas radio message, *AAS*, IL (1957), 6.

"The Freedom of Children of God"

Another type of misunderstanding of the function of tradition and magisterium is that of imagining that they rule out any freedom in research. We saw above that the encyclical *Humani generis* rejected a type of exegesis that claimed to be independent, free of any outside shackle, or exclusively scientific.[84] Bea thus accepts that Catholic exegesis cannot be absolutely "independent" in this sense, for if it were it would no longer be a theological science. Even so, he did uphold its scientific character and thus the need for it to enjoy a just freedom in research.

Bea discusses this subject particularly in his article on biblical studies from Leo XIII to Pius XII, where he sets forth the thinking of the encyclical *Divino afflante Spiritu* in this respect. After warmly encouraging Catholic exegetes to apply themselves wholeheartedly to research, the pope is concerned to protect them against unjust attack, warning everybody in the church that they "should abhor that intemperate zeal which imagines that whatever is new should for that very reason be opposed or suspected"; in positive terms the pope impresses on everybody that the efforts of those carrying out such research "should be judged not only with equity and justice, but also with the greatest charity."[85] In this way the pope wants to guarantee that "these resolute laborers in the vineyard of the Lord" enjoy the "true liberty of the children of God, which adheres faithfully to the teaching of the church, and accepts and uses gratefully the contributions of profane science."[86] The pope adds that this freedom "is the condition and source of all lasting fruit and of all solid progress in Catholic doctrine."[87]

For his part Bea adds the following reflection: "Here we can see the same deep religious spirit of the pope, linked to a great breadth of vision, which can also be seen in all the innumerable speeches in which Pius XII strives to place all the true treasures of human knowledge at the service of religion, the faith, and the good of individuals and of all humanity. He is not afraid of any true, solid science: Leo XIII's saying that 'verum vero adversari haud quaquam potest' is a fundamental truth for him in all his doctrinal activity."[88]

This same line of Pius XII regarding freedom of research is also noted in Bea's comments on other papal documents. He observes that the letter of the Pontifical Biblical Commission to Cardinal Suhard once again confirms the freedom guaranteed in *Divino afflante Spiritu*,[89] and indeed he states that the same situation is also found in *Humani generis*. He challenges certain people's

---

84. Cf. *Humani generis*, English translation, p. 9.
85. *Divino afflante Spiritu*, English translation, p. 24; cf. Biblio. 126, p. 613. Cf. also Biblio. 109, p. 72.
86. *Divino afflante Spiritu*, English translation, p. 24.
87. *Ibid.*
88. Biblio. 126, p. 613. The Latin phrase means that two "truths" cannot contradict one another; the practical meaning of Leo XIII's words is that authentic results of the sciences that allow us to know the secrets of the creation cannot be in contradiction with the truths revealed by God, the Author of the creation.
89. Biblio. 109, p. 77; for the letter to Cardinal Suhard, see *EB*, no. 578.

claims that in this document the pope took back with one hand what he had given with the other—i.e. freedom of research—in *Divino afflante Spiritu*: "The principles of both encyclicals are the same; but it must be remembered that what is known as 'new theology' had not yet developed in 1943 as it had by 1950, and also that in the meantime experience had shown that the principles laid down in the encyclical *Divino afflante Spiritu* had been subject to certain distortions."[90]

Bea comments on the attitude of *Humani generis* in the field of philosophy, stressing that it does not insist on any specific philosophical system, and still less on any specific form of the philosophy of St. Thomas Aquinas, despite the existence of certain tendencies of this type in the Catholic world.[91]

In his address to the Roman Pontifical Theological Academy he observes: "Nobody will therefore be surprised to find various schools of theology and speculative currents peacefully represented in our academy; indeed, this fact will be seen as a great advantage for theological work and a pressing exhortation for each person to strive in his own way, within the limits of the freedom granted by the church, to solve contemporary problems, starting from his own point of view and on the basis of his fundamental principles."[92]

The breadth of the freedom left to Catholic exegetes can be illustrated with various examples. Exegetes must of course respect the interpretation set forth by the church, particularly the holy fathers. Bea, however, draws our attention to the statement of *Divino afflante Spiritu* that there are few texts of the Bible "whose sense has been defined by the authority of the church, nor are those more numerous about which the teaching of the holy fathers is unanimous." Thus he concludes, still with the encyclical: "There remain therefore many things . . . in the discussion and exposition of which . . . Catholic commentators may contribute . . . to the advantage of all, to the continued progress of the sacred doctrine."[93]

The situation is similar with regard to theologians' fidelity to "the great doctors, such as St. Augustine and St. Thomas." In this connection Bea refers back to one of Pius XII's speeches which throws considerable light on the question. In this speech the pope certainly taught "on the one hand the authority" of such great doctors, but also recalled that "none of the great doctors is infallible, that their writings contain elements resulting from their limited and imperfect knowledge of the sciences, both natural (physics, chemistry, biology) and other, and that we must thus strike a harmonious balance between fidelity to the great doctors, especially St. Thomas, and the precious freedom that personal investigation requires, carefully distinguishing between (i) Catholic doctrine and truth connected with it, and (ii) whatever is either a result of attempts at explanation on the part of learned authors or a specific and distinctive element of any of the various philosophical or theological systems."[94]

90. Biblio. 126, pp. 631-632.
91. Cf. Biblio. 83, pp. 47-48.
92. Biblio. 114, p. 43.
93. *Divino afflante Spiritu*, English translation, p. 24, quoted in Biblio. 126, p. 612.
94. Biblio. 114, p. 42. Cf. also Nm 68 (1958), where Bea notes that as concerns the "guarantees"

Personal investigation carried out with a vigilant critical sense should also be the rule in study of statements of the magisterium of the church, and this is how Bea approaches study of the teaching of Pius IX's bull *Ineffabilis Deus* on the mariological sense of the protogospel (Genesis 3:15). He comes to the conclusion that the pope clearly means that in the light of the fathers of the church the protogospel is to be understood in a mariological sense. He then considers the question of whether this means that the problem is settled and can thus no longer be discussed by Catholic exegetes. He answers that the problem can be freely discussed, but that Catholic exegetes must take account of the aforementioned teaching of the bull.[95]

We can give a further example. Authentic mariology and devotion to the Blessed Virgin were very close to Bea's heart, but he wanted to see the subject treated according to strict theological method. When asked if the definition of the universal mediation of the Virgin (or what other theologians call the doctrine of Mary as co-redemptrix) as a dogma of faith could be expected soon, he answered that it was out of the question because this doctrine was still the subject of too much debate among theologians and thus not ripe for definition.[96] In his study on sacred scripture as the "ultimate foundation" of the dogma of the assumption, he discusses the various biblical arguments that had been advanced in favor of the assumption, also referring to that taken from the twelfth chapter of the Book of Revelation, which speaks of the "woman clothed with the sun." In this connection he quotes the words of St. Pius X in the encyclical *Ad diem illum*: "So John saw the Most Blessed Mother of God already in eternal joy." He then asks whether this is a biblical argument in favor of the assumption, and he says no. Why? First of all, it refers to a vision that could also be purely symbolic; and secondly, many exegetes think that the woman more probably symbolizes the church.[97] All this explains why one of Bea's letters speaks of his wish to see mariology resting on solid theological foundations, and also why he indicates his intention of speaking directly with Pope Pius XII about this matter.[98]

These examples show that there truly are spaces for freedom of research. However, they also show that the practical application of this freedom sometimes requires a great deal of perspicacity and precision. Let us give two examples.

The first concerns the application of evolutionism to the origins of the human body. Here the encyclical demands "that the reasons for the two opinions [that of the descent of the human body from preexisting organic material, and that of its immediate creation] be 'weighed and adjudged with all seriousness, fairness, and restraint' and that 'there must be a readiness on all sides to accept the

---

over baptism and education of children that are usually required of Catholics contracting marriage with non-Catholics, we must not speak too easily of divine "law." In this connection he refers to the fact that in China and Japan, for example, such explicit guarantees are not usually demanded.

95. Cf. Biblio. 104, p. 7, note 22, in which detailed reasons for this response are given.

96. Cf. N 1954/72; 1953/60; 1958/99.

97. Cf. Biblio. 82, p. 549.

98. Cf. N 1953/60.

arbitrament of the church as being entrusted by Christ with the task of interpreting the scriptures aright, and the duty of safeguarding the doctrines of the faith.' "[99] We cannot simply act as if "the sources of divine revelation contained nothing that called for the greatest moderation and prudence in this matter."[100]

The second example concerns "the scientific hypothesis closely connected with interpretation of sacred scripture—that of polygenism—which teaches 'the existence, after Adam's time, of some earthly race of men, truly so called, who were not descended ultimately from him, or else supposes that Adam was the name given to some group of our primordial ancestors.' " The encyclical states that such views cannot be embraced by the faithful because "it does not appear how they can be reconciled with the doctrine of original sin, as this is guaranteed to us by scripture and tradition, and proposed to us by the church."[101]

Prudence and Courage

It often requires courage—a great deal of courage—to take up the spaces of freedom that the church leaves its members. However, it also requires prudence, in order to safeguard fidelity to Catholic principles and the church in practical terms.

1. Let us start by taking a look at some *small but significant examples.* We have already seen the situation that publication of the encyclical *Humani generis* created for many people, including certain members of the Society of Jesus. In the face of these difficulties, Bea did what he could to help his brother Jesuits, advising them to avoid behavior or involvements that could in practice compromise important scientific undertakings.[102]

In this context the question of the best way of dealing with the Holy Office often arose. I remember that Bea told me more than once that when people came to complain about difficulties with the Holy Office, he always advised them to contact Cardinal Ottaviani directly, and that so far as he knew things had then gone well.[103]

Prudence was indeed particularly necessary in that period. For example, when a correspondent says that he intends producing an Italian translation of a biblical study by a German Catholic author, Bea advises him to desist, observing that it is also in the author's own interests that his work should not be translated.[104] In such cases, he is very careful to bear in mind the psychological and cultural situation in the countries in question. Referring to the situation in a certain country, he observes

99. Biblio. 109, p. 78, quoting *Humani generis*, English translation, p. 21. Cf. Biblio. 83, p. 52.
100. Biblio. 126, p. 626.
101. Biblio. 109, p. 78, quoting *Humani generis*, English translation, p. 22. Cf. Biblio. 83, p. 52.
102. Cf. N 1951/55; N 1953/52; Nq 8 (1951); out of respect for people who are still alive, we avoid giving any more precise details on this point.
103. Cf. Nq 9 (1951).
104. Cf. N 1953/99.

that it is a very delicate matter to publish things there that could be published elsewhere without hesitation. This is because there are people there who have remained several decades behind the times, and that when someone publishes anything different from what they learned in their time—if they learned anything at all—they automatically hold that it is contrary to the faith; prudence is thus vital.[105] This may seem a harsh view, but it was certainly an accurate evaluation of certain situations. We shall see a specific example below.

2. Bea's prudence and *above all his courage* can be seen in the full stories of two important "cases," both connected with the field of biblical studies.

(a) The first is that of the famous *1948 letter of the Pontifical Biblical Commission to Cardinal Suhard* concerning the literary mosaic authenticity of the Pentateuch and the historical character of the first eleven chapters of Genesis. We have already referred to this in connection with Father Bea's time as Rector of the Pontifical Biblical Institute, using it to throw light on the question of how conservative he in fact was or how open to progress. We shall therefore refrain from describing the background to the letter again or discussing Bea's decisive influence on its orientation.[106] Here we shall take a closer look at its content and the further developments it gave birth to in the field of biblical research.

The document is a striking example of the aforementioned method of "defense" by positive means, in other words by providing a fuller explanation of the various aspects of the question and suggesting the direction in which a solution should be sought.

The *gist* of the document can be described as follows. It starts by reiterating the freedom of research as this was set forth in the encyclical *Divino afflante Spiritu.* Then it explains that the "responses" of the Biblical Commission concerning the question of the literary mosaic authenticity of the Pentateuch and the historical character of the first eleven chapters of Genesis "are in no way opposed to further truly scientific examination of those questions, in line with results attained over the past forty years. This means that it recognizes that those decrees also contain assertions that were based on the scientific situation at the time of their publication, and that are thus subject to modification and change. This was the first time that this point of view concerning the responses of the Pontifical Biblical Commission was officially expressed and confirmed—with the approval of the Supreme Pontiff—by the same commission."[107]

What was the *principle underlying* this decision of the commission? Bea replies that "it is simply an application of the teaching of theologians on the value of doctrinal decisions of the magisterium of the church that are of their nature not infallible."[108] And the explanation is as follows. Although it does

---

105. Cf. N 1958/131. A similar opinion is expressed when he says that in the 1920s "the situation was not very encouraging, especially since there was no lack of minds that were closed to any progress and blind to the serious difficulties that Catholic biblical science had to face" (Biblio. 126, p. 608).

106. Cf. pp. 118 above.

107. Biblio. 109, p. 77.

108. Biblio. 126, p. 623.

indeed concern decisions on the doctrine of the church on faith and morals, as well as matters closely connected with such doctrine, these decisions—and this is particularly true of the responses of the Biblical Commission—"not infrequently speak on questions the solutions of which depend on historical, critical, philological and archeological assumptions, etc., that can obviously change, and in fact often do, in the course of later discoveries."[109] Consequently, the relative doctrinal decision must also change. This applies, for example, to the question of the authenticity and composition of the Pentateuch, which was answered in 1906 and 1909, prior to many new discoveries and much research.[110] This is the light in which we must understand the statement in the letter that the responses are not opposed to truly scientific examination in the light of the results of research carried out over the last forty years.

Nor is this all. Bea stresses that the importance of the letter in question goes far beyond the three responses directly concerned. Thus he says that it "is certainly of supreme importance . . . also as regards . . . decrees of the Biblical Commission *in general* insofar as these deal with matters that are not *de fide et bonis moribus*[111] or connected with such matters."[112] And there was in fact a sequel to the whole affair. In 1955, on the occasion of a new edition of the collection of church documents concerning biblical studies (the *Enchiridion Biblicum*, which we have already cited a good many times in the present work), the then Secretary of the Pontifical Biblical Commission, Father A. Miller, O.S.B., and its Vice-Secretary, Father A. Kleinhans, O.F.M., published two articles that were in such close agreement that it was clear that this was an unofficial but certainly prearranged step. These two articles state in general terms that such decrees are strictly concerned with teaching on faith and morals, but that "insofar as they express opinions that are *not* connected either directly or indirectly with truths of faith and morals, interpreters of sacred scripture are left complete freedom to pursue their own scientific research, while always remembering that the last word in this connection lies with the teaching authority of the church."[113]

Bea explains the caveat that the last word lies with the teaching authority of the church as follows: "It should not be forgotten that the connection between the historical, philological and archeological facts, etc., which are adopted or presumed in a decree, and the doctrine expressed in the same document, is not the same in every case, and that in the last and decisive instance, judgment on how to proceed is up to the Holy See and not to individual scholars."[114]

We could then wonder why the Biblical Commission should have given responses in which the doctrinal elements were so closely linked with assump-

---

109. *Ibid.*, p. 624, note.
110. Cf. *ibid.*
111. In other words questions not concerning faith and good morals.
112. Biblio. 126, p. 623.
113. A. Kleinhans, "De nova Ench. Biblici editione," *Antonianum*, XXX (1955), 63ff, reproduced in *Biblica*, XXXVI (1955), 565. Cf. also A. Miller, "Das neue biblische Handbuch," *Benediktin Monatsschrift*, XXXI (1955), 49ff.
114. Biblio. 126, p. 624, note.

tions that could change—or, more generally, why the magisterium of the church chose this way of proceeding. The answer is implicit in the two articles mentioned above: in the struggle in defense of the faith this is practically speaking the only way possible. Moreover, we must remember that today it is difficult to imagine the situation Catholic exegetes found themselves in fifty years ago, and the danger that Catholic doctrine on sacred scripture ran when liberal and rationalistic criticism tried to break all the bounds of traditional doctrine. Today, when the fight is for the most part over and many things have been clarified, it can certainly seem that there was a lack of openness and breadth of vision in those days, but it would be wrong to judge the latter against the yardstick of our present situation.[115]

(b) The second case may have had a narrower impact, but the course it took is still very interesting, and it is revealing to see the role played by Bea. The subject in question is the French work *Introduction à la Bible*, which first appeared in the fall of 1957. It was a general introduction to sacred scripture of a new kind, and it therefore immediately came in for attack from certain quarters in Rome—attacks that Bea describes as "disgraceful" in a letter from that period.[116] Attacks from other countries followed in due course. In these circumstances, someone laid a complaint to the Holy Office against the work, and in view of the general alarm aroused it is not surprising that the Holy Office agreed to take the matter in hand.

Although Bea's role in this whole affair was, as always with the Holy Office, subject to total secrecy, our witness attests his constant concern, and also the guidance and encouragement given to the director of the work throughout the whole story—and this is also confirmed by the relative correspondence.

(i) The difficulty sprang partly from the fairly new character of the book, and partly from misunderstandings created by the preface, which seemed to say that the work had been conceived as a text-book for exegesis courses in seminaries and theological faculties. There were also, of course, criticisms as to content. Be this as it may, the first decision of the Holy Office was to inform the two Vatican departments concerned with the training of future priests—the Congregation for Seminaries and the Congregation for Religious—that for reasons connected with teaching methods, the book could not be used as a text-book in the training of future priests. Apart from this, both the publisher and the author were warned that for the sake of prudence the work could not be translated into any other language unless the Holy See made fresh dispositions.

We would observe that as early as this first involvement of the Holy Office in the case, Bea was advising the director of the work to prepare a preface for the next edition that would explain that it was not a text-book for the training of

---

115. Cf. Kleinhans, "De nova Ench. Biblici editione," as cited in *Biblica*, XXXVI (1955), 565.

116. Cf. N 1958/55. H. Cazelles, who succeeded A. Robert as director of the work in question, contributed a detailed account of the whole affair to our archives, together with the relative written exchange between Robert and Father Bea, and authorized us to make immediate use of it if we wished.

future priests, and also providing an outline of the corrections and improvements to be made in the new edition.

It is instructive to see how the two congregations in question approached the matter. That for religious confined itself to informing religious superiors of the relative decree of the Holy Office, whereas that for seminaries drew up a decree of its own, in which it not only gave the reasons connected with teaching methods, which were mentioned in the decree of the Holy Office, but added that the use of the work in seminaries was *also* forbidden for other reasons, including doctrinal ones; the implication was that its use was forbidden not only as a text-book, but even as an auxiliary or supplementary teaching aid. In order to draw more attention to its own decree, it had a semi-official commentary published in the *Osservatore Romano* on 2 July 1958, in which the tone was even more uncompromising.[117]

(ii) While certain people in the Catholic world were so impressed by this measure that they did what they could to spread the news,[118] both the Holy Office and the Biblical Commission were annoyed because the additions meant that the Congregation for Seminaries was trespassing on their territory. The Holy Office therefore took the matter in hand once again. A decision on the case was delayed, both because of the death of Pius XII, and also because of the fact that the main "godfather of the case," Father Bea, was sick for almost two months. Finally, in February 1959, the director in charge of the work received instructions to be followed in preparing a new edition: thus he was told that the preface must point out that the work was *not* intended as a text-book, and was also given various guidelines on the content of the work. The instructions were accompanied by advice to submit the manuscript of the new edition to the censorship of a competent, reliable person, who should preferably be sought in the Roman universities. The person chosen was Father Bea, who not only set to work with a will, but also agreed that his name—together with that of the Secretary of the Biblical Commission, Father A. Miller, O.S.B.—should be mentioned in the preface to the work. And this is the tale of how Bea become "involved" with this particular publication.

Awareness of His Own Limitations and Those of Science

We have already discussed Bea's sober-minded critical sense, and this quality went hand-in-hand with another marked characteristic of Bea as theologian: his modesty. This latter quality was based on a clear-sighted awareness of the inherent limitations of his own work, and more broadly of those of science and human knowledge in general.

117. None of the documents connected with this case—not even those involved in the second stage of its consideration by the Holy Office, which we shall consider below—is found in the official publication *Acta Apostolicae Sedis*.
118. Cf. N 1958/287.

1. First of all there was his *personal modesty*. When somebody sent him a study on the question of whether Adam was "the first man" (*Urmensch*), he said that he was not competent to judge it, pointing out that the subject called for two types of skill, for apart from knowledge of sacred scripture, any competent judge would need to know about paleontology as well, and he said that he had been unable to keep up with the latter for ten years now.[119] On another occasion, he wrote that he did not know enough about the field of the New Testament, and that the Book of Revelation in particular had always been "a sealed book" for him.[120] When he had prepared the second edition of his study on the origin of the human body according to science, reason and revelation, he sent the manuscript to a fellow Jesuit, almost thirty years his junior, who was a specialist in anthropology and paleontology, explaining his reasons as follows: "I have tried to be as objective as possible and to set forth the facts as they are; but I realize that a specialist sees many things and circumstances in a light different from that of a mere amateur like myself. I should therefore be grateful if you would be so kind as to note anything that you think should be changed, added or omitted."[121] Nor was this the only case in which he asked for a similar favor from someone else; indeed, we could say that when he was writing for publication, he followed this procedure quite regularly.

2. Then we come to his awareness of the *inherent limitations of science and knowledge in general*. Despite his close involvement with the question of the origin of the Pentateuch, even in 1952 he was writing that there was still no solution that corresponded to all the facts and answered all the problems.[122] As we have seen in the course of this chapter, he had great admiration for the encyclical *Divino afflante Spiritu*, but this did not stop him from writing: "Rather than providing solutions, it indicated tasks for us."[123] Joining his voice to that of the encyclical, he tells scholars not to lose heart "if the wished-for solution be slow in coming."[124] In this connection the encyclical recalls a view expressed by St. Augustine: "God wished difficulties to be scattered through the sacred books inspired by him, in order that we might be urged to read and scrutinize them more intently, and, experiencing in a salutary manner our own limitations, we might be exercised in due submission of mind."[125]

3. More generally, there is the limitation inherent in *any human knowledge*, and in this context we find a very striking reflection in a letter to a young Dominican friend. We should first explain that since the seventeenth century

---

119. Cf. N 1959/32.

120. Cf. N 1954/57.

121. N 1954/116. When he received a wealth of observations from the other man, he thanked him, saying: "Really I could not and should not have expected such a huge effort on your part" (N 1954/150).

122. Cf. N 1952/119; also N 1958/55.

123. N 1958/126.

124. *Divino afflante Spiritu*, English translation, p. 23.

125. *Ibid.*, pp. 23-24.

there had been a controversy between the Jesuits and the Dominicans over the question of reconciling the work of divine grace with human freedom.[126] Thus the young student wrote to Bea, probably jokingly, that, having finished his philosophy studies, he was about to become Bea's "bitter opponent." To judge by the fairly lengthy reaction, it would seem that Bea was touched to the quick: "Becoming 'a bitter opponent of the Jesuits'!" he wrote. "In my view there should never be 'bitter opponents' among us children of the church. You see, . . . every matter and every question has so many different aspects, that it looks different according to your vantage-point. I can certainly understand and respect the point of view of a philosopher who, for example, represents the school of *praemotio physica*,[127] but still say to myself that the matter also has another aspect and that it might be explained better in some other way. I therefore have as much respect and appreciation for the representatives of one school as for those of the other. Both are gropingly striving, from different sides, to draw closer to a truth that is fully known only to God. When they do this, they gain direct experience of the narrow, limited nature of human knowledge, and of the fact that only the infinite wisdom of God penetrates the deep essence of things. So why should we be opponents, let alone bitter ones, if all the registers of the great organ of human knowledge go together to create a harmonious concerto? In this perspective, which I have taken from my earliest years, all the disagreements between various schools seem a waste of time and energy. Even if people may have varying opinions on specific points, I think it is better that we should all work together in charity and harmony for the great cause of the 'kingdom of God,' *dummodo Christus praedicetur.*[128] It seems to me that this is much more important than trying to make our point in arguments between different schools, arguments in which human reason never finds a complete solution, precisely because of its limited nature."[129]

This long, friendly "lesson" throws considerable light on Bea's thought as expressed in the plan of work he set for the Roman Pontifical Theological Academy: "We all know that when the human mind—even the wisest and most profound—investigates the divine nature and its action, at a certain point it finds itself faced with a *limit* beyond which it cannot go, whichever line of approach it takes. Others have made and are making similar attempts from other directions, but they too are unsuccessful. The long history of theology clearly shows where these limits lie and also tell us about the various attempts that have been made to move beyond them. Contemporary theologians who are aware of the incapacity of the human mind to penetrate the immense depths of God and the

---

126. Cf. *EncCatt*, XX, 784-785; VIII, 1221-1224; *LThK*, VII, 527-530; I, 220-221.
127. On the concept of "physical pre-motion," that is, the "previous and immediate influence of God on the activity of every creature and especially on human action even when free, according to the teaching of St. Thomas," cf. *EncCatt*, IX, 1950-1952.
128. The thought is that of St. Paul in the letter to the Philippians—"that in every way . . . Christ is proclaimed" (1:18)—although it is not quoted literally here.
129. Ni 21 (1953); we apologize for the long citation, but it seemed worth giving in full.

ultimate, deepest forces that the Creator has placed in his creatures, will sincerely respect all the efforts made by others."[130]

More Extensive Cooperation with a View to "an Integrated Synthesis of Theological Knowledge"

Awareness of the limitations both of individuals and of human knowledge in general leads Bea to call for harmonious collaboration between theologians, between the various theological disciplines, and indeed between the various branches of human knowledge.

First of all, theologians of all schools must work together under the guidance of the teaching authority of the church.[131] "It is all too clear that this complex task of biblical and patristic research, philosophical and theological speculation, and study of allied and connected profane sciences cannot be carried out by *one theologian alone*, but requires the *wise fraternal collaboration of many people*."[132]

Then comes collaboration between the various branches of the theological sciences: "In order to solve contemporary theological problems, by mutual consent biblical studies, historical and patristic studies and dogmatic and moral speculation will work together, always in faithful dependence on the living magisterium of the church and in full awareness that none of them *on their own* will be capable of performing the great task."[133]

Bea stresses one particular aspect of such collaboration—that of mutual fraternal supervision. When they collaborate in this way, theologians will feel that their work is "checked by skilled colleagues who are specialized in other sectors of sacred science. . . . I use the word 'checked' advisedly, for I know all too well, even from personal experience, that every specialist needs checking: he may be a man of science and be thoroughly familiar with everything in his own sector, but too often he is closed in this sector and thinks that he can talk about things found outside its confines with the same certainty with which he speaks of his own affairs. Fraternal checking is of real benefit for him and is an inestimable advantage for science."[134] Bea does, however, note that such collaboration in no way detracts from the original nature of the research of each expert, saying that they all collaborate "while retaining their individual scientific characteristics," and citing the eminent examples of St. Thomas and St. Bonaventure in this connection.[135]

130. Biblio. 114, p. 42. Bea refers to the 1953 speech that Pius XII made to the Pontifical Gregorian
        University; cf. *AAS*, XLV (1953), 685-686.
131. Cf. N 1959/49; Biblio. 4, p. 43.
132. Biblio. 114, p. 41.
133. *Ibid.*, p. 40.
134. *Ibid.*, pp. 41-42.
135. Cf. *ibid.*, pp. 42-43.

Now that the world "has grown smaller," a truly universal collaboration, both geographically and culturally speaking, is needed, in other words a collaboration that involves different nations and cultures. The different regions of the world present "new problems in history and religious psychology, new aspects of the religious and social heritage of those peoples who glory in this age-old possession. If we are to integrate these new elements into the general framework of our doctrinal system and judge them according to the norms of our absolute truths as revealed by God, we also need the collaboration of those whose education, past, and knowledge of the language and customs of their forebears mean that they are particularly well-placed to provide us with secure foundations for a scientific investigation and a serene examination."[136]

When Bea talks about collaboration between different nations and cultures, he makes it clear that in calling for collaboration between the various disciplines he is in no way confining this to the theological disciplines and is aware that these in turn depend on the results of various other branches of science: "When we consider the present life of other nations we often see new questions arising there as a result of new discoveries and experiences of scholars from that region, especially in the fields of biology, surgery, psychology, psychopathy and similar disciplines. In such cases the academics of those nations will often be the most suitable people to inform the theological world about these new problems and their scientific underpinnings."[137]

Bea's call for collaboration between theologians and between the different branches of the theological sciences is made with a view to "the unity and harmony of all theological knowledge."[138] Only through such collaboration "are the elements gradually created that are needed in order to produce, in our days too, an *integrated synthesis of theological knowledge* built on solid positive, speculative and scientific foundations."[139] Such elements of synthesis obviously encompass not only the results of research from the specific period of each theologian. "It is clear . . . that here we cannot disregard work already carried out in past centuries and strike out along totally new paths. We must combine *nova* and *vetera* harmoniously in a measured and well-considered synthesis."[140]

* * *

---

136. *Ibid.*, p. 43.
137. *Ibid.* In this context it is interesting to see the joy with which Bea greeted the creation of the "Institute of the *Goerres Gesellschaft* for the Meeting between Science and Faith." In a letter about this initiative, he also gives advice on how to request and organize audiences for its members with Pius XII. Then, observing that the relative memorandum repeatedly mentions "Christian humanism" with reference to the "western world," Bea takes the liberty of expressing the hope that the institute will become effectively "universal, or if you prefer, international" (cf. Nv 29/1956).
138. Cf. Biblio. 114, p. 4.
139. *Ibid.*, p. 45.
140. *Ibid.*, p. 38.

In 1952 Bea wrote as follows to a German professor of Old Testament exegesis: "Your students will certainly be grateful to you if you open up the treasures of the Old Testament to them and accustom them to draw on it also for the material for their sermons and catechetical instruction."[141] This was precisely what Bea had tried to do right from the very first years in which he taught Old Testament exegesis; in the 1960s, one of his students from those early years would thank him because his lessons on Isaiah had borne good fruit in the man's work as priest and preacher. In a similar perspective, for several decades Bea gave a course at the Biblical Institute on the methodology of teaching sacred scripture in seminaries, drawing to a great extent on the relative norms handed down by the Holy See, starting with St. Pius X, who provided the first regulations in this connection, thus revealing "the expert pastor of souls." In these regulations "the main concern of the pope is that in the course of his theological studies every seminarian should have the possibility of receiving all the biblical teaching necessary to a priest in order to permit fruitful exercise of his ministry of 'instructing people to eternal salvation through word and example'; thus he stresses the explanation of the dogmatic and moral doctrine contained in the holy books, prescribes daily reading of sacred scripture, and institutes yearly examinations in the biblical disciplines too."[142]

Bea's study on progress in the interpretation of sacred scripture is pervaded by a similar approach. Its underlying principle is drawn from the encyclical *Divino afflante Spiritu*, according to which sacred scripture must become "for the future priests of the church a pure and never-failing source for their spiritual life, as well as food and strength for the sacred office of preaching."[143] In this way sacred scripture will also help the faithful "to lead a life that is holy and worthy of a Christian."[144]

Bea undoubtedly saw the task of every theologian in similar terms: "If pastors of souls must 'penetrate ever more deeply into the sublimities and profundities of supernatural truth,' and with ardent words and devotion proclaim the sublime truths of religion to peoples threatened by the most serious of dangers, theology must provide them with the necessary weapons, itself penetrating ever more deeply into the treasury of divine revelation, pointing out all the elements that can today help to provide light and guidance for humanity in its state of wretchedness."[145]

These last words clearly show that broad collaboration between the various sciences, nations and cultures also has the same basic aim, and all his explanations in fact show this concern. This is why he calls for theologians to concentrate all their efforts "on the tasks we are set *today* by the major problems of *our*

---

141. N 1952/34.
142. Biblio. 90, p. 53.
143. Biblio. 89, 104, quoting *Divino afflante Spiritu*, English translation, pp. 26-27; cf. also Biblio. 126, pp. 622, 633.
144. Biblio. 126, p. 633, quoting *Divino afflante Spiritu*, English translation, p. 17.
145. Biblio. 114, p. 38, quoting Pius XII's address to the Pontifical Gregorian University in 1953 (*AAS*, XLV [1953], 685).

own times and by the *present* needs of the church."[146] The aim is thus that of building up the kingdom of God, so that the church can be, to use the words of the Council, "in the nature of sacrament—a sign and instrument, that is, of communion with God and of unity among all men."[147]

---

146. *Ibid.*, p. 42.
147. *LG*, 1.

CHAPTER 4

THE LITURGIST

We have it on expert authority that the work for the reform of the liturgy carried out in the ten years prior to the Council in fact laid the foundations for the conciliar Constitution on the Sacred Liturgy.[1] For his part, Bea said more than once that in the ten years under consideration here, apart from his work at the Holy Office, his collaboration in this sphere accounted for the major part of his commitments.[2]

We have already seen *how* Bea entered this field.[3] Although he was not a "professional liturgist," he was given the opportunity to give a decisive spur to the beginning of liturgical reform. And this was one of the reasons why Pius XII assigned him to the "Commission of Eight" which was responsible for this reform in the ten years prior to the Council. This said, we have already explained the sense in which we shall be talking about Bea as liturgist; in other words, while recognizing the fact that he was not a liturgist by profession, we shall be considering the important work he performed in this field and the considerable credit he must be given in regard to liturgical reform.[4]

Moreover, this activity allows us to understand Bea's contributions to the conciliar discussions on liturgical reform and shows that these were not some kind of "improvisation," but that the groundwork had been laid in this period, when he was extensively reflecting on and working with the various problems in this field. We would add that this chapter will also provide a clearer view of the close link between Bea the exegete and Bea the liturgist.

In more general terms, if contemporary readers, who take for granted the great reforms brought about by the Second Vatican Council, are to appreciate the beginnings of this reform and thus also Bea's contribution, they must put themselves in the shoes of those living at that time. In 1951 Bea wrote: "The great reform is far off; I shall not live to see it," then went on to describe the renewed Easter vigil as "a fairly audacious step."[5]

Before we go on to give details of Bea's activity in the liturgical sector, we shall provide a *general view* of the framework in which he moved and worked, in other words the plans for reform and their development in the ten years under consideration.

The Commission of Eight started work in 1947, and in the years between 1947 and 1950 it drew up "the complete plan for reform of the calendar, missal, breviary, pontifical, ritual and martyrology."[6] First to appear, in 1951, was the

---

1. Cf. the well-known German liturgist J. Wagner, in BM, p. 208.
2. Cf. N 1955/94.
3. Cf. pp. 145-146 above.
4. Cf. A. Bugnini, "Ricordo del Cardinale Bea," *Notitiae*, IV (1968), 361; J. Wagner, in BM, p. 208.
5. N 1951/11.
6. Cf. Bugnini, "Ricordo del Cardinale Bea," p. 361. Cf. also A. Bugnini, *La Riforma liturgica*

renewed liturgy of the Easter vigil, but only in optional form; the reform of the whole Holy Week liturgy was published in 1955, and this was followed by a "general decree" on simplification of the rubrics.[7] Apart from this, with the constitution *Christus Dominus* Pius XII not only reformed the eucharistic fast, but gave the church the gift of evening mass. Such concessions were then considerably extended in 1957 with his motu proprio *Sacram Communionem*.[8]

Reform of Holy Week

The overall task of reform was far from easy. It was therefore decided to begin with a "test" in a particularly delicate and demanding sector, Holy Week—and indeed only one part of it, Holy Saturday. Prior to this, the corresponding service was held early in the morning, and although it had retained elements of the celebration of the Lord's resurrection, these had been to a large extent obscured both because of the time assigned to the celebration and also because of the progressive addition of other elements. The reform thus brought the celebration back to its original time during the night, so that it became the "Easter vigil." A number of extraneous elements were removed that tended to obscure the central idea of Christ's resurrection, which was symbolized by the Easter candle, and the number of readings was reduced for pastoral reasons. Then, recalling that from ancient times this night had been dedicated to the solemn conferral of baptism on catechumens, the renewal of the baptismal promises was introduced for all the faithful. After the "test case" of the Easter vigil had received a very positive reception, the commission prepared the reform of the whole of Holy Week, publishing it in 1955.[9]

Bea mentioned this reform fairly often in his letters. Referring more specifically to that of the whole of Holy Week, he noted that it had cost considerable effort, and expressed the hope that it would bear rich fruit for souls.[10] In 1951 he was almost nervously concerned to see how successful the test would be (in other words the reform that was published simply as an optional form) and was delighted that it had been well received.[11] We can imagine how delighted he must have been when he learned about the enormous success of the reform of the whole Holy Week liturgy in Germany. Although there had been very little time to prepare the relative books, the whole text had somehow been published

---

(1948-1975) (Rome, 1983), pp. 18-25. For an overview, cf. Ferdinando Antonelli, O.F.M., "Pio XII e la riforma liturgica," in *Pius XII, in memoriam* (Rome, 1984), pp. 139-142; by the same author, *Memoria sulla riforma liturgica*, S. Rituum Congreg., Sectio historica, no. 71; also A. Bugnini, *Documenta Pontificia ad instaurationem liturgicam spectantia: Pio XII*, I (1953), 72-194; II (1954), 1-102.

7. On 9 February 1957; cf. Antonelli, "Pio XII e la riforma liturgica"; also *LThK*, VII, 1278.
8. Cf. Nl 63 (1958).
9. Cf. *AAS*, XLVII (1955), 842-847; *LThK*, VII, 1278; for history prior to the reform, cf. *EncCatt*, IX, 448-453.
10. Cf. Nc 19 (1955); Ni 38 (1956).
11. Cf. N 1951/11.

in three different editions, making up a total of a million copies, which sold like hot cakes.[12] When he received this good news, Bea wrote back that on the basis of information received to date it could be said that in general terms Holy Week had been a great success that year.[13]

However, it must be added that with his usual realism he remained open to observations on any residual difficulties. When a bishop wrote to him from Germany saying that reactions to the new Holy Week had been in general positive, but that the Easter vigil seemed too long, he answered that similar observations had come in from other quarters, and that the matter would have to be discussed again before the definitive reform of the Roman Missal.[14] Two years later, when another German bishop reported a whole series of difficulties that the Easter vigil in particular was encountering in practical pastoral terms, it is interesting to see Bea answering that the reform of Holy Week had "obviously aimed at the ideal situation, but we were aware that in practice all kinds of difficulties would arise, so that it is no surprise to hear about them. . . . Such observations are not placed on the record, but we try to bear them in mind. It would therefore be most helpful if Your Excellency would set these matters out in detail, and if you would formulate a precise request as regards the hour to be assigned to the vigil . . . ; it is equally important to indicate difficulties connected with the use of Latin . . . ; it would be helpful if you would point out that it would be a good thing if Rome made certain concessions; otherwise, under pressure of circumstances, the clergy will go ahead on their own, making cuts and starting to use the vernacular."[15] It is easy to imagine what a pleasant surprise such a letter was to a pastor of souls who had previously apologized for his frankness in describing the various difficulties. In those times at least, people did not tend to expect "Rome" to show such comprehension of practical pastoral difficulties, and particularly not over the thorny problem of liturgical *language*.

Eucharistic Fast and Evening Mass

In order to understand the question under discussion here, we must remember that until 1953 there was a centuries-old rule in the church that mass could be celebrated only in the morning, or at least prior to midday. The Code of Canon Law promulgated by Benedict XV had ruled that it could be celebrated until 1 p.m.[16] Moreover, in preparation respectively for mass and communion, both priest and faithful had to abstain from any food or drink, including water, from midnight on; this was called the "eucharistic fast."[17]

---

12. Cf. Nz 50, 52 (1956).
13. Cf. Nz 52 (1956).
14. Cf. N 1956/140.
15. N 1958/324. We shall discuss the question of the use of the vernacular in the liturgy in due course.
16. Canon 821, no. 1.
17. Cf. Canon 808.

Due to circumstances that involved not only soldiers at the front but also other members of the faithful who were exposed to night-time bombing raids and similar difficulties, between 1940 and 1945 various exceptions had been made to this rule. For example, permission had in general been given to celebrate mass, and thus receive holy communion, in the afternoon, observing four hours of eucharistic fast beforehand.[18] These concessions had then been extended in various ways in view of specific situations and the applications of different bishops. When many of these special concessions were withdrawn at the end of the war, the difficulties inherent in the ancient legislation were felt all the more keenly. The rhythm of modern life made it difficult for many people to attend mass in the morning, or at least prior to midday, and also made the obligation to fast from midnight onward a particularly heavy burden. On the other hand, Pius XII's encyclical *Mediator Dei* on the liturgy (1947) exhorted all Catholics to frequent and full participation in the eucharistic sacrifice, including holy communion.

1. In this situation a German layman, Werner Maurenbrecher, a textile magnate from Krefeld, took the initiative in starting a campaign in favor of evening mass, underwriting it with his own funds and name. As early as 1944 he had started by appealing to the majority of German bishops, asking them to try to have the concession of evening mass maintained. Although he received a number of positive replies, many of his letters remained unanswered in the years 1945 and 1946, and many diocesan curias tended to be irritated by his campaign, feeling that it was enough that priests who applied could obtain permission to celebrate evening mass once a week. Maurenbrecher, however, insisted on daily evening mass.[19]

2. One of Maurenbrecher's closest advisors, Mons. Theodor Schnitzler, thinks that the industrialist's activity was one of the decisive factors leading to a change in the traditional legislation of the church in this area, and says that *Bea* was Maurenbrecher's *"most important and effective dialogue partner"* concerning this activity.[20] In 1954 Maurenbrecher thanked Bea for the help that he had given him "over a period of years" with advice on his work in support of evening mass.[21] The files contain a voluminous correspondence (sixty-six entries) between Maurenbrecher and Bea.

In 1948 Maurenbrecher managed to persuade various eminent figures in Catholic life in Germany to address an appeal to Pope Pius XII in favor of evening mass. This appeal explained that the situation was in many ways still similar to that of the war period. On the basis of experience, it pointed out how impossible it was for people such as manual workers and clerks to attend mass

---

18. Cf. Theodor Schnitzler, "Ein Laie für die Abendmesse. Ein Kapitelchen Kirchengeschichte 1940-1964," *Heiliger Dienst*, XXV/4 (1971), 1.

19. Theodor Schnitzler published extracts from many letters in his booklet, *Florilegium betreffend actio, Siegeszug der Abendmesse* (Cologne, 1972); the booklet also reproduces the article cited in our previous note.

20. ArchWit.

21. Cf. Nl 44 (1954).

in the morning or prior to midday, and also spoke of the particular difficulties of modern-day "night people." The appeal therefore requested general permission to celebrate mass in the evening. On 17 August 1948 the Congregation of the Holy Office gave a firm refusal.[22]

A short time after this, Bea (who at the time of the refusal was not yet a consultor to the Holy Office) decided to take a hand in the matter. In September 1949, he sent Maurenbrecher the following words of encouragement: "There seems to me no doubt that the goal will be achieved in time. . . . So you should continue to work calmly for this cause, but without pushing too hard. Your work will not be in vain."[23] Bea did not confine himself to words of encouragement, but added practical advice on the most effective means of achieving his goal, advising Maurenbrecher to try above all to provide irrefutable statistics. "Facts are always more impressive than a multitude of words and expressions of hope."[24] He also advised him that if a certain bishop concerned himself with the question, it would be in the best possible hands, adding: "I have always stressed that the initiative in this matter must come *from bishops.*"[25]

3. Nor was a positive decision too long in coming. On 6 January 1953, Pius XII published the constitution *Christus Dominus,*[26] which gave permission for the celebration of evening mass on Sundays, feast-days that fell during the week, the first Friday of the month, and once during the week. With regard to the obligation to observe the eucharistic fast, it laid down that water did not break the fast, in other words that it could certainly be taken; apart from this people had to abstain from food and drink for three hours prior to mass (for priests) or holy communion (for the faithful). The pope then entrusted the Holy Office with the task of drawing up detailed regulations for the application of this ruling on the eucharistic fast.

In his correspondence Bea described the pope's step in very positive terms, saying that it represented the radical reversal of a tradition at least fifteen hundred years old,[27] and that such a concession would have been unthinkable twenty years earlier.[28] He explained that the change had sought the best possible balance, taking pastoral needs into account, although without retaining all the concessions made in the very special circumstances of the war.[29] Bea had no doubt that the step would constitute a major, lasting blessing for the church.

Bea's joy was such that he showed keen interest in how the concessions were applied in different places. He sent Maurenbrecher reports on this on several occasions. In the course of 1953, for example, he wrote: "There are nineteen

---

22. Cf. Schnitzler, "Ein Laie für die Abendmesse," p. 1.
23. Cf. Schnitzler, *Florilegium betreffend actio*, p. 17; the letter is not found in our files. However, this is no reason to question Schnitzler's reference, for Bea could easily have placed it in some restricted file, so that it ended up in the Secret Vatican Archives, or somewhere else.
24. Nl 14 (1952); cf. Nl 17 (1952).
25. Nl 7 (1951); cf. Nl 15 (1952); 17 (1952).
26. *AAS*, XLV (1953), 15-32; the relative instruction of the Holy Office is found in *ibid.*, pp. 47-56; cf. *LThK*, I, 35-36.
27. Cf. Nl 50 (1956).
28. Cf. N 1953-119.
29. Cf. *ibid.*

churches in Rome where mass is celebrated in the evening on Sundays and feast-days, and in some of these churches all the seats are taken half an hour before the service starts. The movement is making headway." Evidently in reference to Maurenbrecher's desire for evening mass every day, Bea added: "It remains to be seen whether further concessions are useful or necessary. In any case, things have got off to a good start."[30] A few years later he reported that there were now fifty-two churches in Rome where evening mass was celebrated, and that such masses were announced in the *Osservatore Romano*.[31]

Bea also continued with his work as advisor. A few days after the publication of the apostolic constitution, he wrote to Maurenbrecher saying that a certain kind of propaganda could now be suspended, and that he should instead concentrate on persuading people who could not attend mass in the morning that they should make use of the concession and attend in the evening.[32] He did, however, note that the measure was dictated by necessity, and that it could also entail risks for the sanctification of the whole of the Lord's day, in other words the day could be used simply for personal pleasure, so that the Lord was given nothing but that half hour in the evening.[33]

4. Various problems very soon started to appear. On the one hand, it became increasingly clear that it was not enough to have evening mass only once a week. On the other hand, the regulations concerning the eucharistic fast were soon seen to be too complicated for the majority of Catholics. When someone asked for Bea's advice, he replied that the rules in force reflected "the specific will of the Holy Father, who undoubtedly expressed it deliberately in order not to break with a centuries-old tradition," and added: "For the time being no congregation can change it."[34] On another occasion he said that in view of the fact that a radical change in a very ancient tradition was involved, they must move very cautiously and examine practical results before taking further steps. However, he immediately referred to such further steps: "The main thing is that the stone has been set rolling; everything else is simply a question of time. We must earnestly pray that the development will not take too long."[35]

5. Less than six months after this last letter, on 19 March 1957 Pius XII published a motu proprio entitled *Sacram Communionem*, in which he authorized bishops to allow the celebration of evening mass every day if a considerable number of the faithful wanted this; and as regards the eucharistic fast, he ruled that solid foods must be abstained from for three hours, and liquids for one.[36]

---

30. Nl 33 (1953).
31. Cf. Nl 50 (1956).
32. Cf. Nl 28 (1953); also Nl 49 (1956). In 1955 Bea reassured Maurenbrecher over a "warning" from the Holy Office (cf. *AAS*, XLVII [1955], 218), saying that it in no way intended limiting the concession granted, but merely wanted to warn people that it was granted for the spiritual good of the faithful and not for the solemnization of congresses and similar events.
33. Cf. Nl 35 (1953). We can of course wonder if the same danger does not also exist for anyone who gives the Lord nothing but half an hour in the morning.
34. N 1956/50. Bea advised other people to apply for an indult; cf. N 1953/119.
35. Nl 50 (1956).
36. Cf. *AAS*, IL (1957), 177-178.

"This is a great and decisive step on the part of the Holy Father," wrote Bea. "It is his wish that in the interests of the faithful evening mass should be permitted everywhere." He went on to encourage Maurenbrecher to work for a positive attitude toward evening mass among the faithful, and the fervent use of holy communion, "so that the fruit may correspond fully to the Holy Father's courageous step."[37] When Bea was told about difficulties and resistance, even on the part of certain bishops, he answered: "The will of the Holy Father is now clear, and all we need is patience. With time things will settle down on their own, and evening mass will become an established fact. We must allow enough time for people to get used to it, and for things to develop."[38]

To conclude this section, we would note that a few weeks after the death of Pius XII, Bea wrote to Maurenbrecher as follows: "With the apostolic constitution *Christus Dominus* and the motu proprio *Sacram Communionem*, the late pontiff built a monument for himself that will withstand the centuries."[39]

The Question of the Use of the Vernacular in the Liturgy

In order to illustrate the attitude found in certain official quarters in Rome concerning the use of the vernacular in the liturgy, I would refer back to an episode mentioned in a previous chapter. At the First Pastoral-Liturgical Congress, which was held in Assisi in 1956, the Prefect of the Congregation of Rites was irritated by the applause that greeted requests for reform as concerns language, which led Bea to omit the passages in his own paper that would have elicited similar applause.[40]

To tell the truth, certain concessions did already exist, for example that of having the readings in the vernacular, maybe after they had first been heard in Latin. There were also concessions concerning the use of popular hymns, but apart from this, mass was celebrated in Latin, from start to finish. Let us give an example provided by G.A. Martimort. In 1949 a French bishop obtained permission from Rome to have the readings in the vernacular as well as Latin. Indeed, in view of the lack of clarity over the areas of competence of the various Vatican departments, he obtained *two* sets of permission: the Holy Office granted a simple, straightforward one, while the Congregation of Rites (which was then the department in charge of liturgical matters) gave its permission in the form of an indult that was valid for three years and entailed the condition that the reading in French should be made by a cleric and not by a deacon or subdeacon. After this all the French bishops obtained the same faculty one by one, so that it was eventually decided to publish a bilingual lectionary for the whole of France. In order to make sure of obtaining approval for its publication,

---

37. Nl 51 (1957).
38. Nl 52 (1957); cf. 64 (1959).
39. Nl 63 (1958).
40. Cf. pp. 147-148 above.

Martimort himself suggested that the Bishop of Rouen, J.-M. Martin, should not apply to the Congregation of Rites, but to the Holy Office, using "the good offices of Bea" for this purpose.[41] This was the situation, and it is against this background that we must see and evaluate what we shall be saying about Bea's attitude in this matter.

1. A first glimpse of Bea's views on this subject is found in 1953. A strong supporter of the vernacular had written to him, saying, among other things, that for anyone who did not have the German Schott missal the Latin mass was simply a familiar but incomprehensible ceremony, whereas in the vernacular the mass would become a living thing, almost "a television." Bea answered: "I am less in agreement with what you write about mass in the vernacular. The question is much more complicated than you seem to think. When we come down to it, it is not so easy to ignore the fact that the church is a world-wide church, and if science and technology are currently searching for a language that can be understood internationally and does not raise barriers between different countries and peoples, we must consider whether it is reasonable for the church, today of all times, to give up the advantage it already has. If an Italian goes to Germany today and goes to mass, he knows that it is the mass and can follow it as he does at home; this would not be possible if the mass were in German. And just think how widespread travel has become today. Various other considerations should be added that make it advisable to proceed very very slowly in this matter."[42]

Although Bea's reaction was not completely negative and was elicited partly by the over-enthusiastic and radical suggestion put forward by his correspondent, who did not seem to realize the problems involved, it is certainly surprising. In order to avoid misunderstandings, we should immediately add a thought expressed in another letter written the same year. Bea is commenting on the liturgical exaggerations of a German priest who, he says, has made the faithful lose their taste for mass because they feel forced to "participate." An elderly woman has reacted by saying: "Leave us to pray in peace." And Bea adds that, even so, the use of the vernacular need not be eliminated to too great an extent; indeed, the so-called "German sung mass"[43] is "tolerated with a very benign eye" by the Holy See, and there is no longer such opposition to it in Rome. "At a time when people are being so much subjected to the seductions of radio and movies, we must make an effort to grow closer to the soul of the people."[44]

2. Later on, Bea had to deal with the same question in two practical contexts: firstly, to defend the specific concessions that the Holy See had made to the dioceses of Germany in this sphere; and, secondly, to help find a solution to the problems that Latin caused in mission lands.

First let us describe the *concessions that the Holy See had granted in Germany.* These involved various forms of active participation of the faithful

---

41. Cf. ArchWit.
42. N 1953/80b; cf. also N 1958/88.
43. We shall discuss this in due course.
44. N 1953/148. For Bea's reaction to excesses in this area, see also N 1958/88.

in the mass. The first form was what was known as the "simple dialogue mass," where all the people gave the Latin responses that the servers normally gave; then, while the priest read the variable parts and the readings in a lower tone, a reader said them in German.[45] In another form, popular hymns were sung in German during the introit, offertory, "Sanctus" and distribution of communion, and after the blessing.[46] Similarly, in the sung mass, instead of singing the "Gloria," Creed, "Sanctus" and "Agnus Dei" in Latin, texts with the same content were sung in German.[47] Lastly, there were popular German hymns which used Gregorian melodies, or else hymns composed in the Gregorian style.[48] All these forms of use of the vernacular had been examined in Rome in 1943, and in view of their relative antiquity and the pastoral good they produced, the Holy See had allowed the bishops the freedom of retaining them.[49] It should be added that Pius XII was personally familiar with the situation because of the ten years he had spent as nuncio in Berlin. Moreover, it should be borne in mind that it was particularly in Germany that Lutheranism had so strongly encouraged the liturgy and popular hymns in the vernacular.

However, certain liturgists, especially experts in sacred music, saw such usages as contrary to the authentic spirit of the church and the liturgy, and felt they had a vital duty to uphold the exclusive use of Latin and Gregorian chant. Not content with this, they worked behind the scenes to persuade the Holy See to cancel the indult, and even spread rumors that a measure of this kind was already in the pipeline. For their part, the German bishops pointed out the harm this would do the liturgical movement in general and religious life in particular; this applied especially in East Germany, because under the communist regime the activity of the church was strictly limited to liturgical celebrations. Abolition of the indult would also seriously undermine the authority of the bishops, who had been publishing new official prayer and hymn books in those post-war years, encouraged precisely by the concessions contained in the indult.[50]

Bearing in mind what we said in a previous chapter about Bea's participation in the Assisi congress,[51] it is easy to see which camp he belonged to. In particular, his letters reflect the anxieties of German and French liturgists with regard to the congress on sacred music that was to be held in Paris in 1957. It was feared that difficulties could arise similar to those met with at the previous congress (which was held in Vienna) and that the congress could be exploited to the

---

45. *Gemeinschaftsmesse* in German. Cf. *LThK*, IV, 655-656, with bibliography.

46. *Betsingmesse* in German; cf. *ibid.*

47. *Deutsches Hochamt* in German; cf. *ibid.*

48. Cf. "Deutsche Gregorianik," *LThK*, III, 265.

49. For the relative indult, cf. *Liturgisches Jahrbuch*, III (Trier, 1953), 108-110. Ample information on the structures of these different forms is found in N 1958/301. For the sake of brevity and ease of reference, we shall use the term "the indult" to cover all such concessions.

50. Cf. N 1954/165. We shall in due course discuss the deeper reasons behind the attitudes of the two sides in the debate. According to G.A. Martimort, the representatives of the pastoral-liturgical approach used to refer to their opponents simply as "musicians" since they were often experts in sacred music.

51. Cf. p. 147 above.

detriment of the liturgical-pastoral movement. Bea was kept informed of developments, and his advice and assistance were sought. He felt that the danger was far from negligible, and he therefore insisted that the French bishops should make their authority felt. He repeatedly advised that the bishops' representative for the liturgy should come to Rome to discuss the question with officials at the Holy Office and the Congregation of Rites.[52] G.A. Martimort says that the danger was in fact averted. The organizers of the congress received detailed instructions in this connection, and a letter from the Secretariat of State—obtained, in Martimort's opinion, through Bea's good offices—warned that discussions harmful to the liturgical movement were to be avoided at the meeting.[53]

3. At about the same time Bea also became involved in the problems of the *liturgy, particularly the use of Latin, in mission lands.* He was told about preparations for the missionary liturgical congress to be held at Nijmegen in 1959. Some anxieties were being expressed in this connection: people said that the missionary religious congregations had insufficient grounding in the relative questions, and it was also feared that the congress might impede the granting of indults on the part of the Congregation of Propaganda Fide, the Vatican department responsible for missions. It was therefore suggested that the congress should be postponed for one year and then take place within the framework of the international eucharistic congress to be held in Munich in 1960, since "that would stir up less controversy."[54] Bea answered that one of the organizers had been to see him and gone over the whole program with him, and that it appeared that "technical and financial preparations for the Nijmegen congress are too far advanced to be suspended at this point." In order to reassure his correspondent, he added: "The program itself, which has also been definitively fixed and approved [by the organizers], contains nothing alarming, and has been 'almost approved' even here in Rome." As regards the attitude of the missionary religious congregations, he observed: "Of course, I cannot say what they think about this matter."[55]

This first contact soon offered an opportunity for a further step. Those in charge of the Institute for Mission Apologetics asked Bea to present the pope with the book by the Jesuit Fathers J. Hofinger and Kellner, on liturgical renewal in the missions.[56] A distinguished figure at the Congregation of Rites, they said, had studied the book in detail, and realizing the importance of the questions considered, had made two strong recommendations: first, it should be translated at least into French, if not also into Italian, and second, it should be presented to the Holy Father. Bea (who, as we know, was not new to such requests) willingly agreed, submitting it, as usual, together with a written appraisal of his own. The pope was pleased to accept the gift, and entrusted Bea with the task of thanking the authors. In the relative letter Bea wrote: "The Holy Father is

52. Cf. N 1957/70, 72, 87, 128.
53. ArchWit. For the further developments, cf. N 1957/260, 262.
54. Cf. N 1957/260.
55. *Ibid.*
56. The original title was *Liturgische Erneuerung in der Weltmission.*

very happy over your intention of having the sacred liturgy bear fruit for the great cause of the missions, insofar as actual situations permit and in conformity with the directives issued by the Holy See for the liturgical movement. With this understanding, the Holy Father invokes the rich blessings of the Lord for your initiatives, and expresses best wishes for their success."[57] Bea added his own thanks for the copy of the book he had received, saying that he would study it carefully and that he hoped it would provide him with helpful elements for the work of the commission in charge of liturgical reform.[58]

The question of the use of Latin in the *Roman Breviary* was a separate problem, and arose from the fact that a knowledge of Latin was on the steady wane among priests. A well-known catechetical expert approached Father Bea, explaining the difficulties that the lessons in the breviary raised so far as comprehension was concerned—with the inevitable effects on fruit. Although Bea recognized the problem, he also appreciated the reasons normally advanced in favor of retaining Latin. In conclusion, however, he advised the man to try to interest the bishops of mission lands, for the problem was certainly more keenly felt and pressing there; and Rome would certainly be more willing to listen and have the question studied in greater depth if applications came from that quarter.[59]

The Problems Raised by the Instruction on the Liturgy and Sacred Music

We now return to the problems raised by the "musicians." One of the rumors they spread was that an instruction on the sacred liturgy and sacred music was being drafted in Rome which would abolish the indult in all its various forms as these affected the life of the German dioceses. It was in fact true that the Congregation of Rites was preparing an instruction, and Bea was therefore bombarded with letters asking if there was any truth in these rumors.[60] Bea went straight to the horse's mouth, and received the very encouraging information that special indults were explicitly recognized and safeguarded in the instruction. He was therefore able to calm his correspondents' fears.[61]

1. The instruction was eventually published on 1 October 1958, a few days prior to the death of Pius XII.[62] There was immediate alarm in Germany. Although the instruction did contain a passage stating that specific exceptions to the general rule on the use of Latin should remain in force,[63] there was another

---

57. N 1958/60. We can see that congratulations and good wishes are cautiously formulated: "insofar as actual situations permit" (in order not to import European and western problems into mission lands) and "in conformity with the directives issued by the Holy See."

58. Cf. *ibid.*

59. Cf. N 1959/56.

60. Cf. N 1958/122.

61. Cf. N 1958/122, 123, 124, 176.

62. Cf. N 1958/236.

63. Cf. *AAS*, L (1958), 636 (para. 13c).

passage that said that it was severely forbidden for the "commentator" or the faithful to say parts of the proper and canon out loud together with the priest, either in Latin or in translation.[64] And this latter passage had been approved by the pope "in specific terms in all its parts," a formula that gave it special force.[65] If we recall what was said above about the content of the indult granted to Germany in 1943, it is not difficult to see that this formula withdrew what the indult had granted. On the other hand, the first formula in the instruction stated that already existing exceptions to the general rule on the use of Latin should remain in force. The problem was therefore that of which of the two formulae was to be given precedence.

2. Bea was seriously sick when the instruction was published, and did not recover fully until the end of October. As soon as he could, however, he did all he possibly could, starting with the specific case of Germany. In less than two months, there were ten letters devoted to this question, accompanied by various documents. Let us now take a look at developments.

As early as 4 November, Bea says that he had discussed the question with Cardinals Frings and Wendel, and learned that in the course of the recent conclave (which elected John XXIII) they had spoken about it with Cardinal Ottaviani, who had seemed very well-disposed and had invited them to make precise proposals. And here Bea advances the pastoral reasons in favor of retaining the indult.[66]

In the same letter Bea also clears up the question of areas of authority, saying that the language to be used in the liturgy customarily comes under the Holy Office, whereas the Congregation of Rites is responsible for the liturgy as such. Bearing this situation in mind, he undertakes to obtain the necessary clarification. In a letter addressed to the most influential person at the Congregation of Rites, he explains the juridical basis of the indult granted to Germany in 1943, then, appealing to the passage in the instruction that said that existing legitimate exceptions to the rule on the use of Latin should remain in force, he concludes with the proposal that the indult should thus be retained, while making sure that it is not extended, and also that practice should not vary too widely from one German diocese to another.[67]

A week later he reports that the person he has applied to has fully accepted his suggestions and that the Cardinal Prefect of the Congregation of Rites also seems disposed to see things in the same light.[68] Even so, in the same letter, he tells his correspondent that it might be helpful if he sent Bea a statement on the pastoral (not juridical!) reasons in favor of retaining the indult in Germany, and says that this could possibly prove helpful to him in the future.[69]

The situation in Germany was eventually solved according to hopes, with a

---

64. Cf. *ibid.*, pp. 636-637 (para. 14b-c).
65. Cf. N 1958/301.
66. Cf. N 1958/282; also 1958/301, 308.
67. Cf. N 1958/293.
68. Cf. N 1958/301.
69. Cf. *ibid.*

letter of 23 December 1958 (almost a Christmas gift) in which the Holy Office fully confirmed the 1943 indult, with the sole proviso that the concessions should not be further extended.[70] Reporting this on 28 December, Bea observes: "I hope that a solution will also be found for other countries with similar situations." Then he adds a piece of news that is like an foreshadowing of further progress: "You will be happy to learn that the mass celebrated at eleven o'clock in St. Peter's[71] took the form of a dialogue mass with singing. . . . This is surely not insignificant."[72]

In the meantime, Bea had received similar requests for assistance and advice from *Switzerland*. He answered by describing what the German bishops had done, although he did stress that the situation was different in Switzerland, since this country could not appeal to an indult. Despite this, he said they should not give up hope, but should address an inquiry to the Holy Office as to whether they should consider numbers 14a-b of the instruction as abolishing the type of simple dialogue mass and dialogue mass with singing that had been prescribed in the official prayer and hymn books of the Swiss dioceses for a long time now. They should add that there were many pastoral reasons against such an abolition, and specify these reasons. They should conclude by pointing out that it was not a question of the sung mass, but of various forms of participation in the read mass, for which no norms yet existed.[73]

3. The instruction raised much greater problems in *mission lands*, and Bea received letters saying that Germany could at least appeal to an indult, whereas the missions had never had one, so that the rigid rule of Latin weighed on them doubly. Moreover, the liturgical movement had already been in existence for thirty years in Germany and they had missals with parallel translations and explanations, etc., while the mission lands had none of these advantages. The situation was aggravated by the fact that their pastors of souls tended to hold closely to the saying "Roma locuta, causa finita," to the serious detriment of souls; in other words, the faithful attended mass mechanically, instead of "with adoration in spirit and truth." "If," said one correspondent, "we are not even allowed the possibility of introducing people into a full awareness of the mass through intelligent participation in the low mass, we shall be lost." The correspondent in question gave a practical example. That year a liturgical conference for the whole of India had been held under the aegis of the bishops. This conference had drafted a text for a dialogue mass of the type needed in mission lands, and the relative booklet was about to be published. And now the instruction was ruling out such a thing.[74]

Bea's reaction to this last letter was almost immediate: "I am not surprised by your complaints, and they are not the only ones I have heard. It is clear that the faithful, especially in mission lands, should accompany low mass with

---

70. Cf. N 1958/330.
71. This was almost certainly the mass celebrated by the pope.
72. N 1958/331.
73. Cf. N 1958/308.
74. Cf. N 1958/311.

prayers in the local language. The question does not concern the Congregation of Rites, but the Holy Office. Cardinal Ottaviani, who was asked about this by two German cardinals during the conclave, and then again by Bishop Landers-dorfer (relator for liturgical questions at the Fulda Episcopal Conference) about two weeks ago, has given questioners the most reassuring answers—although without referring to the indult. In view of the fact that the reasons given as regards Germany are all the more valid in mission lands, the Holy Office should consider the question even without reference to the German situation. The simplest way would be to raise the matter with Cardinal Agagianian as soon as possible, sending him a written memorandum and asking him to submit it to Cardinal Ottaviani. In this way the question will soon be cleared up."[75] In another letter he added that Cardinal Agagianian, who would be attending the Conference of Bishops in Manila as Papal Legate, would certainly bring suggestions in this connection. "It is probably a special disposition of providence that the instruction should involuntarily have provided an opportunity for a question that is important for all the members of the church to be studied in a broader context."[76]

The Liturgy for the Good of Souls

We have repeatedly referred to the "conflict" between experts in sacred music and the supporters of a more pastoral approach to the liturgy, and we should now take a slightly closer look at these two ways of viewing the liturgy, for it is only

---

75. The cardinal was Prefect of the Congregation of Propaganda Fide, as the department responsible for missions was then called.

76. N 1958/314. The well-known German moral theologian Bernhard Häring describes the following episode: "Several times in the years 1948-1951 I tried to sponsor the cause of the use of the vernacular in the liturgy with the relevant section of the Congregation of Rites. My confrere, who was vice-relator general of the liturgical section of the congregation, finally asked me to draw up a memorandum on the question, because he had obtained Father Bea's agreement to present it to Pope Pius XII. We agreed to exclude the canon of the mass from the request for the vernacular. Indeed, we both felt that the question of the vernacular concerning the canon would remain taboo for a long time, and that it would therefore be imprudent to try to push too far. When Bea saw the memorandum to my surprise he observed that he saw no reason to exclude the canon from the request; indeed, the canon concerned the whole community of participants in a special way. It seems that Bea also had the impression that the exclusion of the canon had been due to an misplaced sense of diplomacy. However, the requests contained in the memorandum were not in fact granted" (BM, p. 206). We confine ourselves here to reporting the evidence that concerns us, leaving aside the conclusions the witness drew. In his interview "Fede, Storia, Morale" (Rome, 1989), Häring also explains that Bea had simply encouraged him to express himself "frankly" (p. 50) and does not mention the canon of the mass. Anyone who bears in mind the amount of ground we have covered in explaining Bea's complex attitude to the vernacular in the liturgy will certainly understand why we simply say that these statements leave us puzzled, for how can they be made to fit in with everything else we know about Bea's attitude in this connection?

within this framework that we can understand what Bea really means when he speaks about the *"pastoral* value of the word of God in the liturgy."[77]

Roughly speaking, the experts in sacred music claimed that the liturgy is essentially praise of God, and that placing it "at the service of human beings" means debasing it—or, rather, perverting it. Of course not all of these experts expressed the theory of their conception in these terms, but they did *in practice* approach the liturgy, inasmuch as it is praise of God, as something divorced from pastoral considerations, and from what it means and should mean for souls. The group of "musicians" who, as we have seen, created difficulties for the supporters of a pastoral approach to the liturgy were motivated, at least in practice, by a similar view. On the other hand we should recall that in the storm aroused by the instruction on the liturgy and sacred music, those who defended the use of the vernacular placed particular stress on pastoral reasons, in other words, the need for the faithful to be able to participate actively in the liturgy and thus obtain the maximum fruit. Even prior to the problems raised by this instruction, this view had predominated at the pastoral-liturgical congress held in Assisi. It was in this context that Bea developed his own thinking on the pastoral aspect of the liturgy, so that the present explanation provides the indispensable *background or basis* for the subject as he approached it, in other words, from the perspective of the *pastoral* value of the word of God in the liturgy.

Bea starts with the beginnings of the reform in those years, saying that "anyone who analyzes the several steps taken by the Holy See in the field of the liturgy in the last decade will easily recognize that common to all of them is the urgent desire to draw the greatest possible pastoral benefits from each of these elements."[78] Sometimes this intention on the part of the church is mentioned explicitly, for example in the reform of Holy Week and in the introduction to the new Latin translation of the psalter.[79] In other cases, the actual initiative taken by the church can in various ways show the intention of obtaining the maximum benefit for souls; this is the case, for example, with the time factor in the granting of evening mass, the approval of the rituals in the vernacular, and also the warm recommendation of popular religious singing found in the encyclical *Musicae sacrae* of Pius XII.[80]

It is not difficult to see that the above-mentioned facts indicate a very definite *general manner of viewing the liturgy.* Bea himself defines this when he draws the following conclusion from his line of reasoning: "The emphasis is not therefore everywhere and always solely on the praise of God, but, as the Holy Father says in the encyclical *Mediator Dei,* also on 'the union of our souls with Christ, and their sanctification by the divine Redeemer, so that Christ will be glorified, and through him and in him, the most holy Trinity.' "[81]

77. Biblio. 111.
78. *Ibid.*, p. 632.
79. Cf. *ibid.* For the new Latin psalter, cf. *AAS*, XXXVII (1945), 67, and *EB*, no. 575.
80. Cf. *AAS*, XLVIII (1956), 5-25.
81. Biblio. 111, p. 633, quoting *Mediator Dei*; cf. *AAS*, XXXIX (1947), 583.

Bea realizes full well the fundamental importance of this statement, and in order to clarify it further he raises the following *objection*: "Does not all this mean *depriving the sacred liturgy of its sublime dignity* of divine worship and putting it instead at the service of men?"[82] The objection seems all the more serious in that Bea has spoken of the pastoral value of the word of God precisely within the framework of the eucharistic liturgy, so that he seems to be placing the eucharist itself, the climax and center of the liturgy, at the service of humanity.

He answers in the first place by referring back to the historical part of the address.[83] "If holy church," he says, "guided by the Holy Spirit, has taken this course from her very first days, certainly the course is not erroneous and is not contrary to the dignity of the liturgy."[84] This way of acting on the part of the church is described as follows in the liturgical encyclical of Pius XII, *Mediator Dei*: "Whenever their pastors can summon a little group of the faithful together, they set up an altar on which they proceed to offer the sacrifice, and around which are ranged all the other rites appropriate for the saving of souls and for the honor due to God." Among these "other rites" the encyclical includes "the reading of the law, the prophets, the gospel and the apostolic epistles; and last of all the homily or sermon in which the official head of the congregation recalls and explains the practical bearing of the commandments of the divine Master and the chief events of his life, combining instruction with appropriate exhortation and illustration for the benefit of all his listeners."[85] Can we doubt, asks Bea, that if people listen devoutly to the word of God in order to accept it readily and gratefully into their hearts and prepare themselves to put it into practice with an authentic Christian life, this constitutes authentic and valid worship of God?[86]

In this connection, Bea refers to the internal structure of the eucharistic celebration itself, which is not only sacrifice, but also "communion": while we offer God the sacrifice of his Son in it, God responds by giving himself to us as nourishment for our souls. Through the goodness of God we therefore have a giving and a receiving: people who have been prepared by listening to the word of God and its explanation offer God the perfect sacrifice of his Son, and in holy communion receive the bread of life, the pledge of eternal life, in exchange.

Let us close this section by recalling the above-cited words of Pius XII, who said that the liturgy aims *also* at uniting our souls with Christ and sanctifying them. This does not, however, mean simply subordinating worship of God to human beings, for our union with Christ and our sanctification in turn have a view to the glory of Christ and of the most holy Trinity.

---

82. Biblio. 111, p. 644.
83. Cf. *ibid.*, pp. 633-637.
84. *Ibid.*, p. 644.
85. *Mediator Dei*, English translation, p. 10; cf. Biblio. 111, p. 644.
86. Cf. Biblio. 111, p. 644.

The Pastoral Value of the Word of God in the Liturgy

Having thus cleared up the question of principle, Bea applies his conception of the pastoral effect of the liturgy to that important element of the liturgy represented by the reading and explanation of the word of God. He takes the teaching provided by the *history of the church* as a solid starting-point, summarizing his explanations in this connection by saying that the nourishment that the church, in her maternal concern, offered her children in the times of persecution and the great doctrinal struggles was the *lectio continua* of sacred scripture and its explanation; in other words, their nourishment was, "besides the eucharistic bread, the bread of the word of God, which had to fortify them, arouse them and strengthen them."[87] The fortitude of the martyrs and the steadfastness of their faith were in the first place the fruit of the Lord's grace; but their doctrinal basis was undoubtedly the teaching drawn from the ever-living source of the reading and explanation of the holy books.[88]

This said, Bea goes on to wonder about "the most profound and decisive reason for this marvelous efficacy of holy scripture." He answers in the light of the teaching of the church on the inspiration of sacred scripture, saying that its efficacy lies in the very fact that it is the word of God himself, and he explains that he is not saying simply that it *contains* the word of God—as is the case with the catechism or a manual of religious teaching—but that it *is* the word of God. In virtue of the charism known as inspiration, God, the eternal Truth, uses the faculties of the human author in a truly exceptional manner as instrument; without depriving him of his personality, nature and character, he makes him express "all those things and only those things which he himself should command." Here it is no longer the person who speaks, but the Holy Spirit, "who spoke by the prophets," "the Spirit of truth" (John 14:17), who teaches the truth by means of the sacred books.[89] This is why, to use the words of Pius XII in the encyclical *Divino afflante Spiritu*, "the sacred pages, written under the inspiration of the Spirit of God, are of themselves rich in original meaning; endowed with a divine power, they have their own value; adorned with heavenly beauty, they radiate of themselves light and splendor, provided they are so fully and accurately explained by the interpreter that all the treasures of wisdom and prudence, therein contained, are brought to light."[90]

In order to provide a more precise explanation of this efficacy of the word of God, some people have tried to describe it as a sacrament in the strict sense of the term. Bea rules this out, although he also rules out the other extreme, in other words, the view that compares this efficacy with that of the sacramentals, which is drawn from the accompanying prayer of the church. Rather than giving

---

87. *Ibid.*, p. 637.
88. Cf. *ibid.*
89. Cf. *ibid.*, pp. 639.
90. *Divino afflante Spiritu*, English translation, p. 18. Cf. Biblio. 111, p. 639.

a definition of his own, Bea simply indicates the words that the priest says after the reading of the gospel: "By the words of the holy gospel may our sins be blotted out."[91]

The efficacy of the word of God as such is not the only thing involved here. In our case there is also the fact that the reading and explanation of the word of God *within the framework of the eucharist* are positioned in a particularly privileged setting—precisely that of the eucharistic sacrifice. There are a number of elements at work here: the atmosphere of the community celebration; the priest who speaks as the master sent by God and the church to guide consciences, or the pastor entrusted with the task of leading people to eternal salvation; special preparation through the penitential act and prayers; and, last but by no means least, the fact that this reading and explanation are linked to the eucharistic sacrifice, in other words to its unique efficacy in obtaining special graces. All these elements mean that the reading and explanation of sacred scripture within the eucharistic celebration are certainly much more effective than any other form of teaching or study that may take place outside the liturgy.[92]

Having mentioned the ancient use of the *lectio continua* of sacred scripture in the liturgy, Bea comes to the specific problem of reform of this part of the liturgy. We do know that in the ancient church such continuous reading was interrupted only for the great feasts. Bea also emphasizes the special place that the *homily* had in ancient times, in other words the explanation of the passage of sacred scripture, particularly the gospel, that had been read—as opposed to homilies on freely chosen subjects. Thus he also mentions the pressing hopes expressed by "zealous pastors of souls" that the fairly limited number of suitable readings from scripture should be increased in some appropriate form, for example with a three-year or four-year cycle.[93] And here he also points out the importance of the vernacular, so that the faithful can receive and understand the actual reading first-hand, inasmuch as it is made in the framework of the liturgy.

In conclusion, Bea stresses the *intimate relationship* between reading and explanation of the word of God and the eucharistic sacrifice. In the historical part of his address he shows that both paganism and Israel kept sacrificial worship and teaching of doctrine separate, whereas from the earliest days of the church both elements were found united in the one eucharistic celebration (cf. Acts 20:7-12; also John 14–17), which represents a completely new departure and indicates the unique character of the worship of the church.[94] Bea therefore finds it *licit to conclude*: "This mystical union of the word of God and the bread of life which is wonderfully realized in the sacred liturgy is . . . a special gift, rather a unique gift, which the divine Spouse has given his immaculate bride, the church."[95]

Bea then applies the above-cited principle of "giving and receiving" found

91. Cf. Biblio. 111, p. 640.
92. Cf. *ibid.*, pp. 641-644.
93. Cf. *ibid.*, p. 643.
94. Cf. *ibid.*, p. 635.
95. *Ibid.*, p. 645.

in the liturgy, and shows that the union of the two elements is not something extrinsic but concerns the very essence of the elements in question. In other words, when Christians hear and receive the word of God, prepare their souls to adore God, their Lord and Creator, "in spirit and in truth," and offer him the perfect gift of the infinite sacrifice of the God-Man, in exchange they receive from God the precious gift of grace which flows from the eucharistic sacrifice and helps them to carry out the will of God ever more perfectly, as this is manifested to them in the word of God.[96]

The Priest, "Minister of the Word"

Bea takes this mystical union between word of God and bread of life as the basis for a particular *theology of the priesthood*, in which the priest is not only "minister of the sacrament" but also essentially "minister of the word." In him, the word of God must therefore become, so to speak, flesh of his flesh and spirit of his spirit, just as the eucharistic bread becomes flesh of his flesh and spirit of his spirit. In him, the liturgical movement and the biblical movement must meet, merge, and so to speak find their completion. "A priest who knew well how to celebrate the holy sacrifice, the 'breaking of bread,' but did not know how to break the bread of the word of God to the faithful, would be only half a priest."[97]

In this context Bea explains the vital importance of biblical studies for future priests and their liturgical pastoral ministry. Pius XII's document on the most fitting way of promoting biblical studies also provides an outline liturgical-pastoral program for this purpose, saying that a deep knowledge and love of sacred scripture are the best way of preparing priests to understand the liturgy correctly and celebrate it worthily.[98]

The *training* received in seminaries must then continue throughout a priest's whole life. "And if in the many labors of today's apostolic ministry there may not be time enough for a deep and fairly broad study of the holy books, the priest always has one thing, his *breviary* with the scriptural lessons which the church puts into his hands with the precise obligation of making use of them every day."[99]

Approving the new Latin translation of the psalter for use in the breviary, Pius XII had this to say: "Out of our pastoral concern and our fatherly charity toward those, both men and women, consecrated to God, it is our earnest hope that from now on they should daily draw more copious light, grace and consolation from recitation of the divine office, and that in these times that are so difficult for the church this should imbue them with enlightenment and strength for an ever closer imitation of the models of sanctity that so clearly shine forth in the Psalms, and

---

96. Cf. *ibid.*
97. *Ibid.*.
98. Cf. *ibid.*, p. 646. The author is referring to the instruction of the Pontifical Biblical Commission on the method of teaching sacred scripture; cf. *AAS*, XLII (1950), 495; *EB*, no. 592.
99. *Ibid.*, p. 647.

that they should feel moved to nourish and foster in themselves the affections of divine love, courageous fortitude and devout penitence that the Holy Spirit kindles within us through the reading of the Psalms."[100]

This context explains the keen spirit in which Bea set about the task received from Pius XII of preparing the new Latin translation of the Old Testament readings, and then the corrected version of a new choice of New Testament readings for the Roman Breviary. As we know, this latter work, which was carried out under Bea's chairmanship, took ten whole years (1949-1959). Here it is particularly easy to understand his insistence that the choice of biblical readings in the breviary should be recast in a way that would not only offer a greater variety and wealth, but would also include all the essential texts of the history of salvation. In the address under consideration here, he says that "a suitable choice of biblical passages, which would be useful at the same time to the priest's ascetical life and to his pastoral ministry, a choice which is desired by many ministers of God, is certainly one of the wishes of the church. It was already one of the objectives of the breviary reform projected by Pius X, but only begun by him."[101]

* * *

Let us conclude by quoting the words of the distinguished German liturgist J. Wagner: "I can certainly suppose that two great services and thus merits [of Father Bea] as concerns the liturgical renewal are known to wider circles: his leading position in preparing the new Latin translation of the psalter, which set consideration of the reform of the breviary in motion, and then his work concerning the reform of the Easter vigil, which acted as a signal for the general liturgical reform." The author adds: "In the ten years preceding the Council, when (although we were not aware of this) the foundations of the conciliar constitution on the liturgy were being laid through worldwide collaboration, Father Bea was always our friend and advisor in our problems and sometimes in our major difficulties."[102] These last words in particular reflect the specific features of this aspect of Father Bea's activity as it is found in his letters from these years. This correspondence contains such a wealth of information that we were able to use it as a foundation for the whole of the present chapter. It shows that Father Bea was not satisfied simply with working with the respective commission, but that he placed much of his precious time at the service of the reform, acting as a living link between those responsible for reform and the actual circumstances of the church. He explained the reform, provided encouragement over its implementation, accepted further suggestions and ideas, and reassured those who became impatient. The vast scope and fruitfulness of this activity will be appreciated fully only when we are able to read and comment on these letters in the light of the complex and intense spiritual activity of those years.

100. Pius XII, Motu proprio *In cotidianis precibus*, in *AAS*, XXXVII (1945), 67; *EB*, no. 575. Cf. Biblio. 111, pp. 632-633.

101. Biblio. 111, p. 647.

102. BM, p. 208.

CHAPTER 5

THE ECUMENIST

This chapter is certainly of central and major importance in the perspective of the mission that Bea would perform as cardinal during and after the Council, for we shall be considering what specific preparation he himself brought to it.

In previous chapters we have already seen what can be described as the more general and distant preparation, beginning with his studies at Constance High School,[1] continuing with his studies in the pluralistic environment of three German-language universities, and coming to a certain maturity in the study and teaching of sacred scripture, first at Valkenburg and then at the Pontifical Biblical Institute in Rome.[2]

However, the essential question considered in the present chapter is that of whether this was maybe all, or whether there was also some more immediate and specific preparation. If we then want to be more precise, it is helpful to recall that ecumenism has a theoretical (or, more precisely, theological) aspect, and a practical aspect. With regard to the former, the present chapter takes up points from the chapter on Bea as theologian, so that we shall be considering how Bea used his theological approach to throw light on the specific questions of ecumenism—the various parts of what the Council called "the Catholic principles of ecumenism." With regard to the practical aspect, ecumenism entails contacts with other Christians and their communities, dialogue, cooperation, etc. We shall thus be considering what we know about Bea's activity in these areas.

The answers to these questions are all the more important if we consider certain special circumstances connected with Bea's activity as first President of the Secretariat for Christian Unity. How, for example, are we to explain the fact that the creation of the secretariat and the nomination of its first president were viewed with such favor and confidence by other Christians? Although it is true that Bea was well-known among specialists in biblical exegesis, including non-Catholics, this was a relatively closed world. Moreover, such people also knew that Bea had been a trusted advisor to Pius XII, who was in general seen as fairly "conservative," and the negative impression this created could have been considerably reinforced by the fact that he had been a consultor at the Holy Office for ten years. So how are we to explain the fact that despite all this he and the secretariat were greeted with such great confidence?

---

1. See pp. 33-35 above.
2. See pp. 97-98 above. Cf. also J. Höfer, "Das geistliche Profil des Kardinals Bea," *Catholica*, XXVI (1972), 53: "In conversation with me Cardinal Bea stressed that his was not 'a late vocation' to the field of ecumenism, for his academic work had already made him familiar with the thinking of other Christians and with their desire for unity." (We shall speak about J. Höfer below.)

Sources and General Framework

Before launching into our subject, we would point out that we have excellent sources for these aspects of Bea's activity. His correspondence contains over one hundred and eighty letters dealing in one way or another with ecumenical questions—and often in considerable depth. If we bear in mind that Bea was involved in many other activities and that ecumenism was not his main concern, the number is all the more remarkable. A certain number of his publications are also concerned with this field. If we consider his letters and the information they offer in the living context of his correspondents, we obtain a picture of a broad and fairly substantial network of ecumenical contacts, which in turn throws light on his attitudes in this area, together with the underlying principles and convictions. Lastly, we would observe that in the last four years of our period, the number of such letters increased considerably, so that we find fifty-one in 1958 and forty-two in 1959.

As concerns the *general context* in which Bea approached the question of Christian unity, we must start with an observation that will surprise more than one reader: the immediate context that led to Bea's increasingly close involvement in ecumenism was in fact his work at the Holy Office. As we have already said, at that time (i.e. prior to the creation of the Secretariat for Christian Unity), this Vatican department had exclusive authority in all questions concerning other Christians ("heretics" or "schismatics" as they were then called). Bea's relations and contacts, both official and non-official, with brethren in other churches or ecclesial communities were thus occasioned by his position as consultor to this congregation. We can go further and say that it was Bea's experience in this context that convinced him of the need for the Holy See to set up another department—be it a commission or a simple office—to which such brethren could turn without difficulty or fear. It was certainly reasonable to wonder how they could be expected to feel comfortable when approaching a department that was by its nature a court, and that had, moreover, borne the redoubtable name of "Inquisition" until the quite recent reform of St. Pius X.

Apart from this, and in order to avoid any possible misunderstandings, we should immediately add that it was during the first months of Bea's work at the Holy Office that the latter had issued its first positive document on the ecumenical movement, in the form of the instruction of December 1949.[3] A bare year previously, with a view to the first (and constituent) assembly of the World Council of Churches in Amsterdam, the same Vatican department had issued a sharp and decidedly negative "warning" that anyone wishing to attend such ecumenical gatherings had to have explicit authorization from the Holy See,[4] and even if they obtained such permission Catholics could only attend in the neutral guise of "journalists." The new instruction, on the other hand, recognized that the ecumenical movement had been born under the inspiration of the Holy Spirit, and gave positive instructions concerning conversations between theo-

3. Cf. *AAS*, XLII (1950), 142-147.
4. Cf. *AAS*, XL (1948), 257.

logians and cooperation with other Christians in the social field, etc.—although all this was still hedged about with numerous precautions. The number of constructive elements contained in the instruction can also be seen from the fact that after the secretariat was set up, Bea used to take it as the main basis for his ecumenical activity,[5] and continued to do so more or less until November 1964 when the conciliar decree on ecumenism was promulgated.

If we bear in mind the fact that Bea entered the Holy Office in March 1949 and that this instruction was published in December of the same year, we naturally wonder whether it bore the marks of his influence, and what these were. Bea was always extremely careful in observing the total secrecy of the Holy Office, so that we have no information on this point. However, one thing is clear: his participation in the drafting of this document meant that he had to study and reflect personally on the whole ecumenical question.

There was yet another element that led to Bea's involvement with ecumenism—an element that applied throughout his time as consultor at the Holy Office—and this was the fact that he was assigned particular responsibility as concerned German affairs.[6] Given the religious situation of Germany as the primary Reformation country, contacts with other Christians and ecumenical efforts were particularly marked. As we know, such contacts had received a particular boost in the context of joint resistance to the Nazi regime and had then developed further after the war.[7]

Contacts with Ecumenical Circles

As introduction I should like to stress the essential role of *mediator* played by Mgr. J. Höfer, a priest of the Archdiocese of Paderborn, a professor of pastoral theology, and then for fourteen years ecclesiastical counselor at the embassy of the Federal Republic of Germany to the Holy See.[8] On the one hand he himself sought both advice and assistance from Bea, while on the other he provided precious assistance in establishing contacts with the non-Catholic world for Bea and also for many other ecclesiastical circles in Rome. Drawing on a wealth of experience gained in Germany while teaching pastoral theology in Paderborn, he managed to combine the duties and opportunities entailed in his position of ecclesiastical counselor with concern over the highest religious and ecclesiastical interests. Thus he helped Bea to establish contact with a great many non-Catholic figures—or perhaps we should say that he helped these

---

5. Cf. for example *The Unity of Christians*, pp. 25 (note), 29 (note), etc.

6. Cf. p. 144 above.

7. Cf. J. Höfer, "Una-Sancta-Bewegung," *LThK*, X, 464. An exhaustive overview can also be found in Fey (ed.), *A History of the Ecumenical Movement*, II, 316-322. In connection with this latter publication, I must, however, observe that in my opinion, were the 1949 instruction viewed in the context of its time, it would deserve a more positive evaluation as leading, among other things, to extensive cooperation in the political and social fields.

8. He held this position from 1954 to 1968. Details of his life are found in R. Baümer and H. Held (eds.), *Volk Gottes. Zum Kirchenverständnis der katholischen, evangelischenn und anglikanischen Theologie, Festgabe J. Höfer* (Freiburg im Breisgau, 1967), pp. 743-760.

non-Catholic figures to establish contact with such an important figure as Bea, who was, of course, consultor to the Holy Office and confessor to the pope.

The extent of Höfer's activity cannot be judged simply from the relatively few letters found in the archives,[9] and I in fact know much more about it from conversations I had with Bea in that period, for Höfer tended to operate more through personal contacts than through letters. His main sphere of mediation involved contacts with the ecumenical movement in Germany, although he also had good relations with the Anglicans.[10]

1. Let us start with contacts with the Catholic ecumenical movement in *West Germany*. Most important among these were relations with the Archbishop of Paderborn, Dr. Lorenz Jaeger, who was responsible for ecumenical affairs, and more generally for relations with other Christians, on behalf of the West German Episcopal Conference. Together with the well-known Lutheran Bishop Wilhelm Stählin, Archbishop Jaeger had, for example, started the only interconfessional theological dialogue existing in Germany at that time, and it was known as the "Jaeger-Stählin Group" after the names of its two creators.[11] Mgr. Höfer, who was also a member of the group, kept Bea informed of its work, which the latter watched with a keen and optimistic eye.[12]

The correspondence between Jaeger and Bea on ecumenical questions began a little later, but soon became fairly frequent, covering a number of important subjects as these arose. Their letters thus eventually came to deal with all the various aspects of Catholic and non-Catholic ecumenism on the national and international levels, and long conversations on the same subjects also took place during the archbishop's various visits to Rome. Bea was particularly interested and encouraging over Jaeger's plans to found an ecumenical institute in his archdiocesan headquarters. Frequent and fruitful contacts in due course developed between Bea and those in charge of this institute, which was named after the famous nineteenth-century German theologian, J.A. Möhler.[13] In 1957 Bea wrote to the head of the institute, Dr. Eduard Stakemeier, as follows: "It seems that [with the institute] the Holy Spirit wants to lay the groundwork for something that nobody would have thought possible even a few decades ago."[14]

For a while there were also frequent letters to those responsible for the special ecumenical activity of the Benedictine Abbey of Niederalteich, and also a number of personal visits. The correspondence speaks specifically about the ecumenical review *Una Sancta-Briefe* (or "Letters for *Una Sancta*") on several occasions, and also about the interconfessional retreats organized at the abbey.[15]

---

9. Twenty-eight in all.

10. In order to place the relative facts found in Bea's correspondence in context and comment on them, I shall be making use in particular of Höfer's article "Una-Sancta-Bewegung."

11. Cf. especially *ibid.* in this connection.

12. Cf. for example Nk 16 (1956).

13. On J.A. Möhler (1796-1838), cf. *LThK*, VII, 721-722. For the correspondence with the heads of the institute, cf. N 1957/131; 1957/136; 1957/148; 1957/152; 1957/257; 1957/316; 1958/201; 1958/268; 1958/323; 1959/43; 1959/116.

14. N 1957/152.

15. Cf. N 1951/17; 1957/83; 1957/237; 1959/146; Nm 27 (1957); 34 (1957).

Bea's contacts with the non-Catholic ecumenical movement in West Germany were connected with the Evangelical movement known as Sammlung. This movement was founded by H. Asmussen, E. Fink, M. Lackmann and W. Lehmann, with the aim of providing a dogmatically clearer witness to the truth of the Bible and the Reformation, returning to the tradition of the early church.[16] About ten letters are devoted to contacts with various representatives of this movement, including Asmussen,[17] although it is also mentioned in quite a number of those addressed to other people. We would simply note a few facts in this connection.

At a certain point Bea had decided to introduce the movement to a wider audience through an article to be published in a Catholic review, but the plan was scrapped for various reasons.[18] Bea also received suggestions—and sometimes requests—that one or another representative of the movement should be received by the pope in private audience, but he would reply that it was more prudent to be satisfied with a distinguished place at a general audience, and in fact arranged such audiences in certain cases. When Max Lackmann published his study on "The Catholic Reformation" Bea thought it best not to offer the book to Pius XII, because he could see that it still contained considerable lacunae in knowledge of Catholic doctrine; he suggested instead that conversations should be organized between representatives of the Sammlung Movement and various Catholic theologians.[19]

I would add a number of facts concerning H. Asmussen in particular. In 1956 Bea wrote that he was reading the latter's book *Rom, Wittenberg, Moskau*, and said that the author seemed right on a number of points, but that his knowledge of the Vatican was not full enough.[20] When Asmussen visited Rome he had a meeting with Bea, who impressed him deeply, according to Höfer's account.[21] Asmussen then wrote a detailed report on his visit to Rome, sending fifty copies to various leading figures, including Bea. "To keep the dialogue going," Bea responded with eleven pages of reflections on various points in the report.[22]

16. Cf. J.P. Michael, "Sammlung," *LThK*, IX, 298; H. Asmussen, "Zur Vorgeschichte der katholisch-evangelischen Berührungen und Annäherungen," in Baümer and Held (eds.), *Volk Gottes*, pp. 731-742.
17. On Provost H.C. Asmussen (1898-1968), cf. George Zenk, *Evangelisch in Katholizität* (Frankfurt, 1977); Gustav Huhn, *Es begann mit Hans Asmussen. Ein Bericht auf dem Wege zur einen Kirche* (Munster, 1981), esp. pp. 201-204 (although this work was in part received very critically); Enno Konukiewitz, *Hans Asmussen, ein lutherischer Theologe im Kirchenkampf*, Lutherische Kirche, Geschichte und Gestalten 6 (Gütersloh, 1984); Wolfgang Lehmann, *Hans Asmussen. Ein Leben für die Kirche* (Göttingen, 1988). This latter biography is particularly interesting and profound. I would, however, point out that "Bea and Leiber" were not "Pius XII's confessors" (p. 121); nor can it be claimed that the encyclical *Mystici corporis* of Pius XII was "elaborated by Father Bea" (p. 173).
18. Cf. Nw 49 (1958); 50 (1959).
19. Cf. Nk 16 (1956); for the overall context of the publication, cf. Lehmann, *Hans Asmussen*, p. 244.
20. Cf. Nk 8 (1956).
21. Cf. Nk 10 (1956).
22. Cf. N 1956/182, where we find both the report and Bea's reflections. Lehmann, *Hans Asmussen*, pp. 121-122, does not mention Asmussen's report, but says that in 1947 Asmussen posed Bea

When the Sammlung Movement published a series of "theses" that condensed the theological principles of the movement, and distributed twenty thousand copies, Bea devoted a great deal of time to studying it carefully, and then discussed it in a number of contexts, as well as drawing up a list of observations running to seven pages.[23]

Later on, in 1962, when Bea was already a cardinal and was visiting Heidelberg as President of the Secretariat for Christian Unity to give a lecture at the university on the subject "The Council and Christian Unity," he also met with Hans Asmussen, who told him with great simplicity and modesty (I quote from memory here): "Now that your secretariat is undertaking what I was aiming at, I can retire." And the movement was in fact disbanded in 1963, although certain sectors of its work were continued to some extent by the Association for Evangelical-Catholic Reunion.[24]

There was a certain amount of contact with the ecumenical movement in Switzerland through correspondence with the distinguished Swiss ecumenist Dr. Otto Karrer, who had been a friend of Bea since student days. Precisely because they were such old friends, their letters ranged over a wide variety of subjects, but ecumenism was one that recurred repeatedly.[25]

2. There were particularly useful contacts with the *Catholic Conference for Ecumenical Questions* which was founded by the then professor of philosophy at Warmond in the diocese of Haarlem in Holland, Johannes G.M. Willebrands, who also acted as its secretary. This channel allowed Bea at least a certain contact, if only indirect, with a good number of ecumenists of various nationalities, particularly French, who were connected with the association.[26] Willebrands himself states that during his regular visits to Rome to keep the various Vatican departments abreast of the activity of the association, he usually called on Bea as well.[27] The correspondence includes a discussion of the meeting that the association held in the Benedictine Abbey of Chevetogne in Belgium, at

---

and Leiber the following question: "Rome is always speaking of the need for the Protestants to 'return.' What would happen if I brought the news that the Protestants were returning tomorrow?" The reply was: "That would be tricky, since Rome is not prepared for it." Asmussen then retorted: "In that case, the appeal to return is an irresponsible, empty formula and the expression of the old lust for power."

23. Cf. N 1957/120; 1957/131; 1957/136; 1957/147; 1957/148. The text of Bea's observations is attached to this last letter. Cf. also N 1958/150. Both Bea's aforementioned reflections on Asmussen's report and his observations on the "theses" represent precious sources of information on Bea's ecumenical ideas. We shall return to this in due course.

24. Cf. Michael, "Sammlung," p. 298. Cf. also Lehmann, *Hans Asmussen*, p. 245: "In 1963, when the Council began, we declared that the work of the Sammlung Movement was finished."

25. Cf. N 1956/177; 1955/121; 1956/110; 1957/3; Nk 13 (1956). Cf. also Karrer, *Strieflichter aus Briefen an mich*, pp. 44-45, 52-55, and the bibliographical notes on pp. 177, 183, 190.

26. On the association, cf. Michael, "Sammlung," note 8.

27. Cf. J.G.M. Willebrands, "Il Cardinale Bea, Apostolo dell'unione," *OssRom* (17 November 1968), p. 3, where he goes on to say: "I started seeing Cardinal Bea in 1951. . . . He had a lively interest in ecumenical questions. . . . On occasions during those years when I came to Rome to ask his advice, he never refused to see me, but would in fact insist that I should visit him, saying: 'Even if I lacked the time to deal with other matters, I would always be available for the cause of unity.' "

which it sought to provide a Catholic contribution to the document of the World
Council of Churches on Christ's lordship.[28]

Bea repeatedly referred to the "conference" and its activities on other
occasions too. Although his ideas sometimes differed from those of its secretary
as to the line the conference ought to follow,[29] he had great appreciation for its
work, and great respect for its secretary. Indeed, some years later this led to
Willebrands' appointment as first Secretary of the Secretariat for Christian
Unity. Furthermore, contacts with the association proved truly providential, for
they meant that Bea found his task much easier when he came to draw up a list
of bishops to be nominated as members of the secretariat, and he also found a
good number of its consultors among those connected with the conference.
Apart from this, the solid studies on major ecumenical problems that the
conference produced from 1952 onward in the framework of its more or less
annual meetings, were then integrated into the work carried out by the secretariat
in preparation for the Council.

Apart from knowledge acquired through various publications, both Höfer
and Willebrands exercised an important influence on Bea's attitude toward the
World Council of Churches. Just as Willebrands had regular contact with the
Roman authorities, especially the Holy Office, he also had regular relations with
the World Council of Churches (which were facilitated by the fact that the
Secretary General of the council, Dr. W.A. Visser 't Hooft, was a fellow
Dutchman). Bea's correspondence with Willebrands thus contains repeated
references to the World Council of Churches and its affairs.[30]

In due course the time for *some personal visits* arrived. The first visit to Rome
by a member of the staff of the World Council of Churches took place in May
1957 and was made by the then head of its study department, Dr. H.H. Harms,
who was later Lutheran Bishop of Oldenburg. As the visitor himself would later
relate, when Bea showed him the library of the Pontifical Biblical Institute, he
pointed out with a smile that it was "a good Protestant library."[31] Prior to this
visit, the question had been raised of whether it was a good idea to ask for a
private audience with Pope Pius XII. Bea did not feel that it was, partly because
of the stir previously raised at the time of the visit to the pope by the then Bishop
of Berlin, Dr. Dibelius.[32] Bea later wrote to Bernard Alfrink, Archbishop of
Utrecht, and Josef Freundorfer, Bishop of Augsburg, both alumni of the Pontifical Biblical Institute, asking them to see Harms.

Bea remained in correspondence with Harms. Thanking him for his report

---

28. Cf. N 1959/268; 1959/276.
29. Cf. Nm 34 (1957); 53 (1958); 58 (1958); 60 (1958).
30. Cf. N 1958/224; 1958/231. Among other things, he discussed the possible consequences of the
    integration of the World Missionary Council into the World Council of Churches; N 1958/309.
    In 1958/2 he clarified the question of whether or not the World Council of Churches had sent
    condolences on the death of Pius XII.
31. Cf. H.H. Harms, "Anwalt der Einheit. Kurienkardinal Augustin Bea," *Sonntagsblatt*, XIX/22
    (1966).
32. Cf. N 1957/76. As regards the audience that Dr. O. Dibelius, then President of the Evangelical
    Church in Germany, had in January 1956, cf. Nm 8 (1956), and *CC*, IV (1960), 346-347.

on his visit to the United States, Bea explained the cool reception that Harms had met with among American Catholics, reminding him of the unpleasant situation in which they had been forced to live for a number of centuries.[33] In another letter to Harms, Bea expressed concern that the absorption of the World Missionary Council into the World Council of Churches, which was then being organized, could provide a boost to the proselytizing zeal of certain American missionaries in Latin America.[34] In 1958 Harms said that he was planning a long visit to Rome, which was to last from 1 to 14 March. However, his health in fact prevented him from making this journey.[35]

In the context of relations with the World Council of Churches, we should also mention that Bea was responsible for arranging for a member of the organization, Dr. Hans Ruedi Weber, to attend the International Congress for the Lay Apostolate held in Rome in 1957. The correspondence shows that this was a far from obvious or straightforward matter, for it even required authorization (although not public) from the Holy Office.[36] Later on Bea showed disappointment over certain aspects of the confidential report on this participation, particularly over the passage where Dr. Weber completely misunderstood the spirit of Catholic marian devotion and expressed alarm over its growth. "Are we *still* at this point?" asked Bea.[37]

3. Let us add *some evaluations* of the Reformation world, especially in Germany, and of the World Council of Churches, as these are found in Bea's letters. They must obviously be judged in the light of the ecumenical situation at that time, for they do reflect the state of mutual relations in the period in question. It is true that at that time a certain number of Catholic theologians, such as J.G.M. Willebrands, Y. Congar and others, were in contact with the World Council of Churches, just as, for the council's part, a figure such as Dr. Harms had the "courage" to visit Rome. Apart from this, however, there was absolutely no contact, and the psychological consequences of such situations are well-known.

Let us first look at his evaluation of the *Reformation world*. We would start with the more positive judgments: "I think it is certain that God's wise providence has set many things in motion in German Protestantism that were not only static, but untouchable, in my now distant youth."[38] "It is also undeniable that there is a tendency toward unity and an intense desire for it among large sectors of Lutheran Evangelicals."[39]

Then come the less positive judgments. Even in July 1959, less than one year prior to the creation of the secretariat, Bea writes that the developments of recent months "show with sad clarity that we are further than ever from unity."[40] At

---

33. Cf. N 1957/323.
34. Cf. N 1958/173.
35. Cf. N 1958/35; 1959/35. Nm 74 (1959) tells us that the visit—probably the one planned for 1959—was cancelled for health reasons.
36. Cf. N 1957/11; 1957/135; 1957/143.
37. Cf. N 1957/316; 1957/322; Nm 34 (1957).
38. Nm 18 (1956); cf. also N 1956/179.
39. Nm 80 (1959).

about the same time, he expresses his conviction that Protestantism in Germany is not ripe for unity "as we understand it."[41]

So far as the *World Council of Churches* is concerned, Bea moves between a positive view and reservations, although the reservations and diffidence are prevalent. He thinks, for example, that instead of concerning itself with doctrinal unity the council is busy trying to become "a world church."[42] Similarly, he is worried that the plan of integrating the World Missionary Council into the World Council of Churches means that the latter's main concern is that of placing the whole mission field under its own influence. On another occasion he thinks that the council is trying to prevent any rapprochement between Rome and Constantinople, and that with its own rapprochement with the Russian Orthodox Church it is trying to set up an anti-Roman ecumenism and isolate Rome.[43] Bea's letters also reflect the unease caused in Catholic quarters by an article that was certainly written without any ill intentions by the Secretary of the World Council of Churches, Dr. W.A. Visser 't Hooft, on the attitude of the Catholic Church toward the ecumenical movement, under the title "Super-Church and the Ecumenical Movement."[44]

4. Bea's relations in the ecumenical field often involved *various types of assistance* to brethren from other churches or their initiatives, or to Catholic initiatives on their behalf. A willingness to help others was a key-note of Bea's character, and we shall give a few examples in this connection. Such assistance often entailed a helping hand in cases that were either pending at the Holy Office, or were yet to be proposed for its consideration. In this way Bea lent his assistance with regard, for example, to various applications from German bishops for authorization to ordain converted Evangelical pastors to the priesthood despite the fact that they were married.[45] Bea corresponded with a number of pastors who had entered the priesthood in this way.[46] We find an example of another form of assistance in the successful last-minute rescue-attempt he made in 1951 to ensure a significant Catholic participation in the Christological Congress organized at Oxford by the well-known Anglican theologian Dr. Cross.[47]

---

40. Nm 78 (1959); cf. also N 1958/309.
41. Cf. Nm 84 (1959); N 1958-201; 1958/253. If we remember both the positive and negative aspects, it would seem that Bea's attitude is more balanced than it would appear from the article of H. Bacht, "Kardinal Bea: Wegbereiter der Einheit," *Catholica*, XXXV (1981), 176-178.
42. Cf. N 1956/85; Nm 72 (1959); 73 (1959).
43. Cf. N 1958/174; 1958/195; 1958/224; 1958/253; 1958/309; 1959/42; 1959/78; 1958/144; Nm 35 (1958); 85 (1959). Cf. also Bacht, "Kardinal Bea," p. 175.
44. Cf. W.A. Visser 't Hooft, "Super-Church and the Ecumenical Movement," *Ecumenical Review*, LVIII (1957), 365-385. Bea speaks about this in N 1958/195; 1958/224.
45. Cf. N 1954/49.
46. Cf. N 1952/89; 1953/48.
47. Cf. N 1951/55; 1951/59; 1951/71; Nq 5 (1951); 6 (1951). This concerned the paper given by A. Grillmeier, S.J., who had published a monumental three-volume work on the Council of Chalcedon and spoke on the same subject at the Oxford meeting.

Protestants and the Definition of the Assumption

Before moving on to a discussion of Bea's views on ecumenism, let us take a look at the practical illustration of his ecumenical attitude provided by the very significant case of his Italian-language article on "The Definition of the Assumption and Protestants."[48] We should recall that the news of Pius XII's intention to define the bodily assumption of Mary into heaven as a dogma of the faith gave rise to some lively polemics, which sometimes lapsed into bitter tones, on the part of other Christians, especially in the western sphere—although they were not limited to the Reformation world.[49] Bea was thus faced with a challenging situation in which it was all too easy to strike polemical attitudes. Let us therefore try to provide a step-by-step analysis of the positions he in fact took. Such an analysis is all the more interesting for our purposes inasmuch as the article in question appeared at the beginning of the period now under consideration.

In the first place, the article reveals deep concern over the question of union. It opens with the words of the constitution *Munificentissimus Deus* with which Pius XII promulgated the relative definition, words that express the hope that the definition will help foster union.[50]

The article is also anxious to point out the ecumenical intentions behind the writings of other Christians on this subject. They are free of the "tendency to attack the Catholic Church"[51] and "more than one author, inspired by the ideal of union of all the Christian churches, says that today all Christians feel responsible for what is done in any sector of Christianity, especially when this involves questions that can have a favorable or unfavorable effect on relations between the various churches."[52]

Bea steers well clear of all exaggeration or over-simplification, and is concerned to present an honest and nuanced view of the mariological attitudes of the founders of the Reformation: "The veneration of the Blessed Virgin Mary was not rejected out of hand by the Protestants, at least not by all of them, and especially not by the Anglicans." The difficulty sprang more from the fact that this devotion "has never been carefully and fully explained . . . in Protestant-

---

48. Cf. Biblio. 99.
49. We said that the opposition came "especially" from the western sector, for the east in fact shares the relative doctrine, and the earliest witnesses among the fathers of the church on this point are in fact found in the east. The east does not, however, share the Roman definition, because of the well-known differences on the dogmas of the primacy and infallibility of the Roman pontiff.
50. Cf. Biblio. 99, p. 75. And Bea's article is permeated with these hopes and concerns from beginning to end. For example, after noting the generally "moderate and conciliatory" tone of the writings of other Christians with regard to the definition, Bea concludes: "We offer heartfelt tribute to this spirit of Christian charity, and join our separated brethren in hoping that the noble efforts to implement ever more fully the 'Ut omnes unum sint' of the divine Founder of the Church, may be blessed by God and brought to a successful conclusion (*ibid.*, p. 79).
51. *Ibid.*, p. 78.
52. *Ibid.*

ism."[53] Here the author refers in particular to Luther's commentary on the *Magnificat* and similar attitudes on the part of Zwingli, but says that the situation changes radically in Calvinism.[54] Indeed, the actual fact of the bodily assumption of Mary into heaven did not at first meet with any great opposition on the part of Protestants. In rules drawn up in 1539 "for the County of Lippe, which were examined diligently, reflected on and found just and Christian by Luther, Bugenhagen and Melanchthon, we find the assumption included among the feasts of the blessed Mother of God."[55] A decided difficulty would spring from the ecclesiological principle that sacred scripture is the sole source and norm of faith, since, according to the Protestants, sacred scripture does not provide any evidence on the assumption of Mary.[56]

Understanding is not, however, everything. We must also make an effort "to explain our principles with both clarity and charity."[57] Here Bea recalls that the encyclical *Humani generis* "rejected any false irenicism."[58] The sincerity of the Catholic Church is such that it had to issue the definition, and thus destroy "any false hopes that may have been cherished in some quarters that an understanding could be reached by emphasizing first and foremost the points common to everyone, while ignoring or setting aside the others. . . . In this way a solid basis has now been created on which the important work of mutual contact can continue in truth and charity."[59]

Now we come to see how Bea pursues this dialogue "in truth and charity" in practical terms. While not accepting the Reformation principle of sacred scripture as the sole source and norm of faith, he adjusts to it, and as a first step sets about demonstrating *also* on the basis of sacred scripture that the assumption is in no way contrary to sacred scripture (as some people claimed), but that the latter can also be seen to contain elements supporting it.[60]

Bea does not stop here, however, but goes on to explain the whole of Catholic teaching on the assumption, together with its basis. The doctrine of the assumption is based on an element that is "absolutely certain in the elaboration of any Catholic dogma, in other words the illumination of the Holy Spirit, who brings us to contemplate 'in an ever clearer light the wonderful harmony' that exists between the various truths of the faith, and shows how this harmony, in our case, has been seen and understood increasingly clearly, since the Spirit of truth lives in the church and leads it infallibly to knowledge of revealed truth."[61] This development is then verified through the work of the magisterium of the

---

53. *Ibid.*, p. 81.
54. Cf. *ibid.*, pp. 81-82.
55. *Ibid.*, p. 83.
56. Cf. *ibid.*
57. *Ibid.*, p. 90.
58. *Ibid.*, p. 91.
59. *Ibid.*, p. 92.
60. A fuller demonstration of the biblical basis of the dogma is found in Bea's study "La Sacra Scrittura 'ultimo fondamento' del domma dell'Assunzione" (Biblio. 82). The term "ultimate foundation" is taken from the constitution *Munificentissimus Deus* itself.
61. Biblio. 99, p. 89.

church—which in practice means through consultation of all Catholic bishops, in which the *sensus fidei* of the faithful also plays an important role.[62]

Lastly, Bea speaks about the ecumenical implications of the definition, saying that in it "the Catholic Church, while wholeheartedly desiring the unity of all Christians, has had the courage to make a frank public profession of its faith and principles on a point that unfortunately separates us from contemporary Protestantism, and has done so not in order to obstruct or prevent efforts to reach unity, but in order to offer faithful obedience to a law intrinsic in its doctrinal development as inspired and guided by the Holy Spirit. . . . Such frankness could not but impress all those who sincerely seek union."[63] At this point Bea notes two significant facts, the first of which involves the theological conversations of the above-mentioned Jaeger-Stählin Group. A short while before the definition, the Evangelical party warned the Catholics "that the meetings would probably have to stop, both for political reasons and also because of the definition of the assumption. Four months later, however, in March 1951, on the request of the Protestants themselves, the meetings were resumed in a calm, friendly atmosphere and with excellent results."[64] The other fact is of a similar nature: "In Switzerland, too, where the discussions were at first suspended because of the definition, those concerned got in touch again after a short break."[65]

The Unity of the Church and the Path toward This

Having examined a practical example of Bea's ecumenical attitudes, we shall now try to examine them in greater depth, filling out the picture as we consider the principles on which they are based.

First there is the question of the perspective in which we are to view *the aim* of the ecumenical movement, in other words *the unity* to be brought about. Bea is aware of the fundamental problem here: "The deepest and most decisive element in all the points of disagreement is the difference in ecclesiology."[66] In the ecumenical movement "unity is sought—though not the unity of the one true, holy, catholic church, but an ideal invisible unity."[67] Questions connected with the ecumenical movement therefore "require a fresh and fuller examination of doctrines on the church, and one that takes account of the new objections raised against the unity and oneness of the church founded by Christ, against its hierarchical structure and juridical character, and against the primacy and infallibility of the Roman Pontiff."[68]

62. Cf. *ibid.*, p. 90.
63. *Ibid.*, pp. 91-92.
64. *Ibid.*, p. 91.
65. *Ibid.*
66. Biblio. 126, p. 634.
67. Biblio. 114, p. 34.
68. *Ibid.*, pp. 38-39.

In his reflections on Hans Asmussen's report on his visit to Rome, Bea describes unity *in positive terms*, saying that threefold unity is necessary, in other words unity in doctrine, in sacraments and in government of the church under the primacy instituted by Christ and realized in the pope. No unity based on compromises on these points is possible.[69] Even so, he does add that "for Catholics unity in doctrine does not mean uniformity in life and spirituality."[70] In this light he speaks—using the term adopted by Asmussen himself (*evangelisches Sondergut*)—of certain features proper to the Evangelicals which concern the fields of liturgy, discipline and personal piety. He would also see the same category as including the permission to go on living their marriages which is given to married pastors who have converted to Catholicism and been ordained.[71] In the same context Bea observes that if the introduction of the *Filioque* into the Creed "in a liturgy already established for centuries" creates difficulties, the church can forego it with no difficulty, since the profession of implicit faith is admissible in this case as in many others.[72]

We hardly need to emphasize Bea's *firm wish to foster unity*, a wish he shows in practice, rather than simply stating it in theory, as was seen very clearly in our previous section on Protestants and the definition of the assumption. His article on the subject closes by saying that the Holy Spirit kindles the desire for unity, and "it is up to us to provide our humble collaboration in the great work and to pray ever more intensely" that he will bring it about.[73] We would, however, add an explicit piece of evidence. After noting the various difficulties and obstacles (including the recent manifestation of strong anti-Catholic attitudes in Switzerland, the country of his correspondent), Bea states: "None of this should prevent us from seeking and promoting the unity that the Lord has wanted and wants." And he adds: "We must leave it up to him to decide on the results he is pleased to grant our work."[74]

Among the ways and means of bringing about unity, we shall in the first place mention Bea's ideas on *dialogue*. Firstly, he asserts the *need* for dialogue, saying that it is necessary precisely with a view to clarifying doctrine: "Understanding cannot be reached without dialogue."[75] "Where is the unity that the Lord desires to come from if we do not talk to one another?"[76] The *qualities* of such dialogue are often stressed. Thus he says that it must be conducted with objectivity, mutual trust, charity and patience.[77]

Bea's letters also tell us about *underlying motivations* for this attitude to

---

69. Cf. N 1956/182, p. 4.
70. *Ibid.*, p. 2.
71. Cf. *ibid.*, p. 10.
72. Cf. *ibid.*, pp. 5-6.
73. Cf. *ibid.*
74. N 1953/177.
75. Nm 178 (1956).
76. Nm 80 (1959). In a similar context Bea speaks of the need for dialogue in order to dispel prejudice (N 1953/177); cf. also N 1958/65.
77. Cf. Nm 43 (1958); also Nm 44 (1958). In Nm 46 (1958) and Nm 51 (1958) he also mentions calm and serenity.

dialogue, motivations that are drawn partly from his long experience as a scholar, but more especially from theology. He explains that it is certainly not true that there is nothing but error "on the other side"; nor can we *a priori* be sure that our understanding of the viewpoint of the others is always correct.[78] "Only the Lord possesses the absolute truth."[79] And here we see how this applies to our subject: in such a complex matter as ecumenical work, there are obscure points that can be clarified only if we proceed calmly and objectively.[80] In conclusion, as we shall see, he says that doctrinal differences must be frankly noted, but that we must also show the maximum respect and charity for the others, and leave the necessary time for grace and intelligence to operate, just as the Lord God does.[81]

All this means that first and foremost dialogue requires a *constructive* rather than a polemical attitude.[82] Thus, patience and charity will make it possible to recognize the truth contained in the position of the others, and such shared elements are the only possible starting point for ecumenical dialogue.[83] In this way all those who have ecumenical dialogue at heart can and must complete and correct one another.[84] In this context Bea says that he is anxious to reinforce the elements in the ecumenical movement that are positive and of goodwill.[85]

The quality of such dialogue on which Bea places most stress is the *frank and clear statement of the whole of Catholic doctrine.* We spoke at length about Bea's active fidelity to the teaching of the church in our chapter on Bea as theologian. Here we shall consider the application of this principle to the ecumenical field, and particularly to theological dialogue. Bea speaks about this question more specifically in his commentary on the encyclical *Humani generis*, where he in fact considers the document in the ecumenical context.[86] Let us summarize his explanations in this connection. The third root of modern errors, says Bea, and the one that the encyclical describes as the most dangerous, is the tendency to dilute the doctrines of the faith or change their sense by reinterpreting them in order to obtain a basis for a meeting between Catholics and non-Catholics. Now the church certainly encourages the search for union, as can be seen from the instruction on the ecumenical movement issued by the Holy Office less than one year prior to the encyclical. However, this instruction also contains the following warning: "It is necessary to make sure that a spirit that is today called 'irenic'[87] does not lead Catholic teaching—whether dogma

---

78. Cf. Nm 18 (1956).
79. Nm 46 (1958).
80. Cf. *ibid.*
81. Cf. Nm 18 (1956).
82. Cf. Nm 15 (1955).
83. Cf. Nm 17 (1956).
84. Cf. *ibid.*
85. Cf. Nm 22 (1956).
86. Here we are therefore completing what we said on this encyclical in Part II, Chapter 3, pp. 195-197 above.
87. For the sake of precision, Bea usually speaks of *"false* irenicism," a term that the conciliar decree on ecumenism adopted (cf. *UR,* 11).

or truths connected with dogma—to be so conformed or accommodated to the doctrines of the dissidents—under the pretext of comparative study and in the vain desire for progressive assimilation of the different professions of faith— that the purity of Catholic doctrine is harmed and its genuine and certain meaning is obscured."[88]

In his commentary on *Humani generis* in relation to biblical studies, Bea also refers to the positive section in which the same instruction states: "The whole of Catholic doctrine must be expounded in its entirety . . . both because they themselves [non-Catholics] seek the truth, and also because no true union can ever be attained outside the truth."[89] Bea immediately mentions various subjects to which this method of procedure is sometimes applied, such as the attempt to reduce Christ's presence in the eucharist to some kind of symbolism, or that of reducing the principle "Extra ecclesiam nulla salus"[90] to a formula without content.[91]

The encyclical, and Bea with it, also touches on another important principle of recent ecumenism which can give rise to misunderstandings: the *return to the ancient sources*. This principle has sometimes been formulated in the following terms: in disputed questions, theology must return to the ancient sources and evaluate more recent declarations of the magisterium of the church in the light of these sources. Bea answers with the encyclical, saying that theologians certainly have the task of studying the sources, but pointing out that the encyclical also warns that theology must not be identified with history. Alongside the sources of revelation, God has given the church a living magisterium, and wherever the sources are unclear or inexplicit, it is up to the magisterium of the church to interpret and explain them. The encyclical expressly states: "The task of interpreting the deposit aright was not entrusted by our divine Redeemer to the individual Christian, nor even to the individual theologian; it was the church's teaching that must be decisive."[92]

In the foregoing, Bea is commenting on the encyclical *Humani generis*, and thus is primarily concerned with setting forth the thought of this document. However, he does so with conviction, and his explanations and reasoning clearly show that he is completely at one with this line of thinking. This is further confirmed, if such confirmation were needed, by remarks on this question in his letters, and we shall now give a series of examples. Bea writes that where and when principles concerning the method of theology are at stake, ecumenical concerns do not count.[93] Elsewhere he says that the definition of the doctrine of

---

88. *AAS*, XLII (1950), 144. It should be noted that the conciliar decree on ecumenism adopted the last words of the citation (cf. *UR*, 11).

89. Cf. Biblio. 80, p. 421.

90. The principle "There is no salvation outside the church" expresses the view that membership in the church is indispensable for the eternal salvation of human beings.

91. The conciliar decree on ecumenism stresses that in dialogue the Catholic faith must be explained "in such a way and in such terms that our separated brethren can also really understand it" but also "more profoundly and precisely" (*UR*, 11). It therefore rules out any indefinite and imprecise language, just as the encyclical does.

92. *Humani generis*, English translation, p. 12. Cf. Biblio. 83, p. 44.

93. Cf. N 1955/121. This is the light in which we must understand Bea's warning that Catholics

the bodily assumption of Mary into heaven at least had the merit of clearing up a good many questions, for we must frankly face up to our differences.[94] He therefore writes that he does not like the method of the Sammlung Movement in which differences are glossed over, even though this may be done in good faith.[95] It is better if both sides openly uphold their own points of view.[96] In line with this, Bea repeatedly stresses the need for Catholics to take a critical stance: "Catholic 'criticism' is vital for any fruitful ecumenical work."[97] For the same reason he emphasizes the need for clarity and precision in terminology, saying that a lack of these is responsible for the lack of clarity in the statements of the Sammlung Movement.[98] Bea also observes that a number of the concepts expressed in the document of the World Council of Churches on the lordship of Christ need clarification.[99] A lack of Catholic criticism and clarity leads to a danger of indifferentism and the watering down of Catholic doctrine.[100]

The instruction of the Holy Office on the ecumenical movement may be fairly unforthcoming on many points, but it does unequivocally accept "mixed gatherings of Catholics and non-Catholics . . . which discuss the way in which they can join forces in order to defend the fundamental principles of natural law or of the Christian religion . . . or which are concerned with the restoration of the social order or similar matters."[101] Thus Bea also recommends collaboration of this kind. For example, when speaking of certain timid and narrow-minded souls, he observes that while strictly pastoral work should be carried out by each confession separately, ecumenical collaboration over the problems of miners "is legitimate and fruitful."[102] Elsewhere he extends this collaboration in a general way to cover the tasks common to all Christians.[103]

Ecumenical collaboration also gives us another interesting case of cooperation in the field of doctrine itself. A German publishing house had organized a joint Evangelical-Catholic work on the subject of "The Christian Religion."[104] This work offered Catholic authors an opportunity to present Catholic teaching in a book produced by a publishing house whose readers were for the most part Evangelicals. The first edition was a great success, with sales of over one hundred thousand copies. When the question of a second edition was raised, the superiors of the Society of Jesus raised objections. Bea stepped in very firmly

must not give up their own convictions, spirituality, etc., out of respect for Protestants; cf. N 1953/182; 1954/64; 1954/216; 1956/110; 1956/114; 1956/196.
94. Cf. Nm 18 (1956); 35 (1956).
95. Cf. Nm 47 (1958).
96. Cf. N 1953/162.
97. Nm 34 (1957); cf. 45 (1958); 51 (1958); N 1957/310.
98. Cf. N 1957/148; 1957/316.
99. Cf. N 1957/268.
100. Cf. Nm 21 (1956); 2 (1955).
101. *AAS*, XLII (1950), 144.
102. N 1956/43.
103. Cf. N 1956/85; 1956/182, pp. 4-5. Nm 6 (1956) appeals to the instruction in this connection, stating that cooperation over the problem of atomic weapons also falls under the subjects covered by the instruction.
104. This is the work *Christliche Religion* edited by O. Simmel and R. Stählin (Frankfurt, 1961).

in support of the move, with advice on how to get around the problem. Later letters indicate that the attempt was successful.[105]

The Achievement of Unity: Supernatural Means

In the first place we should note that Bea often stresses the extreme difficulty of reaching full unity. When referring to the Reformation world his letters often contain such thoughts as: "Except for a miracle of grace," conversions of individuals or small groups may take place, but not mass conversions.[106] Or the observation that we cannot hope for mass conversions or "re-unions" (*Wiedervereinigung*).[107] The number of references shows that this view runs through all the correspondence like a thread.[108]

Let us try to give a more precise picture of Bea's thinking in this connection. It is not surprising that he *also* thinks of conversions. We shall recall here the principle laid down by the Second Vatican Council in its decree on ecumenism: "However, it is evident that the work of preparing and reconciling those individuals who wish for full Catholic communion is of its nature distinct from ecumenical action. But there is no opposition between the two, since both proceed from the marvelous ways of God."[109] The distinguishing element in Bea's approach is the fact that he uses "conversions" and "re-unions" in parallel, as if conversions were the only way of restoring full communion.

However, there is a text from the second half of 1959 in which Bea moves beyond this view when formulating the problem of the *restoration of unity with groups or associations (Verbände)*: "A serious problem exists for the authorities of the church, and that is the question of what can or should be done in order to obtain not only individual conversions, which as such will never lead to reunion [*Wiedervereinigung*], and what can be done in order to offer larger associations [*Verbände*] the possibility of being united with the church of Christ and to facilitate such union."[110]

Bea finds a certain *answer* to these questions in the light of the various historical cases of restoration of union of eastern churches with the Catholic Church. He speaks of this in the aforementioned reflections in connection with Hans Asmussen's report on his visit to Rome, explaining his ideas on the restoration of full communion with the example of the restoration of full communion with a bishop

---

105. Cf. Nw 50 (1959); 51 (1959). For the successful outcome, cf. Na 634 (1959).
106. N 1959/84.
107. Cf. N 1953/177; N 1956/118; 1956/264; Nm 23 (1956); 27 (1956); 35 (1958); 43 (1958); Nw 49 (1958). Cf. also N 1956/179; 1956/206; 1956/212.
108. Although Bea speaks only of the Reformation world and of mass conversions, it seems reasonable to set his thought alongside that of *UR*, 24: "Further, this Council declares that it realizes that this holy objective—the reconciliation of all Christians in the unity of the one and only church of Christ—transcends human powers and gifts." We shall now go on to speak of the relationship between conversion and the restoration of full unity.
109. *UR*, 4.
110. Nm 80 (1959).

or patriarch of an eastern church who is in the apostolic succession. Such a bishop is the legitimate representative of his flock, and union is therefore concluded directly and immediately with him, and hence also with his flock—although it is true that individual members may refuse their assent, thus excluding themselves from such union. However, the assent of the faithful does not affect the validity of the act of the legitimate representative of the hierarchy.[111]

Given this approach, the difference in the case of the Reformation communities is immediately clear, inasmuch as there we have the problem of ministry and apostolic succession. Bea in fact goes on to point out that the difference between a bishop or patriarch who is in the apostolic succession and an Evangelical bishop lies in the fact that the apostolic succession is lacking in the latter case. As the head of his group, an Evangelical bishop can be authorized to represent it on the human level, but not in virtue of the sacred ministry.[112]

We would conclude by observing that when the Second Vatican Council speaks of ecumenism it is clearly aiming not at conversions but at reconciliation between the Catholic Church and other churches. Although it describes ways of preparing for this,[113] the problem of the actual restoration of full communion is left wide open.

We would also add that here too Bea strongly stresses the *specific responsibility of local churches*, and in particular of *bishops*, just as he does in other contexts.[114] Referring to a plan that someone had sent him for a possible "United Evangelical Church" (analogous to the United Oriental Churches), Bea observes that such a suggestion must be made and handled through the bishops of the territories in question.[115] When Bea refers to the Sammlung Movement, he follows exactly the same line, saying that in these matters no one should go over the bishops' heads and make a direct approach to Rome.[116] In his reflection on Hans Asmussen's report on his visit to Rome, Bea applies this teaching to the ecumenical field, so that although he does stress the limits of the bishop's authority when dealing with real negotiations on unity, he states: "In his own diocese the bishop can, of course, do a great deal in favor of reunion."[117]

References to the *role of the Holy Spirit* in the restoration of full communion are fairly infrequent, but Bea's views come through clearly. Although he confirms the need for a commitment to ecumenism, he is fairly restrained—sometimes maybe even pessimistic—in his appraisal of the prospects of ecumenical work, partly because of his own nature and partly because of experience. His commitment therefore rests on the sole solid foundation: trust in the action of the Holy Spirit. After explaining the need for dialogue, the method to be followed, and our absolute dependence on grace, he concludes: "In the final analysis it is the Holy Spirit, the Spirit of Pentecost, who moves and guides everything in this field."[118]

---

111. Cf. N 1956/182, p. 7.
112. Cf. *ibid.*, p. 8.
113. Cf. *UR*, 3-4, 12, 19-23.
114. For such cases, see Part II, Chapter 3 above, where we discussed Bea's work at the Holy Office.
115. Cf. N 1959/71.
116. Cf. N 1958/47.
117. N 1956/182, p. 9.
118. N 1956/18. Here too Bea's thinking is in line with that of *UR*, 24, on the role of the Holy Spirit.

Referring to certain anxieties, he says: "As is generally the case, so too in the ecumenical sector the church puts its trust much less . . . in worldly propaganda and human means, and more in its own inner strength and in the protection and guidance of the Holy Spirit, who is the soul of the mystical body of Christ and thus gives it its life and energy."[119] We would add that the article on Protestants and the definition of the assumption ends with the words: "The Holy Spirit, who has kindled in many souls a lively desire that all those who are called Christians should be united again in the fold of Christ, . . . also decides the ways in which this desire inspired by him can be fulfilled."[120]

These last words make it clear that, alongside the decisive role attributed to the Holy Spirit, Bea asserts the need for our cooperation, and also the *major role that prayer plays* in this. After speaking about various obstacles to union, he concludes: "We can and must pray [for union], and we can also work for it with love and patience, but it is the Lord who makes it grow [cf. 1 Cor. 3:6-7]."[121] In reply to a letter from a representative of the Sammlung Movement who stresses the need for an intensification of prayer, Bea writes back saying that he is in complete agreement and promising that he will immediately ask for the support of the head of the Apostleship of Prayer, an association run by the Society of Jesus, and having, Bea says, between thirty-seven and thirty-eight million members throughout the world.[122]

This is the correct context in which to understand Bea's thinking on *the role of the Blessed Virgin* in the great question of union. In this connection, Bea quotes and adopts two points from the apostolic constitution *Munificentissimus Deus* with which Pius XII proclaimed the dogma of the assumption: Mary "has maternal tenderness toward all the members" of the mystical body of Christ, which leads to the hope that other Christians will also desire "an increase in their own love" for Mary.[123] Still more specifically, he says: "Mary, who lives in heaven, [is] the bond of union for the mystical body of Christ, as the new Eve and new mother of the living."[124]

Answering the difficulties expressed by certain Protestants concerning this role, Bea explains it as follows: "Everybody knows that when Catholic theology" speaks about Mary's mediation it is "certainly not placing Mary 'on a par with Christ,' or seeing her as acting independently and in coordination, but that it sees the mother's action as *sub*ordinate to the Son's, as willed and established by God himself. Nothing is therefore being taken away from the dignity of Christ who is the sole Mediator and Savior and for whom, as the Holy Father says, Mary is, rather, 'minister and dispenser.' "[125]

---

119. N 1956/182, pp. 4-5.
120. Biblio. 99, p. 92.
121. Nm 17 (1956).
122. Cf. N 1957/147. On the subject of prayer, cf. also N 1956/132; 1957/267; 1958/36.
123. Cf. Biblio. 99, p. 75.
124. *Ibid.*
125. *Ibid.*, p. 88. The last words are taken from a speech Pius XII gave on 21 April 1940. It should be noted that these words to some extent foreshadow the thinking of the Council in its constitution on the church (*LG*, 60-62).

Despite this explanation, we should note that Bea realizes that Catholic doctrine needs further explanation and clarification on this point. After studying the draft program for the mariological congress to be held at Lourdes in 1958 he points out that the wording of one title, "Mary and Christians Separated from the Church," would concentrate the attention mainly on the attitude of other Christians toward Mary and devotion to her, and he therefore suggests that it should be changed to "Mary and the Unity of the Church," a modification that was in fact accepted.[126] As we can see, there is a basic shift in perspective here: instead of considering the attitude of other Christians toward Mary, the question is that of the role and thus the attitude of Mary in the plan of salvation willed by God. We therefore move from the purely historical perspective to the strictly theological one. Whoever redrafted the program for the congress emphasized this perspective, very rightly linking Mary with the subject of the church—an approach that would then be adopted by the Second Vatican Council in the last chapter of its constitution on the church.[127]

* * *

We can summarize and conclude this chapter as follows. Leaving aside Bea's more general and distant ecumenical grounding, which has been seen throughout our study, we can now say that in the ten years considered here he acquired and showed considerably more specific preparation for ecumenical work. This was formed firstly by a good and fairly wide network of direct or indirect contacts with the ecumenical movement of those times. When he decided to take a hand in the very instructive debate that had arisen in the ecumenical world following the definition of the bodily assumption of Mary into heaven, Bea not only showed that he was generically committed to ecumenism, but also took up certain very clear ecumenical attitudes. His various articles and letters also contain a great deal of ecumenical teaching on many fundamental subjects: the question of unity, ecumenical dialogue and its various attributes, particularly the need for it to be carried out in both truth and charity, as well as collaboration between Christians, the role of the Holy Spirit, and lastly the need for prayer.

It would certainly be an exaggeration to claim that this period gives us a full portrait of the Bea we would know as first President of the Secretariat for Christian Unity, for it simply provides the preparation and still lacks the breath of the Holy Spirit provided under the papacy of John XXIII. Even so, it was certainly a noteworthy and solid preparation, and was there, ready and waiting to be placed at the service of the Spirit at the moment decided by the Lord of the church.

---

126. Cf. Nd 13 (1956).
127. Cf. *LG*, 63-65.

CHAPTER 6

ALWAYS READY AND WILLING TO SERVE HIS
BROTHERS AND THE CHURCH

In his spiritual notes Bea describes correspondence as an important part of his apostolate, saying that alongside his work in the Roman congregations, consultations, etc., it enables him to "dispense light and awaken life . . . and thus do much good in silence."[1] And, indeed, although the aspects of Bea's life that we have seen in previous chapters—relations with Pope Pius XII and his work as theologian, liturgist and ecumenist—may be varied and wide-ranging, they in no way exhaust the wealth of information found in his letters. If we look through the correspondence we find a broad variety of cases in which Bea in his own way "dispenses light" and tries to "awaken life"—by providing information, advice and various types of practical assistance, by showing concern over pastoral problems both large and small, or by acting as a peace-maker. We shall attempt to give an idea of these various new aspects of his personality in the present chapter.

Pastoral Concern over Individuals

When we reread his letters we are always struck by the amount of time and attention this busy man devotes to individuals, often to people with whom he has no particular connection and whom he knows barely, if at all, people who come to him with their modest problems and anxieties, or simply with requests for information.

1. First of all we find a type of activity that has a large place in Bea's letters: his activity as *a gifted advisor or counselor*. Someone who was in contact with him for a number of years describes an experience shared by many: "My conversations with you were among the deepest experiences of my time in Rome . . . and represented a profound human joy for me."[2] Bea is very aware of the trust shown him, and encourages people to speak freely and frankly.[3] However, it is not simply a question of open and frank conversations, for there are many cases in which people turn to him for practical advice and assistance.

A fellow Jesuit confides his bitterness over the fact that "some Roman censor" of the order is hostile to the works of certain people and has been preventing their publication. Bea answers with a long letter, saying that it is not a question of hostility or ill-will, but rather of the fact that we are still in the shadow of the encyclical *Humani generis*, and that since the order has suffered

---

1. Cf. Exercises 1958/VIII/3.
2. N 1956/91.
3. Cf. N 1956/155.

considerably from its effects, the superiors—and consequently also the censors—must be doubly prudent and cautious.[4] When another Jesuit complains about the arbitrary opposition of censors and superiors to his publications, Bea encourages him not to lose heart, saying that having dedicated so much time and energy to the works in question, he should bring into play all the rights that the regulations of the order grant him in this respect.[5]

Another Jesuit, a classics professor, writes to him in disappointment, saying that he has been offered a chance (moreover without any cost to his community) of visiting Rome, which would be of very fundamental assistance in his teaching work, but that his superiors have refused their permission. Bea cheers him up, suggesting the form in which his request should be reworded, an attempt that in fact proves successful.[6]

A theologian refers to an article by a Catholic author, describing it as "fairly minimalist" in the area of mariology, and asking for "action from Rome." Bea answers that it would be more profitable if a competent theologian were to intervene with a calm critique of the article.[7] Another correspondent complains about an unjustly critical intervention on the part of a well-placed Roman theologian with regard to the studies of a mariological society, and here again Bea dissolves misunderstandings and irons out difficulties.[8]

One person writes to him to recommend the insertion of the name of St. Joseph into the canon of the mass. Bea replies that applications by individuals do not have much effect in this area, and that his correspondent should try to get such an addition requested by his own episcopal conference.[9]

A pastor of souls tells Bea that the question of the nomination of an auxiliary bishop for his diocese is dragging on; Bea answers with suggestions as to what he can do to move things ahead, and promises that he himself will do what he can to help.[10]

On the basis of his personal experience in Rome, Bea also provides assistance in some more thorny matters. Thus he gives advice on the best steps to be taken in order to obtain permission for a priest who has previously been "laicized" to say mass in private.[11] Similarly, for years he shows concern over the case of a scholar whom the Holy Office has previously forbidden to publish scientific works, and suggests what steps should be taken to obtain his rehabilitation; unfortunately, the man in question is too embittered and refuses to accept certain conditions, so that the attempts prove vain.[12]

These and similar cases show how people turned to Bea in many difficult circumstances for advice, and also explain what he meant when he said that his

---

4. Cf. N 1951-62.
5. Cf. N 1958/169.
6. Cf. N 1954/5; 1954/23; 1954/58.
7. Cf. N 1955/68.
8. Cf. N 1955/176; 1956/5b.
9. Cf. N 1955/69.
10. Cf. N 1955/23; 1955/50.
11. Cf. N 1954/14; also N 1956/195.
12. Cf. N 1956/158.

position entailed a duty to show particular concern over people in trouble and distress.[13]

2. Another of his characteristics is connected with the previous point, and this is the fact that he was always ready and willing *to be of help and service.*

The present author remembers how Bea offered to stand in for him in Rome during his summer leave and correct the proofs of the *Acta* (the official annual publication of the Pontifical Biblical Institute).[14] In the same way Bea offers to stand in for Father A. Miller, O.S.B., Secretary of the Pontifical Biblical Commission, during the summer months.[15] When a fellow Jesuit's manuscript has run into problems with the order's censors, he steps in and gives his assistance.[16] He searches in Lebanon for an important theological work for the daughter of a friend, the well-known Old Testament scholar, Professor W. Kahle.[17] Similarly, he searches all over Italy for a certain drug for someone who is seriously sick.[18] In the years after the Second World War he establishes contact with the "Associatio Perseverantiae Sacerdotalis," which has headquarters in Feldkirch, Austria, and has the aim of helping the clergy in communist countries; and on a number of occasions he does what he can to tell others about it and also to provide other forms of assistance.[19] A member of the ecclesiastical court of a major diocese submits certain difficult matrimonial cases to Bea, and he takes the time to examine them and also has various canon law experts do the same.[20] He is even asked to do what he can at the court of the Sacra Rota in connection with certain matrimonial cases; he answers that unfortunately he does not know any of the rota judges personally, but that in any case an official word from the ordinary of the diocese will be much more effective.[21]

A form of spiritual comfort with which he helped many people was that of obtaining a "special blessing" for them from the pope.[22] His letters contain a particularly touching example of understanding and affection for a fellow Jesuit who was suffering a period of painful trial. A very famous theologian, the man had been hard hit by the measures taken in the wake of the encyclical *Humani generis.* He had every wish to be sincerely and wholly faithful to the church, so that when he was seen as a representative of the "new theology," which was so severely criticized by the encyclical, this was a source of deep distress to him. Following a request from his religious superior, Bea stepped in with his good offices, arranging for the theologian's profession of full fidelity to the church to reach the hands of Pope Pius XII. And the pope in turn had Bea convey his

13. Cf. N 1955/180.
14. Cf. N 1954/99.
15. Cf. N 1958/154.
16. Cf. N 1954/8.
17. Cf. N 1952/83.
18. Cf. N 1956/40. Other cases of such help are found in N 1958/24; 1954/147.
19. Cf. N 1954/75; 1954/87; 1957/28; also 1958/19.
20. Cf. N 1954/162.
21. Cf. N 1954/233. See also the cases of help with other departments of the Roman curia: N 1954/90; 1957/193; 1958/78; 1958/147-147b; 1958/182; 1958/190.
22. Cf. for example N 1954/82; 1956/28; 1956/31; 1957/82; 1958/62; 1958/209.

special blessing to him, together with an assurance that he could be totally at peace with his conscience.[23] The files contain an expression of the theologian's deep gratitude to Bea for helping him at that crucial moment.

We have already seen in our chapter on Bea's activity as Rector of the Pontifical Biblical Institute that a habit of encouraging and supporting other people's work was a marked feature of his whole approach. This applies particularly in the period under consideration here and to relations with alumni of the institute, to whom he was generous with advice and encouragement over methods to be used in teaching, study and scientific work.[24] His correspondence also contains a number of examples of authors who say that they are greatly in his debt, and this applies in the cases of various commentaries on individual books of sacred scripture,[25] a short commentary on the whole of sacred scripture, and also an archeological dictionary.[26] Similar advice and encouragement are also mentioned in connection with the scientific works of fellow Jesuits[27] and others—for example, the English-language *Catholic Commentary* on the whole of sacred scripture.[28]

Within this same context of encouragement of other people's work, he sometimes took on heavy or irksome tasks. Thus he agreed to check the Italian translation of a work on Christ[29] and also that of the German catechism for adults (which we have already mentioned),[30] as well as providing assistance for the publication of a Slavonic psalter.[31] He also agreed to carry out a detailed appraisal of the writings of an Italian archeologist with a view to posthumous publication.[32] And when pressing commitments meant that on one occasion he was not able to go over a manuscript as soon as expected, he apologized to its author.[33]

3. We shall add one last category of "concern over individuals," which is in a way more surprising than any of the others, in other words the various *letters providing information*—information without any particular importance in itself, and quite often sent to people with whom he had no particular link.

Since he had been Rector of the Pontifical Biblical Institute and editor of the review *Biblica* for almost twenty years, it is easy to understand why people went on turning to him with a wide variety of questions in some way connected with biblical matters: the curriculum of the institute and the conditions for enroll-ment, problems with study and research, the rules for publication of books of sacred scripture, and so on. Bea could quite easily have passed such letters on

---

23. Cf. N 1957/324; 1958/66.
24. Cf. for example N 1958/159; 1953/171.
25. Cf. Ny 61 (1953), N 1953/28.
26. Cf. N 1956/38; Ny 61 (1953); 55 (1952).
27. Cf. N 1958/222; Nz 55 (1956).
28. Cf. N 1953/33; also Nz 21 (1952); N 1958/81; 1958/172.
29. Cf. N 1958/216.
30. Cf. Nz 61b (1957); 63 (1957).
31. Cf. N 1958/215.
32. Cf. N 1959/72.
33. Cf. N 1958/93.

to those in charge of such matters, but for one reason or another, and out of due regard for his neighbor and in particular for the authors of such letters, he very often answered them himself.[34] Indeed, we have one case in which he provides a totally unknown correspondent with detailed information on the authenticity of the Qumran (or Dead Sea) scrolls.[35] On another occasion he writes at length to an unknown intellectual, explaining what is meant by such terms as "soul and body" and "intellectual and instinctive life."[36]

He also receives questions and requests concerning other unconnected fields. A stranger asks him not only for a photograph of the deceased Pope Pius XII but also that he should go and pray at the pope's tomb, in his name.[37] Others ask about the cost of papal titles, or how to obtain a papal blessing for newly-weds.[38] Another total stranger asks for information on an apparently famous organ in St. Peter's and on the "two hundred bells of the same basilica."[39] Someone else asks for assistance in a case he has pending with an Italian government department, while another asks him to get him a pass for reduced railroad fares.[40] Although Bea declines to help with the government departments concerned, he does take the trouble to answer, albeit briefly.

References and recommendations were a similar matter. In Italy, and particularly in Rome, these were a constant nuisance, and Bea was exceedingly careful and reserved in such matters. Even so, in cases of true necessity and when he was personally familiar with the situation, he would sometimes agree to act, especially if a greater good was at stake.[41]

4. However, his attention to others was not only seen in special or in some way exceptional circumstances, but also affected his everyday life in various ways, as some examples will at once show.

His kindness and attention to individuals meant that in the community where he lived he was always careful to remember his confreres' anniversaries (namedays, birthdays, and so on), and his correspondence also contains a number of letters in this connection. He even recalled the special anniversaries of other members of the order who had been in the novitiate with him, or had studied or worked with him, but had been far away for many years, maybe even in another continent—for example, men who had left to work as missionaries in North America or Brazil at the end of the last century or the beginning of this.[42] This same regard for his confreres meant that he often set about answering certain

---

34. Cf. N 1954/22; 1954/105; 1958/78; 1958/160.
35. Cf. N 1957/178; also N 1958/213, where he writes to someone he does not know, giving archeological information on the method of crucifixion, or where to find the Latin text of the encyclical *Rerum novarum* of Leo XIII.
36. Cf. N 1953/152.
37. Cf. N 1958/280.
38. Cf. N 1953/161; 1957/18.
39. Cf. N 1958/8.
40. Cf. N 1953/153; 1958/217.
41. Cf. for example N 1954/13; 1954/44; 1954/88; 1954/124; 1958/127; 1958/289.
42. Cf. N 1952/132; 1956/130. Such attention to other people's anniversaries is found in N 1954/86 and 1954/200.

letters personally when he could quite justifiably have entrusted this to others. He used to tell me: "How can I give other people things to do that I can do with less effort and less sacrifice of time, given my experience and the ease with which I work?"

We have already had several occasions to note the affection he had for alumni of the Biblical Institute,[43] and he in turn remembered his own teachers—for example, Professor Martens, his history teacher from Constance, and Father A. Merk, S.J.—with a mixture of gratitude and veneration. After he was introduced to the daughter of his history teacher Martens, during the period under consideration here (and thus many years after his Constance days), he used to see her and help her during her various visits to Rome.[44]

The same sensitivity and kindness led him to concern himself with people who had been at school with him and with distant members of his family; for example, he would tell them how to organize a visit to Rome, where to stay, and how to obtain tickets for a papal audience,[45] although when dealing with relatives and acquaintances, he did not confine himself to plain information, but would also set about finding a small hotel in the right price-bracket, obtaining tickets for audiences or other ceremonies in St. Peter's, and so on.[46]

His kindness and goodness of heart were the source of the great increase in the volume of his correspondence with his large family, including fairly distant members, after the visit he made to his home town in 1950. In view of his numerous commitments and the many calls on his time, he did all he could to cut down on his correspondence, and also made use of cyclostyled letters which would be sent to a number of families. Even so, the letters under this heading run into several hundreds in the period under consideration.[47] He concerned himself over everything, trying to help his relatives in their various difficulties with advice and encouragement, assuring them of his prayers and of being remembered at mass. As we can see, his letters were not only concerned with more practical affairs, but were written with a view to the spiritual good of the recipients; thus they were in fact an apostolate.

One last feature can be seen in the fact that at the end of his letters, having provided the necessary information, explanation or advice, the writer used to close with phrases that expressed his *readiness to provide further service, clarification or assistance,* for example: "If I can do anything else for you, I am always here," "If I can sometimes be useful in some way, I am always available," "You can count on me," and "Remember that I am completely at your disposal."[48]

It is easy to see that all this used to entail a number of commitments. Of course

---

43. Cf. pp. 114-115 above.
44. Cf. N 1954/15; 1954/48; 1958/119. In a similar way he helped the niece of his teacher Father Merk (cf. N 1954/16), and their correspondence then continued for a number of years.
45. Cf. for example N 1954/81; 1954/104; 1954/129; 1954/130; and various of his letters to relatives.
46. There are a great many such cases, and it is therefore unnecessary to give individual references.
47. The precise number of entries is 240.
48. Cf. for example N 1953/2; 1958/99; 1957/125; 1953/48; 1954/173; 1956/91; 1953/17.

these were not usually particularly time-consuming matters if taken individually, but anyone who has had a very busy life knows how much of a burden a rise in the number of such "small" services can represent for a man as busy as Bea certainly was. (He would sometimes say that he had so much to do that he did not know where to begin.[49]) We should also point out that he personally typed most of such letters on his Erika typewriter (which is now found in the museum in his home town), for he did not have a secretary of his own but had to make do with part-time assistance when available, since the person in question was involved in many other matters.

So *how can we explain* this aspect of Bea's life? I think that the explanation lies in a combination of factors. The first is that Bea had a particular sensitivity to human relations. Another is that he was deeply conscious of the trust with which people turned to him for advice and assistance,[50] and he would thus respond generously. The last factor—and in my opinion the most fundamental one—was his true goodness or charity, which had obviously been developed and expanded through his training as a priest and Jesuit. We shall see this aspect more clearly in the next chapter.

Concern over Pastoral Problems

In our previous chapters we have repeatedly seen how in Bea's activity he paid special attention to the pastoral aspects of the various questions he dealt with. We saw this in his work at the Holy Office,[51] and also more explicitly in the practice and theory of his work as liturgist, particularly in his commitment to the use of the vernacular in the liturgy, both in German-speaking countries and in mission lands, which was based first and foremost on reasons of a pastoral order.[52]

1. We have seen that after 1950 he repeatedly visited his home town during the brief vacations he was granted, although we should note that these were neither solely nor even mainly visits to his own relatives. In other words, he did not go as a university lecturer seeking a little quiet and relaxation, and *concern over the spiritual well-being of the faithful* was a constant feature of his visits. He was always involved in preaching, instruction, liturgical services, etc., and even the relative letters are pervaded with pastoral considerations: for him it is a source of the greatest joy if the Christian life flourishes in the parish community; it is for the good of the community that he agrees to celebrate the fortieth anniversary of his priestly ordination there; on various occasions he recalls his visits and talks about the serious spiritual needs he has found in the parish; in one letter, he uses his knowledge of things to give a new parish priest advice on

---

49. Cf. N 1953/159.
50. Cf. for example N 1952/161.
51. Cf. N 1951/29; also pp. 194-198 above.
52. Cf. pp. 222-226; 229-231 above.

a constructive approach to work in the parish.[53] When church authorities decide to entrust a more important job to the parish priest who has just made a very promising start, and the town applies to Bea for assistance, Bea certainly responds—although, instead of upholding the claims of his own little town, he recognizes the justice of the decision taken by the authorities and confines himself to asking them to make sure that the pastoral welfare of his town is adequately catered for.[54]

Similarly, he took a very lively interest in the life and activity of the archdiocese where he was born and his home town, showing concern over its problems and the worries of its bishops, and saying that he was always willing to provide any help he could. A large number of letters are thus devoted to such matters, but since the events in question are relatively recent, we shall refrain from giving further details.[55]

2. It is interesting to see how Bea viewed a *bishop's position* with regard to pastoral tasks and questions. He writes to the pastor of a great archdiocese in West Germany, expressing the hope that he will soon obtain "a good auxiliary bishop" so that he will not be swamped by more "exterior" tasks such as confirmations and other formal appearances, but be freed to devote himself to taking care of the vast number of difficult pastoral problems that tend to arise throughout the church today—as he himself sees again and again in his work at various Roman congregations.[56] These observations must obviously not be understood as meaning that Bea in some way looked down on the work of auxiliary bishops as being of minor importance. For example, he writes to one of the latter, saying that basically the auxiliary bishop is always in the thick of things and therefore gets a closer view of problems and is in a position to set things on the right path, often simply with his presence. And maybe, says Bea, this explains the great importance of the position of auxiliary bishops: the ordinary is taken up with many tasks that oblige him to remain in his office, so that the auxiliary bishop has to maintain personal contacts, an activity that seems especially important in the large German dioceses, which have millions of souls. Bea therefore feels that such "decentralization" must become increasingly the norm.[57]

3. The complex, serious nature of the problems besetting any bishop today (and here Bea is thinking particularly of the large German dioceses) convince him of the importance, or rather the compelling need, for all the bishops of a given country to act in a united way within the framework of *the episcopal conference*. Only in this way is it possible to gain a full picture of problems and work out a coordinated pastoral approach, so that the clergy, not only in the

---

53. Cf. N 1951/48; 1951/70; 1957/274; 1953/148.
54. Cf. N 1955/104; 1955/105; 1955/113; 1955/143.
55. It is significant that his ecumenical commitment did not mean that he closed his eyes to various very questionable forms of proselytism that were practiced by certain Protestant movements in Italy and represented a serious danger to ordinary members of the faithful; cf. N 1953/51.
56. Cf. N 1955/23.
57. Cf. N 1955/187.

individual dioceses but also in the whole country, can follow an integrated line. In order to enable an episcopal conference to organize the effective implementation of such a plan, Bea suggests that as a first step a secretariat should be set up; and here he refers to the practice followed in France. This secretariat would have the task of arranging for experts from a variety of sectors and with a variety of mental approaches—and in consultation with the offices of the Roman curia—to draft studies enabling the episcopal conference to weigh up the situation and choose the best ways and means of solving the major problems common to all the dioceses. In this context Bea suggests that the relative studies could lead to the publication of a pastoral directory along the lines of the French pastoral directory for social problems. This would be very helpful to the clergy, facilitating their work, and also helping to ensure a more homogeneous style of procedure in the different dioceses. When making this suggestion, he says that he is well aware of the objections that could be raised to the creation of such a secretariat, for example that the secretary could become too powerful and pursue "his own policy," but that despite this he thinks the advantages far outweigh any possible disadvantages.[58]

We have already seen how he was particularly concerned over the various problems of Germany, and all the more so inasmuch as he had special responsibility for this sector in his work at the Holy Office. A number of his letters speak about the division of certain dioceses in West Germany, which were too large both geographically and numerically, so that contact with clergy and people was very difficult for their bishops. When such a division was made and the diocese of Essen came into being, Bea watched developments with lively interest.[59] He also took a close interest in the new German catechism for adults, observing that in recent decades there had been too many changes in this connection, so that greater stability was now needed.[60] And he corresponded with a German bishop on problems connected with the practice of children's communion.[61]

In this context it is interesting to note that in 1957 he started to play an active part in the great cause of helping Poles and Germans to get to know one another with a view to reconciliation.[62]

4. Among the numerous serious problems facing the pastoral ministry today, Bea also touches on the question of the collaboration of lay people. Taking his cue from the pastoral letter of a German bishop, he says that in the pastoral ministry people often still tend to work according to the ideas and approaches current in the "pre-motorization era." Today a priest can no longer do many

---

58. Cf. N 1956/85; 1956/97b; 1957/125. I have preferred to summarize the line of thinking found in various letters, rather than giving individual quotations, partly also because of the need for discretion in order not to reveal the specific situations and people concerned. In N 1957/168 Bea expresses similar views with reference to the position of the father general of his own order, saying that he must be relieved of his involvement in details in order to allow him to have an intellectual picture of the overall situation.

59. Cf. N 1955/145; 1958/259.

60. Cf. N 1954/117.

61. Cf. N 1953/162; 1953/181.

62. Cf. N 1957/94; 1957/98.

things that a priest could and maybe should have done thirty years ago, or else lay people can do them better. If the laity say that they have now reached adulthood, this is not simply some "revolutionary" claim but is a sign that they are concerned over the good of the church and realize that something in it is not working as it should. The best way of keeping pace with these trends is that of integrating lay people into the apostolate, after providing them with the necessary training.[63] This indicates the great importance of energetic cooperation between episcopal authority and associations for the lay apostolate, cooperation that should take place under the guidance of clergy and well-trained lay people, while basic orientations should come from the bishop.[64]

In the context of the participation of lay people in the apostolate of the church, Bea also speaks of the question of *worker-priests*, which had been the cause of great concern in many quarters in those years. After receiving a booklet issued by the Schonstatt Movement on pastoral work in the labor sphere entitled "Let down your nets for a catch," Bea writes that its approach seems right to him: "It is not the task of priests to go into factories; rather, they should send well-trained, zealous, capable lay people. This kind of apostolate will certainly bear much more fruit than that of worker-priests, who have in practice achieved very little, and certainly much less than could have been expected from the relative outlay."[65]

His correspondence also contains an interesting example of the extent to which Bea felt this involvement of lay people could be taken. A German bishop with a widely scattered diocese told him of a problem raised by his clergy concerning the more outlying "stations" which priests could visit only every two or even four weeks. Since it is, however, precisely in such situations important for the faithful to be able to approach the eucharist, the clergy brought their bishop the following question: In such outlying places would it be possible, on the Sundays when the priest cannot get there, for a service to be celebrated under the leadership of lay people, who would also be authorized to distribute holy communion? It is revealing that the bishop even tells Bea about such a question. Bea answers that there is probably nothing against lay people leading such a service, so long as the priest also comes to say mass when he can. However, it will be more difficult to obtain permission for the distribution of communion. Having explained the various possibilities that the canon law then in force offers, he advises the bishop to submit the case to the pope himself, orally in the first place; indeed, if the bishop likes, Bea is ready to sound the pope out personally.[66]

5. His pastoral concern also covered *wider problems*, as well as questions connected with *more distant regions*. When a fellow Jesuit sends him the gift

---

63. Cf. N 1957/125; Nm 60 (1958).
64. Cf. N 1956/85.
65. N 1955/145. We do not know if the Holy Office had yet turned its attentions to the question of worker-priests, and if this meant that Bea had had to study it. In any case, he is here following the well-known decision of Pius XII on this question.
66. Cf. N 1958/40.

of a book he has published on priestly vocations, Bea answers: "This is a world-wide problem today, and many efforts will be needed merely in order to maintain the number of priests at the present level. This is a great source of anxiety to the Holy Father."[67]

The happy development of the "Sophia" Catholic University in Tokyo and the Hiroshima Mission—with which he had been concerned as visitator once upon a time—lead him to forecast that it will not be long before Japan receives its own cardinal, as has now happened with Cardinal Gracias for India.[68]

He speaks about Latin America in one letter, saying that it represents a major problem today. "I hope that after the conference of bishops convened by Cardinal Piazza in Rio de Janeiro, bishops will tackle this problem energetically, prudently and generously. May the Lord grant that we are still in time to save Catholicism in Latin America."[69]

In this way his correspondence throws light on the pastoral concerns of Augustin Bea. Obviously we are dealing here mostly with clues and casual indications, and in numbers that are limited by his extreme discretion in matters connected with his relations with Pope Pius XII. However, the spontaneous tone of the letters is what in fact shows that they concern matters close to the writer's heart, so that a mere reference is sufficient to give us an idea of his usual line of thinking. The facts mentioned here provide practical illustrations of the following statement: "Without seeking it, I have been moving further and further away from the Old Testament and placed within the more recent history of the world and the church, so that I must do all I can to keep myself truly up to date on what is happening."[70] We have already cited some similar words written to a fellow Jesuit: "I shall soon have to say that I am occupied in caring for the church in all its aspects,[71] particularly the suffering church and people in distress. This is a fine activity; there are other people who can do exegesis."[72]

* * *

If we consider this chapter as a whole, we can reasonably wonder whether it does not already contain a rough sketch of the first President of the Secretariat for Christian Unity, with certain of his marked characteristics: a very strong pastoral sense; an openness of mind and heart to the great problems that the Second Vatican Council then considered; but above all the goodness and charity that witnesses almost unanimously indicate as his most striking feature right from their first meeting.

---

67. N 1953/19.
68. Cf. N 1953/10. Cardinal Valerian Gracias (1900-1978), Archbishop of Bombay. The nomination of a Japanese cardinal—Tatsuo Doi, Archbishop of Tokyo—took place in March 1960 and was made by Pope John XXIII.
69. N 1955/145. The fruit of this meeting was the creation of the Latin-American Council of Bishops (CELAM), the twenty-fifth anniversary of which was celebrated in Rio de Janeiro in July 1980, within the framework of the pastoral journey of John Paul II to Brazil.
70. N 1956/85; cf. 1955/187.
71. The expression is taken from 2 Cor. 11:28 ("anxiety for all the churches").
72. N 1955/180.

CHAPTER 7

THE SPIRITUAL MAN

While examining the various aspects of Bea's life and many-faceted activity in the previous chapters of this second part, we also received glimpses of the deep spiritual motivations that underlay his whole approach and constitute the true, though often hidden, foundations of his life and activity. In the chapter on his relations with Pius XII we felt called upon to investigate these motivations in some depth, and thus saw that the abundant notes that Augustin Bea left us from his spiritual exercises allow us to look into his interior life, understanding his spiritual world "from inside," and gaining an idea of the true source from which all we have so far studied flowed in the final analysis. We shall now try to fill out our previous remarks in the light of these spiritual notes.

The foregoing provides a reasonably clear indication of the parameters of the present chapter. We do not intend reproducing the full spiritual portrait that we can contemplate by reading and studying these spiritual notes, for such a task would require much more space[1] and would take us too far afield. We shall therefore follow the methodological principle laid down at the beginning of our work, where we said that we shall not aim at presenting a full-scale investigation of his spiritual life as it appears in these notes, but shall simply use them to fill out the study we have already made, indicating the spiritual foundations of his life and activity in the period under consideration.

An Apostle, Sent by Christ

The reference point here is the sending out of the apostles by Jesus, and thus the biblical concepts of "mission" and "apostle," together with the "apostolate" derived from the latter. These concepts are considered most specifically in the meditations on the choosing and on the calling or sending of the apostles. "I must be aware that it is a great grace from the Savior that he allows me to share in his work and mission. Whatever it may be, my work is nothing profane: it means always and everywhere being an ambassador for Christ, representing him, acting in his name; 'for Christ' also means for his interests."[2] "Any task I

---

1. Readers can consult the attempt at a *Spiritual Profile* (Biblio. 191a), which runs to about one hundred pages.

2. 1953/IV/4. We would remind readers of the system used in references to the retreat notes: the first figure obviously indicates the year of the retreat; the second, the day (out of the eight days that the retreat lasts); and the third, the relative meditation (out of the four daily meditations). This system is used by the author of the notes. (*Translator's note.* The original German extracts cited in this chapter, from which the English translation is taken, can be found in the German version of the present biography, *Augustin Bea. Der Kardinal der Einheit* [Graz, 1989], pp. 341-364.)

267

am given by the superiors of the church contains something of the authority of the Savior himself, who says: 'As the Father sent me, so too I send you.' What I do is therefore not simply a 'business' but has something divine about it. . . ."[3] The following text should be understood in the same light: "Having been called to the same office and to the same dignity as that of the apostles, I must also strive after the same perfection. The older I get and the more important my position and the more I am respected, the more my life must be that of a true apostle."[4]

Let us now take a closer look at the role played by the concept of mission. "All my work in the Society of Jesus—all I have done so far and all I shall do in the future—constitutes a *missio*, a sending out to an apostolate, and is an expression of the great love that the Savior has for me."[5] "Everything I do in my profession, in my various positions, is based on this mission, on the sending out on the part of the divine Savior; in everything it is a question of the fulfillment of his mandate and not of a choice or preference of my own."[6] "Every call to take part in a meeting, give a lecture, and similar things, means a 'mission' for me, and I must not see it as a nuisance or disturbance."[7] "The Lord has placed the future of his kingdom in the hands of men and has given them an enormous responsibility in this connection."[8]

The object of the mission is explained not only in the meditation on the call of the apostles, but above all in the contemplation on the kingdom of Christ. The mission concerns the kingdom of Christ, the interests of God, the fulfillment of the plan of salvation.[9] The apostle lives for God and for souls; he does not live for himself, but for immortal souls, for the kingdom of God; all outward activity must be imbued with zeal for souls.[10] In other words, we must cooperate in the specific task of the church; all we do is part of the great apostolic work of the church.[11] In this way we reach formulations that sum up everything: daily work, and thus also all the work of one's life, with its sacrifices and its full commitment, are performed for the kingdom of God, for the glory of God, for the church and for souls.[12]

Sharing in the Great Task of the Hierarchical Church

The apostle's position as part of the church requires further clarification: it can be described as an integration in the hierarchically ordered church, in the

---

3. 1949/VI/1.
4. 1949/V/2.
5. 1950/V/4.
6. 1952/V/3.
7. 1955/V/4.
8. 1952/IV/3.
9. Cf. 1955/V/4; 1953/I/3; 1953/III/4.
10. Cf. 1957/V/2; 1953/V/1; 1955/V/2.
11. Cf. 1952/VIII/3; 1952/IV/3.
12. Cf. 1953/VI/3; 1951/II/4; 1954/I/4.

church which is both human work and mystery in the strict sense of the word because Christ himself lives and works in it. And the fundamental law of the church is love. Let us illustrate this approach step by step.

In the context of the scene of Christ before Pilate we read: "The Savior is king and possesses a kingdom, and under certain aspects this is similar to a kingdom of this world: it is hierarchically organized; it is visible from outside, so it is not a purely spiritual kingdom; it is in this world, although it does not have its origins *in* this world."[13]

In his appearances after the resurrection "Christ institutes the church with its means of grace (baptism, the sacrament of penance), with its doctrine and its magisterium, with its jurisdiction, with its hierarchy with Peter and his successors at its head. . . . But the law of love must reign in the church, and whoever is placed in the highest position must love more than all the others. Thus all the forces are united in the church, because it is basically nothing other than Christ who continues to live and work."[14] "The church is basically nothing other than Christ who continues to live; it is his mystical body. This is why there have always been persecutions; and the more the church grows and the more powerful it is in its doctrine and activity, the more gigantic become the attacks against it. . . ."[15]

This "structure" of the church is retained throughout its journey through history. Considering the function of the apostles in the feeding of the five thousand, the retreatant writes: "The twelve apostles have now become thousands of bishops, on whom Christ confers the same mandate to govern the people (*potestas gubernandi*), teach (*potestas docendi*) and nourish with the bread of life, the holy eucharist (*potestas ordinis*). And all this *flows from the goodness and love of his heart.* This is the original source of the church and of all the church has to give. If I want to be an *authentic and worthy servant of the church*, I too must do everything *in kindness and love,* in the charity of the heart of Christ."[16]

Referring to the appearance in which the risen One entrusts the keys to Peter, thus giving him the authority to feed the whole flock, Bea writes: "How true those words have become since then! The little church of the upper room gave birth to the present world-wide church, and all peoples and races come to St. Peter's successor, the Roman pontiff. He feeds them in the authority of Christ, but in love: 'Simon, do you love me, do you love me more than these?' The kingdom of God has now become a kingdom of love, and whoever works for this kingdom must do so for love and in love."[17]

A number of the texts cited have already shown that the retreatant meditates on these truths in the perspective of his own life, *in order to set his own position*

---

13. 1950/VII/3.

14. 1949/VIII/3.

15. 1953/V/2. For the idea that Christ continues to live in the church (in German "Kirche ist der fortlebende Christus"), cf. 1951/III/3; 1949/VIII/3; 1955/VIII/3.

16. 1954/V/4.

17. 1954/VIII/3.

and activity in their proper context. Let us add one or two more examples. One of the basic texts closes with the words: "I must recognize as a great grace that I can serve this church and work for it."[18] After referring to the world-wide proportions the activity of the church has taken on today, he observes in regard to his own work: "To collaborate in this work in a central position is an apostolate that is the lot of only a few and that I would never have been able to imagine. And it demands all the more total commitment on my part."[19]

From what we have seen, it is clear that Bea certainly does not see the apostolate as limited to what is usually referred to as "direct pastoral work," in other words preaching, catechizing, administering the sacraments, and so on. In this connection he observes succinctly that his "apostolic work involves the lecture podium, the typewriter, study, publications, correspondence. . . ."[20] His whole view of the apostolate provides a clear basis for the following statement: "Everything I do has its foundation in the mission I have received, and with everything I do I am carrying out the mandate received from Christ; everything is part of the great apostolic work of the church. Yes, in view of its final purpose, all my work is apostolic, and it is very often eminently apostolic."[21] "A city set on a hill cannot be hidden. And the Lord has not lit this lamp in order to put it under a bushel. But this means that it is my duty truly to be a 'light': with my teaching, but still more so with my life, with the good example of virtue, of perfection and holiness, an example that I must give to all, without being too 'precious' about it."[22]

In the Service of the Truth

The threefold power—government, teaching and priesthood—that Christ confers on the apostles, and thus on their successors, and also on those who work with the latter, means that they share in the threefold office of Christ as King, Prophet and Priest. In this connection, the notes contain the following words: "I must not ignore the fact that I have a task that is in many ways *important*. It is that of sharing in the office of Christ as Pastor and Teacher, and doing so at the center of the church."[23]

It is quite natural in view of his position that our retreatant should place particular stress on the office of teacher, and hence on the aspect of doctrine, and more generally the service of truth: "As concerns the *magisterium*, the Savior has called me to a position of primary and very great responsibility in relation both to lecturing and to the rest of my activity."[24] "First, I must imbue

---

18. 1958/VIII/3.
19. 1954/V/2.
20. Cf. for example N 1951/127; 1951/147.
21. Cf. 1952/V/3; 1950/V/4; 1952/IV/3; 1955/V/2; 1956/V/4.
22. 1949/V/3; cf. 1957/V/4.
23. 1958/I/2.
24. 1955/V/2.

myself (*the salt!*) with the great truths, and then devote myself with all my strength to working to enable these truths to be recognized in the *world* through my teaching, my publications, and my work of counseling and direction, according to the opportunities presented by the circumstances."[25] "The teaching and guidance, in the broadest sense of the word, that I can offer people is offered not in my own name, but in the name of Christ, following his mandate. I must therefore not set forth my personal ideas or want to impress people with my own thoughts, but must set forth the word of God, in the name of God. 'So that I may be found faithful'!"[26]

The *gospel concept of "salt"* (cf. Mt. 5:13) leads the retreatant to reflect on various aspects of authentic service of the truth: "I am *the salt of the earth*, which is expected to safeguard sound principles and teaching. I must therefore myself *be inwardly true, strong and authentic*, for this is vital for the performance of my task. I must be *light*, and must thus be lit by the truths of the faith, so that I can also give light to others."[27] "I must be *salt*, upholding the principles of the faith with clarity and energy—even if salt corrodes. I must bear witness to the truth, even if such witness is not always pleasant."[28] "I must be *salt*, upholding *the principles of our holy faith*, wherever I am called to do so. I must uphold them without opportunism, without diplomacy, with firmness and clarity, albeit in an engaging and kindly form. In *personal contacts*, too, I must not allow a tendency to be accommodating to lead me to keep quiet about considerations of principle or minimize them."[29]

Let us make a few more observations on the same subject. Meditating on the *progress* of Jesus to Nazareth, he says: "This is how my progress should be manifested *outwardly*: while remaining basically firm, I must always strive to be more composed, balanced and benign, trying to be understanding and helpful."[30]

Under the heading "Intellectual Shortcomings" we find the following recommendations: "Modesty and calmness in discussions, without escalation or exaggeration; I must make an effort to see every side of questions; I must accept and examine *criticism* willingly; as likely as not, it contains at least a grain of truth."[31]

"The Apostolate of Example"

We saw the retreatant's view above that he must be a "light" by his teaching, but even more by his life. "The apostolate of example" is one of the most

---

25. 1950/V/3.
26. 1949/VI/2; the quote is from 1 Cor. 4:2.
27. 1956/I/3.
28. 1955/V/3.
29. 1957/V/4; cf. 1957/VII/3.
30. 1957/IV/4.
31. 1954/V/3.

frequently recurring thoughts in the notes, and is in fact often mentioned in first place.[32] "Maximum fidelity wherever the will of God is shown to me: command-ments, rules, the orders and wishes of superiors. Here I can exercise the apostolate of good example."[33] Under the heading "Fidelity in Small Things" we read: "My position (past and present) demands that I give my brother Jesuits and all those with whom I have dealings the perfect example of perfect observance of all the constitutions of the order; this is a form of *apostolate* for me. This also applies to the trifling inconveniences connected with the infirmi-ties, the aches and pains, of old age and ill-health. I must make a constant effort to ignore these, and never to be moody, bad-humored, etc., but always to be kindly, considerate and obliging."[34] "In my last years I can still perform a notable apostolate in the *family of the community*. First of all, the apostolate of good example. Although I may be one of the oldest fathers, I must not expect special treatment, unless it is imposed by higher authority; I must thus be punctual in everything, faithful to the rules, conscientious in work, edifying in all my behavior. Example of *modesty*: great simplicity, without pretensions, indeed being content if I have the impression that people forget or neglect me."[35] "I must be aware that . . . people expect a good example, edification, prudence and kindness from me."[36]

"Before sending the apostles out, the Savior himself gives them his *example*. . . . I too must act above all with my *example*: to those with whom I live, who must see in me a model of fidelity and fraternal charity; to students: solid preparation, serious scientific commitment and religious spirit; in the [Roman] congregations: serious work, dispassionateness and kindness, linked to firm principles."[37] "Outside the community too I must set a good example and fearlessly take up clear positions in support of what is good. I am not to seek my own interests, but those of the Father. In the church and the society I have nothing to gain and nothing to lose, but I do have a great responsibility."[38]

Commitment in Favor of Unity and Love

In this same context we should highlight references in the notes to the duty of fostering harmony or "the spirit of unity and peace," partly because they are of special interest concerning the future apostle of ecumenism. "Obliging toward my neighbor, *compassionate* and helpful; fostering *peace and harmony* wherever I can, being a mediator and reconciler."[39] In 1948 in a meditation

32. Cf. 1953/IV/3; 1955/I/4; 1956/V/1; 1957/IV/3.
33. 1951/V/1.
34. 1955/I/4; cf. 1952/II/3.
35. 1953/IV/3; cf. 1950/IV/3.
36. 1955/IV/3.
37. 1958/V/2.
38. 1957/V/4.
39. 1957/V/3.

entitled "The Bond of Charity" he writes that he must foster love "in the place that obedience has assigned to me: . . . in the church, ironing out conflicts wherever I can exercise an influence (but without sacrificing principles); . . . in the institute [the Pontifical Biblical Institute], cultivating and promoting a spirit of love between professors and students whenever possible, proceeding in all circumstances according to the principles of love, mutual understanding, the mutual settling of conflicts."[40]

In 1949, we find the following remarks in connection with the calling of the apostles: "The third thing that my apostolic vocation suggests to me is a great unity of love with my fellow apostles, my confreres. I am united with them in a special way in the Savior's heart, since we are all privileged members of his mystical body. . . . It is therefore my duty—and particularly because I am more influential and because of the greater respect I enjoy—to cultivate and promote most particularly the unity and harmony of all; 'the spirit of unity and peace.' "[41] We would observe here that although he speaks of the unity of the mystical body of Christ, the retreatant applies this solely to unity within the Catholic Church, while other Christians do not yet appear on the horizon.

The following year, in his meditation on the high-priestly prayer of Jesus, his thought deepens and his perspective widens. He starts with a psychological analysis of the prayer: "The high-priestly prayer of the Savior is permeated with a subdued pain: concern over *unity* and *love* in his church. With the apostles he had already experienced the difficulty entailed in preserving unity and love in the apostolic college; the washing of the feet was a last attempt to show them that unity and love can prosper only where authentic humility reigns. However, he foresees how things will go in the future, he foresees the divisions and internal strife. Hence his ardent prayer: 'That they may be one even as we are one.' . . . If I can contribute a little—with my prayer, my work and my sacrifices—to unity and love in the church, in some ecclesial community, this will be a great consolation for the Savior's heart."[42]

We would add a reflection: although the meditator also mentions "divisions and strife" in the church, other Christians do not appear in his application, unless we can see the expression "in some ecclesial community" as referring to them, which is possible but not very clear. The retreatant again meditates on the high-priestly prayer of Jesus in his 1958 retreat, but as concerns unity he confines himself to saying that the prayer of Jesus has assured unity to his church, without considering divisions or commitment in favor of the unity of the followers of Jesus.[43]

---

40. 1948/V/4.
41. 1949/V/2.
42. 1950/VII/2; cf. 1957/V/3.
43. Cf. 1958/VII/1.

The Love That "Believes All Things, Hopes All Things, Endures All Things"

"If I want to be *an authentic and worthy servant of the church,* I must act in all things with kindness and love, in the love of the heart of Christ."[44] With reference to the words of Luke's gospel that Jesus grew in grace before men (cf. Luke 2:52), we read: "Show a great supernatural love toward all, a truly paternal kindness, which is composed of great simplicity and which wins people over."[45] "I must surround myself with a certain atmosphere of fatherly benevolence toward everybody, regardless of natural sympathies or antipathies. Benign in judgments, in helping others; no harshness in words, no criticism of others; calm, serene and spiritual in all things."[46] "I must grow day by day in authentic supernatural love, and thus in friendliness, patience, readiness to help, understanding for the concerns and needs of confreres."[47]

Again in the context of the school of Nazareth, the retreatant learns "a benign, selfless, friendly nature, without any egoism, an attitude that does not give way in the face of the errors of others, but benignly excuses everything, presumes the best of brother Jesuits, and bears all things with patience."[48] The attitude of high regard and readiness to serve is also applied to relations with other religious orders—a field in which there have sometimes been weaknesses in other periods: "I must not forget that others are instruments of Christ too, and in a special sense other religious orders. Thus I must have a high opinion of them, esteem them, love them, encourage them."[49]

The texts we have quoted do in themselves provide an idea of the more profound *motivations* for this love, but we shall now add a few others in order to explore this aspect further. Under the heading "The Savior and Love of Neighbor" we read: "Love is the distinguishing mark of disciples; it is his *commandment.* 'It is the Lord's commandment.' . . . If this applies in general terms, it applies in the first place to the religious house, which must be a hearth and a focal point of love. . . . I shall therefore devote myself as much as I can to actualizing this ideal and helping it to be ever more fully realized in our community."[50]

The retreatant draws his inspiration not only from the Lord's commandment, but also—and I would say even more so—from the *example of kindness* and love *of Christ himself.* On the occasion of the miracle of the feeding of the five thousand, Christ "shows all the love of his heart for humanity: he is concerned over the exhaustion of the apostles; he is compassionate toward people who

---

44. 1954/V/4.
45. 1949/IV/3.
46. 1951/IV/2; cf. 1951/II/2.
47. 1952/IV/1.
48. 1951/V/3; cf. 1954/IV/4.
49. 1951/VIII/2. Other similar texts on various aspects of brotherly love: 1950/II/3; 1950/VI/1; 1951/IV/2; 1951/V/2; 1952/I/4; 1951/IV/1; 1952/V/1; 1953/II/3; 1955/I/4; 1957/V/3.
50. 1951/V/3; cf. 1956/IV/2.

have no shepherd. He shows kindness and friendliness in his dealings; in involving the apostles as assistants he shows an extraordinary generosity."[51] "This event [the feeding of the five thousand] shows me first and foremost the kindness of Jesus toward all: toward the tired apostles, toward the crowd which is anxious to hear his words, toward the sick whom he heals, toward the hungry whom he feeds with miraculous bread. . . ."[52]

Lastly, he notes how it is a truly *supernatural* love, so that we see and love God himself in our neighbor.[53] "How great brotherly love is when practiced for a supernatural motive! It is not selfish like earthly love; without any self-interest, it is willing to perform any service; it ignores imperfections; it does not allow disregard or neglect to upset it; it shows concern over everything. And all this because it sees *the supernatural side in the confrere*."[54] This "supernatural side" is the fact that confreres are adopted sons of God and in this sense brothers of Christ, members of the mystical body of Christ, instruments of the Holy Spirit, etc.[55]

Modesty and Humility

In one of the texts quoted above on the way of fostering unity and love, Bea said: "Unity and love can prosper only where authentic humility reigns."[56] And this is why humility occupies a central position in the spiritual notes, alongside love.

First of all we have a *general* reflection, in the meditation on the birth of the Lord: "The greatest event in the history of the world takes place in unseen seclusion, and the only people aware of it are Mary and Joseph, and the angels in heaven. Indeed, not only in seclusion but in grinding poverty and penury, despised and disregarded. . . . The Savior's manner of entry into the world set the tone not only for his own life, but also for the lives of all those who want to be his fellow-workers. The salvation of souls, the glory of God, are brought about through *silent, unsung work, full of renunciations*, performed far from the noise and bustle of the world. And this is *how I too must operate*."[57]

Work performed away from other people's eyes is particularly stressed in reference to his special situation in those years. For nineteen years he had held the important position of Rector of the Pontifical Biblical Institute, and had through force of circumstances always been much in the public eye; after leaving this position, the work he did was for the most part secret, so that he

---

51. 1958/V/4.
52. 1950/VI/1. Cf. 1955/VI/1: Jesus treats the apostles as friends, and "here he is a magnificent model for me as to how to treat my brother Jesuits."
53. Cf. 1957/I/2; 1952/IV/1; 1953/I/4; 1949/IV/3.
54. 1952/I/4.
55. Cf. 1949/V/2; 1951/VIII/2.
56. 1950/VII/2.
57. 1952/III/3; cf. 1949/IV/3.

lived a particularly retired life. He repeatedly declares that he accepts this life, or rather that he loves it: "My Nazareth is now, for my last years, the calm religious house, where I retire without wanting to recall the more brilliant days of my public activity. I appear in public only when *duty* calls me, and I am happy if I can be hidden."[58] In the meditation on Mary's visit to Elizabeth we read: "I do as Mary did: when she is no longer necessary, because other women come to give their help, she returns home; she does not seek to be honored."[59]

The retreatant does not stop at general principles, but goes into details. Speaking of the aim of his life and work, he writes: "My aim is not honors, nor positions of honor, because I do not want them; God's gifts are received in order to serve the kingdom of God and souls, not in order to shine and draw attention to myself; the Lord's crown of thorns helps me to renounce honors and accept unseen, unsung work."[60] The author of the notes adopts St. Bernard's principle: "Great things can only be attained through humility."[61]

Then there is humility in his attitude *toward others*: simplicity without pretensions, grateful for everything, not making his position felt; reacting against his tendency to assert himself, willingly listening to others; not seeking special recognition; recognizing others with sincerity and joy; always being ready to learn; allowing younger people to teach him something.[62] Referring to modesty in speech, the retreatant notes that he has a tendency to be self-satisfied, to parade his knowledge, and thus to give in to a spirit of criticism, and he therefore makes a resolution to place himself in second place, not to put himself forward, to step aside for others; even if success favors him, not to put himself forward; if, on the other hand, people ignore him, to be kind and courteous despite this.[63]

Ever since the New Testament, *patience and meekness* have always been closely linked to love and meekness,[64] and we find this reflected in the retreat notes. When they talk about love, patience and meekness are added almost at once.[65] Let us give a few explicit examples: "I must not moan about small discomforts, but bear them with patience"[66]; "I must not become irritated or nervous and brusque if someone contradicts me or disagrees with me, or when faced with a less enjoyable task; if people interrupt my work, I must be friendly and pleasant despite this."[67]

---

58. 1951/IV/2.
59. 1954/IV/1.
60. Cf. for example 1950/I/3; 1951/Iv/4; 1958/VII/3. Here and in other places where we deal with Bea's less specific thoughts, we confine ourselves to summarizing his thought without quoting individual texts in full; in such cases, passages in quotes should be seen as a collage of thoughts from a number of different texts.
61. 1953/II/2. The original Latin of St. Bernard is found in *Sermo* 34:1 (*PL*, CLXXXIX, 960): "Nisi humilitatis merito, maxima minime obtinentur."
62. Cf. 1951/V/2; 1958/IV/4; 1957/V/3; 1957/IV/4; 1955/IV/3.
63. Cf. 1957/III/2; 1949/IV/3; 1955/IV/3.
64. Cf. 1 Cor. 13:4, 7; Mt. 11:29.
65. Cf. for example 1951/V/3; 1952/IV/1; 1952/V/1.
66. 1951/VII/2; cf. 1956/IV/3.
67. Cf. 1951/V/2; 1951/VII/2; 1956/IV/2.

In the meditation on the Sermon on the Mount we read: "As concerns relations with our neighbor, Christ demands that we be meek and merciful, peace-loving, and also that we promote peace among men, while expecting persecution as our recompense."[68] "This is how I must be toward those who work with me, if I want to follow the Master's example: I must not lord it over other members of the clergy (cf. 1 Peter 5:3), but be meek, mild, kindly—in a word, *like the heart of Jesus.*"[69]

"The Decisive Question for the Apostle Is His Attitude to the Cross"

We all know the place that self-denial and the cross hold in the Christian life according to the gospel, and this is obviously all the truer of the life and activity of an apostle. We shall therefore now consider how Bea sees this element in the context of his own life.

In the retreat notes, self-denial has the primary function of *freeing him* from everything that could prevent full dedication to the mission received from Christ, so that he can give himself unreservedly to the specific apostolic tasks in which that mission is manifested day by day. Observing phenomena of egoism in himself, and also the tendency to seek his own convenience, the retreatant repeatedly resolves that he must seek only the will of God and forget himself; give himself unreservedly without concern for self, honor or advantage; not avoid unpleasant jobs or disagreeable situations; seek nothing for himself but solely the salvation of souls, the kingdom of God, the glory and interests of God.[70]

It was life itself that trained him in such renunciation and total daily self-dedication to the will of God. In the 1954 notes we read: "In my life, the Lord God has disposed things in such a way that I have increasingly had to abandon or subordinate my own preferences and plans. Today I am at the point that I am hardly left any choice in the things I do, but must day by day accept things as they come. Thus now my *great passion must be to fulfill the will of God, in whatever manner it is presented,* without seeking anything for myself or for my preferences."[71]

A practical form of the exercise of self-denial is the *offering up of everyday difficulties* for the kingdom of God and for souls: "*Christ redeemed the world* with *sacrifice*; each day I can unite my small sacrifices to *his great sacrifice* in holy mass; in this way troubles, setbacks, aches and pains, etc., take on a higher meaning and value."[72]

However, it is not simply a matter of resigning himself to the cross when it presents itself, and offering it up for the kingdom of God, but of seeing the hand

---

68. 1958/V/3.
69. 1956/VI/2.
70. Cf. 1957/V/2; 1958/I/3; 1958/II/2; 1958/IV/4; 1956/III/3; 1958/III/4; 1956/III/2; 1957/I/4.
71. 1954/I/4.
72. 1956/V/4; cf. 1955/V/2.

of God in the cross, *the Spirit of God who guides things*. In the meditation on the difficulties the holy family met when obeying the decree of Caesar Augustus, we read: "This total self-dedication to the will of God, letting myself be guided and led as he wants, even through sufferings, hardships, sickness and setbacks: for me all this also represents the service of God. . . . But the Savior walks this path *before* me . . . and *for* me."[73] In the following meditation on the presentation in the temple, this thought is still more clearly articulated: "If the Holy Spirit guides me, he guides me toward the cross and suffering, toward mortification and self-denial, but I must offer it up in union with the sacrifice of the Savior and with Our Lady of Sorrows."[74]

Thus the Holy Spirit guides the retreatant to find *the supreme model* of love in the very person of the crucified Redeemer. In the meditation on the subject of "The Crucified One, Synthesis of My Exercises," we read: "It is above all here that I see what *love* is. Not affections and gentle feelings, but *sacrifice*, and sacrifice that goes as far as the third degree of humility. The heart of Jesus is circled by a crown of thorns, it has the cross over it, and it is pierced with the spear; this is authentic and solid love."[75]

This meditation has led saints and devout souls to ask the Lord to allow them to bear "heavy crosses." Our retreatant "does not dare" ask this. In 1954 he writes: "Truly, so far I have suffered so little for the Savior. But maybe he is still reserving me a share in his cross prior to my death. I do not dare ask him for this; he knows best. I ask him only the grace of accepting what he sends me with *love*, with authentic, true love of the cross, and of carrying it in love with Jesus, through Jesus, for Jesus."[76]

When meditating on the passion in 1950, he writes: "Truly, I have borne few heavy crosses in my life; now at the end of my days, I am almost concerned and pained by this, when I think that true love for the Savior is really shown only by sharing in his cross. Or maybe he still has a heavy cross in store for me for my last years. Whatever the case may be, whatever he may send me, I shall accept it with supernatural joy from his hand. Hail, O blessed cross!"[77]

"For *the apostle* the decisive question concerns his attitude toward the cross and suffering of the Savior. The apostles were the ones to whom Christ in the first place said: 'If anyone wants to follow me, let him take up his cross and

---

73. 1954/IV/2.

74. 1954/IV/3.

75. 1956/VII/4. "The third degree of humility" is a distinctive feature of the Spiritual Exercises of St. Ignatius and it is attained when, "in order to imitate and be in reality more like Christ our Lord, I desire and choose poverty with Christ poor, rather than riches, insults with Christ loaded with them, rather than honors; I desire to be accounted as worthless and a fool for Christ, rather than to be esteemed as wise and prudent in this world" (Spiritual Exercises, 167). We would also note that in the description of the heart of Jesus Bea draws his inspiration from the very well-known image that shows the Sacred Heart as the great apostle of this devotion, St. Margaret Mary Alacoque, saw it in her revelations.

76. 1954/VII/3. I remember that in his last days the cardinal said to me: "I have suffered so little in my life." At that time I had not of course seen the notes on which we are drawing in this chapter.

77. 1950/VII/4.

follow me.' "[78] We have seen that Bea takes these words seriously whatever the specific form such following of the crucified Redeemer assumes in his life—and not only as religious but also, and above all, as apostle; it is truly an essential part of his apostolic commitment.

Accepting the Cross Calmly and Serenely

In the texts cited above, when speaking of the cross that the Lord could still send him the retreatant says that he accepts it "with supernatural joy" or else asks the Lord to enable him to accept it "with authentic, true love of the cross."[79] We would note that these are fairly unusual expressions, for the retreatant normally tends to assume an attitude of "composed calm and serenity" before the cross.

A first example of this more usual attitude is found in the meditation on the Beatitudes, where he says that calamity and suffering entered the world with sin, "and we cannot make them disappear from the world; on the other hand it is possible to cultivate a spirit with which to bear them. And this spirit is the spirit of Christ, which he himself showed us by his own example when he was faced with poverty and hardship, and with bullying and violence on the part of his fellow human beings. . . . It is the spirit of *full loving abandonment of self to the will of God*, as this is seen in the various destinies of our lives; it is thus the spirit of composed calmness and serenity with which we accept all things."[80]

The second example is found in the meditation on Jesus' discourse after the Last Supper (John 14–16). Just as Christ suffered and was persecuted, so the cross, sufferings, tribulations and persecutions "will be the lot of all his disciples, his church and all those who serve the church. In the world we must have tribulations, but 'in me *you shall have peace*': *his* teaching, principles and example give us the inner tranquillity, calmness and contentment that we admire in the saints, the martyrs and the great servants of the church. It is the *gift of the Holy Spirit* who lives in us and teaches and trains us; it is the *gift of the intellect* that allows us to see the meaning and purpose of sufferings and the cross, and the *gift of fortitude* with which we bear all things."[81]

These thoughts are then illustrated with Jesus' example. In the meditation entitled "From Gethsemane to Golgotha" we read: "After the Savior has pronounced his 'Thy will be done' he goes to meet his passion with admirable *serenity, calm, patience and majesty*, and these qualities accompany him throughout. . . . This is the power of his will, but also the power of the Holy Spirit who lives in him, the *Spirit of fortitude*. How much I have to learn from him on this point! . . . I must let myself be trained by the calmness and serenity

78. 1956/VII/2.
79. 1950/VII/4; 1954/VII/3.
80. 1952/IV/4.
81. 1951/VI/3.

of the Lord, which never leave him, so that he remains equanimous in all situations; thus he keeps silent where this is necessary, and speaks where this is necessary, while always remaining the serene, calm master of himself."[82]

In the texts cited we have seen that "serenity and calmness" are linked with abandonment to the will of God and with the gifts of the Holy Spirit. In other texts, the same two qualities are linked with *trust in God*. In the meditation on the storm on the Sea of Tiberias, we read: "The fundamental fact that I must remember in all difficulties and storms—whether of a personal nature or whether concerning the church or the society—is that the Lord is always present with his power and goodness. I am never alone, and the church is never alone. 'I am with you until the end of the world.' This must give me great calmness and serenity in all situations. Storms and difficulties can take various forms: sickness, an inability to work, misunderstandings, etc.; in the end, the name is unimportant. . . . Here the only correct attitude is trust, . . . a trust that is accompanied by *prayer*, work, struggle, a trust that bears in mind that the Lord is in the boat with us."[83]

The concept of *active trust* is described further in another text, where Bea says that God's intervention "does not dispense me from faithful use of all *human means*: study, advice, method, prudence, care and attention: as though everything depended on me, and only on me. I am an instrument, and the instrument must use all its inherent quality. Disappointments and setbacks must not depress me. . . . Everything of value in the kingdom of God has been won at the price of much patience and self-denial."[84]

The path and means to obtain serenity and calmness, and also what they presume, is *prayer*. In one of the texts we read: "The Savior goes 'as was his custom' (Luke 22:39) to pray on the Mount of Olives, although he knows it is *here* that Judas will look for him and find him. He says in advance [in the prayer], 'Thy will be done,' remaining calm and serene. Constancy in prayer!"[85] Prayer is also indicated in the following text as the source of serenity and calmness: "After the Savior has pronounced his 'Thy will be done,' he goes to meet his passion with admirable serenity, calm, patience and majesty, and these qualities accompany him throughout"[86]; we should note that this 'Thy will be done' was not only spoken by the Savior in the long prayer of the agony, but is its true and precious fruit: "After the Savior knows that he must accept the passion, he does not hesitate a moment longer. Every trace of despondency has vanished; with admirable decisiveness and energy—and not with sighs and whining—he goes out to meet his enemies."[87] The "decisiveness and energy" are obviously parallel to the "serenity and calmness" and are the fruit of the prayer in the Garden of Gethsemane.

---

82. Cf. 1951/VII/2; 1953/VI/1. We find similar thoughts in 1951/VII/1; 1953/VII/3; 1954/VII/1.
83. 1949/V/4. Trust in God is also a fundamental element of support for the servant of the Lord; cf. Is. 49:4.
84. 1950/V/4.
85. 1951/VII/1.
86. 1951/VII/2.
87. 1954/VII/1.

"There Is No Retirement from God's Service"

We still have to see the zeal of our retreatant, in other words his practical commitment to implementing the wide-ranging, articulated resolutions we have described. However, we are not dealing with zeal in general, but zeal in the practical context of advancing age and diminishing energies, for we should remember that we are studying a period when the retreatant was already over seventy.

We have a fairly general text to start with. In a meditation on the creation of human beings, we read: "I am his [God's] creature and am therefore *his*, and so I am in his hand. This holds good in every dimension—both as regards time and as regards strength. As regards *time*: I can give up this or that position, but I cannot give up God's service. Right up to my last breath I am and remain bound to God with all my forces and faculties, even now in my old age. It is not licit for me to let any of my faculties retire, so long as I have them and so long as I am able to use them. Thus for me 'being old' does not mean the right to rest; . . . rather it means exploiting all that God has given me up to the last moment, without any slackening off. . . ."[88]

In 1952, in the meditation on the parable of the talents (Mt. 25:14-30), the retreatant refers to the fact that he is now in his seventy-second year, and applies the thoughts described above most specifically to the commitment to *holiness*: "One thing is certain: I must exploit the time I still have left *with much greater commitment and energy for my spiritual life*. This talent is particularly important for me, and, however my life goes, I can exploit *this* talent in a special way. . . . If I do this I shall be ready whenever, wherever and however the Lord comes."[89] In other words, this is the best "preparation" for death. "Work up to the last day, even in sickness and infirmity."[90] "There is no retirement from God's service: so long as he gives me strength, I must work for him and for his kingdom."[91]

It is not surprising that this commitment is sometimes a burden. For example, in the meditation on the kingdom of Christ, we read: "For many years he [Christ] has placed me where practically all my energies, all my time and all my strength are involved in his service, so that there is in fact nothing left for myself. It is not surprising that this sometimes weighs on me. However, this does not mean that I intend to hope or pray for things to change. On the contrary, I hope and pray that they may remain like this up to my blessed end, so that my old age may consist in burning myself down gradually, like a candle on the altar."[92]

In the light of such texts we can understand the retreatant's statements on his "ideal death," which would be that of dying in harness, while working for Christ. In the meditation on preparation for death we read: "My ideal would be for God to call me suddenly, in the midst of my work; but I must leave this up to him."[93]

---

88. 1949/I/1.
89. 1952/II/4; cf. 1951/I/2.
90. 1958/II/4; cf. 1951/IV/2.
91. 1958/IV/4.
92. 1949/III/2.
93. 1950/III/1.

Or again: "The most beautiful thing would be if I could die working for the Lord; however, I leave this too up to him."[94]

"Love Must Be at the Center of My Life"

Here we come to the thought or theme that undoubtedly holds the central position in the notes and is the basis of everything else—the thought to which everything can be reduced, the spring that in the final analysis sets everything else in motion.[95] In the meditation on love we read: "The whole of my exercises are really concerned with love, and here it is simply a question of gathering together in the election[96] what I have already resolved."[97] "Loving God through Jesus is the formula in which I can sum up the aim of my spiritual life, and the fruit that I hope to receive from these exercises with the grace of God."[98] Again we read, still in the meditation on love: "My exercises have as a whole been tuned to love; in fact my main resolution is the following: *'to permeate all my thought and activity with a truly great love of God.'* It is now a question of putting this into practice day by day."[99] "I only have a short time left for work; maybe also to suffer for him. In any case, what remains must be a 'Take, Lord, and receive,' spoken and practiced unreservedly, in the love and for the love of him who has loved me and given himself for me."[100]

The extent to which love is at the center of the exercises and thus of the spiritual life of our retreatant can be seen in the light of an unusual and therefore significant fact. Following the order of the book of St. Ignatius' Spiritual Exercises, retreatants usually meditate on love in the last meditation of the eighth day. In our case, however, the same subject also appears in various other meditations where the book does not envisage it, for example in the meditation on the creation, or on the end for which man was created,[101] in those on the Lord's nativity, transfiguration and discourse after the Last Supper,[102] and even in the context of the struggle against disordered inclinations and against sin.[103]

---

94. 1952/II/4.
95. The subject of love has been seen repeatedly in the preceding sections, precisely because it holds a central place in Bea's life, but here we want to examine it in greater depth. It should be observed that the section "The Love That Believes All Things . . ." was devoted to relations with one's neighbor and not to love in general.
96. The "election" is a distinctive concept in the Spiritual Exercises of St. Ignatius, and indicates the central point of the retreat, when a choice is made or a decision taken which is of fundamental importance for the life of the retreatant. Likewise in Bea's notes, the term indicates the central resolution, or the group of central resolutions, of a specific retreat.
97. 1954/VIII/4.
98. 1952/VIII/4.
99. 1953/VIII/4; cf. 1949/VIII/4.
100. 1951/VIII/4. The formula "Take, Lord, and receive" is taken from the opening words of the prayer with which the retreatant expresses a total gift of self to God at the end of the first point of the meditation on love.
101. Cf. 1952/I/1; 1955/I/1; 1956/I/1; 1958/I/1.
102. Cf. respectively 1951/III/4; 1951/V/4; 1955/VI/3.
103. Cf. respectively 1958/I/4; 1951/II/1.

In order to understand this love more fully, let us take a look at its *motivation*. In the first place the retreatant is following the suggestion of the book here, with its recommendation to meditate on "how much the Lord has given me of what is his," in other words on the benefits received from God: "I shall sing of the mercies of the Lord for ever. I have let my whole life unfold before me and have understood very deeply the words 'all that I have and possess, you have given me.' . . . Now I find myself at the end of a life full of God's graces and gifts. What else can I do but give thanks and repent of having so often collaborated so little with these graces, and above all dedicate the days of life that are still left to me to the Lord God and his glory, with a full and complete 'Take and receive.' This is in practice the content of my 'election.' "[104]

However, it is not only a question of special gifts and graces that the Lord has given to the retreatant personally. There are also the great benefits of the creation and redemption and the love that is seen in these. Thus the retreatant thinks "of the love of God, one and three, that is seen in the creation, but above all in the plan of redemption, . . . of the love of the Savior's divine and human heart which has suffered so much for humanity—and for me in particular; . . . the love of the Holy Spirit that has been poured out over me—over *me*—with such an extraordinary fullness of favors and graces."[105]

We have already said that in the spiritual notes love is seen as the *ultimate basis of various aspects* of the spiritual life that we have considered previously. The following are a few examples.

Love and service of God. " 'Serve God for love and in love' is the fundamental principle of the exercises I am ending. Perhaps I have never before understood so clearly the need for love: love of God, love of Christ, love of souls and love of these around me, or, quite simply, of my neighbor."[106] "I must constantly strive harder to make my life a service of God, wholly bathed in love. In this way my love will be a truly *effective* love and not simply an affective one."[107]

"It is a consolation for me to know that love does not consist of sweet sentiments or expansive words, nor again of a specific position or office. . . . Now in these grace-filled exercises I have reached a very deep understanding of what God wants of me, right down to the details and all the aspects of my daily life. Now I must strive with all my forces to *fulfill this will of God: this will be true love*."[108] "Love [of God] pushes me to do everything as well as I can, indeed in the very best way possible, so as to please him. Such love means that all I do—even the smallest of things—takes on a supreme value, with everything being transformed into gold. Indeed, if I do it in union with the

---

104. 1949/VIII/4; cf. 1951/VIII/4. The words "all that I have and possess, you [O God] have given me" are taken from the aforementioned prayer "Take, Lord, and receive. . . ."
105. 1958/I/4.
106. 1954/VIII/3.
107. 1953/VIII/4.
108. 1955/VI/4.

Savior, *love 'divinizes'* my work and gives it a completely new value, a great, incomparable value, indeed its true value in the eyes of God."[109]

Love and trust in God. In the 1954 meditation on love we read: "Whatever he [Christ] sends me in the forthcoming year, I shall accept it all from his loving, paternal hand, and try to use it for his glory: everything is good and a grace for me, and will help me to grow in his love."[110] In 1957, again in the meditation on love, he resolves to seek and find God in everything: "I must find God even in bitter and unpleasant things; it is his wisdom that sends them to me or allows them for my good, for the salvation of souls."[111]

The *link between love and prayer.* Prayer is the indispensable presupposition and nourishment: *"Without fervent prayer, my spiritual life will always remain cold, dissatisfied, superficial*; and without fervent prayer, *love* will never become the center of my whole spiritual life."[112] And this also applies to *all forms of prayer.* Meditating on his own sins, the retreatant reproaches himself for not having made good use of the many graces received from the Lord, and then resolves: "If I want to attain the true and authentic *love* of God, from now on I must correct myself on this point and make faithful use of everything: meditation, holy mass, visits to the blessed sacrament, examination of conscience. . . . Otherwise I can never hope to obtain a great love for God."[113]

The *connection between love and self-denial and the struggle against sin* is stressed particularly often: "After baptism, the threefold concupiscence is not dead: it makes itself felt wherever it can, preventing the good that I have resolved to do. If I do not struggle day by day to *master myself*, defects that I want to avoid will continue to manifest themselves. In my view the *principal means* of achieving this are not so much theoretical considerations, however good, but above all *love.* 'Who shall separate me from the love of Christ? . . . But in all these things we are more than conquerors through him who loved us' [Romans 8:35, 37]."[114]

Love and the acceptance of sacrifice and the cross. The Lord's nativity "is a scene of *love*: 'for us and for our salvation.' . . . Because it was necessary to us, he [Christ] did not draw back from any sacrifice. If *love must be the center of my spiritual life*, I too must not draw back from *any* sacrifice, but must accept them all with the same generosity and joy, just as the Savior did."[115] Elsewhere the retreatant resolves to seek "a love that faithfully carries out all that grace

---

109. 1955/I/3. Here we shall not consider the connection between love of God and love for one's neighbor, for in our section on love for one's neighbor this link, which is all too obvious, was seen clearly enough. We would recall that in the notes the motivation of brotherly love is seen in the fact that his confreres are members of the mystical body of Christ, favored sons of the heavenly Father; cf. also 1951/V/3.
110. 1954/VIII/4.
111. 1957/VIII/4.
112. 1951/V/4.
113. 1951/II/1.
114. 1958/I/4; cf. also 1953/VIII/4 on love and the purification from disordered love of creatures and self.
115. 1951/III/4.

asks of me, that faithfully makes use of all the graces that God gives me, that faithfully bears all that the Lord sends me (indispositions, ailments, weakness, failure, and so on) with patience and joy, all this in the union of love with the crucified Savior."[116]

"The coming year must therefore be for me—with the grace of God—a year of *intense* love for God and the Savior, *active* love, made up of *work* and *sacrifice*. May this be the fruit of these holy exercises."[117]

In a meditation on God, we read: "Infinite majesty, infinite holiness, infinite love. This is God." After meditation on what God has done for him, the retreatant resolves: "In these exercises I must make an energetic effort—with the grace that will not be lacking—to become a truly *interior* man: seeking God in all things, seeing God in all things, loving God in all things."[118]

In the meditation on the appearance of the risen One to Mary, a meditation suggested by the exercises of St. Ignatius, we read: "Contemplation of the risen Savior must fill me with the same sentiments with which Mary was filled when he appeared to her: joy for his glory, faith in his promises, but above all *love* that was ready for joyful sacrifice and self-donation, together with readiness to do his will also in the future, how, where, and so long as he wants, and thus readiness to pronounce an *unconditional 'Thy will be done . . . ,' inspired by love* in a full gift of self, without reserve, to his holy will."[119]

---

116. 1951/II/1. Cf. 1956/VIII/4: "My exertions and work done in union with the Savior's cross."
117. 1953/VIII/4.
118. 1952/I/1.
119. 1955/VIII/2.

PART THREE

THE COUNCIL

CHAPTER 1

MOVING OFF QUIETLY INTO THE SUNSET?

Early in the fall of 1958 came an event that had far-reaching effects on Bea's life: the fairly sudden death of Pope Pius XII, whose service had given his life a special rhythm for over thirteen years, involving him increasingly in various fields of the life of the church. The repercussions were magnified by various other circumstances, particularly the fact that a little prior to this, he himself had fallen seriously ill, so that he had not been able to offer the pope his assistance in his last days and hours. Although such assistance was obviously fully ensured by other people, Bea suffered at his own inability to give his "august penitent" any help at all, precisely when his ministry was most urgently needed. And what made the break all the more painful was the fact that his health made it totally impossible for him to share personally in the pope's last farewell.

Apart from his immediate pain at the pope's death, Bea now lost that awareness of being in the close service of the pope which had been the special keynote of his life for over thirteen years. It is true that he still had the many commitments he had gradually accumulated as a result of his special relations with Pius XII, but now that those relations had come to an end, it was as if the life had gone out of these commitments—even though it was always of course work performed for the church. He also seemed to be surrounded by a growing silence. The work entailed by the commitments that were still left were a burden, partly because it was many months before he was able to shake off the effects of his sickness, so that he reached the end of the academic year 1958-1959 in a state of near collapse. The whole combination of circumstances made it licit to wonder if this was simply the start of the slow decline of a life that was still active but that was moving ineluctably toward its close.

Two Blows in Quick Succession

On Saturday, 20 September 1958, a Vatican car collected Bea as usual, and drove him to Castel Gandolfo to hear the pope's and the sisters' confessions. Since Bea was planning to make his annual retreat, after hearing the confessions he asked Pius XII if he could be released for the following Saturday, and it was thus arranged that he would not come back until 4 October. The pope gave him a special blessing for his retreat, and then the same Vatican car took him straight to Holy Shepherd Villa near Gallicano, a house belonging to the German-Hungarian College in Rome and where he had already taken his vacation and made his annual retreat a number of times.[1]

The notes from this retreat close with the entry: "The last meditation is

---

1. Cf. N 1958/226; 1958/307.

missing because of sickness." What happened was that on the last day of the retreat he was taken ill, and hurried back to Rome with a temperature of 101. Two weeks later he wrote to a physician who had previously been his student: "The next day my temperature rose even higher, and I had serious diarrhoea. The doctor was very worried and thought it might be typhoid or paratyphoid, although this in fact seems not to be the case. The full results of a blood test have not come in yet, but it has shown a sharp fall in white blood corpuscles. In any case, it is obviously some kind of infection, and it has greatly weakened me."[2] The last diagnosis read: "Severe intestinal infection."[3] When the pope was told about the sickness, he repeatedly sent him his apostolic blessing.[4]

In these circumstances it was out of the question for Bea to return to Castel Gandolfo on 4 October—which was in fact the very day when the first symptoms of the pope's own sickness appeared. At the end of an audience granted to a group of pilgrims in the courtyard of the papal palace, Pius XII had difficulty raising his hand to give his blessing, and forty-eight hours later, on 6 October, he was struck down by the sickness that would bring him to his grave in the space of three days.[5]

Bea was later to comment on those days as follows: "It was a tragedy that I could not be at his death-bed."[6] And: "Naturally, I suffered a great deal from my inability to be at his side in his last hours. However, everything possible was done to give him spiritual assistance—so far as was possible in view of the fact that he was unconscious."[7] Bea was reassured by the knowledge that the dying man had the benefit of "the best spiritual assistance" and that he himself could not have done more than was in fact done.[8] The assistance in question was provided by Father Robert Leiber, S.J., who had been private secretary, first to Eugenio Pacelli and then to the pope, for forty years.[9]

We would add that this very rapid decline in the pope's life was less surprising to Bea than to others. Some months later he wrote: "For you, the death of the Holy Father was of course a surprise. I saw him very often and had been concerned about him for a long time because I could see how weak he had become. Of course I never said anything about it, since there was nothing that could have been done. His whole physique was worn out and it was clear that he would be unable to survive any relatively serious illness. And he in fact died after a bare three days of sickness."[10]

Bea spent the days of the interregnum in the infirmary, and then also those of the conclave. On 13 October he wrote: "I hope to be able to resume work in

2. N 1958/251; also 1958/249; 1958/254; Ni 57 (1958).
3. Cf. N 1958/238; 1958/239; 1958/242; 1958/249; 1958/254; 1958/255; 1958/259; 1958/332; 1959/7.
4. Cf. N 1958/253; 1958/254.
5. Cf. pp. 184-185 above.
6. N 1958/301.
7. N 1958/249; cf. also 1958/251.
8. Cf. N 1958/253; 1958/325.
9. Bea himself told me this; cf. also 1958/325.
10. Nb 159 (1958); cf. also N 1959/6.

the course of this week."[11] However, these proved to be the vain hopes of the kind sometimes cherished by the sick, for he was unable to leave his bed for a whole month. Later he would write that he had thus been forced to take almost four weeks of vacation.[12] I remember that on 28 October, the day of Pope John XXIII's election, I took a radio to his room, so that he could receive the new pope's blessing at least in this way. When I went back to find him after the *urbi et orbi* blessing in St. Peter's Square, he told me in delight that he had seen the whole ceremony on a fellow Jesuit's television and received Pope John XXIII's blessing in that way.

The New Situation

Some months after the death of Pius XII, Bea wrote to one of his relatives as follows: "My work has not lessened. Of course, I am not confessor to the new pope. But that goes without saying, for every pope has his own confessor: that was the case for Pius XII just as it had been for Pius XI. The same goes for private secretaries. . . . The present pope has brought his own secretary with him, so that Father Leiber no longer holds the office—and not because there is a desire to drive the Jesuits out of the Vatican (as certain journalists seem to think), but simply as a consequence of the circumstances."[13] When one correspondent expressed concern that the dead pope's advisors might receive short shrift at the hands of the new administration, Bea reassured him, saying that there was no danger of such a thing happening.[14]

Bea was certainly not shunted onto the sidelines, and his work-load decreased very little.[15] He was happy to be relieved of the unenviable position of confessor to the pope,[16] and it also meant that he no longer had to go to the Vatican every Saturday. However, he did retain all his other tasks.[17] His correspondence was lighter, but to make up for this he had received other tasks, so that his work-load was much the same as before, "and really too much for a man of seventy-nine."[18] "I have so much on my hands that I barely manage to deal with everything that is asked of me."[19] However, he was especially happy that he could now enjoy his vacations in peace.[20]

At the end of December he was writing that since the end of October he had been working as before, and that his health problems had completely cleared up.[21]

11. N 1958/251.
12. Cf. Ni 57 (1958); Nb 342 (1958); 384 (1958).
13. Nb 159 (1958).
14. Cf. Nm 62 (1958).
15. Cf. Nb 384 (1958); N 1958/332.
16. Cf. N 1958/305.
17. Cf. Nb 385 (1958); Nm 73 (1959).
18. Ni 60 (1959); cf. Np 16 (1959).
19. Nb 173 (1959).
20. Cf. Nc 41 (1959).
21. Cf. Nb 384 (1958); 69 (1958).

Let us take a closer look at his work. As had been the case for some years now, *teaching* accounted for the smallest part: in the first semester, he had two hours a week for the course on the inspiration and hermeneutics of sacred scripture, and one hour for the methodology of biblical studies; and in the second semester, he had one hour a week (and for only two months) for the methodology of teaching sacred scripture. Apart from this, he was very probably president of the internal commission entrusted with preparing a new Latin translation of the Old Testament readings for the breviary—for the correspondence shows that John XXIII had confirmed the task that Pius XII had given the Pontifical Biblical Institute in this connection.[22]

Apart from this work, there was also the task of editing the section concerning the Old Testament of a large scholarly publication that the Biblical Institute was preparing in celebration of the fiftieth anniversary of its foundation.[23] In the same period he was also supervising a commentary running to two thick volumes on Pius XII's encyclical *Haurietis aquas* on devotion to the Sacred Heart.[24]

We have little information on his work in the field of *liturgical reform*, although we do know that the most important part of the struggle in favor of the vernacular in the liturgy[25] took place in these months. His activity at the *Holy Office* represented the major part of his work: apart from the regular weekly meetings, the register of his correspondence contains four special "opinions" for the last months of 1958, and ten for the first nine months of 1959.

Then there was his *correspondence*: 1958 ends on 19 September with the number 411, followed by a large gap until the end of the year, except for the numbers 500-503, which refer to four "opinions" for the Holy Office.[26] Regular entries are resumed on 1 January 1959, continuing until 15 October, when we find number 333.[27]

Naturally he also had to make or receive the more usual routine visits, as well as those marking more special occasions. And one "special occasion" is also mentioned in his correspondence, where he speaks about the consistory of December 1958 at which Pope John XXIII created twenty-three new cardinals. In a letter of 20 December 1958 we read that in recent weeks he had had little time left over, for he had had to attend a great many celebrations and gatherings.

---

22. Cf. N 1959/55; 1959/58; also N 1959/55: "Pope John XXIII does *not* want to return to the old psalter."

23. Cf. N 1959/43; 1959/54; this was the volume *Studia Biblica et Orientalia edita a Pont. Inst. Bibl. ad celebrandum annum L ex quo conditum est Institutum. Vetus Testamentum*, Analecta Biblica 10 (Rome, 1959). Strange to say, Bea's name is not found in the work as editor or director, so it may be that his sickness had forced him to leave the work to others.

24. Cf. A. Bea *et al.* (eds.), *Cor Jesu. Commentationes in Litteras Encyclicas Pii Papae XII "Haurietis aquas"* (Rome, 1959); also Nh 17 (1959): "I am simply expected to supervise it. . . ."

25. Described in Part Two, Chapter 4, of the present work.

26. This does not mean that Bea wrote no letters in this period, but simply that he had no time to enter them in the register.

27. We shall return later to the content of these letters, particularly as concerns the ecumenical aims of the Council announced by Pope John XXIII.

Apart from this, the new cardinals were in Rome, and he knew some of them very well. There were also a good number of German bishops. And on top of this there was also his ordinary work.[28]

After Pius XII's death, Bea lived even more out of the limelight than before—at least so far as lay within his power.[29] Thus he wrote in one letter that he did not know the new pope personally and had naturally made no effort to approach him, adding: "I already have enough to do."[30] However, his work itself led to two meetings. The first took place in January 1959, when the pope received the personnel of the Holy Office, and thus also its consultors, in audience. When Bea was presented, the pope, who did not know him, merely said: "I have read some of your publications; keep it up." Four months later, Bea was presented for a second time, together with the members of the Pontifical Biblical Commission. In the meantime he had arranged for the pope to receive an "opinion" on the use of the *Piiano* translation of the psalter in the liturgy.

Conjectures on the Ecumenical Prospects of the Council

In the midst of all this activity, on 25 January 1959, came a bolt out of the blue when Pope John XXIII announced that he was planning to convene an Ecumenical Council. The aims were described as follows in the relative press release: "As concerns the celebration of the Ecumenical Council, the Holy Father does not intend it only as a means of building up the people of Christ, but also as a call to the separated communities for a search for unity, which so many souls today are yearning for in every part of the world."[31]

It is well-known that this announcement raised many hopes, but also gave rise to certain misapprehensions, or at least reflections and conjectures on its ecumenical aim. It is very interesting today to look back at the echoes of such discussions in Bea's correspondence, for they throw some significant light on the uncertain atmosphere in the months following the announcement. And they are particularly important for us, since they give an idea of their author's attitudes at that time, especially toward the ecumenical aims of the Council, allowing us to see whether and to what extent they provide any clue that here we have the future President of the Secretariat for Christian Unity.

The letters reveal lively participation in the relative discussions, as he studies, and indeed carefully sifts through, all the pope's statements in this connection, even the slightest passing reference. The various positions of other Christians and representatives of the ecumenical movement are also observed and noted, particularly those of the World Council of Churches.[32]

In more general terms, the letters bear fairly clear evidence to the fact that

28. Cf. Nb 384 (1958).
29. Cf. Nm 78 (1959).
30. Nb 384 (1958); cf. 69 (1958).
31. *OssRom* (26/27 January 1959); cited in Caprile I/1, p. 51.
32. Cf. N 1959/22; 1959/36; 1959/43; 1959/85; 1959/88; 1959/107; Nm 74 (1959).

all available material on the declarations and stated positions of other Christians was being systematically collected in Rome by those responsible for the Council, so that when the time came to take decisions in this area all the necessary information would be on hand.[33]

Indeed, in a certain sense Bea took the initiative, writing a memorandum of several pages which summarized his "reflections" on the Council and its ecumenical aims, and sending it out to various correspondents so that they could use it, although without saying who had written it. It is a pity that no copy of this memorandum is attached to any of the covering letters,[34] although the loss would not appear irreparable, for if we amalgamate the statements found in various letters we can produce a clear and fairly exhaustive summary.

In the first place, Bea is careful to warn people that too much emphasis is being placed on unity, while there are many other pressing problems. Then, as concerns aims of union, he says that we must neither be pessimistic nor kindle false hopes,[35] but think realistically and objectively.[36] Here the author says very definitely that the Council will not be a Council of union,[37] and points out that the pope has clearly indicated the fact.[38] Apart from this, the question of such aims of union has not yet been resolved; thus the text of the pope's address to the cardinals[39] is markedly more reserved than the press release cited above.[40] The question of unity is an age-old problem and cannot be solved at a single stroke; we cannot humanly hope that the Council will bring about immediate unity—except for some great miracle of the Holy Spirit.[41] "In recent months I have carefully studied the views of Catholics and other Christians, and I must say that people's minds are not yet ready for the establishment of unity."[42] "Today the climate is different from that on the eve of Vatican Council I [1869], but reactions to the announcement of Vatican II have not been very promising, and are sometimes indeed cold and opposed to it, and there is an impression that there is some kind of wish to discredit the Council as 'non-ecumenical' from the outset."[43]

Almost as if to quash any false hopes, one letter emphasizes the fact that the Holy Father has stated that the Council is "an internal affair of the church,"[44] and it is therefore important to stress the meaning that it will have for the internal life of the church; and he adds the somewhat harsh observation that it will be up to

33. Cf. N 1959/46; Nm 74 (1959).
34. These "reflections" are mentioned in N 1959/22; 1959/43; Nm 74 (1959).
35. Cf. N 1959/42; 1959/43.
36. Cf. Nm 74 (1959).
37. It is interesting to see how often this view is reiterated: cf. N 1959/98; 1959/101; 1959/102; 1959/107; Nm 73 (1959); 74 (1959); 74bis (1959); 77 (1959).
38. Cf. N 1959/101; Nm 77 (1959).
39. Published in AAS, LI (1959), 69.
40. Cf. N 1959/66; 1959/90; 1959/116. For the two texts see Caprile, I/1, pp. 50-51.
41. Cf. Nm 73 (1959); 74 (1959).
42. N 1959/107.
43. N 1959/36; 1959/76; 1959/88.
44. N 1959/78; cf. 1959/78bis.

other Christians to seek the path of "rapprochement" and "coming closer together"—concepts used by the pope in connection with the question of union,[45] although they probably do not in fact apply to relations with the West.[46] Again, we find him saying that the Council will strive to solve problems that exist within the church, even if it also takes advantage of the experiences of ecumenism; however, for this it is not necessary for representatives of the World Council of Churches to be present at the Council; their opinions are already known.[47]

What are these "internal problems" of the church? In general terms, the writer thinks that there is much confusion in the doctrinal field, and thus a need for clarification.[48] There are problems over ecclesiology and more especially over relations between church and state.[49] When considering such ecclesiological problems in more specific terms, the author writes: "The most important question is certainly doctrine concerning the church, especially the position of bishops. In my opinion, bishops must be involved to a greater extent in government both of the universal church and more specifically of their own dioceses. It should not be possible for an order to be given or a decision taken on a question concerning a diocese without consulting the local ordinary. Such centralization is certainly not a blessing for the church." Bea continues: "Another point linked to this last one is the composition of the Roman curia, especially the Roman congregations. It is absolutely vital to have a specialist at the head of each congregation, even if he is not a cardinal. And the consultors should be an international body. Furthermore, it would be easy nowadays for cardinals who belong to a congregation but live abroad to take part annually or bi-annually in meetings [of the congregation] when important church interests are at stake." Then he returns to questions of doctrine: "In ecclesiology, the question of Christ's royal dominion seems to me important. Apart from this, the idea of the Holy Spirit as the leading and illumining principle of the life of the mystical body of Christ needs considerable development in order to justify the church's teaching authority from within."[50]

If the Council was thus to be seen as an internal affair of the Catholic Church, and was to devote itself to internal problems, did this maybe mean that it would not be concerned with the question of unity? Far from it. For years *the question of unity* had been one of those facing the church, and Bea indeed states: "I am convinced that even if the Council is not a 'Council of union,' it will contribute a great deal to the cause of unity."[51] "It seems certain to me that it can lay the general groundwork for gradual reunion."[52] "Commissions for contacts will

45. Cf. Nm 76 (1959). Translator's note: *both* of the Italian words—*riavvicinamento* and *riaccostamento*—are most accurately rendered into English with the phrase "coming closer together again."
46. Cf. N 1959/88.
47. Cf. Nm 77 (1959).
48. Cf. Nc 44 (1959); N 1959/42.
49. Cf. N 1959/116; 1959/101.
50. N 1959/127.
51. N 1959/98; 1959/107; on these aspects, cf. also Bacht, "Kardinal Bea: Wegbereiter der Einheit," p. 179.

spontaneously come into existence, once we are in clear agreement about the basic questions."[53] He is therefore sorry that the hopes aroused by the announcement of the Council have since then lost their momentum,[54] and warns that we must avoid anything that could spoil the good atmosphere: "It seems to me that for our part we should abstain from everything that might spoil the atmosphere, since it is wholly in the interests of the church that the decisions that will undoubtedly be taken, on the basis of the wish to advance the cause of unity, should also be received favorably by the other side."[55]

However, he also notes that a fairly large number of questions on the ecumenical aim of the Council have not yet been cleared up; for example, it is not yet possible to say whether the Orthodox will be invited to the Council, and the same applies to representatives of the ecumenical movement.[56] So far the pope has spoken only about the Orthodox, and has not mentioned the West.[57] As regards the World Council of Churches, Bea thinks that it does not even want to be invited, since it does not consider itself authorized to speak in the name of its member churches, and it is therefore merely hoping that during the preparatory period there should be conversations on common problems between competent figures from both sides—and there are no problems over such a suggestion.[58]

Waning Powers?

We must not, however, allow Bea's lively and active interest in reactions to the announcement of the Council and the evolution of its ecumenical prospects to mislead us as to his state of health or his reserves of strength. In these months, members of the community at the Biblical Institute did remark on the fact that his strength seemed to be on the gradual wane.

At least in the first months after his sickness, he was himself fairly optimistic. Although admitting that his sickness had been a warning not to rely too much on his strength, and not to expect too much of it,[59] he wrote to his relatives about the possibility of visiting them in the summer of 1959.[60]

In April, however, his doctors started prescribing various courses of treatment for problems with his heart and liver. We find him noting that he had been

52. Nm 74 (1959).
53. N 1959/85.
54. Cf. N 1959/78bis.
55. Nm 74 (1959); cf. N 1959/22.
56. Cf. Nm 73 (1959); also N 1959/46.
57. Cf. Nm 73 (1959); 76 (1959); N 1959/78bis.
58. Cf. N 1959/46; Nm 74 (1959).
59. Cf. Nb 70 (1959); N 1959/106 notes that out of the fifty-four people who had studied theology with him at his home town, only six were still alive, and four of these had retired.
60. Cf. Nb 69 (1959); 384 (1959).

feeling the effects of the winter and spring more than in previous years: his bout of sickness in the previous fall had in fact had more lasting consequences, so that he still did not feel one hundred percent fit.[61]

The situation worsened further in June, so that we find him saying that he is in ill-health, worn out and exhausted with work, and that he has lost all enthusiasm.[62] He therefore canceled the visit he had planned to his home town. I remember him telling me, "You know how much I've traveled in my life, but I've lost any wish to move. The very thought of packing scares me, let alone the journey itself."[63] And although he had previously thought of going to rest in some peaceful place in northern Italy,[64] he finally decided to stay in Rome, where he had himself given a relatively airy and quiet room in the old part of the house. Most important of all, the room was well away from other people's quarters, so that it would be unlikely that visitors would find him, and he could sleep and relax as much as he wanted. The doorman received instructions to tell visitors, "Father Bea is on vacation," which was of course true, although people usually took it to mean, "Father Bea is *away* on vacation."[65] At this point I left for my own vacation, although with some apprehension over whether he would still be there when I returned, and if so in what state.

Early in September, when my vacation was almost over, I had to go to Constance to visit with his old friend of student days, Dr. Fridolin Amann. On my way there, I wondered what I should tell his friend about Bea's health, but as soon as I got there, Dr. Amann surprised me by saying that he had received a letter from Bea saying that anything I might tell him about Bea's health was no longer true: "I am over everything now, and I feel like another person." I have found the relative letter in the files. It is dated 11 September, and after thanking his friend for his good wishes for his name-day Bea writes: "I was absolutely right to stay here this summer, for in the peace of August (when the house is empty, and nobody imagines that anyone might be here) I have had such a wonderful rest and recovered from almost all the aches and pains brought on by exhaustion, that I can now start again with renewed strength. . . . So if Father Schmidt tells you about my lack of energy and the weakness brought on by my age, you can tell him that I am over all that and have regained my youth."[66]

I wondered whether this letter was not a way of sparing his friend from worry. I do not remember the impression Bea made on me on my return to Rome, so that all I can say here is that in the letters from this period there is a whole series of statements similar to the ones given above: "It was a good thing that I did not go away"; "In this way I have shaken off my aches and pains"; "I am very well"; "I am in good form"; etc.[67] There is also the fact—as we shall see in due

61. Cf. Nb 385 (1959); 387 (1959); 388 (1959); Nh 17 (1959); Ni 60 (1959); Np 16 (1959); Nb 390 (1959).
62. cf. Nb 71 (1959); 289 (1959); N 1959/97.
63. Cf. also Nc 47 (1959).
64. Cf. Np 16 (1959).
65. Cf. Np 17 (1959); Nr 29 (1959).
66. Nc 50 (1959).
67. Cf. Np 17 (1959); Nr 29 (1959); Nb 118 (1959); 161 (1959); 225 (1959); 289 (1959); 391

course—that three months later he bore up very well under the strain of all the events connected with being made cardinal: receiving congratulatory visits, preparing a new home, the various ceremonies, etc.

* * *

I shall end with a letter dated May 1959, which on the one hand reflects the situation we have described, but on the other also casts a somewhat enigmatic glance at the future, for as he sets about a major retrospective reflection on his life, he throws some surprising light on the events that were to follow in a few months. I shall thus give a summary of the content of the letter in question.

Thanking a young religious for the good wishes offered for his seventy-ninth birthday, Bea writes: "It is no longer permissible to wish me 'many happy returns' on my birthday, for the psalmist rightly says: '[The sum of our years is seventy, and] if we are strong, eighty. And most of them are toil and vanity, for soon they pass and fly away.'[68] At my age one has no right to forget this. That 'we are strong' is, so far, more or less true, although I am still suffering somewhat from the aftermath of last fall's sickness; this does not prevent me from working, but it does limit my movements and make physical effort difficult. This is why I shall not go north this year, despite the fact that my fellow townsmen in Riedböhringen are anxious to see me. Instead of this, I shall withdraw to somewhere perfectly calm and have a thoroughgoing rest for a few weeks. After all, we can never know what new things the coming year may bring."[69]

Bea then refers to his young correspondent's future, adding the following reflection on his own life: "We can tranquilly leave the future up to God's providence. In my case it has always decided differently from what my superiors had planned, but in the final analysis something good came of it. For me it would have been infinitely more comfortable if—as my superiors had decided—I had taught Greek and Latin at Feldkirch High School, and it might also have involved less fires of purgatory for me. However, God decided that things should go otherwise, and that is fine."[70] When Bea wrote this, he certainly had no inkling that a few months later providence would be proceeding along similarly unforeseen lines yet again.

(1959); N 1959/134.

68. Bea is citing the psalm according to the *Piiano* psalter (the translation commissioned and published by Pius XII), but he quotes only part of it: "Si validi sumus octoginta anni . . . et plerique eorum sunt labor et vanitas, nam cito transeunt et nos avolamus." In order to make the sense clearer, we have added in brackets the part not quoted.

69. We can certainly rule out any suspicion that Bea is thinking here that he may be made a cardinal, for this came as a complete surprise to him, as we shall see in our next chapter. It seems to me most probable that he was thinking of preparations for the Council, and assuming that the Holy Office—and therefore himself, as consultor—would be particularly closely involved.

70. Ni 60 (1959).

CHAPTER 2

"A CATEGORICAL ORDER" LIKE A BOLT FROM THE BLUE

On 16 November 1959, a Monday, life was going on as normal at the Pontifical Biblical Institute. After the end of morning lectures, the community gathered in the refectory for lunch at 12:45. The rector of the community and another father were absent, but nobody attached much importance to the fact. The custom on ordinary working days at that time was for a book to be read out loud during the meal, while the others ate in silence. On this particular day, after the usual opening prayer the others saw the minister (the rector's chief assistant) leave the room and then come back. To start with, there was a Bible reading, after which the reader would normally have moved on to the book that was at present being read. However, the minister told him to move straight on to the martyrology of the saints,[1] which usually brought the meal to an end. The others looked at one another in surprise because this was a sign that something special had happened and that conversation would be permitted in place of the reading. After the martyrology had been read, the minister said: "We have just received news that the Holy Father plans to create a number of new cardinals, including Father Bea. Thanks be to God."[2]

Later we learned how the institute had first received the news. A little after noon, while the examination of conscience was being made in the community in accordance with the usual practice, the director of the news broadcasts of Vatican Radio telephoned Father Pietro Bocaccio, asking him for a short biography of Father Bea. Father Bocaccio answered that at that moment he was supposed to be concentrating on his examination of conscience, but he was then told that the matter was urgent, because the biography was to be broadcast at half past two, since Father Bea was among the people the Holy Father was shortly to make cardinal. This put a very different complexion on things, and Father Bocaccio hurried to find the rector. Since Father Bea was absent for a meeting at the Holy Office, the two men set to work to assemble the necessary information.

On more than one occasion the person most directly involved described how he himself learned the news, so we know about that in considerable detail.[3] At about 9:30 that day, a car from the Holy Office came to take him to the usual meeting of consultors. While he was sitting in the car outside the Pontifical

---

1. A kind of amplified "calendar" listing the names of the martyrs and saints whose martyrdom or death is celebrated that day, together with their place of death. A number of such calendars have existed since early times, but today the official edition or *Roman Martyrology* is most widely used; cf. *EncCatt*, VIII, 244-258.
2. The formula "Thanks be to God" is the usual signal that conversation can begin, and was therefore not intended as an expression of thanksgiving for the good news.
3. Cf. also JI, pp. 33-34.

Gregorian University on the other side of the square, waiting to collect another consultor, Father Franz Hürth, a car with a Vatican registration drew up outside the Biblical Institute, and an official of the Secretariat of State, Monsignor Angelo Di Pasquale, got out and told the doorman that he had to speak to Father Bea. "He just left. . . . Ah: the car's still outside the Gregorian University," he was told. Monsignor Di Pasquale walked over to the car, and told Father Bea that he had to talk to him. "I'm afraid it's not possible right now, Monsignor. I have to be at the Holy Office meeting, and we're late already." "But I've come from the Holy Father," answered the other. When Bea got out of the car, Monsignor Di Pasquale handed him a large sealed envelope with the words: "My congratulations and best wishes, Your Eminence. But not a word until one p.m." And he took his leave.

Since he was alone in the back of the car, Bea could open the envelope without fear of giving anything away. He found a personal letter from Pope John XXIII, dated 12 November, the central section of which said: "This letter is to advise you that in the forthcoming consistory we shall make you a member of the Sacred College of Cardinals of the Holy Roman Church, in order to express our special benevolence to you and to reward the sterling work you have done for the church with this high honor."[4] The letter closed with a warning that the news was to be kept secret until it had been officially announced.

Bea's account continued as follows: "After reading the letter, I went to the meeting at the Holy Office, doing my best to remain calm and give nothing away. During the meeting, at about eleven o'clock, someone left the room; and when he returned, he came over to me with the words, 'Your Eminence, my best wishes.' 'Shh,' I said, 'it's a secret until one o'clock.' 'Everybody outside is talking about it already,' he answered. Apparently the journalists had received a tip-off, so that news of the announcement was given earlier than intended."

To end with, let us see how the news was received by another person who was fairly closely involved, the Father General of the Society of Jesus, Johannes-Baptist Janssens,[5] who was summoned by the Cardinal Secretary of State Domenico Tardini, the day before the official announcement was made, in other words the Sunday. The exchange between the two went more or less as follows. Cardinal Tardini: "Father General, the Holy Father would also like to see the religious orders represented in the sacred college, and he wants to make a start with the Society of Jesus." Father Janssens reacted as he had in 1953 when Pius XII wanted to make Father Bea a cardinal, and as the constitutions of the order require. The latter lay down that the Father General must draw attention to the relative legislation of the order, and particularly to the vow made by all those in solemn vows that they will never accept ecclesiastical honors, unless the pope

---

4. The Latin original is as follows: "Tibi per has litteras significamus in proximo Concistorio Nos esse te cooptaturos in Sacrum S.R.E. Cardinalium Collegium, ut peculiarem benevolentiam Nostram tibi pandamus, utque tua erga Ecclesiam promerita huius insignis dignitatis praemio decoremus." The letter is reproduced in BM, p. 87.

5. We report this episode as Bea himself described it on a number of occasions, for it is practically certain that he heard it from Father Janssens himself; cf. also JI, p. 34.

orders this under pain of sin. The general must also do all he can to prevent any such step. However, as soon as Father Janssens began to speak, Cardinal Tardini cut in: "Father, it's no good going on. The Holy Father knows your constitutions, and he has therefore issued a categorical order that must be accepted; the announcement will be made tomorrow."

This is how Cardinal Bea described the meeting more than once, and the substance of his account is also found in the letter Father General wrote on 15 November, which Father Bea received the following day on his return from the meeting at the Holy Office. The letter says: "Having received a categorical order from the Holy Father—the notification that the deed had been done, despite my well-known objections—I thank the Lord that it is Your Eminence who has been chosen."[6] Father Bea went to see Father General on 17 November, and the latter confirmed things and told him about his meeting with Cardinal Tardini.

This knowledge was also important for Father Bea, for without it his first duty would have been to let the Holy Father know that in view of the aforementioned vow, he could not accept the nomination—unless the pope ordered him to do so under pain of sin. However, the "categorical order" meant that there was no choice but to obey.

"Like a Bolt from the Blue"

The difficulty that the newly elected cardinal had in adjusting to his changed situation sprang in large part from the fact that the whole thing was totally unexpected. A bare three months earlier, at the beginning of August, he had categorically ruled out any such possibility. A correspondent had written to him, saying that he had "a vague idea—and I only mention it in passing to amuse you—that you are gradually getting ready to become a curia cardinal, as is wished for you by Roman rumor-mongers. This is a rhetorical piece of news to which I do not expect any reply." Bea did, however, reply: "As concerns the news you sent 'to amuse me,' you can set your mind at rest. Rumors of this kind have been around for twenty years; but I am sure that they are now even more on the wrong track than ever."[7]

We can thus certainly believe what he wrote to confreres and friends after the announcement, when his letters repeatedly said the same thing in various forms: "You will believe me when I say that the call to the College of Cardinals not only came to me as a complete surprise, but that it also means not a few sacrifices, especially that of my academic work"[8]; "The news that I was to become a cardinal was totally unexpected for me, even though it had often been discussed previously"[9]; "The announcement was like a bolt from the blue for

---

6. Na 323a (1959); in other letters—Na 371 (1959) and Na 374 (1959)—Bea also speaks of the "categorical order."

7. Nm 79 (1959).

8. Na 352 (1959); this is a letter to O. Karrer, the German original of which was published in Karrer, *Streiflichter*, pp. 45-46.

9. Na 374 (1959); cf. 379 (1959).

me"[10]; "The news of my reception into the College of Cardinals came as a total surprise to me, and also to Father General, who was presented with the *fait accompli* of a 'categorical order' only one day before the announcement (15 November), whereas the letter giving me the news was dated 8 November![11] Thus there was nothing else for us to do but say, 'I promise special obedience to the Supreme Pontiff,' and accept the situation."[12]

A Great Many Things to Organize

It is very interesting to see how calmly Bea faced the new situation, even in the midst of all the excitement of congratulations and good wishes. As we have said, it was a Monday, and for ten years he had been in the habit of taking a pause to draw breath on that day after the heavy morning meeting at the Holy Office, which always cost him some days of preparation; thus he used to go out with the present author for a walk in the more peaceful parts of the city. That day, the meeting at the Holy Office had gone on beyond the usual lunch-time of the community. When Bea finally got back and I asked him what we would do that afternoon, he said that there was no reason why we should not go out for our walk, after he had finished with an appointment he had given a photographer.

It was a grayish November day. First we went to the General Curia of the Order, because he wanted to see Father General, whose letter of good wishes had been waiting for him on his return from the Holy Office. Having learned that Father General was out of Rome, we took a walk over the Gianicolo hill, discussing the various problems now facing him, and making plans. On our way back, we bought the *Osservatore Romano*, and found the announcement of the forthcoming consistory and the names of the eight newly announced cardinals, which also included two alumni of the Pontifical Biblical Institute, Giacomo Testa, a previous Apostolic Nuncio in Switzerland, and the Archbishop of Chicago, Albert Meyer, who had in fact studied under Bea.

The same day the rector of the institute, E. Vogt, wrote the Holy Father a letter expressing deep gratitude for the honor paid to the institute with the choice of one of its professors and two of its alumni, an honor all the more significant in that it coincided with the fiftieth anniversary of the institute. A few days later the Cardinal Secretary of State answered on behalf of the pope: "In calling three such distinguished and worthy men of the church to become part of the sacred college, he [the pontiff] wanted to offer a major mark of recognition to the institute, to which they bring honor."[13]

The numerous expressions of congratulation, however, did not blind the newly elected cardinal to the other side of things: the deep changes that all this

---

10. Na 634 (1959); cf. 203 (1959).
11. Here the cardinal has suffered a lapse in memory, for the letter is dated 12 November.
12. Na 371 (1959).
13. The letter is published in the *Acta Pont. Instituti Biblici* (Rome, 1960), VI, 312-313.

would make in his life, the tasks awaiting him, and more immediately the many preparations to be made prior to the two consistories (one secret, one public), which were to take place in about a month's time. Two weeks later, he wrote as follows to a fellow Jesuit: "It is no easy matter to start on a new life-style at seventy-nine. It takes a good deal of time, energy, and also money, to settle the material side of things to some degree. However, I have now dealt with the most pressing of such practical details with the help of my secretary. . . . I already have a driver, and a lay brother [from the province of Upper Germany] will be coming soon, which will complete this cardinal's 'family.' "[14]

This letter gives a glimpse of some aspects of the preparations, but there were a great many more. There was the question of finding an apartment suitable for the cardinal and his "family," and maybe also the relative furnishings. Then there was the question of the necessary assistance, as already mentioned above: secretary, driver, and a lay brother to act as manservant. Lastly, he had to obtain all the outfits a cardinal needed, with all the various vestments and other garments that were much more complicated then than they are today. And all this also entailed considerable financial costs. Although the Holy See did in fact assure each cardinal's keep, responsibility for these preparations and the relative expenses fell completely to each of the newly-elected cardinals.

In this situation Bea received enormous and very practical support from the Father General of the Society of Jesus, who showed a striking sense of the church and great generosity, as we can see in the letter that he had delivered to Bea on that fateful 16 November, prior to the latter's return from the meeting at the Holy Office. The whole text reads as follows: "Reverend and dear Father: *Pax Christi*. Since this is the last time that I can address you in this simple and familiar way, allow me to offer you my very warm wishes for your new position in the service of the church. Having received a categorical order from the Holy Father—the notification that the deed had been done, despite my well-known objections—I thank the Lord that it is Your Reverence who has been chosen. I am immediately applying five hundred holy masses for your intentions. The Society is fully at your disposal: residence, household personnel, finance. Your Reverence will tell me what you want, and in your person we shall be whole-heartedly serving the church. His Eminence the Cardinal Secretary of State has been so good as to assure me that they will also leave you the possibility of continuing with your academic work. *Sit nomen Domini benedictum*. I would ask you to bless this least servant of Christ, Joh. B. Janssens, S.J."[15]

The strong sense of the church underlying this letter should be particularly stressed. In various letters to the Society of Jesus, Father Janssens had repeatedly emphasized the fact that the society did not exist for itself, for its own glory, etc., but for the service of the church. Thus, the offer of assistance to the new cardinal was not made with a view to making sure that the cardinal would represent the order worthily, or anything of this kind. "In your person we shall

14. Na 613 (1959).
15. Na 323a (1959).

be wholeheartedly serving the church." When Father General met the newly elected Bea on 17 November, he made the same point, after which the various details were discussed: if Bea wanted to live at the general curia, he was certainly welcome, and the general was also ready to put a father at his disposal as secretary, and also any necessary financial assistance. In connection with this last point, on this and other occasions when Bea said he was ready to make repayment, Father General would not hear of it. There is no need to say how relieved the newly-elected cardinal was by such general assistance, which resolved many of his not inconsiderable problems at a single stroke.

However, there were still a number of decisions to be taken. The problem of a secretary was resolved sooner than expected by a combination of circumstances, which there is no need to describe here. When the announcement was made, the rector of the institute had provisionally placed the author of the present lines at his disposal, and before the end of the month Father General made this definitive.

The question of living quarters was a little more complicated. Bea did not want to accept hospitality at the general curia of the order, in order to make sure that he was not seen as an exponent or representative of the order in his work. Similarly, he did not want to live at the German College, in order to avoid giving the impression of representing German interests. In these circumstances, the offer of hospitality at the Pontifical Brazilian College was providential. The college had a number of cardinals' apartments and was only too pleased to make one available to him. However, the apartment needed decorating and furnishing, with special provisions being made to house the large libraries of the cardinal and his secretary. A switchboard was installed, which also linked the cardinal's apartment with his secretary's office.

At the outset, Father General had offered to get him a Mercedes, but a friend stepped in and obtained a Fiat 1800 from the president of the Fiat company, Professor Vittorio Valetta.

While these decisions were being taken and carried out, the days were full of both ordinary and more exceptional commitments. Bea continued to give his lectures on the inspiration of sacred scripture until 5 December, just a short time before the move to the Brazilian College. A considerable amount of time was also taken up with replying to messages of congratulations and good wishes. The relative file in the archives holds 736 letters.[16] Many of them could wait for an answer until after the consistories, but those from important figures in the worlds of both church and state—mostly from Germany—required a more immediate response. Visits took up a considerable amount of time, and there were also quite a number of invitations from Jesuit communities in Rome which wanted to express their congratulations and fraternal joy—and in the new situation any refusal could have been taken amiss. Lastly, there was the far from easy task of organizing the move to the Brazilian College, especially in view of all the manuscripts and books involved.

---

16. The collection is indexed as "Na."

Almost immediately after the announcement was made, he started arrangements with a "papal tailor" for preparation of the necessary wardrobe and vestments, for he needed many things and there was not much time until the consistory. Then there were of course all the relative fittings. It is worth noting that Bea was perfectly happy to use some of the clothes left by the Jesuit Cardinal Archbishop of Genoa, Pietro Boetto, after the necessary alterations had been made.

At that time, a portrait of the titular cardinal had to be exhibited in the church chosen for him—in our case the ancient church of St. Sabas on the Aventine hill. Very soon after the announcement Bea commissioned his portrait from Mrs. Michael Durach, a painter of German origins. Unfortunately this entailed fairly frequent sittings, which took up a considerable amount of his time.

He devoted special care to the question of a *motto and coat of arms*. The motto was to express his membership in the Society of Jesus, and was taken from Colossians 3:17: "And whatever you do, in word or deed, do everything *in the name of the Lord Jesus.*"[17] The coat of arms was to express both his membership in the Society of Jesus, and also a life devoted to sacred scripture. For the former concept, he took the arms of the society, but in the special form found on the seal used by St. Ignatius, which is kept in the archives of the general curia; and for the latter concept, he took a book bearing the letters *alpha* and *omega*, with a dove hovering over it, symbolizing the Holy Spirit. Bea used to explain this last element by referring to the great biblical encyclical of Pius XII, *Divino afflante Spiritu.*[18] On the basis of these indications, Dr. Mario Belardo of the Secretariat of State of His Holiness produced a coat of arms according to the rules of heraldry.

Bea dedicated great care and considerable time to *study of the various complicated ceremonies* connected with his creation as cardinal: the presentation and reading of the relative documents of the Secretariat of State and the Apostolic Chancery, the formal congratulatory visits, the ceremonies for the bestowal of the biretta and mozzetta, and, finally, that for the cardinal's hat in the public consistory. The files contain his notes in this connection, together with explanatory sketches where necessary, and more specific details on points that he himself was expected to perform.

In due course, a farewell meal was given at the Biblical Institute on the Feast of the Immaculate Conception, and the next day the move to the Brazilian College took place. His departure was arranged so that all the students could see him off in the courtyard of the institute during a break between lectures.

---

17. Only later was it noticed that it was very similar to the motto of Cardinal G.B. Montini (the future Pope Paul VI), which was "In nomine Domini."

18. *Divino afflante Spiritu* (= "Inspired by the Holy Spirit") are the opening words of the encyclical. A photograph of the coat of arms is found in BM, p. 85.

What Is a Cardinal, and How Does a Person Become One?

Now that we come to the solemn ceremonies for Bea's creation as cardinal, I would start by noting the limitations of the following explanations. We shall not consider the history of the position of cardinal, because this can easily be found in an encyclopedia.[19] Nor shall we give detailed descriptions of the relative ceremonies, which were particularly complicated at that time but which have been considerably simplified since then.[20] We shall simply give a short run-down on the main steps involved, and then try to explain a cardinal's position and function.

The cardinals are the highest dignitaries of the Catholic Church after the pope, and act as his advisors and closest assistants in governing the universal church.[21] They share in the general government of the church as heads or members of the various departments, especially the sacred Roman congregations, which could be described as the government ministries of the universal church. One of the specific marks of their position is the reddish purple color used for their clothes. Special significance is attributed to this color in the rite of bestowal of the cardinal's hat, when it is said that the blood-red color signifies fidelity to the faith and the church even to the point of the sacrifice of their lives.[22] Their choice and nomination are made freely by the pope, and thus we talk about the "creation" of cardinals. This time the creation itself took place in what is called the secret consistory, with only the College of Cardinals taking part.[23] After announcing the names of those chosen, the pope asks the cardinals: "What is your opinion?" However, the question is purely formal, and the cardinals express their reverent agreement by standing up and replacing their skull-caps.

Their closeness to the pope and his ministry is also seen in the relative ceremonies. They were informed of their "creation" with a "note" from the Secretariat of State and a "brief" from the Apostolic Chancery. It is the pope who bestows on them the insignia of their rank. At the time with which we are concerned, this meant the imposition of the mozzetta and biretta, and the symbolic imposition of the large cardinal's hat, which was the specific sign of his position, and finally the bestowal of the ring. Lastly, in the name of the pope a member of the papal household, who is known as *Monsignor Guardaroba* because of his special tasks, delivers the personal cardinal's hat to each new cardinal.

We saw above that when Pope John XXIII informed Father Bea that he

---

19. Cf. *EncCatt*, III, 779-784; *LThK*, V, 1342-1344.
20. A description of the 1959 ceremonies is found in JI, pp. 37-40.
21. Cf. *EncCatt*, III, 779; *LThK*, V, 1342.
22. In Latin: "usque ad effusionem sanguinis" (= "up to the shedding of one's own blood"); cf. *LThK*, V, 1344.
23. In 1959 there were two consistories, one secret and the other public. Pope John Paul II changed the practice, so that there is now only one; both the creation and the bestowal of the insignia thus take place in the same consistory. The special hat, or *galero*, is no longer bestowed.

planned to make him a member of the sacred college, he stressed the fact that this was also intended as recognition of his special service to the church, and the pope also spoke in similar terms in his address to the secret consistory.[24]

However, this was the usual language used in such circumstances, so that leaving aside such ritual phrases, we should now consider whether there was some *special reason for the nomination*, and whether the pope had some special plans for the new cardinal. A certain amount of conjecture was in fact made about this. I remember that at that time some journalists asked me whether it was true that the pope had nominated Bea because he wanted to entrust him with some important work in connection with preparations for the Council. Among the letters of congratulations, there is one dated 8 December 1959 that refers to such a task: "We have learned from the press that His Holiness John XXIII has been pleased to entrust Your Eminence with heading and coordinating the preparatory work of the Ecumenical Council. . . . I offer my congratulations and am very happy to promise you the support of my prayers."[25] Personally I had to say even then—as I repeat today—that I had heard nothing about such a thing. However, even the person most closely involved knew nothing about it, and on 31 December of the same year he was writing as follows to a fellow Jesuit: "I do not yet know what role I am to play in it [the Council]. As the Holy Father went around to speak to all the cardinals after delivery of the Christmas greetings, he told me that he would like to talk to me soon. I shall ask for an audience as soon as the visits of the diplomats are over."[26]

So what was the reason for his nomination? The question must be asked all the more because it appears that John XXIII did not even know Bea, having met him for the first time in January 1959, when Bea was presented to him together with the staff of the Holy Office.[27] About four months later, Bea was presented to him again at an audience for the consultors of the Pontifical Biblical Commission. One of the consultors, Father G. Duncker, O.P., recalls that occasion as follows: "We were all presented to the Holy Father by our President, Cardinal Tisserant; but it was immediately clear that the pope did not catch our names as the cardinal gave them. And indeed, when the pope was talking with us in his typically simple way and he heard the name 'Bea' he asked; 'Is one of you called Bea?' 'Yes, me, Your Holiness,' answered Father Bea. 'But do you mean there are two Beas in Rome?' asked the pope. 'Not that I know of,' said Father Bea. 'I've been here for many years, but I've never heard of any other Bea.' 'Then you must be that Bea!' exclaimed the pope. It is clear that the pope

---

24. Cf. *AAS*, LII (1960), 11; the same formula was also used in the consistories of 1958 (cf. *AAS*, L [1958], 986) and 1960 (cf. *AAS*, LII [1960], 326).

25. Na 171 (1959).

26. Na 318 (1959); the audience took place on 9 January 1960.

27. In his statement (ArchWit, p. 1), Monsignor L.F. Capovilla mentions that "in the early days of his papacy, John XXIII granted a private audience, and spent a long time talking with the Jesuits who had been responsible for Pius XII's personal library and worked directly for him in the mezzanine of the private apartment." These were Fathers W. Hentrich and R. Leiber, S.J. The witness does not recall whether or not Father Bea was included in this audience, but I am sure that he was not, for he was still sick.

did not know Father Bea until our audience. Although he had heard of a certain Bea who had been his predecessor's confessor and was apparently a well-known figure, he did not know that this was the man he was now talking to."[28]

Certain letters of congratulation linked the nomination with the veneration that Pope John had for his predecessor, and more specifically with the position Bea had held with Pius XII and the services he had rendered him.[29] Bea himself confirmed this connection in a television interview in the spring of 1960.[30] In the light of what Bea told me personally, I think that his meaning was that the pope wanted to offer the Society of Jesus some recognition for the great services that some of its members had rendered his predecessor.[31]

Now, out of the three people who were most closely linked to Pius XII—Father Bea, confessor, Father Robert Leiber, private secretary, and Father W. Hentrich, librarian—Pope John XXIII chose the one whose work with the pope was least well-known, and with whom there was thus least risk that people might imagine that his nomination as cardinal represented special recognition of his previous activity.

We find the *background* to the nomination described in the statement of Monsignor L.F. Capovilla, private secretary to Pope John XXIII. In preparing for the consistories for the creation of new cardinals, the pope also returned to the criterion "of paying honor to the great religious families, with the aim of making use of their experience to help in governing the church, and at the same time encouraging the spread of the specific spirituality and culture of each. He therefore asked for a list of names of Jesuits of different nationalities. He spoke about this specifically in an audience with Father General Johannes B. Janssens. I do not know if the general himself accepted an invitation from the pope to give his views, and thus expressed a preference for Bea as candidate. Apart from this, the pope liked the annotation on Bea's name made by Cardinal Tardini, Secretary of State: 'German, biblicist, was confessor to Pius XII.' The first two elements were of considerable interest in the perspective of internationalizing the curia and with a view to reorganizing the biblical commission (one of the first and most constant concerns of John XXIII, although one that did not unfortunately receive much support); then the third element meant that this choice would have the value of offering homage to the memory of his predecessor."[32]

When the list of the *Roman congregations assigned to the new cardinals* was published on the day of the public consistory, there was still no clue that the

---

28. Duncker, "Ricordando il Cardinale Agostino Bea," p. 53. This account indicates that J.M. Oesterreicher's description of the episode (in *Simposio*, p. 30) is incorrect.

29. Cf. Na 324 (1959); 354 (1959); 434 (1959).

30. Television interview with Dr. Brobeil of the West German company Süd-West-Funk; a copy is found in the archives.

31. Details of these services are found in the present author's article in *Arch. Hist. Pont.*, XVI (1978), 333, note 100.

32. ArchWit, pp. 1-2. Since this evidence is more than a little vague, it should be read in the light of some definite facts given above, i.e. Father General's audience with Cardinal Tardini, and his letter of 15 November to Father Bea.

pope had any immediate special plans for Bea. As said above, the cardinals perform their task of advisors and assistants to the pope in practical terms as members of the Roman congregations. Bea was made a member of the Congregation of Rites, the Congregation for Seminaries (for the training of future priests) and Institutes of Study, and finally the Pontifical Biblical Commission, which has authority in the field of biblical studies. As we can see, there is no connection with preparations for the Council or any special task of this kind.

Let us add a word of comment and clarification on the three areas assigned to the new cardinal. It was natural and predictable enough for him to be appointed to the Congregation of Rites, with which he had been so actively involved for over ten years in connection with liturgical reform, although apart from this work there were now the causes for beatification and canonization with their bulky files. Then again, Bea had also been consultor to the Pontifical Biblical Commission for a quarter of a century, and this was in any case his special field of expertise. Similarly, for over twenty years he had now been a consultor to the Congregation for Seminaries and Institutes of Study, although in fact his opinion had not been very frequently sought.

Some of the letters of congratulation expressed the hope that he would continue to work at the Holy Office,[33] and maybe Bea himself expected to. When he discussed his future work with the Cardinal Secretary of State a few days after the announcement of his creation, Bea did mention that he had been a consultor at the Holy Office for over ten years, but the cardinal simply said that the Holy Office "was already at full strength." When Bea talked to me about this, he sometimes expressed his impression that they did not want him at the Holy Office. Did this suspicion have any basis in fact? Somebody who had worked in the department for many years pointed out that there was an unwritten rule that consultors who became cardinals never became members. And I myself have noticed on occasions when other cardinals were created that the Holy Office is not one of the departments normally assigned to new cardinals. We could add that another consultor of the Holy Office who was created cardinal at the same time as Bea, Francesco Morano, did not become a member. Four years would pass before Bea was made a member of the department in the fall of 1963.

Taking Possession of the Church of St. Sabas as Titular Cardinal

A last act in the succession of ceremonies connected with the creation of a cardinal is that of entry into the "titular church" assigned to him. It is in virtue of this connection that he is incorporated into the *presbyterium* of the Church of Rome,[34] for in formal terms the cardinals are advisors and assistants to the pope as members of this body of clergy.

---

33. Cf. Na 681 (1959).

34. For the history of the institution of titular churches of cardinals, cf. *EncCatt*, III, 780; *LThK*, V, 1342-1343.

Ancient historical churches are chosen for this purpose. St. Sabas had not previously been a titular church, but was raised to this honor on the present occasion. When Pope John XXIII created the new cardinals, he exceeded the number of seventy cardinals fixed by Pope Sixtus V in the sixteenth century, so that he then had to create new titular churches, and these included St. Sabas.

Let us first take a look at *its history* as our cardinal himself described it in the homily given when he took possession of the church.[35] In the first place this church "reminds us of the great figure of the Pontiff St. Gregory the Great, whose Mother St. Sylvia lived on this site and had converted one of the large rooms into a prayer hall."[36] Then there is the connection of the church with St. Sabas. And here the cardinal started by recalling his visit to the original monastery of St. Sabas in Palestine: "In the summer of 1934, as Rector of the Pontifical Biblical Institute, I was the leader of a study expedition in Palestine, and on an incredibly hot day we went down from Jerusalem into the Valley of the Kedron in order to visit the famous monastery of St. Sabas—known as 'Mar Saba' in those parts. After we had been following the valley of the Kedron for about nine miles, we saw the monastery high up on our left, perched on the steep cliffs like a swallow's nest."[37] Then there was the migration of the monks from this monastery to Rome: "In the first half of the sixth century, the monks from the monastery of Mar Saba left Palestine, partly because of doctrinal disagreements, and partly because of the savagery of the Persian invasion. . . . When they reached the eternal city, they settled down beside this already venerated oratory, and there they stayed until the tenth century."[38] Then came other monks: "In the tenth century Benedictine monks followed, probably from Monte Cassino, and in the twelfth century monks from Cluny, who built the present church over the old oratory. . . . After a number of changes in ownership, in 1573 Gregory XII finally assigned the church to the German College, which has remained in possession until today."[39] We would add that in 1931 Pope Pius XI founded a parish here, entrusting it to the Society of Jesus.[40]

Looking back over this history, he observed: "So very many reflections are aroused by the fact that the Holy Father chose to raise a church of such venerable origins to the high dignity of a cardinal's 'title,' thus crowning a history of more than thirteen centuries, and then conferring the title on someone who has had so much to do with Palestine and its age-old history, and in particular with its revered Christian monuments, especially those in the cradle of Christianity, the Holy City *par excellence*, Jerusalem."[41]

---

35. Cf. the relative manuscript, R 1960/5.

36. *Ibid.*, p. 2.

37. *Ibid.*, p. 1.

38. *Ibid.*, p. 2.

39. *Ibid.*

40. Various points in this history also indicate why this particular titular church was assigned to Bea, in other words the fact that the church was the property of the German College, together with the fact that the parish that had been established there had been entrusted to the Society of Jesus.

41. R 1960/5, pp. 1-2.

While the cardinal could point out how appropriate the choice of his titular church was in view of his previous studies, we can now note the connection between this choice and his future activity. Certainly at that moment the new titular cardinal could not foresee that the secretariat he would be called to head would be the chosen and providential instrument in bringing about the truly historic undertaking of the return of the relics of St. Sabas to the original monastery of Mar Saba in the Valley of the Kedron after fourteen centuries—an event that took place toward the end of the Council, in October 1965.[42] Broadening our gaze, it must be admitted that the choice of titular church was in a sense symbolic in view of his future ecumenical mission, and the cardinal himself pointed out its ecumenical significance in the homily he gave in German when he took possession: "This church is a symbol of the unity that is the great desire not only of the church of Rome and its children, but also of so many non-Catholic Christians, indeed of humanity itself, which longs more than ever today to leave its splintering behind it and reach unity—although it will never do so without him who prayed to the Father 'that they may all be one, just as we are one.' "[43]

* * *

As we said above, the cardinals are the highest dignitaries of the Catholic Church after the pope, so we should take a look at the practical expressions of the new cardinal's attitude toward his position. We find him writing as follows to a fellow Jesuit who had been in the habit of writing to him about various problems, including those in the liturgical field: "I assure you that I do not float in some 'purple-tinged unapproachability,' but still have my feet firmly on the ground of everyday life. . . . So go on writing me as before, and I shall try to reply, or have a reply sent to you by my secretary except in the case of personal matters."[44]

Similarly, only six days after the fateful announcement, when he was "practically inundated with cables and letters from all over the world," he found time to write a cyclostyled letter to his relatives, thanking them for their good wishes, explaining the celebrations they would be attending, giving advice over their journey, describing the correct form of dress, and explaining how and where they could see him. He even offered to find accommodations in Rome for them, and he ended by answering their query as to how they would be expected to address him in future: "You will write to me exactly as you used to. For you I am and remain 'Cousin August.' Only on the envelope you must write: 'His Eminence, the most excellent Lord Augustin Cardinal Bea.' "[45]

Nor is this all, for he saw the position of cardinal itself purely and simply as a service of God and the church. The first thing he did the day after receiving

---

42. Cf. *Ecumenism*, pp. 190-193.
43. Cf. the relative manuscript, R 1960/5, p. 6. The cardinal is referring to John 17:22.
44. Na 371 (1959).
45. Na 120 (1959).

THE COUNCIL

the news from the pope was to write him a personal letter. In order not to be disturbed, he sought refuge in my room, where he sat down and wrote the letter for himself. The aim was not so much that of thanking the pope for the "undeserved favor" and so forth. Rather, he took up the subject of the special Jesuit vow not to accept honors in the church unless the pope ordered this under pain of sin. Having heard from Father General of the pope's "categorical order," the newly-elected cardinal told the Holy Father that he accepted the nomination in the spirit of obedience, and therefore wanted to place himself completely at his disposal for any service of the Holy See.[46]

These were not mere ritual phrases or a show of modesty. Even more explicit expressions are found in various letters from those days, especially those to priests and bishops whom he could have expected to understand this attitude. Thus he wrote to a priest friend in Germany: "I would have far preferred to pass the days of my old age in peaceful, unassuming work; but now all I can say is, 'I do not refuse the task.' Help me with your prayers, so that my work may be to the profit of the church and souls."[47] He also wrote to a bishop as follows, referring to the response bishops give at their consecration: "I too have had to pronounce my 'Here am I' for a task that will not be easy, especially since many hopes are pinned on my work. I shall need a great deal of light and strength from on high for this."[48]

He developed this theme still further when writing to the well-known founder and head of the Movement for a Better World, Father Riccardo Lombardi, S.J.: "I thank you most particularly for your prayers, for I know only too well how much divine assistance I shall need in the new position in which I have been placed by that same obedience that we professed members of the society promise with the solemn vow concerning any 'mission' that the Vicar of Christ may entrust to us."[49] Clearly, then, the new task is seen as a mission received from the pope and linked to the fourth vow of the professed members of the order, which obliges them to accept and perform without delay or questioning any task that the pope might entrust to them for the good of the church and souls. In other words, after the pope gave his categorical order, thus removing the obstacle of the vow not to accept ecclesiastical honors, rather than being free to accept the appointment, in virtue of the fourth vow Bea was in fact obliged to accept it as a mission entrusted to him by the pope. In this way he linked his creation as cardinal with the essential aim of the Society of Jesus as expressed in the *Formula of the Institute*, the very first official document of the order, as accepted and approved by Pope Paul III. In this document the aim of the society is expressed in terms typical of those times: ". . . serve as a soldier of God beneath

---

46. Here I am correcting my earlier statements because in the meantime I have found a considerable proportion of the draft letter; cf. Arch. J 112.

47. Na 374 (1959); cf. also Na 681 (1959). The phrase in quotes is taken from the reading of the Liturgy of Hours, for the feast of St. Martin, first Bishop of Tours in France.

48. Na 531 (1959); cf. also Na 681 (1959).

49. Na 420 (1959); similar reference to the fourth vow about "missions" is also found in Na 371 (1959).

the banner of the cross . . . and serve the Lord alone and the Roman pontiff, his vicar on earth. . . ." A formula approved ten years later by Pope Julius III reads: ". . . serve the Lord alone and the church, his spouse, under the Roman pontiff, the vicar of Christ on earth."[50]

---

50. Cf. *Constitutiones Societatis Jesu et Epitome Instituti* (Rome, 1943), pp. XXXVII-XXXVIII.

CHAPTER 3

THE PROSPECTS FOR THE NEW CARDINAL

At the moment when Bea became cardinal, quite a number of people—especially among those closest to him—wondered whether the purpose of this honor was simply to allow him to enjoy a well-deserved prize within the framework of a calm old age. Apart from his age, which was a far from negligible factor even on its own, the question seemed all the more reasonable in view of his state of health after the sickness of fall 1958 and semi-collapse of the following spring.[1] The question was all the more comprehensible inasmuch as most people were unaware of his unexpected recovery during the following summer.[2]

Taking the question of his health first, we must note that his letters from the period starting in December are fairly encouraging in this regard, and we find repeated assurances that the tasks connected with his creation as cardinal—the practical preparations for his new life, with the organization of accommodation, the move, etc., as well as all the complicated ceremonies—had been hard, but that he had come through them without any ill-effects for his health.[3] He also said that the formal congratulatory visits were much more tiring, so that in the evening, after receiving visits from about twenty cardinals and as many ambassadors, he was totally exhausted. Despite everything, however, "I am well and I feel well."[4] And this state of well-being continued. In February he wrote: "Everybody tells me that I am looking better than before."[5] And in April: "Praise be to God I am very well and everybody is astonished that I shall be entering my eightieth year. . . . On the other hand, there is also more variety in my tasks, since I have to receive and make many visits; and I have had to accept various commitments for the International Eucharistic Congress in Munich. Of course it is difficult to say no in many cases."[6]

Summarizing these observations on his good health, the cardinal wrote to his trusted friend Dr. Amann: "I have the strong impression that my erstwhile exalted penitent is watching over the health of his confessor from heaven. Considering the many graces that he grants and the miracles he performs, such care would not in fact be so impossible."[7]

---

1. In this connection Monsignor L.F. Capovilla relates the following exchange with a Jesuit: "When I exclaimed: 'The order will be happy to have a member in the sacred college again,' I was met with a knowing smile and a disarming and not exactly ironic phrase: 'Well, they chose an old man who no longer counts for much among the Jesuits' " (ArchWit, p. 2).
2. The impressions and views of people close to him were thus quite different from the expectations expressed by some of Bea's correspondents in connection with his creation as cardinal, as we saw in the previous chapter.
3. Cf. Nb 192 (1959); 291 (1960); Na 666 (1959).
4. Na 16 (1959).
5. Nb 393 (1960); cf. 394 (1960).
6. Nb 447 (1960).
7. Na 16 (1959).

Another more convincing answer to the question we asked at the start soon came from the increasing range of activities performed by the new cardinal.

Daily Life and Priestly Activity

We can obtain some idea of the cardinal's intense activity from the following statistics drawn up on the basis of the cardinal's and his secretary's diaries for *the first seven months of 1960*: the cardinal presided over seventeen religious services and attended another thirty; he had thirteen official meetings of the Roman congregations, including nine of the Congregation of Rites, which usually has very bulky files; he granted 270 audiences to one or more people; he took part in public events, often giving addresses, on thirty occasions; he wrote about seven hundred letters, not counting straightforward routine matters and good wishes; added to this were forty-four occasions of a more social nature, with invitations to receptions, etc.

1. This considerable work-load is also reflected in the daily schedule to which the cardinal subjected himself despite his age. He would get up at 4:30 a.m. for Lauds and Prime.[8] An hour of meditation followed. At 6:15 came mass in his private chapel, after which he attended the second half of the mass said by his private secretary. Then came breakfast in his own apartment, followed by the Little Hours of the Divine Office, and then to work. Halfway through the morning, and also halfway through the afternoon, he took a little coffee with some biscuits. He took his main meals—lunch at 1 p.m., and dinner at 8 p.m.—with the community of Jesuits who ran the Brazilian College. He wanted to live so far as possible in community, and this was why he had chosen the Brazilian College. He particularly wanted to hear the reading at table, which was still the custom at that time. Since his working day entailed constant contacts with other people, he preferred not to have to speak at table, but to listen to the reading of some interesting book, especially since his many commitments meant that he had little time for reading and it was an occupation he had always enjoyed. After lunch he made the usual visit to the Blessed Sacrament with the community, and then spent between fifteen and twenty minutes in conversation with his confreres, walking along the broad corridors of the college.

In the afternoon he allowed himself a siesta of about forty-five minutes, after which he anticipated Matins, and returned to work, receiving visitors, etc. He had planned to go out for a walk at least once a week, but receptions and similar commitments very soon frustrated this intention. Dinner was followed by the usual visit to the chapel; then, at least in the first years, he watched the television news. This was followed by preparation of his meditation for the next day, the examination of conscience, and a last visit to the Blessed Sacrament in his private chapel, after which he retired for the night, usually sleeping for about seven hours. By nature he was more of a morning worker than an evening or night-time one. Years before this he had made a resolution not to work after

8. Before the liturgical reform the breviary was longer, and its structure was somewhat different.

dinner, saying that he was usually so tired that he would be incapable of doing anything worthwhile in any case.

2. On 20 December 1959, a few days after the consistory, the newly elected cardinal celebrated mass in the German national church in Rome, Santa Maria dell'Anima. The homily he gave reveals his *deeply religious and apostolic view* of his task as cardinal. It was based on the reading of the day, which was taken from the First Letter to the Corinthians, and particularly St. Paul's words: "This is how people should regard us, as servants of Christ and stewards [or ministers] of the mysteries of God" (1 Cor. 4:1). Referring to the ceremonies of the consistory, he said: "Although the ceremonies linked to the creation of a cardinal are very lavish, they can hardly be said to express what he must be in reality: 'a minister of the mysteries of God.' He should not seek splendor and brilliance and riches, but rather to administer generously the holy mysteries of God, the mysteries of doctrine, the mysteries of the word and the mysteries of the holy sacraments, the seven sacraments of the church."[9]

We should not imagine that these words were simply a preacher's rhetoric. Although the letters quoted above still sometimes mention the thought and wish to find time for study and academic work, from the first months of his life as cardinal, we find him extensively involved in the various forms of administration of the mysteries of God: administration of the doctrine with talks, administration of the sacraments, and religious celebrations with homilies. The collection of his manuscripts contains as many as twenty for the first six months of 1960 alone, and particular mention should be made of a number of public talks of various kinds and on various subjects: the law in sacred scripture, the priest as minister of the sacrament and minister of the word, and the excavations at Teileilat-Ghassul.[10] His address given in the presence of Pope John XXIII for the celebration of the fiftieth anniversary of the Pontifical Biblical Institute is particularly important, and we have already drawn on it at considerable length when describing Bea's work as rector of the institute.[11] This activity of lecturing and preaching would continue, but on a decreasing scale, until mid-1961, in other words until his work for Christian unity came to take up all his time and energy.

3. It is surprising to see the extent to which the cardinal was involved in the celebrations marking the *nineteenth centenary of St. Paul's arrival in Rome*, from a first lecture given at the Pontifical Lateran University on the subject "Paul Taken by Christ," including one given in the Christological course at Naples under the title "The Path of the Church through History according to St. Paul," and through the last one, on "The Priest, according to St. Paul: Minister of Christ."[12] It is interesting that the author then chose to publish these lectures in the form of articles in order to reach a wider audience.[13]

---

9. The cardinal spoke without a written text, but we have the transcription of a tape recording; cf. R 1959/60/2, p. 1.

10. Cf. manuscripts R 1960/12 and Biblio. 130; R 1960/16; 1961/29.

11. Cf. Biblio. 129.

12. Cf. *CC*, 1961/IV, 337-349.

13. Various articles on St. Paul reappear in Biblio. 187.

4. Certain homilies deserve special examination, partly because of the stir they caused in the press. This applies to the homily given at a celebration for "the church of silence" organized in the Church of St. Mary Major by the International Pontifical Marian Academy of Rome.[14] The well-known Cardinal Alfredo Ottaviani, who was then Secretary of the Holy Office, and was "patron" of the academy, had given the homily at a similar celebration two months earlier. On that occasion, the preacher had referred to the forthcoming official visit of the President of the Italian Republic, Giovanni Gronchi, to Moscow, and made a strong attack on politicians who have no scruples over shaking hands dripping with blood—a clear reference to the Russian leaders.[15] In *his* homily, our cardinal stressed the fact that the persecutions to which *the church of silence* was subject "have reached proportions, violence and atrocity such as have maybe never before been seen in history,"[16] and added that, while praying for the great needs of the contemporary world and particularly for peace, we must not forget "the terrible situations in which many of our brethren in the faith still live: their sufferings, their anxieties, the Calvary they are undergoing."[17] He ended by listing the graces we must pray for, for these brethren. Public opinion saw the homily as an implicit rectification; hence the great stir it caused. The main passages of the homily were carried by the Italian news agency ANSA, both in its general service as well as in its religious newsletter.[18]

Another homily that raised some echoes in the press (although of a different kind) was given during a mass celebrated *for Silesian refugees* at the tomb of Pope Pius XII.[19] The homily met with an unpleasant reaction from the official Polish press, which misquoted certain expressions about the sufferings of the Silesian refugees. The cardinal had referred, for example, to the painful exile of these people from their country, trying to see it in the light of Jesus' words, "If a grain of wheat falls into the earth . . . and dies, it bears much fruit" (John 12:24), and commenting: "This saying about the grain of wheat applies to *all* those who share the lot of our Savior. They are grains of wheat which are buried in the earth and die, but which bear rich fruit—a hundredfold—for Christ, for souls, for the church, but also *for themselves*. As the apostle says, they have shared in Christ's sufferings. And they will therefore also share in his glory."[20] These innocent words were grossly misquoted by the Polish press as: "The grain that has fallen into the ground, together with the blood of martyrs and those who have suffered persecution, will bear fruit one hundredfold." It obviously wanted to give the impression that the cardinal had spoken in support of possible German territorial claims. Bea went to great trouble to counter the insinuation, but most importantly he wrote a letter to Cardinal Wyszinski. And it should be

14. Cf. the unpublished text, R 1959/60, no. 6.
15. For the circumstances and atmosphere, cf. *CC*, 1959/IV, 320-321; for the visit itself, cf. *CC*, 1960/I, 541ff.
16. R 1959/60, no. 6.
17. *Ibid.*
18. *ANSA*, LXXV (4 February 1960); and *ANSA Informazione Religiosa*, (6 February 1960).
19. Cf. manuscript R 1960/8.
20. *Ibid.*

noted that this distasteful episode never clouded relations with the Cardinal Primate of Poland in the future.

5. We would also mention two further episodes from this period, both concerned with the field of biblical studies. Winding up the Italian Bible Week of 1960, the cardinal offered some reflections on "The Present State of Biblical Studies, and of Teaching in Seminaries and Publications." We should start by referring to the particular context of the talk, for a painful polemic had already begun, with a Roman university accusing the Pontifical Biblical Institute of lacking in orthodoxy, so that there was now considerable anticipation over what the cardinal would have to say. While refusing to become embroiled in the argument,[21] he started significantly by saying that in interpreting sacred scripture we must always bear in mind the souls for whom God gave us the scriptures, and then "*the magisterium of the church* in all its forms: tradition, and also the present living teaching authority of that church to which God entrusted the explanation and interpretation of his word."[22] The speaker then entered into greater detail, stressing on the one hand the need to "pursue progress and foster it,"[23] and on the other the need to realize the real dangers here: "a certain impatience and a resulting lack of thoroughness and care in work"[24]; the danger "of setting forth problems and difficulties without attempting any solution to them"[25] and "an overly uncritical acceptance of non-Catholic academic work."[26] In connection with this last point, the cardinal explained that it was important to remember "the tradition of the fathers of the church and the declarations and decisions of the magisterium of the church."[27] Lastly, "we must take special care to uphold the inerrancy of sacred scripture, particularly in connection with statements of an historical nature."[28] Given the present situation and the fact that this was the cardinal's special province, these words were widely quoted.[29]

The cardinal did not stop at theory, and certain circumstances led him into more practical action. The Archbishop of Chicago, Cardinal Albert Meyer, who had studied under Bea at the Biblical Institute, now asked for his help, saying

---

21. The cardinal kept a careful eye on the attacks against the Pontifical Biblical Institute, but judged it best not to enter the fray. However, I know that he sent a strong letter to the rector of the university from which the attacks came, pointing out that an institute that was "pontifical" in every way was involved in the question. I think that a copy of the letter will be found among the official correspondence kept in the Secret Archives.

22. The address was published, and we are quoting from that publication; cf. Biblio. 131, p. 292.

23. *Ibid.*

24. *Ibid.*, p. 293.

25. *Ibid.*

26. *Ibid.*.

27. *Ibid.*, p. 294.

28. *Ibid.*

29. The address had a considerable impact at the Sacred Congregation for Seminaries and Institutes of Study. According to the official volume *L'attività della S. Sede* (1960), p. 221, the text was to be sent out to bishops as part of a circular on this subject. From later correspondence with the secretary of the congregation, it appears that although this had been the plan "this was in fact never done, out of fear that it could lead to inferences harmful to the good cause" (cf. the letter 1961/154).

that he would soon have to speak to his clergy on the question of the synoptic gospels, and asking for some guidelines. The cardinal answered with twenty-four pages on the subject, entitled "Contemporary Problems in Exegesis of the Synoptic Gospels." Having explained and carefully assessed the "school of the history of forms," Bea drew conclusions regarding the "historical" character of the synoptic gospels and their interpretation, referring to the intention of the evangelists, the degree of accuracy over chronological details, and the differences between the individual gospels; this indicates how we are to understand and protect the inerrancy of the gospels. The paper closed with some guidelines on how to approach these questions, saying that this should be done with truth, prudence and pastoral charity. In connection with this last point, the cardinal stressed that "it is especially important in theological schools to tell students about the problems that are being raised today, so that when they hear about them later on in practical pastoral life, they are not caught unprepared"; however, solutions must also be suggested so far as possible.[30]

The cardinal left the Archbishop of Chicago full freedom as to how he would use the document. The archbishop, who was startled to receive such detailed guidelines, answered that he would frankly tell people where the paper had come from, and would present it as it was, without change.[31]

Possible Prospects for the New Cardinal

Apart from the activity described in the preceding pages, it should be noted that from the time he was raised to the purple, many people wondered if some special tasks were in store for him, for example in the perspective of preparations for the Council. And such a view was not unreasonable. It does in fact seem that the Secretary of State thought that his work at the Roman congregations would still leave Bea time for his academic work; and in his letter of congratulations, Father General Janssens said that he had asked the Cardinal Secretary of State for Bea to be allowed the possibility of continuing with his academic work, and he thought that this request had been successful: "His Eminence the Cardinal Secretary of State was kind enough to promise me that you would be allowed the possibility of pursuing your academic work."[32]

Bea also repeatedly mentions this subject in his letters, especially in those to ex-colleagues, where he usually starts with the reflection that he would rather have spent the days of his old age in calm academic work, while now everything has changed. He then goes on: "Even so, I have been promised that I will not be too overloaded with official duties which would leave me no time for study and academic work. May God grant that these good intentions are put into

30. Cf. manuscript R 1960/14, p. 24; the document as such was never published.
31. This document would lead to some important developments, as we shall see in due course.
32. Na 16 (1959).

practice."[33] "So I hope that despite my new position I can still get something done."[34] Elsewhere he is less hopeful, observing: "It remains to be seen whether it will be so simple to keep them [these promises]. I am not in the same situation as the good Cardinal Mercati who spent his years as cardinal in the Vatican Library, continuing his 'hidden life' there."[35] Again we find: "I am not very optimistic in this respect, but I shall do what I can. I still have several unfinished studies, and maybe I shall be able to finish them."[36] On other occasions he is maybe more far-sighted and realistic: "Despite all the promises to the contrary, I shall no doubt have to consign my biblical studies to definitive burial."[37]

We may wonder why he was so convinced that he was not in the happy position of Cardinal Mercati, so that he would be unable to continue his academic work and would have to bury his biblical studies. He was probably thinking in the first place of his experience over the past ten years, when a number of departments of the Roman curia had taken such abundant advantage of his knowledge and experience that the number of such tasks had gradually cut him off from his academic work. As we have already said, this was a particular sacrifice for him in these ten years. He obviously felt it improbable that his work-load would decrease now that he had been placed in as official a position as that of a curial cardinal.

Apart from his past experience, there was also the extraordinarily *positive reaction* to his nomination from many quarters, particularly *in Germany*, and also the hopes that it raised. On the very first day, the then Archbishop of Paderborn, who had expert knowledge of the situation in Germany, wrote to him as follows: "The echo in Germany will announce loud and clear the trust and veneration you enjoy here, not only among the bishops, but also among the clergy and ordinary members of the faithful."[38] Some days later Bishop H. Tenhumberg, who was the head of the Catholic Office of Bonn, an excellent vantage-point for observation of life in Germany, wrote as follows: "The news has unleashed great joy throughout Germany, as you have certainly seen in the press."[39] At the end of November, Hans Struth, who published the very successful illustrated review *Fuerreiter* and was another attentive and knowledgeable observer, wrote: "As Your Eminence has certainly learned from the German

---

33. Na 192 (1959).
34. Na 571 (1959).
35. Na 352 (1959); cf. 203 (1959); 347 (1959). Cardinal Giovanni Mercati (1866-1957) was Prefect of the Vatican Library, succeeding Achille Ratti, the future Pius XI; when Pius XI wanted to make him cardinal in 1936, it was agreed that he could continue his scholarly life, which is what he did for over twenty years as "Librarian of the Holy Roman Church"; cf. *LThK*, VII, 303-304.
36. Na 291 (1959). The author was probably thinking of the new edition of his manual on the inspiration and hermeneutics of sacred scripture. On the other hand, he had almost immediately given up any idea of revising his *Il problema antropologico in Gen. 1-2. Il Trasformismo* (Biblio. 10), because he felt that his new position made it impossible to speak on such a delicate matter; cf. Na 503 (1959).
37. Na 221 (1959); cf. also Na 352 (1959).
38. Na 328 (1959).
39. Na 681 (1959).

press, there is generally great joy that a German has been called to become a member of the College of Cardinals."[40]

For his part Bea himself wrote: "I am deeply touched by all the expressions of warm good wishes that I have received from every side."[41] However, he immediately realized how great a responsibility this joy and hope imposed on him: "I too have had to pronounce my 'Here am I' for a task that will not be easy, especially since many hopes are pinned on my work. I shall need a great deal of light and strength from on high for this."[42] Or again: "Let us hope and pray that in my new position I manage to some extent to fulfill the expectations people everywhere have of me, especially in Germany. . . . I take consolation in the thought that he who gives us a task also grants us the grace needed to perform it."[43]

What was the precise nature of people's hopes in the future activity of the new cardinal? Some hoped that Bea would continue with his work at the Holy Office, in the wish, for example, to have his support for the Schönstatt Movement,[44] a wish that was not fulfilled in this form, since Bea did not become a member of the Holy Office. Other people hoped that they would find an effective sympathizer for the problems of German Catholicism in the new cardinal,[45] while the expectations of others concerned preparations for the Council,[46] or liturgical renewal and reform.[47]

We also find a reference to *the question of the Jewish people*, and although this may still be indirect, it does seem almost symbolic. The President of the World Jewish Congress sent a cable to the Jesuit Father General, expressing the hope that the nomination would help strengthen the church, whose well-being was of great concern to all men of good will in these turbulent times.[48] Although it was submitted to him through an intermediary, the cardinal received a query from Jewish quarters in Switzerland as to whether it would be possible for Pope John XXIII not only to convene the Council but also to "call a joint meeting of the peoples of the Old and New Testaments."[49]

The practical hopes that had decided pride of place were those concerned with the cause of Christian unity.[50] The Archbishop of Paderborn, whom we have already quoted above, wrote: "I am particularly happy [over the nomination], in view both of the preparations for the forthcoming Council and also of

---

40. Na 659 (1959); an indication of the joy of German Catholics is given by the fact that the President of the Central Committee of German Catholics, Prince Karl zu Löwenstein, asked to be present at the ceremonies for the creation as "an honorary member of the cardinal's family." Cf. Na 415 (1959).
41. Na 624 (1959).
42. Na 531 (1959).
43. Na 681 (1959).
44. Cf. *ibid.*
45. Cf. Na 308 (1959).
46. Cf. Na 27 (1959); 89 (1959); 171 (1959); 308 (1959); 328 (1959).
47. Cf. Na 281 (1959); 308 (1959); 341 (1959).
48. Cf. Na 335 (1959).
49. Na 430 (1959).
50. Cf. Na 26 (1959); 40 (1959); 518 (1959).

reunion in faith, for now you can raise your voice to greater effect in advising and helping people to deal with this difficult problem so that its solution may be brought closer to fulfillment."[51] Another West German figure wrote: "I am among those most delighted over your nomination; for a long time I have been praying that God might give our Pope John the right assistants in his efforts in favor of the reunion of separated Christianity. Now the Holy Father has called Your Eminence to help him in this difficult work. We know how close to your heart this cause has been for many years now."[52]

For his part, Bea said that he was ready to commit himself most especially to this cause. A message from Rastatt High School, where he himself had studied, linked its good wishes to him with the cause of Christian unity; and he declared himself in decided agreement.[53] He wrote as follows to his friend Otto Karrer, whom he had known since they were young men: "You are not the only one who is concerned that I should continue to work for the cause of union; I shall naturally do so, and even more than I have done until now."[54] Nor was this all. According to Johannes Willebrands, the new cardinal told Pope John XXIII himself: "I am particularly happy to have been chosen because with the new authority and responsibility entrusted to me with this position of dignity, I should like to work above all for the great cause of the reunion of Christians."[55]

The Pontifical Commission for Promoting Christian Unity

In August 1959, a meeting of the Central Committee of the World Council of Churches was held on the island of Rhodes. Professor Johannes Willebrands and Father Christophe Dumont, O.P., were present for the Catholics, as "journalists"—at that time the only guise in which the Catholic Church permitted attendance at such gatherings. Father Dumont thought he would take advantage of the occasion to organize a friendly meeting with some Orthodox theologians. The initiative was misunderstood both by the press and by the leaders of the World Council of Churches as an attempt to draw the Orthodox away, and there was a strong reaction on the part of the World Council. A consequence of this misunderstanding was the cancellation of a special ecumenical meeting with the Orthodox, which had been planned to take place in Venice that fall. This situation brought home to people how vital it was to have a Catholic office that could intervene in official terms to clear up such misunderstandings.[56]

---

51. Na 328 (1959).
52. Na 292 (1959); cf. Na 60 (1959).
53. Cf. Na 270 (1959).
54. This is the letter to O. Karrer from which we have already had occasion to quote: Na 352 (1959).
55. We find this in his funeral oration for the cardinal; BM, p. 312. Y. Congar (ArchWit, p. 3) says that J. Willebrands told him the same thing on 28 February 1965.
56. In this connection, cf. J. Willebrands, in *Simposio*, pp. 2-3; W.A. Visser 't Hooft, *Die Welt war meine Gemeinde. Autobiographie* (Munich, 1972), pp. 394-395; *The Ecumenical Review* (October 1959), p. 103; and Fey, *A History of the Ecumenical Movement*, II, 293.

1. This incident led the Archbishop of Paderborn, Dr. Lorenz Jaeger, to write to Father Bea as follows on 8 November 1959: "The Vatican should face up to these dangers and create a specialized office in Rome, with a press bureau attached."[57] Bea moved from the specific case to the broader problem in his answer of 30 November, in other words two weeks after the announcement of his nomination as cardinal: "The most important question is certainly that of having the ecumenical movement represented in Rome. As soon as the celebrations are over, I shall speak directly with the Holy Father about it. Just as a commission *pro Russia* was created at the time, one *pro promotione oecumenica* could be set up now."[58]

Until a few years ago we did not know what took place in this field after this latter letter of 30 November, but the question was cleared up when H. Bacht published some of the cardinal's letters.[59] In the first of these, dated 1 January 1960, the cardinal wrote to E Stakemeier, head of the Johann-Adam Möhler Institute in Paderborn as follows: "A variety of people have asked me about the possibilities for the creation of a commission for the ecumenical movement. The best approach will probably be to deal with it in the framework of the conciliar theological commissions, although these have not yet been formed. However, I shall take advantage of the next opportunity to discuss the question with the Holy Father too. Would it not be useful for the Möhler Institute, which has such experience in this area, to submit a formal request, giving explicit reasons and referring to the importance of the matter?" And the cardinal adds: "If you care to let me have the draft, I shall be very happy to take a look at it, and complete it where necessary. . . . You could then send me the request itself, and I would forward it to the competent authorities with a note in support."[60]

The institute immediately took up the suggestion and sent the cardinal the relative draft, so that as early as 20 January the cardinal was able to write back to the director: "No doubt you have been waiting for a long time for me to return the request for the creation of a pontifical commission for ecumenical matters (as I would call it) here in Rome. I have examined the draft in detail . . . and have suggested a series of modifications, additions and omissions. In the meantime I have also spoken about it with Monsignor J. Höfer, who is as interested in the question as I am. . . . Naturally, the request should be addressed to the Holy Father himself, and I shall forward it to him, with a note in support. The Holy Father knows that I am deeply involved in the ecumenical question, and he is very much in favor."[61]

We would make one observation before continuing. In the letter of 1 January, the cardinal wrote, "I shall take advantage of the next opportunity to discuss the

---

57. N 1959/144.

58. *Ibid.* Although the statement that the ecumenical movement "should be represented in Rome" is in itself ambiguous, the context makes the sense perfectly clear. (*Pro promotione oecumenica* = "for promoting ecumenism.")

59. Cf. Bacht, "Kardinal Bea: Webereiter der Einheit," pp. 183-184. These are letters from the period as cardinal, which is why they are not found in our files.

60. *Ibid.*, p. 183.

61. Bacht, "Kardinal Bea," p. 183.

question with the Holy Father," whereas in the following letter (20 January) we find: "The Holy Father knows that I am deeply involved in the ecumenical question, and he is very much in favor." Between the two letters—on 9 January—the cardinal had his first audience. It seems more than probable that on this occasion his interest in unity was discussed, and that he received the pope's approval and blessing. In this light, the fact that he came out of the audience looking very happy and told me, "We understood each other perfectly," takes on particular significance.

Over a month later, in the letter of 28 February, the cardinal referred to the project again, explaining: "I have taken into account the experience I have gained in and with the Roman congregations over the years, in order to avoid anything that could give offense to anyone or occasion criticism. I have therefore . . . purposely omitted a more detailed description of the aims and tasks of the commission in order to avoid treading on the toes of other departments and creating difficulties for the project. . . . After long reflection we have formulated the title in such a way as to avoid the word 'ecumenical,' since it can be interpreted in different ways, as discussions with the World Council of Churches have shown. The present title of 'for Promoting Christian Unity' is based on . . . article 381 of the Roman Synod of 1960, which says: 'by baptism a man . . . is made a member of the mystical body of Christ the Priest *with the general title of Christian.*' In this formulation the title avoids any question of a 'return' and suchlike." The cardinal observes in conclusion: "I think that in this way the draft duly takes into account everything essential that should be respected, so far as we can judge from our vantage-point [in Rome]. However, there may be other considerations that you [in Paderborn] would like to see incorporated. We shall naturally leave that up to the judgment of those in charge there. . . . The most important thing is that everything should be expressed in such a way as to appear convincing."[62]

This information clarifies Bea's role in the institution of the Secretariat for Christian Unity. It was he who instigated the proposal from the Möhler Institute and worked on it. Archbishop L. Jaeger was only too happy to take over the project, and could do so all the more easily inasmuch as the formal petitioner was the Archbishop of Paderborn, while the Möhler Institute simply appended its name to the request. And there is no doubt that the proposal that Archbishop Jaeger spoke of at Riedböhringen at Bea's funeral[63] was the very petition that we have just been describing. The files contain a photocopy of the petition signed by Archbishop Jaeger together with a copy of the draft as amended by Bea,[64] and a comparison reveals that the archbishop simply copied Bea's draft

---

62. *Ibid.*, pp. 183-184.
63. Cf. BM, p. 317. On this occasion Archbishop Jaeger mentioned two letters from Bea that referred to this proposal; they were dated 1 January and 20 January. We must therefore assume that in this case too, the director of the institute acted in close contact with the archbishop, just as he usually did.
64. Photocopies of the petition and the covering letter are attached to Monsignor L.F. Capovilla's statement (ArchWit).

without any change.[65] The archbishop then sent the petition to the cardinal on 4 March, asking him to submit it to the pope with a note expressing his own support.

2. *What precisely did the document say?* It started with a description of what was already being done in the field on the Catholic side, listing the work of the Johann Adam Möhler Institute of Paderborn, the Catholic Conference for Ecumenical Questions, the Unitas Association of Rome, a center in Paris, and Chevetogne Abbey in Belgium. "Now it is easy to appreciate," continued the petition, "that in as arduous a field as this such bodies need the supreme concern and vigilance of the Apostolic See. Moreover, the initiatives of the various bodies in different countries and regions need to be helped to work together harmoniously in the service of their final aim of Christian unity, helping one another, exchanging ideas and experiences, and cooperating fully with one another. It is obvious that all this can be truly and effectively ensured only with the intervention and authority of the Apostolic See."[66]

The document therefore suggested that a "pontifical commission to promote Christian unity" should be created.[67] Its aim would be that of "watching over and assisting" all initiatives, research and work concerning Christian unity in different countries, providing orientations and giving suggestions, which would also take account of experiences elsewhere, while bearing in mind differences in time and place.[68] The petition closed by stating that if such an office were set up it would be greeted with great joy by Catholics, and indeed "also by Protestants who are well disposed toward the Holy See." Such a move would encourage Catholics to pray and work for Christian unity and would make it easier for "non-Catholics of good will" to find the right path; lastly, it would help us move closer to fulfillment of the desire of Christ the Lord that "there shall be one flock, one shepherd" (John 10:16).

3. The cardinal submitted the petition to the pope, *together with a letter from himself* running to two and a half pages, dated 11 March 1960, in which he said that he wanted to "make a brief statement" of his own "humble opinion" on this matter.[69] He started by saying how often he had heard "even non-Catholics deplore the fact that the Holy See has no official department to take care of the whole complex question of the unity of all Christians, which is so important

---

65. The German translation of the petition is found among the writings of Archbishop L. Jaeger, *Einheit und Gemeinschaft. Stellungnahmen zu Fragen der christlichen Einheit* (Paderborn, 1972), pp. 139-142. There is no basis for H. Bacht's suppositions ("Kardinal Bea," pp. 182-183) that Archbishop Jaeger had already submitted a similar proposal before Bea became cardinal, that Bea was made cardinal in connection with this proposal, or that this proposal received a negative response.

66. Lc 2/3, p. 3.

67. The Latin name of the commission was: "Pontificia Commissio de Unitate Christianorum Promovenda."

68. We leave aside the structures suggested for the new body: a cardinal as president, a secretary, members and councilors. However, we would note one element unusual at that time in the departments of the Roman curia: the fact that it envisaged councilors who were not resident in Rome, for example the directors of various ecumenical institutes.

69. Cf. Lc 2/5.

today. . . . On the other hand, the ecumenical movement, among both Catholics and non-Catholics, has now assumed such dimensions that the church cannot ignore it." And here the letter referred to the World Council of Churches and the wide effects of its activity on public opinion, mentioning the Rhodes incident and its consequences. The letter also referred to the differences of opinion sometimes existing between Catholics involved in the ecumenical movement, which could be so serious that "the Supreme Sacred Congregation of the Holy Office has had to take a hand in things." There was therefore a need for a special "central, official department which would watch over all Catholic ecumenical activity and provide any necessary guidelines and instructions as and when required, when appropriate dealing on its own initiatives with the sacred congregations responsible for the relative sectors (for example the Holy Office, the Sacred Congregation of Rites, the Sacred Congregation for the Oriental Churches)." Lastly, "the question is all the more important in view of the imminent Ecumenical Council so felicitously announced by Your Holiness. Even if the Council will not itself be able to bring about union, it will be able to take account of the present situation concerning the various disputed questions, and thus indirectly pave the way for closer contact between the interested parties, and encourage initiatives aimed at a greater mutual understanding and trust." He also added: "On the Protestant side, a great deal has been written about the hopes and also the fears that are felt concerning the Council; but an office is needed in order to collect all this material, sift through the suggestions offered, and provide a clear response to the criticisms and difficulties expressed. This office would systematically collect all the relative material, examine it, or have it examined and evaluated by experts in these matters, and take or propose necessary or opportune measures."[70]

4. *The pope's reaction* to the petition was positive and surprisingly fast. The cardinal himself wrote about this later, saying that the petition was submitted with his letter on 11 March, and "a bare two days later, on 13 March, the pope had me informed of his general approval and his wish to discuss it in greater detail, which was in fact done at the audience I had that same day."[71] We would now provide some further details in this connection. On 13 March, a Sunday, the cardinal was to be received as an honorary member of the Marian Congregation of Nobles, which was based at the Gesù Church in Rome. A little before he left for this ceremony, he received a telephone call from the pope's private secretary, Monsignor Loris F. Capovilla. I put it through to the cardinal, who later told me about the conversation. Apparently the pope had read all the material submitted and was in agreement, and had therefore invited the cardinal for an audience in order to discuss some details. When the cardinal said that he had a prior engagement for that morning, he was asked to come later, and the audience therefore took place after the pope had recited the Sunday Angelus at his window.

---

70. *Ibid.* It should be noted that unlike the petition, the perspective has been considerably broadened here to include the whole ecumenical movement, and particularly to take into account what other Christians think and do.

71. Cf. Biblio. 285, p. 632.

At the audience the pope started by saying that the Cardinal Secretary of State Domenico Tardini was also in agreement with the suggestion. He said that for the time being he envisaged a body to be set up in the service of the Council, while they could think of turning it into a permanent department of the Roman curia at a later date. In this perspective, the pope then entrusted the cardinal with the task of drawing up a kind of "statute" for the new commission.

5. Apart from these details, which the cardinal gave me immediately after the audience, there was apparently a little more. The files contain a faithful transcription of two notes made by the pope on this matter. In a personal note dated 13 March 1960, the day of the audience, we read: "Yesterday evening visit to Cardinal Tardini: good. May the Lord preserve him and grant him life. This morning I received Cardinal Bea here in the private apartment, and entrusted him with the task of organizing a commission to promote the union of Christians, of which he was to be *the head, nominated by me.*"[72]

The pope wrote his own observations across the top and bottom of the letter with which Cardinal Bea had enclosed Archbishop Jaeger's petition: "Consulted with Cardinal Secretary of State and Cardinal Bea (12-13 March). The suggestion is to be implemented. Cardinal Bea to be president of the proposed pontifical commission, and to answer and take up contact with the Archbishop of Paderborn. Everything is to be organized, but any official announcement is to wait until after Easter, in line with the other commissions that will be appointed for the various subjects of the Council. 14 March 1960, John XXIII."[73] In short, in the space of forty-eight hours the pope had made up his mind not only about the creation of the commission, but also about the nomination of Cardinal Bea as its president. The new president himself commented later: "The speed of this decision seems to indicate that ever since the announcement of the Council the pope had perhaps been looking for a practical way of pursuing the ecumenical aim that he had allocated to the Council, and that he had seen the suggestion to create an appropriate body as the providential path toward this objective."[74]

Pope John XXIII's private secretary also tells us about a supernatural aspect of the speed with which the suggestion was accepted: "When he received a proposal that represented a practical response to the appeal contained in the announcement of the Council . . . the pope felt very happy, for it was as if he had received a new sign from heaven, and it was all the more welcome in that it came from a country where Catholics and Protestants had already set in train observance of the gospel norm of tolerance. . . . The suggestion was handed on to him by a Jesuit cardinal for whom he had great respect. . . ."[75]

The speed seems all the more significant if we reflect that in 1959 *a similar*

---

72. Cf. Lc 2/6 (our italics). Monsignor Capovilla says that "the pope met with no objections to the appointment of Cardinal Bea as president of the new body" (ArchWit, p. 7). In a private conversation, he explained further that Cardinal Tardini had observed in this connection: "Yes, he is a peaceful man who will not cause us problems. . . ."

73. Lc 2/5. The note was published in *Giovanni XXIII, Lettere 1958-1963*, ed. Loris F. Capovilla (Rome, 1978), pp. 495-496.

74. Biblio. 285, p. 632.

75. ArchWit.

proposal had been made by a very authoritative figure, but had not met with success. On 23 May 1959, the well-known Greek Melchite Patriarch Maximos IV submitted a document to the pope in which he and his synod suggested the creation of "a new congregation or special Roman commission for the whole field of relations with Christian churches that are not in communion with the Holy See and for all initiatives aimed at fostering unity."[76] Why then did the pope act so differently and so quickly in our case? We would hazard a guess that the reason is to be sought in the already cited words that Cardinal Bea said to me as he came out of his first audience: "We understood each other perfectly." I think that a spirit of understanding and trust was born between the two men of God at this time, which would only grow and would ensure the future secretariat that vigorous support of the pope without which it would have moved forward much more slowly. This element and the fact that Archbishop Jaeger's suggestion was supported by Cardinal Bea meant that the pope found himself presented with both the proposal and the man he could trust to implement it. Hence his speed in accepting the suggestion and entrusting the new department to Cardinal Bea.

6. It took a considerable amount of time to draft the statute of the new commission, so that it was not submitted until 23 April, in other words almost a month and a half later. We shall confine ourselves to a few brief observations, since the text of the document has not yet been released.[77] The passage on the theological basis of the name of the new commission deserves particular mention. In connection with Christian unity, it refers to Canon 87 of the 1917 Code of Canon Law and to Article 372 of the Constitution of the First Synod of Rome. The canon in question states: "Through baptism man is constituted a person in the church of Christ with all the rights and duties of Christians, unless, in the case of rights, there is some impediment which prevents their exercise." The article of the Synod of Rome, on the other hand, draws its inspiration from the encyclical *Mediator Dei* of Pius XII, and says that with baptism, "through the general title of Christian, man becomes a member of the mystical body of Christ the priest." Here the cardinal gives a foretaste of one of his great contributions to ecumenism, in other words his work on "the theology of baptism," a subject he was to explain to the general public of the Church better maybe than anyone else.[78]

---

76. *Le Lien. Bulletin du patriarcat grec-melkite catholique*, XXXIII/5-6 (November-December 1968), 64-65. As can be seen, the news of this suggestion was not published until much later. Indeed, in the article we have already cited a number of times, the cardinal explicitly states: "I do not know if such a body has also been requested from other quarters" (Biblio. 285, p. 632). L.D. Pivonka, *The Secretariat for Promoting Christian Unity: A Study of a Catholic Response to the Modern Ecumenical Movement* (Washington, D.C., 1982), pp. 71-84, summarizes the considerable number of suggestions made in the ante-preparatory stage concerning the creation of some kind of office for the ecumenical question or movement. Some people envisaged this as an association, others as a scientific institute, a "bureau," a pontifical commission, or even a congregation.

77. Cf. Lc 2/7-1, and Lc 2/7-2.

78. We shall discuss this in Chapter 5 of this third part of our work.

A note must still be added on the name of the new body. Since both Archbishop Jaeger's petition and the draft statute referred to the new body as a "commission," how did the name "secretariat" come to be used? The cardinal refers to this in a 1965 article in Italian on "The Secretariat for Christian Unity," where he writes: "Some weeks later [after the audience of 13 March], after a meeting of the Sacred Congregation of Rites, which was held in the presence of the Holy Father, he called me to tell me that he thought it best for the new department to be called a 'secretariat' rather than a 'commission'; in this way, he said, it could have greater freedom of movement in the fairly new and unusual field assigned to it."[79] I would say that the cardinal seems to have altered the style of the pope's words here, for I remember that in conversation he quoted the pope as follows: "Commissions have their own tradition. We shall call the new body a secretariat, so that you are not bound by any tradition and can be freer."

The Secretariat Is Set Up: The First Steps

On 30 May 1960, after the semi-public consistory for the canonization of Blessed John de Ribera, the pope gathered the cardinals in his private library in order to inform them about the forthcoming announcement of the preparatory commissions for the Council. He also mentioned the setting up of "some secretariats," first of all that for Christian unity, adding that he thought that Cardinal Bea would certainly be a good head for the new body. This was the only name mentioned in the whole address, and moreover it is not found in the official published text, which means that the pope had added it spontaneously— a sign that the question was particularly dear to him.[80]

The preparatory conciliar commissions, and hence also the secretariats, were announced on 5 June, the day of Pentecost, with the motu proprio *Superno Dei nutu*.[81] The names of the presidents of the conciliar commissions and secretariats were published the next day, including those of the president of our secretariat. The secretariat and its task were described as follows in this document: "In order

---

79. Biblio. 285, p. 632. I must add that there is another version of the story of this change of name. Monsignor V. Carbone, who at that time worked at the General Secretariat of the Council, told me that the Cardinal Secretary of State Domenico Tardini proposed the change, giving the following reason: "It's something rather new. Let's call it a secretariat: that way, it will be easier to eliminate it, if it does not go well." I have no reason to doubt this version. The pope and his secretary of state were obviously in agreement on the name, but the pope gave a kinder reason—and one that was probably more in line with his trust in Cardinal Bea.

80. Cf. *AD*, I, 89-92 (it is not found in *AAS*). I was told about the mention of Bea's name immediately after the meeting by the cardinal himself, and it is confirmed in J.-F. Arrighi, "Le Cardinal Augustin Bea premier Président du Secrétarit pour l'Union des Chrétiens," *OssRom*, French edition (7, 14 and 21 February 1969); also in Caprile, V, 711-722, p. 2. The latter heard it from the Cardinal Deacon E. Tisserant (although the meeting in question took place in May and not in March, as is erroneously stated in the article in question).

81. Cf. *AAS*, LII (1960), 433-437.

to show in a special way our love and our benevolence toward those who bear the name of Christians but are separated from this Apostolic See, and in order that they may watch the work of the Council and more easily find the way toward that unity that Jesus Christ implored from the heavenly Father with ardent prayer, we have set up a special committee [Latin = *coetus*] or secretariat."[82] As can be seen, the description was fairly terse and general, a fact that would later give rise to some ambiguities concerning the authority of the secretariat to draw up drafts for the Council. On the other hand, however, it must be noted that apart from the name, the secretariat is placed on the same level as the other preparatory commissions, for like them it had a cardinal as president, and it was explicitly stated that its composition was similar to that of the commissions.[83]

Here we must add a word of explanation on *the delimitation of the authority* of the secretariat. *Superno Dei nutu* placed no limitations, so that its responsibility covered all non-Catholic Christians, both eastern and western. On the other hand, it is a fact that until Christmas 1961 and the bull convening the Council, *Humanae salutis*, responsibility for non-Catholic eastern Christians was entrusted to the preparatory commission for the eastern (Catholic) churches. Cardinal Bea later explained this situation by saying: "When the Secretariat for Christian Unity was set up, the pope's intentions with regard to eastern Christians was to entrust the whole field of non-Catholic Christians to the secretariat. However, this field seemed too broad to me, and in particular I did not feel ready to deal with the complex field of the Christian East."[84] However, experience would later take care of correcting things, as the cardinal went on to explain: "Experience quickly showed that the non-Catholic Christians of the East preferred to remain in the sphere of the secretariat. When I later told Pope John about this state of affairs, he replied with his customary simplicity: 'Then take them, Your Eminence!' This decision was then confirmed by the bull convening the Council."[85]

It is worth noting how quickly the new president set to work; indeed, to some extent he moved ahead of schedule. On 2 June, three days prior to publication of the relative motu proprio, he received Professor Johannes Willebrands, Secretary of the Catholic Conference for Ecumenical Questions, and in confidence told him the news of the creation of the secretariat and his own nomination. In view of the fact that his visitor was leaving for Geneva, he asked him to give the news in confidence to the Secretary General of the World Council of Churches, Dr. W.A. Visser 't Hooft, and to tell him that the president of the secretariat would like to have a private, unpublicized meeting with him.[86] It

82. *Ibid.*, p. 436.
83. *Ibid.*
84. *Ecumenism*, p. 35, note 32 (ct).
85. *Ibid.* (ct). J. Willebrands indicates the underlying reason why the actual situation meant that the secretariat had to take care of the whole field: "It is clear that, despite its twofold aspect of separation and the restoration of full unity, the problem is only one and cannot be divided. Just as unity embraces all Christians, so every division concerns them all" (*Simposio*, p. 6). It is interesting to observe that in the motu proprio *Superno Dei nutu*, which brought the secretariat into being, no limitation is placed on its field of activity.
86. Cf. *Ecumenism*, p. 33; A. Bea and W.A. Visser 't Hooft, *Der Friede zwischen Christen* (Freiburg

should not be imagined that such an idea was in the normal run of things, and the cardinal himself commented on it later as follows: "About the time when preparations for the secretariat were being made, I once asked Pope John XXIII if he thought it a good idea to contact the World Council of Churches. He replied in a way that reflected the general situation at that period: 'The time does not seem ripe.' For my part, I concluded from this that we must 'ripen' it."[87] As we shall see, the meeting would take place about three months later.

Another initiative taken immediately after the announcement of his appointment was a press conference on the tasks and plans of the new secretariat. The cardinal had been in New York from the evening of 5 June to receive an honorary degree in law from the Catholic University of Fordham. After news of his nomination as president of the secretariat was published on the evening of 6 June, some journalists asked if they could meet him in a press conference, and the cardinal accepted, unaware that the nomination had already been published. He was therefore taken by surprise when a journalist handed him a paper bearing the news, and asked him for his comments. He had to speak off the cuff, but everything went well, and the conference was well received.[88]

As concerns the *organization* of the secretariat, the new president found himself faced with the task of preparing two lists of names: three suggestions for the position of general secretary, and a list of possible members and councilors—both of which had to be submitted to higher authority. He had most probably already reflected on the first list even prior to publication of *Superno Dei nutu*, which would be why the secretary was nominated a bare three weeks after the motu proprio. On the eve of the feast of St. Peter and St. Paul, we were about to go to St. Peter's for the first vespers of the feast, when the *Osservatore Romano* was delivered, with the names of the secretaries of the commissions, including that of Professor Johannes Willebrands as general secretary of the secretariat. That same evening, after the service, the cardinal sent the new secretary a cable of congratulations, and on the day of the feast itself, the new secretary telephoned the cardinal to thank him for the cable, and tell him that he would reach Rome on 7 July, when he would place himself at his service in order to draw up the list of members and councilors of the secretariat, and anything else necessary.

On 7 July, I went in the cardinal's car to collect the new secretary at Rome's Ciampino Airport, where he had arrived on a Super Constellation of the Dutch airline KLM. Work started the next day and took up six mornings in all between 8 and 20 July. However, it should be observed that the cardinal had already given consideration to the various candidates, or at least for the commission as a permanent body, so that when he sent the pope the draft statute in April he

---

im Breisgau, 1966), p. 12. The dates in this latter account of J. Willebrands require some correction: the institution of the secretariat could not have been "communicated" to Dr. Visser 't Hooft on 8 June, because the news had already been published on 5 June—or indeed on the evening of 4 June.

87. *Ecumenism*, p. 33 (ct).

88. For a summary of this press conference, see Biblio. 134a.

was able to tell him: "The list of people to whom the various tasks of the commission should be entrusted . . . is almost ready and can be presented as soon as the statute is approved."[89] However, Willebrands' nomination was certainly providential. Since 1951 he had been Secretary of the Catholic Conference for Ecumenical Questions, which had a membership of seventy or eighty Catholic theologians interested in ecumenical matters, and he therefore personally knew the whole of that world of experienced Catholic pioneers of ecumenism, and indirectly also the bishops who were interested in the question. It therefore turned out that most of the councilors of the new secretariat were members of this association.[90]

The Question of Relations with the Jewish People

The secretariat had barely been set up and its president nominated when a further important sphere of activity was already being prepared for it—that of relations with the Jewish people. The biblical image of the mustard seed can very aptly be applied to the birth of this sector. At the beginning of such an historical undertaking, there were neither large organizations nor mass movements, but three old men: Jules Isaac, Pope John XXIII and Cardinal Bea.[91]

1. The path began on Good Friday 1959, and the relative episode is described by Cardinal Bea as follows: "It was on that day, during the solemn liturgy, that Pope John had given the order to omit the painful adjective 'perfidious' from the customary prayer for the Jews. Although this adjective has an extremely pejorative ring to modern ears, in the medieval Latin in which the prayer was first composed it simply meant 'unbelieving.' The gesture excited Jewish public opinion and raised many hopes."[92]

2. This gesture on the pope's part should not, however, be taken as meaning that he was already thinking that the Council should undertake some initiative in this connection, for it appears that there was no thought of such a thing until June 1960.[93] However, it did give rise to many hopes, and especially in a man who was to become the providential instrument in setting things moving and leading the pope and Cardinal Bea to do something about the situation, *Professor Jules Isaac.*

---

89. Lc 2/7-1.

90. Cf. the article in *Simposio*, pp. 5-6.

91. We are referring here to the thrust that in fact decided the first decisive steps. We do not intend to minimize, for instance, the proposals or suggestions made in this connection during the ante-preparatory phase of the Council (for example the suggestion of the Pontifical Biblical Institute to "avoid antisemitism"—see below, note 116, pp. 336-337; and also the suggestion of J.M. Oesterreicher dated 24 June 1960—cf. *The New Encounter between Christians and Jews* [New York, 1986], p. 117). However, such suggestions would not be studied until the time of the preparatory conciliar commissions. As regards Pope John, it is sure, as we shall see, that even if he had maybe already had news of similar proposals, prior to Jules Isaac's audience he had never thought that the Council should address this subject. I cannot therefore agree with J.M. Oesterreicher (*New Encounter*, p. 114) when he describes J. Isaac's intervention as "secondary." Certain major Jewish organizations stepped in much later.

92. *Church-Jews*, p. 22.

93. Statement of the pope's private secretary, Monsignor L. Capovilla, in a note, Lf 6/4.

(a) He was a man of over eighty, an ex-university professor, co-author of a history textbook used in the high schools of France in the 1930s, an inspector of the teaching of history in schools, and a high official in the government of Léon Blum.[94] When the racial laws were passed in 1940, he was dismissed from the Ministry of Culture and from every other public position, and thrown into the street with his whole family. In 1943 he lost his wife and daughter in the concentration camps, although he himself escaped death almost by miracle. Then, in his despair, he discovered that he had a mission, "and I clung to it with desperation and with all my waning forces stretched to the utmost."[95] Professor Vingiani described this mission in the following terms: "He chose to commit himself to a truly *heroic mission*, working against time—for he was over sixty; against his health, which had been definitively compromised; against the serious deafness that had struck him; and against age. And he asked himself: 'But must I still accept such a challenge at my age? Will I manage to get anything done?' "[96] He tried to take positive action, becoming honorary president of the Jewish-Christian Friendship Association.

As he moved further into this battle, which he waged above all with his writings, he became increasingly aware of the enormous difficulty of the whole undertaking. "Habit is a truly immense burden, and it will not be easy for people to throw it off! What is needed is a true conversion, . . . a radical change."[97] He gradually came to the conviction that so far as the Catholic world was concerned "changes must start from the top, . . . and an idea ripened and took root in him: 'What we need is a pope: only in that way can things change.' "[98] He himself explained the origin of this idea in a 1962 interview, saying that Pope John XXIII's gesture at the Good Friday service in 1959 had given him sudden hope: "For the first time, contrary to what I had thought prior to then, I considered the possibility of an approach at the highest level."[99] The professor, who lived in Aix-en-Provence, received encouragement in this connection from the local bishop, C. de Provenchères.[100]

(b) His training and experience as a high-level government official meant that he laid the groundwork very methodically: "As early as a lecture at the Sorbonne, I addressed a call to the pope. Friends asked me to go to Rome as honorary president of the Jewish-Christian Friendship Association, and my

---

94. Autobiographical details of J. Isaac are found in "Le Vatican et nous," *Arche*, LXIX (October 1962), 26-31. The observations of M. Vingiani are particularly helpful: (a) "Jules Isaac. Il promotore del dialogo ebraico-cristiano a venti anni della morte," in *Ecumenismo Anni '80. Atti XXI Settimana di formazione ecumenica 1983* (Verona 1984), pp. 323-338; and (b) "Jules Isaac e il dialogo ebraico-cristiano," *Vita Monastica*, CLXVI-CLXVII (1986), 93-112. M. Vingiani knew J. Isaac very well for a number of years, so that his account is particularly valuable. We shall quote from his first article. Cf. also Arrighi, "Le Cardinal Augustin Bea"; Caprile, V, 715. The present author met J. Isaac during the latter's visit to Rome.
95. Vingiani, "Jules Isaac. Il promotore," p. 330.
96. *Ibid.*, pp. 331-332.
97. *Ibid.*, p. 332.
98. *Ibid.*
99. Isaac, "Le Vatican et nous," p. 30.
100. Cf. Arrighi, "Le Cardinal Augustin Bea."

reply was: 'Yes, but I want to be certain of an audience.' Once I had gained this certainty, the necessary financing was found. I prepared texts and documents, assembling documentation and drawing up a memorandum. Everything was printed in French and Italian. The journey was organized methodically." Its precise aim was "the revision of Christian teaching about the Jews."[101]

He wrote as follows about the difficulty of the undertaking: "We must realize how very difficult and daring the whole enterprise was. The problem of Catholic teaching with which I was dealing was infinitely more complex than the problem of the liturgy. Seen in this specific perspective [that of Israel], although it did not involve the actual data of faith and dogma, it did concern at least a centuries-old—or, rather, age-old—tradition which went back to the fathers of the church, from St. John Chrysostom to St. Augustine. Hence the need to make sure that these Roman conversations combined the greatest prudence with the greatest frankness. I realized that it was an immensely demanding challenge, and that in some cases there would be a true abyss for me to cross."[102]

(c) As soon as he reached Rome, on 8 June, he found himself in an apparently desperate situation. He had been asked to put his application in writing and submit it together with the relative background material to Cardinal Alfredo Ottaviani, Secretary of the Holy Office. Here, however, he was told that the audience with the pope was *not* possible, and the atmosphere, which had previously shown a certain warmth, suddenly froze. Professor Vingiani describes the situation as follows: "On 9 June I was summoned by an urgent note which a hotel bellboy brought to me. I found him [Isaac] in the lobby of the Commodore Hotel with tears in his eyes: 'At eighty-four years! At my age! I came all this way, and now they send me back. I can't go back, because this is the last chance I'll have. I must see the pope. Here they don't want me to see the pope.' "[103] After Professor Vingiani had done her best to calm him down, "he took both my hands in his and told me that he would trust himself to me. I embraced him like a father—which he was for me—and left, determined to do something about things."[104]

The professor's account continues: "It was now up to me to play my small part in events, and I did what I could, with prudence but also with the impassioned sense of urgency that the situation demanded, knowing that it was not so much that Isaac had to see the pope, but that the pope had to see Jules Isaac, talk to him, see the document that had been prepared for him, and learn about it on behalf of the church. I was sure that Pope John still knew nothing about what

---

101. Isaac, "Le Vatican et nous," p. 30. The review *SIDIC*, III (1968), 10-12, published a "previously unpublished report" produced by J. Isaac immediately after the audience that Pope John XXIII granted him; this report is henceforth cited as *SIDIC*. However, it must be noted that various essential points of this report are reproduced in Jean Toulat, *Juifs, mes frères* (Paris, 1962), p. 152. Cf. also the Italian translation, Jean Toulat, "Una visita a Jules Isaac (da J. Toulat, *Juifs, mes frères*)," *Rassegna mensile di Israele* (November-December 1972; Koslev-Tevet, 5733), pp. 3-13.

102. *SIDIC*, p. 10.

103. Vingiani, "Jules Isaac. Il promotore," pp. 333-334.

104. *Ibid.*, p. 334.

was happening, but while Isaac could not reach the pope, if the latter could be told about the situation in some way, he could very well have him invited and receive him. . . . My Venetian friendships were of use here, and this is what happened."[105] Indeed, in a marked about-turn of a kind not unusual in those circles, "suddenly the very curial offices that had prevented the meeting had to facilitate it. Everything was soon ready, and Isaac was in the Vatican on 13 June 1960, unaware of the amount of resistance that had been overcome."[106]

(d) The following are the salient points of the audience of 13 June 1960 as described in Jules Isaac's account: "I slept very little on the night of 12 June; I put the finishing touches to the 'Complementary and Conclusive Note' with a view to lending it maximum effectiveness in a short form. I also honed the essential subjects that were to be stressed."[107]

The audience began at 1:15 p.m. "I introduced myself as a non-Christian, a promoter of the Jewish-Christian Friendship association in France, and as a very deaf old man. We settled ourselves close to one another beside the desk in three chairs; I was beside the pope, who is truly simplicity personified, and this simplicity is in striking contrast with the sumptuousness of the furnishings and the pomp of the ceremonial that had gone before."[108]

The conversation is described as follows: "As I had foreseen, he started the conversation, speaking in lively fashion of his devotion to the Old Testament, the Psalms, the Prophets, the Book of Wisdom. He mentioned his name, saying he had thought of France when he chose it. He asked me where I was born. . . . For my part, I was looking for some opportunity to lead him onto the ground I wanted. I told him about the great hope that the measures he had taken so spontaneously had raised in the hearts of the people of the Old Testament, and said that if we were looking to him for still more, surely he was himself responsible for this through his great goodness. This amused him."[109]

Then they got to the point: "I explained my request concerning teaching, starting with its historical basis. But how could a few minutes be enough to make anyone understand the spiritual ghetto to which the church had gradually consigned the biblical Israel—just as it had consigned it to a more physical ghetto? . . . Today there is fortunately a purifying counter-current, which is growing stronger by the day. Even so, recent surveys have shown that 'the teaching of contempt' still exists, and Catholic opinion remains divided between these two opposing trends. This is why it is vital for a voice to be raised from above, indeed from the highest point—the voice of the head of the church—in order to point out the right path to everybody and solemnly condemn 'the teaching of contempt' which is anti-Christian in its very essence. . . .

"I then presented my *Conclusive Note*, together with the suggestion of setting up a sub-commission with the task of studying the question. The pope reacted

---

105. *Ibid.*
106. *Ibid.*
107. *SIDIC*, p. 11.
108. *Ibid.*
109. *Ibid.*

immediately, saying: 'I have been thinking of that from the beginning of this meeting.' He had demonstrated his understanding and sympathy several times during the course of my brief explanation."[110]

The audience was over: "Expressing all my gratitude for the welcome received, I asked if I could take away some grain of hope, and he exclaimed: 'You have the right to more than hope!' Then he added, with a smile: 'I am the head, but I have to consult other people, and have various offices study the questions raised; this is not an absolute monarchy.' And we parted with another firm handshake."[111]

Here, however, we must add something to the professor's account. Pope John's private secretary gave me written confirmation that the pope also told his guest to go to Cardinal Bea "whom he trusted and on whom he relied."[112] And I do remember that the person who asked for an audience for Professor Jules Isaac told me that the pope himself had sent the professor to Cardinal Bea.

(e) What was the *outcome*? Let us first consider Pope John. In his note, Monsignor Loris Capovilla states: "Until that day, it had not crossed John XXIII's mind that the Council should also deal with the Jewish question and antisemitism. However, he was firmly behind such an idea from that day on. It was vital to clear the church of charges of having sat on the sidelines and defended only baptized Jews (as Isaac seemed to insinuate), and to proclaim once for all that Christians have no right to take the phrase 'His blood be on us' as indicating condemnation."[113]

As concerns Cardinal Bea, the only thing that I remember is that after the visit he told me, with a mixture of amazement and joy: "Just think: the Holy Father told Jules Isaac to come to me."[114] In J. Toulat's account, Isaac spoke of his meeting with the cardinal as follows: "I spent over an hour with Cardinal Bea, who is considered 'the prince of sacred scripture.' This German Jesuit with an open and intelligent face, who speaks French perfectly, showed himself completely *au fait* with the problems facing us. He is in contact with German Catholics who are doing the same work as our Jewish-Christian Friendship groups. In him, I found a providential aid."[115]

(f) It should be said that this was not the first time that the problem had been brought to Bea's attention. We are not referring to the proposal for the Council made by the Pontifical Biblical Institute under the heading "Avoid antisemitism," since it does not seem that the cardinal knew about this.[116] We are thinking

---

110. *Ibid.*, pp. 11-12.
111. *Ibid.*
112. Lf 6/4.
113. *Ibid.*; cf. Mt. 27:25.
114. Cf. the present author's "Bea, le lotte e le sofferenze," in G.F. Svidercoschi (ed.), *Inchiesta sul Concilio* (Rome, 1985), p. 232; in this article, "15 June" should be read for "13 June."
115. Toulat, "Una visita," p. 10.
116. For the proposal, cf. *AD* (1961), I/IV/1, 131-132. (For an explanation of this citation, cf. the list of abbreviations at the start of the present work.) The covering letter of the rector of the institute is dated 24 April 1960, and it gives a list of the professors who worked on the document (*ibid.*, pp. 123-124). Bea's name is not included, which would seem to indicate that the

rather of the message of congratulations he received on being made cardinal, which asked whether he could do something for a rapprochement between those who believe in the Old and New Testaments. Bea answered as follows: "So far as I am familiar with the situation, little attention has yet been paid to attempts at a rapprochement between Judaism and the church. It would therefore be useful if we could discuss it face to face on some occasion, since it is difficult to talk about such matters in writing."[117]

We can therefore appreciate what a deep impression the meeting with Jules Isaac made on him. And we do have a very definite piece of evidence to the fact that the audience, and thus the cause pleaded by Isaac, had stamped itself firmly on his mind: about two months later, he spoke about it in his retreat notes, linking the subject with the task awaiting him as President of the Secretariat for Christian Unity, explaining the spirit in which he intended to perform his ecumenical task and also that regarding the Jews, if the latter were also definitively entrusted to him.[118]

3. In keeping with his usual approach to things, *the cardinal soon got down to the practical details* of the question of the Jews. A little after his return from his summer vacation, on 14 September 1960, he wrote to the pope, saying that he would like to have a personal meeting with him "on certain questions concerning the Secretariat for Christian Unity, of which Your Holiness has been so gracious as to make me president. I would particularly like to bring up the question of responsibility concerning relations between Jews and Catholics, on which I am frequently consulted."[119] He was then received in audience on 18 September, when the pope formally entrusted him with responsibility concerning relations with the people of the Old Testament.[120]

A little over a month after receiving this task, and without waiting for the preparatory commissions (and therefore also the secretariat) to begin their work, the cardinal had a first important meeting with a view to the new task. Nahum Goldman, who was then President of the World Jewish Congress, describes this meeting in his memoirs. I cannot confirm all the details, because I was not present at the meeting, but the account is undoubtedly interesting, and gives a good idea of the situation at that time. The cardinal had let Mr. Goldman know that he would like to meet him, and the audience was therefore arranged for 26 October 1960, when Goldman was passing through Rome. "This was," Goldman says, "the beginning of my relations with Cardinal Bea, one of the most tolerant, understanding, humanly kind, and above all most courageous leaders of the Catholic Church in our time. He was of German origin, and our conversation was conducted mostly in German. He said that he had asked me to come to see him since the pope wished to place the question of relations between

---

document was drafted, at least in its definitive version, after Bea was made cardinal. Cf. also Oesterreicher, in *Simposio*, p. 68.

117. Na 430 (1959).
118. Med. 1960/VI/2; *Der Mensch Bea*, p. 85.
119. Arch. Lf 6/7.
120. Cf. *Church-Jews*, p. 22.

Christians and Jews on the agenda of the ecumenical council . . . and had given him [the cardinal] the task of working on this. The cardinal told me that he had hesitated for a long time over whom to invite to represent the Jews, since of course the Jewish religion possesses neither a pope nor a Vatican, and also since, according to his information, . . . Judaism was divided into a number of groups. He had therefore asked for advice from the Society of Jesus, to which he himself belonged, and he had been advised to invite me in my capacity as President of the World Jewish Congress. From that very first meeting, he showed his deep understanding of the historical and political significance of relations between Christians and Jews, along with his conviction that a radical change in these relations was needed on the part of the church, however difficult and lengthy this process might be; despite the fact that he foresaw determined opposition from many of his colleagues in the curia, he would do all he could in order to bring the ecumenical council to a new and positive stance. In his opinion, the first step must be of the Jewish organizations to submit a memorandum to the pope—through his good offices—asking for this question to be placed on the agenda for the Council. He asked me to try to produce a united Jewish front as comprehensive as possible, in order to avoid having a plethora of Jewish organizations each undertaking its own steps, which would result in chaos and place major difficulties in the path of a solution to the problem. He especially asked me to induce even those Jewish organizations that do not belong to the World Jewish Congress to support the memorandum. I pointed out that this would be a difficult task, and I told him in particular about my concern that Jewish orthodoxy might be opposed to such a step on the part of world Judaism addressed to the Vatican; this would not only make everything more difficult, but if a violent polemic were to break out among Jews it would have the effect simply of prejudicing the attempt at achieving closer mutual relations. Nonetheless, I promised him that I would do my best and that I would keep in touch with him."[121]

The cardinal also took a second step. Since the members and consultors of the secretariat had been nominated before the secretariat was given responsibility for the Jewish question, he now set about the nomination of supplementary specialists for this field.[122]

* * *

At the start of the present chapter we considered the forecasts made for the new cardinal's future. Contrary to all predictions, the cardinal's health enjoyed a remarkable and long-lasting recovery, so that from the very beginning he was able to engage in an active pastoral mission. Nor was this all. Although Pope John did not have any specific plans for him at the time of his creation as cardinal, Bea was very soon playing an effective part in preparations for the

---

121. Nahum Goldman, *Staatsmann ohne Staat. Autobiographie* (Cologne/Berlin, 1970), pp. 378-379.

122. Cf. *LThK: 2. Vat. Konzil*, II, 415.

Council. Thus his nomination as cardinal truly meant a new beginning, with the start of an activity completely different from his previous work.

Nor was he the only one for whom the task entrusted to him was a great novelty. In many ways the creation of the Secretariat for Christian Unity was a new departure for the Catholic Church itself. The ecumenical intentions that Pope John XXIII had seen from the very start as closely linked to the idea of convening a Council now had their own instrument; and instead of confining itself to calls for unity, the Catholic Church now took up a new attitude toward other Christians and was ready to work with them in the search for full unity. The pope was so aware of the novelty of the initiative that he had changed the name of the new body from "commission" to "secretariat" so that it would not be bound by certain traditions and could move more freely in the field under its responsibility. And this new body was entrusted to the eighty-year-old cardinal.

He was very soon given the additional and equally new task of dealing with relations with the people of the Old Testament. As Jules Isaac rightly observed, this involved age-old Christian traditions which went back to the writings of some of the fathers of the church.

Hence, although at that moment nobody could have predicted the spectacular developments that would occur in the activity of the Secretariat for Christian Unity, it was clear from the start that it had been entrusted with tasks of truly historic importance, which marked a deep change of stance in the church and were pregnant with unforeseeable consequences.

CHAPTER 4

PREPARATIONS FOR THE COUNCIL FROM THE ECUMENICAL VIEWPOINT

Although the creation of the secretariat was certainly an event of fundamental importance, it was merely a start, and there were huge tasks ahead. The motu proprio setting up the secretariat described its task as that of helping other Christians to follow the work of the Council, and in more general terms making it easier for them to "find the way toward that unity that Jesus Christ implored from the heavenly Father."[1] In the context of the creation of the secretariat, we saw various positive reactions from other Christians to the announcement of the celebration of the Council. To start with, the Council had aroused great interest, and indeed enthusiasm, among them, because they thought that it was to be an "ecumenical" Council in the sense that representatives of all the Christian confessions would take part. However, after this misunderstanding had been cleared up and it had been explained that the Council was "an internal church matter," disappointment set in, and the ancient distrust returned to the fore.

As regarded the more general task of fostering the search for unity, it was clear that the Council would be faced with a considerable number of problems connected with existing divisions and with the commitment to work for unity. Before going further, we would consider the precise situation of ecumenism *in the Catholic Church* at that time. Today, the enormous development of relations and dialogue on all sides is taken for granted, but things were very different at that time. A certain amount of work had of course been carried out by pioneers, and Cardinal Bea was the first to recognize this, applying Jesus' words to the work of the secretariat and saying that it had come to reap what others had sown (cf. John 4:38).[2] In this context he mentioned the work for the Week of Prayer for Christian Unity carried out by Paul Wattson and also by the Congregation of the Atonement which he had founded; then there was the apostolate of Abbé Paul Couturier, as well as the work of the Benedictine Abbey of Chevetogne in Belgium and the Catholic Conference for Ecumenical Questions, etc.[3] In 1949 the Holy Office had published an *Instruction on the Ecumenical Movement*, which Bea himself had helped to draft in his capacity as consultor to that department. This document evaluated the ecumenical movement in positive terms, noting that there was a special and powerful breath of the Holy Spirit blowing through the Christian world and rousing a true nostalgia for unity. The instruction also laid down precise rules for ecumenical meetings and interconfessional theological conversations on doctrinal questions, and stressed that even in discussion and collaboration between Catholics and other Christians

---

1. *AAS*, LII (1960), 436.
2. Cf. *Ecumenism*, p. 30.
3. Cf. *ibid.*, p. 31.

over matters not specifically religious in nature—such as questions of social welfare and assistance—the faithful should be careful not to go against revealed doctrine and the norms of the church.[4] All this was very positive, but its implementation, with the establishment of contacts and dialogue, was still waiting.

Then if we move on to consider the Council itself, there is the question of the ecumenical experience and training of the bishops who, as Council fathers, would be called to speak and vote on matters of an ecumenical nature. The same question applies to the theologians who were supposed to assist them. A lengthy paper drawn up for the Council by the steering committee of the aforementioned Catholic Conference for Ecumenical Questions was very cautious in formulating the question of whether the Council fathers would have "sufficient background knowledge" to deal with ecumenical questions in an objective way; it added that the same question applied to most of the theologians, who would certainly include only very few experts in ecumenical matters.[5]

In retrospect and on the basis of the situation revealed at the beginning of the Council, Cardinal J. Willebrands did not hesitate to state: "We should not forget that prior to the Council a great majority of the Council fathers had had no contact or experience of an ecumenical kind, apart from the negative experiences prevalent in many countries."[6]

The First Steps

A great deal of energy was therefore needed, and above all a great deal of faith, in order to face huge tasks in a field where success seemed more than uncertain. And it must be said that the newly appointed president personally faced his task precisely in this way. He was in New York the day that his appointment as president was announced, and the next day he gave his first press conference on the tasks and plans of the secretariat.[7] He gave other interviews of the same kind when he took part in the International Eucharistic Congress in Munich at the beginning of August.[8]

Later on he took advantage of the first chance of contact with Catholic ecumenists, which was offered by the meeting of the Catholic Conference for Ecumenical Questions held in September of the same year at Gazzada near Milan. A large number of personal links already existed between the conference and the secretariat. At the beginning of September, the list of members and advisors of the new body had been published, and in his words of greeting to the participants its president could observe in this connection: "Anyone who

---

4. Cf. *AAS*, XLII (1950), 142-145; cf. also Visser 't Hooft, *Die Welt war meine Gemeinde*, pp. 386-393.

5. Cf. Arch. Lc 1/1, no. 12.

6. Willebrands, in *Simposio*, p. 14.

7. Cf. the summary in Biblio. 134a.

8. See for example the Hamburg daily newspaper, *Die Welt*.

looks at the list of members and consultors of the secretariat will soon see how many of them have already worked for the idea of unity, placing themselves at the service of your conference. The president of the secretariat is delighted to be able to include them among those who will be working with him in the future."[9] The cardinal did immediately add, however, that he hoped that the other participants in this meeting of the conference would also offer contributions to the great cause, each in his own field, and said: "We shall always be extremely grateful for any relative information, suggestion or advice, and also for any criticism."[10] Since many members and consultors of the secretariat were present at the meeting, he took advantage of the opportunity for a first exchange of ideas on an informal basis, so that it could be described as the first meeting of the secretariat, albeit unofficial.[11]

The next day another step of great importance was taken at the St. Fedele Center in Milan: the first meeting with the Secretary General of the World Council of Churches, Dr. W.A. Visser 't Hooft. This event also reveals the youthful spirit and energy with which the new president set about his tasks.

It should first be said that about a month earlier, the executive committee of the World Council of Churches had released a fairly positive statement on the creation of the secretariat, saying that it offered an opportunity for dialogue. Although negotiations on unity fell under the responsibility of the individual churches that were members of the world council, the latter could communicate the declarations on questions of principle of its assemblies or its own central committees to the secretariat; differences still undoubtedly remained, but the atmosphere and whole approach were changing, and dialogue made it possible to share experiences and intuitions that had been maturing in the ecumenical movement.[12]

We have two first-hand accounts of the meeting of the two men: that of Dr. Visser 't Hooft himself, and that of Johannes Willebrands, who was also present. We shall for the most part follow the latter account. Cardinal Bea began by saying that he was delighted by the declaration of the executive committee about the creation of the secretariat, and that he would make sure that the Holy Father also received a copy. Visser 't Hooft said that he was especially confident in the situation because both the president and secretary of the secretariat had already been developing contacts with the World Council of Churches for some time now. They then discussed both the sending of official observers to the assembly of the world council that was to be held in New Delhi the following year, and

---

9. Arch. Lc 3/6, p. 1; on this meeting, cf. also *CC*, 1961/II, 79.

10. *Ibid.*

11. Other details can be found in *Ecumenism*, p. 30. Some components of the ecumenism of the secretariat were to be found in the previous work of the Catholic Conference for Ecumenical Questions, and now the work of the advisors to the secretariat who were also members of that association meant that these elements appeared in the schemata drafted by the secretariat. It would be very interesting to carry out a comparative study of the work of the association and the schemata drawn up by the secretariat.

12. Cf. Willebrands, in Bea and Visser 't Hooft, *Friede zwischen christen* (Biblio. 174), pp. 13-14; also Visser 't Hooft, *Die Welt war meine Gemeinde*, p. 396; and Caprile, I/1, 253-254.

also the question of the invitation of observers from other churches to the Vatican Council. The secretary general said that he was ready to offer his advice and good offices to help Catholics in contacts with the other churches. Since the World Council of Churches was anxious to preserve the unofficial contacts that had been established with Catholics, it was agreed that an unofficial dialogue with theologians of the Catholic Conference for Ecumenical Questions would be held on the question of religious freedom.[13]

It is indicative of the situation at that time that the meeting took place in the greatest secrecy. Dr. Visser 't Hooft often said that the secrecy was such that he said not a word about it either to his colleagues or to his own wife, and that the doorman at the religious house where the meeting took place had been warned not to ask the visitor's name.[14] After the meeting Visser 't Hooft commented to Willebrands about Bea: "This man has not only read and studied the Old Testament; he has truly absorbed the wisdom of the men of the Old Testament."[15]

A Vast and Demanding Plan of Work

About two months later, in mid-November, the real preparatory work for the Council began, in accordance with the pope's wishes. After a solemn liturgical celebration with a homily from the pope, the secretariat held its first plenary meeting, which took up two half days. The records contain the inaugural address with which the president opened the meeting, and although it is only a few pages long, it encompasses a vast plan of work.[16]

After mentioning how the secretariat had come into being, the president very clearly indicated its field of responsibility and authority: it was not, as some people had thought, simply an information bureau.[17] Just like the preparatory commissions, the secretariat had the task of studying the subjects put forward by the pope in the light of the suggestions of bishops and departments of the Roman curia, and drawing up drafts to be submitted to the Council.[18] The brief that nominated the president of the secretariat also conferred on him "all the powers necessary and useful" for his office.[19] He added that this first plenary meeting had the precise aim of establishing the subjects to be considered and the work-method to be followed.

---

13. Cf. Willebrands, in Biblio. 174, pp. 14-15; also Visser 't Hooft, *Die Welt war meine Gemeinde*, p. 396.
14. Visser 't Hooft, *Die Welt war meine Gemeinde*, p. 395.
15. Cf. BM, p. 323; also Visser 't Hooft, *Die Welt war meine Gemeinde*, p. 396; on the meeting, cf. also *Ecumenism*, p. 33.
16. Arch. 3/19 (8 pages in all).
17. It was Father S. Tromp, S.J., Secretary of the Preparatory Doctrinal Commission and J. Willebrands' fellow-Dutchman, who said to the latter: "What do you expect? You're simply an information bureau."
18. Arch. Lc 3/19, p. 2.
19. For the text, cf. BM, pp. 112-113.

THE COUNCIL

1. Here the cardinal explained the limits of the authority of the secretariat so
far as the eastern non-Catholic churches were concerned, saying that it had been
thought best to entrust responsibility in this area of the separated eastern
churches to the Commission for the Eastern Churches, since various of the
questions raised were common to all the eastern churches, both Catholic and
separated.[20] Nonetheless, wherever general ecumenical questions were concerned, these were to be dealt with jointly by the commission and the secretariat.
Apart from this, a number of the subjects that fell within the specific sphere of
the secretariat had points of contact with matters entrusted to other preparatory
commissions, for example those to be dealt with by the Doctrinal Commission,
the Commission of Bishops, and the Commission for the Liturgy; in such cases,
either the suggestions prepared by the secretariat would be handed on to the
relative commission, or the subject would be dealt with in a joint commission
by representatives of the secretariat and the relative commission.[21]

The president then invited all the members and advisors to work with the
maximum commitment, saying that the pope wanted work for the Council to
take precedence over any other task. The cardinal went still further, inviting the
members and advisors not to confine themselves to the official work of the
secretariat, but to do what they could in their own fields to spread the idea of
unity, telling people about the methods to be used, and developing contacts.[22]
The only exception was relations with the World Council of Churches, which
were reserved to the leaders of the secretariat, in view of the delicate nature of
the question. The cardinal ended with an exhortation to pray and have others
pray for the success of the Council and the cause of unity: if the pope had invited
other Christians to pray for the Council, how much more did this apply to
Catholics![23]

2. Let us now consider some specific questions. Toward the end of this
inaugural address, the cardinal referred to the technical aspects of the work,
saying that the individual subjects would be entrusted to small subcommissions,
since it is easier to arrange meetings of small groups, and people work better
that way. These subcommissions were to prepare the material to be submitted
to the plenary meetings of the secretariat.[24]

But what *were* these specific subjects? Our records contain *the draft of a first
circular* to be sent out to members and advisors of the secretariat, which was
probably produced in July 1960. This circular referred to (a) theological and
doctrinal questions, (b) those concerning the liturgy, and (c) those concerning
spirituality, and then talked about (d) suggestions for practical steps to be taken

---

20. Contrary to what is said, for example, by D.A. Seeber, *Das Zweite Vaticanum. Konzil des
Uebergangs* (Freiburg im Breisgau/Basle/Vienna, 1966), p. 45, it was the cardinal himself who
suggested that the non-Catholic eastern churches should be entrusted to the Commission for
the Eastern Churches; cf. *Ecumenism*, p. 35, note 32.
21. Arch. Lc 3/19, p. 3.
22. The cardinal also spoke before the Central Preparatory Commission about this activity of
members and consultors of the secretariat; cf. *AD*, II/1, 166.
23. Cf. Arch. Lc 3/19, p. 7.
24. Cf. *ibid.*, pp. 4-5.

right away in order to help the restoration of full unity.[25] It is clear that the aforementioned "Note" of the Steering Committee of the Catholic Conference for Ecumenical Questions setting out the various aspects of the ecumenical question for the use of the Council made a significant contribution even to this first draft plan of work for the secretariat.[26]

A full list of the ten subjects which were entrusted to the same number of subcommissions and around which the preparatory work of the secretariat centered is found in the official address that the cardinal made to the Central Preparatory Commission six months later, in June 1961: (i) relations of baptized non-Catholics to the Catholic Church; (ii) the hierarchical structure of the church; (iii) how to encourage on the one hand conversions of individuals and on the other unity with communities; (iv) the common priesthood of the faithful, and the position of lay people in the church; (v) the word of God and its significance for the liturgy, doctrine and life of the church; (vi) liturgical questions; (vii) the question of mixed marriages; (viii) how to pray for the unity of Christians; (ix) the general ecumenical question and its importance for the church (with particular reference to the World Council of Churches); and lastly (x) questions concerning the Jewish people.[27]

3. However, this wide-ranging and demanding plan of work soon came up against a serious problem, and one with which the secretariat would repeatedly be faced during the whole preparatory period, and which would not be solved until the start of the Council: the question of *whether the secretariat had the right to prepare schemata to be presented to the Council.* This became doubly serious in the case of subjects involving doctrinal aspects as well as pastoral and practical ones. The problem sprang from the terms in which the body was presented in the motu proprio *Superno Dei nutu,* which allocated the secretariat the primary task of helping other Christians to observe the work of the Council. It is true that the document also added the more general aim of helping other Christians to find the way back to the unity that Jesus Christ implored on the eve of his passion, but it is easy to see that this was a fairly slender basis for the ambitious plan of work that the secretariat had set itself.[28]

We may therefore wonder *what the cardinal was taking as his basis* in his inaugural address when he stressed the equality of the secretariat with the preparatory commissions as concerned responsibility for schemata to be presented to the Council. The answer is found in the address of Cardinal J. Willebrands from which we have already quoted a number of times: "In

25. Cf. Arch. Lc 3/3.

26. Cf. Arch. Lc 1/1, no. 12.

27. Cf. *AD,* II/1, 165-166; we should add the document on the question of the invitation of observers to the Council. It is not clear why the subject of religious freedom is not listed here, but maybe it was considered together with one of the other points mentioned. There were thus eleven subcommissions in all. A twelfth would later be added for the subject of tradition and sacred scripture.

28. We can therefore certainly not state, as Pivonka, *The Secretariat for Promoting Christian Unity,* p. 103, does, that the secretariat "as a preparatory conciliar commission also had the task of drawing up five pastoral schemata."

retrospect, it must probably be said that Bea had taken as his starting point the 'statute' drawn up on the instructions of the pope and then approved by the latter, and that he had thus cleared the question of spheres of responsibility with the pope himself."[29] The cardinal added: "This is also borne out by the method that Bea generally used in his relations with the pope. Prior to every audience, he would submit a detailed agenda, listing between six and eight points. After he had then discussed things in detail with the pope, Bea dealt with the various problems on the basis of these discussions, without allowing juridical problems to stand in his way."[30]

Anyone unfamiliar with the true circumstances could also have been forgiven a doubt, on the basis of the fact that it was a "secretariat" and not a commission. However, Bea knew that the pope had chosen this name simply in order to assure greater freedom of action for the secretariat and not in order to limit its responsibility and authority.[31] The validity of such a view finds further confirmation in the explicit disposition of the motu proprio that the secretariat was to have the same composition as the preparatory commissions, for this would have been excessive had it simply been intended as an information bureau or something of that kind. Implicit confirmation is also found in the fact that, according to Bea, the pope had personally said that certain schemata prepared by the secretariat were to be presented directly to the Central Preparatory Commission; this applied to those on religious freedom and on the Jewish people.[32] The files also contain a note on the audience the cardinal was given (an audience suspended on 16 December 1961 and completed the following day): "The cardinal president of the secretariat has all the faculties proper to his office, like any other prefect of a sacred congregation, and is not dependent on any other Roman department."[33]

Lastly, we should note that in the welcoming address that the cardinal gave the pope in March 1962 when the latter visited the secretariat in its plenary session, he said that this body had drawn up "a considerable number of reports and draft decrees."[34] This clearly indicates that Bea was sure that the pope intended the secretariat to have the right to prepare schemata.

We therefore have more than enough reasons in support of the view that the pope intended the secretariat to have authority to draw up schemata for the

---

29. Willebrands, in *Simposio*, p. 7.
30. *Ibid.*
31. Cf. the cardinal's relative article, Biblio. 285, p. 632; also BM, p. 118.
32. We shall come to these in due course.
33. Arch. Lc 4/9. The original Latin reads: "Em.mus Cardinalis Praeses Secretariatus habet omnes facultates suo muneri inhaerentes, sicut omnis Praefectus alicuius S. Congregationis, nec dependet ab ullo alio dicasterio Romano." We saw above that even at the very first meeting of the secretariat, the cardinal confirmed that the brief nominating him as its president conferred on him "all the powers necessary and useful" for the exercise of this office. In this connection, Father Yves Congar, O.P., says that in an audience of 5 March 1962 the cardinal himself told him: ". . . the pope has informed those concerned that all ecumenical questions fall under the responsibility of Cardinal Bea's secretariat" (ArchWit, pp. 1-2).
34. Arch. Lc 5/3.

Council. However, regardless of all this, the situation was not at all clear from the strictly juridical viewpoint, and was thus the subject of some considerable controversy[35]—as we shall see, for example, in connection with discussions in the Central Preparatory Commission concerning the schema on religious freedom drawn up by the secretariat. Moreover, if we bear in mind the huge dimensions of the Council as an undertaking, the confusion is certainly not surprising. Nor was this by any means the only point where there was uncertainty over spheres of responsibility.

A Rapid Change in the Attitude of Other Christians

In an official address made to the Central Preparatory Commission in mid-1961, the president of the secretariat was able to state in this connection: "The secretariat . . . has been greeted with almost unanimous gratitude, by both Catholics and non-Catholics. Evidence of this is seen, for example, in the fact that the secretariat very soon received a huge number of letters, opinions and articles, expressing wishes, proposals and evaluations, to be submitted to the Council itself."[36] And he could go still further, speaking of concrete facts and actions, and saying that events were succeeding one another with a speed that was clearly the fruit of a special breath of the Holy Spirit.[37]

1. The first such step of truly historic importance was the "courtesy visit" of the Archbishop of Canterbury, Dr. Geoffrey Fisher, to the pope in December 1960. The members and consultors of the secretariat had not yet begun their work when an official communiqué was issued on 2 November by Archbishop Fisher, announcing that within the framework of a pilgrimage he was making to Palestine, apart from visiting Constantinople, he also intended to make a courtesy visit to Pope John XXIII.[38] Two days after the announcement, a service was held in the Sistine Chapel to mark the anniversary of the inauguration of the papacy of Pope John XXIII. When the time came for the usual greeting between the pope and Cardinal Bea, the pope's joy over the news was visible as he observed: "The horizon's getting brighter. Courage."

There is no need to describe all the details of the visit here,[39] and we shall simply note certain features of the ecumenical situation on both sides, but especially in the Catholic Church, and more specifically in official circles in

---

35. The cardinal followed juridical practice of that time as he spoke, proceeding on the basis of the pope's decisions *ex audientia Ss.mi*. However, he did not bear in mind the need for him to communicate such decisions officially to the General Secretariat of the Council, so that they could be taken into account in the general proceedings of the Council. This was the origin of the misunderstandings.

36. *AD*, II/1, 14.

37. Cf. *Ecumenism*, p. 32.

38. Cf. *ibid.*

39. Cf. G.F. Svidercoschi, *Storia del Concilio* (Milan, 1967), pp. 69-74; B. Pawley, *Looking at the Vatican Council* (London, 1962), pp. 16-17. We also find abundant information in Caprile, I/1, 303-304, 316-317, 404-416.

Rome. Preparations for the visit began in the summer, when Johannes Willebrands was in England, attending the meeting of "Faith and Order" as an observer. He had a top secret meeting in a London hotel one night with Canon John Satterthwaite, Church of England Secretary for Interchurch Relations. In August 1962, the same churchman pointed out to me the hotel where the meeting had taken place.[40] At the meeting Satterthwaite told Willebrands of Archbishop Fisher's intention of making a journey that would take him to the Holy Land and Constantinople, and would then end with a courtesy visit to Pope John. Confirmation was received in October, and the news was made public on 2 November.

On the occasion of this visit it became clear how ill-prepared people in Rome were for such visits. Some time later the cardinal would write: "The visit entailed considerable problems with protocol for those responsible for organizing things here in Rome, for it was something new, something we had to get used to, both psychologically and also as regards practical details."[41] The first "incident" concerned the fact that the visit was announced in the *Osservatore Romano* in the smallest type available.[42] Lengthy discussions then followed on details of protocol, and it is interesting here to note a confidential observation of Pope John: "Not everybody here understands these things: they'd like everything to be perfect or nothing. . . ."[43] Pomp and ceremony were cut to a minimum. The official communiqué reports that the archbishop, who is the second most important person in England after the Queen, was received simply by an ordinary official and then ushered into the private library by the chamberlain on duty.[44] This approach was dictated in part by fears that any other treatment of the guest might be interpreted as recognition of his position as bishop and head of the Church of England, or rather of the Anglican Communion.

However, it must also be admitted—and this too is indicative of the general situation—that the archbishop himself had not helped matters. The day before the audience he preached a homily in the Anglican Church of All Saints in Rome, in which the reference to the Church of Rome was clear as he stressed the opposition—"which was then resolved with the Reformation in the sixteenth century"—between "the conception of an imperialistic church and the more ancient and apostolic conception of a commonwealth of churches."[45] He probably felt that he had to reassure members of his own church who were worried over his forthcoming visit to the pope.

Similar precautions were also taken for the visit that Archbishop Fisher made

40. Despite all the secrecy, some information did later leak out; cf. Svidercoschi, *Storia del Concilio*, p. 69.
41. *Ecumenism*, p. 32 (ct).
42. Cf. *OssRom* (2-3 November 1960), p. 1, cited in Caprile, I/1, 408.
43. Cf. Caprile, I/1, 303, note 2.
44. Cf. *OssRom* (3 December 1960), p. 1. Monsignor L.F. Capovilla writes as follows: "I was an eye-witness to that meeting, which took place, one might say, 'on tiptoe.' . . . No protocol was planned for that day. The audience list bore the brief note: '12:15, Dr. Geoffrey Fisher' " (*OssRom* [9 December 1985], p. 8).
45. Cited in Caprile, 1/1, 305, note 3.

to the president of the secretariat at his residence at the Pontifical Brazilian College. The conversation lasted about forty minutes. The archbishop started by asking about the nature and work of the secretariat, and then spoke about possible improvements in relations between the Anglican Communion and the Catholic Church, the possibilities of cooperation, particularly on a national level in England, ways of providing such relations with a more permanent form, and the possibility of inviting Anglican observers to the Council.[46] Cardinal Bea's report ends with the following significant evaluation of the importance of the secretariat: "Dr. Fisher closed our talk by saying that he considered his visit to the Holy Father an event of historic importance, but that the creation of the Secretariat for Christian Unity was much more important: his visit was something ephemeral, while the secretariat is a permanent body which will continue its work."[47]

Some days later, the review *La Civiltà Cattolica* published an article by the cardinal examining and evaluating the event, and including the following statement: "We attach the highest possible importance to it, and we feel that its deep significance is to be found above all in what it reveals and symbolizes: the new atmosphere that now exists between Anglicanism and the Roman Catholic Church. The initiative for the visit came wholly from the Anglican side, and in particular from Dr. Fisher himself."[48]

2. Documents now found in our files show that in these same months the Ecumenical Patriarch Athenagoras I had told a number of private visitors of his desire and intention to pay a visit to the pope, adding, however, that he owed it to his position to ask that the pope return the visit.[49] The same sources show that the pope said he would be happy to receive the patriarch, "and also to find some way in which the visit could be returned, obviously not by himself in person, but by an important representative to be agreed upon in advance."[50] The document adds, however, that the pope felt "that it would be better to postpone it [the visit] until certain questions on the situation in the field of the oriental churches had received further clarification."[51]

3. Returning to the West, we would mention a number of visits that followed that of the Anglican primate. In November 1961 it was the turn of Dr. Arthur

46. Cf. *ibid.*
47. Arch. Lc 3/19, p. 3. Cf. also *The Unity of Christians*, p. 135. Peter Hebblethwaite's statement (*John XXIII, Pope of the Council* [London, 1984], p. 383) that the cardinal was not permitted to see the archbishop is surprising. The whole story of Cardinal Ottaviani's presumed campaign against Cardinal Bea (*ibid.*, pp. 370ff) also seems to be without any true foundation. Whenever anyone spoke to Cardinal Bea about his relations with Cardinal Ottaviani, he invariably answered: "We are good friends."
48. *The Unity of Christians*, p. 71 (ct). Cf. also the evaluation of this visit given by Bea in the context of the visit of Dr. Fisher's successor, Dr. Michael Ramsey, in 1966; *Ecumenism*, p. 262. Some months later the visit had a practical result when Dr. Fisher sent Canon B. Pawley to Rome as his own representative during preparations for the Council; cf. Caprile, I/2, 52-53. Canon Pawley was received by Cardinal Bea on 1 May 1961; cf. also Arch. Lc 4/1/3.
49. Cf. Arch. Lc 4/1/3.
50. *Ibid.*
51. *Ibid.*

Lichtenberger, Presiding Bishop of the Episcopalians, the autonomous branch of the Anglicans in United States. The following month came the visit of Dr. J.A. Jackson, President of the National Baptist Convention, which represents five million black American Baptists.[52]

In the following March (1962), the Evangelical Church of Germany, a federation of twenty-eight Evangelical churches in West Germany, followed Archbishop Fisher's example and sent Dr. E. Schlink to Rome in order to observe preparations for the Council.

In March 1962 there was the visit of the Moderator of the Presbyterian Church of Scotland, Dr. A.C. Craig. The position assumed by his community toward the Catholic Church, together with the fact that the relative decision had been preceded by lively debate, meant that this visit was particularly important. It was announced in advance in a press release of 20 March 1962, which read: "The secretariat had informed the Holy Father that the Church of Scotland—through its combined committee—had decided that a courtesy visit to His Holiness would show Christian charity, encourage good will, and be a step toward more friendly relations between Protestants and Catholics in Scotland and elsewhere. His Holiness deeply appreciated this show of Christian sentiment and answered that for his part he would be only too happy to receive such a courtesy visit."[53] The meeting with the pope took place on 28 March in a very cordial atmosphere. In the afternoon of the same day, the moderator met with Cardinal Bea.[54] In order to complete the picture, we would add that in October 1962 Dr. Pierce Corson, President of the World Methodist Council, attended the opening ceremony of the Council and was then received by the pope.[55]

The Catholic Church Goes Out Toward Other Christians

In this same period it was very soon the turn of the Catholic Church to take some steps toward other Christians, moves that were marked by difficulties similar to those we have already seen in connection with the Archbishop of Canterbury's visit.

1. We have seen that right from the first meeting between the cardinal and the General Secretary of the World Council of Churches, they had discussed the question of the invitation of official Catholic observers to the Third Assembly of the World Council, which was to be held in New Delhi, 19 November—6 December 1961. As had been the case with the visit of the Archbishop of Canterbury, problems of protocol were not the only ones that had to be overcome before it was possible to take this step, which was of such fundamental importance for further developments in ecumenical contacts.[56]

52. Cf. *Ecumenism*, p. 33.
53. Arch. Lc 5/4/2.
54. For details, cf. Svidercoschi, *Storia del Concilio*, pp. 120-121.
55. Cf. *Ecumenism*, p. 33.
56. Cf. *ibid.*, p. 34.

Today there is certainly nothing against revealing the nature of these difficulties. What was then the Holy Office (today the Congregation for the Doctrine of the Faith) had been in agreement with the secretariat that the invitation fell within the latter's sphere of responsibility, but had suggested that it would be useful for it to be informed of the various names in advance, so that the information it had at its disposal could help the secretariat avoid any false moves. However, after this had been done, the cardinal received a solemn letter from the Holy Office, stating that the cardinal members of the Holy Office had decided that the principle in force until now should be upheld; in other words, the people chosen should attend the meeting as "journalists" and not as "observers."

Now it is for many reasons interesting to see how Bea acted at this point. I remember it as if it were yesterday. He read the letter from the Holy Office, folded it, and said: "It won't do." Then he left things as they were for some days. (When he wanted to reflect further on something, he used to say, "Let's sleep on it.") After this he sent a fairly exhaustive memorandum to Cardinal Ottaviani, stressing the new situation brought about by the announcement of the Council and its ecumenical aim, which had then been incarnated with the creation of the Secretariat for Christian Unity. He also referred to the possibility of inviting other Christians to send observers to the Council, and then went on to ask how such an invitation could be issued, having refused the fraternal idea of sending observers to the assembly of the World Council of Churches, whose members were those very churches and ecclesial communities that would be invited to the Council. He sent a copy of the memorandum to the pope "for information." "I do not want to involve him, for he has enough on his hands without this," he said, and I think that he was referring to the difficulties the pope himself had with the head of the Holy Office.

Bea's letter had its effect, and persuaded those involved to reconsider the matter; and this time the decision was favorable. Cardinal Ottaviani informed our cardinal of this, telling him: "We didn't have full details at our first discussions," and adding: "I am happy to have been able to remove this thorn from your side, Your Eminence."[57]

The presence of five official Catholic observers at New Delhi was the great novelty of the assembly. They were greeted with considerable joy, which was a sign of the new situation and atmosphere that were growing up between the Catholic Church and other Christians. It was a step of fundamental importance for further developments, particularly for the future presence of observers from other Christian confessions at the Council.[58]

2. We have already said that Patriarch Athenagoras I had told various private

57. Contrary to what R. Kaiser states, *Inside the Council. The Story of Vatican II* (London, 1963), p. 42, it does not appear that the pope acted in this matter, and Cardinal Bea certainly did not ask him to.
58. Cf. Bea and Visser 't Hooft, *Friede zwischen Christen*, pp. 17-18, for the words of greeting that the Secretary General of the World Council of Churches addressed to the Catholic observers in New Delhi. Cf. also *Ecumenism*, p. 34.

visitors of his interest in the Council, and also of his desire, or rather his intention, to visit the pope. As a result, the Catholic Church was also called on to take some steps forward as concerned the eastern churches—which did not at that time fall under the responsibility of the secretariat. And close to Easter 1961 two members of the preparatory conciliar Commission for the Eastern Churches—Archbishop Giacomo Testa, who had been Apostolic Delegate in Turkey and was at this time President of the Ecclesiastical Academy of Rome, and Father A. Raes, S.J., Rector of the Pontifical Oriental Institute—made *a visit to Patriarch Athenagoras* in order to tell him about preparatory work for the Council. Father Raes said in this connection: "Our mission has a twofold aim: that of showing that the Holy See appreciates the gestures of benevolence performed by Patriarch Athenagoras in various circumstances, and in many statements concerning the Church of Rome; and that of personally telling the patriarch about preparations for the Council."[59]

3. A last and far from insignificant step on the part of the Catholic Church toward other Christians was represented by the *visit of the president of the secretariat to Dr. Michael Ramsey*, Dr. Fisher's successor, at his official residence in Lambeth Palace on 5 August 1962. The cardinal had various engagements in England, and he took advantage of the opportunity to make this visit, which he intended as returning the visit that Ramsey's predecessor had paid him in Rome. The archbishop received the cardinal at the top of the main steps with the words: "Your Eminence, this is an historic moment. No cardinal has entered Lambeth Palace since the time of Queen Mary and Cardinal Pole."[60]

The visit took place in a very relaxed atmosphere, and the cardinal stayed on for lunch. The archbishop had returned the day before from a visit to the Soviet Union, where he had been shaken by the serious religious situation, and he now described his impressions to the cardinal. After this the archbishop showed the cardinal around his palace, including the library, which is also where the Lambeth Conference meets every ten years. Showing him into the chapel, he said: "We celebrate the holy eucharist here every day." They then withdrew to the archbishop's study in order to discuss various aspects of mutual relations.[61] They talked about the problem of mixed marriages, the possible canonization of Catholic martyrs from the Reformation period, and difficulties in relations with the English Catholic hierarchy, particularly the question of rebaptism for Anglicans who were converted to the Catholic Church. In order to improve relations with the Catholic hierarchy, the archbishop suggested the creation of a joint commission to discuss mutual difficulties. In conclusion, the archbishop asked the cardinal to tell the Holy Father of his deep respect and convey his best wishes.[62]

59. Caprile, I/2, 141.
60. Cf. *Ecumenism*, p. 40; cf. also Biblio. 290, p. 30.
61. Our files contain a summary of this conversation: Arch. Lc 5/6.
62. Cf. *ibid.*

A First Evaluation of the Preparatory Work of the Secretariat

While the first practical steps on the path of a rapprochement were being taken, the preparatory work of the subcommissions and plenary sessions was moving briskly ahead, encouraged both by the urgency of things, and also by these same events. We shall now consider the various aspects of this work.

1. In the first place let us say a few words about certain *general aspects*. In the preparatory period the secretariat held six plenary sessions, each one lasting about a week.[63] One of the participants, Monsignor J.-F. Arrighi, spoke about the organization of this work as follows: "During the period prior to the Council, various preparatory meetings of members and consultors were held; in order to make the meetings as productive as possible and help the participants to work better together, the meetings were held in a religious house near Rome [Casa Gesù Divin Maestro near Ariccia, belonging to the Pious Society of St. Paul]. During these days of work, a spirit of brotherhood grew up, which was one of the major features of the secretariat. The cardinal was always with us, in the chapel, in the working sessions, at lunch, during recreation."[64] One of the plenary sessions was in fact held during the summer vacation in August 1961 and took place abroad (in West Germany)—something fairly unusual, if not revolutionary, at that time.

Cardinal Bea spoke twice about the wonderful harmony that reigned at these gatherings. In a speech made to the Central Preparatory Commission, referring to four schemata of a doctrinal nature drawn up by the secretariat—on the church-membership of other Christians, on the hierarchical structure of the church, on the common priesthood of the faithful and the position of lay people in the church, and, lastly, on liturgical questions—he stressed that the voting on these documents had shown "a remarkable unanimity of all the members."[65] Speaking of "accord" the cardinal also stated more specifically that the schemata drawn up by the secretariat had been approved by its members with barely one or two votes against, and often unanimously.[66]

2. Let us now take a look at *the way in which the ambitious plan* drawn up in the first plenary meeting in November 1961 *was implemented*, together with the resulting schemata. I remember that from the very start the president of the secretariat had said that a number of the subjects obviously also involved certain aspects that fell under the competence of other preparatory commissions, and that we would proceed in various ways according as the individual cases dictated. Sometimes the schema would be drawn up by the secretariat in the ecumenical perspective and then handed on to other commissions, while in other

---

63. The dates were as follows: 14-15 November 1960; 6-9 February 1961; 16-21 April 1961; 26-31 August 1960; 27 November—2 December 1961; 6-10 March 1962.

64. Cited in Caprile, V, 716.

65. *AD*, II/1, 1965. The original Latin reads: ". . . in suffragatione . . . mirus omnium Membrorum consensus apparuit."

66. Cf. Arch. Lc 4/3.

cases the material would be considered jointly with the relative commission.[67] We have two major documents that tell us how things really went: first of all, the address the cardinal made to the Central Preparatory Commission,[68] and then the inaugural address with which the cardinal opened the work of the last plenary session of the secretariat.[69]

The former tells us that as early as April 1961 the secretariat had completed its *schemata on four major subjects*: the church-membership of non-Catholic baptized people; the hierarchical structure of the church; the priesthood of all the faithful, and the position of lay people in the church; and, lastly, the ecumenical aspects of certain liturgical problems. The cardinal added: "The papers drawn up by the secretariat are handed on to the relative commissions, so that, if necessary, they can be dealt with in a joint commission according to the norms laid down by the Holy Father."[70] Thus, the schemata on the first three of these subjects were handed on to the Doctrinal Commission, and that on the liturgy to the commission responsible for this field.[71] In due course we shall see how the Doctrinal Commission treated the schemata it received.

The inaugural address, on the other hand, tells us in the first place about *certain decisions of the Holy Father*. (1) The pope reserved to himself study and decision on the question of the continued existence of the secretariat as a permanent body after the Council, so that the relative schema was not to be proposed to the Council. (2) On the other hand, the question of the possible admission to sacred orders of Protestant pastors converted to the Catholic Church was to be proposed to the Council. (3) In the audience the cardinal had on 1 February 1962, the pope had decided that the secretariat should submit the schema on religious freedom and the one on the Jewish people directly to the Central Preparatory Commission, without the intervention of any other commission.[72]

This inaugural address also tells us that the secretariat had already sent a schema on the question of *mixed marriages* (in other words marriages between a Catholic and a member of some other Christian confession) to the commission responsible for the sacraments, and that the latter had "accepted all our sugges-

---

67. For the norms governing the study of "mixed matters," in other words those that fell under more than one commission, cf. V. Carbone, *Gli Schemi*, Monitor Ecclesiasticus 32 (Naples, 1971), p. 29, note 81.
68. *AD*, II/1, 164-166.
69. Arch. Lc 5/1/2.
70. *AD*, II/1, 165.
71. Cf. *ibid.*
72. We are not giving the history of *Nostra aetate* (the Latin title of the document on the Jewish people) here, so we confine ourselves to indicating certain contributions on the part of Jewish organizations. The memorandum that the cardinal had asked for from N. Goldman (cf. our previous chapter) was submitted on 27 February 1962; it was presented by Dr. Goldman of the World Jewish Congress and Label A. Katz of B'nai B'rith, in the name of the World Conference of Jewish Organizations; cf. *Simposio*, pp. 96-97, which gives the text in full. *Simposio*, pp. 99-103, also gives a study-survey published in 1964 by the Anti-Defamation League of B'nai B'rith; cf. also the study of Thomas A. Krosnicki, SVD (USA), "From Reproaches to Psalm 22," *Notitiae*, CLXXXVIII (Rome, March 1982), 156-164. For the history of the schema at this stage, cf. *LThK: 2. Vat. Konzil*, II, 415-426.

tions."[73] Work on the schema on ecumenism was particularly complex, since the same material was also being dealt with by the Doctrinal Commission and the Commission for the Eastern Churches. So far as the Doctrinal Commission was concerned, the secretariat was already in contact with one of the consultors of that commission, whereas the Commission for the Eastern Churches had agreed to consider the question together with the secretariat within the framework of a joint commission.

These various details allow us to summarize the fruit of the preparatory work of the secretariat and its significance in a single framework.[74] Apart from the schema on the Jewish people (which was not strictly speaking ecumenical), those on religious freedom, the admission of Protestant pastors converted to Catholicism to priestly ordination, and ecumenism were sent to the Council—although the way in which the last named of these was actually produced still remains to be seen. The schemata on the word of God, the need for prayer for Christian unity, and the tasks of the secretariat during the Council itself were still being drafted.[75]

3. When we consider the abundant harvest of the secretariat's work during this preparatory stage of the Council, we cannot help but wonder *about the specific elements that can be attributed to its president.* Here we have the particularly well-qualified opinion of Cardinal Willebrands, who was a daily witness both to the work of the secretariat and also to the commitment of its president. He writes as follows: "I have no intention of giving Bea all the credit for this work. The secretariat was lucky enough to have the collaboration of first-rate people, some of whom had already been involved in the ecumenical movement for years. So what was Bea's special contribution in this regard? It lay first of all in his capacity to give the maximum trust to those who worked with him, which of course acted as a stimulus to them; it lay also in the fact that he was very open and had a youthful liveliness of mind. He had often said in reference to his time as a teacher that he had learned a great deal from his students, and now too he was ready to learn and open-minded. This was also reflected in the way in which he chaired the long and by no means easy meetings of the secretariat. He allowed the maximum freedom in discussion, but insisted—gently but firmly—that participants stick to the subject in hand and that discussions move straight toward their aim, while not losing their creativity."[76] While the president provided stimulation for others by giving them his trust, he also encouraged them with his *highly appreciated inaugural addresses,* in which he kept them abreast of how things were going, any decisions of the pope, and (especially in 1962) the progress of the work of the Central Preparatory

73. Arch. Lc 5/1/2, p. 4.
74. Here we shall not speak about the document on the question of inviting observers, since this was a preliminary question and would be dealt with prior to the opening of the Council.
75. It can thus be seen that the results of the work of the secretariat cannot be reduced to the five schemata referred to by Willebrands (cf. *Simposio*, p. 7); in fact he is speaking solely of the schemata that the secretariat presented and upheld in the Central Commission, as we shall see.
76. Willebrands, in *Simposio*, p. 8; cf. also the statement of the consultor of the secretariat, John M. Oesterreicher, in BM, p. 214, and his own *The New Encounter*, p. 134.

Commission, which we shall discuss below. He also encouraged them with his example. We saw that even in his opening address to the first plenary session he had invited everybody, both members and consultors, to introduce people in their own circles to the idea of unity and teach them ways of fostering it, establishing contacts, and praying and having others pray for the cause of unity. In all this, he himself set *an incomparable example*: despite his eighty years, he became a true ambassador of unity, giving talks and interviews, and subjecting himself to many exhausting journeys, as we shall see in the following chapter. In the inaugural address of March 1962, he described the enormous interest he had met, and the success of his talks; however, he was not telling them this "for personal motives," but "as a sign of the times, and of the action of divine providence in support of unity."[77]

We must also remember the great personal commitment with which he directed the work of the secretariat outside the plenary sessions as well. After giving us the statement quoted above, Cardinal J. Willebrands told me in confidence about a personal experience in this connection. When the secretary first took up his position, Bea told him: "I won't mind if you make a mistake sometimes; but I'll take it very hard if you don't work, and if you don't get anything done in practical terms."[78] Let us give an example that shows how much time the cardinal devoted to *meetings with his right-hand assistant*, and how warm his interest was in all his commitments, journeys, etc. The cardinal's diary and my own show that in the period between January and July 1962, when the secretariat was not only dealing with drafting schemata, but was also engaged on the complex and delicate task of inviting other Christians to send observers to the Council, the secretary was received by the cardinal as many as twenty-seven times. In the inaugural address of March 1962, the cardinal also referred to the journeys that the secretary had made or was planning to make in connection with the invitation of observers to the Council.[79] In his own diary Bea carefully noted the days of the secretary's departure and return—obviously not in order to check up on him, but out of affectionate concern, so that he could accompany him in thought, and also, I am sure, in prayer. If we want to appreciate fully what all this meant for the cardinal, we must remember that at the same time, apart from the aforementioned talks, interviews and journeys, he had to take part in long, exhausting meetings of the Central Preparatory Commission, which examined and weighed up the material prepared by all the preparatory conciliar commissions (as we shall see in greater detail below), work that obviously called for much study and reflection.

---

77. Arch. Lc 5/1, p. 3.
78. Willebrands, in *Simposio*, p. 8.
79. Arch. Lc 5/1, p. 1.

The Invitation to Send Observers to the Council: A Decision on the Principle Involved

Some years after the Council, the cardinal wrote as follows about the importance of the presence of observers at the Council: "The presence at the Council of observer-delegates of non-Catholic churches, ecclesial communities and federations was the factor that proved to be decisive for the ecumenical spirit which was predominant at the Council and greatly contributed to its ecumenical results."[80] However, even in the thick of events, the great importance of this factor was already clear. Both the interest that other Christians had shown in the Council since its announcement, and even more so the positive reception of the creation of the secretariat and the practical steps that followed its institution, demonstrated the pressing need to consider whether it would not be a good thing to invite other Christians to send representatives to the Council as observers. Although the habits and attitudes ingrained over many centuries meant that the participation of "observers" at the Council was a very novel idea, the cardinal had raised the question as early as the draft "statute" for the "commission for the union of Christians" that he had drawn up at the pope's request some months prior to the creation of the secretariat.[81]

1. The secretariat itself very soon started to concern itself with the question. In his address to the Central Preparatory Commission in June 1961, the president of the secretariat spoke as follows: "The secretariat has given special care and attention to the question of the admission of non-Catholic observers to the Council—a question that has been brought to it from various quarters."[82] He went on to say that since 15 December 1960 the question had been examined by members and consultors who lived in Rome; then it had been studied at the plenary meeting of February 1961; and it had also been discussed with the Preparatory Commission for the Eastern Churches, insofar as it also concerned their sphere. The schema had been definitively approved in the plenary meeting of the following April (1961) and had already been passed on to the Central Preparatory Commission.[83]

All was therefore now in order for the question to be considered and decided on by the Central Preparatory Commission itself.

2. After the central commission had heard the reports of the presidents on the work of the commissions and other preparatory bodies for the Council at its first session (12-19 June 1961), and had studied various aspects of the regulations, *the first subject* on the agenda of the following session, which began on 7 *November 1961*, was the question of observers. The pope was well aware of the fundamental importance of the matter; he attended the session in person, and in his opening address he listed many "reasons for hope," highlighting the lively and respectful interest that other Christians had shown in the Council: "We

---

80. *Ecumenism*, p. 34 (ct).
81. Arch. Lc 2/7.
82. *AD*, II/1, 165.
83. Cf. *ibid.*, pp. 165-166.

would go further, and are happy to repeat it: the attention of so many separated brethren and many others too must be stressed. . . . This attention, which is made up of respect and expectation, is the very reason for anxious exultation, and cannot leave any member of the Catholic family unmoved."[84]

3. The basis of the discussion was obviously the relative document drawn up by the secretariat,[85] and we would summarize its content as follows. After mentioning the previous statements on the matter by Cardinal Domenico Tardini, then President of the Central Antepreparatory Commission, which had left the possibility open, the document went on to list the various forms and ways in which other Christians had demonstrated their own lively interest in the Council. It then stated the aim of inviting observers to the Council: that of enabling them to know the Catholic Church as it is in its doctrine and its pastoral concern, and also in its love for other Christians.[86]

The proposal as to *the form* in which observers would participate in the Council was particularly important, and here the plan came up against the fact that the structure of the Council, the types of meetings, etc., had not yet been decided. The document therefore suggested in general terms that the observers should attend not only religious ceremonies and public sessions, but also those other sessions where they could observe the real work of the Council, with its debates and voting. The document also suggested that special meetings should be organized for them at which the conciliar theologians and advisors—and maybe even the fathers—would tell them about the progress of work, for example that of the commissions, which they could not personally observe.[87] In conclusion it listed the churches and ecclesial communities to be invited. And in order to facilitate clarity in discussions, all the suggestions were summarized under four "conclusions."[88]

This schema was presented in the first place by the president of the secretariat.[89] In his address Cardinal Bea made a point of the fact that the participation of observers was important not only for the Council, but in a more general way for the great cause of unity as a whole.

Cardinal A. Cicognani spoke about the schema from the viewpoint of the Commission for the Eastern Churches.[90] He started by recalling the similar invitation that Pope Pius IX had addressed to the Christians of East and West on the occasion of the First Vatican Council.[91] He then mentioned some recent statements by heads of Orthodox churches, which showed their interest in the Council, and indeed their wish to attend, should they be officially invited. Apart from this, the speaker was in agreement with conclusions drawn in the document of the secretariat.

84. *Ibid.*, p. 144.
85. Cf. *ibid.*, pp. 449-458.
86. Cf. *ibid.*, p. 453.
87. Cf. *ibid.*, p. 457.
88. Cf. *ibid.*, pp. 457-458.
89. Cf. *ibid.*, pp. 458-463.
90. Cf. *ibid.*, pp. 463-466.
91. For the circumstances of this invitation, cf. Jaeger, *Das ökumenische Konzil*, pp. 149-150.

This was followed by a *discussion* in which each of the seventy-five members of the commission expressed any observations and cast his own vote, in order of ecclesiastical precedence; to be precise, there were forty-four cardinals, two patriarchs, twenty-one archbishops, four bishops and four major superiors of religious orders.[92] Obviously, we cannot go into the details here. It is, however, surprising that the overall result was largely positive: fifty-six in favor, eight in favor with a reservation over some modification, two against, and one abstention.[93] If we bear in mind the situation at the start of preparatory work, this was certainly a more than surprising result. It seems beyond doubt that it was largely due to the influence of Pope John and his orientations, and it represented a good omen for the Council itself.

The Task of Inviting Observers

For the time being, the result of the relative discussion in the Central Commission was secret, and considerable uncertainty reigned in this connection—apart from the fact that the General Secretariat of the Council issued a reminder that the vote of the commission was merely consultative and that any decision was up to the pope.[94] There was therefore great joy the following Christmas, when the bull convening the Council was signed and published, with the title *Humanae salutis*, and it was seen to contain the following reference to other churches: "We also know that the announcement of the Council was not only welcomed joyfully by them, but that many have already promised to offer prayers for its success, and that they hope to send representatives of their communities to observe its work at first hand. All this is a source of comfort and hope for us, and in order to facilitate such contacts we set up a Secretariat for Christian Unity some time ago."[95] As the president of the secretariat had suggested in his report, this was a general statement on the possibility of inviting observers to the Council, while also giving the secretariat the task of organizing this.[96]

The bull also brought another novel element: although Cardinal Bea's report had envisaged collaboration with the Commission for the Eastern Churches on the question of the non-Catholic eastern churches, it had asked that action should be entrusted to the secretariat *alone*.[97] The bull fully accepted this suggestion,

92. Cf. *AD*, II/1, 433.
93. This result is not official, but was made by the present author. Cardinal Ottaviani was the only person who did not vote, feeling that the suggestions were neither clear nor adequately developed; cf. *AD*, II/1, 436, 480. We cannot speak, as Kaiser does (*Inside the Council*, p. 43), of "the opposition of the Roman curia."
94. Pivonka, *The Secretariat for Promoting Christian Unity*, p. 102, note 82, is therefore incorrect when he speaks of the *decisions* taken at this meeting.
95. *AAS*, LIV (1962), 12-13; English translation in *Ecumenism*, p. 36 (ct).
96. It is worth noting the extent to which the text of the bull follows the relative passage in the cardinal's report to the Central Commission; cf. *AD*, II/1, 459.
97. *Ibid.*, p. 460.

entrusting the secretariat with sole responsibility in this area, as we have already seen. From now on, the secretariat had full responsibility for the whole field of other Christians in both East and West, as had originally been envisaged in the motu proprio *Superno Dei nutu.*

1. The secretariat had a very delicate task here. It must not be forgotten that until eighteen months before there had been no relations at all between the Catholic Church and the various other western and eastern churches, so that it was necessary to proceed very carefully in order to avoid treading on toes and compromising everything. Referring to the refusal met with by a similar invitation from Pope Pius IX, Cardinal Bea told a fellow Jesuit: "You can rest easy that we shall be careful not to lay ourselves open to a refusal this time."[98] This was also why his report had suggested *proceeding by degrees.* In the first place they would explore the ground; members of the secretariat and others who already had some acquaintance with the various people to be invited would thus sound out the latter on their attitudes, and on whether and in what form they wished to be invited. Only if this exploratory contact was positive would a formal invitation be issued.[99] The leaders of the World Council of Churches were of great assistance to the secretariat in this delicate task.[100]

So far as the various categories of those to be invited were concerned, the document drawn up by the secretariat had already contained a list, and the president of the secretariat had referred to this in his report. For the *East* this included the four historical Patriarchates of Constantinople, Alexandria, Antioch and Jerusalem; then came the Patriarchates of Moscow, Belgrade, Bucharest and Sofia; lastly came the autocephalous Churches of Greece and Cyprus, and the Catholicosate of Georgia. After this there were the "ancient oriental churches" (also called the "non-Chalcedonians," because they had not accepted the decisions of the Council of Chalcedon): the Coptic, Ethiopian, Syrian and Armenian Patriarchates. For the *West,* since the Council was to be a world-level meeting, the aim was that of inviting the major confessional bodies (what are today called "Christian World Communions"): the Union of Utrecht of Old-Catholics, the Anglican Communion, the Lutheran World Federation, the World Alliance of Reformed Churches, the World Methodist Council, the World Baptist Convention, and the World Convention of Churches of Christ ("Disciples of Christ").[101]

2. In practical terms, the major responsibility for exploratory contacts fell to the secretary, Monsignor J. Willebrands. In his inaugural address to the plenary meeting in March 1962, the president of the secretariat said that the Holy Father has "given his benevolent permission for our secretary to go to Constantinople and Athens, in order to have direct discussions on the question of inviting Orthodox observers to the Council. . . . This journey has since taken place (between 14 and 20 February), and the reverend secretary will be telling you

98. Cf. Bacht, "Kardinal Bea," p. 173.
99. Cf. *AD*, II/1, 459-460.
100. Cf. Visser 't Hooft, *Die Welt war meine Gemeinde*, p. 397.
101. Cf. *AD*, II/1, 460-461.

about it when I have finished. At the end of the present month of March, the secretary will go to England in order to discuss the question of observers with Archbishop Michael Ramsey. He will then go on to Utrecht to talk with the President of the Union of Utrecht of Old-Catholics. At the beginning of April he will then contact the Lutheran World Federation in Geneva, the Reformed Alliance, the Convention of Baptists, and others. Finally he will go to Berlin to meet with the President of the Evangelical Church in Germany. We hope that in this way we shall soon reach a satisfactory solution to the somewhat difficult question of observers."[102]

3. The delicacy of the task of inviting observers is shown up particularly clearly by the difficulties the secretariat encountered with regard to the *Orthodox churches*. The first contacts had gone well, and the Orthodox seemed well disposed and responsive. However, although the official invitation to the Orthodox churches of Byzantine tradition was sent out in July, no reply appeared to be forthcoming. Now, the Moscow Patriarchate had originally assumed a fairly negative position,[103] but in due course "direct" information on the Council was requested, and Monsignor Willebrands was invited to Moscow for this purpose. After this visit they asked to receive an invitation, without informing the Ecumenical Patriarchate. The result was that after the Ecumenical Patriarchate had waited some considerable time in vain for the views of the Moscow Patriarchate, it finally sent a negative reply, because of its concern to safeguard the unity of Orthodoxy. Then at the last moment the Moscow Patriarchate sent two observers. This gave rise to some unpleasant recriminations among the Orthodox, and even to accusations against the secretariat, as if *it* had sought to divide the Orthodox.[104] This whole episode froze relations with the Orthodox for some years, and it was only the historic meeting between Paul VI and Patriarch Athenagoras in Jerusalem in January 1964 that succeeded in unblocking the situation and making it possible for observers from the Orthodox churches to attend the Council starting in the third period (1964).

4. Here we must make a short digression in connection with the *invitation to the Russian Orthodox Church*. It has been said that Metropolitan Nikodim, who was head of the Department of Foreign Affairs of the Russian Orthodox Church, had obtained guarantees as to the *non-political attitude* of the Council from Cardinal E. Tisserant, and that on this understanding he had agreed that someone from the Catholic Church should go to Moscow with the invitation.[105] Since the

---

102. Arch. Lc 5/1, pp. 1-2.
103. The expression used by the Russians was "non possumus." On the rejection encountered by the cardinal's statement in this connection, cf. A. Wenger, *Première Session* (Paris, 1963), pp. 207-221; Svidercoschi, *Storia del Concilio*, pp. 124-130.
104. On this whole painful episode, cf. Wenger, *Première Session*, pp. 222-256.
105. In 1963, Bishop J. Schmitt of Metz gave information on the meeting between Cardinal E. Tisserant, Dean of the Sacred College, and Metropolitan Nikodim, saying that the latter had asked for "guarantees as to the non-political attitude of the Council"; cf. Wenger, *Première Session*, p. 224. This information and the fact that the Russian Orthodox Church decided to send observers to the Council led to the over-hasty conclusion that Cardinal Tisserant had promised—perhaps with authorization from the pope—that the Council would refrain from

question of the attitude of the Council to communism was repeatedly raised in certain quarters both before and during the Council, it would be wise to clarify the circumstances surrounding this invitation to observers. I discussed the question in depth in my study on John XXIII and the Secretariat for Christian Unity,[106] and I shall now summarize the main points.

(a) I find it very significant that Metropolitan Nikodim mentions Cardinal Tisserant as many as fifteen times in his study on John XXIII, but never makes any reference to this meeting—although he speaks at length about Monsignor J. Willebrands' visit to Moscow at the end of September 1962 to bring them "direct" information on the Council. This fact shows that at least for the metropolitan the meeting with Cardinal Tisserant certainly did not have the importance that others attributed to it.

(b) A good two months before the Tisserant-Nikodim meeting, contacts had already been established between the secretariat and Archpriest Vitaly Borovoy, Geneva representative of the Moscow Patriarchate; indeed, there was already an implicit invitation to provide direct information on the Council.

(c) What could Nikodim have meant when he spoke about the "non-political character" of the Council? It seems that while Nikodim also condemned atheistic materialism, for him an "anti-communist" attitude represented hostility to his country. Now in a letter to the aforementioned Vitaly Borovoy, J. Willebrands said that the Council "will *not* speak out against one country, for example England, Germany or Russia. If the church must warn its members against certain errors of our times, . . . in so doing it does not intend to condemn a people or a nation, although the authors of the error may belong to a specific nation."

(d) The attitude of the Central Preparatory Commission of the Council, which had Cardinal Tisserant as its President, throws very interesting light on this whole question. Two preparatory commissions had considered the problem of communism: the commission concerned with bishops and the government of dioceses had prepared a schema entitled "The Pastoral Care of Christians Infected with Communism," while the commission on the discipline of the clergy had prepared one entitled "Pastoral Care and Communism"; the Central Commission had then decided that the two documents should be amalgamated, which led to a single schema entitled "The Pastoral Care of the Faithful So That They May Not Fall into the Errors of *Materialism.*" Thus, had Cardinal Tisserant been faced with a request from Metropolitan Nikodim to confirm the non-political character of the Council, he could simply have pointed out that this was the attitude of the preparatory body of the Council, prior to and independent of any invitation to observers from the Russian Orthodox Church.

In conclusion, we can say that apart from the serious problems encountered in inviting observers from the Orthodox churches, the whole question of invitations went well, both with the ancient oriental churches (the "non-Chalcedonians") and with the great confessional communions of the West. In his

---

speaking out against communism.
106. Cf. "Giovanni XXIII e il Segretariato per l'unione dei cristiani," *Cristianesimo nella storia,* VIII (1987), 102-107.

address, the cardinal had forecast the presence of about fifty observers,[107] and there were in fact forty-eight for the first period of the Council. We can thus see that by and large this very important ecumenical aspect of the Council had also been satisfactorily conducted. Although the secretariat had been faced with a total absence of relations between the Catholic Church and the other Christian confessions at the outset, in two years it had successfully established contacts on all sides, and from the beginning of the Council there were representatives of all the Christian confessions listed in the address of the president of the secretariat—except for Orthodoxy and the Baptist Convention.

In the Central Preparatory Commission: The Cardinal's Work for the Renewal of the Church

It is not difficult to imagine how much time and energy the cardinal needed for the work we have described so far. Even so, this was not all, especially from 1961 onward, for there was also his participation in the meetings of the Central Preparatory Commission for the Council, which had the task of evaluating the schemata produced by the individual commissions and the secretariat. We have already gained some idea of the work of this commission when describing how it examined the schema on the invitation of observers to the Council.

1. Let us first try to see the *breadth or extent of this new commitment* by considering what we can describe as its "external" aspects, starting with some figures. Between November 1961 and June 1962 the meetings of the Central Commission took up sixty mornings in all.[108] The cardinal was so conscientious in his attendance that he was absent on only five occasions, because of journeys or speaking engagements. All the material to be examined was then divided into ninety-one "points,"[109] and the cardinal took part in discussion of eighty-three of these.[110]

In their report of the relative discussions, the official documents distinguish between "observations," which were more expanded opinions and were submitted in advance, and the "votes" or "opinions" (*voti*) with which the one hundred or so members of the commission expressed their thoughts in briefer fashion.[111] Our

---

107. Cf. *AD*, II/1, 461.
108. Sixty-seven days in all, which leaves sixty if we take away the Sundays. However, it should be noted that meetings sometimes also took up part of the afternoon.
109. According to the figures given by Carbone, *Gli Schemi*, p. 24, there were seventy-five schemata in all, contained in 124 files.
110. As concerns the remaining commitments of our cardinal, we should remember his ordinary work in the Roman curia. For the period January-July 1962—when the major part of the work of the Central Commission was taking place—I find the following meetings noted in our diaries: Secretariat, 5; Congregation of Rites, 7; Congregation for the Oriental Churches, 1; Pontifical Biblical Commission, 1. We shall talk about journeys, lectures and interviews in the following chapter.
111. In Latin there is a distinction between *animadversiones* (the longer contributions) and *suffragia* (the brief opinions, possibly with explanations).

cardinal was fairly restrained in the submission of "observations," and produced such papers for no more than thirteen points. However, it should also be pointed out that in the sixty-five cases in which he confined himself to a "vote" together with relative motivations, these brief interventions not only bore witness to careful study of the schema in question, but often contained important pointers.[112]

2. We should also emphasize *the importance* of this work and thus the burden of responsibility entailed for the cardinal. We are not referring here to the obvious importance for the Council as a whole, but more to the importance that the various schemata had for the cause of unity. As we have seen, from the start of its preparatory work the secretariat had included various ecclesiological subjects in its program: the church-membership of baptized non-Catholics, the hierarchical structure of the church, the common priesthood of the faithful and the position of lay people in the church, as well as the fraught subject of mixed marriages. It obviously did not want to trespass on anyone else's territory, and when it sent its drafts on to the various commissions involved, its aim was that of drawing attention to the ecumenical aspect of the matters under consideration. As a member of the Central Commission, the president of the secretariat had the further task of seeing whether the relative commission had borne such points in mind, and then reiterating ecumenical aspects if necessary. When we describe Bea's various interventions, we are therefore not claiming that they all represented original thoughts on his part.[113] However, it *was* the cardinal who defended them with his authority in the Central Preparatory Commission.

3. First we have contributions on *ecclesiological questions*.[114] Even then it seemed clear that a document on the church would have a central place in the Council, and it must be said that as early as this our cardinal was supporting three concepts that were then to become special features of the conciliar Constitution on the Church: the fundamental importance of the concept of the church as the people of God, the substantial church-membership of all validly baptized people, and the concept of the "college of bishops" as the successor of the "apostolic college."

(a) Let us start with the concept of *the people of God*. Referring to the first two chapters of the draft constitution on the church presented by the Doctrinal Commission (under Cardinal Ottaviani), the president of the secretariat started by stressing that the subject was of major importance for all baptized people. The secretariat had therefore studied it very carefully and had several times asked to consider it in a joint commission with the Doctrinal Commission.

---

112. Apart from the subjects we shall consider below, the files contain notes on the following individual subjects: the *Formula professionis fidei* (La 1/2), various contributions on the schema *De fontibus revelationis* (La 1/3/1 and La 1/3/2), the ordination of non-Catholic pastors who have converted (La 1/4), the schema *Ut unum sint* of the Commission for the Eastern Churches (La 1/5 and 6), the schema *De Beata Maria Virgine, Matre Dei et Matre hominum* (La 1/7).

113. Only when the documents of the secretariat are opened for examination will it be possible to see how much is the fruit of the work of the secretariat and how much is Bea's original contribution.

114. We shall discuss the schemata drawn up and presented by the secretariat in due course.

However, the proposal had always been rejected, so that the secretariat had simply let the Doctrinal Commission have all the material it had prepared in this connection. The cardinal then said it was good to see that the schema revealed some traces of this material, although many other things had not been taken into account.[115] Moving on to details, the speaker observed that the schema said little about Christ as Founder of the church, about his conception and his plan, which are elements "of fundamental importance in discussions with the Protestants and the Orthodox."[116] "Apart from this, the texts have a great deal to say about the hierarchy, and little, indeed almost nothing, about the tasks and duties of the faithful themselves. There is no section on the Christian people, as if only the hierarchy had tasks in the church. However, it is the people itself—and each member of the people, according to his or her own position and vocation—that has as such, *as people of God*, received the promises; it is the people of God that has been entrusted with the task of bearing witness to the gospel; it is the people of God that has the task of consecrating the world. This last task *is* mentioned later, in Chapter VI, as a duty of the laity. However, this duty does not apply only to the laity, but to the *whole* people of God."[117]

(b) A second point concerns the question of *the efficacity of baptism* and hence of *the substantial church-membership of other Christians*. As we shall see more fully in our next chapter, the cardinal had already dealt with this question in various public lectures since January 1961, in other words for almost one and a half years. He spoke about the matter in the Central Commission in connection with the schema presented by the Doctrinal Commission, the second chapter of which bore the title "Of the members of the church militant and of its necessity for salvation." This schema upheld the teaching that the only "true" members of the church are those who, having received new life with baptism, profess the true Catholic faith, recognize the authority of the church, and have not been separated from the mystical body of Christ by heresy, schism or very serious sin. Anyone else (and not only catechumens) is "ordered" or "disposed" toward the church through a conscious or unconscious "wish for the church," in other words, either through a conscious desire to belong to the church, or, in the absence of any knowledge of Christ and the church, through a general wish to fulfill the will of God, his or her Creator.[118]

---

115. Cf. *AD*, II/3, 1012.
116. Cf. *ibid.*
117. *Ibid.*, pp. 1012-1013. It should be observed that after the general chapter on "The mystery of the church" the conciliar Constitution on the Church, *Lumen gentium*, in fact dedicates its first chapter to "The people of God."
118. Cf. *AD*, II/3, 990-991. It can be seen that the concept of membership of the church *in voto*, in other words in virtue of a relative desire, is not an easy one. Later on, the question would maybe become a little clearer. It is obvious that for reasons of space we are to a large extent forced to simplify our explanation of the thinking of the schema—although of course avoiding any compromise on substance. On what we shall say below of the cardinal's views as expressed in the Central Commission, cf. the full study of G. Vodopivec, "Card. A. Bea: La prima realtà sacramentale del battesimo come base del genuino attegiamento ecumenico tra cristiani fratelli separati," in *Simposio*, pp. 198-222. As we have said, the cardinal had already dealt with this subject some considerable time before; cf. the basic lecture in *The Unity of Christians*, pp.

In his talks the cardinal had repeatedly examined and interpreted the relative passage from the encyclical of Pius XII, *Mystici corporis*, distinguishing first of all between the statement of the encyclical and the conclusion that has been drawn from it that other Christians belong to the church only *in voto*. He strongly attacked this latter claim, saying that the concept *in voto* is very ambiguous. It cannot be applied in the same sense to a pagan as to a Protestant or Orthodox, inasmuch as a pagan's view of the church, and hence the corresponding "desire," are completely different from those of a Protestant or Orthodox. Furthermore, this doctrine seriously offends other Christians. And here the cardinal quoted a lecture given by a Lutheran professor of dogmatic theology (whom he does not name), who said that no Christian can understand how the aforementioned doctrine of Pius XII on the limits of the church, the mystical body of Christ, could have ignored the salvific efficacity of a validly conferred baptism, and simply have considered it as non-existent. It is impossible to understand how baptism can be valid, but ineffective with regard to salvific incorporation into Christ. The professor in question concluded: "In dogmatic terms, surely this means disparaging a sacrament instituted by Christ?"[119]

Having thus implicitly confirmed St. Paul's teaching on baptism and its effects, the cardinal moved on to a *positive suggestion* as to how to proceed in regard to this difficult question. First of all, he suggested that it might be more prudent to avoid reference to "members" of the church,[120] for although the concept of membership is found in St. Paul, it maybe has a considerably different meaning there. Furthermore, if we are to have any hope of providing an adequate idea of the church, we must not confine ourselves to the concept of the mystical body of Christ, in view of the fact that the New Testament also gives a number of other images: kingdom, vineyard, family, house and people are all used as metaphors to illustrate its various aspects.[121] Indeed, we must be careful not to stop at metaphors, but try to reach the essence of what they actually mean.

However, if we wish at all costs to use the term "members of the church" we can maybe do so as follows: "Those who adhere *completely* to the Catholic Church as means of salvation can be called members in the full and strict sense."[122]

29-37. Cf. also the specific study of E. Lanne, in *Simposio*, pp. 159-185. In view of this whole background and the fact that we shall return to the subject in the following chapter, we shall be fairly brief here.

119. Cf. *AD* II/3, 1014; the author referred to is Peter Brunner, "Die abendländische Kirchentrennung und das kommende Konzil," in *Erwägungen zumkommenden Konzil*, (Würzburg, 1961), pp. 35-50, esp. p. 42.

120. This path was in fact followed, at least in the schema on ecumenism. In article 3, instead of speaking of "members," the document speaks of the "communion" existing between other Christians and the Catholic Church.

121. Cf. *AD* II/3, 1015. Indeed, before the conciliar Constitution on the Church explores the concept of the church as mystical body of Christ, it lists all the various images that the New Testament uses to illustrate the mystery of the church (*LG*, 6).

122. Although he puts a specific interpretation on it, here the cardinal basically accepts the relative text of the encyclical *Mystici corporis* of Pius XII (cf. *AAS*, XXXV [1945], 202-203); cf. also *The Unity of Christians*, pp. 31-34. In the Central Commission, a number of other members had suggested a similar interpretation of the text of Pius XII; cf. *AD* II/4, 1010, 1023, 1026.

It was fortunate that the president of the secretariat was not the only person to react against this doctrine as found in the schema.[123] The Archbishop of Vienna, Franz König, and the Archbishop of Munich, Julius Döpfner, explicitly suggested that a distinction be made between members in the perfect sense and members in a partial sense.[124] We can reasonably wonder whether and to what extent these high prelates were influenced by the talks that Cardinal Bea had given on the subject over a year earlier, especially since these talks had been widely reported and discussed.[125]

(c) The third point that Cardinal Bea raised in the field of ecclesiology concerned the way of seeing the hierarchy, and more specifically *the episcopacy and its relation to the primacy of the pope*. In the draft profession of faith proposed by the Doctrinal Commission, the sole church of Christ was described as that "which he [Christ] gave into the pastoral care of St. Peter, prince of the apostles, and his successors, the Roman pontiffs."[126] The president of the secretariat suggested that this last element should be modified to read: "which he [Christ] gave into the pastoral care . . . of the Roman pontiffs and *of the bishops*, the successors of the apostles."[127]

The first chapter of a schema for the constitution on the church, again presented by the Doctrinal Commission, also contained a similar formula, saying that the risen Christ entrusted the government of the church "to St. Peter and his successors."[128] The cardinal pointed out that Christ did not entrust the government only to St. Peter and his successors, but to St. Peter *with the apostles*. The cardinal therefore criticized the way in which this same schema considered the subject of the episcopacy. He suggested that it would be better to take "the biblical documents of the New Testament as a starting point," and made the following observation: "No mention is made anywhere in this schema of the supremely important text on this subject, Matthew 28:19: 'Go therefore and make disciples of all nations.' . . . Christ did not say these words exclusively to St. Peter. He did not say, 'Now you, Peter, send the apostles out into the world, conferring on them the necessary powers,' but conferred the necessary faculties directly on all of them. It is thus an institution that will last 'until the end of the world': together with St. Peter, head and vicar of Christ, they are apostles, and more precisely they are apostles as a college." And the cardinal drew the following conclusion as to method: "With regard to this whole question, it is necessary to *treat the college of bishops first*, and only move on to consideration of individual bishops after this."[129]

---

123. Fellow objectors included the following, who expressed a variety of approaches: the Bishop of Lille, Cardinal A. Lienart (cf. *AD* II/3, 998), the Archbishop of Vienna, F. König (cf. pp. 1005-1006), the Archbishop of Munich. J. Döpfner (cf. pp. 1010, 1030), the Archbishop of Abidjan, B. Yago (cf. p. 1021).

124. Cf. *ibid.*, pp. 1006 and 1010 respectively.

125. See the following chapter.

126. *AD* II/1, 496.

127. *Ibid.*, p. 519; the same thought is found in *AD* II/4, 456.

128. *AD* II/3, 988.

129. *AD* II/3, 1058. For the actual text of the schema in question, see *ibid.*, p. 1041. His words make it clear that in emphasizing the fundamental importance of the college of the apostles and

(d) Let us refer briefly to how the cardinal drew the *practical consequences* of this doctrine for the episcopacy in a wide variety of contexts. In the discussion on the language to be used in the Council, he pointed out the inalienable right of all the Council fathers to be able to understand the schemata, listen to discussions and take an active part. Since Latin is very little studied today in many parts of the world—especially in the East and in mission lands—those responsible for organizing the Council therefore had the imperative duty of making it possible for bishops from such regions to participate actively in the Council—whatever the technical means used to make this possible.[130] In the same context, the cardinal pointed out that the conciliar commissions must be distinct from those for the preparatory phase, whose members were nominated by the Holy See.[131]

With reference to a schema that spoke of the faculties of papal representatives, the president of the secretariat asked whether it would not be better to grant the greater part or maybe all the faculties in question to the episcopal conferences that had direct knowledge of the situations in question.[132] Again in the context of respect for the field of competence and responsibility of bishops, it is significant to see that on a number of occasions the cardinal asked for various questions to be left up to the decision of episcopal conferences. This applied to the question of the division of dioceses, although bearing in mind the opinion of the ordinary, and also to details concerning Catholic schools.[133] Similarly, he suggested that the Council should open up the possibility of having permanent deacons, even married ones, and then leave it up to bishops and episcopal conferences to try this out, and take a decision on the basis of results.[134]

(e) Certain requests the cardinal made concerning *the work of lay people* in the church are to be linked to what we have already said about his contribution to the subject of "the people of God" and thus the position of "the Christian people" in the church. In the discussion of regulations for the Council, the cardinal asked that apart from theologians and canonists, lay experts should also

bishops, the cardinal has no wish to detract from the position of Peter and the pope. He fully recognizes the position of the pope, head of the apostolic college and vicar of Christ. Indeed, right from the very first meetings of the Central Preparatory Commission, when the rules of the Council were being discussed, he gave the following warning: "What has been said about the *freedom and supreme authority* of the Supreme Pontiff in the Council seems to be of major importance. It might therefore be useful for these things to be clearly set out prior to the Council itself" (*AD* II/1, 305).

130. Cf. *AD* II/1, 306.
131. Cf. *ibid.*, pp. 303-304. As we know, this method was not in fact followed, so that when the Council fathers found that they lacked the necessary information at the first General Congregation, they requested, and were granted, a postponement of the elections of the conciliar commissions for a while, in order to allow them to obtain such information; cf. Caprile, II, 20-21.
132. Cf. *AD*, II/2, 563.
133. Cf. *AD* II/2, 515; II/4, 152. This also applied to the question of the distribution of clergy (cf. II/4, 590), as well as to the question of the reform of the index of forbidden books, which many bishops wanted. On the other hand, it should be borne in mind that the dioceses themselves could help avoid many dangers connected with the publication of books; cf. II/3, 861.
134. Cf. *AD* II/2, 173.

be invited to the Council.[135] In the context of the problem of the shortage of clergy and their distribution, the cardinal suggested that there should be greater recourse to the assistance of lay people.[136] He insisted especially on the need for the cooperation of lay people in the field of the mass media; and here he disagreed with the proposal of the relative commission that the Roman office responsible for this field should be raised to the position of a Roman congregation.[137] What was the reason for this view? Bearing in mind the fact that the Roman congregations are essentially made up of a handful of cardinals, it seems probable that Bea's attitude was based on reluctance to see a field that belonged fairly specifically to the laity pass under the direct control of cardinals.

4. In his interventions our cardinal also stressed various other aspects of *the renewal of the life of the church* in which it must also renew itself in the service of the restoration of the full unity of divided Christians.

(a) He was therefore attentive to its *catholicity or universality*; in other words the Council should not think exclusively of the Latin church, but should also remember the eastern churches. In connection with the schemata that dealt with the sacrament of confirmation, and also that of penance, the cardinal said that the principles valid for both the Latin and eastern churches should be gathered together in a single schema, leaving details up to the respective codes of canon law.[138]

(b) Similarly, in another context, he warned that cultural differences should be borne in mind. In connection with a schema on the way of "preserving the deposit of faith in its purity," he said that it was important that the schema should not be purely negative but should offer solutions to contemporary problems and speak a language comprehensible to people of cultures different from our own.[139]

(c) Having gained an idea of Professor Augustin Bea's mentality in the previous part of the present study, we are not surprised to find him here in the Central Preparatory Commission as the champion of *study and research*, and also of respect for the *freedom* of both. Even so, it is worth noting that his fidelity to his own convictions prevented any hesitation over upholding these principles even in such an exalted gathering.

The first opportunity in this connection was offered by the schema on "The Sources of Revelation" presented by the Doctrinal Commission, when he observed: "This draft constitution is unlikely to give contemporary exegetes much satisfaction, and will not provide them with much help in their difficult task."[140] He objected that the schema did not place sufficient stress on "the task and right of Catholic exegesis to work effectively to foster knowledge and interpretation of the sacred books, a task so strongly insisted on by Popes Leo

135. Cf. *AD* II/1, 300.
136. Cf. *AD* II/1, 590.
137. Cf. *AD* II/3, 563.
138. Cf. *AD* II/2, 113, 135.
139. Cf. *AD* II/2, 301.
140. *AD* II/1, 547.

XIII and Pius XII. Now, such research necessarily follows a path of 'conjecture and testing.' Of course these must not be prematurely or over-hastily placed before the general public, but it is only right that they should be published in scholarly reviews or books addressed to specialists. If it is not permitted to place such scientific work before other specialists, biblical research will remain sterile and unfruitful, to the serious detriment of the church. . . . It is therefore vital to protect the freedom of scientific research, which was so warmly recommended by the encyclical *Divino afflante Spiritu* [of Pius XII]."[141] The schema should therefore be revised in the light of the relative teaching of the Supreme Pontiffs Leo XIII, Benedict XV, Pius XI and Pius XII.[142]

(d) The conciliar schemata also contained a very specific case in this connection: the question of fidelity to the teaching of St. Thomas Aquinas. The first schema in which the question was raised was that on the training of future priests, which demanded that "the method and principles" of St. Thomas Aquinas be followed in teaching philosophy and theology. It did not, however, state to what extent. And in order to eliminate any ambiguity and avoid an overly narrow and inaccurate interpretation, our cardinal stressed that this norm does not extend to points that are the object of discussion among the finest commentators on St. Thomas and among Catholic authors—and he cited the explicit statements of both Pius XI and Pius XII in this connection. On such points, the individual is in fact free to follow the view that seems truest to him. In this way, observed the cardinal, charity would be preserved, and also fraternal collaboration between followers of different "schools."[143]

The subject came up again in a schema presented by the Commission for Studies, which had a third chapter entitled "Holding to the teaching of St. Thomas."[144] The president of the secretariat totally rejected the schema as "unilateral and unrealistic."[145] "A large part of the church cannot either now or in the future observe what is laid down here. I am not referring to the practical difficulties in mission lands, but rather to those in the Greek church, both the united one but also the one in whose union we hope. The East does not know 'scholasticism'[146] or St. Thomas, and indeed does not even understand their language. . . . For them [those of the eastern churches] it is necessary rather to insist on the need for them to study their great Greek Doctors . . . who are their glory and with study of whom they can contribute a great deal to the progress of Catholic theology."[147] The cardinal added: "Nor am I speaking of those others for whose return to the church we hope: the Anglicans and all the Christians of the Reformed tradition, who accept the teaching of the first centuries. With them

141. *Ibid.*
142. Cf. *AD* II/1, 548.
143. Cf. *AD* II/2, 792-793.
144. Cf. *AD* II/4, 165-170.
145. Cf. *AD* II/4, 190.
146. In the broader sense "scholasticism" means "medieval philosophy," but in a more restricted sense the term refers to "that doctrinal movement that proposes a systematic conception of the world and of man in accordance with revelation and faith"; *EncCatt*, XI, 121.
147. *AD* II/4, 190-191.

we must appeal not to scholasticism and St. Thomas, but rather to the early fathers."[148]

The Cardinal as "Ecumenical Conscience" of the Central Preparatory Commission

The specifically ecumenical activity of the president of the secretariat is to be seen in the larger context of his vast activity in the Central Preparatory Commission as we have described it so far.

1. A first kind of action is represented by warnings as to *how to act or the language to use* in order to avoid anything that might offend other Christians, while encouraging anything that might help them understand us better. Thus, in connection with the draft profession of faith—which we have already mentioned above—the cardinal said that out of regard for the Protestants it should speak of Christ as *sole* Mediator in the sense of 1 Timothy 2:5.[149] Elsewhere he asked that the question of the origin of the jurisdiction of bishops (which is disputed even among Catholics) should be avoided, in order to avoid creating difficulties in discussions with the eastern churches.[150] Similarly, we find a warning to avoid the phrase "the so-called Orthodox," which was introduced at the time of Pius XII but which is offensive to them.[151] On another occasion, however, having asked that treatment of the subject of the Blessed Virgin be given a "more attractive" form, he said that we must not be afraid that our teaching in this area could offend the Protestants: "Today many of them sincerely venerate the Blessed Virgin no differently from the way the 'reformers' themselves did, as a Protestant historian has very recently shown on the basis of the sources."[152]

2. It is very interesting to see the way in which the cardinal emphasized the passage in a liturgical schema on *the readings from sacred scripture in liturgical celebrations.* The schema said: "Anglicans and Protestants tend to accuse Catholics of ignorance of sacred scripture, and observe in surprise that there is a certain lack of proportion in the Roman liturgy between the sacramental element and the scriptural element, in other words the proclamation and preaching of the word of God."[153] The cardinal did not hesitate to endorse this criticism of the Catholic liturgy and to stress it as being of major importance. And his observation on preaching is to be linked to his emphasis of this point. In the context of a schema on catechesis, the cardinal said: "It is necessary to speak explicitly of preaching. . . . A great deal is expected of the Council in this area, even by non-Catholics."[154]

---

148. *AD* II/4, 191.
149. Cf. *AD* II/1, 519.
150. Cf. *AD* II/2, 563.
151. Cf. *AD* II/3, 1016. In Latin the author used the expression "orthodoxi qui dicuntur" ("those who are styled orthodox"); the offending terminology often consisted simply in the fact that the word "orthodox" was placed in quotes.
152. *AD* II/4, 781. The work to which the author was referring is W. Tappolet, *Das Marienlob der Reformatoren: M. Luther—J. Calvin—H. Zwingli—H. Bulliger* (Tübingen, 1962).
153. *AD* II/3, 96; the text of the schema is found in *AD* II/3, 39.
154. *AD* II/3, 832.

3. We shall now consider some more direct references to *relations with other Christians.*

(a) In connection with the schema on *the duties of parish priests,* the cardinal suggested that since the pope intended that the Council should also be helpful to our "separated brethren," it "should be recommended that parish priests exercise a certain amount of care for them." He then more practically suggested how this recommendation might be formulated.[155]

(b) We have already seen that the secretariat had considered the question of the admission to sacred orders of Evangelical pastors who had converted to Catholicism. Now, it so happened that the same subject had been considered by the Commission for the Discipline of the Clergy and the Christian People,[156] although without the knowledge of the secretariat. Otherwise, the cardinal observed, the latter would have offered its cooperation. Be that as it may, the cardinal was substantially in agreement with the suggestions made in the schema, inasmuch as they basically corresponded to the relative practice initiated by Pope Pius XII. However, the cardinal did point out how important the language used in this delicate area was, and also said that there was a risk that treatment of this subject could be seen as some kind of "Catholic propaganda" for the conversion of Evangelical pastors. Moreover, since the problem did not concern the whole church, it would be best if the Council were not called upon to consider it.[157]

4. A third series of contributions by the cardinal concerned certain *problems common to both Catholics and other Christians.*

(a) The first question is that of *a common date for the feast of Easter,* a subject that received increasingly lively attention after the Council. In its schema, the Commission for the Eastern Churches expressed the hope of seeing all Christians in both East and West celebrating the feast of Easter on the same day.[158] Now, the delegate of Patriarch Maximos IV Sayegh explained how painfully this problem was felt in the East, and expressed the hope that the pope himself would take the initiative in seeking a solution.[159] The cardinal then declared that as President of the Secretariat for Christian Unity he wholeheartedly supported what the patriarch said, and added: "Such uniformity [in the celebration of Easter] will constitute a first step toward full unity."[160]

---

155. Cf. *AD* II/2, 606. This recommendation is in fact contained in the conciliar Decree on the Ministry and Life of Priests, *Presbyterorum ordinis,* 9.

156. Cf. *AD* II/4, 292-294.

157. Cf. *AD* II/4, 305-308. We saw above that the pope had decided that this subject should be presented in the Council, and we do not know why our cardinal supported the contrary view here. We would note in passing that the Commission for the Eastern Churches had drawn up a schema on *communicatio in sacris* concerning eastern Christians (cf. *AD* II/2, 230-231) and that Bea had expressed his agreement (cf. *AD* II/2, 245). And these proposals were in fact accepted by the Council (cf. the Decree on the Catholic Eastern Churches, *Orientalium ecclesiarum,* 27).

158. Cf. *AD* II/3, 1305.

159. Cf. *AD* II/3, 1314.

160. *AD* II/3, 1319.

(b) Another problem was that of *relations with the missions and missionaries of other confessions*. The commission responsible for the field of missionary activity had presented a schema on "The Government of the Missions." Fully aware that this field involved the sensitive problem of relations between missionaries of the various confessions, the cardinal observed briefly: "I would note that in no part is the very thorny question of relations with the missions of non-Catholics considered." Since we ourselves were barely at the start of ecumenical relations, the cardinal realistically added: "However, it is maybe more prudent that the Council should avoid discussing this for now, and that the question should be approached in some other way."[161]

(c) Another very delicate joint problem was that of *mixed marriages*. Anyone even slightly familiar with religious life in confessionally mixed regions—and this applies to most areas today—knows the difficulties that exist in this field even after the new legislation introduced in 1970 with Paul VI's motu proprio *Matrimonia mixta*. Leaving aside the brief transitional period of 1966-1970, when the matter was regulated on the basis of a special Instruction of the Congregation for the Doctrine of the Faith, we can say that the previous situation—which fell under the 1917 Code of Canon Law—was immensely more difficult. The problem concerned the attitude of the Catholic Church toward the partners in a marriage between a Catholic and someone belonging to another Christian confession. Since the church felt responsible for the faith of the Catholic partner and also for any children born of such a marriage, it granted permission to such a marriage on condition that the Catholic partner promise that he or she intended to remain faithful to the Catholic faith, and also to baptize and bring up any children in the Catholic faith, as well as trying to win the non-Catholic partner to it. Moreover, the non-Catholic partner was required to give a written promise that he or she would respect the Catholic convictions of the partner, and would not prevent offspring from being baptized and raised in the Catholic faith. Lastly, the marriage had to be celebrated before a Catholic priest. Although it is clear that the question of religious freedom was deeply involved here, and thus that of respect for the religious convictions of the non-Catholic partner, there was a very long way to go before the problem could be resolved.

Now, the preparatory commission responsible for the sacraments had drafted a schema on this matter. We have already seen that the secretariat had also studied the question very carefully and had transmitted its own conclusions and suggestions to the commission in question. In his contribution in the Central Preparatory Commission, our cardinal started by stressing the vital importance of the question, which is seen as a kind of test-case by a number of other Christians, in other words as a criterion of good will on the part of the Catholic Church. Furthermore, the president of the secretariat reported that the relative schema of the secretariat had been definitively approved on 30 November 1961 and that it had contained twelve specific suggestions; the aforesaid commission

---

161. *AD* II/3, 206.

had "taken these into account in its schema . . . apart from certain points which I shall now list."[162]

Although we obviously cannot enter into the details of this thorny juridical question here, we would mention one or two points. In those early days, the general ecumenical situation was still such that the secretariat did not think it could suggest more than the following: "The non-Catholic partner should give a serious promise that he or she will not oppose the freedom of conscience and Catholic religious practice of the other partner, either with blandishments or with force, and that he or she will not oppose the baptism and education of all offspring in the Catholic Church."[163] However, the norm of the Code of Canon Law then in force that invited the Catholic partner to try to win the other spouse over to the Catholic faith was toned down in the suggestion of the secretariat to read as follows: "The Catholic partner has the obligation to ensure with his or her own life, example and prayer that the other spouse can obtain a correct evaluation of the Catholic faith."[164]

As can be seen, there was as yet no major progress in the difficult field of mixed marriages, which would in fact require not only the years of the Council, especially with the clarification of the problem of religious freedom, but also a number of years of development after the Council. For now, the cardinal demonstrated his usual pragmatism and had to be satisfied with having stated the problem and offering some suggestions toward a solution.

The Schemata Prepared by the Secretariat Are Examined by the Central Preparatory Commission

1. One of the last sessions of the Central Preparatory Commission, in June 1962, saw an open clash between Cardinal A. Ottaviani's Doctrinal Commission and the secretariat over two schemata: one on "religious *tolerance*," championed by Cardinal Ottaviani's commission, and the other on "religious *freedom*," championed by the secretariat. As had happened in a number of other cases, here again the Doctrinal Commission had rejected the secretariat's collaboration, and the two bodies had each continued on its own, drafting a schema according to its own specific aims. As we have seen, in order to avoid misunderstandings Pope John XXIII had explicitly stated that the schema prepared by the secretariat should be presented to the Central Preparatory Commission without intervention from any other commission.

(a) Before describing the relative discussions in the Central Commission, let us try to give *an idea of the two positions*. When we talk about "religious freedom" we mean recognition of the right of the individual to follow his or her

162. *AD* II/3, 1191.
163. The motu proprio *Matrimonia mixta* of Paul VI (*AAS*, LXII [1970], 257-263) limits the part concerning the non-Catholic partner, asking solely that he or she should be informed about the promises made by the Catholic partner.
164. *Ibid.*

own conscience without being prevented by blackmail, coercion or anything similar. The fundamental problem starts when an erroneous conscience is involved, for there is then the question of whether or not we can recognize the so-called freedom to err. Human beings have received freedom in order to decide freely for the truth, so how can we accept a right not only to profess but also to spread error? When we apply this idea to the religious field, the question then becomes: How can we accept the right to profess and spread a religion that is not true? The supporters of religious freedom answer that even for them error always remains error, but that the person who believes that he or she has found his or her truth in error has the right to say so openly, and must not be exposed to blackmail or any other type of coercion to the contrary, either by individuals or by society itself. The second step is then as follows: What should be the attitude of the state in this matter? The schema of the Doctrinal Commission bore the title "Relations between Church and State, and Religious Tolerance," and considered the problem mainly in this perspective.[165] Indeed, the title itself indicates the direction of the solution proposed, which was that the state must positively protect and foster the truth, in other words the Catholic religion and the church, whereas it can only "tolerate" other religions for reasons of a greater good. The schema of the secretariat, on the other hand, stated that the state must uphold and protect the rights of all citizens, and hence also their right to profess and spread their religious convictions, so long as these do not conflict with certain rights of others persons or of society as a whole.[166]

(b) Let us now take a brief look at *the discussion and its results*. In his address the President of the Doctrinal Commission, Cardinal Ottaviani, bluntly challenged the authority of the secretariat to deal with this purely doctrinal matter, since the Doctrinal Commission had exclusive authority here. Moreover, the schema of the secretariat had suffered very strong influence from contacts with non-Catholics. He concluded by saying that the only schema to be discussed was that of the Doctrinal Commission.[167]

Cardinal Bea answered calmly as follows: "Nobody should be surprised that our secretariat has considered the question of religious freedom. Our secretariat is not at all of the opinion that in dealing with this question it has exceeded the limits of authority conferred on it by the supreme pontiff. We are sorry that just as the Doctrinal Commission has refused to collaborate with other commissions, it has also done so with regard to the secretariat. A joint commission, like those the secretariat has formed with other commissions, would have had no difficulty in preparing a unified schema. However, since this was not done, we must now discuss both schemata."[168]

The president of the secretariat then emphasized the ecumenical importance

---

165. Cf. *AD* II/4, 657-661.

166. In the context of the present work, we obviously cannot go into all the details of this difficult problem, but must simplify things somewhat. We shall in any case have to return to the matter in due course.

167. Cf. *AD* II/4, 684-688.

168. *AD* II/4, 688.

of the subject: "Non-Catholics are most concerned over this problem, and they continue to accuse the Catholic Church of being intolerant where it is in a majority, while calling for religious freedom where it is in a minority. Cases where such intolerance is seen are carefully highlighted and advanced against the Catholic Church. . . . In proposing this schema, the secretariat has therefore shown fidelity to its duty, by bearing these circumstances in mind and considering the task of the church with regard to religious freedom, and also how this freedom must be put into practice."[169] Having described the principles underlying the schema and also the differences between it and that of the Doctrinal Commission, the cardinal stated that the schema had been "*unanimously* approved by all the members of the secretariat."[170]

(c) It is not difficult to imagine the tense atmosphere in which the long debate took place, and the relative minutes take up fifty-four pages.[171] As in other cases, after the full-scale contributions of varying lengths, the individual members cast their votes, adding motivations also of varying lengths. As usual, there were three types of view expressed: positive, negative, and positive with reservations. It is, however, very significant that the schema of the Doctrinal Commission received 19 positive votes, 14 negative votes, and 28 qualified positive votes, while that of the secretariat received 16, 11 and 22 respectively. If we bear in mind on the one hand the novelty of the position upheld by the secretariat and also the novelty of the very body itself, and on the other the fact that many people tended to identify the Doctrinal Commission with the very authoritative department of the Holy Office, especially because of its president, Cardinal Ottaviani, it must be said that this was a more than satisfactory result for the secretariat.[172]

---

169. *AD* II/4, 688-689.
170. *AD* II/4, 689-691. As he did in other cases, here too Cardinal Ottaviani answered the various speakers. In particular he spoke out strongly for the absolute independence of the commission of which he was president, when dealing with doctrinal questions, stating that it was in no way obliged to consider such questions jointly with the other commissions; cf. *Act. praep.* II/4, 691. The difficulty was therefore not peculiar to the Secretariat for Christian Unity. I feel it possible that this attitude had its roots in the mentality that had meant that until the reform of 1965 the Holy Office bore the title "Supreme Sacred Congregation"—a title not in fact envisaged by the Code of Canon Law then in force.
171. *AD* II/4, 692-746.
172. Recently, the well-known Archbishop M. Lefèbvre has compared the Ottaviani draft with the Bea draft, observing that while the former contains sixteen pages referring to the magisterium, the latter makes no reference to it at all; cf. M. Lefèbvre, *Lettera aperta ai cattolici perplessi* (Rimini, 1987), p. 84. What reply can we give? The observation is correct. However, the difference between the two drafts derives from the difference in method. During the preparatory period, and also in the Council, Bea repeatedly reproached the drafts of the Doctrinal Commission for being too closely based on the declarations of the magisterium in recent centuries. (This is also the case as regards the draft in question: the sixteen pages of references are made up exclusively of declarations from the last two centuries.) As against this, Bea observes that Councils have always referred to the ultimate and underlying source of faith. i.e. sacred scripture and the fathers of the church. Thus the draft of the Secretariat for Christian Unity is based above all on sacred scripture: on the profound truths of faith, especially the teaching of scripture on man as the image of God. (The context was not appropriate for a study of the teaching of the fathers of the church.) The draft then justifies its arguments on sound metaphysical and ethical bases (cf. *AD* II/4, 679: "exigentias sanae rationis" or "the demands

(d) There was still naturally the question of *what should now be done*. It was clear that two schemata on the same subject could not be taken to the Council, particularly when they expressed such differing positions. The members of the Central Preparatory Commission were not at all sure what to do. About ten of them wanted to appeal to the pope as supreme arbitrator, while fifteen others called, as seemed logical, for an amalgamation of the two schemata. Some suggested the creation of a joint commission to carry out this task, while Cardinal F. Cento suggested collaboration between the presidents of the two bodies, with the addition of another cardinal to be chosen by them.[173] A variation on this latter suggestion was in fact adopted, with the addition of Cardinal Ciriaci and the secretaries of the two bodies.[174] Unfortunately this decision remained on paper, and the commission in question never met.[175] Thus, the subject does not appear at all in the schemata from which the material for the Council was to be drawn.[176]

2. The secretariat also found itself "in competition" with the Doctrinal Commission on the subject of *ecumenism*, for the latter had considered this at the end of its draft constitution on the church.[177] And just to make things even more difficult, the Central Commission had already discussed another schema on the same subject drafted by the Commission for the Eastern Churches, although this one referred only to eastern Christians.[178] In any case, discussion of the schema of the secretariat went smoothly this time. Its authority in this area was not challenged, maybe because the draft was presented as a "schema for a pastoral decree." In his address, Cardinal Bea pointed out: "The schema is pastoral; hence, it does not consider theological questions *ex professo*."[179] Discussion of the schema was fairly short. Opinions were favorable to both schemata, and neither of the two received any negative votes: that of the Doctrinal Commission received 28 positive votes and 14 qualified positive votes, while that of the secretariat received 30 and 14 respectively. Sixteen members expressed a wish to see the two schemata combined. However, all *three* schemata remained distinct and separate until their discussion in the Council hall, and only there was it finally decided to amalgamate them.[180]

3. There were now two other schemata of the secretariat: that on the need for

---

of sound reason"). Thus, far from neglecting the teaching of the church, this draft seeks absolute fidelity to the most profound truths of faith. It thereby also avoids suspicions that could arise as a consequence of the aforementioned method of the Doctrinal Commission, namely, that the teaching authority of the church over the last two centuries has done nothing but accommodate its own teaching to the development of modern society.

173. Cf. *AD* II/4, 731.
174. Cf. Carbone, *Gli Schemi*, p. 22.
175. Cf. *ibid*.
176. For the schema of the constitution on the church, cf. Series II, 641; for the schemata of the secretariat, cf. Series IV, 373-391.
177. For the schema of the secretariat, cf. *AD* II/4, 785-792; for that of the Doctrinal Commission, cf. *AD* II/4, 792-800.
178. For the schema "De Ecclesiae unitate. Ut omnes unum sint," cf. *AD* II/4, 436-438. The commission intended the schema to refer only to unity with eastern Christians; cf. *AD* II/4, 455.
179. *AD* II/4, 801.
180. Cf. Carbone, *Gli Schemi*, p. 23. We shall discuss this in the context of the Council itself.

prayer for unity, especially in our times, and that on *the word of God*.[181] With regard to the content of the latter, in his presentation the president of the secretariat explained that it was not a doctrinal treatment of the word of God, since this had already been given in the schema of the Doctrinal Commission on the sources of revelation; rather, the text expressed the importance of the word of God for the church, and particularly for its pastoral activity.[182] The discussion was not lengthy, and the outcome was largely positive, with neither of the two schemata receiving negative votes: the first received 36 positive votes and 9 qualified positive votes, while the second received 36 and 14 respectively.[183] In due course these two schemata of the secretariat were united with that on ecumenism, and this was the form in which they appeared in the official *Schemata*.[184]

4. There was still one last schema drawn up by the secretariat—that on *the Jewish people*—and in this connection, there was a real *volte-face* from one day to the next. The minutes of the Central Commission for 20 June contain a cold-sounding report of a proposal of Cardinal Secretary of State Amleto Cicognani: "It was discussed with His Eminence Cardinal Bea whether it was a good idea for the 'Decree on the Jewish People,' which has been prepared with such charity by the same cardinal, to be presented to this Central Commission and included in the Acts of the Ecumenical Council. It seemed untimely. . . . It is therefore proposed that the Council should not take account of this decree and that it should not appear in the conciliar Acts."[185]

How could such a decision have been taken after all the wishes previously expressed by Pope John XXIII and the work of the secretariat for almost two years? When Cardinal Bea spoke about this question in the Council hall itself, in 1963, he said that the schema had been removed from the Council's agenda "not because of the ideas or doctrine set forth in it, but simply because of certain unfortunate political circumstances of those days."[186] The "circumstances" in question were the announcement made by a Jewish organization that it would be sending a person who had previously worked at the Israeli Ministry of Worship to Rome as its special representative in connection with the Council. The announcement raised such a storm of protest from the Arab states that it was thought more prudent to remove the schema from the agenda.[187] After a surprising statement by the Cardinal Secretary of State, which could have given the impression that the decree did not reflect the aims of the Council,[188] the

---

181. Cf. *AD* II/4, 813-816, and 816-819, respectively.
182. Cf. *AD* II/4, 822.
183. The figures are those of the present author; cf. *AD* II/4, 828-834.
184. They appear in this order: prayer for unity, the word of God, ecumenism; cf. *Schemata*, Series IV, 373-391.
185. *AD* II/4, 22-23.
186. *AS* II/IV, 481.
187. Cf. John M. Oesterreicher, "Texgeschichte der Konzilserklärung über das Verhältnis der Kirche zu den nichtchristlichen Religionen," *LThK: 2. Vat. Konzil*, II, 426; cf. also Svidercoschi, *Storia del Concilio*, p. 131. There is no foundation to R. Kaiser's statement (*Inside the Council*, p. 215) that it was the Holy Office that stirred up the Arab nations.

minutes in question do, however, mention the real reasons for the decision, describing these as "present disagreements between Jews and Arabs," and saying that "since this is a political matter, it would be easy to arouse suspicions that we are siding with one party or the other—and there have already been rumors to this effect."[189]

Our files contain the text of the short address in which Cardinal Bea had planned to present the draft decree to the Central Commission.[190] In this text he mentioned the explicit task the pope had given the secretariat, in other words, that of dealing with the many prejudices against the Jewish people, which are also widespread among Catholics, especially the view that Jews are "God-killers" and "cursed by God." The schema prepared by the secretariat simply set forth the relative doctrine of St. Paul and the liturgy. The cardinal then added, obviously with reference to the coming storm: "It is a completely different question whether in the present circumstances it is timely and prudent to propose this decree."[191] He then referred to the enmity between Jews and Arabs, saying that "the Eminent Cardinal Secretary can give further details of this."[192]

It is clear that when the president of the secretariat was preparing his text, he already foresaw what would happen, and he may even have prepared it after his talk with the Secretary of State. However, did he in fact give this address in the Central Commission? The minutes do not mention it, but it is possible that they omitted it in order to strengthen the impression that the schema had simply been ignored, and thus not pour oil on troubled waters.

* * *

In this chapter we have observed the huge amount of ground covered and the very varied aspects of the diligent and complex official activity of the secretariat. There is no need to carry out a full-scale evaluation of the results here, but we would simply observe that the overall results in the preparatory period were largely positive, exceeding even the most optimistic hopes that could have been conceived when it was created. We can in particular emphasize the fruit of the initiatives taken to invite the various Christian World Communions and the World Council of Churches to be represented by observer-delegates at the Council. This same initiative was in fact successful in establishing fruitful contacts with the eastern churches, with all the Christian World Communions and with the World Council of Churches in a short time, so that from the beginning of the Council the great majority of those invited would in fact be represented. There was, however, the failure of the invitation with regard to

---

188. In Latin: "Verum stare debemus fini huius Concilii" (= "But we must keep to the purpose of this Council"), a phrase that seems to suggest that the subject was outside the scope of the Council.

189. *AD* II/4, 22.

190. Arch. Lf 1/6.

191. *Ibid.*

192. *Ibid.*

almost all the Orthodox churches, which meant that apart from the Russian Orthodox Church, the Orthodox would be absent from the Council until its third period. And this failure also gave rise to a painful division between the Orthodox churches themselves—a rift that would be difficult to heal.

The general success of the activity of the secretariat did not prevent its results from being exposed to a number of dangers, and the continuation of its activity in the Council presented some difficult problems, which could possibly have put these results radically in question. For example, at the beginning of this chapter we mentioned the fact that prior to the Council the great majority of the Council fathers had not had any positive contact or experience of an ecumenical kind, while many of them had often been exposed to the negative experiences prevalent in a number of countries.[193] Now the question of the attitude of the bishops was an important consideration from the start of the Council, since it would exercise a decisive influence on the election of the members of the conciliar commissions, whereas in the preparatory period the president himself had been able to draw up the relative lists of names and these had been largely approved by Pope John XXIII. There was thus considerable uncertainty over how things would go when members were elected on the part of the Council, for it is not difficult to see how much the progress of the work of a similar body depends on its composition. Moreover, there was still the difficulty, which we have repeatedly met, of the authority of the secretariat as regards the conciliar schemata, in other words the question of whether the secretariat would be authorized to speak in the Council on behalf of the schemata it had prepared and work with other commissions on matters of concern to both, or whether its schemata would be entrusted to other bodies, with serious and detrimental consequences.

A major *reason for hope* lay in the benevolence and active support that Pope John had given to the work of the secretariat. When Monsignor J. Willebrands accompanied the Presiding Bishop of the Episcopalians, Dr. A. Lichtenberger, to a papal audience in November 1961, the pope observed: "I am always very happy to see Cardinal Bea." On another occasion when Monsignor J.-F. Arrighi of the secretariat was presented to him, the pope said very explicitly: "I watch your work with great interest. Cardinal Bea is very dear to me. You must remember that the pope is with you."[194] Not that he let himself be carried away by uncritical partiality and enthusiasm. As early as September 1960 in a handwritten note we find him saying: "Doubts have arisen over the importance that the secretariat should have alongside the main Central Commission and the individual Catholic commissions, because of the anxiety that is already being betrayed by the separated brethren to speed things up and to press for contacts that could distract the Council fathers and create some disturbance or delay in their own specific work."[195]

Monsignor L.F. Capovilla in turn observes: "The pope carefully read the many 'work sheets' sent in by the cardinal, and found them in full conformity

---

193. Cf. Willebrands, in *Simposio*, pp. 14-15.
194. I heard both these reports from those concerned and immediately noted them down in my diary.
195. L. Capovilla, ArchWit, enclosure, no. 7.

with his magisterial and pastoral line, in spirit and practice, in their implementation of the plan for the Council. He often tried to persuade the doubtful not to be afraid: once every compromise with irenicism was avoided, a start would be made on the recomposition of Christian unity, following the only possible path—that of charity."[196]

The hope of the secretariat was based most strongly on what the pope had already done for it throughout the preparatory period. Cardinal Bea made a very significant statement in this connection when Pope John XXIII visited the plenary session of the secretariat in March 1962. Speaking about what the secretariat had achieved in the preparatory period, the cardinal stated: "All that we have done so far would certainly not have been possible without the benevolence, constant support, assistance and prayers of Your Holiness."[197] This was not some empty compliment, as we have seen from various examples in the course of the present chapter.

---

196. *Ibid.*
197. Arch. Lc 5/3, p. 2.

CHAPTER 5

SENSITIZING CHRISTIANS TO THE CAUSE OF UNITY

Parallel with the work of drafting schemata for the Council, that of contacts with a view to the invitation of observer-delegates to the Council, and that connected with the work of the Central Preparatory Commission, the cardinal also worked hard in order to sensitize public opinion to the ecumenical question, or maybe more accurately in order to satisfy the great interest of vast numbers of Christians in the cause of union. In his book *Ecumenism in Focus* he wrote in 1967: "Almost from the first beginnings of the secretariat, . . . I began to receive requests from radio, television and the press in various countries. It was impossible to satisfy anything like all the requests received. It is sufficient, for example, to say that in the first nine months of 1962 alone I gave twenty-five interviews. Invitations also soon began to arrive for me to give public lectures on the question of ecumenism."[1]

The present chapter intends examining all this work in a twofold perspective. In the first place we shall give a kind of diary of the various public talks, indicating their general subject, and describing the atmosphere, reception and reactions of their audiences and of public opinion.[2] In the second part of the chapter we shall then take a closer look at the teaching the talks proposed on the various aspects of the ecumenical question. We shall introduce the main subjects as they arise, and then watch their development, in order to reach an overall picture of the ecumenical teaching developed by the president of the secretariat starting in the preparatory stage of the Council.

Sensitization in Italy

The lectures started very soon, with the first taking place on 9 November 1960, about one week prior to the official start of the work of the preparatory conciliar commissions. It was given at *Ferrara*, the city where the Council of union with the East—the Council of Ferrara and Florence (1401-1439)—had opened five centuries earlier. The lecture marked the opening of the eleventh year of the Advanced Institute of Religious Education run by the Jesuits. The subject was "Christian Unity: Difficulties and Means,"[3] and the talk aroused considerable interest in university circles in the city.

A lecture that was in part similar followed on 18 December at the *Urbanian*

---

1. *Ecumenism*, pp. 38-39 (ct).
2. As regards the various talks, cf. BM, pp. 141-144, 154-157, 158-161, 164-167.
3. Ms. R 1960/23. On this lecture, cf. *OssRom* (11 November 1960), p. 6; also Caprile, I/1, 315; part of the talk is found in *The Unity of Christians*, pp. 47-53, which also contains publishing information for all these lectures, so that we shall simply indicate the pages of this book for the various texts.

University in Rome, and was given to the Catholic Committee of University Lecturers, on the subject "Christian Unity: Problems, Means, Prospects."[4]

During the Week of Prayer for Christian Unity and within the framework of a series of talks organized by the *Studium Christi* organization to mark the nineteenth centenary of St. Paul's arrival in Rome, the cardinal gave a lecture on the ecumenical question at the *Pontifical University of St. Thomas* (the "Angelicum") on 22 January 1961—a lecture to which the organizers gave the somewhat unfortunate and ambiguous title of "The Great Call to Christ's Fold." It was on this occasion that he spoke for the first time about the question of baptism and its consequences for the church-membership of other Christians.[5] For various reasons of a technical nature—the cardinal's soft voice, combined with problems with the microphone—the lecture was not a great success, although it later had a considerable effect when it was published in the review *La Civiltà Cattolica* under an Italian title that can be translated as "Catholics in the Face of the Question of Christian Unity."[6]

Within the framework of a series of lectures on the Council organized by the *Columbianum Institute* of Genoa, Augustin Bea gave a lecture of a very special kind about one week later. It was entitled "The Council on the Path of the Protestants," and described on the one hand the reactions to the announcement of the Council, indicating both the welcoming attitudes and the difficulties raised on the part of the world of the Reformation, and on the other hand the possible contributions the Council could make to solving the problems raised, and meeting the desires of the Protestants.[7] The lecture then appeared in the review *La Civiltà Cattolica*, after considerable reworking and with the addition of extensive references, and was later translated into a number of languages.[8] In this way it exercised considerable influence, for it not only gave Catholics a clearer picture of the real situation, but also (especially through its vast bibliography) showed Christians of the Reformed tradition that the president of the secretariat was very familiar with their publications, opinions, criticisms and possible wishes.

About two months later a series of three lectures in Milan, Lugano and Turin were organized by the organization known as "Friends of *La Civiltà Cattolica*," and added to these was a fourth for the Marian Congregation of Chieri, near Turin. All these talks dealt with the same subject: "Christian Unity: Problems, Means, Prospects."[9] The Turin lecture provided a real surprise. It took place on

---

4. Ms. R 1960/26; the same text was used for the lecture given on 7 January 1961 to the association "Friends of *La Civiltà Cattolica*," whereas the cardinal spoke more spontaneously on 18 January 1961 to the students of the Pontifical Brazilian College, where he lived (cf. the notes, R 1961/32).

5. Ms. R 1961/4. On this lecture, cf. *OssRom* (27 January 1961), p. 6; this report was made on the basis of a summary produced by myself. Cf. also Caprile, I/2, 72-73.

6. Cf. Biblio. 137 for information on translations.

7. Ms. R 1961/5; a report is found in *OssRom* (1 February 1961), p. 5; Caprile, I/2, 73-74.

8. Cf. Biblio. 142.

9. Ms. R 1961/7. The dates of these lectures were as follows: Milan, 8 March; Lugano, 9 March; Turin, 11 March; Marian Congregation of Chieri, 12 March.

a Saturday evening, and in view of the fact that the weather was already fairly mild and that it was held on a weekend, there were fears that the audience would be small, so that it was thought best to hold it in a smaller hall. However, since the Carignano Theater was already booked, the organizers had to accept the larger Alfieri Theater. Despite this, the theater was completely filled, so that from the point of view of public interest it proved the most successful of all the talks so far listed.[10]

The Field Widens

So far the cardinal had been operating solely in Italian circles, and the lectures had been addressed to an Italian public—and I would include the Lugano lecture here, inasmuch as it was given in the Italian-speaking canton of Switzerland. However, journeys and lectures abroad now gradually began.

1. A start was made with the lecture given at the congress of students of the French minor seminaries, which was also attended by their colleagues from Belgium, Holland, Germany and Switzerland. The invitation had come from the delegate of the French episcopacy for seminaries, Bishop R. Johan of Agen. About seventeen hundred people took part in the congress, and on the last day, 2 September 1961, they made a pilgrimage to Strasbourg to the Shrine of St. Odile. And it was here, during mass, that the cardinal spoke to them about "The Priest: Minister of Christian Unity," in the first part describing the necessary training, both general and specific, and in the second the various aspects of practical action. Probably the talk—which was more of a homily—was a little long for the occasion and for the last day of a demanding congress, especially since those present had walked all the way from Strasbourg to St. Odile. However, the negative aspects were in part made up for when the talk was published in the review of the Movement of Seminarians, and then translated into various languages.[11]

2. Among the fruits of the lecture given in Lugano was the fact that it encouraged the Bishop of Basel, Franz von Streng, to invite the cardinal to give two talks in his diocese: one in the federal capital of Berne, and the other in Basel. And a very fitting occasion was chosen: the Day of Prayer and Penance, which had been a national holiday in Switzerland for over a century, and in which all confessions took part.[12] The first talk took place on 18 September in Berne on the subject "The Council and Christian Unity." Starting with the growing desire for full unity, which had been shown in particular on the occasion of the announcement of the Council, the cardinal explained what the Council could do in favor of union in the context of doctrine, canon law, liturgy and ecumenical work.[13]

---

10. During a visit to the Pontifical Seminary at Cuglieri in Sardinia, the president of the secretariat held a "conversation" on the ecumenical question for the seminarians and the local clergy.
11. Ms. R 1961/18; *The Unity of Christians*, pp. 73-93, with publishing information in note 1, p. 73. An ample summary and quotations in Caprile, I/2, 242-244.
12. Cf. *LThK*, II, 842.
13. Ms. R 1961/19; the text was not published. Cf. Caprile, I/2, 245.

The decision to start talking to the Swiss public in a canton with a Protestant majority certainly entailed some risks, but there was no lack of interest. The President of the Swiss Confederation, Dr. Wahlen, and two Catholic ministers of state were present, and the audience of about eighteen hundred, a good number belonging to other confessions, showed lively interest and listened to the speaker with close attention for a whole hour. The next day, however, it turned out that a number of ecumenists both Catholic and non-Catholic were disappointed: "If that's the way things are," they said, "there's not much hope." The question now arose of whether anything could be done to rectify this impression, especially in view of the forthcoming lecture in Basel. The cardinal left Berne the morning after his lecture, and it is Professor Otto Karrer of Lucerne, a life-long friend of Bea, who must be credited with having had the courage and taken the trouble to go to Basel to tell the cardinal about the reactions and suggest corrections or improvements. Bea accepted the advice willingly, and the crossings-out and corrections in his manuscript show how carefully he revised the talk before giving it in Basel.[14] The main corrections concerned the following points: recognition of the religious life lived by other Christians in virtue of the grace of baptism; the fact that the definitions of Councils are historically conditioned by the circumstances in which they are produced, and thus show only certain aspects and not the fullness of revelation; and the statement that differences in liturgical language, ritual and such things are not essential points, and should not therefore act as obstacles to the realization of full unity. Here we see how the cardinal, who had come straight from a Roman environment, had needed first-hand experience of other environments and mentalities in order to develop not so much his basic convictions as his sensitivity to other Christians' viewpoints and use of language.

The Basel lecture was given on 20 September in the Exhibition Hall, which was the second largest in the city, with 2,400 seats. Even so, according to newspaper reports, several hundred people had to stand in the aisles, or in the entrances to the hall.[15] In a report written immediately after the event, I wrote: "Very great interest also from our non-Catholic brethren in both lectures: they made up about 30% of the audience in Berne, and 25% in Basel." It was observed that it was over five centuries, in other words since the Councils of Basel,[16] since a cardinal had spoken there, and that in this sense the lecture was a truly historic event.[17]

3. Two months later, the cardinal visited Switzerland again to give three lectures which were even more important, because of both the level of their audiences and the places chosen: two at the Catholic University of Fribourg, and one in Zurich.

In *Fribourg*, the president of the secretariat spoke to the people of the town

---

14. The comparison is all the more striking if we compare the text as it was originally drafted for Berne, with the text that resulted after all the changes that were introduced at different stages.
15. Cf. *Nationaalzeitung Basel*, CDXXXVII (21 September 1961); also the archive material, Ra 1961/18/6.
16. These were the Councils held in 1431-1437 and 1448; cf. *LThK*, II, 23-25.
17. Cf. *Ecumenism*, p. 39.

in French on 14 November, on the subject "The Council and Christian Unity."[18] The next day, within the framework of the start of the academic year, he gave the inaugural address to the academic authorities, teaching body and students, on the subject "How University Research and Teaching Can Further Christian Unity." This was the first time that the cardinal had spoken on Christian unity in a university. In his lecture he mentioned the vast range of disciplines—philosophy and the history of philosophy, the history of dogmas, dogmatic theology, exegesis, the history of the church, canon law—and pointed out the considerable number of opportunities the various disciplines had to contribute to the cause of unity. For other branches of study, it was more a case, according to circumstances, of working with other Christians and of joint service of the truth. Obviously there was no intention of denying the individual value of the various branches of study, but rather of indicating the many opportunities they had of contributing to the cause of unity while retaining their own specific viewpoints.[19] On this occasion the cardinal was given an honorary doctorate in theology and elected an honorary governor of the university.

The lecture given on 16 November in *Zurich* in the main hall of the Congress Building—the second largest in the city—was entitled "The Council and Christian Unity,"[20] although it was somewhat different from others in a number of ways. There was an entrance fee for the lecture, maybe to cover the rent of the hall, but despite this fact all 2,300 tickets were sold out two days before the date, and other people were still crowding around the ticket office on the day itself. The Protestant Theological Faculty of Zurich had reserved seats for its own professors. In keeping with the Reformed mentality of the people of Zurich, the setting and approach were extremely austere, so that from this point of view some people observed the resemblance to a Reformed religious service. The meeting opened with a few words of greeting from the Vicar General of the Bishop of Coira for the Zurich area, Monsignor Alfred Teobaldi. This was followed by the lecture itself, and a short closing prayer, after which the audience left in deep silence.

After the lecture there was a reception in honor of the speaker, at which the Dean of the Protestant Theological Faculty introduced the professors to him. A report on the event published in the *Osservatore Romano* says that the Protestant Pastor Peter Vogelsanger "thanked the Catholics for having organized such a useful and fraternal meeting. He then said he felt a little uncomfortable to be addressing a cardinal, because the last greeting of this kind dated back to 1521, when Zwingli, who had not yet joined the Reformers, had addressed words of welcome to Cardinal Schiner."[21]

4. The lecture given in *Paris* on 23 January within the framework of the 1962 Week of Prayer for Christian Unity was a major public demonstration in favor of unity. The invitation had come from the Catholic Center of French Intellec-

18. Ms. R 1961/25.

19. Ms. R 1961/26; published in various languages, Biblio. 154.

20. Ms. R 1961/27.

21. *OssRom* (24 November 1961), p. 2. Cf. also the other material, Arch. Ra 1961/22/13.

tuals, and the cardinal spoke on his usual subject of "The Council and Christian Unity." On this occasion, his treatment of the subject essentially reached the definitive form in which it was then published in the original Italian version and the various translations of *The Unity of Christians*, except for the German edition.[22] The audience was exceptional in many ways. Various neighboring halls were linked up with loudspeakers to the main hall of the Mutualité Building, so that the lecture reached an audience of four thousand, a considerable number of whom had settled themselves on the steps in order to have a place in the main hall. Since a meeting of the French bishops was taking place at the same time, six cardinals and another six archbishops and bishops were present at the lecture.[23] There were also high-level representatives of other Christian confessions: the Orthodox Archbishop Meletios, Pastor Marc Boegner, Honorary President of the Protestant Federation of France, an ex-president of the World Council of Churches, and Pastor Roger Schutz of Taizé.

As an example of the impression made by the lecture, we would cite the testimony of a very well-known figure in French Protestantism, the ecumenist Marc Boegner, who spoke about it some years later in an address of welcome to the cardinal: "I am still stirred by the memory of the lecture you gave prior to the opening of the Council at the Mutualité Building in Paris, a lecture that was very startling from many points of view. At the beginning of it you emphasized in abrupt fashion, if I may put it that way, that in no case should the Protestant churches or the churches separated from Rome expect even the slightest diluting of Catholic doctrine, and I publicly thanked you for this, in the name of all those who had listened to you, and particularly the Protestants, for the frankness with which you had ruled out any possibility of 'confusionism' . . . , saying that you were totally opposed to a sentimental ecumenism of the kind that I myself had always tried to speak out against in my writings and lectures, and pointing out to us the immense difficulties that we would have to face up to and then resolve."[24]

In German-Speaking Countries, Especially in Universities

After invitations started to come in from Germany, I asked someone why it had taken them so long to think of inviting the cardinal, for surely it would have been natural for his own country to be the first to issue an invitation to the President of the Secretariat for Christian Unity. The answer was that they had simply not thought it possible to issue a similar invitation to a cardinal of the

---

22. Ms. R 1962/6; *The Unity of Christians* (Biblio. 169), pp. 111-128.

23. Other details in the article of G.F. Arrighi, *OssRom* (2 February 1962), p. 2; Caprile, I/2, 317-318; other material in Arch. Ra 1962/27/18.

24. This is the lecture given within the framework of Cardinal Bea's official visit to the headquarters of the World Council of Churches on 18 February 1965; cf. *Rencontre Oecuménique à Genève*, Col. oecum. 4 (Geneva, 1965) (cf. Biblio. 290), pp. 40-41; other impressions of the lecture are found in *Inf. Cath. Intern.* (15 February 1962), pp. 26ff.

Holy Roman Church! Be that as it may, this last series of lectures is in certain ways the most important, because five of the eight took place in universities, many of them of ancient foundation and still highly respected.

1. The first group of lectures concerned the famous universities of Heidelberg and Tübingen. At that time the former had about ten thousand students, including three thousand Catholics, and the latter nine thousand, including two thousand Catholics. The former had an Evangelical theological faculty, and the second had two theological faculties, one Evangelical and the other Catholic. It was observed at the time that no cardinal had ever spoken at Tübingen since its foundation in 1477, and at Heidelberg since the time of the Reformation.

The first invitation came from the community of Catholic students at *Heidelberg*, and the lecture took place on 9 February 1962. Although the great hall was not normally made available for events organized by the students, in this case it was the rector himself, an Evangelical, who suggested to the governing body that it should be offered for the lecture, and the suggestion was unanimously approved. Interest in the lecture then proved such that another two lecture halls had to be linked up. The cardinal thus spoke to an audience of about three thousand, who listened with close attention for one and a half hours to his explanations on the subject that had now become *de rigueur*, "The Meaning of the Council for Christian Unity."[25]

Two days later, on 11 February, came the turn of *Tübingen University*. Although the lecture took place on a Sunday morning, not only was the great hall filled, but loudspeakers also had to be set up in another large lecture hall. Apart from the introduction, the text of the lecture was the same as that given in Heidelberg. It was calculated that in both cases over one-third of the audience was made up of Evangelicals. And in both cases, apart from the lecture, there was also an extended discussion with the professors of the Evangelical theological faculty.

I would conclude this subsection by quoting from the overall evaluation found in an account I published immediately after the events: "Those most familiar with the environment of the two universities" considered the lectures "of truly historic importance . . . because of the enormous interest they aroused. They also revealed and strengthened an important change in atmosphere, constituted by a great opening to the prospect and nostalgia for union of all the baptized in Christ. A sign of this atmosphere was also the great interest in these events shown by the media and public opinion: press, radio, etc."[26]

2. The following group of talks—one lecture and two homilies—concerned ordinary members of the faithful. The lecture took place in the city of Essen in the industrial area of West Germany, while the homilies were given in East Berlin and West Berlin.

The diocese of *Essen* had only recently been created, but there was already considerable ecumenical cooperation. Even so, interest in the lecture of 9 April,

---

25. Ms. R 1962/9; the text was not published as such.

26. *OssRom* (22 February 1962), p. 2; although the article was not signed, I am sure that I wrote it; it also contains other details. Other material is found in Arch. Ra 1962/28/26.

which had the usual title of "The Importance of the Council for Christian Unity," exceeded the most optimistic forecasts. A public hall and its adjoining rooms could barely contain the crowd, which was calculated at between four and five thousand, and which listened to the speaker in absolute silence for over an hour and a quarter.[27] In the same city the cardinal also held a dialogue with a group known as *Una Sancta*, made up of about 130 people, including twenty-five Evangelical pastors.

The visit to *East Berlin* on 11 April was a particularly sensitive event, especially at that period. An article I wrote at the time says: "The visit had been meticulously planned and approved through careful consultation with all the parties involved, both ecclesiastical and civil, western and eastern."[28] The high point of the visit was a religious service—the only framework possible in the circumstances at that time—in Corpus Christi Church, where the cardinal spoke to a congregation of two thousand on the subject "The Council and Unity in the Light of Faith."[29] My article ends with the words: "It was the general opinion of those who took part that it [the ceremony] marked a high point and represented very great encouragement for that particular portion of the church, both pastors and laity."[30]

In view of the fact that it was after all the same city, the cardinal's talk in *West Berlin* took the same form as that in the eastern sector. He spoke on 12 April on the same subject of attitudes to the Council and the question of unity, and the ceremony took place in the Cathedral of St. John—one of the largest churches in West Berlin—with a congregation of about two thousand. The talk was recorded by local radio stations, which broadcast it later.[31]

In West Berlin the cardinal had an important meeting with the Evangelical Bishop of Berlin and Brandenburg, Dr. Otto Dibelius, and the President of the Evangelical Church of Germany, Dr. Kurt Scharf. The three men discussed joint problems, and in particular the sending of Evangelical observer-delegates to the Council.

My article stresses the great interest of the media in this series of talks: "There was thus a first interview with the radio station of northwestern Germany, followed by one with the radio station for the American sector of Berlin (RIAS), and one with the West Berlin television station, while various other requests for interviews had to be turned down due to lack of time."[32] Press interest was equally great, so that our files contain a large collection of press cuttings covering this whole journey, including over fifty cuttings about the visit to Essen, and as many about the visit to West Berlin.[33]

We would briefly mention two events from the following month of April. The first was a *press conference given in Rome* on 25 April to the Foreign Press

27. Ms. R 1962/14; cf. my article in *OssRom* (4 May 1962), p. 6 (= Ra 1962/29/15).
28. *OssRom* (4 May 1962), p. 6.
29. Ms. R 1962/16.
30. *OssRom* (4 May 1962), p. 6.
31. Cf. the diary of the Berlin visit, Arch. Ra 1962/29/8.
32. *OssRom* (4 May 1962), p. 6.
33. Cf. Arch. Ra 1962/29/18 and 19.

Association, which is made up of the foreign journalists stationed in Italy. About seventy journalists attended, and since they represented in their own way a particularly specialized audience, the conference had echoes on a truly world-wide scale. The breadth of the audience was also reflected in the ground covered by the conference itself, which is well expressed in the title "A Council for the Whole of Mankind" which was given to the relative text in the book *The Unity of Christians*. The speaker, however, also dealt at some length with various other ecumenical aspects of the Council, beginning with doctrine on baptism and its consequences for the church-membership of other Christians, and stretching to the varied and rich opportunities that were opening up for the Council to promote the full union of all the baptized.[34]

3. For a number of reasons the following three lectures constituted the crowning achievement of the cardinal's work to sensitize public opinion.[35] The first took place on 22 May in *Munich*, on the invitation of the Bavarian Catholic Academy, as usual on the subject "The Meaning of the Council for Christian Unity." The Rector of Munich University, an Evangelical, offered the hospitality of the university for the purpose, thus enhancing the academic standing of the event. The request for tickets was such that three other lecture halls had to be linked up with the great hall, giving a capacity of four thousand, including standing-room. Nonetheless, tickets ran out several days before the lecture, and it was calculated that about two thousand people had to be turned away. The audience was also of a first-class caliber, and included the President of the Sovereign State of Bavaria, with three ministers and five under-secretaries, the Rector of Würzburg University, and representatives of the Bavarian Academy of Science and the Evangelical Theological Faculty of Erlangen, as well as about fifty Evangelical pastors. In his words of greeting, the rector of the university stressed what a very rare event it was for a cardinal to speak at the university in the course of its many centuries of existence.

The lecture itself followed similar lines to those given in Heidelberg and Tübingen. As usual, the cardinal warned against any false hopes that the Council could bring about union with any group, and then mentioned the various practical ways in which the Council could effectively foster union. The lecture provided a kind of overview of all that could be said on the ecumenical prospects of the Council at that time, just a few months prior to its opening. Apart from more normal types of publication, the text was also included in the German version of the book *The Unity of Christians*.[36] Before leaving the university, the cardinal also visited the three other lecture halls linked up with the great hall, in order to speak a few words of greeting to the less fortunate audience there.

After the lecture the Cardinal Archbishop of Munich, Julius Döpfner, gave

---

34. Ms. R 1962/30; published in *The Unity of Christians*, pp. 197-208. Less than a week later, this was followed by a lecture in Padua which, like various others, dealt with the importance of the Council for Christian unity; cf. Ms. R 1962/21; the text was not published.

35. For the following, see my article in *OssRom* (7 June 1962), p. 2 (= Arch. Ra 1962/33/7).

36. Ms. R 1962/24; published in *Der Einheit der Christen* (Biblio. 169), pp. 123-144; the lecture was also recorded on a record by Christophorusverlag of Freiburg im Breisgau in 1962.

a reception which lasted almost two hours and took place in a warm, friendly atmosphere. We shall confine ourselves to two examples of the comments that could be heard on the lecture. Cardinal Döpfner told me in amazement: "Cardinal Bea did nothing but expound Catholic doctrine"—as if to say, "So why all the great fuss?" A Protestant pastor in turn said: "The cardinal said some very hard things to us, but he could have said a great many more, and the way in which he said them meant that we would have had to accept them."[37] There are over forty press clippings referring to this lecture.[38]

Two days later, on 24 May, Bea spoke on the same subject at *Vienna University*, where he had been invited by the Viennese Catholic Academy and the Catholic Theological Faculty, from whom he had received an honorary doctorate in theology ten years or so earlier. The audience was not as large here—only one other hall was linked up with the great hall—but it was a top-level one, including academic authorities and teachers, Catholic and non-Catholic church authorities, ministers, and members of the diplomatic corps.

The aforementioned article in the *Osservatore Romano* has this to say about the third lecture, which was held on 26 May in *Innsbruck*: "The little Catholic city of Innsbruck, where the last lecture took place, showed an interest exceeding any forecast. The invitation had come from the Bishop Administrator of Innsbruck, Paulus Rusch, while the organization had been entrusted to the Catholic Institute of Education. It was originally planned that the lecture should be given in the great hall of the university with another two lecture halls linked up with it. However, it proved necessary to put loudspeakers in the Jesuit church too, thus adding a further 2,500 places—which were also soon accounted for. After the welcome by Bishop Rusch, the audience listened to the cardinal for over an hour and a quarter in the most total silence. The representative of the Catholic Institute of Education later said that this event was the most beautiful that had taken place in the institute's sixteen years of existence."[39]

Lectures and Other Commitments Continue during the Summer Vacation

After the incredible amount of work and activity the cardinal had performed over the past ten months, we would certainly imagine that he needed a good, long rest, particularly in view of the forthcoming start of the Council. However, even the summer months were full of engagements, and apart from the eight days of his yearly retreat and six days of relative rest in the family castle of friends in Germany, he never eased up on his activity. We shall confine ourselves to describing his public speaking engagements.[40]

1. The first event was his participation in the *Ecumenical Conference for*

---

37. Cf. my article, *OssRom* (7 June 1962), p. 2.
38. Ra 1962/33/3-8.
39. *OssRom* (7 June 1962), p. 2.
40. We shall discuss his interviews later. This vacation also coincided with Archbishop Dr. M. Ramsey's visit, which we mentioned in our previous chapter.

Priests of England and Wales, organized by the Archbishop of Liverpool, John Carmel Heenan, a member of the Secretariat for Christian Unity. The meeting was held at Heythrop College, Oxfordshire, from 6 to 10 August, and was attended by about seventy priests. The cardinal gave the keynote talk on "The Priest: Minister of Christian Unity," developing and considerably expanding what he had said to the French seminarians on this subject a year earlier.[41]

A practical problem connected with this particular lecture was the question of the language to be used, since the cardinal did not speak English—although he could read it. The organizers suggested that he should speak in Latin, saying that the priests would certainly understand him, but Bea was not too convinced. It happened that only a few months prior to this he had given an interview for a documentary produced by the National Council of Catholic Men of the United States.[42] The television crew thought that the interview had gone fairly well, so the cardinal took heart and decided to give the present lecture in English. When the organizers were told about this decision, we received a worried answer, begging us not to do it, and explaining that the English were very demanding, etc. However, there was no going back now. The lecture had already been translated into English and there was no time to translate it into Latin. In order to obtain a little practice with the language, the cardinal arrived in England four or five days in advance, so that he was able to practice the lecture with a fellow Jesuit in London. The result was that he now gave his first lecture in English at the age of eighty-one. When he had finished, after one hour and twenty minutes, one of the organizers told me enthusiastically: "He was wonderful. We understood every word." This success was to be the prelude and also the training-ground for the lectures the cardinal would give the following year in the United States.

The president of the secretariat attended all the sessions during the three and a half days of the meeting, and at the end he was asked to summarize the results. Since he had very little time for preparation, he used Latin this time, speaking for about forty minutes.[43]

In a report that Archbishop Heenan wrote for the English bishops he described the impression made by the president of the secretariat as follows: "Those [of the priests] who had come to the conference out of obedience to their superiors and without any great attraction for ecumenical work soon became enthusiastic. This was largely due to the presence of Cardinal Bea. If hitherto any had thought his judgment unsound on English religious affairs they now discovered the cardinal to be a well informed man of balanced views, great learning and evident piety. He guided us magnificently and in the most benevolent way."[44]

2. The talk he was asked to give in the framework of the *Congress of*

---

41. Ms. R 1962/36; publishing details, Biblio. 216, and in *The Unity of Christians,* pp. 73-93. It is also interesting to see how one of the participants looked back on the event: R.L. Stewart, "Ten Years Since Heythrop," *One in Christ,* VIII (1972), 264-276.

42. This was a documentary on various aspects of the Council; Ms. R 1962/26.

43. Cf. Ms. R 1962/37. English translation = Biblio. 216.

44. Arch. Ra 1962/35/31.

Catholics in Hannover was rather different from others, both because of the type of audience and also the subject chosen. Catholics represent a bare thirteen percent of the population in Hannover, and it was the first time since the Second World War—apart from the meeting in Berlin—that a congress of Catholics had been held in such an area. Moreover, there was still some deep-rooted resistance to ecumenism among the Evangelical population. Although it is true that quite a number of Evangelicals had offered hospitality to the Catholics who took part in the congress, the general atmosphere was such that at the reception given by the Evangelical Bishop of Hannover, Dr. M. Lilje, great attention was paid to what the Germans call "confessional arithmetic," in other words, making sure that both confessions were represented with exactly the same number of guests. Bishop Lilje also sent a message of good wishes to the congress, but he received so much criticism from certain circles in his own church both over the reception and this message that he felt called upon to answer his critics in the course of a crowded religious service before the congress was even over.[45]

These were thus the atmosphere and background for an academic meeting held on the subject "Niels Stensen and Our Times." Stensen was a seventeenth-century Danish Lutheran, a scholar of world fame, who converted to the Catholic faith, became a priest, and was nominated Apostolic Vicar for the "northern missions" of Germany in 1677.[46]

Bearing in mind that the subject was a convert, and also the general atmosphere, it is not difficult to imagine the delicate nature of the task entrusted to the cardinal when he was asked to give the keynote paper under the title "Niels Stensen and the Cause of Christian Unity." There was an all-too-obvious danger that the subject could be misunderstood as meaning that the promotion of unity was basically a form of propaganda for conversions.[47] The cardinal was very well aware of the delicacy of his task, but instead of trying to sidestep the issue, he devoted much time and care to study of Stensen in relation to the cause of ecumenism. The archives contain twelve pages of typewritten notes made by the cardinal, which were then used as the basis for the talk.[48]

In the lecture given on 23 August the cardinal thus took this painstaking and in-depth background work as his basis, explaining first of all that the fundamental presupposition in the search for unity was a deep religious spirit of the kind that can be seen in Niels Stensen, starting with the upbringing he received within his Lutheran family. Without this religious life, ecumenism would lack its soul. The second point concerned the path toward unity. In this regard, Stensen allows us to see an example of the concern to recognize all the good that is found in

---

45. Cf. "Im Nächsten der Bruder suchen. Landesbischof Lilje antwortet seinen Kiritikern," *Offiz. Festzeitung des 79. Kirchentages*, 2nd ed., p. 20 (= Arch. Ra 1962/36/38).

46. For Niels Stensen, cf. *LThK*, IX, 1037-1038. In October 1988 Stensen was beatified by Pope John Paul II.

47. Later on the conciliar Decree on Ecumenism would warn that "it is evident that the work of preparing and reconciling those individuals who wish for full Catholic communion is of its nature distinct from ecumenical action," although it immediately added that "there is no opposition between the two, since both proceed from the marvelous ways of God" (*UR*, 4).

48. Arch. Ra 1962/36/12.

our separated brethren, which gives rise to a true and deep respect and love. This is the attitude with which we must set out in search of the truth, seeking to gain a true knowledge of our own faith and also that of other Christians. Hence the importance of theological conversations conducted with deep respect and love for our dialogue partner, and with great care not to use coercion on his or her intelligence or will, aiming at friendly rapprochement, while avoiding the false irenicism that disguises or hides the truth. Lastly, the cardinal used Stensen as an example to describe the way in which all Christians can and must contribute to the cause of unity: prayer, authentic Christian life, and cooperation in various fields not directly concerned with faith. The fruit of such cooperation would then be a growth in mutual knowledge, respect and love.[49]

The lecture received a very positive reception. For example, the next day an important Evangelical figure, an ex-bishop, asked me to convey his thanks to the cardinal for his lecture. When I asked him if he had some particular reason for this gratitude, the answer was: "I have listened to ecumenical talks more than once, and very often I have felt uncomfortable because of the efforts the speakers made to stretch their own convictions in order to meet those of other confessions. The cardinal, on the other hand, was perfectly frank and honest in stating that the dogmas of faith cannot be touched."

As concerns the significance that the lecture had for the Congress of Catholics as a whole, a very highly respected German journalist wrote that Cardinal Bea had made the most important contribution toward giving the congress an ecumenical orientation, especially through his stress on the fundamental importance of the sacrament of baptism, the need to recognize all the good found in other Christian brethren, and the sincere search for the truth.[50]

A Remarkably Far-Reaching Activity

Let us in conclusion try to take an overall look at the activity developed by the president of the secretariat to increase public sensitivity to the cause of unity. In under two years he gave twenty-six public talks in six European countries. Sixteen were to a fairly general audience, while ten were to more specialized or university audiences. Here, however, we must fill out the information provided in our chronological account.

In the first place we would note the care the cardinal devoted to *the clergy*, because of his awareness of their fundamental role in passing on ecumenical ideas and attitudes to their flocks. Thus apart from the two lectures already mentioned on the priest as minister of Christian unity, we would note that during his journeys he often held "conversations" for groups of local clergy—and that

49. Cf. Ms. R 1962/39; for publishing details, cf. Biblio. 163, 215. We have given a fuller summary of this talk because it involved a more difficult subject.

50. Cf. O. Rögele, "Das Ereignis von Hannover," *Rhenischer Merkur*, XXXV (31 August 1962), 2 (= Arch. Ra 1962/36/37).

these groups sometimes exceeded one hundred. My notes show that there were fourteen such meetings, which were maybe in some ways even more effective than the main lectures, because of their more spontaneous and immediate character.

His "comments" on the ecumenical intentions of the *Apostleship of Prayer* represented another form of fairly widespread influence on broad sectors of the faithful. The Apostleship of Prayer is an international association of the faithful that was started in the last century and was led for the most part by the Society of Jesus. During the period in question it was calculated that it had over thirty million members world-wide. Each month a particular general intention and a missionary one, chosen and blessed by the pope himself, were entrusted to the zeal, prayer and sacrifice of these thirty million members. The Roman center and the national and local leaders cooperated on an explanation of these intentions, and this was printed in a hundred publications, most of them bearing the title *The Messenger of the Sacred Heart*, which at that time had a circulation of about two and a half million world-wide. The explanation was also circulated in a condensed form in over fourteen million pamphlets for the use of the association. Starting in 1961, the president of the secretariat agreed that he would personally write the comment for the ecumenical intention, which was usually assigned to the month of January, together with the Week of Prayer for Christian Unity. It is easy to see how this activity enabled him to obtain a grassroots penetration of ecumenical thought among vast sectors of the faithful. And it was not only a case of transmitting an idea, for it also obtained a vast spiritual contribution of prayer and sacrifice in favor of ecumenism—and the importance of such a contribution was always very warmly mentioned in the cardinal's lectures.[51]

Apart from this, there was also the cardinal's concern to obtain the help of *the mass media*. We saw in one of our previous chapters that from the moment it was first suggested that something practical should be done for the union of Christians, emphasis was placed on the need for particular attention to press relations—and relations with the mass media in general. The cardinal always bore this need in mind, and therefore did what he could to ensure that the media were his allies in his ecumenical activity. We have already seen practical examples of this in the bibliographical and other information provided in the course of our chronological account. Effective interaction was developed between the great interest shown by the press on the one hand, and the cardinal's concern to provide them with the necessary material on the other, so that when he gave his lectures he made a point of providing the daily press with a summary of the lecture, and later also with quotes so that journalists would be in a position to produce their own individual reports.[52]

---

51. One such comment is found in *The Unity of Christians*, pp. 54-63. For the manuscripts of other comments, cf. R 1961/1; R 1962/30. We shall speak of the ecumenical significance of prayer and sacrifice later.

52. More than once the cardinal also expressed immediate reactions to events or ecumenical situations; cf. Biblio. 134; Mss. 1962/3; 1962/4; 1962/40.

In this concern over the media, and particularly the press, the cardinal did not think only of his own field of work, but also of the general interests of the Council. Thus he submitted a memorandum to Pope John XXIII in May 1962, listing suggestions for the solution of *the problem of the press in connection with the Council*—suggestions that in a certain way foreshadowed the procedures later laid down by Paul VI for the second period of the Council (fall 1963).[53] And this same concern led the cardinal to agree to take part in a meeting dedicated to this subject, which was held at the end of May 1962 at St. George's Theological College in Frankfurt.

In our account we have repeatedly mentioned the interviews the president of the secretariat granted to press, radio and television. In his book *Ecumenism in Focus* the cardinal observes, as we have seen, that he gave twenty-five in the first nine months of 1962 alone.[54] In the collection of his writings we find twenty-seven manuscripts of interviews for the whole period under consideration here,[55] and apart from these we should add another sixteen interviews he gave without written texts during his various journeys between November 1961 and September 1962. Leaving aside these latter sixteen, which covered the countries where the various lectures were given, we would note that the twenty-seven for which we have manuscripts were divided among various countries as follows: Italy, five; Germany, four; France and England, three each; Switzerland and the United States, two each; and Holland and Spain, one each. We would observe lastly that sixteen of these interviews were for the press, eight for radio, and seventeen for television.

The editor of a well-known English paper referred to the publicity enjoyed by the Secretariat for Christian Unity, observing: "Had they spent a million dollars, they'd never have been this successful." The president of the secretariat had invested no money, but he had known how to take advantage of the very lively interest of the mass media in the Council and particularly in the ecumenical question, and had devoted much time and effort to the matter, establishing an atmosphere of mutual trust, thus stimulating further interest and fruitful cooperation.

How Could the Council Contribute to the Cause of Unity?

As can be seen, we are now moving on to *the content* of the lectures. However, we must start by pointing out that this will be a very much abbreviated survey: since most of the lectures were published by the cardinal himself, all we have to give here are the major points, while anyone who wishes for further information can very easily find it by following the bibliographical indications given in the notes. Obviously, the fact that we are discussing preparations for the Council means that we shall base ourselves chiefly on the large group of

---

53. On the situation concerning the press at that time, cf. Caprile, I/2, 128, 450-452, 455-458.
54. Cf. *Ecumenism*, p. 39.
55. For 1959-1960 there were two; for 1961, eleven; and for 1962, fourteen. Cf. also the list in *L'unione dei cristiani*, pp. 261-262.

lectures that discuss the ecumenical opportunities of the Council[56]—although we shall not of course neglect the others.[57]

As introduction we shall make some fairly general observations, in the first place noting what the Council would *not* be able to do. The president of the secretariat was categorical and vocal in stating—against any over-optimism, not to say false hopes—that the Council would not be able to bring about full union with any given group of Christians.[58] In this connection he was basing himself firstly on the thought of Pope John XXIII, who in various ways spoke only of an indirect contribution.[59] Here we can quote his well-known reference to union with the eastern churches, where he used concepts indicating only gradual union: "Rapprochement, then coming closer together, and finally perfect union."[60] For his part the cardinal did not hesitate to state that the realization of full unity with any group was unthinkable at the present time.[61]

The cardinal organized *the positive opportunities* provided by the Council around three concepts: it would be able to give an indirect contribution in the field of truth, and in that of love[62]; moreover, it would be able to make a direct

---

56. In order to make our summary as rich as possible, we shall base ourselves on all the material of the lectures, including those that were never published, where we shall be referring to their manuscripts. As concerns the published ones, the major part of these are found in the volume *L'unione dei cristiani* and were for the most part originally given in Italian. However, there are some exceptions, and the following is a list giving the language and the relative book, together with the page numbers in the English-language version, *The Unity of Christians*:

1.) The Fribourg lecture, "How University Research and Teaching Can Further Christian Unity" (*The Unity of Christians*, pp. 94-110) was given in German, and the original is found in *Die Einheit der Christen*, pp. 105-122.

2) The Paris lecture "The Council and Christian Unity" (*The Unity of Christians*, pp. 111-128) was given in French, and the original is found in *Pour l'unité des chrétiens*, pp. 123-145.

3) This lecture was given in a different form in Munich, and the German original is found in *Die Einheit der Christen*, pp. 123-144.

4) The Heythrop lecture "The Priest: Minister of Unity" (*The Unity of Christians*, pp. 73-93) was given in English.

When we are not quoting directly from this material but simply referring to it, we shall merely indicate the reference in *The Unity of Christians*, whereas in the case of direct quotes from texts originally in some language other than English, we shall add a reference to the original, so that readers can check the fidelity of the translation if they so wish.

57. The lectures can be grouped under three headings: a first group is made up of the three concerned with specific sectors, on the one hand the priest as "minister of unity" (*The Unity of Christians*, pp. 73-93), on the other academic work in the service of unity (Biblio. 154); a second group of five lectures deals with the ecumenical question without reference to the Council (Biblio. 137, 163, 194, 199); and the third and by far the largest group speaks about the significance of the Council for unity.

58. We find such statements in almost all the talks: cf. R 1960/23, p. 18; R 1961/19, p. 2; R 1961/27, p. 3; R 1962/20, p. 5.

59. Cf. R 1960/23, p. 18 (= *AAS*, LI [1959], 511). The same view is often repeated in the lectures: cf. R 1961/4, p. 1; R 1961/5, p. 1; R 1961/7, p. 7; R 1961/25, p. 4; R 1961/27, p. 3; R 1962/6, p. 5.

60. *AD*, I, 19, cited in R 1960/23, p. 19.

61. Cf. R 1962/9, p. 6; R 1962/14, p. 4.

62. These two ideas of truth and love in their own way constitute the framework of at least some of the lectures in the first group (for example those in Ferrara and at the University of St. Thomas

contribution by exercising considerable influence on the ecumenical movement itself. Our presentation will follow the same approach.

Inasmuch as the concepts of truth and love constitute the corner-stones of the cardinal's thought, let us immediately add a brief explanation. These concepts are drawn from the two key elements of truth and love in the Letter to the Ephesians, and the relative text is cited as follows in the Paris talk: "Doing the truth in love, we are to grow up in every way into him who is the head, into Christ" (4:15). The cardinal immediately comments: "Truth and love are inseparable in this task. Truth without love becomes intolerant and repelling; love without truth is blind and cannot endure. So the Council must keep truth and love closely bound together."[63]

The Contribution of the Council in the Field of the Truth

1. Here too we see first of all what the Council *cannot* do. The speaker is very definite: "It is evident that there can be no question in the Council of seeking a compromise on dogma, on divinely revealed doctrine. We would be showing a very misguided love for unity and our separated brethren if we allowed them to hope that we will not demand of them anything more than the recognition of 'fundamental articles,' that we will no longer require their acceptance of the dogmatic decrees of the Council of Trent, or that we are ready to revise the dogma of the primacy or the infallibility of the pope."[64]

And the *motivation* can be stated very briefly: it was the attitude and practice of the apostles.[65] And the Councils have acted in exactly the same way: "All the Councils have realized this and they have never decreed *new* articles of faith or revised old ones; their role has always been to decide, with the help of the Holy Spirit and in accordance with scripture and the tradition of the church, what is a divinely revealed truth. The Second Vatican Council will act likewise. It will not, through some mistaken idea of irenistic aims, dilute or explain away any truths of the faith."[66]

Put *in positive terms*, it is a question of "determining the truth and bearing witness to it: the whole undivided, undiluted Catholic truth, as made known by

---

in Rome), so that they too correspond to the general approach we have chosen.

63. *Unity of Christians*, p. 115 (ct); *Pour l'unité des chrétiens*, p. 128. In the Padua lecture, his thinking shows some small differences: "the truth . . . intolerant *and divisive*; love . . . *cannot give lasting fruit*" (cf. R 1962/21, p. 5). It is interesting to observe that the two elements with the relative comment appear for the first time in the Zurich lecture (R 1961/27, p. 5), but then return in those in Heidelberg (R 1962/9, p. 8), Essen (R 1962/14, p. 4), Berlin (R 1962/16, p. 6) and Munich (*Die Einheit der Christen*, pp. 126-127).

64. *The Unity of Christians*, p. 116; *Pour l'unité des chrétiens*, p. 129. Cf. also *The Unity of Christians*, pp. 108, 200-201.

65. Cf. Gal. 1:8; 1 Cor. 4:1; *The Unity of Christians*, p. 116. For detailed support from sacred scripture, cf. *The Unity of Christians*, pp. 21-25.

66. *The Unity of Christians*, pp. 116-117; *Pour l'unité des chrétiens*, pp. 129-130. This is why the speaker refutes accusations of guilt on the part of the church in the sense that it has been mistaken in its teaching; cf. for example *The Unity of Christians*, pp. 122-123.

scripture and tradition and laid down by the teaching authority of the church."[67] This attitude springs from a "spirit of zealous love: love of truth, of unity, of the souls of the faithful, and also of those of the wanderers."[68]

2. Moreover, the Council can draw *the elements important for unity* from the fullness of revelation. Starting with the statement in the encyclical of Pius XII *Humani generis* that the sources of revelation "contain treasures so varied and so rich that they must ever prove inexhaustible,"[69] the cardinal explains that for the Council, "Here is a wide field for theological investigation—in this treasury of revealed truth, to search out and find those elements which, in *our* time, are most important for our separated brethren. Thus, in clarifying certain matters that are particularly pertinent to our time, the Council not only can dispel much misunderstanding about Catholic doctrine, but can also draw out from the depths and riches of the truths of faith those truths which are of special concern today."[70] Further, "The Council will be able to take into account the deepest present-day hopes of our separated brethren, their problems and difficulties, and highlight the specific aspects of revealed doctrine that provide a response to these expectations and needs."[71]

(a) And what are the particular points of faith that need more explanation and clarification today? It is surprising to see how much foresight the president of the secretariat showed in discerning even then what more recent developments of ecumenism have described as the crux of the ecumenical problem, in other words, the question of the church, for this "and *not*, for example, the question of justification or of the mass as a sacrifice," is the central problem. "Protestants themselves are becoming more and more aware of this, so much so that nowadays people are speaking of a 'rediscovery' of the church."[72] He says elsewhere that this is the area in which we find the deepest gulf dividing us from our brethren of the Reformed tradition.[73] And the question is also involved to a certain extent in our relations with the Orthodox.[74]

The speaker expands on the questions involved here: "Who holds authority in the church? What is the extent of this authority? Can it oblige the faithful in conscience to believe certain things and to obey certain laws? Is this authority, in certain cases and within certain limits, really infallible; that is, by virtue of the very special help of the Holy Spirit is it preserved from error?"[75] Indeed,

---

67. *The Unity of Christians*, p. 108 (ct); *Die Einheit der Christen*, p. 120.
68. *The Unity of Christians*, p. 24; *L'unione dei cristiani*, p. 9.
69. *AAS*, XLII (1950), 568; English translation CTS (London, 1961), para. 21.
70. *The Unity of Christians*, p. 118; *Pour l'unité des chrétiens*, p. 131. Similarly, cf. R 1961/25, p. 7; R 1962/9, p. 14; R 1962/14, p. 11.
71. R 1962/21, p. 8.
72. *The Unity of Christians*, p. 145 (ct); *L'unione dei cristiani*, p. 154. Similarly, cf. R 1961/19, pp. 8-9; R 1961/25, p. 8.
73. Cf. R 1962/9, p. 16; R 1962/14, p. 13.
74. Cf. *The Unity of Christians*, p. 120; R 1961/19, pp. 8-9. It is interesting to see that although Bea's evaluation here was limited to the ecumenical aspect, it agrees with Paul VI's statement in his inaugural address for the second period, in other words that the church is far and away the main subject of the Second Vatican Council; cf. *CDD*, p. 906.
75. *The Unity of Christians*, p. 203; *L'unione dei cristiani*, pp. 229-230. Cf. also *The Unity of*

"the question of the nature of the church has been posed since the time of the Council of Trent. But neither at that Council nor at the First Vatican Council was it possible to deal thoroughly and completely with that fundamental question. It is for the coming Council to complete the task. . . ."[76]

The path to full consideration of the question of the church has now "been paved by theological study and research, as well as by the directives compiled and authoritatively set out in the encyclical *Mystici corporis* of Pius XII on the church as the mystical body of Christ."[77] This encyclical highlights the fact that the Holy Spirit is the "soul," the vital principle, of this supernatural body; although it is a well-structured human body, it is divinely vivified and guided; and in this light the magisterium of the church can be recognized simply as a vital manifestation, assisted by the Holy Spirit, of that same Christ who gave us revelation.[78]

The speaker also indicates certain facts that help comprehension of *papal primacy* today, for this is "the most difficult point for our separated brethren."[79] These would include the example of Pope John XXIII, who "created a much more favorable climate in showing by his charity, good will and humility that 'the Roman Church understands and exercises the primacy . . . not as an ambition to dominate but, as it ought to be, a service, a *diaconia*.' "[80]

Moreover, the Council can fully expound *the overall idea of the unity of the church*: "Unity of *faith* stands paramount: that is, the profession of the same faith by all who are baptized." However, "Christian unity is concerned also with unity in the use of *the means of grace* which are the sacraments." Lastly, "unity would not be perfect . . . unless it included *submissiveness* to those commissioned by God to guide and rule us in matters of faith and practice, that is, to the shepherds of the flock, successors of the apostles, united among themselves and united with the chief shepherd, the successor of St. Peter, the Bishop of Rome."[81] Here too, concludes the cardinal, "it is for the Council guided by the Holy Spirit, the Spirit of the mystical body of Christ, to speak the decisive word."[82]

(b) Still in the field of truth, it is not simply a case, however, of a commitment

---

Christians, pp. 120-121; R 1961/27, p. 7; R 1962/21, p. 9.

76. *The Unity of Christians*, p. 120; *Pour l'unité des chrétiens*, p. 134.

77. *The Unity of Christians*, p. 146; *L'unione dei cristiani*, p. 154.

78. Cf. R 1961/19, p. 9.

79. *The Unity of Christians*, p. 121; *Pour l'unité des chrétiens*, p. 134.

80. *The Unity of Christians*, p. 121; *Pour l'unité des chrétiens*, pp. 134-135; *Die Einheit der Christen*, pp. 137-138. Cf. R 1962/14, p. 13.

81. *The Unity of Christians*, pp. 80, 81; *L'unione dei cristiani*, p. 75. Cf. *The Unity of Christians*, p. 52; R 1961/7, pp. 2-3; R 1961/18, pp. 4/5.

82. *The Unity of Christians*, p. 124; *Pour l'unité des chrétiens*, p. 138. Cf. also R 1961/27, pp. 10-11; R 1962/9, p. 18. Still within the context of the doctrine of the church, the cardinal often notes that the Council also has the task of clarifying *the position of the laity* in the church: cf. *The Unity of Christians*, pp. 124, 126; R 1961/19, p. 11; R 1961/25, p. 11; R 1961/27, p. 11; R 1962/9, p. 19; R 1962/14, p. 15. Here we could also mention the speaker's clarifications on the question of mariology, but since this subject was considered in only one lecture (cf. *Die Einheit der Christen*, pp. 138-139), the reader can simply read this.

to learning more about revealed truth, but also of overcoming the serious obstacles of *ignorance and prejudice*. Here the speaker quotes Pope Pius XI, who said that "Catholics are sometimes lacking in a due appreciation of their separated brethren" of the East.[83] Bea adds: "We must confess loyally and honestly that in many other countries also, and among Catholics and Protestants, there are on both sides many prejudices, and much resentment and mistrust."[84]

Positively stated, this means that we must learn *how our Christian brethren understand revealed truth*: "In what divides us, it is very often not a case of a difference in doctrine itself, but rather of ignorance and misunderstandings concerning what the other believes and confesses."[85] A methodological principle for this task is borrowed from Karl Barth, who said that study "to attain this goal, the philosophical treatment of a divergent opinion, must not content itself with establishing . . . what is 'said,' but will go beyond the words and make clear what is 'meant,' that is, the content and real significance of the words."[86]

With this aim in mind the cardinal quotes Pope John XXIII's orientation for the Council: "So we must, as the Holy Father says, 'by going back to the pure sources of revelation and tradition, give new value and force to the very substance of Christian thought and living, of which the church has been for centuries the guardian and teacher.' "[87]

However, there is another important element in such a return to the sources: in the effort to give new value and force to Christian thought and living, we must bear in mind the *language* and mentality of other Christians: "The Council can explain Catholic doctrine in a way that takes account of the change in theological language of our separated brethren that has occurred since the days of the separation."[88] Similarly, "Truth can be better explained by taking account of the mentality and language of modern man or of one or another group of our separated brethren in order to enable them to understand it better."[89]

---

83. *The Unity of Christians*, p. 89, quoting Pius XI, Address of 8 January 1927, *Discorsi di Pio XI* (Turin, 1959), I, 671. Similarly, cf. R 1962/9, p. 13; R 1962/14, p. 5; *Die Einheit der Christen*, p. 131.
84. *The Unity of Christians*, p. 89.
85. "Niels Stensen und das Anliegen der Einheit der Christen" (Biblio. 215), p. 290. In a discourse given in Constantinople, Paul VI referred to the efforts of St. Hilary and St. Athanasius to recognize "the identity of faith behind differences in vocabulary"; *AAS*, LIX (1967), 841.
86. *The Unity of Christians*, p. 97; *Die Einheit der Christen*, p. 108.
87. *The Unity of Christians*, pp. 117-118; *Pour l'unité des chrétiens*, p. 131. For the pope's words, cf. *AAS*, LII (1960), 1006.
88. R 1962/21, p. 8. Cf. also R 1961/7, p. 7.
89. *The Unity of Christians*, p. 201; *L'unione dei cristiani*, p. 228. This can be compared with a similar idea found in the address Pope John XXIII gave at the opening of the Council, when he said that we must set forth "the authentic doctrine, which, however, should be studied and expounded through the methods of research and through the literary forms of modern thought." And the pope gave the reasons for this requirement by making an important distinction: "The substance of the ancient doctrine of the deposit of faith is one thing, and the way in which it is presented is another"; *AAS*, LIV (1962), 792; English translation in Walter M. Abbott (gen. ed.), *The Documents of Vatican II* (New York, 1966), p. 715. This distinction then found its place in the conciliar Constitution on the Church in the Modern World (*GS*, 62). The similarity between the thinking of Pope John and Bea has led some people to wonder whether Bea helped

Baptism and Its Effects for Church-Membership

An important point on which Bea hoped the Council would provide clarification was that of the church-membership of Christians separated from us. According to Cardinal Johannes Willebrands, who worked more closely with the president than anyone else and thus had a first-hand view of his activity, the cardinal "worked out and expounded" this point of doctrine "to the general public of the church better maybe than anybody."[90]

We shall first try to give an idea of *the problem* facing the cardinal in this field, and how he set about solving it. For the most part we shall follow the lines of the lecture given in January 1961, where the question was dealt with more fully than anywhere else.[91]

The problem sprang from a solemn passage in the encyclical *Mystici corporis* of Pius XII, which stated: "Only those are to be accounted really members of the church who have been regenerated in the waters of baptism and profess the true faith, and have not cut themselves off from the structure of the body by their own unhappy act or been severed therefrom for very grave crimes, by the legitimate authority."[92]

The president of the secretariat takes various statements of Pope John XXIII as his starting point, particularly a passage from the "programmatic" encyclical *Ad Petri cathedram*, where the pope refers to other Christians as his own children and brethren: "Allow us to express our affection for you and to call you sons and brothers. . . . We address you, then, as brothers even though you are separated from us, for, as St. Augustine said: 'Whether they like it or not, they are our brothers. They will only cease to be our brothers when they cease to say: *Our Father.*' "[93]

In this connection the cardinal formulates the following question: What is the underlying reason for the language used by the pope? And he answers by referring to the doctrine on baptism found in the liturgical encyclical of Pius XII, *Mediator Dei,* which states that with baptism the baptized "become by a common title members of the mystical body of Christ."[94] The speaker adds that

prepare the pope's address. However, to the best of my knowledge there was no question of this. Moreover, we have what I would consider decisive evidence to the contrary in Monsignor L.F. Capovilla's statement that the pope said: "I should like it known—not in order to obtain credit for myself, but more to shoulder my own responsibility—that it [the speech] is my own from beginning to end"; L.F. Capovilla, *Giovanni XXIII, Quindici letture* (Rome, 1978), p. 197.

90. *Simposio*, p. 8; on the same subject, cf. E. Lanne, "La contribution du Cardinal Bea à la question du baptême et l'unité des chrétiens," in *Simposio*, pp. 159-185. The reader will recall that Bea had spoken about this question in the Central Preparatory Commission. Here we shall try to examine it in greater depth.

91. Good summaries of the cardinal's thought in this connection are also found in *The Unity of Christians*, pp. 201-202; *Die Einheit der Christen*, pp. 127-128; R 1962/9, pp. 8-9, R 1962/21, p. 6. On this whole question, cf. also the very full study of Lanne, "La contribution du Cardinal Bea." In our presentation of Bea's thought we shall follow the article of Cardinal J. Willebrands, in *Simposio*, pp. 8-10. since it seems very faithful to Bea's thought.

92. *AAS*, XXXV (1943), 202-203, quoted in *The Unity of Christians*, p. 30.

93. *AAS*, LI (1959), 515-516, quoted in *The Unity of Christians*, p. 26.

this doctrine of the encyclical is simply "the crystalization of the teaching of St. Paul that Christ, though he has many members, is 'a single body,' and this because of baptism. Paul actually says: 'By one Spirit we were all baptized into one body—Jews or Greeks, slaves or free' (1 Cor. 12:13). With baptism, he writes to the Galatians (3:27), we have 'put on Christ' and are all '*one* in Christ Jesus.' "[95] Bea also draws attention to the way in which this New Testament teaching is codified in juridical terms in the Code of Canon Law then in force, which says: "By baptism man is constituted a person in the church of Christ with all the rights and duties of Christians, unless, in the case of rights, there is some impediment which prevents their exercise."[96]

The cardinal then sums up his point, observing: "Now notice that the teaching of *Mediator Dei* and St. Paul is unqualified; it states what is always effected by the actual reception of baptism, provided, of course, that it is valid. So this must somehow hold good for our separated brethren also, even though they are separated from the Holy See as a result of heresy or schism inherited from their ancestors."[97]

In the light of this line of reasoning, the passage from *Mystici corporis* quoted above is interpreted as follows: ". . . the encyclical *Mystici corporis* denies that heretics and schismatics belong to the mystical body, which is the church, *only in the full sense* in which Catholics are said to belong to it. That is, it denies *full* sharing in the life which Christ communicates to his church, and in the divine Spirit of Christ which is the soul and life of the church, . . . but the encyclical *does not by any means rule out* all *forms of membership of the church or deny* all *influence of the grace of Christ*."[98]

This reference to the influence of the grace of Christ paves the way for the following statements: "Because fundamentally, even if not fully, they belong to the church, they also have the benefit of the influence of *God's grace*. . . . The Holy Spirit . . . works in a special and powerful way in them too, although, as we have said, not in such a full manner as in the members visibly united with the Catholic Church."[99]

---

94. *AAS*, XXXIX (1947), 555, quoted in *The Unity of Christians*, p. 30.

95. *The Unity of Christians*, p. 30 (ct); *L'unione dei cristiani*, p. 15.

96. Canon 87, quoted in *The Unity of Christians*, p. 30.

97. *The Unity of Christians*, p. 30; *L'unione dei cristiani*, p. 15.

98. *The Unity of Christians*, pp. 31-32; *L'unione dei cristiani*, p. 17. In other lectures, the speaker draws attention to another passage from the same encyclical, in which Pope Pius XII invited people to pray for those who are separated from the visible body of the church (cf. *AAS*, XXXV [1943], 243); the speaker argues that the use of the adjective "visible" is a fairly clear indication that the encyclical does not consider other Christians as separated from "the body of the church" but only from the *visible* body. In this connection, cf. *Die Einheit der Christen*, p. 127; R 1962/9, p. 8.

99. *The Unity of Christians*, p. 33; *L'unione dei cristiani*, p. 19. In explaining the cardinal's teaching in this area, Romano Amerio, *Jota unum* (Milan/Naples, 1985), p. 466, draws the conclusion (attributing it to the cardinal, and referring to *OssRom* [27 April 1962]) that other Christians "are therefore in a situation of salvation no different from that of Catholics." As we have seen, the cardinal explicitly says that the Holy Spirit does not work in other Christians "in such a full manner as in the members visibly united with the Catholic Church."

Cardinal Willebrands speaks about the impression that the explanation of this doctrine made on other Christians, saying: "Only those who personally witnessed it can appreciate how carefully other Christians listened when Bea expounded these thoughts. They had often complained in the past that Catholics treated them as if they were not baptized, but pagan. And here they were hearing a highly authoritative voice speaking a new language, and they opened themselves up in trust."[100] The words spoken by the Archbishop of Canterbury, Dr. Michael Ramsey, on the occasion of his official visit to Rome in 1966 are significant in this connection: "You, Your Eminence, in your own teaching and writing have emphasized ceaselessly the doctrine of holy baptism and the brotherhood of the baptized. We shall try to learn and to practice the lesson you teach us."[101]

In his study Cardinal Willebrands points out what a novelty the line taken by the president of the secretariat really was at that time: "The idea of our common baptism and its ecumenical consequences has become our natural heritage today, but things were very different then. A respected and influential Roman theologian—not an Italian—publicly stated that Bea's explanations in this connection were 'absolutely untenable.' "[102]

The Nature of Our Love for Other Christians, and Its Consequences

We now come to the second of the two poles of Bea's ecumenical teaching: that of *love*. Here we can note in the first place that certain specific features of our love for other Christians flow from what we have said about baptism and its effects. Commenting on the words he quoted from Pope John's first encyclical, *Ad Petri cathedram*, the cardinal observes: ". . . the love he has in mind is the love that exists among brothers, the love that the pope has as common father of all the faithful, and consequently the mother's love that the church has for Christians who are not Catholics."[103]

---

100. In *Simposio*, p. 10.
101. *Ecumenism*, pp. 264-265.
102. J. Willebrands, *Simposio*, p. 280. What can we say about the origins of the cardinal's thinking in this field? In 1976, the then head of Pusey House in Oxford, Christopher Jones, said that he had personally heard Monsignor Josef Höfer state that he had "converted Bea to ecumenism, that is to recognizing other Christians as Christians" (ArchWit, p. 1). The well-known Lutheran pastor R. Baumann, who had visited Father Bea in 1956, writes that he had repeatedly issued the following call to Father Bea: "Do not address us as pagans or Jews or Moslems, but as persons baptized in the name of the Three-in-One God, in other words bearing in mind our baptism. Baptism is a sacred action conferred in the name of the Trinity; a baptized person is a person in the church. Whatever we non-Catholics may lack must be clarified within the framework of the already existing baptismal communion under the authority of the word of God" (ArchWit, p. 2). The way in which doctrine on baptism and its effects was seen in the Council was explained by the cardinal in his study, "La communio interecclesiale e l'ecumenismo" (Biblio. 436), pp. 1007-1014; the consequences for ecclesiology were discussed in *ibid.*, pp. 1014-1016.
103. *The Unity of Christians*, p. 26 (ct); *L'unione dei cristiani*, p. 11.

This love the church has is the reason why it "will lovingly recognize and willingly leave intact the authentic and precious religious values that are found in our separated brethren, whether these have been drawn from the sacred scriptures with study and prayer, or whether they have become dear to them through the tradition of centuries."[104] Indeed, even in the preparatory stages of the Council the cardinal does not hesitate to state: "It is true that, by baptism, they possess a union of grace with Christ, and this union enables them to have the authentic religious life which we admire in many of our separated brethren; it helps them to develop their life of faith and gives them the strength to overcome difficulties and obstacles to that life of faith."[105]

One particular expression of the *loving attitude of the Council* will be its approach to what are referred to as "disciplinary matters," in other words matters concerning *canon law, the liturgy and various forms of piety.* In this connection the cardinal observes: "Nor will it be forgotten in the Council that all these questions of language, rite, church singing and such things are marginal matters and must not constitute a reef on which the great cause of unity is wrecked."[106]

Now, the attitude of the church and the Council should also be the attitude of Catholics, for they too have the duty to *recognize all the good* and all the treasures that are found in other Christians, all the elements of the Christian heritage that they still preserve and all that Christ and his Spirit perform in them.[107] And, more generally: "Nor should we forget that, in spite of all the differences in doctrine and worship, our separated brethren *still have much in common with us.*"[108]

Love gives birth to the effort to know one another, thus overcoming prejudice, resentment and suspicion.[109] Further, "Love will preserve Catholics from impatience and discourtesy in their relations with non-Catholics, from resentment and prejudices caused by unpleasant events in the past for which the latter are in no way responsible, from uncalled-for judgments and rash generalizations."[110]

The respect that is a fruit of love "will teach us also *the right way to put forward the truth.* Conviction in proposing the truth is proper, but this should not tempt us to despise the convictions of our brethren. Those convictions have been inherited from their ancestors and deepened through their education, and are considered by them as a sacred trust."[111]

An important application of this love and respect concerns the field of past faults, and in this connection the cardinal says: "Let us rather leave the past in

104. R 1961/19, p. 12a.
105. *The Unity of Christians*, p. 122; *L'unione dei cristiani*, p. 123.
106. R 1961/19, p. 12a.
107. Cf. *Die Einheit der Christen*, p. 128; R 1961/19, p. 12; R 1962/9, p. 9; R 1962/14, p. 5; R 1962/16, p. 6; R 1962/21, p. 6; Biblio. 215, pp. 189-290.
108. *The Unity of Christians*, p. 27; *L'unione dei cristiani*, p. 12.
109. Cf. *The Unity of Christians*, p. 89.
110. *The Unity of Christians*, p. 149 (ct); *L'unione dei cristiani*, pp. 157-158. Cf. also *The Unity of Christians*, pp. 56-58, 108; Biblio. 215, pp. 289-290.
111. *The Unity of Christians*, p. 79. For the words of Pius XII, cf. *AAS*, XXV (1943), 243.

peace and busy ourselves in winning back what was lost: the unity of all baptized Christians."[112]

Lastly, the cardinal points to *the example of Pope John XXIII* to show how authentic fraternal love can constitute a sizable contribution to a rapprochement between brethren: "Just as the pope's deep charity in speaking and dealing with our separated brethren has contributed greatly to an improvement in the atmosphere, so also the approach of each one of the faithful has its importance."[113]

The Council Must Provide a Fresh Stimulus for the Ecumenical Movement

Our speaker takes the doctrine on baptism and its consequences as the basis for a view of the unity of the church in its concrete reality, and of the aim of the ecumenical movement. "The unity of the church desired by her divine Founder is, like holiness and catholicity, one of her essential 'marks'; but, in reality, *unity is not yet complete and perfect.* It needs our work in order to become ever fuller." In other words, "according to the will of her Founder," it must become fully "a unity in doctrine, in government and in the means of salvation which are the sacraments, and it is founded on the rock chosen by Christ himself, St. Peter and his successors."[114]

In order to provide a fresh impulse to the ecumenical movement,[115] the Council can issue guidelines.[116] "The Council can above all place strong emphasis on *the great duty* of every baptized person to show concern over everybody else who has been baptized in Christ, and hence over their union. This duty springs from baptism itself."[117] "We cannot say that the consciousness of this duty is very much alive among all Catholics, in every country. There is hope that the Council will awaken consciences in this respect also."[118] Apart from highlighting this duty, the Council can issue instructions with a view to remedying the lack of coordination that still exists among ecumenical initiatives: "Activities for Christian unity—is it possible that they are still, even today, too individualistic and uncoordinated? . . . The Council, without any attempt at centralization or uniformity, can give general directives and indicate attainable objectives."[119]

112. *The Unity of Christians*, p. 123; *Pour l'unité des chrétiens*, pp. 136-137; *Die Einheit der Christen*, pp. 140-141.
113. *The Unity of Christians*, p. 149; *L'unione dei cristiani*, p. 157. For the pope's example of charity, cf. also *The Unity of Christians*, pp. 26, 34; R 1960/23, p. 8.
114. *The Unity of Christians*, p. 35; *L'unione dei cristiani*, p. 21. Cf. *The Unity of Christians*, pp. 80-82.
115. Cf. *The Unity of Christians*, p. 126.
116. Cf. R 1962/21, p. 10; *Die Einheit der Christen*, p. 142; R 1962/9, p. 21; R 1962/14, p. 3.
117. R 1962/21, p. 11. For the duty of the faithful to concern themselves with the question of union, cf. also *The Unity of Christians*, pp. 86-87, 122, 126; R 1962/9, p. 21.
118. *The Unity of Christians*, pp. 86-87. Cf. also R 1961/19, p. 4.
119. *The Unity of Christians*, p. 126; *Pour l'unité des chrétiens*, p. 143. The view that ecumenical

Turning to the practical aspect—the "means"—we have already seen the vital importance of authentic fraternal love, but the cardinal also lists a number of others.

In the first place he strongly emphasizes the need for *prayer for unity*. "Of these means, prayer is the most important, as the Holy Father has repeatedly stressed, and as the World Council of Churches also stated at its New Delhi meeting."[120] Unity is first and foremost a work of grace, and "this grace must be implored with humble, confident, persevering and insistent prayer."[121]

The president of the secretariat usually links prayer and *sacrifice*: "Prayer must be accompanied by *sacrifice*, by the daily offering of our sufferings, difficulties and disappointments, for the great intention of unity."[122]

The cardinal also regularly stresses the ecumenical importance of *a Christian life*. Thus in his lecture on Niels Stensen he notes the role that example played in the spiritual path of this man, who was "deeply affected" by the example set by his Catholic friends in Florence, by the search for Christian perfection that he observed in priests and religious, and by the example of charitable activity seen in hospitals.[123] Elsewhere the speaker goes further, saying that it is not simply a case of a Christian life, but in fact of *the search for holiness*. In this he draws his main inspiration from a significant statement Pope John XXIII made when inaugurating the work of the preparatory commissions for the Council: "We do not hesitate to say that our efforts and study with a view to ensuring that the Council is a great event could all prove vain, if this *collective striving after sanctification* were less than unanimous and resolute. No one element can contribute as much as a holiness sought after and attained."[124] The cardinal adds that the pope's words are also certainly valid for the success of work for unity.[125] Elsewhere he explains this as follows: "The more closely one is united to the Blessed Trinity, to Christ, and to the church, bride of Christ, the more efficaciously will one be able to work with others for unity."[126] Indeed, the attainment of full unity will in the last analysis be the work of the Holy Spirit, who alone can give people the necessary grace.[127]

---

activity is still uncoordinated and that orientations are needed is also found in *Die Einheit der Christen*, p. 142; R 1961/19, p. 15; R 1961/27, pp. 13-14; R 1962/9, p. 21. R 1962/37, p. 4, states: "There is a good hope that the Holy See will publish an 'Ecumenical Directory' that will be fuller and more practical than the Instruction of the Holy Office." (He is referring here to the 1949 Instruction, which we have already mentioned a number of times.)

120. *The Unity of Christians*, pp. 126-127 (ct); *Pour l'unité des chrétiens*, p. 143. Cf. also *The Unity of Christians*, pp. 35-36.
121. *The Unity of Christians*, p. 88.
122. *The Unity of Christians*, p. 127; *Pour l'unité des chrétiens*, p. 143; *Die Einheit der Christen*, p. 142. Cf. also R 1961/7, p. 10; R 1961/19, p. 15; R 1962/16, pp. 9-10; R 1962/21, p. 12.
123. Cf. Biblio. 215, p. 196; also *ibid.*, pp. 288-289.
124. *AAS*, LII (1960), 961; cited in R 1962/21, p. 15. Cf. also Biblio. 215, p. 196; R 1962/16, pp. 9-10.
125. Cf. Biblio. 215, p. 296.
126. *The Unity of Christians*, p. 90. As concerns supernatural means, cf. also *ibid.*, pp. 77-78; R 1962/37, p. 6.
127. Cf. *The Unity of Christians*, p. 35.

There is another means that may not be open to all, but certainly is to many: "... *cooperation with our separated brethren* ... in various social and charitable activities, and in the defense of the human rights and values that are so often disregarded and denied today: the rights of religious freedom, respect for human life, concern for world peace, the means of safeguarding it, and so on."[128]

Such cooperation also and "above all has the great advantage of creating a spirit of brotherhood and fellowship between those who implement it, and this spirit is a fundamental requirement if we are to improve our understanding of each other in doctrinal matters too."[129] Cooperation "contributes a great deal to mutual knowledge, sincere respect and authentic Christian love."[130]

One particular group of people who have very great responsibilities in this field are *theologians*, and what is needed here is "calm and objective study by individuals" and "theological conversations between specialists belonging to different denominations."[131] Emphasis on the need for such conversations is found in practically all the cardinal's talks.[132] Thus he says that he is very pleased that in the Assembly of the World Council of Churches held in New Delhi, "Faith and Order" should have asked for "special provision to be made for conversations with Roman Catholics."[133] The cardinal also stresses, however, that "not all Christians are called upon to take part in theological conversations."[134] Such discussions call for careful advance preparation, and must be conducted by qualified people.[135] And the cardinal cites the example of Niels Stensen in this connection.[136]

A Task to Be Performed with Realism and Calm Confidence

In September 1961, the Mayor of Strasbourg, Mr. Pflimlin, surprised the cardinal with a question: "Your Eminence," he asked, "are you an optimist or a pessimist about the future of ecumenism?" "Mr. Mayor, I'm a realist," replied

128. *The Unity of Christians*, p. 49 (ct); *L'unione dei cristiani*, p. 37. This thought is found in some form in almost all the lectures; cf. *The Unity of Christians*, pp. 89-90, 127, 204; *Die Einheit der Christen*, p. 142; R 1961/19, p. 15; R 1962/9, p. 21; R 1962/16, p. 8; R 1962/21, pp. 12-13. In this connection the speaker mentions the example of Niels Stensen, who had no hesitation over working with Catholics in his scientific research when he was still a convinced Lutheran; cf. Biblio. 215, p. 196.
129. R 1962/21, p. 13. Cf. also *The Unity of Christians*, pp. 204.
130. Biblio. 215, p. 296. Various other possibilities of collaboration are noted in the lecture on "How University Research and Teaching Can Further Christian Unity," for example between exegetes, philosophers and theologians; cf. *The Unity of Christians*, pp. 101-102.
131. *The Unity of Christians*, p. 203; *L'unione dei cristiani*, p. 230.
132. Cf. *The Unity of Christians*, p. 120, 124, 140; R 1961/19, p. 15; R 1961/27, p. 14; R 1962/9, p. 16; R 1962/16, p. 8; R 1962/37, p. 2.
133. *The Unity of Christians*, p. 124; *Pour l'unité des chrétiens*, p. 138; quoting from *The New Delhi Report* (London, 1962), p. 175. Cf. also R 1962/9, pp. 16, 18.
134. Biblio. 215, p. 195.
135. Cf. R 1962/37, p. 2; *The Unity of Christians*, p. 187.
136. Cf. Biblio. 215, pp. 292-293.

the cardinal. Bea himself enjoyed telling this story—an indication that his answer reflected his true attitude on this matter. It may seem obvious and simple at first sight, but if we consider it in the light of his lectures we shall discover its unsuspected complexity and depth.

Let us first take a look at the cardinal's general thinking in this connection: "And now, what are the prospects for the success of the great task? We would have to be prophets in order to provide an adequate answer to this important question, for only God knows the hour he has decided. However, we can at least draw some inferences from present information and evaluations of such information—although we must be careful to steer clear of any excessive pessimism or imprudent optimism when doing so."[137]

In the first place we must avoid *over-enthusiasm* and *false hopes*: "It is all too easy to let oneself be carried away by enthusiasm on the pretext of its being a good and holy matter, and to disregard all caution and prudence. . . . Today when the nostalgia for unity is spreading more and more, even among those strata of the faithful called 'the masses,' we must remember that mass psychoses exist, fraught with illusions which lead to most dangerous delusions."[138]

Let us now return to the cardinal's statement that in the field of prospects "we can at least draw some inferences from present information and evaluations of such information." According to him, the first encouraging factor is the work of grace that is kindling a nostalgia for unity: "The nostalgia for unity, which is displayed not only by many individuals but also by whole groups, shows how powerfully this divine grace is working today."[139] Referring to the efforts being made in the field of union, the cardinal does not hesitate to speak of "a gigantic effort to come at least in some measure nearer to that unity which is so eagerly desired."[140]

However, there is also the other side of the coin, that is, *the serious difficulties and obstacles* that still stand in the way of progress toward full unity. At the end of various lectures, the cardinal makes the same observation that he made at the end of the Paris one: "You will agree, I think, that I have not been starry-eyed, but blunt and realistic. The obstacles are still enormous. Our separated brethren and ourselves stand far apart on many issues. Illusions could be most damaging."[141]

The speaker is so convinced of the size and complexity of the difficulties that he says: "But *the Council* cannot be a finishing point, but rather *a starting point*.

---

137. R 1961/7, pp. 10-11.
138. *The Unity of Christians*, p. 91. The author is referring to a survey carried out by Catholic Action in Bavaria; cf. *Die Einheit der Christen*, p. 123. In connection with the reference to prudence, it should be noted that he rarely speaks of the prudence needed in the ecumenical movement, but only when talking about it to priests who have the task of supervising it; cf. *The Unity of Christians*, p. 91; R 1961/18, p. 11. He recommended it more with his example than with words.
139. *The Unity of Christians*, p. 28 (ct); *L'unione dei cristiani*, p. 13. Cf. also *The Unity of Christians*, p. 51.
140. *The Unity of Christians*, p. 85.
141. *The Unity of Christians*, pp. 127-128; *Pour l'unité des chrétiens*, p. 144. Cf. also R 1961/18, p. 11; R 1961/19, p. 16; R 1961/25, p. 16; R 1961/27, p. 14; R 1962/9, p. 22; etc.

. . . It is clear then that at the moment there is no question of spectacular results, nor of successes in the near future, but of long, patient preparation, to which can be applied the proverb quoted by our Lord himself: 'One man sows, another reaps' (John 4:37)."[142]

The president of the secretariat is *even more explicit* in this connection in his summary of the discussions of the conference of priests at Heythrop: "Lastly, *patience is above all necessary*. What has taken place over centuries cannot be changed in a few years. We must therefore move forward step by step, making a prudent evaluation of the things that are possible at the present moment and those that must be left for better times. Impatience is the defect of contemporary man. Any intemperance and haste are necessarily harmful. The first apostles were sent out to convert the world, but the Roman world needed five centuries for this, and there were also setbacks. It will be like that in our field too."[143]

So what conclusions can we draw? Considering the serious difficulties that are still facing us, "some among us may feel *discouraged* and be tempted to abandon all efforts. Nothing could be worse. It would be a false conclusion to draw, even granted the natural hopelessness of the present situation. To conclude so would indicate excessive trust in mere human resources."[144] "Let us not forget, however, what St. Paul once said to the Corinthians about his apostolic work: 'It was for me to plant the seed, for Apollo to water it, but it was God who gave the increase . . . we are only his assistants' (1 Cor. 3:6-9). The outcome, the increase, is God's business."[145]

"But God is *all-powerful*. Remember our Lord's reply to his disciples who, in their fear, had raised an objection: 'To men,' says the Savior, 'that is impossible, but not to God: for all things are possible to God' (Mark 10:27)."[146]

These are the thoughts that form the basis for supernatural trust and "faith capable of moving mountains" (cf. Mt. 17:20). Such trust is also based on the prayer that Jesus addressed to the Father the night before his passion: "We trust entirely in this prayer of the divine Founder of the church, not letting ourselves be discouraged by the difficulties that still lie between us and the attainment of the precious gift of unity. . . ."[147] All these thoughts give us "an unshakable confidence and an invincible courage."[148]

It is in this perspective that the president of the secretariat closes many of his talks with the words: "That is why we go forth full of confidence and courage,

---

142. *The Unity of Christians*, pp. 36-37 (ct); *L'unione dei cristiani*, pp. 22-23. For the thought found in John 4:37, cf. also R 1961/7, p. 13.

143. R 1962/37, p. 5.

144. *The Unity of Christians*, p. 142 (ct); *L'unione dei cristiani*, p. 149. Cf. also *The Unity of Christians*, p. 128.

145. *The Unity of Christians*, p. 128; *Pour l'unité des chrétiens*, p. 145. Cf. also *The Unity of Christians*, pp. 92-93.

146. *The Unity of Christians*, p. 128; *Pour l'unité des chrétiens*, p. 145. Cf. also *The Unity of Christians*, pp. 142, 153.

147. *The Unity of Christians*, p. 153; *L'unione dei cristiani*, p. 162. Cf. also *The Unity of Christians*, pp. 51-52.

148. *The Unity of Christians*, p. 92. Cf. also R 1961/18, p. 11.

in a spirit of love, prayer, sacrifice and work, along the path that leads to the unity of all who have been baptized in Christ, mindful of the words of St. Paul: 'Both the will to do it and the accomplishment of that will are something which God accomplishes in you, to carry out his loving purpose' (Phil. 2:14)."[149] However, the work of the Holy Spirit also needs our collaboration with prudent, attentive activity, based on love, but above all on faith—a faith capable of moving mountains. This is how we and our separated brethren must prepare ourselves with a view to a Council of union that will take place in the hour of God's mercy, as and when he himself prepares it according to his mysterious plans.[150]

---

149. *The Unity of Christians*, p. 128; *Pour l'unité des chrétiens*, p. 145. In the description of the spirit in which "we go forth" the author adds "repentance" (*Busse*) on a number of occasions, a concept close to that of conversion; cf. R 1961/27, p. 15; R 1962/9, p. 231; *Die Einheit der Christen*, p. 144.

150. Cf. R 1962/21, p. 17. It should be noted that the conclusion of many lectures follows the same lines that we have followed in this last section, in other words: there are many serious obstacles and difficulties, but this is no reason to despair; the result is in fact the work of God; what is important is to build on trust in God, and in this way we can move forward with courage. In this connection, cf. *The Unity of Christians*, pp. 127-128; R 1961/19, p. 16; R 1961/25, pp. 16/17; R 1961/27, pp. 14-15; R 1962/9, pp. 22-23; R 1962/14, p. 9.

CHAPTER 6

THREE YEARS RICH IN COMMITMENTS AND EVENTS

September 1962–December 1965

It is obvious that the three years or so that the Council lasted—with the actual periods of assembly on the one hand, and the preparatory work carried out between these by the various commissions on the other—must be taken together.[1] It is, however, so rich that we cannot describe it adequately except by taking the various aspects one by one. As concerns our particular field of study, these aspects can be divided into the following groupings: the growth of ecumenical awareness and of rapprochement between Christians; a similar growth in understanding and rapprochement between the church and the Jewish people and other non-Christian religions; progressive development on the question of religious freedom; Bea's personal activity as a Council father and his work for the unity of the whole human race. Before considering these individual aspects, we shall give *a general overview* of events in the cardinal's life in these years, for this will provide a setting in which to examine his more specific work for these great causes. This general picture in fact constitutes the concrete background and common context for all his commitments, and should thus be born in mind when studying the individual aspects of his activity.

Let us give some examples to clarify this idea. In the present chapter we shall consider the sickness and death of Pope John XXIII and the election of Pope Paul VI, together with the consequences that these two events had for Bea's life and activity. We shall also give a general idea of the cardinal's activity as a public speaker, indicating the subject of the various lectures, interviews, etc., although leaving any more specific description of content to the following chapters. Similarly, for the twenty or more addresses the cardinal made in the Council hall, we shall simply indicate the conciliar document under discussion and give a very general idea of the subject. In this way, the present chapter will gradually allow the reader to build up a picture of the various subjects on which Bea spoke, although the specific content will be left for study in the following chapters; and this overall picture of his wide-ranging and demanding activity in these three years must be borne in mind when reading the following chapters with their full information on the content of the lectures, interviews, Council interventions, etc.

---

1. Here there was some uncertainty about terminology. To start with, the term "session" covered the whole period of two months or so in which the conciliar meetings took place (this terminology is still used in Bea's work *Ecumenism in Focus*—though mostly because of the wishes of the publisher). Later it was officially suggested that it should be replaced by the word "period," so that we have the first, second and third periods of the Council; we shall follow this latter system, except in direct quotations from works that use the earlier system.

Concerns on the Eve, and Encouraging Beginnings

If we go back a few months, we find an event in the cardinal's life that undoubtedly constituted a deep preparation for the Council, in other words his *ordination as bishop*. Pope John XXIII had decided that in view of their great responsibilities, from now on the cardinal deacons should receive episcopal orders, and had told the twelve cardinal deacons of the time that he would personally confer ordination on them on the forthcoming Holy Thursday (19 April 1962) in his own cathedral, the Church of St. John Lateran. This was a source of great joy to the cardinal, and from then on his retreat notes repeatedly contain the reflection that he must be aware of the new situation created with his ordination as bishop and the serious duties deriving from it.[2]

At this point we must consider the atmosphere and outlook on the eve of the Council. And here we are thinking not so much of general apprehensions, which were more than comprehensible on the eve of an undertaking so unfamiliar, vast and complex. A great deal depended on two particular practical problems, and it was difficult to see how they would be solved.

The first was *the election of the members of the conciliar commissions*, which was on the agenda for the first general congregation, scheduled for 13 October 1962, although no groundwork had been laid in this connection. A general list of the Council fathers and also a more restricted one of those who had been members of the preparatory commissions had been distributed to the electors, but it was unrealistic to suppose that the roughly three thousand Council fathers knew each other and therefore had even the slightest orientation on which to base their vote in these elections. Respect for their freedom also ruled out any suggestion that they should simply cast their vote for those who had been members of the preparatory commissions. People wondered why the individual episcopal conferences had not, for example, prepared lists of suitable candidates who had some special background or training in the various subjects with which the Council was to deal.[3]

A second source of concern was the position that *the Secretariat for Christian Unity* would hold in the Council. While the preparatory commissions had been disbanded on the eve of the Council, the rules of the Council laid down that the Secretariat for Christian Unity—like the Technical and Organizational Commission and the Economic Secretariat—should retain not only its same aims but also the structure and composition it had in the preparatory period.[4] The reasons for this ruling are clear, inasmuch as this was in fact the moment when the secretariat was called on to perform its specific mission of helping other Christians to observe the Council, for example by helping the observer-delegates in their delicate task. However, this did not resolve doubts over its right

---

2. Cf. *Spiritual Profile*, pp. 98, 114, 117, 132; also BM, pp. 99-108.
3. According to Caprile, II, 22-23, the general secretary, Archbishop P. Felici, had suggested that it would be a good idea to invite papal representatives, or better still national episcopal conferences, to present lists of suitable people, but nothing came of this.
4. Cf. *Ordo Concilii*, art. 7, n. 2.

to draft conciliar schemata. Indeed, these doubts were aggravated by the fact that this ruling highlighted the secretariat's position as a *pre*conciliar body, rather than as one elected by the Council. This gave rise to the question of what would happen to the schemata drawn up by the secretariat. Who would present them to the Council, and who would be given the task of explaining, correcting and guiding them through to their definitive approval?

From the very first days there were a number of events that began to dissipate the various apprehensions of the eve. On Thursday, 11 October, the impressive opening of the Council took place in the presence of about two thousand five hundred Council fathers and fifty or so observer-delegates or guests of the secretariat, and with the courageous and illuminated address of Pope John XXIII.[5]

Two days later, on Saturday, 13 October, the first general congregation was held, and to the general surprise, the problem of how members of the conciliar commissions were to be elected was solved in a very short time. After the general secretary had invited the Council to begin voting, the Archbishop of Lille, Cardinal Achille Liénart, took the floor, followed by the Cardinal Archbishop of Cologne, Josef Frings, who also spoke in the name of other German-speaking cardinals. Both asked for time in which to gather information and reflect, and Cardinal Liénart also made the practical suggestion that the episcopal conferences should compile lists of possible candidates. The requests and the relative suggestion were accepted, and the voting was postponed until Tuesday, 16 October.[6]

On the evening of the same day (13 October) there was the memorable audience granted to *the observer-delegates and guests* of the secretariat. We shall be giving further details in another chapter, and would merely mention now that it made such an impression that Bea declared: "It is a miracle."[7]

The postponement of the vote obviously did not resolve all the problems entailed in *preparations for the election* of members of the conciliar commissions, for the amount of time granted was fairly short if we bear in mind the complexity of the whole procedure. The episcopal conferences needed a certain

---

5. Cf. *AAS*, LIV (1962), 786-795; English translation in Abbott (gen. ed.), *The Documents of Vatican II*, pp. 710-719.

6. Cf. *AS*, I/I, 207-208; apart from the official Latin publication, in order to help the reader we shall often add the respective reference from the monumental work of G. Caprile, which is far and away the most detailed and accurate of the vast amount of conciliar literature. In this way any reader who for some reason does not have access to the official publication will find it easier to check any particular point or gain further information.

7. Cf. *Ecumenism*, p. 49. Another high prelate of the Roman curia was also very struck, but drew some surprising conclusions, telling me: "This is the most beautiful thing. We could close the Council now." I was surprised and puzzled, and asked him: "But why close it?" "Didn't you see what happened this morning?" he asked, referring to the first general congregation. "But surely that was to be expected, Your Excellency. How could they elect members of the commissions out of over two thousand bishops if they didn't know them?" He replied firmly: "If I had been in Archbishop Felici's place, I would have told anyone who raised objections: 'Nonsense. We vote now!' " I reflected that this was not a surprising reaction, for he had never taken part in a Council before.

amount of time for consultations, etc., before they could draw up their lists of candidates. There was then the physical question of collecting and printing the lists, etc. The official list drawn up by the General Secretariat was therefore distributed to the Council fathers on the day of the vote itself (16 October).[8] This meant that although the fathers did have a list of candidates at the moment they were called on to make their choices, they had no possibility of seeking further information on individual names, discussing the matter with other colleagues, etc. Fortunately, at least twelve private lists had been in circulation since as early as Saturday, 13 October.[9] In the two or three days available, Bea was thus able to draw up a rough list of those he would vote for, and on the day of the official vote he was able to use this as a basis for his definitive choice when he came to fill out the ten sheets, corresponding to the ten commissions, for each of which each voter had to give sixteen names.[10] All things considered, however, the election of the commission-members went fairly well—all the more so, since at the moment when the results were announced the pope accepted the suggestion made as early as the day of the vote itself that, although the regulations (art. 39) stipulated the contrary, a relative majority was enough to ensure election.[11] Bea liked to point out that things had gone much faster and more smoothly than at Vatican I, when a whole month had been needed for the election of the conciliar commissions, even though there had been less than a third the number of bishops on that occasion.

However, there was now all the more urgency over a solution to the second question of *the right of the secretariat* to present and amend schemata, and during these same days the president of the secretariat thus sent Pope John a memorandum on the subject. It is significant that despite the intense activity of that time, the pope had an affirmative reply sent back to the cardinal through the Secretary of State as early as 19 October, saying that as concerned responsibility for schemata, the secretariat was *on an equal footing* with the conciliar commissions.

We do not possess the cardinal's memorandum on this matter, but I am sure that on 19 October the cardinal transmitted the pope's decision to Cardinal Eugene Tisserant, president of the conciliar authorities, asking that it be officially announced in the Council hall as soon as possible.[12] This announcement was particularly urgent because of its important consequences for the constitution of the conciliar commissions: since no Council father could belong to more than one commission, it followed that those bishops who had been members of

---

8. Cf. Caprile, II, 41.
9. The archives contain (Lb 12/2-16) the privately circulated lists that Bea made use of in drawing up rough lists of the names preferred for each commission, which he then copied out with some corrections when the official voting took place on 16 October. These unofficial lists were drawn up by the following countries or areas (and some of them were truly international in composition): Latin America, Belgium, Brazil, Canada, China, Germany, India, Italy, Spain, Central Europe, and the Chaldean Patriarchate. There was also one drawn up by the Holy Office.
10. Rough copy Arch. Lb 12/18.
11. Cf. *AS*, I/I, 109; Caprile, II, 43, cf. 45.
12. Cf. Arch. Lc 5/9-1.

the secretariat since the preparatory period of the Council could not be elected to any conciliar commission, and this must thus be taken into account in sorting and counting ballot papers.

On the same day that he wrote to Cardinal Tisserant, Bea informed the members and consultors of the secretariat of the pope's decision.[13] It was then announced in the Council hall on 22 October, and the note attached to Bea's letter was also read out, explaining the pope's decision in juridical terms.[14]

Apart from what was laid down in the Council regulations concerning the tasks and composition of the secretariat (art. 8, no. 2) it was laid down that, like the conciliar commissions, the secretariat would have the task described in article 5 of the regulations, in other words that of examining and amending schemata for documents; in the general congregations, too, the secretariat was to proceed like the conciliar commissions in presenting the schemata it had drafted, which were to be treated in every way like those presented by the commissions (arts. 56-61); in cases involving other areas as well as its own specific field the secretariat was also expected to play its part in the joint commissions to which such matters were to be entrusted (art. 58, n. 2). Lastly, the formal juridical basis of the whole announcement was given, by stating that it was a decision handed down by the Pope to the Secretary of State in the audience of 19 October.[15]

The Episode of the Schema on "The Sources of Revelation"

Once the conciliar commissions had been formed, the Council could move on to discussion of the various schemata. The presiding authority of the Council had selected liturgical reform as the first subject for discussion, and this question took up about a month. Then on 14 November the Council moved on to the schema on the sources of revelation drawn up by the Theological Commission.[16] And here the Council came to its first *impasse*. In one of his later publications, the cardinal described the situation as follows: "*The question* was whether the schema, which had been drawn up with a view to seeing scripture and tradition

---

13. Cf. Arch. Lc 5/10, pp. 1-2.
14. For the announcement in the Council hall, cf. *AS*, I/I, 112, 261; for the text of the note, cf. *ibid.*, p. 78.
15. In Latin the technical term was "rescriptum ex audientia sanctissimi" (cf. *AS*, I/I, 112, 161). *At that time* the cardinals had a special privilege according to which if they stated anything in writing, appealing to an audience they had had with the pope, this was to be accepted as law; cf. 1917 Code of Canon law, Canon 239, para. 1, n. 17. In connection with this statement of equality with the commissions, there was what was jokingly referred to as "a palace revolution," and not completely without foundation, for the pope's decision meant that there was a *de facto* conciliar commission with members who had not been elected by the Council.
16. The official title was "Commission for the Doctrine of the Faith and Morals." For reasons of brevity we shall use the term that was then widely accepted of "Theological Commission."

as two independent sources, would be accepted with few modifications, or whether an entirely new schema would be drafted."[17] From the beginning the discussion was fairly lively, with opposing views being expressed. The Italian Cardinals Ruffini and Siri and the Spanish Cardinal Quiroga y Palacios spoke in favor of the schema, while it was strongly challenged by Cardinals Liénart (France), Frings (Germany), Léger (Canada), Alfrink (Netherlands), Suenens (Belgium) and Ritter (United States).[18] Bea also spoke on the very first day of the discussion, stating flatly that he did not like the schema and suggesting that it should be sent back to the commission for a complete redrafting so that it could be made to reflect the aims of the Council.[19] The debate continued for another five days, with diametrically opposed views being expressed, but by this time the subject had been exhausted and the speakers were merely repeating themselves. It was therefore suggested that the debate should be suspended while a decision was reached on how to proceed. A vote was taken on 20 November on whether the discussion should be broken off and the schema sent back to the commission. And this is where the *impasse* arose: although the suggestion to suspend the discussion obtained a very large absolute majority—1368 votes against 822[20]—the regulations required a majority of two-thirds.

Apart from the problem of the lack of a two-thirds majority, another more serious problem now arose. The debate and the vote had in a way shaken the faith of the Council in the Theological Commission which had been responsible for the schema, so that people now wondered how they could ensure that the schema would be redrafted following the lines requested by the vast majority of the Council. In the course of the discussion it had been suggested a number of times that the "ecumenists" should also be involved in the redrafting process.[21] The Archbishop of Toulouse, Gabriel-Marie Garrone, who had been elected to the Theological Commission with a very large number of votes,[22] explicitly suggested that the task should be entrusted to a joint commission made up of the Theological Commission and the Secretariat for Christian Unity.[23] Archbishop Garrone gave us the following very telling statement in this connection: "I wanted to take advice before suggesting it in a public intervention, and I could not see anyone who could be a better advisor for me than Cardinal Bea, especially since the question involved the secretariat. I have a very clear memory of our conversation, and I can still see the cardinal as he reflected on

17. *Unity in Freedom*, p. 54 (ct).
18. For the ten speakers who preceded Bea, cf. *AS*, I/III, 32-48; cf. also Caprile, II, 157-159.
19. Cf. *AS*, I/III, 48-52. As concerns the fairly tense atmosphere of those days, it is interesting to see the extract Y. Congar quotes from his personal notes for 9 November 1962 (p. 130): "The Cardinal [Léger] is very severe over the doctrinal schemata, and is convinced that they should simply be rejected. Cardinal Bea, he says, is still more firmly convinced over this and is ready to throw his life and his position as cardinal into the balance" (ArchWit, p. 2).
20. Cf. *AS*, I/III, 220, 255; Caprile, II, 57.
21. Cf. the suggestion of Cardinal L. Rugambwa, *AS*, I/III, 172; cf. also similar suggestions, *AS*, I/III, 108, 199.
22. Cf. *AS*, I/I, 225; with 1738 votes he received the second largest number of all.
23. Cf. *AS*, I/III, 191.

the prospects of such cooperation, for which he would be bound to bear the burden. I watched him as he turned it over in his conscience, and finally received his encouragement. Looking back, it seems to me that I witnessed one of those 'elections' for which St. Ignatius drew up the rules."[24]

Although a great deal has been written about later developments in this connection, and particularly about Bea's role in these, a good proportion of the facts are still unknown.[25] For a variety of reasons I am in a position to give a number of further details.[26]

On the same day as the fateful vote, there was an official lunch at the Japanese Embassy to the Holy See, to mark the official visit of the Japanese Prime Minister Hayat Ikeda.[27] The guests also included the Substitute of the Secretariat of State, Archbishop Angelo Dell'Acqua, and the Head of Protocol, Monsignor Igino Cardinale. The conversation turned to the vote, which was the burning subject of the day. Apparently they had not heard the result, and when I told them, they both seemed worried and said that it was absolutely vital to find a solution. They must have discussed the matter with Cardinal Secretary of State Amleto Cicognani, who was a fellow-guest, either during or immediately after the meal, for when we left the embassy the Secretary of State invited Bea to join him in his car in order to discuss what could be done. Our car therefore followed them on the journey back to the Vatican.

Having taken his leave of Cardinal Cicognani in the Courtyard of St. Damasus, Bea got back into his own car and told me that he had been asked to talk about the problem with some other cardinals. We went first to the residence of Cardinal Achille Liénart, at the *Procura* of St. Sulpice in Via Quattro Fontane. Cardinal Liénart declared himself in agreement with Bea that the pope should step in to solve the juridical difficulty of the lack of a two-thirds majority and thus suspend the debate. After this we went to the College of Santa Maria dell'Anima, to meet with Cardinal Frings. Although the latter was out at the time, he came to the Brazilian College that same evening, and it was discovered that he was of the same opinion. After dinner, Cardinal Bea received a telephone call from the secretary of state, who was with the pope. Cardinal Bea reported the results of his soundings, and the next day we learned that the pope had accepted and agreed with the opinion of the three cardinals. However, it should

24. ArchWit. The "election" spoken of here refers to a methodical procedure which is given by St. Ignatius of Loyola in his *Spiritual Exercises*, and which is used, for example, in order to choose one's state of life or to make any other important decision.

25. Caprile, II, 181, note 20, refers to the matter only briefly in a note, and none of the authors listed in the bibliography speak about the details. M. Lackmann, *Mit evangelischen Augen. Beobachtungen eines Lutheraners auf d. 2. Vatikan. Konzil*, 5 vols (Graz, 1963-1966), I, 304, does give some details, but is neither accurate nor exhaustive on the whole affair.

26. I in no way intend to attribute all the credit for the pope's decision to Cardinal Bea. Apart from any other contributions, we must consider the kind of contribution made by the Cardinal Archbishop of Montreal, Paul E. Léger, who was received by the pope on the evening of 20 November in an audience that Pope John XXIII himself recalled in an affectionate letter to the same cardinal, when sending him the gift of a valuable pectoral cross; cf. *Giovanni XXIII, Lettere*, pp. 434-435.

27. Cf. the report in *CC*, 1962/IV, 500.

be noted that from what I understood from the cardinal, his inquiries were solely concerned with the question of suspending the debate and sending the schema back to the Theological Commission, and not with any other possible remedy.

Even so, it was not easy to reach a decision. Monsignor Loris Capovilla tells us that on the morning of the following day, 21 November, the cardinal secretary of state had again told the Pope of his uncertainty over the advisability of a papal intervention, but John XXIII had answered firmly: "Your Eminence, you can go and announce it. I have prayed a great deal and thought about it all night. Let's do it without fear."

The pope's decision was therefore announced in the general congregation of 21 November: the discussion was to be suspended, and the schema was to be redrafted by a joint commission made up of the Theological Commission and the Secretariat for Christian Unity, bearing in mind the general principles and taking into account the doctrine expounded in this connection by the Council of Trent and the First Vatican Council.[28] The pope's decision took much of the heat out of the situation.

Bea would later comment on Pope John's decision as follows: "He [the pope] took the greatest pains to see that his new special commission should include representatives of all the main currents of opinion represented in the Council. He overrode the letter of the procedural rules; but he did so only after the Council fathers had discussed freely and fully, and he intervened in order to enable free expression of opinion to be more effective."[29] On another occasion, he also quoted the observation of one of the Orthodox observer-delegates on this episode: "I'd never realized how useful it is to have a pope."[30]

It will be helpful to add a reflection on the repercussions of these events for the secretariat. The pope's decision was certainly evidence of his trust in the secretariat, and in Cardinal Bea in particular, but there was much more to it than that. After various speakers in the Council hall had mentioned the secretariat as a body capable of providing the schema with greater balance and with the elements hoped for by the majority of the assembly, when he announced his decision the pope himself was confirming the secretariat almost as a specially qualified representative of this majority and as guarantor that the schema would include the elements that had emerged during discussions in the Council hall.[31] And the joyful welcome that the majority gave the pope's decision in turn constituted a kind of confirmation of his opinion.

It is easy to see how much extra work this decision would entail for the secretariat, and particularly for Bea. Cardinal Garrone, who was a first-hand witness, describes the difficulty of the undertaking as follows: "After the Holy

---

28. Cf. *AS*, I/III, 259; Caprile, II, 179.
29. *Unity in Freedom*, p. 55 (ct). Cf. also the talk the cardinal gave at Assisi, 18 March 1963; R 1963/18, pp. 11-12.
30. Cf. the Assisi talk, R 1963/18, p. 13.
31. Later on Cardinal G.B. Montini, the future Paul VI, would suggest in the Council hall that the secretariat should also be involved in the task of reworking the schema of the constitution on the church; cf. *AS*, I/IV, 294; and Caprile, II, 252.

Father had accepted the idea of this joint commission, I experienced its laborious progress. It is a very delicate matter to discuss, but the least one can say is that the Secretariat for Unity was not accepted with a good grace by certain members of the Theological Commission. Cardinal Bea must certainly have known some of the harshest trials in his life during those days. There were many of us who shared his trials and fought by his side. I must say in all sincerity that I several times had occasion to feel deep admiration for this man: his calm in the midst of the storm, his unfailing humility, his serene firmness of judgment, and I would even dare say his strength of spirit in forgiving examples of a lack of respect that another man would certainly not have tolerated. The cause was a very important one and it was worth the effort, but I am sure that the cardinal served the church well in those days and that the rules of St. Ignatius on 'the exercise of the virtues' found an outstanding field of application."[32]

It is maybe significant that a few months later, the cardinal himself should have passed over the unpleasant aspects and should have used a good dose of optimism in stressing the success of the work of the joint commission: "Although the commission certainly included representatives of all the main currents of thought and mentalities present in the Council, before the close of the first session of the Council it had already finished and approved with a virtual unanimity four of the five chapters which go to make up the draft. And even as concerns the remaining chapter, which deals with revelation, in the course of these last days the commission has unanimously approved a new text to be proposed to the Council."[33]

Commitments Inside and Outside the Council

Since the previous section has said all that needs to be said here about the work of the first period of the Council, it now seems a good idea to give a brief idea of the amount of work the Council entailed for our cardinal, also bearing in mind his age. The plenary meetings or "general congregations" were held five times a week, lasting three hours and sometimes more. There were thirty-six such meetings in the first period of the Council.[34] Bea watched the debates with close attention, taking notes on large sheets of paper. By chance a certain number of these sheets, dating from the third period of the Council, are now found in our files.[35] The notes become particularly detailed when they deal with the

32. ArchWit. Archbishop Marcos G. McGrath of Panama, who was a member of the Theological Commission, describes one example of what would happen in the meetings of the joint commission, saying that Cardinal Bea was very alert and energetic, but that if the meeting dragged on, this was sometimes too much for his strength, and dangerous situations could arise; ArchWit, p. 2.

33. The Assisi talk, R 1963/18, p. 12. This draft was to encounter a number of further difficulties, as we shall see, and was not approved until 1965, in the last period of the Council.

34. Bea was absent only once, because of a lecture he gave in Venice, as we shall see.

35. Cf. Arch. Lb 1/1; these refer to the general congregations held between 15 September and 19 November 1964.

outcome of votes (which were fairly frequent in this period). We would note one further detail. There were two refreshment rooms, one on either side of the Council hall. The cardinal did not usually patronize either, probably because he did not think it a good idea since there was no scheduled refreshment break and it would have meant leaving his place while the meeting was in session.[36] At a certain point, however, Bea found another way of keeping his strength up, and used to carry some lumps of sugar with him.

Apart from the work of the general congregations there was also that of the secretariat. From the outset it was decided that the meetings of the secretariat would take place regularly once a week on Friday afternoons.[37] In this first period there were six in all. As we shall see, however, from the second half of November a further task was added: that of working with the Theological Commission in joint meetings on the subject of divine revelation; and this added another six afternoon meetings to the score.

Apart from all that we have already said about the work entailed by the Council, Bea also gave seven speeches in the Council in this period. Together with Cardinals Ruffini and Spellman, he was among those who spoke most frequently in the Council debates.[38] Three of these speeches concerned liturgical reform (the liturgy in general, the mass, the divine office), while there was one on each of the following subjects: the sources of revelation, the means of social communication, the cause of unity, and the schema on the church.[39] Apart from the subject of social communications, where there were special reasons for his contribution,[40] the number of his speeches is explained mostly by the fact that the assembly was considering subjects—liturgy, revelation, the church—with which he had been concerned in the past, and with which he was therefore particularly familiar.

And as if the activity connected with the Council were not enough, various circumstances obliged Bea to undertake a number of lectures and other activities. In the first place, on 8 November he gave a press conference in the Council press room. The review *La Civiltà Cattolica* had suggested that such a conference would enable a more general public to learn about the collection of lectures and interviews the cardinal had given in the preparatory period for the Council and had now published under the title *The Unity of Christians*—a book that we used extensively in our previous chapter.[41] However, far from confining itself

---

36. This supposition is confirmed by the fact that in the 1967 Synod of Bishops, when there was a scheduled break for refreshments, Bea did not think twice about availing himself of these.

37. Cf. Arch. Lc 5/10.

38. As concerns the drafting of the various speeches, it must be said that not only did Bea for the most part do this on his own, but that circumstances meant that he also typed the text on more than one occasion.

39. For the list and the sources, cf. Appendix 2, which gives all the cardinal's interventions in the Council.

40. On this occasion he presented certain observations in the Council hall which had come to the surface in the course of a special meeting of the observer-delegates and which he felt were important.

41. Biblio. 169.

to this objective, the press conference gave a kind of overview of the ecumenical situation, and particularly the activity of the observer-delegates.[42]

On the invitation of the Cardinal Patriarch of Venice, Giovanni Urbani, the cardinal gave a lecture in the Fenice Theater on 18 November on the occasion of the local festival of Our Lady *della Salute*. He spoke on the subject of "The Council and Non-Catholic Christians," and the lecture enjoyed considerable success.[43] Bea stayed in Venice no longer than was strictly necessary, so that he only missed a single general congregation, and was back in Rome on 20 November, just in time to play his role in resolving the *impasse* over the schema on the sources of revelation.

He exercised a particularly notable influence in this same period with regard to the thorny question of *the historicity of the gospels*. As happened on many other occasions, the cardinal's action was elicited by a specific situation and by a request for clarification from various quarters, in this case from the Council fathers. Certain groups had been distributing writings to the Council fathers in which they pointed out various serious dangers that they claimed were threatening Catholic doctrine, and especially Catholic exegesis.[44] Thus the cardinal, having been "requested several times by my brothers in the episcopacy—even with insistence," thought it "profitable to put at their disposition" the notes that he had prepared two years earlier for Cardinal A. Meyer and that had now been "brought up to date and completed in the past few months."[45] These notes were then distributed, not only in the Italian original, but also in French, English and Spanish translations.[46]

The Secretariat Reexamines Its Own Conciliar Schemata (February-May 1963)

Bea described the atmosphere of the months that followed the close of the first period of the Council as follows: "But clouds were gathering on the horizon, for the health of the 'Pope of the Council' grew steadily worse due to an illness whose effects were already beginning to be felt toward the end of the first session."[47] Despite this, or maybe for this very reason, these months would be

42. Cf. Ms. R 1962/44.
43. Cf. Ms. R 1962/45.
44. A letter signed by nineteen cardinals and addressed to the pope (cf. Caprile, II, 181-182) also speaks about the denial "of the historical truth . . . of important accounts in the Old and New Testaments." In June 1961, this had been preceded by a "Warning" from the Holy Office on the same question; cf. *AAS*, LII (1961), 507. The problem was thus a very delicate one, and also particularly in the forefront at the time. It was also linked to the campaign against the Pontifical Biblical Institute that was started in 1960 by certain Roman exegetes; cf. Kaiser, *Inside the Council*, p. 156.
45. The quotations are taken from the introduction to the booklet, Biblio. 221, p. 1. Bea also gave a talk to the Brazilian bishops on the same subject; cf. R 1962/46.
46. Only later did we learn that it had been published in Argentina, obviously without permission. We shall return to this booklet in the course of these chapters.
47. *Ecumenism*, p. 56.

full of keen activity and exertion. On the basis of experience gained in the first period, a complete reorganization of the Council's work was drawn up during these months, reducing the seventy or so schemata of the preparatory phase to seventeen main headings and creating a Coordinating Commission to supervise all the work of redrafting and recasting, and to check the results before the new schemata were sent to the Council fathers.[48]

On 21 January 1963, the Coordinating Commission issued precise instructions for the work of the commissions,[49] and this meant that the secretariat too was gradually able to carry out the necessary revision of its own schemata. There were therefore two series of plenary meetings of the secretariat in the period under study here: the first from 25 February through 2 March, and the second from 12 through 19 May.

The first series was concerned chiefly with the draft document on ecumenism, and it included the joy of a visit from the pope. At the end, the revised schema was approved.[50] After it had also been examined and approved by the Coordinating Commission on 13 April, the document could be sent on to the Council fathers, together with a request to them to submit their observations by the end of July.[51]

The second series of plenary meetings was devoted to the other two schemata: one on religious freedom and the other on relations with the Jewish people, for the latter had been put back on the Council agenda following a decision taken by the pope. Almost immediately after the close of the first period of the Council, Cardinal Bea had sent a memorandum to Pope John and had received a positive answer a few days later in a personal note from the pope.[52] A schema that was substantially the same as that of June 1962 was thus taken up again.

Parallel with the first series of plenary meetings there were also four meetings of the joint commission in which the schema that had been called "The Sources of Revelation" and was now entitled "The Schema on Divine Revelation" was to be revised in the light of the instructions of the Coordinating Commission.[53] The revised schema was then examined and approved by the Coordinating Commission on 27 March, but then nothing more was heard about it for some time after this, and only at the end of the second period of the Council did Pope Paul VI himself issue an assurance that the schema would be presented in the hall in the course of the next period of the Council.[54]

In accordance with a decision of the Coordinating Commission, the secretariat was also involved in study of the question of mixed marriages, together

48. Cf. Caprile, II, 325-335.
49. Cf. Caprile, II, 325-327. Since the minutes of the commissions have not yet been published, we shall refer above all to Caprile's work.
50. Cf. W. Becker's commentary on the Decree on Ecumenism in *LThK: 2. Vat. Konzil*, II, 20. On 28 March the schema was examined by the Coordinating Commission, in the presence of the pope; cf. Caprile, II, 377.
51. Cf. Caprile, II, 410.
52. Cf. Arch. Lf 9/1/12; the note bears the date 13 December 1962; cf. also *Church-Jews*, p. 23.
53. The meetings took place on 23 and 25 February, and 1 and 4 March.
54. Cf. *AAS*, LVI (1964), 36.

with the Theological Commission and the Commission for the Sacraments. The relative meetings took place in February and March, although the resulting draft was not examined by the Coordinating Commission until 3 July.[55]

Lastly, there was a *change in the structure of the secretariat*. As early as 30 November, when the cardinal spoke in the Council hall on the schema drawn up by the Commission for the Eastern Churches on the question of unity, he had announced that two sections were to be created in the secretariat, one for the East and the other for the West. This decision was then implemented in January. We find the following passage in the book *Ecumenism in Focus*: "In January by means of a letter from the Secretary of State (14 January), the pope decided that the Secretariat for Unity, 'apart from a cardinal and a secretary, should also have two under-secretaries, one for the West and the other for the East.' New members were later added for the Eastern section."[56] This meant that the responsibility of the secretariat for the whole non-Catholic world, in both East and West, was now a formal fact.

A New Phase Full of Commitments (January-April 1963)

I remember that in a conversation a little before the start of the Council, the cardinal observed that the time for lectures and such activities was past, and that now he had to concentrate on the Council. However, as soon as the work of the first period was over, he resumed this type of activity with a will, and new fields and perspectives started opening up for it too. This activity started with an ecumenical assessment of the first period of the Council—a subject that constituted the material for, among other things, the now customary "conversations" made during the Week of Prayer, both on Vatican Radio and Bavarian Radio.[57]

1. His activity during a *visit to Denmark* in January 1963 was especially demanding. Denmark was a Evangelical stronghold, with only about twenty-six thousand Catholics, and he went on the invitation of the Catholic Bishop of Copenhagen, J. Suhr. In the largest theater in Copenhagen, he gave a talk entitled "The Second Vatican Council and Non-Catholic Christians." The Lutheran Bishop of Copenhagen, Dr. Westergaard Madsen, decided to speak the concluding words. Apart from this talk, the cardinal had to give a press conference, an interview for television and another for Danish Radio. Lastly, the Student Missionary Association, which was holding its annual meeting at Roskilde near the capital, asked him to speak on "Ecumenism and Missionary Thought" and to answer their numerous questions. A recording of the whole of this meeting

---

55. For the decisions of the Coordinating Commission, cf. Caprile, II, 333. According to Caprile, II, 359, the relative meetings took place at the beginning of March, but according to my diary, on 14-15 February. For the examination of the schema on the part of the Coordinating Commission, cf. Caprile, II, 466.

56. *Ecumenism*, p. 56 (ct).

57. Cf. Biblio. 228; for Vatican Radio, cf. R 1963/6 (given in three languages), and for Bavarian Radio, cf. R 1963/5.

was later broadcast by Danish Radio.[58] On this occasion it was also pointed out—rather as had been done in previous years in connection with similar visits to Basel, Heidelberg and Tübingen—that no cardinal had made such a solemn and well-received visit to Denmark since the Reformation in 1536.[59]

2. By far the most demanding journey, and indeed the crowning point of the cardinal's personal activity in this period, was his *visit to the United States of America*, in which we find examples of all the various fields of the activity of the President of the Secretariat for Christian Unity that we have so far described: ecumenism, relations of the church with the Jewish people, and the Agapé meeting.[60]

(a) A first invitation came during the first period of the Council, from the Harvard Divinity School, through Dr. Douglas Horton, a professor at the school, who was an observer-delegate for the International Congregationalist Council. The reason for the invitation was given as follows: "It is the first time that the university, or more precisely its Divinity School, has organized a Catholic-Protestant colloquium. The only way of ensuring its success is the presence of an outstanding figure, and the cardinal is certainly such."[61] Cardinal Richard Cushing, Archbishop of Boston, who had established a close relationship with the cardinal during the first period of the Council and was also a great friend of the President of Harvard University, the Methodist M. Pusey, also assured Bea that the success of the meeting really did depend on his attendance.

The meeting opened on 27 March with a reception, which was followed by the cardinal's first talk, which was addressed (unlike the others) to the faculty members, and was devoted to the subject of "Teaching and Research in the Service of Christian Unity." The Sanders Theater was packed, and another large

---

58. Cf. *Ecumenism*, p. 57. For the manuscript of the various talks mentioned here, cf. (in the order in which they were given) R 1963/11, 10, 13, 9, and 12; for the two talks at Roskilde, cf. R 1963/14 and 15; cf. also the large files Arch. Ra 1963/44 and 45, which also include press clippings.

59. Merely in passing, I would mention the talks that Bea gave in this period in various institutions in Rome: one to the students of the Pontifical Gregorian University, one to the Pontifical College of Propaganda Fide (cf. R 1963/7 and 8); "conversations" at the Pontifical Germanic College and the St. Robert Bellarmine College; a lecture at the Pontifical College of St. Peter on 5 March, under the title "The Priest, Minister of Unity," and another on 4 May to the Verbite Fathers under the title "Ecumenism and the Missions" (cf. R 1963/17 and 33). Lastly, we should mention the talk given at the *Cittadella* in Assisi, to three or four hundred university professors, in the framework of a meeting devoted to "The Greatest Modern Discoveries in the Service of the Moral Progress of Humanity," and in which he spoke about "The Discovery of the Church in the Light of the Second Vatican Council" (cf. Biblio. 227a). There were also various interviews; cf. R 1963/16, 19, and 35.

60. There is a confidential report on the whole journey, but it has not yet been made public (Arch. Lc 6/1); in 1966 the cardinal described the journey in a fairly full article entitled "Aspects of a Peaceful Revolution" (Biblio. 335), to which we shall refer throughout the present section. It is unfortunate that there are various printing errors in the article; for example, the meeting at Harvard took place in 1963, not 1962 (p. 122); the opening took place on 27 March, not May (p. 123), and it was the cardinal, and not Mr. M. Pusey, who spoke about academic teaching (p. 123).

61. This was said at the first discussion of the invitation.

hall had to be linked up with closed-circuit television to allow the many people who had not been able to obtain seats in the theater to see and hear the speaker. On the two following evenings, the cardinal gave two talks for the general public on the subject of "The Council and Non-Catholic Christians." In the first he outlined the preparations and developments of the first period, and in the second he gave an overall evaluation, describing the fruits to date and also indicating further prospects.[62]

Later, the Dean of the Divinity School, Samuel H. Miller, made the following overall evaluation of the colloquium in a letter to Cardinal Bea: "Now that the colloquium has come to a close, we are more persuaded than ever that it far exceeded our expectations in many different ways. The public response to your presence was in itself an extraordinary event of great significance. The public lectures in the afternoons and the concern and interest which they elicited in the life of the university were certainly a most signal success. The four colloquies which were conducted in the morning and which involved something like one hundred and sixty scholars, both Protestant and Catholic, were extremely exciting to men who had been working in this field for many years. . . . The letters of testimony which are coming in to us are without exception full of appreciation for this particular aspect of the work."[63]

(b) A stay in *New York* then followed. The main reason was that he was to attend—and indeed preside over—the Agapé meeting of people belonging to various religious confessions, which we shall discuss in due course. However, in time various other engagements had been added.

The first meeting concerned the representatives of the *World Council of Churches* present in New York, and took place on the afternoon of 31 March at the Lutheran Center. More than ten highly respected representatives attended, and the cardinal was accompanied by the Secretary of the Secretariat, Monsignor Johannes Willebrands: "The conversation dealt mainly with possibilities of collaboration in fields in which the faith was not directly concerned, with particular reference to racial discrimination problems and those of Christian schools in countries which have recently obtained their independence."[64]

The following morning, a meeting with representatives of the *U.S. National Council of Churches* took place at the Interchurch Center. For this second meeting it had been "suggested that the conversation be directed rather toward those points of contrast which create greater difficulty. *Mixed marriages* were first discussed; in fact, due to the brevity of available time, the conversation was limited to this question alone."[65] Bea closes his account with an overall evaluation of these two meetings: "In both of these meetings the general atmosphere

---

62. This and the two talks on the following days were published in *Ecumenical Dialogue at Harvard* (Biblio. 258-260). There is no need to emphasize that there is no foundation whatever to the statement of Kaiser, *Inside the Council*, p. 255, that Bea had some of his statements checked by the Holy Office.

63. Biblio. 335, p. 124; cf. *Ecumenism*, p. 58; Arch. Ra 1963/48-49.

64. Biblio. 335, p. 125; cf. R 1966/9, p. 7.

65. Biblio. 335, pp. 126-127; cf. R 1966/9, p. 8.

was really excellent and fraternal. The Protestant representative presiding over the meeting concluded on both occasions by saying that as a result of these meetings the participants felt themselves closer to the Vatican Council and would pray more fervently for its success."[66]

A third meeting involved *representatives of Jewish organizations* and took place on the evening of 31 March. To use the words of Cardinal Bea, "about a dozen important people from the Jewish religious world took part, being fairly representative of the various existing currents." Since the cardinal was in a delicate situation because of his position at the Council, he started by stating that he could not speak either in the name of the Council or in that of the secretariat; nor could he forecast what the Council would decide in this connection. He was merely expressing his personal opinion on the various questions and on what could be done in the field.

The cardinal summed up the content of the conversation as follows: "In reply to questions which had been included in the program, I first of all clarified from the exegetical viewpoint the matter of the Jews' responsibility for the death of Jesus, that of the meaning of the dispersal of the chosen people among the nations, ruling out, as St. Paul does, any idea that God had rejected or gone so far as to curse his own people."[67] Bea added an overall evaluation: "The atmosphere which prevailed at this meeting also was an excellent and fraternal one. Several of the participants declared that they considered the meeting as an historic date, both by reason of the meeting between Jews and the cardinal, as well as by that between representatives of the various Jewish currents themselves."[68]

The most important meeting in New York—indeed the high point of the whole trip—was the Agapé meeting. This was a new type of event in which the cardinal had first taken part in 1962 at the "Pro Deo" International University of Social Studies in Rome. They were fraternal encounters between members of various religions, nations and races, inspired by mutual respect, and with the aim of overcoming prejudice, suspicion and resentment.[69]

In view of the success of the second Roman Agapé meeting, it was decided that one should be organized in New York, with the cardinal being invited to preside. In the article already quoted a number of times, Bea describes the reason for his participation in this type of event as follows: "I had agreed to preside at this meeting . . . not in my capacity as President of the Secretariat for Promoting Christian Unity, but merely in the personal capacity of one who loves men and mankind and desires to promote brotherhood among men. I did so all the more readily since at that time the two secretariats later instituted by the pope for contacts with non-Christian religions and with non-believers did not yet exist."[70]

---

66. Biblio. 335, p. 127; cf. R 1966/9, p. 9.
67. Biblio. 335, p. 129 (ct); cf. R 1966/9, p. 11.
68. Biblio. 335, p. 130; cf. R 1966/9, pp. 11-12. An important participant in the meeting of the various Jewish currents told me: "It's a miracle, not that these people met with the cardinal, but that they met with each other." On the New York meetings, cf. Arch. Ra 1963, 50-51.
69. Further explanations are found in Chapter 10 of this third part of our study.
70. Biblio. 335, p. 131; cf. R 1966/9, p. 13.

The cardinal then describes the meeting itself: "The meeting was extremely impressive by reason of the large numbers who participated—in spite of all efforts at limitation the numbers swelled to almost one thousand—and also for the quality of the guests. In this respect Nelson A. Rockfeller, Governor of New York State, remarked in his words of greeting that he had never before seen an assembly so imposing for the number of important people present. After a few words of greeting by the president of the American Council, Mr. Peter Grace, and a word of welcome by the Mayor of New York, Mr. R.F. Wagner, and by the Governor of New York State, I spoke on the theme which had been set for the meeting, namely, 'Civic Unity and Freedom under God.' Various aspects of the subject were then commented upon and illustrated in brief speeches by illustrious representatives of various creeds and religions. The first of these was Rev. H.P. Van Dusen, President of the Union Theological Seminary. Next came Rabbi Abraham J. Heschel, Professor of the Jewish Theological Seminary. Then it was the turn of His Excellency Mohamed Zafrulla Khan, President of the United Nations General Assembly, a Moslem. The final speaker was His Excellency U Thant, Secretary General of the United Nations, by religion a Buddhist. The various speeches were then briefly summarized by Rev. Father Felix A. Morlion, O.P., President of the 'Pro Deo' International University of Social Studies in Rome."[71]

(c) Apart from the engagements in New York, there were then others in *Baltimore*, the See of the Primate of the United States, at that time Archbishop L. Shehan, an eminent member of the secretariat. Thus, apart from a high mass in the cathedral, Bea also gave a talk for the clergy and laity on 2 April under the title "The Priest and Ecumenical Work," which was followed the next day by another for seminarians on "The Priest's Preparation to Be a Minister of Unity."[72]

(d) The last stop was *Washington*, where the cardinal had been invited by Archbishop P. O'Boyle, who was also President of the Episcopal Commission for the Catholic University of the United States. The university awarded Bea an honorary degree in theology, and the address listing the candidate's merits, which was spoken before the degree was conferred, was particularly warm. The cardinal spoke on the subject of "The Ecumenical Task of the Catholic Intellectual."[73]

* * *

To conclude this section, we shall make a few general reflections on the visit to the United States. In the first place it showed how remarkably interest in the question of unity had grown in that country—and Bea's popularity with it. After

---

71. Biblio. 335, p. 131; cf. R 1966/9, pp. 13-14. The files contain a large album with all the talks, newspaper clippings and photographs (cf. also Arch. Ra 1963/52). The meeting received extraordinary publicity partly because of the strange coincidence that the New York press had been on strike for some months and had resumed work on 31 March, the eve of the meeting.

72. Cf. R 1963/30 and 31; the talks have not been published. Cf. also Arch. Ra 1963/54.

73. Cf. Biblio. 232; cf. also Arch. Ra 1963/53. Before leaving, Bea held a press conference at the airport to deny the news published by *Time* magazine that Pope John had entrusted him with the mission of explaining to the White House why the pope was ready to talk to the communists.

the cardinal had accepted the Harvard invitation, his host, Cardinal R. Cushing, released a statement to the press saying that Bea would also visit other parts of the United States, accompanied by himself. Alarmed by this announcement, we immediately pointed out that the cardinal's visit was to be fairly short, but despite this invitations poured in from every side: there were about seventy in all, thirty-five from universities and colleges, fifteen of them non-Catholic.[74]

After the death of John XXIII, his faithful secretary, Monsignor Loris F. Capovilla, gave us a photocopy of a sheet from a table calendar, dated 23 March, on which the pope had made the following note: "Always good work from Cardinal Bea, most worthy President of the Secretariat for Christian Unity, and very meritorious, now leaving for America, where opportunities are awaiting him to do a great deal of good. I feel a heartfelt need to accompany him with particular union of spirit and prayer."[75]

The visit called for an enormous expenditure of energy on the cardinal's part. Even setting aside the importance of the engagements and the weight of responsibilities involved, it is enough to consider the fact that in a mere ten days he gave six different major talks, and five full-scale addresses, all in English, a language with which he was not familiar.[76]

Lastly, the cardinal's visit gave birth to a new publication. Following the success of the Agapé meeting in New York, Bea was urged to write a whole book on the subject dealt with in his address at that meeting, and this was given the provisional title of *Unity in Freedom*.[77] The American publisher was sure that he could place half a million copies in the United States alone. After some reflection, Bea accepted the suggestion, and set to work. The fact that he had no other public engagements in those weeks made the task easier. Then when the pope's health began to deteriorate, this acted as a fresh spur to speed things up. Thus, on the eve of the conclave, we were able to send off the manuscript, already translated into English. Although the study would still entail further attention, the back of the task had been broken.

The Whole Church Walks Through the Valley of the Shadow of Death

In one of the last years of Bea's life (I think in 1967) the following exchange took place between him and Pope Paul VI. The pope: "Your Eminence, I would ask you to look after your health and not to work too hard." Bea: "But we are worried too, Holy Father." "Why?" asked the pope in surprise. "Your Holiness works too hard," answered Bea. And the pope: "But I do what I can. When I can't go on any

---

74. Cf. *Ecumenism*, p. 58; also R 1963/35, p. 1, and Ra 1963/55.

75. Cf. ArchWit, statement of Monsignor Capovilla, enclosure 5; cf. also Bea's report, R 1965/25, p. 3.

76. His exhaustion continued even after the trip, and this led his physician to prescribe some radical treatment with an implant of living cells about one month later. The result was excellent and helped Bea over the difficult weeks of the death of Pope John and the successive conclave.

77. Cf. Biblio. 335, p. 132.

more, someone else will take over." Cardinal Bea's answer was significant: "Holy Father, one conclave is quite enough for us." This was one of the rare occasions on which Bea gave any indication of how much the events connected with the death of Pope John and the election of his successor had cost him.

More than once the cardinal had said that one of the first signs that something was amiss, and that therefore marked the start of concern and worry, dated back to about the month of September 1962, when the pope himself had told him about certain problems, adding: "They've advised me to drink certain types of mineral water." At which Bea, who had had health problems himself, and had also gained a great deal of experience, having been a religious superior for most of his life, said that a proper medical check-up was needed. Later on he also told the pope's private secretary the same thing.

During the first period of the Council when the signs became more alarming, Bea had twice—probably the first time in November 1962 and the second in April 1963—had one thousand masses celebrated for the pope's intentions. And he told the pope about this in order to boost his spirits. I think that on the second occasion the pope let him know that he had offered the masses for the Council.

Although these episodes had gradually prepared us for the pope's loss, we had no idea that we would have to face it so soon. The news given on 31 May that the pope had received the last rites came as a thunderbolt. After I heard the news on Vatican Radio, I waited for the cardinal to finish resting, and we then set off for the Vatican. However, the cardinal was not able to see the pope.[78] This condition lasted until the following afternoon, when I received a telephone call after four p.m. saying that the pope had recovered consciousness. We hurried to the Vatican. On a number of later occasions the cardinal described this last, very painful meeting with Pope John: "I came into the room together with Cardinal G. Pizzardo. The pope was awake. We were announced. The pope looked up at the ceiling and tried to say something. The oxygen was removed in order to help him, but despite this all he could make were some unintelligible sounds. . . . That was all."[79]

After this there was nothing to do but pray. When the news finally came on the evening of 3 June, the cardinal watched the whole Italian television program on Pope John. Early the next morning, he went to pray beside the body. On the afternoon of 4 June the bier was transferred to St. Peter's, and the solemn funeral took place on 6 June.

About three months later, speaking on Bavarian Radio on the eve of the second period of the Council, the cardinal spoke about his impressions during those hours: "By the end of the first period of the Council, the shadow of a death was hanging over the Council, and over our hopes and expectations. The pale

---

78. Later on we were told that in such circumstances all authority passes into the hands of the first *cameriere partecipante*, who in this case was the private secretary, Monsignor L.F. Capovilla. And in fact he later said to me: "If you had only telephoned me. . . ."

79. It was in these circumstances that a well-known Roman attorney, Dr. Vittorino Veronese, told me in the antechamber that in an audience a few weeks earlier (20 April) the pope had said to him: "Just think what a great grace the Lord gave me in letting me find Cardinal Bea."

face of the beloved Pope John XXIII increasingly gave rise to anxious questions. Would he still be here for the second period of the Council? Would he be able to see it through to the end? And after many vicissitudes and hours of anxiety, when the final, decisive attack indicated the major crisis and the approach of a painful and sudden end, we—and to some extent the rest of the world with us—became really frightened, for what was to become of the gigantic work of the Council that had only just begun? Much of what had moved us and filled us with joy and happy confidence over these last few years now seemed endangered and seriously compromised by this death.

"The memorable evening mass on St. Peter's Square, with its *Ite missa est* coinciding with the death of the Holy Father, seemed to be a renewal of the sacrifice of Golgotha, not only for the pope, but also for the church and for each one of us; we all felt that God the Father was also demanding that we all assent to this event, accepting it with deep faith, together with all the difficulties this death could entail for the church and the world. The church itself—and we with it—passed through the valley of the shadow of death with its dying head, and took part in spirit in Christ's sacrifice on the cross. . . .

"Yet this Golgotha-event was surrounded by *a special light*, visible only to the eyes of faith, which announced the approach of the resurrection morning. This light was the fact that this unique death, whereby the pope became 'a spectacle to the angels' and—through the modern information media—also 'to men' (cf. 1 Cor. 4:9), was truly worthy of so great a pope. We need think only of the heroic submission to the will of God with which Pope John laid all his plans and wishes, including the Council, and also himself, in God's fatherly hand, saying to all who were offering their trembling prayers for him throughout the world: 'What you should pray for is this: that God's will be accomplished in me, whether this be a return to health and continuation in the high-priestly service, if this be God's good pleasure, or whether it be my death.'

"Another ray of the light that surrounded John XXIII's death was the unparalleled unity of spirit, which had maybe never before existed, with which Christians of all creeds and also many non-Christians joined together in prayer and mourning for the dying pope. Thus they were all, at least in this moment and in this respect, 'one heart and one soul' (Acts 4:32)."[80]

Those who knew Bea and his close ties to this great pope, and especially the way he saw this papacy and the way he had identified himself with its objectives, will easily appreciate that this was not rhetoric but, if anything, a watered-down expression of how the cardinal had personally experienced those painful events. This is confirmed by the rich and detailed testimony that Bea bore to the pope of the Council in his book *Unity in Freedom*.[81]

---

80. This English translation has been made from the German original, which has never been published. Cf. *Ecumenism*, pp. 94-96. Similar thoughts are found in a shorter form in R 1964/3, p. 1, and R 1964/4, p. 2.

81. Cf. Biblio. 170, pp. 50-74.

"The Approach of the Resurrection Morning"

The days preceding the conclave were full ones. Since the College of Cardinals governs the church during any vacancy of the Holy See, plenary meetings of the cardinals present in Rome had been held every day since 5 June, although they only discussed and passed decisions on those questions that could not wait. There were fifteen such meetings before the start of the conclave. Moreover, the novena of masses celebrated for the deceased pope started on 7 June.[82]

In the midst of all these activities, the cardinals also had to prepare for the conclave. The task was facilitated on this occasion by the fact that the first period of the Council had given the cardinals enough opportunity to get to know one another—although this increased knowledge, with all the consequent impressions and judgments, could also make the choice even more difficult. As regards the role played by Bea during this period, one writer, who was more interested in sensationalism than the truth, wrote that the cardinal's office in Via Aurelia was the center of activity prior to the conclave, with constant visits from cardinals of various countries and also from curial cardinals.[83] We would first of all note that, out of a total of about eighty cardinals, the diary notes visits from seven in all, from six countries. Certainly the respect Bea enjoyed would lead to the assumption that many people would consult him, although it should not be forgotten that doctrinal activity in the Council and the highly practical issue of electing a pope are two very different matters. On the other hand, the cardinals saw one another every day in their official meetings, and therefore had enough opportunity to exchange views. Lastly, we must remember the extreme discretion and prudence which were such hallmarks of the cardinal's character. As a member of the Society of Jesus—an order traditionally suspected of secret maneuvers and power-plays—he had to be doubly cautious in expressing his views.[84]

As regards his state of mind during this period, my diary for 7 June bears the following observation: "The cardinal is a little tired, and often preoccupied. I must help him, support him."

---

82. Cf. for example the report in *CC*, 1963/III, 85.

83. Cf. Michael Serafian (a pseudonym of Malachi Martin), *The Pilgrim. Pope Paul VI, the Council and the Church in a Time of Decision* (New York, 1964), pp. 117-118. The cardinal received the book in Boston in June 1964. After reading the many references to himself (in the index of names there are twenty-eight listings for his name!), he smiled as he told me: "There is hardly anything true in the whole thing." Cardinal M. Novak speaks somewhat similarly about the role of the book; *ibid.*, p. 36.

84. And in this very sensitive matter he certainly never indulged in the telephone discussions that R. Kaiser mentions (*Inside the Council*, p. 112). As regards the candidature of the cardinal himself, the following episode is interesting from a number of viewpoints. During that period the cardinal received a visit from Prince Carlo Pacelli, a nephew of Pius XII. While I was accompanying the visitor to the door, we talked about possible candidates, and I observed that the French newspaper *Le Monde* had written that if Cardinal Bea were younger and not a Jesuit, he would have stood a chance. At which the prince said: "And the second impediment is the most serious of the two!"

When the cardinal left the Brazilian College on 19 June to go into conclave, he told the members of the community who had come to see him off: "We'll have a new pope in two days."

For the conclave we had an apartment with a magnificent view out over the Benediction Loggia and St. Peter's Square, while all I had to do was go out into the corridor on the other side of the apartment when I wanted to watch for the black or white smoke. The cardinal was unusually silent during the conclave. This was partly due to his anxiety over how things would go, but also partly to his concern over strict observance of the obligation to secrecy. Although on other occasions he would tell me about even confidential matters, in this case the secrecy was total.

In his diary for 21 June we find the following entry, written in red: "Paulus VI, Papa electus."[85] Later on, he referred to the fact that the election had taken place on the Feast of the Sacred Heart, saying: "The Sacred Heart has given us a great gift."

After the *urbi et orbi* blessing given by Paul VI, I accompanied the cardinal back to our apartment, and he immediately told me that when he had made his first act of homage to the new pope, the latter had told him: "Now Your Eminence can continue the work of the secretariat as you have done until now."[86] This represented immediate confirmation of both the president and the orientation of the secretariat. After lunch, a photograph was taken of the new pope with the cardinals. Bea happened to be close to the pope, and modestly started to move away, but the pope took his hand and kept him beside him.[87] At the second act of homage, which immediately followed this, the pope entrusted the cardinal with the task of sending his greetings and blessing to the Pontifical Gregorian University, where he had studied in 1921.

The cardinal's talk on Bavarian Radio gives us a good idea of how he assessed the pope's election and first decisions: "Surprisingly rapidly elected in one of the shortest conclaves in history, the new pope announced his program to the whole world in a radio broadcast less than twenty-four hours after his election, adopting his predecessor's program in its entirety. In this program the Council is seen as the principal task of the new pontificate. In the thick of untiring activity—in which he gave an important place to the works of mercy so dear to his predecessor—and even prior to his coronation, Paul VI had announced that the Council would be resumed on 29 September, and had already taken numerous measures to facilitate this. . . . We shall not forget what we possessed and lost in John XXIII; nonetheless we can be profoundly glad over the new pope the Holy Spirit has given us, and whose election has found a joyful echo practically throughout the world. This more general joy increases even further when we consider the details of the new pope's program, paying special attention to what is so dear to the hearts of all of us and was a characteristic

---

85. "Pope Paul VI elected."
86. Cf. *Ecumenism*, p. 64.
87. Cf. the photograph in *Diario di un Cardinale* (the Italian version of *Der Mensch Bea* and *Spiritual Profile* = Biblio. 191a), after p. 160.

feature of the first period of the Council: the unity of all who believe in Christ."[88]

On 7 July the cardinal was received in audience by Paul VI for the first time, and the appointment is underlined in red in his diary. He came out of the audience very satisfied, and told me: "The pope had prepared very thoroughly for the audience; he goes straight to the crux of problems and is very open."[89]

* * *

There is not much to relate about the rest of the time prior to the opening of the second period of the Council. We would say first of all that the death of Pope John and the successive events meant that the cardinal had to cancel some talks he was to give in various Italian cities (Florence, Brescia, Trieste) in the month of June.[90] He left Rome on 18 July for a break of about one and a half months, although even this period was by no means devoid of engagements of various kinds. However, after the virtual lack of any vacation in 1962, he now had to allow himself a real rest.

He began with the eight days of his annual retreat in the novitiate of the South German Province of the Society of Jesus, at Neuhausen, near Stuttgart. This was followed by the priestly ordination of fellow Jesuits in Munich. After eight days of relative rest at Moos Castle near Plattling, which belonged to the Arco Zinnenberg family, Bea took part in Salzburg's University Week where, among other engagements, he gave a lecture under the title "The International Character of Science in the Service of Christian Unity." The lecture considered a number of the points discussed in the lecture given two years earlier at the Catholic University of Fribourg in Switzerland, but there was an important new element this time: the suggestion that an international institute should be set up after the Council for scientific research in the field of ecumenism, and that this institute should also publish its own journal.[91]

From Salzburg Bea went to Rorschach on Lake Constance, where he allowed himself three weeks' rest in the Stella Maris Institute of the Teaching Sisters of the Holy Cross of Menzingen. This was the same house where Eugenio Pacelli, the future Pius XII, used to go when he needed a rest, both when he was Apostolic Nuncio in Germany and also after he became Secretary of State. Even this period was filled with work, for he had to deal with the normal business of the secretariat, preparations for the next period of the Council and such things; however, it was work he could take calmly, without too must haste or pressure.

In the course of his journey back to Rome, Bea visited Trent, where he took part in the International Historical Congress dedicated to the subject, "The

88. Here again, the English translation has been taken from the original German, R 1963/41; cf. also *Ecumenism*, p. 96. On the first ecumenical actions of the new pope, cf. *ibid.*, pp. 64-68.

89. Cf. also the evidence of the cardinal in R 1964/9, p. 9. For Bea's views on Paul VI after some months as pope, cf. the portrait he gave in February 1964 in "The Image of Paul VI in the Light of the First Months of His Government" (Biblio. 262); original Italian ms. R 1964/9.

90. These talks were to have taken place on 8, 17 and 19 June respectively.

91. Cf. Biblio. 234, p. 13; in the archives the relative file is labeled Ra 1963/58.

Council of Trent and the Tridentine Reform." He presided over the session of 14 September, giving a brief address.[92] When he reached Rome, there were some public engagements awaiting him, foremost among them a talk on "Journalists and the Second Vatican Council," which he gave to the Congress of the Catholic Union of Italian Journalists.[93]

The Second Period of the Council: Light and Shadow (September–December 1963)

Just as he had done in 1962 on the eve of the opening of the Council, the cardinal now spoke again on Bavarian Radio on the eve of this new period. With his usual sense of realism he gave his listeners a warning which could almost be described as prophetic in the light of later events: "Despite all these favorable prospects we should not, however, exaggerate. We know that, as is the case in the church in general, the Council is also composed of human beings. It is therefore only too natural for us to have to envisage some difficulties and delays; and above all we must accept that not everything that each of us personally hopes for from the Council can be fulfilled."[94]

1. Let us start by looking at the various speeches the cardinal gave in the Council, and in the first place those made in his own name. The first concerned the first chapter of the schema of *the constitution on the church*, which dealt with *the mystery of the church in general terms*. The speaker particularly criticized its method, and asked that the treatment should go into greater depth, drawing not only on sacred scripture but also on the oldest sources of tradition, prior to the divisions between Christians—and not only the divisions of the sixteenth century but also those of the eleventh.[95]

His second intervention concerned the fourth chapter of the same schema, which dealt with *the general vocation to sanctity*. The speaker significantly asked that the text should be made more realistic, distinguishing between the perfect sanctity of eschatological times and the progressive and dynamic sanctity of the pilgrim church.[96]

The third intervention was concerned in a general way with the schema on *bishops and the government of dioceses*. The speaker asked that the field of responsibility of bishops should be fully respected, confirming this in the light

---

92. Ms. R 1963/40; on the meeting, cf. also *OssRom* (7 September 1963), p. 7, and Caprile, III, 19-22; Arch. Ra 1963/59.

93. Ms. R 1963/43; there was also a message for the start of lessons on ecumenism at the University of St. Louis, Mo.; R 1963/44.

94. This translation has been made from the original German, R 1963/41, pp. 5-6; cf. also *Ecumenism*, pp. 97-98.

95. Cf. *AS*, II/II, 20-22; there were also written observations, pp. 23-32; cf. Caprile, II, 39. The cardinal did not speak on Chapters II and III of this schema, but he did present written observations on Chapter II; cf. *AS*, II/II, 643-651.

96. Cf. *AS*, II/III, 638-641; there were also written observations, pp. 641-646. Added to these were written observations on the schema concerning the Blessed Virgin, pp. 677-681.

of what is known as the "principle of subsidiarity." The same principle also means, however, that the good of the church can require that the legitimate freedom of bishops be limited—as can be necessary in order to coordinate the activity of the different members and order it more effectively for the greater or more universal good of the church.[97]

In this same period, a long—perhaps over-long—discussion on the episcopacy, its sacramental character and collegiality took place, and people have often wondered why Bea offered no contribution in this connection. It was probably primarily a result of the changed situation. In the first period, the Council was still in its breaking-in phase, so that it was necessary to ensure that certain of its basic orientations were known and guaranteed, while this was no longer so necessary in the second period.

2. On 8 November came *the great moment for the secretariat: the schema on ecumenism* was distributed in the Council hall. The document was made up of three chapters, with an appendix of a fourth chapter on the relations of the church with the Jewish people. On 19 November, the schema on religious freedom was added as a fifth chapter.

As a number of presidents of conciliar commissions did, Bea entrusted others with the task of presenting the schema on ecumenism in the hall. Since part of the third chapter had been drafted together with the Commission for the Eastern Churches, the general introduction to the schema was made by the president of that commission, Secretary of State Cardinal Amleto Cicognani, while the more detailed speech on the three chapters was made by the Archbishop of Rouen, J.M. Martin.[98] The speech on the fifth chapter, which dealt with the question of *religious freedom*, was entrusted to the Bishop of Bruges, Emile de Smedt.

In view of the delicate nature of the matter, and since it dealt with the biblical field, Bea himself presented the fourth chapter, which dealt with *relations with the Jewish people*. This took place on 19 November, at the seventieth general congregation.[99]

It should be added that later on Bea also *took part in the discussion on ecumenism*, speaking about the first chapter, which was entitled "The Catholic Principles of Ecumenism." His purpose was mainly that of answering various objections that had been raised in the debate: people had said that ecumenism led to indifferentism, interconfessionalism, etc., and the speaker answered that the danger certainly existed, but that the way to avoid it is not that of fleeing ecumenism, but that of having the latter guided and supervised by the bishops.[100]

3. Let us now look at the areas of light and shadow in the specific field of the schemata of the secretariat. The area of *light* was the preliminary vote (a vote

---

97. Cf. *AS*, II/IV, 481-485; Caprile, III, 194.
98. Cf. *AS*, II/V, 468-471 and 472-479.
99. The text of the schema, *AS*, II/V, 431-432; the speech, pp. 481-485.
100. The intervention took place in the 74th general congregation (25 November); cf. *AS*, II/IV, 14-17. At this time the cardinal was also planning to speak on the subject of "ecumenism and the duty of evangelization" (cf. the draft Arch. Ld 1/1), but gave up the idea since there was a general feeling that the discussion had already gone on too long, and people wanted to move on to Chapters 4 and 5 of the same schema.

taken to obtain a general indication of whether the document was acceptable as a basis for discussion) on the schema of the decree on ecumenical work, in which the document was approved with a virtual unanimity, since there were only 86 votes against, out of the 2052 cast.[101] "This was an important and most significant result, which only three years before we could not have dared hope for," wrote the cardinal in this connection.[102]

The *shadows*, on the other hand, concerned the attached chapters dealing with relations with the Jewish people and the question of religious freedom. The facts were as follows. When the preliminary vote on the chapters on ecumenism was announced, it was said that the same thing would be done for the additional chapters too.[103] However, the discussion on the three chapters on ecumenism dragged on much longer than expected, and the agenda for that period of the Council still contained the schema on the apostolate of the laity, so that it was impossible to start discussing the chapters in question, let alone put them to the vote. This was the source of great disappointment and considerable anxiety.

Although the cardinal was the first to feel this, he stepped in firmly in the Council hall in order to *calm people's fears*. I think that it is worth quoting the central part of this speech, since it reveals quite a lot about Bea's character: "We are sorry not to have been able even to start on the discussion—and for no other reason than a simple lack of time! . . . However, I think that we must be grateful to the moderators for having allowed us so many interventions on the first three chapters, thus eliminating any risk of criticism for being over-hasty in voting on these first three chapters and on the other two, which deal with such very serious, new and important questions for the life and activity of the church in our days. . . . We must meditate and reflect deeply and unhurriedly so that we can discuss these and decide on them in the next period, when the question will be ripe for a fruitful debate."[104]

Bea describes the situation at the end of this period as follows: ". . . a certain effort is required to evaluate it [the period] dispassionately. The general atmosphere at the end of the period was not in fact such as to make this kind of evaluation easy. For many Council fathers it was a wearying period, but apart from their tiredness there was the feeling of having achieved virtually nothing, and, particularly toward the end, there were the various frustrations (for example, the lack of a vote on the schemata dealing with the problem of religious liberty)."[105]

Then, a bombshell fell into this atmosphere, changing it completely, when the pope announced in his closing address that he would be making a pilgrimage to the Holy Land. The change was such that some people imagined that the pope

---

101. Cf. *AS*, II/V, 690.
102. *Ecumenism*, p. 77; cf. also R 1964/3, p. 2.
103. Cf. *AS*, II/V, 682; Caprile, III, 313.
104. Caprile, III, 410; *AS*, II/VI, 365-366. It is unnecessary to add that time and events proved the accuracy of what the speaker said. The cardinal continued his efforts to reassure people; cf. for example *Ecumenism*, p. 107; the interview Biblio. 251, p. 108 (cited also in Caprile III, 563); R 1964/36, p. 1.
105. *Ecumenism*, p. 79. Bea thus described this period as "a hardworking seed-time" (*ibid.*, p. 78).

had taken this sensational decision in order to shake people out of their despondency at the way the work of the second period of the Council had gone. However, Bea said that the plan had been conceived much earlier: "The pope had spoken to me about a pilgrimage in the audience he granted me in September, when the work of the Council had not even begun."[106] The cardinal explained the connection between the Council and the pilgrimage as follows: "It would seem more correct to say that the pilgrimage was suggested [to the pope] by the awareness that the Council was and remained an undertaking fraught with serious difficulties, and that it therefore needed prayer and penance. And this view is fully confirmed by the pontiff's own statement."[107]

Months Full of Engagements (December 1963—August 1964)

It might be thought that the exertions of the second period of the Council would be followed by a time of relative calm. However, we find months full of engagements of various kinds, travel and study. We can start with some simple figures: there were almost two weeks of plenary meetings of the secretariat,[108] eleven meetings of the Holy Office,[109] six meetings of the Sacred Congregation of Rites, and eleven of the Council for the Proper Implementation of the Constitution on the Sacred Liturgy,[110] while a further twenty-eight days were taken up with various journeys. There were also a number of demanding public talks and publications.

1. Let us start by looking at the two weeks of *plenary sessions of the secretariat*. In the first place it was necessary to study and weigh up the abundant material on the three chapters on ecumenism, which had been the harvest of the various days of discussion. Moreover, in the aforementioned speech given in order to reassure people over the failure to reach a vote on the fourth and fifth chapters of the schema on ecumenism, Bea had in a way invited the fathers to send in observations on these chapters, for he had said: "So in the forthcoming months, the questions dealt with will be submitted for the study and examination of the fathers."[111] And such observations did arrive in large numbers, so that the two weeks were full of work.

2. However, this period is above all full of *personal engagements* directly connected with the schemata of the secretariat or related problems.

---

106. Cf. *Ecumenismo*, p. 86, note 5. According to the cardinal's diary, the audience took place on 26 September. Later the pope's note on the pilgrimage, dated 21 September, was published; cf. *ibid.*, p. 86.

107. *Ibid.*

108. These meetings took place between 24 February and 7 March 1964.

109. The cardinal had become a member of the Holy Office in September 1963 and had already taken part in eight meetings of this department during the second period of the Council.

110. Bea was appointed a member of this council from the time it was set up following the decision of Paul VI after the promulgation of the conciliar constitution *Sacrosanctum concilium*. There were also two meetings of the Congregation for Seminaries and Institutes of Study (today's Catholic Education), and one meeting of the Biblical Commission.

111. AS, II/VI, 365-366.

(a) The work of the second period of the Council was barely over on 13 December when the cardinal gave an extremely demanding talk in Rome on the question of religious freedom. The date had been set months earlier, but was most timely in the tense atmosphere created by the lack of any discussion or vote on the relative conciliar schema. The importance of this event was highlighted by the fact that the address was given in the Capitol and was the introduction to the annual Conference of Italian Catholic Jurists. There was also the fact that it coincided with the tenth anniversary of the famous speech that Pius XII had given in 1953 to the same association on the subject of religious tolerance.[112] The talk made a remarkable stir in the press. And in order to broaden its audience as much as possible, thus helping develop people's thinking, and preparing the way for the discussion in the next period of the Council, we arranged to have it reproduced in a dozen theological reviews and similar publications in various continents.[113]

(b) Then came a talk involving the question of *the Jewish people*—at least so far as the actual context of the lecture was concerned. Bea took part in a "Fraternity Week" held in Cologne in March to mark the end of the "Monumenta Iudaica" exhibition. On this occasion he gave a talk on what the Council could do to foster mutual understanding and fraternity among human beings, and in particular with regard to relations with the Jewish people.[114]

(c) There was then a whole series of activities concerning ecumenism. In mid-April, we find Bea in Milan, where he and three of his staff had long conversations with representatives of the World Council of Churches.[115]

Catholic mariology is always seen as constituting a major problem for relations with Christians of the Reformed tradition, and this problem had in fact already been raised in the Council. On the one hand there were some theologians who were hoping for a solemn proclamation of the doctrine of Mary as "mother of the church," or even the definition of the doctrine of Mary as mediatrix. Ecumenical circles, on the other hand, bore in mind the beginnings of mariological reflection among Christians of the Reformed tradition, and said that it would be best not to upset this process with new steps but to allow reflection on the ancient fundamental marian dogmas to ripen in them. Bea had already presented a written intervention on this matter during the second period of the Council,[116] but now he dedicated a broader study to the question. This was published in a number of reviews, with the English translation appearing under the title of "Mariology and Ecumenism."[117]

---

112. Cf. *AAS*, XLV (1953), 794-802.
113. Cf. Biblio. 248; also in the booklet, Biblio. 184; cf. also the full collection of forty entries in the files: Arch. Ra 1963/61.
114. The text appeared in the official publication *Monumenta Iudaica* (Biblio. 279), and in a reworked form in various other publications (Biblio. 252); cf. the material for the whole journey, Arch. Ra 1964/66.
115. Cf. *Ecumenism*, pp. 92-93. He also gave a lecture at the Catholic University on "What Christian Unity Expects from the Laity"; cf. Biblio. 257; papers in Arch. Ra 1964/68.
116. Cf. *AS*, II/III, 677-681.
117. Cf. Biblio. 273 for the various translations and publishing information, as well as Biblio. 173.

Another ecumenically important event was the cardinal's presence at Harvard University in June 1964 to receive an honorary degree in law, which was in a certain sense the fruit of the lectures he had given the previous year. The ceremony was attended by twelve thousand students, and a number of important figures from various continents also received honorary degrees on the same occasion, including the German Chancellor, Dr. L. Erhard. The certificate stated that Bea had been awarded this honor for the following reasons: "Among the differences of mankind this revered scholar seeks fraternal dialogue evoking harmony in Christendom."[118] On the eve of the ceremony, the president of the university, M. Pusey, spoke to me in confidence, saying something that explains both the invitation of the previous year and also the award of this honorary degree: "You see, we know that the Spirit of God is working in a special way in the church, and Bea is a vehicle for it. This is why we venerate him."

The homily the cardinal gave at Bernkastel, the birthplace of Cardinal Nikolaus von Kues, was also ecumenically significant. The occasion was a pontifical mass marking the fifth centenary of the birth of this man[119] who was in many ways the forerunner of unity; among other things, it was he who accompanied the members of the Orthodox hierarchy to the "Council of Union" of Ferrara and Florence.[120] In his homily Bea drew a portrait of the cardinal, pointing out the many points of similarity with the modern search for unity and particularly with the activity of the secretariat in the Council.[121] Among the other events connected with this occasion, Bea laid the foundation stone of the Institute for the Study of Anglican Theology in the Benedictine Abbey of St. Matthias.[122]

3. In this period too the cardinal once again had to deal with the question of the *historicity of the synoptic gospels*. Not content with having placed his booklet on the subject at the disposition of the Council fathers at the end of 1962, the cardinal worked hard to have the Pontifical Biblical Commission (of which he was a member) publish an Instruction on the matter, and he played an active part in drafting this document. It was again he who presented the draft at the meeting of the member cardinals on 11 March. And when the Instruction had been definitively approved and published,[123] he prepared a commentary, adapting the text of his booklet for the purpose. The fact that he was able to do so

Cf. also the file, Arch. Ra 1964/72. We would mention in passing Bea's pilgrimage to Fatima in mid-May, which was explained by the fact that this time the pilgrimage was dedicated to prayer and penance for Christian unity and peace; cf. Ra 1964/70. Furthermore, the cardinal saw it as an opportunity to encourage a christocentric marian devotion; cf. R 1964/16 and 17.

118. Arch. Ra 1965/74/9.
119. Nikolaus von Kues (1401-1464), born in the Diocese of Trier, a canonist, mathematician, philosopher, theologian, bishop and then cardinal; cf. *LThK*, VII, 988-991.
120. Held in 1438-1445 under Eugene IV.
121. Cf. Biblio. 278; Arch. Ra 1964/79.
122. Another ecumenically important event was the cardinal's participation in the Congress of German Catholics, held in early September in Stuttgart, where he also spoke the concluding words in the great celebration of the word of God; cf. R 1964/34.
123. The official title was *Sancta Mater Ecclesia*, and it is found in *AAS*, LVI (1964), 712-718. The text of the address with which Bea presented the document in the meeting of the cardinal-members of the commission, 11 March 1964, is found in Arch. Mc 5/8.

without too much difficulty is certainly an indication of the relationship between the two texts. The commentary enjoyed considerable success and was translated into six languages.[124] Together with the Instruction itself, it exercised a considerable influence in the drafting of the parts of the conciliar Constitution on Divine Revelation that deal with this question.[125]

Lastly, in the midst of these various commitments, he made his annual retreat from 1 through 10 August at the Novice House of the Society of Jesus at Neuhausen, and spent a period of rest from 12 through 29 August at the Stella Maris House of the Teaching Sisters of the Holy Cross at Rorschach on Lake Constance. Here too, however, his time was largely taken up with day-to-day affairs of the secretariat and with study of the conciliar schemata in preparation for the next period of the Council.

A Tiring Conciliar Period, Rich in Both Difficulties and Results (September–November 1964)

The third period of the Council was particularly full for many reasons. The Council began to bear its *first important fruit*: the definitive approval and promulgation of the Constitution on the Church, the Decrees on the Catholic Eastern Churches and on Ecumenism, and also the preliminary vote on the schema concerning the relations of the church with the Jewish people. The period was also full of work. Apart from taking part in forty-seven general congregations, twelve meetings of the secretariat, and seven of the Holy Office, the cardinal also made five interventions in the Council hall in his own name and two official speeches, both concerning the schema for the Decree on the Relations of the Church to Non-Christian Religions. The period also brought *some notable difficulties*, which left deep marks. In this connection we shall confine ourselves to those concerning the documents prepared by the secretariat: the difficulties that arose immediately prior to the last vote (in the general congregation) on the Decree on Ecumenism, and the renewed lack of a vote on the schema on religious freedom.

1. Let us first of all take a look at the speeches the cardinal made in his own name in the Council hall. The first concerned Chapter VIII of the *Constitution on the Church*, and specifically its approach to the doctrine of the faith on Our Lady; it obviously followed the same lines as the article he had published on this subject some months earlier, and on the whole it exercised a positive influence on the constitution.[126]

A second speech was concerned with the schema of the *Constitution on Divine Revelation*. This was a somewhat delicate subject for Bea to speak on,

---

124. Cf. Biblio. 171.
125. His critical and ecumenical evaluation of R. Kittel's *Theological Dictionary of the New Testament* also created a certain stir in the academic world; cf. Biblio. 265, 328.
126. Cf. *AS*, III/I, 454-458; Caprile, IV, 16-17. He also gave a talk in Latin on the same subject to the Brazilian bishops; cf. R 1964/37.

since, as we have seen, the secretariat was jointly responsible with the Theological Commission for drawing up this schema. The speaker therefore started by saying that he would not make any distinction between material from the commission and material from the secretariat. He then went on to refer above all to the part concerned with the importance and significance of the Old Testament for Christians, calling for greater clarity and precision in the use of language.[127]

The third speech concerned the schema of the *Constitution on the Church in the Modern World.* The cardinal asked above all that greater use be made of the sources of the written word of God when expounding doctrine, and went on to provide a series of biblical texts in support of the main propositions of the document.[128]

His speech on the schema of the *Decree on the Missionary Activity of the Church* was particularly interesting. Many bishops from mission lands felt that the schema had been cut down too much in the redrafting process,[129] and, apart from appealing to the Secretary General of the Council, they organized a series of speeches by various Council fathers. Bea also agreed to help, and this is how he came to speak in the name of all the bishops of Africa and many Asian bishops, pointing out in particular the need for the missionary work of the church.[130] All this concerted action carried the day, and although Pope Paul VI had personally stepped in, observing that "We feel that the text will easily be approved by you,"[131] the schema was sent back to the commission in the following vote, with 1601 in favor and 311 against.[132]

The last speech was concerned with *the renewal of religious life.* The cardinal asked that the document should be such as to provide religious life with a fresh boost. Instead of confining itself to the juridical aspects, it should therefore explain the underlying bases of religious life in an attractive manner and in conformity with the pastoral aims of the Council.[133]

2. With regard to the field of *the secretariat,* we would mention first of all that in this period the cardinal had the great joy of heading the papal mission that returned the precious relic of the head of St. Andrew to the Greek Orthodox Archdiocese of Patras, after it had been venerated by the Council and by the people of Rome. During this journey, the cardinal was most impressed by the devotion shown by the Orthodox people.[134]

127. Cf. *AS*, III/III, 284-287; Caprile, IV, 133. Bea added detailed written observations for this schema; cf. *AS*, III/III, 287-290.
128. Cf. *AS*, III/V, 272-276; Caprile, IV, 249-250.
129. This abridgement was maybe due to the expectation that the Council would end with the third period.
130. Cf. *AS*, III/VI, 364-367.
131. Cf. *AS*, III/VI, 324.
132. The 118th general congregation, in *AS*, III/VI, 446-457; Caprile, IV, 398.
133. Cf. *AS*, III/VII, 442-446; Caprile, IV, 321. There was also an address on the ecumenical situation, which the cardinal gave before the pope and the college of cardinals on 17 November 1964; cf. Arch. Lc 6/8-10.
134. Cf. the cardinal's address at the audience of the observer-delegates; *Ecumenism*, p. 135. On the

As concerns the conciliar schemata, we should first and foremost note the positive developments regarding the schema on the relations of the church with non-Christian religions, and in particular with *the Jewish people*. Bea gave two official speeches on this subject, one on 25 September to present the new text, and the other on 20 November immediately before the vote on the redrafted text.[135] There were a number of harsh attacks in the press against the document, and also against the cardinal himself.[136] Despite all the opposition from certain quarters, the schema reached its outline vote, when it was accepted as the basis for a definitive document with *a surprising majority* of about ninety-five percent.[137]

The great success of the secretariat in this period was the definitive approval of the *Decree on Ecumenism* and its *promulgation* in public session. Apart from the actual fact of its approval, it should be stressed that the document was accepted almost unanimously.[138] Even so there was one painful note in this connection: twenty-four hours before the document received its first reading and relative vote in the general congregation, the secretariat received thirty-eight "benevolent suggestions expressed by authority"[139]—although it should be noted that the pope left it up to the discretion of the president of the secretariat to decide whether to act on them, and only half of them were in fact accepted. The pope's intervention gave rise to considerable criticism and bitterness, and the cardinal had his work cut out for a number of months to calm things down, especially in ecumenical circles.

The chapter concerning *religious freedom* met with even greater difficulty. In a letter of 9 October 1964, the Council authorities instructed that the schema should be reexamined by a joint commission including some members of the Theological Commission and some other "independent" figures. Moreover, the text was then to be submitted for the evaluation of the Theological Commission.[140] The latter approved the schema on 9 November, although not without some suggested modifications.[141] The schema could therefore not be presented in the Council hall until 17 November, a few days before the close of the period.

---

journey as a whole, cf. *ibid.*, pp. 130-135. See also the file Arch. Ra 1964/86, especially the press clippings (nos. 5-23).

135. Cf. *AS*, III/II, 558-564, and III/VIII, 649-651; English translation in *Church-Jews*, pp. 154-172.

136. Cf. Caprile, IV, 89-90 (esp. note 23). This author would note, however, that the press comments on the debate were in general favorable.

137. Cf. *AS*, III/VIII, 672. There were 1651 in favor, 99 against, and 242 *iuxta modum* (i.e. with reservations).

138. Cf. *AS*, III/VIII, 783: 2137 in favor and 11 against.

139. Cf. *AS*, III/VIII, 422: ". . . suggestiones benevolas auctoritative expressas"; cf. also Caprile, III, 479-480. Surprise was probably the reason why the document received 64 contrary votes at this time (cf. *AS*, III/VIII, 636-637); In the public session these were reduced to a mere 11; cf. also Caprile, IV, 476, 479.

140. On this letter, cf. Pivonka, *The Secretariat for Promoting Christian Unity*, p. 244.

141. Cf. P. Pavan (one of the experts who contributed most to the drafting of this document) in the introduction to the commentary on the same document, in *LThK: 2. Vat. Konzil*, II, 705-706. Similarly, Oesterreicher, in *ibid.*, pp. 448-450; Caprile, IV, 476-479. Arch. Lc 1 contains a series of documents concerning the whole matter.

Although it had been repeatedly announced that the preliminary vote on the schema would be taken on 19 November, it was in fact cancelled on the day itself, because 143 Council fathers had appealed for more time to study the schema, and the authorities had judged it right to grant this. It is not difficult to imagine the upheaval this caused among the majority. Despite the presentation of an appeal bearing 441 signatures in favor of holding the vote, the pope confirmed the decision of the Council authorities, saying that he had to uphold the right of the minority to the time necessary to study the schema—and all the more so since it had been considerably modified.[142] On this occasion too, the cardinal not only remained calm, but—as he had done in the previous period— he spoke in the Council in defense of the actions of the authorities in regard to both the question of amendments to the Decree on Ecumenism and the cancellation of the vote on religious freedom.[143]

Speaking Engagements and Travel Reach Their High Point (January-April 1965)

There were two main features of the months that followed. On the one hand they were still taken up with conciliar activity. Although the Decree on Ecumenism had now been promulgated, the secretariat was still involved in the work—and we might say the struggle—connected with two important schemata: that on the question of religious freedom, which is also of fundamental importance for ecumenism, and that on the relations of the church with the non-Christian religions, in particular the Jewish people. On the other hand, now that it had been promulgated, the Decree on Ecumenism provided a basis on which to start post-conciliar activity in the ecumenical sphere.

As concerns the cardinal's personal activity, for a number of reasons this period saw the high point and then the end of a certain type of activity he had been performing until then, in other words, travel, public speaking and official visits. Although Bea's activity would still be intense after the close of the Council, it would be confined almost exclusively to his many tasks in Rome, with the addition of a great deal of fruitful work as scholar and writer.

1. With regard to *his work in the secretariat*, we should note the two series of plenary meetings: 28 February through 6 March, and 9 through 15 May. There were certainly reasons for concern after the lack of a vote on the schema on religious freedom, but the document on the attitude of the church to non-Chris-

---

142. We shall not go into the details here: for the announcement of the vote, cf. *AS*, III/VIII, 184; after the petition of 143 fathers it was announced that in the general congregation itself a vote would be taken on the preliminary question of whether the schema should be voted on or not (*ibid.*, p. 391). The presiding authorities of the Council then decided that the general congregation was not authorized to make such rulings (*ibid.*, p. 415). For the reply to the petition supported by "over 600 signatures," cf. *ibid.*, pp. 544-545; for the precise figure of 441 signatures, cf. Caprile, IV, 477.

143. For the amendments, cf. *Ecumenism*, pp. 170-171; on religious freedom, cf. *ibid.*, p. 168.

tian religions was the source of even greater anxiety. After the latter had obtained that significant majority in the Council, such a storm of protest and objections broke out in the Middle East that there was cause for concern over the safety of the Catholic minority in that region. Since we shall discuss this in the relative chapter of the present work, for now it will suffice to say that these events would cause the cardinal and his staff considerable headaches for a number of months.

2. Alongside this work, the cardinal was deeply involved in *journeys and speaking engagements*. In the second half of January, he gave a talk in Munich and another at Würzburg University on what the Council had so far attained for Christian unity. He also spoke on the same subject a month later to the students of Cologne University.[144]

In April Bea made his last visit to the United States, where the Fellowship Commission in Philadelphia awarded him the International Brotherhood Prize. He made various other visits and speeches in the course of this trip to the United States.[145]

3. The fact that this period saw the beginning of the cardinal's post-conciliar ecumenical activity was much more important than all these journeys and speeches. Thus we have the two official visits that he made in quick succession to the World Council of Churches in Geneva and the Ecumenical Patriarchate in Constantinople. These two visits marked fundamental steps in the creation of new relations, on the one hand with the Orthodox Churches, and on the other with the World Council of Churches, which was the concrete incarnation of the modern-day ecumenical movement, uniting both the eastern churches and also the churches and ecclesial communities of the Reformed tradition.

(a) *The visit to the World Council of Churches* took place in February, and three main points deserve particular mention: first of all the cardinal was given an official reception at the headquarters of the council; then he announced that the Catholic Church accepted the proposal that the council had formulated at the meeting of its central committee held in Enugu to create a joint working group with the Catholic Church to explore the possibilities and methods for dialogue; and the third element was the public conversation between the cardinal and Pastor Marc Boegner, a previous President of the World Council of Churches. The public conversation took place, most significantly, in the Hall of the Reform, which was not able to hold the huge crowd of people who wished to attend.[146]

---

144. The content of the three lectures was substantially the same, and corresponds to the article "Il contributo del Concilio," *CC*, 1965/I, 422-434; for these three lectures, see also the files Ra 1965/92, 93 and 96.

145. Cf. Ra 1965/99. For the speech in connection with this award, cf. R 1965/21 (Italian original and English translation). For the other speeches, cf. R 1965/22, 23, 24, 25, 26 and 27. A number of speeches are published in the volume *Lectures by Augustin Cardinal Bea during His Visit to Philadelphia* (Biblio. 183). On the journey itself, cf. also BM, pp. 174-179; also the file Ra 1965/99.

146. Publishing information for all the lectures and the text of the public conversation, Biblio. 290-291. An account of the Geneva meeting is also found in *Ecumenism*, pp. 153-157. Cf. also Arch. Ra 1965/97.

Since all these events took place in the city of Calvin, there were also two significant events primarily concerning relations with the Reformed communities: first, a visit to the Protestant Cathedral of St. Peter, and secondly a solemn reception of the cardinal on the part of the Synod of the Reformed Church of Geneva.

(b) A few days before the cardinal left for Geneva, an ecumenical event of vast importance took place in Rome: the visit of a special delegation of the Ecumenical Patriarchate, made in fulfillment of the decision of the Third Pan-Orthodox Conference of Rhodes (fall 1964), which had entrusted Ecumenical Patriarch Athenagoras with the task of informing "the Bishop of Rome" of the results of this conference.[147]

In order to return this solemn visit, the President of the Secretariat for Christian Unity made *an official visit to the Ecumenical Patriarchate the following April*, the first time for many a century that a cardinal had made an official visit to Constantinople at the head of a papal delegation. We shall speak more fully about this visit in the following chapter, but for now we shall note simply in general terms that the visit included a meeting with the Holy Patriarchal Synod, attendance at the solemn liturgy in the Patriarchal Church of St. George, and, most important, detailed conversations on what could be done to advance mutual relations. It was on this occasion that a start was made on preparations for an important event that would take place at the end of the Council: the removal of the mutual excommunications of 1054 "from memory and from the midst of the church."[148]

In conclusion, we would observe that the difficulties that had arisen at the end of the third period of the Council over the Decree on Ecumenism had led many people to believe that from then on ecumenical work would become much more difficult. The sensational beginning made with the two official visits of the president of the secretariat completely gave the lie to these pessimistic forecasts. And other similarly encouraging events would follow in due course.

A Long Illness and Convalescence (June-September 1965)

The intense activity of recent months was followed by a period of ill-health so long and serious that there was some doubt as to whether the cardinal would have the strength to face the exertions awaiting him in the next period of the Council, or indeed whether he had not simply reached the end of his prodigious career.

The crisis did not come without warning. On his return from the United States, he had another cell implant. It was hoped that this treatment would restore

---

147. Cf. *Ecumenism*, p. 158. We shall speak in greater detail about this conference in the following chapter.

148. Cf. *ibid.*, pp. 204-211. A detailed account of the visit is found in *ibid.*, pp. 159-161. For the documents concerning the visit of a delegation to Rome and the return visit, cf. *Ecumenismo*, pp. 194-207; cf. also the file Arch. Ra 1965/98. During the visit Bea had serious health problems, but fortunately they cleared up.

his energy, as it had on three occasions in the past.[149] And for a few weeks he did continue with his usual activity. At the beginning of June he took part in the Italian Eucharistic Congress in Pisa, with a public lecture on the important subject of "The Eucharist and Christian Unity."[150] Then the first problems appeared in the second half of June. Every now and then he had a slight temperature, but the main symptom was a great sense of exhaustion. In early July, his temperature eventually forced him to stay in bed. The state of his heart meant that antibiotics had to be used very sparingly, which in turn made it impossible to keep his temperature down. However, the most serious aspect was that nobody was able to diagnose the basic problem.

In these circumstances Bea remembered a matter that had been worrying him for a number of years, in other words *his will*. Although he had been trying to make his will for some time, the frenzied activity of recent years had never allowed time. In the forced inactivity of these weeks, he returned to the question, and after extensive consultation he was finally successful in drawing up this important document. After signing it on 18 July, he gave a long sigh of relief: "Now I can rest easy."

Vacation time was drawing near and the heat was building up in Rome. It was clear that the sick man could not stay in the city; moreover, it was becoming urgent for him to receive more systematic treatment in a hospital environment. It was therefore decided that he should be taken to the Theodosianum Hospital in Zurich, belonging to the Nursing Sisters of the Holy Cross of Ingenbohl,[151] and the move took place on 19 July, with the kind and efficient assistance of the national airline, Swissair.

His personal physician accompanied him to Zurich in order to brief the staff at the hospital. All the various tests and examinations were then made, but it appeared impossible to reach any sure diagnosis. To start with there was a suspicion of viral hepatitis, but this theory was soon discarded, and both his personal physician and the medical staff of the hospital laid the blame at the door of the cell implant treatment, although for different reasons. The chief physician of the relative ward—who was against this type of treatment on principle—thought that the implanted cells must have come from an animal to which Bea was particularly allergic. On the other hand, his personal physician pointed out the complete success of the three previous implants, and thought that the present problems must spring from the use of infected or deteriorated cells. Whatever the truth of the matter, they were now faced with the task of freeing the sick man of these cells and their effects.

Bea was hospitalized for about a month. The nursing sister who tended him throughout his stay described the patient's attitude as follows: "The first wish he expressed was characteristic of the whole of his stay in the hospital: 'I want

---

149. The previous implants took place in May 1963, January 1964 and December 1964.

150. Cf. Biblio. 299.

151. This was the sister foundation to the *Teaching* Sisters of the Holy Cross of Menzingen, which owned the Stella Maris House at Rorschach, to which we have already referred a number of times.

to be nothing but a patient and be treated the same as all the other patients.' He did not want to be a prince of the church, but simply a human being. We responded to this wish, sharing the ups and downs of his illness. With great modesty he had only one goal: that of recovering in order to be able to serve God and the church for a little longer. He submitted obediently to all instructions. He observed every improvement in his state of health with satisfaction and joy. He had kind words for everyone he met in the clinic, and most of the other patients were unaware that he was a prince of the church. He spoke to them as one human being to another, as one patient to another. He was always pleasant, and his nice sense of humor made him a joy to nurse. His whole inner attitude impressed me deeply. He was richly endowed with God's graces, and he was also able to pass them on to others in the most remarkable way."[152]

On 17 August, the patient left the clinic, cured but still weak. He went straight to Stella Maris House in Rorschach, where he had been taking his summer "vacation" in recent years. He returned to Rome in mid-September, but a good deal of time—as well as the assiduous assistance of his personal physician—was still needed before he regained enough strength to face the exertions of the last period of the Council.

Apart from what we have said about the diagnosis, it must also be said that this whole episode was both a consequence and a symptom of the exhaustion resulting from his almost hectic activity in the years of the Council. Although the sickness had in a certain sense definitively reduced his strength to a considerable extent, it had at least forced him to take two months of complete rest, thus allowing him to recover a part of his powers, as would be seen in his activity during the last period of the Council. The sickness also led him to change his type of activity and his approach to it: the journeys and public speaking engagements now gave way to more static—although no less intense—activity in the secretariat and the other departments of the Roman curia, as well as considerable work as scholar and writer. This latter activity was aimed above all at spreading knowledge of the conciliar documents and encouraging their implementation.

A Period Rich in Toil and Results (September-December 1965)

The fourth and last period of the Council brought a rich harvest, particularly for the secretariat. However, we must at once add that its schemata would still require much work and some tenacious struggle. Bearing in mind his recent sickness and the fact that the cardinal was still convalescing, it is truly extraordinary that he should not only have survived under the pressure of all this work and the agitation and anxiety inherent in certain situations, but in fact have emerged from the period with flying colors.

In the first place let us give some figures on the Council sessions and other engagements of this period: apart from the forty-one general congregations and

---

152. Sister M. Bernadette Achtner, ArchWit.

the four public sessions, there were fifteen meetings of the secretariat, eight meetings of the Holy Office, three of the Council for the Proper Implementation of the Constitution on the Sacred Liturgy, three of the Congregation of Rites (for causes of beatification), two of the Commission for the Neo-Vulgate (which we shall discuss below), and one of the Commission for the Reform of Canon Law.

1. As regards his *personal interventions in the Council hall*, we must observe that in general the Council fathers made many fewer in this period than in the previous three. Even so, Bea did make two, one on the schema of the Constitution on the Church in the Modern World, in order to emphasize the need to base the reasoning more fully on sacred scripture.[153] The second speech concerned the schema of the Decree on the Ministry and Life of Priests, and called for a balanced presentation of priestly celibacy, so that it avoided wronging the married clergy of the eastern churches.[154] On the request of Pope Paul VI, the cardinal also took part, on a personal basis, in the discussions of the Theological Commission on the Constitution on Divine Revelation; these meetings considered the question of relations between sacred scripture and tradition, the doctrine on the inerrancy of sacred scripture, and lastly the question of the historical character of the gospels.[155]

2. The schema on *relations with the non-Christian religions*, especially with *the Jewish people*, also entailed considerable worry and toil. Although the eastern Catholic patriarchs had accepted the revised text of the document in July, this did not mean that opposition was yet at an end. There was also the danger that the ranks of those who had always opposed the document would now be swelled by supporters who felt that the new version had been watered down. In this situation the cardinal gave a talk for the Brazilian bishops on 28 September, which then appeared in a reworked form in the Italian review *La Civiltà Cattolica* and various other journals.[156] On 14 October Bea gave his last speech in the Council hall, explaining the amendments that had been made to the text after the third period of the Council on the basis of suggestions put forward by the Council fathers.[157] In the definitive vote, its opponents were reduced to 250 votes out of the 2023 cast on the first reading, while in the vote in public session on 28 October, the figure fell even further to 88 out of the 2312 cast (or under four percent).[158]

3. The battle over the document on *religious freedom* was more bitter. It was indeed the first item on the agenda for this period, as the pope had promised,

---

153. Cf. *AS*, IV/I, 576-579. Added to this were fifty pages of detailed written observations concerning above all the Latin used in the schema, which had originally been drafted in French; cf. *AS*, IV/I, 579-596.
154. Cf. *AS*, IV/V, 34-36; Caprile, V, 222-229. On this subject too, there were also twenty pages of written observations; cf. *AS*, IV/V, 36-46.
155. Cf. Arch. Lb 3/6/2-3.
156. Ms. R 1965/34; for the reworked version, cf. Biblio. 312.
157. Cf. *AS*, IV/IV, 722-725; English translation in *Church-Jews*, pp. 169-172.
158. For the vote in the general congregation, cf. *AS*, IV/IV, 824, and for that in public session, cf. *AS*, IV/V, 674.

but after six days of discussion the Council authorities decided once again that the assembly should not proceed to the usual preliminary vote. The pope himself had to step in—a little as Pope John had done in connection with "The Sources of Revelation"—before the schema was submitted to the vote on 21 September. It was a happy surprise when it obtained roughly ninety percent of favorable votes.[159] A period of hard work then followed in order to turn the basic draft into a definitive document. And after the latter had been voted on in its individual parts, the sixteen hundred or so amendments proposed in this last vote had to be evaluated.[160] The various processes meant that the definitive vote and the promulgation did not take place until the last public session, on 7 December. On the other hand, there was the satisfaction of seeing the 249 opposing votes of the first reading reduced to a figure of 70 out of 2386, or under three percent, in the public session.[161]

4. We shall mention in passing that in these months, the cardinal was also involved in organizing another important undertaking: *the Commission for the Neo-Vulgate*. We shall speak about this project more fully in another context, so that for now we shall merely say that it involved the revision of the venerable Latin translation of the sacred scriptures known as the vulgate, in order to make sure it reflected the original texts—Hebrew and Aramaic for the Old Testament, and Greek for the New. Preparations for this commission had already been started in the spring, but it was formally constituted with the letter of the secretary of state of 29 November, and Bea became its president.[162]

5. *The close of the Council* was marked by three significant ecumenical events. In the first place, the message prepared by the observer-delegate Dr. Lukas Vischer, with which the observers took their leave of the Council fathers, was read out in the Council hall. In the afternoon of the same day, a liturgy of the word was held in the Church of St. Paul outside-the-Walls, with the observers taking an active part in their formal choir robes, alongside the pope and the Council fathers.[163]

Three days later came the last event, which was a truly sensational ecumenical act: the abolition of the unhappy excommunications of 1054 between Rome and Constantinople, which had been followed by a total break and the start of schism. This abolition meant "removing them from memory and from the midst of the church" (this was the technical phrase) so that they would no longer disturb relations between the two churches. The relative ceremonies took place

159. There were 1997 votes in favor and 224 against; cf. *AS*, IV/I, 434, 564; Caprile, V, 45-46. It should be noted that the decision of the Council authorities not to proceed to the general vote is not found in the *Acta Synodalia*; however, the background is described as carefully as usual by Caprile, V, 45-48.
160. Cf. Caprile, V, 322.
161. In the vote on the first reading, out of 2216 votes cast, there were 1954 in favor, and 249 against; cf. *AS*, IV/VI, 780. In the public session (or second reading), there were 2308 in favor, and 70 against; cf. *AS*, IV/VII, 859-860; Caprile, V, 500.
162. Cf. T. Stramare, "La Neo-Volgata: impresa scientifica e pastorale insieme," *Lateranum*, XLV (1979), 10-35, esp. 13; also Arch. Mb/4.
163. Cf. *Ecumenism*, pp. 201-204.

simultaneously in the Patriarchal Church of St. George in Constantinople and the Basilica of St. Peter in Rome, with the presence of a delegation from the other party in each case. In St. Peter's, the embrace between the delegate from Constantinople and the pope was greeted by the longest applause of the whole Council. It was a very moving moment and provided a worthy conclusion to the whole marvelous development of ecumenism that had taken place in the context of the Council.[164]

* * *

Let us conclude with some figures to give an idea of Bea's commitments in the three years covered by this chapter. We obviously do not see figures as more important than content—indeed, in the following chapters we shall be considering the content in greater detail—but in the present case even the figures are eloquent, particularly if we remember that they refer to a man of over eighty.

In the first place, there were the commitments connected with the Council: attendance, with very few exceptions,[165] at 168 general congregations, as well as nine public sessions. In these congregations Bea gave four official speeches and nineteen personal interventions. The work of the secretariat involved the cardinal in thirty-five full days of plenary meetings, added to which were forty-five individual meetings held in the afternoons during the four periods of the Council. There was also participation in fifteen meetings of various other conciliar commissions.

Bea often said: "The diocesan bishops have left their own dioceses, so that they only have Council work to deal with in Rome, while for us who live here, we have all the *day-to-day work of the Roman curia* as well as the work of the Council." The following are the figures in this connection: forty-one meetings of the Holy Office, twenty-nine of the Congregation of Rites,[166] fourteen of the Council for the Proper Implementation of the Constitution on the Divine Liturgy, and six meetings at various other bodies. Added to these were the fifteen "congregations" of cardinals held during the vacancy of the Holy See after the death of Pope John XXIII.

Lastly, there was a considerable amount of *personal work*. Apart from the numerous audiences granted to groups or individuals, and the fairly large number of engagements of a more social nature, we have the following figures: thirty-four public lectures; thirty-four interviews, press conferences, etc.; eighty homilies, sermons, etc.; 108 days spent traveling.[167]

It is not surprising that at a certain moment the cardinal should have collapsed

---

164. Cf. the full description in *Ecumenism*, pp. 204-209. For the relative documents, cf. *Ecumenismo*, pp. 261-265.

165. It is impossible to state precisely how many these "very few exceptions" in fact were.

166. Although the Congregation of Rites had official responsibility both for the liturgy and for beatifications and canonizations, at this time it only had the latter field, since the postconciliar liturgical reform had been entrusted to a special council.

167. Obviously the latter figure does not refer to the days of absence from Rome, which were many more, but to the actual days spent on the move.

under the burden of such a work-load—even if the immediate cause of his sickness was another. At the end of the Council Bea was so exhausted that his doctor thought it advisable for him not to attend the concluding public session on 8 December. In any case, there would have been a serious risk in exposing himself to the cold and wind during a long open-air ceremony, but the cardinal's state of exhaustion was the decisive point. Apart from the tiredness that had built up in the course of the more than two months of this conciliar period, the last days of the Council had brought an exceptionally large number of commitments.

The cardinal let himself be persuaded, and I do not think he was too sorry to miss the long concluding celebration in St. Peter's Square. It also gave him an opportunity to reflect in silence on the years of the Council, on the many graces that the Lord had granted the church in those times, and in particular on the way in which the Lord had so abundantly blessed the work of the Secretariat for Christian Unity—as we shall see in the following chapters.

CHAPTER 7

DEVELOPMENTS IN ECUMENISM DURING
THE COUNCIL

"Ever since the end of the Council's first period I have repeatedly stated that the fruits of the Council were to be sought, to a large extent, less in the actual documents than in the whole experience the Council represented for those who took part in it and as a result also for Christians who watched the conciliar work. This is especially true in the ecumenical field."[1] These words of the cardinal provide a clue to the orientation of this chapter, for in seeking to describe the surprising progress of ecumenism during the Council, we shall not be referring either exclusively, or indeed directly, to the documents produced and promulgated by the Council, but more to ecumenism in a broad sense—in other words to all the contacts, the process of getting to know one another, the practice of Christian charity, and the mutual rapprochement between Christians of various churches and ecclesial communities.[2] The plans and resolutions expressed in the various documents promulgated by the Council are of course of enormous value, but they have their underlying foundation and draw their inspiration from the ecumenical experience gained during the Council.

In keeping with these same principles we shall not be considering Bea's contribution to the implementation of the Council in the ecumenical field in abstract terms, but shall watch him at work in his lectures and interviews, as he observes and evaluates ecumenical events, spreads information about them, fosters deeper understanding of them, and thus encourages the growth of ecumenical awareness. We have seen that Bea was very active in this field during the Council, as he had been in the period of preparation for it, but there is a notable difference between the two approaches. During the preparatory period he talked about possibilities, hopes and wishes, whereas after the Council had started he drew the attention of his audience to facts and events, commenting on them in order to highlight their underlying significance.[3]

---

1. *The Way*, p. 9 (ct).
2. Many readers are undoubtedly familiar with the volume *Ecumenism in Focus* (which we abbreviate to *Ecumenism*), in which the cardinal described the ecumenical aspect of the Council. This means that we can be fairly brief here, for the reader can turn to this book for any further information and details. (*Translator's note.* The Italian original of this book, *Ecumenismo nel Concilio*, is more complete, and also contains various documents not found in the English version. Although I use the latter wherever possible, in some cases I have had to translate directly from the Italian original, as will be clear from the relative footnotes.)
3. In order to help the reader to grasp the chronology of events, we would note that we shall simply be following the timetable of the Council, with its four periods and the "inter-sessions" between these. The four periods always took place in the fall (1962, 1963, 1964 and 1965), while the "inter-sessions" compromise January through September of the years 1963, 1964 and 1965.

454 THE COUNCILTHE COUNCIL

"It's a Miracle!"

In the press conference held in the press room of the Council on 9 November 1962, Bea summed up the general impression of the ecumenical aspects of the Council during the first period in the following terms: "In the past few days people have been reporting my impression after the audience that the Holy Father granted the observers from the non-Catholic Christian communities, when I said: 'It's a miracle, a true miracle.'[4] However, the phrase was not simply the fruit of my impression of that audience—although it was indeed a unique event, and also deeply moving due to the delicately friendly form that the Holy Father himself chose to give it in his benevolence. No, those words reflect the sum of our experiences in the two years since the secretariat was set up."[5]

The speaker explained this statement above all by referring to the presence of the observer-delegates: "*The first factor* is the presence of over forty observer-delegates and 'guests of the secretariat' who represent almost all the major federations of non-Catholic Christian confessions of the Reformed tradition, as well as a good number of eastern churches."[6] "The presence in the midst of the Council of observers representing non-Catholic Christian communities" is a source of special gratitude to the Lord, "inasmuch as this aim was much more difficult to envisage and attain than that of the Council itself."[7] Moreover, there was clear proof of this difficulty also in the absence (which was also stressed at the press conference referred to above) "of the venerable Orthodox churches." It would still require considerable effort, together with such a remarkable event as the pilgrimage of Pope Paul VI to the Holy Land, before they would send their representatives to the Council.

The second factor leading the cardinal to refer to the situation as miraculous "is even more important in the faith perspective, and is the fact that so many communities of non-Catholic Christians have made repeated appeals, sometimes official ones, to their own members to pray for the Council. I shall give a certain number of names, mainly in order to demonstrate the variety of confession, and the fact that such calls come from most parts of the world. . . . The following have made an appeal for prayer for the Council in one form or another: the Swiss Evangelical Federation, the Austrian Protestants, the Archbishop of Canterbury, Dr. Ramsey, Primate of All England, to the Anglicans of the whole of England, the Swiss Old Catholics, the Council of the Evangelical Church in Germany, the World Council of Churches, the World Alliance of Young Men's Christian Associations." The speaker then listed other calls from the United States, Canada and Australia, adding: "Various communities that for one reason or another have not been able to send observers have also made calls for prayer,

---

4. R 1962/44, pp. 2-3. Such references to a "miracle" are found in many other places; cf. for example R 1962/45, p. 9; 1963/11, p. 9; Biblio. 258, p. 50; *Ecumenism*, p. 49.
5. R 1962/44, pp. 1-2.
6. *Ibid.*, p. 2.
7. R 1962/45, pp. 1-2.

for example the Ecumenical Patriarch of Constantinople and the World Baptist Alliance."[8]

The underlying significance of such calls for prayer is explained as follows: "It is above all this union in prayer that I call a true miracle, if we compare this situation with some of the attitudes assumed at the time of the First Vatican Council. With regard to this union in prayer, the Holy Father found reason to say in his inaugural speech for the Council that the unity that Christ implored with such ardent prayer for his church shines forth among other things in this 'ray'—and here I am quoting literally—'of the unity of prayers and ardent desires with which those Christians separated from this Apostolic See aspire to be united with us.' "[9] The cardinal went on: "This is thus a first *beginning of unity*, and above all a solid basis for our trust in God. If Jesus assured us that prayers would be granted where two are gathered in his name to ask for something, how much more will the prayer of all the baptized in Christ be granted, when from all over the world they join their petition to the prayer of Jesus the High Priest to the Father: 'That they may all be one.' "[10] The idea that this communion of prayer of Christians for the Council represents a start to unity is explained elsewhere as follows: "It is the fact that this union of Christians of various confessions in prayer has undoubtedly created a new awareness—or an increase in the already existing awareness—of the fact that all Christians, despite their membership of different confessions, deep down want to be one, and must become increasingly so."[11]

In the same press conference Bea referred in passing to the impression that the inauguration of the Council had made on the observers: "Many of them were seen to weep, and many have stated and continue to state: 'Unfortunately we did not and do not know the Catholic Church.' "[12] Even more significant, according to Bea, were the words of John XXIII, who said that the sight of the observers at the opening of the Council was a "source of comfort" to him. When he received them in audience on 13 October, two days after the inauguration, the pope in fact said: "In that providential and historic moment, I was concentrating particularly on my immediate duty of praying and thanking the Lord. Even so, every now and then my gaze wandered in search of so many sons and brothers. And when it rested on your group and on each one of you, I found a source of encouragement in your presence. Let us not run away with ourselves, but be satisfied today simply with noting the fact. . . . And for your part I would like you to look into my heart, for perhaps you will read much more there than in my words."[13]

---

8. R 1962/44, pp. 1-2. On the subject of prayers offered for the Council, cf. also R 1963/2, p. 1; R 1963/3, pp. 1-2; R 1963/5, p. 2; R 1963/6, pp. 1-2; R 1963/11, p. 10; R 1963/23, p. 11; Biblio. 258, pp. 50-51. The files also include a list, probably incomplete, compiled at the time; cf. Lc 5, 7-8.

9. R 1962/44, p. 4.

10. *Ibid.*; for the two biblical texts, cf. Mt. 18:19 and John 17:21. Similar views are expressed in R 1962/45, pp. 10-11; R 1963/3, p. 2; R 1963/11, p. 10; Biblio. 258, pp. 51-52.

11. R 1963/6, p. 2. For this new awareness, cf. also R 1963/3, p. 3; R 1963/5, p. 2; R 1963/11, p. 15.

12. R 1962/44.

13. R 1962/45, p. 9. For the official French text of the pope's speech, cf. *AAS*, LIV (1962), 815;

The Life and Work of the Observers

Let us now try to move beyond first impressions. The Council meant a great deal of hard work for the observer-delegates: study of the many lengthy schemata, attendance at the long general congregations, important contacts and discussions with the Council fathers, to the advantage of both sides, and commitment to conscientious performance of the task received from their own church or ecclesial community. Let us see how Bea describes the various aspects of these multiple tasks.

1. In the first place let us see what could be called *the spirit* in which such meetings and discussions took place. When the president of the secretariat welcomed the observer-delegates and guests to a reception that the secretariat offered in their honor a few days after the start of the Council, he started as follows: "My dear brothers in Christ! Instead of a long enumeration of your titles, which I obviously respect, allow me to address you with the simple but very profound words: 'My brothers in Christ.' This title immediately plunges us into a deep awareness of the incomparable grace of baptism, which has established indestructible bonds that are stronger than all that divides us. Christians in every part of the world are daily growing more aware of these bonds, and this is what prompted your church authorities to send you as guests to the Council of the Roman Catholic Church."[14]

Moving on to the practical details of the shared commitment and work, the cardinal said: "I hope that so far as is possible all of you have found in our secretariat all the understanding and all the brotherly help you need to fulfill your task easily and successfully."[15] He then asked the observer-delegates for their trust and frankness: "I would ask you . . . to speak frankly, especially during the meetings organized for you by the secretariat, telling us anything that you do not like, and informing us of any criticisms, suggestions or wishes. Obviously I cannot promise to find a solution to every problem, but I do assure you that we shall be grateful to you for your trust and that we shall do our best to consider everything sincerely in Christ and do anything in our power both now and in the future."[16]

Professor E. Schlink, delegate for the Evangelical Church of Germany, answered on behalf of the observer-delegates: "We see the fact that our meetings at the Council now have an official character as a major step forward, and we realize that it was by no means a matter of course that we should be given the same schemata as are given to the Council fathers, and that Your Eminence gives us the opportunity to express our thoughts on these schemata. We know that we owe these opportunities to His Holiness himself, who has followed the promptings of his heart and brought about a new atmosphere of openness toward the non-Roman churches."[17]

OD, p. 6. Cf. *Ecumenism*, pp. 48-49.
14. *Ecumenismo*, p. 64.
15. *Ibid.*, p. 65.
16. *Ibid.*
17. *Ibid.*, p. 66; original in *Oekumenismus im Konzil*, p. 85.

2. Referring to Professor Schlink's words, the cardinal described *the opportunities for work offered to the observer-delegates* in the following terms, saying that they and "the observers had access to all the documents distributed to the Council fathers. They were also present at all the general congregations, and were therefore able to follow the work of the Council as it developed. Both they and the Council fathers had complete freedom to establish contact with each other, and they soon began to make use of this."[18]

However, it was realized that the material to be studied—and moreover in Latin—was too unfamiliar, and the secretariat therefore offered some additional assistance: "Another important development was the special weekly meeting arranged for the observers by the secretariat, in which they could discuss among themselves the schemata then under discussion in the Council hall. First of all a Council father or a theologian who had specialized in this field would explain the often involved history of the document and its precise meaning. The discussion then opened, and the observers put forward their own doubts, criticisms and difficulties. Members of the secretariat or other experts would then try to clarify their uncertainties. These meetings proved well suited to their special situation and way of thinking, and the observers found them very fruitful."[19] The president of the secretariat added that the discussions in the meetings of the observer-delegates more than once proved helpful to the Council itself, since the points of view put forward at these meetings were later expressed in the Council hall by one or another Council father.[20]

3. The previous points already indicate the interplay and mutual influence between observers and Council, but the subject requires further study. Let us first consider *the influence of the Council on the observer-delegates,* which calls for a very clear picture of the practical situation of the observer-delegates and their participation in the Council: "In comparison with the more than two thousand Council fathers, this group of observers was numerically much smaller—merely a mustard seed, we might say—but even so the aforesaid mutual influence went far beyond all expectations. A number of the observer-delegates have repeatedly, either in writing or orally, expressed their joy at being able to share so closely in the work of the Council, their joy over the freedom that reigned in discussions, as they were repeatedly able to observe, and lastly their happiness over the many private contacts that they were able to establish with a considerable number of the Council fathers, outside the Council sessions as well."[21] Further: "Many of them showed how deeply struck they were, not

18. *Ecumenism,* p. 51. Cf. also Biblio. 258, pp. 52-53; R 1962/45, p. 11; R 1963/11, pp. 11-12. However, since all the texts and all the discussions were in Latin, the secretariat made interpreters available to the observers and guests, so that they could have the Latin translated into the various languages.

19. *Ecumenism,* p. 51.

20. Cf. *ibid.*. Cf. also Biblio. 258, p. 53. An example of this claim is given by the Anglican observer, Bishop J. Moorman, *Vatican Observed. An Anglican Impression of Vatican II* (London, 1967), p. 28, who describes the occasion on which the Archbishop of Chicago, Cardinal A. Meyer, spoke in the Council expressing a thought of the Lutheran observer K.E. Skydsgaard.

21. R 1963/6, p. 2. The Anglican observer Bishop J. Moorman stresses that the joint prayer services

only by the kind welcome and treatment they received, but also by the universality of the church, as this is seen in the variety of nations, colors and continents of the Council fathers. Even more than this, many of them have been much impressed by the freedom of discussion."[22]

4. However, we must also note *the deep and beneficial influence that the presence of the observer-delegates had on the Council fathers*. The cardinal describes this as follows: "In fact it must not be forgotten that the great majority of the Council fathers, through a complex series of circumstances, found for the first time, in the Council, the opportunity to come face to face with the painful divisions among Christians. We know that in St. Peter's the observers were given a central position immediately in front of the table of the Presiding Commission and the Moderators. In the presence of these men the Council fathers must have realized that they represented hundreds of millions of Christians in the world; they were here with them, praying together and present at the holy mass; they had been ceremoniously welcomed by the pope. These men were baptized believers in Christ; they loved Christ and wished to testify to him and serve him. Why then were they separated from us? What were the consequences of this separation for Christianity as a whole and for the world?"[23]

Let us now take a more detailed look at the various *symptoms of this experience* and the new path that had opened up for the Council fathers. In the first place we would note a negative but very eloquent sign: at the end of the first period, Bea quoted the words of Professor James H. Nicols of the Princeton Theological Seminary, an observer-delegate for the World Alliance of Reformed Churches: "During the speeches made in the two months of the Council, there has not been even a single phrase aimed at offending or humiliating the Protestant or Orthodox observers."[24] Then, in positive terms: "Often bishops, after greeting the Council fathers, would greet 'our most welcome guests.' "[25] Nor was this mere politeness or lip service. Rev. George Williams, Professor of Church History at the Harvard Divinity School, substitute observer for the International Congregationalist Council, declared: "It is a new climate, a climate of trust, of mutual respect, which touches on the miraculous. A student of ecclesiastical annals, I have found an atmosphere such as this only at this moment of history, at this first Council of the twentieth century."[26]

Summing up the experience of the whole of the first period of the Council in more general terms, Cardinal Bea observed that "in all the work of the Council a very lively and almost generalized awareness of the ecumenical task of the

---

and especially participation in the eucharistic sacrifice brought the observers closer to the Catholic Church; cf. Moorman, *Vatican Observed*, p. 30.

22. R 1962/45, p. 12. Cf. also R 1962/44, p. 5; R 1963/1, p. 12. Bea develops this idea in various lectures after the close of the first period of the Council, saying that in the Council the observers were able to observe freedom in discussion as well as the exercise of the magisterium and fidelity to tradition; cf. R 1962/44, pp. 5-6; R 1962/45, p. 13.

23. *The Way*, pp. 9-10; cf. also R 1964/46, pp. 9-10.

24. R 1963/3, p. 4; here the cardinal quotes *Ecumenical Press Service*, 2 (18 January 1963), 6.

25. *Ecumenism*, p. 52.

26. Biblio. 258, pp. 58-59.

church could be seen, and this applies to all discussions, both of a doctrinal and of a more practical nature, for example on the liturgy. A number of voices were repeatedly heard—and did not go unheeded—warning that the Council should not close any door that offered the possibility or actual access to contacts with non-Catholic Christians."[27]

On the other hand, from the start of the Council, the secretariat itself made efforts to draw attention to the ecumenical dimension of the various subjects that were to be discussed. Indeed, the president of the secretariat, its members and staff were convinced that *all* the subjects dealt with by the Council had an ecumenical dimension and that the secretariat must thus act as the "ecumenical conscience" of the Council through its various members.[28] Thus the minutes of the meeting of the secretariat held on 19 October 1962 contain the following statement: "The role of our secretariat does not consist solely in preparing its own schemata, but also in making sure that other schemata do not contain anything that could harm work in favor of union. The non-Catholics must realize that the secretariat is doing everything in its power in all matters concerning them." All the vast amount of material of the other schemata was thus divided into twenty-two groups and at the same meeting was shared out among the twelve members of the secretariat who were Council fathers, the ten "experts" and the other collaborators and consultors.[29]

The authority of the secretariat—and thus indirectly the ecumenical conscience—was further confirmed by the pope's decision to have the secretariat work with the Theological Commission in redrafting the schema on divine revelation in order to make sure that it corresponded better to the ecumenical and pastoral aims of the Council.[30]

Evaluation of the First Period of the Council

In the previous pages we have referred to some of the events of this first period of the Council, but let us now attempt to give an overall evaluation.

1. As concerns the observer-delegates, they were fully integrated into the work of the Council. In this connection the cardinal quotes the statement of the

---

27. R 1963/6, p. 4. Similarly, see also R 1963/3, p. 4; R 1963/5, p. 5; R 1963/11, p. 14; R 1963/31, p. 2; R 1963/37, p. 1; *The Way*, p. 10; Biblio. 258, p. 61; *Ecumenism*, pp. 52-53. Cf. extensive confirmation and partial supplement to this observation by the Anglican observer, Bishop J. Moorman, *Vatican Observed*, pp. 26-28. Cf. also the fine and interesting address delivered by the Congregationalist observer D. Horton at the reception offered by the secretariat in honor of the observers, *Ecumenism*, pp. 187-188. Bishop Moorman does, however, make two critical observations, saying that the observers would have preferred (a) to have been consulted concerning questions in which their churches had greater experience (e.g. modern languages in the liturgy), and (b) that some of them had been offered the opportunity of addressing the Council fathers directly; cf. Moorman, *Vatican Observed*, p. 28..

28. Cardinal J. Willebrands later applied the expression "ecumenical conscience of the Council" to Cardinal Bea himself (cf. BM, p. 313), but Bea insisted that all members of the secretariat should act as such, together with him.

29. Cf. Arch. Lc 5/10, pp. 3-4.

30. Cf. *Ecumenism*, p. 53.

Secretary General of the World Council of Churches, Dr. W.A. Visser 't Hooft: "The observers are no longer only observers; many contacts and a true dialogue now exist between them and the Council fathers."[31] This statement is echoed in that of Dr. Lukas Vischer, observer-delegate of the World Council of Churches. When the observers were received by Secretary of State Cardinal Amleto Cicognani in the name of Pope John (whose ill-health prevented him from receiving them personally) at the close of the first period, Dr. Vischer spoke on behalf of the observers as follows: "The past two months have been an extremely rich period for all of us. . . . We have truly lived the work of the Council, taking part in it in spirit. We have had a very special opportunity to learn to know some representatives of your church. We have had free access to all events and have always been able to see the great effort made to understand our beliefs, our character, our hopes and our difficulties. I am convinced that in this way not only have contacts been established—to use an ecumenical expression—but that true friendships have been formed."[32]

2. As concerns the Council itself, it should be noted that it approved virtually unanimously a first, albeit not definitive, document on the question of Christian unity. This was the ecumenical schema *Ut omnes unum sint*, drawn up by the Commission for the Eastern Churches.[33] After it had been presented in the twentieth general congregation, the discussion went on for a further three general congregations, although it was sometimes interrupted by other work commitments. At this point it was agreed that the president of the secretariat, which was the body with specific responsibility for ecumenical questions, should present a proposal that all the elements concerning the question of unity that were contained in the schema under discussion, in that drawn up by the secretariat, and in Chapter XI of the draft constitution on the church drawn up by the Doctrinal Commission, should be combined in a single decree—in other words that the Council should adopt the decision previously reached by the Central Preparatory Commission in this connection.[34] Cardinal Bea's suggestion was approved with virtual unanimity.[35]

In his evaluation of this result, the cardinal looks far beyond the schema in question, for in his view it was in fact an extremely positive vote *in favor of ecumenism as such*, since the schema already contained, "in one manner or

---

31. R 1963/11, p. 12; Biblio. 258, p. 53.
32. *Ecumenismo*, p. 68. Cf. also *ibid.*, p. 53; *Unity in Freedom*, pp. 78-79.
33. For the schema and the relative discussion, cf. *AS*, I/III, text pp. 528-545; discussion pp. 554-837 (with various breaks). The reader will recall that three schemata on ecumenism had been presented to the Central Commission in the preparatory period: one by the Theological Commission, one by the Commission for the Eastern Churches, and one by the secretariat. The Central Commission had decided that the three schemata should be combined, but there had not been enough time to do so, and thus the Commission for the Eastern Churches now presented its own.
34. For Bea's speech, cf. *AS*, I/III, 709-712.
35. Cf. *AS*, I/IV, 9, for the text of the proposal, and 141 for the result; out of 2112 votes, there were 2068 in favor, 36 against, and 8 null. It was the cardinal himself who used the term "virtual unanimity"; cf. R 1963/2, p. 2.

another, many of the general principles of Catholic ecumenism. Now the Council fathers approved this draft decree in general terms with virtual unanimity and with an explicit declaration that it must be merged into a single decree with the other schemata drawn up by the other commissions. . . . In this way the Council assembly has solemnly and with its supreme authority given its outline approval to the fundamental lines of Catholic ecumenism and has also shown its wish to organize and supervise ecumenical work more fully."[36]

3. The third consequence was that "the results of this first session . . . were not limited to the Council assembly or to those who in one way or another shared in its work in Rome." And he explained: "Through the channels of social communication *the Council was having a wider effect on the whole Christian world*. Just as many non-Catholic churches and communities had responded to Pope John's plea for prayers for the Council, they now watched the work of the Council with lively interest."[37]

Elsewhere, Bea finds confirmation of such participation of public opinion in the award of the Balzan Peace Prize to Pope John. Alongside the pope's diplomatic efforts in favor of peace, the citation for the prize also mentions the invitation of observer-delegates to the Council, saying that in this way the pope had helped and fostered "brotherhood among men and peoples" by bringing about "a greater degree of mutual understanding between members of the denominations invited to send observers and members of the Catholic Church, a fact which should have further important repercussions."[38]

As concerns the ecumenical atmosphere of the Council, Cardinal Bea adopted the very authoritative evaluation expressed by Pope John XXIII. In his Christmas radio message a few weeks after the close of this first period, the pope described the ecumenical aspect of the Council as follows: "One of the outstanding results of this session of the Ecumenical Council has been the sense of unity that has risen spontaneously among us, although almost unexpected by many people. We could perhaps more correctly describe it as a process of becoming aware of a movement toward Christian brotherhood, recognizing it and responding positively to it; this brotherhood is expressed, in the words of the Apostles' Creed, in the one, holy, catholic and apostolic church, whose apostolic seal affirms and emphasizes that this church is not to rule but to serve all nations, who though earnestly seeking the fulfillment of Christ's plan still find difficulty in seeing its application in their own society and its progress."[39]

---

36. R 1963/6, p. 4. Cf. also R 1963/2, p. 2; R 1963/3, p. 5; R 1963/5, pp. 4-5; R 1963/11, p. 16; Biblio. 258, p. 63.

37. *Ecumenism*, p. 53 (ct).

38. Cf. *Unity in Freedom*, p. 76.

39. *AAS*, LV (1963), 17-18; quoted in *Ecumenism*, p. 54. We have already spoken about the work of the secretariat and the cardinal in the time between the first and second periods of the Council (in our previous chapter), and we have nothing else to add here.

Ecumenical Aspects of the First Stages of the Papacy of Paul VI
(June–September 1963)

The cardinal writes: "It is obvious that the sad death of John XXIII and the beginning of the reign of Paul VI profoundly affected the course of events, particularly within the Council. For this reason they naturally mark the end of one period and the beginning of another, and so the discussion of the second period of the Council must begin with the election of Paul VI rather than the opening of the second session. This also marks the start of a new period from the point of view of ecumenism."[40]

1. The first noteworthy fact in this new period is the way that other churches and ecclesial communities sympathized and shared with the Catholic Church in its mourning and joy—a completely new element in the history of the church. In this connection, at the reception offered in honor of the observers at the beginning of the second period of the Council, the president of the secretariat addressed the following words of gratitude to these observers and the communities that had sent them: "I should once more like to thank you—although some months have now passed—for what you and the churches and communities you represent did when the Church of Rome was struck by such deep mourning over the death of the august author and father of the Council, Pope John XXIII, and also for what you did when divine providence gave us a new head. Thank you for all those displays of solidarity and those prayers, not only in our sorrow, but also in our joy."[41] Bea immediately laid stress on *the fruits* that this solidarity had brought for mutual rapprochement: "There is nothing that brings people closer together than the union of hearts in suffering and in joy, and this is all the truer, the greater and deeper is the suffering and the stronger is the joy. Thus I dare believe that the lively demonstrations of solidarity in our suffering over the death of Pope John and our joy over the election of his successor Paul VI had vast ecumenical implications, because they brought so many brothers in Christ, who are separated from one another for so many reasons, closer together—and to a considerable degree, I believe."[42]

Bea himself refers as follows to a particular expression of *this sharing in joy*: "Various churches and ecclesial communities who were represented at the first session of the Council had on their own initiative sent their representatives to the coronation. The *Osservatore Romano* . . . notes in this connection that for the first time in history some important representatives of non-Catholic churches and communities were present at the unforgettable ceremony of coronation."[43]

2. The second aspect is the contribution the new pope made to ecumenism from the very first months of his papacy and the inauguration of the second period of the Council. A description of this contribution certainly does not

---

40. *Ecumenism*, p. 63.
41. *Ecumenismo*, pp. 111-112.
42. *Ibid.*, p. 112.
43. *Ibid.*, pp. 75-76, which also gives a list of these representatives.

constitute a digression from our subject, for it provided a remarkable boost to the work of the cardinal and the secretariat.

The first fact is that in a radio message twenty-four hours after his election, the pope declared his commitment to the cause of unity: "Our pontifical service will do its utmost to carry on the great work which our predecessor, Pope John XXIII, set into motion with such hope and in such happy circumstances. The work is directed to the fulfillment of Christ's prayer 'that they may all be one' (John 17:21), a fulfillment which is ardently desired by all, and for which he gave his life. The desire of all for reunion, so sadly crushed in the past, will find an echo in our keen will and fervent prayer, and in our awareness of the task entrusted to us by Jesus: 'Simon, Simon . . . I have prayed for you that your faith may not fail; and . . . strengthen your brethren' (Luke 23:31f)."[44]

A first confirmation of this commitment came some weeks later. His Holiness Alexis, Patriarch of Moscow and of All the Russias, was celebrating fifty years as bishop, and the Holy Synod of the Russian Church had expressed a wish that a delegation of the Catholic Church should also take part. The pope promptly accepted the invitation—a far from automatic and obvious move in the atmosphere of those times, which was still full of diffidence and suspicion. A delegation of the Secretariat for Christian Unity took part: the Bishop of Lausanne, Geneva and Fribourg, François Charrière, and Father C.J. Dumont, O.P. With regard to the significance of this participation, in his speech of greeting to the patriarch, Bishop Charrière explained that it was also to be seen as an expression of gratitude to the Russian Church not only for having sent observers to the Council, but for having sent a representative both to the funeral of John XXIII and to the coronation of Paul VI.[45]

An extremely important element was provided by the fact that in his inaugural speech Paul VI described *the unity of all Christians* in the one church of Christ as *one of the main aims* of the Council: "There is a third purpose which claims the attention of this Council, a purpose which must be considered as of the highest importance among our spiritual concerns, and in this our predecessor John XXIII gave us a prominent lead. We are referring to that concern which looks toward 'other Christians,' that is toward those whom we cannot number amongst those who are joined with us in the perfect unity of Christ—a unity which is due to them by virtue of their baptism, which they so ardently desire themselves, and which the one Catholic Church can certainly offer them."[46]

The pope wondered about *the attitude of the Council* "toward these immense

44. *Ecumenism*, pp. 64-65 (ct); cf. *AAS*, LV (1963), 573-574.

45. Cf. *Ecumenism*, pp. 66-68. Concluding the account of this Catholic participation in Patriarch Alexis' jubilee, Bea mentions another event that represented a further step in the improvement of mutual relations: the visit to Rome made by Metropolitan Nikodim, who was in charge of relations between the Russian Orthodox Church and other churches. Apart from a visit to the president of the secretariat, the metropolitan went to lay flowers on the tomb of John XXIII, where he also sang a short Orthodox prayer for the dead; cf. *Ecumenism*, p. 68; *CC*, 1963/IV, 73.

46. Latin text in *CDD*, pp. 915-916; English translation from *Ecumenism*, p. 69. The pope's thinking was then included in *UR*, 1.

groups of separated brethren" and "the possibility of such variety in unity," and asserted: "The answer is clear. This is one of the characteristic features of the calling of the Council. The Council is striving toward an ecumenism which will be complete and universal; this is apparent at least in its intentions, in its prayers to God, and in its preparation. Today there is a strong and shining hope, tomorrow it may be a reality."[47]

The same inaugural speech also included the passage that was the great ecumenical surprise of this opening ceremony. In it the pope addressed other Christians, *asking and granting forgiveness* for the wrongs done on both sides in the past: "If any blame for this separation can be laid at our door, we humbly beg God's pardon for it, and ask forgiveness from any of our brothers who feel themselves injured. We are ready for our part to overlook the injuries inflicted on the Catholic Church, and to put aside the sorrow caused by the long series of dissensions and separations. May our heavenly Father accept our declaration, and bring us all to a true and fraternal peace."[48]

The decisive importance of this gesture in the concrete circumstances can be seen from the following statement of a Council theologian, W. Becker, an Oratorian Father and a consultor of the secretariat, who said: "Between the first and second periods of the Council I asked the cardinal if the time had not come to include some recognition of the responsibility of the Catholic Church for errors and omissions at the time of the Reformation, in the schema on ecumenism. The cardinal answered: 'We shall never obtain a large enough majority for this in the Council.'"[49]

We can see how deeply the pope felt about this matter from the fact that he himself brought it up again in the audience he granted to the observer-delegates some weeks later: "In our speech of 29 September we ventured before all to have recourse to Christian forgiveness—mutual, if this is possible. 'We forgive and ask forgiveness of one another.'[50] Our spirits need the peace this brings if they are to begin friendly relations and peaceful conversations. First of all because it is Christian: 'So if you are offering your gift at the altar, and there remember that your brother has something against you, leave your gift there before the altar and go; first be reconciled to your brother, and then come back

47. Latin text in *CDD*, p. 915; English translation from *Ecumenism*, p. 70. Cf. also R 1964/1, pp. 13-14.
48. Latin text in *CDD*, pp. 916-917; English translation from *Ecumenism*, pp. 70-71 (ct). Cf. the idea of sins against unity in *UR*, 7.
49. BM, p. 198.
50. A quotation from Horace (*Veniam damus petimusque vicissim*). As concerns the significance of this request for forgiveness, H.-D. Wendland, *Die ökumenische Bewegung und das II. Vatikanische Konzil* (Cologne, 1968), p. 13, observes: "When did anything even slightly similar ever happen in the history of the divided churches?" He concludes: "This plea for forgiveness had unfortunately not yet received a sufficiently clear, sincere and humble response from the Evangelical churches" (*ibid.*, p. 14). Cf. also H. Dietzfelbinger, "The Council and the Churches of the Reformation," in G. Lindbeck (ed.), *Dialogue on the Way. Protestants Report from Rome on the Vatican Council* (Minneapolis, Minn., 1965), pp. 259-260, where in reference to the corresponding statement released by the Evangelical Church of Germany the question is asked: "Is that the right answer?"

and offer your gift' (Mt. 5:23-24). And then it is the best method for us: not looking back to the past, but toward the present and above all toward the future."[51]

A last factor shows how *open and attentive Paul VI was to the suggestions and proposals of other Christians*. At the audience granted to the observers, the Danish Lutheran Professor Kristen E. Skydsgaard spoke in the name of the observer-delegates and guests, suggesting in the course of his speech that greater care should be devoted to study of the history of salvation: "May I be allowed at this point to draw attention to something which seems to me to be extremely important: I am thinking of the role of a biblical theology which concentrates on the study of the history of salvation in the Old as well as the New Testament. The more our understanding of the paradoxical and mysterious history of the people of God grows, the more we begin really to understand the church of Jesus Christ, in its mystery, in its historical existence, and in its unity."[52] In his response to this speech, Paul VI said: "You opened up perspectives on this subject that we should be careful not to neglect. We would willingly support your call for the development of a 'concrete and historical theology centered on the history of salvation,' and the suggestion appears worthy of further study and action. The Catholic Church has institutions which could easily specialize further in this kind of research, and a new institution could even be set up for this purpose if circumstances warrant it."[53]

Two Great Steps Forward

The first step was that during the second period of the Council there was the first general vote on the schema of a Decree on Ecumenism and that it was approved almost unanimously.[54] The second step was Paul VI's pilgrimage to the Holy Land, which took place outside the Council but (a) was announced by the pope in the Council hall, (b) took place a short while after the close of the second period, and (c) was above all closely linked to the Council.

1. Let us first consider *the Decree on Ecumenism*. The reader will recall the decision taken in the first period of the Council that the three schemata dealing

---

51. French text in *OD*, pp. 21-22; English translation from *Ecumenism*, p. 74 (ct). The cardinal repeatedly stresses the pope's request for forgiveness; cf. R 1964/11, p. 1; R 1964/46, p. 12; R 1964/54, p. 6; R 1965/3, p. 9; Biblio. 262, p. XIII.

52. Quoted in *Ecumenism*, pp. 73-74.

53. French text in *OD*, pp. 22-23; English translation from *Ecumenism*, p. 75 (ct). Examination of the possibility of setting up a special institute went so well that in 1966 plans were actually laid for its creation (cf. *Ecumenism*, pp. 250-251), so that it was able to open for the academic year 1972-1973. The cardinal also notes other important ecumenical elements found in this inaugural address of Paul VI; cf. *ibid.*, pp. 71-72.

54. Cf. R 1964/3, pp. 1-2; similarly, R 1964/1, p. 14; R 1964/4, p. 3. In a number of lectures the cardinal also stresses various ecumenically important elements contained in other schemata, especially in that on the church: the subjects of the people of God (cf. for example R 1964/3, p. 2; R 1964/1, p. 14), collegiality (cf. *Ecumenism*, p. 78), and the laity (cf. *ibid.*).

with the ecumenical question should be combined.[55] This was done in the first months of 1963: the schema of the secretariat was taken as the basis, with its two chapters setting forth the principles and then the practice of ecumenism; certain paragraphs from the schema of the Commission for the Eastern Churches were then added, describing specific features of the eastern churches; and a similar description of the western churches and ecclesial communities was therefore also added.[56] The schema was then sent to the Council fathers, asking them to send in their written observations before the end of July. Fifty individual opinions and eight collective opinions had thus been received prior to the second period of the Council, and the secretariat summarized these in a document entitled "Amendments" which was distributed in the Council hall on 18 November together with the new schema.[57]

The schema was presented in the Council hall by three speakers: Cardinal Amleto Cicognani, President of the Commission for the Eastern Churches, made a general introduction; the Archbishop of Rouen, Joseph Martin, presented the whole schema; and the first part of the third chapter, which concerned the eastern churches, was more specifically explained by the Archbishop of Belgrade, Gabriel Bukatko.[58]

The general discussion then began, and this took up four general congregations, in which forty-one evaluations in all were presented, as well as a further forty written evaluations.[59] After the general discussion was over, a vote was taken on the question of whether the three chapters of the schema should be accepted as a useful basis for further discussion. The result was more than satisfactory, for the schema was accepted with virtual unanimity.[60]

Having received the green light, the assembly moved on to discussion of the individual chapters, a task that took up another eight general congregations, with 102 spoken evaluations and 101 evaluations presented in writing.[61] We would add that the collected interventions on our schema, both oral and written, run to about six hundred folio-sized printed pages.[62]

Like many other presidents of conciliar commissions, *Cardinal Bea* had left the task of presenting the schema to other people, but he did feel called upon *to speak twice*: once during these discussions, and once in order to close them.[63]

55. Cf. *AS*, I/IV, 141.
56. Cf. *AS*, II/V, 478; cf. p. 480, no. 2.
57. For the amendments, cf. *AS*, II/V, 442-467; for the text of the relative written contributions, cf. *AS*, II/V, 874-910.
58. Cf. *AS*, II/V, 468-481.
59. Cf. *AS*, II/V, 405-686, 771-833.
60. Cf. *AS*, II/V, the precise question to be voted on p. 682; the result p. 690. Out of 2052 votes cast, there were 1966 in favor and 86 against. Cf. H. Roux, *Détresse et promesse de Vatican II* (Paris, 1967), p. 152, who says that this was a turning point: "Now it was certain that the Council would not end without producing a document solemnly introducing the Catholic Church as such into the 'dialogue.' "
61. For all the material of these contributions, cf. *AS*, II/V-VI.
62. This figure also includes the fifty-eight written opinions sent in prior to the second period of the Council and summarized in the "Amendments" discussed above.
63. Cf. *AS*, II/VI, 14-17, 364-367; cf. Caprile, III, 330, 410.

His first speech was made in order to clear up a number of points raised in the various interventions up to that moment. It had, for example, repeatedly been stated that ecumenical activity creates dangers of "indifferentism, interconfessionalism, false irenicism, religious doubt, etc." The president of the secretariat admitted that these dangers do of course exist, but added that the remedy must not be inactivity, but vigilance, guidance, and if necessary correction, all of which are duties of the sacred pastors, for they are the people primarily responsible for fostering union, just as it is their duty to preach the gospel and feed Christ's flock.[64] Bea also stated that the secretariat would welcome any suggestions; some of these would be included in the schema, whereas the more detailed ones would find their place in the *Ecumenical Directory* that was already in preparation and that would provide further orientations for ecumenical activity.[65] The application of these instructions, however, would fall under the responsibility of episcopal conferences, and it would therefore be a very good idea for the latter to set up special secretariats in the various regions which would have the task of keeping abreast of the ecumenical movement, working in cooperation with our secretariat.[66]

The cardinal would later give the following overall evaluation of *the discussion* on the schema on the ecumenical movement: "The enormous work of examination and study performed by the Council fathers for the schema on ecumenism shows beyond doubt how convinced they were of the historic importance of this subject, both in itself and for the future efforts of the Catholic Church to foster the union of all the baptized."[67]

In conclusion, we would quote the cardinal's evaluation of the fact that in the preliminary vote the schema was approved with virtual unanimity. Speaking on Vatican Radio and comparing the result with the rosiest hopes of the preparatory period, he said: "At that time I could certainly not even dream that less than three years later, over two thousand Council fathers would have almost unanimously accepted a conciliar schema on ecumenical work."[68]

2. The second major step forward was *Paul VI's pilgrimage to the Holy Land.*[69] In order to give an idea of the importance of this event, we must remember the state of relations between Rome and the Orthodox churches. In this connection Bea writes that Pope Paul VI described the past period as a silence: "It has been a 'silence,' resulting from the lack of contacts and the separate life and development of each side, a silence devoid of all charity. All this only broadened the rift which was already wide because of the differences

---

64. Cf. *AS*, II/VI, 14-15; also 365.
65. Cf. *AS*, II/VI, 365.
66. Cf. *AS*, II/VI, 15, 365.
67. R 1964/15, pp. 1-2.
68. R 1964/3, pp. 1-2.
69. Cf. the official publication, Michele Maccarrone, *Il pellegrinaggio di Paolo VI in Terra Santa* (Vatican City, 1964). See also the double issue of *Proche Orient Chrétien*, XIV (1964), entitled *Jérusalem—Paul VI, pèlerin du Christ, pèlerin de l'unité.* The article "Le Cardinal Bea," *Irenikon*, XIV (1968), 492, erroneously states that Cardinal Bea accompanied the pope on this journey.

in mentality, history and culture. And during all the time that each party was developing independently, every kind of tragedy, with very grievous losses of many types, had befallen both the Latin West and the East. Obviously all this had helped to create a psychological barrier which might have seemed, or even was, humanly insuperable."[70] In the period of preparation for the Council serious disagreements had then been added in connection with the invitation of observers, with accusations that the Catholic Church had tried to divide Orthodoxy.[71]

(a) This was the atmosphere at the end of the second period of the Council, when the announcement was made of the pilgrimage of Pope Paul VI to the Holy Land, and of its aims with regard to the church and its unity. In his announcement, the pope said that he was going on pilgrimage "in order to offer Christ's church to him, and to call our separated brethren back to her, as one and holy."[72] This was followed by the generous and courageous reaction of Patriarch Athenagoras to Paul VI's announcement, for a bare two days later, on 6 December, the patriarch invited all the heads of the churches to travel to Jerusalem in order to pray with the pope in a fraternal meeting in the places consecrated by the redemption.[73]

(b) More *direct preparations* went ahead quickly. The cardinal writes: "Events took place with almost dizzying speed. As a pleasant surprise, on Christmas Day itself we received the Ecumenical Patriarch's telegram announcing the arrival in Rome of a delegation from the Patriarchate of Constantinople. And on the Feast of St. John, His Eminence Metropolitan Athenagoras of Thyatira, a monk of Patmos, the island of the great Seer of the Book of Revelation, arrived in Rome, almost as a gift of the beloved disciple. He was received by the Holy Father in a memorable audience on 28 December, when he declared in his short address to the Holy Father: 'I am so deeply conscious of the significance of this historic moment that I am overwhelmed by emotion. After centuries of silence, the Latin West and the Greek East, urged on by the mutual love and respect, which are inspired in them by the gospel and by their Christian hearts, are moving toward a mutual encounter for an exchange of views and fraternal greetings, and in order to begin, if possible, a dialogue of comprehension, for the peace of the world and the progress of the church of God.' "[74]

For his part, *Paul VI cooperated* with exemplary readiness and gospel simplicity. The cardinal also says: "As to the question of protocol the metropolitan was somewhat surprised to see how quickly and easily agreement was reached. Earlier, one of the greatest difficulties in deciding the relative 'proto-

---

70. *Ecumenism*, p. 109 (ct).
71. On these events, cf. A. Wenger, *Deuxième Session* (Paris, 1964), pp. 282-285.
72. *Ecumenism*, p. 80 (ct); original in *CDD*, p. 944.
73. Cf. *THS*, p. 55; *Ecumenism*, p. 81. There had in fact been a prior exchange of letters between the patriarch and Paul VI on the occasion of the latter's election; cf. *THS*, pp. 49-51; *Ecumenism*, p. 80.
74. R 1964/3, p. 2. The remainder of the very beautiful address is found in *THS*, pp. 59-60; *Ecumenismo*, pp. 88-89. Originally the patriarch had wanted to send two metropolitans (cf. *THS*, pp. 57-58), but was unable to do so because of difficulties in obtaining visas.

col' was the custom, which has been in force for centuries, of the pope not returning visits personally, but through his secretary of state. But in this case the Holy Father had quite definitely stated his intention of personally returning the visits of the eastern non-Catholic patriarchs—that is not only the Ecumenical Patriarch of Constantinople, who as we know enjoys a primacy of honor in the East, but also any of the other patriarchs who wished to pay a visit."[75]

In connection with this clarification of protocol, I remember that Cardinal Bea more than once said that the pope had told him: "I am going to Palestine as a simple pilgrim, without either crown or miter; some people have raised objections to the return of the Ecumenical Patriarch's visit, but I see none. Even Jesus visited his own friends, so what is there against his vicar on earth doing the same?"[76]

In this way "in a few days all the details of the planned meeting had been agreed, so that in his New Year's Day homily the patriarch himself could give the solemn announcement that he would be going to Jerusalem to meet with the Holy Father."[77]

(c) We now come to the actual *meeting between the pope and the patriarch.* The cardinal describes it as follows: ". . . the meeting was not only sincere and fraternal, but took place in *an atmosphere of deep spirituality.* There was a recitation, alternating in Latin and Greek, of the prayer that Jesus the High Priest made to his Father after the Last Supper and just before his passion, which contains that most burning plea for the unity of all those who would believe in him; then there was the joint recitation—each praying in his own language—of the prayer to the heavenly Father which Jesus taught to us; and finally the blessing was given to all those present by the pope and the patriarch together."[78]

Let us immediately take a look at the impressions of the meeting expressed by its leading figures. On his return to Rome, the pope addressed the people gathered in St. Peter's Square as follows: "I will say only this to you this evening: this morning I had the great fortune to embrace the Ecumenical Patriarch of Constantinople, after so many centuries, and to exchange words of peace with him, words of brotherhood, of desire for unity, of agreement and love of Christ, and of service to the profit of the whole human family."[79]

The pope's *statement to the Sacred College,* which had come to welcome him back to Rome, was fuller. He started by saying in general terms: "We have now reached a stage, if the initial indications develop as they promise to do, which is really important, and which seems to be cutting across our normal human standards; we are now face to face with something divine and supernatural." The pope than commented on the meeting itself: "Athenagoras, the

---

75. *Ecumenism,* p. 82 (ct).
76. R 1964/46, p. 12. Cf. also the observations on the "simplicity and humility [of the pope] which made him forsake the triple crown . . ." (*Ecumenism,* p. 82), which reflect the same thought. Cf. also *Unity in Freedom,* p. 181: "In returning their visits, the pope followed a protocol which has had no precedents for centuries."
77. R 1964/3, pp. 2-3.
78. *Ecumenism,* p. 110 (ct).
79. Quoted in *ibid.,* pp. 109-110 (ct). Cf. Maccarrone, *Il pellegrinaggio di Paolo VI,* p. 138; R 1964/3, p. 2; 1964/10, p. 3.

Ecumenical Patriarch of Constantinople, along with eleven metropolitans, came to meet me, and he wished to embrace me as one embraces a brother, to take my hand and to lead me by the hand into the room where we were to exchange a few words, as if to say: we must, we must understand each other, we must make peace to show the world that we have become brothers again. The patriarch added, this morning: 'Tell me what we must do, tell me what we must do.' "[80]

In his turn *Patriarch Athenagoras* stated: "For me, the meeting in Jerusalem with the pope was more than a hope fulfilled, more than a dream come true. Two months ago, who would have thought that it could be possible?"[81]

(d) We also have to emphasize *the universalistic nature* of the meetings of Paul VI, for he also met other eastern patriarchs and representatives of other Christian confessions. Bea notes: "The non-Catholic churches and communities are represented as follows: the Greek Orthodox Church by Archbishops Aristovulos, Artemios and Stephanos, Archbishop Jacovos of America, some archimandrites and numerous members of the clergy; the Russian Church by the Archimandrite heading the Russian mission in Palestine, representing the Patriarch Alexis; the Armenian Church by the Patriarch of Jerusalem, with the auxiliary bishop and numerous clergy; the Catholicosate of Cilicia by an archbishop and two archimandrites; the Coptic, Ethiopian and Syrian Churches each by a bishop and members of the clergy; the Anglican Church by Archbishop McInnes, Bishop Cubain of Jordan and numerous clergy; the Lutheran Church by Provost Dr. Malsch."[82]

For his part, when Paul VI told the cardinals about his impressions, he emphasized his meetings with representatives of the whole gamut of churches and ecclesial communities: "The other patriarchs came in the same way, likewise the Anglicans and the Protestants; they came to take my hand and to ask how we could find ourselves together again in the Lord."[83]

(e) Our cardinal also highlights various circumstances connected with the meetings. Patriarch Athenagoras had received the prior assent of almost all the autocephalous churches—with the exception of the Orthodox Church of Greece—for the meeting with the pope.[84] Then there were "the unique circumstances of the meeting, unprecedented in history. Above all, the place: the ground sanctified by the birth, life, passion, death and resurrection of the divine Redeemer—the Holy City. We could borrow the words of the Metropolitan Athenagoras of Thyatira when he greeted the Holy Father: the pope and the ecumenical patriarch had climbed the same mountain of the Lord from different sides, and now had met at the summit, close by the cross of our Lord."[85]

---

80. Quoted in *Ecumenism*, p. 85. Cf. also Maccarrone, *Il pellegrinaggio di Paolo VI*, pp. 140-141; R 1964/3, p. 3.

81. Quoted in *Ecumenism*, p. 109 (ct). Cf. also the significant positive evaluation that Metropolitan Meliton of Helioupolis and Theira gave of the meeting in his position as President of the Third Panorthodox Conference of Rhodes in the fall of 1964; *Ecumenism*, p. 139.

82. *Ecumenismo*, p. 90.

83. Quoted in *Ecumenism*, p. 85; cf. Maccarrone, *Il pellegrinaggio di Paolo VI*, p. 114.

84. Cf. R 1964/10, p. 5.

85. *Ecumenism*, p. 110. The text of the speech of Metropolitan Athenagoras of Thyatira is found

The cardinal also pointed out the great importance of the fact that *large numbers of the faithful had been able to share* in this event. In one of his talks, he stressed: "The Holy Father's pilgrimage was apparently followed by one thousand five hundred journalists from every part of the world, despite the great technical difficulties facing them in their work, especially in transmitting their dispatches."[86] The impact of the event was thus "helped enormously by the press, radio and television bringing the events to such a vast cross-section of the faithful. The joint declaration issued after the meeting [between Paul VI and Metropolitan Athenagoras] stated: 'The feelings that we share are being made known to all the members of the respective hierarchies and to all the faithful so that they may take part and send up a stream of prayer to the throne of God for all Christians to see before them the truth of the one Church of Christ, and of his gospel, the light and salvation of the world.' "[87]

(f) As concerns *the fruits of the pilgrimage and the meetings*, the cardinal notes: "As to the effects on our oriental non-Catholic brethren it can be said that the pilgrimage succeeded in changing at one stroke the relations between the Catholic Church and the oriental patriarchates. . . . The results of the pilgrimage could be felt immediately. For example, the Patriarchate of Constantinople and the Greek Orthodox Patriarchate of Alexandria in due course sent observer-delegates to the third session of the Council. The change in atmosphere could also be felt in the way in which the Third Panorthodox Conference of Rhodes developed."[88]

Lastly, the pope himself started considering the question of *what was now to be done*, and this is seen as early as his declaration to the Sacred College. Referring to Patriarch Athenagoras' request, "Tell me what we must do," Paul VI stated: "We are now faced with this question, a question we must think about and reflect upon a great deal. We must not allow ourselves to be misled by appearances or by momentary flashes of enthusiasm; it is a question which could indeed be an indication of a very different future for the universal church of tomorrow from its situation today in which it is still split into so many fragments."[89] A few weeks later, on 31 January, a meeting was held of the cardinals present in Rome in order to consider the question. And some months later, in his response to the good wishes of the Sacred College on his feast day, the pope again spoke about it, saying: "We are now faced with the task of giving advice, and of working, praying and studying so that the 'signs' that have been so clearly

in *THS*, pp. 59-60.

86. R 1964/10, p. 8.

87. *Ecumenism*, pp. 110-111. Cf. also R 1964/3, p. 4; *Unity in Freedom*, p. 181. A particularly positive observation of the Russian Orthodox Church concerning the Jerusalem meetings should be noted: "We see a possibility for the development of relations between the Roman Catholic Church and the Orthodox Churches in their mutual effort to fulfill the command of Christ the Savior concerning unity in him and between all his followers (John 17:21-23) and in actively translating into practice their joint responsibility for the reconciliation of the human race" (quoted in Biblio. 251, p. 913, note).

88. *Ecumenism*, p. 86 (ct). Cf. also R 1964/50, p. 3; R 1965/5, p. 1.

89. Quoted in *Ecumenism*, p. 85 (ct); cf. Maccarrone, *Il pellegrinaggio di Paolo VI*, pp. 140-141.

visible may be fulfilled, so that the seed that has sprouted from the previously hard, unyielding soil may come to flower and bear the fruit so ardently yearned after. We watch and shall continue to watch the development of this demanding and complex question with immense spiritual interest according to the spirit of Jesus Christ."[90]

Other Steps Follow on Various Fronts (April-November 1964)

1. The cardinal writes as follows about a first initiative taken by Paul VI: "A fine example of the truly new spirit can be found in *the Easter greetings* which the pope sent to our non-Catholic Christian brethren on Maundy Thursday from his cathedral, the Lateran Basilica."[91] This greeting drew its inspiration from the new commandment given by the Lord within the framework of the Last Supper, and thus the pope introduced it by speaking about fraternal love: "To all who can hear the echo of our celebration of the passover supper, in the faith of Christ and in his charity, we address the words of the apostle Peter, "May you be pleased to be brothers' (1 Peter 2:17)."[92]

The pope went on to list the recipients of these wishes: "Maybe for the first time on an occasion as sacred as this, we send our Easter greetings and good wishes to the eastern churches who are separated from us, but who are already so close to us in faith."[93] The pope explicitly named Ecumenical Patriarch Athenagoras, then "the other patriarchs we met on the same occasion [his pilgrimage to Jerusalem]; peace and good wishes to the other members of the hierarchies of those ancient and venerable churches who have sent their representatives to the Ecumenical Vatican Council."[94]

The cardinal continues his account of the pope's speech: "Peace and good wishes to the whole of the Anglican Church, while with sincere love and the same hope we wish one day to see her once again as an honored member of the one universal fold of Christ." Lastly, the pope addressed the other ecclesial communities of the Reformed tradition: "Peace and good wishes to all the other churches that originated in the Reformation in the sixteenth century, which separated them from us. May the power of Christ's passover show the right path, however long, back to perfect communion; meanwhile, in mutual respect we are already seeking ways of narrowing the gap and practicing charity in the hope that such charity may one day be truly victorious."[95]

---

90. *AAS*, LVI (1964), 585. Further developments would take place especially in the fourth period of the Council with the abolition of the excommunications of 1054, followed in 1967 by Paul VI's visit to Constantinople and the return visit on the part of the patriarch.

91. *Ecumenism*, p. 86.

92. *AAS*, LVI (1964), 361.

93. *Ibid.*, quoted in *Ecumenism*, p. 86 (ct).

94. *Ibid.*, quoted in *ibid.*, pp. 86-87 (ct).

95. *Ibid.*, p. 362, quoted in *ibid.*, p. 87 (ct). Cf. also R 1964/14, p. 8. On the ecumenical importance of these greetings, cf. R 1964/18, p. 10; R 1964/46, p. 12; R 1965/2, p. 3; R 1965/5, p. 3; Biblio. 261, p. 912.

The initiative in addressing these greetings to other Christians, "maybe for the first time on an occasion as sacred as this," was of major importance. However, it is in a certain sense even more important that the pope should have so to speak institutionalized it by reviving the ancient custom of sending Easter letters of greeting and communion to the heads of other churches. The cardinal explains this custom as follows: "In the early centuries of the church the exchange of letters on the occasion of the Easter festivities was one of the ways in which the bishops and patriarchs expressed their unity in the celebration of the mystery of the risen Christ. . . . The Holy Father wished to revive this tradition."[96]

In the case of Ecumenical Patriarch Athenagoras, however, the pope did not stop at sending Easter letters. On the occasion of the eastern feast of Easter a special delegation was sent from Rome, headed by a member of the secretariat, Archbishop Joseph-Marie Martin of Rouen, who was accompanied by the secretary, Monsignor Johannes Willebrands, and by Father Duprey. The delegation delivered a personal letter from Paul VI, in which the pope said that the delegation had come "to tell you how vividly we recall our blessed meeting in Jerusalem, and how we feel that it has marked the beginning of a new period in the relations of the Holy See and the venerable Ecumenical Patriarchate. . . . We would be happy, too, if this visit provided an opportunity to strengthen the bonds which we have already tied, and make them firmer still."[97]

2. For its part, the secretariat took a major step on another front, with the aim of clarifying and advancing ecumenical relations with the World Council of Churches. In this connection Bea writes: "The speed with which relations began to improve during these months, especially with our eastern brethren, did not prevent attention from being given to a further deepening of relations with Christians of the Reformed tradition, and in particular with the World Council of Churches, who had been sending observer-delegates to the Council from the beginning. Now it was a question of trying to make the dialogue deeper and more intense."[98] This was the purpose of the "private and confidential" meeting held in Milan in April 1964, which was the first of such importance for both the status and the number of those taking part: "Those taking part, apart from Dr. Visser 't Hooft, the Secretary General, were Dr. Lucas Vischer and Dr. Nikos Nissiotis from the World Council of Churches; from the secretariat, besides the president and Monsignor Willebrands, the secretary, there were Fr. Jerome Hamer, O.P., and Fr. P. Duprey."[99]

So far as the subjects and the results of the meeting were concerned, Bea observes: "Whilst the participants agreed that the time for making decisions had not arrived, at least until after the Decree on Ecumenism had been promulgated, nevertheless they reached a better understanding of the situation and the various

---

96. *Ecumenism*, p. 89, quoting Vatican Radio. Since then similar letters have been regularly sent each year to all the heads of churches or ecclesial communities, etc.

97. *AAS*, LVI (1964), 423; English translation in *THS*, p. 72; cf. also *Ecumenism*, p. 88.

98. *Ecumenism*, p. 92 (ct).

99. *Ibid.*

possibilities." He adds that together with further consultations that took place during the third period in Rome, the meeting would bear its fruits in the forthcoming year, after the promulgation of the Decree on Ecumenism.[100] We now know that these meetings laid the groundwork for the developments that took place early the following year with the creation of the Joint Working Group.

3. Here we come to another initiative of Paul VI: *the return of the precious relic of the head of the apostle Andrew* to the Orthodox Church of Patras in Greece.[101] Like the pilgrimage to the Holy Land, the pope's announcement of this caused a considerable stir. In his response to the good wishes of the Sacred College on his feast day, the pope said: "In accordance with a request made by Constantine, the Orthodox Metropolitan of Patras, the Basilica of St. Peter will restore to his see a reliquary of inestimable value—that containing the sacred head of the apostle St. Andrew." The pope immediately explained the background: "This precious relic was given into the care of our predecessor Pope Pius II, the famous Enea Silvio Piccolomini, who received it on 12 April 1462 in particular historical circumstances, so that it might be fittingly guarded next to the tomb of his brother the apostle St. Peter, on the understanding that it would be sent back one day, if God saw fit."[102] And here we see the spirit in which this gesture was to be performed, for the pope said that the return had "a great significance for us: that of bearing witness to our veneration for the Greek Orthodox Church, and of our intention to open our heart to them in brotherhood, and in the faith and love of the Lord."[103]

The communitarian and ecclesial manner in which the relic was actually returned was also full of significance.

As a first act, the relic was venerated on 23 September in the presence of the pope and the Council fathers. In his address on this occasion, the Cardinal Archbishop of Vienna, Franz König, explained the significance of the return of this precious relic as follows: "By sending it [the relic] back we are testifying to our charity, and, at the same time, we are expressing our strong desire and hope that reunion will one day be accomplished."[104] Commenting on the act of veneration of the whole Council, Cardinal Bea writes: "In this way the whole [Catholic] church, through its most qualified and legitimate representatives, is associated in the Holy Father's brotherly gesture to the Greek Orthodox Church."[105]

The second act was its veneration on the part of the people of Rome: from the evening of the same day, 23 September, until the morning of 26 September, the relic was exposed for the veneration of the Christian people of Rome in the great

---

100. Cf. *ibid.*, p. 93. On the meeting, cf. also Fey, *A History of the Ecumenical Movement*, II, 339.
101. In order not to abandon a subject in mid-stream, here and in the following point (the Rhodes Panorthodox Conference) we move ahead to events that took place in the third period of the Council. This is easier in these cases because they have only an indirect connection with the Council.
102. *AAS*, LVI (1964), 586, quoted in *Ecumenism*, p. 91 (ct).
103. *Ibid.*, quoted in *ibid.*
104. *AS*, III/II, 285-287, quoted in *Ecumenism*, p. 131.
105. *Ecumenism*, p. 132.

church of St. Andrew della Valle.[106] On the afternoon of 25 September, a delegation of the Archdiocese of Patras arrived in Rome: the vicar general, accompanied by an archimandrite and by the priest in charge of Patras Cathedral. The delegation was received by the pope that evening.[107] "On 26 September, after a pontifical mass attended by the delegation from Patras and the observers at the Council who represented the Patriarchates of Constantinople, Alexandria and Moscow, the representatives of the Vicariate of Rome entrusted the precious relic to the President of the Secretariat for Christian Unity, who was to lead the special papal delegation entrusted with taking the precious relic to Patras in the pope's name. When the cardinal had received the relic, he left on a special Olympic Airways flight, accompanied by the Orthodox delegation from Patras."[108]

The third act was the reception and delivery in Patras. The aircraft had barely come to a standstill, when the Metropolitan of Patras came aboard, deeply moved. Having exchanged a brotherly kiss with Cardinal Bea, the metropolitan welcomed the papal delegation with the words: "We welcome you with feelings of great joy and warmth, but also with the most sincere fraternal charity, and we give glory to the triune God, who has brought about our holy meeting under such favorable and happy auspices."[109]

The center of all this was naturally Patras itself. Here "a large crowd had gathered in the streets and in King Constantine Square, where a platform had been set up with a small altar. The platform was surrounded by twenty-three Greek metropolitans dressed in liturgical vestments, including seven members of the holy synod, who were there as the official representatives of the Church of Greece (about twenty others had sent their excuses); there were also numerous members of the clergy and tens of thousands of members of the faithful."[110]

When he handed over the precious relic, the president of the secretariat explained *the meaning of the gesture* as follows: "For centuries we have lived as strangers to one another, whereas a common baptism had made us children of God in Jesus Christ, and brothers of one another. . . . But from now on, charity can and must reign in mutual respect, frankness, sincerity, and the wish for a progressive restoration of this brotherhood which has been forgotten and wounded for centuries. This brotherhood—the brotherhood of Peter and Andrew—is very closely united in the charity and service of Christ, and must be a model for all of us in the efforts required of us for the presentation of the gospel in the contemporary world."[111]

---

106. Cf. *Ecumenismo*, p. 166. On the whole question of the return, cf. also Agostino Pertusi, "Da Roma a Patrasso con la reliquia dell'Apostolo Andrea," *Vita e Pensiero*, XLVII (1964), 773-781.

107. Cf. *Ecumenismo*, p. 167.

108. *Ibid.*, pp. 167-168.

109. *Ibid.*, p. 168.

110. *Ibid.* In R 1964/46, p. 13, defending the Greek *people* against the accusation of being anti-ecumenical, Bea stresses this presence of so many metropolitans, saying that it was all the more significant if we bear in mind that certain quarters had issued a call for a boycott of the ceremony.

111. *Ecumenismo*, p. 170; cf. also *ibid.*, p. 137.

After the Greek translation of the cardinal's speech had been read, and after the words of greeting from the Metropolitan Constantine of Patras, the papal brief of Paul VI was read in Latin. In the course of this document, the pope addressed the following prayer to the apostle Andrew: "Through your intercession may these famous relics, which had found so noble a haven beside your brother's tomb, become the pledge and spur to fraternity in a single devotion and faith in Christ, in mutual charity."[112]

After this the relic was borne in procession to the cathedral, where the ceremony ended with an anthem of thanksgiving. The next day the papal delegation attended the solemn liturgy concelebrated by the Greek metropolitans in the Orthodox cathedral. After an exchange of gifts and souvenirs, the delegation left Patras.[113]

4. *The significance of the Third Panorthodox Conference in Rhodes.* Confirmation of the fact that the return of the relic of St. Andrew "contributed in an essential way" to consolidation of the new atmosphere created by the Jerusalem meetings could be seen fairly "clearly on the occasion of the Third Panorthodox Conference, which was held in the first half of November in Rhodes, and which was particularly concerned with relations between Orthodoxy and the Roman Catholic Church."[114]

(a) With regard to *the atmosphere* of the conference, we should note the terms in which some of its main figures spoke about the ecumenical efforts of the Catholic Church. The representative of the Ecumenical Patriarchate and President of the Conference, Metropolitan Meliton of Helioupolis and Theira, stated: "It is only right to acknowledge that the venerable Roman Catholic Church has done a great deal, for her part, to promote union with our Orthodox Church, by creating a favorable climate for a more rapid development of reconciliation than we could ever have hoped for between the churches of old and new Rome with a view to Christian unity."[115]

The delegation of the Patriarchate of Jerusalem in turn described the meeting between the pope and the ecumenical patriarch as "that great world event," and stated: "This meeting must be considered as an important leap forward and as the real beginning of dialogue between the churches of the East and West."[116]

(b) However, the exchange of messages between the pope and the conference was a new factor. In his message, Paul VI wrote as follows: "Thoroughly seized as we are by the importance of this venerable assembly, with fervent prayer we call down on it the light of the Holy Spirit. Please accept our assurance that we ourselves, together with the Council gathered together at this very moment, and

112. *Ibid.*, p. 172; cf. the, note that the document is found in *OssRom* and not in *AAS*.
113. Cf. *ibid.*, pp. 173-174. The cardinal took advantage of the journey to make a visit in Athens to the head of the Greek Orthodox Church, His Beatitude Archbishop Chrysostom, to whom he presented a pectoral cross as a gift from the pope; cf. *ibid.*, p. 175.
114. R 1965/5, p. 1. Cf. also R 1965/2, p. 1. On the conference, cf. F.W., "'La 3e Conference panorthodoxe de Rhodes," *Proche Orient Chrétien*, XV (1965), 93-105; also Caprile, IV, 190-192, 536-539; and A. Wenger, *Troisième Session* (Paris, 1965), pp. 274-302.
115. *Ecumenism*, p. 139 (ct).
116. *Ibid.*, p. 141 (ct).

the whole Catholic Church, will follow with a very special interest the progress of your labors. . . . We make bold to count on the aid of your prayers."[117]

The response of the conference, writes Bea, "required a great deal of preparation, first of all within the committee for the actual text, and then in the general assembly," because the conference wanted—and was successful in this—that the message should be approved and passed by a unanimous vote. The essential passage is as follows: "We sincerely appreciate the expressions of love and peace in the one same Lord, which you were good enough to send to us on your own behalf, as well as that of the Second Vatican Council and the whole Roman Catholic Church. By a unanimous decision we send Your Holiness our heartfelt thanks."[118]

With regard to the decision of the conference on dialogue with the Catholic Church we would quote the following passage: "The Third Panorthodox Conference renews the desire already expressed by the Orthodox Church concerning the theme of this dialogue; but having studied the details of such a dialogue, it has decided that if there is to be a truly fruitful theological dialogue, a certain amount of preparation and the creation of suitable conditions appear to be necessary. This does not mean to say that each one of the separate Orthodox Churches is not free to continue to engage in fraternal relations with the Roman Catholic Church on its own behalf. . . ."[119] The cardinal writes about this decision as follows: ". . . it is understandable that, while the dialogue of the Orthodox Church with the Catholic Church came up against more serious obstacles of an historical and psychological nature, it also perhaps had to take into account the concerns of the churches in communist countries over the possible attitudes of their governments."[120]

With regard to the impression left by the return of the relic of the head of the apostle Andrew, apart from the statements quoted above we should also note the fact that at the end of its work all the members of the conference made a pilgrimage to Patras. On this occasion Metropolitan Meliton of Helioupolis and Theira (who had been president of the conference) said that the return of the relic was "an example of how much could be achieved through charity."[121]

An Ecumenical Assessment of the Third Period of the Council

The cardinal writes as follows: "The central ecumenical event of this period, and it could be said of this year, was undoubtedly the definitive approval and *promulgation of the conciliar Decree on Ecumenism.* This decree shows the

---

117. *THS*, pp. 80-81.
118. *THS*, p. 81; original Greek text and French translation in *TAG*, pp. 158-159.
119. *Ecumenism*, pp. 144-145 (ct).
120. *Ibid.*, p. 144 (ct).
121. *Ibid.*, p. 133 (ct).

Catholic Church as such taking up an official position in theory and in practice in the cause of unity and in the ecumenical movement. This significance of the approval of the decree was almost universally recognized."[122]

1. However, before talking about this event, we must refer to *the vast amount of work* that was carried out between the second and third periods in order to produce this document. The reader will recall that we have already mentioned the very large number of interventions, both spoken and written, concerning the document. And after the close of the second period of the Council, a further fifty written interventions were added, making up 185 pages.[123] The first task facing the staff of the secretariat was that of carefully sorting all this material according to the articles in the text of the schema. An interview given by the president of the secretariat tells us that the observations sorted out in this way made up "two volumes of 226 pages in all of *general* observations on the schema; then a volume of 340 pages of observations on the first and second chapters; and a volume of 145 pages on the third chapter."[124]

The same interview also tells us about *the method* used in revising the text of the schema in the light of these observations: "*Twenty experts* worked with immense patience but also with love, from 4 to 21 February, on that enormous number of opinions to which I have referred. In order to be able to devote the greatest possible amount of time to this work, they all lived together in a religious house during this period, holding meetings every morning and afternoon, and often again after dinner in the evening. In this way we obtained a revised text of all the chapters of the schema."[125]

The next step is described as follows: "This new text was then weighed up by almost all *the members of the secretariat* (except for some who were prevented for reasons of ill health) between 24 February and 7 March, always with the help of very diligent experts. For this purpose, we all lived in the 'Gesù Divin Maestro' House of the Society of St. Paul near Ariccia, outside Rome. There were about fifty of us in all, bound together by a true family spirit." Here too the cardinal describes *the method* followed: "After hearing a general report on the relative part of the text, any difficulties entailed, and suggested solutions, etc., we divided up into three large groups to make discussion easier, and studied the material in question. The results of the group discussions were then reported

122. *Ibid.*, p. 147 (ct). Obviously the central fruit of the period was the promulgation of the Constitution on the Church, which is also in its own way of great importance for ecumenism, but here we are talking about the result that *directly* concerns the question of unity.

123. It is not possible to establish the precise number, since *AS*, III/III, 621, simply reviews all the written interventions sent in between 10 December 1963 and 21 May 1964 as a single whole, thus making no distinction between those submitted before the official closing date, i.e. the end of January, and those that arrived later. Now, as we shall see, reexamination of the schema by the secretariat was completed at the beginning of March, so that it was impossible to take account of written interventions sent in after 21 May 1964 (cf. *AS*, III/II, 850-876) or even after 14 September 1964 (cf. *AS*, III/II, 896-918).

124. Biblio. 251, p. 907; cf. also Caprile, III, 561. The volumes are found in the archives of the secretariat; cf. the precise figure in *AS*, III/II, 330, where the second figure is given as 341 pages and the third as 144.

125. Biblio. 251, pp. 911-912; cf. Caprile, III, 565-566.

at the plenary meetings in the afternoons, when we tried to clear up any doubt or lack of clarity that might still remain."[126]

Once the successive technical and editorial work had been completed and the text had been printed and sent out to the Council fathers, the Secretary General of the Council announced on 7 July that the draft Decree on Ecumenism had been placed on the agenda for the next period of the Council.[127]

2. On 6 October *the Council* started considering this new text,[128] although we would point out that this time it was no longer a question of discussion; the revised document had to pass through a complicated process of voting, almost article by article. Once all the articles in a given chapter had been dealt with, the chapter was then voted on as a whole, and in this last vote the fathers were allowed to cast not only simple votes in favor or against, but also a favorable vote "with reservations," in other words a positive vote accompanied by some suggested amendment which would later be evaluated by the secretariat. This voting process took place from 6 through 8 October, and the document obtained a very high average of about 98% favorable votes.

The voting did, however, leave the secretariat with the further major task of examining the very numerous amendments suggested: for the three chapters of the schema, the secretariat in fact received over one thousand favorable votes "with reservations."[129] The amendments were first examined by groups of consultors, whose conclusions were then evaluated in the plenary meetings of the Council fathers who were members of the secretariat. The result of this painstaking work was then condensed into detailed reports called "Examination of Amendments,"[130] to be put to the vote in the Council hall. In these reports the amendments proposed were listed one by one, with a note as to whether they had been accepted or not, and the reason why. According to the *Acta Synodalia*, there were 449 such amendments proposed in all, grouped under various headings.[131] Lastly, this "Examination of Amendments" was also approved by the Council with a vast majority.[132]

3. The path now seemed clear for the Council to move on to vote on the first reading of the whole document, but at this point there was a bombshell. On 19 November, twenty-four hours before this vote was taken, the Secretary General of the Council informed the Council fathers that *after* the vote on the "Examination of Amendments" the Secretariat for Christian Unity had made further

---

126. Biblio. 251, p. 912; cf. Caprile, III, 566.

127. Cf. Caprile, III, 459.

128. The text is found in *AS*, III/II, 296-317.

129. For the figures, cf. *The Way*, p. 38. See also the very detailed official reports that give first the outcome of the vote and then an examination of the proposed amendments; for the first chapter of the document, cf. *AS*, III/VII, 12-47; for the second, *AS*, III/VII, 412-421; and for the third, *AS*, III/VII, 669-702.

130. In Latin "Expensio modorum."

131. The reports mentioned in note 129 give the following figures: Chapter I, 207 amendments; Chapter II, 86 amendments; and Chapter III, 156 amendments.

132. The votes on the "Examination of Amendments" took place in the general congregations of 10, 11 and 14 November; cf. *AS*, III/VII, 59, 451, and 711.

modifications to the text, incorporating nineteen "benevolent suggestions" that had been made on the part of higher authority in order to lend the text greater clarity.[133] It is easy to understand how this intervention by "authority" caused a certain amount of dismay for a moment.

What had in fact happened? Later, the cardinal himself explained the matter as follows: "Due to an error in transmission or delivery, at the last minute (during the period between voting on the modifications and voting on the text as a whole) the higher authorities found themselves obliged to send in a series of fresh amendments which were to be taken into account. . . ."[134] However, Bea immediately notes that the amendments were "*not* to be imposed without prior examination. In fact nineteen, that is about half the modifications suggested, were incorporated into the text."[135]

4. Fortunately, there were twenty-four hours between the bombshell and the voting on the first reading, which gave the Council fathers time to calm down. The day after the incident, the document received 2054 votes in favor and 64 against. It is possible that the relatively large number of contrary votes was at least partly due to this incident, particularly since the document received *2137 votes in favor and only 11 against* in the vote on the second reading, which took place *in the public session* a further twenty-four hours later.[136]

5. Despite the "incident," the cardinal still emphasizes *how remarkable the result was.* A few weeks after the decree had been promulgated, he wrote as follows in an Evangelical journal: "If we look at things calmly and objectively, the decree represents a truly great and very important result of the third period of the Council."[137] Even a few years earlier such a decree would have been impossible; for example in 1962 there was still considerable concern that confessionally mixed countries, and thus their bishops, constituted a minority in the Council, and that it was therefore more than doubtful whether ecumenism would manage to make any headway.[138]

Further, "The particular *persuasive force* of all the teaching and the practical

---

133. Cf. *AS*, III/VIII, 422; the secretariat had accepted "suggestiones benevolas auctoritative expressas." For details, cf. Caprile, IV, 479-482, 460; also Svidercoschi, *Storia del Concilio*, pp. 490-493.

134. *Il cammino*, p. 43. Bea told me: "Paul VI spoke about it with me, saying, 'We have had a breakdown.' "

135. *The Way.* For the whole of this question, cf. R. Rouquette, *Vatican II. La fin d'une chrétienté*, 2 vols. (Paris, 1968), II, 542-544, 555-557. H. Fesquet, *Diario del Concilio. Tutto il concilio giorno per giorno* (Milan, 1967), p. 732, is incorrect in stating that the cardinal was "forewarned" of the amendments made to the text. Cf. also O. Cullmann, "The Bible in the Council," in Lindbeck (ed.), *Dialogue on the Way*, pp. 142-143; and W. Dietzfelbinger, "The Council Continues: Third Session," in *ibid.*, pp. 92-93 (in this last case, a calmer presentation would have been preferable).

136. Cf. *AS*, III/VIII, 783. E. Schlink, "The Decree on Ecumenism," in Lindbeck (ed.), *Dialogue on the Way*, p. 186, clearly through an oversight gives only the results of the vote on the first reading.

137. Biblio. 288, p. 11.

138. Cf. R. 1964/46, pp. 1-2; R 1965/23, p. 3; *Ecumenism*, p. 166. This lack of preparation is also rightly emphasized by Roux, *Détresse et promesse de Vatican II*, p. 147.

instructions of this decree lies especially in the fact that it received practically unanimous approval in a secret ballot. . . . Such unanimity clearly shows that the Catholic Church, through its highest representatives, was now pledging itself to promote with all the means at its disposal the unity of all those who believe in Christ and who have been baptized in his name. It is easy to understand how one of our non-Catholic brothers could have said that the Decree on Ecumenism constituted a milestone on the road to unity."[139]

6. With regard to the intervention on the part of "higher authority" described above, the cardinal had his work cut out in the following months, as we shall see, to pass on his own serenity to others in order to prevent the incident from making people lose sight of the importance of the overall result. He was too closely in contact with the observers not to feel the dismay it also caused among them and among the churches and ecclesial communities they represented.[140]

In the first place he rejected the claims of those who said that the amendments involved had been presented after everything had already been decided: no such final decision had been made because, according to the doctrine of the church, the pope has the last word even in a Council.[141]

With regard to the amendments themselves, the cardinal was especially concerned over one that had particularly upset and saddened Christians of the Reformed tradition, and that referred to the reading of sacred scripture and the fruit derived from this. The cardinal explained the question as follows: "Originally the text ran: 'Moved by the Holy Spirit they [Christians originating from the Reformation] find God in scripture as he speaks to them in Christ.' The text was changed to read; 'By invoking the Holy Spirit, they search in the sacred scriptures for God as the one who speaks to them in Christ.' "[142] In this connection, the president of the secretariat said that he was "genuinely sorry that this change has caused so much regret to our non-Catholic brothers," but assured them: "Knowing the situation, I can say that there was no intention of offending anyone, and further that this new text, given calm consideration, contains nothing offensive. In its present form the decree does not deny the doctrine of the New Testament—and could not do so—that our non-Catholic brethren, like all baptized people in general, are under the guidance of the Holy Spirit ('are moved by the Holy Spirit'), and that this is especially true in such a holy activity as reading the word of God in sacred scripture."[143]

7. Lastly it should be noted that Bea stated a number of times that the observer-delegates had "contributed in a decisive way" to the Decree on Ecumenism, saying this, for example, at the reception the secretariat gave in honor of the observers,[144] in an official address given before the pope and the

---

139. *Ecumenism*, p. 147 (ct).
140. Cf. Visser 't Hooft, *Die Welt war meine Gemeinde*, p. 401, who says that they wondered whether after this event it would still be possible to continue with the dialogue.
141. Cf. *Ecumenism*, pp. 170-171.
142. *Ibid.*, p. 173.
143. *Ibid.*, pp. 173-174 (ct). Cf. also R 1965/1, p. 5; R 1965/3, pp. 17-18; R 1965/8, p. 17; *Rencontre oecuménique*, pp. 65-66; *The Way*, p. 49; also an unpublished note, Arch. R 1965/45.
144. Cf. *Ecumenismo*, p. 182.

cardinals,[145] and in various conversations and interviews.[146] He also wrote that the very presence of the observers and "their participation in the Council in prayer and in work placed the problem of the division of Christians squarely and vividly before the Council fathers. The many lively contacts between them and many Council fathers every day produced an increasingly deep awareness on the one hand of our union in Christ, which already exists and is the work of the Spirit of Christ in us and our shared faith and our shared love of Christ, and on the other hand of the painful wound of our divisions."[147]

* * *

In conclusion, the evaluations quoted enable us to see ecumenism as a kind of "peaceful and constructive revolution in the life of the church."[148] The cardinal hence has no hesitation in stating: ". . . so we can begin to see already something of the abundant influence it [the decree] is likely to exercise in the church in years to come. Only the actual development of the movement for Christian unity in the decades and centuries ahead will show posterity the full measure of its beneficial influence on the church and the whole of Christianity."[149]

The Cardinal Makes an Official Visit to the World Council of Churches

So far as the ecumenical situation after the third period of the Council is concerned, it is helpful to see the picture painted by the Secretary General of

---

145. Cf. R 1964/50, p. 2.

146. Cf. R 1965/5, p. 2; R 1965/3, p. 3; R 1965/8, p. 3; *Ecumenismo*, p. 185; *Der Friede*, p. 56.

147. *Ecumenismo*, p. 182. The observer H. Roux has a whole chapter in his book (*Détresse et promesse de Vatican II*, pp. 19-33) entitled "The 'Critical' Position of the Observers," and in it he indicates in comprehensive and detailed fashion the numerous circumstances that made the observers' work considerably more difficult: without any specific prior preparation, they found themselves faced with copious documents dealing with subjects with which most of them were completely unfamiliar; there was no dialogue among the observers themselves; apart from the long sessions they were very taken up with contacts and invitations, and of course with the regular reports that had to be made to the communities that had sent them. It may therefore be reasonable to wonder whether at least some of them were really able to master the enormous quantity of material, or whether too much had not been asked of them. In this respect it will no doubt be interesting to study the accounts and reports of the observers, once the conciliar and other archives are accessible. And the final words of the cardinal's explanations cited here take on their full meaning in this light. The major fruit of the observers' participation in the Council has been the post-conciliar development of the ecumenical movement, for this participation meant that they—and, through them—their churches and ecclesial communities—became convinced that a dialogue with the Roman Catholic Church was possible, useful, and indeed urgently necessary. This produced the truly creative post-conciliar development of ecumenism, as we shall see again later.

148. *The Way*, p. 58.

149. *Ibid.*, p. 34.

the World Council of Churches, Dr. W.A. Visser 't Hooft, in January 1965, in his speech to the Central Committee of that association, which was meeting in Enugu, Nigeria. After stressing the problems there had been at the end of the period in question, he pointed out that a new situation had been created with the promulgation of the Decree on Ecumenism, for the Catholic Church had officially stated its wish to enter into dialogue with other churches or communities, and thus become part of the ecumenical movement.[150] The Central Committee received this evaluation positively, and then resolved to give a practical form to the intensification of dialogue with the Catholic Church, along the lines discussed at the secret meeting in Milan in April 1964. It thus *approved the following declaration*: "In the light of the above considerations it is proposed that a working group be established consisting of eight representatives of the World Council of Churches and six representatives of the Roman Catholic Church. The task of this group will be to work out the principles which should be observed in future collaboration and the methods which should be used. . . . The working group shall have no power to take decisions, but must work out suggestions to be submitted to the churches represented, and communicate them to the member churches."[151]

A combination of circumstances meant that the acceptance of this proposal on the part of the Holy See took place within the framework of an official visit of the President of the Secretariat for Christian Unity to Geneva, and in particular to the general headquarters of the World Council of Churches, in February 1965. The visit had two high points: the solemn reception offered to the president of the secretariat by the World Council of Churches, and the public conversation between the cardinal and Pastor Marc Boegner, ex-president of the World Council of Churches.[152]

1. In *the words of greeting* addressed to the president of the secretariat, the secretary general highlighted the various circumstances that made this reception truly memorable: "This present time—some months after the promulgation of the conciliar Decree on Ecumenism and a few weeks after the decision of the Central Committee of our council concerning the deepening of the dialogue with the Catholic Church—is singularly propitious."[153] The speaker immediately amplified on this "deepening of the dialogue with the Catholic Church," saying that it was not a question of "entering into negotiations with the Roman Catholic Church concerning the union of churches," since such tasks lay outside the sphere of the world council, but that it was more a question of "the problems that have caused, and continue to do so, serious tension between the churches,

---

150. A German translation of this report is found in *Der Friede*, pp. 114-118. In *Ecumenismo*, the cardinal observes that this report represents an example of a "serene and fraternal discussion of difficulties" (p. 153, note 9).

151. *Ecumenism*, p. 152 (ct). On the Enugu meeting, cf. also Fey, *A History of the Ecumenical Movement*, II, 339-340.

152. Details of these two important events are found in the volume we have already cited a number of times, *Rencontre oecuménique à Génève* (Biblio. 290-291); the cardinal's address is also found in *Der Friede*, pp. 49-54; cf. also Caprile, IV, 540-550; BM, pp. 168-171.

153. *Ecumenism*, p. 153 (ct); original French in *Rencontre oecuménique*, p. 23.

although we are also concerned with the possibility of collaboration in the practical sphere. . . . In the world that is being born before our eyes, churches can only help the nations in their spiritual and moral perplexity and loss of bearings by cooperating with one another."[154]

Replying to this speech, *the president* of the secretariat stated: ". . . today's meeting can be considered to have a truly historic importance. We are aware that there has been nothing of this kind for many decades. . . . It is enough to say that we all know that things were very different for a very long time."[155] The importance of the meeting also lay in the fact that it was the fruit of long preparation, which had begun with the creation of the secretariat and been developed in the three periods of the Council, culminating in the approval of the Decree on Ecumenism with only eleven votes against: "This vote, in its turn, is a sign of an increasingly intense ecumenical atmosphere in the Council."[156]

In this context, the cardinal referred to the proposal made by the Central Committee at its Enugu meeting, and said that "the Holy See greets with joy and fully *accepts the proposal made by the Central Committee* of the World Council of Churches last month at Enugu to set up a joint committee, consisting of eight representatives of the World Council and six representatives of the Catholic Church, to explore together the possibilities for dialogue and cooperation between the World Council and the Catholic Church. As we know, the task of this committee is not to make decisions on these matters, but only to study methods and principles for an eventual dialogue and cooperation. The results of the work of this committee will go for further examination and decision to those in authority on both sides."[157]

The secretary general then briefly expressed his gratitude for this response: "But we thank you above all for having officially informed us that the Catholic Church accepts the proposal made by the Central Committee of the World Council of Churches at its meeting in Enugu. . . . The fact that your church and the world council have now publicly expressed their desire to develop their contacts is *an historic event*. Now the work can begin."[158]

2. Let us now take a look at the other high point of the visit, i.e. *the public conversation*. The very fact that it should have taken place in the "Hall of the Reform" (built in the nineteenth century) was already a very significant element,

---

154. *Ecumenism*, pp. 153-154 (ct); original French in *Rencontre oecuménique*, p. 27.

155. *Ecumenism*, p. 154; original French in *Rencontre oecuménique*, p. 30.

156. *Ecumenism*, p. 155; original French in *Rencontre oecuménique*, pp. 30-31. Many steps in this long preparation, as concerns direct contacts with the world council, are described by J. Willebrands on the basis of his own experience in the introduction to the book *Der Friede*, pp. 11-25.

157. *Ecumenism*, p. 155 (ct); original French in *Rencontre oecuménique*, pp. 32-33.

158. *Ecumenism*, pp. 155-156 (ct); original French in *Rencontre oecuménique*, p. 36. For reasons of brevity, we shall not quote from the very beautiful "message" of Pastor M. Boegner (cf. *Rencontre oecuménique*, pp. 37-43), especially since we have already quoted certain significant extracts in other contexts. We would add that the joint working group met for the first time the following May (cf. *Ecumenism*, p. 158); in this context Bea says that at about the same time a similar group was set up with the Lutheran World Federation.

but it took on an ever wider significance through the fact that it was held in Geneva, which had in the past been called "the Rome of the Reformation," and with a dialogue partner who was the Honorary President of the Reformed Church of France and also one of the founders of the World Council of Churches. Describing the event, the cardinal notes various details: "The conversation itself was framed in a particularly significant way by anthems, which were sung first separately and then together by two choirs, one Protestant and the other Catholic; and the occasion closed with the recitation of the Lord's Prayer in unison. The hall was incredibly full, and a large number unfortunately had to remain outside because of lack of space."[159]

We shall not linger over the content of this discussion. Bea began by relating the results obtained in the ecumenical field since the creation of the secretariat, especially in the Council. He went on to speak of the main subjects to be dealt with in future dialogue: on the one hand, the question of the church, which should be studied in the light of sacred scripture, the fathers of the church and the liturgy, and, on the other, various practical problems. After the other speaker had stated his position on these same subjects, the cardinal referred more particularly to the question of the difference between the apostolic and the post-apostolic traditions, problems concerning mariology and those concerning the unity of the church.[160]

* * *

In conclusion, we would give *an overall evaluation*, particularly of the visit to the World Council of Churches and the creation of the joint working group. In the first place, we can cite the on-the-spot comment of Pastor Marc Boegner, who said that the visit "marked the beginning of a new era in the contemporary history of ecumenism."[161] For his part, the cardinal stated: "I have no doubt that this step will bear excellent fruit, both in the field of cooperation in solving the major pressing problems of our times, and also in that of theological dialogue as such."[162]

Exchange of Official Visits between Orthodoxy and Rome

Parallel with developments in relations with the World Council of Churches, there were also important developments in relations with Orthodoxy.

---

159. *Ecumenism*, p. 157 (ct). It had been suggested that the hall, which had 2,600 seats, should be linked up with a nearby church, but this was not done because it was not imagined that there would be such a huge crowd.

160. Cf. *Rencontre oecuménique*, pp. 47-52, 63-68, 77-85. For an evaluation of the *fact* of this public conversation on the part of Pastor Boegner, cf. *ibid.*, p. 54. The cardinal's evaluation is found in R 1965/11, p. 1; *Rencontre oecuménique*, p. 47.

161. *Rencontre oecuménique*, pp. 69-70.

162. R 1965/16, p. 4; cf. also R 1965/12, pp. 3-4.

1. On 15 February 1965, three days before the Geneva meeting described above, an official delegation from the Ecumenical Patriarchate arrived in Rome, in accordance with a resolution of the Third Panorthodox Conference of Rhodes, which had entrusted the Ecumenical Patriarchate with informing "the Bishop of Rome" of its decisions. The delegation consisted of two metropolitans: Metropolitan Meliton of Helioupolis and Theira, president of the conference, and Metropolitan Chrysostom of Myra, its secretary.

When they were received in audience by Pope Paul VI, Metropolitan Meliton first of all transmitted "the kiss of peace" of the Ecumenical Patriarch to the pope. He then explained the decisions of the Rhodes conference—which we have already seen above—and concluded by expressing the hope that this mission "may be the blessed beginning of a regular well-planned fostering of brotherly relations between our two churches in a sincere dialogue of charity. By means of this dialogue may we labor together, removing the accumulated obstacles that stand in our way and preparing the ground on all sides, so that we may be soon brought into theological dialogue." In this way we shall move toward the final objective, which is full communion in eucharist and faith, in other words "the dawn of that bright day of the Lord, in which those of the West and those of the East, after the ancient fashion of our common martyrs, confessors and fathers, will eat the same bread and drink from the same chalice and confess the one faith 'in one Spirit,' and again 'with one mind strive side by side for the faith of the gospel' (Phil. 1:27). . . . "[163]

Apart from the document containing the decisions of the conference, the delegation also handed the pope a personal letter from Patriarch Athenagoras, which included the following passage: "Indeed it is with joy that . . . we see clearly displayed on an ever wider scale the desire and readiness of the local Christian churches for cooperation and for a joint progress toward the fulfillment of the Lord's will for the unity of all who believe in him."[164]

The pope thanked them, exclaiming: "Yes, this day is one that the Lord has made; let all be given over to thanksgiving and joy." Then he said: "In the future people will be able to say: here centuries of history reached their term; here a new stage in the relations between the Catholic West and the Orthodox East began." The pope went on to say that for his part he was determined to put the dialogue of charity into practice: "We must, by means of more numerous and fraternal contacts, restore step by step what the time of isolation has undone, and recreate anew, at all levels of the life of our churches, an atmosphere that will allow us, when the time comes, to set about theological dialogue likely to yield good results."[165]

The cardinal concludes his account of this event with the following observation: "This first official visit of a special delegation from the Ecumenical Patriarchate of Constantinople took place in such a friendly atmosphere that Metropolitan Meliton was able to say as he took his leave at the end of his stay

163. THS, pp. 86-87.
164. Ibid., p. 84.
165. Ibid., pp. 87-88.

in Rome: 'Your Eminence, we are going with the feeling of leaving our own home.' "[166]

2. *This visit* of the delegation from Constantinople was then *returned* in the following April by the *President of the Secretariat for Christian Unity*, who headed a special papal delegation, which included Bishop J. Willebrands and the under-secretary of the secretariat, Father P. Duprey.

In his greetings to the Ecumenical Patriarch, the cardinal explained *the aim* of the visit as follows: "Our visit today is meant to return that of your own delegation, and to continue the dialogue of charity already entered upon, with a view to drawing closer still the bonds which link us each to each like brothers."[167] He then said that this visit was the cause of joy for a great many people: "What joy, in the kingdom of eternity, for the blessed soul of Pope John. What joy for the whole Church of Christ both in East and West. What joy, too, all this must bring, I am sure, to Your Holiness, you who have for many years spoken and labored, have prayed and suffered, to hasten the longed-for hour when we shall open our arms once more to each other like brothers, and set out on the same road toward the goal of our yearnings—the unity willed by Christ."[168]

The president of the secretariat delivered a *personal letter from Paul VI* to the patriarch, in which the pope referred to the decisions of the Third Panorthodox Conference of Rhodes, saying: "The program there outlined seems to us to meet the requirements of the actual situation which history has bequeathed us, and by the same token those of our common advance toward the unity willed by the Lord, the desire for which has been so marvelously enkindled by his Spirit of love in the hearts of the Christians of our times. . . . Surely the happy harmony easily perceived between the decisions of the Conference of Rhodes and those of the Vatican Council is a fresh sign of the action of the Holy Spirit."[169]

The patriarch in turn greeted the papal delegation with the words: "Truly your visit to us is a matter of joy in the Lord on both sides, and we hail it as a new and significant stage in the period of the Christian history of East and West which is now being opened up."[170] Then, referring to the aim of the visit, the patriarch continued: "You are here to manifest to our Orthodox Church, in a more concrete form and within the context of sacred historical responsibilities, *the positive response* of the venerable Roman Catholic Church to the recent official communication, through our patriarchal delegation, of the decisions of the Third Panorthodox Conference. These in a similar concrete fashion expressed the desire of the Orthodox to carry out the dialogue of charity without delay, and to make a careful preparation for the theological dialogue."[171]

We shall not stop to give a detailed account of the whole visit, but merely

---

166. *Ecumenism*, p. 159.
167. *THS*, p. 92.
168. *Ibid.*
169. *Ibid.*, p. 91.
170. *Ibid.*, p. 95.
171. *Ibid.*

quote the cardinal's description of a significant episode that took place on 5 April: "Before going to the airport, the delegation visited St. Sophia (which was once the cathedral of the ecumenical patriarchate). The head of the delegation purposefully went straight to the place where the altar had once stood on which, in the ill-omened year of 1054, the papal legate Humbert had placed the bull of excommunication against Patriarch Cerularius (to which the patriarch had in turn replied by excommunicating the pope). This was a symbolic gesture. Knowing that he was the first cardinal sent to Constantinople by the pope since the time of the papal legate Humbert,[172] the president of the secretariat wanted his gesture to indicate that the present efforts of the Catholic Church were aimed at wiping out this sad past."[173]

Concluding his account, the president of the secretariat says: "It must be borne in mind that no words can reproduce the atmosphere and the way in which the visit took place; it was easy to see the genuine nature and the depth of the rapprochement that has been brought about between the Catholic Church and the Ecumenical Patriarchate after the meeting in Jerusalem. Eloquent evidence of this change is also the way in which the visit was seen by the press, whose reports were all in all unanimously favorable. The press also quoted long extracts from the Holy Father's letter, and also from speeches of the patriarch and the head of the delegation."[174]

The Council Closes with Some Important Ecumenical Acts

In the fourth period of the Council various important documents of great ecumenical relevance were approved and promulgated, for example *Dei verbum* on divine revelation and *Dignitatis humanae* on religious freedom. We shall be talking about these in due course, but for the moment we are thinking (1) of the date of 4 December, which was a very great day, especially for the observers, since it was then that the message from the observer-delegates to the Council fathers was read out in the Council hall and that the joint prayer service of the observers with the pope and the Council fathers was held at St. Paul's Outside-the-Walls. We are also thinking (2) of the solemn return of the relics of St. Sabas, one of the famous fathers of eastern monasticism, to the Patriarchate of Jerusalem; and above all (3) of the mutual abolition of the excommunications of 1054 on the part of the Catholic Church and the Ecumenical Patriarchate.

1. *"A great day lived with the observers."* We would start by noting the great increase in the number of observers and guests of the secretariat: ". . . the number of observer-delegates and guests of the secretariat who attended the last session

---

172. Here it must be noted that this statement is not strictly accurate. Cf., for example, for the missions of the fifteenth century, Joseph Gill, *The Council of Florence* (Cambridge, 1958), pp. 349-380. This does not, however, detract from the deep value of the cardinal's symbolic gesture.
173. *Ecumenismo*, p. 207.
174. *Ibid.* In a note the author refers to the review of press cuttings published in *Proche Orient Chrétien*, XV (1965), 187ff.

amounted to one hundred and three, more than double the number at the first session. They represented twenty-nine churches, ecclesial communities and federations."[175] The cardinal observes that we could almost say that the various churches and ecclesial communities were anxious not to miss this last opportunity.

As concerns the day itself, the cardinal writes as follows: "4 December will remain a particularly memorable one in the story of the Second Vatican Council from the point of view of ecumenism. The day was dominated by three events: in the morning Dr. Lucas Vischer, observer-delegate for the World Council of Churches, read a message from the observers to the Council fathers during the general assembly.[176] In the afternoon the liturgy of the word was held in St. Paul's Basilica in which, besides the Holy Father and the Council fathers, the observers took an active part in their formal choir dress. After this solemn service the pope received the observers in a final audience."[177]

(a) So far as the message is concerned, it should be noted that this was the only time during the Council that the whole assembly listened to a speech—indeed a solemn message—from the observers. The value of the message, which was fairly short, lies in the fact that it was given in the name of all the observers and guests and the fact that it sums up the experience of the four conciliar periods. We shall quote only two basic extracts. First of all let us see the remarks on *relations* between the observers and the Council fathers: "We were welcomed with great kindness in all quarters. We experienced innumerable signs of respect, charity and friendship. The dialogue so often spoken of remained no empty word. Again and again we were given a chance for formal discussion and personal conversation. Although the Council fathers and the experts were all occupied with a vast amount of work, they were full of concern for us, and were anxious to acquire a deeper knowledge of the opinions of other churches. Personal bonds and relationships begun in these years have enriched us greatly, and we shall carry them with us when we go."[178]

The message then refers to *the great earnestness and zeal* with which the observers had followed the course of the Council: ". . . there is one thing which we wish to express firmly to the Council fathers: we have followed the labors of the Council not just by observation, as though from a great distance, but by a true participation in its spirit. For what takes place in one church also concerns the others. This much certainly became clearer as one session succeeded another. Despite separation, the various churches are nevertheless united in the name of Christ. We observers are firmly convinced that the communion achieved so far can grow further, and will certainly increase."[179]

---

175. *Ecumenism*, p. 187.
176. The text is unfortunately not found in *AS*; the minutes of General Congregation 167 merely say that the address was read by the Secretary General of the Council (and thus not by Dr. Vischer!); cf. *AS*, IV/I, 117.
177. *Ecumenism*, p. 201 (ct).
178. *Ibid.*, p. 202 (ct).
179. *Ibid.* (ct).

(b) As concerns *the liturgy of the word*, we must above all note that it was held on *the initiative of the pope himself*. The cardinal writes as follows: "Paul VI had in fact made it known at the beginning of this session that he did not simply intend to repeat the audiences of past years, but that he wanted to do something special. It was his idea to take part in a solemn prayer and Bible service with the observers."[180] Today's readers, who are now quite used to such joint services, must try to carry themselves back in spirit to the situation at that time, when such a thing was an absolute novelty—and one that was all the more significant inasmuch as the pope and the whole Council took part. Furthermore, it took place virtually at the end of the Council and therefore "not only the pope, but also the Council fathers were able to take leave of the observers. The service was made more moving by the fact that observers belonging to different churches and ecclesial communities took an active part in the readings from the scriptures and in the chanting of the prayers."[181]

The service was given the following form: a psalm was sung as an introduction; then followed an Old Testament reading (1 Chron. 29:10-18), a reading from the Letter to the Romans (15:1-6), and finally the Beatitudes from St. Matthew's Gospel; after the pope's homily and the prayers of the faithful, "the service ended with the recital—with each speaking in his own language—of the Lord's Prayer, and the singing of the *Magnificat*."[182]

This initiative on the pope's part constituted a *clear signal to the whole church*, and the president of the secretariat comments as follows: "With this service of prayer the Holy Father gave a shining example of the recommendation formulated a year earlier in the council Decree on Ecumenism: 'In certain circumstances, such as in prayer services for unity and during ecumenical gatherings, it is allowable, indeed desirable, that Catholics should join in prayer with their separated brethren' (no. 8). The service turned out, in fact, to be one of the finest ecumenical experiences of the whole Council."[183]

2. *The return of the relics of St. Sabas*. St. Sabas was the founder of the famous eastern monastery of Mar Saba above the valley of the Jordan. Following a series of vicissitudes, his relics, like those of so many others, ended up in Venice, where they had been preserved for a number of centuries now.[184] After various negotiations it was eventually agreed that they should be solemnly returned to their place of origin.[185] The relics were taken out on 25 October 1965 and handed

---

180. *Ibid.*, p. 203.

181. *Ibid.*

182. *Ibid.* We would add that after the service the pope received the observers; when Cardinal Bea had made the introductions, the Anglican Bishop of Ripon, John Moorman, spoke in their name; the text is found in *OD*, pp. 49-72, and Moorman, *Vatican Observed*, pp. 211-213. The pope gave each of them a bronze bell cast by one of the foremost contemporary Italian artists, explaining that it was a symbolic souvenir because the bell calls us to the divine office, to charity and to prayer; cf. *Ecumenismo*, pp. 257-260.

183. *Ecumenism*, pp. 203-204 (ct).

184. Cf. *ibid.*, p. 190; *EncCatt*, X, 1505-1506.

185. The return did not take place at the end of the Council, but at the end of October (always of course *close* to the end of the fourth period of the Council), and we consider it here so as not

over to a high-ranking delegation from the Patriarchate of Jerusalem, which was accompanied back to Jerusalem by a delegation from the Catholic Patriarchate of Venice. When the relics reached Athens on 25 October, "Chrysostomos, Archbishop of Athens and of all Greece, accompanied by a large number of clergy, came to venerate them on board the aircraft itself. . . . During the night there was an unbroken flow of faithful venerating the relics. On Tuesday, 26 October, the plane was met at Jerusalem Airport by Patriarch Benedictos and the Synod together with the Governor of Jerusalem His Excellency Daud Abu Ghazaleh, the Consul General of Greece in Jerusalem, and civil and military authorities of the district. The procession reached the Jaffa Gate where numerous clergy of all rites and a considerable crowd of faithful welcomed and accompanied the relics to the Basilica of the Holy Sepulchre."[186] A solemn doxology of thanksgiving was celebrated here. The crowds who had come to venerate the relics then started to file past, and this continued for a number of days.[187]

The deep-lying significance of the event was stressed as follows by the Orthodox Patriarch of Jerusalem, Benedictos: "This event will give to the church, especially at this time when the spirit of ecumenism is developing, a new impetus toward charity, mutual respect, reconciliation and sincere collaboration between the two great churches, Catholic and Orthodox, for the good of the church of Christ and the whole of humanity."[188]

3. *The abolition of the excommunications of 1054* undoubtedly constitutes the crowning moment of conciliar events from the ecumenical point of view, and even the assembly of the Council fathers felt and expressed this when it greeted the embrace between the pope and the representative of the ecumenical patriarchate with what was described as "the longest applause of the whole Council."[189]

(a) Let us first consider *what these excommunications had actually meant.* The cardinal explains that they were "related to the well-known and unhappy events which took place in June 1054 when the papal legates with Cardinal Archbishop Humbert at their head placed the bull which excommunicated the Ecumenical Patriarch Michael Cerularius and his followers on the altar of St. Sophia, just as the sacred liturgy was about to be celebrated. In reply the patriarch, with a solemn synodal act, excommunicated all those who had published, written or given their consent or encouragement to the bull of excommunication delivered by the papal legate. This took place on 24 July of the same year."[190]

---

to leave this particular thread hanging in mid-air.
186. *Ecumenism*, p. 192 (ct).
187. Cf. *ibid.*
188. *Ibid.*, p. 193.
189. R 1966/6, p. 10; cf. also R 1966/2, p. 6; *Der Friede*, p. 36. The event is fairly extensively described in *Ecumenism*, pp. 204-211. The main documents are found in *Ecumenismo*, pp. 261-265; cf. also BM, pp. 242-244. Many documents regarding the planning and execution of this abolition are found in *THS*, pp. 115-133.
190. *Ecumenism*, p. 205 (ct). Cf. note 9 on the same page for bibliographical information on the texts

How did the idea arise of abolishing these excommunications, and how precisely was it to be implemented? The president of the secretariat tells us that the relative discussions had begun in July that year, with a conclusion being reached during the fourth period of the Council, at the end of November. The actual instruments were, on the one hand, a *joint* act of the two sides, and, on the other, a separate act on the part of each. As the joint act, *a joint declaration of intent* of Pope Paul VI and Ecumenical Patriarch Athenagoras I was drawn up, expressing their wish to wipe away those sad events and their consequences so far as possible. "No tribunal is erected nor does a historical judgment emerge, but, as in a family which comes together after an old and painful feud, there is solemnly shown the will to commit it to oblivion, and remove it from memory and from the midst of the church."[191] Each of the two sides would then put this will into action with a document of its own, which would be drawn up according to the juridical structures and customs of each.

(b) *The implementation* of this joint decision took place simultaneously in Rome and Constantinople on 7 December, in both cases in the presence of a delegation from the other side, and comprising two stages: the reading of the joint declaration, and then the reading of the individual document of the relative side with which the act of abolition was performed in the name of that church.

Let us start with the essential passage from *the joint declaration*, which said that both parties "declare in mutual agreement: (a) that they regret the offending words, the baseless reproaches, and the blameworthy symbolic acts which on both sides marked or accompanied the sad events of this time; (b) that in the same way they regret and remove from memory and from the midst of the church the sentences of excommunication which followed, the remembrance of which acts right up to our own times as an obstacle to our mutual approach in charity, and they condemn these to oblivion; (c) that they deplore, finally, the troublesome precedents and the further happenings which, under the influence of various factors, including misunderstanding and distrust on both sides, eventually led to a real rupture of ecclesial communion."[192]

(c) Now we come to the salient moments of *the service that took place in Rome*. As the cardinal observes, the reading of the joint declaration "preceded the celebration of Holy Mass, and in this way it could be said that the pope and the conciliar assembly placed this holy and generous proposal on the altar next to the divine victim."[193]

The act of abolition, on the other hand, was formally performed *after* mass, with the reading of the papal brief *Ambulate in dilectione*.[194] The document was read out by the President of the Secretariat for Christian Unity, while "beside the pope was Meliton, Metropolitan of Helioupolis and Theira, the head of the

of the relative documents.
191. *Ibid.*, p. 206. Here the cardinal for the most part follows the report in *CC*, 1966/I, 78ff; cf. Caprile, V, 506-512.
192. *THS*, p. 127.
193. *Ecumenism*, p. 207.
194. Or *Walk in love*.

delegation from Patriarch Athenagoras."[195] The brief first referred to the sad events of 1054, and then stated: ". . . being anxious to make further progress along the road of brotherly love, by which we could be led into perfect unity, and to remove obstacles and shackles, in the presence of the bishops gathered together in the Second Ecumenical Vatican Council, we declare that we regret the words and deeds that were said and enacted at that time and cannot meet with approval now. Furthermore, we wish to cancel out from the memory of the church and remove from its midst the sentence of excommunication then pronounced, and to have it buried in oblivion."[196]

At the end of the service, "when the reading of the brief was finished, the pope received the original of the letter from the master of ceremonies. This was written on parchment. Opening the scroll he gave it to Metropolitan Meliton, and then he rose and embraced him fraternally amidst the applause of the assembly. Cardinal Bea and the other two cardinals also embraced him."[197]

(d) Now let us see the cardinal's description of the parallel *celebration in Constantinople*: "At the same time a similar ceremony was taking place in the patriarchal church of Phanar in Constantinople in the presence of a papal delegation sent from Rome the evening before under the leadership of Cardinal Shehan, Archbishop of Baltimore, U.S.A., and a member of the Secretariat for Unity. In the course of the solemn liturgy in honor of St. Ambrose and before a crowd which filled and overflowed the church, the reading of the gospel text on the Good Shepherd was followed by the reading of the joint declaration in Greek. When the time for the Lord's Prayer came the patriarch invited the delegation to recite it in Latin. When this had ended he himself read the *tomos* (a document similar to the papal brief) which had been signed by himself and the members of his synod. At its central point the document read: 'Accordingly we, that is to say our humble self, together with the very venerable and highly honored metropolitans, our beloved brothers and colleagues, . . . declare and set down in writing that the anathema pronounced in the main Chancellery of the Great Church in our part of the world, in the year of salvation 1054, in the month of July, of the seventh indiction, is henceforth removed from memory and the midst of the church, and is to be regarded as such by all. And this by the mercy of the God of all pity.' "[198]

The cardinal's account closes as follows: "Amidst the enthusiasm and the acclamation of those present Patriarch Athenagoras and Cardinal Shehan, head of the papal mission, blessed the crowd many times together, both inside and outside the church."[199]

"The *precise value* and significance" of this "act of abolition" is explained as follows in the joint declaration: "In carrying out this symbolic action,

195. *Ecumenism*, pp. 207-208.
196. *THS*, p. 129; cf. *Ecumenism*, p. 208.
197. *Ecumenism*, p. 208 (ct).
198. *Ibid.*, p. 209 (ct); the translation of the document in question is taken from *THS*, p. 131, and not from *Ecumenism*.
199. *Ibid.*, pp. 209-210.

however, they [Pope Paul VI and Patriarch Athenagoras I] hope that it will be acceptable to God, who is quick to pardon us when we pardon one another, and that it will be appreciated by the whole Christian world, but above all by the general body both of the Roman Catholic Church and the Orthodox Church, as the expression of a sincere mutual desire for reconciliation, and as an invitation to follow up, in a spirit of trust, esteem, and mutual charity, the dialogue which will lead them with the help of God to live afresh, for the greater good of souls and the coming of God's kingdom, in the full communion of faith, of brotherly harmony, and of sacramental life, which obtained between them throughout the first thousand years of the life of the church."[200]

The foregoing has already given a very good idea of the dimensions of this historic act, but the cardinal further highlights them in the following extract: "It was no accident that the reading of the joint declaration and the embrace between the pope and Metropolitan Meliton was greeted by what was almost certainly the longest applause of the whole Council. This applause and the deep and widespread echo which this twofold act created in the East and the West showed how the faithful—and to some extent world public opinion—were aware of the great significance of this act, which took its place in the history of the gradual creation of an atmosphere of authentic brotherhood and charity in Christ among all those who were baptized in him and imbued with his Spirit—the Spirit of unity."[201]

An Ecumenical Assessment of the Council

Throughout our whole account of the Council we have obviously provided many elements that must of necessity enter into the overall evaluation, and we do not intend to repeat them here. Rather, we shall report some views expressed by the leading figures in the context of the end of the Council, taking our lead from an observation of the cardinal which distinguished between the fruits incarnated in people and those fixed on paper in the conciliar documents.

1. As concerns *the first category* of fruits of the Council, we would first quote two statements by observer-delegates which can in general terms be taken in the name of all the others.

(a) The first comes from Rev. Dr. *Douglas Horton*, observer for the International Council of Congregationalists, in reply to the greeting of the president of the secretariat at a reception on 18 September. He expanded on the thought that "you have opened many doors for us," saying that the most important of these was "the door of your friendship," and then going on: "There are various

---

200. *THS*, p. 128; another translation is found in *Ecumenism*, pp. 210-211.

201. *Ecumenism*, p. 210 (ct). We would note another touching gesture by the head of the delegation from Constantinople, Metropolitan Meliton of Helioupolis and Theira, who went to pray at the tomb of Pope John XXIII, and also placed nine roses on the tomb of Pope Leo IX (the pope of the 1054 excommunication) in memory of the nine centuries of separation; cf. *Ecumenismo*, p. 265.

differences in theology and organization that have developed between the Roman Catholic Church and us over the centuries, in which we have striven to remain apart. We shall have to wait generations, if not centuries, in order to resolve them, but clearly the friendship that you have shown us has prepared the ground in which reconciliation can grow. As theologians you may call friendship a non-theological factor, but, theological or not, friendship must have a part to play in the future of the church. The historian can easily show that unhappy non-theological factors led to the great division of the church—economic and political rivalries and the like—and if that is the case then the happy non-theological factor of friendship can play its part in the reintegration of Christendom."[202]

(b) The second statement was made at the farewell reception given by the observers and guests, and was made by Monsignor *Karekin Sarkissian*, observer-delegate for the Armenian Orthodox Church (non-Chalcedonian), who is now Armenian Catholicos of Cilicia: "And now we are going our separate ways with a far deeper understanding, a more intimate knowledge, as well as wider horizons. . . . Throughout the four sessions over these past three years, we have been presented with every opportunity to acquire a real understanding of the Roman Catholic Church, and the effort it is making to discover the most efficient way of achieving the mission that God has given it in the modern world." The speaker ended by declaring: "I am certain that our presence as observers at the Second Vatican Council and our relationship with the Secretariat for Christian Unity has made even clearer our firm conviction that it is through common prayer, joint study and concerted action that we will be able the better to serve the cause of Christian unity."[203]

(c) For his part, the president of the secretariat described the influence exercised by the observers' presence at the Council. Replying to Monsignor Sarkissian's speech, Bea said: "There have been increasingly deep-ranging repercussions. Much of all this is already known, but much still rightly remains the secret of those concerned, or is still covered by the discretion so vital in this sphere. What we can say for the moment is that only gradually as time passes shall we come to realize fully the breadth of the grace that the Lord has granted the church in this field."[204]

(d) In his homily at the joint prayer service held at St. Paul's Without-the-Walls on 4 December, Paul VI gave a particularly detailed and touching evaluation of the *mutual enrichment*. We shall confine ourselves to a few phrases: "We can first of all note an increased awareness of the existence of the problem itself, which concerns us all"; "we can add another fruit, which is still more precious: the hope that the problem—not today of course, but tomorrow—can be resolved, slowly, gradually, frankly, and generously; this is something wonderful"; "we have learned to understand each other a little better"; "we have recognized certain shortcomings and certain mutual feelings that were not

---

202. Partly in *Ecumenism*, p. 187; fully in *Ecumenismo*, p. 248.

203. *Ecumenism*, pp. 188-189 (ct).

204. *Ecumenismo*, p. 251. Other extracts from this address are found in *Ecumenism*, pp. 189-190.

good"; "we want to restore a situation of relations that are human, serene, benevolent and trusting"; "we can chalk up a gain at the end of the Council: we have begun to love one another again; and may the Lord grant that at least in this the world can see that we are truly his disciples."[205]

(e) The *wish or intention* formulated by Cardinal Bea—but certainly express- ing a generalized attitude—was certainly a significant fruit of the Council. He expressed the wish "that the experience of these years should be continued and, if I dare say it, be further developed. . . . We have tasted the rich happiness of being brothers in Christ beyond all our divisions. We have also experienced how fruitful it can be for all of us to meet as brothers in the love of truth, in humility and in charity. Now this experience, the result of Christ's grace and so a completely free gift of God, imposes serious and binding obligations on us. It creates, I could almost say, a new vocation, which is a variation of our vocation as Christians and is the vocation I would call ecumenical: that of devoting ourselves with all our strength to bringing about the unity of the church, which Christ wanted and prayed for, and which God decidedly desires."[206]

2. Let us now—again with just a few phrases—give an idea of the cardinal's views on the conciliar documents that had particular ecumenical relevance.

The Constitution on the Church: "In order to understand the general ecumeni- cal importance of this document, it is enough to recall that the problem of the church undoubtedly encompasses the main divergences existing between the Catholic Church and Christians of the Reformed tradition, and to a large extent also those existing between the Catholic Church and non-Catholic eastern Christians."[207]

The Constitution on Divine Revelation: ". . . this constitution has been described by non-Catholics as the most important document of Vatican II for ecumenical purposes."[208]

The Declaration on Religious Freedom: the promulgation of this document "cleared the air in the field of the delicate relations between the various confessions or religions."[209]

The Constitution on the Church in the Modern World: ". . . it is symptomatic that this document in particular should have been warmly greeted by our non-Catholic brethren almost from the beginning. It in fact offers an important platform for cooperation between Christians of any denomination, in the joint fulfillment of our responsibility before the world and for the world."[210]

---

205. *Ecumenism*, p. 204 (ct); cf. *OD*, pp. 60-62.
206. *Ecumenism*, pp. 189-190 (ct). On this occasion the observers offered the secretariat publications describing the life of each of their churches. The cardinal in turn said that he would in due course send the observers and guests copies of his publications in various languages; cf. *Ecumenismo*, p. 252.
207. *Ecumenismo*, pp. 149-150.
208. *The Way*, p. 20.
209. *Ibid.*, p. 22.
210. *Ecumenism*, p. 213 (ct). The ecumenical dimension of this latter document and of that on divine revelation is dealt with more fully in *The Way*, pp. 82-99, 229-247.

The Cardinal's Contribution to Developments in Ecumenism during the Council

Let us state immediately that we are not concerned here with some kind of eulogy of the cardinal, which would above all be against his own wishes, for we have seen how often he reiterates that in everything that has taken place we must see the gift of God and the wonderful work of the Holy Spirit. As concerns human cooperation with the work of the Spirit of Christ, we must also remember the activities of the cardinal's assistants and fellow-workers on many fronts. We shall not repeat here what we have already said, either concerning his work within the secretariat,[211] or his activity to spread ecumenical awareness and attitudes, which he continued with great commitment during the Council. Our intention here is more that of considering *the secret of the deep and wide influence* that Bea exercised on Catholics and other Christians through his activity, both official and personal.

We shall start by quoting various statements from other people,[212] starting with one from Paul VI when the cardinals came to welcome him back from his pilgrimage to the Holy Land. When it came to Bea's turn, the pope told him with great modesty: "I have followed in the footsteps of Pope John and Your Eminence."[213]

In more general terms, Patriarch Athenagoras bore the following testimony to the cardinal on the occasion of the latter's visit to Constantinople in 1965: "... we know well that since the time when Pope John XXIII, that unforgettable and inspired herald and worker for Christian peace and unity, summoned you to be responsible for the promotion of Christian unity, you have been the best and most diligent interpreter of the spirit and the sincere dispositions both of that late holy pope and of our brother gloriously exercising the chief priestly office in Rome today. You have been the faithful and tireless worker for the ideal of unity, and have contributed greatly, in cooperation with the devoted helpers who are standing here at your side, both to the cultivation of this ideal within the domain of your own church, and to its promotion in dealings with our church, and more generally with the whole Christian world."[214]

Dr. W.A. Visser 't Hooft, who was Secretary General of the World Council of Churches for eighteen years, starting at its foundation, spoke as follows on the occasion of Bea's visit to the headquarters of the council in 1965: "Your secretariat has had the great and beautiful responsibility for drawing up the schema *De Oecumenismo*. We know that this was not an easy task, and entailed

---

211. Cf. pp. 355-356 above.
212. We shall confine ourselves to a few brief statements. Numerous other statements from highly qualified people can also be found in BM, pp. 331-376, and of course in the whole of the volume *Simposio*.
213. The cardinal was visibly moved as he told me about this observation immediately afterwards, and I noted it in my diary at once.
214. *THS*, pp. 95-96.

pioneering work. However, now that this schema has become a conciliar decree, allow us to tell you that we honor the man who is its spiritual father."[215]

Cardinal Johannes Willebrands in turn writes: "The most important aspect of Bea's personal contribution to the Decree on Ecumenism is contained in the following observation of the Patriarch of Venice, Cardinal Urbani: 'I cannot say that I trust all the ecumenists, but I do place my blind trust in Bea.' These words in fact indicate the cardinal's decisive contribution, for with his authority he made ecumenism credible and acceptable to many Council fathers. We must not forget that prior to the Council a great majority of the fathers had had no contact or experience of an ecumenical kind, not to mention the negative experiences prevalent in a number of countries. Some powerful influence in favor of ecumenism was therefore needed, and apart from the attitude of Pope John XXIII and the presence of observer-delegates, this came from Bea's authority and personal commitment."[216]

In considering the *underlying basis of this trust*, I should like to recall some words of Patriarch Athenagoras that certainly reflect the opinion of many people. The patriarch described the cardinal as "the best and most diligent interpreter of the spirit and the sincere dispositions both of that late holy pope [John XXIII] and of our brother gloriously exercising the chief priestly office in Rome today."[217] Certainly, when Pope John appointed Bea first President of the Secretariat for Christian Unity, he was in a way investing him with some of the trust that he himself enjoyed among both Catholics and other Christians, and especially the trust aroused among the latter with the announcement of the ecumenical aims of the Council. However, I do think that this conviction was also born and nourished by the *method* the cardinal followed in his activity as publicist. Just as he had followed the lines of the supreme magisterium of the church in his teaching at the Biblical Institute, so now he took the teaching and declarations of "the Pope of the Council" as his basis and starting point. We would cite a single but very eloquent example: when the cardinal expounded the doctrine on baptism and the church-membership of other Christians, he very clearly took the declarations and teaching of John XXIII as his starting point.[218] And he did the same thing later with regard to the teaching of Paul VI. It is obvious that this special reputation as a faithful interpreter was particularly important, and maybe indeed decisive, in establishing that trust of the Council fathers that we saw reflected in the words of Cardinal Urbani quoted by Cardinal Willebrands in the extract above.[219]

---

215. *Rencontre oecuménique*, p. 25. Similarly, cf. Visser 't Hooft, *Die Welt war meine Gemeinde*, p. 403.
216. *Simposio*, p. 14. Concerning the prestige enjoyed by the cardinal, cf. also the statement of the theologian Y. Congar, in *ibid.*, pp. 27-28.
217. *THS*, p. 96.
218. See, for example, *The Unity of Christians*, p. 26.
219. Cf. *Simposio*, p. 14. We should of course also bear in mind certain other factors which had a greater or lesser importance according to the particular sector involved; for example the facts that Bea had dedicated his life to the study of sacred scripture, had been Rector of the Pontifical

So it would seem that the cardinal's special contribution to the remarkable development of ecumenism within the framework of the Council is to be sought in the deserved trust people had in him, for he knew how to preserve and nourish trust, and make it grow. If the divisions between Christians begin with distrust, the path toward reconciliation begins with the rebirth of trust. Thus, the progressive mutual rapprochement between Christians, both before and during the Council, was based above all on the rebirth and growth of mutual trust; and this also applies in its own way to the Catholic field itself, particularly the Council fathers.

* * *

Here, however, we must once again turn to the "Giver of every good thing" (cf. James 1:17). Trust is one of the great fruits of the love that is poured into our hearts through the Holy Spirit who has been given to us (cf. Rom. 5:5). This is why the cardinal spoke out about the need for prayer, attributing the developments in ecumenism to the prayers offered by many Christians for dozens of years, and asked for the support of people's prayer; and also why during the years of the Council he asked for the support of the offering of mass by thousands of his fellow priests, thus making them co-workers with God for the great cause of unity.

Biblical Institute in Rome for nineteen years, and had been confessor of Pope Pius XII for thirteen years.

CHAPTER 8

THE DEVELOPMENT OF THE CHURCH'S RELATIONS WITH THE JEWISH PEOPLE

As we know, "The relation of the church with the Jewish people is a two thousand year old problem as old as Christianity itself. It became much more acute, particularly in view of the ruthless policy of extermination inflicted upon millions of Jews by the Nazi regime in Germany. And so it has attracted the attention of the Second Vatican Council."[1] The Second Vatican Council dealt with this subject in its declaration *Nostra aetate*, and Cardinal Bea writes that this document "has been widely acclaimed as a milestone in the history of the relations between the church and the Jewish people," and adds: "That it does deserve such a description emerges firstly from the fact that it was the first time that an ecumenical council had considered the problem in so explicit a manner. Furthermore, instead of confining itself to a purely practical decree or a simple condemnation of anti-semitism, the Council approached the problem in the wider context of the relations of the church with non-Christian religions in general, while proposing a solution based on deeply biblical foundations."[2]

The difficulties that marked the laborious process of drafting and approval of the document were in keeping with the serious nature of the "two thousand year old problem," and it is interesting to see what the cardinal once told someone in confidence after the document had been approved and promulgated: "If I had been able to foresee all the difficulties we would have encountered, I do not know whether I would have had the courage to undertake this task."[3]

Let us at once explain the subject of the present chapter. We are making a distinction between the history of the document and its content. The present chapter will describe the history of the development of the *whole* document inasmuch as this cannot be divided up. However, as concerns its *content*, it must be borne in mind that *Nostra aetate*—apart from a general introduction and conclusion—deals not only with the relations of the church with the Jewish people, but also with those with Hinduism, Buddhism, Islam, and lastly with the general brotherhood of all men. This chapter will be dedicated *exclusively* to the theology of the part concerning the Jewish people, and we shall deal with the rest in a subsequent chapter concerning the unity of the human family. This is because, on the one hand, these questions too are of great importance and deserve more specific attention, and, on the other hand, the original task given by Pope John concerned relations with the chosen people of the Old Testament,

---

1. *Church-Jews*, p. 7. For the sake of brevity we shall refer to the conciliar Declaration on the Relation of the Church to Non-Christian Religions by its Latin name, *Nostra aetate*.
2. *Church-Jews*, p. 7 (ct).
3. Schmidt, "Il Cardinale Agostino Bea," p. 10.

500

which occupy a very special position within the framework of the relations of the church with non-Christian religions in general.

No Discouragement, Despite Repeated Setbacks

When studying preparations for the Council, we saw how the difficulties raised by the Arab countries in June 1962 were able to bring to nothing almost two years of work on the part of the secretariat, so that the schema on relations with the Jewish people was simply deleted from the Council agenda. This was a symptom and a symbol of the huge difficulties and obstacles that would be raised to prevent the Council from making any statement on so sensitive a topic.

As if this were not enough, another blow followed almost at once. When the first setback occurred, the cardinal was working on a study aimed particularly at Catholic circles, with the intention of helping people to understand the heart of the problem. The title was: "Are the Jews a 'Deicide' People and 'Cursed by God'?", and the article was to be published in the well-known journal of the Italian Jesuits, *La Civiltà Cattolica*, which had a circulation of about sixteen thousand at that time. The second proofs were already being checked when Cardinal A. Cicognani, the Secretary of State, asked Cardinal Bea to suspend publication in order to avoid irritating the Arab States further. Cardinal J. Willebrands, who has recently revealed the facts about the whole episode, describes Bea's reactions to this request as follows: "Now at that time the secretariat was a very new department in the Roman curia, and it also had to defend the vast subjects of ecumenism and religious freedom, so that it was thought better to bow to the anxieties of the Secretariat of State, at least for the moment."[4] We shall study the actual ideas of the article later, but would note here that it had already had the positive effect of inducing the cardinal to study the most difficult points of the problem from the very outset.[5]

---

4. Willebrands, in *Simposio*, p. 79. We shall take our translation from the original Italian manuscript of the study; the proofs in the archives bear the code R 1962/29; on the centenary of the cardinal's birth, the article was published in its entirety in *CC*, 1982/I, 430-446 (Biblio. 441).

5. It is particularly instructive to compare the article with the first official speech with which Bea presented the schema on the Jews in the Council hall in 1963. However, the cardinal's thinking, which is summarized in this study, received a certain degree of indirect publicity even then, coming to exert its influence more fully when the Council began to deal with the subject of relations with the Jewish people in 1963. In the article cited above, Cardinal Willebrands says that the cardinal's study was scheduled for publication not only in *La Civiltà Cattolica*, "but also in the German review *Stimmen der Zeit* and the Belgian *Nouvelle Revue Théologique* published in Louvain. After its publication was blocked in *La Civiltà Cattolica*, the editors of *Stimmen der Zeit* insisted on having the text. They were told that it would be made available to them if someone else agreed to sign the article. Thus it was that Father Ludwig von Hertling, S.J., a member of the board of editors—and formerly Professor of Church History at the Pontifical Gregorian University—accepted. He reorganized the material in accordance with his own style, but the basic content remained. The article was published in October 1962. Later, Father von Hertling said that he had never received so much reaction to an article as he did on

The declaration the cardinal made one month later in London to Mr. Joel Cang, the editor of *The Jewish Chronicle*, shows how little the cardinal allowed himself to be discouraged by this twofold setback. After stating that he did not intend giving an interview as such, he said he was "willing to . . . explain why and how the Catholic Church, at this juncture in history, is determined to deal with matters affecting the Jewish people. In the course of his explanation, he said the following: "The World Council of Churches at its meeting in New Delhi last autumn, at which the Catholic Church had observers, came out strongly in denouncing this evil. This was a worthy demonstration, and the Catholic Church will certainly not be behind in this regard." Bea ended the conversation by observing with a smile that the incident concerning the sending of Dr. Vardi to represent Jewish organizations at the Council "should in no way affect the basic attitude and policy of the Catholic Church."[6]

A short time later (on 26 October) the cardinal expressed himself in equally decided terms during one of the first meetings of the secretariat after the inauguration of the Council. In the minutes of the meeting we read: "As concerns the schema on the Jews, His Eminence thinks it will be possible to include in a suitable place what has been stated in our schema."[7]

With the firmness seen in these declarations, and not content with including the schema "in a suitable place," the president of the secretariat took up the matter again immediately after the close of the first period of the Council. In this regard but at a later date, he would state the following in the official address with which he presented the schema on "The Attitude of Catholics toward Non-Christians and Principally the Jews" in the Council hall in November 1963: "In December of last year I gave the Supreme Pontiff, Pope John XXIII of happy memory, a written study on this whole question of the Jews. After a few days the Holy Father indicated to me his full approval."[8] As we see, the pope replied

---

this occasion. Nor did things stop here, for the article was unearthed by a Jew from Genoa, Mr. Raffaele Nahum, who obtained permission to have it translated and published in various languages. He had it translated into English, French and Italian, and in the fall of 1963 it was distributed to the Council fathers. In this way, the essence of the cardinal's work did in fact exercise an important influence on the basic orientation of the Council fathers" (*Simposio*, pp. 82-83).

6. *Jewish Chronicle* (10 August 1962), in Arch. Lf 1/7 and 8. Cf. also Caprile, III, 418.

7. Arch. Lc 5/11, p. 1; the expression "our schema" naturally refers to the one that was not accepted by the Central Preparatory Commission. During the first period of the Council there was also an appeal on the problem of antisemitism from the Bishop of Cuernavaca in Mexico, Mendez Arceo; cf. Caprile, III, 255. Cf. also John M. Oesterreicher, "Textgeschichte der Konzilserklärung über das Verhalten der Kirche zu den nicht-christlichen Religionen," *LThK: 2. Vat. Konzil*, II, 427; this study has recently been republished in Oesterreicher's book *The New Encounter between Christians and Jews* (New York, 1986), pp. 183-295, and we shall base ourselves on this English version. Oesterreicher, *The New Encounter*, p. 161, also mentions the appeal of "the Chief Rabbi of Rome," but it is not clear whether this refers to Professor D. Lattes of the Italian Rabbinical College: "Un appello al Concilio Ecumenico," in L. Sestieri and G. Cereti (eds.), *Le Chiese cristiane e l'Ebraismo 1947-1982, Raccolta di documenti* (Casalmonferrato, 1983), 346-348.

8. *AS*, II/V, 485; English translation, *Church-Jews*, p. 159. Cf. also Arch. Lf 1/1. Oesterreicher, *The New Encounter*, p. 162, gives the impression that Cardinal Bea immediately applied to the

as promptly as he had when dealing with the question of the institution of the secretariat and that of giving it a status equal to that of the conciliar commissions. In a personal letter on official stationery, dated 13 December, the pope wrote: "Having read attentively this report by Cardinal Bea, we are in entire agreement concerning the seriousness and the responsibilities of our involvement. The expression 'His blood be on us and on our children' [Mt. 27:25] in no way dispenses any believer in Christ from involving himself in the question and in the apostolate to save all the sons of Abraham as well as every person living on the earth.

"'We therefore pray thee, help they servants, whom thou hast redeemed with thy precious blood.' John XXIII PP."[9]

It is true that the pope's reply contains certain points that might upset a Jewish reader, but we should remember that the document was intended strictly for internal use among Catholics. And anyone who knew Pope John XXIII will certainly realize that it was an expression of his charity, formulated with his customary simplicity, and far removed from any proselytizing aim.[10] In any case, the important point is that with this simple letter Pope John XXIII restored the problem to the Council agenda, thus becoming for the second time the true spiritual father of the future conciliar document.

The Council Considers the Question of the Jews for the First Time (Fall 1963)

After this generous act on the part of the pope, performed only a few months before his death, work was resumed in order to reach the desired goal of a solemn document promulgated by the conciliar assembly. The secretariat also dealt with this subject at its plenary meetings of February 1963, although without making any significant changes to the schema prepared in spring 1962; indeed, in the speech with which he presented the schema in the Council hall in November 1963, the president of the secretariat declared that the document was substantially the one that had been completed in May 1962.[11]

1. Meanwhile, the interest of the Jewish world was growing, and this involved numerous highly demanding contacts for the secretariat with various Jewish organizations. The files contain a list of these contacts for the years 1960-1964, which shows over thirty personal contacts, with individuals or groups, representing various Jewish organizations. This list was prepared on the basis of the diaries of the cardinal and his private secretary.[12] The most important and significant meeting was of course that already mentioned in one of our foregoing

---

pope, whereas in fact this did not take place until six months later.

9. Capovilla, ArchWit, enclosure 8; cf. also Capovilla, *Giovanni XXIII, Lettere*, pp. 561-562. The closing phrase is taken from St. Ambrose's hymn *Te Deum*.

10. See the explanation of Oesterreicher, *The New Encounter*, p. 164.

11. Cf. *AS*, II/V, 481.

12. Arch. Lf1/4.

chapters, which took place on 31 March 1963 at the headquarters of the American Jewish Committee in New York, and which involved ten representatives of civil and religious Jewish organizations of various shades.[13]

This interest was linked with hope—and also to some extent with gratitude for the steps already taken in this direction by Pope John XXIII. Tangible evidence of this was the fact that during the days when the great pope was dying, the crowd of Christians assembled in prayer in *St. Peter's Square* was joined by a clearly recognizable and *distinguished delegation* from the Jewish community in Rome.[14] In his autobiography, the Chief Rabbi of Rome Elio Toaff tells how "on a Saturday in springtime" Pope John XXIII was driving along the bank of the Tiber and made the motorcade stop so that he could bless his "Jewish brothers," who had surrounded him after a moment of uncertainty, applauding enthusiastically. He then goes on to say: "The night that John XXIII was on his death-bed, I felt the pressing need to join the large numbers of Catholics who were keeping a prayer vigil in St. Peter's Square, in order to do what I could in return for that unforgettable blessing."[15]

It can even be said that interest was spreading among public opinion in general. In his second address in the Council hall, Bea was thus able to state that it was a "fact that this declaration is one in which public opinion has shown the greatest interest. There is scarcely any other schema about which so much has been written in the press of the world and in newspapers of wide circulation and influence."[16] Corresponding with this interest there was extensive press coverage of news, rumors and conjectures concerning this aspect of the Council's work. Although this sometimes had a positive aspect and could have the effect, so to speak, of spurring the Council fathers on,[17] it also often had the effect of slowing down progress, inasmuch as it provoked reactions from those who were opposed to the schema. Personally, the cardinal would often have preferred silence on the part of the press in order to be able to work more calmly.

However, since it was impossible to obtain press silence, *the secretariat repeatedly issued press releases* in order to clarify matters. Following various rumors, a press release was issued on 18 June 1963, reassuring the public that "the text in question is still being studied and thus has not yet been sent to the Council fathers. If modifications have to be made, their aim will be to harmonize the form of expression with all the other doctrinal conciliar schemata."[18] Four

---

13. Cf. Biblio. 335, pp. 128-129.
14. I base this on a statement by the well-known Italian ecumenist Professor M. Vingiani, who was told about it directly by the Chief Rabbi of Rome E. Toaff.
15. Elio Toaff, *Perfidi Giudei—Fratelli maggiori* (Milan, 1987), p. 220.
16. *AS*, III/II, 558. We shall be taking the English translation of the cardinal's four official speeches in the Council hall from *Church-Jews*, pp. 154-172; since these speeches are relatively brief, we shall not give the page of the translation each time, but only that of the original in *AS*; if we have corrected the translation we shall indicate this as usual with the abbreviation "ct."
17. Cf. Oesterreicher, *The New Encounter*, p. 165.
18. Caprile, III, 432; it should be borne in mind that at this time the schema of the Decree on Ecumenism had already been sent to the Council fathers with a request to send in any observations in advance.

months later, on 18 October, another press release declared that "the final text [of the schema] was submitted in June of this year to the competent conciliar authorities, who have not yet made any decision concerning the distribution and presentation of the document to the Council fathers."[19]

It is significant that there were several phrases in Paul VI's address inaugurating the second period of the Council, in which the pope himself emphasized the church's attention to non-Christian religions, speaking of "the other religions that preserve the sense and notion of God, who is One, the Creator and Sustainer, the supreme, transcendent Being, that profess worship of God with acts of sincere piety, and that found the principles of moral and social life on these beliefs and practices."[20] For obvious reasons, the pope's phrases are selected to include Islam, but the reference nonetheless constitutes confirmation of the Council's open attitude concerning the question of the Jews, all the more so in view of the fact that at this time the schema already spoke of Catholics' attitude "toward *non-Christians*, especially the Jewish people."

2. On 8 November, a press release from the secretariat announced that the schema had been distributed and that it formed the fourth chapter of the schema on ecumenism, and also gave a detailed explanation of the various aspects of its content.[21] A particularly finely nuanced summary of the schema had been prepared for the press of the Arab countries.[22]

Before moving on to the discussion of the document in the Council hall, we must mention a providential incident concerning the text of the speech with which the president of the secretariat was to present the document in the hall. The day before the document was distributed in the hall, I received a telephone call from the offices of the secretariat, saying that they had received the proofs of the cardinal's address, but that the Secretariat of State had asked that certain small passages be omitted because of the sensitivity of the question. The cardinal was attending a meeting of the Sacred Congregation of Rites in the Vatican, so I went to the secretariat offices to collect the proofs. I saw that the main passage in question concerned the Nazi genocide of the Jews in Germany. In reply to the question "Why is it so necessary precisely today to recall these things?" the speech stated: "The reason is that antisemitism, as it is called, had already been rampant for some decades in various regions and in a particularly violent and criminal form, especially in Germany under the National Socialist regime, which through hatred for the Jews committed frightful crimes, extirpating several million Jewish people—it is not our task to seek the exact number. Moreover, this whole activity was supported and accompanied by very powerful and effective 'propaganda,' as it is called, against the Jews."[23]

---

19. Caprile, III, 420.
20. *AAS*, LIX (1963), 857-858; also *CDD*, p. 925.
21. Cf. Caprile, III, 420-421.
22. From notes for a letter of the cardinal dated 7 December 1964 we learn that this summary "was also delivered privately to the representatives of countries concerned before the release was published"; cf. Arch. Lf 1/18, pp. 1-2.
23. *AS*, II/V, 483 (ct).

I took the proofs and went to the fourth floor of the Apostolic Palace, where the meeting of the Congregation of Rites was being held, and asked to speak to the cardinal. After examining the request of the Secretariat of State, the cardinal agreed, obviously in order not to compromise the delicate progress of the schema. I then went to the General Secretariat of the Council to tell them of the cardinal's consent. While I was still there, the official on duty, Monsignor Vincenzo Fagiolo, telephoned the Vatican press and told them which passages were to be omitted.

Our surprise can well be imagined when we received the printed text and saw that the passage in question was still in the text! Later, after the cardinal had given the speech in the Council hall, I learned that that very passage had made a great impression in diplomatic circles, especially German ones. The fact that a cardinal—and a German one, too—had made a solemn declaration of this kind before representatives of over 140 countries seemed a true and worthy act of reparation for the crimes committed by National Socialism.[24]

3. General discussion of the schema on ecumenism began on 18 November, and the cardinal delivered his speech explaining the schema the following day, in the seventieth general congregation.[25] He started with a brief reference to the history of the schema, and then stated *its subject and purpose*: "There is no national or political question here." Rather, the purpose of the schema was to recall what was contained in the deposit of faith concerning relations with the Jewish people.[26] He then emphasized the topical and urgent nature of the question following the recent crimes committed by National Socialism, but also in view of the fact that elements of antisemitism are always cropping up afresh in the church in various forms and places. Furthermore, reflection on this question was part of the effort the church was making in the Council to renew itself and to "seek again the feature of its most fervent youth." For the church, it was a question of conforming itself to the attitude of Jesus and the apostles with regard to relations with the Jewish people, as in other fields, and this attitude was one of meekness and forgiveness.[27]

It is interesting to take a brief look at *the points that emerged during the discussion*, for although it was only the general discussion of a schema that contained three chapters on ecumenism and another on religious freedom as well as considering the question of the Jews, from the very beginning we can

---

24. I was told of this impression by Monsignor J. Höfer, who was at that time Ecclesiastical Counselor to the Embassy of West Germany to the Holy See; however, I have never heard that any of the Germans felt offended.

25. Cf. *AS*, II/V, 481-485. We would recall, as we explained in Chapter 6 of this third part of our work, that the cardinal had left the presentation of the schemata on ecumenism and religious freedom to others, but had reserved for himself the presentation of the schema on the Jews, both because it dealt with biblical matters and also because of the sensitive nature of the question.

26. When presenting the content of the speech, we shall not go into details of a doctrinal nature, as these will be discussed in the second part of this chapter.

27. Cf. Wenger, *Deuxième Session*, p. 178: "This address had an enormous effect in the Council and an even greater one in the world."

see all the points that would later dominate the scene in this regard.[28] It is important to grasp these orientations if we are to understand subsequent developments.[29] The first thing we should note is that there were very few people who thought it inappropriate for the council to consider this question.[30] Quite a large number considered that it should *not* be treated in the context of ecumenism,[31] and there were fairly numerous requests that the treatment be extended to all the non-Christian religions.[32]

Thus, the schema had basically been received positively and prospects did not seem bad. At the end of the *general* discussion on the schema as a whole (including ecumenism and religious freedom) the presiding moderator proposed *an outline vote* to the fathers, to decide whether *the first three chapters*—that is to say, those dedicated to ecumenism proper—could be accepted as a basis for further discussion. The general secretary stressed that the vote concerned *only* the first three chapters on ecumenism, adding that "in the next few days" the same question would be voted on for Chapters IV and V, which dealt with the Jews and religious freedom.[33] No explanation was given as to why these two chapters were excluded from the present vote.

Although it was hoped that they *would* be voted on in a few days, *this never happened*: after the vote on the part dealing with ecumenism proper, which had obtained a very large majority, the detailed discussion began, and this took a great deal of time. However, the schema on the apostolate of the laity was also on the agenda for this period of the Council, and the conciliar authorities considered it preferable to move straight on to this subject, leaving aside the vote on Chapters IV and V. This produced a great deal of anxiety. We saw in one of our previous chapters how the cardinal took pains, when closing the discussion on ecumenism, to calm the atmosphere,[34] explaining that the vote had not taken place "because of a lack of time and for no other reason,"[35] and

---

28. We would start by saying that six weeks earlier, during the discussion of the schema on the church, voices had been raised asking for clarification of the close links existing between the church and the Jewish people. Thus we find, for example, the request made in the name of the Dutch bishops by Bishop J. van Dodewaard, and that made in his own name by the Archbishop of Zagreb, the future Cardinal Franjo Seper; the former spoke on 2 October (cf. *AS*, II/I, 433), and the latter on 3 October (cf. *AS*, II/II, 32). Cf. also Oesterreicher, *The New Encounter*, pp. 168-169.

29. We shall limit our survey to the addresses delivered in the Council hall, leaving aside observations made only in writing (cf. *AS*, II/V, 771-836), and we shall not tire the reader with lists of names of those who supported one view or another, for we are concerned here with general tendencies and not with the people involved. For details, cf. Oesterreicher, *The New Encounter*, pp. 169-170, 175-176.

30. These were three Eastern patriarchs who live in Arab countries: the Syrian Patriarch Tappouni (cf. *AS*, II/V, 527-528), the Coptic Patriarch Sidarouss (cf. *AS*, II/V, 541-542), and the Greek Melkite Patriarch Maximos IV (cf. *AS*, II/V, 544).

31. Cf. *AS*, II/V, 527, 533, 541, 543-544, 551, 560, 598, 608, 666, 672, 746.

32. Cf. *AS*, II/V, 529, 540, 544, 557, 598, 601, 617, 744; also the summary in the official report by the secretariat, *AS*, III/II, 333.

33. Cf. *AS*, II/V, 682.

34. Cf. p. 437 above.

35. *AS*, II/VI, 365; cf. also R 1963/51, p. 1.

winding up his speech with a request to the fathers to send their observations on these two chapters to the secretariat before the following 31 January. This was a way of declaring publicly that there could be no doubt that the two chapters remained on the agenda of the Council.[36]

The statements the cardinal made in calmer circumstances some months later show that this had not been simply a point of strategy. I think it is worth looking more closely at *the reasons why the vote was not taken*. While admitting that some people were less than happy concerning these two chapters—for reasons that are in fact easy to understand—the reasons events took the turn they did were not those claimed by rumor and hearsay. The truth of the matter is chiefly that it was considered—and rightly, I believe—that *a general vote on all five chapters of the schema, en bloc*, might have caused the Council fathers considerable uncertainty over how to act, and made the results very difficult to interpret. For example, should those fathers who doubted the advisability of including the chapter on the Jews in the schema nonetheless accept it, or should they reject it? Was it right to reject the whole schema simply because of a doubt of this kind, which was really of a technical nature? On the other hand, if the schema was accepted in general, did this not mean definitive acceptance of the retention of the chapter on the Jews in the schema on ecumenism? So how were they to express any reservations they may have?[37] The cardinal also mentioned another possible source of doubt: "Then, as concerns *the results* of the vote, would some doubt not have been left as to whether and to what extent any votes against the schema referred only to a single chapter or even to the technical side of a chapter, or whether they referred to the whole schema? Although the various subjects dealt with in the schema had internal links, they were too disparate to be voted on in this way *en bloc*."[38]

It was then decided that these chapters should be *voted on separately*, and once this decision had been taken there was then "the custom that the vote on acceptance of a schema as a basis for discussion was held immediately before moving on to the detailed discussion."[39] However, since there was no time left for the detailed discussion of Chapters IV and V once the detailed discussion of the three chapters on ecumenism had been concluded, this principle or custom meant that there was no reason to vote straightaway on whether these last two chapters could be taken as a basis for detailed discussion.

Referring to possible claims that certain people might intentionally have dragged out the discussion on the three chapters, the cardinal observed that "all in all, it was neither longer nor slower than that on the other schemata discussed previously in the second period. And the material was certainly neither easier nor more familiar than that of the other schemata."[40] Bea therefore concludes by saying: "The truth is that serious efforts were made, and also by the Council,

---

36. Cf. *AS*, II/VI, 365.
37. Cf. Biblio. 251, p. 909.
38. *Ibid.*
39. *Ibid.*
40. *Ibid.*

to find the time to hold a well-prepared general vote on these last two chapters as well. So why try to see intentional delays, resistance or pressure here?"[41]

Laborious Preparatory Work for the Third Period of the Council

Since our schema had not been discussed in detail, it might be imagined that there was no reason to revise it. However, we should recall that the president of the secretariat had asked the Council fathers to submit their observations on this schema by 31 January, thereby giving rise to a kind of discussion by correspondence. In this way the secretariat received a whole series of opinions and suggestions. The official report in which, in the third period, the secretariat explained the method adopted to revise the document tells us that when the various observations—both those made in the hall during the second period and those sent in later and received in time—had been sorted into the same order as the material dealt with in the schema, they made up a volume of seventy-two typed pages, by no means a negligible amount for a document of less than two printed pages.[42] So far as the quality of the opinions received was concerned, we read: "The written observations of the fathers were so numerous and well reasoned that it seemed best to revise the text even before the third period. We hope that this will facilitate the discussion and pave the way for the final text."[43]

1. Thus, after these observations had been meticulously arranged in the same order as the text, they were first studied by the experts of the secretariat in the meeting held between 4 and 21 February 1964.[44] The new text prepared by them was then examined in the plenary session held between 24 February and 7 March. The following are the conclusions reached and the nature of the revision: (a) despite the fact that a few people felt that it would be best to avoid discussion of this question, the schema should be retained, both on account of the intrinsic importance of the material and on account of the great expectations expressed in this connection throughout the world; (b) the schema has been revised and abridged; (c) in view of the particular relationship between the church and the chosen people of the Old Testament, the schema must remain linked to that on ecumenism, but as an appendix rather than a chapter; (d) this schema will also include the question of relations with other religions, particularly Islam.[45]

2. We find further important information on the revision in the speech with which the president of the secretariat presented the new text in the hall during the third period of the Council. There is firstly a significant reference to the

---

41. *Ibid.*.
42. Cf. *AS*, III/II, 330; Biblio 251, p. 907. All the observations received up to the date of the plenary session on 24 February were taken into account.
43. *AS*, III/II, 331 (ct).
44. Oesterreicher, *The New Encounter*, p. 183, notes that not all the collaborators were convened for this work who had previously worked on this schema; we do not know why this form of procedure was adopted.
45. Cf. *AS*, III/II, 334.

contribution of *the Coordinating Commission*: "The members of the Coordinating Commission of the Council also know that they have had to spend a great deal of time on this short document."[46] It was of course normal procedure for this commission to examine texts before they were sent on to the Council fathers. However, in the present case this cost them a great deal of time. The cardinal further explained that many discussions were held on the question of whether—and if so how—to deal with the matter of "deicide," in other words the question of whether, when the authorities of Jerusalem of the period condemned Jesus and had him killed, they became guilty of "deicide."[47] Part of the cardinal's reason for raising this point was a procedural consideration, as he explained: "These deliberations took a long time. Consequently we were unable to submit this part of the declaration for examination by the members of the secretariat. Since the secretariat had dealt with all its other business at its March session, it was decided not to recall the members to Rome to discuss this one section."[48] This meant, said the cardinal in conclusion, that the Council fathers must examine this part of the question all the more carefully.

A similar situation had also been created concerning the second part of the schema, i.e. that concerning the non-Christian religions, and the cardinal explained: "When our secretariat first started considering this subject, there was no other commission or secretariat that could deal with it, for the Secretariat for Non-Christian Religions was not set up until May of this year. The only solution, then, was for our secretariat to undertake the task. We therefore set about drafting a schema with the help of some of the Council experts."[49] *The Coordinating Commission* also took a hand in this case too: "After carefully examining it the Coordinating Commission sent a letter on 18 April, stating that three ideas should be set forth in this part: (1) God is the Father of all men, and they are his children; (2) all men therefore are brothers; and (3) consequently all types of discrimination, violence and persecution directed against anybody at all for national or racial reasons must be condemned. The secretariat set about acting on this decision as best it could."[50] It had been impossible to submit this draft too to the members of the secretariat: "Since all the other matters before the secretariat were finished by the end of March, we could not submit this part to the members. This will now be possible, Venerable Fathers, after you have expressed your views on the schema."[51]

Although we cannot give all the details here, it can be seen that the progress of the schema was laborious and complex.[52] All this meant that the new schema

46. *AS*, III/II, 559 (ct).
47. This term presented one of the greatest problems until the very end.
48. *AS*, III/II, 561 (ct); this explains the impassioned terms in which certain Council fathers who were members of the secretariat expressed themselves, for example Archbishop C. Heenan; cf. Oesterreicher, *The New Encounter*, pp. 193-194.
49. *AS*, III/II, 561 (ct).
50. *Ibid.*, pp. 561-562 (ct).
51. *Ibid.*, p. 562.
52. Cf. Oesterreicher, *The New Encounter*, p. 183. While it would obviously be possible to compare the text of November 1963 with that of the beginning of the third period of the Council, it is

did not receive the pope's approval until 3 July, after which it could be sent to the Council fathers.[53]

New support for the cause proposed by this schema—and more explicitly than in the speech opening the second conciliar period—was given by Paul VI himself in his encyclical *Ecclesiam suam* in which he set forth a plan for the church's future. Speaking of the various partners with whom the Catholic Church was entering into dialogue, the pope mentioned those who believe in God as "the second circle." Here, explicit mention was made of Jews and Moslems, saying that this is the circle "made up of the men who above all adore the one, supreme God whom we too adore. We refer to the children, worthy of our affection and respect, of the Hebrew people, faithful to the religion which we call that of the Old Testament."[54]

Unhoped-for Fruits (Fall 1964)

The third period of the Council opened with the discussion of subjects that were not only demanding but also thorny and hotly debated. Alongside the discussion on the document on the pastoral office of bishops, the controversy on the collegiality of bishops reappeared in the context of the draft Constitution on the Church; shortly after this the discussion on religious freedom began, and finally that on the document concerning the non-Christian religions.

In view of his mission to Patras to return the relic of the head of the apostle Andrew, the cardinal delivered his introductory speech to the schema on the non-Christian religions in advance, on 25 September.[55] He started by claiming that it was impossible "for this question to be completely eliminated from the agenda of the Council," and saying that "a favorable or unfavorable judgment of the whole Council will largely hinge on the approval or disapproval of this declaration."[56] He then went on to explain that the schema consisted of two equal parts: one dedicated to the non-Christian religions, and the other to the chosen people of the Old Testament. He then tried to clarify the issues involved in the controversial concept of "deicide."[57]

As concerns the part dealing with *relations with the Jewish people*, this was an important aspect of the renewal that the church was trying to bring about in the Council: "Such renewal is so important that it is even worth exposing

---

not possible for the present—or until such time as the archives of the work of the commissions are opened—to know which elements of the 1964 text came from the secretariat and which from the Coordinating Commission.

53. Cf. *AS*, III/II, 327. We would merely mention in passing the talk the cardinal gave in Cologne, in the context of Brotherhood Week (Biblio. 279); in this talk, Bea referred only briefly to the content of the schema, not wishing to go into detail out of respect for the Council.

54. For the text of the encyclical cf. *AAS*, LVI (1964), 654-655; English translation, N.C.W.C. (Boston, Mass.: St. Paul Editions, 1965). In his address, Bea pointed out this example of the pope to the Council fathers; cf. *AS*, III/II, 563.

55. Cf. *AS*, III/II, 558-564.

56. *Ibid.*, pp. 558-559.

57. Cf. *ibid.*, pp. 559-561.

ourselves to the danger that some people might prevent this declaration for political ends. It is a case of our duties to truth and justice, our duty to be grateful to God, our duty to imitate faithfully and as closely as possible Christ our Lord and his apostles Peter and Paul. In fulfilling those duties the church and this Council can never allow any political influence or motive to find a place."[58]

2. *The discussion* of the document started on 28 September and occupied two general congregations.[59] Thirty-five speeches were made in the hall, and twenty-seven written memoranda were received for this document, which covered a mere two printed pages.[60] Later, the results of the discussion were summarized as follows in the official report of the secretariat: a small number had asked that the schema be removed from the Council agenda and that the relative questions be dealt with in other schemata, either in that on the church or in that on the church in the modern world; a good number of fathers had asked that the section concerning relations with non-Christians be broadened so as to include not only Islam and Judaism but all the great world religions; indeed, some of them felt that the African and Asian religions are sometimes closer than Islam to the Catholic Church; they therefore thought that the title of the schema should be simply: "On Non-Christian Religions."[61]

With particular regard to *the section dealing with the Jews*, a certain number of fathers felt that the text presented in the previous conciliar period had been "better and more suited" to the purpose, inasmuch as it was more clearly motivated by the spirit of love and the condemnation of the persecutions against the Jews was stronger. Many fathers asked that greater details should be given of "the religious values of the Jews of today and thus the heritage we have in common with them." Some fathers also asked that the wrongs committed by Christians against Jews be recognized. On the other hand, others asked that the language of the schema be more moderate and cautious.[62]

3. Once the discussion was over, the secretariat set to work to *revise the text* in the light of the opinions expressed both orally in the Council hall and in writing. This work was in full swing when a bombshell fell in the form of a letter dated 8 October from the Secretary General of the Council, reporting various decisions that the Council authorities had taken concerning this schema. It explained that the *Declaratio de Judaeis et de non Christianis* had been examined in the joint session of the Presiding Council, the Coordinating

---

58. *Ibid.*, p. 564 (ct).

59. We should observe that this discussion was *not* preceded by the usual outline vote. The reader will recall that in 1963 a *general* discussion was held on the three chapters on ecumenism and on those on the Jews and religious freedom. This was followed by an outline vote on the chapters concerning ecumenism *alone*. Logically speaking, there should have been a similar vote before moving on to the discussion under consideration here.

60. For the speeches in the Council hall, cf. *AS*, III/II, 581-607 and III/III, 11-55; for the written observations, III/III, 155-178. We are not taking into account here the thirty written observations sent in *before* the third period of the Council; cf. III/II, 783-849 and 877-881.

61. Cf. *AS*, III/VIII, 643; it is not our task to go into details concerning the opinions expressed and those who expressed them.

62. Cf. *ibid.*, p. 647.

Commission and the Cardinal Moderators on 7 October, with the following outcome: after a report by the Most Eminent Cardinal Secretary of State and in view of the opinions expressed during the discussion, it had been decided that the question of the Jews should be dealt with in the second chapter of the schema on the church, where the people of Israel is already mentioned in number 16 (*De non christianis*). The following *operative* decision had therefore been taken: a commission would be formed of some members of the secretariat and others from the Theological Commission in order to draft the new text, bearing in mind the content of the declaration recently discussed in the Council hall and the observations made on this subject by the fathers. The new text was to be presented by the 20th of the present month.[63]

It goes without saying that this letter created a great deal of anxiety and apprehension. Was this basically an attempt to make the schema disappear? And what did the task of "drafting the new text" really mean? Did it amount to shortening it, diluting it or depriving it of its "bite"? It was later learned from a confidential note that this decision was inspired by concern over *the reactions of the Arab world* to the part concerning the Jews, and it was hoped to avoid such reactions by giving less weight to discussion of the question of the Jews inasmuch as the subject would not have a special document dedicated to it and its insertion in a dogmatic constitution would give greater emphasis to the purely religious character of the statement of the Council.[64] Material in our archives shows that the cardinal saw no obstacle to the document's being inserted into the Constitution on the Church, but that he preferred this operation to be brought about simply by a conversation with certain members of the Theological Commission, without the formal creation of a joint commission.[65]

4. After this letter, *we possess no information* on further developments *until 20 November* when *a revised version* of the document was presented in the Council hall to be put to the vote. The following is the story behind this event.

We learn the facts from the address in which the president of the secretariat presented the reworked text for voting. In the first place he informed his listeners of the decision on the part of the authorities to insert the document into the Constitution on the Church, an action "suggested partly by the present title of this declaration, speaking as it does of the attitude of the *church* to non-Christian religions."[66] However, he at once went on to speak of *the practical manner* in which

---

63. Cf. Arch. Lf 2/11-1; this letter makes it clear that it is not correct to say, as Oesterreicher does (*The New Encounter*, p. 215), that the origin of the decision taken was indicated with the general formula that it came from "higher authority"; the author probably confused this decision with the letter of the same date concerning the schema on religious freedom. Pivonka's account (*The Secretariat for Promoting Christian Unity*, pp. 219-220, 244) also needs to be reevaluated, since he simply follows Oesterreicher. On the whole question and its further developments, cf. Raniero La Valle, *Fedeltà del Concilio. I dibattiti della terza Sessione* (Brescia, 1965), pp. 246-255, 265-268, 581; Fesquet, *Diario del Concilio*, pp. 557-559, 566-567, 571 (including the history of the letter about the schema on religious freedom).

64. Cf. Arch. Lf 2/11-14.

65. Cf. Arch. Lf 2/11-2.

66. *AS*, III/VIII, 649 (ct).

this insertion was to take place: "In order to avoid any interruption to the flow of the argument of the constitution and any delay to its early vote and promulgation because of this new declaration, it seemed best to attach the declaration to the end of the Constitution on the Church as an appendix."[67] The cardinal emphasized another positive result of insertion of the declaration into the Constitution on the Church, saying that it "has the further advantage that its purely religious character would be emphasized, and any political interpretation would thereby be prevented."[68] Furthermore, contrary to the view of others that the declaration would now carry less weight, Bea added: "At the same time, the weight and impact of the declaration are all the greater inasmuch as it is added to a dogmatic constitution, even though the aim of the declaration is pastoral rather than dogmatic."[69]

Above all, the cardinal was very firm in stating *the need for a declaration* concerning relations between the people of the Old Testament and the church, despite the risk that it might be misunderstood and misused: "It is a question of recognizing the salvific plan of God and his benefits, condemning absolutely hatred and injustice, and avoiding them in the future. The church—and thus also the council—therefore had and has to be faithful to its charge, and cannot keep silent." On the other hand, "it was impossible to draw up a declaration that would not be open to misinterpretation by anyone at all in any of its statements." Bea then added with his customary realism: "Besides, it must be borne in mind that it is more important to have such a solemn declaration by the Council than to satisfy everyone, even were that possible."[70]

In conclusion, Cardinal Bea referred to the forthcoming journey of Paul VI to the Eucharistic Congress in Bombay in India, and emphasized *the burningly topical character* of the part of the document concerning the non-Christian religions: "At this historic moment, when Christ's vicar on earth is about to travel to visit that great people who, as he himself said, represent the innumerable races and peoples of the whole continent of Asia for him, it would certainly have been most appropriate if, by the grace of God, this declaration could have been definitely promulgated. . . . Nonetheless, even what has been possible to prepare is of great importance."[71]

After these explanations, it is easy to understand the notes that accompanied the text and highlighted the following three important points: (a) the questions dealt with are so special and urgent that a separate declaration is necessary, and it is not sufficient for the material to be dealt with in the course of some other schema; (b) given the nature of the question, which is fairly different from that of ecumenism, the document on the non-Christian religions will not take the form of an appendix to the document on ecumenism; the church must speak explicitly of

---

67. *Ibid.* (ct).
68. *Ibid.*
69. *Ibid.* (ct). Cf. similarly R 1965/7, p. 1. We should note the difference between the address as printed by the secretariat and that of its president, which I am unable to explain.
70. *AS*, III/VIII, 650 (ct).
71. *Ibid.*, p. 651 (ct); here the text actually read in the hall differs from the manuscript, and thus our translation is also different from that published in *Church-Jews*.

its relations with the other religions, and the world is waiting for such a declaration; and (c) the secretariat has adopted the opinion of those who demanded that the schema be extended in such a way as to include all religions, while still retaining the explicit and separate treatment of relations with the Moslems and the Jews.[72]

5. Thus *the vote* was finally taken, with the document being divided into two parts for this. The first part, concerning the various non-Christian religions (with the exception of Judaism) received 1,838 votes in favor and 136 against,[73] while the part concerning the Jews and the conclusion of the document received 1,770 votes in favor and 185 against.[74] The vote on *the entire text*, in which votes with reservations were permitted, gave the following result: 1,651 in favor, 99 against, and 242 favorable votes with reservations.[75] At this point Bea stated: "According to the Council ruling, 'Yes with reservations' is counted as basically positive, so that the text obtained nearly 95% of the votes in its favor."[76] This is the only evaluation that we find in the cardinal's speeches and writings at this stage. He evidently preferred to await the definitive approval, maybe because he had an inkling of the storm that had yet to be undergone.[77]

At this point, certain *reflections* seem to be in order. In the first place, it would seem that the decision to insert the document into the Constitution on the Church worked to the advantage of our document in a number of ways, for this is why the outline vote was omitted, and also why the secretariat was able to draft the new text and have it *voted on* in the same period in which it was discussed in detail. It is quite likely that this decision was taken not only because the document was so short, but above all in order to speed up the conclusion and make it possible for it to be inserted into the Constitution on the Church, which was promulgated during this same period.

One final question: as we know, *Nostra aetate* was published as a separate document, but how was this result obtained? The fact is that serious practical difficulties prevented its insertion into the Constitution on the Church, which was about to receive its final vote, while our document had yet to be voted on for the first time, after which amendments would have to be examined, before it could receive *its* final vote.[78] On the other hand, since the Council was already in its third and certainly penultimate period, everyone was anxious to move ahead and show the world some practical results, and was thus concerned not to hold up publication of the major, fundamental document on the church on account of a relatively small appendix. The decision to insert the document into this constitution was therefore simply cancelled out by events.[79]

---

72. Cf. *ibid.*, pp. 643-644.
73. Cf. *ibid.*, pp. 651 (the question voted on) and 661 (the result).
74. Cf. *ibid.*, pp. 654 (the question) and 661 (the result).
75. Cf. *ibid.*, pp. 661 (the question) and 672 (the result).
76. *Church-Jews*, p. 24.
77. The archives contain a series of positive reactions from Jews following the first voting, Lf 4/27-35; cf. also *Freiburger Rundbrief*, XVI-XVII/61-64 (1965), 21-25.
78. The schema on ecumenism was also in a similar situation, so that the same technical reasons made it difficult to see how the schema on the non-Christian religions could be united to it.
79. It is strange that in January 1965, when the Constitution on the Church had already been

The Storm (December 1964—June 1965)

A few days after the schema was voted on, the *Osservatore Romano* published *a note signed by the president of the secretariat*, in which he referred to this vote, saying that it was impossible to give the declaration "any political interpretation. . . . Just as the passages on the Hindus, the Buddhists and the Moslems quite obviously have no connection with politics, the passage on the Jews is entirely foreign to any political interpretation. . . . The exclusively religious character of the document is still further emphasized in the text proposed for the vote by the fact that it had meanwhile been decided that it was to form an appendix to the Constitution on the Church"; the document was "inspired by motives of truth, justice and Christian love, clearly in full accord with the gospel."[80] The Secretariat of State had asked for the note because dangerous signs of anxiety had begun to appear in the Middle East, and it was thus an attempt to prevent further growth of such anxiety. However, hostility to the document grew steadily to the point where it was possible to speak about "a holy war" waged against it.[81]

1. In the following months the situation became more and more threatening, with declarations from political and religious figures, including heads of churches, being added to press and radio attacks. People claimed that if the Catholic Church and the Council absolved the Jews from the charge of deicide, they were betraying historical truth and the gospel; a conciliar declaration of this kind was a threat to ecumenism; and the document was the fruit of a plot on the part of international Zionism, which had bribed bishops from certain countries to speak in favor of the Zionist government and the policies of Israel. Public demonstrations and marches were organized; Catholics were invited to go into schism and "break with the Vatican"; there were warnings that if the document was approved it would have serious consequences for Catholic minorities in Arab countries, for example the occupation of Catholic schools, the withdrawal of the privileged positions of these schools, and the refusal of land to build churches; and there were even threats to set fire to churches.[82]

It is true that from the very start, but especially in June 1962, it had been foreseen that the schema would cause difficulties in Arab countries, and in particular that if a document of this kind were approved, it might create difficulties for Catholics living in those countries.[83] However, difficulties for Catholics were now assuming increasingly threatening forms, and to a degree that it would have been difficult to forecast, so that the problem of the conse-

---

promulgated for two months, in an interview which was not in fact published (R 1965/7, p. 1), Bea still spoke of the document on non-Christian religions as though it were an appendix to this constitution.

80. Caprile, IV, 500.
81. Cf. Oesterreicher, *The New Encounter*, p. 236; Willebrands, in *Simposio*, p. 19.
82. Cf. Oesterreicher, *The New Encounter*, pp. 237-243, 248-249; *Freiburger Rundbrief*, XVI-XVII/61-64 (1965), 24-25.
83. Cf. Arch. Lf 1/10, p. 3.

quences the promulgation of the document would have for Catholic minorities in the East had become much more acute and dramatic for the president of the secretariat. On the other hand, at this point the document was not solely an initiative of the secretariat, even though Pope John XXIII had assigned this task to it; it had now been approved, albeit with only a preliminary, and hence non-definitive, vote, with an overwhelming majority by the bishops of the whole of the Catholic world assembled in an ecumenical council. So what was to be done?

2. The various documents in the archives for *January 1965*—the very weeks when the troubles and demonstrations were taking place—*show the cardinal's views very clearly*. The general agitation could not be taken lightly, for it could be very dangerous and harmful for the church, especially for Christians in Arab countries. On the other hand, the difficulties were no reason for the Council to give up and abandon the document, nor even for it to be watered down and made more "prudent." However, it must be written with maximum precision of language in the light of the observations made by the Council fathers. Furthermore, the eastern world, both Arab and Orthodox, must be carefully prepared with a view to introducing and voting on the document during the fourth period of the Council.[84]

3. Despite this clear view of how to proceed, Bea was fully aware of the difficulty entailed in correcting the schema according to the indications given by the Council fathers, and this is why he left plenty of space to the Council fathers who were members of the secretariat, allowing great freedom for discussion and voting. This was the approach followed in the plenary sessions of the secretariat of 3 and 4 March, which made *a preliminary examination both of the amendments* proposed by the 242 Council fathers who had cast favorable votes "with reservations," and also of those proposed by others. In order to make sure that the members of the secretariat had all the necessary information at their disposal, they received not only a list of the proposed amendments, but also adequate information drawn from the reports of papal representatives on the reactions there had been in the Middle East. In examining suggested amendments, as much prominence as possible was given to the religious purpose of the document, thus obviating to the greatest possible degree any political interpretation on the part of Arab countries. There was also the intention of eliminating any misunderstanding concerning the responsibility of the Jews for the death of Jesus, without embarking on the difficult and controversial question of "collective responsibility." However, a definitive decision was postponed until the following plenary sessions, which were to take place in May, since this would allow more time for reflection, the collection of information, and the preparation of public opinion.[85]

4. Then came the decisive *plenary sessions* of the secretariat in *the month of May*, which obviously took place in an atmosphere that was far from calm or

84. Cf. Arch. Lf 1/22.
85. Cf. Oesterreicher, *The New Encounter*, pp. 246-248.

free of worry. We would leave aside rumors of disastrous decisions that it was claimed the authorities had taken on the document,[86] but refer rather to the bad news from the Middle East which had been confirmed during a journey the secretary, Bishop Johannes Willebrands, had made with Father P. Duprey after the meetings in March, in order to collect first-hand information. In all the countries they visited the tension was almost as high as if there were a war on, and the authorities were not always able to control the situation. There was a risk of violence toward Christians or even of persecution, and although it might not in fact have come to this, the danger was real.

The responsibility of the members of the secretariat was all the greater inasmuch as the president had assured them that *the pope was leaving them total freedom*. In view of the situation, it was necessary to give serious consideration to the various suggestions that had been made, especially by those who would have to bear any painful consequences of approval of the document. A first suggestion was that the Council should entrust the whole matter to the pope, as had been done in the case of the schema on mixed marriages. A second suggestion was that if the document were approved, it should not be promulgated, but be entrusted to the relative departments of the Holy See, for example the Secretariats for Christian Unity and Non-Christians. Another suggestion was that the document be reduced to general principles without mentioning any of the non-Christian religions.[87]

In these May discussions of the secretariat, the starting point taken was an important and *fundamental distinction between the two tasks* to be faced: on the one hand, drawing up the final version of the document, and on the other, the question of the advisability or timeliness of the declaration. The Council fathers who were members of the secretariat agreed that their task, according to the Council regulations, was strictly speaking only that of amending the text itself in accordance with the "reservations" expressed by the Council fathers either when voting or subsequently. However, as regarded the question of timeliness— and all the above-mentioned suggestions concerning some other location for the document referred to this—the same fathers felt that at the present moment (i.e. after the declaration had been voted on by the Council) they had no other choice but to offer their opinion to the highest authorities, almost in a private capacity, leaving any decision up to these authorities.

---

86. For example, a rumor circulated that the pope had entrusted the schema to a commission composed of four persons, including the Bishop of Segni, Luigi Carli, who had written various articles against the ideas of the schema, or even that the schema had been removed from the Council agenda (cf. *ibid.*, pp. 252-253).

87. Thus the well-known theologian Y. Congar had proposed "a new text" which would be "short and general," although he himself observed: "Cardinal Bea tells me he would smile at a solution of the kind I have proposed." We find this in an extract from Father Congar's diary, which has kindly been made available to us, and which is now found in the archives with his other evidence. The later note of the same author (in *Simposio*, p. 27) is therefore inexact, when he states that it was Bea who canvassed a suggestion of this kind. The archives contain a document (Lf 2/18-20) giving the reasons for and against this abridgement, and also a practical outline by an unknown author.

We shall discuss *the corrections* to the text in the context of its presentation in the Council hall during the next period of the Council. Here we shall simply note that the major part of this work obviously concerned the statements on the Jewish religion found in the document. The most difficult point, and the one that required the longest discussion, was the question of whether the Jews were guilty of *deicide*. It was judged that the *expression* "deicide" did not as such belong to the substance of the text, whereas it was in fact the major source of misunderstanding. It was therefore decided by a majority of almost seventy-five percent that this term should be avoided because of its ambiguity.

As concerns the question of timeliness, bearing in mind the initial observation, it was agreed that this question lay outside the field of competence of the secretariat, inasmuch as it was a conciliar commission, and *no vote* was therefore taken on the question. Any views expressed by a number of fathers and not on the whole contradicted by the others were simply recorded.[88]

". . . and there was a great calm" (Fall 1965)

On 1 July, the cardinal was received in audience by Paul VI. Among other things, he asked that papal representatives in the Middle East should set to work to prepare the ground for the decisions of the Council as to the document on the church's attitude to non-Christian religions.

However, it is significant that after so much human progress and effort, Bea was also concerned to employ *supernatural aid*. Addressing the Sisters of Our Lady of Sion at a later date, he told them: "The difficulties and opposition in the Middle East continued during the month of July 1965, and it was therefore decided to have two thousand holy masses celebrated for this great intention. Toward the end of the month, we had the first signs that the Lord had heard this prayer, for the eastern Catholic patriarchs accepted the new text in general terms, albeit with certain reservations."[89] We would add an immediate explanation concerning the celebration of masses: it was a remedy that the cardinal had employed on several occasions during the Council, and basically it involved asking thousands of priests to cooperate by offering the holy sacrifice of the mass.

The "first signs that the Lord had heard this prayer" refer to the fact that around the middle of July a delegation from the secretariat—the Bishop of Bruges, Emile de Smedt, the secretary, Bishop Johannes Willebrands, and Father Duprey—traveled to the Middle East in order personally to present the amended text of the declaration to the eastern Catholic patriarchs. For the first time, the reaction was positive, apart from requests for certain small changes.[90]

---

88. Cf. Arch. Lf 1/36.

89. R 1966/31, p. 4.

90. The good news reached the cardinal on about 24 July in Zurich, where he had been hospitalized for a week in connection with the long illness he suffered in the summer of 1965, which we described in an earlier chapter.

Not only was the text accepted, but the patriarchs went further, saying that it was now up to them to support this amended text, for otherwise there was the risk of a return to the more difficult text of the previous period of the Council.

Naturally, not all the difficulties had vanished. It seems that during the month of September an Arab delegation came to Rome to present their objections to the document to the pope and the Council authorities.[91] In his talk to the Sisters of Our Lady of Sion, the cardinal also mentioned that on 10 September "the bells were rung in Jordan against the declaration."[92] G. Caprile tells us that as late as the eve of the last vote on the document in general congregation (14-15 October), Cardinal Marella had received "a letter in German, with certain parts in French, threatening 'death and destruction' to the Council fathers who played Israel's game; and another letter signed by about thirty leaders of self-styled Catholic or Christian organizations was also sent to the fathers, inviting them to abstain in the final vote."[93]

However, those in charge were also pursuing their positive activity to prepare the ground in the Middle East. I have been told that during this period (some time in the first half of September), the new text was confidentially passed to the Arab embassies to the Holy See, and that the reaction was in general fairly positive. The various governments thus accepted the possibility of informing their populations, and in these circumstances the Arabic section that had been created in the conciliar press room was able to work to good effect.

Within the new period of the Council, Bea himself made a great effort to provide the Council fathers with further information, for example giving a talk on 28 September, principally for the Brazilian bishops, entitled "The Question of Our Attitude toward the Jewish People."[94]

1. On 30 September, *the revised text* was distributed to the Council fathers with the corresponding *Examination of the Amendments* suggested by the Council fathers. The first thing to note is the vast quantity of work that had been faced, almost requiring the fineness of filigree. In order to make it easier for the reader to follow the text, it was presented in two columns, the first giving the text approved in the previous period of the Council, and the second giving the amended text, with the corrections shown in italics.[95] All this was then explained in a full, precise report, the main part of which consisted of a detailed analysis of the amendments suggested by the Council fathers. These had been condensed into ninety points and arranged according to the numbers in the margin of the text, and were then evaluated individually, giving reasons for the decision that had been taken.[96] For greater clarity, a complete list of the amendments accepted and introduced into the text was added at the end.[97]

---

91. Cf. Caprile, V, 282; this author doubts whether the visit did in fact take place. Our diaries show, however, that the delegation fixed the appointment with the cardinal for 25 September.
92. Cf. R 1966/31, p. 4.
93. Caprile, V, 275, note 6; cf. also Svidercoschi, *Storia del Concilio*, pp. 531-532.
94. Cf. ms. R 1965/34; the talk was later reworked and published in the journal *CC* (Biblio. 312).
95. Cf. *AS*, IV/IV, 690-696.
96. The document covers twenty printed pages, *ibid.*, pp. 698-717.
97. Cf. *ibid.*, pp. 717-720.

2. On 14 October, the president of the secretariat presented the new text, with *an address* of his own.[98] He began by stating the criterion that had governed the revision of the text: "that the schema should as far as possible become clearer and more accurate, but in such a way that *the tone of the text*, which you approved last year by a large majority [i.e. with only 99 votes against, out of 1,996 votes cast], *should be faithfully retained*."[99]

(a) With regard to the first part, which dealt with *considerations of principle*, Hinduism, Buddhism and the Islamic religion, the cardinal observed gratefully: "The amendments and observations which you proposed have greatly helped us, so that now this declaration, by which the Catholic Church for the first time proposes fraternal dialogue with the great non-Christian religions, better fulfills its purpose."[100]

(b) With regard to the part dealing with *the Jews*, the speaker mentioned not only the work of revision but also the journeys undertaken to countries where the document had provoked the greatest difficulties, saying that these two initiatives aimed at clarifying the correct interpretation of the theological doctrine of the document and emphasizing its purely religious character.[101]

The effort at theological clarity was concerned principally with "the most difficult point of the schema: the question of *the responsibility of the Jews* for the acts committed in the Lord's passion." The address first of all quoted the new text: "Although the Jewish authorities and those who followed their lead pressed for the death of Christ (cf. John 19:6), nevertheless what happened in his passion cannot be attributed indiscriminately to all Jews then alive, or to the Jews of today. Although the church is the new people of God, the Jews should not be presented as rejected by God or accursed, as if this follows from the holy scriptures." The cardinal continued: "From this text it appears clear that: (i) the schema completely preserves and expounds the truth of the gospel; (ii) at the same time it rules out unjust statements and accusations made indiscriminately against all Jews then living and against the Jews of today—namely, that all of them are guilty of condemning the Lord and are therefore rejected by God and accursed; (iii) the Council exhorts everyone to make sure that in this connection catechetics and preaching correspond to the truth of the gospel and the spirit of Christ."[102]

(c) It is here that the cardinal reached the crucial point, namely the *omission of the expression "guilty of deicide."* He gave the reason for this decision as follows: "It is known that the difficulties and controversies—in other words as if the schema might be seen as contradicting the gospel—in fact arose chiefly from the use of this expression. On the other hand, it is obvious to anyone who

---

98. Cf. *ibid.*, p. 722.

99. *Ibid.* (ct). We have taken into account the additions made when the speech was made in the Council hall. Although the text of the address is given as an appendix to the cardinal's commentary on *Nostra aetate* (Biblio. 172), we shall give slightly longer quotations in order to highlight the precise strategy employed by the cardinal at so crucial a moment.

100. *Ibid.*

101. Cf. *ibid.*, p. 723.

102. *Ibid.*, pp. 723-724 (ct).

reads the text that has just been read out and explained that *the substance* of what we wished to express by this word [deicide] in the earlier text is still precisely and fully expressed in the new text."[103]

Although this would appear to have clarified matters, there was also an important *psychological element* here, and the cardinal addressed this immediately: "I am well aware that some people give great psychological importance to this word. However, I say that if this word is misunderstood in many regions, and if the same idea can be expressed by other more suitable words, then surely pastoral prudence and Christian charity forbid us to use it, and in fact require us to explain the matter in other words."[104] The speaker then continued by recalling the original assignment received from Pope John XXIII: "I say that this is required by that same 'religious, evangelical love' that led John XXIII to order that this declaration itself be prepared and that last year inspired you to approve it. Our secretariat judged this amendment to be of great importance in order that the declaration itself be everywhere rightly understood and accepted, in spite of the various difficulties. Thus, I strongly urge you to consider this amendment in the light of pastoral prudence and evangelical charity."[105]

3. The complex procedure of voting then followed. The whole text and the corresponding examination of the amendments was divided into eight sections, each of which was voted on separately. This division was important in order to achieve a clear picture of the situation, since it was obvious, for example, that the section dealing with the Jewish religion created greater difficulty than the others. And this section was in fact subdivided into four parts, which were voted on separately. Thus the overall voting on *the examination of the amendments* produced the following results: out of 2,108 votes cast, there were 1,856 in favor, and 243 against. And the voting on *the whole text* produced the following result: out of 2,023 votes cast, there were 1,763 in favor, and 250 against.[106]

Although it is certainly true that in comparison with the results generally obtained in the Council there was a fairly high number of votes against, we should bear in mind first and foremost the difficulties the document had met with from the beginning. In the present case, it was also very likely that the contrary votes came from two very different quarters, in other words not only from those who were simply against the document, but also from those who felt that the part concerning the Jewish religion had been watered down by omission of the term "deicide" and by the fact that it no longer "condemned" antisemitism but merely "deplored" it.[107] There was an even greater sigh of relief when the

---

103. *Ibid.*, p. 724 (ct).
104. *Ibid.* (ct).
105. *Ibid.* (ct). The official report of the secretariat observes that the term "deicide" should disappear from Christian terminology; cf. *ibid.*, 715. We should bear in mind that the Jews—and also a good number of the Council fathers—considered the question of "deicide" an extremely important one.
106. Cf. *ibid.*, 800 (vote no. 404) and 824 (the vote was not numbered).
107. Those who maintained the latter opinion forgot that the Latin *deplorat* does not have the weaker meaning of the English "deplore"; cf. Oesterreicher, *The New Encounter*, p. 269, and *Freiburger Rundbrief 1966*, p. 35. On the other hand, we must agree that the motive adopted

second reading, in *the public session* of 28 October, produced a far better result: out of 2,312 votes cast, there were 2,221 in favor and only 88 against.[108] Thus there was a massive *increase* of 458 in the votes in favor, both on account of a more numerous participation of the Council fathers, and also because of a reduction in the contrary votes,[109] meaning that the document had been accepted by ninety-six percent of the Catholic bishops of the whole world.

4. Satisfaction over this unhoped-for result was further increased by the fact that the negative reactions that had been feared in the Middle East did not then take place, and everything stayed calm. In his talk to the Sisters of Our Lady of Sion, the cardinal said: "Another no less surprising result was that *the whole of the East stayed calm.* It is true that one Orthodox patriarch spoke out, but it remained an isolated voice."[110]

On another occasion, the cardinal mentioned a factor that had helped the document to be accepted calmly: "By a providential coincidence—which was not foreseen, let alone calculated—the final vote and promulgation of this document occurred on 28 October, that is, in the very period of rejoicing for the happy return of the relics of St. Sabas; and this meant that the approval of the controversial decree received considerably less attention."[111] Indeed, on this very occasion, those in charge of the region had many words of gratitude and praise for the Catholic Church. The Greek Orthodox Patriarch of Jerusalem said: "This event will give a new impetus to the church, especially at this time when we are witnessing the development of the spirit of ecumenism, love, mutual respect, rapprochement and sincere cooperation between the two great churches, the Catholic and the Orthodox, for the good of Christ's church and of the whole of humanity."[112]

The Governor of Jerusalem, Daud Abu Ghazaleh, declared at the official banquet: "I, a Moslem, feel an immense joy at the fraternal and friendly gesture made by the Catholic Church in restoring the holy relics of St. Sabas to the Orthodox Church. This gesture is certainly a new testimony to the peace and love that inspire all men, and especially Christians."[113]

As concerns the other party—*the Jews*—the cardinal observed in the same talk: "At first the Jews were in general not too satisfied. They felt that the declaration had been excessively watered down by the omission of the word 'deicide' and the replacement of the word 'condemns' by 'deplores'; it was not what they had been expecting. However, they too gradually calmed down."[114]

---

for substituting *deplorat* for *damnat*—that is, that the latter term is normally reserved for doctrinal errors (cf. *AS*, IV/IV, 725)—could seem less than convincing. Indeed, in a declaration of the Holy Office dated 1928 it was stated that the church *damnat* hatred directed against the Jewish people; cf. *Church-Jews*, p. 12, note.

108. Cf. *AS*, IV/V, 674.
109. Cf. also the comparison with the 1964 vote in *Church-Jews*, p. 24.
110. R 1965/37, p. 5.
111. *Ecumenismo*, p. 223, note. Cf. pp. 490-491 above.
112. *Ecumenism*, p. 193 (ct).
113. *Ibid.* (ct).
114. R 1965/37, p. 5.

In illustration of this statement, we shall quote what Mr. Nahum Goldman wrote to the cardinal in the name of the World Conference of Jewish Organizations a few days after the promulgation of the document: "Now that the Ecumenical Council is coming to an end and the declaration on relations with the Jewish people has been approved with such a resounding majority, I feel the need to express to you both personally and in the name of the organizations I represent our gratitude for the wise yet also courageous manner in which you and your secretariat have brought this far-from-easy declaration to success. I am sure that Your Eminence knows that we are not happy about several changes in respect to the previous draft, but in this sinful world nobody ever gets everything he wants, and there can be no question that taken as a whole and viewed in its historical perspective, we consider this declaration to be of major importance, and we all, with a few exceptions, assess it in this way."[115]

* * *

The day after the promulgation of the document, the cardinal made a statement to the Italian news agency ANSA, referring to the surprising coincidence that the document had been promulgated exactly seven years since the election of Pope John XXIII to the see of Peter: "I believe that he too is happy about this fruit, which I hope is not an unworthy one, of his initiative, and that with that unforgettable smile of his he is saying to us, 'Courage!', as he said to me personally so many times. For the declaration is a very important and promising beginning—but only a beginning—of a long, demanding path toward the arduous goal of a human race in which all men will really feel and behave as sons of the same Father who is in heaven."[116]

The Basic Points of The Church and the Jewish People

Not content with what he had done until then, shortly after the promulgation of the document *Nostra aetate* the cardinal set to work to write a commentary on it. This work explained the whole document, but obviously the greater part of it, or five out of its eight chapters, was dedicated to the most difficult section, in other words the relations of the church with the Jewish people. And this explains why the book was entitled *The Church and the Jewish People*. First published in 1966, it was translated into six languages[117]—a fact that could

---

115. Letter of 3 December 1965, Arch. Lf 4/40. Cf. also the above-mentioned talk, R 1965/37, p. 4: "The text as promulgated fully satisfied neither the Jews nor certain others. . . ." Other Jewish evaluations of *Nostra aetate* are found in Sestieri and Cereti (eds.), *Le Chiese cristiane e l'Ebraismo*, pp. 349-363.

116. Lf 1/38, p. 2.

117. Cf. Biblio. 172. The original Italian was translated into French, English, Dutch, Portuguese, Spanish and German. In order to understand the commentary, it is vital to remember that the author is explaining a Council document and is thus addressing Catholics, and maybe other

reasonably lead us to wonder whether we now need to present a summary of the cardinal's thinking on the question of relations between the church and the Jewish people. I do, however, think that it will prove useful, although I shall be as brief as possible, presenting the cardinal's main statements and conclusions almost *in the form of theses*, since the substance of his thought is in fact concentrated in the commentary in question. A more complete study based on all the cardinal's publications on the subject[118] would undoubtedly be very interesting, if only in order to follow the continuity or otherwise of his think-ing.[119] However, any reader who so wishes can study this subject in greater depth both in the commentary under consideration here and also in the fuller Italian edition of the biography.

1. *The basis*: the people of God of the New Testament is *spiritually linked* to the stock of Abraham. In this connection, the cardinal proposes "the interpreta-tion that is placed upon them [the texts in Genesis concerning Abraham] under the guidance of the Holy Spirit in the New Testament, and especially by St. Paul. In the Epistle to the Romans, when St. Paul speaks of Christians in general— many of whom, if not the majority, were at that time non-Jews—he does not hesitate to say that Abraham 'is the father of us all, as it is written: "I have made you the father of many nations"—in the presence of the God in whom he believed, who gives life to the dead' (Rom. 4:16-17)."[120]

Furthermore, according to St. Paul, "Christ is the link which enables the gentiles to be numbered among the inheritors of the promises. . . . Faith creates so close a union between Christ and those who believe in him that they form one mystical person with him. It is in virtue of this union with Christ that like him they become the descendants of Abraham, and therefore sharers in the promises made to Abraham and his posterity: . . . 'You are all *one* in Christ Jesus. And if you are Christ's, then you are Abraham's offspring, heirs according to the promise' (Gal. 3:26-29)."[121]

In a further passage, the cardinal points out the links of the church *with all the offspring of Abraham*: "Christ cannot be isolated from the offspring of

---

Christians, but *not* Jews. Had he been addressing the latter, his approach would have had to be totally different. (From this point of view, the English translation created misunderstandings by giving the impression on p. 17 that the cardinal was writing for the Jews.)

118. I am referring in particular to the article "Sono gli ebrei un popolo 'deicida' e 'maledetto da Dio'?" (or "Are the Jews a Deicide People, Accursed by God?") (Biblio. 441).

119. For Bea's complex thinking, cf. also Biblio. 317 and 334, and the manuscripts R 1966/12 and R 1966/13. For a summary of his thinking, cf. also B. Dupuy, "Augustin Bea, cardinal de l'Eglise catholique et l'ami du peuple juif," *Rencontre, chrétiens et juifs*, III (1969), 33-45, and F. Mussner in *Simposio*, pp. 110-115. I shall mention only in passing the extensive study of Cesare Manucci, "Storia e teologia dell'antisemitismo cristiano: l'odio antico," *Comunità*, XXVI/166 (1972), 9-123; this work deals (pp. 53-71) with the history of *Nostra aetate* and the cardinal's commentary on this document; the study is based on various prejudices and deals with the subject in a somewhat polemical manner; since the contributions of the Council and the cardinal have been widely recognized also by Jews, there is no need to respond to such polemics.

120. *Church-Jews*, p. 55 (ct).

121. *Ibid.*, p. 56.

Abraham as a whole. *He* is the preeminent offspring but not the only one. It is not without reason that God allowed two millennia to elapse between Abraham and Christ. This long lapse of time allowed for the period of long and arduous preparation which God willed."[122] Thus, if the entire history of the Jewish people essentially constitutes the preparation for the coming of Christ and the slow preparation of the church, it follows that all this preparation, and hence the history of the Jewish people, concerns the whole church and all Christians.[123]

This explains the Council's statement that "the church acknowledges that the beginning of her faith and her election, according to God's saving design, are found already in the patriarchs, Moses and the prophets."[124] "On this account the church cannot forget that she received the revelation of the Old Testament by way of that people with whom God in his inexpressible mercy established the ancient covenant. Nor can she forget that she draws nourishment from that good olive tree onto which the wild olive branches of the gentiles have been grafted."[125]

2. *The religious motivations for antisemitism.* In the first place, the cardinal states that antisemitism "has many other causes arising from racial, economic and social factors as well."[126] It is well-known that, starting in the time of the Emperor Claudius (Acts 18:2) and continuing throughout the centuries, motives of a social and economic order also played their part.[127] However, the fact remains that antisemitism has *also* been fed from religious sources.

(a) In the accusation directed at the Jews, the guilt of the Jerusalem authorities is expressed in the term "deicide." Now, "objectively speaking, the condemnation and crucifixion of Christ constitutes the crime of deicide, since according to Christian teaching Jesus was certainly Man-God."[128] The author then contin-

122. *Ibid.*, pp. 58-59.
123. Cf. *ibid.*, p. 59.
124. *NA*, 4, quoted in *Church-Jews*, p. 60. On pp. 60-61, the author cites the fundamental texts of the conciliar Constitution on the Church (*LG*, 2 and 9) as confirmation. The author reminds those who might see these explanations as an undue panegyric of the Jewish people that it is not a case of the people's merits but of God's freely given gifts: "The choice of Abraham, and thus of the Jewish people, is an entirely gratuitous gift of God and is not the fruit of human genius or merits" (*Church-Jews*, p. 62 [ct]). Cf. Biblio. 441, p. 444.
125. *NA*, 4; cf. *Church-Jews*, pp. 60-61. With reference to the cardinal's words, "the gentiles . . . are now grafted on to the *good olive*, the *new people of God*," Mussner observes (in *Simposio*, p. 112, note 1) that "the good olive-tree" in St. Paul's thinking is and remains the Jewish people. He is perfectly right, and this is a simple oversight on the part of the cardinal. For further explanations, see the Italian edition.
126. *Church-Jews*, p. 66. We speak of "antisemitism," as does the present document, because this term has become current. In Biblio. 441, p. 431, note 5, the cardinal observes: "More precisely speaking, we should speak of anti-Judaism, since, at least in recent times, there has not been a movement against Semites in general, but solely against Jews."
127. Cf. Biblio. 441, p. 431; R 1963/25, p. 6; *Church-Jews*, p. 158. A survey carried out about twenty years ago in the United States stated similarly: "Obviously, religious motives are far from being the only, or perhaps even the major, source of support from these anti-semitic stereotypes held by Catholics" (quoted in *Simposio*, p. 102).
128. *Church-Jews*, pp. 68-69 (ct). Cf. Biblio. 441, p. 432. On the theological meaning of the term "deicide," cf. also Oesterreicher, *The New Encounter*, pp. 254-255, who cites an article by the

ues: "On the other hand, we must immediately add that *true guilt* of deicide can be imputed only to those who have committed the crime in the clear knowledge of Christ's human-divine nature."[129] However, in declarations by St. Peter and St. Paul in the New Testament (Acts 3:15, 17; 13:27) it is stated that these authorities "acted in ignorance." In saying this, the two apostles are simply following the example of meekness given us by Jesus himself, who prayed on the cross: "Father, forgive them, for they know not what they do" (Luke 23:34).[130] What is the precise meaning of these texts? On the one hand, "they cannot possibly be regarded as completely exonerating those responsible for the death of Jesus. There would have been no need, for example, for Christ's request for forgiveness had their ignorance been complete and their lack of guilt consequently equally complete. On the other hand, we cannot treat these words as an empty, meaningless formula. Especially in Jesus' prayer, it is clear that he supports his supplication for their pardon with a genuine excuse in favor of the Jews."[131]

Even though the guilt of "deicide" proper is ruled out, "there still remains the more general responsibility of the Jerusalem authorities for *the condemnation of an innocent man, known as a holy teacher and even as a prophet,* indeed even as *the* Prophet, the promised Messiah."[132] However, even with regard to guilt in this connection, "we must still ask to what extent the Jews of Jerusalem fully understood what they were doing and acted in full liberty, not blinded or carried away by passions, circumstances or concrete situations."[133]

(b) The decisive *question* is whether *the Jewish people are involved* in this responsibility as defined.[134] "Even at the time of Christ, the majority of the chosen people did not cooperate at all with the leaders of the people. . . . Indeed, even those who cried 'Crucify him!' to Pilate represented a tiny part of the chosen people. Is it not true that the leaders of the Jews did not want to kill the Lord 'during the feast, lest there be a tumult among the people' (Mt. 26:5)?"[135] Furthermore, the gospels specifically state that the people who were present and who consented to the condemnation of Jesus "had been seduced and persuaded by their leaders." All of this leads the author to conclude: "The circle of the true authors of the tragedy is thus *restricted* above all to the members of the Sanhedrin, a very influential although not very numerous group."[136]

---

well-known Swiss theologian C. Journet according to whom the term is not part of authentic Christian tradition. Cf. also J.M. Oesterreicher, "Deicide under Microscope," in his book *The New Encounter,* pp. 375-393.

129. *Church-Jews,* p. 69 (ct). Cf. Biblio. 441, p. 432. In order to avoid misunderstandings over this text, we should bear in mind the footnote added by the editors of the journal: "Obviously when the author speaks of the human-divine *nature,* he means to refer to Christ's human-divine *reality.*"

130. Cf. *Church-Jews,* p. 69; also Biblio. 441, pp. 432-433; Biblio. 312, p. 213.

131. *Church-Jews,* pp. 69-70 (ct).

132. *Ibid.,* p. 71 (ct).

133. Biblio. 441, p. 436.

134. Cf. *Church-Jews,* p. 70.

135. First address to the Council, *AS,* II/V, 484 (ct).

136. Biblio. 441, p. 435.

(c) Does there exist *a collective responsibility* of the people as such?[137] There are texts which would seem to say so. Thus St. Peter, St. Paul and St. Stephen reproach certain groups of Jews, "You crucified him," "You killed the author of life," etc.[138] Indeed, while St. Paul "speaks primarily of the Jews of Thessalonica and then of those of Jerusalem, he subsequently refers to the Jews *in general* in view of the fact that he has been persecuted by the Jews in many of the cities and places where he has preached."[139] However, this is *not* how things really are. We should note the following facts: "In none of the texts cited above does the speaker (St. Peter, St. Paul or St. Stephen) include *himself* among those responsible for the crucifixion of Jesus. Their rebukes are always addressed to someone else, whether it be the Sanhedrin, the crowd involved in the trial, the inhabitants of Jerusalem or Jews in general. Now if these texts referred to a collective responsibility and guilt of the entire Jewish people as such, that is of all members of the people of Israel, then in all honesty the speakers would have been obliged to use the pronoun 'we' and to include themselves."[140]

In the texts cited above which speak of the responsibility of the Jews for the condemnation and death of Jesus, we have to conclude that they do *not* speak of a collective responsibility of the people as such. "Here, then, we find ourselves involved *not* in a nationalistic frame of reference, so to speak, but in an *exclusively religious* context. We are confronted with a biblical concept according to which there exist in the world *powers that are hostile to God....* It is for this reason that St. Peter advises the people: 'Save yourselves from this perverse generation' (Acts 2:40)."[141] Obviously guilt acquired simply by membership of a certain people cannot be removed by repentance and conversion.[142]

(d) On these bases it is easy to reach a further *conclusion.* If it is impossible to take the New Testament texts as indicating a collective guilt of the Jewish people of Jerusalem and of Palestine, what can we say of *the Jews of the time who were scattered throughout the world*? "Statistics show that in the apostolic age, the Jews dispersed throughout the Roman Empire numbered about four and a half million."[143] Now if even the Jews of Jerusalem had no collective responsibility, this obviously applies all the more to the scattered Jews. And it would be even more mistaken to try to attribute such guilt to the descendants of the

---

137. The author does not deal with the philosophical aspect as such, but does sometimes touch on it: "Everyone finds it normal, for example, to enjoy the advantages obtained by our leaders, to boast of the glory of famous men and illustrious forebears. Furthermore, it is a fact that we often have to suffer because of their misdeeds. Up to a certain point this is considered fairly normal, and nobody would dare deny it. However, all this is valid within certain limits" (*ibid.*, p. 441; cf. also Biblio. 312, p. 226). Nevertheless, in his second address to the Council, the cardinal observed: "Can any other case be found anywhere in which we blame a nation for the actions of its ancestors over nineteen centuries ago?" (*Church-Jews*, p. 162).

138. Cf. *Church-Jews*, pp. 73-74, referring to the following texts: Acts 2:22-23; 3:15; 7:52; 13:27-28; 1 Thess. 2:15.

139. *Ibid.*, p. 74, referring to the following texts: Acts 9:23; 13:45, 50; 14:2, 5, 19; 17:5, 13; 18:12.

140. *Ibid.*, p. 77. Cf. Biblio. 312, p. 217.

141. *Church-Jews*, pp. 79-80. Cf. Biblio. 312, p. 217.

142. Cf. *Church-Jews*, p. 77; Biblio. 312, pp. 217-218.

143. Second address to the Council, *AS*, III/II, 560.

Jewish people throughout history and in our present times.[144] Elsewhere the cardinal says: "Anyone acquainted with the historical facts and with the attitudes of mind that have arisen among Christians from time to time will appreciate the historic importance of this solemn statement by the Council."[145]

3. Even after the events of the passion, *the Jewish people retained its position as the chosen people whom God loves.*

As in the question of collective responsibility, here too Bea starts with some *facts* given in the New Testament. The first, which shows that the people was not repudiated by God, is that *God continued to offer them his gifts,* offering them the gospel of salvation. For several decades the apostles continued to address their preaching to the Jews of Palestine, and even when they left Palestine, they spoke firstly to the Jews of the diaspora. "Thus, when together with Barnabas he [St. Paul] speaks to the Jews of Antioch in Pisidia, he states that God himself has decreed that his ministry should follow this pattern: 'It was necessary that the word of God should be spoken first to you . . .' (Acts 13:46). And in the Epistle to the Romans he declares that the gospel 'is the power of God for salvation to every one who has faith, *to the Jew first* and then to the Greek' (Rom. 1:16)."[146]

If this is so, it leads to the question of how we are to explain the fact that the majority of the people did not accept the gospel. The author replies: "The fact is that the various Jewish communities in Palestine and the diaspora gradually succumbed to the influence of social factors and ties, particularly the influence of the community at Jerusalem and its leaders."[147] This maybe became even more marked when the Sanhedrin began to take measures against the apostles, arresting them, threatening them and beating them, and later on persecuting Christians.[148] Things took a similar turn in the diaspora. St. Paul "regularly encountered the hostility of the leaders of the Jewish communities, and very often either he himself or his neophytes were subjected to persecution."[149]

Lastly, the cardinal searches with St. Paul for *the psychological motives* that led the majority not to believe in the gospel, and indicates as *the immediate cause* "the idea that the Jews had formed of salvation. They claimed to work out their salvation themselves through their own works and the observance of the law, and not through faith in Jesus Christ, through whom salvation came as a free gift of God."[150]

A final question arises: Can it, perhaps, be that their persistent incredulity led God to reject his people?[151] The cardinal replies: "St. Paul categorically denies any such conclusion: in spite of everything, in spite of the majority's lack of faith, God has not rejected his people: 'I ask then, has God rejected his people?

---

144. Cf. *ibid.*
145. *Church-Jews*, p. 86 (ct).
146. *Church-Jews*, p. 84.
147. *Ibid.*, p. 91 (ct).
148. Cf. *ibid.*, p. 92, referring to the following texts: Acts 4:1-21, 5:17-41; 8:1-3; 9:1-2; 12:1-2.
149. *Ibid.*, referring to the following texts: Acts 9:23, 29; 13:45, 50; 14:2, 5, 19; 17:5, 13; 18:12; 20:3; 21:7; 23:12.
150. *Ibid.*, p. 97 (ct).
151. Cf. *ibid.*, p. 93.

By no means. . . . God has not rejected his people whom he foreknew' (Rom. 11:1-11). A little later on he develops this theme still further when he says: 'As regards election they [the Jews] are loved for the sake of their forefathers. *For the gifts and the call of God are irrevocable*' (Rom. 28:28-29)."[152]

The following objection is often raised against the interpretation given to the words "the gifts of God are irrevocable": "Israel according to the flesh is no longer the chosen people of God, since this is now 'Israel according to the spirit,' that is, the church." In other words, the people has been rejected by God. What can we say in the face of such a line of reasoning? The author replies by making a distinction: "Evidently it is true that the Jewish people is no longer the people of God in the sense of an *institution for the salvation of humanity*. The reason for this, however, is not that it has been rejected, but simply that its function in preparing for the coming of the kingdom of God finished with the advent of Christ and the founding of the church" (*Church-Jews*, p. 96 [ct]).

4. "No one can take from the Jewish people the honor arising from the part played in the past in the preparatory stages of the work of redemption. In addition, it is indisputable that the church was grounded on this people and on individual members of it. Christ, the head of the church, was the preeminent descendant of Abraham. From Abraham's stock came also his blessed mother, the apostles, who were the foundation of the church, and the first communities who made up the church. True, the founding of the church constituted an entirely new beginning, wholly due to Jesus Christ who founded it on *his* apostles, chosen and taught by him. This new start was manifested to the world by the descent of the Holy Spirit on the day of Pentecost. Nevertheless, this *new beginning* came from the people of the old covenant. The apostles were so very much Jews—and felt themselves to be so—that although they had an embryonic liturgy of their own in 'the breaking of bread' and 'the teaching of the apostles,' they continued to visit the temple and to pray there and, as we have seen, for decades they preached to Jews."[153]

5. *Life and action.* After having thus cleared the ground of prejudices, the cardinal then stated: "It remains to summarize the practical measures necessary to develop *relations between Christians and Jews* in a constructive manner."[154]

---

152. *Ibid.*, pp. 93-94. Speaking of the present situation of the Jewish people, *Nostra aetate* employs a negative formula, saying that they should not be presented as rejected by God and cursed. However, before this they are also referred to in a positive formula: "God holds the Jews most dear for the sake of their fathers; he does not repent of the gifts he makes." Nevertheless, the report of the secretariat states that it does *not* intend defining *the sense* in which the Jewish people remains, according to the Dogmatic Constitution on the Church, "a people according to their election most dear on account of their fathers"; cf. *AS*, IV/IV, 715. In the light of this teaching it is easy to understand the cardinal's indignation at the accusation that this people has been "cursed" by God. "This is a very grave offense, not just to the chosen people and to truth itself, but above all to God's faithfulness and to the Lord's promises, infinite mercy and love" (Biblio. 441, p. 440).

153. *Church-Jews*, pp. 99-100 (ct). As confirmation of the apostles' manner of acting, the author cites Acts 2:46; 3:18; 5:20-21; 21:26; 24:12, 18; 22:17. The apostles used the expression "the breaking of bread" to indicate the celebration of the eucharist.

154. *Ibid.*, p. 116.

In broad terms, practical consequences must be drawn from what has been stated above concerning "the common spiritual heritage" of Christians and Jews. This does not provide a complete plan of action, for "we shall have to wait for cumulative experience gradually to lay bare the various possibilities."[155]

(a) First of all, there is what we can call the *negative* part, which is nevertheless extremely important. Before energetically decrying "hatred, persecutions and manifestations of antisemitism, directed against Jews at any time and by anyone," the Council document addresses the following admonition to the whole church: "All should see to it, then, *in catechetical work and in the preaching* of the word of God that they teach nothing save what conforms to the truth of the gospel and the Spirit of Christ."[156]

(b) We then come to the *positive* part: "The first, essential task, which will certainly be rewarding, is to realize . . . how many paths we tread as fellow-pilgrims with them [the Jews] in the daily practice of our religion."[157] The conciliar Constitution on Divine Revelation tells us that "the books of the Old Testament have been caught up as a whole in the proclamation of the gospel."[158] "We are made very vividly aware of this by the sacred liturgy, especially during the seasons of Advent and Lent."[159]

Of course, there are certain *difficulties* involved in employing and living the Old Testament: "Christians often complain of the difficulty they experience in trying to understand and love the Old Testament in view of the very obvious differences between it and the New Testament."[160] The *remedy* is as follows: "It is necessary, therefore, to know how to read the Old Testament intelligently, in order to be able to identify *the permanent elements* which concern every man, particularly every Christian. The constitution summarizes these very valuable elements and values of the Old Testament in a few brief words. After exhorting the faithful to look upon the books of the old Testament with great respect and devotion, it adds the following reason: 'They express a very lively sense of God'; in them is contained 'sublime teaching about God, and wise and salutary guidance for the conduct of life together with marvelous treasures of prayer'; finally, in them 'lies hidden the mystery of our salvation' (*DV*, 15)."[161]

It may be added that "Christians and Jews also encounter one another at the point on which they are so sadly divided, i.e. in their differing concepts of *the divine plan of salvation*. Thus, in spite of this painful and distressing fact, it is

---

155. *Ibid.*, p. 129 (ct).
156. *NA*, 4; cf. *Church-Jews*, p. 118. In the 1963 talk in New York to which we have referred on several occasions, with reference to teaching the cardinal further specifies the tasks of moral theology, and also the education of consciences both by means of teaching and by the ministry of confession; and lastly the revision of the Code of Canon Law; cf. R 1963/25, pp. 5-7. In the interview he gave to *The Jewish Chronicle* in 1962, he emphasized the need to correct history textbooks; cf. Arch. Lf 1, 7 and 8.
157. *Church-Jews*, p. 129.
158. *DV*, 16.
159. *Church-Jews*, p. 125.
160. *Ibid.*, p. 121.
161. *Ibid.*, pp. 122-123.

true that from the very beginnings of the church, Christians have been gradually instructed in the mystery of salvation and prepared to admit Christ the Savior to an ever-growing intimacy in their own lives by means of the writings of the Old Testament."[162]

The cardinal asks how this is possible, and replies: "*This is made possible* by the fact that although Christians believe that Christ has already come and has fulfilled his part in the work of redemption, they *also* believe that he will come again in glory at the last day. They look forward to his second coming with a great longing because they live 'awaiting our blessed hope, the manifestation of our great God and Savior Jesus Christ' (Titus 2:13). . . . Their desire for the second coming of Christ in glory and their preparation for it find apt expression and firm support in the books of the Old Testament, especially in the Psalms and in the prophecies of Isaiah."[163]

(c) What has been said leads to the following important "obvious principle": "Christians or Jews will come together and become more capable of still closer association, the more thoroughly they understand and live the word of God as contained in the Old Testament in all its fullness and richness with regard to their own lives, their relationship to God and their salvation."[164]

(d) In *Nostra aetate*, the Council particularly recommends "mutual understanding and esteem. This will be the fruit above all of *biblical and theological studies and of brotherly dialogues*."[165] Bea makes the following comment: "For the task of bringing Jews and Christians together more closely, great importance must be attached to cooperation in biblical and theological research."[166]

(e) Another task is that of *working together in order to* "*bring to mankind all that God has given them in the revelation of the Old Testament*, to enable them to live in accordance with it and to understand it. In the first instance, we shall do this best if we ourselves bear witness to it through living our own lives according to its precepts. To this we can then add all those other fresh undertakings which will be seen to be necessary in the light of actual circumstances." Nevertheless, the rules for such cooperation must be borne in mind: "The common effort should be made in an atmosphere of freedom, in absolute fidelity to the truth and in a spirit of mutual respect, esteem and goodwill."[167]

Apart from cooperation in bringing the riches of the Old Testament to humanity, in another context the cardinal emphasized the need for *more general cooperation* in order to uphold religious and moral values, for example, the natural ethics of the Old Testament, and also in charitable and welfare activities.[168] Joint work in the service of the same great ideal will have the effect of

---

162. *Ibid.*, p. 126.
163. *Ibid.*
164. *Ibid.*, p. 129 (ct).
165. *NA*, 4.
166. *Church-Jews*, p. 130 (ct).
167. *Ibid.*, p. 133.
168. Cf. *ibid.* Cf. also the talk to the Sisters of Our Lady of Sion: ". . . as far as is possible, working with the Jews themselves, in all fraternity, to proclaim religious and moral values" (Biblio. 246, p. 8); furthermore, cooperating in "charitable and welfare activities" (*ibid.*). Cf. also the New

bringing men together, and they will thus learn to know one another better, respect one another, and love one another.[169]

The final goal, "the lofty ideal," of all this is that of "hastening the approach of that wonderful day foretold by the Old Testament in the prophecy of Zephaniah and quoted in the declaration: 'That day when all peoples will address the Lord with a single voice and service him with one accord' (Zeph. 3:9)."[170]

* * *

Let us now cast a look back over all we have seen in this chapter in order to summarize Bea's *specific contribution* in this particular field. There is no need here to give even a brief account of all the tributes he received, both after the promulgation of *Nostra aetate* and after his death.[171] He was called one of the architects, or quite simply *the* architect, of *Nostra aetate*.[172] One of those mostly closely involved in drafting the declaration, Monsignor John M. Oesterreicher, wrote of Bea as follows: "He is to be considered the most important advocate and the true father of this document."[173] It is most significant that the cardinal's foremost assistant throughout the history of this document, Cardinal Johannes Willebrands, ratifies this judgment.[174] Nevertheless, we should also recall that the aim of such evaluations, as Willebrands has written, is not "to attribute all the merit to Bea" for what was done in support of *Nostra aetate*, for we must bear in mind, among other things, that "the secretariat was lucky enough to have collaborators of the first order at its disposal."[175] Bea was always the first to recognize this. Thus, if we try to highlight Bea's specific contribution, we do not intend to minimize the large amount of work performed by his collaborators, but simply to illustrate the various aspects of the cardinal's work by summarizing the results of this chapter.

The first contribution we should mention concerns *the field of thought* and doctrine. In this connection, the study he prepared toward the middle of 1962 is particularly significant. While it is true that this was published only twenty years later, the corrected proofs were dated 1962, and thus the text gives a faithful picture of his thinking at the time. This study shows that at a time when the

---

York talk (R 1963/25, p. 7), where in a similar context the cardinal suggested the creation of an interreligious institute or study center in order to solve the major problems facing humanity today.

169. Cf. *Church-Jews*, pp. 133-134.

170. *Ibid.*, p. 134.

171. In this context, cf. "Augustin Kardinal Bea in jüdischen und israelischen Nachrufen," *Freiburger Rundbrief*, LXXIII/LXXVI (1968), 54-56; *Bea-Preis*, pp. 145-149; Dupuy, "Augustin Bea," p. 45; J. Lichten, in *Simposio*, pp. 89-94; S. Talmon, in *Simposio*, p. 107.

172. Cf. *Bea-Preis*, pp. 145-146; *SIDIC*, special issue, *In memoriam Cardinal Augustin Bea* (1969), p. 8.

173. Oesterreicher, *The New Encounter*, p. 162: *Pate* (or "godfather") in the German version of this study, but "father" in the English version.

174. Cf. *Simposio*, p. 20.

175. *Ibid.*, pp. 7-8.

schema on this subject as prepared by the secretariat consisted of a single printed page, the cardinal's thinking on the question was already well developed. Comparison of this study with the first two speeches he made in the Council hall shows how far these were the expression of his personal views and convictions. After *Nostra aetate* was promulgated, he further developed his thinking in his lengthy commentary on this document in which, as we have seen, he provided a vast and deep scriptural basis for each of the points.

An attentive observer of Bea's activity in support of *Nostra aetate* has written that the general public never realized *how much energy and time* the cardinal dedicated to this document, for their knowledge was almost exclusively limited to his activity in the ecumenical field.[176] This is a very astute observation. Indeed, before the document was promulgated, Bea had hardly referred to it at all in public,[177] a policy dictated by the special nature of this work, in which publicity inevitably provoked disruptive activity on the part of its opponents. Bea dedicated all the more time and energy not only to preparation of the schema, but also to personal meetings and contacts, as we have seen above.

It has rightly been emphasized that all Bea's activity was characterized by the two qualities of *flexibility and perseverance*.[178] In June 1962, when it was asked that the schema and its subject be removed from the Council agenda, he had evidently felt that at the moment resistance was so great that it was best to give in. Nevertheless, a few months later, he launched a counter-attack with the memorandum he presented to Pope John XXIII the following December; and he won the battle. He also accepted the decision to make the schema an appendix to the Dogmatic Constitution on the Church—which had the providential effect that the schema was voted on before the storm of protest broke out into a full-scale crusade, while in the end, despite everything, the document became a special, separate declaration. With regard to Bea's prudence and flexibility, one author has wondered whether they may not have impaired the prophetic spirit which was originally the keynote of the schema.[179] Here we have to say that he acted deliberately, for in his address of 20 November 1964 he declared: "It must be borne in mind that it is more important to have such a solemn declaration by the Council than to satisfy everyone, even if that were possible."[180]

Apart from working and fighting for *Nostra aetate*, the cardinal also suffered insults and derision on its account, repeatedly being attacked in various publications as a freemason, an enemy of the church, a heretic, and as having tricked

---

176. Thus E.E. Ehrlich in *Neue Zürcher Nachrichten*, LII (31 December 1968), supplement.

177. In the press conference of 25 April 1962 he was surprised by a question and hardly mentioned this. He later spoke on the subject during "a conversation" reported in *The Jewish Chronicle* (cf. above). In the talk given on 15 March 1964 in Cologne he only mentioned in passing the content on the schema presented to the Council. Only the ideas of his 1962 study, reworked in the article by L. Hertling cited above (cf. above) exerted a certain influence "in incognito."

178. Cf. *SIDIC, In memoriam Cardinal Augustin Bea*, p. 15.

179. Cf. S. Talmon, in *Simposio*, p. 107; against this, J.L. Lichten, in *ibid.*, p. 95, considers that Bea and his collaborators had an extraordinary grasp of what was and was not possible in this extremely sensitive task.

180. Address to the Council immediately prior to the first vote on the schema, *AS*, III/VIII, 650.

Pope John XXIII and hatched a "plot against the church."[181] However, I never heard him complain of this, or indeed even mention it. In the face of such things, he maintained the attitude he had described in his retreat notes when meditating on the Sermon on the Mount: "And in the face of all this: braced against ill-will, scorn, slander and calumny 'for my sake' [= for Christ]. And not only being 'braced' against it, but 'rejoicing and being glad.' The Savior refers to the lot of the prophets; I also have in mind the lot of the apostles and all apostolic workers. 'Blessed are you!' "[182]

However, just as we noted when speaking of his contribution to the Decree on Ecumenism, the most important and decisive contribution sprang from the fact that he had placed all the capital of his prestige and of the trust he enjoyed with the Council fathers at the service of this document. Indeed, he exerted himself on behalf of this document in the Council even more than he had for the one on ecumenism, insisting on presenting it personally in the Council hall *four* times. In this case, the fact that he had dedicated a whole life to study of the sacred scriptures, and particularly the Old Testament, carried special weight.

A French bishop wrote: "For history Cardinal Bea will doubtless be seen as the man chosen by providence who put all his efforts into reconciling the Catholic Church with Judaism, and who set a definitive goal for this movement within the church."[183] I do not think I am wrong in thinking that the most important influence on Cardinal Bea in his performance of this historic task was his relationship with Pope John XXIII. It was the pope who sent Professor Jules Isaac to him in June 1960, asking him to see what could be done. It was also the pope who gave him the formal assignment on 18 September of the same year. And it was again the pope who renewed the assignment in December 1962, restoring the subject to the Council agenda. In this way, the task became a kind of spiritual heritage for the cardinal, and was all the more sacred inasmuch as it had been entrusted to him by the vicar of Christ. Thus it seems right to see Augustin Bea's persevering fidelity in the light of what he wrote in his retreat notes: "I consider the task that has been entrusted to me as the 'mission' given to me by the Savior, which I shall perform with the fullest dedication."[184]

---

181. During the first period of the Council, the fathers were sent the gift of a book of several hundred pages entitled *Plot against the Church* by an author using the pseudonym of Maurice Pinay; cf. Caprile, II, 255, note 14. *Two* translations were published in German, and the campaign continued in various forms right up to the promulgation of the document. For details, cf. ol pp. 467-470; *Freiburger Rundbrief*, LXI-LXIV (July 1965), 19; also Caprile, IV, 89-90.

182. Cf. Med. 1961/V/2; for the original German, cf. *Der Mensch Bea*, p. 112. Although these notes are from his 1961 retreat and are thus prior to the events we are discussing, we can see that Bea was already prepared for such events.

183. Arthur Elchinger, Bishop of Strasbourg, in BM, p. 212. Cf. also the evaluation of the illustrious Jewish exegete, Professor A.J. Heschel: "The rare combination of wisdom, learning, and saintliness of this very great man have made him one of the most outstanding sources of spiritual comfort in an age of so much darkness" (*Bea-Preis*, p. 148). This famous scholar was received repeatedly by the cardinal in Rome from November 1961 onwards, and also in Boston in 1963, and exercised an important influence on the development of *Nostra aetate* as the cardinal's erudite colleague; cf. *America* (10 March 1973), a whole issue dedicated to Rabbi A.J. Heschel.

184. Cf. Med. 1960/VI/2; original German in *Der Mensch Bea*, p. 84.

CHAPTER 9

COUNCIL FATHER

The title of this chapter will undoubtedly have the reader asking in astonishment why there should be yet another chapter on the cardinal as Council father. Surely we have given a sufficient account of his work in the previous chapters, describing all he did for the Decree on Ecumenism and the Declaration on the Relation of the Church to Non-Christian Religions, especially the Jewish people. This is certainly true, but we should bear in mind that there is still a much larger series of contributions to the discussions of the Council than those we have seen so far: leaving aside the contributions considered in the two preceding chapters, there are sixteen further items, including speeches made in the Council hall and lengthy written observations. The speeches amount to about sixty folio-sized pages, and the written observations to over eighty.[1]

Let us once more make some general remarks about the vast range of Council documents to which all this material refers. These contributions concern the liturgy, the Constitutions on Divine Revelation, the Church, and the Church in the Modern World, the Decrees on the Pastoral Office of Bishops, the Church's Missionary Activity, the Up-to-Date Renewal of Religious Life, the Ministry and Life of Priests, and, lastly, the Means of Social Communication. In other words, they concern all the documents except for the Decrees on the Catholic Eastern Churches, the Training of Priests, Christian Education, and the Apostolate of Lay People.[2]

The Impression Made by Bea as Council Father

As *a kind of introduction* to our study of these contributions, we shall first note what other Council fathers have to say about the impression made by the cardinal under various aspects during the course of the Council.[3]

Let us start with a series of very *general* observations. "After Pope John XXIII, he [Cardinal Bea] will live on in the memory of many as the most impressive figure of the Second Vatican Council," according to the Lutheran observer Professor E. Schlink.[4] ". . . by the end, he was generally recognized to

---

1. Cf. the list in Appendix 2; items 1-4, 10, 18 and 19 should be excluded from this calculation.
2. We shall of course leave aside the interventions we have already described, in other words, those concerning the schemata prepared and proposed by the secretariat.
3. There is no need to emphasize that statements of this kind are always somewhat relative; and although the evidence comes from different countries and cultural contexts, we shall try to remain objective.
4. BM, p. 357.

be, if not the most eloquent, certainly the most practical and persuasive speaker in the Council," says Cardinal J.C. Heenan, Archbishop of Westminster.[5] The Bishop of Casale, G. Angrisani, was asked the following question in an interview he gave in 1963: "Out of all the Council fathers, was there one in particular who impressed you with his strong personality and his influence over others?" The interviewee replied: "Many of them impressed me for various reasons. But, for me, pride of place must go to Cardinal Augustin Bea for his combination of moral qualities, long experience, deep culture and human qualities, which were the reasons why the pope rightly chose him to head the Secretariat for Christian Unity."[6] A similar tribute was expressed by the Archbishop of Siena, Mario Castellano, O.P., who came to know Augustin Bea when they both served in the Holy Office in Rome: "I admired Cardinal Bea's interventions, which were courageous, well researched, and heartfelt. Along with his vast cultural background, he possessed a no less vast experience of problems and of people, and along with his knowledge of the Roman world in which he had spent the greater part of his life, he possessed a knowledge of the German world from which he came and with which he had resumed very close contacts."[7]

The well-known Dominican theologian Yves Congar writes: "Cardinal Bea exercised a great influence on the Council (I only knew him during the Council). He enjoyed great prestige on three accounts: (a) because he had been confessor to Pius XII; (b) because of his biblical scholarship; and (c) because of his sincere, peaceful, measured, prudent yet courageous character."[8]

We would now add certain other observations on the impression made by the cardinal's *contribution to Council discussions*. They were "always keenly awaited and decisive, because they had been carefully pondered and were inspired by love for God, the church and souls. . . ."[9] Monsignor Arrighi, who spent decades as Under-Secretary of the Secretariat for Christian Unity, writes: "Before and after the sessions, the fathers vied with one another to approach him and ask for advice; every time he spoke, the Council hall filled up, the refreshment rooms emptied, and everybody listened intently to his words."[10] One of the observer-delegates of the World Lutheran Federation, Professor Kristen Skydsgaard, writes: "When Cardinal Bea addressed the general congregations in St. Peter's, his words received close attention. He spoke elegant Latin, and he was calm, to the point and persuasive."[11] One of the Council fathers

---

5. Homily delivered at the mass for the cardinal on 4 December 1968; ArchWit.

6. ArchWit. I would, however, hesitate to adopt W. Becker's judgment (in BM, p. 195), which places the cardinal immediately after Popes John XXIII and Paul VI.

7. ArchWit.

8. ArchWit. Cf. also *Simposio*, p. 28.

9. The Italian M. Tinti, Bishop of Fabriano, ArchWit; likewise Claudio Gaddi, Bishop of Bergamo, ArchWit.

10. J.-F. Arrighi, "Il Cardinale Agostino Bea, primo Presidente del Segretariato per l'Unione dei Cristiani," in Caprile, V, p. 716. I recall having heard a number of remarks from participants in the general congregations to the effect that when a speech by Cardinal Bea was announced the refreshment rooms emptied because people wanted to hear him.

11. The Danish Professor K.E. Skydsgaard, in BM, p. 360.

writes that he had only "occasional personal contacts with him in the context of the Council, but these were enough to make me feel the Johannine qualities of the man, his priestly meekness and his prophetic certainty."[12]

In view of these observations, it is easy to see that the cardinal's *interventions* constituted *a reference-point* and provided orientation for a number of Council fathers. One of the observer-delegates tells us that they had heard that when the Council fathers were aware of the difficulty of certain problems, quite a number of them would try to find out how Cardinal Bea would vote in order to obtain guidance.[13] Yves Congar describes the influence exerted by the cardinal in the Council as follows: "He also influenced the Council with his whole manner of being, his personal style. He was thin, with rounded shoulders, and gave an impression of transparency. He greeted people affably and kindly. I think that if the president of the secretariat had been a violent, impetuous man, he would have aroused equally violent opposition. Cardinal Bea's meekness and obstinate patience served his cause better than any aggressive kind of force would have done."[14]

His *open attitude* to problems is often emphasized. Cardinal Bea was "almost the representative or symbol of the open current in the Council."[15] An Italian bishop, who had been Father Bea's student at the Pontifical Biblical Institute, notes the difference between the "revered teacher" of his student days and the Council father: "The teacher rigidly bound to tradition, albeit with an openness to what were sometimes innovations, had given way to a Council father with a very open—almost avant-garde—perspective, who was attentive to the signs of the times."[16] This openness was in surprising contrast with his age. The Cardinal Archbishop of Munich, Julius Döpfner, one of the four Moderators of the Council, declared in a homily that the cardinal was "one of the oldest of the Council fathers, yet, very admirably, one of the most youthful."[17]

Various people emphasize *the prestige* the cardinal enjoyed, and also *its spiritual basis*. Thus an Italian bishop writes: "I approached the prelate, and greatly appreciated the affability that put everyone at their ease. His speeches and contributions to the Council were marked by such great humility that they were accepted even by those who might have held divergent opinions."[18] The then Archbishop of Santiago de Veraguas (now of Panama), Marco McGrath, writes: "I was surprised by the profound kindness that he could demonstrate toward people whose points of view he obviously could not share and which he considered to be seriously harmful to the church, along with a firmness in

---

12. B. Fratteggiani, Archbishop of Camerino (Italy), ArchWit.
13. Cf. J.R. Nelson, in *Christian Century* (11 December 1968), p. 1563; cf. also the well-known Swiss ecumenist, L. Vischer, in BM, p. 368.
14. ArchWit. In *Simposio*, pp. 27-28, the same theologian compares him with various leading personalities who exercised a major influence in the Councils of past centuries.
15. This is once again Yves Congar, ArchWit.
16. T.G. Cioli, O.Carm., Bishop of Arezzo, ArchWit.
17. ArchWit. The conciliar theologian and consultant Hans Quasten writes: "Rarely have I seen such mental clarity at such an advanced age. In him this was something charismatic" (ArchWit, to be found under the name J. Schmitz).
18. Paolo Ghizzoni, Bishop of San Miniato, ArchWit.

maintaining the position that he was convinced was right. It was an exercise of true Christian charity that I shall never forget."[19] The above-cited Archbishop Castellano of Siena writes in similar terms in connection with the cardinal's attitude in the face of contradiction from others: "Even after being created cardinal, he remained a humble, reserved, simple and sincere religious, who drew on prayer and listening to the word of God for the strength of faith and love he needed in order to serve the church he loved so much, and serve it despite all the trials and opposition that he too had to face."[20]

In his brief portrait of Cardinal Bea, the English Jesuit theologian Bernard Leeming cites an English Council father: "An English bishop of whom I asked some account of Cardinal Bea said this: 'He is a man who thinks things out in the presence of God. He speaks measuredly and with balanced charity. He has a mind of his own and can speak it. He weighs up everything, but I feel that before speaking he has weighed up everything in the chapel.' And the bishop added that Bea is a holy and a priestly man."[21]

Let us conclude this introductory section by repeating what we said at the outset, namely that our purpose was not that of using the tributes we cite to produce a full portrait of the cardinal as Council father. The number and breadth of these statements was too restricted for this, and our intention was rather that of offering the reader an introduction in the form of a series of impressions. The portrait itself will be the result of the chapter as a whole.

At this point we must consider *how best to proceed* in order to give an idea of the rich, complex spectrum of the cardinal's spoken and written contributions. It may be helpful to make a distinction between specific content, in other words the cardinal's ideas on various subjects, such as the liturgy, the church or the ministry of bishops, on the one hand, and the more constant features that we can observe in a number of his interventions (if not all), on the other. Both aspects are important and informative in their respective ways. We shall therefore start by describing his specific ideas on *individual subjects*, and then move on to consideration of certain *more general aspects* of his contributions.[22]

As regards *the first question*, it seems obvious that we cannot go into this fully, as it would in a way call on us to give at least a summary of the whole complex development of the numerous documents to which the cardinal contributed. *The second question* puts us in a similar position: in order to reply, we would have to carry out an extremely detailed study for each individual point, comparing the various stages in the development of each document with the very numerous speeches and written opinions of the Council fathers; above all,

19. M.G. McGrath, C.S.C., Archbishop of Panama, ArchWit.
20. ArchWit.
21. B. Leeming, *Agostino Cardinal Bea* (Notre Dame, Ind., 1964), pp. 47-48. The author told me privately that this statement came from F.J. Grimshaw, Archbishop of Birmingham.
22. The setting forth of the individual subjects would lead us to ask the following questions for each intervention: (a) How did it fit into the general context of conciliar discussion on the schema in question? (b) What were its results, i.e., to what extent were the cardinal's suggestions taken up in the drafting of the final texts of the various documents?

we would have to have at our disposal the minutes of the meetings of the commissions responsible for the various documents.

In certain exceptional cases we do have statements that enable us to assess the influence exercised by the cardinal. In other cases, we are able to observe that a suggestion made by the cardinal found its way into the final text of a document; however, when we mention this, it is a simple observation, and is not intended as a claim that the modification was solely or even in part due to the cardinal's contribution.

In Support of Liturgical Renewal

As can be seen from the list given in Appendix 2, the cardinal spoke about the liturgy on three occasions: first, on general principles,[23] then on the chapter concerning the eucharist, and lastly on that concerning the divine office (or what is now called the liturgy of the hours). His observations on general principles were for the most part concerned with questions of method,[24] and we shall deal with them in another context, so that here we shall be concentrating on the two latter subjects.

1. His intervention concerning *the eucharist*[25] was particularly rich in pointers. We shall try to collect these elements under various headings, starting with some major doctrinal elements. The cardinal observed in general that the schema was "much less clear and precise" than the equivalent text of the Council of Trent. The schema spoke of the eucharist as "paschal banquet," but we should remember that the eucharist is also a sacrifice.[26] Furthermore, "the Council of

23. Cf. *AS*, I/I, 407-408. We should bear in mind the method followed in the *Acta Synodalia*: first they give the text of the speech as transcribed from the tape-recording; this is followed by a list of variations from the written text submitted to the secretariat of the Council, although if the differences are too great, the entire written text is given. When giving the content of the cardinal's speeches, we shall follow the spoken text as a general rule, and if we take a point from the written text we shall make explicit mention of this fact.

24. For example, the author observed that four preparatory bodies had dealt with the liturgy: apart from the Commission for the Liturgy, those for the Eastern Churches and the Missions, and also the Secretariat for Christian Unity. It would therefore appear necessary to coordinate this work, or else to draw up a schema confined to the general principles of the liturgy of the church (and not only of the Latin rite!), leaving the field clear for the various bodies to set forth the parts that involved each of them.

25. We would observe that here the cardinal was not referring back to the contributions of other fathers, but was expressing his own remarks on the schema. For the individual speeches, we shall give not only the bibliographical reference, but also indicate the general congregation and the date; the speech in question is GC 10 (30 October), *AS*, I/II, 22-26. In view of the relative brevity of the speeches, when describing their content we shall indicate the precise page only in the case of direct citations. For the convenience of readers who do not have access to the original text, we shall also indicate the summary published by G. Caprile; for example, for the speech in question, Caprile, II, 104-105. Translations do exist of some of the contributions, and these are indicated in the appendix giving the list of the cardinal's contributions.

26. This request was accepted, and the final text takes as its starting point the eucharist precisely as sacrifice (no. 47); cf. *AS*, I/I, 279. The cardinal was certainly aware that these remarks on

Trent strongly stresses the fact that the mass is not only a sacrifice of praise, but also a propitiatory sacrifice."[27]

Speaking on various aspects of *the liturgy of the word*, the cardinal drew on the pre-conciliar experience he had acquired in the context of the Commission for Liturgical Reform, and also on the talk on the pastoral importance of the word of God in the liturgy that he gave in Assisi in 1956, at the 1st Congress on Pastoral Liturgy.[28] With regard to the suggestion made in the schema that the faithful should be offered more of the treasury of the word of God in the readings, the cardinal emphasized the need to make *a real change* in the present choice of *passages to be read*.[29] He also called for the homily to be *mandatory* rather than simply being recommended, and in support of this request he cited the decisions of the recent Synod of the Diocese of Rome.[30] The cardinal also insisted that *the prayer of the faithful* should be made by the celebrant *together with* the faithful before the offertory; this could replace the so-called "Leonian prayers" which were "not very liturgical, to say the least."[31]

The subject of *concelebration* provoked some particularly impassioned discussion. Cardinal A. Ottaviani spoke just before Bea, in energetic opposition to what was proposed in the schema.[32] Cardinal Bea simply stated his support for the statement in the schema that concelebration was "an ancient practice both of the Latin and of the Eastern Church," but he did demand that the list of reasons for concelebration should avoid the impression that it was being allowed simply in the case of a lack of time or availability of space when there were numerous celebrants.[33]

Even stronger passions were aroused by the subject of *communion under both kinds*. Cardinal A. Ottaviani had spoken just before him, appealing to the fact that this proposal had been "almost unanimously rejected" in the Central Preparatory Commission.[34] Cardinal Bea, however, chose to refer to what had been said the day before by Cardinal E. Ruffini, Archbishop of Palermo, who had cited all the edicts of former centuries forbidding this practice, in order to defend the *status quo*.[35] Bea's speech was quite long, partly because it involved an eminently ecumenical subject. He made a survey of all the historical docu-

---

the mass as sacrifice (and the following one on the mass as propitiatory sacrifice) would upset certain observers from the Reformed tradition, but for him it was a question of frankly setting forth the whole of Catholic truth.

27. *AS*, I/II, 22.
28. Cf. Biblio. 111, and pp. 145-148 above.
29. Cf. *AS*, I/II, 23.
30. The final text of no. 52 accedes to the request in part, stipulating that the homily should not be omitted on Sundays and holy days of obligation, except for serious reasons.
31. These were certain prayers prescribed by Leo XIII which were recited at the end of the mass.
32. Cf. *AS*, I/II, 19-21.
33. Cf. *ibid.*, 23.
34. Cf. *ibid.*, 18. The well-known German liturgist, J. Wagner, who had considerable dealings with Cardinal Bea over liturgical questions, states, in BM, p. 209, that the latter had prepared his contribution in the night before the general congregation in question, and that he saw it as a kind of closing word to the whole discussion.
35. Cf. *AS*, I/I, 600-601.

ments and events in order to show that, on the contrary, there were serious reasons why the previous dispositions could be changed. He began by observing: "Providing the presence of Christ under both kinds is accepted, the question is not doctrinal but disciplinary. The Council of Trent clearly recognizes this point when it states that the change in custom was introduced for serious and justified reasons, and that its dispositions on this point cannot be changed arbitrarily without its authority." The cardinal at once drew the conclusion that "these dispositions can be changed for serious reasons,"[36] and then continued his line of reasoning as follows: "In the Council of Trent itself, the votes of the two papal legates were cast in favor of granting the chalice; in 1564, two years after the decree, Pius IV granted the use of the chalice to various German provinces; and at the Council the votes in favor of granting the chalice were seventy, with eighty-seven against, so that the latter had a very small majority. Hence, if the question is brought up again today, this is in no way contrary to the teaching of the church or any unchangeable ruling. The Council of Constance, which was referred to here yesterday [by Cardinal Ruffini], condemned the dogmatic error of the Hussites, but did not teach that communion under both kinds was illicit. In the same fifteenth century during which the Council of Constance was held, on Easter Day the popes used to give communion under both kinds to lay people as well, in their private chapel. In 1548, Paul III granted, for Germany, the use of the chalice to those who asked for it with devotion and explicitly professed their faith in the real presence in both kinds. This is the mind and the tradition of the church."[37]

2. The well-known liturgist, Josef Jungmann, S.J., tells us that the cardinal made a particularly fortunate observation concerning *the comprehension of the rites*.[38] The schema spoke of the church's concern that the faithful should not be passive, silent spectators at the eucharist, "but should have a good understanding of the rites and the prayers, and thus participate actively, consciously and piously."[39] The cardinal suggested the wording "so that they may have a good understanding of the rites, the prayers and *the mystery they express*."[40] The above-mentioned liturgist observes: "The commission jumped at this suggestion, and in this way the definitive text of no. 48 was attained."[41] This same liturgist continues his account as follows: "I myself, in Group X which was entrusted with reform work after the Council, repeatedly referred to this expression, emphasizing that it meant that something should also be done about the

36. *AS*, I/II, 23.
37. Cf. Caprile's summary, II, 104-105, which is basically faithful. It is well-known that communion under both kinds was subsequently authorized, and it is now becoming more and more frequent.
38. ArchWit. This is the author, among other works, of the classic *Missarum Sollemnia*.
39. *AS*, I/I, 279.
40. *AS*, I/II, 22. We have cited the written text here, since the spoken text is less clear.
41. ArchWit. Cf. the original Latin text of *SC*, 48: "... per ritus et preces id [mysterium] bene intellegentes. . . ." This element is not brought out in either of the English translations normally used, which should read as follows: "... through a good understanding, they should comprehend the mystery and so take part. . . ."

canon of the mass. . . . This eventually led to the vernacular (for the canon too) and to new eucharistic prayers."[42]

3. The cardinal's intervention concerning *the divine office* was of a different kind. He took as his starting-point the observation that the present context was that of an Ecumenical Council. This meant that the fathers should bear the whole church in mind, and not just the West and the Latin rite; furthermore, given the numerous serious problems to be faced by the Council, it should avoid going into too much detail, but leave this to a post-conciliar commission and the work of specialists. He went on to clarify the matter with a few examples, saying that it was not the Council's task to deal with the restoration of the hymns in their original form, however necessary this might be, or with the revision of the readings for the saints so as to bring them into line with historical truth, or with the revision of the psalter of Pius XII, inasmuch as this revision had already been decreed by the pope three years previously. The Council should instead concentrate on principles and general norms—and all the more so in view of the fact that there were various forms of the office in existence in the Latin church itself, for example, the monastic and Ambrosian traditions. There were also various forms of the office in existence that were proper to the eastern churches, whereas the schema dealt almost exclusively with the Roman breviary.

Cardinal Bea then explained his ideas in greater detail: the Council should lay down *the general norms that are valid for all forms of the divine office* in both West and East, in other words, those concerning its nature as a prayer performed by priests and religious in the name of the whole church, its merits, and its usefulness and necessity for the whole church, particularly for the priestly and apostolic life. There should then be a word about spreading the prayer over the course of the day in order to sanctify the whole day. Mention should be made of the obligation to recite the divine office, either in choir or outside it. The relation between private prayer and recitation of the divine office should be dealt with, whereas this was hardly mentioned in the schema, despite the fact that, as Cardinal Lefèbvre had observed, this was of supreme importance at the present time.[43] Lastly, the participation of the faithful should be spoken of.[44]

4. At this point, the cardinal touched on the question of the reform of *the divine office of the Latin rite*, referring to the enormous quantity of preparatory work that had been done from the time of Pope Pius XII onward. In point of fact, in 1956 a survey of Catholic bishops had been made in this connection, and in 1957 the 341 replies received had been condensed into a 136-page memorandum.[45] These replies had shown that there was a general agreement on the need for revision but very great disagreement on details. Since it would be difficult for a discussion in

42. ArchWit.

43. The contribution of Cardinal Joseph Lefèbvre is found in *AS*, I/II, 396-397. (The cardinal should not be confused with the traditionalist archbishop whose Christian name is Marcel.)

44. Cf. *AS*, I/II, 412.

45. On this detail, cf. also Caprile, II, 135, note. A.-G. Martimort remarks that this was the first time that official mention had been made of this work, and it had the helpful result that this preparatory work was placed at the disposal of the conciliar commission; ArchWit, p. 10.

the Council to add any new elements, the work should be entrusted to *a post-con-ciliar liturgical commission*, which should be set up as soon as possible.[46]

The well-known German liturgist *J. Wagner*, for his part, writes: "It was an unforgettable moment for me when he [Bea], during the discussion of the *Ordo Missae* and the need for reform of the Roman canon, stated with total clarity and without beating around the bush that the vernacular was also necessary in the context of the eucharistic prayer—and this was before anything of this kind had even been imagined" (BM, p. 209).

Divine Revelation: Support for a Pastoral and Ecumenical Approach

Here we are dealing with the schema *On the Sources of Revelation*, which was the subject that provoked the most discussion in the first period of the Council, as we saw in one of our previous chapters.[47]

1. Let us start by taking a look at the cardinal's *first intervention*, which was made *prior* to the pope's decision to entrust the schema to a joint commission composed of the Theological Commission and the secretariat for reworking.[48]

The speaker began with a brief word of praise for the work that had gone into the preparation of the schema, but immediately went on to state: "I regret that I am forced to say that I cannot accept the text in its present form." He then gave the reasons for this statement. In the first place, it "does not correspond to the aim the pope set for the Council," and the speaker cited the message the Council fathers addressed to the whole world at the beginning of their work, underwriting the pope's ideas.[49] He also cited what Pope John XXIII had said in his speech at the opening of the Council: ". . . from the renewed, serene, and tranquil adherence to all the teaching of the Church in its entirety and preciseness, . . . the Christian, Catholic and apostolic spirit of the whole world expects a step forward toward a doctrinal penetration and a formation of consciences in faithful and perfect conformity to the authentic doctrine. . . ."[50] The cardinal observed that "this is the pastoral aim," and then went on to say that the pope had added that this doctrine "should be studied and expounded through the methods of research and through

---

46. We would give two further evaluations of Bea as a liturgist in the Council. The well-known French liturgist *A.-G. Martimort* writes that the cardinal's contributions to discussion on the liturgy were sometimes disappointing, and he cites the following example: "The cardinal complained that the mass was being presented as the presence of the paschal mystery" (ArchWit, p. 9); if we examine the exact terms of the cardinal's observation, we see that it was solely to the effect that the Christian people would find it difficult to understand the expression, inasmuch as the term "paschal" is nowadays used only to refer to the resurrection (cf. *AS*, I/II, 22).

47. Cf. pp. 416-419 above.

48. GC 19 (4 November), *AS*, I/III, 48-52; Caprile, II, 159 (rather brief). Although various other fathers had made speeches before the cardinal spoke, he did not refer to what they had said, but simply moved on to a direct assessment of the schema.

49. Cf. *AS*, I/I, 254; Caprile, II, 50.

50. *CDD*, p. 864. English translation in Abbott (gen. ed.), *The Documents of Vatican II*, p. 715.

the literary forms of modern thought, . . . everything being measured in the forms and proportions of a magisterium which is predominantly pastoral in character."[51]

The speaker moved on to *an examination of the schema* in the light of these principles: "It is completely lacking in pastoral character. . . . It is not written with a view to contemporary men and women, to the souls entrusted by Christ to the church today, but rather to theological schools, or sometimes even . . . (as I shall say later) to a single theologian who may have said something erroneous."[52]

The speaker then gave examples in support of his statement, starting with the following observation: "The schema begins by speaking of the sources of revelation without any introduction on revelation as such; now, unless I am mistaken, today's world is so full of atheism that it desperately needs to be told about revelation and its importance."[53]

Another example is then given: "Almost nothing is said about the fundamental importance of revelation and holy scripture, especially for the church, for the life of the faithful and for all people today," whereas the schema repeats things that are no longer even questioned in the church,[54] or things that are only of interest to schools of theology and cannot be defined by a Council.[55]

Lastly, "the schema in no way takes the ecumenical question into account. It is not enough to state Catholic doctrine. It must be stated in such a way that our non-Catholic brethren can understand it and also its underlying reasons."[56]

The cardinal spoke of another point that he found important as a professional exegete: "The schema speaks a great deal about exegetes, especially in connection with the New Testament. There is only one mention that can be construed as recognition of the work accomplished by modern exegesis, whereas, as Pope Pius XII stated in his encyclical *Divino afflante Spiritu*, the work performed in the past fifty years has been really immense—as is also recognized by non-Catholic authors. However, the schema speaks with some degree of suspicion, and is motivated by a certain fear of errors, without really giving detailed consideration to the problems involved."[57]

The speaker *concluded* as follows: "Unless we are to replace this schema entirely, the text must be reworked in great—very great—depth. It must become shorter, clearer, less ambiguous, more pastoral and more ecumenical. If this is done, the schema can certainly constitute a great benefit for the modern world."[58]

---

51. *Ibid.* Here we are not following the official Latin text, but the original Italian text as published in the *OssRom* and cited in Caprile, II, 4-5, since this appears to be the original.

52. *AS*, I/III, 49.

53. *Ibid.*, p. 50.

54. For example, the question of the authors of the gospels, or the doctrinal authority of the Latin Vulgate translation.

55. For example, the question of the nature of the inspiration of sacred scripture, a treatise found in theology manuals.

56. *AS*, I/III, 50.

57. *Ibid.*, pp. 50-51.

58. We have followed the spoken text here, which in this case shows such considerable differences from the written text that instead of using their usual system of listing differences, the editors

2. During the third period of the Council *the revised text* reached the Council hall. It now bore the simple title *Divine Revelation*. The various speakers included Cardinal Bea, who dealt particularly with the last three chapters, which speak of the Old and New Testaments, and also of the position and function of the scriptures in the life of the church.[59]

In the first place, the speaker informed his listeners of what had happened to the schema immediately after it was first discussed. He explained that, as was generally known, the text the fathers had before them was in part the work of the joint commission composed of the Theological Commission and the Secretariat for Christian Unity, and in part the work of the Theological Commission on its own; in point of fact, the joint commission had completed its own work in the spring of 1963.[60] The resulting draft had been sent out to the Council fathers for a preliminary examination, but the observations sent back had been examined by the Theological Commission *alone*, as was explicitly stated in the general report.[61] On this basis, the speaker made a preliminary statement about his approach: "In what I have to say, I shall take no account of whether the passages that seem problematic to me are the work of the joint commission or of the Theological Commission on its own. I shall present my ideas on the text as we have it before us, without taking into account who drafted it."[62]

The speaker *began his assessment* with the following words: "I am sincerely happy to be able to state that I very much like the schema as a whole. It is most important to preserve the praiseworthy qualities of the text."[63] The cardinal went on to list these qualities.

(a) "The fundamental elements of doctrine on divine revelation, scripture and tradition are very well expounded. It is unnecessary to emphasize that in the present world-situation this is of major importance. . . . Thus the schema is extremely useful for the pastoral ministry."[64]

(b) "The *positive tone* of the presentation must be praised. . . . In my humble opinion, the best way of refuting errors is to give a positive presentation of Catholic doctrine."[65]

(c) The text very properly avoids going into questions that are still under discussion among Catholics, and presents what is common to all.

(d) "Lastly, a major quality of the presentation is that the points are demon-

---

of the *Acta Synodalia* first gave the spoken text in its entirety and then the written text. With regard to the latter, the most important point is that it gives a nineteen-line list of the points that ought to be taken into consideration when redrafting the schema; *AS*, I/III, 52.

59. GC 94 (5 October), *AS*, III/III, 284-287; Caprile, IV, 133.

60. Cf. p. 420 above.

61. Cf. *AS*, III/III, 70, note. It should be observed that one and a half years had passed between the conclusion of the work of the joint commission and the discussion we are now examining. In our presentation of the cardinal's contribution we shall combine elements of the spoken text with those of the written text, inasmuch as neither of the two is complete.

62. *AS*, III/III, 284.

63. *Ibid.*, p. 285.

64. *Ibid.*.

65. *Ibid.*.

strated above all with proof-texts from sacred scripture and from the earliest tradition. Indeed, the whole presentation is expressed for the most part in biblical language, and many biblical texts or at least expressions are cited. All this makes it easier for our non-Catholic brethren to understand the doctrine presented, and—at least in part—to accept it."[66]

Despite the praise, various aspects of the schema needed *improvement*. Leaving aside the minor points, we shall concentrate on the main one, which concerned the Old Testament. "I feel that *the importance of the books of the Old Testament* has not been presented in a happy or complete manner, when it is stated [in the schema] that disciples of Christ must read them above all because they express a lively sense of God, who is most holy and clement."[67] In point of fact, the Old Testament contains much other teaching on subjects that are more typical features of it: the justice of God, his providence, his omniscience, his power, etc.; in the didactic books we also find rich teaching on the religious and moral life of human beings, on virtues and vices, on sin and its punishment. Lastly, the Old Testament is "a school of prayer unique of its kind, offering us that marvelous collection of prayers that constitutes the psalter."[68] The cardinal's written text also states: "We must also add the pastoral importance of this point [the teaching on the qualities of the Old Testament], because the Old Testament is often disparaged and neglected as being less perfect—not to mention what the propagators of antisemitism have to say about it."[69]

3. We have not yet come to the end of our account of Cardinal Bea's contribution to this important conciliar document. Following the order of the document itself, we must now consider his role in the formulation of three important points: the question of scripture and tradition (no. 9), that of the inerrancy of sacred scripture (no. 11), and, lastly, that of the historical character of the gospels (no. 19). However, since the cardinal's contribution to this latter point was the fruit of study covering several years, we shall consider it first.

(a) The subject in question was as follows. The schema on divine revelation, no. 19, established *the historical character of the four gospels* and also explained that this is a particular type of historical character. We should start by saying that although the cardinal's contribution was fairly *indirect*, it was still extremely important and valid. On this particular point the Council document in fact drew to a large extent on the instruction of the Pontifical Biblical Commission *Sancta mater ecclesia* of 21 April 1964, "on the historical truth of the gospels."[70]

---

66. *Ibid.*
67. *Ibid.*, pp. 285-286. Compare with the text of the schema in *AS*, III/III, 94.
68. *AS*, III/III, 286.
69. For criticism of antisemitic positions, cf. the article the cardinal published in the 1940s, Biblio. 42. The suggestion was favorably received, inasmuch as a phrase was inserted in *DV*, 15, saying that the books of the Old Testament "are a storehouse of sublime teaching on God and of sound wisdom on human life, as well as a wonderful treasury of prayers." The cardinal also added two and a half pages of written remarks on minor points.
70. *AAS*, LVI (1964), 715. It is interesting to note that although the Council document is prior to the instruction, the article in question (no. 19) begins with the same words.

We shall now give the main points that the Council document drew from the instruction. If we compare the definitive draft of the document with the preceding version, we find a series of changes—printed in italics—which describe the principles that throw light on the particular historical character of the gospels,[71] namely: the fact that the apostles handed down the deeds and words of Jesus with the enhanced understanding they possessed after the resurrection and the ascension of the Lord and the coming of the Holy Spirit; furthermore, the fact that when writing the gospels, their authors selected, summarized and explained with reference to the situation of the churches. Now these points were derived from the instruction in question.

In one of our previous chapters, we saw the fundamental influence exercised by the cardinal on the development of the instruction in question and above all the deep influence his little book *The Historicity of the Gospels*, produced in 1962, had on it.[72] Stanislas Lyonnet has made a comparative study of *The Historicity of the Gospels* and the instruction *Sancta mater ecclesia*.[73] He observes in the first place that the cardinal showed that it is legitimate to apply the doctrine of Pius XII's encyclical *Divino afflante Spiritu* on literary genres to the New Testament as well,[74] a question that was the subject of much controversy at the time. Since the encyclical mentioned the historical genre as one of the literary genres, this naturally suggested the possibility of a special historical genre for the gospels. Furthermore, the cardinal's study explicitly established the principle we saw above: ". . . the apostles explained the message of Christ and the events after the gift of Pentecost, and this explanation was clearly made in the light of the mature faith they possessed at that time."[75] Almost immediately after this, Bea also established the second of the above-mentioned principles, that concerning "the application of the accounts, and especially of the teaching, to the needs of the audience."[76] As can be seen, the cardinal had to a great extent prepared *the basic principles* on which the instruction rests.

(b) During the last period of the Council, the cardinal was once more involved in discussion of the schema on divine revelation, this time on the direct request of the pope. The schema had now been definitively examined by the Theological Commission, but there were three points that the pope considered in need of more satisfactory formulation: apart from the question of the historical character of the gospels, there was the question of the relationship between scripture and tradition, and the manner in which the inerrancy of the scriptures was defined. After a great deal of personal study and consultation of theologians,[77] he decided

---

71. Cf. *AS*, III/III, 98.
72. Cf. Biblio. 221. For the cardinal's influence on the instruction, cf. pp. 440-441 above.
73. S. Lyonnet, "Le Cardinal Bea et le développement des études bibliques," *Rivista Biblica* (1968), 371-392.
74. Biblio. 221, pp. 14-15.
75. *Ibid.*, p. 34.
76. *Ibid.*
77. Cf. the article by Caprile, V, 325-340, entitled "Tre emendamenti allo schema sulla rivelazione" (= "Three Amendments to the Schema on Revelation"); I believe the author is writing on the

to ask the commission to reexamine these points. The pope was very well aware of the sensitive approach required if he was to intervene in this way, and he thus gave his reasons in detail in a letter dated 18 October, the content of which is summarized as follows by G. Caprile in his detailed study of the matter: the pope gratefully recognized what had been accomplished and had no intention of making substantial alterations to the work of the commission, "but simply of improving it on certain points of great doctrinal importance, so that he could serenely pronounce the approval required in order for the decree in question to be promulgated, for the subject entailed very great responsibility to the church and his own conscience. The Holy Father also desired that Cardinal Bea, President of the Secretariat for Christian Unity, who was formerly a member, as joint president, of the special joint commission set up by John XXIII, be invited to the next meeting of the commission."[78]

Even though the request came from on high, it was still a rather unpleasant task for the cardinal. It was true that he was not being sent in as a kind of papal plenipotentiary, since the pope also sent a series of statements that reflected his thought on controversial points. Despite this, the cardinal's presence in a way symbolized the pope's intervention, and despite the invitation of the letter to the commission to "consider the suggestions freely," there was a general fear that the pope wished to impose something.[79] The cardinal followed the pope's wishes, but was careful to declare to the commission that he was taking part in it in an exclusively personal capacity, since the questions on the agenda had not been discussed by the secretariat.[80]

(i) The first point to be discussed concerned the relation between *scripture and tradition*. The question was whether sacred scripture contained, at least implicitly, *the whole* of revelation, so that tradition simply interpreted this deposit, or whether there were some truths found only in tradition.[81] This question was the subject of much discussion among Catholics, which was why Pope John XXIII had decided when creating the joint commission that the Council was *not* to deal with the matter but to leave it open. The problem was that of finding a suitable way of expressing this. No less than seven alternatives had been suggested to the commission. The cardinal declared "in a personal capacity" that he preferred the third, which read: "Thus the church derives its certainty concerning all revealed things, not from scripture alone." After various vicissitudes, this formula obtained two-thirds of the votes.[82]

(ii) The second point under discussion concerned *the inerrancy of sacred scripture*, or, as it is often expressed, the truth of sacred scripture (no. 11), in other words, the fact that since the Bible is the inspired word of God, it teaches

---

basis of documents and specific information. For the consultations made by the pope, cf. *ibid.*, p. 326.

78. *Ibid.*, p. 331.

79. Cf. *ibid.*, p. 332, note 9bis.

80. After an incorrect item of information was published by the French newspaper *La Croix*, we sent them a correction; cf. Caprile, V, 332, note 8.

81. For a more precise explanation of this simple formula, cf. *ibid.*, pp. 327-333.

82. Cf. *ibid.*, p. 332.

faithfully and "without error" the truth that God wished to communicate to us by means of it. The commission had formerly adopted the expression: "It must be held that the books of sacred scripture . . . teach in an unblemished and faithful manner, completely and without error, *the salvific truth*," in other words, the truth about our salvation.[83] Various Council fathers, and also the pope, felt that this expression was open to misinterpretation, so that people could claim that scripture is immune from error only where it teaches truths concerning our salvation, thus limiting its inerrancy and admitting the possibility of error in matters not concerning our salvation.

As he had done on other points, the pope had consulted various theologians on this point,[84] including the cardinal. In his letter to the commission, the pope stressed that his worries on this point were even greater than those concerning the relation between scripture and tradition.[85] The cardinal felt personally involved in this question, because it touched on a subject that he had taught for several decades at the Pontifical Biblical Institute in the context of the question of the inspiration of sacred scripture. He stated his *total opposition to the expression*, asking that the word "salvific" be omitted. He explained that it was true that sacred scripture was given to men for their salvation. It was also true that the commission had explicitly rejected the interpretation of the expression "the salvific truth" as meaning that its inerrancy was restricted to matters of faith and morals. However, the expression was still ambiguous and was too open to subsequent misuse by people who could claim that it meant that these were the limits of the inerrancy of scripture.[86] Nevertheless, part of the commission was anxious that it should be stated that sacred scripture was given for man's salvation. After a series of votes, a new expression was therefore agreed on, and this is now found in the final text, which reads as follows: ". . . the books of scripture, firmly, faithfully and without error, teach that truth which God, for the sake of our salvation, wished to see confided to the sacred scriptures."[87]

(iii) The last point raised by the pope concerned the section on the historical

---

83. For the text, cf. *AS*, IV/I, 355.

84. On the consultation of theologians, cf. Caprile, V, 332.

85. Cf. *ibid.*, p. 335.

86. According to *ibid.*, among the arguments used by the cardinal was the fact that the expression "*salvific* truth" was not found in the text formerly approved by the joint commission. For the cardinal's opinion, cf. Arch. Lb 3/6/2 and 3/6/3.

87. *DV*, 11. Cf. Caprile, V, 335-336. In passing we would note the statement of Yves Congar on this point. He speaks of the echo created by the contribution of the cardinal who, he says, launched a severe attack against the expression "salvific truth" and also told Father S. Tromp, S.J., Secretary of the Theological Commission, that he [Bea] had fought all his life against the idea he believed lay behind the expression. According to Congar, this contribution was judged harshly even by the cardinal's close collaborators (ArchWit, diary entry for 24 October 1965, p. 757). Lyonnet, "Le Cardinal Bea et le développement des études bibliques," p. 391, is of a different opinion in the final analysis: "Even those to whom the cardinal's contribution could have seemed somewhat untimely later recognized that it had in fact produced a happy result: while the formula proposed and adopted by the commission did, as the cardinal had requested, avoid the expression 'salvific truth,' it maintained the link between biblical truth and the plan of salvation very clearly and less ambiguously."

character of the gospels, where he questioned the phrase chosen to express the intention of the authors of the gospels to relate *the objective truth* about the life and preaching of Jesus. The expression adopted by the commission, which stated that the authors' account was "true and sincere,"[88] seemed weak, inasmuch as it might be taken as referring only to the authors' *subjective* honesty and sincerity. The pope suggested that the words in question should be changed to read that the authors relate "things that are true and worthy of historical faith." Cardinal Bea spoke in favor of this suggestion. Others observed against it that many Protestants, especially Rudolf Bultmann and his followers, identify historical faith "with the act of the believer who projects his existential experience onto a fictitious account, from which it is then the task of the learned exegete to expurgate all mythical elements."[89] It was therefore proposed that the words "true and sincere" be preserved, but that the following phrase be inserted a little earlier in the text: "*the historicity* of which it [the church] unhesitatingly affirms." This suggestion was adopted.[90]

We can *in conclusion* say that it has been a lengthy matter to follow the cardinal's various contributions in connection with the conciliar document on divine revelation, from the first negative assessment of the initial schema through to the last minor but doctrinally important finishing touches. We can maybe claim that apart from the three documents proposed by the secretariat itself, the conciliar Constitution on Divine Revelation was the one that most exercised Cardinal Bea, and also the one to which he made the greatest contribution, not only as joint president of the relative joint commission,[91] but also personally.

Bea's Work for the Schema on the Church, the Central Subject of the Council

In his inaugural address for the second period of the Council, Paul VI stated that the first aim of the Council was "the church's knowledge, or, if you prefer, consciousness of self."[92] As we shall see, Cardinal Bea had sensed this central position that the subject of the church occupied in the Council as early as his intervention of December 1962, and this is why he dedicated four speeches and thirty-eight pages of detailed written observations to this schema alone.[93]

---

88. According to the classical meaning of the words, "true and authentic things."
89. Caprile, V, 338.
90. Cf. *ibid.*. Thus the commission showed that it felt truly free in its decisions, introducing an alternative solution, after a serene examination and comparison. To some extent something similar also occurred concerning the question of "the salvific truth."
91. We did not feel that our task extended to explaining the specific contribution of the secretariat to this important conciliar document. In this connection, the reader can consult the extremely authoritative study by a very close collaborator of the secretariat at this time: J. Feiner, *La Révélation divine* (Paris, 1968), I, 119-153.
92. Cf. *CDD*, p. 906.
93. Fifty-four pages in all.

1. The first schema on this subject presented to the Council in 1962 was produced by the Theological Commission and—like the schema on the sources of revelation—it was the subject of hot debate from the very beginning. The cardinal did not contribute to the discussion until the third day, after about thirty other Council fathers had spoken.[94] He started with a reflection on *the importance* of the schema, first what could be called its historical importance, and then its importance for the Council. As regards *the historical aspect*, he recalled that the subject had first been raised in the sixteenth century, but that unfortunately the Council of Trent had met with numerous difficulties and had been unable to clarify it sufficiently. The First Vatican Council had also dealt with the question and had made important statements about it, but had been unable to complete its work before it was suspended. "This question is all the more urgent inasmuch as it is also of major concern to our non-Catholic Christian brethren, especially Protestants, and to such an extent that there has been considerable talk amongst them of a 'rediscovery of the church.' " All this led him to the important conclusion: "From what we have said, it is clear that this schema occupies a very central position in our Council."[95]

The speaker began his assessment of the schema by recognizing the commitment and hard work that had gone into its preparation, as can be seen in the rich selection of biblical texts and even more in that from the magisterium of the church. However, we had to consider whether the schema really offered what we can and must expect from a document of such commitment and weight. By way of a reply, the speaker set about examining it from various points of view.

In the first place, as concerns *the subject*, it was clear that this must be the church *in all its being*. However, the schema confines itself from the outset to the church "militant," which is moreover a rather unfortunate expression. Thus we do not have "those beautiful and profound reflections that we find in sacred scripture and in the fathers on the fulfillment and glorification of the church. Now, it is clear that this fulfillment is an essential aspect of the church, providing the pilgrim church in this world with all its light."[96]

He then brought up another point. Once the nature of the church had been explained, one would have expected an explanation of its purpose, that is, its teaching and priestly mission. However, the duty to proclaim the gospel to all nations is dealt with only in the penultimate chapter, while the teaching office of the church is dealt with in Chapter VII in a manner which is far too

94. GC 33 (4 December), *AS*, I/IV, 227-230; Caprile, II, 247-248. Concerning these contributions, cf. Caprile, II, 238-246; and D.A. Seeber, *Das Zweite Vaticanum. Konzil des Uebergangs*, Herderbücherei, 260/261 (Freiburg im Breisgau/Basel/Vienna, 1966), pp. 115-116. As usual, the cardinal did not refer to these contributions but directly to the schema.

95. *AS*, I/IV, 227. The president of the secretariat had thus grasped the central importance of this subject from the very beginning. This point deserves particular emphasis inasmuch as the cardinal made *relatively* few contributions to certain discussions on this schema; for example, he spoke neither on the subject of the episcopate nor on that of collegiality. It is well-known that at a later date Paul VI emphasized the central position of the subject of the church in his opening address for the second period; cf. *CDD*, p. 906.

96. *AS*, I/IV, 228.

disconnected from the nature of the church, from which this office receives its whole meaning. "The natural and biblical order would be to start with the college of bishops, as the New Testament does, where we first see the apostolic college being instituted by Our Lord Jesus Christ, and exercising the teaching office both in an ordinary and in a solemn form (in the Council of Jerusalem). We would then move on to speak of Peter, the head of the apostolic college, and of his successors. In this way, the Roman pontiff would not be separated from the apostolic college, but would appear as its apex, as he is in fact. Furthermore, in this way the presentation of the whole question would become much more natural and persuasive."[97]

As was the case for the schema on divine revelation, the speaker also considered this schema in the perspective of *the task* that the pope had entrusted to the Council, in other words that of presenting the substance of Christian life in the light of the pure sources of sacred scripture and tradition. Bea stated that the dogmatic constitutions of Councils had always taken the greatest care to prove their statements from scripture and tradition. Was this the case in the present schema? In order to reply, it would be enough to examine, for example, the notes in the margins of Chapter VII in order to see that it appealed solely to the tradition of the last century or two.

In the last analysis, the reason for all the elements that seem unacceptable is that "the schema does not correspond to the aim that the Holy Father assigned to the Council and that our Council underwrote in its message addressed to all men, in other words that of speaking not to professors of theology, nor only to priests, nor even only to members of the Catholic Church, but to all Christians, indeed to all men, and of explaining the teaching of Christ to them in a comprehensible and acceptable manner, so that they may understand, love and accept it—as I explained on a previous occasion."[98]

"From what I have said, it is clear that the schema is not acceptable as it stands, and in my opinion it needs a very thorough reworking."[99]

2. The cardinal set such great store by the success of this important schema that, taking advantage of the opportunity to submit observations in the months following the first period of the Council,[100] he found the time to draw up a ten-page *written memorandum on the nature of the church* in which he summarized all the relative biblical theology of the New Testament. He send this memorandum to the Cardinal Archbishop of Munich Julius Döpfner, a member of the Coordinating Commission for conciliar work, on 30 January 1963, explaining its purpose in a covering letter[101]: he wished to present the church in such a way that its nature could be concluded directly from sacred scripture; not only was this particularly important for dialogue with other Christians, but he

97. This method was in fact adopted in the final text; cf. *LG*, Chapter III, "The Church Is Hierarchical."
98. *AS*, I/IV, 228.
99. *Ibid.*, p. 230.
100. Cf. Caprile, II, 279.
101. The written opinion and covering letter, Arch. Lb 2/2 and 3.

also wanted to present it in such a way as to bring out all that is contained in the New Testament and not only certain aspects, for example the hierarchical structure, or membership of the mystical body of Christ; in this way the Council document would avoid being one-sided, and would present all the fullness of the idea of the church as found in the New Testament.[102]

3. As in the case of the schema on divine revelation, the cardinal was able *to check* how far the observations made during the first discussion of the schema on the church had been taken into account. In the second period of the Council he therefore spoke about *the first chapter* and partly also about the second in this perspective,[103] starting by summarizing his assessment by saying that he must reply as follows to the question of whether the chapters in question corresponded to the purpose of the Council as established by Pope John: "In many points they correspond, and very closely too, but in numerous others, less closely. It is my modest opinion that the biblical texts must be carefully revised, as Cardinal Ruffini has already observed. The same goes for the citations taken from tradition. Both these points are particularly important today, since the Council also intends showing our non-Catholic Christian brethren the nature, unity and task of the church. Now the sources they have in common with us are sacred scripture and early tradition; and if we are to start a dialogue with them, it must rest on these bases . . . ; we must propose proof-texts that are suited to the present situation."[104]

Here he indicated points where this requirement had not been borne in mind: for example, the schema made no effort to prove the oneness of the church in this manner; the same applied to the concept that Christ also entrusted the church to the bishops as successors of the apostles[105]; and when proof-texts were drawn from tradition, recourse should be made to sources prior to the sixteenth-century separation, indeed prior to the eleventh-century separation, thus seeking the earliest tradition.[106]

4. During the second period, the cardinal made a further contribution to the discussion of the schema on the church, speaking about *Chapter IV, on the universal vocation to holiness* in the church.[107] After paying tribute to the positive aspects of the chapter, the speaker observed that "it is not realistic enough. Anyone who looks at the church with open eyes—whether over the course of past centuries, or today—will certainly realize that alongside the saints

---

102. We heard nothing more about the subsequent history of these observations. Since they do not appear in the *Acta Synodalia* it seems clear that they were not considered to be a written opinion on the conciliar schema itself, and were therefore simply made available to the commission in question.
103. GC 40 (3 October), *AS*, II/II, 20-22; Caprile, III, 39.
104. *AS*, II/II, 20.
105. *Ibid.*
106. The cardinal added some remarks concerning certain details: ten pages for Chapter I (*ibid.*, pp. 23-32), and nine for Chapter II (*ibid.*, pp. 643-651); later five pages followed for Chapter III (*AS*, II/III, 393-397).
107. In the final text, this became Chapter V; GC 58 (30 October), *AS*, II/III, 638-641. More written remarks are found in *ibid.*, 641-646.

it has many sinners amongst its members. If the church were purely and simply holy, there would have been no reason for the so-called Reformation of the sixteenth century. Although it *is* fully and perfectly holy in an eschatological sense, the pilgrim church . . . tends by its nature toward the sanctification of its members, but never attains this goal in a perfect manner. In this perspective the holiness of the pilgrim church is therefore dynamic and not static."[108]

"When speaking of the church, the terms 'perfection' and 'perfect' should thus be employed with caution, particularly since they are unattractive to contemporary men and women, who see the world in a realistic fashion."[109]

As elsewhere, the speaker criticized the reasoning drawn from sacred scripture: "An almost complete teaching on the holiness of the faithful can be drawn from the New Testament."[110]

The teaching on the holiness of the church is also very important from an ecumenical viewpoint: contrary to those—less numerous today, however—who still hold that human nature is so corrupt as to be incapable of any good work, and that justification is simply an external imputation of Christ's justice, we must emphasize the ontological holiness conferred in baptism.[111]

5. In his first intervention on the Constitution on the Church, the cardinal had already also touched on the chapter concerning *the eschatological character of the church*, and in the third period he presented some written observations on the subject,[112] although we would mention only the observation concerning the veneration of saints. This was a very important subject in dialogue with the Protestants who, as is well-known, have difficulties with this point, for it seems to them that the practical forms of such veneration among Catholics often offend the infinite dignity of Christ and do not take into account humanity's absolute dependence on God's grace. It is indeed very easy for the faithful to lose sight of our underlying dependence on God and on Christ's grace. And it is therefore necessary for our faithful to become accustomed, when venerating the saints, to praising Christ and the triune God above all else, attributing the virtues and merits of the saints to Christ's grace, and also attributing the protection and help of the saints not to any particular power that they are claimed to possess, but solely to their intercession with God and with Christ, who is the sole Mediator.[113]

6. The president of the secretariat dedicated great attention not only to the first two chapters of the Constitution on the Church, but also to its last chapter, which deals with "*The Blessed Virgin Mary*, Mother of God, in the Mystery of Christ and the Church."

---

108. *Ibid.*, p. 639; in this connection the speaker recalled the gospel parables on the fishing-net that catches both good and bad fish (Mt. 13:47-50), and on the wheat and the tares (Mt. 13:24-30).

109. *Ibid.*

110. *Ibid.*, p. 640; in note 24 references are given to twelve texts from St. Paul and three from 1 Peter.

111. Cf. *ibid.* We would mention only one point from the six pages of remarks: no mention is made in the schema of abnegation and mortification, or the duty to carry one's own cross (cf. Mt. 16:24-25).

112. Cf. *AS*, III/I, 479-481.

113. *Ibid.*, p. 481.

(a) In *the second period* of the Council, he had already submitted some lengthy written observations on this subject,[114] in the first part of which he offered a critical assessment of the schema, and in the second a constructive suggestion on how to organize the chapter as a whole.

The assessment is severely negative. As in other cases, the author refers back to the purpose of the Council, and notes that the schema does not correspond to this, attempting more than anything else to summarize the teaching of the most recent popes, starting with Leo XIII. Furthermore, the schema does not take account of other Christians—eastern Christians and above all Protestants. It is well-known that the Christian East has a great veneration for the blessed Virgin. And today Protestants are also coming to recognize that the sixteenth-century reformers still had a veneration for Our Lady, which was eclipsed only at a later period, so that they are now trying to reestablish this veneration through study of scripture and early tradition. It is therefore a very serious duty of charity to help rather than hinder these promising developments, by giving an account of marian doctrine as found in scripture and early tradition.

As usual, Bea wanted his contribution to be constructive, and he therefore included *an outline proposal on how to organize the chapter*. After the introduction, it should be shown how Mary is closely linked with Christ on the one hand, and with the church on the other. This should be followed by an account of the principles in the light of which the facts should be interpreted, in other words the early teaching of St. Irenaeus on the parallelism between Mary and Eve, and on the blessed Virgin as "partner" of the new Adam and as "mother of the living." The facts should then be interpreted in this light, confirming the teaching with other texts, especially those of St. Augustine on Mary as mother of humankind. In the light of this account, it should be explained how Mary is "full of grace" and also her extraordinary holiness: on the one hand, it is all a splendid fruit of Christ's redemption, and on the other hand, the preparation for Mary to be a noble first-fruit of the church and a chosen assistant to Christ in the work of redemption. Lastly, in the light of ancient tradition it should be shown how Mary is intimately united to Christ after her glorification—*also* in the continuation of his work by means of the church, particularly with her motherly intercession.

(b) As he had done for other subjects on which he was an expert, in the months following this intervention, the cardinal also tried *to influence public opinion*, and particularly the Council fathers. He wrote a lengthy article on the harmony of marian doctrine and devotion with the ecumenical spirit, which was first published in the large encyclopedic work entitled *Marie*, edited by H. du Manoir, and also obtained a wide readership in various church reviews.[115] The

---

114. Cf. *AS*, II/III, 677-681; the text was written during the summer vacation and submitted on 16 September. On the mariological discussions in the Council in general, cf. A. Wenger, *Deuxième Session* (Paris, 1964), pp. 123-126; for the third period, cf. A. Wenger, *Troisième Session* (Paris, 1965), pp. 96-107, and R. La Valle, *Fedeltà del Concilio. I dibattiti della terza Sessione* (Brescia, 1965), pp. 20-23. As we shall see, it was mainly a question of the titles "Mediatrix" and "Mother of the Church."

115. Cf. Biblio. 273, and *The Way*, pp. 160-173; our citations are taken from the latter publication.

author stated the need for a mariology based on the principles spoken of in the intervention we have just discussed: in other words, a mariology that is based on sacred scripture and the earliest tradition, and that takes account of the elements and developments already present in the heritage of other Christians.[116] Inasmuch as the article was published in various church reviews immediately prior to the third period of the Council, we may reasonably imagine that it made an important contribution to preparing the Council fathers for discussion of the question in the Council itself.[117]

(c) During the third period of the Council, the cardinal made *a speech* on this same chapter of the constitution.[118] After recognizing that the schema certainly contained a very valuable "mariological treatise," he stated that the observations he was about to make were not concerned with his personal devotion or that of others, but simply with the question of whether the schema corresponded to the well-being of the church and of souls, and whether it was sufficiently mature and tested to be proposed by the highest authority of the church, namely an Ecumenical Council.

In this light he assessed the thinking of the schema concerning the Blessed Virgin as *mediatrix*, and observed: "It is more prudent that the term 'mediatrix' be avoided in a conciliar document: not only is there a danger that Catholics themselves might misunderstand it, but it also creates serious, indeed very serious, difficulties for Christians separated from us."[119] He added the observation that it would be a good idea to recommend that "in their words and actions, theologians and preachers should avoid anything that might lead our separated brethren into error concerning the true teaching of the church. However, in the very interests of unity a more positive recommendation is required: that marian doctrine be presented according to the bases of scripture and tradition, and that marian devotion be more christocentric."[120] He added: "This chapter on the Blessed Virgin should set the standard in this field by its own example."[121] However, this was not always the case: for example, the schema had interpreted the annunciation very well in the light of the witness of Saints Irenaeus, Cyril, Epiphanius, etc., "but on many other points of great importance it has not done so, for example, when explaining the Virgin's participation in the sacrifice of Christ on the cross, and in its explanation of the theological and ecclesiological

116. Cf. *The Way*, pp. 167-171.
117. With the same aim of providing the Council fathers with guidelines, he gave a public talk on 22 September 1964, intended first and foremost for the Brazilian bishops; in this talk he spoke about Chapter VIII; ms. R 1964/37.
118. GC 81 (16 September), *AS*, III/I, 454-458; Caprile, IV, 16-17.
119. *AS*, III/I, 456. This point had already been made in the above-mentioned written contribution, *AS*, II/III, 680. Likewise, it was observed that the schema was not faithful to its declared purpose of avoiding questions that had not yet been settled among theologians; on the contrary, several of these were introduced in the schema, for example the mariological interpretation of the "woman" of Genesis 3:15, and the episode of Our Lady and St. John beneath the cross (cf. John 19:25-28).
120. Summary in Caprile, IV, 17.
121. *AS*, III/I, 456.

significance of the words Our Lord addressed to the Blessed Virgin and St. John who were present beside the cross."[122]

(d) We would complete our account with *two items of information*. The first concerns the cardinal's views on *whether he was successful* in his battle in support of the ecumenical character of this chapter. He himself gave us an answer when he published the volume *The Way to Unity after the Council*, which included the article we referred to on the harmony of marian doctrine and devotion with the ecumenical spirit. In his words of introduction, he assessed the method employed in the definitive version of the mariological chapter of the Constitution on the Church as follows: "The Council's manner of proceeding is therefore the best confirmation of the explanations in this chapter which, in turn, constitutes an indirect commentary on the brilliant mariological synthesis achieved by the Constitution on the Church, and thus on the importance of this synthesis for ecumenism."[123]

The other item of information concerns the history of the papal proclamation of Mary as *Mother of the Church*. In the written observations quoted above, the cardinal had cited "the little-used title of Mother of the Church" as an example of doctrines that were still debated among theologians but had been proposed in the schema.[124] Pope Paul VI later saw fit to grant the request of many bishops to attribute this title officially to the Virgin.[125] It is important to see how the cardinal reacted to this in one of his publications. Commenting on the ecumenical results of the third period of the Council, he wrote: "It is true that I have maintained both inside and outside the Council that there was no need to use relatively new titles or ones that might be less comprehensible for some people, thus making the way to a genuine veneration of Mary more difficult for our non-Catholic brethren. . . . I know, however, that though this aspect of the problem is very important, it is not the only one that must be taken into consideration. There are also many other reasons that could have led the Holy Father to take this step. Be that as it may, once taken, the principle must be observed according to which Christian unity can ask for sacrifices, not of the truth, but of the individual personal opinion. Unity really is worth the greatest sacrifice—provided that it is compatible with conscience—as is evident if one looks at the sad division among Christians today."[126]

---

122. *Ibid.* To the objection that the schema had to be brief and could therefore not take all the observations into account, the speaker replied that for this very reason it could not go into too many details that could not be explained sufficiently; it should confine itself to setting forth the principles. The speaker concluded mercilessly that the schema needed "fairly radical" revision if it was to correspond to its purpose (*ibid.*, p. 457).

123. *The Way*, p. 161 (ct).

124. Cf. *AS*, II/III, 678. I cannot see which of the cardinal's texts Romano Amerio is referring to in *Jota unum* (Milan/Naples, 1985), p. 82, when he states that the cardinal claimed "that the whole of the mariological doctrine developed in the constitution implicitly contained the title *Mater Ecclesiae*." I can find nothing of this kind in the conciliar contributions that I have consulted.

125. Cf. *CDD*, p. 985. For the long and complex development leading up to this proclamation, cf. V. Carbone, "Maria Madre della Chiesa," *OssRom* (3 February 1988), p. 5, which is a very interesting study with precise, detailed references.

126. *Ecumenism*, pp. 172-173 (ct). It is interesting to observe one detail. After his death I found a

The Pastoral Office of Bishops

Cardinal Bea made a very telling speech on the schema *On Bishops and the Government of Dioceses*,[127] which was rather surprising since he had never been a residential bishop, and also since he might have been expected to express quite a different type of opinion on account of his experience in the Roman curia. It was not customary to applaud in the Council hall, and the authorities had several times asked the fathers to refrain from doing so. The fact that the cardinal's speech was greeted by applause despite this fact is maybe an indication that he had expressed the unspoken thoughts of many of the fathers.[128]

The speaker stated that he agreed that the schema did not have the task of presenting theological doctrine on relations between the pope and the bishops, for this subject had its place in the Constitution on the Church. However, certain principles could be deduced from the doctrine presented in the latter document which were of fundamental importance for the schema under discussion. "The principles governing the organization and action [of the church] must be drawn from divine revelation. And these principles are much more important for us than certain practical applications that vary according to circumstance. . . ."[129]

1. Thus, according to the written text, the first part is dedicated to the presentation of these *revealed principles*.

(a) "The first and basic principle revealed by God is that the church . . . is a living body, endowed with a variety of members, by means of which, as the apostle says, the church builds itself up in love 'according to the specific energy of each member,' i.e., to the extent needed by each member for its own specific task.[130] It should be noted that, according to the apostle, this building up is achieved not only by the work of the hierarchy or of the supreme authority, but by the work of each member. If one or several members are . . . prevented from performing their specific part, the church itself is seriously harmed. . . ."[131]

(b) "Since the church is a body, all the members are intimately linked to one another and must also work united in this way. . . . However, in the church the members are free; indeed, Christ has called them to freedom. As a result, all the

---

holy picture in his personal prayer-book with the prayer to the Blessed Virgin, "Mother of the Church." This all goes to show that his contributions in this connection were dictated exclusively by regard for other Christian brethren.

127. GC 61 (6 November), *AS*, II/IV, 481-485; Caprile, III, 194. We should also add the written remarks on the same schema. Chapter I: *AS*, II/IV, 657-658. Chapter II: *AS*, II/V, 97. Chapter III: *AS*, II/V, 271. Chapter IV: *AS*, II/V, 358.

128. Rather than joining in the discussion of any particular point, the speaker went into greater depth, indicating the ecclesiological bases of the subject, along with the principle of subsidiarity. His contribution was rather long, but its content was so consistently rich that any shorter account would run the risk of reducing its precision and clarity.

129. *AS*, II/IV, 482.

130. These are the well-known Pauline texts: 1 Cor. 12:12-31; Rom. 12:4-5; Eph. 4:16.

131. *AS*, II/IV, 482.

members must act with the greatest care, both for the good of the other members and also for the good of the whole body."[132]

(c) "Inasmuch as the church is a visible society, the supreme authority in it has been given to the college of apostles, to whom Christ gave Peter as its head; the college of bishops succeeded this college, and its head is the Roman pontiff. In the course of time, the church has also created certain other organs, under the guidance of the Holy Spirit: patriarchates, ecclesiastical provinces, national and international episcopal conferences, and central government by means of the holy Roman congregations. It is evident that all these organs are also members of the church, each in its own way; they must therefore serve the building up of the church, and the Holy Spirit acts in them. The doctrine presented above concerning the members and their reciprocal relations must also be applied to them."[133]

(d) "As in any other society, in the church it is *not* the task of authority *to replace* the individual members in what they can do, but only *to supplement* what they are not capable of doing; it can help them to operate in such a way that individual action is coordinated and directed toward the common good. The same holds good, by analogy, for every kind of superior authority with respect to inferiors."[134]

2. This is where *the application of the principles to the subject in question* begins, according to the written text.

(a) All the members must work for the good of the others and for the good of the whole body; however, it is clear that in certain matters their freedom of action must be limited so that it may be harmonized with the actions of the others and of the whole body.

(b) It is clear that this holds good in a very special way for those eminent members of the mystical body, the members of the college of bishops. "Thus they must work with the utmost mindfulness also for the good of the whole church, indeed of the whole world, since they have been sent to preach the gospel to every creature. Every bishop is not only permitted, but obliged to perform the functions proper to him and assume responsibility for them. . . ."[135]

(c) This free commitment of individual members for the good of the whole church must be respected with supreme reverence. The reason for this is given in the written text, although not in reference to individual members of the church, but to bishops. This text reads as follows: "Here we are dealing not only with the dignity of the human person, but even more with the respect due to the action of the Holy Spirit, which must always be presumed and recognized, unless in some particular case it be truly demonstrated that the superior acted under some other influence. Authority too must respect this freedom, and indeed protect it, by reason of its very office."[136] "And if the supreme authority places restrictions on some particular freedom, this too must be greatly respected; indeed, it must be recognized that, by reason of its office, it must safeguard and

132. *Ibid.*
133. *Ibid.*
134. *Ibid.*, pp. 482-483.
135. *Ibid.*, p. 483.
136. Caprile, III, 194, who follows the written text for the most part (notes 46 and 47).

bring about the good of the church. Hence, the only reason for which this freedom can and must be limited by direct or indirect authority is that of safeguarding the good of the church, for which freedom was in fact given."[137]

"Some principles concerning *the so-called faculties* dealt with in Chapter I follow from what I have said. If I am not mistaken, in their own dioceses, bishops can perform everything that falls within their task and is their duty by virtue of episcopal consecration and their membership of the college of bishops, with the sole exception of anything that, for the greater common good, is better exercised only together with some higher direct or indirect authority, such as the provincial or national episcopal conference. . . . By acting in this way, each in his own diocese, the bishops work through this very fact for the universal good of the church."[138]

(d) "However, in order to show the fraternal collaboration of the episcopal college with the Roman pontiff outwardly as well, it will be well for a number of bishops from different nations to be called to share the concern of the Roman pontiff in a practical manner, in ways that the pontiff himself considers most appropriate to the various questions and circumstances."[139]

Lastly, the cardinal emphasized *the ecumenical importance* of what he had explained: "It is well-known that the Roman Catholic Church is often accused of a desire—indeed an ambition—to dominate, of so-called imperialism, of excessive centralization, curialism, etc. Words will not suffice in the face of such accusations, nor will the uttering of bland phrases of charity about help that must be given to bishops by higher authority, etc. The only effective remedy is profound respect for the rightful responsibility and freedom of individuals, of all lesser authorities, and above all of bishops."[140]

The Church in the Modern World

As is well-known, this schema arrived rather late on the Council's agenda, and therefore also in the Council hall. The cardinal intervened in the debate on two occasions, but he also dedicated numerous detailed written observations to the subject,[141] which indicates that he had realized the vastness and the serious

---

137. *AS*, II/IV, 483.
138. This is the spoken text, *ibid.* Elsewhere, the cardinal gave a more detailed account of his thinking on these "faculties," saying that the term implies that these matters normally fall under the pope's responsibility, and that he grants the bishops the "faculty" to do them. However, the fact that until that moment the matter was reserved to the pope is no proof that it is necessarily in itself reserved to him; *AS*, II/IV, 657.
139. Caprile, III, 197. In his written remarks, the cardinal added that something ought to be said here about the collaboration of the bishops in the government of the universal church (and not only collaboration in one or another of the Roman congregations); in other words, something ought to be said about the central council that was to be set up in Rome in order to coordinate the work of the individual congregations more effectively and deal with questions of major importance; *AS*, II/IV, 658.
140. Caprile, III, 197, with a few corrections by the present author.
141. For the two oral contributions (nine pages), cf. *AS*, III/V, 272-276; *AS*, IV/I, 576-579. For the twenty-four pages of written remarks, cf. *AS*, IV/I, 579-596; *AS*, IV/III, 299-303; *AS*, IV/III, 407; *AS*, IV/III, 757.

nature of the problems dealt with in this schema, and therefore also his personal responsibility to contribute to its success.

1. In his first speech in the third period of the Council,[142] the speaker started by recognizing that the schema had given an excellent, concise account of a very difficult subject. The main aspect under which the schema needed improvement was that the profound principles that must enlighten practice required better demonstration on the basis of sacred scripture. "The document is first and foremost addressed not to non-believers, to the world, . . . but to believers, who must be instructed as to how they should behave in the world, on the basis of the sources of faith, and not only by means of philosophical arguments."[143]

The cardinal's first example of how such principles should be illuminated by scripture was *"the universal dominion of Christ* over the whole of creation, and social, economic and political life."* It must be demonstrated explicitly "that this dominion is intimately connected with the work of redemption, and more precisely with Christ's resurrection from the dead and his ascension—as is stated, for example, in the Letter to the Ephesians: 'God raised him [Christ] from the dead and made him sit at his right hand in the heavenly places, far above all rule and authority and power and dominion, and above every name that is named, . . . and he has put all things under his feet' (1:20-22)." Another very important principle is also closely connected with this teaching: "that *all things,* and especially all things created inferior to man, *are ordered toward the good of man* and of society, according to the vigorous words of St. Paul: 'All things are yours, . . . the world or life or death or the present or the future, all are yours; and you are Christ's; and Christ is God's' (1 Cor. 3:21-23)."

A further example concerned a doctrine that is even more typical and important, but may be less well-known and thus in need of clearer explanation; *the twofold character of the life of the Christian,* which is at the same time earthly and heavenly, together with the tension that this generates and the consequences it produces. This teaching is important, and we find it set forth explicitly and clearly in the New Testament.[144] This characteristic of the life of man extends to the whole of creation, even that which is inferior to man.[145]

This teaching has *important practical consequences* for the Christian's behavior in the world. The speaker was thinking above all of 1 Corinthians 7:29: "The appointed time has grown very short; from now on, let those who have wives live as though they had none, and those who mourn as though they were not mourning, and those who rejoice as though they were not rejoicing, and those who buy as though they had no goods, and those who deal with the world as though they had no dealings with it. For the form of this world is passing

---

142. GC 106 (21 October), *AS,* III/V, 272-276; Caprile, IV, 249-250.
143. *AS,* III/V, 273.
144. The speaker refers to elements from the letters of St. Paul: Col. 3:3; Eph. 2:19; Phil. 3:20; Heb. 13:14; 12:12.
145. Cf. Rom. 8:20-22: "The creation was subjected to futility . . . in hope . . . [that it] will be set free from its bondage to decay. . . . The whole creation has been groaning in travail together until now." Cf. also 2 Peter 3:10, 13.

away."[146] This teaching can be misunderstood, as it was even in St. Paul's day, which led the apostle to emphasize the need to work conscientiously, giving his own example in this connection, and citing his own exertions.[147] "The difference between the sons of light and the sons of this world is not a question of how hard they work and how deeply they are committed in their work when it also concerns the things of this world, but, rather, the motivation of the person who works. Now, the Christian's motive is heavenly, and thus infinitely more sublime than the reasons that motivate the sons of this world; hence, his industriousness and commitment must be infinitely greater." The speaker added: "It seems to me that this teaching derived from biblical theology constitutes an extremely solid basis for illustration of the Christian's behavior in the world."[148]

2. As was the case for various other schemata, the cardinal's *second spoken intervention*, which he made in the fourth period, consisted of a kind of examination of the progress made in connection with the document in question.[149] The speaker recognized that the text had been greatly improved. "It seems that the commission has now found the right language for this exceptional schema, and this is very important."[150]

He then stated that the schema required *improvement* in three ways. In the first place, certain general principles were repeated too often, whereas they ought to be given in Chapter I and the first section of Chapter II, after which the reader should be referred back to them every time the material under discussion required this.

Furthermore, *the teaching* and the manner in which it is set forth requires revision at various points, for example in the passage speaking of the various meanings of the word "world." Another example given by the cardinal was as follows: with the aim of proving that the church does not seek dominion in temporal matters, it is claimed that "Christ himself renounced any earthly authority for himself"—whereas this is an indefensible claim that flies in the face of Christ's very words that "All authority in heaven and on earth has been given to me" (Mt. 28:18), as well as what is said about Christ in the liturgy of the feast of Christ the King, where his dominion in the temporal order is affirmed.[151]

The Latin was also of great importance. The first part was in particular need of linguistic revision, "because incorrect terms frequently occur, as well as some fairly obscure expressions. The ambiguity derives from the effort to use classical

---

146. Cf. 1 Cor. 7:29-32. The speaker also cited 2 Peter 3:11-12.
147. Cf. 2 Thess. 3:11-13; Gal. 6:9-10.
148. *AS*, III/V, 274-275. The speaker at once made it clear that it was not a question of making the Latin more elegant, but clearer; otherwise it would not be comprehensible. He returned to this point in his second contribution.
149. GC 132 (21 September), *AS*, IV/I, 576-579; Caprile, V, 70.
150. *AS*, IV/I, 576.
151. This refers to the sixth reading of the Roman breviary prior to the reform. These readings were taken from the encyclical *Quas primas* of Pope Pius XI, instituting the feast of Christ the King; cf. *AAS*, XVII (1925), 600.

Latin, whereas it would be preferable to employ or even create simpler and more comprehensible expressions."[152] "We must beware of the opinion that it is enough to give the Council fathers the text in French or some other modern language. The official text of the Council, which must be understood and approved by the fathers, is not some modern translation but solely the Latin text, rendered fully comprehensible. . . . Otherwise, endless discussions will arise as to the meaning of the words, and the uncertainty of the text will seriously compromise the actual doctrinal authority of the document."[153]

Some Specific Aspects of the Life of the Church

1. Missionary Activity

As we said in a previous chapter, the cardinal intervened in this case in response to outside promptings. Many Council fathers from mission lands felt that the schema in question was too undeveloped and was concerned almost exclusively with juridical aspects, and they therefore approached both the General Secretary of the Council and also various Council fathers with a view to putting this right. The cardinal was one of those approached in this way,[154] and he was glad to accept, speaking very vigorously in the third period.[155]

The starting point was as follows: since the Council was seeking the renewal of the church, as Pope John XXIII had stated, "there can be no doubt that it must give *a new impulse* to the missionary activity of the church. Indeed, this activity must be included among the most essential tasks of the church. 'Giving a new impulse' means fostering new missionary vocations and new fervor, not just drawing up a new juridical order."[156] It was in fact a well-known fact that missionary vocations had declined, and doubts were gaining ground in various quarters as to whether missionary activity could still be considered relevant or opportune.

This first thing to do in this context was to highlight *the aim* of missionary activity. "We are dealing with God's great plan for the temporal and eternal destiny of the whole of humanity, in other words his plan to unite all peoples very closely with Christ in his mystical body, and thus also with each other."[157] In this way, people will see the good news as it is, and those who proclaim it

---

152. Caprile, V, 71, with a few corrections by the present author. "For the first fourteen or so pages of the first part alone, I have been obliged to fill twenty pages of remarks," wrote the cardinal. It should not, however, be imagined that these detailed observations were all concerned with the Latin of the document, for after about fifteen pages concerning the Latin *among other points*, the author declared that it was not possible to continue at this rate, and he would therefore deal *only* with the content from then on; cf. *ibid.*, p. 592.

153. *AS*, IV/I, 578.

154. Cf. various documents on these passages, Arch. Lb 9; also Caprile, IV, 386, note 11.

155. GC 120 (11 November), *AS*, III/VII, 364-367; Caprile, IV, 385. He began with the words: "For me it is a great honor to be able to speak on behalf of all the bishops of Africa and many of the bishops of Asia."

156. *AS*, III/VII, 364.

157. *Ibid.* The speaker cited Eph. 1:10; 2:11, 15-16, 19; 1 Cor. 12:12-13; Gal. 3:28; John 17:1-3.

will not be seen as preachers of an invention of the white race, some foreign culture or western civilization, but as ministers of Christ, who is the Head of humankind, and as dispensers of the mysteries—that is, the gifts of God—which transcend nature and human knowledge. The new peoples will then see this plan not as something unworthy of them, but rather as doing them great honor, since it makes them full members of the kingdom of God and calls them to share in building up a new humankind in Christ.[158] It is therefore obvious that this activity is to continue until the end of the world.[159]

Here, the speaker recalled "the basic truth" set forth in the Constitution on the Church, namely, that all the members of the college of bishops must together care for the whole church and have the serious duty of proclaiming the gospel to all humanity. "This same task also involves all the members of the same mystical body of Christ in some way, according to the words of St. Paul: 'The members [should] have the same care for one another. If one member suffers, all suffer together; if one member is honored, all rejoice together' (1 Cor. 12:25-26)."[160]

In his written text, the cardinal closed with a *suggestion* that at the beginning of the schema (in no. 1) greater stress should be laid on the need for missionary activity, and this should be done in a manner more in keeping with the mentality of contemporary people. He also stated that he was presenting a draft text in this connection, and although it does not appear in the *Acta Synodalia*, a copy *is* to be found in the archives.[161] This draft text contains what amounts to a summary of St. Paul's teaching, which the cardinal had, as we have seen, set forth in his speech, and the due consequences are drawn from this teaching.

As in the case of other schemata, in the fourth period of the Council the cardinal submitted a written contribution containing a survey or examination of the progress that had been made on this document.[162] He observed with satisfaction that the schema had now become excellent: "It indicates the theological bases along with the essential principles of missionary activity."[163] The author then stressed that it was necessary in some way to prove the statement that *all* the faithful have a duty to take part in missionary activity, and he suggested that this be done with the help of two texts from St. Paul: the teaching on the mystical body of Christ (1 Cor. 12), and Ephesians 4:16.[164]

2. The Religious Life

As had been the case for the schema concerned with missionary activity, there was a feeling of dissatisfaction over the schema dedicated to the religious

---

158. The idea of "building up a new humankind" is found in *AS*, III/VII, 365, note 23.

159. Here the author cited claims that missionary activity is no longer necessary, since throughout mission lands a hierarchy composed of members of the native clergy is now established; to this objection he replied that the hierarchy is not equal to the enormous task of evangelization and is in urgent need of outside assistance; furthermore, the church has always particularly cherished the first proclamation of the gospel to those who have never known it.

160. *AS*, III/VII, 366; the speaker was interrupted because his time was up.

161. Arch. Lb 9/1.

162. *AS*, IV/IV, 397-401.

163. *Ibid.*, p. 397.

164. Cf. *ibid.*, p. 398.

life, especially among the thousand or so Council fathers who were members of various religious orders and congregations. This was seen clearly in the voting following the discussion. While it is true that the schema was not sent back to the commission as had been the case for missionary activity, the result was far from brilliant: the introduction to the schema did not attain the necessary proportion of votes, while the various separate parts received hundreds of votes with reservations, accompanied by suggestions for improvement.[165]

The cardinal's intervention was certainly one of his most profound and vigorous speeches.[166] With figures to prove it, he started by stressing the great importance of the apostolic work of male and female religious, and, more generally, the influence they exercised in the church. On the other hand, he observed, vocations had fallen off to such an extent that we could almost speak of a crisis. "It is therefore vital that the Council should provide this institution with *a new and effective impulse*. . . . The renewal of the church brought about by the Council must also exert its influence on the various religious families."[167] Although the schema did emphasize the need for renewal, it tried to foster it mostly through juridical dispositions, while "almost completely omitting to propose the principles and religious bases of such renewal and the internal, spiritual means of bringing it about. Now these are the primary things that are required, although juridical norms are also necessary."[168]

"*Among the means* the Council should employ, pride of place undoubtedly goes to that of proposing *the nature and the purpose* of religious life to the faithful and to religious themselves, in the light of the pure sources of faith, especially the New Testament and the writings of the apostles, and in a manner that corresponds to the mentality of contemporary people."[169]

As usual, the speaker at once indicated *the main elements* of this teaching on the nature and purpose of the religious life. The act whereby religious consecrate themselves to Christ refers by its nature not only to the physical and individual Christ, but "to the total Christ, that is, the church and its purpose, for the mystical body of Christ cannot be separated from Christ himself. This consecration therefore refers to the continuation of the work of human redemption, and thus to the whole of humanity."[170]

This relation to the total Christ has two aspects. The first concerns the specific spirit and purpose of the individual institute: "It is the task of the individual orders and congregations to preserve faithfully the gifts they have received from their respective founders, and to act in such a way that they may render fertile

---

165. Cf. the general vote, *AS*, III/VII, 555, with 882 contrary votes; cf. also the votes on individual sections, *AS*, III/VII, 714, 717-718, etc.; also Caprile, IV, 421.

166. GC 120 (11 November), *AS*, III/VII, 442-446; Caprile, IV, 411.

167. *AS*, III/VII, 442-443.

168. *Ibid.*, p. 443.

169. *Ibid.* The Constitution on the Church did deal with this subject, but not with the aspect that is proper to this schema; moreover, the practical pastoral decrees of the church usually give a brief indication of the spirit that gave rise to them.

170. *Ibid.*

the life of the church, so far as the circumstances of the moment permit and demand. . . ."[171]

On the other hand, "while they live the life proper to each individual institute and act in conformity with this life, they must feel that they are united, and, *all the more so as members of the total Christ*, they must live and work as such, and be aware that with Christ they are destined to serve the whole human family, . . . like the Son of man who 'came not to be served but to serve, and to give his life as a ransom for many' (Mt. 20:28). Hence, with ardent charity they should embrace the whole church, indeed the whole of humankind, suffering and rejoicing with it (cf. 1 Cor. 12:25)."[172]

However, religious should beware of the tendency to cultivate the spirit and activity proper to them in a way that does not *take into account*—or does so only insufficiently—*developments and changes* in the situation obtaining both in the church and in the world. Now, the best way of avoiding this danger is to cultivate intensely the awareness that they are members of the church, and only members, and that their own consecration and the search for perfection also involve the perfection of their relations with the whole church; in this way each religious will seek renewal with the church from day to day. Religious should therefore take part in the biblical and liturgical renewal, in the spirit of the apostolate, and in the missionary and ecumenical spirit, thereby embracing all human beings, whether Christians or non-Christians, believers or non-believers.

The speaker *concluded* by suggesting that the ideas he had set forth be expressed in a condensed form and be used as an introduction to the schema. He also submitted a draft text along these lines.[173]

It is interesting to see that this latter suggestion met with total success. Whereas the schema at that stage had said nothing about the spirit inspiring the decree, in the final text two lengthy paragraphs have been inserted which give the various ideas suggested by the speaker, albeit in a more condensed form.[174]

3. *The Ministry and Life of Priests*

The cardinal's intervention on this subject was dictated above all by ecumenical motives, but was delivered in a decidedly disturbed atmosphere. Earlier on, during the discussion of the schema on missionary activity, a letter dated 10 October from Pope Paul VI and addressed to the president of the presiding authorities of the Council, Cardinal Eugene Tisserant, had been read in the Council hall. This letter expressed the pope's wish that the fathers should refrain from dealing with clerical celibacy in the forthcoming debate on the ministry

---

171. *Ibid.*, pp. 443-444. The written text added that the perfection to which religious must aspire in virtue of their particular state does not concern only the charism proper to each institute, but also, and to a greater extent, the relations that are common to all institutes, in other words, relations to the mystical body of Christ which is the church, and hence the perfection of relations with all the members of the church; cf. *ibid.*, p. 444, note 17.

172. The citation from Mt. 20:28 and what follows are taken from the *written* text of the contribution.

173. Cf. *AS*, III/VII, 445-446.

174. The text of the schema during this phase (*AS*, III/VII, 85) should be compared with the final text of the decree *Perfectae caritatis*, 1. We obviously do not intend to ascribe all the credit to the cardinal's contribution.

and life of priests, and said that those who had suggestions or objections should submit them in writing and the pope would examine them conscientiously before God.[175] In the general atmosphere that this brought into being, the cardinal was misunderstood as saying that he was against celibacy, whereas he explicitly stated the opposite, as we shall see.

The speaker started by expressing delight that a Council was now for the first time dealing so fully and positively with the priestly life and ministry.[176] There was just one point he wished to raise, and that concerned *the manner in which celibacy was spoken of.* What the text stated about the motivations, advantages and fruits of priestly celibacy (in no. 14) was excellent and should all be approved without any further discussion. It was also correctly stated that the priesthood did not of its very nature *require* celibacy. However, in the following sentences it was put forward in such an absolute fashion that celibacy appeared to spring from the very nature of the priesthood. Thus the text stated that the priest's mission is totally dedicated to the service of a new humanity, and concluded: *"Hence, by means of celibacy, priests become a living sign of this future world."* Where did this leave the married priests of the eastern churches? Were they not priests in the full sense of the term? The schema admitted that there were worthy married priests in the eastern churches, almost as though this could happen as an exception.

The speaker then moved on to suggest what action could be taken. "Unless I am mistaken, our ecumenical—and I say *ecumenical*—Council ought to speak *of both priestly states*: the state of perfect continence in celibacy and the state of perfect (I would almost say 'ideal') matrimony of the married priesthood, and this perfect model is of very great importance for the eastern churches. It should be shown how candidates should be selected, educated and trained for the two states, according to the situation of each, and how they should each be trained to protect themselves effectively against the dangers threatening them. By acting in this way, our Council would also be most useful to our very dear eastern brethren."[177]

It is not difficult to see from the very structure of this part of his contribution that the cardinal was not in fact casting any doubt on the legitimacy of celibacy in the Latin church, but was insisting that the Council should bear both models in mind and make provision for both celibate and married priests.[178]

* * *

175. Cf. *AS*, IV/I, 40; Caprile, V, 222-223; cf. also pp. 222-229, where various opinions and documents are listed which illustrate the situation.
176. GC 151 (16 October), *AS*, IV/V, 34-36; Caprile, V, 261-262.
177. Apart from minor corrections we have followed Caprile's summary. The speaker also observed: "The material is often poorly organized, and certain important points, such as mental prayer, penance and study, do not occupy the position they logically deserve, and hence their value is not shown in its correct light" (Caprile, V, 262).
178. It is also clear that the speaker did not touch on the question of the possible ordination of married men, which was fairly often discussed in those days; cf. *ibid.*, pp. 223-229.

As a kind of postscript we would make brief mention of two written "opinions" of the cardinal, the precise content of which is still reserved information. The first concerned *the doctrinal agenda of the Council.* On the occasion of the twenty-fifth anniversary of the first announcement of the Council, a letter from the then Archbishop of Milan, Cardinal G.B. Montini, was published. This letter was dated 18 October 1962, and was addressed to the Cardinal Secretary of State. One passage read as follows: "I am taking the liberty of drawing your attention to a matter that seems very serious to me and other Council fathers, namely, the lack—at least so far as is publicly known—of an organic, ideal and logical plan for the Council."[179] Now, three days prior to this, Cardinal Bea had sent the Secretariat for Extraordinary Affairs, which was presided over by the same Secretary of State, a written opinion in Latin entitled *The Need to Discuss and Specify the Doctrinal Agenda of the Council.*[180]

In *a second written opinion* presented to the authorities about ten days before the end of the first period of the Council, the cardinal set forth detailed suggestions as to how best the months preceding the next period could be used.[181] Now, in the general congregation of 6 December a document signed by the Secretary of State, Cardinal Amleto Cicognani, and confirmed by the pope, was read out in the Council hall, giving the dispositions for the nine months' work between the first and second periods.[182] And if we compare this document with the written opinion submitted by the cardinal, we can see that various points correspond. We would confine ourselves simply to noting this fact.[183]

* * *

In order to sketch *a rough portrait of Bea as Council father* it will suffice to recall very briefly the characteristic features of his work as we have described it.

(1) His concern to bear the universal church in mind at all times, with the well-being of all Christians, indeed of the whole of humankind.

(2) His insistence that the task of the Council was to propose "the substance of human and Christian thought and life" in the light of "the pure sources of revelation and tradition," which meant that he stressed the need to draw on the ultimate sources of faith, in other words, sacred scripture and tradition, and, in the case of the latter, earlier tradition—that prior to the sixteenth or even the eleventh century.

(3) This task must be matched by the way in which doctrine is set forth, and indeed the whole way of speaking; in other words, it must correspond to the mentality of contemporary people, so that they can understand the teaching.

(4) Great concern that formulation be correct and precise. This is eloquently

179. *OssRom* (26 January 1984), special supplement.
180. Cf. Arch. Lb 13/2.
181. Cf. Arch. Lb 13/3.
182. Cf. *AS*, I/I, 96-98; Caprile, II, 257-259.
183. We do not mean to claim that the cardinal's suggestions were decisive, and we do in fact know that similar suggestions were also made by others; cf. Caprile, II, 257.

borne out by the more than eighty pages of detailed observations concerning various schemata. The cardinal explained that the Council had to limit itself to the substance, that is, to major principles, without going into excessive detail, but that it also had to take the greatest care that *what was said* was comprehensible to contemporary men and women, correct and precise.

(5) When stressing this point, the cardinal pointed out that these were not his own ideas, *but those of Pope John XXIII*: it was he who had said that the Council wanted to speak "to all people"[184]; it was he who had specified that the Council's task was that of setting forth "the substance of human and Christian thought and life"[185]; and it was he who had emphasized that doctrine "should be studied and expounded through the methods of research and through the literary forms of modern thought,"[186] and that the formulation of this doctrine must be treated with great care and "patience."[187]

When considering the work of Bea as Council father we quite naturally wonder where this man who had spent his life in the lecture hall and within the walls of academic institutions obtained this surprising capacity for such a thorough grasp of the vast and demanding pastoral agenda that Pope John XXIII had given the Council, embracing it with such great energy. Here we should recall the period between 1949 and 1959, which we described as that of "immediate preparation" for his future mission, especially due to the fact that he was confessor to Pope Pius XII. As we have seen, this latter position was in no way limited to the sacramental ministry, but involved him in many problems concerned with the government of the universal church. In an interview on the doctrinal work of Pius XII and its importance for the Council, he himself explained what had most impressed him as the "breadth [of Pius XII's work] which takes into account every single one of the problems of humanity today and seeks to solve them in the light of the gospel as it is preserved and taught by the church."[188] It was this example and teaching of Pope Pius XII that had profoundly marked—maybe we can say shaped—his pastoral attitude and his openness to the major problems of the church and the world.

After this basic training, the extraordinary mutual understanding that existed between the pope of the Council and the cardinal further helped the cardinal to absorb the pope's plan in such depth and commit himself totally to its implementation.

---

184. Opening speech to the Council, *CDD*, p. 855; English translation in Abbott (gen. ed.), *The Documents of Vatican II*, p. 713.

185. Speech inaugurating the work of the preparatory commissions, *AAS*, LII (1960), 1006.

186. Opening speech to the Council, *CDD*, p. 865; English translation in Abbott (gen. ed.), *The Documents of Vatican II*, p. 715.

187. Cf. *ibid.*

188. *The Unity of Christians*, p. 207.

CHAPTER 10

ONE HUMAN FAMILY, FREELY UNITED IN TRUTH, JUSTICE AND LOVE

A rapid look back over the most important events of the three years of the Council, as we described them in order to provide an introduction to the whole work of the Council,[1] is enough to show that there are certain other aspects of the cardinal's activity that still require examination. The first of these is his thinking on religious freedom, together with his contribution to the Council document devoted to this subject. The second aspect concerns the "Agapé meetings," two of which were held in Rome, and one in New York. As in his ecumenical activity, his participation in these meetings had the aim of helping to overcome certain divisions existing between human beings. For example, the subject of the 1962 meeting was "Racial Prejudices: The Reason for Religious, Political and Cultural Incomprehension." The objective was thus that of overcoming such obstacles with the help of dialogue, thereby promoting human unity on the purely human level.[2]

The basic concept of the Agapé meetings as applied to the immediate interests and needs of various contexts was broadened at the New York meeting in April 1963 to a global vision of the purely human unity of the entire human family. And this Agapé meeting in fact provided the opportunity and motivation for development of this approach in the volume entitled *Unity in Freedom. Reflections on the Human Family*.[3] In our previous chapter we saw that it was Pope John's intention, and thus also the cardinal's, that the Council itself should contribute to the well-being of the whole of humankind, by placing the latter, with all its problems and needs, in living contact with the life-giving forces of the gospel. In this context, it was explicitly stated on several occasions that human beings will find the solution to their problems and the means for overcoming their divisions and rifts, as well as *their full unity, solely in Christ*. This leads to consideration of the relation between this "unity in Christ" and the above-mentioned purely human unity of humankind.[4]

We should also mention *the novelty of the subject, and thus the place it holds* in the work of Cardinal Bea. In the first place, we shall note that, generally speaking, this aspect of his activity has been almost completely ignored. For

---

1. Cf. Part III, Chapter 6, pp. 412-452 above.

2. Connected with these initiatives of the cardinal were those that had been secret until then in favor of the creation by the Holy See of a "secretariat for non-Christians" and another "for non-believers." In the same context we should also see the cardinal's role in various little-known contacts with official circles of the Soviet Union.

3. Biblio. 170.

4. Here we find a certain problem over terminology in distinguishing between the two types of unity. In order to provide a certain variety, we shall call the former "human unity" or "purely [or simply] human unity" or "unity on the human level"; the second, which is easier, will be referred to as "unity in Christ," "Christian unity," or "specifically Christian unity."

example, it is not even mentioned in the major existing work on the cardinal, the illustrated volume edited by M. Buchmüller, which we have cited so frequently. Nor is the subject referred to in any of the statements that are found in the archives and that we have repeatedly consulted.[5] And in practice it is not even mentioned in the many tributes paid to the cardinal during his lifetime or after his death.[6] Maybe the sole examination of this aspect is to be found in the introduction to the book *The Augustin Bea Prize*.[7] This introduction was written by Cardinal Johannes Willebrands, who succeeded Bea as President of the Secretariat for Christian Unity, and who does not hesitate to state: "Even in his ecumenical work, Cardinal Bea did not hold only Christians in mind; he always had the whole of humankind in view. Tirelessly he emphasized the fact that Christian unity is not an end in itself, but that it is in the service of humankind."[8]

Contrary to first impressions, the material is vast and complex. I think the best way to understand it will be to start with a brief account of the facts: the talks and articles dealing with various aspects of the subject of this chapter, as well as the special initiatives we have mentioned, which had the aim of creating institutions—the secretariats we have mentioned—that would be dedicated to dialogue at various levels. In this way we shall indicate both the various sources on which we shall draw in a second section in order to show the line of thinking underlying this activity, and also the precise context of these sources.

Activity in Support of the Conciliar Declaration on Religious Freedom

When speaking of the work of the secretariat, its first president often said that it had not started with major plans and blueprints for action, but that it tried to deal with suggestions and tasks as they arose. This is particularly true of the initiative to draft a Council document on religious freedom. According to Cardinal Willebrands, this was first discussed about three months after the secretariat had been created, in the course of the first meeting between the President of the Secretariat and the General Secretary of the World Council of Churches, Dr. W.A. Visser 't Hooft, during which they agreed to organize an informal meeting on the subject between representatives of the World Council of Churches and the Catholic Conference for Ecumenical Questions, of which Willebrands was secretary at the time. Another reason for such a meeting was the fact that the next meeting of the World Council of Churches, which was scheduled for November 1961, was to deal with the same subject.[9] In this connection, I recall a detail mentioned to me by Willebrands: he and the visitor

---

5. These are the statements which are found in the archives and from which we cited a certain number at the start of our previous chapter.

6. The largest collection of such tributes is found in *Bea-Preis* (or *Bea Prize*), where the texts of these is always given in the original language.

7. Cf. *ibid.*, pp. 7-21.

8. *Ibid.*, p. 7.

9. Cf. *Friede*, p. 15.

had been so filled with enthusiasm by their conversation with Cardinal Bea that they jotted down some ideas concerning religious freedom during the lunch they had together immediately after the meeting.

It is somewhat difficult to define *the cardinal's contribution* to the document on religious freedom, for his commitment in support of this document is not nearly as clear as in the case, for example, of the document on ecumenism or that on the non-Christian religions which the cardinal went so far as to introduce and defend personally in the Council hall. The question of this contribution has been carefully studied by Cardinal P. Pavan, who can speak on the basis of his own experience, since he and Father J.C. Murray, S.J., were the members of the secretariat principally involved in drafting *Dignitatis humanae*.[10] Pavan stresses that Bea's first important contribution was his activity in informing and enlightening public opinion.[11] Bea spoke on the subject for the first time at the Rome Agapé meeting in January 1963, where his address had a sensational effect, with the press agencies reporting it all over the world.[12] The talk he gave at the New York Agapé meeting[13] had similar effects, because of the special circumstances. However, the talk he gave in the Capitol in Rome in December 1963 on "Religious Freedom and Social Transformations" was of particular importance. This talk was delivered only a few weeks after the first introduction and a partial general discussion of the relative schema in the Council hall, in other words when public opinion, especially the Council fathers, had begun to consider the question and realize its importance. Subsequently, during the months when preparations were being made for the full-scale discussion of the problem in the Council, the talk was published in fourteen reviews in the various continents of the globe.[14] Given the topical nature of the question and the identity of the author, it is reasonable to suppose that in this way the talk will have played a considerable role in preparing the Council fathers for the discussion that was to take place in the third period of the Council.[15]

Cardinal Pavan also emphasizes *a special aspect* of this activity of the cardinal in the sphere of public opinion: "It is noteworthy that the basic line seen in these initiatives of the cardinal with regard to public opinion is in full harmony with the basic line followed by the secretariat in its progressive development of

10. Cf. *Simposio*, pp. 116-147.

11. Cf. *ibid.*, p. 144.

12. Cf. Biblio. 227. The cardinal had already treated the subject *in part*—although not in the context of the Council—in the article "San Paolo araldo ed eroe della libertà" (Biblio. 127; cf. also 187).

13. Cf. Biblio. 231.

14. Cf. Biblio. 248 (fourteen reviews in seven languages). We would note in particular that while the talk was being prepared somebody (without authorization) distributed in the Council hall ten cyclostyled pages listing all the objections to the schema on religious freedom. This meant that they could be taken into account in the talk.

15. Cf. W. Kasper, "Wahrheit und Freiheit. Die Erklärung über die Religionsfreiheit des II. Vatikanischen Konzils," *Sitzungsberichte der Heidelberger Akademie der Wissenschaften. Philosophisch-historische Klasse. Jahrg. 1988*, IV (Heidelberg, 1988), 19, note 56: "Cardinal Bea also considerably contributed to the success of the conciliar declaration through a series of talks, which attracted a wide audience."

the declaration *Dignitatis humanae*, and this is also true of the various stances the secretariat adopted during this process with regard to three questions that were very hotly debated by the Council fathers, namely, the basis and the object of the right to freedom in religious questions, and the role of the state with regard to this freedom."[16] After examining some details of these questions, the author concludes: "The total agreement, even as concerns time-tables, between the doctrinal statements made by the secretariat and those made by its president Cardinal Bea with regard to the drafting of the conciliar document—statements that were adopted one by one by the secretariat when drafting its schemata, and by the cardinal in his public talks on the same subject—reflects the active role played by the cardinal in the work of the secretariat, and show that he felt called upon to inform the public about the most important steps taken by the secretariat in this work."[17]

After emphasizing these major contributions, the author says that in his view Cardinal Bea "played a role of the greatest importance, . . . maybe all the more so on account of the weight his prominent personality brought to bear in the life of the church." He then expands on this in the following description of the cardinal's personality: "Open and undisputed faithfulness to the church, exceptional theological and biblical learning, a wealth of knowledge in a series of more profane spheres, breadth of vision, nobility of behavior and aspect, serenity and openness of spirit, a disposition for dialogue that was a gift of nature and also the fruit of training, and a great understanding of others, combined with an inflexible regard for truth. And everyone recognized these natural gifts and moral virtues in the cardinal."[18]

In order to understand the full weight of this last contribution, we should recall the tortuous progress of the document, which was certainly the most contested of the conciliar documents, so that we see from the *Acta Synodalia* that 98 speeches and 194 written opinions were dedicated to it.[19] *Nostra aetate* also had a prolonged and difficult development, but in the case of the schema on religious freedom there was also the very serious obstacle that on two occasions the conciliar authorities refused to allow the vote to be taken. The situation was eventually resolved through a personal intervention on the part of

16. *Simposio*, p. 144.

17. *Ibid.*, p. 145. A detailed comparison between the cardinal's statements and the various stages in the drafting of the conciliar document would carry us too far afield, although it would provide an interesting subject for special research at some later date. Cf. *ibid.*, p. 135.

18. *Ibid.*, p. 143. This analysis of the reasons for the influence exercised by the cardinal reminds us of the tributes of Council fathers and theologians cited at the start of our previous chapter, and also represents noteworthy confirmation of these.

19. These figures are not easy to calculate. In the first place it is practically impossible to work out the number of interventions in the first period of the Council, since these were made in the context of the general discussion on the whole schema on ecumenism (and the question of the Jewish people was also included here). Following the index in the *Acta Synodalia* we obtain the figures we have cited, although the official spokesman stated in the Council hall on 25 September 1965 that 218 written documents had been received (cf. *AS*, IV/I, 196). In any case, the 120 oral contributions and 600 written contributions mentioned in an address in the Cardinal A. Bea Symposium represented a decided exaggeration (cf. *Simposio*, p. 148).

Pope Paul VI, similar to the well-known one that Pope John XXIII made concerning "The sources of revelation" during the first period of the Council.[20] In view of these facts, we may well wonder how so many major obstacles could have been overcome, and we can understand how Cardinal Pavan himself could have summarized his thoughts on Cardinal Bea's specific contribution as follows in a private conversation: "It is beyond doubt that without the cardinal's active presence, we should never have obtained the Declaration on Religious Freedom."[21]

Activity in Favor of Harmony and Unity among Human Beings

In a previous chapter we described the context and background to the three Agapé meetings at which the cardinal made major speeches,[22] but here we shall be concentrating on the content of these speeches. Although the subjects dealt with at the various meetings were not identical, they were all concerned in one way or another with the unity that must be achieved among human beings.

1. *The Agapé meeting held in January 1962 in Rome* had the following subject: "Racial Prejudices: The Reason for Religious, Political and Cultural Incomprehension." The cardinal's speech was fairly brief. He took as his starting-point the fact that this was a meeting between people who believed in God and wished to work together for the major interests of humankind, particularly for peace. In the face of the divisions caused by racial prejudices, they intended this meeting to manifest and strengthen their common basis, that is, faith in God, and love for God and human beings.[23]

The second Agapé meeting was held in Rome in 1963, and its subject was expressed in a more positive and general manner: "The Love of Truth, Practiced in Charity, as the Way to Harmony between Individuals and between Groups."

20. Cf. pp. 416-419 above. The facts are as follows. In the third period, in *AS*, III/VIII, 184 (= GC 124 of 17 November) it is announced that the vote is to be taken the next day. In *ibid.*, p. 391 (= GC 125 of 18 November) we find the announcement that a preliminary vote is to be held on the question of *whether* the schema is to be voted on. In *ibid.*, p. 415 (= GC 126 of 19 November), the Council authorities state that the assembly is not competent to decide on whether or not the vote should be taken, and thus announce their own decision that the schema will not be put to a vote. In the fourth period of the Council, although the decision of the Council authorities is *not* found in the *Acta Synodalia* (cf. note , p. 449 above), the facts are certain. For the background, cf. Caprile, V, 45-48. To the best of my knowledge, a specific and providential circumstance played a particular role here: the fact that this was the eve of Pope Paul VI's visit to the United Nations, and the pope felt it would be difficult to appear before such a gathering if at that moment, in the last period of the Council, the draft on religious freedom had not even reached an initial vote; the pope therefore intervened indirectly, and the vote was taken. This is reported by Monsignor Vincenzo Carbone, an official at the General Secretariat of the Council.

21. Cardinal Pavan said this to the Under-Secretary of the Secretariat for Christian Unity, Monsignor J.-F. Arrighi, in 1980, and Monsignor Arrighi repeated it to me almost immediately afterward.

22. Cf. pp. 427-428 above.

23. Cf. Biblio. 227, pp, 75-78, 109-110.

The cardinal gave the inaugural key-speech,[24] starting by describing the often tortuous path that people follow in search of the truth. Thus he made particular reference to the sad phenomenon of wars over religion, when people try to impose certain convictions on others by force, in the name of truth, forgetting that human freedom is no less fundamental than the love of truth.[25] He went on to explain the nature of human freedom, and then asked: "What is the best way to avoid the pitfalls we have listed and all the others that threaten the love and the search for truth?" His reply was as follows: "The best way is without doubt authentic love of one's neighbor."[26] He explained the concept of love of neighbor, but immediately felt called on to make the following warning in this connection: "Beware of snares and aberrations."[27] He then summarized his stance as follows: "The love of truth, without love, becomes intolerant and repels. Love without truth is blind, and cannot last. . . . They must be combined harmoniously, each in its place and according to its own weight. When they are united in this way, they can be effective in uniting people and creating harmony."[28] However, people find it all too easy to separate these two factors and all too difficult to unite them harmoniously. This led him to consider where we are to seek help in order to avoid separating truth and love, and to ensure their harmony among people. And he replied as follows: "It is in recourse to God, our Creator, that we shall seek the harmony that is so difficult to achieve between the love of truth and charity."[29]

The subject of *the Agapé meeting held on 1 April 1963 in New York* was "Civic Unity in Freedom under God,"[30] and we shall summarize the content of the cardinal's speech. He started by observing that the subject certainly encompassed the two deepest trends and anxieties among contemporary people, although there was a vast tension between the two. Today the urge toward unity is very powerful, but if this unity is to be truly human it must be the fruit of a free decision on the part of human beings. The law that guarantees that true unity is achieved in true freedom is the law of truth, justice and love. Nonetheless, humankind is also conscious of its very deep relations with a supreme personal Being who is at the beginning of its temporal existence, and who guides human events and human destinies; people feel related to him because they are made in his image. He is the supreme guarantor of the law of truth, justice and love, which rests on his authority—an authority that is both paternal and just.

Cardinal Bea concluded with the hope that meetings of this kind "between people of good will who love man and the human family, whatever nationality or faith they belong to," may be held increasingly often: "This is an extremely

---

24. Cf. Biblio. 227.
25. Cf. *ibid.*, p. 6.
26. *Ibid.*, pp. 6-7.
27. *Ibid.*, p. 7.
28. *Ibid.*
29. *Ibid.*, p. 8.
30. Cf. Biblio. 231. The original Italian manuscript (R 1963/28) has never been published as such, since the version found in the Italian translation of the book *Unity in Freedom* is simply a translation of the official English text found there.

important and urgent task. In point of fact, it is not only the material peace of the world at stake here, but also the well-ordered and harmonious development of mankind and its worldly and other-worldly destinies."[31]

2. A few days after the New York Agapé meeting, certain influential circles in the city asked the cardinal to expand his address into a book; and they quickly found a publisher who was prepared to publish it, and who calculated that he could place at least half a million copies in the United States alone. The proposal offered unexpected opportunities to fulfill the hope with which the cardinal had concluded his speech, and he therefore accepted.

He started on the task almost immediately after his return to Rome. The book went through two major drafts. The first of these was originally written in Italian and then translated into English in Rome; however, for various reasons, probably including the fact that the translation was inadequate, the publisher was not satisfied. Assistance was then sought from a fellow-Jesuit, B. Leeming, who taught at Heythrop Theological College in England, and who had supervised the English edition of *The Unity of Christians* (a book that became almost a best-seller) a few months earlier. The cardinal therefore had great faith in him, and the resulting very productive collaboration meant that this new book reached completion by the end of December 1963.[32]

Let us now take a brief look at *the content and structure* of the book. The first chapter introduces the subject and is for the most part the text of the speech the cardinal gave at the New York meeting. The second chapter is devoted to the basic law of "encounters of free men,"[33] that is, the dual law of truth and love; this is for the most part the talk he gave at the January 1963 Agapé meeting. The third chapter deals with the means of social communication in relation to the general theme of the book. The fourth chapter takes the example of Pope John XXIII, particularly his last encyclical *Pacem in terris*, to illustrate the basic concepts of the book. The next chapter shows how the Second Vatican Council intends moving in the same direction.

The six following chapters deal with various aspects of both unity and freedom in the life of the church. Thus, the first is entitled "The Dynamic Unity of the Church." The next two deal with freedom—the need to defend it, and its practice in the church. The next three chapters speak of the unity of the church, describing (a) the problem of the division of Christians and the significance of the ecumenical movement, (b) what the Council will be able to do in order to further Christian unity, and (c) what the church is already doing. The last chapter

---

31. *Ibid.*
32. Our files contain the manuscript of the first draft (both the original Italian and the English translation—Rbd 6, 4-15) and also a photocopy of the manuscript of the second draft (Rbd 10). The accompanying correspondence indicates an initial intention to give a short introductory note saying who had helped in preparing the second draft, but this in fact came to nothing. We leave it up to later research (when the files become generally available) to carry out a detailed comparative study of the two versions of this book. For our purposes it is sufficient to observe that B. Leeming was always scrupulously faithful to the cardinal's thinking, and that the cardinal was no less attentive in evaluating the suggestions of his collaborator.
33. This is the title of the first chapter of the book.

is entitled "A Twofold or a Single Unity?" and provides a concluding summary of the whole book.

3. A very important contribution to the subject in question is provided by the conciliar declaration *Nostra aetate*, which we have discussed in considerable detail in one of our previous chapters. It begins by recalling the fact that in our times "men are drawing closer together, and the bonds of friendship between different peoples are being strengthened."[34] Consequently, the church, "ever aware of her duty to foster unity and charity among individuals, and even among nations, reflects at the outset on what men have in common and what tends to promote fellowship among them."[35] Referring to these last words, the document states that on account of their common origin and their common goal who is God, "All men form but one community."[36] The document closes with an affirmation of *universal brotherhood*: "We cannot truly pray to God the Father of all if we treat any people in other than brotherly fashion, for all men are created in God's image."[37] These themes are therefore reflected in the cardinal's commentary on *Nostra aetate*, which is entitled *The Church and the Jewish People*. One of the chapters has the title "Living and Working Together" and another "All Men Are Brothers, and Children of the Same Heavenly Father."[38]

In a similar way, the cardinal set about commenting on the conciliar declaration on *religious freedom* and publicizing its line of thought. Like his December 1963 talk, his commentary "The Church and Religious Freedom" received a wide readership, for it appeared in eight reviews in six languages on various continents.[39]

One Secretariat for Non-Christians, and Another for Non-Believers

True to the character we have come to know, the cardinal was too practical a man to stop at mere concepts, and we therefore find the various ideas set forth in the Agapé meetings and in the successive publications reflected almost at once in suggestions as to how they could be put into practice.[40]

As early as April 1962—and therefore prior to the two 1963 Agapé meet-

---

34. *NA*, 1.
35. *Ibid.*
36. *Ibid.*
37. *Ibid.*, 5.
38. The following articles should also be mentioned here: Biblio. 252; Biblio. 183 (cf. also *The Way*, pp. 248-254); Biblio. 317 (also found in *The Way*, pp. 214-228, and we shall cite from this book); Biblio. 334 (translator's note: the English version of this article is used in all successive citations, except when otherwise stated).
39. Cf. Biblio. 320 (translator's note: the English version of this article will be used in all successive citations); also *The Way*, pp. 184-214.
40. If anybody wonders about the connection between the subject of this chapter and the initiatives that we are about to describe here—those concerning the secretariats for non-Christians and for non-believers and others—he or she should simply remember that they were all concerned with serious divisions that are found among humankind and that we must try to bridge.

ings—the cardinal gave a press conference in Rome for the foreign press corps entitled "A Council for the Whole of Humanity." After speaking of the broad-based cooperation of all Christians, he went on as follows: "Mention may perhaps be made of another possible step forward. Pius XII and the present pope have appealed on more than one occasion to *all men of good will* for the good of humanity and particularly for peace. The problems confronting humanity at the present time are indeed so urgent that it is absolutely indispensable to mobilize all those forces that are in agreement at least in their general ideas about religion and God and the existence of a moral order. In these spheres they can and ought to try to make headway, wherever they can and as far as possible, by working together for the good of humankind. Perhaps also, in the same order of ideas, the Council will be able to give a more concrete form to the reiterated appeals of recent popes, thus contributing effectively to the good of human-kind."[41]

We should note *the basis* of the desired meeting with representatives of the non-Christian religions, in other words "their ideas about religion and God." This of course recalls the cardinal's declaration in January 1962 at the *first* Agapé meeting, where he spoke of the cooperation of "all those who believe in God," who have as their "common basis faith in God"[42]; nor, however, should we lose sight of the appeals made "to all men of good will" by John XXIII and, even earlier, by Pius XII.

During the press conference given in New York on 1 April 1963, the same day as the Agapé meeting, the cardinal was asked whether the secretariat was also concerned with relations with non-Christians, and especially with the organized non-Christian religions. He replied that the secretariat as such was not responsible for this field: "This would create dangerous and harmful confusion. However, inasmuch as representatives of the various non-Christian religions have also demonstrated great interest in the Council,[43] and inasmuch as relations with them are also encompassed in that unity of all men of good will for the good of humankind, which we discussed earlier, it is certainly to be hoped that a practical form may be found in order to cultivate these contacts too. I myself expressed this hope during a press conference a year ago. The favorable echo produced by this declaration leads us to suppose that here too we have a mature situation and spirits that are already open or are opening up to broader views and energetic action to make humankind truly a family of brothers and sisters, united in fraternal love and in effective cooperation under the eye of God the Father of all men, who are made in his image and likeness, and in union with him."[44]

---

41. *Unity of Christians*, p. 195 (ct).
42. Cf. Biblio. 227, pp. 76-77.
43. We would recall the announcement made in June 1962 on the part of a *Jewish* organization that it planned sending a representative to Rome for the Council (cf. *Simposio*, p. 18). Similar intentions were expressed in certain Moslem circles.
44. R 1963/27, pp. 6-7; this passage is also published in Caprile, II, 501; cf. also *ibid.*, pp. 415-416, which lists various similar suggestions, all of them, however, as Caprile observes, made after those of the cardinal.

In a letter of 12 September 1963 addressed to Cardinal Eugene Tisserant, Dean of the Sacred College of Cardinals, Pope Paul VI made various announcements concerning the Council, including the following: "We also saw fit to concern ourselves with the secretariat that is to be constituted in due course for those who belong to the non-Christian religion."[45] In view of the fact that Bea had been hoping for some time for an initiative of this kind, it is easy to understand how he greeted the pope's announcement. Moreover, in January 1964, several months before the pope actually created the secretariat in question (which was on 17 May 1964), he made an active contribution by defining the tasks and structure of the future body.[46]

We saw above that the cardinal did not confine himself to the religious sphere in his suggestions, but took his inspiration from certain appeals made by Pius XII and expressed the hope that all "men of good will" would work together to resolve the major problems of humankind, with especial emphasis on peace. In due course, he developed these seed-ideas, so that as early as February 1964— over a year prior to the creation of the Secretariat for Non-Believers—he was advocating the institution of a body for contacts with people who are without a religion or opposed to all religions.[47] The phenomenon of unbelief and atheism had by now assumed such proportions that it was vital that the church as such, from its center to its grassroots, should play a serious role here.

It was fairly natural that in this context the cardinal also felt the need for the Council to do something about the serious problem of *atheism* in the broadest sense of the term, ranging from theoretical to practical atheism, and without excepting any country or regime. In his view, this should be done with full respect for the freedom of all, with the arms of truth, justice and love alone, and with the sole intention of serving the well-being of the individual and of humanity as a whole.[48] It is well-known that the conciliar Constitution on the Church in the Modern World deals with the problem of atheism in three paragraphs,[49] and this leads us to deduce that the higher authorities decided to place the above-mentioned suggestions in this particular schema, where the subject could be dealt with in a broader and deeper context.

Some Steps Achieved in a Difficult Dialogue

Between December 1962 and April 1963, the cardinal was involved, through no initiative of his own, in some difficult contacts with the Soviet Union. The whole question is obviously complex and extremely sensitive. The leading actor

---

45. *AS*, II/I, 12; Italian translation in Caprile, III, 6. The singular "non-Christian religion" in this text is surprising, since there are in fact more than one. However, the original text speaks of "those whose religion is not included among the *professiones christianae*."

46. Cf. Arch. Me 1/3. The necessary discretion forces us to confine ourselves to this brief observation.

47. Cf. Arch. Mo 18/4.

48. Cf. *ibid.*; Mo 18/7; and Mo 18/8.

49. *GS*, 19-21.

and witness in this affair, Norman Cousins, has described it in detail in one of his books,[50] and I have personal proof of the trustworthy nature of his statements and thus have great respect for him.[51] Our files contain over twenty items concerning this episode, and I have myself already described it in an article of over thirty pages, which is still on the reserved list. In point of fact, I do not believe the time is yet ripe for revealing all the background information. I shall therefore confine myself to an unadorned presentation of the facts; and, for the reasons given above, I shall not footnote them individually but simply make a general reference to the relative file which is found in our archives.[52]

In October 1962 the Council had only just started when the Cuban crisis came to a head,[53] with the attempt of the Soviet Union to install missiles in Cuba, and President Kennedy's ultimatum. The world thus seemed to be on the brink of a new world war, with incalculable effects. Confidential consultations with the leaders of the parties to the dispute on the one hand, and the Secretariat of State on the other, indicated that the parties would be well-disposed toward a mediating appeal from Pope John XXIII. Monsignor Loris F. Capovilla, the pope's secretary, spoke of this mediation twenty years later as follows: "In the night between 23 and 24 October 1962, he [the pope] wrote his call for peace at his prie-dieu and his desk, and the following morning it was handed to the ambassadors of the major powers. *Pravda* published it, very unusually, on its front page, stressing that John XXIII was right to call for negotiations. Talks were duly organized between Khrushchev and Kennedy, and the Soviet ships took the nuclear war-heads home with them."[54]

In his Christmas message, Pope John XXIII referred to his "invitation" to the two parties, saying: "We are all the more pleased to recall this invitation, venerable brothers and beloved children, since unmistakable signs of deep understanding assure us that these words were not spoken in vain, but touched minds and hearts, thus opening up new prospects for fraternal trust and the first glimmers of a calm future with true social and international peace."[55] We should

---

50. Cf. Norman Cousins, *The Improbable Triumvirate. An Asterisk to the History of a Hopeful Year 1962/1963* (New York, 1972).

51. On the other hand, the account found in Giancarlo Zizola, *Utopia di Papa Giovanni* (Assisi, 1973), is far from objective, and is marred particularly by the incorrect preconceived view that the "Secretariat of State" was opposed to Pope John's plans. Zizola takes no account, for example, either of the well-known division at that time of the Secretariat of State into a "first" and a "second" section (respectively the Sacred Congregation for Extraordinary Affairs and the "Secretariat of State"), or of the fact that the attitude of the two sections was very different. Moreover, he appeals to secret documents, while making no mention at all of the articles that the leading figure, N. Cousins, had published on the whole episode nine years earlier. (Nor does he do so even in his "second, revised edition," despite the fact that this had been specifically brought to his attention.) For full details in explanation and confirmation of this opinion, cf. Arch. Mh 10/2.

52. Arch. Mp 19.

53. Cf. Cousins, *The Improbable Triumvirate*, pp. 13-19.

54. Recollections of the encyclical *Pacem in terris* on Vatican Radio, 30 March 1983, found in *Studi*, X (year XXVII), 5.

55. *AAS*, LV (1963), 15.

note the clear tone of optimism pervading the pope's words: not only had the invitation "touched minds and hearts," but it was "opening up new prospects . . . and the first glimmers of a calm future with true . . . peace." These words clearly go beyond the solution of the Cuban crisis and refer to certain further developments, which we shall now consider.

The success of the pope's appeal led one of those who had taken part in the aforementioned confidential consultations, Norman Cousins, to conceive a plan for further contacts, and in particular a personal journey to Moscow in order to promote peace, and also religious freedom in the Soviet Union if possible.[56] He came to Rome to find out what requests might be made to Moscow. In view of the delicate nature of the matter and also the fact that a few months earlier the Secretariat for Christian Unity had succeeded in receiving approval for observer-delegates of the Russian Orthodox Church to be sent to the Council, Cardinal Bea's name sprang to mind. I can state that it was Pope John himself who made this decision, telling some of his collaborators: "Give him my warmest greetings. When I am in Cardinal's Bea's hands, I need not worry." The cardinal thus received this very important task directly from the pope.[57]

Cousins visited the cardinal on 10 December. The requests, which had of course been agreed upon with those responsible for the relative spheres, were the liberation of the Ukrainian Archbishop of Lvov, J. Slipyi, who had been imprisoned in Soviet labor camps for eighteen years, and permission to send religious publications to the Soviet Union for various categories of believers, in line with the concept of religious freedom.

After the meeting with Cousins and while the latter was in Moscow, the cardinal paid a visit to the Cardinal Secretary of State on 11 December, and was then received in audience by Pope John XXIII on 16 December. Cousins returned to Rome on 19 December, and was received by several people, including Cardinal Bea, but most importantly by the pope himself. With regard to the case of Archbishop Slipyi, Cousins thought that there would soon be some news.[58] Apart from reporting on his conversations, Cousins brought the pope a greeting card from Khrushchev.[59] It was thus this series of initiatives on the part of Cousins, and their results as reported on 19 December, that were behind the reference to "new prospects" and "first glimmers of a calm future" in the pope's Christmas message.

The pope replied to Khrushchev, using the diplomatic mail to send a greeting card and a copy of his Christmas message in the original Italian together with a Russian translation.[60] And on 24 January we received the first news of the liberation of Archbishop Slipyi, who arrived in Rome on 9 February.

56. Cf. Cousins, *The Improbable Triumvirate*, pp. 20-21.

57. It is surprising that Hebblethwaite, *John XXIII*, p. 467, makes no mention of Bea's role.

58. Cousins, *The Improbable Triumvirate*, p. 64.

59. Italian translation of the card in Capovilla, *Giovanni XXIII. Lettere*, p. 439. For Cousins' conversation with Khrushchev on the case of Archbishop Slipyi, cf. Cousins, *The Improbable Triumvirate*, pp. 47-53, and for his audience with Pope John XXIII, cf. *ibid.*, pp. 62-65.

60. The original Italian text of the covering letter is found in Capovilla, *Giovanni XXIII. Lettere*, p. 438.

The day after this arrival, the pope revealed his deep feelings, confiding: "From the very region of eastern Europe we received a touching consolation yesterday, and we humbly thank the Lord for this as something that in God's secret plans may provide the holy church and righteous souls with a new impulse of sincere faith and apostolic work. . . . Let us not disturb the mysterious design in which God calls everybody to cooperate, by drawing together the threads of a fabric that is woven by his grace and by the ready service of innocent souls—of meek and generous souls."[61]

Even before reception of this news, it seemed clear to us that Khrushchev had specific aims in view with his improvement in relations with the Vatican; in other words, he wanted to establish diplomatic relations with the Holy See. On 7 February 1963—two days before the already liberated Archbishop Slipyi actually arrived in Rome—Cardinal Bea received a visit from S.P. Kozyrev, the Soviet ambassador to Italy. At this meeting, the cardinal tried to "move very, very cautiously," in keeping with the instructions he had received, without pushing anything. It is interesting that despite all the discretion that we for our part observed, there was a news leak, so that an Italian magazine was even able to report that there were rumors in diplomatic circles that the Soviet Union was sounding out the ground with a view to establishing diplomatic relations.[62]

Three months later, in April, Norman Cousins undertook a further journey to Moscow, traveling via Rome as he had done on his first journey. Two points were especially recommended to his attention: possibilities for the higher authorities of the Catholic Church to contact their faithful in the Soviet Union, and the liberation of the Archbishop of Prague, Joseph Beran. Without going into details, we would simply state that on 2 October of the same year Archbishop Beran and other Czechoslovakian bishops were freed,[63] although it is not possible to establish a specific link with the initiatives of Cousins.

Let us conclude this section with the following remarks:

(a) The cardinal always acted on higher orders, and he did his homework very thoroughly, asking for orientations and following them, and also keeping the authorities that had entrusted him with the task abreast of events.

(b) The task the authorities had entrusted to him in this field was certainly a sign of great trust. For the cardinal, it entailed both sacrifice and considerable risks, and it was no light matter for a man of his authority to be willing to assume these risks. And he did in fact do so, not only in a spirit of obedience to the pope, but also in consideration of the great profit to the church that was at stake.

After an overview of the initiatives connected with the subject of this chapter, a first general contact with the cardinal's thinking, and some information on the sources on which we shall draw in order to gain a more thorough understanding of this thinking, we shall now take a closer and more detailed look at the latter as it was revealed in the various sectors. From the very beginning of the chapter we have seen how he spoke of two kinds of unity: one that is purely human, and

61. *Discorsi, messaggi, colloqui del Santo Padre Giovanni XXIII* (Vatican City), V, 123.
62. Cf. the magazine *Vita* (of Rome) of 21 February 1963.
63. Cf. *OssRom* (5 October 1963), and *CC* (1963/IV), 193.

the other specifically Christian. We saw the same thing when indicating the main points of the book *Unity in Freedom*. Our presentation of his ideas will therefore be divided into three sections: (A) the concept of human unity; (B) the concept of Christian unity; and (C) the relations between the two.[64]

A. Purely Human Unity

1. *The Situation of Humanity Today.* In an attempt to establish a diagnosis, the cardinal remarked that in this world of ours there are *very many factors at work, urging us toward unity.* In the address he gave at the New York Agapé meeting, the cardinal stated in this connection: "In the modern world there are a number of factors, and of causes, which have tended and continue to tend to produce a certain unity among the inhabitants of the world: quick and easy travel, and so contacts with many people; mass communication which informs about events in every part of the world; an increasing interdependence caused by political and economic necessity; cultural and scientific developments which directly or indirectly affect all peoples."[65]

At the same time, contemporary people feel pain in the face of *the divisions that split humanity.* Indeed, the harder they seek unity, the more aware they become of the forces opposing it. We would recall that the subject of the first Agapé meeting the cardinal attended was "Racial Prejudices: The Reason for Religious, Political and Cultural Incomprehension."[66] Would that this were the only such reason! Elsewhere, the author gives an even more dismal account of the situation, recalling "politico-economic estrangements, with the consequent armaments race. . . . The complete banning of nuclear weapons, much more general disarmament, seems outside the range of practical possibilities.[67] Consider the prejudices and antagonisms which spoil or ruin human relations between different races and nations, between different classes of society and between economic groupings. Even in the domain of religion, which should be sacrosanct and unifying, there are divisions, ignorance, prejudices, resentments and aversions, the practical consequences of which are endlessly ramifying."[68]

Furthermore, the author indicates the paradoxical function exercised in this

---

64. In 1967 the subject of relations between the churches and the unity of humanity was taken as the subject of a study by the Faith and Order Commission of the World Council of Churches. The general project that was born from this study was then studied in further depth by various groups. Cf. for example Josef Schubert (ed.), *Zum Thema Eine Kirche—Eine Menschheit. Eine ökumenische Arbeitsgruppe unter Leitung von Peter Bläser und Hans Heinrich Wolf* (Stuttgart, 1971); also J.R. Nelson and W. Pannenberg (eds.), *Um Einheit und Heil der Menschheit* (Frankfurt, 1973).

65. *Unity in Freedom*, p. 3; cf. also *The Way*, p. 248. Cf. also the more detailed description of economic interdependence (*Unity in Freedom*, p. 60). For the general movement toward unity, cf. *The Way*, p. 248. For the "nostalgia for unity," cf. R 1963/21, p. 1; R 1964/28; *The Way*, p. 217.

66. Cf. Biblio. 227, p. 69.

67. We would note in passing that in the twenty years following publication of the cardinal's book the situation progressively deteriorated, becoming increasingly grim.

68. *Unity in Freedom*, p. 2.

field by the means of social communications: "These modern wonders by which news is rapidly transmitted—newspapers, cinema, radio, television—could tend to mitigate or correct this deplorable state of affairs; but rapid dissemination of 'news' may even aggravate the evil, since closer contact is made between people of differing cultures, differing standards of living and differing political, social and religious outlooks, and the closeness and vividness of the contact increase the frequency and violence of the contrasts, even the clash, between them."[69]

2. Passing from diagnosis to practical treatment, the first question concerns *the precise basis* on which the edifice of unity is to rest, and the cardinal replies: "The first rock that is alone capable of bearing the grand and imposing structure of the unity of the whole human family . . . is the noble and great dignity of the human person, his nature as a being endowed with intelligence and free will, with the laws that are impressed within it. Notwithstanding the natural differences in talent and quality which exist between individuals and between nations, by far the most important element is this fundamental dignity of the human person, which is common to all."[70]

3. On this basis, we must then ask *what precisely freedom is*, and the cardinal replies: "Every affirmation of liberty must bear in mind two elements. The first is man's noble and awe-inspiring power to be master of his own actions and to build up his personality, step by step, with conscious and free acts which will eventually also go to decide his destiny beyond the grave. The second consists in the fact that the exercise of this power is not and cannot be completely free, for it has its own law in the reality of man's own nature."[71]

This law inherent in human nature is more clearly defined as "what St. Paul said was written in man's heart; even when he is without the law given by divine revelation man does God's will if he follows the natural light which illuminates his conscience (cf. Rom. 2:14-15)."[72]

Neglecting either of the two elements that are essential to any freedom "means harming man's dignity as a person in one way or another, and making him a slave to his lowest instincts or an unhappy being who is egotistically confined within the narrow bounds of self, a slave to the law which he indeed accepts but in a servile manner rather than freely and deliberately."[73]

4. Once again taking the fundamental dignity of the person as our starting-point, let us ask more *precisely what unity is*, and we find the following reply: "It is the conscious, *free* decision taken by responsible persons to enter into union with other responsible persons. It is a conscious and responsible encounter of free persons and consists of *a mutual exchange*, of giving and receiving what each one possesses, not solely or mainly as regards material goods, but above

---

69. *Ibid.*

70. *The Way*, p. 251 (ct). Cf. also *Unity in Freedom*, p. 3.

71. *The Way*, p. 187 (ct). Cf. also *Unity in Freedom*, p. 112: "A self-restraint, a self-control," makes the human being not less but more human.

72. *The Way*, p. 187 (ct); cf. also *ibid.*, p. 186. We shall discuss the relation between freedom and God below.

73. *Ibid.*, p. 188 (ct).

all spiritual goods; this exchange is also a symbol of the mutual, reciprocal giving of self, as occurs in authentic love, whether between man and woman or in authentic friendship."[74]

"Indeed, nature itself inserts man, from the moment of his birth, not only into the family and into various forms of religious and civil society, but also into the great family of nations, or rather, into the whole of mankind. And man is able to achieve his development only in such conscious encounters with other individuals and groups in society."[75]

It is obvious that this mutual exchange must also take place between peoples and nations. "Even though human beings differ from one another in their ethnic characteristics, they all possess certain essential common characteristics and are inclined by nature to meet each other in the world of spiritual values, in which progressive unifying development opens to them the possibility of improvement without limits. They have the right and duty, therefore, to live in communion with one another."[76] In this way the vast areas of potential latent in humanity are gradually developed, and its profound unity grows, above all in spiritual terms.

5. The "polarity" that exists between unity and freedom is all too well-known[77]—as is the difficulty entailed in harmoniously combining the practice of both. This leads to *the problem* of "whether there is a principle which can guide man's conduct in such a way as to guarantee both the unity of man with other men, and the freedom of every person."[78] We have already seen this principle when speaking of freedom: it does not only mean having dominion over one's own acts, but also means following one's own conscience, for only in this way can freedom avoid degenerating into anarchy or ending up in discord and the destruction of unity. The principle we seek is "the law that comes from the very nature of man."[79] In other words, it is "the law written in man's heart to do good and to avoid evil." In point of fact, each of us experiences daily what the non-Christian poet Ovid confessed: "I see the things that are better and I approve them, but I follow those that are worse."[80]

The principle of "doing good and avoiding evil" is then more precisely defined: "Pope John XXIII once said of himself that for his part he tried always to give weight to that which united and to go the same way with everyone as far as was possible, without impinging on the rights of justice and truth. The firm

74. R 1963/28, p. 2.
75. *Unity in Freedom*, p. 5.
76. *Ibid.*, p. 49, citing the words of John XXIII in the encyclical *Pacem in terris* (*AAS*, LV [1963], 284-285). I would recall that Chapter 4 of *Unity in Freedom* is in fact devoted to showing that this is not merely the cardinal's own personal view, but the teaching of the Catholic Church.
77. Cf. R 1963/28, p. 1; *Unity in Freedom*, pp. 5-6.
78. *Unity in Freedom*, p. 6.
79. *The Way*, p. 187.
80. Cf. R 1963/28, p. 3 (quoted in Latin: "Video meliora proboque deteriora sequor"). At this point in *Unity in Freedom*, it is shown that "every man has a conscience and must follow it," and it is concluded that "so long as men are men, they will praise or blame one another, which is an implicit acknowledgment of freedom and of conscience" (p. 7).

and constant norm for the constitution of unity is hence given by truth and justice—and, we can add, also by love."[81]

Here we should refer back to the reflections expressed in the cardinal's address to the second Agapé meeting held in Rome (1963), "The Love of Truth, Practiced in Charity, as the Way to Harmony between Individuals and between Groups,"[82] when he summarized the dialectic existing between these two tendencies in the phrase: "The love of truth, without love, becomes intolerant and repels. Love without truth is blind and cannot last."[83] The cardinal could therefore conclude that truth and love are unifying virtues *par excellence*, provided that they are both united in a well-based balance.[84] "Indeed, what greater union is possible than when one spirit sparks off the other and one is lit by the flame of the other, when one heart warms another and is warmed by the spirit of the other and by his love."[85]

6. There is one final element essential for the construction of unity in freedom, namely *the idea of God*, and the cardinal presents this in two ways: first from the viewpoint of man, and secondly from the viewpoint of God himself.

(a) Relations with God are an essential part of *the total dimension of human life*.

A first approach here takes as its starting-point the difficulty cited above of obtaining a balance between truth and love. Indeed, "one of the sorry consequences of original sin is man's very capacity to dissociate truth from love."[86] So where is aid to be sought for this search and battle? The cardinal replies as follows: "Every religion that knows authentic prayer directs man to search in his Creator, God, not only for material goods but also—and above all—for those goods that are the deepest and most essential for the soul: the intelligence and wisdom that will aid him to conduct his life well. It is thus in recourse to God our Creator that we shall seek the harmony that is so difficult to obtain between the love of truth and charity."[87]

The second, more profound, approach is as follows: "Where man has preserved himself in the healthy and original freshness of his being, where he preserves a spontaneous and profound vision of the whole of life as it really is and not falsified by blindness or by results claimed by philosophy and science, he has *the sense and awareness that his personal relations extend beyond purely human society*."[88] In this connection, the cardinal appeals to the witness "of the most ancient cultures and religions" and to "science, especially history and ethnology."[89] The cardinal described this personal relationship with the supreme

81. R 1963/28, p. 3; cf. *Unity in Freedom*, p. 7.
82. Cf. Biblio. 227.
83. *Ibid.*, p. 8.
84. Cf. *ibid.*, pp. 6-7.
85. *Ibid.*, p. 7.
86. *Ibid.*, pp. 7-8.
87. *Ibid.*, p. 8.
88. R 1963/28, p. 3; here we cite the original text of the address rather than the reworked version found in *Unity in Freedom*, pp. 10-14.
89. *Ibid.*, pp. 3-4; cf. also *Unity in Freedom*, pp. 10-11, while on p. 11 we find an answer to possible

Being as follows: "According to the well-known dictum of the non-Christian poet cited by St. Paul at the Areopagus in Athens, 'we are indeed his [God's] offspring' (Acts 17:28); the human creature feels in some way related to this mysterious and supreme personal Being, because he is made in his likeness.[90] Hence, the human person knows that mutual exchanges of giving and receiving exist between him and this Being, similar to those that the person has with other people."[91]

Going into greater detail, it is obvious that it is precisely our faithfulness to the law of our conscience that also defines our relations with this Being and thus our final destiny: "Inasmuch as man . . . feels that he is placed under the just and fatherly authority of this supreme personal Being—although, despite this authority, he still retains the freedom to decide his own destiny for himself—his actions, depending whether they are good or bad, inevitably affect his relationship with this supreme Authority, and it is in this way that our final destinies beyond the grave are forged and decided for each one of us."[92] Here we can clearly see the unshakable foundation of rock on which this law of truth, justice and love rests: "It is not an abstract law, floating in the air, as it were; on the contrary, it rests on the fatherly yet just authority of this supreme personal Being."[93]

(b) How can we present the essential significance of the idea of God for the building up of the unity of the human family, as it were *from God's point of view*? The cardinal replies by quoting the introduction to *Nostra aetate*: "All men form but one community. This is so because all stem from the one stock which God created to people the entire earth, and also because all share a common destiny, namely God. His providence, evident goodness and saving designs extend to all men."[94] These words, the cardinal observes, "could well be branded in letters of fire on every international organization."[95]

In his commentary on *Nostra aetate*, the cardinal discusses these words of the Council at some length,[96] indicating in particular their biblical foundations, partly because several elements in the text are taken directly from sacred scripture.[97] For *the common origin* of all peoples, reference can be made

objections of "agnostics, atheists, dialectical materialists."
90. Cf. also *Unity in Freedom*, p. 213.
91. R 1963/28, p. 4.
92. *Ibid.*
93. *Ibid.* The essential elements of this conception are already seen in the short address to the 1962 Agapé meeting; cf. Biblio. 227, pp. 76-77, 110. As on other points, the cardinal confirms these statements on the basis of the encyclical *Pacem in terris* (cf. *AAS*, LV [1963], 266-271); cf. *Unity in Freedom*, p. 63.
94. *NA*, 1. The same concept is found in *GS*, 24.
95. *Church-Jews*, p. 30. Cf. also *NA*, 5, which speaks of God as Father of all mankind and of fraternity; however, the underlying thought here is different, and we shall hence deal with it in another context.
96. *Church-Jews*, p. 31-37.
97. To avoid any possible misapprehension, we would state that although we are drawing on revelation here, we are doing so in order to speak about purely human unity, and that we are therefore keeping to our stated subject.

primarily to Acts 17:25-26, which in turn echoes many Old Testament texts.[98] He then considers the statement that all people "share a common destiny, namely God,"[99] and finally the words: "His [God's] providence, evident goodness and saving designs extend to all men."[100]

* * *

Let us summarize this whole account of *unity on the human level* by citing a very helpful résumé made by the cardinal himself: God's plan and will are to make "humanity into a true family of brethren, united in fraternal union and in effective cooperation under the watchful eye [of God] and in union with God, the Father of all men, who are made in his image and likeness."[101]

B. Specifically Christian Unity

In this connection, the cardinal explains: "The Christian teaching, however, while accepting this natural unity of mankind, holds that God, without in the least lessening or harming this natural unity, has lifted it to a higher plane. God has freely given to mankind a new vital principle of unity, a transfusion into human nature of the very life-blood of God himself—insofar as one can use such language of God."[102] We are thus faced with the question of the more precise nature of this specifically Christian unity.

1. *Christ's work of redemption* lies at the basis of this new unity. The cardinal explains this in most detail when commenting on the words that the Council addresses to those who wrongly accuse the Jewish people: "The church always held and continues to hold that Christ out of infinite love freely underwent suffering and death because of the sins of all men, so that all might attain salvation."[103] Here the Council reminds everybody of "the fundamental truth of Christianity, which, as St. Paul points out, belongs to the rudiments of Christian teaching: 'I have delivered to you as of first importance what I also received, that Christ died for our sins in accordance with the scriptures' (1 Cor. 15:3)."[104] "St. Peter reminds his readers: 'You were ransomed from the futile ways you inherited from your fathers, not with perishable things such as silver and gold, but with the precious blood of Christ, like that of a lamb without blemish or spot' (1 Peter 1:18-19). The metaphor of the lamb recalls the idea of sacrifice,

---

98. For example Ex. 20:11; Ps. 145:6; Is. 42:5; Wis. 9:1-2; Ps. 115:16, cf. Is. 45:18. Cf. *Church-Jews*, pp. 31-32.
99. Cf. Sir. 17:6, 9-10; Wis. 15:3. Cf. *Church-Jews*, p. 32.
100. Cf. Wis. 11:24; Ps. 145:9, cf. Sir. 18:13; Wis. 8:1: 14:3, cf. Prov. 16:1, 9; Acts 14:17. Cf. *Church-Jews*, p. 36.
101. R 1963/27, p. 7; this is the text of the press conference given in New York in April 1963.
102. *Unity in Freedom*, p. 91.
103. *NA*, 4.
104. *Church-Jews*, p. 105.

as it is expressed in the Epistle to the Ephesians: 'Christ loved us and gave himself for us, a fragrant offering and sacrifice to God' (Eph. 5:2)."[105]

2. This immediately shows us *the situation of humanity* prior to the work of redemption wrought by Christ.

(a) In the first place, humankind was *divided from God* its Creator, and Christ's work thus means reconciliation of humankind with God: "It pleased God to reconcile all things with him, whether on earth or whether in heaven, by means of the blood of Christ (cf. Col. 1:20). It was thus God himself who 'was in Christ reconciling the world to himself, not counting their trespasses against them' (2 Cor. 5:19; cf. Eph. 2:16)."[106] This is because when people commit sin, they become "enemies" of God (cf. Rom. 5:10). St. Paul can thus state about himself and his readers: "We too were once 'children of wrath, like the rest of mankind' (Eph. 2:3), because we were sinners and we have been saved only by the undeserved gift of the grace of God."[107]

(b) Humankind was also divided internally: "In order to give us a concrete and very vivid idea of our state prior to the redemption wrought by Christ, sacred scripture frequently returns to the subject. Thus Isaiah in the celebrated Song of the Suffering Servant says: 'All of us like sheep have gone astray; we have turned every one to his own way; and the Lord has laid on him [the Suffering Servant] the iniquity of us all' (Is. 53:6)."[108] This context also allows a very clear explanation of St. John's statement that "Jesus should die for the nation, and not for the nation only, but to gather into one the children of God who are scattered abroad" (John 11:51b-52).

3. Apart from healing the divisions afflicting humankind, Christ's work also gives people *a basis for a new, supernatural unity* that is specifically Christian, in other words the transformation through which people become adoptive children of God. "God's plan is to offer to every man, as a gratuitous gift in Christ, the possibility of becoming the adopted child of God. In fact, as St. Paul tells us, God has 'predestined them to be conformed to the image of his Son, in order that he might be the first-born among many brethren' (Rom. 8:29), the eldest of a family of many brothers. Christ, by coming into this world, 'gave to all those who received him and believed in his name the power to become children of God; who were born, not of blood nor of the will of the flesh nor of the will of man, but of God' (John 1:12-13). For this reason St. John speaks of Christians as children (Greek *tekna*; Latin *nati*) of God."[109]

Let us try to explain this even more precisely: "Here we are concerned with a sonship that is usually called *adoptive*, in order to distinguish it from natural sonship, which is proper to the Word alone. All the same this gift must not be considered as a mere legal act and token of affection; as will be seen, it entails

105. *Ibid.*, pp. 105-106.
106. *Ibid.*, p. 106 (ct).
107. *Ibid.*, p. 90.
108. *Ibid.*
109. *Ibid.*, pp. 138-139. Cf. John 11:52; 1 John 3:1-2; 5:2. Similarly St. Paul: Rom. 8:16-17; Eph. 5:1; Phil. 2:15.

a true inner transformation in the person, giving him a likeness to God which transcends his human nature and is therefore called '*super*natural.' "[110] "Man's individual personality is not destroyed, but is amplified, expanded, lifted up to new heights, given a share in the very life of Father, Son and Holy Spirit."[111]

We can therefore say that just as purely human unity has its basis in our nature as intelligent, free beings, so specifically Christian unity has its basis in the transformation through which we become partakers in divine life itself. This transformation enables Jesus in his high-priestly prayer to compare the unity of his disciples with his own unity with the Father: "I . . . pray . . . also for those who believe in me through their [the disciples'] word, that they may all be one; even as thou, Father, art in me, and I in thee, that they may also be in us, so that the world may believe that thou hast sent me" (John 17:20-21).[112] In this connection, the cardinal recalls the words of the conciliar Constitution on the Church in the Modern World, which states that in this prayer Jesus "has opened up new horizons closed to human reason by implying that there is a certain parallel between the union existing among the divine Persons and the union of the sons of God in truth and love."[113]

4. Apart from providing a new basis for unity, Christ not only respects our freedom, but guarantees our freedom from the wounds inflicted by sin.

(a) With regard to *respect for freedom*, the cardinal points out Christ's manner of action: "Christ, during his lifetime, did indeed lament the hard-heartedness and pride which led some to reject his message; but he never forced men to believe him. He relied upon the power of truth and of goodness and the evidence he gave that God was with him."[114]

This is echoed in the conciliar document on religious freedom: "One of the key truths in Catholic teaching, a truth that is contained in the word of God and constantly preached by the Fathers, is that man's response to God by faith ought to be *free*, and that therefore nobody is to be forced to embrace the faith against his will."[115] And the document continues with the following statement: "The act of faith is of its very nature a free act. Man, redeemed by Christ the Savior and called through Jesus Christ to be an adopted son of God, cannot give his adherence to God when he reveals himself unless, drawn by the Father, he submits to God with a faith that is reasonable and free."[116]

---

110. *Ibid.*, p. 139.
111. *Unity in Freedom*, p. 214. On the mystery of the incarnation as the basis of the gift of divine adoption, cf. *ibid.*, p. 90.
112. Cf. *ibid.*, p. 218.
113. *GS*, 24, referred to in *The Way*, p. 216, note 2.
114. *Unity in Freedom*, p. 106. Later on, *Dignitatis humanae*, 11, would propose the same line of reasoning.
115. *DH*, 10. Cf. Biblio. 320, p. 270. It is particularly worth noting the wealth of references from the fathers of the church and church documents given in notes 8 and 9 to this conciliar text (including one to Pius XII's classic encyclical *Mystici corporis*).
116. *DH*, 10. Cf. *Unity in Freedom*, p. 121: Faith, "involving a personal relation to God, is . . . necessarily a free act." *Dignitatis humanae* also takes up a position on possible ways of acting against this doctrine as these have been seen in the history of the church; cf. *DH*, 12.

(b) Christ *heals wounded freedom*.[117] St. Paul explains this point in a well-known passage in his Letter to the Romans: "I am carnal, sold under sin. I do not understand my own actions. For I do not do what I want, but I do the very thing I hate. . . . For I know that nothing good dwells within me, that is, in my flesh. I can will what is right, but I cannot do it" (Rom. 7:14b-15, 18). In various places, the cardinal explains that this liberation occurs by means of *the gift of the Spirit*, and cites the following chapter of the Letter to the Romans: "For the law of the Spirit of life in Christ Jesus has set me free from the law of sin and death. For God, . . . sending his own Son in the likeness of sinful flesh and for sin, . . . condemned sin in the flesh, in order that the just requirement of the law might be fulfilled in us, who walk not according to the flesh but according to the Spirit" (Rom. 8:2-4).[118] In another context, the cardinal explains: "That 'Spirit of life' is the Spirit of God, brought and given by God incarnate; and the Spirit of God is charity. It is this Spirit which can heal the split in the human psychological make-up, can overcome the rebellion of the lower self, bring unity to the whole man, and light and warm his life with the fire of charity."[119]

5. It is hardly necessary to say that in the new order too, *the threefold law* of truth, justice and love remains in full force, and is indeed reinforced. As regards *truth*, we should recall Christ's declaration before Pilate (John 18:37), as well as his earlier statement that "I am the Way, the Truth and the Life" (John 14:6)[120]; the Holy Spirit is the "Spirit of truth" (John 16:13). As regards *love*: "Through love be servants of one another" (Gal. 5:13); "He who loves his neighbor has fulfilled the law" (Rom. 13:8); thus the practice of love of neighbor undoubtedly encompasses the practice of *justice*. And, as we have seen, the Christian actually receives a new "Spirit" in order to be able to live out this threefold law in its fullness.

6. The unity that Christ creates among his disciples is so close that he can compare it to his own unity with the Father: ". . . that they may all be one; even as thou, Father, art in me, and I in thee" (John 17:21). Now this divine gift is *offered and intended for the whole human family*. In order to understand this, we must take as our starting-point *Christ's link with the whole of humankind*, which can be seen in the clear teaching of St. Paul. In order to explain this, the cardinal takes as his basis the words of *Nostra aetate*: "The church believes that Christ who is our peace has through his cross reconciled Jews and Gentiles and made them one in himself."[121]

(a) St. Paul described the *former* situation of the *non-Jewish peoples* when he wrote to the Ephesian Christians, who had come from paganism: "Therefore remember that at one time you Gentiles in the flesh, called the uncircumcision by what is called the circumcision, which is made in the flesh by hands—re-

---

117. Cf. *CC* (1960/IV), 3-14; this article is also reproduced in the booklet, Biblio. 187; cf. also *Unity in Freedom*, pp. 114-118.

118. Cf. *Church-Jews*, pp. 58-59. We cannot enter into the complicated question of the precise explanation of the Pauline concept of "liberation from the law."

119. *Unity in Freedom*, p. 117.

120. Cf. *ibid.*, pp. 224-225.

121. *NA*, 4.

member that you were at that time separated from Christ, alienated from the commonwealth of Israel, and strangers to the covenants of promise, having no hope and without God in the world" (Eph. 2:11-12).[122] All this was because they did not share in the revelation of God and in the promises he had made directly to Israel.

(b) The great change is described as follows: "But now in Christ Jesus you who once were far off have been brought near in the blood of Christ" (Eph. 2:13). And this miracle was brought about as follows: "It pleased God to reconcile to himself, through Christ, all things whether on earth or in heaven, making peace by the blood of his cross (cf. Col. 1:20). In order to bring this about, Christ, 'our peace,' has broken down the dividing wall of hostility, abolishing through the sacrifice of his flesh the law made up of commandments and decrees (cf. Eph. 2:14-15), in other words, the former, so-called 'ritual law'; and he has done all this in order—and here we come to the words of St. Paul which are used in the conciliar document itself—'that he might create in himself one new man in place of the two, so making peace, and might reconcile us both to God in one body through the cross, thereby bringing the hostility to an end. And he came and preached peace to you who were far off and peace to those who were near; for through him we both have access in one Spirit to the Father' (Eph. 2:15-18)."[123]

The author *concludes* with the following observation: "Obviously a great deal more would have to be said to explain these texts in detail, but since that is not practicable here, it will suffice to bear in mind the principal idea: by the sacrifice of his life on the cross Christ, as the new Head of the human race, has united in himself both Israel and the non-Jewish peoples, reconciling both to the Father. He is our 'bond of peace' and has come to spread the joyful news of the peace concluded between God and mankind."[124]

(c) As we have seen, Christ creates a unity between peoples that *transcends all differences* of nationality, race, social class, or even sex. In this connection, the cardinal cites a significant statement made by St. Paul in his Letter to the Galatians: "In Christ Jesus you are all sons of God, through faith. For as many of you as were baptized into Christ have put on Christ. There is neither Jew nor Greek, there is neither slave nor free, there is neither male nor female; for you are all *one* in Christ Jesus" (Gal. 3:26-28).[125] Here we should note that St. Paul does not say, "You are all *one thing* in Christ Jesus." This is because he is thinking of his teaching on the church as *the mystical body of Christ*, which is also why he writes in his First Letter to the Corinthians, addressing his words directly to this community: "You are the body of Christ and individually members of it" (1 Cor. 12:27). Let us now examine this teaching in greater detail.

First of all, we have *the general principle*: "For just as the body is one and has many members, and all the members of the body, though many, are one

---

122. Cf. *Church-Jews*, p. 58.
123. *Ibid.*, pp. 52-53 (ct).
124. *Ibid.*, p. 58; cf. *ibid.*, p. 37.
125. Cf. *ibid.*, p. 57.

body, so it is with Christ" (1 Cor. 12:12); in other words, Christ too, although he is one, has many members, and all the members, though many, are one body. Paul answers the question of how this can be achieved, by referring to baptism: "For by one Spirit we were all baptized into one body—Jews or Greeks, slaves or free—and all were made to drink of one Spirit" (1 Cor. 12:13). By means of baptism, all the baptized have become "one body," which is vivified "by one Spirit." Hence this is no lifeless corpse, but a body vivified by the Holy Spirit. And since this Spirit is the Spirit of Christ, St. Paul can state that Christ is the Head of the church, which is in turn the body of Christ, "the fullness of him who fills all in all" (Eph. 1:23).[126]

Thus we become members of the mystical body of Christ through baptism. However, a body also needs to be fed if it is to grow, and in our case this is achieved through the sacrament of *the eucharist*: "As a natural body needs food for sustenance and health, so, too, does this body of the church; and St. Paul tells us of this food: 'The chalice of benediction, which we bless, is it not the communion of the blood of Christ? And the bread which we break, is it not a partaking of the body of the Lord? For we, being many, are one bread, one body, all that partake of one bread' (1 Cor. 10:16-17)."[127]

Thus, by virtue of faith, and by means of baptism and the eucharist, people become one, just as the Father is in Christ and Christ in the Father (cf. John 17:21), and share in the mystical divine unity "that is impenetrable to human reason" and for which Christ prayed in his high-priestly prayer.[128]

7. After considering unity on the human level, we moved on to consideration of the relationship of human beings to the supreme Being, and similarly we shall now consider what kind of *image of God* and of his relationship with humankind we obtain from all that Christ has done and continues to do for the unity of the human family, and in particular the image of God and his relationship with humankind that we obtain from the words and teaching of Christ, the only-begotten Son of God.[129]

(a) In the first place, we should note *Christ's solidarity with suffering humankind*, which is seen most sublimely in the mystery of his death on the cross. The cardinal speaks of this most particularly when commenting on what *Nostra aetate* says in this connection: "The church always held and continues to hold that Christ out of infinite love freely underwent suffering and death because of the sins of all men, so that all might attain salvation.[130]

"First of all, there is Christ's spontaneity and freedom of choice in his submission to his passion and death. . . . Christ himself also expresses the same idea very forcefully: 'For this reason, the Father loves me, because I lay down

---

126. Cf. *Unity in Freedom*, p. 95. To obviate any possible misapprehension, it must be stated that the very close union of the members of the mystical body of Christ in no way eliminates the independence and freedom they possess as human beings.
127. *Ibid.*, p. 95.
128. Cf. *GS*, 24.
129. This will therefore be a reflection on facts that we have already described, although it will be filled out further with the words of Christ himself.
130. *NA*, 4.

my life, that I may take it up again. No one takes it from me, but I lay it down of my own accord. I have power to lay it down and I have power to take it up again' (John 10:17-18)."[131] Furthermore, "This liberty is both apparent and explicitly affirmed in the gospel account of the passion."[132]

The reason was "because of his immense love." He was too humble and reserved to speak of it to his disciples very often or in explicit terms, but on one occasion he did say it, albeit in a rather roundabout fashion: "Greater love has no man than this, that a man lay down his life for his friends" (John 15:13).[133] However, his disciples do speak of it in the New Testament on the basis of their own experience: "Christ loved us and gave himself up for us, a fragrant offering and sacrifice to God" (Eph. 5:2).[134]

(b) From Christ, we must then take one further step: *Christ's work* is God's work, and *reveals God*. As *Nostra aetate* goes on to state: "It is the duty of the church, therefore, in her preaching to proclaim the cross of Christ as the sign of *God's universal* love."[135] The cardinal comments as follows: "The whole work of the redemption flows from it [God's love] and is borne up and carried on its tide. Here, too, the New Testament prefers to tread the firm ground of fact rather than to rely on words to demonstrate God's love: 'God so loved the world that he gave his only Son, that whoever believes in him should not perish but have eternal life' (John 3:16). And in another place St. John points out: 'In this the love of God was made manifest among us, that God sent his only Son into the world that we might live by him' (1 John 4:9)."[136]

On the basis of all the foregoing, the cardinal can thus conclude as follows: "How wonderful is the light that comes to mankind from the cross, which is the tangible proof that we have a God who is not only gracious, patient and merciful but whom St. John indeed describes as love personified, when he solemnly states: 'God is love' (1 John 4:8). What encouragement we find here! What a reason for a serene and optimistic view of the life and destiny of the human family!"[137]

(c) Although this is a magnificent view, it is also a great deal more. We have already seen that God gives men an incredible gift, making them become "conformed to the image of his Son, in order that he might be the first-born among many brethren" (Rom. 8:29), and that Christ gives human beings the power to become "children of God" (John 1:12); thus we can truly say that the baptized are "born" of God "and become partakers of the divine nature" (2 Peter 1:4). This means that *God becomes the "Father" of human beings in real terms*, inasmuch as he transmits to them participation in his own divine nature and a likeness to his own being. On this basis, all that the New Testament has to say

---

131. *Church-Jews*, p. 108.
132. *Ibid.*; cf. Mt. 26:52; John 18:6.
133. Cf. *ibid.*
134. Cf. *ibid.*. Cf. also 1 John 3:16; Gal. 2:20; 2 Cor. 5:14-15; Rom. 8:35-37.
135. *NA*, 4.
136. *Church-Jews*, p. 110.
137. *Ibid.*, p. 113 (ct).

about his relationship with us human beings appears in a new light, for example Jesus' use of such expressions as "our heavenly Father."[138] In this light, the whole of humankind is seen as a real family of which God is the Father and all human beings are members and therefore brothers and sisters to one another.[139]

C. The Real Situation: More Divided than Ever?

We have shown the twofold unity that opens up prospects for the human family: purely human unity and specifically Christian unity. However, it is apparently precisely here that new reasons for divisions appear. We need only think of the scandal of the divisions among Christians, who are split into many confessions and denominations. This leads us to consider whether the very appearance of Christianity is not maybe the source of a new division among humankind, that is, between the world of Christians and that of non-Christians—and also that of non-believers, today. This leads us to the third part of our study, which will consider the relationship between purely human unity and Christian unity, and we shall start once again with the divisions that exist among humankind.

1. We have spoken at considerable length about *the divisions among Christians* throughout our work, so that here we shall simply give a very brief overview to highlight the aspects touching on the subject of the present chapter, the unity of the human family.[140]

The fact of these divisions and their depth are too well-known for us to need to discuss them here.[141] In the course of our book we have, however, seen how much stress the cardinal—like the Council itself—placed on baptism, which creates a communion among Christians that is deep and true, although imperfect and not full.[142] Nevertheless, we shall try to define the situation in greater detail. We are divided from the eastern churches, both those of the Byzantine tradition and the "ancient oriental churches" (or "non-Chalcedonians"), above all by certain aspects of the teaching on the church, especially that on the primacy of the pope; on the other hand, we have the creed, the sacraments and the hierarchy in common. We are widely separated from Christians of the Reformed tradition in the teaching on the church and the ecclesiastical ministry, but we have in common not only the reality of baptism, but also "some, even very many, . . . most significant elements and endowments which together go to build up and give life to the church itself."[143]

---

138. Cf. Mt. 6:32; 6:4, 6; 5:45. Cf. *Church-Jews*, p. 137. In another context, the cardinal adds those incredible words of Jesus: "You, therefore, must be perfect, as your heavenly Father is perfect" (Mt. 5:48); cf. *ibid.*, pp. 139-140.

139. Cf. *ibid.*, p. 143.

140. Cf. also *Unity in Freedom*, Chapters 9-11.

141. Cf. *ibid.*, pp. 136-137.

142. The division is thus much more serious where there is no baptism, which is the indispensable basis of ecclesial communion.

143. *UR*, 3. Fuller details are found in *Unity in Freedom*, pp. 150-157.

These divisions are very detrimental to the sacred cause of proclaiming the gospel. Indeed, according to Christ, the unity of his followers should be the sign by which the world recognizes his divine mission and believes in him (cf. John 17:21). The divisions are therefore a serious obstacle, preventing Christians from fulfilling their mission of communicating to all humankind the riches that Christ has brought them. Awareness of the harm that is being done to the gospel and to humankind has been shaking Christians for several decades, and has given rise to the ecumenical movement, which has set itself the task of remedy- ing the scandal of divisions.[144]

This development is a major new boon granted by the Spirit of God, but it should not give rise to illusions over the ease of the enterprise. The Second Vatican Council declared very frankly that it realized "that this holy objective— the reconciliation of all Christians in the unity of the one and only church of Christ—transcends human powers and gifts," and immediately followed this profession of our powerlessness with an indication of Christian hope: "It [the Council] therefore places its hope entirely in the prayer of Christ for the church, in the love of the Father for us, and in the power of the Holy Spirit. 'And hope does not disappoint, because God's love has been poured forth in our hearts through the Holy Spirit who has been given to us' (Rom. 5:5)."[145] Now one of the features of Christian hope is that of awaiting *what is not seen*, so that St. Paul writes: "Now hope that is seen is not hope. For who hopes for what he sees?" (Rom. 8:24). Hope therefore does not deny the size of the divisions, and also recognizes responsibility for the damage that the divisions cause to the gospel and to the unification of the human family in Christ. Hope lies precisely in this confident expectation of God's activity, despite the clear obstacles standing in its way.

2. The second question is that of whether there is *a gulf dividing purely human unity from Christian unity*. Our starting-point here is the conclusions deduced from our considerations on purely human unity on the one hand and specifically Christian unity on the other. We observed that they are two different types of unity, situated on different planes: "The first unity, the natural one, is based on a common possession of intelligence and free will, and upon their derivation from the ultimate Intelligence and Freedom, God."[146] In contrast, "the other unity, that of 'the new people of God' gathered in the church of Christ, is based not only upon a new revelation of God's intimate nature, but also upon a new communication of God's very being to men"[147]; in other words, it is based on sharing in God's life in Christ and through Christ. There is thus a clearly defined distinction between the two. However, we must ask whether this distinction entails division in the circumstances of real life, so that people who share in one or the other have nothing in common and are inevitably and completely divided from one another.

144. Cf. *Unity in Freedom*, pp. 144-148.
145. *UR*, 24.
146. *Unity in Freedom*, p. 213.
147. *Ibid.*

In order to reply to this question, we could examine the way in which the church has acted in the course of history, with special attention to its charitable work. However, instead of this, we shall follow the cardinal in referring simply to the attitude of recent popes, starting with John XXIII. In order to demonstrate "that the church is genuinely and wholeheartedly working for the achievement of a united human family—not limiting her vision only to baptized Christians who are already members of her family," the cardinal writes as follows: "Pope John XXIII declared, a month before the Council opened, that one of the things it intended to proclaim was the requirements of that fraternity that is itself a natural need of mankind. The pope on this occasion said that 'the Council will be concerned to praise, also in more sacred and solemn forms, the deepest applications of the fraternity and love that man's nature demands, while they are also obligatory for Christians as rules for relations between individuals and peoples.' "[148] The other example the cardinal gives is that of Pope Paul VI, who consecrated the whole of his 1964 Christmas message to the subject of human brotherhood.[149] Later, when he was about to leave for Bombay, Paul VI declared "that this pilgrimage, so unusual for a pope, was conceived as 'a journey of peace and love to strengthen the bonds of mutual understanding and friendship between all peoples, reminding them of their binding duty to learn to know one another, love one another and help one another effectively according to the variety of gifts received from God.' "[150] *Nostra aetate* speaks along identical lines, saying that the church has a duty "to foster unity and charity among individuals, and even among nations."[151] And the reason was simply that unity on the human level is no extraneous matter for the church. Indeed, before it became a human task, the unity of the human family "was God's plan, conceived by him for the whole human race."[152]

This approach on the part of the church is easier to understand if we bear in mind the effects of baptism on *the human nature* of the baptized person. For centuries, Catholic theology has upheld the principle in this connection that "grace supposes [human] *nature, but does not destroy it.*" The cardinal's explanation is as follows: "Christ makes man 'a new creature,' 'a new creation,' a brother of Christ through the Spirit of sonship within man's being, capable of living a new life in union with the self-giving of Christ."[153] The cardinal's next words explain what happens to human nature then: "Man's individual personality is not destroyed, but is amplified, expanded, lifted up to new heights, given a share in the very life of Father, Son and Holy Spirit."[154] A little later, the cardinal reiterates this principle, and also deduces its consequences: "Christians

---

148. *The Way*, p. 248, citing *AAS*, LIV (1962), 683.
149. Cf. *Unity in Freedom*, p. 216, citing *AAS*, LVII (1965), 176-183. This attitude on the part of the church obviously does not prevent individual Christians from assuming closed attitudes toward the world, as if the natural and supernatural spheres were radically incompatible.
150. *The Way*, p. 249, citing *AAS*, LVII (1965), 114.
151. *NA*, 1.
152. *The Way*, p. 216; cf. *ibid.*, p. 215.
153. *Unity in Freedom*, pp. 214-215.
154. *Ibid.*, p. 215.

do not lose their humanity, but on the contrary become more human, and, being such, are more aware of their obligations to work for justice and charity in the whole human family."[155]

By way of conclusion, we can cite the following words of the cardinal: "There is not, nor can there be, any conflict between this purely human unity and specific church unity: the church recognizes with sober equity of judgment the good that is in all men, even when they do not believe in its message. It gladly acknowledges the dignity and the nobility in all men, and their inalienable rights as men, and endeavors to protect and to foster this dignity and nobility and to maintain men's rights."[156]

The Attitude to Non-Christian Religions

The church does not confine itself to solidarity with men and women on the level of purely human unity, but also adopts a specific attitude of solidarity with the various *religions in their own field*. Its attitude involves "two equally essential elements: first of all there is the attitude of the church insofar as other religions are directly concerned; secondly, there is the attitude of the church to the commandment she has received from Christ to preach the gospel."[157]

1. *Nostra aetate* has the following to say concerning the church's attitude so far as *other religions are directly concerned*: "The Catholic Church rejects nothing of what is true and holy in these religions. She has a high regard for the manner of life and conduct, the precepts and doctrines which, although differing in many ways from her own teaching, nevertheless often reflect a ray of that truth which enlightens all men."[158] The cardinal explains the reasons behind the expressions "rejects nothing" and "high regard" as follows: "This respect arises from her recognition of the dignity of the human person and of what is due to him, especially in all that he holds as most sacred, as is the case with religion; it also arises from a consideration of the actual content of individual religions, that is from the second of the two elements mentioned above—the sincere acknowledgment of the treasures of truth and holiness contained in each of the various religions. The serious and genuine nature of the church's esteem for these treasures of truth and holiness is guaranteed by the motive which prompts it: for her they are reflections of that eternal truth that enlightens every man, that is to say, they reflect the work of God in Christ."[159]

The underlying *theological motivation* for this latter idea is then given: "The church firmly believes as a truth of divine revelation that men who profess religions other than her own were also created by God in his own image. Even though it is true that in all men God's image has been damaged by original sin, it is equally true that Christ died for all men and that . . . God does not abandon

---

155. *Ibid.*, p. 216.
156. *Ibid.*
157. *Church-Jews*, p. 45.
158. *NA*, 2.
159. *Church-Jews*, pp. 45-46 (ct).

men who, through no fault of their own, have no knowledge of him, but vouchsafes to them also the help of his grace."[160]

After the above-cited description of the church's attitude, *Nostra aetate* adds a direct exhortation to all the faithful: "The church, therefore, urges her sons to enter with prudence and charity into discussion and collaboration with members of other religions. Let Christians, while witnessing to their own faith and way of life, acknowledge, preserve and encourage the spiritual and moral truths found among non-Christians, also their social life and culture."[161] *The cardinal* gives the following analytical *comment* on this text: "So the duty incumbent upon the faithful is to recognize, safeguard and foster the progress of the spiritual and moral values as well as the social and cultural values to be found in the various religions with which they come into contact. The means for doing this are dialogue and cooperation with the followers of other religions. Obviously, they must employ these means with prudence and above all with charity."[162] Elsewhere, he gives further details concerning the means to be employed: "They are the same means that the Council recommended also in the ecumenical field . . . : in other words, the means amply dealt with by His Holiness, Paul VI in the programmatic encyclical *Ecclesiam suam.*"[163]

The fruits that will be obtained *for humanity* once this exhortation of *Nostra aetate* is followed are explained as follows in another context: ". . . little by little, humanity will be enriched with infinite numbers of men all trying to understand, to respect and to show good will toward those millions who belong to faiths other than their own, particularly toward what these men hold as most sacred, their religious faith. Thus a deep spiritual encounter will become possible . . . ; such a meeting . . . naturally leads to exterior expression in the exchange of spiritual treasures . . . and so in a real communion of spiritual life. One could hardly hope for a greater contribution toward the construction of the unity of the human family."[164]

2. The second element of the church's attitude toward non-Christian religions is *fidelity to the mandate received from Christ*: "Yet she proclaims, and is duty-bound to proclaim without fail, Christ who is 'the way, the truth and the life' (John 14:6). In him, in whom God reconciled all things to himself (2 Cor. 5:18-19), men find the fullness of their religious life."[165]

The cardinal comments as follows on this idea expressed by the Council: "*This aspect* of the church's attitude is of course likely to be harsher for the representatives of other religions, and also in a certain way for the church itself."[166] The following reason is given: "It is all too easy for non-Christians to

---

160. *Ibid.*, p. 46.
161. *NA*, 2.
162. *Church-Jews*, p. 49 (ct). Cf. also *The Way*, p. 220. Similarly, cf. the conciliar Decree on Missionary Activity, *AG*, 11. *Nostra aetate* speaks both of "the witness of faith and of Christian life," and we shall discuss this element in due course.
163. Biblio. 334, p. 15. For the encyclical, cf. *AAS*, LVI (1964), 609-659.
164. *The Way*, p. 227 (ct). Cf. also Biblio. 334, p. 15.
165. *NA*, 2.
166. *Church-Jews*, p. 44 (ct).

gain the impression that they are dealing with people who are insufferably arrogant and claim to be the sole possessors of the fullness of truth. The church, too, is well aware that fidelity to her own mission inevitably exposes her to this odious suspicion."[167]

In order to clear the ground immediately of *psychological difficulties* of this kind, the cardinal first of all observes: "The church does *not* put forward her message as *something that she has herself discovered* as a result of her own efforts and merits, which might justify her in claiming superiority over others from a *human* point of view. On the contrary, she presents it exclusively as a message received from God through Christ, a gratuitous gift of God to mankind which confers no merit on the church herself but simply makes it incumbent on her to transmit it, not in her own name but in the name of Christ and of God."[168] And not only do those who proclaim this message have no merit of their own, but they recognize that they are *unworthy sinners*: "As far as any individual messenger charged with the duty of handing on the message is concerned, she humbly and sincerely echoes St. Paul in saying: 'The saying is sure and worthy of full acceptance, that Christ Jesus came into the world to save sinners. And I am the foremost of sinners' (1 Tim. 1:15)."[169]

This is where we see *the motivation* proposed by the church for its mission, a motivation that has a positive and a negative aspect. Let us first consider the *positive* aspect: the church is aware of an "inexorable command which she has received from Christ and because of which she says with the apostle: 'For if I preach the gospel, that gives me no ground for boasting. For necessity is laid upon me' (1 Cor. 9:16). This obligation has its underlying reason in the fact that Christ died for all men, without any distinction, and by doing so reconciled them all with God (cf. 2 Cor. 5:14-21)."[170]

Let us now consider the *negative* aspect, which is the reverse of the coin of the attitude of the church toward non-Christian religions, as described above. While it is true that not only does the church not reject but actually recognizes all that "is true and holy in these religions," it is also convinced "that *in Christ alone* can men find *the fullness* of the life of religion and reconciliation with God, which God has brought about through Christ and through him alone. 'For there is no other name under heaven given among men by which we must be saved' (Acts 4:12)."[171] In other words, apart from its awareness of its own mission, the church is also motivated by sincere love for the followers of non-Christian religions: it desires to transmit to them the immense treasures which are brought to us by Christ and which they can obtain only in and through Christ.

167. *Ibid.*, p. 47. In *Unity in Freedom*, pp. 218-219, Bea presents the suspicion of arrogance with a nuance, saying that some people see it almost as the racial pride of members of the white race; he then points out that Christianity is in fact semitic in origin.
168. *Ibid.* (ct); cf. also *Unity in Freedom*, p. 219.
169. *Church-Jews*, p. 48; cf. also *Unity in Freedom*, p. 219.
170. *The Way*, p. 220 (ct).
171. *Ibid.* (ct).

Obviously the church is fully aware that anybody who presents himself as being "sent" must offer sufficient *credentials*. Hence it "cannot refuse to make *its own specific mandate the object of dialogue* and discussion and to furnish proofs of its authenticity."[172] We must add that when the church meets representatives of other religions in dialogue it "demands nothing more from them than the attitude it itself adopts . . . with regard to them: an attitude of respect involving serious consideration of the content of its message, together with readiness to admit candidly the presence of anything good or true or holy which they may succeed in discovering in it, especially with the aid of dialogue. Lastly, it asks them for genuine respect for the sincerity of its convictions, and in particular for its conviction that it has received a mandate from Christ, and its fidelity to this."[173]

There is still one further element to be stressed. When *Nostra aetate* exhorts all the faithful to engage in dialogue and collaboration, it adds an important phrase, saying that this must be done *"while witnessing to their own faith and way of life."*[174] In point of fact, the obligation to proclaim the gospel extends to *all the members* of the church, each according to his or her position. The document adds that this must be done "with prudence and love."[175]

3. Inasmuch as the church's attitude to non-Christian religions also involves the proclamation of the gospel and of "the fullness of Christ," it raises in various ways the problem of *religious freedom*, which is dealt with in the conciliar document *Dignitatis humanae*. This document found itself in a similar situation to that of *Nostra aetate*: after clearly and strongly proclaiming the right of the individual and of communities to freedom in religious matters, it felt called on to bear witness to the mission of the church, and hence to affirm its right to proclaim Christ, to show that this is in harmony with the general principles of religious freedom, and, lastly, to indicate to the members of the church how this mission is to be fulfilled in harmony with these same principles.

(a) In the first place, let us see the witness to *the church's mission* in religious matters. In its introduction, *Dignitatis humanae* states: "We believe that this one true religion continues to exist in the Catholic and Apostolic Church, to which the Lord Jesus entrusted the task of spreading it among men."[176] Even more explicit is the witness given at the end of the document: "In order to satisfy the

---

172. *Church-Jews*, p. 47.
173. *Ibid.*, p. 48 (ct). Elsewhere the cardinal observes that *the way* God has chosen to communicate to men his own gifts which bear the fullness of religious life *is in full keeping with human nature* and human life: "Men are interdependent on the natural level, dependent upon their ancestors since they live in a world in so many ways conditioned by the ideas, the institutions and the almost unrealized psychological and communal inheritances from the past; men are likewise dependent on other men for knowledge, instruction, and the ordered society in which they live. It is not then strange that God should give his greater gift of a share in his own intimate life by ways in accordance with man's intelligence and freedom, and in accordance with human interdependence" (*Unity in Freedom*, p. 220).
174. *NA*, 2.
175. Cf. *Church-Jews*, p. 49. We shall return to various aspects of this witness in due course.
176. *DH*, 1.

divine command: 'Make disciples of all nations' (Mt. 28:19), the Catholic Church must spare no effort in striving 'that the word of the Lord may speed on and triumph' (1 Thess. 3:1)."[177]

The cardinal summarizes as follows the teaching in the document on the church's *right to freedom* in fulfilling its mission: "Conscious of her mandate regarding those who belong to her and those who do not, the church, both as a religious communion and also because of the command she has received from Christ, lays claim in this document to religious freedom. In doing so she appeals to the special titles to freedom conferred upon her by Christ. It is a 'sacred freedom with which the only-begotten Son has endowed the church redeemed with his blood' (no. 13). This freedom is due to her 'as to a spiritual authority established by Christ the Lord, and upon which she has placed the obligation to go out into the whole world and preach the gospel to every creature' (*ibid.*)"[178]

However, there is then the question of whether this claim is in harmony with the principles proclaimed in *Dignitatis humanae*: "It will . . . be asked whether the church, in proclaiming the truth of the one true religion and of its own mission as the only true way to God—with consequent obligations binding on men's conscience—is not perhaps arrogating to itself a special and privileged position, with exclusive rights (as discussed in no. 6 of our document), to the detriment of the notion of equality with other religious communities.

"This is our reply: when the church affirms its mission to be the one true way to God, it does not do so with a view to special rights and immunities, or a favored position in relation to religious freedom, but seeks only to show the special (supernatural) *title-deeds* of its freedom to transmit to all men the gospel it received from Christ. It is basically a question of a special *justification* for its claim to freedom, not one of claiming some special privilege with regard to freedom."[179]

(b) Performance of the church's mission, whether by the clergy or the faithful, entails the obligation to combine the greatest respect for human dignity and freedom with the greatest fidelity to the mission received from Christ to proclaim the gospel. This explains the instructions given by the Council in the document in question and summarized by the cardinal as follows: "Here, then, is *the principle* which the faithful will bear in mind: 'All is to be taken into account—the Christian's duties to Christ, the life-giving Word which must be proclaimed, and the rights of the human person' (no. 14)."[180] In the first place, there are the Christian's *duties toward Christ*: "Moreover, the members of the church are recommended to 'show a wise tolerance—"in the Holy Spirit, in unaffected love, in the word of truth" (2 Cor. 6:6-7)—toward those who do not

---

177. *Ibid.*, 14.

178. Biblio. 320, p. 275.

179. *The Way*, p. 212 (ct) (emphasis ours). This statement is further supported by the following consideration: if "another religious community were to come forward with a similar claim to represent the one true religion—and this in fact often happens—then the church would not contest the right to make such a claim but would only reserve its own right *to question the truth of the claim itself*—nothing more" (*ibid.*, p. 213).

180. Biblio. 320, p. 276.

share their faith, and let them set about their task of spreading the light of life with all confidence and apostolic courage, even to the shedding of their blood' (no. 14)."[181]

Then comes *respect for the freedom of individuals*: "This they will do fully respecting the freedom of others, 'never at any time having recourse to methods which are incompatible with the spirit of the gospel.' Indeed, 'the charity of Christ urges his followers to treat all who are in error or ignorance about the faith with loving prudence and patience' (no. 14). The same document goes on to enunciate another profound *theological principle*: 'They must always take into account the measure of grace granted by God through Christ to men who are invited freely to accept and profess the faith.' "[182]

The Church as the Sacrament of the Unity of the Human Family with God, and Also of Its Own Internal Unity

We saw above that the divine gift of unity brought by Christ is offered and destined to all people, in other words to the entire human family. Christ united all in himself in order to reconcile them with God in one body, by means of the cross (cf. Eph. 2:15-16). This is why the Council clearly states: "All men are in fact called to one and the same destiny, which is divine."[183]

Now, from this point of view the immense field of those who belong to the various non-Christian religions raises a new problem that fills us with anguish, for "isn't the number of people reached by missionary activity like a drop of water in the vast sea of the non-Christian populations of the world?"[184] This leads the cardinal to ask whether the gifts brought by Christ remain the exclusive privilege of those who are formally and publicly Christians. This is the question that is expressed in theological terms as follows: What must we say of *the eternal salvation of those who do not know Christ and the church*?

1. By way of a reply, the cardinal starts by making the following *general remark*: "The divine plan of salvation in Christ is open to *all men* without distinction. It is the goal appointed for all mankind by God 'who desires all men to be saved' (1 Tim. 2:4). The proof that this is indeed the divine will lies in the fact that God our Father and Christ our Lord have already done everything that depends on them for the realization of this end. The death and resurrection of Christ were accomplished for the benefit of all mankind."[185]

---

181. *Ibid.*

182. *Ibid.* (ct); in this way the cardinal sums up the very rich conciliar doctrine. The author also recalls that the conciliar Decree on the Pastoral Office of Bishops recommends that the latter should "explain . . . how high a value, according to the doctrine of the church, should be placed on the human person, on his liberty . . ." (*CD*, 12). Cf. also *The Way*, p. 211.

183. *GS*, 22. It should be noted that the reference here is to men's *final* destiny. This does not exclude, but indeed presumes, the *natural* destiny inherent in their nature as intelligent and free human beings; however, they cannot stop at this natural destiny, thus excluding the ultimate and supernatural one.

184. Biblio. 334, p. 11.

185. *Church-Jews*, pp. 141-142 (ct). The author uses the phrase "everything that depends on them,"

Here we find *the nub of the argument*: "The unceasing operations of God, of the grace of Christ and of the Holy Spirit *affect* all men, *including those who through no fault of their own are ignorant of Christ and his church.*"[186] In order to prove this, the cardinal cites the specific doctrine of the Second Vatican Council in its Dogmatic Constitution on the Church: "Those who through no fault of their own do not know Christ or his church but who nevertheless seek God with a sincere heart, and, moved by grace, try in their actions to do his will as they know it through the dictates of their conscience, can obtain eternal salvation."[187] The cardinal makes the following comment: "Nor does this refer solely to an abstract possibility which in practice does not produce any effect. The constitution goes on to say that they can actually be saved because God gives them the necessary help: 'Nor shall divine providence deny the assistance necessary for salvation to those who, without any fault of theirs, have not yet arrived at an explicit knowledge of God, and who, not without grace, strive to lead a good life.' "[188]

Do we also have *proof* of this action on God's part? "The Council replies, 'Yes': the proof of it lies in all that is good and true which is found among them. All this is indeed the gift of God who has a care for them and guides them. 'Whatever good or truth is found amongst them is considered by the church to be a preparation for the gospel and given by him who enlightens all men that they may at length have life.' "[189] The cardinal adds the following remark which sheds a great deal of light on the matter: "The work of the church for the salvation of souls is certainly bound up with particular ways and means, among the chief of which are the sacraments. But God is not so bound and does not limit his activity to these means. This divine activity is unceasing."[190] The cardinal observes that the church "opens, as it were, the eyes of the soul and of faith so that in our own times we may contemplate the prophetic vision of Isaiah," who saw the peoples walking toward the light that came from the mountain of the Lord.[191]

On the basis of this teaching, the cardinal deduces an important consequence as regards a *brotherly attitude* toward "the others"—those who do not know Christ and the church. Thus he says that the teaching on the salvation of these brethren "should suffice to lead every Christian to see all his fellow men through the eyes of God and of Christ and to realize the sublime dignity to which every man is called in Christ, and toward which men are guided by grace in a manner which God alone knows. *It is not our business to judge* to what extent others may be achieving it, or who does or does not. All should consider themselves brothers and treat one another as such. Otherwise we may find ourselves in the

---

for there is also the question of the individual's free acceptance of salvation.
186. *Ibid.*, p. 142.
187. *LG*, 16.
188. *Church-Jews*, p. 38, quoting *LG*, 16.
189. *Ibid.*, quoting *LG*, 16.
190. *Ibid.*, p. 39.
191. *Ibid.*, p. 40 (ct).

situation described by St. Augustine: 'You have hated your brother without knowing it.' "[192] The cardinal becomes even more explicit elsewhere, stating: "Let us therefore hold as a general principle that we must recognize all people, without any exception or discrimination, as adopted children of God and our brethren, and hence the whole human family as the family of the heavenly Father, and the family of brothers and sisters in Christ."[193]

2. Certain people might imagine that this teaching could be taken as an excuse or a reason for the church and its members to commit themselves less to cooperating with Christ for the salvation of these brethren. Nothing could be further from the truth, for this very work of God constitutes the most sublime *example for the church to imitate*. And the very *nature* of the church demands this commitment. Indeed, the Council stated this in several contexts, such as the following: "The church, in Christ, is in the nature of sacrament—a sign and instrument, that is, of communion with God and of unity among all men."[194] The cardinal then expands on this conciliar teaching with a series of citations from the same constitution: "That messianic people, although it does not actually include all men, and at times may appear as a small flock, is, however, a most sure seed of unity, hope and salvation for the whole human race."[195] Hence, the church "ceaselessly and efficaciously seeks to bring all humanity with all its riches back to Christ the Head in the unity of his Spirit."[196]

(a) The church must therefore adopt the words of the apostle: "The love of Christ controls us, because we are convinced that one has died for all" (2 Cor. 5:14). There must thus be maximum commitment to the proclamation of the gospel. However, we must ask if this is all. Here it would seem that respect for "all that is true and holy" in the non-Christian religions, the fostering of these values, and dialogue and collaboration with non-Christians open up new perspectives. Such an approach is undoubtedly very effective in preparing the way toward knowledge of the church and the gospel,[197] but independently of this point, and prior to it, this action *constitutes in itself a contribution toward the eternal salvation* of the followers of non-Christian religions. Although this may seem a paradox, it is perfectly true. According to what we saw above, "These men obtain salvation, in fact, by seeking God sincerely and by carrying out his will, known to them through the dictates of conscience. It is clear that this happens, above all, when they put into practice those elements in their religion which are true and holy. If therefore the faithful foster and promote these values, *they are actually helping the non-Christians to obtain eternal salvation*."[198]

In this light, we can see the full urgency of the recommendation from *Nostra aetate* that we cited above, and this is why the cardinal writes as follows in his

---

192. *Ibid.*, p. 142. For the text of St. Augustine, cf. *PL*, XXXVI, 630.
193. Biblio. 334 (Italian version), p. 463.
194. *LG*, 1; cf. also *ibid.*, 9 and 48. Cf. *The Way*, p. 248.
195. *LG*, 9.
196. *Ibid.*, 13.
197. Cf. Biblio. 334, p. 15; also *The Way*, p. 226.
198. Biblio. 334, p. 15; cf. also *The Way*, p. 227.

reflections on the tasks of the Secretariat for Non-Christians: "Since in the normal way of things the conversion of non-Christians is a very difficult task, which is slow and often concerns relatively few converts,[199] it follows that *in actual fact* for many people—in practice, for the majority—the only way to salvation is that of living in good faith according to the religion they have inherited from their fathers, and of following the moral code they know.[200] Hence, if the church wishes to help them—as is its duty, by reason of its mission to be the salvation of all people—on the basis of the *real* possibilities, the work it performs through the new secretariat will concentrate on confirmation of what is naturally good, true and morally honest and healthy in the religions and practical life of these non-Christians. . . . This is all the more urgent inasmuch as these non-Christians are also besieged by modern materialism, which poses a serious threat to their religious spirit and moral life."[201]

After these explanations, it is no surprise to find the cardinal stating that *Nostra aetate* "opens up *new dimensions for fulfilling the church's mission.*"[202] He explains this statement as follows: "In this way, the church is already carrying out her salvific mission to those men, by means of her faithful, in the way that is concretely possible for her, although they do not actually arrive, in this life, at knowledge of the gospel and of the church. This thought, which is a clear consequence of the doctrine set forth, is explicitly affirmed, moreover, in the conciliar Decree on Missionary Activity: 'Closely united with men in their life and work, Christ's disciples hope to render to others true witness of Christ, and *to work for their salvation, even where they are not able to proclaim Christ fully*' (*AG*, 12)."[203] In a reflection on the tasks of the Secretariat for Non-Christians, the cardinal thus states that this body, "although it does not directly preach Christ, shares fully in the essential mission of the church—and not only by preparing paths for the gospel among non-Christians, but also by helping them to attain salvation by truly practicing their own religion in good faith."[204]

(b) *Nostra aetate* speaks only of the followers of non-Christian religions. However, the teaching set forth above concerning the salvation of those who do not know Christ and the church is a general doctrine and is not limited to

---

199. Here we can see clearly that Bea is not an optimist at any cost in his considerations on the salvation of non-Christians, for he also sees the other side of the coin, in other words the major obstacles that are strewn along the path of non-Christians, as *Lumen gentium* itself explained, saying that, "deceived by the Evil One, men have become vain in their reasonings, . . . living and dying in this world without God" (no. 16); cf. also Biblio. 334, p. 15.

200. The cardinal had stressed the same point when speaking before the Central Preparatory Commission of the Council in its discussion of Chapter 2 of the schema on the church, which dealt with the necessity of the church for salvation. On that occasion he had stated that it is difficult to deny ("vix negari poterit") that even today the majority of people are saved outside the "normal" means which is the church ("extra medium normale i.e. Ecclesiam"); *AD*, II/3, 1014.

201. Arch. Me 1/3, p. 2. In the same context the author warns of the importance of avoiding any form of indifferentism.

202. *The Way*, p. 319.

203. Biblio. 334, p. 15. Similarly, Arch. Me 1/3, p. 2.

204. Arch. Me 1/3, p. 3.

followers of non-Christian religions. The cardinal is very explicit on this point, and appeals to the Pastoral Constitution on the Church in the Modern World, which explains the continuous and universal action of God and the work of Christ's grace, before going on to state: "All this holds true not for Christians only but also for *all men of good will* in whose hearts grace is active invisibly. For since Christ died for all, and since all men are in fact called to one and the same destiny, which is divine, we must hold that the Holy Spirit offers to all the possibility of being made partners, in a way known to God, in the paschal mystery."[205]

The cardinal is therefore fully justified in taking the above-cited considerations and applying them by analogy to dialogue and general collaboration with people with no faith or religion, so that he writes as follows: "Turning . . . our gaze to the whole world and to every form of religionlessness, we can say that in today's world there are vast masses of people without religion, if they are not indeed opposed to religion. There are millions of Catholics who have lost their faith; there are enormous masses of non-Catholic Christians in the same condition; and there are also very extensive masses of non-Christians—Moslems or followers of various other major religions—who find their religiosity incapable of bearing the impact with the world of modern culture, and thus abandon the religion of their forebears, after which their lack of religion exposes them to the risk of falling prey to practical materialism, if not indeed to organized atheism."[206] The means and methods used here will undoubtedly be at least in part different, and may still need to be invented. However, for the cardinal the most important task here is that of "fostering in all the members of the church an *awareness of their serious duty* to concern themselves with the non-Christians who are in such extreme need of the church's effective help."[207]

We can truly say that the teaching of the Council on this subject, the considerations found in Paul VI's encyclical *Ecclesiam suam* on the various facets of the dialogue, and the institution of the Secretariats for Non-Christians and for Non-Believers offer the church new possibilities for fulfilling its mission even where the gospel cannot be proclaimed, and for being for all people a "sacrament of unity" with God and each other.

The Arduous Path to Fulfillment of the Divine Plan for Unity

The sublime vision of the unity given to humankind in Christ in no way changes the fact that the path to bringing this sublime unity into being is fraught with extremely serious shadows. We have already pointed out the very grave scandal of the divisions among Christians themselves. And what are we to say about the fact that after twenty centuries of Christianity this divine plan has not

---

205. *GS*, 22; cf. *The Way*, pp. 226-227. Similarly, *AG*, 7.
206. The cardinal's observations on the Secretariat for Non-Believers, Arch. Mo 18/6, p. 2.
207. *Ibid.*, p. 8.

in fact reached even one-third of humankind, so that there are major continents—for example, Africa and Asia—where Christians are like a drop in the
great ocean of non-Christian peoples? As early as 1960, the cardinal discussed
this problem in extensive detail,[208] and in fact added other disconcerting facts
to those we have just cited: "the scandals caused so often by those whose lives
should have been models of holiness and integrity; and still today there are all
those children of the church who have been baptized and yet remain oblivious
of their Christian duties and live in apathetic indifference or complete worldli-
ness, as if supernatural realities simply did not exist."[209] All these facts could all
too easily lead us "to doubt the authenticity of the mission of the church, its truth
and holiness."[210] So what are we to say about this whole situation?

In the study in question, the cardinal begins by mentioning the experience of
the great apostle to the Gentiles himself in this area: the failures of his apostolate,
the scandals and divisions that erupted for example in his beloved Corinth, the
relentless persecutions from his fellow Jews, etc.[211] Nonetheless, all these
painful elements were unable to dishearten the apostle. On the contrary, it is he
who gives us an ecclesiology that shows that all these elements reflect specific
laws established by God, which govern the church and its growth in this world.

1. The first law is that of *organic growth*: "The church is *a living organism*
and hence is subject to the laws of all created life. . . . Right from its birth out
of the pierced heart of the divine Redeemer, the church has possessed its nature,
its essential marks of holiness, oneness, and catholicity. But these properties
must be understood not in a static but in a dynamic sense: while always
remaining the same in substance, they must grow, develop, and attain their
perfection."[212]

If only this growth could occur in ideal conditions! Unfortunately, however,
growth is considerably *hindered by various factors*. In the first place, "Paul is
not unaware that Christians, while by the power of grace they are free from the
tyranny of sin, are *not* for all that *immune from relapsing into sin* if they relax
their effort in the ceaseless struggle against the passions and the desires of the
flesh (Rom. 8:9; 6:14; cf. Gal. 5:13; Rom. 6:12; 8:13; Gal. 5:24). It is no wonder,
then, that throughout the whole time of its development here on earth the church
has so often found itself sullied by the weaknesses, imperfections and sins of its
members."[213]

Next we have to consider the unfavorable influences of *the environment*—the
environment that the Lord himself calls " '*the world*,' which, as St. John says,
'lies in the power of evil' (1 John 5:19). St. Paul knows this: he admonishes the
Corinthians to protect themselves against the evil influences which come from

---

208. Cf. Biblio. 141; this study is also published in *The Unity of Christians*, and we shall therefore
    quote from the latter work.
209. *Unity of Christians*, p. 211.
210. *Ibid.*, p. 220.
211. Cf. *ibid.*, pp. 212-214.
212. *Ibid.*, p. 215 (ct).
213. *Ibid.*

without. . . . He knows that this world is dominated by the spirits of darkness and by their prince, the devil."[214] The consequences are described as follows: "The difficulties and the dangers that the flesh and its lusts raise against the life of Christ in man are notably aggravated by the pernicious influence of the world and its crafty prince, who seek to overthrow man with their attacks, or at least to damage him by flattery, by intimidation, by attrition. It is true that Christ has triumphed over all the powers of the enemy (Col. 2:15), freed man from the powers of darkness (Col. 1:13) and taken him out of the wicked world (Gal. 1:4), but he has neither taken away, nor wished to take away, from his followers and his church the law of struggle against the powers of darkness (Eph. 6:12)."[215]

2. To this we must add *the law of the cross*, in other words, that of humiliation and suffering. The life of the Master was marked by persecutions and humiliations, and this also holds good for his church: "Christ did not choose for himself an ordinary and peaceful human existence but a life that was exposed to all kinds of adversity: opposition, persecutions, painful defeats and humiliations from the world and its prince, as long as 'the hour of the powers of darkness' should last, according to the plans of God (Luke 22:53). In the same way he has also placed his church in the midst of the world and wills that it should live in hiddenness, that it should conquer through defeat, that it should become great through deep humiliations."[216] St. Paul also gives us *the underlying reason* for this strategy on God's part: "The life and work of the church is sealed with the cross so that the work of redemption may be seen not as a human work, but as a work of the mercy of God: 'If anyone boasts, let him make his boast in the Lord' (1 Cor. 1:31)."[217]

3. However, the greatest difficulty still remains. In other words, we can understand that the Lord permits humiliations and defeats, but how can he permit evil and sin? In the case of Christ, it is true that the law of development and that of persecutions and humiliations applied, but sin was always completely ruled out (cf. Heb. 4:15). So *"how is it and why is it that God permits sin* even in his church, which is redeemed by the blood of his Son and given life by his own Spirit?"[218] The cardinal starts by defining the meaning of the term "permits": "When we say 'permits,' our meaning is clearly not that he approves it, but only that he tolerates it, in other words, that he respects the free will given to men and thus does not prevent sin by making use of all the means that are open to his omnipotence and by which he would certainly be able to prevent it."[219]

After establishing the precise meaning of the term "permits," the cardinal begins by giving *a general reply*, taking his inspiration from St. Augustine, who "says that God has judged it better to draw good out of evil, rather than to permit

---

214. *Ibid.*, p. 216.

215. *Ibid.*, pp. 216-217 (ct).

216. *Ibid.*, p. 222 (ct).

217. *Ibid.*, p. 218 (ct).

218. *Ibid.*, p. 222.

219. *Ibid.* The painful problem of the division of Christians is also basically reduced to this same problem of the "how and why" of sin in the church; cf. *ibid.*

no evil.[220] In the omnipotent hand of God's all-wise Providence, weaknesses and even sins are transformed so that they can *serve* and benefit the church."[221]

We would now mention some of these ways in which God, by not preventing sin, renders it of service to the church. The primary aspect is as follows: "God's will is that no one should glory in himself, but that he who glories should glory in the Lord (1 Cor. 1:29, 31; cf. 2 Cor. 10:17). He wishes, then, to teach men not to trust in themselves, nor to attribute to themselves the good that they possess or that they have done, but to put their trust in God alone and to attribute success to him alone. Now for this purpose there is no means more efficacious, nothing that more humiliates man, detaches him from himself, and casts him into the arms of the merciful heavenly Father, than sin admitted, repented, pardoned and atoned."[222] Another aspect is also described: "A great good which he can draw from sin is to restore to modern men *trust in the mercy of God our Lord.* Too often the man of today thinks that after his worst falls and most grievous offenses against God nothing remains but to flee like Cain before the wrath of an outraged God. The man who can preach the mercy of God because he has experienced it himself, and who, like the church, tries to be merciful according to the example of our Lord, is a benefactor to humanity."[223]

4. Very well, will be the response, but does all this—growth in the midst of persecutions, weaknesses and sin—not *endanger the actual fulfillment of God's plan of unity*? This would no doubt be so in human terms, in other words if matters depended on human beings alone. However, there is also the guarantee of God's promise. The final words of St. Matthew's Gospel are those of the risen Lord to the apostles: "Lo, I am with you always, to the close of the age" (Mt. 28:20). Speaking to the apostles of the persecutions to come, Jesus said: "In the world you have tribulation; but be of good cheer, I have overcome the world" (John 16:33). When constituting Peter as primate in the church, he said to him: "You are Peter, and on this rock I will build my church, and the powers of death shall not prevail against it" (Mt. 16:18).[224] It is firm faith in these promises that sustains the church, and this is a substantial part of Christian hope.[225]

---

220. Cf. *Ench. de fide, spe et caritate,* in *PL,* XL, 245.
221. *Unity of Christians,* p. 223.
222. *Ibid.* (ct).
223. *Ibid.*
224. Cf. *Unity in Freedom,* p. 228, where the cardinal appeals to the texts cited; cf. also *ibid.,* pp. 96-97.
225. For those who maybe do not share this faith, the cardinal points to some facts that show the reliability of this promise: "Granted all the sins and deficiencies in the church, is there any other institution which can show such love for men, can give such cogent reasons for sincere concern for the great human family and can offer such founded hopes for peace and true brotherhood among men? Is there any other system of thought which can satisfy the mind and give adequate motives to the mass of men for a life in justice and freedom and charity? Is there a real alternative to the church?" (*ibid.,* p. 229).

The Unity of the Human Family: The Final Prospect

However, let us return to the promise cited above. Accepting it and basing ourselves on it means living from Christian hope. In this connection we have already cited the words of St. Paul: "Now hope that is seen is not hope" (Rom. 8:24). Since we hope for what is not yet seen, hope too bears the seal of the arduous path we have described, but by its very nature and by the infallible authority of him who made the promise it also gives us serene confidence and courage. This is all the more so inasmuch as the promise is not limited to the assurance we cited above. The word of God has been at pains to portray for us the final goal to which Christ leads us, and hence also the fulfillment of the unity of the human family, in terms so splendid that they would seem completely utopian, were it not a case of the word of God.

Let us first consider *the final goal of individuals*. Having said that by faith and baptism people become truly adoptive children of God and sharers in the divine nature, it is easy to understand the importance of the prospects that the New Testament opens up for them: "St. Peter writes: 'God, the author of all grace, has called you to his eternal glory in Christ' (1 Peter 5:10; cf. 1 Thess. 2:12). In the last hours of his life, when speaking of his mission and addressing his Father who gave him power over all men so as to give eternal life to all those entrusted to him, Jesus would say: 'And now this is eternal life, that they may know thee, the only true God, and Jesus Christ whom thou hast sent' (John 17:2ff). . . . To every man without distinction is given the ineffable greatness of becoming like God, of becoming a son of God, as we are told by the apostle John: 'Beloved, we are God's children now; it does not yet appear what we shall be, but we know that when he appears we shall be like him, for we shall see him as he is' (1 John 3:2)."[226]

The depth of faith in this prospect is shown in a special manner when Christians, like their crucified Master, are *confronted with suffering*. In the light of the hope of heavenly glory, "pain and suffering lose their sting. In fact, 'if we are children, then we are heirs, heirs of God and fellow heirs with Christ, provided we suffer with him that we may also be glorified with him' (Rom. 8:17). From this St. Paul triumphantly concludes: 'I consider that the sufferings of this present time are not worth comparing with the glory that is to be revealed to us' (Rom. 8:18)."[227]

Nor is this all. Since Christ's glorification also includes his *resurrection*, Christians' glorification also extends to their bodies. The life of grace of God's adoptive children "will blossom into divine life itself, in which the whole man will share after the glorious resurrection of the body. 'Christ has been raised from the dead, the first fruits of those who have fallen asleep. For as by a man came death, so also by a man has come the resurrection of the dead' (1 Cor. 15:20-21)."[228]

---

226. *Church-Jews*, p. 32.
227. *Ibid.*, p. 113.
228. *Ibid.*, p. 35.

The cardinal writes about the glorious resurrection of the body as follows: "*Belief in the resurrection* after death . . . is a revelation of the nature of God, who approves and loves the whole material creation and wants man, the noblest in that creation, to be everlasting." The resurrection of the body "means that man's spiritual horizons are not bounded by death but are opened to limitless personal and bodily existence. It means that the death-principle rules only for a time but is conquered in the end: 'Then shall be brought to pass the saying that is written: "Death is swallowed up in victory" ' (1 Cor. 15:54). The Christian martyrs did not fear to die, for they knew that death is not the end."[229]

So far, it might seem that Christianity recognizes an eternal destiny only for individuals. However, it is perfectly clear that this destiny also includes *the collectivity—peoples and all humankind*. In Isaiah we read the account of a great vision of Christ the Prince among humankind: "It shall come to pass in the latter days that the mountain of the house of the Lord shall be established as the highest of the mountains, and shall be raised above the hills; and all the nations shall flow to it, and many peoples shall come, and say: 'Come, let us go up to the mountain of the Lord, to the house of the God of Jacob, that he may teach us his ways and that we may walk in his paths.' . . . He shall judge between the nations, and shall decide for many peoples; and they shall beat their swords into plowshares, and their spears into pruning hooks; nation shall not lift up sword against nation, neither shall they learn war any more" (Is. 2:2-4). The underlying reason for this universal pacification is indicated elsewhere in the writings of the same prophet: "They shall not hurt or destroy in all my holy mountain; for the earth shall be full of the knowledge of the Lord as the waters cover the sea" (Is. 11:9).[230]

Certainly, this advance of the peoples toward the mountain of the Lord takes place throughout the whole of human history, but ultimately the prophet here opens up the prospect of a humankind that is perfectly fraternal and peaceful because it is perfectly united with God—a prospect that is not of this world and does not correspond to the painful path of humankind throughout history. In other words, it refers to the humankind that corresponds to "the glorious advent of the messianic kingdom when . . . 'the elect will be united in the holy city, the city ablaze with the glory of God, and the nations will walk in his light.' "[231]

And the prophet's vision here is neither an allegory nor an illusion: the word of God and all that God has already done guarantee that it will come to pass in the hour known and prepared by God.[232] We have solid *confirmation* of this in the teaching of the New Testament according to which *the whole creation will be transformed* in order to share in "the glory of the children of God." St. Paul gives us a guarantee of this when he writes to the Romans as follows: "The creation waits with eager longing for the revealing of the sons of God; for the creation was subjected to futility, not of its own will but by the will of him who

229. *Unity in Freedom*, pp. 229-230.
230. Cf. *ibid.*, p. 231; also *Church-Jews*, p. 145.
231. *Church-Jews*, p. 145.
232. Cf. *Unity in Freedom*, p. 231.

subjected it in hope; because the creation itself will be set free from its bondage to decay and obtain the glorious liberty of the children of God" (8:19ff). St. Peter in turn declares: "According to his promise we wait for new heavens and a new earth in which righteousness dwells" (2 Peter 3:13).

The final touch is given by "the seer of Patmos," who writes as follows in the *Book of Revelation*: "Then I saw a new heaven and a new earth; for the first heaven and the first earth had passed away, and the sea was no more. And I saw the holy city, new Jerusalem, coming down out of heaven from God, prepared as a bride adorned for her husband; and I heard a great voice from the throne saying, 'Behold, the dwelling of God is with men. He will dwell with them, and they shall be his people, and God himself will be with them; he will wipe away every tear from their eyes, and death shall be no more, neither shall there be mourning nor crying nor pain any more, for the former things have passed away.' And he who sat upon the throne said, 'Behold, I make all things new' " (Rev. 21:1-5).[233]

At that time the division between the chosen people of the Old Testament and that of the New Testament will come to an end.[234] At that time the scandal of the division of Christians will cease and they will be "perfect in unity," just as Christ is one with his Father and the Father with Christ (cf. John 17:23). And at that time there will also be an end to all the other painful divisions of humankind. Indeed, to use the words of *Nostra aetate* once again, "Together with the prophets and that same apostle, the church awaits the day, known to God alone, when all peoples will call on God with one voice and 'serve him shoulder to shoulder' (Zeph. 3:9)."[235] "The Christian knows that Christ is not only 'the Prince of Peace' (Is. 9:6) but is 'our peace' (Eph. 2:14), the peace of the whole of mankind, for he is its Savior and its peace through time and eternity."[236]

---

233. Cf. *ibid.*, p. 230.
234. On the subject of the ceasing of the divisions between the chosen people of the Old Testament and that of the New, cf. *Church-Jews*, pp. 98-99.
235. *NA*, 4; the conciliar text also appeals to Is. 66:23; Ps. 65:4; Rom. 11:11-32.
236. *Unity in Freedom*, p. 231.

PART FOUR

THE LAST THREE YEARS OF THE CARDINAL'S LIFE

In the notes from the retreat he made in January 1966, a short time after the close of the Council, the cardinal cast a look over the immediate future, in the context of his meditation on Jesus' hidden life in Nazareth, writing: 'The hidden life. The time has now come when I can in a special way imitate the Savior's hidden life. God's will is revealed in the waning of my powers. He could have called me away definitively. If he did not do so, this means that I must still go on working for his kingdom, even in the hidden life. This is therefore not a time of inactivity, but one of intense interior and exterior work." As concerns the latter, he added: "The fact that I live a more retired life does not dispense me from apostolic activity. I can and must perform this not only through prayer and sacrifice, but also through practical assistance in the form of advice, planning, and consultation. In this way I can still do a great deal in the many tasks that I still have: through study and information, and also by continuing with publications." [1]

To what extent do these forecasts give an accurate picture of the last three years of the cardinal's life? Following his long bout of sickness in the summer of 1965, the first element, "waning powers," was certainly a factor, and it meant that he had above all to avoid physical exertion, so that he gave up journeys for public speaking engagements, etc. When the cardinal mentioned "a retired life" he was probably referring to the fact that the close of the Council meant the end of the period in which his life and activity took place to a large extent in the general view; a more "hidden" activity now began, and in this sense a retired life. The cardinal certainly did a great deal of such hidden work, both within the secretariat and in the various other departments of the Roman curia to which he belonged. However, apart from these two aspects, the forecast was not particularly accurate. In the post-conciliar period ecumenism developed at such a rate that the spotlight of public opinion was still repeatedly turned on the cardinal. In addition, he was able to perform a great deal of personal work, particularly in the field of publications, producing no fewer than six books in this period.[2] And all this activity continued until the onset of his last illness, less than three months prior to his death.

---

1. Med. 1966/III/2; original German in Der Mensch Bea, pp. 210-211.
2. Biblio. 172, 173, 175, 189, 190, 191.

CHAPTER 1

THE RAPID POST-CONCILIAR DEVELOPMENT OF ECUMENISM

Although the book that we have cited many times now, *Ecumenism in Focus*, was intended primarily as a record of ecumenism in the Council, the author did not stop with the close of the Council, but continued until the exchange of visits between Rome and Constantinople in 1967. He himself explains the reasons as follows: "With the account of the fourth session one would perhaps consider this study concluded. However, there are several events after the closing of the Council which deserve to be included, since they developed from moves initiated during the Council period. In this way too we can trace concretely the future prospects for ecumenism after the Council; indeed, the events to be described in this chapter are a good example both of the great variety of problems posed by ecumenism, and of the means taken to overcome them. In this way the present chapter is a practical commentary on the Decree on Ecumenism, and while opening new horizons it also synthesizes the numerous elements we have seen as we followed the surprising progress of ecumenism in Vatican II."[1]

In the post-conciliar period we find two particular series of factors that were of decisive importance for the development of ecumenism. In the first place there was a remarkable burst of initiatives on the part of other Christians, which was no less lively and active than the one that constituted the great surprise of the preparatory period of the Council. These brethren had inevitably had a prevalently passive role in the Council, in other words that of observing the Council and what was taking place in the Catholic Church with and through the Council. Now, however, they had the opportunity and the great desire to assume an active role in trying to develop relations with the Catholic Church and dealing with the problems entailed.

The second factor concerns the Catholic Church itself. It was now vital to implement the decisions of the Council concerning ecumenism—both those contained in the conciliar decree on the subject and also those found in other conciliar documents.[2] However, it was not only, or even directly, a question of fulfilling an obligation, albeit one imposed by a Council. The fervor born with the Council led to a holy impatience to put into practice the ecumenical experience acquired in the Council, and this impatience led to a translation into the life of the Catholic Church on all its levels—central government, episcopal conferences, dioceses, down to ordinary members of the laity—of what the Council had decided on the question of relations with other Christians, so that

---

1. *Ecumenism*, p. 221.

2. In *The Way* the cardinal commented on the ecumenical aspects of a number of these documents: those on divine revelation, the church, and the church in the modern world.

Catholics would be as ready as possible to respond to the initiatives of other Christians.

So far as *method* is concerned, our account will be limited to the essential elements, partly because the period in question was full of major events, and partly because the cardinal has already described it fairly fully in his publications, particularly in the last part of *Ecumenism in Focus*. However, apart from describing the events, we shall follow the method used in our previous chapter on the developments of ecumenism in the Council, adding elements from the cardinal's own evaluation of these events. For our purpose it is particularly interesting to see how the cardinal viewed these post-conciliar developments of ecumenism. In other words, our aim is an overall picture of ecumenical developments and how the cardinal saw them.[3]

Dialogue Starts with the World of the Reformed Tradition

Since the secretariat is a department of the Holy See, it was clear from the outset that it would leave initiatives on the local or national level to the relative episcopal conference. Its obvious dialogue partners in the world of the Reformed tradition were the great confessional families that are today referred to as "Christian World Communions," and in this first section we shall be speaking about dialogue with these.

1. *An energetic start to relations with the Anglican communion.* About one month after the close of the Council, on 13 January 1966, it was announced that the Archbishop of Canterbury, Dr. Michael Ramsey, was to make an official visit to Rome about two months later in his capacity as President of the Anglican Communion.[4] During the visit, the illustrious guest met with Paul VI three times: first at a solemn reception in the Sistine Chapel, in the presence of a number of cardinals and the diplomatic corps, then in a private audience, and lastly at the prayer service held in the Church of St. Paul's Outside-the-Walls. The archbishop also took advantage of the opportunity to open the "Anglican Centre" in Rome, which was to help Anglicans and Catholics to get to know one another better.

The impressive solemnity of the meeting in the Sistine Chapel "was maybe increased by the simplicity and brevity of the occasion," wrote the cardinal.[5] The archbishop spoke in English, explaining the purpose of his visit as follows: "I have come with longing in my heart which I know to be in your heart also, that we may by our meeting together help in the fulfillment of the prayer of our Divine Lord that all his disciples may come to unity in the truth." Then, after

---

3. We shall not proceed in chronological order, partly because the various subjects often overlap, and it would make us lose sight of the development of the various threads. We shall instead try to group the material under some major headings: the Reformed tradition, the East, the World Council of Churches, and work within the Catholic Church.

4. The visit has been amply described in *Ecumenism*, pp. 221-228, 258-267.

5. *Ibid.*, p. 223.

expressing recognition and admiration for the ecumenical work of Pope John XXIII, who was "so greatly loving and greatly loved," he concluded with the prayer: "May the grace of God enable us to serve his divine purpose by our meeting, and enable Christians everywhere to feel the pain of their divisions, and to seek unity in truth and holiness."[6]

The pope answered in Latin, beginning with the following greeting: "We dearly hope that your first impression on crossing the threshold of our residence will not be that you are entering a strange house, but a home which for ever-valid reasons you can call your own. . . ." The pope then emphasized the *historic quality* of the meeting: "We realize that this event has various aspects. We have no hesitation in putting the main emphasis on the historical importance of this hour. We see it as a great and blessed moment and one which is deeply moving, especially if we think of the long and sorrowful story which it is its purpose to bring to an end, and of the new developments which could begin at this time, between Rome and Canterbury. From now on we must be ruled and guided by friendship." In addition, the pope described the nature of the meeting *in theological terms* as follows: "In the realms of doctrine and ecclesiastical law there is still a great difference and distance between us; and that is the way things must remain at present, as we must recognize out of respect for truth and freedom, until such time as we merit the supreme grace of true and perfect unity in faith and communion. However, from now on charity can and must be exercised amongst us; it must show forth its mysterious and tremendous strength: 'Where there is charity and love, there is God.' "[7]

The joint declaration of the pope and the archbishop was of fundamental importance, and was read out in Latin and English during the prayer service at St. Paul's.[8] It closed the sad accounts of the past and drew up a basic plan of work for the future. With regard to the past, the two leaders declared that with the Lord's help, "they wish to leave in the hands of the God of mercy all that in the past has been opposed to this precept of charity," while in regard to the future, they start by expressing, in this same spirit of love, the desire "that all those Christians who belong to these two communions may be animated by these same sentiments of respect, esteem and fraternal love." With this aim, "they intend to inaugurate between the Roman Catholic Church and the Anglican Communion a serious dialogue which, founded on the Gospels and on the ancient common traditions, may lead to that unity in truth for which Christ prayed." Apart from such dialogue there will be various forms of cooperation in the vast field of "the great problems that face those who believe in Christ in the world of today."[9] It was a magnificent plan for the future, and the archbishop was right to say that the document "could serve as a model for church relations."[10]

---

6. *Ibid.*, pp. 258-259.

7. *Ibid.*, pp. 260-261 (ct); original in *AAS*, LVIII (1966), 306-307.

8. The text is given in both languages in *AAS*, LVIII (1966), 286-288, while the English is found in *Ecumenism*, pp. 265-266.

9. *Ecumenism*, p. 266.

10. *Ibid.*, p. 228; the archbishop made this declaration to the World Council of Churches; cf. *CC*,

While this visit was being planned, Pope Paul VI referred to the embarrassed and embarrassing way in which Archbishop Ramsey's predecessor Archbishop Fisher had been received in Rome in 1960, and said half-jokingly and half-seriously: "We need to recover our reputation." After the visit the cardinal was able to sum it up very positively: "It has been said, and justly in my opinion, that the visit exceeded all expectations. Its primary importance is that it has opened a new and extremely fruitful stage in the long development of relations between the Church of England, the Anglican Communion, and the Catholic Church, in accordance with a wide-ranging, long-term plan."[11]

The resolutions expressed in the joint declaration did not remain empty words, and both parties soon moved into action.[12] In the first place a Joint Preparatory Commission was set up, with ten members from each side, and it held its first meeting in January 1967. The second meeting took place the following August, and the last in December 1967—January 1968.[13] At the second meeting (in August 1967) it was decided that a subcommission should be set up to study the theology of marriage and its applications to the question of mixed marriages,[14] and this subcommission held its first meeting in April 1968.[15] The Joint Preparatory Commission wound up its work at its third meeting, which was held in Malta, so that its report was known as *The Malta Report*.[16]

In due course, specific practical suggestions were extracted from the report to be submitted to the authorities on both sides. On the Anglican side, these suggestions were submitted to the Lambeth Conference, the supreme organ of the Anglican Communion, which met in London, 25 July—25 August 1968. Apart from various guests, eight official Catholic observers attended this meeting, and Pope Paul VI himself sent a personal message of good wishes.[17]

1966/II, 191.

11. *Ecumenism*, pp. 227-228 (ct); this is an extract from an interview given to the Italian newspaper *La Stampa* of Turin, and to *The Times* of London; the original Italian manuscript is R 1966/40. Cf. also the cardinal's evaluation on Vatican Radio (R 1967/3, pp. 1-2) and his interview to *La Rocca* of Assisi (Biblio. 323); also the declaration made by Pope Paul VI in the general audience (*Ecumenism*, p. 228). On the subject of the visit, we can also see the study of someone who worked with the secretariat, J.F. Long, "Il significato della visita dell'Arcivescovo Ramsey," *CC*, 1966/II, 108-116.

12. Cf. *Ecumenism*, pp. 229-231. This account stops, however, in mid-1967, so after that we shall follow the bulletin that the secretariat started to publish in 1967, the English version of which is entitled simply *Information Service*, abbreviated to *IS*. There is also a French edition entitled *Service d'Information*, abbreviated to *SI*. The dates are not consistent in the early issues, and in order to avoid confusion we shall give first the number of the issue, then the year and the month (where the latter exists). The two editions usually correspond, and, except in special cases where the original texts were French, we shall follow the English edition, which was also (apart from these exceptions) the original version.

13. Cf. *IS*, 1 (1967), 6; 3 (1967), 4; 4 (March 1968), 5.

14. Cf. *IS*, 3 (1967), 5.

15. Cf. *IS*, 5 (June 1968), 6.

16. This report should not be confused with the 1972 report on the Catholic-Lutheran dialogue, which goes by the same name.

17. There is some uncertainty over the number of observers. *IS*, 4 (March 1968), 5, speaks of six,

After careful study of The Malta Report, the conference accepted its conclusions, approving the creation of the subcommission on marriage, and deciding that a new permanent commission should be set up in charge of dialogue with the Catholic Church.[18]

In conclusion, we must stress above all the clarity with which the two sides saw *the aim of dialogue*. It was not simply a case of reaching some degree of understanding or general rapprochement. The joint declaration explicitly expressed the hope that this dialogue "may lead to that unity in truth for which Christ prayed."[19] And the Joint Preparatory Commission also spoke along similar lines, starting at its very first meeting. The statement issued by the meeting begins with the words: "After four hundred years of separation between the Roman Catholic Church and the Anglican Church, official representatives of both have taken the first steps along the road to the restoration of *full unity.*"[20]

2. *Dialogue with the Lutheran World Federation.* In June 1965, a short time after the World Council of Churches had done so, the Lutheran World Federation also decided to set up a joint working group, and this met for the first time the following August.[21] It should be recognized that this federation was in fact the first non-Catholic Christian grouping to offer the Catholic Church an official dialogue. This was a result of its meeting at Reykjavik in Iceland, in September 1964, when its executive committee decided to suggest to the Catholic Church that "official talks be inaugurated in the near future."[22]

Immediately after the conciliar Decree on Ecumenism had been promulgated, a joint group was created with the task of exploring the ground, and seeing what should be done, and how. Immediately after its second meeting (in April 1966) it was able to present the authorities on the two sides with an official report, which was then published a short time later with the approval of both.[23] Our cardinal summarizes the content of the report as follows: "The document emphasizes the importance of a regular exchange of observers and advisors, and recommends the creation of two joint study groups, one on 'The Gospel and the Church,' and the other on 'The Theology of Matrimony and the Problem of

---

the pope's message (*IS*, 6 [January 1969], 20) speaks of seven, while the report of the observers (*IS*, 6 [January 1969], 15-16) gives eight names.

18. It can certainly be assumed that there was similar approval from the Catholic side, although the bulletin does not mention it; cf. *IS*, 6 (January 1969), 19.

19. *Ecumenism*, p. 266.

20. *IS*, 1 (1967), 6. We do not have any full-scale evaluation of these events on the part of the cardinal. The ecumenical survey he made in 1967 on Vatican Radio mentions the meetings of the joint preparatory commission (R 1968/3, p. 4), and in his diary he entered the dates of the Lambeth Conference and noted the presence of Catholic observers. In the message sent to the plenary meeting of the secretariat at the beginning of November 1968 he mentioned "the new fact" of the presence of Catholic observers at the Lambeth Conference (cf. R 1968/17a, p. 3).

21. At that time the federation covered fifty-nine Lutheran churches, with fifty million members, out of a total of about eighty million Lutherans in the world; cf. *IS*, 1 (1967), 5-6.

22. Cf. *Ecumenism*, p. 239.

23. Cf. *ibid.*, pp. 239-240; English text in *IS*, 3 (1967), 26-28; original German in *Lutherische Rundschau* (1966), pp. 560ff. In presenting this report the cardinal follows the presentation made by Monsignor J. Willebrands in *OssRom* (23 July 1966); cf. also *IS*, 1 (1967), 5-6.

Mixed Marriages.' "[24] It also clearly stresses the spirit and method of this dialogue: "Further, it demands an honest reappraisal of divergences and an in-depth examination of both points of view, with a constant shift of the dialogue from the academic to the spiritual level, and with a spirit of patience and open-mindedness."[25]

The first of these international study commissions mentioned—that for dialogue on "The Gospel and the Church"—was set up fairly soon, with six members from each side, and held its first meeting in Zurich in November 1967, which was devoted mainly to the biblical and exegetical aspects of the subject.[26] Less than a year later (in September 1968), the second meeting was held at Bastad in Sweden, dedicated particularly to relations between the church, the world and the gospel.[27]

The new spirit animating relations between the Catholic Church and the Lutheran World Federation can be seen very clearly in the exchange of messages between the cardinal and the president of the federation on the *450th anniversary of the Reformation*. After expressing gratitude to God for the positive changes in mutual relations in and after the Council, the cardinal wrote: "The decisive element for you, as for us, is faith—faith in Jesus Christ, our God and Savior, as this has been delivered to us by the apostles and is alive in the church. This faith is threatened in our world as never before—a faith under attack. At this point we would like to underline the words of the report of the Evangelical Lutheran/Roman Catholic Working Group and pray that together we might succeed in giving 'a more effective witness to the world where so many feel incapable of faith in the gospel of our Lord Jesus Christ or even of accepting the existence of a personal, living God.' "[28] And the cardinal adds that the Year of Faith proclaimed by Pope Paul VI aims precisely at this.[29]

In his response, F.A. Schiotz, President of the Lutheran World Federation, above all rejects any triumphalistic tones in connection with the anniversary, and then quotes a declaration of the 1957 Assembly of the Lutheran World Federation as an indication of the spirit in which the celebrations should be held: "From the very beginning the church was called to be the herald of the truth, receiving and delivering the apostolic message of the mighty deeds of God in the history of salvation, supremely the life and earthly ministry, death and resurrection of Jesus Christ, and calling men to repentance and faith. This

---

24. *Ecumenism*, p. 240; cf. also *IS*, 3 (1967), 27.

25. *Ibid.* (ct).

26. Cf. *IS*, 3 (1967), 3-4, which also gives a list of members of the commission; cf. also BM, pp. 364ff.

27. Cf. *IS*, 7 (May 1969), 6. On the other hand the subject of "the theology of marriage" would not be discussed until 1970, and then only in a single dialogue with the World Alliance of Reformed Churches.

28. Since the German original has not been published we follow the English translation found in *IS*, 3 (1967), 21.

29. "Year of Faith" 1967-1968 was proclaimed by Pope Paul VI on the nineteenth centenary of the martyrdom of the apostles Peter and Paul, so that the church should follow the example of their faith and renew herself in strong, living faith.

apostolic tradition, in which the living Lord himself reigns and acts, remains sovereign and unchangeable throughout all ages. In every generation the church must be confronted and judged by this apostolic message. This is her ongoing reformation."[30]

In conclusion, the letter returns to the reference in the cardinal's message to the Year of Faith and says: "The federation's member churches will welcome participation in the 'Year of Faith' proclaimed by His Holiness Pope Paul VI on this 1900th anniversary year of the martyrdom of the apostles Peter and Paul."[31]

3. *Dialogue with the World Methodist Council.* Here too the preparations began soon after the Council.[32] In October 1965, the President, F. Corson, had said that its executive committee wanted the creation of a joint working group with the Catholic Church. This was then confirmed in March 1966, after the publication of the joint declaration of the pope and Archbishop Ramsey. In April 1966, Pope Paul VI had given his agreement, but the Methodists decided to wait until the end of their congress held the following August. The final message of this congress spoke about ecumenism as follows: "In the brief five years since our last conference amazing progress had been made in courtesy and coopera-tion between the Christian denominations. The most remarkable is the lowering of the barriers of suspicion and ignorance that have divided us from our brethren in the Roman Catholic Church and them from us. The Commission on Methodist Ecumenical Relations is to give particular attention to exploratory talks with representatives of the Vatican Secretariat for Christian Unity."[33]

The first meeting of the joint working group was held at Ariccia, just outside Rome, in October 1967, and was taken up for the most part with getting to know one another and, as was the case with other similar groups, exploring possible subjects and methods for dialogue. The following subjects were decided on for the next meeting: the eucharist, and authority and ministries in the church. So far as the general method was concerned, the working group stressed the need for the results of its meetings to be subscribed to by the respective communities and also for the subjects to be linked with contemporary life and problems.[34] The second meeting was held at the end of August and beginning of September 1968 in London, and was devoted, as planned, to the subjects of "the eucharist" and "authority in the church."[35]

4. Possibilities for a dialogue with the World Alliance of Reformed Churches

30. *IS*, 3 (1967), 21-22.

31. *Ibid.*, p. 22.

32. Cf. *Ecumenism*, p. 240. The World Methodist Council comprises the majority of the Methodist churches in the world and has twenty million members; cf. *IS*, 1 (1967), 8. David B. Barrett, *World Christian Encyclopedia* (Oxford, 1982), p. 14, gives the figure of twenty-six million. Other sources give "twenty-one million members and forty-nine million children and friends"; cf. H. Krueger, W. Loeser, W. Mueller-Roemheld, *Oekumenelexikon -Kirchen-Religionen-Bewegungen* (Frankfurt, 1983), p. 801.

33. *Ecumenism*, p. 241, and *IS*, 1 (1967), 8.

34. Cf. *IS*, 3 (1967), 6-7 (which also gives the names of the members of the commission).

35. Cf. *IS*, 5 (June 1968), 8; *IS*, 7 (May 1969), 9.

also opened up in this period. In its meeting in June 1968, the executive committee of the association decided that "it is necessary to explore the elements of the new situation that suggest that it would be timely to begin a dialogue" with the Catholic Church. The Catholic Church judged this decision to be in line with the orientations of the Second Vatican Council, particularly those expressed in the Decree on Ecumenism, and put into practice by the Secretariat for Christian Unity. These two factors led to a joint exploratory meeting, which was held in Geneva, 27-29 November 1968, a few weeks after the cardinal's death, although the decision to hold it obviously dated back to the previous months and thus to the cardinal himself.[36]

Remarkable Broadening of Relations with the World Council of Churches

The reader will recall that one of our previous chapters described the creation of the joint working group of the Catholic Church and the World Council of Churches in spring 1965, with the task of exploring the ground and examining possibilities for dialogue and cooperation, as well as the method to be used. In this connection, it was stated that "The joint working group shall have no power to make decisions but must work out suggestions to be submitted to the churches represented, and communicate them to the member churches."[37] The joint working group would produce periodic reports on its activity, together with any suggestions. These reports are therefore one of the main sources of information on developments in relations between the Catholic Church and the World Council of Churches. As usually happens in the early years, the group met fairly frequently, so that between May 1965 and May 1968 there were no fewer than seven meetings.[38] After the fifth meeting, which was held near Rome, the group was received in audience by Pope Paul VI, an occasion the cardinal describes as follows: "There was one important new aspect to this meeting. The entire group was received in audience by the pope; the representatives of the World Council were led by Dr. Carson Blake, its Secretary General. In accordance with the express wishes of both parties the audience did not take the usual solemn form but that of a free conversation on various problems of interest to both sides."[39]

This intense work rhythm brought further developments within the group itself. Thus the sixth meeting, which was held at Assisi, the city of St. Francis, on the request of the representatives of the World Council, was concerned primarily with reorganizing the group itself, so that relations between the World Council and the Catholic Church could become more dynamic. The an-

---

36. For the two factors, cf. *IS*, 7 (May 1969), 8.

37. Cf. pp. 482-485 above.

38. The full list is found in *IS*, 7 (May 1969), 2.

39. *Ecumenism*, p. 238 (ct); cf. also R 1968/4, p. 5.

nouncement explained that until then the group had had a more or less exploratory task, although it had already fostered a whole series of initiatives. Now,
however, the time had come for the group to take on "a more positive function
of coordinating such initiatives, and others too, although without abandoning
its exploratory function."[40]

1. Now that we have taken a look at the main instrument of development of
relations between the Catholic Church and the World Council of Churches, we
can move on to its plans and their implementation. The first report of the group
sets out a very broad plan of work.[41] Bishop J. Willebrands described the various
points, saying that it encompassed "the various questions raised by dialogue
between the Catholic Church and the World Council of Churches, as well as
those that have arisen in direct discussions between the Roman Catholic Church
and the other churches (what are today referred to as bilateral conversations),
the exchange of observers at study meetings and events of ecumenical importance, possibilities of practical cooperation in social work, prayer for unity,
specific problems of the laity in the Christian world, and the role of women."[42]
These few lines already indicate almost all the main subjects that we shall see
gradually developing in the next two years.

2. Moving on now to the practical implementation of its plans, at this third
meeting (in May 1966) the joint working group set up various groups and
commissions, etc., among them a small group with the task of drafting a study
document on the nature of *ecumenical dialogue*. Apart from this, "the decision
was also taken for a special theological commission which will study *'catholicity and apostolicity,'* since this is a fundamental problem that was continually
arising in the dialogue between the Roman Catholic Church and the member
churches of the World Council of Churches. A second commission was established to study the *nature and task of ecumenism*, and a third to deal with the
problems of *proselytism* in the light of the duty of the church to bear witness,
the principles of religious freedom and the shared ecumenical task. The theology
of *marriage* and the question of mixed marriages will also be studied."[43]

Let us immediately take a look at how far the *work of these subcommissions*
had proceeded in our period, in other words during the cardinal's life. The
subcommission on marriage met in February 1967 and drafted a document,
although this paper remained reserved for internal use and was not published.[44]
Work on the subject of ecumenical dialogue proceeded so fast that the relative
document could be published in the course of 1967.[45] With regard to the activity
of the other two subcommissions, the summary of the official reports presented
to the plenary meeting of the secretariat held in the last days of the cardinal's
life gives us all the information we need. The subcommission concerned with

40. *IS*, 4 (March 1968), 3.
41. Original English text in *IS*, 1 (1967), 18-21.
42. *Ecumenism*, p. 231 (ct), quoting an article in *OssRom* (24 February 1966).
43. *Ibid.*, p. 237 (ct); cf. also R 1968/4; *IS*, 1 (1969), 4-5.
44. The meeting took place 28 February—4 March 1967.
45. Original English text in *IS*, 1 (1967), 33-36.

the catholicity and apostolicity of the church had drawn up a working paper and "a decision will be taken about the future of this at the next meeting of the working group. It is not planned to publish it, but various other ways of using it are under consideration."[46] Work on the document on Christian witness and proselytism was on course, and efforts were being made to improve it, "but it is a complex problem, and the intention is that of giving it all the attention it deserves."[47]

3. Apart from dialogue on various important subjects, *practical cooperation in charitable and welfare activities* in various spheres was very soon established between the World Council of Churches and the Catholic Church.[48] In the aforementioned article, Bishop Johannes Willebrands, who was then secretary of the secretariat, gives a practical example of cooperation in relief work at the time of the publication of the first report of the group: "A concrete example of collaboration has already been given by Caritas Internationalis and the department of Inter-Church Aid of the World Council of Churches, who have joined together in an appeal against the famine in India."[49] He also says: "As a result of a joint action it was recently possible to send an aircraft load a bare two hours after the request in order to help the victims of the flood in Portugal." And the report adds: "The sufferings caused by the Vietnam war also offer an opportunity for concerted action between Roman Catholic bodies and those belonging to the World Council of Churches."[50]

4. Efforts were also being made to increase cooperation "in seeking *justice*, and in the *development of international affairs* and *world peace*." This work took two factors as its starting point: on the one hand, the fact that the World Council had successfully organized a conference on "The Church and Society," and on the other hand, the fact that the Holy See had set up the Justice and Peace Commission. It was thus decided "to hold joint specialist consultations on these matters,"[51] and soon after this, in June 1967, the World Council and the Pontifical Commission for Justice and Peace set up a joint commission known as *Sodepax*, which was to help the church "to develop a world-level plan with which to mobilize public opinion in support of practical action to overcome the increasingly wide gulf between rich and poor nations." The commission had a full-time secretary.[52]

The first major action undertaken by Sodepax was the *Conference on World Cooperation for Economic Development* which was held in Beirut, 21-27 April

---

46. *IS*, 7 (1969), 3.
47. *Ibid.*. Cf. also *IS*, 5 (June 1968), 3-4. The document was in fact not published until 1970; cf. *IS*, 14 (April 1971), 19-24.
48. Cf. *Ecumenism*, p. 231.
49. *Ibid.* (ct). The news was taken from the French paper *La Croix* (12 February 1966), p. 4.
50. *IS*, 4 (March 1968), 3.
51. *Ecumenism*, p. 238. These discussions would continue at the sixth meeting of the group; cf. *IS*, 4 (March 1968), 3.
52. Cf. *IS*, 5 (June 1968), 5. Sodepax (abbreviation for Society, Development, Peace) continued its work until 1980. On the reasons for its replacement by the "Consultative Group of Social Thinking and Action," see the fifth report of the joint working group, *IS*, 53 (1983/4), 110-111.

1968. This was the first joint effort of Catholics, Protestants and Orthodox to explore what could be done to reach a more just distribution of the riches of the earth.[53]

5. An important form of cooperation, this time in the spiritual field, was that of preparing the material for the *Week of Prayer for Christian Unity*, and the cardinal describes this as follows: "In October 1966 . . . there was a meeting at Geneva between various Catholic ecumenical centers and the Faith and Order section of the World Council of Churches. The theme under discussion was the celebration of the week of prayer for unity. During this meeting the important decision was taken that from 1968 onward a mixed working group would prepare a common text for the week each year, so that it could be used by both Catholics and non-Catholics." And the cardinal explains the importance of this cooperation: "Indeed, the use of the same prayers and scripture readings by Christians of the various confessions is a visible sign of the union that already exists among them, and without denying the differences that still exist it deepens the awareness of this union among those who pray in this way."[54]

6. This development in mutual relations was demonstrated very clearly by the Catholic presence at certain major events of the World Council of Churches.

(a) The first such occasion took place in the summer of 1966 when the World Council organized a huge international conference in Geneva under the title "The Church and Society," with the subtitle "The Task of the Christian in the Technological and Sociological Revolution of Our Time." Eight Catholic observers attended this meeting, and the cardinal later wrote about the event as follows: "The press office of the World Council commented that the conference, as well as being the largest ever organized by the council, also had more Catholic observers than ever before."[55] Nor was this all, for one of the observers, Monsignor Charles Moeller, Under-Secretary to the Sacred Congregation for the Doctrine of the Faith, also took an active part, with a paper on the conciliar Constitution on the Church in the Modern World. "It is an event that needs no comment," said the cardinal in the course of a conversation on Vatican Radio.[56]

(b) The second event was even more important, and was the *Fourth Assembly of the World Council of Churches*, which was held at Uppsala, 3-19 July 1968. Fifteen Catholic observer-delegates and six guests took part. Let us immediately see how these observers felt about their attendance and its effects on relations between the World Council of Churches and the Catholic Church. Their official report begins with the statement: "The Uppsala assembly represents, without any doubt, a step of prime importance in the dialogue between the Roman

---

53. Cf. *IS*, 5 (June 1968), 5. Cf. also *Documentation Catholique*, LXV (1968), 973-980. Similar cooperation was developed with the Council for the Laity, particularly on the occasion of the Third International Congress for the Apostolate of the Laity, which was held in Rome in October 1967. We shall return to this in due course. Cf. also *IS*, 4 (March 1968), 3; *IS*, 7 (May 1969), 3.

54. *Ecumenism*, p. 236 (ct); cf. also R 1967/3, p. 3; *IS*, 1 (1967), 11.

55. *Ecumenism*, p. 234 (ct); cf. press release NB/10/66 of 1 July 1966.

56. Cf. *Ecumenism*, p. 234; for the statement on Vatican Radio, cf. ms. R 1967/3, p. 4.

Catholic Church and the World Council of Churches."[57] Practical confirmation of this statement is seen in the fact that the assembly greeted the pope's message with applause that was not simply an expression of courtesy, but "reflected the feeling and the hopes which we had all sensed in private conversations from the moment of our arrival."[58] The report then continued: "Moreover we might add that every reference to a closer cooperation between Rome and the World Council of Churches was greeted with joy and with the desire, sometimes openly expressed, that this cooperation might lead to a deeper association."[59] As concerns the future, the observers state: "It appears that this insistence will demand that in the near future the question of the Catholic Church's entry into the World Council be studied seriously."[60]

For its part, the assembly took *three decisions* with regard to the Catholic Church: (i) the admission of a certain number of Catholic theologians into the Faith and Order section; (ii) the ratification of the activity of the joint working group; and (iii) approval of the report on Sodepax, with its secretariat being strengthened.[61]

Pope Paul VI's message to this gathering is also extremely significant. It starts by saying that the presence of observer-delegates and a certain number of guests "is a sign for our times. It confirms in happy fashion the mutual will to continue and extend the cooperation already existing between the World Council and the Catholic Church. It is also the expression of the lively interest that we take in your gathering. We pray to the Holy Spirit to inspire your work and ensure its full success."[62]

The message of the president of the secretariat is fuller: "This gathering is undoubtedly of major importance, in the first place for the member churches represented by delegates, but also for all Christians, and indeed all mankind."[63]

Reflection on progress in mutual relations "must not make us lose sight of

---

57. The whole report is found in *IS*, 6 (January 1969), 5; various items on the contribution of the secretariat to the meeting are found in Arch. Ma 4/15-18.

58. *IS*, 6 (January 1969), 6-7.

59. *Ibid.*, p. 6.

60. *Ibid.*

61. Cf. *ibid.* Later on the question of the *participation of Catholic theologians in Faith and Order* was clarified further. According to the general regulations of Faith and Order, such theologians must enjoy the trust of their own church, which must agree to their appointment. They are elected by the Faith and Order department from names put forward by the various churches. Nevertheless, they do not operate as delegates of their own church, but simply on a personal basis. Nine Catholic theologians were elected in this way after the assembly; cf. the list in *IS*, 7 (May 1969), 3-4. Bishop J. Willebrands described the history of Faith and Order, and the participation of Catholic theologians, in an article in *OssRom* (1 September 1968); a summary is found in *IS*, 7 (May 1969), 3-5.

62. French original in *OssRom* (7 July 1968) and *Documentation Catholique*, LXV (1968), 1473; I do not know why neither the pope's message nor that of Cardinal Bea—which we shall discuss below—was given in the bulletin of the secretariat. An English translation is found in the official report of the meeting, *The Uppsala Report 1968*, ed. Norman Goodale (Geneva, 1968), p. 403.

63. French original in *OssRom* (7 July 1968), and *Documentation Catholique*, LXV (1968), 1474-1476; here 1474. An English translation is found in *The Uppsala Report 1968*, pp. 403-404, although it is incomplete.

the divisions which, sad to say, exist among us; they go to the very heart of our faith and our Christian life. And this is why brotherly love must take on the character of joint repentance before God. Unanimity in repentance must mark the start of unity in the fulness of faith and life."[64]

The message then indicates *the objectives*: "Pastoral concern is no less important than theological reflection, joint prayer, and cooperation for the development of peace among peoples, for it will guide and help to extend the movement toward Christian unity to local communities."[65]

"We all labor side by side in the ecumenical field, and thus we keep our eyes on the importance of our task rather than the difficulty involved. The Lord desires all Christians to be gathered and united in the communion of a single church, as scripture tells us. Thus we cannot rest from our exertions so long as we have not brought about, by the grace of God, the ecclesial unity of all the disciples of Christ."[66]

Cooperation with the Bible Societies

Staying in the West a moment more, we still have to describe a very important ecumenical development born after the Council. The Bible societies have a certain similarity to the World Council of Churches inasmuch as according to their statutes they have members of different confessions; moreover, although they devote themselves to a single sector—that of the spread of sacred scripture—their activity is of fundamental importance, just as the written word of God is for Christians, and they thus have a very wide evangelizing influence among Christians and non-Christians.

Let us first of all see exactly what the Bible societies are, and also the organization of the United Bible Societies (or UBS) to which they belong. The cardinal writes about them as follows: "The UBS is a group of national Bible societies—the most important being Britain and America—and the members belong to various different confessions. The purpose of the Bible societies is quite simply to foster translation and distribution of the Bible. Altogether the UBS have a membership of about three thousand experts, both clerical and lay, and publish the scriptures in six hundred and fifty languages. Work on the first translation or revision of existing translations is in progress for a further five hundred—half of these being the first translations of the Bible in the respective languages."[67]

When these societies first started about one hundred and fifty years ago, they were in friendly relations with the Catholic Church. The British Bible Society and the Foreign Bible Society were in frequent contact with leaders of the

---

64. *Documentation Catholique*, LXV (1968), 1476.

65. *Ibid.*, p. 1475.

66. *Ibid.*

67. *Ecumenism*, p. 248 (ct). Ample information is found in *IS*, 1 (1967), 8-9, and the following explanations by the cardinal are based on this study.

Catholic Church, and distributed eight of the latter's translations of the sacred scriptures in the main European languages. Similarly, representatives of the Catholic Church were invited to the founding in New York of the American Bible Society, which is a very powerful body today. Unfortunately, things later changed, with generations of suspicion, and in certain cases hostility, setting in.[68]

1. As in many other fields, Vatican Council II made a change possible. *It was the UBS that took the first step* when some of its representatives wrote to Cardinal Bea and the secretariat in February 1963, asking if it would not be possible to take up contacts in order to discuss how they could work together in translating, publishing and distributing the scriptures throughout the world.[69] Although Cardinal Bea decided that more formal negotiations should wait until the publication of the conciliar Constitution on Divine Revelation, he did agree that a small group should meet in Crêt-Bérard in Switzerland in order to work out certain principles on which such cooperation should be based.[70] In March 1965, Dr. O. Béguin presented a report on the results of this meeting to the headquarters of his organization, and in the months that followed this report was examined by the various national Bible societies.[71]

On 4 April 1966, Cardinal Bea presented Pope Paul VI with a suggested plan for such cooperation, stressing that it was basically a question of implementing numbers 22 and 25 of the conciliar constitution *Dei verbum*. As usual, he sent the pope a memorandum on the question prior to the audience. The pope's reaction was as rapid as that of Pope John XXIII on the question of the creation of the secretariat. I remember that immediately after the audience the cardinal told me how, as soon as he entered the private library, Paul VI told him: "Well, I'm in complete agreement over cooperation with the Bible societies." The pope also entrusted the secretariat with the task of putting the project into operation.[72]

The agreement of the UBS was equally decided. Its council met the following May under the chairmanship of the Anglican Archbishop of York, and *unanimously* voted to accept cooperation with the Roman Catholic Church in translating and distributing the scriptures in line with what is laid down in the conciliar constitution *Dei verbum*, nn. 22 and 25.[73] Bearing in mind the specific

---

68. Cf. *IS*, 1 (1967), 10.

69. Cf. *IS*, 5 (June 1968), 13. There were two letters, one from the Secretary General of the UBS, Dr. Oliver Béguin, and one (and this is worthy of note!) from Lord Fisher of Lambeth (retired Archbishop of Canterbury, who had made the famous visit to Rome in 1960) in his capacity as President of the British and Foreign Bible Society, the oldest member of the UBS.

70. The meeting took place on 10-13 November 1964; cf. *Ecumenism*, p. 248; *IS*, 1 (1967), 9.

71. The member societies of the UBS are autonomous.

72. Cf. *IS*, 5 (June 1968), 14. This assignment was not publicly announced until seven months later (cf. *OssRom* [12 November 1966], p. 2) since the episcopal conferences were to be informed first (cf. *ibid.*).

73. Cf. *Ecumenism*, p. 249, and *IS*, 1 (1967), 9. *DV*, 22, states above all the principle that "access to sacred scripture ought to be open wide to the Christian faithful," and then speaks about translations "made in a joint effort with the separated brethren," saying that such translations "may be used by all Christians." *DV*, 25, on the other hand, broadens the perspective and states that "editions of sacred scripture . . . should be prepared for the use even of non-Christians, and

structure of the UBS itself, its council added that this decision must be successively examined in the continental meetings of the national Bible associations.[74] These rapid decisions on both sides were a result of the fact that such cooperation was in the interests of all concerned.

We would cite an example of how Cardinal Bea explained the immediate interest of many sectors of the Catholic Church. In many mission lands, he says, "the bishops found themselves in the difficult situation of introducing the vernacular in the sacred liturgy, in accordance with the spirit of the Council, but then having the problem that there are no Catholic translations of sacred scripture in the local language, while there are on the other hand those of the Bible societies. It has therefore been agreed with the Bible society in question that the existing translation should be revised in such a way that it can be used in the liturgy, maybe even deciding to produce a new translation together in due course."[75]

However, there are far greater interests at stake in the field of spreading the good news, as we can see from the following figures. In Asia, excluding China and Japan, out of 331 million children of school age in 1960, about 67 million went to school; however, in this same year no more than 3 million copies of the New Testament were distributed. The Bible societies are therefore faced with an enormous task and are delighted with the renewed interest of the Catholic Church in sacred scripture.[76]

2. The secretariat now set to work, first of all "informing episcopal conferences of the opportunities offered in this field, and asking them for information on the number of translations already existing in their areas, the extent of their distribution, and what was being done to encourage their distribution, etc."[77] This survey provided a very useful general picture of outdated or inadequate translations, sometimes in course of revision; there was also information on plans for new translations, with or without the cooperation of others. It also became clear that very little was on the whole done to encourage people to read the Bible. Many bishops said that a great deal needed to be done, and expressed their desire to change this situation with the help of the Bible societies.[78]

At the beginning of January 1967, a meeting was held at the secretariat with the representatives of the UBS. The cardinal opened the meeting, saying: "It does not seem to be an exaggeration to say that the possibility of our cooperation is one of the most important developments in contemporary Christian history. It challenges decades, even generations of suspicion and, in some cases, hostility. It draws us into deeper probing and more honest appraisal of our different attitudes. We stand on the threshold of a great enterprise."[79]

---

adapted to their circumstances"; and these translations "should be prudently circulated, either by pastors of souls, or by Christians of any rank." With regard to the history of this cooperation, cf. Biblio. 354, which also refers to these dispositions of the conciliar document.

74. Cf. *IS*, 1 (1967), 9.

75. Biblio. 354.

76. Cf. *IS*, 1 (1967), 9.

77. Biblio. 354.

78. Cf. *IS*, 1 (1967), 9-10.

79. Original English text, R 1967/1. *IS*, 1 (1967), 10-11, reports the meeting held at the secretariat,

The meeting was told about the results of the survey of episcopal conferences, together with details of various initiatives already being undertaken. Norms for cooperation in translating the scriptures were also discussed, and also those for the publication of joint translations. Thus a fuller and more precise form was given to the draft principles drawn up in 1964,[80] and these were in due course examined by various national Bible societies.[81] So far as the Catholic side was concerned, after it had passed examination by the Pontifical Biblical Commission and other departments of the curia, instead of giving it his own formal approval, Pope Paul VI said that since it was a biblical matter, Cardinal Bea's approval was good enough for him. The document was presented to the public, most significantly, on the Feast of Pentecost 1967, for according to an ancient tradition of the fathers of the church, the Holy Spirit had begun to remedy the confusion of languages of Babel on the first Pentecost.[82]

3. The secretariat did not stop here, however. Cooperation with the Bible societies in translating and publishing the Bible was obviously not all that was entailed in implementing the decisions of the Council with regard to spreading knowledge of the scriptures. The Catholic Church also needed special bodies to promote the biblical apostolate, concerning themselves with the publication, distribution and knowledge of the Bible, as well as scriptural training for priests and lay people. A similar body could also take charge of contacts with the non-Catholic Bible societies over the various projects for joint translations and any problems that might arise. In April 1968 the secretariat therefore organized a meeting of representatives of Catholic Bible societies to be held at its offices, which was also attended by representatives of the UBS. The various participants, who came from nine European countries, the Americas, Canada and India, told the meeting about their own work, and there were also some written reports from the Philippines and Africa.[83]

It was at this meeting that the idea took root that the Catholic societies in the various countries should join together to form a federation. We would add that in April 1969, after the cardinal's death, another meeting was held at the secretariat at which this federation was in fact formed.[84]

We would conclude by emphasizing the ecumenical importance of cooperation with the Bible societies, particularly because of the fact that these societies do not as such represent any particular confession but are interconfessional.[85]

but does not, for some reason, give the text of the cardinal's address. On cooperation with the UBS, cf. also Biblio. 354.

80. Cf. the joint declaration, *IS*, 1 (1967), 10.

81. Detailed reports on this process can be found in *IS*, 3 (1967), 7; and 4 (March 1968), 6.

82. For this interpretation of Pentecost, cf. the conciliar Decree on the Church's Missionary Activity, 4. The text of the document is found in *IS*, 5 (June 1968), 22-25. Cooperation with the UBS developed a great deal after this, so that by 1985 over one hundred and sixty interconfessional translations of the Bible, either partial or whole, were already under way; cf. *OssRom* (30 September/1 October 1985).

83. Cf. *IS*, 5 (June 1968), 12-13.

84. Cf. *IS*, 7 (May 1969), 10.

85. Cf. *IS*, 1 (1967), 9. A very positive evaluation is also found in R 1967/3, p. 3.

This fact meant that such cooperation opened up a new field for contacts that had not yet been reached in dialogue with the individual Christian confessions.[86]

The First Visit of the Head of an Eastern Church to Rome

When we speak about the eastern churches, we must distinguish between two major branches: on the one hand there are the "ancient oriental churches" which split from the rest of Christendom over the Christological definitions of the Council of Chalcedon in 451, and on the other the eastern churches of Byzantine tradition. After the painful division of the fifth century, the "ancient oriental churches" had practically no further relations with the Catholic Church. And this made their great readiness to send observer-delegates to the Second Vatican Council all the more surprising. It was, moreover, the spiritual head of one of these churches who made the first official visit of a head of an eastern church to Rome, when the catholicos of the Armenian Church of Cilicia, Khoren I, came to visit the pope in May 1967.[87] The catholicos had already met Paul VI at Beirut Airport in November 1964, during the pope's journey to Bombay, but the present visit was an official, solemn one.

An idea of the spirit and atmosphere of the occasion can be seen from the statement the catholicos made during his speech of greeting to the pope: "We rejoice wholeheartedly and give thanks to the Lord for this blessed moment of our meeting with Your Holiness—a meeting in which we find ourselves with the most profound joy at the very heart of our brotherhood and of our spiritual communion in the only Son of God, the incarnate Word."[88] The catholicos went on to stress the contribution of the Second Vatican Council to the spirit of brotherhood among Christians: "This spirit and the efforts which follow, which

---

86. The importance of these developments can also be seen from *the immensity of the task* facing Christians in the field of spreading the scriptures. In this connection, the cardinal gave the following figures: "The complete Bible exists in about two hundred and fifty languages; the New Testament alone in about three hundred. Just over seven hundred . . . have at least one book of the Bible. But there are still a further thousand or so languages which as yet have no translation at all, not one book, not even a page" (*Ecumenism*, p. 249, citing the very worthy assistant to the secretariat in this field, W.M. Abbott, "Alla ricerca di una Bibbia comune," *CC*, 1967/1, 331-338, esp. 336.

87. On account of various complicated historical events, there are two Armenian churches: apart from the Church of Cilicia, which is referred to here, there is another with headquarters at Etchmiadzin, the head of which bears the title "Supreme Catholicos of the Armenians." When the cardinal welcomed Catholicos Khoren I to the secretariat, he noted that the Armenian Church of Cilicia "was one of the first of the eastern churches to accept our invitations, and it sent observers to every one of the Council sessions" (*Ecumenism*, p. 274).

88. We follow the French translation published in *SI*, 3 (1967), 4, which was provided by the Catholicos' own group, and is also found in *OssRom* (10 May 1967), and *Documentation Catholique*, LXIV (1967), 992-994. The visit is fully described and the various speeches are found in *Ecumenism*, pp. 268-276. Probably due to an oversight, the English-language bulletin of the secretariat does not mention this visit. An English translation is, however, found in *Ecumenism*, pp. 268-270.

we call the 'ecumenical movement,' have been given a completely new dimension by the Second Vatican Council, which marked a turning point not only in the life of the Roman Catholic Church but also in the Christian world in general."[89] In conclusion, he prayed that the Lord would "deign to strengthen the bonds of spiritual communion in the hearts of all Christians; that by the action of his grace he will prepare people to understand one another; that he will lead all men to unity and to a common witness in charity and in truth."[90]

In his response, the pope started by expressing gratitude to the catholicos for sending observers from his church to all the periods of the Council,[91] then stressed *the urgent need for the search for full communion*: "We venture to say that we are constrained to strive to restore this perfect communion not only because it is the will of Christ, but because the holy eucharist which we celebrate also demands this of us. St. Paul teaches us: 'The cup of blessing which we bless, is it not a participation in the blood of Christ? The bread which we break, is it not a participation in the body of Christ? Because there is one bread, we who are many are one body, for we all partake of the one bread' (1 Cor. 10:16-17). How then could we ever not strive with all our might to clear away the obstacles and to resolve the differences which still prevent our celebration from becoming a concelebration?"[92] Referring to the Council the pope also stressed *the norm of the unity* to be sought: "The recent Vatican Council in its Decree on Ecumenism gave us a valuable guiding principle on this subject: 'In order to restore communion and unity or preserve them, one must "impose no burden beyond what is indispensable" (Acts 15:28).' What is indispensable is charity without any pretense, identity of faith, and submission to the essential order which Christ desired for his church."[93]

The next day Cardinal Bea welcomed the guest to the secretariat, explaining the thinking of the secretariat with regard to *the practical path* to be taken in the search for full unity as follows: "I am thinking here especially of theological dialogue, but also of dialogue on important problems over a vast field which were brought to light by the Second Vatican Council. I am also thinking of dialogue at the practical or pastoral level."[94] Having emphasized an important consideration which did not exist with other eastern Christians, in other words the fact that the Armenians celebrated Easter on the same day as the Catholics,

89. English translation taken from *Ecumenism*, p. 269.
90. English translation taken from *Ecumenism*, p. 270 (ct).
91. Cf. *Ecumenism*, pp. 271-272; the original French is found in *AAS*, LXIX (1967), 510-512, and also in *SI*, 3 (1967), 5-6. When the Catholicos visited the secretariat, Cardinal Bea noted that in the meantime these "very worthy observers had since been raised to the dignity of the episcopate." In 1977 one of them, Karekin Sarkissian, became coadjutor, succeeding Khoren I as Catholicos in 1983, and in fact making an official visit to Rome in 1983 as such; cf. *IS*, 51 (1983), 37-41.
92. English translation taken from *Ecumenism*, pp. 272-273.
93. *Ibid.*, p. 273, quoting *UR*, 18.
94. *Ibid.*, p. 274 (ct). The official French text of the speeches of Cardinal Bea and the Catholicos is found in *OssRom* (11 May 1967), and the Catholicos' response is also found in Arch. Md/2. The original Italian of the cardinal's speech is found in R 1967/14.

the cardinal concluded: "May this unity in relation to the great feast be the symbol of the profound bonds that unite us in Christ, despite the factors that separate us; the symbol also of our common desire to go forward together in every sphere where this is possible, so as to present ever more effectively to the world that vision of unity in which they ought to recognize Christ and his mission."[95]

For his part, the guest expressed warm gratitude for the work of the secretariat, stressed the commitment of his church to move forward, wherever possible, in fraternal union, and concluded: "We are firmly convinced that the churches cannot remain isolated from each other when the awareness of their calling to the same mission is opening out in their souls. In our own time, the twentieth century, the most authentic expression of our fidelity to the word and to the life which Christ has called us to serve and to live is to pray together, to discuss things together, and to work together."[96]

The cardinal referred repeatedly to this important visit, stressing that it was the first visit of the head of a non-Catholic eastern church, and that the catholicos had thus played a pioneering role.[97] He also stressed the spiritual atmosphere of the visit, quoting the words, "We find ourself ... at the very heart of our brotherhood,"[98] although he could just as well have quoted from a number of the passages we have given here, for they all bear witness to the extraordinary spiritual attitude and the firm ecumenical commitment shown during this visit. These qualities made it an excellent beginning and first fruits of the various visits that would follow.[99]

Still remaining in the field of relations with the ancient oriental churches, we would also mention the exchange of visits between Paul VI and the *Armenian Patriarch of Constantinople*, Kalustian, of the Armenian Church of Etchmiadzin, Head of the Armenians of Turkey. At the time of Paul VI's visit to Turkey (which we shall discuss below), Patriarch Kalustian came to visit him. In his speech of welcome,[100] the pope sent a cordial greeting also to the Supreme Catholicos of the Armenians, Vasken I, and went on to recall the great fathers

---

95. *Ecumenism*, p. 275 (ct).

96. *Ibid.*, p. 276.

97. Cf. R 1968/1, p. 1; R 1968/3, p. 7; R 1968/4, p. 2.

98. R 1968/4, p. 2.

99. In 1968 the Coptic Church of Egypt celebrated the nineteenth centenary of the martyrdom of its patron, St. Mark the Evangelist. On this occasion, Kyrillos VI, Patriarch of the See of St. Mark, who bears the title of Pope, inaugurated the new Cathedral of St. Mark, inviting Pope Paul VI to the ceremony. Since the latter was unable to accept, he sent a special delegation made up of Cardinal L.E. Duval, Archbishop of Algiers, with the Auxiliary Bishop of Venice, G. Olivotti, and Bishop J. Willebrands; cf. *IS*, 5 (June 1968), 11. The following is a list of the successive visits of the heads of the ancient oriental churches: in 1970 the Supreme Catholicos Vasken I (cf. *IS*, 11 [July 1970]); in 1971, the Syrian Orthodox Patriarch Jacob III (cf. *IS*, 16 [January 1972]); in 1973, the Coptic Patriarch Shenouda III (cf. *IS*, 22 [October 1973]); in 1981, the Patriarch of the Church of Ethiopia, Tekle Haimanot (cf. *IS*, 47 [1981], 100-101); and lastly, in 1983, the Catholicos of the Syrian Orthodox Church of India, Mar Baselios Marthoma Mathews I (cf. *IS*, 52 [1983]).

100. Original English in *AAS*, LIX (1967), 842-843, and *IS*, 3 (1967), 13.

and doctors of the Armenian Church "who are our shared doctors of the faith."
Referring to his forthcoming visit to Ephesus, the pope stressed that the faith
proclaimed at that Council constituted the joint heritage of both churches.
Lastly, he pointed out how urgent it was to strive for the restoration of full unity
in love and truth.

The following day, the pope returned the visit, and in his speech of welcome
the patriarch said that this city had been waiting for a visit from the Roman
Pontiff for almost one thousand years, and also passed on the "fraternal greetings" of the Supreme Catholicos of the Armenians Vasken I. He said that when
it began, the Armenian Church had close links with the Church of Rome, and
even if factors beyond our control then disturbed these, "the spirit of charity has
never been completely extinguished" on either side. He thus expressed the hope
that this visit would bring blessings "on us all."[101]

An Exchange of Official Visits between Rome and Constantinople

Moving on to relations with the Orthodox churches of Byzantine tradition,
there are a number of events to be recorded,[102] as well as various ecumenical
initiatives on the part of Paul VI.[103] So far as these latter initiatives are concerned,
we shall, however, confine ourselves to the most central and courageous of
these, in other words his visit to Patriarch Athenagoras I. And so far as the
Orthodox side is concerned, we shall concentrate on the same patriarch's return
visit.

A. Paul VI Visits Constantinople

With one of those unexpected decisions of his, of which we have already
seen a number of examples, on 15 July 1967 the pope announced that he planned
to visit "Istanbul, the ancient Constantinople, among the various famous cities,
to pay our respects . . . to the memory of the important ecumenical councils
which were held there." He added: "Then we want to pay a visit to His Holiness

101. Cf. *IS*, 3 (1967), 14-15.
102. As concerns relations between *Rome and Constantinople*: (a) the fact that the abolition of the
      excommunications at the end of the Council was deeply appreciated by the other churches of
      Byzantine tradition (cf. *Ecumenism*, p. 210); (b) the fact that the Ecumenical Patriarchate sent
      a large delegation to Rome for the opening of the Year of Faith on the nineteenth centenary of
      the martyrdom of St. Peter and St. Paul. There was also the beginning in 1967 of pastoral
      conversations with *the Russian Orthodox Church* on Catholic social thinking, and, on the other
      hand, Catholic participation in the fiftieth anniversary celebrations of the reestablishment of
      the Patriarchate of Moscow; cf. *IS*, 4 (March 1968), 17-18; 5 (June 1968), 9.
103. We are thinking especially of the pope's efforts to encourage progress toward the establishment
      of a date for Easter that would be shared by all Christians (cf. pp. 766-767 of the Italian edition
      of this work; *Ecumenism*, pp. 243-244), and also of his active concern over the Ecumenical
      Institute on the History of Salvation (cf. p. 513, Italian edition) and the excellent way it
      developed (cf. pp. 767-768, Italian edition).

Patriarch Athenagoras, anticipating in this way the visit which he has so often manifested the desire to pay to us."[104]

We do not intend providing a detailed description of the journey itself, for the reader can find this both in *Ecumenism in Focus* and in the official publication about the whole journey.[105] We would simply say that the two leaders met—apart from an unscheduled meeting at the airport—in the Patriarchal Church of St. George, and later in the Latin Cathedral of the Holy Spirit. Our main concern is that of highlighting the elements that indicate the state of relations between the two churches and the prospects for their progress toward full unity, especially since we can truly say that the speeches of the two leaders contain valuable pointers for a whole authentic ecumenical program.[106]

In Paul VI's speech of greeting to the patriarch at their meeting in the Patriarchal Church of St. George, he issued an invitation to recognize the identity of faith uniting the two churches: "In the light of our love for Christ and of our brotherly love for one another, we are making further discovery of the profound *identity of our faith*." And he added: ". . . the points on which we still differ ought not to hinder us from seeing this deep unity."[107] The pope then referred to the example of St. Hilary and St. Athanasius who, helped by a spirit of charity, were able "to recognize the identity of the faith beyond *variations of vocabulary*, at a time when serious differences were dividing the Christian episcopate. Was it not the practice of St. Basil himself, in his pastoral charity, to defend authentic faith in the Holy Spirit while avoiding the use of certain words which, for all their accuracy, could have acted as a stumbling block for one part of the Christian people?"[108] Here the pope also referred to the attitude of the fathers of the church such as St. Basil and St. Cyril, concluding: "Surely there is here a domain in which *the dialogue* of charity can be profitably carried further by putting to one side quite a number of obstacles, and by opening up ways leading to full communion of faith, and doing this in the truth. To find ourselves again one in a combination of fidelity and diversity can only be the work of the spirit of love. If unity of faith is required for full communion, a diversity of customs is no obstacle—rather the reverse."[109]

How far does this unity in faith allow us to go? Here the pope mentioned *the concelebration* of the eucharist—an ideal very dear to the patriarch: "Charity allows us to become more aware of the very depth of our unity, while at the same time making us feel greater pain at the fact that this unity cannot yet reach fulfillment in concelebration, and it urges us to try all possible means to hasten the day of the Lord's coming."[110] The pope's words indicate a burning desire to hasten the moment of concelebration, but also an awareness that this is as yet

---

104. *Ecumenism*, p. 278 (ct); *AAS*, LIX (1967), 804.
105. Cf. *Il viaggio di Paolo VI a Istanbul e a Efeso* (Vatican City, 1967).
106. We feel that this wealth of pointers both explains and justifies the length of the quotations we shall be giving.
107. *THS*, p. 157. The whole address is found in *AAS*, LIX (1967), 840-842.
108. *THS*, p. 157.
109. *Ibid.*
110. *Ibid.*, p. 158.

impossible. He pointed out the responsibility of church leaders and members of the hierarchy who, "out of recognition and respect for the fact that they are pastors of the part of the flock of Christ entrusted to them," must avoid "everything that could scatter it or cause confusion in its ranks." The pope concluded by mentioning the part that faith and charity play in the movement toward full unity: "Charity is that living context necessary for the ripening of the faith, and communion in the faith is the condition for the full manifestation of charity expressing itself in concelebration."[111]

If we compare these thoughts of Paul VI with *Patriarch Athenagoras' speech*, we can see the underlying points of agreement, along with a certain difference in emphasis.[112] Recalling their common responsibility toward both the church and the world, the patriarch described the aim toward which they should be moving: "submissive to his words and will, we look toward the union of all, to the full communion of charity and faith expressed in concelebration with the common chalice of Christ, in a common expectation of and hope for the One who will come again to bring time and history to fulfillment and to judge the living and the dead."[113]

In order to reach this objective, in the first place "let us make every possible sacrifice, and with full self-abnegation do away with everything on either side which in the past had the appearance of contributing to the integrity of the church, but in fact only helped to produce an almost unbridgeable division."[114] Therefore, "Let us join together what was divided, wherever this is possible, by deeds in which both churches are involved, giving added strength to the matters of faith and canonical discipline which we have in common."[115] *Theological dialogue* should then be started according to the principle of "full community in the fundamentals of the faith, liberty both in theological thought, where this is pious and edifying and inspired by the main body of the fathers, and in the variety of local customs, as was favored by the church from the beginning."[116] In this whole undertaking we must bear in mind "our role of service on a wider scale, offering ourselves singly and together to all other beloved brothers of the Christian world as examples and agents in the full carrying out of the Lord's will for the unity of all, so that the world may believe that Christ was sent by God."[117]

During the meeting in the Latin Cathedral of the Holy Spirit, the pope presented the patriarch with two finely illuminated parchment scrolls with the Latin and French texts of the papal brief *Anno ineunte*,[118] which represented a

---

111. *Ibid.*
112. Cf. *TAG*, pp. 379-383, for the Greek and French versions, and *THS*, pp. 158-161, for the English translation.
113. *THS*, p. 160.
114. *Ibid.*
115. *Ibid.*
116. *Ibid.*
117. *Ibid.*
118. Cf. *AAS*, LIX (1967), 852-853; *TAG*, pp. 386-393, with the French and Greek versions; *THS*, pp. 161-163, for the English translation. A brief summary of these documents is found in R 1968/4, p. 14.

kind of *practical suggestion* as to the path to be followed. The starting point is the profound concept of *sister churches*. "By baptism 'we are one in Christ Jesus' (Gal. 3:28). In virtue of the apostolic succession, we are united more closely by the priesthood and the eucharist. . . . In each local church this mystery of divine love is enacted, and surely this is the ground of the traditional and very beautiful expression 'sister churches,' which local churches were fond of applying to one another."[119] This concept is applied as follows in the present case: "For centuries we lived this life of 'sister churches,' and together held the ecumenical councils which guarded the deposit of faith against all corruption. And now, after a long period of division and mutual misunderstanding, the Lord is enabling us to discover ourselves as 'sister churches' once more, in spite of the obstacles which were once raised between us."[120]

On the basis of these concepts, the brief puts forward a suggested plan as to how we can live the deep identity of our faith in a fraternal spirit: "On both sides we profess 'the fundamental dogmas of the Christian faith in the Trinity, in the Word of God who took flesh of the Virgin Mary,' as these 'were defined in the ecumenical councils held in the East' (cf. *UR*, 14), and we have the true sacraments and a hierarchical priesthood in common. In view of these facts it behooves us in the first place to work together in a fraternal spirit in the service of our faith, to find the appropriate ways which will lead us further on as we try to develop and make real in the life of our churches the communion which, although imperfect, exists already." This process requires the progressive renewal of both churches: "Next we must on either side, by making the most of our dealings with one another, deepen and adapt the formation of the clergy, and the education and the life of the Christian laity." Then there is the question of theological dialogue: "What we are concerned with is, by means of a sincere theological dialogue, itself made possible by the reestablishment of fraternal charity, to come to know and respect one another amidst the legitimate variety of liturgical, spiritual, disciplinary, and theological traditions (cf. *UR*, 14-17), in order to reach agreement in a sincere profession of every revealed truth. To restore and maintain communion and unity we must indeed be careful 'not to impose anything which is not necessary' (cf. Acts 15:18; *UR*, 18)."[121]

It is significant that the pope wanted to avoid any accusation of "exclusivism" in connection with this journey. Therefore when he went to Ephesus in order "to pay our respects . . . to the memory of the important ecumenical councils which were held there," he sent a message of greeting to "*all the patriarchs and primates* of the Orthodox churches": "This pilgrimage to the places blessed by the undertakings of the fathers of the great ecumenical councils has offered us the opportunity to understand better that, despite the real differences that divide us, we do enjoy a deep unity in faith, as preached and proclaimed by those fathers and doctors whom we have in common. . . . With full respect for your customs and legitimate traditions, we wish for our part to let you know of our will to

---

119. *THS*, p. 162; cf. *UR*, 14.
120. *Ibid.*
121. *Ibid.*, p. 163.

carry forward the dialogue of the truth in charity (cf. Eph. 4:15)." The pope concluded by expressing the hope that, through the intercession of the holy fathers of the church, "the successors of the apostles" can make the greatly desired day draw closer when "we shall all be united in the celebration of the eucharist of our one Savior."[122]

We shall close with two observations taken from Cardinal Bea's evaluation of this visit. The cardinal said that with these journeys the pope had performed *an act of truly historic importance*, inasmuch as no pope had visited the Ecumenical Patriarchate of Constantinople since the eighth century, in other words since the time of Pope Constantine I (708-715).[123]

Moreover, "non-Catholics have remarked with regard to the visit of Pope Paul to Istanbul that its most important spiritual contribution to the cause of unity lay in the fact that it was an outstanding act of charity and humility." The visit was made in "the same spirit which had marked the pope's pilgrimage to the Holy Land and the meetings in Jerusalem. Perhaps this was more obvious in the 1967 journey." The pope did indeed state that in going to Istanbul he wanted to "anticipate" the visit that the patriarch had several times expressed the intention of paying him, thus putting into practice St. Paul's instruction to "outdo one another in showing honor" (Rom. 12:10).[124]

B. Patriarch Athenagoras I Returns the Visit

In his speech inaugurating the work of the Synod of Bishops, Pope Paul VI recalled his visit to Constantinople "with great emotion," adding: "We are now in a position to be able to tell you that the venerable patriarch has announced *his return visit*, which is intended to take place at the end of the forthcoming month of October. You, venerable brothers, can form the crown to this new meeting, which will fill the churches of East and West with exultation and an ineffable hope."[125]

The visit took place from 26 through 28 October 1967, and its high points were the joint prayer service in St. Peter's, the private and public audiences, and the final leave-taking audience. These events were then framed by various others in this "pilgrimage of love," for the patriarch had explicitly stated his intention of "excluding from his visit every thought and element of mere sightseeing, so that it should remain simply and exclusively a pilgrimage to the holy places in the eternal city."[126] In his first address, which was given during the prayer service in St. Peter's, he had thus expressed his great joy at being "in this eternal city of Rome, the home of the two chief apostles Peter and Paul and the glory of the

---

122. *AAS*, LIX (1967), 851-852; *IS*, 3 (1967), 15 (which does not correspond to the original French at certain points); cf. also *Il viaggio di Paolo VI*, pp. 105-106.

123. Cf. R 1968/3, p. 2; also R 1968/4, p. 3.

124. Cf. *Ecumenism*, p. 308.

125. *Ibid.*, p. 290 (ct). Original in *AAS*, LIX (1967), 974. Cf. also the patriarch's letter of 6 October and the pope's reply of 17 October, *THS*, pp. 169-170 and 171-174. Various papers concerning the visit are in Arch. Md/3. Cf. also "Athénagoras I rend visite à Paul VI (Questions d'actualité)," *Proche Orient Chrétien*, XVIII (1968), 1-24.

126. *Ecumenism*, p. 301.

Christian world," where, he went on to say, "we hear at this extraordinarily holy moment the blood of the apostles Peter and Paul crying out, we hear the voice of the church of the catacombs and of the martyrs of the Colosseum," calling on us to work for the cause of unity.[127]

A visit to the tomb of Pope John XXIII in the crypt of St. Peter's was another of these acts of pilgrimage. Here the patriarch performed a gesture pregnant with meaning, placing three small gold ears of wheat on the tomb, together with a parchment scroll bearing the words: "Unless a grain of wheat falls into the earth and dies, it remains alone; but if it dies, it bears much fruit" (John 12:24).[128]

The joint prayer service "was certainly the climax of his stay in Rome. Despite the fact that it was a working day, a huge crowd packed the basilica, and apart from the seventy-five members of the Sacred College of Cardinals and the fathers of the Synod of Bishops, there were the parish priests of Rome, male and female religious, and many representatives of various Catholic associations."[129] And this impressive quality was not confined to appearances, for *the content itself was unique*. The prayer service was different from those on similar occasions in the past—both the one that took place with the observer-delegates at the end of the Council, and also the one celebrated with the Archbishop of Canterbury, Dr. Michael Ramsey. Some extremely significant elements were added to those used on these previous occasions: ". . . there was also a Preface. This was followed by the singing of the *Sanctus*; to some extent this part of the service resembled the Canon—but without the consecration—then the Lord's Prayer was said; and finally, the fraternal kiss of peace." After listing these elements, the cardinal goes on to explain their underlying importance: "Such a structure showed both the ardent desire of the two participants to celebrate the eucharist and to take communion together, and the present unfortunate impossibility of satisfying this desire."[130]

Now that we have a general picture of events, we can move on, as we did in the case of the pope's visit to Constantinople, to those elements from the various speeches that help give a picture of the situation and ecumenical commitment of the two sides, avoiding repetition so far as possible.

1. In the first place, we have *the greetings the patriarch* addressed to the pope at the end of the prayer service.[131] Having stated that for a long time his heart had nurtured the desire for this visit, the patriarch paid homage to the Church of Rome, which is "the first in honor and rank in the ordered whole of Christian churches throughout the world," and then went on to indicate first and foremost *the objective* toward which we must strive. "We stand in this holy place, . . . preparing ourselves

---

127. *THS*, pp. 171-172. The patriarch spoke similarly at the start of his address in St. Peter's, referring to Rome as "the dwelling place of the apostles Peter and Paul" and to the pope as "the successor to a pleiad of wise and holy men" (*THS*, p. 172).

128. Cf. *Ecumenism*, p. 303.

129. *Ibid.*, p. 290 (ct).

130. *Ibid.*, 291.

131. Cf. *TAG*, pp. 410-417, for the Greek and French texts; *THS*, pp. 171-174, for the English translation; cf. also *Ecumenism*, pp. 292-295 (although we shall be using the translation found in *THS*).

in heart and spirit for the future advance to a common eucharist, as we carry out in our souls the service of the washing of the feet, . . . to leave no ways and means untried to complete the holy work that has been begun—that of the perfect recomposition of the divided church of Christ—so that the will of the Lord may be fulfilled, and the world may see the first mark of the church according to our creed, namely that she is 'one,' shining forth brilliantly."[132]

And *the path toward unity* was described as follows: "In the course of this common advance—which will be an advance toward the truth, an advance toward 'what was believed always, everywhere, and by all'—we are called upon to continue and intensify the dialogue of charity, so as to make this a reality antecedent to theological discussion. As for the theological dialogue properly so called, let us by common consent conduct this with a view, on the one hand, to the interpretation of what we both already live out in common in our church life, and on the other, to the exploration of the truth in a spirit of charity and edification, and its formulation in a spirit of service."[133]

And *the result* was seen in the following terms: "Thus we hope to be brought to an exact appreciation of those principal matters of faith which it is absolutely necessary that we profess in common, and to distinguish these from the other elements of the life of the church, which, since they do not affect the faith, can find free expression in the usages and characteristics proper to each church according to its tradition—and these things should be respected on both sides."[134] He then considered how long this is likely to take: "Obviously we cannot determine in advance the length of the journey. This is a matter of faith in the ultimate issue, of many prayers, of holy patience, of diligent work, but above all it is a matter of charity."[135]

2. In *his reply*, which was spoken in Latin,[136] *the pope* stressed the fact that the prayer service was taking place in the immediate context of the Synod of Bishops, which was a sign of *the renewal of the Catholic Church*. Having mentioned the parallel commitment to such a renewal among the Orthodox, especially through panorthodox conferences, the pope expressed the following hope: "We must courageously follow up and develop this effort on both sides, being as far as possible in contact with each other as we do so, and cooperating in ways that should be discovered by joint effort."[137]

He then pointed out the vital, pressing need to work for the restoration of unity, saying that we are urged to this not only by the spirit, but also by *the situation of humanity*: ". . . does not the modern world, too, invaded by unbelief in many different forms as it is, remind us in a pressing manner of the need for unity between us?" This task, "this common testimony, one and varied, definite

132. *THS*, p. 172.
133. *Ibid.*, p. 173.
134. *Ibid.*
135. *Ibid.*
136. Cf. *AAS*, LIX (1967), 1048-1053, for the original Latin text; *TAG*, pp. 418-435, for the Greek and French translations; and *THS*, pp. 174-178, for the English translation; cf. also *Ecumenism*, pp. 195-300 (although we shall be using the translation found in *THS*).
137. *THS*, p. 176.

and persuasive, to a faith humbly sure of itself, breaking forth in love, and casting rays of hope round about—is it not this that the Spirit is asking first and foremost of the churches today?"[138]

This renewal gives fresh life to faith, hope and charity, and brings us *to live the deep communion* already existing between the two churches, making use of all the means the Spirit uses "to make us tend with our whole being toward the fullness of that communion, already very rich but still incomplete, which unites us in the mystery of the church." Another condition "fundamental to the progressive closing of our ranks" is implicit in what has been said: "This is *conversion of the heart*, which makes us listen to the Holy Spirit in our personal lives and carry out with ever increasing sensitivity and openness whatever he demands of us. . . . This striving toward sanctity, on the other hand, brings into play the whole of that spiritual patrimony which we mentioned a little while ago, and which the Second Vatican Council took pleasure in recalling at some length."[139]

3. *The joint declaration*[140] summarizes the main results of the public declarations and private discussions of the two church leaders. The salient points are as follows:

"*A renewal* of the church and of Christians, in fidelity to the traditions of the fathers and to the inspirations of the Holy Spirit, who remains always with his church."[141]

The dialogue of charity: "They recognize that the true dialogue of charity which must underlie all the relations between themselves and between their churches must be rooted in a complete fidelity to the one Lord Jesus Christ, and in a mutual respect for their own traditions."[142]

Cooperation on many fronts: "They are convinced that the dialogue of charity between their churches should bring forth fruit in an unselfish collaboration and common action upon the pastoral, social, and intellectual levels, with a mutual respect for the fidelity of members on either side to their own church. It is their wish that regular contacts may be made in depth between Catholic and Orthodox pastors for the good of their faithful. The Roman Catholic Church and the Ecumenical Patriarchate are ready to study practical measures for solving pastoral problems, particularly as regards marriages between Catholics and Orthodox. They would hope for a better collaboration in works of charity, to

---

138. *Ibid.*

139. *Ibid.*, p. 177.

140. Cf. *AAS*, LIX (1967), 1054-1055; *TAG*, pp. 444-447, for the French and Greek texts; *THS*, pp. 181-182, for the English translation; cf. also *Ecumenism*, pp. 304-306 (although we shall be using the translation found in *THS*). Cardinal Bea speaks of the "joint *communiqué*," while *IS*, 3 (1967), 18, speaks of the "joint *declaration*." In my opinion it is not to be understood as a "joint declaration" in the solemn sense of that made with Archbishop Ramsey, which was a document drawn up in Latin and English, with both versions being solemnly signed by both parties; cf. *Ecumenism*, pp. 265-266; *AAS*, LVIII (1966), 287-288. However, since the official publication of the present text in *AAS*, LIX (1967), 1054-1055, describes it as a "joint declaration" (as does *THS*, p. 181), we shall follow this terminology. A summary of the document is found in R 1968/4, p. 4.

141. *THS*, p. 181.

142. *Ibid.*

help refugees and those who suffer, and to promote justice and peace in the world."[143]

Special cooperation between Catholic and Orthodox professors: "By way of preparation for fruitful contacts between the Roman Catholic Church and the Orthodox Church, the pope and the patriarch give their blessing and pastoral support to every effort of collaboration between Catholic and Orthodox professors in the study of history, of the traditions of the churches, of patristic and liturgical matters, and in a presentation of the gospel which would correspond at one and the same time to the authentic message of the Lord and the needs and hopes of today's world. The spirit which should inspire these efforts is a spirit of loyalty to the truth and of mutual comprehension, with a real desire to avoid the rancors of the past and every kind of spiritual or intellectual domination."[144]

4. We shall make two brief observations on *the importance of the visit.* Cardinal Bea described it as "*a gesture unique* in history. Indeed, since the foundation of the Patriarchate of Constantinople, no Patriarch of Constantinople in office had ever paid an official, solemn visit to the Bishop of Rome."[145]

This importance is all the greater inasmuch as "the meetings in Rome were preceded by an important visit which the patriarch made to the autocephalous Churches of Serbia, Rumania and Bulgaria. These visits were geared to a coordination of Orthodox activity in general and with regard to unity in particular. If it is true that a projected visit to the Russian Orthodox Church had to be cancelled at the last moment, it remains true that such a visit—which should be made in the near future—is certain to be made, in the light of the events which took place during his days in Rome."[146]

Commitment to the Cause of Unity Involves the Whole Church

When speaking of the features of the ecumenical movement, the cardinal warned that we must not commit "a mistake made repeatedly in past centuries, when earlier 'unions' were concluded between the authorities without the necessary preparation of the people as a whole—witness the reconciliation at Lyons in the thirteenth century, or that at Ferrara-Florence in the fifteenth. These unions were unable to withstand the onslaught of events. An outstanding break-through of the modern ecumenical movement is precisely this awareness of the necessity of preparing the faithful, the necessity of the participation of the whole church; and this participation is clearly present already."[147]

This thought was very much to the fore in the Council, which "ordered a full-scale mobilization of all the members of the church in the cause of unity when it proclaimed in the Decree on Ecumenism that 'concern for restoring

---

143. *Ibid.*, pp. 181-182.
144. *Ibid.*, p. 182.
145. R 1968/3, p. 2.
146. *Ecumenism*, pp. 309-310 (ct).
147. *Ibid.*, pp. 252-253 (ct).

unity pertains to the whole church, faithful and clergy alike. It extends to everyone, according to the potential of each, whether it be exercised in daily Christian living or in theological studies' (no. 5)."[148]

The Council did not, however, confine itself to general statements, but went into greater detail in its Decree on Ecumenism: "In ecumenical work, Catholics must assuredly be concerned for their separated brethren, praying for them, keeping them informed about the church, making the first approaches toward them."[149] Further, our ecumenical duty calls on us "to make 'an honest and careful appraisal of whatever needs to be renewed and achieved in the Catholic household itself, in order that its life may bear witness more loyally and luminously to the teachings and ordinances which have been handed down from Christ through the apostles' (no. 4). From this follows the necessity of personal renewal, and the same decree thus continues: 'Every Catholic must therefore aim at Christian perfection (cf. James 1:4; Rom. 12:1-2) and, each according to his station, play his part so that the church, which bears in her own body the humility and dying of Jesus (cf. 2 Cor. 4:10; Phil. 2:5-8), may daily be more purified and renewed, against the day when Christ will present her to himself in all her glory, without spot or wrinkle (cf. Eph. 5:27).' "[150]

Nor is this all. The cardinal is also happy to see that today, by the grace of God, "the energetic appeal" referred to above "has reached the hearts of large numbers of the faithful"; in other words, the "*full-scale mobilization*" of the whole church to work for unity *is already taking place*. This general mobilization "has shown itself most clearly in the fervor with which the week of prayer for unity is celebrated. Also of great significance is the increasing number of ecumenical centers, commissions and secretariats, both on the diocesan level and on the national episcopal level. Another sign of the growing interest of the faithful in ecumenism is the increase in publications of every kind—reviews, commentaries on the Decree on Ecumenism, etc.—not to mention the articles on ecumenism that appear in publications at every level. More and more ecumenical institutes are also being founded in universities and theological colleges."[151]

Nonetheless it is clear that there was a great deal still to be done: there were entire regions not yet reached by this mobilization; the large numbers of initiatives needed a steering hand; since the Catholic Church had only recently entered the ecumenical movement through the decisions of the Council, there was still a great deal to be learned; and it had to be ensured that ecumenical activity was in line with the relative Catholic principles laid down by the Council. In other words, apart from contacts and dialogue with other Christians, the Secretariat for Christian Unity was faced with the enormous task of implementing the great ecumenical design of the Council *within the Catholic Church itself*. Let us examine at least some aspects of the work that was done in this connection during the cardinal's life.

---

148. *Ibid.*, p. 253.
149. *Ibid.*, quoting *UR*, 4.
150. *Ibid.*
151. *Ibid.*, pp. 253-254 (ct).

1. The first and fundamental service that the secretariat wanted to offer to the ecumenism of the Catholic Church was an *Ecumenical Directory*, giving detailed instructions and orientations. It is worth noting that even before the end of the Council the secretariat realized the need to distinguish between the major principles, which were the proper field and subject of the Council, and the more detailed instructions on specific, practical aspects which should be the task of a "directory." During the first discussion of the conciliar schema on ecumenism, the cardinal pointed out this distinction, announcing that the secretariat intended drawing up a more detailed directory in due course.[152] And the secretariat set to work on this task immediately after the promulgation of the conciliar Decree on Ecumenism.[153]

As the cardinal explained, "It was a delicate, complex task demanding long, patient work, first on the part of experts, and then on the part of the secretariat, so that it was decided to take the work in stages. In the first part a series of directives was given on the most urgent questions, for example: the organization of diocesan and regional ecumenical work (ecumenical commissions); various problems concerning baptism, particularly 'conditional' baptism, when an adult non-Catholic is received into the church and makes a profession of faith; prayers for unity both for Catholics alone and also jointly with our separated brethren; and finally the problem of taking part in the liturgical celebrations of our non-Catholic brethren (*communicatio in sacris*). The writing of this first part required a whole series of meetings, first of the experts and then of the members of the secretariat, which had itself already begun work on the publication between the third and fourth sessions and continued during the fourth session."[154]

Although the secretariat worked hard and very conscientiously, it never sought to act solely according to its own lights. Thus it had its work checked by various bodies—and not only by different departments of the central church authorities, but also, and very significantly, by the episcopal conferences of the whole world: "The finished text was submitted to the conciliar Commission for the Doctrine of the Faith, and then sent to episcopal conferences throughout the world for their comments. By June 1966 these were in the hands of the secretariat and were being carefully studied by the experts, and then by a plenary session of the secretariat."[155]

Finally, after much work and the various examinations, in the audience granted to the plenary meeting of the secretariat on 28 April 1967, the pope announced: "We are happy ... to grant the desire expressed to us and to announce to you publicly that the first part of the Ecumenical Directory will be published in a few days' time."[156] The pope's interest in the directory can also be seen from the fact that a few months later he spoke of it again in his response

152. The cardinal spoke about this on two occasions; cf. *AS*, II/VI, 15 and 365.
153. For the history of the directory we shall confine ourselves to the essential elements given in *Ecumenism*, pp. 254-255. More details can be found in the text of the press conference Bishop J. Willebrands gave to present the first part of the Directory to the press; *IS*, 2 (1967), 13-15.
154. *Ecumenism*, p. 254 (ct).
155. *Ibid.* (ct).
156. *Ecumenismo*, p. 326, note; cf. *AAS*, LIX (1967), 494. The Latin text of the directory is found in *AAS*, LIX (1967), 574-592; the English translation is found in *IS*, 2 (1967).

to the good wishes of the Sacred College on his feast day: "We are sure that the principles and norms laid out in this document will help to spread among the faithful a healthy ecumenical spirit that calls firstly for the renewal of Christian life, that excludes any false irenicism, indifferentism or compromise on the truth, and that entails a spirit of charity and fidelity to the lines laid down by the Council."[157] When the president of the secretariat spoke about the publication of the directory on Vatican Radio in January 1968, he stressed the pope's respect for the document: "In his speech opening the work of the Synod of Bishops, the pope even referred to it as 'our directory.' "[158]

As concerns the cardinal's specific view of ecumenism, which stressed the direct responsibility of local churches, it is worth quoting the following passage from the press conference in which Bishop Johannes Willebrands presented the document to the public: "The directory, the first part of which is published today, is not intended to cover every possible situation and case. It does not preclude further developments under the direction of the appropriate ecclesiastical authorities. It is to be completed by directives for each particular locality, and is simply intended as a service to the holy cause of the reconciliation of all Christians in the unity of the church of Christ."[159]

As we said above, the published document was only the first part of the directory. Thus the cardinal wrote in *Ecumenism in Focus*: "While the first part of the directory was still being examined by the Congregation of the Faith, the Secretariat for Unity had already begun work on the second part, which deals with various aspects of dialogue and the considerable number of complex problems of ecumenical training."[160] Continuing with his account of the undertaking, the cardinal went on to say: "These questions were first discussed at length by the various experts and then in April 1967 by the plenary meeting of the secretariat."[161]

The bulletin of the secretariat also tells us that the subject was subsequently considered at the plenary meeting of the secretariat in November 1968, which the cardinal was unable to attend. At this point the material had grown to such an extent that it was decided to divide it into two documents, the first dealing with dialogue in general, while the other dealt with ecumenical training on the academic level.[162] This division was subsequently retained, so that two documents were published in September 1970 still with the same titles.[163]

2. An initiative on the level of the universal church was the organization in Rome of a *Congress of Delegates for Ecumenism* of episcopal conferences

157. Quoted in *Ecumenism*, p. 255 (ct); cf. *AAS*, LIX (1967), 788-789.
158. R 1968/3, p. 6. Similarly, cf. R 1968/1, p. 6; R 1968/4, pp. 8-9; *Ecumenismo*, p. 340. For the pope's speech, cf. *AAS*, LIX (1967), 971.
159. Quoted in *Ecumenism*, p. 255 (ct); *IS*, 2 (1967), 15.
160. *Ecumenism*, p. 255 (ct).
161. *Ibid.* (ct). For the work of the plenary meeting, cf. also the cardinal's introductory report (R 1967/9, p. 2), and the interview given to the *Osservatore della Domenica* (Biblio. 354).
162. Cf. *IS*, 7 (May 1969), 5.
163. For the document on dialogue in general, cf. *IS*, 12 (December 1970); and for that on ecumenical training on the academic level, cf. *IS*, 10 (June 1970).

throughout the world.[164] This took place from 29 May through 3 June 1967, and was attended by fifty-two people representing forty-two episcopal conferences—for the most part the presidents or secretaries of ecumenical commissions. The main subject discussed was the newly-published first part of the Ecumenical Directory, especially in the perspective of the responsibilities and tasks of diocesan ecumenical commissions. The meeting also discussed the question of mixed marriages, partly in view of the fact that the relative Instruction of the Sacred Congregation for the Doctrine of the Faith (1966) was provisional, and the subject had been placed on the agenda of the first General Synod of Bishops which was to be held a few months later.[165]

In his opening speech to the meeting, the cardinal strongly stressed that *the immediate responsibility* for unity lay with the particular or local churches: "From the ecumenical viewpoint, it is you who have direct, on-the-spot responsibility; it is you who must deal with the wide variety of situations, which are often new and complicated. The experience that you have acquired in daily life is thus extremely precious to us. . . . Our aim is to give you a chance to speak so that you can tell us about this experience, and also exchange information with one another. If the church is a communion, then this mutual exchange is indispensable and is a sign of an authentic life of the spirit of the Council."[166]

Looking *to the future*, he then stated: "We want to remain in permanent contact with ecumenical commissions throughout the world. I hope that our meeting will fulfill your expectations, and ours too. I have already received some excellent reactions. However, we would ask you to let us know any wishes you may have, and indeed also any criticisms. Full frankness in an open, honest context in which the responsibilities of all parties are recognized is part of the atmosphere of communion which is indispensable to us."[167]

Satisfaction on both sides was so great that the cardinal could say, a little optimistically: "With the grace of God we plan to organize a similar meeting each year. For my part I should like to see such meetings taking place in other countries and other regions too."[168] The bulletin of the secretariat, however, tells us that the participants decided that it would be difficult to organize such a meeting each year, and that it would be better to hold meetings on the regional level, not organized by the secretariat but under its auspices.[169]

3. In spring 1967 the secretariat also started producing its own bulletin in French and English, with the intention of providing regular information on ecumenical matters, and particularly that of publishing any relevant documents.

4. Another part of the secretariat's activity was that of making sure that initiatives on the universal church-level should take account of the ecumenical

---

164. Cf. *IS*, 3 (1967), 9-10.
165. We shall discuss the question of mixed marriages later.
166. Ms. of the speech, R 1967/31. *IS*, 3 (1967), 9, carries a report on the meeting, but does not give the speech. We shall discuss the meeting itself later.
167. R 1967/31, p. 1.
168. *Ibid.*
169. A further three world-level meetings were then organized in 1972, 1979 and 1985.

dimension. A very good example of this is *the Third International Congress for the Apostolate of the Laity*, which was held in Rome in October 1967, and at which the ecumenical consciousness of the Catholic laity was shown remarkably clearly. The cardinal repeatedly mentioned this in the annual "ecumenical survey" that he made on the occasion of the Week of Prayer for Christian Unity, both on Bavarian Radio and Vatican Radio, describing the congress as "important" inasmuch as "a hundred non-Catholic observer-consultants took part, representing many churches and federations of churches." He added: "It was an event that could hardly have been imagined a few short years ago. And the involvement of the non-Catholics was so close that a number of the observer-consultants expressed surprise that it had been possible. There was no problem over their participation in group discussions, and one of them, Klaus von Bismarck, superintendent of the German Radio in Cologne, chaired one of the plenary sessions. In the ecumenical prayer service, a number of them read either prayers or Bible readings."[170]

5. The secretariat was also involved in supporting the cause of unity *within the Roman curia*. The introductory report for the 1968 plenary meeting tells us how the cardinal saw the position and task of the secretariat after the reform of the Roman curia had come into force in March 1968.

In the first place he noted that with the reform the secretariat had become a department of the Roman curia, "and it has been given its precise position among the Holy Father's collaborators, and has received legal confirmation of the activity that it has in fact been performing for a number of years now."[171] This new status also made it possible to set up joint commissions with other departments of the Roman curia to ensure useful and fruitful cooperation between the various departments.[172]

A second aspect that he stressed is that a number of appointments had been made in response to the need for cooperation within the Roman curia, inasmuch as certain cardinals of the Roman curia had been assigned to the secretariat "who were not official members until now." And the speaker explained this further: "How can we not mention the Prefect of the Sacred Congregation for the Doctrine of the Faith in this connection? The same spirit guided the appointment of new consultors, just as, on the other hand, members of the Secretariat for Unity have been appointed members or consultors of other Roman departments."[173]

170. R 1968/3, pp. 1-2. Similarly, cf. R 1968/1, pp. 1-2; R 1968/4, p. 2. On the congress itself, cf. *CC*, 1967/IV, 295-296. Readers will recall that at the first such meeting, in 1957, it was only with infinite precautions and after the mediation of Father Bea, as he then was, that a total of one representative of other Christians (Mr. Hans-Ruedi Weber of the World Council of Churches) was able to attend, and even then only as a "journalist." Cf. S. Schmidt, "Il Cardinale Bea: sua preparazione alla missione ecumenica," *Archivum Hist. Pontificiae*, XVI (1978), 322-323; cf. also pp. 243 above.
171. R 1968/17a, p. 2 (the text has not been published).
172. It is in this context that the report mentions the multi-faceted cooperation that had been received for the second part of the Ecumenical Directory. It could maybe be said that in a sense the reform of the curia had an importance for the secretariat similar to that of the act with which Pope John XXIII placed it on an equal footing with the conciliar commissions on 22 October 1962. Cf. pp. 415-416 above.
173. R 1968/17a, p. 2.

In order to explain this need for cooperation, the cardinal made the following fairly significant statement, which also throws light on the spirit in which he himself worked with the many departments of the curia of which he was a member: "While each department of the Roman curia has specific fields of responsibility, the complexity of the various problems and questions involved means that these fields inevitably overlap, so that cooperation is necessary. And this is all the truer where our secretariat is concerned."[174]

Here the cardinal indicated how he saw the ecumenical task within the framework of the Roman curia: "Ecumenism must not be some separate activity in the life of the church: it is *a new dimension* which must be borne in mind in all matters, perspectives, plans and solutions."[175] It would be difficult for either the ecumenical dimension of the whole life of the church, or the need for the practical application of the truth of ecclesial communion to the activity of the Roman curia, to be stated more clearly or more strongly.

We have two fairly striking examples of cooperation within the Roman curia. The first concerns the second part of the Ecumenical Directory. The manuscript of the cardinal's introductory speech to the 1968 plenary meeting—which was read in his absence by the vice-president of the secretariat—tells us that the secretariat had sought the cooperation of other departments of the central government of the church for this part too. Indeed, the manuscript says that when it came to the subject of "ecumenical education," the secretariat received the assistance of *four* sacred congregations: those for Catholic Education, the Oriental Churches, the Evangelization of Peoples, and Religious.[176]

Another example is the complicated subject of legislation on the thorny question of *mixed marriages*. The problem is that of reconciling on the one hand the necessary protection of the faith of the Catholic party and the values of the family, including the education of children, and on the other the necessary respect for the freedom of conscience of the non-Catholic or non-Christian party. After the respective schema had been considered in the preparatory phase of the Council—with the assistance of the secretariat—in the Council itself it was entrusted to the pope. An Instruction from the Congregation for the Doctrine of the Faith then followed in 1966. Since this document was judged unsatisfactory, the subject was submitted for the consideration of the First General Synod of Bishops in 1967, the result of which was in turn entrusted to a commission

---

174. *Ibid.*
175. *Ibid.*
176. Cf. *ibid.* Such cooperation can of course entail problems. In his opening address to the 1967 plenary meeting of the secretariat, the cardinal felt called upon to explain the delay that had taken place in the preparation of the first part of the Ecumenical Directory after the meeting of June 1966: "The long delay was not our fault. After that meeting, in the same month of June we produced the final draft, and then, in accordance with the wishes of the pope, we sent the manuscript for examination by the Sacred Congregation for the Doctrine of the Faith. The latter kept this manuscript from June until the following March without an answer. After various efforts, including some by the pope himself, the directory was eventually returned to us with its approval" (R 1967/9, p. 2).

of cardinals, including Cardinal Bea. This finally led to the motu proprio *Matrimonia mixta* of Paul VI in 1970.[177]

6. After speaking so much about the activity of the secretariat, let us take a closer look at this *instrument of providence* itself, and particularly at how it sees its identity and task. We shall as usual let our cardinal speak about this.

(a) A first pointer is seen in the agenda for the 1967 plenary meeting. Apart from the various subjects that we have already mentioned, this meeting also studied the ecumenical situation in the Catholic Church on the basis of a full nineteen reports, and since some of the member cardinals or bishops were in a position to offer reports on neighboring countries as well, we find descriptions of the ecumenical situation in twenty-one countries in five continents.[178] Close contact was clearly being sought with the practical situation of the local churches, which have immediate responsibility for ecumenism. The same concern is also seen in the methodical principle established at that time that, alongside subjects of a doctrinal nature, as we have seen in a number of examples, discussions should also be held on the "activity reports" of the secretariat, in other words on the reports on various dialogues, relations with other churches, etc. Here too, we can therefore see close contact with the real-life situation of the various churches.[179]

The secretariat had one very special opportunity to act as a "bond of communion" with local churches through its *member cardinals and bishops*, the great majority of whom came from different countries, representing every continent. And when Pope Paul VI confirmed the secretariat as a permanent department of the central government of the church in his motu proprio *Finis Concilio* of 3 January 1966, he also stated that it should retain the composition it had during the Council.[180] Hence, unlike the Roman congregations,[181] it had members from every part of the church,[182] and through them it was in direct contact with the true ecumenical situation in local churches—as was seen in the agenda for the 1967 plenary meeting. This feature of the secretariat was retained after the reform of the Roman curia,[183] so that in his introductory report to the 1968 plenary meeting the cardinal observed: "More members of the secretariat have been appointed. These appointments had the purpose of ensuring that the universal church was represented in the secretariat."[184]

---

177. The details can be found in the two unabridged editions of the present biography: the Italian version, pp. 730-735, and the German version, pp. 816-822.

178. List in *IS*, 3 (1967), 8-9.

179. This method is still followed today.

180. Cf. *AAS*, LVIII (1966), 40: "... iisdem viris constabit, quibus per Concilii celebrationem constabat" = "... it will have the same members as during the Council."

181. Only in August 1967 did the pope introduce the new idea that seven residential bishops should form part of each congregation, alongside the cardinal members; cf. motu proprio *Pro comperto sane*, in *AAS*, LIX (1967), 881-884.

182. It will suffice to look at the aforementioned list of cardinals and bishops, each of whom reported on the ecumenical situation in his own or neighboring countries.

183. Cf. Apostolic Constitution *Regimini ecclesiae universae*, in *AAS*, LIX (1967), 885-928; for the secretariat, see pp. 918-919.

184. R 1968/17a, pp. 1-2. The report was read by the vice-president, Monsignor E.J. De Smedt, due

A similar representation of the universal church, and thus a "bond of communion," gradually began to be seen in the composition of the staff at the *offices of the secretariat*. The cardinal's introductory report to the 1967 plenary meeting also tells us that *the work of these offices* was on the constant increase, so that it had been necessary to take on more personnel. Following the generosity of the General Master of the Dominicans, the secretariat obtained the assistance of Father Jerome Hamer, O.P., who became deputy general secretary, so that he could supervise the running of the office during the frequent absences of the secretary, Bishop J. Willebrands. Various specialists were also taken on for different sectors: the English canon William A. Purdy, for relations with the Anglicans; the Swiss Dr. A. Hasler, for relations with the Lutherans and Reformed churches; the American Jesuit W.A. Abbott, for relations with the Bible societies; and the Dutch professor C. Rijk, for relations with Judaism.[185]

(b) As concerns *the spirit* with which the secretariat works, we should first note the spirit of *service*. When the cardinal spoke to the delegates of the ecumenical commissions in 1967, he said: "So far as we at the secretariat are concerned, we intend placing ourselves modestly at your service. We do not have ready-made solutions. By listening to you and discussing things with you, we want to seek the path that we must tread together. A moment ago I recalled that the church is a communion. Here at the secretariat we intend to be *the bond of communion* with regard to ecumenism—that living bond that must make it possible for the whole communion to coordinate its efforts and thus reach some tangible results."[186]

If it is to be a "bond of communion" it must enjoy the trust of those for whom it works, and the cardinal therefore closed this address to the delegates with the following words: "This morning I united my intention to that of your concelebrated mass. One of the greatest graces that the Lord has granted the secretariat is that of allowing it to bring an atmosphere of trust into being around itself. I have asked the Lord to preserve in all of us this priceless gift for the service of the cause of unity, and to grant it further growth. In this spirit of trust, I thank you wholeheartedly and say goodbye."[187]

Lastly, there is *an authentic trust* based on "the certainty that we shall not lack divine assistance, that the Father is a father for us, that Christ is with us, that the Holy Spirit is still bountiful in working wonders, comforting us, freeing us, and giving us interior encouragement to continue along the path on which we have set our feet."[188] This trust received broad support and confirmation from the observation that "the Holy Spirit is largely and intensely at work within

---

to the cardinal's ill-health.

185. Cf. R 1967/9, pp. 1-2.

186. R 1967/31, p. 1.

187. *Ibid.*, p. 2

188. Paul VI, Address to the Plenary Meeting of the Secretariat (28 April 1967), quoted in *Ecumenismo*, p. 331.

Christians. When we look at the many events, both great and small, described in this chapter, the influence of the grace of Christ is almost tangible, so that we are forced to exclaim, 'Here is the finger of God! It is a change wrought by the hand of the Most High' (cf. Ps. 76:11)."[189]

189. *Ecumenism*, p. 257 (ct).

CHAPTER 2

SPREADING KNOWLEDGE AND ENCOURAGING IMPLEMENTATION OF THE COUNCIL

In our previous chapter we described the Secretariat for Christian Unity, its structure and its activity in promoting ecumenism within the Catholic Church— and this in itself gave us considerable insight into the work of its president. However, this was by no means his only field of activity. If we open the official publication *Annuario Pontificio*, which provides a list of the various positions in the Holy See and their holders, we find that, apart from being President of the Secretariat for Christian Unity and the Commission for the Neo-Vulgate, in 1968 Cardinal Bea was also a member of five sacred congregations,[1] two commissions,[2] and, lastly, of the Council for the Proper Implementation of the Constitution on the Sacred Liturgy. We would add that alongside all this work, he still found time to give lectures and publish articles; and in the period after the Council alone, he also published six books.

The First Synod of Bishops—Activity in the Roman Curia

1. The cardinal's participation in *the First Synod of Bishops* (1967) deserves separate and fuller attention, both because it was the first meeting of this new body created by Paul VI, and because of the quality of Bea's contribution. The cardinal took part in his capacity as president of the secretariat. The fact that the meetings took up three hours a day also represented a *physical challenge*, but the cardinal survived this very well. He did his homework carefully, studying all the relative papers during his summer vacation.

Apart from the important subject of legislation on mixed marriages,[3] the first subject on the agenda was of particular gravity—"Dangerous Contemporary Opinions and Atheism"—and was to be discussed on the basis of a paper drawn up by the Congregation for the Doctrine of the Faith.[4] If my memory serves me well, the cardinal drafted his speech during the summer vacation, although he then had to alter it afterward. Since the synod was first and foremost a meeting of residential bishops, their contributions took precedence over those of members of the Roman curia; thus, what the cardinal felt to be the fundamental defect

---

1. Those for the Doctrine of the Faith, the Oriental Churches, the Evangelization of Peoples, Rites, and Catholic Education; cf. *Annuario Pontificio* (1968), p. 89.
2. Those for Biblical Studies and the Revision of the Latin Code of Canon Law; cf. *ibid.*
3. Cf. pp. 622 above.
4. Cf. the basic work in this connection, G. Caprile, *Il Sinodo dei Vescovi* (Rome, 1968), pp. 146-155. Except in the case of Cardinal Bea's intervention, for which we shall base ourselves on the manuscript found in our files, we shall always refer to this very complete work, citing it simply with the name of the author.

of the basic document, in other words its overly abstract and negative character, was pointed out by the many speakers who preceded him. He therefore changed his text, concentrating on positive suggestions as to ways of remedying errors and deviations. We can now move on to consider the main elements of this contribution.[5]

In the first place, the cardinal stressed that "it is more important for our present discussion to bear practical fruit, . . . since it is of little good to the church simply to concentrate on the dangers, albeit with fear and trepidation. Such dangers have existed in the church since the days of the apostles, as St. Paul bears witness. . . . They spring from human weakness, and from human sins, and are permitted by Divine Providence so that the true teaching may be seen more clearly—as has been the case in almost every Council—and so that the faithful may be tested and purified."

In evaluating dangers and errors, "it is very important to distinguish those concerning the universal church from those that are found only in certain regions, or in one region alone. There is no need to generalize, and it serves no useful purpose. Remedies must correspond to the situation of both the universal church and the individual region.

"In seeking and indicating remedies, we must therefore distinguish those that must be indicated by the central government of the church for the good of the universal church, from those that must be undertaken by individual bishops, or by the episcopal conferences of one or more countries or even an entire continent." Moreover, if we are to understand the true situation of the church and decide on remedies, we must make use of the copious light received from the Holy Spirit in the documents of Vatican Council II.

After these preliminary remarks, the speaker gave certain practical remedies, starting with what needed to be done for *the universal church.* As soon as they appear, problems of a biblical nature are to be submitted for careful analysis by the Pontifical Biblical Commission and by other experts, both exegetes and theologians, to reach a positive solution which should not be confined to a simple condemnation of the errors. Similarly, doctrinal problems are to be studied by the Congregation for the Doctrine of the Faith. "Indeed, it would maybe be helpful—as a number of fathers have suggested—to set up a truly international *theological commission* here in Rome which, like the biblical commission, would examine theological questions, and promote and supervise their study."[6] The Congregation for Seminaries can also provide some useful remedies, encouraging a wise reform of studies in seminaries and theological faculties, and fostering cooperation between the various disciplines that are taught in Catholic faculties and universities, particularly in order to examine theological and philosophical problems in the light of data from the positive sciences.

5. Cf. Arch. Mk 1/1. For the sake of convenience, we shall use Caprile's broad summary (pp. 188-189), filling this out in various places by highlighting the observations dictated by good sense, which are not found in Caprile.

6. One of the important fruits of this discussion was in fact Pope Paul VI's creation of the International Theological Commission in April 1969.

As regards *individual bishops and episcopal conferences*, the speaker pointed out above all that bishops have the very serious duty of watching over the doctrine of the faith, as is highlighted in the conciliar Constitution on the Church.[7] Since they are often taken up with many other obligations, it would be helpful to *set up a commission* in the individual dioceses and in the episcopal conferences which would not only try to prevent errors, but would positively foster study and investigation of the true doctrine.[8] Wherever possible these should seek the assistance of theological faculties and of professors who teach theological and related subjects in the major seminaries. "Bishops must maintain good contacts with those who teach in theological faculties and seminaries, showing trust in them, helping them as much as they can, and paternally encouraging their studies. In this way they will always be able to turn to them for advice and assistance in doctrinal difficulties."

Having emphasized (in the light of the Council) the need and major importance of a solid training for priests, the speaker pointed out the need "for a solid and progressive *education of the laity*, in order to train them for the apostolate too. How can we entrust increasingly important tasks in the field of apostolic work to lay people if they have not been trained for this? Apart from ordinary preaching, there is thus a vital need for a solid *catechization of adults.* . . . The means of social communication are also very helpful in this context. So far as I know, in many regions these instruments are not yet being sufficiently cultivated and used."[9]

In conclusion we can say that instead of stopping at worried warnings and accusations, the cardinal faced deviations and dangers in practical pastoral terms, bearing in mind the source on which to draw for light to clarify problems and also the many forces in the church that can help on various levels, pinpointing problems, bringing light to bear, and taking practical pastoral provisions.

2. The cardinal's work within *the Congregation for the Doctrine of the Faith* requires a special word of explanation. We have seen the work that Father Bea had performed in the ten years up to 1959 in what was then called the Supreme Sacred Congregation of the Holy Office. Since then, however (in December 1965), Pope Paul VI had reorganized this department, not only changing its name, but also its aims. Thus the relative motu proprio says that promotion is the best way of guarding and protecting doctrine in our times, so that apart from the task of correcting errors the department was also given that of promoting doctrine, for example with meetings for experts and scholars.[10]

---

7. Cf. *LG*, 25.

8. The creation of such a commission had already been suggested prior to this by the Sacred Congregation for the Doctrine of the Faith with its letter of 23 February 1967, which was not published in *AAS*; Italian translation in Caprile, pp. 625-626.

9. The synod also discussed the reform of the liturgy; cf. Caprile, pp. 471-490, 497-515. The cardinal did not speak in this discussion because he thought it best that the residential bishops should speak about this matter, and that it was important for the relative council to hear their opinion. For similar reasons, he did not take part in the discussion on the reform of the Code of Canon Law (cf. Caprile, pp. 87-136): he was a member of the commission in question, and was more concerned to hear from the residential bishops who were involved in pastoral work.

10. Cf. *AAS*, LVIII (1966), 935-954. This reform was then encompassed in the Apostolic

We do not know a great deal about content, in other words the actual subjects it dealt with. In the previous chapter we mentioned the instruction on mixed marriages.[11] And we have just seen that this congregation was responsible for the basic document for the First General Synod of Bishops on "Dangerous Contemporary Opinions and Atheism."

In the same year the congregation published an important statement intended to resolve the thorny problem of the "Index" of forbidden books. Readers will recall that Father Bea had already considered this question in the ten years prior to 1959.[12] Now, however, a declaration was published on the question, stating that the Index retained its *moral* value, inasmuch as it reminded the faithful of their duty to avoid anything that could endanger their faith, or more generally their spiritual good; on the other hand, it was no longer a matter of *ecclesiastical law with consequent ecclesiastical penalties*; lastly, the document reminded the bishops of the need to encourage a "sacred culture."[13]

We have another example from the same year, in the shape of a letter that this department sent out to episcopal conferences, drawing attention to various serious errors that were spreading in the church with regard to *interpretation of the conciliar documents*.[14] In 1967 the department published a formal "profession of faith" to be used in certain circumstances of an administrative nature, instead of the old "Tridentine profession of faith" and the "antimodernist oath."[15]

3. Then there was work with *the Council for the Proper Implementation of the Constitution on the Sacred Liturgy*. This constitution, which was promulgated during the second period of the Council in the fall of 1963, laid down *the main principles* for the reform in general, and also those for the reform of the individual sectors: the eucharistic mystery, the other sacraments, the divine office, the liturgical year, and sacred music. The aforementioned council was then set up in order to implement this whole reform. It had forty-eight members (eleven cardinals, thirty-six bishops, and one abbot) from all over the world, who were backed up by two hundred experts, divided into forty-two study groups. Between the first months of 1964 and 1 May 1967, 228 draft documents had been drawn up in this connection,[16] and in the three years between 1964 and

Constitution *Regimini ecclesiae universae* on the reform of the Roman curia; cf. *AAS*, LIX (1967), 897-899.

11. Cf. *AAS*, LVIII (1966), 235-239. Cf. p. 622 above.

12. Cf. p. 198 above.

13. Cf. *AAS*, LVIII (1966), 445. The penalty involved was of course excommunication. The congregation returned to the problem once more; cf. *AAS*, LVIII (1966), 1186.

14. Cf. *AAS*, LVIII (1966), 659-661; Italian translation in Caprile, pp. 623-624. This was also one of the main subjects at the 1967 Synod of Bishops, as we have seen, and the same congregation had prepared a document on the subject which was taken as the basis for discussion.

15. Cf. *AAS*, LIX (1967), 1058. The "antimodernist oath" was imposed at the beginning of the century by St. Pius X in order to preclude the dangers of the errors of modernism, and it had been in force for almost half a century.

16. Cf. the speech of the president of the council, Cardinal Giacomo Lercaro, in Caprile, p. 447, inasmuch as the liturgical reform was one of the subjects of the 1967 synod.

1967, the council held eight plenary meetings, each of them lasting several days.[17]

To what extent did our cardinal take part in the work of this body? One of the consultors, the well-known French liturgist Canon A.-G. Martimort, says that he attended the meetings with praiseworthy regularity considering his many other commitments.[18] The same witness says that he does not remember the cardinal's speeches in detail, but mentions two that "disappointed" him. In discussions on the reform of the mass, the cardinal had supported the plan of the council, although "above all *in a devotional sense* which did not correspond very closely to the concerns of most of the bishops and experts," and generally speaking "he gave me the impression of being more concerned with the devotional aspect of the mass than its traditional liturgical structure." Moreover, in connection with the ceremonial of bishops, "he disappointed me by the way in which he dismissed the line of reasoning . . . coming from the East."[19]

For his part, the secretary of this council, Bishop A. Bugnini, writes: "People looked forward to his presence at the meetings; and he was assiduous in his contributions, despite the fact that in the last years this cost him considerable sacrifice. . . . But he was always anxious not to miss a meeting, if for no other reason, he used to tell me, than that of giving 'a witness of solidarity and friendship in these difficult moments.' "[20] Bishop Bugnini then speaks of the cardinal's general influence: "He was listened to and loved. His contributions bore a very special decisive weight."[21]

4. *In conclusion*, let us cast a general look over all the cardinal's work within the central government of the Catholic Church. In the first place we can look at the figures in order to obtain an idea of the amount of work he performed in the five congregations and two commissions to which he belonged. The figures are based on entries in our diaries and certainly err on the side of under-estimation.[22] For the three years 1966-1968, in addition to the work of the Secretariat for Christian Unity,[23] and a month of daily meetings of the General Synod of Bishops in 1967,[24] we find almost one hundred other meetings of various kinds.[25]

---

17. Ill-health prevented the cardinal from attending the plenary meeting that began on 21 November 1967.

18. Cf. ArchWit, p. 11.

19. *Ibid.* So far as the last observation is concerned, I must say that I personally noticed that the cardinal was allergic to a mixture of elements from different rites.

20. Quoted in the review *Notitiae*, IV (1968), 362. Given the cardinal's numerous obligations, it was inevitable that his various engagements should sometimes clash.

21. ArchWit, p. 7. From my own observation, I would add that people liked to turn to the cardinal privately for advice on questions that were particularly hotly debated. A special aspect of the work of the council was the revision of the Latin psalter, and we shall discuss this below.

22. For example, the Sacred Congregation for the Doctrine of the Faith held its meetings fairly regularly every Wednesday, and this regularity may explain why they are not always entered in the diaries, which note only twenty-six meetings for the three-year period.

23. Here we would note particularly the two plenary meetings—June 1966 and April 1967—each of which entailed eight full days of meetings.

24. We saw this at the beginning of the present chapter.

25. Doctrine of the Faith, 26; Rites, 23; Neo-Vulgate, 24; Reform of the Liturgy, 25 others, 9.

Apart from the sheer number of meetings, as also the time needed to prepare for them, we must obviously take account of the importance of all this work for the universal church, and hence the responsibility entailed. So far as such preparation is concerned, we can take as an example the meetings of the Sacred Congregation of Rites (which was called "for the Causes of the Saints" after the 1967 reform), which almost always entailed study of bulky files in connection with the various causes for beatification or canonization. The meetings of the Sacred Congregation for the Doctrine of the Faith also very often called for prior study of large amounts of paper work.

Let us also consider *the spirit* in which the cardinal approached all this work, for he saw it in two perspectives, both fairly demanding. In the first place there was the question of making a contribution to the central government of the universal church, but added to this general aspect there was that of the particular task he had been assigned with regard to Christian unity, which meant that he saw his special task as that of being "the ecumenical conscience" at the center of the church—not as if other people should not think about it too, but as a specific institutional task as president of the secretariat. As concerns the importance that the cardinal attributed to ecumenism in the central government of the church, we would recall the forceful statement quoted in our previous chapter and contained in the message he sent to the plenary meeting of the secretariat a few days before his death: "Ecumenism must not be some separate activity in the life of the church: it is a new dimension and must be borne in mind in all matters, perspectives, plans and solutions."[26]

The Neo-Vulgate: Origins and Developments

In his response to the Christmas wishes of the Sacred College in December 1966, Pope Paul VI announced that a new commission had started work within the Roman curia, "presided over by Cardinal Augustin Bea, for the preparation of a new Latin-language Bible, the neo-vulgate as it is already called; the desire for such an edition has arisen from the progress of biblical studies and the need to give the church and the world a new and authoritative text of the sacred scriptures."[27] The pope immediately gave details of this task, explaining in what way it was a "new Latin-language Bible": "The aim is a text in which that of the vulgate of St. Jerome will be respected to the letter wherever it faithfully reflects the original text, as this is seen from present-day scholarly editions; it will be prudently corrected wherever it differs from this or does not interpret it correctly, using the language of *Latinitas biblica* for this purpose. In this way respect for tradition and the healthy critical requirements of our day will be combined."[28] To put it briefly, the aim was that of bringing St. Jerome's text

26. Ms. R 1968/17a, p. 2.
27. *AAS*, LIX (1967), 53-54.
28. *Ibid.*

fully into line with the original texts, correcting it wherever necessary, while using the same Latin as St. Jerome in the correction—in other words not classical Latin, but traditional "biblical and Christian" Latin.[29]

1. Let us first of all consider *the origins* of this project, examining how it was born and who first had the idea for such a revision—not out of some concern over prestige, but simply in order to establish the historical facts. And the first fact is as follows. From my notes I see that on 27 February 1965 Cardinal Bea reported to the pope on "the new Latin translation of sacred scripture: work completed to date." It should be noted that at this point there was no mention of a "revision" of the vulgate, but of a "new translation," and, moreover, of work *already* performed. Readers will recall that some years after the publication of the new Latin translation of the psalter, which had been produced by the Pontifical Biblical Institute on the instructions of Pius XII,[30] the latter gave the institute the task of continuing this work and translating a selection of original Old Testament texts into Latin so that they could be used in the divine office. Bea's personal notebook tells us that this task was started, again under his chairmanship, in May 1949. Work continued until November 1959, when it was suspended because Father Bea was made a cardinal.[31] When the cardinal reported to the pope on 27 February 1965 on "the new Latin translation of sacred scripture: *work completed to date*," he was thus referring to work performed between 1949 and 1959 on this task of translating a selection of Old Testament texts.

Therefore at this point there was no mention of any revision of the vulgate. This is all the more significant inasmuch as an at least partially new situation had been created by the Council as long ago as the end of 1963, for in the Constitution on the Sacred Liturgy, which was promulgated on 4 December 1963, it had stated: "The task of revising the psalter, already happily begun, is to be finished as soon as possible. It shall take into account the style of Christian Latin, the liturgical use of the psalms—including the singing of the psalms—and the entire tradition of the Latin Church."[32] The Council thus gave precedence to Christian Latin and tradition, in other words the fifteen hundred years of use of the vulgate, over the classical Latin of the *Piiano* translation, and at the beginning of 1964 Pope Paul VI had in fact appointed a subcommission within the framework of the Council for the Proper Implementation of the Constitution on the Sacred Liturgy, which was to take care of the desired revision of the *Piiano* psalter.

We can add that the cardinal had to some extent announced these developments as early as the preparatory phase of the Council. The records of the Central Preparatory Commission show that Pope John XXIII had approved the *Piiano*

29. Cf. S. Schmidt, "Il primo libro della Neo-Volgata, il Salterio," *CC*, 1969/IV, 356-360.
30. Cf. pp. 101-104 above. This translation was published in 1945. People came to refer to it as "the *Piiano* translation," from the name of Pius XII, and for brevity and clarity we use this term, although it was also sometimes known as "the Bea translation."
31. Cf. p.103 above.
32. *SC*, 91. We shall discuss the implementation of this instruction later.

translation much earlier, while admitting that "certain opportune improvements can be made to this version." Having reported this decision of the pope in his speech, the cardinal added: "As the Supreme Pontiff explained to me orally, it is above all a question of the Latin language. So far as this is concerned, there was an almost unanimous desire that Christian Latin should be used so far as possible. And this desire will be satisfied."[33]

It appears that after the pope's decisions, Father Bea had been in contact with the Abbot Primate of the Benedictines, Benno Gut, since 1959, and had said that he was only too willing to take account of Christian Latin and the liturgy.[34] Given this background, it is all the more surprising that the cardinal should have suggested the old project of Pius XII to Paul VI. Maybe he thought that there were some special reasons in favor of the Latin of the psalter "as the prayer-book *par excellence* of the church," so that the decisions of the Council were to be limited to the psalter. Or maybe he felt obliged to continue with it until instructed to the contrary. Or maybe he was simply taking this project and the work completed to date as a starting point.

However, certain other facts indicate that the cardinal also had a second, more hidden attitude, which was willing, and indeed secretly prepared, for the revision of the vulgate. I remember that when he was drawing up the plan for the revision of the vulgate, he asked me to read it. After doing so, I returned it, remarking: "I have no observations, but I wonder if you realize that these norms are diametrically in opposition to the line followed to date"—in other words, for the translation of the psalter and the Old Testament texts. He answered imperturbably: "I know, but it's what the pope wants, and I agree. In fact, I would have personally preferred it even for the psalter, instead of a new translation in classical Latin." He had already told me more than once that he would have preferred it to be closer to the vulgate, but out of obedience he had accepted Pope Pius XII's decision to prepare a new translation into classical Latin. And we also have confirmation, dating back to a time free of all suspicion, that Father Augustin Bea would have preferred a revision of the vulgate, for in 1952 he wrote almost prophetically to a university professor in Germany: "When 'a new translation' of the whole Bible is undertaken at some future date, as will certainly have to be done sooner or later, this 'new translation' will certainly be 'an amended vulgate.'"[35]

Bearing in mind the cardinal's whole background in this matter, let us try to imagine what took place when he reported, as we have seen, on the "new Latin translation" ordered by Pius XII and already largely completed by the Biblical Institute.[36] The cardinal inevitably had to remind the pope that he had some time before personally approved the criteria for the revision of the psalter on the basis of the aforementioned conciliar norms, and that this revision aimed at safeguard-

---

33. *AD*, II/III, 354.
34. Cf. Na 1959/622.
35. N 1962/144; the original German phrase is: "wird . . . sicher eine Vulgata emendata sein."
36. We obviously cannot rule out the influence of other considerations or facts, such as that mentioned in the statement of A.-G. Martimort, which we shall give below.

ing the traditional Christian Latin of the psalter.[37] It was maybe obvious in this context for the pope to ask the cardinal whether the decision of the Council did not constitute a signal for the whole of the vulgate. This question could easily have brought Bea's second, hidden, attitude into play. And it cannot be ruled out that he told the pope in confidence that he had accepted Pius XII's instruction to translate the psalter into classical Latin simply out of obedience, whereas he would personally have preferred a revision of the vulgate. He could also have added that in the case of the New Testament, Pius XII himself had envisaged a simple revision of the vulgate and had even approved the relative guidelines.[38] We would add that it was all the easier for the cardinal to accept the planned revision of the vulgate inasmuch as the first essential element of this project came from Pope Pius XII himself in the basic idea of bringing the vulgate into line with the original, scientifically established texts, in other words those produced under the immediate inspiration of the Holy Spirit.

2. Thus the idea was born. The pope entrusted Cardinal Bea with the job of drawing up a detailed plan with guidelines, etc. This task was much facilitated by a measure going back to Pius XII, that is *the guidelines* for the revision of the Latin text of the vulgate of *the New Testament*. This came about because in the context of the translation of the Old Testament texts for the divine office it was realized that the New Testament readings must also be considered for the same purpose; and it was suggested to Pius XII that a new translation should *not* be made but merely a revision or correction of the text of the vulgate to make it fully faithful to the original Greek. The pope had at once accepted the suggestion and also approved the relative guidelines, the practical application of which was demonstrated on two practical examples: the revision of the Letters of St. Paul to the Philippians and the Colossians. Thus in 1965 there were already some practical and very authoritative guidelines for revising the vulgate which were now applied to the *whole* Latin translation of the Bible.[39]

Once the first detailed plan and particularly the guidelines had been approved, the pope entrusted the cardinal with *organizing the undertaking* through the creation of the necessary structures. The cardinal began with various exegetes from the Roman universities and consultors of the Pontifical Biblical Commission. It was decided to divide the work between an *on-the-spot commission* in Rome, and *outside collaborators* abroad. Each of the members of the commission would choose the book in which he was particularly well qualified and would undertake its revision according to the approved guidelines. He himself would find the most skilled exegetes from different countries, who had already worked on the book in question, and would carry out its revision with them, using all the critical, philological, exegetical and theological aids available. The translations already made by the Biblical Institute would also be

37. Cf. Caprile, p. 449; the pope approved these criteria on 15 February 1964.
38. We shall speak about this last element shortly.
39. A speech by the cardinal in the course of discussions on the liturgy in the Central Preparatory Commission indicates that Pope John XXIII had approved both the assignment given to the Biblical Institute and also the guidelines for revising the New Testament; cf. *AD*, II/III, 355.

placed at the disposition of the individual groups. Once the work had been completed, the text of the individual books would be submitted to the Roman commission, which would examine and judge it. In other words, the revision of each book would have *two stages*: the first work would be done by a small group of specialists, and the results would then be examined collegially by the "Roman commission." The following terminology was in due course adopted: the components of the Roman commission would be "members," while the outside collaborators would be "consultors."[40] The whole plan was approved with a letter of the Secretary of State of 19 November 1965, which also set up the commission, nominating the cardinal president, its eleven members and its secretary.[41] A few days later, the revised "amended" vulgate which was to be born was given its official name of "Neo-Vulgate."[42]

The work of the commission moved fast. In a press conference in March 1967, the secretary, Monsignor P. Rossano, could report: "The commission . . . has already prepared the new texts of the Gospel of St. Mark, while those of Matthew and John, the Book of Revelation and the prophets Jeremiah and Isaiah are well on the way to completion."[43]

In March 1968 Pope Paul VI took a decision that lent a *highly ecumenical tone* to the new undertaking. Our files contain the following note on this decision: "With a view to the creation of a neo-vulgate which should also have an ecumenical character, the Holy Father has graciously instructed that after the revision of the various books has been completed, they should each be sent for examination and an opinion to a certain number of non-Catholic scholars, leaving the practical implementation of this instruction to those in charge of this commission."[44] Thus the proofs of the various revised books were sent to dozens of non-Catholic scholars for examination.[45]

In June 1968, a release from the Press Room, obviously based on information received from the commission, gave the following report on the state of work: "The work of the Commission for the Neo-Vulgate is proceeding smoothly, despite some difficulties, which were in any case predictable. . . . At this

---

40. Cf. Schmidt, "Il primo libro," p. 359. This structure was also retained later; cf. T. Stramare, "La Neo-Volgata: impresa scientifica e pastorale insieme," *Lateranum*, XLV (1970), 10-35, esp. 13-14.

41. Apart from the brief note in *AAS*, LVIII (1966), 112, no published document exists. Even when the work was finished and Pope John Paul II officially approved the neo-vulgate in his Apostolic Constitution *Scripturarum thesaurus* (*AAS*, LXXI [1979], 558), when he mentions the creation of the Commission for the Neo-Vulgate, the only reference given is the date of 19 November 1965, without mention of any document.

42. Cf. Arch. Mb 1/3. A little later the question was also raised of whether the result of the work of the commission should not be subject to examination by the Congregation for the Doctrine of the Faith, given the close link of the vulgate with dogma. However, it was decided that the Pontifical Biblical Commission should be entrusted with such supervision, as the department most qualified for such a task.

43. Cf. the press conference of 17 March 1967, in *OssRom* (18 March 1967); Arch. Mb 7/38.

44. Arch. Mb 1/16.

45. Cf. Piero Rossano, "Le Epistole di S. Paolo e Cattoliche," *OssRom* (18 October 1970), p. 5. Arch. Mb 7/41 says that this was done for the psalms and the gospels.

moment the revision of the four gospels, the psalter, the Book of Isaiah and some of St. Paul's Letters, is complete. The texts of the gospels will thus be sent to the Vatican Polyglot Press by the end of the summer, and the psalter by the end of October. In keeping with the express wishes of the Holy Father, the proofs of these, and also of the other books that will be printed in due course, will also be sent to a group of non-Catholic scholars who are experts in the text and in ancient versions of the Bible, to obtain their opinion."[46]

3. *The revision of the psalter.* Here we have a special case, not only or even chiefly because of the complicated textual state of the book, but because at the beginning of 1964, when the revision desired by the Council was started, the plan for the neo-vulgate did not yet exist, and there were therefore no guidelines to provide a more detailed explanation of the general conciliar decision. The Council wanted Christian Latin to be restored in the *Piiano* translation, bearing in mind "the liturgical use of the psalms—including the singing of the psalms— and the entire tradition of the Latin Church."[47] In this way the Council wanted to take account of the insistent criticisms to which the *Piiano* had been subject because of the type of Latin adopted. The Secretary of the Commission for the Neo-Vulgate, Monsignor P. Rossano, writes in this connection that the criticisms "were aimed essentially at the type of language used; for basically they expressed regret that a 'classicalized' and artificial Latin had replaced the ancient Christian Latin, with its spiritual connotations, its pure poetry, its depth of meanings, and its link with the Greek version of the Septuagint and the reading of the Bible in the early church."[48] As can be seen, although the aim was clear, the way was less so, and it is thus hardly surprising that some considerable effort was needed before the right road was found.

With a view to implementing the instructions of the Council, a subcommission for this matter was appointed at the beginning of 1964, within the framework of the Council for the Proper Implementation of the Constitution on the Sacred Liturgy. The report made to the 1967 synod by the president of this council, Cardinal G. Lercaro, describes the position of the work of the commission as follows: "After the Holy Father had confirmed the criteria for the reform (15 February 1964), the whole psalter was revised once. A second revision was carried out after receipt of observations from about thirty experts from various parts of the world."[49]

Things are described rather differently by one of the consultors of the council.[50] In the statement on Cardinal Bea from which we have already quoted, the liturgist Canon A.-G. Martimort says that the relative commission was set up without consulting the bishops and consultors of the council: "The member

---

46. *OssRom* (8 June 1968); Arch. Mb 7/39.

47. *SC*, 91.

48. Piero Rossano, "Il 'Liber Psalmorum' della Neo-Volgata,' *OssRom* (10 August 1969); Arch. Mb 7/40.

49. Caprile, p. 449.

50. In order to avoid giving the names of the persons involved, we shall give this evidence for the most part in a summarized form, rather than quoting verbatim.

bishops of the council were not allowed to know who its members were, and its work was kept secret." When they came by chance into possession of the text of a certain number of psalms, "we realized that, contrary to what the Council had expressly asked, the commission had returned to a translation that was basically an improved version of Father Bea's translation." Various members of the council became alarmed and asked for details. Bishop Bugnini then asked Father Duncker, Canon Wambacq and some other members of that commission to provide the council with some explanations. "This meeting was very heated," notes Canon Martimort, and then says that he thinks that after this meeting Bishop Guano of Livorno, "a personal friend of Paul VI," went to see the pope. "To put it briefly, the commission was disbanded, and since people always know how to find a solution in Rome, it was announced that the pope did not want the work to be confined to the translation of the psalter but that a commission would be set up for the translation of the *whole* Bible."[51] As can be seen, this statement draws attention to a number of aspects of the matter. However, it does have the serious drawback that no dates are given, so that it does not offer a sufficient basis for a full clarification of precisely how things went. We shall try to describe the facts on the basis of documents in our possession.

In the first place, we have the clear statement of the secretary of the council, Bishop Bugnini, on the role the cardinal played from the beginning with regard to the revision called for by the Council. In his written statement we find the following: "Direct more personal contact [with the cardinal] came when the study group was set up for the revision of the psalter on the basis of article 91 of the constitution. I went to see the cardinal several times at the Brazilian College to submit all the details of the undertaking to him: names, guidelines, method. Everything was agreed with him, and I wanted to do nothing without him."[52] However, we would also note the following observation on the cardinal's feelings in this matter: "I could see that even when he showed interest and gratitude for this thoughtful treatment, it was basically painful to him, even if he did not show it. When everything had been settled and he was escorting me to the door after we had discussed the matter for the last time, he said: 'Now don't go spoiling my work too much.' "[53] However, we should also recall the above-mentioned statement of the president of the liturgical council that the norms for the revision had been approved by the pope himself. Although we do not know what the norms and criteria in question were, on the basis of Bishop Bugnini's evidence and also of later developments it is clear that the basic concept was that the *Piiano* translation was to be taken as the basic text, with its language being corrected in keeping with the instructions of the Council.[54]

---

51. ArchWit, pp. 12-13. I do not see how the statement that "the commission was abandoned" can be reconciled with the previously cited statement of Cardinal Lercaro that the commission had revised the psalter not once but twice.

52. ArchWit, p. 7.

53. *Ibid.*

54. It is not surprising that the norm given by the Council should have been interpreted in a number of different ways. The Council does not use the technical language of specialists and is thus open to a variety of interpretations.

A very recent statement by the President of the "Study Group for the Revision of the Psalter," G. Duncker, O.P., does give us a better idea of the work of the group and all the difficulties it encountered.[55] He writes: "One day Bishop Bugnini spoke to me about a subcommission of the Commission for the Neo-Vulgate which was to be set up for the revision of the psalms according to the express wishes of Vatican II, and said that Cardinal Bea had told him that he wanted me as chairman, in the hope that under my supervision something of the *Piiano* translation could be saved. I accepted the task solely to please Cardinal Bea, for I did not feel I was at all the right person for the job. Wambacq, Mackenzie, Castellino and Gribomont were appointed members, with me as president. Abbot Egger was added as a Latinist, but without voting rights." Difficulties soon arose: "A marked division in the subcommission was clear from the outset: Wambacq and Mackenzie were always in favor of a Latin translation that was closer to the Hebrew, while Castellino and Gribomont assiduously supported a version much closer to the Latin of the vulgate, often preferring the Septuagint for liturgical use; and Egger held similar views. Since Egger could not vote, it was left to me to decide, and my decision was generally in favor of the text presented by Wambacq and Mackenzie." In these circumstances the president felt still greater need of orientation, and the statement thus continues: "You will recall that I came regularly to report to Cardinal Bea on our discussions."

Here a new factor appears, for the statement continues: "In the first months he [Bea] generally approved the decision taken, but then, even on points that he had previously approved, he began to show a change of mind. . . ." What had happened? This commission had been at work for almost a year and a half when the commission for the revision of the vulgate was set up. In this new context, writes Monsignor P. Rossano, Secretary of the Commission for the Neo-Vulgate, "it was clearly a good idea to coopt the subcommission for the psalter into it, unifying the method and guidelines for the work."[56] I know that the problem was submitted to the relative authorities in February 1966, and then again at the beginning and in the course of the month of the following April. Monsignor Rossano states baldly: "*It was he* [Cardinal Bea] who handed the subcommission for the psalter the practical guidelines which articulated the wishes of the Council fathers in the complex and delicate textual situation of the Book of Psalms, and also the orientations that the Holy Father had expressed for the whole undertaking of the neo-vulgate in his speech to the Sacred College on Christmas Eve 1966."[57]

In this connection we also have a statement that goes back to Paul VI himself.

---

55. Letter of 19 February 1988.

56. Rossano, "Il 'Liber Psalmorum.' " As can be seen, the method followed in revising the psalms was changed because the context had been changed, for the revision was now to be seen in the context of the revision of the whole vulgate. This change does not allow conclusions to be drawn as to the validity or otherwise of the criteria *previously* laid down for the revision and, as we have seen, approved by the pope.

57. *Ibid.*

When the revised psalter was published in 1969, the pope demonstrated his usual sensitivity, telling Monsignor Rossano that he was concerned that some people could see the revision of the psalter as being directed against Cardinal Bea's work, *whereas it had been he who suggested it.*[58]

In fact, in a letter of 23 May 1967 to the President of the Subcommission for the Revision of the Psalter, Father G. Duncker, O.P., the cardinal explicitly states that in accordance with the "wishes of the president of the liturgical council and of the Holy Father himself" he (Bea) had been entrusted with making sure that the revision of the psalter corresponded to the norms laid down for the neo-vulgate.[59] The letter goes on to give precise instructions. As concerns *the question of principle*, or of which text was to be taken as the basis, the letter says: "I agree completely with what you say about a compromise between the Gallican Psalter and the *Piiano* Psalter, so long as it is understood as meaning that the Gallican version should have preference, and the *Piiano* version should be adapted to the norms valid for the neo-vulgate. This will ensure fulfillment of the Holy Father's wish that the translation of the psalms should be in keeping with that of the other biblical books of the neo-vulgate." What about cases where the text of the Gallican version does not correspond to the original Hebrew? "Then the correction that has already been made in the *Piiano* version is to be used. The *Piiano* text should be changed, so far as necessary, as concerns the Latin; in other words, the sense of the *Piiano* version should be retained, but this sense should be expressed in Christian biblical Latin."[60]

The remainder of Father Duncker's account is probably to be located at this point: "I felt I could no longer continue in this way, and asked to be relieved of the position of chairman. Wambacq and Mackenzie soon followed my example." And thus the revision of the psalter moved into the general framework of the revision of the vulgate.

The introduction to the new psalter, which was published in 1969, tells us that after the relative subcommission had finished its work of revision at the beginning of January 1969, in accordance with the aforementioned instructions of Paul VI the new text was sent to over one hundred scholars in every part of the world who were experts in exegesis, liturgy and Christian Latin.

$$* * *$$

Let us now conclude the subject of the revision of the psalter, and also that of the vulgate in general. Work continued for a little over ten years after the cardinal's death, and the officially authorized edition of the neo-vulgate was published by Pope John Paul II on 25 April 1979 with the apostolic constitution

---

58. I heard this directly from Monsignor Rossano. In connection with this decision of Bea, Father G. Duncker writes that "by submitting in total simplicity, humility and sincerity," the cardinal "signed the cancellation of his previous work, his *Piiano* Psalter" (*ibid.*; Duncker, Archwit, p. 49).

59. Cf. Arch. Mb 1/11, p. 2.

60. *Ibid.*

Scripturae thesaurus.[61] This represented the fulfillment of the hopes expressed by Pope Paul VI when he announced the whole plan in December 1966: "The Latin liturgy will thus have a unified, academically unimpeachable text, in keeping with tradition, hermeneutics and Christian language, which will also serve as a reference point for versions in modern languages."[62]

Cardinal Bea must be credited with having provided the spur for the plan, albeit indirectly, when he again raised the possibility of "a new translation" of the Bible. Apart from the question of the origin of the idea of revising the vulgate, it is certain that he was psychologically well prepared to embrace the project fully. And the then Secretary of the Commission for the Neo-Vulgate testifies that he in fact did so: "The present writer can testify that despite the time-consuming commitments and responsibilities binding him to the ecumenical movement, the venerable cardinal set to work with sincere conviction and extraordinary dedication."[63] In this way he laid the groundwork for the task, giving it guidelines and organizing it, and setting it firmly on its way.

Scholarly Work and Writing

The common feature of all the work we shall deal with in this section is the aim of spreading knowledge of the Council and encouraging its implementation. A first group of writings is concerned directly with the ecumenical aspects of the Council, and a second with more general subjects, although always in the context of the Council and its documents.

We shall confine ourselves to books, leaving aside lectures, articles, etc.[64] *Our aim* is obviously not that of producing a full, detailed study, but more than anything that of giving an idea of the general purpose and content of each work.

1. *Publications concerning ecumenism.* Taking the books in chronological order, the first is *The Way to Unity after the Council*,[65] which is made up partly of writings published previously in the form of articles (for example the commentary on the Decree on Ecumenism and the article on religious freedom), while the chapters on the ecumenical significance of the Dogmatic Constitution on the Church, the Constitution on Divine Revelation and the Pastoral Constitution on the Church in the Modern World are essentially new material. There are also quite a few sections on specific aspects of work for Christian unity.[66]

Ecumenism in Focus certainly needs no introduction here, having accompa-

61. Cf. *AAS*, LXXI (1979), 557-559.
62. *AAS*, LIX (1967), 54.
63. Rossano, "Il 'Liber Psalmorum.' "
64. Anybody who wishes can easily find these in the bibliography for this period.
65. Cf. Biblio. 173.
66. Here we would note the following: the common heritage; the Old Testament as bridge; the eucharist and Christian unity; the unity of the church in the variety of gifts; the harmony of doctrine and marian piety (cf. Biblio. 273); the church and non-Christian religions (cf. Biblio. 317); ecumenism and the building up of the unity of the human family.

nied us throughout our present study. We would say briefly that it describes ecumenical facts and events during the Council and for roughly two years after the close of the Council, together with Bea's evaluation of these, and that it also contains the various documents issued in this field.[67]

2. The main feature of the second group of books written by the cardinal after the Council is that they are all based in varying ways on the conciliar documents, and are all linked to varying degrees with the subject of the unity of the human family, which the cardinal dealt with most specifically in *Unity in Freedom*.[68]

(a) *The Church and Mankind*[69] is a book of about three hundred pages, and its "Preface" links it directly with *Unity in Freedom*: "Both these books deal with the destiny and especially with the unity of the human family in the varied aspects of its concrete reality."[70] However, as we have said, this book is based on the Council, and in particular on the Dogmatic Constitution on the Church and the Pastoral Constitution on the Church in the Modern World,[71] although it should be observed that the relative conciliar texts are scattered throughout the book rather than examined in a systematic order.

This book thus aims at producing a synthesis encompassing the multiple aspects involved. "The most important thing is *to point out the sources*, that is, to show how these ideas are drawn directly from our faith. We are not dealing with ideas which are more or less marginal to our faith. On the contrary, they coincide with the main ideas of Christianity itself."[72] One last point: although it is true that the subject is considered in the light of the Council, "nevertheless, the book does not set out just to give a commentary on the appropriate texts of the Council documents, but follows *in a systematic way* the order suggested by the subject itself."[73]

The question the book seeks to address is expressed as follows: "Can the church help contemporary men to resolve the basic and serious dilemma in which they struggle, aiding them to achieve a genuine and deep sense of society, in free encounter and interior communion with other men?"[74]

The book starts from the fact that people have their first and fundamental experience of society in the family, and that this experience is then gradually broadened until it reaches the level of their own nation and people. This can also be applied analogously to the religious field: "First of all, in all that concerns the idea of the *family*. The very first elements of religious instruction teach this.

---

67. This latter point applies more specifically to the Italian version, *Ecumenismo nel Concilio*, since the English version *Ecumenism in Focus* was somewhat abridged.
68. *The Church and the Jewish People* (Biblio. 172) would also be included in this second group, but since we have already dealt with it at some length both in the chapter on relations with the Jewish people and in that on the unity of the human family, there is no need to consider it again here. The same applies to the various writings on non-Christian religions (Biblio. 317, 334).
69. Cf. Biblio. 175.
70. *Church and Mankind*, p. 1.
71. Cf. *ibid.*, p. 28.
72. *Ibid.*, p. 19.
73. *Ibid.*, p. 20.
74. *Ibid.*, p. 13 (ct).

A man is taught that with baptism he has become an adopted son of God, that God is therefore his Father, and from his first prayers he learns to address himself to God with the words, 'Our Father, who art in heaven.' In other words the church teaches man from the very beginning that even in the religious field he is part of a family, of *God's family.*"[75]

"The second step originates in the concept of *the people of God*, which was of course abundantly illustrated in the Council's Constitution on the Church, of which it forms the second chapter."[76] The study starts with the preparation of salvation through the chosen people of Israel, and then examines the complex content of the concept of the people of God of the New Covenant.[77] This is followed by consideration of the "internal structure" of the people of God, "especially the balance between the individual and society, between authority and liberty."[78] Then comes consideration of *the universality* of this people, "since it 'transcends at once all times and all racial boundaries.'"[79] In speaking of the *horizontal* universality it will be a case of showing how all men of whatever nation, race or color are called to be members of God's people. . . . Then we will turn our attention to the *vertical* universality, by virtue of which this people includes all peoples at all times; we will try to show the union of the people of God, in pilgrimage on earth, with all the elect, from the time of Adam and the just man Abel, who have already passed from this life and already enjoy the glory of heaven."[80] There is then a chapter considering its eschatological fulfillment.[81]

"The world of good and evil spirits" must undoubtedly be included in any consideration of the social situation in which we are immersed. "It is true that the sources of our faith do not teach us all that there is to know of that world of spirits, but it is still true that often, along our way, we come across its representatives and realize their various and manifold influences, good and bad, on our lives. Faith and a healthy realism require us, therefore, to take cognizance of them."[82]

It may seem surprising to find a chapter on *the sacred liturgy* at this point (Chapter 8), but the author explains this as follows: "The inspiring and wonderful reality in which every member of the church, every son of God, is immersed by baptism, and by which he is carried and sustained and lives from day to day, ought to be lived in a clear and conscious way. Now this can be done in a fundamental manner through the liturgy. It is here that the Christian lives out and translates into practice his relationship with Christ, and with his heavenly Father in the Holy Spirit; he is also united with his brothers in Christ who are already glorified—the Holy Mother of Christ, the saints, and in varying ways all the members of the

---

75. *Ibid.*, p. 16. This corresponds to Chapter 2, "In the Family of God."
76. *Ibid.*, p. 17 (ct).
77. Cf. Chapter 3, "The Mystery of the People of God."
78. *Ibid.*, p. 17; cf. Chapter 4, "A Difficult Balance."
79. *LG*, 9.
80. *Ibid.*, p. 18. Cf. Chapter 5, "Beyond the Boundaries of Peoples and Times."
81. Cf. *LG*, 7; Chapter 6, "A Final Goal."
82. *Ibid.*, p. 18.

people of God who have passed from this life, whether they are still being purified, or whether they already rejoice in the intuitive vision of God. Finally in the liturgy the Christian feels himself closely united with all the brothers who like himself are on pilgrimage on this earth, and indeed with all mankind. He is aware of being, with Christ and like Christ, at the service of all humanity, indeed of being an instrument of Christ for the redemption of mankind."[83]

(b) *The Word of God and Mankind*[84] is a broad commentary (roughly three hundred pages) on the conciliar Constitution on Divine Revelation. It should be noted that the cardinal had been concerned with various aspects of this subject for several decades,[85] and had also made some considerable contributions to the discussion of the relative schema both in the preparatory phase and in the Council itself.[86]

The conciliar document itself establishes the link with "humanity" in the "Prologue," which states that "in the steps of the Councils of Trent and Vatican I, this synod wishes to set forth the true doctrine on divine revelation and its transmission. For it wants *the whole world* to hear the summons to salvation, so that through hearing it may believe, through belief it may hope, through hope it may come to love."[87] After quoting these words, the cardinal states: "So, by expressly assigning to this document the purpose of seeking that all people may believe and be saved, the Council fathers have set upon it the characteristic seal of the Second Vatican Council, namely, the church's constant desire and aim to bear the whole of humankind in mind, to be at its service and to act for the good of the whole human family."[88]

The cardinal starts his commentary by observing: "The document we are now studying frequently indicates *its theme* in the term 'reveal' or 'revelation,' but at other times uses the truly biblical expression '*word of God.*' This latter term owes its origin to the fact that God revealed himself by *speaking* to humanity through the prophets, and then in his Son.[89] . . . Consequently, the term 'word of God' is very common in scripture, and may be considered as God's own description of his self-revelation to humanity. Psychologically speaking, this term enables us to understand, almost as if by intuition, *the nature* of the divine gift constituted by God's revelation of himself to humanity."[90]

Taking this description of the subject as his starting point, and having further explained the biblical concept of the "word of God," the author describes the whole problem addressed in the conciliar document, the various aspects of

---

83. *Ibid.* (ct).
84. Biblio. 189. As concerns this work, cf. S. Schmidt, "L'impegno ecumenico biblico del Cardinale Bea," *Biblica*, LXIII (1982), 1-21, which also considers other publications by the cardinal, but is based particularly on the book we are discussing here.
85. Cf. Biblio. 2, 53, 54, 57, 80, 86, 89, 104, 126, 135.
86. Cf. Part III, Chapters 4 and 9, of the present biography, and also Appendix 2, which gives a list of interventions in conciliar discussions.
87. *DV*, 1.
88. *The Word of God*, p. 10 (ct).
89. Cf. Heb. 1:1-2.
90. *The Word of God*, p. 11 (ct).

which are expressed as follows: "How can we understand this manifestation of God? How can we listen to his speech? What precise forms does the word of God assume? And since this treasure is essential for the life of humanity in time and in eternity the following question is vital: How does this message of life reach the generations who came after God revealed himself and spoke to humanity? Who is or are the guardians of the word of God, guaranteeing its authentic and integral transmission in the midst of human vicissitudes, as generations pass away and new ones come into being?"[91]

Nor is this all. There is not only the question of handing on the word of God, but "also that of *explaining* God's message. It came from God in times that are removed from our own by thousands of years, and it has come down to us from a world with cultures very different from our own. Therefore, if it is really intended for all humanity it must be understood in all cultures and traditions, even if these are very different from that in which it was first received and formulated. Moreover, is it not possible that with the transmission of this word of God from one generation to another, from one culture to another, it may have been distorted, even to the point of becoming unrecognizable, of losing its vital force, or even becoming harmful? What guarantee have we that we still possess the authentic word of God?"[92]

(c) We now come to the third volume in the series, which is entitled *We Who Serve. A Basic Council Theme and Its Biblical Foundations.*[93] The starting point is provided by the roughly 190 passages in the conciliar documents that speak of "service," either that of the hierarchy—bishops and their assistants, priests—or that of the laity and the church in general.[94] We would start with a particularly clear example. Speaking of the church in general, it is not rare to find the statement that the whole church is and must be at the service of humanity, because "the church desires nothing more ardently than to develop itself untrammelled in the service of all men."[95] The Council thus issues the following call to all Christians: ". . . and let us pattern ourselves daily more and more after the spirit of the gospel and work together in a spirit of brotherhood to serve the human family which has been called to become in Christ Jesus the family of the sons of God."[96]

---

91. *Ibid.*, p. 17 (ct).

92. *Ibid.* (ct).

93. Cf. Biblio. 191. The book was prepared during the last months of 1967, but was not issued until after the cardinal's death.

94. Cf. *ibid.*, p. 11, note 2. The texts are distributed as follows through the various documents: Constitution on the Church, forty; Decree on Ecumenism, eight; Decree on Bishops, seven; Decree on the Up-to-Date Renewal of Religious Life, eleven; Decree on the Training of Priests, eight; Decree on the Apostolate of Lay People, fourteen; Decree on the Church's Missionary Activity, twenty; Decree on the Ministry and Life of Priests, forty-two; Pastoral Constitution on the Church in the Modern World, thirty-three; Constitution on Divine Revelation, five; Declaration on Christian Education, one; Declaration on the Relation of the Church to Non-Christian Religions, one; Declaration on Religious Liberty, two. We should also bear in mind p. 12, note 1, which describes the criteria used in counting these texts, for the author does not count texts which simply use the normal technical terms "minister" and "ministries."

95. *GS*, 42.

96. *GS*, 92. Cf. Chapter 3 of *We Who Serve*, "Service by the Whole People of God."

However, the texts are generally less explicit, and the connection between this "service" and the "*human family*" is for the most part implicit insofar as they are texts in which the Council calls people to place themselves at the service of Christ "the Servant" and his work, in other words the salvation of mankind. Thus, for example, the Constitution on the Church speaks about the service of *bishops* as follows: "In order to shepherd the people of God and to increase its numbers without cease, Christ the Lord set up in his church a variety of offices which aim at the good of the whole body. The holders of office, who are invested with a sacred power, are, in fact, dedicated to promoting the interests of their brethren, so that all who belong to the people of God, and are consequently endowed with true Christian dignity, may, through their free and well-ordered efforts toward a common goal, attain to salvation."[97] Thus, "In its vigorous and insistent attempt to awaken Christians to an awareness of their duty of service, the Council aimed precisely at mobilizing all available energies and inducing them to concentrate entirely on the realization of *God's great design for mankind* which is revealed in Christ. Service, in point of fact, understood in the full and specifically Christian sense, aims at nothing less than the fulfillment of this divine plan."[98] This is the aim of the mission of *Christ "the Servant"* who is "sent by the Father in view of the creation of a new humanity, and in serving God he is at the same time completely at the service of men, to the point of giving his life for them."[99]

In the light of the figure of Christ "the Servant" we immediately see "*the specific character of the service* which, according to the Council, the Christian renders to his own brethren and to all men—the character that distinguishes it from any purely natural humanism. In point of fact, to serve, as we have seen, means to cooperate with Christ in the divine design of salvation. Hence, not only does service aim at a goal which is, in the last analysis, ultramundane and supernatural, but the very spirit in which it is practiced is essentially a religious one."[100]

Here the author at once realizes that this aspect of "service" raises various problems for contemporary men and women, and he does not hesitate to face up to these. People today are ready to accept a certain type of what might be called "secularized" service. "But when there is a question of 'service' in the religious sense, and primarily service of God, contemporary man no longer understands. Or he may even reject the idea of such service as a residue of bygone times, an image of religious life drawn from types of culture altogether foreign to him and from outmoded social situations in which there were 'masters' who had 'servants.' Even those who do not go so far in their objections are inclined to wonder if there can be any sense today in the biblical notion of 'service of God,' whether it can be reconciled with human dignity, or whether it ought not rather to be abandoned or at least interpreted in a manner corre-

---

97. *LG*, 18.
98. *We Who Serve*, p. 9.
99. *Ibid.*
100. *Ibid.*, p. 20 (ct).

sponding to the solemn recognition—professed by the Council—of the eminent dignity of the human person. For these and similar reasons people today are not disposed to view under the aspect of service that which they hold most sacred, namely, their relationship with God or their religious spirit."[101]

Examination of the interior attitude of the person who "serves" his neighbor also raises the further question of the element of "humility" contained in placing oneself at the service of one's brothers and sisters: "In what sense and to what extent can he agree to consider himself 'inferior' to others or even as the 'last' among the brethren, and how does this attitude fit in with the conviction that all men are equal?"[102]

The study closes with reflections on the kingdom of God, which, both in its temporal phase and in its eschatological fulfillment, constitutes a deep synthesis of the service of God and humanity.[103]

* * *

We would conclude with three evaluations indicating how the cardinal's work was viewed in the circles in which it was performed. First of all we have a statement from Prof. F. Alessandrini, who was Deputy Editor of the *Osservatore Romano* for several decades. He talked with me about the cardinal in Greece during the journey to return the relics of St. Andrew to the Orthodox Archdiocese of Patras, and he said something like the following: "You know that I've known Pope Paul VI for about forty years now,[104] and also that I'm very familiar with things in the Vatican. Well, bearing all this in mind, I tell you: if I were Cardinal Bea, I'd be in the pope's antechamber, so to speak, every day. You probably haven't the slightest idea of the extent of the various pressures to which this poor man is exposed every day, and how much he therefore needs someone who will give him sincere assistance, seeking nothing for himself. And Cardinal Bea is such a man. That is why I said that he should be with the pope so to speak every day."

---

101. *Ibid.*, p. 20 (ct). Cf. Chapter 5, "What Does Serving God Mean?" See also *ibid.*, p. 21, for the connection of service of God with humility and obedience, with humble submission to God, even to the very harshest trials and sufferings of the "cross."

102. *Ibid.*, p. 21. Cf. Chapter 6, "The Spirit in Which Men Are to Be Served."

103. After the book *We Who Serve*, the cardinal began a new study under the provisional title of *A Pauline Council* (cf. Arch. Rbm 30), although it was clear that the name was decidedly ambiguous. The idea was to produce a summary of Pauline thought as it is found in the conciliar documents. The draft manuscript of six chapters is found in the archives: (I) "Reuniting Everything in Christ, the Son of God, Head of the New Humanity"; (II) "The Mediator, the Fullness of Revelation, the High Priest"; (III) "Reconciliation of All Things through the Cross of Christ"; (IV) "He Empties Himself for Love"; (V) "Christ Constituted 'Lord' in order to Bring All Things to Fulfillment"; (VI) "Dying with Christ to Live with Christ." As can be seen, a better title would have been *Christ and Humanity*, and the work would have been a further sequel to the three we have just described.

104. I think that he met G.B. Montini in the Italian Catholic University Federation, for Montini had been ecclesiastical assistant to this federation for a considerable period of time; cf. Mario Casella, "Federico Alessandrini: Una testimonianza ecclesiale vissuta nel giornalismo," *OssRom* (29-30 April 1985).

It is surprising how well this evaluation fits with an observation made by one of Pope Paul VI's closest assistants. I think that it was the then Substitute of the Secretariat of State, Archbishop Angelo Dell'Acqua, who told me: "We have noticed that after seeing Cardinal Bea the pope is always happy and serene." And if we want any proof that this was not an empty compliment but a serious observation, we have it in the fact that the speaker followed it up with the invitation: "The cardinal should ask for an audience regularly each month."[105]

We should also consider the attitude of the pope himself, and although it is obviously not easy to find out about this, we do have information on two significant episodes. The first dates to the fall of 1967, when Cardinal Bea had heard indirectly that the pope perhaps intended replacing certain heads of congregations who were getting on in years, possibly by placing a pro-prefect or pro-president alongside them. The cardinal thus offered his resignation, believing these were the pope's wishes. The only reaction was that at the beginning of his next audience the pope told him: "You have not persuaded me"—as if to say that he was unconvinced by the reasons for the resignation. And the cardinal remained president of the secretariat until his death.[106]

The other episode in a way carries even more weight because of the solemn circumstances in which it took place. When the pope granted an audience to the full secretariat—cardinals, bishops and staff members—on 28 April 1967, in a long speech he referred to "the many aspects of your activity" and then went on: "And you know the multitude of problems it raises, faces, and must resolve. Each of these aspects would in itself suffice to provide the subject for broad and helpful reflections. We shall confine ourselves simply to noting the studies to which Catholic ecumenism has given rise, confirming, if there was any need, the importance and urgency of the question." And here the pope added: "And among so many publications, we shall be satisfied to recall those of your venerable president, the Most Eminent Cardinal Bea, which point out the complexity of the subject, draw a sure and wise picture, and do honor to the lucidity of mind and the greatness of spirit of their eminent author."[107]

---

105. And in the first half of 1966, for example, the cardinal was in fact received in audience practically every month (3 January, 24 February, 3 April, 28 April, 26 May, 4 July).

106. The pope's decision seems all the more significant if we consider the fact that a fair number of replacements were made in those months. In 1967 the Archbishop of Toulouse, G.M. Garrone, had been appointed Pro-Prefect of the Congregation for Catholic Education; and in 1968 the President of the Liturgical Council and the Prefects of the Congregations of Rites, the Oriental Churches and the Doctrine of the Faith were all replaced.

107. *AAS*, LIX (1967), 494; also *Bea-Preis*, p. 134, for the original French text.

CHAPTER 3

THE LIGHT OF SUNSET

The previous two chapters showed us the rapid development of relations with other churches and ecclesial communities, and then the cardinal's tireless activity to help spread knowledge and implementation of the decisions of the Council. Now we are simply left with the task of describing the various aspects of the cardinal's personal life in the three years after the Council: events both public and private, happy and sad, until that very personal one of his last illness and his departure from the stage of this world. These events too throw a light of their own and have their own language, speaking to us about the cardinal as religious and priest, and showing us his personality, sometimes even better and more fully than we have been able to do in our previous account.

A Series of Awards

1. On 12 May 1966, news came from Frankfurt that the Council of the Foundation for the *Peace Prize* of the Association of German Publishers had decided to award the prize that year jointly to Cardinal Augustin Bea, President of the Secretariat for Christian Unity, and Dr. W.A. Visser 't Hooft, retiring Secretary General of the World Council of Churches. The press release gave the following citation for the award: "The erudite Roman cardinal from Baden and the Dutch theologian who was for almost thirty years Secretary General of the World Council of Churches have, with their personal activity and publications, helped ensure that the renewed encounter between separated Christians should cease being a utopian dream and that a central area of life should be cleared for joint work."[1]

We would add a word on the history and standing of this prize, which was first awarded in 1950. It is awarded each year to a person—with no distinction as to nationality, race or religious faith—who has rendered some very special service to the cause of peace and understanding between peoples. In the past it has been awarded to such figures as the great philanthropist Albert Schweitzer, the Catholic priest Romano Guardini, the well-known Jewish scholar Martin Buber, the poet Reinhold Schneider, the philosopher, statesman and President of India Sarvepalli Radhakrishnan, and the famous French philosopher and writer Gabriel Marcel.[2]

---

1. This is the information issued officially; cf. Arch. Ra 119/60. The citation is very similar to that given when the Balzan Foundation awarded Pope John XXIII its International Peace Prize; cf. *Unity in Freedom*, pp. 89-90. This citation—like those we shall see in connection with other awards—shows that this section is in no way some sort of attempt at glorifying the cardinal, but that we simply intend relating events of ecumenical importance. On this award in general, cf. H. Fries, "Ein Freidenspreis für ökumenische Arbeit," *Stimmen der Zeit*, XCI/178 (1966), 161-170.

2. Cf. Arch. Ra 119/66; cf. also the ample information provided by the association itself, Arch.

Before publishing the news, the foundation had made sure that those chosen would accept. With ecumenical thoughtfulness they had sent the Catholic publisher H. Herder of Freiburg to Dr. Visser 't Hooft, and the Evangelical publisher, F. Wittig of Hamburg, to the cardinal. The cardinal was very hesitant over accepting, partly out of modesty and partly because of the various engagements and exertions it would entail, with a journey to Frankfurt, extra correspondence, etc. However, he was persuaded for a number of reasons connected with the ecumenical importance of the nomination: the award ceremony amounted to a symbol of ecumenical dialogue; the prize came from an association in which religious publishers made up a bare ten percent of the members; moreover, it had a truly international dimension because it took place at the close of the World Book Fair, which is maybe the foremost event of its kind in the world.

The announcement of the award naturally led to a flood of congratulations, added to which were the greetings and wishes for the cardinal's eighty-fifth birthday, especially since news of the latter had been published in the official newsletter of the Association of German Publishers. The cardinal was not very pleased about this, partly because he immediately thought of the amount it would add to his already voluminous correspondence. On the other hand, the reactions did provide an idea of the esteem the cardinal enjoyed in the very highest spheres of public life in West Germany, and not only in church circles, but also in cultural, and even political ones.[3] However, we would cite only the content of the personal letter in Latin that the cardinal received from Pope Paul VI on this occasion. The pope offered the cardinal his congratulations "for the long life in which, as a good soldier of Christ, you have not spared any effort—despite increasing age—to fulfill the tasks entrusted to your wisdom and concern; thus you have acquired remarkable merit, which won you the special benevolence of our predecessors and our own." After the good wishes and congratulations the letter continued with an invitation to continue "the path started on, and show forth the Holy Church with ever more shining virtues."[4]

When we came to organize the cardinal's journey to receive the prize, we did all we could to limit his engagements. In the circumstances he would obviously be expected to visit the book fair, and particularly the stands of the Catholic publishers who had published a number of his books. He also attended the presentation of the German translation of his book *Unity in Freedom*.[5] The

---

Ra 119/58-65.

3. Cf. Arch. Ra 113/1-23 (twenty or so letters or cables from important figures).

4. The letter is dated 14 May; cf. the original Latin in *Bea-Preis*, pp. 132-133; it was *not* published in *AAS*; cf. also Arch. Ra 113/24-80, which provides an idea of press reports from various countries and in various languages. It was on this occasion that the book *Friede zwischen Christen* (Biblio 174) was published in paperback form, with a print-run of twenty thousand copies, with contributions from the two prize-winners.

5. This was produced by the highly respected publishing house of W. Kohlhammer, which had been producing the monumental biblical work *Theologisches Wörterbuch zum Alten Testament* for over thirty years. The manuscript of the presentation = R 1966/24; cf. also Arch. Ra 118/1-6. On the request of the niece of Cardinal F. Ehrle, Dr. Gertrud Ehrle, President of the Catholic Women of West Germany, he celebrated mass in the Regina Pacis Church in Frankfurt,

central event was of course the award ceremony, which took place on 25 September at the close of the fair, in the *Paulus-Kirche*, a church that had been used exclusively for civil purposes since the previous century. It had been destroyed during the Second World War and had just been completely rebuilt. The President of the Federal Republic of Germany, Dr. H. Luebke, and representatives of the government, the host city and the various churches were also present at the ceremony. After some words of greeting from the President of the Association of German Publishers, Friedrich Georgi, the mayor of the city, Dr. Willi Brundert, spoke.

The speech listing the prize-winners' merits was given by Professor Paul Mikat, Minister of Education for the Rhineland, who introduced the two winners and described their contribution to the cause of peace.[6] Despite the major differences between the activity of the two, there is a vital common feature in their work for the unity of Christians, who are still so painfully divided: "The work of both prize-winners concerns the church. Its peace-making power, however, extends beyond the sphere of the church to the community of all mankind. This solidarity of all men has its basis in the fact that God became man and thereby the brother of us all. In his Letter to the Ephesians, St. Paul writes: 'But now in Christ Jesus you who once were far off have been brought near in the blood of Christ. For he is our peace.' "[7]

An identical reason for the prize is found on the certificates presented to the two award-winners: "Both have worked in an exemplary spirit for religious peace; by their theological writings and speeches they have prepared the way for interconfessional dialogue, and have thus made a decisive contribution to the dawning reconciliation of Christians. They have understood their work for unity in faith as being also *a service to peace in the world*, and thus each has become in his own way a precursor of peace among men." The certificate immediately goes on to state the purpose of the award in this case: "This award is intended to encourage all those who strive to bring about peace between religions, world views and peoples based on mutual esteem."[8]

In his speech expressing his thanks, the cardinal first of all described the development of relations between the Catholic Church and the World Council of Churches, showing that all this work represents a service to the cause of peace. The speaker then went on to explain how work in the cause of peace springs from the interior nature of the church, which is the peaceful kingdom of the Messiah King, and ended by complimenting the Association of German Publishers for having given recognition with this award to the great importance that spiritual values have for the preservation and promotion of peace.[9]

---

preaching a homily on "Women and Peace"; cf. R 1966/25; Arch. Ra 118/7-20.

6. All the speeches at the award ceremony are found in the official publication *Börsenblatt für den Deutschen Buchhandel, Frankfurter Ausgabe*, XXII/78 (1966), and were also published in booklet-form: Augustin Kardinal Bea & Willem A. Visser 't Hooft, *Ansprachen anlässlich der Verleihung des Friedenspreises des Deutschen Buchhandels* (Frankfurt, 1966).

7. Bea & Visser 't Hooft, *Ansprachen anlässlich der Verleihung*, p. 39; cf. Eph. 2:13-14.

8. *Ibid.*, p. 5.

9. Cf. *ibid.*, pp. 43-47.

When his turn came, Dr. Visser 't Hooft described how from its very beginnings the ecumenical movement had also kept in mind the aim of bearing witness before the world to justice and peace. And this was not only a witness in words, for it wanted first and foremost to place itself at the service of the world, and hence at the service of peace. This is the cosmic task of the people of God who see themselves as the salt of the earth and the light of the world; in following Christ they feel responsible for the whole human race.[10]

A prayer service organized jointly by Evangelical and Catholic religious publishers was held the same evening in the Evangelical St. Peter's Church, led by the two prize-winners. This service was filmed, and then shown later on television. The cardinal spoke on the beautiful exhortation to unity in Ephesians 4:1-7,[11] while Dr. Visser 't Hooft spoke on the passage in the Book of Revelation on the new world and the new Jerusalem (21:1-7), and the service ended with a blessing given by the two prize-winners. "I would never have dreamt," Dr. Visser 't Hooft commented immediately afterward, "that the day would come when I would lead a prayer service and give the blessing together with a cardinal of the Roman Catholic Church." Later on he added in more general terms that during this ecumenical prayer service "all those present felt that despite all the differences we had already been given a deep unity."[12]

The event received great attention from the press, and not simply for the curiosity value of its more striking outward aspects, with the presence of top-level figures from political, religious and cultural life. If we take a look at the press survey given in the official publication of the Association of German Publishers, it is surprising to see how deeply the press had grasped the significance of the event, and how aware it was of the importance of inter-church dialogue for the harmony of human society and for peace between nations.[13]

Some months later, the same official publication of German publishers printed a letter from the cardinal to the president of the association, Friedrich Georgi, containing a noteworthy *personal evaluation* of the event. The cardinal wrote that the journey and the ceremony had certainly represented "a great exertion" for him, but that he was happy to have undertaken it: "When I now think back to the celebration, I must say that it was not only very impressive, but that now I see it in all its deep and broad significance. It was an extremely serious and moving public affirmation of the concept of peace. Moreover, it was an expression of the conviction that lasting peace can be built only on spiritual foundations. All these ideas were, furthermore, carried to very large numbers of people through the modern communications media.

"Thus I should like—quite aside from personal considerations—to thank you

---

10. Cf. *ibid.*, pp. 51-56.
11. Cf. ms. R 1966/27; on the prayer service as a whole, cf. Arch. Ra 118/24-37 (with press clippings).
12. BM, p. 370.
13. Cf. *Börsenblatt für den Deutschen Buchhandel, Frankfurter Ausgabe*, XXII/95 (1966), 2500-2505 (= Arch. 119/64). Arch. 119/70-134 contains a rich harvest of over sixty press clippings.

and the Association of German Publishers for this whole demonstration and the contribution it made to reinforcement of the idea of peace and the will for peace in broad circles of people.

"In the same context, the ecumenical prayer service too can certainly be seen as a living and moving example of 'peace among Christians'—an example that was all the more impressive inasmuch as it consisted not of some form of consensus, but rather of shared, united listening to the word of God, in common repentance and prayer to God."[14]

2. Some months later came an award of quite a different kind, given by the French President, General Charles de Gaulle. I had already heard how much the general admired the cardinal, whom he had once described as "a great man." In the spring of 1967, he decided to decorate the cardinal with *the Grand Cross of the Legion of Honor*, and wanted to bestow it personally during a visit to Rome. The same day that he was received in audience by Pope Paul VI there was an official lunch at the French Embassy in Rome. Before the meal, the president withdrew to another room, together with Prime Minister Georges Pompidou, Foreign Minister M. Couve de Murville, and the French Ambassador to the Holy See (who invited me to join them), and bestowed the decoration on the cardinal with the following simple but significant words: "Your Eminence, this is the highest decoration that the French Republic can give you for your ecumenical work." The cardinal expressed his thanks, observing that he had found great support for his work among the French bishops.

3. About six months later, the Society for the Family of Man, which has its headquarters in New York, awarded the cardinal *the Family of Man Prize "for human relations."* This society is an interconfessional, non-profit association with the basic idea that all humanity constitutes a family under the sovereignty of God, and that each individual has a personal responsibility to work to make this idea a reality. The society is concerned over the human person as a whole, encompassing his or her moral, spiritual and physical well-being, and seeks to provide support to people who have leadership qualities in the business world in order to help them to fulfill a specific role in favor of the human family. Apart from its main prize, the association also awards special prizes each year in the field of human relations, science, communications, education and the arts.[15]

The aims of the society are obviously closely related to the ideas that the cardinal expressed and upheld at the Agape meetings and in his various books, especially *Unity in Freedom*. After some initial hesitation the cardinal accepted the prize, thinking that it basically represented recognition of the work of the church and would make this contribution better known to the general public. He asked Father T. Stransky, C.S.P., one of the collaborators of the secretariat, to represent him at the award ceremony, which took place in New York.

The citation for the prize emphasizes "the dedication and purpose" the cardinal had brought to his task as President of the Secretariat for Christian

---

14. *Börsenblatt für den Deutschen Buchhandel, Frankfurter Ausgabe*, X (3 February 1967), 233; Arch. Ra 119/95.

15. Cf. information material, Arch. Ra 132/16.

Unity, and then continues: "He is a major figure in what is surely one of the most significant movements of the twentieth century—the quest for nothing less than the reunion of all Christians. Under his diplomatic guidance historic changes in the relations between fellow Christians and Christians and Jews have come about in our time."[16]

Father Stransky read a brief statement from the cardinal, expressing his gratitude for the prize and saying: "I accept it wholeheartedly, because I regard it as an expression of appreciation, not primarily for whatever I have done to help foster a love of truth and charity, especially among Christian communities, in the building up of religious fellowship, but appreciation primarily for the thousands of Christians, known and unknown, who in recent years have stirred up a dynamic and active yet reflective concern for that divine reconciliation within the Christian family which today is still burdened by tragic and scandalous divisions."[17]

4. A few days before the cardinal received the Family of Man Prize, *Oxford University* wrote him a letter on 14 November 1967, saying that they wanted to grant him an *Honorary Degree of Doctor of Divinity*.[18] The cardinal had a reply sent, expressing his grateful acceptance and saying that he saw the university's decision as "one of the many signs of the new spirit that is inspiring Christians throughout the world, particularly in the academic sphere." He also saw it as "the expression of the urgent need for cooperation between Christians, particularly in the field of theological studies."[19]

With regard to more practical details, in view of the need to cut down on travel, the cardinal then wanted to know whether it was necessary for him to receive the degree in person. The university replied that although this would normally be expected, there had been two recent cases in which the university had voted to give a degree to people who could probably not have received them personally; in these cases, the people in question would at least have had the pleasure of knowing that the university had taken the relative decision. If His Eminence preferred, the university was therefore ready to follow the same course, resolving to confer the degree and publishing its decision, and then leaving open the possibility of actual conferral.[20] The cardinal accepted the suggestion, and the *Oxford University Gazette* of 1 February 1968 stated that in its "convocation" of 30 January 1968 "it was resolved (*nemine contradicente*) to confer degrees, *honoris causa* upon the following persons. Degree of D.D.: His Eminence Cardinal Augustin Bea." The reason was given as follows: "Cardinal Bea is a distinguished biblical scholar and has made an outstanding contribution to Christian unity."[21]

---

16. Thus the official citation; cf. Arch. Ra 132/15.
17. Cf. ms. R 1967/24; also Arch. Ra 132/5 and 18.
18. Cf. the whole file, Arch. Ra 137; the correspondence covers 19 entries.
19. Arch. Ra 137/1.
20. Cf. the letter of 8 December 1967, outside the file, Arch. P 1968/13.
21. *Oxford University Gazette* (1 February 1968), p. 40. (*Nemine contradicente* = without any contrary vote.) Cf. Arch. Ra 137/21.

A letter was written on 2 March in the cardinal's name, telling the university that there was a good possibility that the cardinal would be able to receive the degree in person. At the same time the apostolic delegate in Great Britain was asked to get in touch with the university authorities in order to agree on a date. It was thus in due course agreed that the degree would be conferred on 16 November of the same year. A whole series of letters then followed in order to work out the details and arrange some other important meetings—first and foremost a meeting with the Archbishop of Canterbury, Dr. Michael Ramsey. In mid-August, measurements for the cap and gown to be worn at the ceremony were also sent to Oxford.

However, at the end of August, the cardinal fell seriously ill, and although he was apparently better after two weeks, his doctors insisted that he should curtail his activities as much as possible, particularly travel. On 24 September, we therefore informed the university of the cardinal's definitive decision against receiving the degree in person. Both the university and the apostolic delegate were very sorry to hear the news. Then on the day that he had been supposed to receive the degree, 16 November, the cardinal left this earth in order to receive the eternal degree.

Relations with His Home Town Become Closer

On 16 February 1965, the parish priest of the cardinal's home town of Riedböhringen, Paul Sumser, wrote to me as follows: "Given the mutual extremely cordial relations between the cardinal and his home town, we should very much like to have our honorary citizen linked with us not only during his life." After saying how awkward it would be to approach the cardinal directly about the matter, he asked me to take advantage of some "suitable opportunity" to let the cardinal know "that his home town is very happy to reserve him *an honorable last place of repose*. We should be happy if this thought reflected a secret but never yet expressed wish of His Eminence." The letter added an ecumenical reason: "It would undoubtedly constitute a most permanent and beautiful expression of the ecumenical orientation of his work, if his memory were in this way to remain visibly rooted in his German homeland."[22]

1. Knowing the cardinal's mentality, I handed the letter on to him without more ado. He smiled over the embarrassed tone of the letter and said that he would accept at once, adding that people would undoubtedly pray more for him in Riedböhringen than in the Roman cemetery. However, he made one condition: he wanted to have his grave beside that of his parents. Since it was already fifty years since his father's death (in 1912) and little less since his mother's (in 1918), their graves would normally have been due for elimination very soon, but the cardinal wanted to have them preserved so that he could be buried beside them.

22. Arch. P 1965/126.

His home town was perfectly happy to accept the cardinal's condition, and things in fact took a turn that he had not even imagined. He had envisaged being buried in the town cemetery, whereas the town reasoned that a cardinal could be buried in the church, and that this would also apply to his parents, since he wanted them with him.

When the archbishop of his home town, H. Schäufele, was told about the plans for the cardinal's burial, he not only gave his approval, but also offered to shoulder the considerable expenditure entailed in preparing a tomb. Indeed, when the authorities started on the project, it was discovered that the bell-tower would need large-scale shoring up before the tomb could be built. Even so, everything was ready by July 1967.

2. However, another link with his home town was also very soon added. With considerable financial sacrifice, the town had built *a new school*, and the cardinal was asked if it could be *named after him*. The cardinal agreed, and on 17 July 1966 he attended its *inauguration*. In the course of the ceremony, he made an impromptu speech, and we have a transcript of the tape-recording.[23] He started by complimenting the town authorities, saying that the sacrifices undertaken in order to build a new school showed their respect for culture. He also urged teachers to discover the children, both boys and girls, with talent and the will to study; and he took advantage of the occasion to give public expression to his gratitude for what the parish priest T. Joholzer and the schoolmaster L. Herzog had done for him in this regard. He encouraged parents to accept the sacrifices connected with their children's education: "I know very well from personal experience and the experience of my family—my late father and mother—that it is no easy matter to have a boy or girl study, and if means are also scarce, as they were in my family, then of course the sacrifice is all the greater."[24] In this connection the cardinal pointed out that so far as finances were concerned, his fellow townsmen must be credited with having given him considerable assistance. He also said that in speaking about education he was certainly not thinking only of religious vocations: "Not everybody is called to the priesthood. There are many other fields in which we can be active and can work, for example as jurists, doctors or teachers." He was in fact keen to emphasize the education of girls: "In the various fields involved in my work I have known women who I must say have done truly great work for the church and the world."[25]

3. In his diary for this visit to his home town, we find the entry "burial" on 19 July. This referred to a meeting with the parish priest and the mayor in order to finalize plans for his tomb. They visited the church and saw that a worthy tomb for the cardinal and his parents could be made in the solid bell-tower, and they also decided how this should be done. Since it seemed that the necessary work could be carried out before the summer of 1967, it was planned that the mortal remains of his parents should be moved to their new burial place in July 1967, and that the cardinal would attend.

---

23. Ms. R 1966/18; the text in BM, pp. 284-285.

24. R 1966/18, p. 3.

25. *Ibid.*, p. 4.

Another idea was also discussed as an expression of the same bond between the cardinal and his home town. In 1965 the cardinal—probably as a further response to the wish expressed by the town—had the authorities informed of his willingness to leave some personal objects, for example liturgical vestments, to the parish as personal mementos.[26] And he had then taken account of this when he made his will in July 1965. Later on, when the cardinal was in a Zurich hospital in the summer of 1965, he talked about the matter with the Riedböhringen parish priest, according to a letter I wrote on 11 February 1966.[27] In his reply of 7 April 1966, Paul Sumser explicitly spoke of "a small museum."[28] The various possible ways of implementing the idea were then discussed in July 1966.[29]

4. It was arranged that his parents' mortal remains would be moved on Sunday, 16 July. When the graves were opened the day before, their remains were found to be in a good state, for not only were there pieces of clothing, but the main bones were also well preserved. These were laid in two small boxes, which were placed in the chapel at the cemetery. On the Sunday morning there was a concelebrated mass, while the actual move took place in the afternoon.

In the course of the ceremony the cardinal was seated beside the tomb, and he spoke to the congregation in a homily obviously centered on his parents— although not in order to give some kind of panegyric, but rather to offer that family with its exquisite pastoral sense as an example of a true "domestic church," to use the expression of the Second Vatican Council in the Constitution on the Church.[30] When speaking of his parents, I remember that apart from a brief moment of emotion, he retained his serenity throughout. He began with the words: "This is now the third time that I have accompanied my parents to their grave." Having recalled the dates of the two deaths, he added: "In both cases I had the joy of being beside my parents in their last hours and accompanying them to their grave. And now I have been able to accompany them for the third time." He went on to explain how the decision for his own burial and the translation of his parents' remains had been reached, saying that he had also requested the necessary permission from the pope, who had agreed on condition "that it will be a long time until then." He then described what he had received from his parents, giving the various details we have already described in our section on his family background and his childhood. He also said how his parents had cooperated at the birth and development of his priestly vocation, and he recognized the generosity with which they had left him free to embrace the religious life, giving up any hope of the support they could have expected from him in their old age. He concluded by exhorting the congregation to pray to the

---

26. Cf. P 1965/126.
27. Cf. P 1965/135.
28. Cf. P 1966/346.
29. After the cardinal's death a combination of circumstances provided another possible solution, and the museum was set up in two of the classrooms in the Cardinal Bea School and opened on 31 May 1970; cf. BM, p. 383.
30. Cf. *LG*, 11. The text of the homily is found in BM, pp. 287-289.

Blessed Virgin and St. Joseph "that on the present occasion they may once again create a great and deep understanding of this task of parents in all your hearts, and make all your families true domestic churches in which the word of God is proclaimed and in which sacrifice and work are offered to the Lord God."[31]

The next day a mass was celebrated for his parents.

Advantage was also taken of his visit to Riedböhringen to decide on the type of inscription to be placed on the cardinal's tomb. A few months earlier he himself had composed the text and sent this to the parish priest, who had had designs made by an artist named A. Riedel from hometown, so that it was now a question of choosing one of these. The cardinal took part in the discussion very calmly as if they were discussing somebody else's burial place. Later on, the chosen design had to be altered again in order to make the cardinal's coat of arms stand out clearly enough.

Thus, two years after the cardinal had drawn up his will, all the necessary preparations had also been made for his burial—although nobody at that moment imagined that it would be needed only a little over a year later.

"I want to be freed of my body in order to be with Christ"

On 28 April 1968, Bishop J. Willebrands told me of the following episode. He had been received by the cardinal together with the Anglican Bishop Dr. J. Moorman, who had been an observer throughout the Council. In the course of the meeting Bea referred to "we poor old people," using an expression dear to Pius XI. Bishop Willebrands retorted quickly: "Your Eminence is neither poor nor old." However, the cardinal observed seriously, "My thoughts and inclinations are going in the direction of being freed from my body in order to be with Christ."[32]

1. When Bishop Willebrands told me this, although I noted it in my diary, I must confess that I neither took it very seriously, nor did I consider that it reflected the *true state of the cardinal's health*. The reader will recall the long bout of ill-health suffered in 1965; and the last period of the Council, full of work and tensions, had not only been decidedly unfavorable for convalescence, but had also considerably sapped the cardinal's strength. However, with the return to a somewhat calmer (although by no means gentle) work rhythm, he did recover his strength in the first half of 1966, so that in the second half of the year he allowed himself some journeys outside Italy. Apart from the visit to Frankfurt for the peace prize, there was a visit to Taizé,[33] and also attendance at the opening of the restored Rastatt High School, where he himself had received his high school diploma in 1900.[34]

---

31. BM, pp. 287-288.
32. Here the cardinal cited Phil. 1:23 in the Latin of the vulgate.
33. Cf. Arch. Ra 116.
34. Cf. Arch. Ra 129. Cf. also Ludwig-Wilhelm-Gymnasium Rastatt, 1715-1965, *Fundatio Rastadiensis 1742-1967. Festschrift* (commemorative issue on the occasion of the reopening

On the whole, however, he was very wary of undertaking journeys, and we find an example of this in connection with Pope Paul VI's visit to Turkey to see Patriarch Athenagoras. When the pope's journey was being planned, I received a telephone call one afternoon from the Substitute of the Secretariat of State, Archbishop Angelo Dell'Acqua. Since the cardinal was out at the time, the caller wondered if I would ask him if he would be able to accompany the pope. Now at that particular time, the cardinal was suffering from a health problem which was not serious but which gave him considerable discomfort in view of his age. I went to find him, and jokingly said: "Your Eminence, now I know why the Lord has sent you this problem." He looked at me in bewilderment, and I explained: "That way you have a valid excuse for not accompanying the pope on his next journey." The cardinal certainly did not like refusing the pope, but in view of his doctor's insistence on the need to husband his energies, and also the considerable exertions the journey would have entailed, it was not too difficult to persuade him that it was best to ask the pope to excuse him.

However, *an accident* in the first half of November 1967 did not pass off so easily. One afternoon I went to see him at 4:15 to invite him to come out for our regular little walk. I was worried to see that he had a number of band-aids on his head, as well as what appeared to be bruises, but when I asked what had happened, he told me with no apparent concern: "Oh, I had a little accident after my rest. I was lacing my shoes, with one foot up on a chair, but the chair slipped so that I fell on my side and hit my head on the floor." He led me into his bedroom, where there were some blood-stains on the floor. Not wanting to disturb anyone, he had medicated himself. And he was so sure that this was the end of the matter that we went out for our usual walk. However, after about a quarter of an hour, he felt tired and wanted to go back.

On our return I contacted his personal physician, who arrived very fast, worried mainly about the effects of the shock on his heart. The cardinal did in fact have a slight temperature, and more worryingly he also had a pain in his side, although an X-ray reassured us, for it showed nothing but a hair-line crack in his pelvis (!). The pain was caused simply by a bruised nerve. The cardinal suffered from this for a few weeks, especially when walking, but then recovered completely.[35]

2. In July 1968 he again spent some days in his beloved *Riedböhringen*, which provided an opportunity for another meeting with R. von Thadden-Trieglaff, founder and for many years president of the Evangelical Church Days.[36] The then Chancellor of West Germany, Dr. Kurt Kiesinger, also wanted to meet him,

---

of the renovated school building and official celebrations of the 250th anniversary of the school on 23-24 September 1967); also August Grosskinsky, "Das Ludwig-Wilhelm-Gymnasium Rastatt einst und jetzt," *Heimatbuch des Landkreises Rastatt*, VIII (1968), 55-74.

35. This accident prevented him from attending the plenary meetings of the Liturgical Council which were held in this period.

36. *Evangelischer Kirchentag* (Evangelical Church Day) was an institution parallel with *Katholikentag* (Catholics' Day); it had been instituted after the Second World War, while the Catholic one dated back to the previous century. On R. von Thadden-Trieglaff, cf. G. Gloede, *Oekumenische Profile*, II (Stuttgart, 1963), 223-235.

and after a private discussion and a visit to the church, the statesman also accepted an invitation to lunch with the parish priest Paul Sumser.[37]

3. The cardinal spent the second part of his vacation with the Teaching Sisters of the Holy Cross at Menzingen in Switzerland, and it was here, on Sunday 18 August, in the restricted circle and calm atmosphere of the convent, that he celebrated *the golden jubilee* (or fiftieth anniversary) *of his solemn religious profession.* In order to avoid being exposed to some indiscreet panegyric, he asked me to give the homily at mass. Taking the liturgical texts as my starting point, I gave a kind of meditation on how, through the many events of his long life, Divine Providence had guided and prepared him for the task that the church would entrust to him in the last ten years of his life.[38] He was happy with this.

The personal letter that Pope Paul VI had written him for his jubilee was also read out at this service. The pope wrote as follows: "Not wanting to let this occasion pass, we want our congratulations and assurance of our good will to reach you. We are happy to look back with you over that great space of time in which you have been allowed to serve God and the church 'in the name of the Lord Jesus,' as you wrote on your coat of arms when you were made a cardinal. This memorable anniversary will undoubtedly spur you to offer God your heartfelt thanks—almost with the joy of a spiritual harvester—and hurry on along the path of perfection, aware as you are of the wonderful gift represented by the divine vocation to the religious life."[39]

The text of the cardinal's cable of thanks was then read out: "During the celebration of mass on the occasion of the golden jubilee of my solemn religious vows, I and all those who took part in the celebration prayed for Your Holiness and all your intentions. Most especially, we entreated God that the new encyclical[40] may be received by the whole church with humble faith and great trust in God, and that Your Holiness' forthcoming journey to Bogotá may bring rich blessings to the church. I have the honor of expressing to Your Holiness our deep gratitude for the apostolic blessing imparted to myself and the whole community."[41]

4. When we were least expecting it, *ill-health* struck, with a first, painful warning. For some weeks the cardinal seemed very well. Immediately after the jubilee his personal physician had examined him and pronounced him to be in good health. On 20 and 21 August he went to Germany on the other side of Lake Constance to visit a convent of Dominican Sisters in Constance and see a benefactor. The weather was very beautiful, and it was quite warm. After his return, he said that he was feeling tired, but we paid little attention. His spiritual notes show that on *Sunday, 25 August,* he had made his monthly retreat. This

---

37. Cf. BM, pp. 289-291.
38. Text in Arch. Ra 134. The substance of this meditation was published on the thirtieth day after the cardinal's death in *OssRom* (16-17 December 1968); cf. also Schmidt, "Lebenslange Vorbereitung," pp. 9-32.
39. The original Latin is found in *OssRom* (18 August 1968), p. 2; *AAS*, LX (1968), 522.
40. He is referring to the encyclical *Humanae vitae* on birth control; cf. *AAS*, LX (1968), 481-503.
41. Text in Arch. Ra 134.

was fairly unusual, since he had made his yearly retreat only two weeks earlier,[42] and he normally made his monthly retreat either on the first Friday or the first Sunday of the month.

At ten o'clock in the evening he called me, complaining that breathing difficulties were keeping him awake. I at once called the sister on night duty, and she gave him some medication to help his heart, then called the doctor. The latter was absent, but arrived after half an hour, diagnosed a pulmonary edema, and gave the necessary treatment. He told me later: "If I'd come half an hour later I could have done nothing for him."

After a while the patient felt well enough to be moved to the closest hospital, which was in Zug. In order to keep his spirits up, I sat beside him in the ambulance, and then stayed on at the hospital until the initial examinations and tests were complete. The results were reassuring. He had a peaceful night, and the next morning I found him unusually calm, and indeed happy—although I did wonder whether he was not making an effort in order to spare us too much worry.

I thought that the presence of his personal physician, who had been looking after him for six years now, might prove important in the circumstances, so I made a number of attempts to reach him and have him come. However, after I had given him the first news, we were cut off, and I was unable to speak with him again. Unfortunately, somebody was not as discreet as could have been wished, and the news got out, so that a Catholic news agency even announced that the cardinal was dead.

After the first improvement, various complications arose. Despite all the attention and loving care of the staff, the patient suffered from depression, partly because he had excruciating fits of coughing when he ate, which not only stopped him from taking nourishment, but were very exhausting. However, this condition did gradually improve, and he left the hospital on 7 September.

We organized his journey back to Rome with every possible care, and arranged that his personal physician would accompany him. When the latter arrived in Switzerland and examined the cardinal for the first time, I watched him carefully, unsuccessfully trying to gauge his reaction. Later he told me: "I found him so much weaker that I was afraid I would not get him back to Rome alive." However, with every possible care and attention, the journey went better than he had feared, so that when we got home on 12 September and the doctor examined him, he was able to give a sigh of relief.

5. In the following days, we tried to combine the necessary convalescence with *the work that was awaiting his attention*. Apart from the correspondence that had accumulated during his absence, I see from my notes that he took an active hand in various questions concerning the Secretariat for Christian Unity: preparations for the plenary meetings planned for the beginning of November, which were to consider the second part of the Ecumenical Directory, a document on joint witness and proselytism, and one on *communicatio in sacris*. He was

---

42. Cf. *Spiritual Profile*, p. 189.

also concerned with relations with the Old Catholics in Switzerland and Germany, as well as with the lack of sufficient personnel in the secretariat's offices.

During these same days he also had various public engagements closely linked with his work in previous decades. On 25 September, on the twenty-fifth anniversary of Pope Pius XII's encyclical *Divino afflante Spiritu* on sacred scripture, he spoke on Vatican Radio "on the significance of the encyclical in the light of the past twenty-five years."[43]

On 28 September there was the annual meeting of *the Italian Biblical Association*, which was celebrating its twentieth anniversary, and which he had helped found. He spoke on the subject of "The Background to the Italian Biblical Association and Its Birth in 1948."[44] Realizing how weak he was, the organizers had suggested that someone else should read his address, but he wanted to do it himself. The following words from the address deserve special emphasis, for they can be seen as his legacy to the association: "My wishes on this twenty-fifth anniversary of the encyclical and the twentieth anniversary of the Italian Biblical Association are that your association should continue the biblical apostolate with solid and prudent work, with exemplary fidelity to the magisterium of the church, with energy and perseverance, following in the footsteps of the encyclical *Divino afflante Spiritu* and in the light of the Second Vatican Council, helping, as the Council says in the aforementioned constitution, 'the whole world to hear the summons to salvation, so that through hearing it may believe, through belief it may hope, through hope it may come to love.' "[45]

Lastly, on 1 October he recorded some brief *Memories of Pope Pius XII* for the Bavarian Radio, to mark the tenth anniversary of the death of Pius XII.[46] The significant central portion is as follows: "When dealing with him when he was pope, I repeatedly noticed how cautious he was when making decisions. He sought much advice, but preserved his independence and kept for himself the freedom to make the decision personally. In general, this was no easy matter for him. Yet once he had made his resolve, he held to it uncommonly firmly, and it would have been almost impossible to make him change his mind."[47]

On 29 September he made his last monthly retreat, the fruits of which he summarized on a sheet of paper as follows: "(1) Do the will of God, as actual circumstances require; (2) Personal prayer of the heart (holy mass, visits); (3) Serve all disinterestedly; (4) Try to bring joy to all."[48]

6. Despite this resumption of work, the cardinal was under no illusion about the state of his health. The head of the Zug Hospital had summarized his diagnosis as follows: "I should like to emphasize that the cardinal, who is over eighty years old, now has only very slight reserves as regards his heart and his circulation. The patient must therefore cut down his physical and intellectual

43. Cf. BM, pp. 265-268, esp. p. 267.
44. Cf. *Rivista Biblica Italiana*, XVI (1968), 354-360; also various material in Arch. Ra 135.
45. *Ibid.*, pp. 359-360, quoting *DV*, 1.
46. For the text, cf. BM, p. 268.
47. *Ibid.*
48. *Der Mensch Bea*, p. 284.

activity to the indispensable minimum." It is worth noting that for the first time the cardinal raised no objection to following the instructions based on this diagnosis.

At the beginning of October he therefore approached the Holy Father to ask to be *relieved of the burden of his commitments in the Roman curia.* With a view to an audience, he submitted a request to be relieved of the meetings of the Sacred Congregations for the Doctrine of the Faith and Catholic Education, and the Commission for the Revision of the Code of Canon law; so far as the Congregation of Rites (today's Congregation for the Causes of the Saints) was concerned, he would participate only in cases when he was the official representative for the cause. He saw no problem over continuing his involvement with the Commission for the Neo-Vulgate and the Biblical Commission, since these concerned strictly biblical matters. When he had been freed in this way from many commitments, he would be able to devote himself completely to the secretariat, while he would take part in meetings of the Sacred Congregations for the Oriental Churches and for Evangelization (he was an *ex officio* member of both) only when the interests of the secretariat were involved. The petition was accompanied by a certificate from his personal physician which included the following statement: "An immediate, broad and permanent reduction in the rhythm of his life and work is called for." It also said: "A considerable reduction in the number of meetings is particularly necessary, since these are especially tiring for the heart."

For a number of reasons—the Holy Father's commitments, and a deterioration in the cardinal's health—the audience did not take place, and thus the petition was never answered, so that he was left with all his duties—although ill-health in fact prevented him from performing them.

Alternating Fears and Hopes

Despite various types of treatment, the cardinal was suffering from great physical exhaustion, especially in his legs, so that he had difficulty walking, and he felt tired out by the time evening came. His doctor tried to build up his strength with transfusions, but the treatment exhausted him not only at the time, but also in the long run. Maybe in order to reassure me, the doctor told me: "This is a somewhat stormy period, but conditions will stabilize." However, in mid-October his patient was then struck down by a bout of influenza—what was known as "Asian flu"—which tended to affect the digestive tract in particular. This weakened him considerably, but above all there was the question of whether his heart would be able to bear the strain. The doctor spoke to me about the anointing of the sick, saying that "it would help the cardinal to hold out."[49]

1. The antibiotics had brought the patient's temperature down by the next

---

49. From now on I shall base my account mainly on a long circular letter that I sent out to the cardinal's friends and acquaintances a few days after his death: Arch. A 2/65.

morning, although the heart specialist found his heart very weak. "The situation is still critical," said the doctor, "especially if his temperature goes up again." And it did indeed start to rise again on the morning of the following day, 17 October. When the doctor again mentioned the anointing of the sick, I went to the cardinal and cautiously suggested it. His only reaction was to ask me: "Can you give me it?" "Of course, if Your Eminence wishes." Everything was soon prepared, and the only people present were his confessor, Father Giuseppe Danti, S.J., and Brother K. Burth, S.J., who served.[50]

To my great surprise, the cardinal was radiant with joy after the ceremony. I have often wondered about the precise reason for this, but I felt it would be indiscreet to ask him at the time. I think that the explanation may lie in the sheet of paper, yellowed with time and use, and entitled "Preparation for Death," which I found in his personal prayer-book after his death. It read as follows: "O Lord, my God, even now I take death obediently and willingly from your hand, with great pleasure and joy, however it comes to me, with all its anguish, suffering and pain." This prayer is basically a formula that was often, at least at that time, found in prayer-books, although the cardinal had added the words "with great pleasure and joy," which he had taken from the Exercises of St. Ignatius.[51] He had later added the following resolution on the same sheet of paper: "Every day, until death, make progress in virtue."[52] Later on I discovered in his spiritual notes that the use of this prayer went back to his 1950 retreat,[53] so that he had been using it for eighteen years, reciting it every day after mass. In his 1961 retreat notes he wrote: "Now that I am eighty-one, death can no longer be seen as a stranger, but as a dear guest whom I await daily." He had prepared himself in this way, and the Lord had truly given him the grace of accepting the prospect of death with joy.

I asked the cardinal if we should maybe not inform the Holy Father and the Father General of the Society of Jesus of the situation, since the cardinal was still of course a member of the order. He did not want the pope to be told, for he wanted to spare him any worry, and also avoid a visit that would have given rise to premature public concern. However, he did agree that the Father General should be informed, and the latter came to visit him that same evening, accompanied by one of the fathers; the cardinal was very pleased and grateful over this.[54]

---

50. BM, p. 294, states incorrectly that Father Danti administered the sacrament.
51. The expression is taken from "the second way of making a healthy and good choice," the fourth rule for which reads as follows: "Imagining and considering my state on the day of judgment, I shall think of how at that time I would like to have decided in the present matter, and the rule that I would then like to have followed I will now adopt, in order to have *great pleasure and joy* at that time" (*Spiritual Exercises*, 187).
52. In Latin: "Cotidie progredi in virtute usque ad mortem."
53. Cf. ms. of his 1950 retreat notes, 1950/III/1 (i.e. the first meditation for the third day).
54. We would note another small detail. The cardinal had been supposed to give evidence in the cause for the beatification of Pope John XXIII on the afternoon of this day, 17 October. I think that he had in fact done some careful homework for this, and that he would have testified with great joy. However, we had been forced to cancel the appointment two days earlier, and he thus

2. The following days were difficult ones for the cardinal's "family." The obvious course would have been to move him to a clinic, but it was feared that this would cause premature public alarm—which would have been particularly unfortunate, in view of the fact that the plenary meetings of the secretariat were to begin on 4 November. On the other hand, his home was not equipped for such a situation.

The patient's temperature was again normal on 18 October, and it stayed down for a few days. The doctor tried to persuade him to get up to attend my mass, but this proved too tiring. After two days, his temperature went up again, and then came down, staying normal for another four or five days. My notes say that on 24 October the doctor told me: "The strophanthin treatment has helped. His pulse is good. However, there is still that arterial blockage, and his heart could stop at any moment. We could simply find him dead one morning. That was a very bad attack he had in Menzingen, and it's a miracle he survived."

After 27 October his temperature went up again, and we realized that we had to take a decision. After some discussion we decided that he should be moved to a nursing home. The Villa Stuart Clinic of the Handmaids of the Holy Spirit on Monte Mario was chosen, because of its high, secluded position, which would guarantee the necessary privacy. When I suggested the move to the cardinal, he hesitated to start with, and since he had no temperature that day I told him that he would receive better treatment in a clinic and be able to recover better; I also said that I would be with him every day, both morning and afternoon. At this point he agreed.

However, we now had to inform the Holy Father, for we could not let him hear about the cardinal's hospitalization from other sources. Thoughtful as ever toward the pope, the cardinal insisted: "We must tell him the move was made to allow me to convalesce better"—which in fact reflected his condition at that moment and also the reasons I had myself used to persuade him to move. As soon as Paul VI received the letter he asked if a visit would be welcomed. Following instructions from the cardinal, we answered that he was obviously very grateful for the thought, but that he begged the Holy Father not to consider a visit for the moment, because we did not want to cause any public alarm. A few days later, the pope asked Bishop Johannes Willebrands the same question, and when the latter also mentioned the danger of alarming people, the pope answered that he understood this, but that he had asked again because he did not want to be discourteous.

Once he was settled in the clinic, the cardinal really did seem to feel much better, accepting all the various treatments prescribed—drip-feeds, etc.—with no problem. On 31 October the doctor reported that the cardinal was "decidedly improving . . . ; he will be able to return to work at a quieter pace, and also take regular walks." The doctor was so sure about this that he planned to spend a few days away from Rome for the Feast of All Saints.

3. During these days the cardinal still had one particular task on his mind: on

---

definitively lost the opportunity of giving his evidence, although he still had the satisfaction of having borne Pope John very personal and eloquent testimony in the book *Unity in Freedom* (cf. Chapter 4, "The Impact of Pope John XXIII," pp. 54-62).

4 November the plenary meetings of the secretariat were to begin, and he did not want them to start without *his usual inaugural speech*. After some discussion with him, we managed to draw up a draft, which was then corrected and redrafted. When the final, corrected version had been read to him, he approved it and heaved a sigh of relief.

In this speech he gave the members of the secretariat the following noteworthy instruction: "It is necessary to move forward prudently but resolutely, for this is the only way of influencing and guiding a movement. If you hang back and put on the brakes, you often run the risk of causing skids and wrong turns. Let us listen to St. John's exhortation which the Holy Father took up as the *leitmotiv* of the speech he made in St. Peter's when he received Patriarch Athenagoras: 'He who has ears, let him hear what the Spirit is saying to the churches,' what the Spirit is today asking of the church."[55] He then kept abreast of events in the meetings, asking Bishop J. Willebrands for news.[56]

The Rapid Sunset

During these days, we had the impression that he was getting steadily stronger. On the insistence of his doctor, he agreed to get up and walk in the corridor, and later on even ventured into the garden. If not before, he certainly attended my mass on 3 November, seated in a chair. After the mass he visited two sick friends: the German Ambassador to the Holy See, Dr. D. Sattler, and his confessor, Father Giuseppe Danti, S.J., who were both patients in the same clinic. All in all, there seemed to be good prospects for a recovery, although it was likely to be slow.

On the afternoon of Sunday, 3 November, however, the cardinal raised more objections than usual to taking the walk ordered by his doctor, and even became impatient. On his return, he apologized to me, and said, referring to the rule of the Jesuits, that in sickness one must obey one's doctor no less than one's superior: "I want to be clear about this: I do want to obey." A few hours later we realized the reason for his objections, for his temperature was up again. And this time it stayed up for quite a while, despite the antibiotics prescribed.

1. I think the reader might be interested to know *how the cardinal used to spend his days* at this time. In the morning, after he had been brought holy communion, the various treatments started, with transfusions, etc. During these he was attended by his personal physician, Professor A. Amadei, who would pass the time by reading, but would often have the great joy of talking with the cardinal on various topics, including certain episodes in his life.

I would personally spend most of the morning and afternoon in his room, and if he was not too tired I first of all would tell him the news from the church and the world. On other occasions, I would read to him from his book of media-

---

55. Ms. R 1968/17a, p. 3.
56. Cf. the inaugural speech to the 1969 plenary meeting, *IS*, I (1970), 4ff.

tions,[57] or sometimes something lighter that might be of interest to him. This reading sometimes used to prompt personal reflections. Thus on one occasion he said: "They say that in order to become a saint, you must have suffered a great deal; but I have suffered very little." Later on I found the same thought in his 1959 retreat notes: "And although I have not lacked crosses and difficulties—really they were very few, almost too few."[58]

2. During these days I myself had another serious worry related to *the legal aspect of the cardinal's will.* The reader will recall that the cardinal had drawn this up and signed it in July 1965. He had then placed it in the central drawer in his desk. However, it was not handwritten but typed, so that there was no juridical guarantee that it would be recognized. After consulting the governing authorities of Vatican City, it was agreed that it should be deposited with them as a "secret will." The authorities were so helpful that the whole operation was carried out on 5 November. After the cardinal had signed all eighteen sheets and also the document certifying the act by which it was deposited with the authorities, he smilingly asked the notary: "Can I die now?"

Once again the patient's condition improved. The temperature he had had since 3 November finally responded to the antibiotics, staying down for about three days from 10 November, and he was also in good spirits. On 12 November the doctors said that the patient was relatively well. That same day I sent his friends and acquaintances a circular letter on his condition, speaking of a "convalescence" that was "somewhat prolonged."

3. On the morning of Wednesday, 13 November, Pope Paul VI granted an audience to those taking part in the plenary meetings of the secretariat. He very thoughtfully started by recalling the cardinal president: "Our first thought when receiving you, our venerated brothers and dear sons, at the end of your work meetings, concerns the president of your secretariat, our dear and revered Cardinal Bea, who is kept away from us by a slight indisposition. If he is not able to be with us in person today, we are pleased to consider him present in spirit, and send him, in your name and ours, our greetings and heartfelt wishes in the Lord."[59]

4. On the afternoon of that same day the final crisis started. The cardinal had various problems, and I also saw that his doctor was worried. When I asked the latter his opinion, he answered: "I'll come to your mass tomorrow morning and we can talk then." After the mass he told me without beating about the bush: "There's no more hope. I've done all I could, but yesterday afternoon his heart started giving out, and I had to accept that we cannot fight against nature. It's a matter of about forty-eight hours." Later I learned other medical details of those

57. I think that it was the book by the Benedictine, Benedikt Bauer, on the saints of the day.

58. 1959/IV/4; cf. *Der Mensch Bea*, p. 52.

59. *AAS*, LX (1968), 794; we have cited the text as it appeared in *OssRom* (14 November 1968), which spoke of "a *slight* indisposition"; in the light of the information then in his possession (and partly of the situation itself), the pope could not speak otherwise. However, the text in the *AAS* has been modified, in the light of the crisis of the afternoon of 13 November and the successive events, to read "a *serious* indisposition."

last days, starting on 3 November. His blood tests showed that he was suffering from Pfeiffer's disease (mononucleosis), and in the last days they also discovered localized pneumonia—which was of course the reason for the fever. And then his heart had finally been unable to withstand the antibiotics.

After my talk with the doctor at 8:30 in the morning, I informed the Substitute of the Secretariat of State, Archbishop Giovanni Benelli, asking him to give the Holy Father the news. "Would a visit from the Holy Father be welcome now?" he asked. "Definitely—and it would be a great joy for the cardinal."

I hurried to the clinic. And at 9:45 Pope Paul VI was already at the cardinal's bedside. The patient was fully conscious, and the two men remained alone for a short while; the cardinal was visibly moved, thanking the pope for his kindness. The pope's private secretary, the cardinal's private secretary, and one or two others were then admitted to the room. After making sure that the cardinal had received the last rites, the pope imparted holy absolution again. Then all those present recited the Lord's Prayer and an Ave Maria together. Before leaving, the pope placed a farewell kiss on the patient's forehead and gave him his apostolic blessing. Those who met the pope as he was leaving the clinic found him visibly moved.[60]

A little later, the sick man received a visit from the Father General of the Society of Jesus, Pedro Arrupe, accompanied by some of his General Assistants. The patient was very touched and grateful for this attention.

The Secretary of the Secretariat for Christian Unity, Bishop Johannes Willebrands, also came, bringing the sick man the greetings, best wishes and assurance of prayers of all those attending the plenary meetings of the secretariat. When the meeting ended that morning, various cardinals and bishops came to visit the sick man and take their leave. The staff of the secretariat's offices also came, and although he was very tired the cardinal not only recognized everybody, but had a special word of greeting and thanks for a number of his visitors.

All the staff had met the evening before the cardinal's death in the Roman church of St. Susanna to celebrate the eucharist for the cardinal and his intentions.[61]

5. On the last two days, the Thursday and Friday, the dying man had great difficulty swallowing, so that all he could take was a few teaspoons of water. Apart from this he slept much of the time. I repeatedly asked him if he was in pain, and each time he told me he was not, but that he was simply very tired. His rising temperature meant that both nights his sleep was fitful. In view of the uncertainty of the situation, I spent these last two nights in the clinic, and I was therefore able to lend my assistance on the Friday morning when he was brought holy communion. He had such difficulty in swallowing that we gave him a very small piece in a teaspoon of water. This was his last communion.

Pope Paul VI repeatedly asked for news of the sick man. I was told that about an hour after visiting him, he was already asking those around him if there was

---

60. Cf. the photograph in BM, p. 295.
61. Cf. IS, 9 (1970), 5.

any news. On the Thursday evening he had his private secretary telephone to find out how the cardinal was. On the Friday morning the Prefect of the Apostolic Palace, Bishop Mario Nasalli Rocca di Corneliano, came to visit the cardinal, and told me: "The Holy Father keeps asking me for news, so I must be in a position to tell him." On the Friday afternoon the patient was much more lucid than on the previous afternoon. Touched by their kindness, he thanked three cardinals who visited him, and asked for their prayers: Secretary of State Giovanni Villot, the Dominican Cardinal M. Browne, and Cardinal Pietro Parente who had been Secretary of the Sacred Congregation for the Doctrine of the Faith. The patient recognized and greeted various other visitors with clear joy, including the secretary Bishop Johannes Willebrands and the deputy secretary Father J. Hamer, O.P. However, he was again very tired by about six in the evening.

In one of these last visits, the cardinal told Bishop J. Willebrands: "I'm infinitely grateful." These were his last words to the man who had shared his concerns and exertions in building up the secretariat from its beginning. Bishop J. Willebrands explains this brief phrase as follows: "By means of these words he opened his whole soul to God for what he had been able to give and receive as president of the secretariat."[62]

In order to help him breathe, the head of the clinic, Dr. Canizzaro, gave orders that he should be placed in an oxygen tent. "We can still try this. In any case, it will make the patient feel more comfortable," he told me. Personally I had the impression that the cardinal found it more uncomfortable, since it cut him off from those around him.

6. It was feared that the Friday night could be his last, and the mother superior of the religious community of the clinic decided to keep vigil by his bedside. The next morning she told me that at about midnight she had asked him how he was, and he had replied simply: "I am dying." However, he had said it with a particularly matter-of-fact tone, as if to say: "Just as you might expect. I'm dying."

At one in the morning the mother superior called me, thinking that the end was near. Brother Konrad Burth, S.J., the chaplain of the clinic, and the patient's personal physician were also present, as well as his confessor, Father Giuseppe Danti, S.J., who was ninety-three years old and was also a patient in the clinic, but was already able to get up. At about one o'clock we started the prayers for the dying. Since those present came from various countries, we prayed alternately in Latin and German, reciting some of the prayers twice.

During the prayers the mother superior held his left hand and I held the right, and every now and then I would suggest short ejaculatory prayers to him in a low voice. Then Brother Konrad Burth had the happy idea of taking the patient's personal prayer-book from the night-stand. The book contained various prayers written in the cardinal's own hand which he was accustomed to recite after communion, and we recited a number of these. Since he had prayed them so

---

62. This is taken from the inaugural speech to the 1969 plenary meeting, *IS*, 9 (1970), 5.

many times, it was enough for him to understand a word here and there, in order to remind him of the rest.

He said nothing more during the prayers, but several times as we prayed, and particularly when I suggested ejaculatory prayers in his ear, I had the impression that he was following the prayers inwardly. The mother superior also told me that every now and then she felt a very slight squeeze on her hand, a sign that the sick man was accompanying us in spirit.

His breathing gradually became slower and more difficult, and at about 2:30 it seemed to have stopped, although it began again for a few minutes, to finish at 2:37. His death was very serene, and it could be said that he went out like a candle that has burnt down.

* * *

I would close with some reflections and observations. In the first place, I would recall that in his retreat notes the cardinal repeatedly expressed the wish that death should call him "in the midst of work." In 1959 he wrote explicitly: "May it call me in the midst of work."[63] And we can say that this wish was basically granted, for although death did not surprise him at work, he *was* able to work fully well beyond his eighty-seventh birthday, until a bare month before his death.

I would also note certain coincidences—although without trying to read any mysterious connections into them. The cardinal died on the precise day that he had originally been going to receive his degree at Oxford University. It was also exactly nine years since the day on which Pope John had informed him that he was going to make him a cardinal. Lastly, his death came on a Saturday. I emphasize this detail because I have reason to believe that it was in line with his wishes, and indeed in his notebook *The Dates of My Life* he stresses the fact that he was born on a Saturday, and also the fact that his beloved mother died on a Saturday.[64] It is a fact that he had a deep devotion to the Blessed Virgin, and for a number of years he was a member of the commission of theologians who worked on the definition of the assumption of the Blessed Virgin Mary into heaven. In the Council he did all he could to make sure that in the field of mariology the Council acted in a way that would make it easier for separated Christians of the West to rediscover the role of Mary in the work of redemption. In the notes made during his yearly retreat in 1959, when meditating on death, he wrote with trust: "At that moment, Mary will benevolently turn her eyes on me."[65]

---

63. 1959/II/4; cf. *Der Mensch Bea*, p. 44.

64. Cf. *Dates*, pp. 1, 13. We shall see later that his funeral in his home town would take place on the Feast of the Presentation of the Virgin in the Temple.

65. 1959/II/4; cf. *Der Mensch Bea*, p. 45. This is a reference to the words of the well-known marian prayer, *Salve Regina*: ". . . illos tuos misericordes oculos ad nos converte."

CHAPTER 4

"WE MUST THINK OF CARDINAL BEA AS EVER-PRESENT"

One of our first concerns at this point was a practical one regarding the cardinal's person. We had been wondering for some time about how he should be dressed for burial. Church regulations prescribe the reddish violet pontifical vestments for cardinals, but these are worn over the cassock, which would mean choral dress for a cardinal. However, we were fairly certain that the cardinal would have preferred to be clad in his religious habit, especially since when he was still alive and used to go out, for example for a walk, he preferred to wear his Jesuit habit. This also had an underlying symbolism: he was still a member of the Society of Jesus, as he had asked to have written on his tombstone. We proceeded accordingly, and he therefore rests in the Jesuit cassock that was so dear to him.

While Brother Konrad Burth, S.J., and the sisters of the clinic were offering the cardinal this last service of veneration and charity, I personally took care of informing the press and radio through the good offices of a friend. I also telephoned the parish priest of Riedböhringen, who was therefore able to give the parish the sad news when the bell was rung at six that morning.[1]

After some hours of rest, I continued with my task of telling people the news. I telephoned the General Curia of the Society of Jesus, but the porter told me that they had already heard, and indeed that Father General Pedro Arrupe had already been to visit the body. Later on I learned that the general had heard the sad news over the radio while he was shaving at five in the morning. He immediately went to the clinic to pray beside the body, but was considerate enough not to want to disturb those of us who had been up for most of the night.

I then gave the news to Archbishop Herman Schäufele of Freiburg im Breisgau, the cardinal's original diocese. I learned later that Archbishop Schäufele was at that moment preparing for mass and was therefore able to offer it for the dead man's soul. At 6:45 I was able to inform the Substitute of the Secretariat of State, Monsignor Giovanni Benelli, asking him to tell the Holy Father, since I knew that the pope usually celebrated mass at seven o'clock.

The Vatican department responsible for providing flowers and the necessary furnishings for such occasions had also been told as early as possible, so that it was able to use the early hours of the morning to prepare everything needed for the funerary chamber. According to custom, an altar for the celebration of mass was set up in the same room. At 8:30 everything was ready; the body was moved, and the masses and visits began, with visitors being received by officials of the Secretariat for Christian Unity.[2]

A short time later, I received a telephone call from the Vatican asking me to

1. Cf. BM, p. 196.
2. A photograph of the cardinal on his catafalque is found in *ibid.*, p. 299.

698

offer any assistance necessary to the representatives of Vatican City who were to seal the cardinal's apartment at the Brazilian College. (This was a normal security measure so that in those critical days everything in the cardinal's apartment should remain intact until it could be sorted out under official supervision.) A representative of the Secretariat of State and another of the Tribunal of Vatican City were sent to take care of this matter. After telling me to take whatever I would need in the way of money and other things in the forthcoming days, they removed the cardinal's seals and stamps, and then placed seals on all the doors. Lastly, a report of the whole operation was drawn up and signed by all those present.

Knowing from experience how anxious for material the mass media are on such occasions, the office of the secretariat had previously produced a considerable number of copies of a detailed curriculum vitae of the cardinal in various languages, together with the expanded biography entitled *An Eminent Figure in the Council,* which had been written by a member of Vatican Radio for the cardinal's eighty-fifth birthday. Now everything was placed at the disposal of journalists in the Press Office of the Holy See.

After these and other things had been dealt with—particularly the question of transporting the body to Riedböhringen—the Sunday was fairly calm from this point of view, although a very large number of people came to pay their respects to the body. For the two nights that the body was on view in the clinic, some German sisters of the Congregation of the Missionary Handmaids of the Holy Spirit, which owns the clinic, generously volunteered to keep vigil.

It had been decided that the funeral should take place in St. Peter's on Tuesday, 19 November, at ten a.m., and the Riedböhringen service was therefore fixed for Thursday, 21 November, the Feast of the Presentation of the Blessed Virgin in the Temple. *The "rogito" ceremony*—the closing of the coffin and related matters—was held at five p.m. on Monday, 18 November, the day before the funeral in St. Peter's. As is usual, a very restricted number of people was present at this ceremony: Father General Pedro Arrupe of the Society of Jesus, with some members of the General Curia, some members of the Secretariat for Christian Unity, and a few other people who had been specifically invited. The central element of the ceremony was the reading of the *rogito,* an official document listing the details of the life and merits of the dead man.[3] The College of Apostolic Protonotaries is responsible for drawing up this document, and it usually entrusts the task to the member who acted as the cardinal's "master of papal ceremonies." His position means that this man is in fact considered a member of the cardinal's "family" and is therefore presumed to be familiar with the dead man and his work. In the present case the lot fell to Monsignor Angelo Di Pasquale. After the document had been read, it was signed by the most important people present, and was then sealed into a lead case and placed beside the body, rather like an identity document.

---

3. A *rogito* is a special type of public document received from a notary. Its specific form in the present case will now be explained.

According to normal custom, it was left to me to cover the dead man's face with a chalice-veil in the same color as the chasuble the cardinal was wearing. I had a spontaneous urge to kiss the cardinal's hand for the last time, and all those present then did likewise.

After the coffin had been hermetically sealed, we accompanied it to St. Peter's under a heavy rain. Here we found *a completely new type of arrangement*. Until then it had been usual—if not actually obligatory—for cardinals to be placed on a high catafalque surrounded by no less than one hundred candles. People in the offices of the secretariat had been worried over the negative impression that this could make on the numerous representatives of other churches and ecclesial communities who would be attending the funeral. We do not know the line of reasoning followed by the Chief Papal Master of Ceremonies, Bishop Annibale Bugnini. Perhaps he too was thinking of the representatives of other churches and ecclesial communities, or perhaps he simply wanted to take advantage of their presence to implement a reform that he felt was in any case necessary. Whatever the case, Bishop Bugnini told the then under-secretary of the secretariat, Monsignor Gianfrancesco Arrighi, that he personally took the initiative to reform things. However, he had some difficulty at the outset, and the usual black and gold decorations started going up over the altar and the seats. At this point Bishop Bugnini applied directly to Pope Paul VI's private secretary, Monsignor P. Macchi. The pope's personal intervention obviously carried the day, and the decorations that had already been put up were removed. Moreover, as a sign of humility and penitence, instead of being placed on a high catafalque, the coffin was placed *simply on the ground*, on a large Persian carpet; this also gave the feeling that the dead man was more directly in the midst of the community as it prayed. At the foot of the coffin was his cardinal's hat, and at its head, as sole ornament, was a large lit paschal candle, symbol of the resurrection.[4]

The funeral took place in the right transept, which is dedicated to Saints Processus and Martinian, and which is, incidentally, where the First Vatican Council was held. The requiem mass was celebrated by Bishop Johannes Willebrands, Secretary of the Secretariat for Christian Unity, with Monsignor Gianfranco Arrighi, Under-Secretary of the Secretariat, as assistant priest, Father B. Lachenschmidt, S.J., as deacon, and Monsignor E. Salzmann of the secretariat as sub-deacon. Twenty-five cardinals also attended the service. The absolution was imparted by the Camerlengo of the Holy Roman Church, Cardinal Aloisi Masella, in the name of Pope Paul VI.[5]

However, *the ecumenical character* of the funeral is the aspect that deserves particular emphasis, and in the circular letter I wrote a few days after the funeral I said: "Like his death itself, his funeral also constituted an ecumenical event of the first order. You will of course understand that in those days I was unable to

---

4. When I returned home after the service I found the first copies of the German translation of the volume *We Who Serve* (*Zum Dienen gerufen*). The original Italian (*Servire*) would not appear until later (cf. Biblio. 191).

5. Cf. BM, pp. 300-301, with a very lovely photograph.

read the papers or listen to the radio. However, everything I heard from various people, both at the time and afterward, on the reactions of the press, radio and television in the various countries shows that there was a vast and deep sympathy—I would say on a world-scale—over this death. It seems that on this occasion the world relived in summary form what the Lord had performed in the church in recent years in connection with the Council. This was also seen in the way in which the world of Christians of other churches and ecclesial communities was represented at the mass in St. Peter's."[6]

Let us give a list of the representatives of other churches and Christian communities.[7] From the Ecumenical Patriarchate of *Constantinople*: His Eminence Metropolitan Meliton of Chalcedonia, representing His Holiness Patriarch Athenagoras; His Excellency Chrysostom, Metropolitan in Austria; the Rev. Archimandrite Basilios, parish priest of the Greek Orthodox Church of Rome. From the Patriarchate of *Moscow*: His Excellency Bishop Vladimir of Zvenigorod, representing His Holiness Patriarch Alexis; the Reverend Archpriest Vladimir Roskov; the Reverend Archpriest Peter Raina. From *the Anglican Communion*: the Right Rev. Dr. Allison, Lord Bishop of Winchester, representing the Archbishops of Canterbury and York; the Rev. Canon John Findlow, Director of the Anglican Centre in Rome. From *the World Council of Churches*: the Rev. Dr. W.A. Visser 't Hooft, ex-Secretary of the Council. From the World Lutheran Federation: the Rev. Dr. Carl Mau, Deputy Secretary of the Federation. From the World Reformed Alliance: the Rev. Dr. Neri Giampiccoli, Moderator of the Waldensian Table. From the National Council of the Churches of Christ in the USA: Mr. Robert Dodds. Also present were the Rev. Pastor M. Sbaffi, President of the Protestant Federation of Italy; the Rev. Brother Roger Schütz, Prior of the Taizé Community; the rectors of the churches and Christian communities of Rome—the Rev. Canon Wanstall of the Church of England, the Rev. Canon Woodhaus of the Episcopalian Church, and the Rev. McLean of the Church of Scotland. The Secretary of the Israeli Embassy to Italy and the European Director of the American Jewish Committee, Dr. Z. Shuster, also attended.

In view of the presence of so many exalted representatives, the pope received them in audience at one o'clock that day in the *Sala del Tronetto*. In the name of all the representatives, Metropolitan Meliton of Chalcedonia, representing Patriarch Athenagoras, addressed a speech to the Holy Father expressing their respects and also a reverent thought for the holy memory of the deceased Cardinal Bea, whose lively and constant concern for the cause of Christian unity he remembered so well. The pope warmly thanked the metropolitan and all those present for their sympathy over the great loss of the Catholic Church.

---

6. Arch. A 2/65, p. 7.

7. Cf. *ibid.*, pp. 301-302, which is not, however, totally accurate, inasmuch as it includes the representatives of the World Lutheran Federation, the World Reformed Alliance, etc., in the list of representatives of the World Council of Churches.

Cardinal Bea Seen in the Light of the Messages of Condolence

I think that it would be useful at this point to take a look at the various expressions of condolence over the cardinal's death, some of them telegrams and some letters. The author of the present work published a broad selection in his book *Augustin Bea-Preis*.[8] Others are found in the archives. Since a rich selection of the most important of these messages has already been published, there is no need to repeat them here. On the other hand, it does seem a good idea to examine their content further from four points of view: (a) the enormous variety of people and organizations represented; then what they say about (b) the cardinal's work, (c) the man himself, and (d) the legacy he left.[9]

As an exception, we would start by citing the central part of two telegrams from Pope Paul VI. The first is addressed to the Archbishop of Munich, Julius Döpfner, President of the Episcopal Conference of West Germany, and places special stress on the ecumenical work of the president of the secretariat: "With Cardinal Bea the Holy Church loses an illustrious member of the Sacred College, and the Secretariat for Christian Unity its first and very outstanding President who, with deep doctrine, tireless activity and rare personal gifts, managed to provide efforts for Christian unity with orientations capable of assuring their fruitful development."[10]

In the second telegram, which is addressed to Father General Pedro Arrupe of the Society of Jesus, the pope speaks above all about the cardinal as a religious and as a faithful servant of the church, then goes on to say: "We raise our prayer to the Lord, beseeching the eternal prize for one who has earned it with deep doctrine, exemplary zeal and devout fidelity in the long-lasting service of the holy church, in a many-faceted activity that was always marked by humility and self-abnegation and that made him dear to our predecessors and ourselves, in particularly appreciative memory of the illuminated and diligent action that he performed as apostle and animator of the ecumenical cause. . . ."[11]

1. Moving on now to study the material under the four aspects mentioned, we shall first of all consider its *source*. A first group comes from the various churches, Christian World Communions and, more in general, *the ecumenical movement*:

---

8. Cf. *Augustin Bea-Preis*, pp. 119-157. We refer in our notes to the German edition, for the page numbers are different in the English edition, although the material is identical, with the various messages being given in their original languages in both.

9. Cf. Arch. Pa 28/278-324, where there are photocopies of the letters and telegrams cited in note 7, as well as others. For the former we shall give the reference from *Bea-Preis*, for the latter the file reference.

10. *Bea-Preis*, pp. 135-136 (but see our next note).

11. Reproduction in BM, p. 298; other declarations of Paul VI are found in *Bea-Preis*, pp. 136-137. Since I did not have the originals when I was editing the latter work, I was misled by *CC*, 1968/IV, 493, which combined the essential passages of the telegram to Cardinal Döpfner with that of the one to Father Arrupe. Examination of the reproduction in BM, p. 298, makes it easier to separate the two telegrams: the first part, up to the word *sviluppo* (= development), is from the telegram to Cardinal Döpfner, while the remainder, starting with the word *eleviamo* (= we raise), is from the telegram to Father Arrupe.

Ecumenical Patriarch Athenagoras I; Patriarch Alexis of the Russian Orthodox Church; the Archbishop of Canterbury and President of the Lambeth Conference, Dr. Michael M. Ramsey; the World Council of Churches; the World Methodist Council; the Conference of European Churches. This group also includes various national church bodies: the Evangelical Church in Germany, the National Council of Churches in USA; the British Council of Churches.[12]

Another large group is that of the various *Jewish organizations* throughout the world: the World Jewish Congress, the Anti-Defamation League of B'nai B'rith, the American Jewish Committee, the American Jewish Congress, the Council of the Synagogues of the USA. There were also various continental or national Jewish organizations: the South American Executive of the World Jewish Congress, the Representatives of French Jews, the Canadian Jewish Congress, the United Community of Italian Jews. We would also add the significant presence of some local Jewish communities in this group: that of Barcelona and that of Beirut.[13]

Simply in passing we would note some messages of condolence from *the civil authorities*: the President, Chancellor and Interior Minister of the Federal Republic of Germany,[14] the President of the French Republic,[15] and the Academy of Athens.[16] We would also add the condolences of the International League against Racism and Antisemitism.[17]

2. Let us take a brief look at how the cardinal's ecumenical work is seen in the various messages. He is referred to as an "inspired worker of unity,"[18] the "wise workman of the church."[19] "With cautious, patient work, step by step Cardinal Bea opened many doors to the new encounter between confessions in truth and charity."[20] "The work that the cardinal, of everlasting memory, performed by the side of Pope John XXIII and Pope Paul VI is of inestimable value."[21] "The cardinal was one of the greatest friends of Christian unity and his work in that cause will prove to be of immense importance in history."[22] "It is

---

12. Cf. *Bea-Preis*, p. 136. For the World Methodist Council, cf. Arch. Pa 28/58; for the World Baptist Alliance, cf. Arch. Pa 28/309. These messages are additional to the fact of the attendance of representatives at the funeral in St. Peter's, which also included those of the World Alliance of Reformed Churches and of the various Christian communities of Rome; cf. BM, p. 302, where these representatives are mistakenly mentioned under the heading "World Council of Churches."

13. Cf. *Bea-Preis*, pp. 145-153. For the Council of the Synagogues of the USA, cf. Arch. Pa 28/316; for B'nai B'rith, cf. also Arch. Pa 28/319.

14. The text in BM, p. 308; various others in Arch. Pa 28.

15. Cf. Arch. Pa 28/292.

16. Cf. *Bea-Preis*, pp. 150-151.

17. Cf. *ibid.*, p. 152.

18. Patriarch Athenagoras I, in *ibid.*, p. 137.

19. Russian Patriarch Alexis, in *ibid.*, p. 139.

20. The President of the Evangelical Church in Germany, Bishop Hermann Dietzfelbinger, in *ibid.*, p. 141.

21. Patriarch Athenagoras I, in *ibid.*, p. 138.

impossible to evaluate too highly the personal work of His Eminence and of the secretariat under his guidance. Especially in Europe, where we have suffered so long from ecclesiastical barriers which seemed insurmountable, the new spirit of fraternal understanding brought by and personified in His Eminence has opened new possibilities of contact of which few dared to dream only ten or fifteen years ago."[23] "He was the symbol of sincere Christian understanding. His name is bound up with the complete turn-about performed by Rome and its dynamic entry into the ecumenical movement."[24] The cardinal "during his lifetime became a symbol of the search for unity within Christendom."[25] His work in a specific but not very large field is also emphasized: "It is primarily due to him and his collaborators that a new era has been opened up in relations between the Bible Societies and the Catholic Church."[26]

Therefore "the death of Cardinal Bea is a loss not only for the Roman Catholic Church but for the whole of Christendom."[27] "The whole of Christendom is in mourning for him."[28] Indeed, "Cardinal Bea will be mourned by all men of good will, for essentially that is what he was, a man of good will and deep humanity."[29]

Then there is *his work concerning relations with the Jewish people.* "His historic contribution to the opening of fraternal communication with our people in the service of our common ideals will remain a source of guidance."[30] "His unique contribution to the opening of avenues of communication between our people and the Catholic Church is and will remain in the future a living monument to all fair-minded people throughout the world."[31]

Next comes his specific work concerning *the conciliar Declaration on the Relation of the Church to Non-Christian Religions*: "We render deep homage to the leading role that the lamented cardinal played at the last Council, battling heroically against prejudices, a struggle issuing in the historic declaration in favor of a rapprochement between Jews and Christians on the religious level"[32];

---

23. The Secretary General of the Conference of European Churches, Dr. Glen Garfield Williams, in *ibid.*, p. 141.
24. The review *Klirononia* of the Thessalonica Patriarchal Academy for Patristic Studies in the news section of its issue number 1 of 1969, cited in *Bea-Preis*, pp. 155-156. Cf. also Prof. Amilkar Alivisatos of the Academy of Athens, in *ibid.*, p. 151.
25. Dr. E. Carson Blake, Secretary General of the World Council of Churches, in *ibid.*, p. 139.
26. Dr. Olivier Béguin, Secretary General of the United Bible Societies; Arch. Pa 28/283.
27. Dr. E. Schlink in the name of the Evangelical Church in Germany; cf. BM, p. 320. Through a misunderstanding this message was not read out at the funeral in Riedböhringen. Cf. also *Bea-Preis*, pp. 144-145; similarly, Prof. Panayotis Bratsiotis of the Academy of Athens, in *ibid.*, p. 152.
28. These are the words of Dr. Fred P. Corson in the name of the World Methodist Council; Arch. Pa 28/50.
29. The Anti-Defamation League of B'nai B'rith, in *Bea-Preis*, p. 153.
30. Dr. Nahum Goldmann in the name of the World Jewish Congress, in *ibid.*, p. 145. As concerns the historic role played by Bea, cf. also Pierre Bloch, President of the International League against Racism and Antisemitism, in *ibid.*, p. 152. As concerns improved relations with the Jewish people, cf. also the telegram of the American Jewish Congress, in *ibid.*, p. 145.
31. Telegram of Monroe Abbey, President of the Canadian Jewish Congress, in *ibid.*, p. 149.
32. Dr. Joseph Attie, President of the Jewish Community of Beirut, in *ibid.*, p. 149.

Cardinal Bea "was one of the main architects of the important pronouncements that were issued by the Vatican Council"[33]; "Cardinal Bea . . . [will] be remembered by Jewish history as the architect of the Declaration on Non-Christian Religions passed by the Vatican Council in 1965. . . . [This historic work] has provided the foundation for an unprecedented improvement in relations between Catholics and Jews throughout the world."[34]

However, *the perspective repeatedly becomes broader.* Thus the World Baptist Alliance sees in Bea "the sincere defender of religious freedom, human rights and freedom of conscience."[35] The cause of the Jewish people is also seen in a broader perspective, with Bea being described as "the champion of religious freedom and the brotherhood of men of every faith who seek to re-establish the historical truth against the iniquitous accusations launched against the Jews."[36] Similarly, the leaders of the Jewish community of Barcelona consider Bea "an eminent champion of the new relations between the Church and Jews, which is a model of so many other fraternal affections of our times."[37] "His courageous and devoted dedication to the cause of universal brotherhood, and more particularly to the improvement of Catholic-Jewish relations has won for him a lasting place in the affections and memory of the Jewish people."[38]

If we broaden our perspective still further, the cardinal is seen as "the indefatigable defender of social peace and justice, and promoter of the Declaration on Non-Christian Religions, who did so much in favor of a rapprochement between the different spiritual families."[39] And we find an even more explicit statement: "His leadership of the ecumenical movement opened doors that had been shut for centuries. Men of differing religions have as a result been enabled to reason with each other, to understand each other and to respect and appreciate each other."[40] The National Council of Churches in the USA thanks the Lord for a variety of qualities, including "his historic contribution to understanding and reconciliation among all mankind."[41]

3. His work allowed an idea of what lay behind it, in other words of Bea *the man and the Christian*: "We personally had the good fortune of maintaining relations with Cardinal Bea and of deeply respecting the clarity and sincerity of his thinking, his deeply Christian simplicity and his courage," says Patriarch Athenagoras I.[42] The element of *courage* is also described by Dr. Eugene Carson Blake, Secretary General of the World Council of Churches: "He was a man of

---

33. Telegram of the American Jewish Congress, in *ibid.*, p. 145.
34. The American Jewish Committee, in *ibid.*, p. 146.
35. The Secretary General of the World Baptist Alliance, Josef Nordenhaug; Arch. Pa 28/309.
36. Mr. Piperno, President of the United Community of Italian Jews, in *Bea-Preis*, p. 148.
37. In *ibid.*, p. 149.
38. Council of the Synagogues of the USA; Arch. Pa 28/316.
39. Telegram of Dr. Modiano, President of the Representative Council of French Jews, in *Bea-Preis*, p. 148.
40. Telegram of the Anti Defamation League, New York, in *ibid.*, p. 153.
41. In *ibid.*, p. 141.
42. In *ibid.*, p. 138.

great courage and always prepared to take responsible risks, at times even going beyond the law of prudence, to further the search for unity."[43]

The same author adds: "In Cardinal Bea's life the power of *hope* always found new ways to overcome seemingly insurmountable obstacles to a fuller expression of the essential unity of the whole people of God."[44] Others describe the cardinal as *a spiritual figure* as follows: "Intellectually vigorous despite his advanced age, modest despite his exalted office, his saintliness and humaneness were the indelible hallmarks of his character."[45] The well-known Jewish scholar, Professor Abraham J. Heschel, for his part writes: "The rare combination of wisdom, learning, and saintliness of this very great man have made him one of the most outstanding sources of spiritual comfort in an age of so much darkness. He taught his contemporaries that we must understand the doctrines of faith in the context of love."[46]

The well-known Protestant exegete, Professor Oscar Cullmann, expands on the quality of *wisdom* as follows: "A great wisdom acquired in contact with the Bible. He knew how to preserve a sense of reality, holding back those impatient people who wanted to act too fast, ignoring the differences in view that do exist. Such differences will be resolved only if Christians concentrate on the foundations of faith."[47]

Dr. E. Carson Blake stresses another element: "But more than his knowledge, it was his *friendship*—because friendship is an art—that led him to follow one path rather than another, and to find the way of good relations."[48] The Lutheran observer at the Council, Dr. E. Schlink, states: "Yet anybody who turned to him with regard to a question of the unity of the separated churches of Christ was struck even more deeply by Bea the man, with his loving and humble availability to others and his intellectual alertness, than by the actual conciliar decisions."[49] Dr. Friedrich Georgi, President of the Association of German Publishers, which had awarded the cardinal its Peace Prize in 1966, writes: "The wisdom of age and the kindness of heart—combined with his firm wish to work for the unity of the Christian churches—impressed me very deeply and filled me with veneration and respect for this great personality."[50] The quality of goodness is also stressed by Professor Oscar Cullmann: "Then a great goodness. The trust that his presence inspired was able to dissipate the atmosphere of distrust that had predominated in relations between the various confessions in the past."[51] And again: "God had given him a heart and spirit large enough to include all of us," writes the President of the World Methodist Council, Fred P. Corson.[52]

43. In *ibid.*, p. 139.
44. In *ibid.*, pp. 139-140.
45. The American Jewish Committee, in *ibid.*, p. 146.
46. In *ibid.*, p. 148.
47. In *ibid.*, p. 162.
48. In *ibid.*, p. 140.
49. In *ibid.*, p. 145.
50. Arch. Pa 28/1-3.
51. In *Bea-Preis*, p. 163.
52. Arch. Pa 28/58.

Various messages have already mentioned the quality of *holiness*, and this is described in greater detail as follows: "Cardinal Bea . . . possessed the energy and spirit of sacrifice of an extended youth. His knowledge, his holiness of life, his obedience, his understanding, made him an excellent instrument in the hands of the popes in their activity in bringing Christians closer together."[53]

Dr. E. Carson Blake stresses the cardinal's *fidelity to Christ and the church*: "He was capable of doing what he did because he was faithful to Jesus Christ and to his church. When I say 'faithful to his church,' I mean that even if he was one of the progressive theologians of the curia, he was always faithful to the Roman church; and his fidelity was not restricted but was as great as his love for Christ."[54]

4. The work and example of his life are in themselves a precious legacy to the future. Various messages of condolence, however, speak *more explicitly of what the cardinal left to the future*. First of all there is a precious memory: "His personality also made an unforgettable impression on innumerable Evangelical Christians, who remember him with love and veneration," writes Dr. Edmund Schlink, observer-delegate at the Council for the Evangelical Church in Germany.[55] "Let me state that apart from Pope John XXIII no other Catholic personality of our time has enjoyed such unreserved veneration and gratitude within Protestantism as the deceased Cardinal Bea," writes the retired Evangelical Bishop of Vienna, Dr. G. May.[56]

Similar expressions are also used by various Jews. The cardinal's memory "will remain honored and blessed amongst the Jewish people all over the world."[57] In several of these texts the perspective broadens from the specific context of the Jewish people to all men of good will: "His name will be cherished by the Jewish people as well as by all people of good will as an inspired architect of interreligious understanding and will remain a blessing forever," writes Professor Abraham J. Heschel of the Jewish Theological Seminary of America.[58] "Mutual understanding and mutual respect will always be associated with his name."[59]

We can understand the words of Patriarch Athenagoras in the same light: "We consider his death a personal loss, but we also consider the work that he has left us as *our own possession*."[60] "To all men of every religious creed he was a symbol of the true ecumenical spirit and set an example for all of us."[61] In this

---

53. Maximos V Hakim, Melchite Patriarch of Antioch, in *Bea-Preis*, p. 138. In the specific tradition of Judaism, the idea of the cardinal's holiness is also expressed by recognizing Bea as "one of the truly righteous men among the peoples of the earth" (the American Jewish Committee, in *ibid.*, p. 147), and as "one of those righteous men that the nations give to us" (*Tribune Juive* of Strasburg, in *ibid.*, p. 164).
54. In *ibid.*, p. 140.
55. In *ibid.*, p. 145; cf. BM, p. 320.
56. In *Bea-Preis*, p. 142.
57. American Jewish Congress, in *ibid.*, p. 146.
58. In *ibid.*, p. 148.
59. Hon. Monroe Abbey, Q.C., President of the Canadian Jewish Congress, in *ibid.*, p. 149.
60. In *ibid.*, p. 138.
61. Telegram of the American Jewish Congress, in *ibid.*, pp. 145-146.

spirit the President of the World Methodist Council, Fred P. Corson, makes the very practical suggestion of creating a "Cardinal Bea Memorial Lecture," which would keep the memory of his life alive, as well as his leadership in the ecumenical movement.[62] Professor Oscar Cullmann writes: "We must meditate on the significance of the cardinal's work in order to continue his activity."[63]

The idea of drawing *inspiration* from the cardinal's work is found in a large number of these texts. The cardinal "nurtured a spontaneous charismatic love for Orthodoxy, and his example will inspire generations of servants of reconciliation."[64] Thus also the National Council of Churches in the USA writes: "We shall always be inspired by his spirit."[65] And we find similar expressions in messages from various Jewish quarters: "His historic contribution . . . will remain a source of guidance."[66] The American Jewish Committee expresses the following hope: "May his memory be an inspiration for all future generations who seek to build a more humane world based on mutual trust and understanding."[67]

Journey to the Last Resting Place

After the funeral in St. Peter's the coffin had to be taken back to the cardinal's own home town in southern Germany. Some people thought that it should be taken by air, and in fact Dr. Franz H. Röttsches of the Information Office of the Federal Republic of Germany, whom I had known since the years of the Council, told me later that his office had expected us to ask for the use of an aircraft, a request that would obviously have been granted. However, such an idea did not cross our minds. A journey by road was more modest, and thus more fitting for a cardinal who was a member of a religious order; moreover, the various stops along the way gave it a much more human touch.

1. A little after the end of the solemn funeral in St. Peter's, the cardinal's coffin left for Germany, escorted throughout the journey by the members of the cardinal's "family," together with Monsignor Gianfrancesco Arrighi of the Secretariat for Christian Unity. Various members of the General Curia of the Society of Jesus, representatives of the West German Embassy to the Holy See, members of the secretariat and members of the Pontifical Brazilian College also accompanied it to the outskirts of Rome. We were no longer bothered by the rain that had gone on for most of the morning, and there was even some weak sunshine.

---

62. Cf. Arch. Pa 28/58.
63. In *Bea-Preis*, p. 162.
64. The review *Klironomia* of Thessalonica, in *ibid.*, p. 156. In its obituary, the review *Pandainos* of the Greek Orthodox Patriarchate of Alexandria also recalls a detail of Cardinal Bea's visit to Constantinople in 1965, "which we Orthodox have not forgotten": the fact that on that occasion "he asked to visit Saint Sofia, the place where the holy altar had previously stood on which the misled and violent Cardinal Humbert had placed his unrighteous hands, leaving the anathema of 1054. When they showed him this place, he knelt and prayed with tears in his eyes"; in *ibid.*, p. 156.
65. Edwin Espy, in the name of the National Council of Churches in USA, in *ibid.*, p. 141.
66. Nahum Goldmann, President of the World Jewish Congress, in *ibid.*, p. 145.
67. In *ibid.*, p. 147.

At 8:15 that evening the cortège reached the Aloisianum, the Jesuit house of studies at Gallarate, near Milan, where it was to stop for the night. As soon as the coffin had been placed in the adjoining church, the local archpriest started a mass, which was concelebrated with another six priests and attended by Cardinal Giovanni Colombo, Archbishop of Milan. At nine o'clock Cardinal Michele Pellegrino, Archbishop of Turin, concelebrated another mass, also giving a short homily.

We left for Switzerland at 8:45 the next morning, after a mass concelebrated by ten priests. The sky was completely clear, and since it had snowed the day before, the pines clad in their fresh blanket of white sparkled like so many Christmas trees, creating a festive atmosphere. Mount Rosa and the whole chain of snow-covered mountains stood out very clearly. The weather was clear and sunny almost all the way across Switzerland, and we therefore had no difficulty on the road.

We stopped for ten minutes at the mother house of the Sisters of the Holy Cross of Ingenbohl. Since the cardinal had been official representative in the cause for beatification of Mother Theresia Scherer, foundress of this congregation, and also of the Servant of God Ulrike Nisch of the same congregation, it was a special joy for the sisters to be able to pay him their last respects and speed him on his way with their prayers.

We made a longer stop at the mother house of the Teaching Sisters of the Holy Cross of Menzingen, where the cardinal had spent his summer vacations in the latter years of his life. The stop lasted about one and a half hours, with the sisters praying silently around the dead cardinal.

At seven in the evening we reached the German border, where the cardinal's relatives were waiting for him, just as they used to do when he visited his home town during his lifetime. Since we had a little time to spare, the customs officers gave us the use of a room where I was able to give his relatives a little first-hand information on the cardinal's last days and death, partly in order to bring them some comfort. When they had learned about the last crisis in his health, some of them had in fact wanted to come to Rome to see him one last time and take their leave of him, but things had happened too fast for them to do so.

2. Riedböhringen is close to the border, and a little later the procession therefore entered the town with a police escort. After the coffin had been removed from the hearse outside the church, *the mayor, Mr. M. Buri*, made a short speech expressing the town's respects.[68] He stressed the fact that the cardinal's family had been in the town for many generations and could be traced back to the first half of the eighteenth century. Although he was a great churchman and had visited so many countries, he had always remained attached to the town where he had been born, and had felt increasingly drawn to it in his last years. Although he was a man of learning and diplomacy (in the best sense of the word), he had always retained a genuine simplicity in contacts with

---

68. For the events in Riedböhringen we follow BM, pp. 303-320, which also gives the texts of all the speeches and homilies, as well as some beautiful illustrations. For the mayor's speech, cf. *ibid.*, pp. 303-304

everybody in the town. "His tongue is silent now, but his life still speaks to us." As a final legacy he had left his mortal remains to his fellow townsmen. And when the latter went back to their homes, they would assume the sacred commitment of never forgetting him, so that even a long time later they would tell their children and their children's children about their cardinal.

A prayer and Bible-reading service was then held in the parish church, with a homily by *the parish priest Father Paul Sumser*.[69] The preacher took the miraculous catch of fish (Luke 5:1-11) as his text, describing the cardinal's life and the lesson that Christians could draw from it in the light of this gospel episode. "The fishing is over, the boat has returned to its original moorings," but the great task of fishing—the mission entrusted by the Lord—must continue. Father Sumser said that the one who had now returned and around whom they were gathered was still the great fisher of men, and that what he had begun in the night, following the Lord's command, in an apparently hopeless situation, had become irreversible. The path of Christians toward their own unity was continuing irresistibly. The fact that this had happened in our times, after centuries of separation, was a miracle in no way less than that of the miraculous catch of fish. And our cardinal had placed himself at the service of this miracle, with modesty and faith, with simplicity and courage, just as the fishermen on Lake Gennesaret had done in their age.

And now the cardinal would rest among them until the final day of judgment, close to the altar on which they celebrated the sacrifice of the Lord and proclaimed his death until his coming in glory. The tomb that they had prepared for him should not be seen as recalling the past with sadness, but as a place of contact between his life and theirs.

Like Pope John, the cardinal had not left a completed work to posterity, but had broken ground for them, leaving them a start. "And now, dear Cardinal, you are handing over the full net to us. Help us not to tire when the night seems endless in our lives. Tell us it is worth continuing the long struggle for peace and unity. Walk with us and the coming generations of your home parish toward the day when the tombs will open and we shall be united and blessed for ever."

After this and throughout the night the fire brigade and the cardinal's relatives formed a guard of honor to keep vigil around the bier. The following day too, during the periods when there were no services being celebrated, his relatives took turns keeping vigil until the morning of Friday, 22 November, when the niche was finally closed. Some people spent the whole night praying beside the coffin, together with the guard of honor.

On the morning of Thursday, 21 November, I concelebrated mass at 7:30 with Monsignor Arrighi. At 8:30 Bishop Willebrands and Father Stransky of the secretariat concelebrated. Throughout this time, many members of the faithful came to pay their respects at the coffin and pray, especially since they knew that the large number of important personages attending the service in the

69. Cf. *ibid.*, pp. 304-309.

afternoon would mean that there would be very little space left for *them* in the church, since it was not very large.

3. In the afternoon *the solemn pontifical funeral* was celebrated by the Archbishop of Freiburg im Breisgau, Dr. H. Schäufele, with the assistance of the parish priest, Rev. P. Sumser, and one of the cardinal's relatives, the Dominican Father Odilo Kaiser. The church was decked out with red carnations, a gift of Prince Joachim zu Fürstenberg.

Many important figures attended the funeral.[70] On the Catholic side, there were the Apostolic Nuncio in West Germany, His Excellency Archbishop Corrado Bafile; Cardinal Julius Döpfner, Archbishop of Munich and President of the German Episcopal Conference; Cardinal Dr. Lorenz Jaeger, Archbishop of Paderborn and a member of the secretariat from the very start; and various other archbishops, bishops and abbots from Germany, France and Switzerland. There were also representatives of the Lender Institute of Sasbach, the city of Rastatt and Rastatt High School.

So far as other Christians were concerned, the service was attended by Hans Katz, Chief Counsellor, representing the Lutheran Bishop of Karlsruhe; Professor Dr. W. Küppers in the name of the Old-Catholic Church of West Germany; and Professor Dr. E. Schlink, in the name of the Evangelical Church in Germany. And Rabbi Levinson of Heidelberg was also present for the Jews.

So far as the civil authorities were concerned, there were the Federal Minister Krone, representing the Chancellor Dr. Kurt Kiesinger; the President of the Regional Parliament of Baden-Württenberg, C. Wurz; and the Finance Minister, R. Gleichhauf, in the name of the government of the same region.

(a) *The very rich homily* on the gospel was given by Bishop J. Willebrands,[71] and we shall quote a few short extracts concerning the cardinal's personality and work, and also the heritage he left us. When Pope John XXIII created him cardinal, Augustin Bea told Willebrands: "If I am pleased by this decision, it is particularly because I want to use the new authority and responsibility conferred on me by this dignity to work for the great cause of the reunification of Christians." He had received a remarkable training for this work, and from that moment onward all the experience and wisdom acquired during a long life became visible and operative in the pursuit of this great task. After Dr. W.A. Visser 't Hooft met the cardinal in Milan in 1960, he told Willebrands: "This man has not only read and studied the Old Testament, he has truly absorbed the wisdom of the men of the Old Testament."

As the head of the secretariat, the cardinal provided an essential contribution in pressing for the Council to define the Catholic principles of ecumenism. Although he left us the gift of the unity of the church, it is still our task to bring it about.[72] He also worked for a Christian understanding of the Jewish people

---

70. Cf. *ibid.*, p. 309.

71. Cf. *ibid.*, pp. 310-314; also *Bea-Preis*, pp. 164-169.

72. The original German of this difficult phrase is as follows: "Er hat die Einheit der Kirche als Gabe hinterlassen, eine Gabe, die auch immer unsere Aufgabe bleibt." There is thus a pun on the two words *Gabe* (= gift) and *Aufgabe* (= assignment).

and of the task that it had performed in the history of salvation, as the Bible bears witness.

His work in the Council was not confined to leading the secretariat: "He took upon himself the task of bringing out the ecumenical dimension of all the conciliar texts and resolutions, and explaining them on the basis of the present situation and the future of the church. We can say that in this connection his voice was the conscience of the Council."

Winding up his homily, the preacher wondered about the "spiritual motivations" that guided the cardinal in his work. Referring to the paschal candle which had been the only ornament by the dead man's coffin during the funeral in St. Peter's, the preacher explained: "The paschal candle is the sign of Christian hope. Cardinal Bea was not an optimist in the superficial sense that this word has in current usage. He preferred to say that he was a realist. But many people would certainly see his realism as an optimism with its basis in Christ. His hope was based on the promises of Christ given to the whole of humanity. . . . He had the conviction of faith that the gifts of God, the gifts of unity and of peace, are already operative amongst us through the Spirit of God. 'The kingdom of God is in your midst.' The kingdom of God is within us. The earthly form of the kingdom of God is rendered visible in a special way in the church of Christ; even so, it is in a mysterious way already operative throughout the world." Indeed, the cardinal's influence extended beyond the limits of the church, for "he has given the whole of humanity a new courage and a new faith in order to recover its own peace."

(b) *After the mass* various other people spoke, and we shall try to give an idea of the most salient observations on the cardinal's personality and work. *Archbishop Dr. H. Schäufele* summed up his views on the cardinal in the succinct phrase: "Fidelity to origins and courage to launch out broadly."[73] After describing how these qualities were seen in various periods of the dead man's life, the speaker described his ecumenical contribution to the Council: "Cardinal Bea made a decisive contribution to the present face of the church as modeled by the Council. He represents the ecumenical openness and impetus which have awakened a kind of new Pentecost in the Catholic Church after years, indeed decades, of distance. The legacy the cardinal left us can be expressed as follows: 'Fidelity to the origins and ecumenism as a task.' The spirit he has awakened must be preserved: the spirit which gives us life and makes us free, the spirit which renews, the spirit which believes, hopes and loves, the spirit of Pentecost."

Cardinal Dr. Lorenz Jaeger, Archbishop of Paderborn, then spoke.[74] His testimony is particularly telling, because his contacts with Augustin Bea went back to long before the Council, which meant that he was in a position to declare: "His thinking and work had assumed ecumenical dimensions long before the ecumenical opening in the church took place." And he went on as follows: "We

---

73. The German phrase is not easy to translate: "Oeffnung zur Weite und Treue zum Ursprung" or in other contexts: "Treue zum Ursprung und Mut zur Weite."

74. Cf. BM, pp. 316-318.

must thank Bea's caution, intelligence and perseverance that the great church assembly of the Second Vatican Council came to support the cause of ecumenism. . . . This personality that won people over with the light it radiated, its readiness to understand and its selfless service, succeeded in opening doors that were formerly tightly shut, and began conversations between confessions on a world level."

The funeral orations made frequent mention of ripe fruit that is harvested into the storehouse, and certainly a life as full as the cardinal's is a ripe fruit: "However, here I should like to compare the cardinal's life and work to *excellent seed* sown in God's field. This seed will certainly grow and bear fruit for a very long time yet. . . . Although hurdles, resistance and disappointment were not lacking on his path, no difficulty was capable of discouraging him or making him waver. He was certain of the will of God, and thus he followed his path, firm and determined as he moved toward his goal, in the unshakable trust that God in his mercy will grant unity to the church at the time that his wisdom has decided. We are all called to continue his work in the same spirit and in the same unshakable trust. This hope will not be confounded."

(c) Various representatives of the civil authorities then spoke. *The President of the Regional Parliament of Baden-Württemberg, C. Wurz,*[75] stated: "If in these days and at this hour the entire Christian world takes its leave of Augustin Cardinal Bea, its mourning for his death is outshone by the radiation of his life's work, which has given new hope to countless people in a world of contradiction, disorder and division. . . . Recognizing the needs, hopes and longings of an era is one of the talents of a great man. Thus Cardinal Bea courageously and unhesitatingly opened long-closed gates before which people were waiting— people who also had confidence in the good news. Within the organization of his church and in the service of the supreme pontiff, he himself built bridges so that he could go across and talk to others. In doing so, he did not make use of human instruments of power, nor did he seek them. . . . His work has no need of our praise, but of the collaboration of all of us, so that it may live on. He has no need of our thanks, but we need him as a model in this sadly disordered and disturbed world."

The Finance Minister, R. Gleichhauf, spoke in the name of the Regional Government of Baden-Württemberg,[76] stressing above all what the dead man had meant for contemporary society: "The deep longing of peoples in this time of conflict and tension is directed more than ever toward unity and comprehension. The last and certainly the most significant portion of the life of this great man was dedicated to this major goal of a humankind that has become uncertain and full of anxiety. . . . He sought and also—we all hope—smoothed the way to the unity of Christians, not with human instruments of power or with overbearing argumentation, but with understanding love and in brotherly dialogue. In his last work he once again made a heartfelt appeal to all of us to

---

75. Cf. *ibid.*, pp. 318-319.
76. Cf. *ibid.*, pp. 319-320.

concentrate more strongly on the true sources of our Christian faith, and to use this as a basis for contributing to the solution of the many practical tasks that call for the joint activity of Christians in our world. The life of our great fellow countryman Cardinal Bea is over. His work must be continued. And we are all called to this."

(d) The various funeral orations[77] were followed by absolution at the tomb, which was imparted by the Archbishop of Munich, Cardinal Julius Döpfner, President of the Episcopal Conference of West Germany.

The coffin was then placed in the niche that had been ready since the previous year, and at eleven o'clock the following day, 22 November, the niche was walled up in the presence of a restricted number of people. The wall was temporarily covered with the slab that had covered the niche while it was still empty, and the shield with the cardinal's coat of arms—which had until then hung over the door of the parish church—was fixed to this slab.

A few weeks later, the great stone slab was put in place, bearing *the inscription* that the cardinal himself had chosen.[78] Beside the cardinal's coat of arms, first come the words of the Letter to the Colossians from which the cardinal's motto was taken: "And whatever you do, in word or deed, do everything in the name of the Lord Jesus" (3:17). This is followed by a verse from Jesus' high-priestly prayer for the unity of his followers: "That they may all be one, even as thou, Father, art in me, and I in thee, that they also may be in us, so that the world may believe" (John 17:21). Then come biographical details: "Augustin Bea, member of the Society of Jesus, Cardinal of the Holy Roman Church." Finally there is the closing request: "Pray for his eternal rest."[79]

* * *

Before closing, let us take another brief look at *the cardinal's will*, which was signed on 18 July 1965. It is a longish document, composed of a fairly lengthy introduction and eight enclosures, making up a total of eighteen typewritten pages. There is obviously no need to go into great detail, and we shall simply list the various legatees to show that the cardinal wanted to take into account the many different relations he had had in the course of his long life. Obviously he thought of the supreme government of his own order, and also the Province of Southern Germany, to which he belonged, in particular leaving the private part of his papers to the latter. As a mark of gratitude, he then left some things to the Pontifical Brazilian College, where he had lived after he was made

---

77. Due to a deeply regretted misunderstanding, Dr. E. Schlink's homily, which is given in *ibid.*, p. 320, was not in fact spoken.

78. A reproduction is found in *ibid.*, p. 317. Cf. also *ibid.*, p. 321.

79. I would mention in passing that a short time after my return to Rome, the cardinal's apartment was opened and his belongings officially sorted. The official section of his papers was removed and deposited in the Secret Vatican Archives, where it was decided that it should be kept together as the "Cardinal Bea Collection." Later on, when I was sorting out the section that was considered private, I discovered the "spiritual notes" of his retreats, which I published in *Der Mensch Bea (Spiritual Profile* in English).

cardinal. Nor did he forget the Pontifical Biblical Institute, where he had spent such a large part of his life. He left the ecumenical part of his library to the Secretariat for Christian Unity, and the more theological or more specifically Catholic part to the Harvard Divinity School, in view of the fact that the contacts he had had at this institute had marked an important stage in the development of his ecumenical work. He left a small souvenir to the Seminary of the Archdiocese of Freiburg im Breisgau where he had studied for two years before entering the Society of Jesus. He left a series of personal objects to his home town of Riedböhringen, with a view to the possible creation of a museum, as we have already mentioned.

The most interesting part of the cardinal's will for us is *the introduction*, in which he took leave of this life.[80] The full text is as follows:

"In the name of the Lord Jesus! Amen.

"Having reached the end of a long life I can only thank the Lord for what he has given me, and humbly beseech his forgiveness and the forgiveness of all those I have grieved and offended during my life.

"The Lord in his infinite goodness called me from humble conditions to the religious life, the priesthood and episcopate, and the closest collaboration with his vicar on earth, and all this out of sheer grace and without any merit on my part. May he be thanked for this and also accept, in humble thanksgiving, whatever I have been able to do, with his grace, in his service for the good of his holy church and the salvation of souls.

"I also thank in a special way my dear Society of Jesus, superiors and subjects, for the vast good done me in my religious life with the example of a holy life and apostolic zeal.

"I humbly pray the Lord to forgive all my shortcomings, defects and failures committed in his service, not looking to my sin, but to his immense goodness and mercy. I also beg all those who have felt offended by me to grant me their forgiveness and to pray for my soul. I too wholeheartedly forgive those who have maybe offended me.

"And now I commend to the Lord's mercy my poor soul, redeemed by him and filled with so many precious graces. 'Into thy hands, O Lord, I commend my spirit.' "[81]

* * *

When Pope Paul VI received the representatives of other Christian confessions in audience after the funeral in St. Peter's, he said that Cardinal Bea "must be considered as ever-present, and his prayers will help all those who labor for this high mission of faith, hope and brotherhood." These words indicate the underlying dimensions of the cardinal's presence, or his presence in virtue of

---

80. Reproduced in BM, p. 322, which gives only the first page, while we also quote three lines from p. 2.

81. Luke 23:46; the cardinal gives the phrase in Latin ("In manus Tuas, Domine, commendo spiritum meum").

"the communion of saints" that we profess in the creed. The following passage from the conciliar Constitution on the Church explains this concept as follows: "So it is that the union of the wayfarers with the brethren who sleep in the peace of Christ is in no way interrupted, but on the contrary, according to the constant faith of the church, this union is reinforced by an exchange of spiritual goods. Being more closely united to Christ, those who dwell in heaven fix the whole church more firmly in holiness, add to the nobility of the worship that the church offers to God here on earth, and in many ways help in a broader building up of the church (cf. 1 Cor. 12:12-27)."[82] The liturgical Preface of Holy Men and Women, in turn, praises God in his saints, and summarizes our relation to them as follows: "In their lives on earth you give us an example. In our communion with them you give us their friendship. In their prayer for the church you give us strength and protection." In this light all the ways in which the cardinal is present among us—as example, stimulus and encouragement—are seen on a new and deeper level. Since we are united with the cardinal in Christ, his example and teaching, and also his intercession, work in us *in Christ and through Christ*. In the mystical body of Christ as a whole, which includes both the pilgrim church as well as the church in glory, it is a constant law that "the different members have the same care for one another" (1 Cor. 12:25), each in his own place and order. In this perspective there is a living presence of Cardinal Bea among us, and in his own way and in his own order he therefore continues his work in the church in Christ and through Christ.

---

82. *LG*, 49.

EPILOGUE

SOME ELEMENTS FOR A PORTRAIT

A short while after the cardinal's death, the present author tried to sketch a portrait on the basis of his own memories.[1] Since then a considerable number of publications have appeared with the aim not only of giving the essential facts about the cardinal's life and work, but more specifically of trying to provide an overall picture of this great personality,[2] and we have certainly taken these studies into account. As is natural for a biography, our study has so far followed the various stages of the cardinal's life and the various aspects of his thought and activity. It is true that we have quoted other people's views on the cardinal's personality—as man, priest, Council father, or president of the secretariat.[3] However, rather than giving a portrait as such, so far it has been simply a question of collecting the relative material, which means that closer, more specific study is now needed. Lastly, such a study is also required as a necessary complement to the present biography. At the end of the long path on which readers have seen the cardinal's life, thinking and activity, they will obviously still be wondering about the precise identity and personality of this man who was responsible for such an enormous amount of work for the church.

I would start with some observations on *the method* to be used.

(1) In order to reach a true understanding of the cardinal, it is not enough to carry out an almost static study of how he appeared in the last stage of his life when he was at the height of his activity as a cardinal. Every now and then we shall therefore cast a brief look back in order to show the development of the various aspects of his character.

(2) Only occasionally, and with a view to considering a specific aspect in greater depth, shall we draw on the cardinal's retreat notes, which were published in the volume *Spiritual Profile*,[4] and we shall therefore not be simply repeating the various aspects of the spiritual portrait we sketched in the second part of that book. We see the latter as a study complete in itself, but in many ways different from that of the present chapter.

---

1. Cf. S. Schmidt, "Il Cardinale Agostino Bea," *CC*, 1969/I, 8-20. Cf. the section of our bibliography giving details of publications *about* the cardinal.
2. We would mention in particular the interesting attempt of K.H. Neufeld ("Wirksame Oekumene. Kardinal Beas Einsatz für Einigung der Christen," *Catholica*, XXXV [1981], 189-210) to produce a portrait of the cardinal as ecumenist on the basis of an analysis of his writings. The present attempt is based, as will be seen, on different and broader foundations, although it does inevitably have points of contact with Neufeld's study.
3. We spoke about this in Part I, Chapters 3 and 4, in the context of the tasks entrusted to him from the start of his activity as priest up to his time as Rector of the Pontifical Biblical Institute; for the latter part of his life, reference can be made especially to Part III, Chapter 9, on Bea as Council father, and Part IV, Chapter 4, which quotes various messages of condolence on his death, funeral orations, etc.
4. Cf. Biblio. 191a.

(3) In quoting the statements of others, we shall be careful not to break them up and note only the specific aspect at present under examination; we shall instead quote them with their surrounding context and in all their wealth, therefore including certain elements that are not immediately under consideration. This should not prejudice the clarity of our description, so long as the reader remembers the specific quality being studied at any given moment.

Bea's Most Striking Feature

We would start with a little episode that contains a revealing comparison by no less a personage than Pope John XXIII, to whom people had, it will be recalled, given the title of "the good pope." One day the pope was talking with Bea, and explained his own optimism by saying that it was a well-based optimism, an optimism reached after due consideration. Then he told the cardinal: "They say that you are too good . . . but they say the same thing about me."[5]

I think that here the pope in fact pinpointed the element that made the first and most striking impression when meeting the cardinal. The closest of his collaborators, Johannes Willebrands, stresses "his incomparable kindness and amiability, his availability and his understanding for every individual."[6] Monsignor Igino Cardinale, then a high official in the Secretariat of State, writes: "His smiling goodness, his deep serenity, his spontaneous humility, his untiring availability to others: . . . these are the qualities of Cardinal Bea that have remained alive in my memory."[7] Father Pedro Arrupe, the Jesuit General, also stresses this point: "The first thing that one felt on meeting him—I am talking about the period when I was often fortunate enough to meet him—was his authentic humanity: he was sympathetic, open, kindly, understanding and available. He radiated amiability and thus elicited respect and veneration."[8]

The well-known Reformed exegete, Oscar Cullmann, a guest-observer at the Council, wrote as follows , after mentioning Bea's wisdom: "Wisdom must go hand in hand with *kindness*. No one who knew Cardinal Bea will ever forget the kindness his nature radiated; it was written all over his face. *This* was the basis for the great trust that his nature inspired in all—Catholics, Orthodox and Protestants alike."[9] After the German writer Alexander Stoll had visited the cardinal and been given a copy of *Unity in Freedom*, he wrote: "I read it during the next few days of my journey, and have read it and re-read it here at home a second and third time. And I found that the same wisdom and kindliness shone

---

5. The cardinal told me this, and I immediately noted it in my diary.

6. Cf. manuscript of the homily given in the Gesù Church in Rome, and the homily given at Riedböhringen, in BM, p. 310.

7. ArchWit.

8. BM, p. 16. The collection of statements by various people published in BM is particularly helpful for our study, and we shall make considerable use of it.

9. *Ibid.*, p. 341.

forth from every one of the three hundred or so pages as from the author's eyes when I looked into them."[10]

In view of these and similar statements, the observation of the Italian Catholic writer, Igino Giordani, seems particularly apt: "At meetings, even those at a distance looked at that lean face with its sunken eyes, and saw in it the face of the Catholic Church," which he presented from its most attractive side.[11]

And lest it be imagined that this was the cardinal's attitude only when meeting with important people, the following statements are made by people who worked with him in the offices of the secretariat. E. Fortino declares: "We who were close to him will never be able to forget the kindly and paternal air with which he was able to head and supervise the task entrusted to him."[12] The statement of Gianfrancesco Arrighi, then Under-Secretary of the Secretariat for Christian Unity, is much more detailed: "It is true that the cardinal was very reserved, but his person emanated goodness; he was deeply sensitive toward others, a quality expressed in very thoughtful gestures and words. When he came to the office he had a smile for everybody; he asked our doormen about their families; he shared in the joys and sorrows of each of us. He always had time for those who worked with him, and treated them with fatherly affection but also, I would like to say, with friendship." And Arrighi adds that working with others "was translated, not only into the love and goodness I have mentioned, but also into the great trust that the cardinal had in his collaborators, whom he had made into a family as their number grew."[13]

Various statements emphasize the cardinal's "smiling goodness" and recall that he "had *a smile for everybody*." N. Zupcich, Bea's driver during the nine years he was cardinal, writes: "I had the job of going to collect and drive people of every race, color and activity, and then showing them into the cardinal's office. The cardinal welcomed everybody with a smile (excuse me if I insist) but a Christian smile, not a 'diplomatic' smile; and I would return happily to my other tasks."[14] The Lutheran observer at the Council, K.E. Skydsgaard, stresses "this convincing and warming smile, which meant that personal contact was rapidly achieved."[15] The European Director of the World Jewish Congress, Dr. G. Riegner, states: "His greatest gift was his smile, which showed the deep goodness of the man and opened every heart to him."[16]

10. Quoted by H. Guske, *Augustinus Bea (Alle Menschen sind seine Brüder*, Christ in der Welt, 12 (Berlin, 1967), p. 33.

11. I. Giordani, "Agostino Bea, il tessitore dell'unità," *Città Nuova*, X (December 1968), 16-17.

12. Cyclostyled ms. of a homily; Arch. U 3/32.

13. G.-F. Arrighi, "Il Cardinale Agostino Bea, primo Presidente del Segretariato per l'Unione dei Cristiani," in Caprile, V, 720. Cf. other similar statements: E. Schlink, in BM, p. 359; O. Cullmann, in *ibid.*, p. 340; P. Vogelsanger, "Wahrheit und Liebe. Zum Lebenswerk von Augustin Kardinal Bea," *Materialdienst d. konfessionskundl. Instituts Bensheim*, XIX (1968), 111; P. Gordan, "Das ökumenische Gewissen der Kirche. Kardinal Augustin Bea zum Gedenken," *hometowner Rundbrief*, LXXIII/LXXVI (1968), 4. Among the statements found in the archives, cf. those of A. Gosskinsky and H. Tenhumberg.

14. ArchWit.

15. BM, p. 360.

16. G. Riegner, in *Simposio*, p. 149.

In the light of these statements we can understand the ease the cardinal had in establishing human relations, indeed in creating friendships. The exegete and oriental scholar, T. Federici, who had known the cardinal since he was at the Biblical Institute, writes: "With innumerable Protestants—some of whom were famous—he formed a faithful friendship which was truly a beginning of communion in faith in the one and only Lord. The capacity to establish human relations was a clear gift of Cardinal Bea. . . . However, it has been rightly observed that this unique capacity to give birth to a human, sincere and generous friendship would suddenly be transformed into an invitation toward the opening up of a true spiritual communion."[17] K.E. Skydsgaard can state in more general terms: "In the eyes of the observers, of whatever tendency, he was quite simply a friend."[18]

In his statement G.-F. Arrighi talks about the "*great trust* that the cardinal had in those who worked with him." F. Thijssen, who was a consultor of the secretariat for many years from its beginnings, describes the cardinal's attitude toward people considered "progressive": "In this respect, Cardinal Bea not only reassured us, he stimulated us. He was not only magnanimous, but he also had trust in us. So I always gained fresh courage to speak completely frankly with him. Particularly at the beginning, I even dared to contradict him directly in personal discussion because at that time, as was also the case for Msgr. Willebrands, I could speak from personal experience."[19] As we have seen elsewhere, Cardinal Johannes Willebrands sees this point as one of the "specific merits" of the cardinal in connection with the accomplishments of the secretariat. These merits lay "above all in his capacity to grant his fellow workers the maximum trust, thus encouraging them."[20]

Thomas F. Stransky, who worked at the secretariat for ten years from the time it started, writes: "I never felt in the office a spirit of being judged only the executors or instruments of the President of the Secretariat. He respected our feelings and our skills, and considered us as mature priests who had no need to be treated as adolescent clerks."[21]

Conservative Reformer

We now move on to Bea's specific qualities as ecumenist. Here we find a series of attitudes that are often, at least apparently, opposed to one another, and the various statements reflect this fact. In any case, it is not easy to combine them harmoniously in a single person.

The first of these pairs of contrasting qualities is seen in the question that

---

17. T. Federici, "Une occasion exceptionnelle. Le Concile Vatican II: Le rôle joué par le Cardinal Bea et le Secrétariat dans sa préparation et réalisation," *SIDIC*, special issue (1969), 6.
18. BM, p. 360. Cf. also the statement of Dr. E. Carson Blake on the role of friendship in his ecumenical commitment, in *Bea-Preis*, p. 140, already quoted above, p. 678.
19. ArchWit.
20. Cf. pp. 355-356 above.
21. ArchWit, p. 5.

various authors wonder about: that of how the cardinal could be so open to renewal of his own church and also open in the face of other churches, while still remaining so firmly faithful to his own church, its tradition and its magisterium. The Old-Catholic observer-delegate, Dr. W. Küppers, admiringly recalls the cardinal as "the guardian angel of the spirit of the Council," and says that he was "conservative and yet keenly set on what was new, striding out in the vanguard, and showing the way for ecumenism. While firmly claiming that he was anchored to his own church, he was able to work for the hope of the great and truly ecumenical renewal of the church in our time."[22] The Lutheran Bishop W. Stählin says that one of Cardinal Bea's basic concerns was that of "linking reliable fidelity to the tradition of his own church with openness to the life that God has given rise to in the other churches."[23] The well-known Reformed theologian L. Vischer, an observer-delegate at the Council, finds his own memory of Cardinal Bea summarized in the small Latin word *attamen*[24] which appears so frequently in the Decree on Ecumenism: "He was very deeply rooted in his own church. People were sometimes in fact surprised at the extent to which he was in agreement with traditional convictions. However, his personality and work were imbued with *attamen*, and this made it possible for new openings and new initiatives to be taken so many times in his circle."[25] The Lutheran observer at the Council, E. Schlink, analyzes the cardinal's attitude as follows: "Certainly he was on the whole theologically conservative, and he never abandoned or even questioned any of the teachings that had been formally declared a dogma in the history of the Roman church. But in him there burned a love for all who confessed the name of Christ, and this love opened his eyes to the possibilities that the very extensively fixed dogma of his church still left open for greater closeness between the separated churches—possibilities that had not for the most part been recognized until then."[26]

After stressing the openness that Bea showed in biblical studies, the Archbishop of Canterbury, Dr. M. Ramsey, goes on to say that this same openness could be seen in his ecumenical attitude: ". . . and this openness showed itself . . . pre-eminently in his desire to understand Christians of other Churches. He was open, too, to the need for reforms in the Church which were in accordance with the mind of the Council. It was this open-mindedness that has in fact produced a revolution in ecumenical thinking which is by no means confined to the Roman Catholic Church."[27] Professor K.E. Skydsgaard describes the

---

22. BM, p. 334.
23. *Ibid.*, p. 361.
24. = nonetheless, yet, however.
25. BM, p. 369. Cf. also the statement of Dr. E. Carson Blake, in *Bea-Preis*, p. 140.
26. BM, p. 357. We can also consider the statements of various Catholic witnesses concerning his fidelity to the church, for example: P. Pavan, "Il Cardinale Bea e la libertà religiosa," in *Simposio*, pp. 120-121; Fortino, cyclostyled ms. of a homily, p. 3; A. Hasler, "Die ökumenische Bedeutung von Kardinal Bea," *Oekumenische Rundschau*, XVIII (1969), 257-258; G. Vodopivec, "Il Cardinale Agostino Bea: Testimone a servizio dell'unità cristiana," *Ut unum sint* (March-April 1969), p. 55; B. Wambacq, O.Praem., ArchWit.
27. BM, p. 336.

impression that the cardinal made on him at the time of the Council as compared with that of his first meeting with him in 1955: "He had become visibly older, but was completely youthful in spirit. His open, positive attitude, his clarity and wisdom, and his love for the common cause almost increased as he grew older."[28]

Monsignor Josef Höfer, who was for many years Counselor at the German Embassy to the Holy See, and who knew the cardinal well, coined the apparently paradoxical formula of "conservative reformer"[29] to express this complex dual quality of fidelity to the church and its magisterium on the one hand, and openness to necessary clarifications of doctrine and to reform—and also to other Christians—on the other. It seems to me that this expression very nicely sums up what we have been saying about this particular aspect of the cardinal's character. It has also rightly been observed that this characteristic enabled him to be in various ways a mediator between "conservatives" and "progressives,"[30] if we want to use a terminology that is in fact so ill-suited to the religious and ecclesiastical sphere. Moreover, this attitude fully reflects what Pope John XXIII expressed in his special term *aggiornamento*.[31] Indeed, according to the pope's private secretary, Monsignor L.F. Capovilla, the pope had used the phrase "fidelity and renewal" in order to explain the concept of *aggiornamento*—a phrase that was later taken up by Pope Paul VI.[32]

Wisdom, Realism, Courage and Perseverance

Dr. W. Küppers admires the cardinal because he combined wisdom and dynamism.[33] Dr. W.A. Visser 't Hooft, for many decades Secretary General of the World Council of Churches, also speaks of the cardinal's wisdom, describing the impression he had of the cardinal at their first meeting in September 1960: "In all gratitude I may say that it was in no way a diplomatic conversation, but a conversation of the kind that should and can be held between Christians. I at once had the impression that I was speaking with a very wise and very mild

---

28. *Ibid.*, p. 360. We would recall that we have repeatedly noted this quality in the course of our biography: from our description of his work as exegete, in particular in studying literary genres in sacred scripture, to his public lectures given to prepare people for the Council, which were then collected in the book *The Unity of Christians.*
29. *Konservativer Reformer*: the term is mentioned by Vogelsanger, "Wahrheit und Liebe," p. 111, and by G.F. Svidercoschi, in *Il Tempo* (29 September 1985), and also by W. Becker, "Augustinus Bea, Kardinal der Einheit," in G. Gloede (ed.), *Oekumenische Profile. Brückenbauer der Einen Kirche* (Stuttgart, 1963), p. 169, who however uses the German word *Reformator*, while the original expression used the word *Reformer*. I have been assured that the term was coined by J. Höfer, although I did not hear this personally from him.
30. Cf. Vogelsanger, "Wahrheit und Liebe," p. 111.
31. = updating, renewal (although the Italian word *aggiornamento* has itself often been used in English in this connection).
32. Cf. Svidercoschi, in *Il Tempo* (29 September 1985).
33. Cf. BM, p. 334.

person."[34] As we saw in our previous chapter, Visser 't Hooft used the following words to summarize his impressions of that encounter to Monsignor Johannes Willebrands, who was accompanying the cardinal: "This man has not only read and studied the Old Testament; he has truly absorbed the wisdom of the men of the Old Testament."[35]

The Italian Catholic publicist, I. Giordani, writes: "When you met Augustin Bea, you did not know whether to admire more his goodness (we can say: holiness) or his intelligence (we can say: wisdom). You had the impression that his was a light that had been made prophetic and far-seeing by the power of love, and that his was a love illuminated by genius."[36] And he adds: "The cardinal attracted everybody with his candor and his wisdom."[37]

The well-known Reformed theologian O. Cullmann links the cardinal's wisdom with *a sense of reality and balance*, writing: "Ecumenism today would be in even greater need of Cardinal Bea's wisdom. No one can reproach him for having had too little enthusiasm or for having betrayed his convictions. Yet he had a lively sense for realities, which derived from his love for truth. This preserved him from all exaggeration and radicalism. In the ecumenical field his wisdom found expression in his efforts to moderate impatience and any attempt to advance too rapidly and to bring into being a unity that was not anchored in faith, as well as any attempt to pass over in silence the differences that still separate the confessions."[38] Professor K.E. Skydsgaard writes similarly that the cardinal "was well aware of the serious difficulties and certainly did not indulge in any naïve or imprecise form of ecumenism. He was a man of clarity."[39] The Lutheran Bishop W. Stählin writes: "The sober sense of reality that was such a hallmark of his character, meant that he never indulged in any kind of ecumenical romanticism."[40] His sense of realty was also closely linked to a very lively sense of what was possible and of the need for a gradual approach. Just as in his life as a teacher he had realized what his students could understand and absorb, so he knew that in life in general, and hence also in scholarship and in the church, we must move gradually, by steps, taking into account people's capacity for assimilation.

He himself spoke about his own *sense of reality* in his autobiographical reflections in 1967, referring to his remark that so far as the prospects of

---

34. *Ibid.*, p. 369.
35. *Ibid.*, p. 313.
36. Giordani, "Agostino Bea," p. 17. His wisdom is also stressed by O. Cullmann, in BM, p. 340; and by A. Stoll, quoted by Guske, *Augustinus Bea*, p. 33.
37. Giordani, "Agostino Bea," p. 17.
38. BM, p. 340. On the subject of his sense of balance, cf. also Arrighi, "Il Cardinale Agostino Bea, primo Presidente," p. 720; Fortino, cyclostyled ms. of a homily, p. 3; Hasler, "Die ökumenische Bedeutung," p. 293; *Irenikon*, p. 489. For the fact that he did not level down differences, cf. Vogelsanger, "Wahrheit und Liebe," p. 111; J. Frings, in BM, p. 13; Y. Congar, in *Simposio*, p. 27.
39. BM, p. 360.
40. *Ibid.*, p. 361; cf. also L. Vischer, "Kardinal Augustin Bea S.J. zum Gedenken," *Offen*, XXVII/2 (1969), 10; Hasler, "Die ökumenische Bedeutung," p. 258; Arrighi, "Il Cardinale Agostino Bea, primo Presidente," p. 720; R. Baumann, ArchWit ("sober").

ecumenism were concerned he was neither pessimistic nor optimistic, but simply realistic, and explaining: "If anyone who heard me talk about respect for other people's opinions, the necessary effort to understand one another, etc., thought that I was an optimist at any price, or that I wrap myself in illusions that man is 'by nature good,' and disguise difficulties and obstacles, he would be mistaken." And he expanded on this as follows: "In speeches and in my books I have always tried to guard against every illusion that ecumenical work is easy. When we are concerned with understanding and unity on the merely human level, difficulties increase immeasurably and the limits of human possibility are more restricted."[41]

His wise sense of balance and his realism were combined with another quality which at first sight could seem to be in opposition to them: *courage* in all its aspects, that of being able to conceive and launch out into far-sighted plans, working toward their accomplishment despite all obstacles. Igino Giordani writes that the cardinal was able to "interpret the greatest aspirations of contemporary ecumenism and was able to articulate and defend them with prudence combined with a unique courage."[42] The Lutheran Bishop W. Stählin writes: "Bea and Pope John XXIII shared the boldness of perspicacious advance planning, and foresight of a future not yet tangible."[43] Dr. W.A. Visser 't Hooft writes: "In Bea one found a happy mixture of prudent foresight and dynamism. He was able to wait, but when he was sure that the time was ripe for the next step, he went ahead courageously."[44] Dr. G. Riegner in turn writes: "With his deep religious faith he possessed the gift of calm resolution; . . . he had enormous will-power and uncounted reserves of energy and patience, for which many decades passed in the service of the church had prepared him, but which were astonishing at his age."[45]

Courage also includes *perseverance* in difficulties and also in possible defeats, and E. Schlink writes about this point as follows: "In the various setbacks he experienced in the often dramatic course of the Council, he never lost heart, but perseveringly kept the ecumenical goal before his eyes, and in the end, through kind and supple constancy, he attained goals that had been formerly considered unattainable."[46] Dr. A. Hasler, who was responsible for the "Lutheran and Reformed Churches" section of the secretariat after the Council, writes: "The third basic attitude that led Cardinal Bea to success was the *tenacity* with which he pursued a goal upon which he had once fixed his sights. This attitude could be described as patience, stamina, and a fighting spirit. He was

---

41. Biblio. 363 (in *What I Have Learned*), p. 19. In the course of our study we have repeatedly encountered examples of this sense of reality and the reasons on which it was based: the teaching of sacred scripture on the presence of the forces of evil in this world, and on man's weakness and sinfulness, etc.
42. Giordani, "Agostino Bea," p. 16. Cf. also Arrighi, "Il Cardinale Agostino Bea, primo Presidente," p. 720.
43. BM, p. 362. Thus also Fortino, cyclostyled ms. of a homily, p. 3: "uncommon farsightedness."
44. BM, p. 370.
45. Riegner, in *Simposio*, p. 149.
46. BM, p. 359.

able to accomplish his plans through great skill and circumspect prudence. He knew how to give way in minor matters in order to push through his essential ideas in due course. There is no need to emphasize how much courage and steadfastness this required at the Roman curia, especially in pre-conciliar times."[47] In the context of the vicissitudes of the schema on the Jews, the Lutheran writer J.C. Hampe writes: "During the tragedy that struck the schemata on the Jews, his back slumped into an ever more hunched position. However, anyone who imagined he would not survive a rejection of his draft on the part of the Council was far from the truth, even though this was never put to the test. He always had enough strength of spirit in him to parry the worst setbacks and to make the best out of the evil that threatened."[48]

If we seek *the deep roots* of this courage and perseverance, I think that the cardinal himself indicates it when he describes *Pope John's courage* as follows: "It has been very truly said, by a writer well acquainted with the circumstances and the situation, that the Council was first of all, and above all, an act, and the fruit, of Pope John's faith and confidence in God. No other explanation meets the facts. He succeeded in inspiring others with this faith and his courage. How often have I heard him utter the word 'Courage'—for he was not spared opposition and resistance, which he felt acutely, above all when they impeded and planned to obstruct his pastoral efforts."[49] The cardinal adds: "Because of this humility, and humble trust in God, he was lion-hearted in facing the gigantic problems of the modern world, in seeking a solution to them; he had a dynamic yet sober optimism and a surprising youthful zest."[50]

Prudence, Simplicity, Humility, Meekness and Patience

1. It is perhaps worth noting that A. Hasler mentions *skill and circumspect prudence* alongside courage, for it is not in fact so normal for prudence to go hand in hand with courage. Monsignor Josef Höfer, who knew Father Bea and then Cardinal Bea closely for more than ten years and was impressed by the mature Bea, imagines the young Bea as follows: "I would hazard a guess that the characteristics of objective intelligence in the choice of means and methods of work, in relations with his school companions, and in his manner of resting and relaxing could already be discerned early on. With respect to the tasks assigned to him and in dealings with others, the young Father Bea already clearly showed the developing virtue of prudence in the choice and use of the necessary means in order to achieve his goal."[51] Thus, M. Zerwick, who worked closely with Father Bea during the latter's time as Rector of the Pontifical Biblical Institute, speaks of what Father Bea accomplished in this post, saying that his

47. Hasler, "Die ökumenische Bedeutung," p. 258; cf. also *Irenikon*, p. 480 ("patience and daring").
48. BM, p. 347.
49. *Unity in Freedom*, p. 61.
50. *Ibid.*
51. Höfer, "Das geistliche Profil des Kardinals Bea," *Catholica (Paderborn)*, XXVI (1972), 60.

"unusual prudence, astonishing self-control and never-failing kindness" played a decisive role in his successful maneuvering between conservative and more open currents.[52]

So far as Bea's ecumenical work is concerned, Dr. E. Carson Blake writes that maybe the major contribution of the first president of the secretariat to ecumenism was "the persistence with which he was able to stop short the more imprudent or reactionary movements which naturally were implicit, if not explicit, in so much of the post-conciliar situation. Here it is hard indeed to measure the extent of his work, but one is instinctively sure that *the quality of prudence*, which so generally was a hallmark of his life's work, must have had considerable influence on so much of the work which went on around him."[53] The same witness adds: "To the gift of prudence he grafted the firm will of persistence, a combination which made him a singular advocate for ecumenism."[54] I. Gordan, who worked for Vatican Radio and thus observed the cardinal's work for many years, writes as follows about his activity in support of the declaration *Nostra aetate*: "Cardinal Bea, an expert in biblical theology and an ecumenist, did not allow himself to be confounded by the many attacks he had to endure because of his fight for a just word addressed to Israel, a struggle fought with prudence, tenacity and mildness."[55] The Bishop of Münster, H. Tenhumberg, who had to negotiate complicated and delicate questions with Bea, evaluates Bea's sense of prudence and diplomatic skill as follows: "In these talks I also immediately realized that although Father Bea had a very fine feeling for all the rules of diplomacy and tactics, he himself was above all suspicion of manipulation. On the contrary: when negotiating with him I received a deep, indelible impression that his whole way of thinking and acting was *religiously inspired*. He saw all things in their religious and ecclesial dimension, and was ready to commit himself in favor of the victory of truth and justice even in situations where there was really no way out."[56]

The Lutheran scholar, J.C. Hampe, who observed and studied the Council at close quarters, describes the cardinal in the following terms: "He was not a revolutionary, but rather *a diplomat of goodness* like John XXIII. . . . He was an ecumenical diplomat, but never solely a diplomat."[57] The same author goes on to expand on his statement in this way: "Guileless as a dove and wise as a serpent, this man stood firm amidst the waves of the Council and was often practically alone in the innermost circle of cardinals around Pope Paul VI. Without him, the whole Council would have followed a different course, and a worse one, just as without John XXIII it would never have got under way at all."[58]

---

52. Cf. M. Zerwick, "Kardinal Bea und die katholische Bibelwissenschaft," *Bibel und Kirche*, XXIV (1969), 18.
53. E. Carson Blake, in *Diakonia*, p. 4; cf. also W.A. Visser 't Hooft, in BM, p. 370 ("a happy mixture of prudence and dynamism").
54. E. Carson Blake, in *Diakonia*, p. 4.
55. Gordan, "Das ökumenische Gewissen der Kirche," p. 4.
56. ArchWit, p. 1.
57. BM, p. 347.
58. *Ibid.*, p. 348.

Professor G. Vodopivec, who was a consultor to the secretariat for many years starting from its beginnings, writes: "Objective sobriety is also the only way of worthily commemorating this man who sought in all things to be completely sincere and frank, sincere with himself and with others, with his church and with other believers, his Christian brethren. Nothing was more foreign to him than deceitful and insincere bowing and incense, for he had an instinctive repugnance for obsequiousness without true substance or triumphal formulae without any basis in reality. He was a man of truth and always sincerely bowed before the truth, because he saw in it a reflection of the supreme Truth."[59]

2. We have already met the word *simplicity* in the extracts we have quoted, and in this connection the famous French theologian Yves Congar writes that when he visited the cardinal "he made me sit beside him, on the same couch, and we could talk freely. The cardinal was simplicity itself. You could talk with him like a friend."[60] The German writer Alexander Stoll describes his visit with the cardinal as follows: "Stefan Zweig has coined the telling expression 'astral hours.' On this occasion, I experienced one of these astral hours, yet I had written to an acquaintance about this meeting on a postcard and she replied: 'I'm sure you weren't able to think of the Council and Bea jokes during that hour.' She was wrong. I even told them, but they fell flat, as in every case the cardinal knew better variants, for despite all the awards and recognition he has received, he had kept his Swabian sense of humor."[61]

Simplicity was so much a hallmark of the cardinal's personality that it was incarnated in his *literary style*, as has been noted by various completely independent commentators. Thus a well-known Swiss journalist, G. Huber, writes: "The cardinal was eloquent in his own way, with the type of eloquence which Pascal says scorns eloquence. His eloquence lay in the vigor of his convictions, the clarity of his thinking, the sincerity of his explanations and reasoning, and the simplicity of his style."[62] Monsignor Josef Höfer analyzes this feature as follows: "The artlessness of his speech aroused and riveted attention even in large halls. What he had to say did not always sound like a new message, but it did always sound like a statement of truth and opinion as the audience imagined it should ideally be expressed. This led to trust, not only in the speaker's reliability, but also in the validity of what he was saying."[63] Dr. L. Vischer writes as follows: "Cardinal Bea had the gift of expressing the imperative nature of the ecumenical movement with great courage and in the

---

59. Vodopivec, "Il Cardinale Agostino Bea," p. 48; cf. also O. Cullmann, in BM, p. 340, who says that he did not hide points of disagreement; similarly, H. Dietzfelbinger, in BM, p. 341.

60. *Simposio*, p. 26. The cardinal's simplicity is stressed in various statements found in the archives, for example those of Cardinal F. Seper and the Swiss Sisters Johanna Schmidlin and Irene Sganzini. Cf. also P.G. Duncker, "Ricordando il Cardinale Agostino Bea," *Angelicum*, LIX (1958), 57; and Höfer, "Das geistliche Profil," p. 58.

61. Cited by Guske, "Augustinus Bea," p. 32. Cardinal Bea's former driver, N. Zupcich, relates how once in his home town the cardinal stopped perfectly naturally to talk with a peasant beside his cart laden with manure; ArchWit, p. 2.

62. G. Huber, in *La Liberté* (29 November 1968), p. 2.

63. Höfer, "Das geistliche Profil," p. 58.

simplest of words. He could speak so convincingly of unity and of the need to manifest it that he was understood by everyone. He had the gift of the simple word, and, of course, it is true time and time again that simple words are the most effective."[64]

3. What we have said about his style is also a sign of the cardinal's *modesty*, the mark of someone who does not seek the limelight, but tries to efface himself behind the task of serving the truth, justice and love. The English Catholic Bishop of Leeds, W.G. Wheeler states: "Those of us who knew him will never forget the inspiration of this deeply humble and profoundly learned man whose resources were so essentially spiritual. And he will always, to my mind, be remembered for his stress on the twin importance for ecumenism of truth and love."[65] The then President of the World Methodist Council, Dr. F.P. Corson, describes the cardinal's work method in unusual terms, comparing it with that of the apostle Andrew: "Cardinal Bea was a humble and practical man, like Nathanael, an Israelite in whom there is no guile. He confronted the miracles which had to be performed, especially in the areas assigned to him and, like St. Andrew, quietly he always set about finding the resources, meager as they might be, with which to begin. So we who worked with him often thought of him as St. Andrew."[66]

The well-known ecumenical review *Irenikon* writes about the cardinal's position in the Roman curia in the following terms: "Lastly, if the spirit of domination often reigns in the departments close to his own, his *humility* always kept him on the straight and narrow. This freedom and independence certainly contributed considerably to his prestige and authority."[67] The Argentinian ecumenist Jorge Mejía, who had known Father Bea from his time as a student at the Pontifical Biblical Institute, stresses his modesty and then writes: "I must mention his *humility*. Had the cardinal not become Cardinal and President of the Secretariat for Christian Unity, and hence the bearer of a papal commission to draw up a plan of ecumenical strategy and implement it, he would never have shown what he was. And why? Because his position in the church—even when he was Rector of the Pontifical Biblical Institute—did not call for it, or even permit it. He felt no prophetic impulse until he received a true mission as prophet in the context of church communion. Had he not received it, we would all have been the poorer, except for him, because he had no motivation for pushing himself beyond what his conscience asked of him."[68]

---

64. Vischer, "Kardinal Augustin Bea S.J.," p. 9. Similarly, cf. J.C. Hampe, in BM, p. 347, who says that he spoke modestly, not brilliantly, but that he struck home; cf. *Irenikon*, p. 489, which refers to reducing things "to simple formulae."

65. W.G. Wheeler, Bishop of Leeds, Sermon in Westminster Cathedral (25 January 1969), cyclostyled ms. Cf. also F.P. Corson, in BM, p. 338, and N. Zupcich, ArchWit, p. 2.

66. BM, p. 338.

67. *Irenikon*, p. 490. Federici, "Une occasion exceptionnelle," p. 5, also talks about Bea's humility.

68. J. Mejía, "El Cardenal Bea," *Confraternidad Judeo-Cristiana de la Republica Argentina* (November-December 1968), p. 3. For his modesty, cf. also J.C. Hampe, in BM, p. 348, who says that the cardinal never sought the limelight. L. Rood, S.J., ArchWit, wonders why the cardinal should have planned a museum in his home town, but we have explained the origins

4. Josef Höfer stresses yet another aspect of the cardinal's humility: that of *the spirit of service.* He speaks about the book *We Who Serve,* observing that the cardinal wrote it after a long life spent "in the service of the holy scriptures and of the visible Roman Catholic Church"; he describes the book as the cardinal's "testament" and then concludes: "Cardinal Bea's service was the basis of his authority. His spiritual profile, like his physical profile, is marked by service."[69]

In this context, the terms in which the Lutheran theologian E. Schlink sees the cardinal and his ecumenical influence seem particularly noteworthy, for Schlink says that the cardinal placed himself at the service of Christian unity "and did so not only as a prince of the church and as a theologian, but as a simple Christian, who was *always there for others,* who never avoided conversing with his neighbor, wherever the latter might seek him out, and who encountered his neighbor in these conversations as one who himself had questions and hopes. As this humble, fatherly and brotherly figure, he broke through all the ramparts of alienation and mistrust between the churches, and rendered the new ecumenical orientation of the Roman Church credible for others."[70]

5. *Meekness* goes hand in hand with humility, and we shall introduce our consideration of this quality with a text in which the cardinal expresses admiration as he recalls the personality of Pope John XXIII: "In his coronation address he asked his children throughout the world to pray that God might give him a special gift during his pontificate; and the nature of the gift he wanted caused surprise to some. He said this: "Now the divine teaching and its great school are summed up in his words: 'Learn from me, for I am gentle and lowly in heart' (Mt 11:29). This is the great principle of gentleness and lowliness. We beseech all of you throughout the world, devout and 'fervent in spirit' (Rom. 12:11), to pray assiduously to the Lord for your pope, with this intention, that he may advance more and more in the practice of gospel meekness and humility."[71]

The reader will obviously not have missed the admiration with which the cardinal wrote these words. Various witnesses confirm that such *meekness* was also one of the cardinal's qualities. From his very first meeting with him, Dr. Visser 't Hooft had the impression of talking "with a very meek man."[72] The famous theologian Yves Congar writes as follows about the cardinal's speeches in the Council hall: "He spoke calmly, in a gentle, unimpassioned voice. This way of speaking carried more weight than some impassioned or commanding speech, which would have aroused defensive reactions."[73] In the same context,

---

and reasons for this idea in one of our previous chapters; cf. p. 656 above.

69. Höfer, "Das geistliche Profil," p. 60.

70. BM, p. 358. This passage contains a very difficult phrase to translate: ". . . und der ihnen in diesen Gesprächen als einer begegnete, der selber ein fragender und Hoffender war."

71. *Unity in Freedom,* p. 60. We have slightly corrected the translation of the pope's words to bring them into line with the official Latin text; cf. *Discorsi, messaggi, colloqui del S. Padre Giovanni XXIII,* I, 13.

72. BM, p. 370.

73. *Simposio,* p. 27. In our chapter on Bea as Council father, we quoted a similar statement by

Congar describes the answer the cardinal gave him to the question of how he had become an ecumenist: "I have always been a man of peace and encounter. When, for example, there was some misunderstanding and tension between the Dominican Biblical School of Jerusalem and the Biblical Institute of Rome, which had set up a branch in Jerusalem, I stepped in so that we could clarify our positions and reach an agreement."[74]

6. Thomas F. Stransky, C.S.P., who worked in the offices of the secretariat, writes: "The cardinal possessed an extraordinary sense of timing. He was too experienced not to know how slowly human beings and structures change, but he did not want change at the price of destroying people. He *accepted others as they were.* He certainly had long-range plans of what had to be done through the secretariat, and knew with serpentine wisdom that although we could not avoid stepping on toes, we should prevent public screaming. He patiently accepted the impatience of his staff. Yet I respected his timing—when to take the initiative with the pope, other curial organs, ecumenical organizations, etc.—because of his gift of knowing the moods and understandings of others."[75]

Patience has rightly been described as an "ecumenical virtue." The Bishop of Münster, H. Tenhumberg, describes the impression that Father Bea made on him after he had become cardinal: "There was practically no change in his basic life-style. He remained a simple son of St. Ignatius, always available for everyone—insofar as time permitted—with *boundless patience* and kindness."[76] The German Evangelical review *Materialdienst* speaks about the qualities that the different popes had appreciated in Bea, and says: "In Bea, John XXIII found a man of love and patience—two qualities that were essential for Bea's dialogue with non-Catholics."[77] The Italian exegete T. Federici describes the various contributions the cardinal made "to the Council and in the Council," saying that these included "invincible tenacity and patience, before which the most redoubtable opponents had to admit defeat; there was also a generosity that meant that he never took advantage of a situation, but left the door open to the possibility of reaching an understanding with opponents. In him, boundless patience and humble tenacity were the weapons of sure success."[78]

On the basis of decades of ecumenical experience, Dr. Visser 't Hooft writes that the cardinal had the special charisms that are hallmarks of a true ecumenist, including that special type of patience that is able to wait patiently for visible results.[79] Similarly, the then President of the Evangelical Churches in Germany, the Lutheran Bishop H. Dietzfelbinger, writes: "In the final analysis, his great

Father Congar which is found in our files. Sister I. Sganzini also speaks of his meekness; ArchWit.
74. *Simposio*, p. 26.
75. ArchWit, pp. 3-4.
76. ArchWit, p. 2. T.F. Stransky, C.S.P., speaks of the cardinal's patience with those who wasted time in meetings with pointless digressions; ArchWit, p. 6. Cf. also *Irenikon*, p. 489; Hasler, "Die ökumenische Bedeutung," p. 258.
77. Vogelsanger, "Wahrheit und Liebe," p. 111.
78. Federici, "Une occasion exceptionnelle," p. 5.
79. Cf. *Simposio*, p. 25; also BM, p. 370.

merit was that of showing far-sighted patience in ecumenical matters. . . . From the start of our conversations we were in agreement that it would be a long path, and that the promise of full truth and love could be seen only in this context, and not in some hasty covering of gulfs that have not yet been legitimately filled in. Action must of course be taken, but during such action we must be capable of waiting for the fruit, for it needs time to ripen."[80]

7. There is one more quality closely linked with the previous ones: that of *serenity and calmness*. The Bishop of Münster H. Tenhumberg writes: "Although he had an enormous workload in his service of the church, . . . he never seemed harassed, but always composed, relaxed, calm, and happy."[81] Sister Heribert Ross, General Superior of the Secular Institute of the Marian Sisters of Schönstatt, who had had repeated contacts with Father and then Cardinal Bea for many years, states: "His contacts with others were inspired with deep respect, which did, however, contain a quality of warm and relaxed humanity. He could sometimes also joke and accept a more informal kind of conversation."[82] Thomas F. Stransky writes about what he had observed during the eight years he worked at the secretariat: "A man who never lost his serenity or calmness, . . . which was a clear charismatic quality in that period of extreme nervousness in the church."[83]

Dr. G. Riegner, then European Director of the World Jewish Council, speaks about the stormy waters through which the document on the Jews passed, and writes as follows: "The stormier the times became, the calmer, the more serene and the more self-confident he showed himself to be. . . . But each setback only stimulated his iron will-power to overcome the new difficulties and in the end his determination and his flexibility prevailed."[84]

The Trilogy of Faith, Hope and Love

The German ecumenist H. Fries concludes his portrait of Cardinal Bea by expressing the following hope: "May the testament and work of this amiable and modest man, whose faith, hope and love were so great and moved all those who had the good fortune to meet him, remain as a good spirit watching over ecumenism in the universal church and in the church of his and our people."[85] Here faith, hope and love are rightly seen as inseparable, as they are in reality. Thus they are all visible to varying degrees even in statements where only one of them is more specifically emphasized.

A. Hasler writes: "In the first place, it seems to me to be basic to stress that

---

80. BM, p. 341.
81. ArchWit, p. 2.
82. ArchWit, p. 2. Cf. also A. Stoll, cited by Guske, "Augustinus Bea," p. 32.
83. T.F. Stransky, "Deux pionniers. Le pape Jean XXIII et le Cardinal Bea, le Secrétariat et les Juifs," *SIDIC*, special issue (1969), p. 2.
84. Riegner, in *Simposio*, p. 150.
85. H. Fries, "Ein Pionier der christlichen Einheit. Leben und Werk von Kardinal Augustin Bea," ms. Bayerischer Rundfunk (24 November 1968), p. 13.

Bea possessed unshakable faith and invincible confidence. He was absolutely convinced that God desires the unity of Christians, and that he is already visibly at work in order to bring it about. On the basis of this fundamental conviction he was able to deploy his already failing powers entirely for a movement whose fruits he knew for certain he would not reap. Thus he was not afflicted by discouragement, nor by fear or anxiety as to where this movement might lead the church or what changes and disturbances it could arouse. Here he was on the same wave-length as Pope John XXIII, who spoke against the prophets of doom of our time."[86]

Professor G. Vodopivec writes in very similar terms: "His firmness in going into things in depth came to him from an unshakable basis of faith, of hope that the 'holy cause of the gospel and of unity' deserves any effort, any humiliation and any sacrifice of patience."[87] Cardinal Johannes Willebrands recalls Bea's "deep understanding and hope, which had their roots in faith."[88] The three statements quoted here link faith with hope. The then President of the Evangelical Church in Germany, H. Dietzfelbinger, gives his testimony the title "A Model of Ecumenical Hope and Patience."[89]

The various statements show that the cardinal also drew *the practical consequences* of faith and hope for ecumenical work. The Lutheran Bishop W. Stählin writes: "The Christian unity that Bea wished to serve can of course not be achieved without human prudence, theological consideration and organizational work; however, Bea never tired of emphasizing that this hoped-for unity is fundamentally the work of God's creative power and that prayer for the coming and action of the Holy Spirit must therefore be the supreme concern of the ecumenical movement. For, as Bea himself wrote, 'in the last analysis, unity will be a work of the Holy Spirit.' "[90]

We have an eloquent confirmation of the cardinal's convictions in this regard in what he wrote about Pope John XXIII: "He was well aware that it was an enormous and risky task to call an Ecumenical Council. In the audiences he gave, the constant theme was prayers for the success of the Council. It was astonishing how insistent he was about it, as well as how felicitous he was in finding ways of bringing home his request not only to mixed assemblies of people in general audiences, but to each group in the smaller audiences—children, the sick and suffering, professional people, theological students, nuns and priests. He always found a special reason why each group should pray for the Council and for trust in God's help."[91]

The cardinal followed the same line of procedure, and I can draw on my own

86. Hasler, "Die ökumenische Bedeutung," p. 256. The author is referring to Pope John's speech at the opening of the Council (11 October 1962), in *AAS*, LIV (1962), 789.
87. Vodopivec, "Il Cardinale Agostino Bea," p. 56. Cf. also *Irenikon*, p. 489, which says that Bea was supported by a great faith. Federici, "Une occasion exceptionnelle," p. 5, speaks of his "unshakable faith."
88. *Simposio*, p. 21.
89. BM, p. 341.
90. *Ibid.*, p. 362. Cf. also E. Schlink, in *ibid.*, p. 358.
91. *Unity in Freedom*, pp. 60-61.

personal memories in this connection. When the cardinal visited religious communities he would say that he was only too happy to do so "out of egoistic reasons," since it meant that he could ensure the prayers of many souls for his work and that of the secretariat: "We live from the prayers of all those people throughout the world—including many non-Catholic brethren—who accompany and support us with the Lord, through their prayers and their self-sacrifice." He explained this further: "Of course the secretariat has worked a great deal, but we should not attribute this labor with credit for the wonderful things that have taken place in the ecumenical field during recent years. In our work we can see particularly clearly the need for grace, and hence also the work of Christ: it is the Spirit of God that works and has created the great ecumenical events of these years."[92] For the same reason he used to send financial assistance to twelve of the poorest cloistered communities in Italy several times a year, telling them how his work was progressing, and commending the special intentions of the moment to their prayers. And on a more personal level, for many years he held to the decision to celebrate the votive mass of the Holy Spirit on the first day of the week when this was allowed "because," he would say, "I always have great need of the Holy Spirit."

He had great trust above all in the effectiveness of the eucharistic sacrifice. When anyone came to him with some difficulty, burden or great spiritual need, and asked for the help of his prayers, he believed he could offer no greater comfort or more effective help than to promise: "Tomorrow I will say mass for your intentions." Such trust, combined with faith in church communion and in the solidarity that exists in the mystical body of Christ, led him to ask many fellow priests for the help of their mass, in this way making them his fellow workers in regard to God for the great ecumenical cause. These were the decisive means that allowed the Secretariat for Christian Unity to accomplish its arduous tasks in the Council. More than once the situation seemed hopeless in human terms. At such times, a call for the cooperation of thousands of fellow priests through the infinite efficacy of the mass was always the prelude to a satisfactory solution, which would sometimes be found within the space of very few days.

2. And now we come to *love*, in the first place that for human beings. From the outset we have seen that this was the first thing that struck people about the cardinal—his amiability, kindness, understanding, and availability to others. We shall add a few more statements from various witnesses.

The Danish Lutheran theologian K.E. Skydsgaard saw Cardinal Bea again seven years after their first meeting at the Biblical Institute, and found him full of "an authentic Johannine love for brothers in other churches."[93] The Evangelical review *Materialdienst* describes the cardinal at the moment when Pope John took him up as an instrument of his action as "a man of love and patience."[94] And various people stress the sense of delicacy which prevented the cardinal

---

92. The phrases in quotes are not verbatim statements of the cardinal, but do indicate thoughts that the cardinal expressed various times in similar circumstances.

93. BM, p. 360.

94. Vogelsanger, "Wahrheit und Liebe," p. 111.

from judging people who held other opinions or made difficulties for him.[95] In this connection, Monsignor L.F. Capovilla, who had been secretary to Pope John XXIII, speaks of the cardinal's "heroic exercise of charity toward all," writing: "Before and after the death of John XXIII, I often had occasion to speak with His Eminence, to tell him about a papal audience, saying that it had been very easily granted, or to encourage him to ask for one, maybe because I was aware that there were some clouds on the horizon. I always admired the dignity of the man, the clarity of his thought, the *heroic* exercise of charity toward all, the boundless trust in the Lord, the humility lived out to an eminent degree."[96]

E. Schlink links this virtue with ecumenical dialogue, observing that love made the cardinal far-sighted about previously unnoticed possibilities for a rapprochement with other Christians.[97] And he recalls that it was Bea himself who several times stressed the application of love to ecumenical dialogue, following the famous principle in the Letter to the Ephesians which refers to "speaking the truth in love" (Eph. 4:15). The Lutheran historian P. Meinhold considers this question in greater depth, linking love with faith: "Rarely have I come across anyone in so exalted a position in the church with such a readiness to listen and to understand, with an infinite kindness that ruled his words and behavior, and with that invincible freshness of faith that is found wherever love is the seal of knowledge. Cardinal Bea himself therefore described the ecumenical dialogue as being a conversation 'about truth, carried out in love,' thus marking the dialogue with a new blazon that committed and united both partners."[98]

A particular aspect of this virtue of Bea as priest and bishop was the love that is expressed in *a pastoral sense*. In this connection we have an extremely authoritative witness in Pope John XXIII. After his first meeting with Father Bea, the pope confided to his secretary: "This Father Bea is a man and religious of great value. He inspires confidence simply by looking at him: so learned and humble, ascetical and scholarly, capable of coming down from the lecture platform to become a catechist. He has the material of a pastor of souls. I feel I should open myself to him confidentially, and I shall do so. It will be very useful to me. . . ."[99]

In our biography we have seen how Bea's activity as teacher always had a pastoral accent, an observation that also applied to his work as consultor to the Holy Office. This spirit was what prepared him for wholehearted acceptance of the instruction given by Pope John XXIII that the Council was to be above all a pastoral one. His eighteen speeches in the Council hall were inspired mainly

---

95. Cf. the statements in the archives of H. Ross, p. 2; T. Stransky, p. 4; N. Zupcich, p. 2; and K.E. Skydsgaard, in BM, p. 361.

96. ArchWit, p. 9. It should be noted that although this witness was not secretary to Pope Paul VI, he was a member of the latter's household, receiving visitors who came to see the pope, and was thus able to speak about the papacy of Paul VI.

97. Cf. BM, p. 357.

98. *Ibid.*, p. 350.

99. ArchWit, p. 3. The President of the World Methodist Council, P.F. Corson, in BM, p. 338, compares the cardinal with no less a figure than St. Paul, saying that both had "a pastor's heart."

by this same spirit, particularly his contribution to discussions on the constitutions on the liturgy, the church and divine revelation. It was in this same spirit
that he did what he could to make sure that the Council documents would be
permeated with the written word of God, and indeed that they would make use
of the language of the Bible so far as possible.

3. *What was the spirit* and underlying motivation of this love for his brethren?
O. Cullmann stresses that it was "a convincing kindness," and adds that it was
"anchored in love for Christ."[100] However, in order to receive a more complete
answer we must draw on Bea's retreat notes. Meditating on the sending out of
the apostles, the cardinal writes: "I consider my task in this entirely apostolic
spirit: for souls, for the building up of the body of Christ. I must therefore do
everything to render unity an attractive goal for them, and to offer them every
kind of help in order to achieve it. Above all, I must show my *love*: in daily
contacts, in discussions, in letters, and in negotiations. They [the separated
brethren] must recognize that I am driven on solely by the love of Christ. I shall
do all I can to inspire all my collaborators with this same attitude. My work must
be done with *interiority* and in the spirit of fortitude: with supernatural power.
Everyone must see that here there is no lust for power, no earthly interest, no
simple 'activism,' no routine, but the authentic spirit of Christ."[101] Here the
cardinal's pastoral love is seen in all its purity and wealth. And above all we can
see how deeply rooted it was in the spirit and love of Christ.

It was precisely this deeply spiritual attitude that struck a considerable
number of our witnesses. Professor Johannes Willebrands describes Father Bea
before he became cardinal in the following terms: "In the various visits I made
to Rome, Father Bea, S.J., was undoubtedly the man who made the deepest
impression on me and to whom I returned most willingly. This . . . was above
all due to the spiritual attitude with which he approached the mystery of the
unity of the church and the problem of the division of Christians."[102]

The Dutch exegete Father G. Duncker, who was a long-standing friend of
Father Bea, writes: "Apart from his honesty, fairness, frankness, simplicity,
affability and other human gifts, there was undoubtedly his true and deep
spirituality which was seen in every aspect of his ecumenical apostolate, in his
contacts with non-Catholic Christians." And the author refers to the cardinal's
retreat notes as published in *Spiritual Profile*, adding: "When a man has such
true spirituality in him, it must obviously manifest itself in some external
way."[103]

The Archbishop of Canterbury, Dr. Michael Ramsey, links this aspect
directly with the ecumenical cause, writing: "Then there was the cardinal's
insistence that *spirituality* and unity go hand in hand. Those who met him found

---

100. BM, p. 341.

101. Med. 1960/VI/2; *Der Mensch Bea*, p. 85.

102. Introduction to *Spiritual Profile*, p. VIII. Cf. also Bishop Wheeler, ms. of sermon (*op. cit.*), who
    says that the cardinal's "resources" were essentially spiritual.

103. Duncker, "Ricordando il Cardinale Agostino Bea," p. 57. Cf. similarly the German Sister
    Sigmunda of the Sisters of Christian Charity; ArchWit.

the humility of a man who walked with God. In his many writings and speeches on unity he constantly stressed the fact that unity and holiness go together, and that the church's holiness should be as visible as her unity."[104]

Sister H. Ross speaks as follows about the impression made by Father and then Cardinal Bea: "Through an intense (official) correspondence and several personal meetings, I came to know and respect Father Bea as a deeply pious priest and religious. . . . His supernatural attitude appeared clearly when it was a question of shedding God's light on earthly events."[105]

A German lay brother, Brother F. Spohn, S.J., summarizes his judgment as follows: "Father and Cardinal Bea was a quite exceptional, rare and grace-filled personality given to us by the Lord. He was called to great things and did great things, but, astonishingly, he did not forget minor matters and minor people, encouraging them throughout his life. In my eyes he was and is a saint of our time."[106] Similarly, the Dutch priest Father Thijssen says: "I can only say that Cardinal Bea was an erudite man, who knew men's souls; he was a saint."[107] The Bishop of Münster, H. Tenhumberg, describes the effect that visits to Cardinal Bea made on him in the following terms: "Every time I left Cardinal Bea, I had a feeling of profound gratitude and religious joy. No doubt this is the feeling that comes over one in the presence of a holy person."[108]

A Charismatic Man

There is yet another way of viewing the whole of the cardinal's life and personality, in other words by comparing the two great periods of his life—the first devoted to biblical studies, and the second, when he was cardinal, encompassing ecumenism, his contributions to the Council, etc. In this connection the question has sometimes been raised of whether there was a true continuity in his life or whether the last period—that of his ecumenical work and contributions to the Council—represents something completely new, if not indeed a real break with his whole past.

The difference between the two periods is brought out very clearly by E. Schlink, who says that before meeting Cardinal Bea for the first time, in the fall of 1961, his Catholic friends had described him as "a very old, conservative theologian." Even after this, in the first period of Schlink's activity in Rome, "I was asked in slightly surprised tones with a hint of concern, by those who knew him from his earlier work in the order and in the Biblical Institute, as to how the ecumenical conversation was going with him." To which the author adds: "The personality I came to know and then repeatedly encountered over a period of

104. BM, pp. 335-336. P.F. Corson, in *ibid.*, p. 337, includes the cardinal among "the patron saints" of the Council.
105. ArchWit, p. 1.
106. ArchWit, p. 3.
107. ArchWit, p. 2; cf. also Giordani, "Agostino Bea," p. 1.
108. ArchWit, p. 3.

years . . . was to an astonishing degree different from the way he had been represented to me."[109] The judgment of Schlink's Catholic friends is seen repeatedly in the statements of other witnesses and in writings on Cardinal Bea.[110]

We would also recall the observation of K.E. Skydsgaard on how different his impressions were when he met the cardinal during the Council than those when he visited Father Bea in 1955.[111] Jorge Mejía, who had studied under Father Bea at the Pontifical Biblical Institute in Rome, writes about Cardinal Bea in the following terms: "Father Bea had given way to a new man, in whom his old students would have had difficulty recognizing him. . . . For those of us who had known him earlier he seemed a new man."[112]

The problem is expressed in similar but broader terms by a layman, Professor P.G. Camaiani, according to whom Bea "managed to reconcile apparently irreconcilable experiences while remaining faithful to himself: a member of the Society of Jesus, the order dedicated to the anti-Protestant struggle during the Counter-Reformation, he became the leading Catholic figure in the ecumenical movement; President of the Secretariat for Christian Unity from 1960 until his death, he had previously been Rector of the Pontifical Biblical Institute from 1930 to 1949, but also consultor to the Holy Office for the next ten years; lastly, he became the most influential of Pope John XXIII's assistants in the work of reform, having been confessor to Pius XII."[113]

1. The obvious starting point is *the new elements*, and E. Schlink describes these as follows: "Many considered this personality to be a puzzle—and the immense amount of work performed in so few years was in itself enough to give rise to such reflections. At the age of eighty, when most people have long since given up their professional activity, he launched into a new task—ecumenism— with youthful fervor and vigor. And one had the impression that his life, which was already almost over, had only now come to its real life's work. It was as if something had broken through within him that had not previously been able to work its way out, but that now thrust forward with elemental power to express itself."[114] Although Schlink does not use the term "charism," his description implies it. On the other hand the Reformed theologian O. Cullmann does use it when he writes: "Two exceptional qualities . . . enabled Cardinal Bea in a particular way to fulfill his great ecumenical task: his wisdom and his goodness,

109. BM, p. 357.
110. Cf. Hasler, "Die ökumenische Bedeutung," p. 257. J.C. Hampe, in BM, p. 347, describes him as "a complete conservative"; and Vogelsanger, "Wahrheit und Liebe," p. 11, describes him as a theologian who was "fairly conservative by nature."
111. Cf. BM, p. 360.
112. Mejía, "El Cardenal Bea," pp. 1 and 3; cf. also Hasler, "Die ökumenische Bedeutung," p. 253.
113. P.G. Camaiani, "Agostino Bea," *Critica Storica*, I (31 January 1969), 109-115. In his last words here, the author highlights a particular aspect of our problem: the special relations that Augustin Bea enjoyed, first with Pope Pius XII, and then with Pope John XXIII. How could the same man have been such a trusted advisor to two popes who were so different? We shall return to this question in due course.
114. BM, p. 358.

which struck everyone who met him. They were truly charisms, gifts of God, but Cardinal Bea also nurtured them and developed them in daily contact with the holy scriptures, which were the source of his personal piety."[115] He seems to me more than justified in talking about charisms, for without them there is no explaining the cardinal's prodigious activity, with all the circumstances mentioned by E. Schlink—still less its extraordinary breadth of influence.[116]

The concept of this charismatic character is further expanded on and enriched by J. Höfer, who starts from the fact that a number of Evangelical theologians see the cardinal as "a charismatic" and explains the fact as follows: "He prayed for illumination for his faith and through his faith—and certainly not only during his retreats. He looked for progress in the visible unification of divided Christians through the gift of grace. In prayerful contact with his Lord, he performed the ecumenical work that had been entrusted to him. The whole of his personality was inevitably marked by this. Evangelical theologians were thinking of this when they called him a charismatic."[117] Returning to this same idea, the author agrees with the Evangelical authors who call Bea "a charismatic personality," explaining it as follows: "His charism did not cancel the natural, acquired gifts, but gave his calmness, prudence and patience a spiritual stamp and manner of acting—and the father or cardinal was unaware of this. He lived in prayer, and was not far from contemplation of the will and model of Christ in the midst of demanding work. The spiritual, supernatural dimension had become natural to him."[118]

We would lastly recall what we said at the beginning of this chapter when explaining the principal quality that immediately struck those who met the cardinal—his amiability, humanity, goodness—and quoted the very apt expression used by Dr. K.E. Skydsgaard that "the cardinal appeared to be animated by an authentic Johannine love.[119]

2. Let us now consider this particular aspect in connection with Father Bea, in other words before he was made a cardinal and before he was appointed president of the secretariat. Of course, from the time of the first statements on his activity as priest at Aachen (1914-1917), as professor, and then as provincial and as rector of the Biblical Institute, his readiness to help, his humanity and benevolence, and his serene and cordially welcoming attitude are always recognized. Some more critical statements do, however, note some other and less attractive aspects, connected with his strong, severe character. Father H. Koffler, S.J., who lived with the young superior Augustin Bea at Aachen in

---

115. *Ibid.*, p. 340.
116. Two other witnesses also speak of charisms in a certain sense. W.A. Visser 't Hooft, in *Simposio*, p. 25, writes that the cardinal possessed "the charisms that are features of the true ecumenist: readiness to listen, capacity for friendship, patience as concerns visible results." And Stransky, "Deux pionniers," p. 2, sees "a clearly charismatic quality" in the fact that during the time of the Council, which was so full of tensions, the cardinal never lost his calm or serenity.
117. Höfer, "Das geistliche Profil," p. 53; in this connection the author refers the reader to his article in *LThK*, X, 465.
118. *Ibid.*, pp. 58-59. J. Mejía also speaks of charisms, as we shall see in due course.
119. BM, p. 360.

1914-1915 as a novice, says that his relations with his superior were "very stiff and formal," and that "an icy atmosphere" reigned, and then goes on to say: "I came from a family of Prussian government officials, and dealing with authority was nothing new to me. If Father Bea was formal, I was far more so as a result of my education." Father Koffler adds, however, that Father Bea soon realized that this was not the right way to behave with fellow religious, and thus one day he invited the novice to walk with him. This walk "remained unforgettable" to the novice in question. "En route . . . Father Bea talked of his teachers in Berlin, and asked about my personal situation and interests, and was glad to learn that I was interested in oriental languages and so on. The ice was thus broken. After that Father Bea became a fatherly friend to me, and remained so until the end."[120]

We have another statement about the same period, which on the one hand corrects Koffler's harsh judgment, but on the other indicates character traits that explain the facts described. The witness in question is another Jesuit, Hermann Huber, who succeeded Koffler as assistant to Father Bea: "As superior of the house, Father Bea was strict and set store by punctuality and order. . . . The confreres coming to the house—from Valkenburg and from the front—were received by Father Bea most cordially, and he was always willingly at their disposal." Huber adds a general observation: "Although he had a strong temperament, I cannot remember ever having seen him overbearing or angry. . . . He used to talk willingly during recreation after the midday meal, but he was impersonal and serious rather than light-hearted and entertaining."[121]

The observation that Bea was impersonal and serious rather than lighthearted and entertaining explains how Father Koffler can comment as follows about Bea in his later position as Prefect of Studies at Valkenburg (1917-1921): "I cannot claim that Father Bea was particularly popular. He was too impersonal for that, not to say 'business-like.' "[122]

During his time as Rector of the Biblical Institute in Rome, his cordiality and kindliness in dealings with other people are also stressed, and we read that he was always smiling, that he was a good listener, and that he was understanding, welcoming, and gave fatherly encouragement.[123] However, one witness who recognizes that Bea was "always very polite and friendly and almost always smiling" does observe: "He had so much to do that I rarely had a personal conversation with my rector."[124]

Two episodes from this period give a glimpse of the traits noted above by H. Koffler. The lay brother B. Hagemann was Bea's typist for almost the whole of his time as rector, and I believe that Bea had great respect and appreciation for his reliability and fidelity. Despite this, relations were not particularly warm. Hagemann had received permission to smoke from the major superior, and when the rector learned about this he was not very happy. And Hagemann himself

120. ArchWit, pp. 1-2.
121. ArchWit.
122. ArchWit, p. 2.
123. Cf. p. 111 above.
124. L. Rood, S.J., student at the Pontifical Biblical Institute from 1932 to 1935; ArchWit.

confided to me once: "In all the years that I worked with Bea, he almost never addressed a personal word to me."

I would also describe my own experience of my first meeting with the then Rector of the Biblical Institute. I came to Rome in the fall of 1941 and my professor of sacred scripture in Croatia, who knew Father Bea, asked me to take him his greetings. I went to the institute, gave the rector the message, and told him that my provincial had decided I was to pursue biblical studies. I asked for any helpful advice and possibly the name of some book I could read in this connection. Upon which he asked me to tell him precisely what I wanted. Then, since the conversation had gone on long enough for him, he told me with a smile: "And now we'll send you home." I cannot say that I was very favorably struck by this gesture. However, I must add that about one month later I received a note in which he offered to lend me a certain biblical commentary, obviously in answer to my request at our meeting. It would seem that he had since realized that all was not well and was trying to make amends. I accepted his offer, and relations were smoothed out.

We find a similar situation in *the ten years prior to his creation as cardinal.* The well-known Lutheran Pastor R. Baumann, who met Father Bea on various occasions starting in 1956, writes about him as follows: "He is straightforward, honest, convivial, indeed brotherly and fatherly. . . . He is kind and helpful."[125] A somewhat different impression is described by K.E. Skydsgaard whom we have quoted a number of times and who met Augustin Bea for the first time in 1955: "When I think back, I see the image of a serious, friendly, somewhat cautious, prudent man. He hardly smiled; and if he did, it was only the hint of a smile."[126]

J. Höfer was understandably puzzled by the opinions on Bea that could be heard among his acquaintances in the mid-1950s and that seemed "contradictory": "He is described as friendly, tirelessly ready to help, but also as unapproachable—the latter meaning that one can approach him in a conversation only concerning the matter in hand, but not in personal terms; he remains inscrutable."[127] The well-known Jesuit Father R. Leiber, private secretary first to Cardinal Pacelli and then to the latter as Pius XII, spoke to Höfer as follows about Bea: "Look out! Father Bea is made of steel!"[128]

In summary, we can certainly accept the presence of kindliness and affability, although they are not given free rein because of other traits—force of character, seriousness, severity, a sense of order—which have an even more marked influence because of the number of his commitments. The inaccessibility referred to by J. Höfer could also come from the fact that Father Bea was a superior of religious communities almost throughout his life, often in fairly difficult positions, so that he perhaps felt he had a duty to hold himself at a certain distance from people.[129] However, we are still left with the huge

---

125. ArchWit.
126. BM, pp. 359-360.
127. Höfer, "Das geistliche Profil," p. 54.
128. *Ibid.*
129. Moreover, in the retreat notes of the cardinal himself, we find incontrovertible evidence that

difference between the image of Father Bea and that of the cardinal as described above and at the beginning of the present chapter respectively. We are thus faced with the question of how statements about the cardinal are all so unanimously positive, without a trace of the reservations that were glimpsed to some extent in all the previous periods in the life of this man. It seems to me that the answer lies in what more than one of the authors quoted holds to be a "charism."

A similar observation could be made with regard to the reflections made in the section entitled "Conservative Reformer" above. Certainly in our chapter on Father Bea's activity as professor and Rector of the Pontifical Biblical Institute, we saw that in that period, too, alongside the "conservative" element there was a clearly visible openness to new things, to discoveries and to anything that such discoveries could contribute to a better understanding of the word of God.[130] However, in the president of the secretariat the openness toward others and toward the necessary renewal of the Catholic Church was such that it surprised and aroused admiration—so much so that Archbishop Ramsey was able to say that this openness had created a whole revolution in ecumenical thinking, a revolution that has not remained confined to the Catholic Church.[131] The surprise and admiration were all the greater because the cardinal was also clearly very firmly rooted and anchored in his own church, and his openness went hand in hand with a marked fidelity to the church and to its tradition and magisterium.

In conclusion, we can note that not everything is clear in descriptions and explanations of the presumed charism: the authors do not all follow the same line of reasoning, so that they describe and explain things in different ways. However, there is always the fact of the presence of charismatic gifts in the cardinal. On this basis, we can give a first answer to our original question of whether there was a continuity or a break in his life. There was neither a simple continuity, nor a true break, but rather a line of development—though one where there was an extraordinary intervention of the Holy Spirit at a certain moment, bringing about a leap in quality. However, this intervention did not constitute a break, because it was harmoniously grafted onto the long preparation, so that (to use the words of J. Höfer) although its effect was supernatural, it seemed like second nature.[132]

Deep Links with the Church

In our section entitled "Conservative Reformer," we saw how various non-Catholics emphasize the cardinal's deep link with the church in one way

---

he was aware that he had something "stiff" in his character that had to be kept in check. In his 1964 retreat, meditating on the marriage feast of Cana, he draws the following lesson: "I must always be attentive to the needs, difficulties, etc., of my neighbor, particularly of the people around me. I must do this out of love or for other lofty reasons; *thus I must not be stiff*" (1964/IV/3; *Der Mensch Bea*, p. 185).

130. Cf. pp. 119-122 above.

131. BM, p. 336.

132. Cf. Höfer, "Das geistliche Profil," p. 59.

or another, saying that he was firmly anchored in his own church,[133] that he was a faithful son of his church,[134] and that he was deeply rooted in the church.[135] We shall now examine this aspect of our portrait in greater depth.

1. Let us first of all consider his *fundamental concept*: for him, it is Christ himself who lives and works in the church.[136] This aspect of Bea's underlying ecclesiological convictions was clearly—and I would say authoritatively—described by John Paul II himself on the basis of the retreat notes I published in *Spiritual Profile*. The pope said: "This sense of the church as vivified by Christ is in fact seen in all the activities that I have mentioned, and this is expressed in two phrases drawn from his spiritual notes: 'The church is not simply a pious association, but Christ himself who continues to live, with all his gifts and graces' (cf. 1 Cor. 12:12-17), which has the following consequence: 'My work must always proceed from participation in the life and destiny of the church; the church must provide the form.' "[137] After giving examples of this attitude of the cardinal in his work in the church and for the church, the pope describes another aspect: "The depth of these links with the church—his feeling with the church in the deepest sense of the word—also opened him up to the needs of the world, so that he observed and interpreted the signs of the times, in order to understand what the Spirit is saying to the churches today (cf. Rev. 2:7)."[138]

2. This also explains *his love for the church*, which is described by a number of people. The Lutheran Pastor J.C. Hampe writes: "He loved his church, he inclined himself before it, whether he understood or disapproved of its decisions."[139] "The cardinal's human qualities were rooted in a deep sense of the priestly life and of love of the church," writes Gianfrancesco Arrighi.[140] After describing the cardinal's loyalty and fidelity to the church, G. Vodopivec wonders how he could have been so explicit, and at times almost harsh, in stating this fidelity. "The answer is that his statements did not sound offensive precisely because he also gave an almost transparent witness of convinced and total fidelity to his own church and to his Christian brethren, trusting and expecting the will of the Lord of all to be accomplished." The author then explains: "Two fidelities and two loves, both of which came from the Bible, from the same word of God: 'That they may be one.' He often also repeated the instruction to 'do the truth in love' (Eph. 4:15) as a favorite golden rule."[141]

One last observation on this point is made by the Jesuit Father General Pedro Arrupe: "Augustin Bea is a man of the church. He thought ecclesially; he loved

133. Cf. the Old-Catholic Professor W. Küppers, in BM, p. 334.
134. Cf. the retired Lutheran Bishop W. Stählin, in *ibid.*, p. 361.
135. Cf. L. Vischer, in *ibid.*, p. 369.
136. Cf. *Der Mensch Bea*, pp. 326-327.
137. *Simposio*, p. VII. For the two texts cited, cf. 1963/VIII/1 and 1966/IV/3; *Der Mensch Bea*, pp. 168, 232.
138. *Ibid.*, p. VIII.
139. BM, p. 347.
140. Arrighi, "Il Cardinale Agostino Bea, primo Presidente," p. 720.
141. Vodopivec, "Il Cardinale Agostino Bea," p. 55.

the church; he committed himself to its renewal; he suffered with the church, above all on account of the division of Christians and continuing injustice."[142]

4. This love was also the underlying reason for his *submissiveness and obedience* toward the church. A. Hasler writes: "For decades he had shown himself to be a faithful and trustworthy servant of his church. Although he had a critical mind, he kept an almost childlike submissiveness to the decisions of the supreme church leaders, a submissiveness so total that it would be very difficult to equal."[143] As an example the author cites the fact that the cardinal had repeatedly asked that out of regard for other Christians the Council should not proclaim any new titles for the Blessed Virgin, but that he then fully accepted Paul VI's proclamation of Mary as "Mother of the Church."[144]

E. Fortino describes the cardinal as follows: "A great and faithful servant of the church, deeply attached to the Holy See and the Roman Pontiff."[145] The Superior General of the Secular Institute of Schönstatt, H. Ross, writes: "A profound religious attitude of obedience permeated all Father Bea did. Once the church had established dispositions through its representatives, he stood upon the ground of obedience, and saw to it that these dispositions were carried out and observed. However, when he saw human error at work, this attitude did not stop him from seeking ways and means—with illuminated prudence and great humility—of preventing disaster and helping the truth to come to light."[146] Lastly, a Dominican sister writes: "In the replies he gave to my questions concerning topical religious events, I was most impressed by his compassionate love for the Holy Father, his childlike love for the Mother of God and his clear, faithful support for his church, which was in no way in contradiction to his ecumenical thinking and indefatigable ecumenical activity."[147]

The Role of Pope John XXIII

In the context of the cardinal's relations with the church, we still have to describe and explain Bea's specific links with Pope John XXIII.

We can start by looking at the opinions of *two observer-delegates, both Lutherans*. In his statement, E. Schlink mentions various elements in Bea's ecumenical preparation, but thinks that the decisive factor was his meeting with Pope John: "However, the encounter with Pope John XXIII must have been decisive for him. His plan of renewal was taken up by him and thought through ecumenically, and he totally dedicated the rest of his life to this."[148] Similarly, K.E. Skydsgaard writes: "I was often with Cardinal Bea in the years 1962 to

142. BM, p. 16.
143. Hasler, "Die ökumenische Bedeutung," p. 257.
144. Cf. pp. 529-530 above.
145. E.F. Fortino, "Agostino Bea: rivoluzione ecumenica non violenta," *Ricerca*, XXXIV/22-23 (15 December 1968), 3. Cf. also Cardinal P. Pavan, in *Simposio*, p. 120.
146. ArchWit, p. 1.
147. This was the Prioress of Zoffingen Convent at Constance, Magdalene Israel, O.P., ArchWit.
148. BM, p. 358.

1965 in my capacity as Council observer for the World Lutheran Federation. He was the same man [as the one I had met in 1955] and yet—it seems to me—another. Pope John must have elicited qualities that were found in him only potentially until then: a surprising liberty and openness."[149]

One of the authors who speaks of Bea as "charismatic," J. Mejìa, also considers this gift in relation to the church as institution: "In him there is no opposition between institution and charism. Should we say (as I believe) that he always enjoyed charisms, but that he put them to their full use only when he was called to this by the institution? Or should we say that he received his charisms when the institution placed him in a situation that called for charisms? It basically amounts to the same thing. The fact remains that one of the most charismatic men of the contemporary church owes his prophetic effectiveness to his living link with the institution of the church. I say one of the most charismatic men, and the other (for it is difficult to find a third) with a similar history and development is Angelo Roncalli, John XXIII."[150]

Let us see if we can reach a deeper understanding of this influence exercised by Pope John and his papacy on the cardinal. Monsignor L.F. Capovilla gives us some precious clues: "The fairly lengthy conversations [with Bea] were a comfort to the Supreme Pontiff, who drew inspiration from them for further impetus in his apostolic commitment, bolstered by the support of a man of such stature."[151] Capovilla then goes on to explain relations between the two personalities, distinguishing four categories of people with whom John XXIII had "confidential relations": "immediate high collaborators," "friends and old acquaintances from Bergamo and Rome," "collaborators and assistants," and "*soul friends.*" He speaks about the last category, observing: "These were the few people with whom he opened himself completely. His confessor, Monsignor Alfredo Cavagna, should be included among these. Cardinal Bea was also a member of this group. He felt at ease with him. He had a kind of feeling that he had always walked with him. He sensed the contact with the master who did not like to assert himself or impose his views."[152]

Conversations with the pope had a similar effect on the cardinal. I remember the first meeting between John XXIII and Augustin Bea, who was already a cardinal, which took place on 9 January 1960. The cardinal came out of the private library radiant, and told me: "We understood one another perfectly." In a note made in 1965, the cardinal wrote: "My personal contacts with Pope John were always a deeply personal and joyful feast of the spirit for me. They allowed me to enter into his innermost religious life and see that his judgments and his actions sprang from this hidden source."[153] We find the following statement in

---

149. *Ibid.*, p. 360. We are obviously referring not to the very great assistance that Pope John gave the secretariat in various ways, but to the influence he exercised on the cardinal himself.

150. Mejìa, "El Cardenal Bea," p. 3.

151. ArchWit., p. 3.

152. *Ibid.*, pp. 3-4. Capovilla finds proof of the fact that the pope opened himself with Cardinal Bea in the portrait that the latter made of him in the volume *Unity in Freedom*, pp. 59-61.

153. Ms. R 1965/48.

the cardinal's short portrait of Pope John: "I never came out of an audience with him without being deeply impressed by his character; he was so large-minded, so tolerant and so forbearing, and yet so strong, so inflexible in his principles and in his purposes. Such he was as I knew him, and I admired him as a man great in his humility and humble in his greatness."[154]

There is no doubt that this deep understanding—which can be called a spiritual friendship—is of major importance in explaining Pope John XXIII's influence on Cardinal Bea. But is it all? I do not think so. In this connection it is extremely instructive to draw a comparison between the spirit of Father Bea's relations with Pope Pius XII and that of his relations with Pope John XXIII. In the relative chapter we used Father Bea's retreat notes to show that the spirit of his relations with Pius XII was a deeply religious one. He saw the pope as "the vicar of Christ on earth": "And the closer my task lies to the vicar of Christ, the more is the question 'Do you love me *more than these*?' applicable to me."[155] In the pope Bea loved and served Christ himself.

If we now examine Bea's retreat notes from his time as cardinal, and hence from the time of Pope John XXIII, we find exactly the same spirit and reflections. During the very first retreat, the cardinal writes in his meditation on the kingdom of Christ: "This meditation now takes on an entirely new meaning for me. The King and Lord of all things is now the only one who can give me orders through his vicar. Thus I am his most immediate and close instrument, and I remain here only in order to follow him as directly and closely as possible."[156] Three years later, almost identical reflections are found as those we saw for the time of Pius XII: "The closer I am to the successor of St. Peter, the more is the question 'Do you love me? Do you love me more than these?' valid for me too, and I must be able to reply humbly: 'Lord you know all things; you know that I love you!' "[157] The foremost element—and in the final analysis the decisive one—in his relations with Pope John XXIII is therefore not friendship, but the deeply religious, christological and ecclesiological view that sees the pope as Christ's vicar on earth.

In 1969 Cardinal Bea's successor, Johannes Willebrands, spoke about the cardinal in the presence of Patriarch Athenagoras I, saying that Cardinal Bea had accepted the tasks entrusted to him by Pope John as "a new vocation."[158] And the cardinal himself did in fact see it as a vocation. Reflecting on the events of his life, he said: "My whole life has been a preparation for this task." However, his faith, which meant that he saw the pope as Christ's vicar, meant that in a new way he became sure that it was a mission entrusted to him by Christ himself. And this awareness, which was drawn from faith, unleashed and elicited new energies in him.[159]

---

154. *Unity in Freedom*, pp. 59-60.
155. Cf. pp. 186-188 above.
156. 1960/III/2; *Der Mensch Bea*, p. 329.
157. 1960/VIII/3; *Der Mensch Bea*, p. 325.
158. We quote from the manuscript, since for some unexplained reason the passage concerning Cardinal Bea was omitted from the speech as published in *SI*, IX/I (1970).
159. The cardinal's contribution to the implementation of Pope John XXIII's plan has often been emphasized. The foregoing shows how necessary it is to see also the essential contribution of

An Instrument in God's Hand

We have already referred to the question of whether Bea's time as cardinal, with all its relative work, represents a continuity or a complete break with his previous life, and we still have to consider two interesting attempts at an answer. The first is that of the Bishop of Münster, H. Tenhumberg, who considers the more specific question of how the same man could have been a trusted advisor to both Pope Pius XII and Pope John XXIII, two so very different popes. He writes that when the cardinal assessed the Council, or more generally any events in the life of the church, he was "extraordinarily sober." "I often had the impression," writes Bishop Tenhumberg, "that he was congenial not only to Pope Pius XII but also to Pope John XXIII and Pope Paul VI. The reason for this impression was probably not so much a particularly marked capacity to adapt to various people—although he certainly possessed this faculty—but more an availability that was a gift of the Spirit and was impressed by Jesuit spirituality."[160]

However flattering it may be to Bea, let us leave aside the statement that he was congenial to the three pontiffs, and try instead to follow the clue of the spirituality of the Society of Jesus and in particular the concept of "openness" or "availability." It is very interesting, and maybe significant, that G. Camaiani should have sought a solution along the same lines. Starting in general terms with the question of a continuity or a break between the two periods of Augustin Bea's life, he suggests the following solution: "The key to an explanation of this exceptional capacity for synthesizing and grasping the most varied situations as elements to move in the same direction can be found both in the man's personal gifts and in the features typical of more 'progressive' Jesuits, whose best exponents are sometimes able to reach the most difficult of balances: that between *total ascetical availability* to the wishes of the order, and the spirit of personal initiative; and that between submissive obedience to the tradition of the church and the instructions of the pope, and a critical commitment that is very open to the suggestions of contemporary thinking. In this way, and with obedient shrewdness, they are able to move as far ahead as is permitted within the structures of the church in the various circumstances involved. Bearing this aspect in mind, we can solve the major problem in evaluating our portrait of Cardinal Bea, or that of the 'continuity' or 'newness' in the historic task performed after 1959 in the period of his life richest in innovating contributions."[161]

We would start by noting that these two authors make special mention of Jesuit spirituality, and in this connection we would quote the words of Father General Pedro Arrupe, who states very explicitly that the cardinal lived this spirituality in great depth: "Bea lived from the spirit of the Ignatian Exercises

Pope John XXIII to what Cardinal Bea accomplished.

160. ArchWit, pp. 2-3.

161. Camaiani, "Agostino Bea," pp. 109-110.

and the Constitutions of the Society of Jesus. In the order he was always ready for ever greater service for the glory of God and the salvation of his fellow men, and felt himself very deeply bound to it until the end of his life."[162]

Taking this as our starting point, let us turn our attention to the element that is common to both attempts to consider the cardinal's personality in greater depth, in other words his "availability" or "ascetical availability." I think that this concept points fairly clearly toward a particular hallmark of the Constitutions of St. Ignatius: the idea that in his apostolate each member of the order is "an instrument in God's hand," as a classic passage in the Constitutions states.

In Part Ten of the Constitutions we read: "For the preservation and development not only of the body or exterior of the Society but also of its spirit, and for the attainment of the objective it seeks, which is to aid souls to reach their ultimate and supernatural end, the means which unite the human instrument with God and so dispose it that it may be wielded dexterously by his divine hand are more effective than those which equip it in relation to men. Such means are, for example, goodness and virtue, and especially charity, and a pure intention of the divine service, and familiarity with God our Lord in spiritual exercises of devotion, and sincere zeal for souls for the sake of glory to him who created and redeemed them and not for any other benefit."[163]

Let us be clear about *the intention* of this passage. The author stresses that in order to preserve the order and pursue its goals, supernatural means are more effective than natural gifts, for they ensure the union of man the instrument with God, and also his compliancy. The idea that the order, and thus its individual members, are "instruments in God's hand" is not so much the object of this passage, but almost an assumption or self-evident truth.

To avoid any misunderstanding, we must point out that when it is stated that man is an "instrument" in the hand of God, we are certainly not thinking of some kind of lifeless or mechanical instrument, but always of a living, intelligent and free instrument. And all these human faculties cooperate in the action of the instrument; and they do so freely. The idea that man is an instrument in God's hand does not refer simply to the fact that he is a wretched creature whom the Creator can make use of as he pleases, but is above all an expression of the faith-based awareness that salvation is essentially an undeserved gift of God and a work of grace, and that whoever cooperates in it must always say with St. Paul: "I worked . . . though it was not I, but the grace of God which is with me" (1 Cor. 15:10).

Thus we are dealing with *a truly biblical concept*. We are thinking of the gospel parable of the vine and the branches, which is so true that Christ states categorically that in this order of divine life begun by him "apart from me you can do nothing" (John 15:5). And when St. Paul speaks about the variety of divine gifts (or charisms) he says: "There are varieties of working, but it is the same God who inspires them all in every one. . . . All these are inspired by one

---

162. BM, p. 16.

163. *Constitutions*, Part X, no. 2 (813). The concept of being an instrument is also found in Part VII, chap. 4, no. 3.

and the same Spirit, who apportions to each one individually as he wills" (1 Cor. 12:6, 11). And this is how the mystical body of Christ is built up and grows: Christ "is the head . . . from whom the whole body, joined and knit together by every joint with which it is supplied, when each part is working properly, makes bodily growth and upbuilds itself in love" (Eph. 4:16).

The retreat notes published in *Spiritual Profile* show that the cardinal *lived this principle in great depth*. The concept of being simply an instrument in the hand of God is reiterated a number of times. Indeed, the cardinal enriches the Ignatian concept with christological and ecclesiological elements. He feels that he is an instrument not only in *God's* hand, but more specifically in the hand of Christ and thus that of the church, in which Christ himself lives and works.

In his meditation on the kingdom of Christ, the retreatant paraphrases the final prayer in the Ignatian meditation ("Take, Lord, and receive") as follows: "Thus my watchword can only be: 'Accept, Lord, the whole of my will. . . . All I have and possess is yours, and I give it back to you.' Thus *an instrument* ever and totally devoted to him—following his own example."[164] Similarly, in the meditation on the feeding of the five thousand, he writes: "The example of the Savior: he does not set himself in the foreground, and yet he is the center from which all else flows. We are his *instruments*: nothing else. Am I always a good instrument? I shall take pains to be so more and more."[165] The retreatant also sees the celebration of the eucharist in the same light, so that in his meditation on the Last Supper, he writes: "I must constantly renew this thought within me, so that I do not go to the altar as a matter of routine, cold and indifferent, but am aware that as an *instrument* of the Savior I renew his sacrifice of praise, thanksgiving, intercession and propitiation every morning."[166]

And this attitude of placing himself totally in Christ's hands springs *from love*. Meditating on the calling of the apostles, the retreatant writes: "For me he has been everything he was for his apostles, but I have not yet attained what I might call that 'blind' love of the Savior, which places itself *exclusively and without reservation* at his service, and seeks and desires nothing other than to be his instrument, an instrument in the sense of the sixteenth rule."[167]

A fuller explanation is found when the concept of instrument is linked to the very similar one of *service*: "However, I have a special debt of gratitude toward God for all he has done for me, and for all the special graces he has given me, not on account of my merit, but exclusively out of his will that I should become a special instrument of his salvific will. In a very special way, he has placed the accomplishment of his salvific will in my hands. . . . 'O Lord, I am thy servant, the son of thy handmaid' (Psalm 116:16)."[168]

---

164. Med. 1965/II/3; *Der Mensch Bea*, p. 209.

165. Med. 1967/V/3; *Der Mensch Bea*, p. 257.

166. Med. 1961/VI/3; *Der Mensch Bea*, p. 115.

167. Med. 1962/V/3; *Der Mensch Bea*, pp. 139-140. The "sixteenth rule" states that the interior life and holiness, and thus love, are much more important than natural and human gifts for the fruitfulness of apostolic work.

168. Med. 1964/I/2; *Der Mensch Bea*, pp. 177-178. Cf. also Med. 1960/I/2; *Der Mensch Bea*, pp. 71-72.

It is noteworthy and typical of the cardinal that this idea is also linked to *service of the church and of the vicar of Christ*. After he has said, "I am his most immediate and close instrument," he continues: "This is part of my position, but it must also be present in my will: 'I must be set on fire with greater zeal and must distinguish myself in every service of the eternal King.' "[169] Again, when meditating on how much Christ has done for his church, the retreatant concludes: "It is this church that I am allowed to serve in an eminent position."[170] "It must be an honor and a joy to me to work for the successor of St. Peter."[171]

What do these observations add to our spiritual portrait of the cardinal? A first reflection is that the belief that he was an instrument and nothing but an instrument in God's hand gave the cardinal above all a great interior freedom and a great openness to any type of cooperation. This is where we should seek *the true basic explanation* of Bea's close relations of trust with both Pope Pius XII and Pope John XXIII. Apart from his gift of adaptability and other factors that facilitated understanding and cooperation,[172] the spiritual and supernatural element was decisive for Father Bea as it later was for Cardinal Bea: for him both popes were the vicar of Christ, and he was at their service; he was their instrument, and hence absolutely compliant.

However, the spirituality of being an instrument in God's hand leads us to a much deeper level of the cardinal's portrait. It gives us an idea of *the internal bond that united all the elements of the portrait* described in our study. They all received their orientation and cohesive force in the cardinal's awareness and wish to be simply an instrument in God's hand—or, as the cardinal writes, an instrument in the hand of Christ who lives and works in and through the church. It is not hard to see how this conviction provides further confirmation of his deep links with the church, and thus explains his fidelity to the church, and to its tradition and magisterium, all qualities that very deeply impressed Catholics and other Christians alike.

This same spirituality also helps us understand the cardinal's deep spiritual life. With the aim of bringing men to God constantly before his eyes, and his awareness that he was Christ's instrument in this task, the cardinal cultivated anything that could foster closer union of the instrument with God and dispose it to allow him to guide it well, in other words deep union with God in Christ, the trilogy of faith, hope and love. The same thing should also be said of the other qualities noted in this chapter: goodness, understanding, love, wisdom and a sense of reality, courage and perseverance, prudence, simplicity, humility, meekness, and patience.

To summarize, this study has certainly revealed the great wealth and consid-

---

169. Med. 1960/III/2; *Der Mensch Bea*, pp. 77-78; quoting *Spiritual Exercises*, 97.

170. Med. 1962/VIII/3; *Der Mensch Bea*, p. 146.

171. Med. 1959/VI/1; *Der Mensch Bea*, p. 55.

172. For example, Bea's admiration for Pius XII, which meant that he called him "my august model" (cf. Nc 25/1956; N 1953/73) and in fact considered him his spiritual model (cf. Höfer, "Das geistliche profil," p. 57). Another factor was the spiritual friendship that linked Bea and John XXIII, as we saw above.

erable complexity of the cardinal's personality. However, in the light of the spirituality of being an instrument in God's hand, the many elements of our portrait come together and are knitted into one complex but integrated whole. Referring back to the title of this biography, we could say that Augustine Bea was "the cardinal of unity" partly, or indeed primarily, because he was a personality deeply united within himself. The fact that he saw himself simply as an instrument of God to bring men to God and God to men gave his personality a deep interior unity and ensured his deep union with God in Christ; and this made him a compliant instrument in Christ's hand. It is here that we should seek the secret of the incredible effectiveness of his proclamation and activity in favor of unity in the broadest sense of the word.

* * *

In conclusion, on 20 April 1963, less than two years prior to his blessed death, Pope John XXIII told an Italian layman in a private audience: "Think what a great grace the Lord gave me in finding Cardinal Bea."[173] This was an expression of humble gratitude for what the cardinal had done above all in furthering the ecumenical aspect of the pope's plan of renewal. The cardinal himself, looking back over the almost nine years of his activity as first President of the Secretariat for Christian Unity, could equally well have said that the papacy of Pope John, particularly the fact of having made him president of the secretariat, had been a great grace of the Lord for him. There was a very special reason for this, for Augustin Bea said that this task had enabled him to understand the often enigmatic way in which the Lord had guided his life along paths that sometimes seemed tortuous to human eyes. And he explained that it was precisely this great variety of experiences, which were frequently difficult, and the need to keep beginning again in new situations, that had given him a firmness, combined with a necessary flexibility, two qualities that were indispensable for the person chosen by providence to take charge of the ecumenical aspect of the Second Vatican Council and pave the way for the official entry of the Catholic Church into the ecumenical movement. At the vital point on the road from the long period of preparation to the fulfillment of this divine plan stood Pope John XXIII with his personality, with his plan for the Council as inspired in him by the Lord and with the serene energy with which he implemented it. In other words, through Pope John the Lord had enabled the cardinal to discover and fulfill the true vocation of his life—his ecumenical mission.

In both cases, the grace given by the Lord to these two men of the church was also a great gift to the whole church.

---

173. The phrase was said to Vittorino Veronese, former Director General of UNESCO, who told me this in the antechamber of the dying Pope John XXIII on 1 June 1963.

APPENDICES

APPENDIX 1

SELECT BIBLIOGRAPHY
OF CARDINAL AUGUSTIN BEA

The *full* bibliography and the criteria followed in its composition are found in the two unabridged versions—Italian and German—of this biography, while a reduced bibliography seemed sufficient and preferable for the present abridged version. The principles followed in preparing this select bibliography are as follows.

1. *The aim* governing the choice is twofold: that of providing the reader with the essential information, and that of facilitating citation in the course of the biography by referring simply to the various numbers of this bibliography, which means that footnotes can be much shorter.

2. In our choice we have dealt differently with the part concerning *academic* publications (roughly the first 130 entries) and those that are *for the most part* (although not exclusively) *aimed at a broader audience* and date from the time when he had been created a cardinal. We felt it was right to give preference in a way to the former category, both because of its very nature and also because of the essential role it had in preparing and shaping Bea as ecumenist. The latter category allows greater cuts, both because not all the publications are of equal importance, and also (and above all) because many articles were later included in the cardinal's books.

3. Obviously *the books* cannot be treated in the same way as the articles, interviews, etc. Thus, in the case of books, we give not only the original, but also *all the translations*, which will give an idea of the readership the individual works reached in various countries.

4. The *criterion* for the inclusion of an entry in the bibliography is the importance that an article, interview, etc., had in the preparation of an idea, the development of a line of thinking, or more generally in historical terms.

5. Although it might have seemed reasonable to renumber the entries in the present bibliography, we have preferred to retain the entry numbers used in the full bibliography as found in the Italian and German versions. This means (a) that if the reader so wishes, he or she can consult one of the latter for further information, and also (b) that we have been able to avoid confusion in our footnotes.

Abbreviations of Frequently Cited Reviews, Dictionaries, etc.

Bib	*Biblica*, Pontifical Biblical Institute, Rome
CC	*La Civiltà Cattolica*, Rome
DocCath	*La Documentation Catholique*, Paris
EncCatt	*Enciclopedia Cattolica*, Vatican City
Greg	*Gregorianum*, Pontifical Gregorian University, Rome
KIPA	*Katholische Internationale Presse-Agentur*, Geneva
KNA	*Katholische Nachrichten-Agentur*, Bonn
LThK	*Lexikon für Theologie und Kirche*, Freiburg im Breisgau
Month	*The Month*, London
NRT	*Nouvelle Revue Théologique*, Louvain
Oik	*Oikumenikon*, Fiano Romano
OssRom	*L'Osservatore Romano*, Vatican City
RazFe	*Razon y Fé*, Madrid
StiZt	*Stimmen der Zeit*, Freiburg im Breisgau
TDig	*Theology Digest*, St. Mary's, Kansas
VD	*Verbum Domini*, Pontifical Biblical Institute, Rome

A. Books

1. *De Pentateucho. Institutiones biblicae scholis accommodatae.* Vol. II, *De libris V.T. Ia pars.* Rome: Pontificium Institutum Biblicum, 1928; VI + 185 pp. 2nd ed.: Rome, 1933; VIII + 245 pp.

2. *De inspiratione Sacrae Scripturae, quaestiones historicae et dogmaticae. Quas accommodavit in usum privatum auditorum.* Rome: Pontificium Institutum Biblicum, 1930; VII + 102 pp. 2nd ed.: *De Scripturae Sacrae inspiratione. Quaestiones historicae et dogmaticae. Quas in usum scholarum accommodavit.* Rome: Pontificium Institutum Biblicum, 1935; VIII + 150 pp.

2a. *Quaestiones litterariae, criticae, historicae in Librum Danielis et in Scripta Apocalyptica Veteris Testamenti. In usum privatum auditorum.* Cyclostyled. Rome: 1933; 58 pp. 2nd ed.: "Retractata." Rome: 1937; 67 pp.

3. *Pontificii Instituti Biblici de urbe prima quinque lustra, 1909 - VII Maii - 1934.* Rome: Pontificium Institutum Biblicum, 1934; 77 pp., 19 tab = (*sine illis tab.*) *Miscellanea Biblica.* Rome: Pontificium Institutum Biblicum, 1934; 1-52.= *Bib*, XIV/2-3 (1934), 121-172.

4. *Archaeologia Biblica. In usum privatum auditorum.* Cyclostyled. Rome: Pontificium Institutum Biblicum, 1939; 39 pp. + charta geogr.

4a. *Geographia Palaestinae Antiquae. Notae in usum privatum auditorum.* Rome: 1940; 63 pp.

5. *De effossionibus in Palaestina factis, quae Sacram Historiam illustrant.* Fasc. 1: *A tempore Patriarcharum ad regnum Salomonis. In usum privatum auditorum.* Cyclostyled. Rome: Pontificium Institutum Biblicum, 1941; 27 pp.

6. *Liber psalmorum cum Canticis Breviarii Romani. Nova e textibus primigeniis interpretatio latina, cum notis criticis et exegeticis, cura professorum Pontificii Instituti Biblici edita.* Rome: Pontificium Institutum Biblicum, 1945; XXIV + 350 pp. 2nd ed.: 1945; XXXI + 350 pp. Translated into various languages a number of times.

7. *La nuova traduzione latina del Salterio. Origine e spirito.* Rome: Pontificium Institutum Biblicum, 1945; 37 pp. (Cf. nos. 59a, 64.)

8. *Il nuovo Salterio Latino. Chiarimenti sull'origine e lo spirito della traduzione.* (1st ed. = no. 7.) 2nd ed.: Rome: Pontificium Institutum Biblicum, 1946; IV + 180 pp.
   In French: *Le nouveau psautier latin. Eclaircissements sur l'origine et l'esprit de la traduction.* Paris: Desclée de Brouwer, 1947; 210 pp.
   in German: *Die neue lateinische Psalmenübersetzung. Ihr Werden und ihr Geist.* Freiburg im Breisgau: Herder, 1948; VII + 171 pp.
   in Spanish: *El nuevo Salterio latino. Aclaraciones sobre el origen y el espíritu de la traducción.* Barcelona: Herder, 1947; 186 pp.
   In Portuguese: *A Nova Traduçâo Latina do Saltério.* Evora: 1946.
   In Polish: *O nowym Psalterzu Lacinskim. Geneza i duch przekladu.* Posnan: Pallottinum, 1955; VII + 122 pp.

9. *Liber Ecclesiastae qui ab Hebraeis appellatur Qohelet. Nova e textu primigenio interpretatio latina cum notis criticis et exegeticis.* Rome: Pontificium Institutum Biblicum, 1950; XIV + 30 pp.

10. *Il problema antropologico in Gen. 1-2. Il Trasformismo.* (= *Questioni Bibliche alla luce dell'Enc. "Divino afflante Spiritu,"* Part II.) Rome: Pontificium Institutum Biblicum, 1950; 68 pp.

11. *Canticum Canticorum Salomonis quod hebraice dicitur "Sir Hassirim." Nova e textu primogenio interpretatio latina cum textu masoretico ac notis criticis ac exegeticis edita.* Rome: Pontificium Institutum Biblicum, 1953; VI + 66 pp.

12. *Kleines Marianisches Offizium. Erweiterte Ausgabe.* Latin/German text. Regensburg: Pustet, 1953; XII + 510 pp.
   Latin text only: *Officium parvum Beatae Mariae Virginis. Ed. amplior.* Turin/Rome: Marietti, 1955; VIII + 373 pp.
   In French, with Latin text: *Petit Office de la Bienheureuse Vierge Marie.*

Ed. ampliée. Paris/Louvain: Lethielleux/Mont César, 1955; XII + 498 pp.
In Spanish, with Latin text: *Oficio Parvo de la Santìsima Virgen Maria*.
Ed. ampliada. Barcelona: Herder, 1957; 514 pp.
In Slovenian, included in: Dr. F. Zakelj. *Zdrava Marija, Milosti Polna*.
Adrogueja, Argentina: Ed. Marian Congregation of Slovenian Theologians, 1960; pp. 96-241.
In Japanese, with Latin text: *Officium parvum Beatae Mariae Virginis. Ed. amplior*. Sapporo: 1961; X + 607 pp.

12b. *L'unione dei cristiani. Problemi e principi. Ostacoli e mezzi. Realizzazioni e prospettive*. Rome: Ediz. CC, 1962; XI + 266 pp. (For English version, cf. no. 169.)

B. Articles

13. "In einer rückläufigen Bewegung zur Tradition: Zur Orientierung über A. Harnacks neueste Schrift: 'Neue Untersuchungen zur Apostelgeschichte und zur Abfassungszeit der synoptischen Evangelien.' Leipzig 1911." *StiZt*, LXXX (1911), 591-598.

14. "Deutsche Pentateuchforschung und Altertumskunde in den letzten vierzig Jahren." *StiZt*, XCIV (1918), 460-470.

15. "Neue Wege in der Pentateuchforschung." *StiZt*, XCIV (1918), 584-594.

16. "Antisemitismus, Rassentheorie und Altes Testament." *StiZt*, C (1920), 171-183.

17. "Die grosse Tauschung" (Zur gleichnamigen Schrift von Friedrich Delitzsch, Stuttgart 1920). *StiZt*, IC (1920), 472-477.

18. "Biblische Kritik und neuere Forschungen." *StiZt*, CXIV (1928), 401-412.

19. "P. Leopoldus Fonck S.J. + 19 oct. 1930 (Necrologio et bibliografia P. Fonck)." *Bib*, XI (1930), 369-372.

20. "Constitutionis Apostolicae 'Deus scientiarum Dominus' momentum pro studiis biblicis." *Bib*, XII (1931, 385-394.

24. "Lucrari mundum - perdere animam. Disquisitio exegetica in Mt 16,26." *Bib*, XIV (1933), 435-447.

25. "Der heutige Stand der Pentateuchfrage." *Bib*, XVI (1935), 175-200.

26. "Die Bedeutung der Ausgrabungen von Teleilat Ghassul für die Frühgeschichte Palästinas." In: *Werden und Wesen des Alten Testaments*. Beiheft 66 zur Zeitschr. f. d. Atl. Wissenschaft. Berlin: 1936; pp. 1-12.

27. "Praehistoria et exegesis libri Genesis (Haec referunt magnam partem quae de eodem argumento Auctor secunda die VII Hebdomadae Biblicae coram Pontifice Maximo Castrigandulfi disseruit)." *VD*, XVII (1937), 344-347, 360-366; XVIII (1938), 14-20.

29. "Kinderopfer für Moloch oder für Jahwe? Exegetische Anmerkungen zu O. Eissfeldt, Molk als Opferbegriff. Halle 1935." *Bib*, XVIII (1937), 95-107.

30. "Ras Samra und das Alte Testament: Zur neueren Literatur um Ras Samra." *Bib*, XIX (1938), 435-453.

30a. "Marie-Joseph Lagrange O.P." *Bib*, XIX (1938), 474-476.

30b. "Neuere Arbeiten zur biblischen Archäologie und Palästinakunde." *Bib*, XX (1939), 327-341.

32. "Pius PP. XI, quantopere de studiis biblicis meruerit. In memoriam." *Bib*, XX (1939), 121-130.

35. "Archäologisches und Religionsgeschichtliches aus Ugarit-Ras Samra." *Bib*, XX (1939), 436-453.

37. "Die Texte von Mari und das Alte Test." *Bib*, XXI (1940), 188-196.

40. With A. Ferrua. "Neueste Literatur zur Dura-Europos." *Bib*, XXI (1940), 312-320.

41. "Archäologische Beiträge zur israelistisch-jüdischen Geschichte: 1. Beth Semes-'Ain Sems; 2.''Esiongeber-'Elath: Tell el-Helefi." *Bib*, XXI (1940), 429-445.

42. "Das Zeugnis des Spatens." *StiZt*, CXXXVII (1940), 284-290. In Danish: "Hvad Spadestikker vidner om." *Credo*, XXI (Uppsala, 1940), 276-287.

43. "P. Paulus Joüon + S.J. In memoriam." *Bib*, XXI (1940), 234-237.

44. "La Costituzione Apostolica 'Deus scientiarum Dominus': origine e spirito." *Greg*, XXII (1941), 445-466.

45. "Ghassulkultur und Bandkeramik." *Bib*, XXII (1941), 433-438.

46. "Neuere Arbeiten zum Problem der biblischen Chronikbücher." *Bib*, XXII (1941), 46-58.

47. "Hummelauer, François de." *Dictionnaire de la Bible, Suppl.*, fasc. XVIII (Paris, 1941), 144-146.

48. "P. Vincentius Scheil O.P. +." *Bib*, XXII (1941), 96-97.

51. "La Compagnia di Gesù e gli studi biblici, Roma 1942." In: *La Compagnia di Gesú e le scienze sacre. Conferenze commemorative del IV centenario della fondazione della Compagnia di Gesù, tenute alla Pontificia Università Gregoriana (Roma 1941).* Ed. 1942; pp. 115-143.

52. "König Jojachin in Keilschrifttexten." *Bib*, XXIII (1942), 78-82.

52a. "Neuere Literatur zur Palästinakunde (Recensiones: Fr. Nötscher, "Biblische Altertumskunde," Bonn 1940; M. Noth, "Die Welt des A.T.," Berlin 1940; Cl. Kopp, "Grabungen und Forschungen im hl. Land," Köln 1939;

A. Scharff, "Die Frühkulturen Aegyptens und Mesopotamiens," Leipzig 1941). *Bib*, XXIII (1942), 83-94.

53. "L'enciclica''Divino afflante Spiritu.' " *CC*, XCIV (1943/IV), 212-224. (Italian translation of the encyclical in *ibid.*, pp. 193-211.)

54. " 'Divino afflante Spiritu,' De recentissimis Pii Papae XII litteris encyclicis." *Bib*, XXIV (1943), 313-322.

55. "La Palestina preisraelitica. Storia, popoli, cultura.' *Bib*, XXIV (1943), 231-260.

57. "Deus auctor S. Scripturae. Herkunft und Bedeutung der Formel."*Angelicum*, XX (1943), 16-31.

58. "Neuere Probleme und Arbeiten zur biblischen Urgeschichte." *Bib*, XXV (1944), 70-87.

59. "P. Robertus Köppel + 22 apr. 1944 (Necrologio e bibliografia)."*Bib*, XXV (1944), 254-256.

59a. "La nuova traduzione latina del Salterio. Origine e spirito." *Bib*, XXVI (1945), 203-237. (Cf. no. 7.)

59b. "P. Bernardus Allo O.P. +." *Bib*, XXVI (1945), 151.

60. "P. Augustinus Merk S.J. + 3 apr. 1945 (Necrologio e bibliografia)." *Bib*, XXVI (1945), 310-315.

62. "Die Entstehung des Alphabets; eine kritische Uebersicht." *Miscellanea Giovanni Mercati*, vol. VI. Studi e Testi 126. Vatican City: 1946; pp. 1-35.

64. "The New Psalter: Its Origin and Spirit."*Catholic Biblical Quarterly*, VIII (1946), 4-25.

65. "Institut Biblique Pontifical." *Dictionnaire de la Bible, Suppl.*, fasc. XX (Paris, 1946), 559-561.

66. "Das Marienbild des Alten Bundes." In: P. Sträter (ed.). *Katholische Marienkunde*. Paderborn: F. Schöningh, 1947; I, 23-43.
In Spanish: "Imagen de Maria en la Antigua Alianza." *Revista Biblica (Buenos Aires)*, XVI (1954), 13-16, 50-52, 88-89, 122-124.
In Italian: "La figura di Maria nell'AT." In: P. Sträter (ed.). *Mariologia*. Turin: Marietti, 1952; pp. 41-80.

67. "Il problema del Pentateuco e della storia primordiale. A proposito della recente lettera della Pont. Comm. Biblica (al card. Suhard)." *CC*, IC (1948/II), 116-127.
In French: *DocCath*, XXX (1948), 717-726.

71. "Anima. II: L'Anima nella Sacra Scrittura."*EncCatt*, I (1949), 1307-1310.

72. "Alfabeto, Origine." *EncCatt*, I (1949), 1824-1831.

73. "Archeologia Biblica." *EncCatt*, I (1949), 1798-1802.

74. "Biblos." *EncCatt*, II (1949), 1620-1621.

75. "De manuscriptis hierosolymitanis recens inventis." *Bib*, XXX (1949), 128-129, 293-295, 474-475, 546-548.

76. "Epistula aramaica saeculo VII exeunte ad pharaonem scripta." *Bib*, XXX (1949), 514-516.

77. "I manoscritti ebraici scoperti nel deserto di Giuda." *CC*, CI (1950/I), 480-494, 612-624.

77a. "Canaan e Cananei." *EncCatt*, III (1949), 480-486.

78. "De genuinitate manuscriptorum in caverna Ain Fesha inventorum." *Bib*, XXXI (1950), 242-245.

79. "Cronologia Biblica (Vecchio Testamento); Dagon: Fenicia e Fenici; Filistei; Fonck; Ghassul." *EncCatt*, IV (1950); 1011-1014; 1111-1112; V (1950), 1152-1155; 1332-1334; 1471-1472; 1958.

80. "L'enciclica''Humani generis' e gli studi biblici." *CC*, CI (1950/IV), 417-430.

82. "La Sacra Scrittura 'ultimo fondamento' del domma dell'Assunzione." *CC*, CI (1950/IV), 547-561.

83. "Die Enzyklika 'Humani generis.' Ihre Grundgedanken und ihre Bedeutung." *Scholastik*, XXVI (Freiburg im Breisgau, 1951), 36-56.

84. "Neuere Werke zur biblischen Einleitung." *Bib*, XXXII (1951), 273-280.

85. "Karge (Paul); Kennet (Robert Hatch); Knabenbauer (Joseph); Kraetzschmar (Richard); Kugler (François-Xavier)." *Dictionnaire de la Bible, Suppl.*, fasc. XXIV (vol. V) (Paris, 1951), 3-4; 7; 188-189; 198; 199-200.

86. "Die Instrumentalitätsidee in der Inspirationslehre." *Studia Anselmiana*, XXVII-XXVIII (Rome, 1951), 47-65.

88. "Pontificio Istituto Biblico; Messina Giuseppe." *EncCatt*, VII (1951), 377; VIII (1952), 870.

89. "Il progresso nell'interpretazione della Sacra Scrittura." *Greg*, XXXIII (1952), 85-105.
    In English: *TDig*, I (1953), 63-71.

90. "Il Beato Pio X, gli studi biblici e l'Istituto Biblico." In: *In onore del B. Pio X*. Rome: Pontificio Istituto Biblico, 1952; pp. 93-107. (Cf. no. 105.)

91. "'Erant perseverantes ... cum Maria Matre Iesu ... in communicatione fractionis panis' (Atti 1,14; 2,42)." *Alma Socia Christi. Acta Congressus Mariologici-Mariani Anni MCML*, VI/I (Rome: Academia Mariana Internationalis, 1952), 21-37. (For Portuguese version, cf. no. 106.)

92. "Nuova luce sui manoscritti ebraici recentemente scoperti." *CC*, CIII (1952/IV), 128-142.

93. "Maria Santissima nel Protovangelo." *Marianum*, XV (Rome, 1953), 1-21.

95. "Der heutige Stand der Bibelwissenschaft." *StiZt* (1953), 91-104. (For English version, cf. no. 103.)

96. "I nuovi manoscritti del Mar Morto." *Atti della Pontificia Accademia Romana di Archeologia, Rendiconto*, XXVII/1-2 (Rome, 1953), 17-28.

97. "L'idea della pace nel Vecchio Testamento." *XXXV Congreso Eucaristico Internacional, Sesiones de Estudio*, I (Barcelona, 1952, ed. 1954), 49-59. In Spanish: "La idea de paz en el Antiguo Testamento." *Revista Biblica*, XVIII (1956), 4-14.

98a. "Maria e i Protestanti." *Enciclopedia Mariana "Theotocos."* (Genoa/Milan, 1954), pp. 367-373.

99. "La definizione dell'Assunta e i Protestanti." *Echi e commenti del domma dell'Assunzione*. Studia Mariana, 8. Rome: Academia Mariana Intern., 1954; pp. 75-92.

100. "I primi dieci anni del nuovo Salterio latino." *Bib*, XXXVI (1955), 161-181.

103. "Biblical Studies Today." *TDig*, XXX (1955), 51-54. (Cf. no. 95.)

104. "Bulla'Ineffabilis Deus' et hermeneutica biblica." *De Immaculata Conceptione Mariae in Sacra Scriptura = Virgo Immaculata. Acta Congressus Intern. Mariologici 1954*, III (Rome, 1955), 1-17.

105. "Il B. Pio X, gli studi biblici e l'Istituto Biblico." *San Pio X, Promotore degli studi biblici, Fondatore del Pontificio Istituto Biblico*. Rome: Pont. Istituto Biblico, 1955; pp. 43-57. (Cf. no. 90.)

109. "Pio XII e gli studi biblici." *Pio XII, Pont. Max. postridie Kalendas Martii 1876-1956*. Vatican City: 1956; pp. 65-80.

111. "The Pastoral Value of the Word of God." *Worship*, XXX (Collegeville, Minn., 1956), 632-648.
Also in: *The Assisi Papers, Proceedings of the First International Congress of Pastoral Liturgy (Assisi-Rome, Sept. 18-22, 1956)*. Collegeville, Minn.: The Liturgical Press, 1956.
Original: *Die seelsorgliche Bedeutung des Wortes Gottes in der Liturgie*. Leipzig: St. Benno-Verlag, 1957; 28 pp.

112. "Nova psalterii translatio latina statistice illustrata (B. Steiert)." *VD*, XXXIV (1956), 181-186. (For Spanish version, cf. no. 118.)

113. "La rinascita di una vetusta Accademia." *Ecclesia*, XVI (Vatican City, 1957), 110-113.

114. "Discorso inaugurale: La Pontificia Accademia Teologica Romana nel nostro tempo." *Divinitas*, I (Rome: Pontifical Lateran University, 1957), 31-46.

119. "Cento anni di una enciclopedia ecclesiastica (*Lexikon für Theologie und Kirche*)." *OssRom* (3 April 1958), p. 3.

120. "Il Modernismo Biblico secondo l'enc. 'Pascendi.' " *Divinitas*, II (1958), 9-24.

121. "Date a Cesare quel che è di Cesare, e a Dio quel che è di Dio." *CC*, CIX (1958/III), 572-583.

123. "L'enc.''Pascendi' e gli studi biblici." *Bib*, XXXIX (1958), 121-138.

124. "Pio XII di s(anta) m(emoria) e la S. Scrittura.' *Bib*, XL (1959), 1-11.

125. " 'Religionswissenschaftliche' oder 'theologische,' Exegese?" *Studia Biblica et Orientalia*, I (= *Analecta Bibl.*, X), 186-207, = *Bib*, XL (1959), 322-341.

126. "La scienza biblica da Leone XIII a Pio XII." *Divinitas*, IV (1959), 590-634.

129. "Discorso per il 50° dell'Istituto Biblico, tenuto davanti al S.P. Giovanni XXIII, 17 febbr. 1960." *Bib*, XLI (1960), 9-16.

130. "Law and the Sacred Scriptures." *Thought*, XXXV (1960), 325-330. (For Italian version. cf. no. 140.)

130a. "Inspiration (der Hl. Schrift)." *LThK*, V, 703-711.

131. "Parole di chiusura alla (XVI) Settimana Biblica italiana, 24.9.1960." *CC*, CXI (1960/IV), 291-295. Also in *Atti della XVI Settimana Biblica*. Rome: Associazione Biblica Italiana, 1961; pp. 97-103.

133. "Diener des Sakramentes und Diener des Wortes." *Liturgisches Jahrbuch*, X (Trier, 1960), 193-199. (Cf. no. 144.)

134. "A proposito della visita di Sua Grazia il dott. G. Fisher." *CC*, CXI (1960/IV), 561-568.
In English: *Month*, XXV (1961), 133-150.

134a. "Conferenza stampa del Card. Bea a New York." *CC*, CXI (1960/III), 89-90).

135. "Libri sacri Deo dictante conscripti." *Estud. Eclesiast.*, XXXIV (Madrid, 1960, ed. 1961), 329-337.

137. "Positions of Catholics regarding Church Unity." *The Ecumenical Council and the Laity*. New York: Paulist Press, 1961; pp. 3-23.
Original: "Il cattolico di fronte al problema dell'unione dei cristiani." *CC*, CXI (1961/I), 113-129.

139a. "La Chiesa di Cristo è ormai superata?" *Rocca (Assisi)*, XX (15.1.1961), 12-13. Also in: *La Chiesa di Cristo non sarà mai superata*. Assisi: Ediz. pro Civitate Christiana, 1961; pp. 117-127.

142. "Il Concilio sulla via dei Protestanti: I. Consensi e difficoltà." *CC*, CXII

(1961/III), 561-572. "II. I suoi possibili contributi." *CC*, CXII (1961/IV), 3-13.
In English: "The Council and Church Unity." *The Second Vatican Council.* New York: The America Press, 1962; pp. 68-79.

142a. "Il sacerdote secondo S. Paolo: ministro di Cristo." *CC*, CXII (1961/IV), 337-349.

144. "Word and Sacrament." *Doctrine and Life*, XI (Dublin, 1961), 174-180.

150. "Geistiges Bildnis Johannes' XXIII." Chrysostomus Dahm. *Johannes XXIII.* Offenburg: 1961; pp. 9-14.

154. "Akademische Forschungs- und Lehrtätigkeit im Dienste der Einheit der Christen" (Freiburger Universitätsreden). Fribourg: Universitätsverlag, 1962; 31 pp.

158. E.C. Bianchi. "A Talk with Cardinal Bea: What are the problems that will be discussed at the coming Vatican Council?" *America*, CVII (1962), 584-590 = no. 2773 (11 August 1962).

163. "Niels Stensen und das Anliegen der Einheit der Christen" (Konferenz auf dem Katholikentag, Hannover 1962). *KNA, Sonderdiest Zweites Vatikanisches Konzil*, VI (30.8.1962), 2-3; XII (4.10.1962).

164. "Am Vorabend des 2. Vatikanischen Konzils." *StiZt*, CLXXI (1962-1963), 1-4.

167. *Apostleship of Prayer, Monthly Intentions. Commentary-Documentation.* General Intention of the Month (January 1963): "That the existing desire of Church unity among Protestants may lead to the knowledge of the true Church of Christ." I (January 1963, ed. 1962), 1-7. Also in *Unitas*, XV (1963), 48-55, and *Unity in Christ*, Unity Studies, 35; Graymoor Garrison; 8 pp.

A. Books

169. *L'unione dei Cristiani.* Rome: La Civiltà Cattolica, 1962; 266 pp. (Cf. no. 12b.)
The Unity of Christians. London/New York: G. Chapman/Herder and Herder, 1963; 231 pp.
Pour l'unité des chrétiens. Paris: Ed. du Cerf, 1963; 278 pp.
Die Einheit der Christen. Freiburg im Breisgau: Herder, 1963; 278 pp. Abridged paperback version: Freiburg im Breisgau: Herder-Bücherei, 1963; 159 pp.
La unió dels cristians. Barcelona: Edit. Estela, 1963; 359 pp.
La unión de los cristianos. Barcelona: Ed. Estela, 1963; 398 pp.
De Eenheid der Christenen. Hilversum-Antwerp: P. Brand, 1963; 171 pp.
A uniâo dos cristâos. Petropolis, Brazil: Vôzes Limitada, 1964; 303 pp.

170. *Unity in Freedom. Reflections on the Human Family.* New York: Harper and Row, 1964; 272 pp. (Various previous writings or addresses were used for the first chapters: Chapter 1 = no. 231; Chapter 2 = no. 227; Chapter 5 = no. 213.)
Einheit in Freiheit. Stuttgart: W. Kohlhammer, 1965; 304 pp.
Unidad en la libertad. Buenos Aires: Ed. Troquell, 1965; 293 pp.
Unità nella libertà. Brescia: Ediz. Morcelliana, 1965; 295 pp.
L'unité dans la liberté. Paris: Fayard, 1966; 293 pp.
Eenheid in vrijheid. Utrecht-Antwerp: Aula Boeken, 1966; 250 pp.
Rozwazania rodzinie ludzkiej. Krakow: Spoleczni Institut Wydawniczy ZNAK, 1967; 255 pp.
Unidad en la libertad. Madrid: Ed. Euramerica, 1967; 302 pp.

171. *La Storicità dei Vangeli.* 2nd ed. Brescia; Morcelliana, 1964; 86 pp. (Cf. no. 221.)
The Study of the Synoptic Gospels. New York/London: Harper and Row/Chapman, 1965; 95 pp.
La historicidad de los Evangelios. Biblioteca "Razòn y Fé" cuestiones actuales, 57. Madrid: RazFé, 1965; 141 pp.
Evandjelja u svjetlu povijesti i vjere. Znanstveni pogledi na sinopticka Evandjelja. Zadar: 1966; 77 pp.
Die Geschichtlichkeit der Evangelien. 2nd ed. Paderborn: Schöningh, 1966, 101 pp.
A historicidade dos Evangelhos. S. Paulo: Ediçôes Paulinas, 1967; 55 pp.
De historiciteit van de synoptische Evangeliën. Bilthoven: H. Nelissen, 1967; 111 pp.

172. *La Chiesa e il popolo ebraico.* Brescia: Morcelliana, 1966; 166 pp. (Cf. no. 312.)
Die Kirche und das jüdische Volk. Freiburg im Breisgau: Herder, 1966; 167 pp.
The Church and the Jewish People. London/New York: G. Chapman/Harper and Row, 1966; 172 pp.
L'Eglise et le peuple juif. Paris: Ed. du Cerf, 1967; 179 pp.
De kerk en het joodse volk. Concilieverklaring over de Joden. Tekst en commentaar. Collez. Vaticanum 2, 4. Hilversum/Antwerp: P. Brand, 1967; 135 pp.
La Iglesia y el pueblo judío. Colección compromiso cristiano, 16. Barcelona: Ediciones Peninsula, 1967; 168 pp.
A Igreja e o povo Judeu. Coleçâo Sinais do tempo, 3. Petropolis, Brazil: Ed. Vôzes limit., 1968; 147 pp.

173. *Il cammino all'unione dopo il Concilio.* Brescia: Ediz. Morcelliana, 1966; 360 pp. (This book includes the substance of nos. 293, 329, 299, 297, 273, 248, 317, 183).
Der Weg zur Einheit nach dem Konzil. Freiburg im Breisgau: Herder, 1966; 340 pp.

The Way to Unity after the Council. London/New York: G. Chapman, Deacon Books/Herder and Herder, 1967; 256 pp.
Le chemin de l'unité. Paris: Desclée de Brouwer, 1967; 320 pp.
El Camino hacia la unión despues del Concilio. Colección Pensamiento cristiano, 11. Barcelona: Edicions 62 S.A., 1967; 310 pp.

174. With Willem A. Visser 't Hooft. *Friede zwischen Christen.* Herder-Bücherei, 269. Freiburg im Breisgau: Herder, 1966; 172 pp. (This book is made up, either literally or in substance, and in the following order, of nos. 315, 309, 288, 290, 277, 304, 324, 330, 320, 300.)
Peace among Christians. New York: Association Press/Herder and Herder, 1967; 236 pp.
Vrede tussen Christenen. 's-Gravenhage: Boekencentrum N.V., 1967; 190 pp.
Kristen enhet i sikte? Stockholm: Verbum, 1968; 285 pp.

175. *La chiesa e l'umanità.* Brescia: Ediz. Morcelliana, 1967; 325 pp.
Die Kirche und die Menschheit. Freiburg im Breisgau: Herder, 1967; 279 pp.
The Church and Mankind. London: G. Chapman, 1967; 280 pp.
L'Iglesia y la humanidad. Barcelona: Ed. Peninsula, 1968; 285 pp.

183. *Lectures by Augustin Cardinal Bea during His Visit to Philadelphia in April-May 1965.* Philadelphia: printed as a public service by Fidelity-Philadelphia Trust Company, 1965; 24 pp.

187. *Personalità e pensiero di Paolo e Concilio Vaticano II.* Rome: Città Nuova Editrice, 1967; 126 pp. (Cf. nos. 127, 128, 141, 142a.)

189. *La Parola di Dio e l'umanità. La dottrina del Concilio sulla Rivelazione.* Assisi: Cittadella Editrice, 1967; 322 pp.
The Word of God and Mankind. London: Chapman, 1967; 318 pp.
Das Wort Gottes und die Menschheit. Stuttgart: Katholisches Bibelwerk, 1968; 271 pp.
La Parole de Dieu et l'humanité. Tours: Edit. Mame, 1968; 179 pp.
La Palabra de Dios y la humanidad. Madrid: RazFé, 1968; 337 pp.

190. *L'Ecumenismo nel Concilio. Tappe pubbliche di un sorprendente cammino.* Coll. La ricerca religiosa, Studi e Testi. Milan: Bompiani, 1968; 365 pp. (This book contains, either literally or in substance, nos. 218, 219, 236, 247, 283, 284, 289, 305, 357.)
Ecumenism in Focus. London: Geoffrey Chapman, 1969; 311 pp.
Der Oekumenismus im Konzil. Freiburg im Breisgau: herder, 1969; 496 pp.

191. *Servire. Un'idea-forza del Concilio e le sue basi bibliche.* Modena: Ed. Paoline, 1970; 7/IV + 185 pp. (Due to a change in publisher, the Italian original of this work was not issued until after two translations.)
Zum Dienen gerufen. Ueberlegungen zur Lehre des Konzils und der Schrift über das Dienen. Meitingen/Freising: Kyrios Verlag, 1968; 196 pp.

We Who Serve. A Basic Council Theme and Its Biblical Foundations.
London: Geoffrey Chapman, 1969; 192 pp.
Servir. Idéia vital do Concilio. Seus fundamentos biblicos. Sâo Paulo:
Ediçôes Paulinas, 1971; 196 pp.

191a. *Der Mensch Bea. Aufzeichnungen des Kardinals 1959-1968.* Ed. Stjepan
Schmidt. Trier: Paulinus Verlag, 1971; 421 pp.
Diario di un Cardinale. Alba: Ed. Paoline, 1970; 468 pp.
Augustin Cardinal Bea; Spiritual Profile. Notes from the Cardinal's Diary.
With a Commentary. London: G. Chapman, 1971; 298 pp.
*Augustin Bea, Ma vie pour les frères. Notes spirituelles 1959-1968, avec
le profil spirituel de l'auteur par les Bénédictines de Lisieux.* Lisieux:
Apostolat des Editions, 1971; 414 pp.
Augustyn Kard. Bea, Ut unum sint. Wydawnictwo Apostolstwa Modlitwy.
Krakow: 1973; 383 pp.
Kardinal Augustin Bea, Duhovni dnevnik. Zagreb: 1974; 423 pp.

B. Articles

201. "The Council and Christian Unity." *The Second Vatican Council.* New
York: Paulist Press, 1962; pp. 3-24. (Cf. no. 153.)

213. "Aspetti Internazionali del Concilio ecumenico Vaticano II (Conf. tenuta
4.10.1962 all'Istituto per gli Studi di Politica Internazionale, Milano)."
Relazioni Internazionali, XLI (1962), 3-16.

215. "Niels Stensen und das Anliegen der Einheit." *Glauben, Danken, Dienen.
Gesamtbericht des 79. Deutschen Katholikentages, Hannover 1962.* Paderborn. (Cf. no. 163.)

216. "The Priest: Minister of Unity." *Christian Unity: A Catholic View.* London:
Stagbooks, 1962; pp. 51-81.

217. "Concluding Reflections." *Christian Unity: A Catholic View.* London:
Stagbooks, 1962; pp. 185-194.

219. "Parole di saluto agli Osservatori Delegati al ricevimento offerto in loro
onore dal Segretariato per l'unione, 15.10.1962." *OssRom* (18.10.1962),
p. 1; also in *DocCath* (1962), pp. 1423-1424.

221. "The Historicity of the Gospels." Cyclostyled notes on the serious problem
of the history of forms, placed at the disposition of the Council fathers for
private use. 59 pp. (Original: *La Storicità dei Vangeli*; cf. no. 171.)

223. "Reazioni dei cristiani non cattolici al Concilio—le impressioni riportate
dagli Osservatori Delegati." Press conference given on 8.11.1962 at the
Press Office of the Council. Manuscript.

227. "L'amore della verità, praticato nella carità, via all'armonia tra gli indi-

vidui e tra gruppi." Address to VII Agape. *Aggiornamenti sociali*, XIV (February 1963), 3-8.

227a. "La scoperta del Concilio." *La Rocca (Assisi)* (1.4.1963), pp. 14-15.

228. "Der ökumenische Aspekt des Konzils (Rückschau)." In: W. Seibel (ed.). *Zwischenbilanz zum Konzil. Berichte und Dokumente der deutschen Bischöfe*. Recklinghausen: Paulus Verlag, 1963; pp. 112-116.

229. "Sister Formation and the Ecumenical Movement." Letter to the 59th Annual Convention of the National Catholic Educational Association; Section: Sister Formation Conference. *National Catholic Educational Association Bulletin: Proceedings and Addresses, 59th Annual Meeting*, pp. 215-218. Also in *Sister Formation Bulletin*, VIII/4 (1962).

230. Talk at Boston College Convocation, March 26, 1963. Manuscript.

231. "Civic Unity in Freedom under God." Address to IX Agape (New York City, April 1st, 1963). Manuscript.
"Einheit in Freiheit unter Gott." In: *Führung und Bildung in der heutigen Welt*. Stuttgart: Deutsche Verlags-Anstalt, 1964; pp. 109-112.

232. "The Ecumenical Tasks of the Catholic Intellectual." *The Catholic University of America Bulletin*, XXI (July 1963), 3-4, 7-9.

234. "Die Internationalität der Wissenschaft im Dienste der Einheit der Christen" (Vortrag bei den Salzburger Hoschschulwochen, 11.8.1963). Manuscript.

235. "La Chiesa martire di fronte al Concilio." *Fede e Civiltà*, VIII (October 1963), 9-12.

236. "Vigil des Konzils." Talk on Bavarian Radio, 22.9.1963. Manuscript published by *KNA Sonderdienst z. Konzil*, XXXVIII (25.9.1963).

238. "Parole di saluto al ricevimento offerto in onore degli Osservatori Delegati, 19.10.1963." *DocCath* (1963), pp. 1427-1428.

240. "Kirche auf dem Weg. Das Konzil endete im Vertrauen auf die Güte und Barmherzigkeit Gottes." *Rheinischer Merkur*, LI (20.12.1963). Also in *KNA Sonderdienst z. II. Vatik. Konzil*, XCVII, 2-5.

246. "Aux religieuses de ND de Sion." Talk given on 15.1.1964 to the General Chapter of the Sisters of Our Lady of Sion with regard to their mission after the Council. Publication for private use. 16 pp. Also in: L. Sestieri and G. Cereti. *Le Chiese cristiane e l'Ebraismo*. Turin/Rome: Marietti, 1983; p. 51-62.

248. "Libertà religiosa e trasformazioni sociali." *Aggiornamenti sociali*, XV (1964), 3-17.
In English in *Month* (1964), pp. 197=210. Also in *Catholic Mind* (May 1964), pp. 4-17.

251. "Problemi conciliari ed ecumenici." *CC*, 1964/II, 172-187.
In French in *DocCath* (17.5.1964), pp. 635-642.

252. "Il Concilio e la fraternità fra gli uomini." *CC*, 1964/II, 213-224.

257. "Quello che l'unità dei cristiani attende dai laici." *Rivista del Clero Italiano*, XLV (1964), 363-376. Also, separately, under the same title; Milan: Conferenze dell'Università Cattolica, Sezione religiosa, 1964; 27 pp.

258. "The Academic Pursuits and Christian Unity." In: S.H. Miller and G.E. Wright (eds.). *Ecumenical Dialogue at Harvard. The Roman Catholic-Protestant Colloquium*. Cambridge, Mass.: Harvard University Press, 1964; pp. 27-39.

259. "The Second Vatican Council and Non-Catholic Christians: preparation and the work in the first period." In: S.H. Miller and G.E. Wright (eds.). *Ecumenical Dialogue at Harvard. The Roman Catholic-Protestant Colloquium*. Cambridge, Mass.: Harvard University Press, 1964; pp. 40-54.

260. "The Second Vatican Council and Non-Catholic Christians: Evaluation and Prognosis." In: S.H. Miller and G.E. Wright (eds.). *Ecumenical Dialogue at Harvard. The Roman Catholic-Protestant Colloquium*. Cambridge, Mass.: Harvard University Press, 1964; pp. 55-67.

262. "The Image of Paul VI in the Light of the First Months of His Government." In: *The Mind of Paul VI on the Church and the World*. London: Chapman, 1964; pp. IX-XVI.

263. "Clarifications [on the schema *De Oecumenismo*]." In: Y. Congar, H. Küng and D. O'Hanlon (eds.). *Council Speeches of Vatican II*. Glen Rock, N.J.: Paulist Press, Deus Books, 1964; pp. 165-169. British edition: London/New York: Sheed and Ward, 1964; pp. 109-111.

264. "Catholics and Jews." In: Y. Congar, H. Küng and D. O'Hanlon (eds.). *Council Speeches of Vatican II*. Glen Rock, N.Y.: Paulist Press, Deus Books, 1964; pp. 254-261. British edition: London/New York: Sheed and Ward, 1964; pp. 169-174.

265. "Gedanken zum Theologischen Wörterbuch zum Neuen Testament, Beilage zu G. Kittel." *Theologisches Wörterbuch zum Neuen Testament*, VII/17-18. Stuttgart: Kohlhammer Verlag, 1964; 4pp. Also in *Neue Zürcher Zeitung* (12.8.1964), supplement. (Cf. no. 328.)

273. "Doctrine et piété mariales en accord avec l'esprit oecuménique." Preface to: H. du Manoir (ed.). *Marie*, vol. VII. Paris: Beauchesne, 1964; pp. III-XIII.
"Mariology and Ecumenism." In: *Commentaries by Cardinal Bea*. Unity Studies, 45; Graymoor Garrison; pp. 51-63.

277. "The Church in New Directions. Interview with a Member of the Protestant Press Service." *Peace among Christians*, pp. 127-137.
Original: "Die Kirchen auf neuen Wegen (Interview mit dem Evang. Pressedienst." *Evang. Welt*, XVIII (1964), 695-700.

278. Homily for the 5th centenary of Nikolaus von Kues (11.8.1964 in Bernkastel-Kues). in: *Cusanus-Jubiläum*. Trier: Paulinus Verlag, 1964; pp. 50-54.

279. Address at the conclusion of the *Woche der Brüderlichkeit*, Cologne, 15.3.1964. in: *Monumenta Judaica, Fazit—2000 Jahre Geschichte und Kultur der Juden am Rhein* (1964), pp. 169-175. (Cf. no. 252.)

280. "Die Vigil des Konzils." Talk on Bavarian Radio, 9.9.1964. *KNA— Dokumentation*, XXXIV (20.8.1964). Also in *KNA—Sonderdienst zum 2. Vatik. Konzil*, XXXVIII/XXXIX (1964), 14-15.

284. Words of greeting at the reception in honor of the observer-delegates, 22.10.1964. Manuscript.

285. "Il Segretariato per l'unione dei cristiani." *Rivista del Clero Italiano*, XLVI (1965), 631-639.

288. "Die Einheit der Christen im Oekumenismus-Dekret." *Christ und Welt*, V (29.1.1965), 11.

290. "Characterization of the Present Situation: Address at the Ecumenical Center in Geneva, February 18, 1965. In: *Peace among Christians*, pp. 121-126. Also as "Brothers in Christ." *Social Digest*, VIII/3-4 (March/April 1965), 71ff.
     Original: "Addresse de Son Em. le Cardinal Augustin Bea." In: *Rencontre Oecuménique à Genève*. Collection oecuménique, 4. Geneva: Ed. Labor et Fides, 1965; pp. 29-35.

291. "Dialogue with Pastor Marc Boegner (Geneva, 19.2.1965)." In: *Rencontre Oecuménique à Genève*. Collection oecuménique, 4. Geneva: Ed. Labor et Fides, 1965; pp. 47-91.

292. "Ciò che si può fare subito, ciò che si vedrà." Interview on the importance of the Geneva meeting. *VITA*, XIII/307 (3.3.1965), 42-43.

294a. "The Building of the Unity of the Human Family Seen in the Light of Ecumenism." Acceptance Remarks at International Fellowship Award Dinner, Philadelphia, April 1965. In: *The Way to Unity*, pp. 248-254. (Cf. also no. 183.)

295. Interview given to *The New York Herald Tribune* (13.6.1965), p. 21. In French in *DocCath* (1965), pp. 1312-1314.

296. "Più uniti per il bene dell'umanità." *Yomiuri Shimbun* (a major Tokyo newspaper) (June 1966).

299. "Eucaristia segno dell'unità alla luce dell'Ecumenismo." Talk given in the main lecture hall at Pisa University, 9.6.1965. In: *Atti del XVII Congr. Eucar. Nazionale, Pisa, 6-13.6.1965*; Pisa; 1966; pp. 198-202. Reworked version: "L'Eucaristia e l'Unione dei Cristiani." *CC*, 1965/III, 401-413.

304. "Orthodoxy and the Catholic Church. Interview with a Greek Journalist." In: *Peace among Christians*, pp. 138-150.
     Original: "Le cardinal Bea répond aux questions d'un journaliste hellène." Interview to the Greek journal *To Vima*, 12.5.1965. *Proche Orient Chrétien*, XV (1965), 246-253. Also in *DocCath* (1965), pp. 1299-1306.

305. "Parole di saluto agli Osservatore Delegati in occasione del ricevimento offerto in loro onore, 18.9.1965." *OssRom* (20/21.9.1965), p. 3. Also in *DocCath* (1965), pp. 1801-1804.

307. "Interventus Card. A. Bea ad schema 'De ministerio et vita Presbyterorum.' " Manuscript of the intervention in the Council hall, 16.10.1965. In French in *DocCath* (1966), pp. 333-334.

309. "Farewell Address to the Delegated Observers." In: *Peace among Christians*, pp. 49-52.
     Original: "Parole di congedo durante il ricevimento offerto dagli Osservatori Delegati, 6.12.1965." Manuscript.

312. "The Jewish People and Salvation." *Thought* (1966), pp. 9-32.
     Original: "Il popolo ebraico nel piano della salvezza." *CC*, 1965/IV, 209-229.

314. "Bilancio ecumenico del Concilio, 1965." Talk on Vatican Radio for the Week of Prayer for Christian Unity. *Rivista delle Religiose*, V (1966), 266-270.

315. "Die ökumenische Bilanz des Konzils 1965." Talk on Bavarian Radio. Manuscript distributed by the radio company. Also published in *KNA* (26.1.1966), no. 5: "Konzil-Kirche-Welt." Also in *Theodosia (Ingenbohl)*, LXXXI (1966), 164-170.

317. "The Church and Non-Christian Religions." In: *Commentaries by Cardinal Bea*. Unity Studies, 45; Graymoor Garrison; pp. 51-63. Also in *Direction, National Magazine for Adult Sodalists*, XIII/4 (1967), 11-18. Also in *Month* (1966), pp. 10-20.
     Original: "L'atteggiamento della Chiesa verso le religioni non-cristiane." *Rivista del Clero Italiano*, XLVII (1966), 4-14.

320. "The Church and Religious Freedom." *Month* (1966), pp. 267-277.
     Original: "La Chiesa e la libertà religiosa," *Rivista del Clero Italiano*, XLVII (1966), 266-277.

324. "Rome Promises More Talks on Mixed Marriages." Interview on the occasion of Archbishop Ramsey's visit. *The Times* (26.3.1966).

328. "Gedanken zum Theologischen Wörterbuch zum Neuen Testament." In: *Hundert jahre*. Stuttgart: W. Kohlhammer Verlag, 1966; pp. 277-283. (Cf. no. 265.)

330. "Die Mischehe und die Einheit der Christen. Eliteartikel Deutsche Presseagentur." Manuscript. 1966.
     In French in *DocCath* (1966), pp. 1093-1097.

332. "Der Schmerz der Trennung ist gross. Die Erfahrung ist ein Schritt zur Einheit." Homily at the ecumenical liturgy of the word at Frankfurt, 25.9.1966. *KNA, Konzil-Kirche-Welt*, XLI-XLII (29.9.1966), 11-12.

334. "La Chiesa di fronte alle religioni non-cristiane." *CC*, 1966/III, 454-464.

335. "Aspects of a Peaceful Revolution." *Chicago Studies*, V (1966), 121-133.

336. "Dankansprache bei der Freidenspreis-Verleihung." Frankfurt, 25.9.1966. in: Augustin Kard. Bea and Willem A. Visser 't Hooft (eds.) *Börsenverein des deutschen Buchhandels*. Frankfurt: 1966; pp. 43-47.

345. "The Growth of the Ecumenical Movement during the Past Year." *Unitas*, XIX (1967), 3-7.
     Original: "Il Movimento ecumenico è cresciuto in ampiezza e profondità." Manuscript of the talk on Vatican Radio, 14.1.1967. *Radio Vaticana Studio*, X/9, no. 5.

346. "Wege zur Einheit." Manuscript of the talk on Bavarian Radio, 18.1.1967. Also in *KNA Am Wege der Zeit*, II (19.1.1967). Also in *Theodosia (Ingenbohl)* (1967), pp. 101-104.

350. "Die göttliche Inspiration der Heiligen Schrift und ihre Auslegung." Talk on Bavarian Radio, 12.3.1967. In: *Die Kirche und das Wort Gottes*. Arena Taschenbuch, 131. Würzburg: 1967; pp. 63-76.

354. "Lavoro del Segretariato. Lavoro per la Neo-Volgata. Collaborazione nella traduzione della Bibbia con i non cattolici." Interview in *OssRom* (14.5.1967), pp. 2-3.

357. "Paul VI on Ecumenism." *Month* (July-August 1967), pp. 25-34.
     Original: "Un luminoso consuntivo ecumenico." *CC*, 1967/II, 525-533.

362. "Pope and Patriarch." *Month* (1968), pp. 49-51.
     Original: "Il significato dello scambio di visite tra Roma e Costantinopoli." *Rivista del Clero Italiano*, XLVIII (1967).

363. "Paths to Ecumenism." (In the series "What I have learned.") *Saturday Review* (July 8, 1967), pp. 8-11. Also in: *What I have learned. A collection of twenty autobiographical essays by great contemporaries, from the "Saturday Review."* New York: Simon and Schuster, A Saturday Review Book, 1968; pp. 13-23. Also, partially abridged, in *Catholic Digest* (November 1967), pp. 20-24. Cf. also *The Beacon*, XLII (1967), 190ff. (For original, cf. no. 409.)

364. "Parole di saluto e incoraggiamento ai partecipanti alla XIX Sett. Bibl. Ital., in *San Pietro*." *Atti della XIX Sett. Bibl. Ital.* Brescia: Paideia; pp. 19-25.

365. "La valeur oecuménique du Tourisme." Closing address to the World Congress on the Pastoral Care of Tourism, 18-21.4.1967. In: *Les valeurs spirituelles du tourisme*. Rome: Coletti, 1967; pp. 187-198.

369. "Oekumenische Bilanz 1967." Manuscript of talk on Bavarian Radio, 21.1.1968, for Week of Prayer for Christian Unity. Also in *Der christliche Osten*, XXIII (1968), 27-31.

C. Prefaces, Introductions, etc.

389. New message to the Sisters of Our Lady of Sion, 13.11.1965, manuscript for private use.

405. Preface to the prayer book: Alois Spindeler (ed.). *Eins vor Gott. Gebete für konfessionsverschiedene eehen.* Cologne: Verlag Wort und Werk, 1967.

406. "Bilancio ecumenico 1967." Talk on Vatican Radio for Week of Prayer for Christian Unity, 13.1.1968. In: *Radio Vaticana Studio*, XII/4 (manuscript).
Also in French, in interview form, in *DocCath* (March 1968), pp. 439-444. (Cf. no. 369.)

407. "Parole di saluto alla Conferenza delle Società Bibliche cattoliche, Roma, 22.4.1968." Manuscript.

409. "Camminare insieme verso la grande mèta." This is the manuscript of the Italian original of article no. 363.

Various Contributions That Appeared or Were Discovered After the Bibliography Had Been Compiled

418. "I pregiudizi razziali motivo di incomprensioni religiose, politiche e culturali." Address to VII Agape. In: *Per una sempre maggiore diffusione della verità nella carità—Atti della VII Agape "Pro Deo."* Rome: 1962; pp. 75-78.

426. Preface to: Michael Hurley, S.J. (ed.). *John Wesley's Letters to a Roman Catholic.* London: Geoffrey Chapman, 1968; pp. 15-21.
Also in Swedish translation of the same book. Stockholm: 1968; pp. 14-22.

427. Presentation of: Norbert Calmels. *Concile et vies consacrées.* Robert Morel (ed.). Forcalquier: Le Jas, 1968; pp. 9-13.

428. Presentation of: R.E. Brown, J.A. Fitzmyer and R.E. Murphy (eds.). *The Jerome Biblical Commentary.* Englewood Cliffs, N.J.: Prentice-Hall, 1968; pp. VII-VIII.

431. "La 'Dei Verbum' nel Concilio." *Pubblicazioni Religiose*, XX (1968), 253-263.

432. "The Bible in the Life of the Church." In: R.C. Fuller, L. Johnston and C. Kearns. *A New Catholic Commentary on Holy Scripture.* London: 1968; pp. 3-13.

435. Presentation of: Jacques Desseaux. *Consacrate ed Ecumenismo.* Alba: Ed. Paoline, 1970; pp. 5-8.

436. "La Communio Interecclesiale e l'Ecumenismo." *Communio*, XIII (Rome, 1972) = *Comunione Interecclesiale—Collegialità—Primato—Ecumenismo*, 1003-1019.

438. "Interview with Archbishop Paul J. Hallinan, 13.6.1963." In: *Georgia Bulletin*. Also in: *Days of Hope and Promise. The Writings and Speeches of Paul J. Hallinan.* Collegeville, Minn.: The Liturgical Press, 1973; pp. 41-48.

440. "I precedenti dell'Associazione Biblica Italiana e la sua nascita nel 1948." *Rivista biblica italiana*, XVI (1968), 354-360.

441. "Sono gli ebrei un popolo 'deicida' e 'maledetto da Dio'?" *CC*, 1982/I, 430-446. (On this article, cf. *Simposio Card. A. Bea*. Rome: 1983; pp. 79-83.) Also in: L. Sestieri and G. Cereti. *Le Chiese cristiane e l'Ebraismo.* Turin/Rome: Marietti, 1983; pp. 25-43.

442. "Geleitwort zu Benedicta M. Kempner." In: *Priester vor Hitlers Tribunalen (Lizenzausgabe für Bertelsmann, Reinhard Mohn OHG).* Gütersloh: 1966.

443. "Vorwort zu Benedicta M. Kempner." In: *Nonnen unter dem Hakenkreuz. Leiden—Heldentum—Tod.* Würzburg: Naumanverlag, 1979; pp. 9-10.

APPENDIX 2

CONTRIBUTIONS TO THE WORK OF THE COUNCIL

A. In the Central Preparatory Commission

I. *Official Reports to Introduce the Schemata Drawn up by the Secretariat, etc.*

1. Report on the preparatory work performed by the secretariat, June 1961, *AD*, II/I, 164-166.

2. Regarding the invitation of non-Catholic observers to the Council, November 1961, *AD*, II/I, 458-463.

3. Introduction of the schema on religious freedom, June 1962, *AD*, II/IV, 688-691.

4. Introduction of the schema on ecumenism, June 1962, *AD*, II/IV, 801-804.

5. Introduction of the schema on the need for prayer for Christian unity, June 1962, *AD*, II/II, 819-821.

6. Introduction of the schema on the Word of God, June 1962, *AD*, II/IV, 821-822.

II. *Interventions in a Personal Capacity*

N.B. The *Atti* make a distinction between "observations" (*animadversiones*) and a simple vote (*suffragium*) possibly with the addition of a short motivation. We list *only the "observations."*

7. On various questions on the Council, *AD*, II/I, 302-307.

8. On "the sources of revelation," *AD*, II/I, 541-548 (with various interruptions on the part of Cardinal Ottaviani).

9. On relations between bishops and the Roman congregations, *AD*, II/II, 562-563.

10. On the obligations of parish priests, *AD*, II/II, 606.

11. On states of perfection, *AD*, II/II, 675.

12. On Catholic universities, *AD*, II/II, 806, 838-839.

13. Liturgy: the divine office, *AD*, II/III, 354-355.

14. Constitution on the Church, chaps. I-II, *AD*, II/III, 1012-1016.

15. Constitution on the Church, chaps. III-IV, *AD*, II/III, 1058.

16. On mixed marriages, *AD*, II/III, 1191-1194.

17. On fidelity to the magisterium: on the way of teaching sacred scripture and on the way of following St. Thomas, *AD*, II/IV, 189-194.

18. On the ordination of non-Catholic pastors, *AD*, II/IV, 305-308.

19. On the unity of the church, *AD*, II/IV, 455-456.

B. In the Council Itself

Official Reports and Interventions in a Personal Capacity, Both Spoken and Written

N.B.
1. First we list the official reports given in the name of the Secretariat for Christian Unity.
2. Interventions made in his own name are mostly spoken contributions, although in certain cases Bea adds a series of written observations on specific points.
3. In a few cases, Bea confines himself to a written contribution.
4. For ease of reference, both reports and interventions are given progressive numbers.

I. *Official Reports Made in the Name of the Secretariat for Christian Unity, in order to introduce or accompany the various stages of the document "Nostra aetate" on the attitude of the Church to non-Christian religions*

1. The first report, GC 70 (19 November 1963), *AS*, II/VI, 481-485.

2. The second report, GC 88 (25 September 1964), *AS*, III/II, 558-564.

3. The third report, GC 127 (20 November 1964), *AS*, III/VIII, 649-651.

4. The fourth report, GC 149 (14 October 1965), *AS*, IV/IV, 722-725.

II. *Interventions in a Personal Capacity*

(a) In the first period of the Council (1962)

5. Sacred liturgy: *proemio* and chap. I (general principles), GC 6 (24 October), *AS*, I/I, 407-408.

6. Sacred liturgy: chap. II (holy eucharist), GC 10 (30 October), *AS*, I/II, 22-26.

7. Sacred liturgy: chap. IV, on the "divine office" (today the "liturgy of the hours"), GC 15 (9 November), *AS*, I/II, 411-413.

8. The sources of revelation, in general, GC 19 (14 November), *AS*, I/III, 48-52 (cf. *ibid.*, 51-52, the written text, which is somewhat different).

9. Means of social communication, GC 26 (24 November), *AS*, I/III, 465-466.

10. The unity of the church (schema "Ut omnes unum sint" presented by the Commission for the Oriental Churches), GC 30 (30 November), *AS*, I/III, 709-712.

11. Constitution on the church (in general), GC 33 (4 December), *AS*, I/IV, 227-230

(b) In the second period of the Council (1963)

12. Constitution on the church, chap. I (and in anticipation, also chap. II), GC 40 (3 October), *AS*, II/II, 20-22; also *written* observations on chap. I, *ibid.*, 23-32, and chap. II, *ibid.*, 643-652.

13. Constitution on the church, chap. III, *written* observations: *AS*, II/III, 393-397.

14. Constitution on the church, chap. IV (on the universal vocation to holiness in the church), GC 58 (30 October), *AS*, II/III, 638-641; also *written* observations on the same chapter, *ibid.*, 641-646.

15. Schema on the Blessed Virgin, *written* observations, *AS*, II/III, 677-681.

16. The pastoral office of bishops (in general), GC 61 (6 November), *AS*, II/IV, 481-485.

17. *Written* observations on the pastoral office of bishops:
    a. Chap. I, *AS*, II/IV, 657-658;
    b. Chap. II, *AS*, II/V, 97.
    c. Chap. III, *AS*, II/V, 271.
    d. Chap. IV, *AS*, II/V, 358.

18. Ecumenism, chap. I, GC 74 (25 November), *AS*, II/VI, 14-17.

19. Ecumenism, conclusion to the discussion, GC 79 (2 December), *AS*, II/VI, 364-367.

(c) In the third period of the Council (1964)

20. Constitution on the church, chap. VII, *written* observations, *AS*, III/I, 479-481.

21. Constitution on the church, chap. VIII (on the Blessed Virgin), GC 81 (16 September), *AS*, III/I, 454-458.

22. Divine revelation, chaps. IV-VI, GC 94 (5 October), *AS*, III/III, 284-287; also *written* observations, *ibid.*, 287-290.

23. Divine revelation, *written* observations (presented prior to the third period), *AS*, III/III, 792.

24. The church in the modern world (in general), GC 106 (21 October), *AS*, III/V, 272-276.

25. The missionary activity of the church (in general), GC 116 (6 November), *AS*, III/VI, 364-367.

26. The religious life (in general), GC 120 (11 November), *AS*, III/VII, 442-446.

(d) In the fourth period of the Council (1965)

27. The church in the modern world, GC 132 (21 September), *AS*, IV/I, 576-579; also *written* observations, *ibid.*, 579-596.

28. Constitution on the church in the modern world, *written* observations:
    a. second part, chap. II, *AS*, IV/III, 299-303;
    b. second part, chaps. III/IV, *AS*, IV/III, 407;
    c. second part, chap. V, *AS*, IV/III, 757.

29. The missionary activity of the church, *written* observations, *AS*, IV/IV, 307-401.

30. The ministry and life of priests, GC 151 (16 October), *AS*, IV/V, 34-36; also *written* observations, *ibid.*, 36-46.

APPENDIX 3

SELECT BIBLIOGRAPHY
ON CARDINAL AUGUSTIN BEA

N.B. The full bibliography is found in the two unabridged versions—
Italian and German—of this biography, while a bibliography reduced
to the essential elements seemed sufficient and preferable for the
present abridged version.

ABBOTT, Walter M. "The Cardinal of Unity." *America* (April 13, 1963).

ARMAOS, A. "Kardinalios Aygost, Mpea." *Katholiki* (Athens) (2 February 1971).

ARRIGHI, Jean-François. "Le Cardinal Augustin Bea premier Président du
Secrétariat pour l'Union des Chrétiens." *OssRom*, French edition (7 February, 14 February, 21 February 1969). Also in Caprile, V, 710-722.

*Augustin Cardinal Bea (1881-1968). Thoughts on His Centenary. Christian
Jewish Relations. A Documentary Survey*, XIX/4 (77). Published by the
Institute of Jewish Affairs in association with the World Jewish Congress,
December 1981.

"Augustin Kardinal Bea in jüdischen und israelitischen Nachrufen." *Freiburger
Rundbrief*, LXXIII-LXXVI (1968), 54-56.

BACHT, Heinrich. "Kardinal Bea: Wegbereiter der Einheit." *Catholica* (Paderborn), XXXV (1981), 173-188.

"Bea, Augustin, Cardinal." *Current Biography*, XXV/8 (September 1964), 7-10.

BECKER, W. "Augustinus Bea, Kardinal der Einheit." In: Günther Gloede
(ed.). *Oekumenische Profile. Brückenbauer der Einen Kirche.* Stuttgart:
1963; pp. 167-178. Also in: *Theol. Jahrbuch.* Leipzig: 1965; pp. 114-132.

BLAESER, P. "Augustin Kardinal Bea zum Gedächtnis." *Bibel und Leben*, X
(1969), 1-8.

BLAKE, E. Carson. "In memoriam: Cardinal Bea." *Diakonia*, IV (1969), 1, 3-5.

BUCHMUELLER, Maria (ed.). *Augustin Kardinal Bea. Wegbereiter der Einheit. Bearbeitet und herausgegeben unter Mitarbeit von Mariette Held und
Friedrich Buchmüller.* Augsburg: 1972; 391 pp.

_____, Friedrich BUCHMUELLER and Gustav WALSER. "Kurien-
kardinal Augustin Bea aus Riedböhringen, Landkreis Donaueschingen."
Ekkhart-Jahrbuch 1977 of the "Badische Heimat," pp. 38-84.

BUGNINI, Annibale. "Ricordo del Cardinale Bea." *Notitiae* (Vatican City)
(November-December 1968), pp. 360-362.

CAMAIANI, Pier Giorgio. "Agostino Bea." *Critica Storica* (Messina-Florence)
(31.1.69), pp. 109-115.

"Cardinal Bea." *Jewish Chronicle* (London) (22 November 1968).

CAVALLARI, Alberto. "Giovane Curia: Bea e la nuova frontiera." In: *Il Vaticano che cambia*. Milan: 1966; pp. 175-180.

DORN, Luitpold A. "Augustin Kardinal Bea." In: *Porträts katholischer Bischöfe Deutschlands*. Osnabrück: 1963; pp. 39-46.

DUNCKER, P.G. "Ricordando il Cardinale Agostino Bea." *Angelicum* (Rome), LIX (1982), 45-58.

DUPUY, B.L.D. "Augustin Bea, cardinal de l'Eglise catholique et l'ami du peuple juif." *Rencontre, chrétiens et juifs*, III (1969), 33-45.

_____. "Jules Isaac et le Cardinal Bea." In: *Jules Isaac, Actes du Colloque*. Paris: Classiques Hachette, 1979; pp. 104-112.

EHRLICH, E.E. "In Verpflichtung zur Wahrheit, in Gerechtigkeit und Liebe." *Neue Zürcher Nachrichten*, LII (31 December 1968).

ERNST, Josef. "Bea, Kardinal Augustin." *Theol. Realenzyklopädie*, V, 390-393.

FAIRLIE, Gerard. "I knew I was in the presence of a great man." *News of the World* (17 October 1965), p. 19.

FEDERICI, T. "Une occasion exceptionnelle. Le Concile Vatican II: Le rôle joué par le Cardinal Bea et le Secrétariat dans sa préparation et réalisation." *SIDIC* (Rome), special issue (1969), pp. 4-6, 14.

FORTINO, Eleuterio F. "Agostino Bea: rivoluzione ecumenica non violenta." *Ricerca* (Italian Federation of Catholic University Workers), XXXIV/22-23 (15 December 1968), 19.

FRIES, Heinrich. "Ein Pionier der christlichen Einheit. Leben und Werk von Kardinal Augustin Bea." Manuscript, Bayerischer Rundfunk, 24 November 1968.

GALBIATI, Enrico. "Il Card. Agostino Bea (in memoriam)." *La Scuola Cattolica* (Brescia), XCVII (1969), 153-155.

GILBERT, Maurice. "Le Cardinal Augustin Bea 1881-1968. La Bible, rencontre des chrétiens et des juifs." *NRT*, CXV (1983), 369-383.

GIORDANI, Igino. "Agostino Bea, il tessitore dell'unità." *Città Nuova* (Rome), (10 December 1968), pp. 16-17.

GOLDMANN, Nahum. "Recollections." In: *Augustin Cardinal Bea (1881-1968)*, pp. 18-20.

GORDAN, P. "Das ökumenische Gewissen der Kirche. Kardinal Augustin Bea zum Gedenken." *Freiburger Rundbrief*, LXXIII-LXXVI (1968), 3-4.
In Italian: "Ricordo del Cardinale Bea." *Bollettino dell' "Amicizia ebraico-cristiana" di Firenze* (May-June 1969), pp. 3-5.

GORRESIO, Vittorio. "Il Cardinale Bea, gesuita e confessore di Pio XII, e l'infaticabile pellegrino del dialogo ecumenico." *La Stampa* (Milan daily) (17 November 1965).

GUSKE, Hubertus. *Augustinus Bea (Alle Menschen sind seine Brüder)*. Christ in der Welt, 12. Berlin: Union Verlag, 1967.

HAINES, B. Aubrey. "Augustin Bea: Ecumenical Cardinal." *The Lamp—That all may be one* (Graymoor), LXXI (April 1973), 20-23.

HAMPE, Johann Christoph. "Augustin Kardinal Bea—Willem Visser 't Hooft,

Friedenspreisträger 1966." *Börsenblatt für den deutschen Buchhandel* (29 August 1966), pp. 5-18.

HARMS, Heinrich Hans. "Anwalt der Einheit. Kurienkardinal Augustin Bea." *Sonntagsblatt* (Hanover, ed. H. Lilje), XIX/22 (29.5.1966).

HASLER, August. "Die ökumenische Bedeutung von Kardinal Bea." *Oekum. Rundschau*, XVIII (1969), 252-258.

HÖFER, Josef. "Das geistliche Profil des Kardinals Bea." *Catholica* (Paderborn), XXVI (1972), 50-62.

HONOLD, Lorenz. "Jugend und Anfänge. Erinnerungen an Kardinal Augustinus Bea." *Almanach '77, Schwarzwald-Baar Kreis*, pp. 21-23.

"In memoriam Augustin Cardinal Bea." *Mission and Development*. Cardinal Bea Studies, 1. Manila: 1970; pp. 13-28. (With contributions from: Horacio de la Costa, S.J.; Jesus Dias, O.P.; Rev. Cirilo A. Rigos; Bishop Mariano G. Gaviola; C.G. Arevalo, S.J.)

JUNG-INGLESSIS, E.M. *Augustin Bea, Kardinal der Einheit*. Recklinghausen: Biographie und Dokumentation, 1962; 152 pp.
In French: Paris: Ed. de St. Paul, 1963.

KAGAN, Rabbi Henry Enoch. "Augustin Cardinal Bea." *Sinai Temple Bulletin* (Mount Vernon, N.Y.), XV/5 (1969).

KALINIKOS, Konstantinos. "Augustinos Kardinalios Bea, Lutti Ecumenici." *Gregorios O Palamas* (Salonika) (1969), pp. 313-325, 406-416.

Kardinal Augustin Bea: Die Hinwendung der Kirche zur Bibelwissenschaft und Oekumene. Freiburg im Breisgau: 1981.

KLEIN, Charlotte L. "Pioneer of a New Age." In: *Augustin Cardinal Bea (1881-1968)*, pp. 27-30.

KOENIG, Cardinal Franz. "Freedom in Unity, Love in Truth." In: *Augustin Cardinal Bea (1881-1968)*, pp. 21-26.

LANDAU, Lazare. "Le Cardinal Bea Jésuite révolutionnaire." *Tribune Juive* (Strasbourg) (29 November - 5 December 1968), pp. 12-13.

LANNE, D. Emmanuel. "La contribution du Cardinal Bea à la question du baptême et l'unité des chrétiens." In: *Simposio Card. Agostino Bea*, pp. 159-185.

_____. "L'architecte de Nostra Aetate. Le Cardinal Bea et la Déclaration conciliaire sur les rapports entre l'Eglise et le judaïsme." *SIDIC* (Rome), special issue (1969), pp. 7-9, 14. (Article signed by the editors.)

LEEMING, B. *Agostino Cardinal Bea*. Notre Dame, Ind.: University of Notre Dame Press, 1964; 48 pp.
In German in: *Männer des Konzils*. Würzburg: 1965; pp. 13-52.

LICHTEN, Joseph L. "Augustin Cardinal Bea and Christian-Jewish Relations during the Second Vatican Council." In: *Simposio Card. Agostino Bea*, pp. 89-103.

LOHFINK, Norbert. "Augustin Bea und die moderne Bibelwissenshcaft." In: *Kardinal Augustin Bea: Die Hinwendung*, pp. 56-70.

LYONNET, S. "Le Cardinal Bea et le développement des études bibliques." *Rivista Biblica* (Italy) (1968), pp. 371-392.

_____. "L'orientamento dato dal P. Bea agli studi biblici: un contributo all'Ecumenismo." *CC*, 1981/II, 550-556.

MAHONSKI, Thomas J. "Guardians of Sacred Scripture." *Roman Echoes* (North American College, Rome) (1957), pp. 61-66.

MARON, G. "Augustin Kardinal Bea. Porträt eines Konzilsvaters." *Materialdienst des Konfessionskundliches Instituts, Bensheim*, XIV (January-February 1963), 7-8.

MARTIN, M. *Three Popes and the Cardinal.* New York: 1972; 295 pp.

MATABOSCH, A. "Acción e influencia del Cardenal Bea en el campo del Ecumenismo." *Boletin Informativo del Secretariado de la C.E. Relaciones Interconfesionales* (May-September 1981), pp. 3-10.

McGURN, Barrett. "The Cardinal of Reunion." *The Sign* (July 1962), pp. 11-13.

_____. "Vatican Insight through Eyes of Father Bea." *New York Herald Tribune* (13 June 1965).

MEJIA, Jorge. "El Cardenal Bea." *Confraternidad Judeo-Cristiana de la Republica Argentina* (November-December 1968). Also in *Criterio* (Buenos Aires), no. 1560.

_____. "Charisma." In: *Augustin Cardinal Bea (1881-1968)*, pp. 31-35.

MUSSNER, Franz. "Die Kirche und das jüdische Volk in der Sicht des Kardinals Bea." In: *Simposio Card. Agostino Bea*, pp. 110-115.

NEUFELD, Karl H. "Wirksame Oekumene. Kardinal Beas Einsatz für die Einigung der Christen." *Catholica* (Paderborn), XXXV (1981), 189-210.

NICODIM, Metropolitan of Leningrad and Novgorod. "Il Cardinale Agostino Bea." *Giornale del patriarcato di Mosca*, II (1969), 57-58.

OESTERREICHER, John M. "Cardinal Bea: Paving the Way to a New Relationship between Christians and Jews." In: *Simposio Card. Agostino Bea*, pp. 29-78.

_____. "Paving the Way. Cardinal Bea's Life and Work." In: John M. Oesterreicher. *The New Encounter between Christians and Jews.* New York: 1986; pp. 27-99.

PAVAN, Pietro. "Il Cardinale Bea e la libertà religiosa." In: *Simposio Card. Agostino Bea*, pp. 116-147.

PAWLEY, B.C. "Cardinal Bea (1881-1968). An Address Given in Westminster Abbey, on Sunday 24 November 1968." *One* (Westminster Abbey), II, 2-6.

PURDY, W.A. *Cardinal Bea.* London: 1981; 17 pp.

QUASHA, W.H. "A Tribute to Augustin Cardinal Bea." *Philippines Studies* (Manila), XVIII (1970), 645-653.

RIEGNER, Gerhart. "Comunicazione sul contributo del Cardinale Bea al 'Dignitatis Humanae.' " In: *Simposio Card. Agostino Bea*, pp. 148-154.

ROOT, Howard E. "Some Reflections on Cardinal Bea's Defence and Justification of Religious Liberty." In: *Simposio Card. Agostino Bea*, pp. 154-158.

RYNNE, Xavier. "Letter from Vatican City 26/4/1963." *The New Yorker* (11 May 1963), pp. 120-145. (The entire letter is devoted to the cardinal.)

SASSE, H. "Salvation Outside the Church? In piam memoriam Augustin Cardinal Bea." *The Reformed Theological Review*, XXVIII (1969), 1-16.

SCHLINK, Edmund. "Kardinal Augustin Bea zum Gedächtnis." *Ruperto-Carola* (Heidelberg), XX (1968), 70-72. Also in the German Catholic weekly *Publik* (22 November 1968). (The content is basically that of BM, pp. 357-359.)

SCHMIDT, Stjepan. "Il Cardinale Agostino Bea." *CC*, 1969/I, 8-20. Also in *DocCath*, 1533 (1969), 125-131.

_____ (ed.). *Augustin Bea-Preis. Einheit der Menschheit in Freiheit.* Lugano: Intern. Stiftung Humanum, n.a.; 186 pp.
In English: *The Augustin Bea Prize.* Lugano: Intern. Stiftung Humanum, n.a.

_____ (ed.). *Der Mensch Bea. Aufzeichnungen des Kardinals 1959-1968.* Trier: 1971; 421 pp.
In English: *Augustin Cardinal Bea, Spiritual Profile. Notes from the Cardinal's Diary. With a Commentary.* London: 1971.

_____. "Il Cardinale Bea: sua preparazione alla missione ecumenica." *Archivum Hist. Pontif.* (Rome), XVI (1978), 313-336.

_____. "Lebenslange Vorbereitung auf die Sendung des letzten Lebensjahrzehnts." In: *Kardinal Augustin Bea: Die Hinwendung,* pp. 9-32.

_____. "L'impegno ecumenico biblico del Cardinale Bea." *Biblica,* LXIII (1982), 1-21.

_____. "Ein grosser Geist in einem schwachen Körper." *Almanach 1982, Heimat-jahrbuch Schwarzwald-Baar Kreis* (1982), pp. 17-19.

_____. "L'opera del Cardinale Bea per la creazione del Segretariato per l'unione dei cristiani." *OssRom* (3.2.1984), p. 6.

_____. "Bea, le lotte e le sofferenze in nome di una grande causa." In: G.F. Svidercoschi (ed.). *Inchiesta sul Concilio.* Rome: 1985; pp. 232-236.

_____. "Giovanni XXIII e il Segretariato per l'unione dei cristiani." *Cristianesimo nella storia,* VIII (1987), 95-117.

Simposio Card. Agostino Bea (16-19 dic. 1981). Rome: 1983,; 234 pp.

STRANSKY, T.F. "Deux pionniers. Le pape Jean XXIII et le Cardinal Bea, le Secrétariat et les Juifs." *SIDIC* (Rome), special issue (1969), pp. 2-3, 13.

_____. "The Foundation of the Secretariat for Promoting Christian Unity." In: Albert Stacpoole (ed.). *Vatican II by those who were there.* London: 1986; pp. 62-87.

TALMON, Shemarjahu. "Cardinal Bea and the Christian-Jewish Dialogue." In: *Simposio Card. Agostino Bea,* pp. 104-110.

TANENBAUM, M.H. "Jewish Reaction to Catholic Positions in Vatican II." *21st Conv. Cath. Theol. Soc.,* pp. 303-313.

TILLARD, J.M.R. "A propos du baptême: deux regards différents du Cardinal Bea." In: *Simposio Card. Agostino Bea,* pp. 186-194.

TOLEDANO, Benzaquen Samuel. "Acción e influencia del Cardenal Bea en las relaciones judeo católicas." *Buletín Informativo del Secretariado de la C.E. de Relaciones Interconfesionales* (May-September), pp. 11-16.

VISCHER, Lukas. "Kardinal Augustin Bea S.J. zum Gedenken." *Offen* (Zurich), XXVII/2 (1969), 9-11.

VODOPIVEC, Giovanni. "Il Cardinale Agostino Bea: Testimone a servizio dell'unità cristiana." *"Ut unum sint"* (March-April 1969), pp. 48-57.

_____. "Card. A. Bea: La piena realtà sacramentale del Battesimo come base del genuino atteggiamento tra fratelli cristiani separati." In: *Simposio Card. Agostino Bea*, pp. 198-222.

VOGELSANGER, Peter. "Wahrheit und Liebe. Zum Lebenswerk von Augustin Kardinal Bea." *Materialdienst d. konfessionskundl. Instituts Bensheim*, XIX (1968), 111-114.

WERBLOVSKY, Zwi R.J. "Broad-minded Narrow-mindedness." In: *Augustin Cardinal Bea (1881-1968)*, pp. 36-39.

WHEELER, W.G., Bishop of Leeds. "Sermon in Westminster Cathedral, 25 January 1969, for Unity Week." Cyclostyled.

WILLEBRANDS, Johannes. "Il Cardinale Bea, apostolo dell'unità." *OssRom* (17 November 1968).
In English: *OssRom*, English edition (19 January 1969), p. 2.

_____. "Omelia per il Cardinale Agostino Bea, 26 nov. 1968, Chiesa del Gesù." *Notizie dei Gesuiti d'Italia* (December 1968), p. 35.

_____. "Discours prononcé devant le Patriarche Athenagoras I, 30 nov. 1969." Manuscript.

_____. "Augustin Bea, der Kardinal der Einheit. Eine Würdigung." In: Schmidt (ed.). *Bea-Preis*, pp. 7-22.

_____. "Augustin Bea—Vorkämpfer für die Einheit der Christen, für die Religionsfreiheit und ein neues Verhältnis zum jüdischen Volk." In: *Kardinal Augustin Bea: Die Hinwendung*, pp. 33-55.

_____. "Il Cardinale Agostino Bea: Il suo contributo al movimento ecumenico, alla libertà religiosa e all'instaurazione di nuove relazioni con il popolo ebraico." In: *Simposio Card. Agostino Bea*, pp. 1-23. Also in *DocCath*, no. 1824 (21 February 1982).
Partially reproduced in English as "Champion of Christian Unity and of a New Relationship to the Jews." In: *Augustin Cardinal Bea (1881-1968)*, pp. 3-17.

_____. "Cardinal Bea's attitude to relations with the Jews—Unpublished details." In: *Simposio Card. Agostino Bea*, pp. 79-83.

WILLIAMS, George H. "Introduction to 'The Charles Chauncey Stillmann Lectures on the Unity of Christians.' " In: S.H. Miller and G.E. Wright (eds.). *Ecumenical Dialogue at Harvard. The Roman Catholic-Protestant Colloquium*. Cambridge, Mass.: Harvard University Press, 1964; pp. 3-24.

WITTE, Johannes L. "The Question of Baptism and the Unity of Christians." In: *Simposio Card. Agostino Bea*, pp. 223-230.

ZERWICK, M. "Kardinal Bea und die katholische Bibelwissenschaft." *Bibel und Kirche*, XXIV (1969), 17-19.

ZIEGLER, Josef. "Erinnerungen an Kardinal Bea." *Würzburger Kath. Sonntagsblatt*, 115 (18 and 25 December 1968).

APPENDIX 4

GENERAL BIBLIOGRAPHY

N.B.
1. Out of all the very rich harvest of publications on the Council, we confine ourselves here simply to those of which we have made particular use. We feel that the vast amount of information found in the volumes of G. Caprile dispense us from consulting many volumes, especially since we are working on the sources and it is not our task to indicate or correct all the mistakes, errors, and lack of precision of authors when speaking of Cardinal Bea.
2. On the other hand, we do give all the publications by representatives of various Christian World Communions that we were able to consult, because they bear witness to the vast interest that the Council elicited in those circles.

ALIVIZATOS, Hamilcar. "Le Deuxième Concile du Vatican et l'orthodoxie. Point de vue d'un théologien orthodoxe." *Proche Orient Chrétien*, XII (1962), 333-345.
BARTH, Karl. "Thoughts on the Second Vatican Council." *The Ecumenical Review*, XV (1963), 357-367.
BROWN, McAfee Robert. *Observer in Rome*. New York: 1964.
_____. *The Ecumenical Revolution. An Interpretation of the Catholic-Protestant Dialogue*. Garden City, N.Y.: 1967; 388 pp.
BRUNNER, Peter. "Die abendländische Kirchentrennung und das kommende Konzil." In: *Erwägungen*, pp. 35-62.
_____. "The Mistery of Division and the Unity of the Church." In: Skydsgaard (ed.). *The Papal Council and the Gospel*, pp. 170-209.
BUCHMUELLER, Maria (ed.). *Augustin Kardinal Bea, Wegbereiter der Einheit*. Augsburg, 1971.
CAPOVILLA, Loris F. *Giovanni XXIII. Lettere 1958-1963. In appendice documenti e appunti vari*. Rome: 1978; 609 pp.
CAPRILE, Giovanni. *Il Concilio Vaticano Secondo*. 5 vols. Rome: n.a.
"Concilio Ecumenico e unità delle Chiese cristiane (I problemi di Ulisse)." *Ulisse* (Florence), XV/7 (September 1962), 160 pp.
CONGAR, Yves; KUENG, Hans; and O'HANLON, Daniel (eds.). *Discours au Concile Vatican II*. Paris: 1964; 300 pp.
Konzilsreden. Einsiedeln: 1964; 217 pp.
Council Speeches of Vatican II. Glen Rock, N.J.: 1964; 288 pp.
Concilie Toespraken. Hilversum/Antwerp: 1964; 198 pp.

CULLMANN, Oscar. "The Bible in the Council." In: Lindbeck (ed.). *Dialogue on the Way*, pp. 129-144.

_____, and VISCHER, L. *Zwischen zwei Konzilssessionen*. Polis 15. Zurich: Evangel. Zeitbuchreihe, 1963; 62 pp.

DIETZFELBINGER, Hermann. "The Ecumenical Responsibility of the Reformation." In: Skydsgaard (ed.). *The Papal Council and the Gospel*, pp. 1-11.

_____. "The Council and the Churches of the Reformation." In: Lindbeck (ed.). *Dialogue on the Way*, pp. 253-268.

DIETZFELBINGER, Wolfgang. "The Council Continues: Third Session." In: Lindbeck (ed.). *Dialogue on the Way*, pp. 72-94.

DORN, L.A., and DENZLER, G. *Tagebuch des Konzils. Die Arbeit der dritten Session*. Nürnberg/Eichstätt: 1965; 453 pp.

Erwägungen zum kommenden Konzil. Studien und Berichte der Kath. Akademie in Bayern, 15. Würzburg: 1961; 145 pp.

FAIRWEATHER, Eugene R. "The Church." In: Pawley (ed.). *The Second Vatican Council*, pp. 54-84.

FESQUET, Henri. *Diario del Concilio. Tutto il Concilio giorno per giorno*. Milan: 1967; 1198 pp. (I had only the Italian translation of this work at my disposal.)

FEY, E. Harold (ed.). *The Ecumenical Advance. A History of the Ecumenical Movement*, vol. II, 1948-1968. Geneva: 1986. (Not having the original of this work at my disposal, I used the Italian translation: *L'avanzata ecumenica*. Bologna: 1982.)

FINDLOW, John. "The Church in the Modern World." In: Pawley (ed.). *The Second Vatican Council*, pp. 206-232.

GRANT, C. Frederick. "Divine Revelation." In: Pawley (ed.). *The Second Vatican Council*, pp. 28-53.

HAMPE, Johann Christoph. "Das Konzil und die Protestanten." In: Meinhold and Roegele. *Christenheit in Bewegung*, pp. 108-144.

_____. *Ende der Gegenreformation? Das Konzil. Dokumente und Deutung*. Stuttgart/Berlin/Mainz: 1964; 445 pp.

_____. *Die Autorität der Freiheit. Gegenwart des Konzils und Zukunft der Kirche im ökumenischen Disput*. Munich: 1967; I, 630 pp.; II, 703 pp.; III, 733 pp.

HEBBLETHWAITE, Peter. *John XXIII, Pope of the Council*. London: 1984; 550 pp.

HELBLING, Hanno. *Das Konzil und christliche Kirche*. Zurich: 1964; 31 pp.

HORTON, Douglas. *Vatican Diary. A Protestant observes the first/second/third/fourth session of Vatican Council II*. Philadelphia/Boston: 1964/1965/1966; 206/203/205/202 pp.

JAEGER, Lorenz. *Das ökumenische Konzil, die Kirche und die Christenheit*. Erbe und Auftrag, 4. Paderborn: 1961; 181 pp.

KAISER, Robert. *Inside the Council. The Story of Vatican II*. London; 1963; 250 pp. U.S. edition: *Pope, Council and the World. The Story of Vatican II*. New York: 1963; 266 pp.

KINDER, Ernst. "Will the Council be Ecumenical?" In: Skydsgaard (ed.). *The Papal Council and the Gospel*, pp. 12-26.

KUNST, Bischof Hermann. *Der Katholizismus nach dem Konzil. Evangelische Sicht*. Evangelisches Verlagsw.: 1966; 24 pp.

LACKMANN, Max. *Mit evangelischen Augen. Beobachtungen eines Lutheraners auf d. 2. Vat. Konzil*. I: Erste Session; II-III: Zweite Session (Bd. II: *Die innere Reformation der Kirche*; Bd. III: *Der kath. Oekumenismus*); IV: Dritte Session; V: Vierte Session, *In der Welt für die Welt*. Graz: 1963-1966.

LA VALLE, Raniero. *Coraggio del Concilio. Giorno per giorno la seconda sessione*. Brescia: 1964; XII + 574 pp.

_____. *Fedeltà del Concilio. I dibattiti della terza sessione*. Brescia: 1965; 760 pp. (Including a letter from Cardinal A. Bea.)

LINDBECK, George A. "Roman Catholicism on the Eve of the Council." In: Skydsgaard (ed.). *The Papal Council and the Gospel*, pp. 61-92.

_____ (ed.). *Dialogue on the Way. Protestants Report from Rome on the Vatican Council*. Minneapolis, Minn.: 1964; 270 pp.

In French: *Le dialogue est ouvert*. Neuchâtel: 1965.

_____. "Pope John's Council: First Session." In: Lindbeck (ed.). *Dialogue on the Way*, pp. 18-46.

_____. "Church and World: Schema 13." In: Lindbeck (ed.). *Dialogue on the Way*, pp 231-252.

MARON, Gottfried. *Evangelischer Bericht zum Konzil, Zweite Session*. Göttingen: Bensheimer Hefte, 1964; 65 pp.

MEINHOLD, Peter. "Die Kirche und die Kirchen. Evangelische Stellungnahme zur zweiten Konzilssession." *Wort und Wahrheit*, XVIII (1964), 329-341.

_____, and ROEGELE, Otto B. (eds.). *Christenheit in Bewegung. Eine Bestandsaufnahme der Konfessionen*. Hamburg: 1964; 320 pp. (Contributions from various Evangelical and Catholic authors.)

MOORMAN, John, Bishop of Ripon. *Vatican Observed. An Anglican Impression of Vatican II*. London: 1967; 213 pp.

_____. "The Ministry, the Papacy and Collegiality—Bishops—Priestly Training—Deacons—Clergy Training—The Lay Apostolate—Religious Orders." In: Pawley (ed.). *The Second Vatican Council*, pp. 85-111.

NELSON, Claude. *The Vatican Council and All Christians*. New York: 1962; 126 pp.

NISSIOTIS, A. Nikos. "Die Ekklesiologie des Zweiten Vatikanischen Konzils in orthodoxer Sicht und ihre ökumenische Bedeutung." *Kegygma und Dogma*, X (1964), 153-168.

NOVAK, Michael. *The Open Church. Vatican II. Act II*. New York: n.d.; 370 pp.

OESTERREICHER, John M. "Textgeschichte der Konzilserklärung über das Verhalten der Kirche zu den nichtchristlichen Religionen. Kommentierende Einleitung." *LThK: 2. Vat. Konzil*, II, 406-478.

_____. *The New Encounter between Christians and Jews*. New York: 1986; 470 pp.

OUTLER, Albert C. *Methodist Observer at Vatican II*. Newman Press: 1967; 189 pp.

PAWLEY, Bernard. *Looking at the Vatican Council*. London: 1962; 136 pp.

_____. *An Anglican View of the Vatican Council*. New York: 1962; 116 pp.

_____. "Ergebnisse des Zweiten Vatikanischen Konzils für die Einheit der Christenheit in anglikanischer Sicht." In: Meinhold and Roegele (eds.). *Christenheit in Bewegung*, pp. 65-77.

_____ (ed.). *The Second Vatican Council. Studies by Eight Anglican Observers*. London/New York/Toronto: Oxford University Press, 1967; 262 pp.

PEDERSEN, Gerhard J. "Structure and Procedures of the Council." In: Lindbeck (ed.). *Dialogue on the Way*, pp. 3-17.

PELIKAN, Jaroslav. "Luther's Attitude toward Church Councils." In: Skydsgaard (ed.). *The Papal Council and the Gospel*, pp. 37-60.

PIVONKA, Leonard D. *The Secretariat for Promoting Christian Unity: A Study of a Catholic Response to the Modern Ecumenical Movement*. Dissertation. Washington, D.C.: Catholic University of America, 1982; 405 pp.

QUANBECK, Warren A. "Problem of Mariology." In: Lindbeck (ed.). *Dialogue on the Way*, pp. 175-185.

_____, and LINDBECK, George A. "Paul VI Becomes Pope: Second Session." In: Lindbeck (ed.). *Dialogue on the Way*, pp. 47-71.

ROOT, Howard E. "Ecumenism in the Dogmatic Constitution on the Church and in the Decree on Ecumenism." In: Pawley (ed.). *The Second Vatican Council*, pp. 112-148.

_____. "The Church and Non-Christian Religions." In: Pawley (ed.). *The Second Vatican Council*, pp. 233-239.

ROUQUETTE, Robert. *Vatican II, La fin d'une chrétienté*. Chroniques I-II. Coll. Unam Sanctam, 69a-69b. Paris: 1968; 713 pp.

ROUX, Hébert. *Détresse et promesse de Vatican II*. Paris, 1967; 206 pp.

RYNNE, Xavier. *Letters from Vatican City, First Session*. New York: 1963; 289 pp.

Second Session. New York: 1964; 390 pp.

Third Session. London: 1965; 399 pp.

Fourth Session. London: 1966; 368 pp.

SASSE, Hermann. "The Ecumenical Movement in the Roman Catholic Church." *The Reformed Theological Review*, XXIII (1964), 1-15.

_____. "The Ecumenical Challenge of the Second Vatican Council." *Lutheran World*, XII (1965), 107-119.

SAVRAMIS, Demosthenes. "Die griechisch-orthodoxe Kiche und das Zweite Vatikanische Konzil." In: Meinhold and Roegele (eds.). *Christenheit in Bewegung*, pp. 78-107.

SCHATZ, Werner (ed.). *Was bedeutet das Zweite Vatikanische Konzil für uns*. Basel: n.d.; 217 pp. (Contributions from O. Cullmann, Protestant; J. Feiner, Catholic; H. Aldenhoven, Old-Catholic; P.C. Rodger, Anglican; N.A. Nissiotis, Orthodox; E.L. Ehrlich, Jewish.)

SCHLINK, Edmund. "Das Ringen um einen römisch-katholischen Oekumenismus im II. Vatikanischen Konzil." *Kerygma und Dogma*, X (1964), 169-191.

_____. "Bericht über das II.Vatikanische Konzil vor der Synode der Evangelischen Kirche in Deutschland." *Kerygma und Dogma*, XII (1966), 235-254.

_____. *Nach dem Konzil*. Munich/Hamburg: 1966; 253 pp.

_____. "The Decree on Ecumenism." In: Lindbeck (ed.). *Dialogue on the Way*, pp. 186-230.

SCHWEIGART, Hans G. *Evangelischer Bericht über das römische Konzil bis zur Wahl Pauls VI*. Frankfurt: 1963; 134 pp.

SEEBER, David Andreas. *Das Zweite Vaticanum. Konzil des Uebergangs*. Herderbucherei, 260/261. Freiburg im Breisgau/Basel/Vienna: 1966; 413 pp.

SEIBEL, W., and DORN, L.A. *Tagebuch des Konzils. Die Arbeit d. Zweiten Session*. Nürnberg/Eichstätt: 1964; 286 pp.

SESTIERI, L., and CERETI, G. (eds.). *Le Chiese cristiane e l'Ebraismo, 1947-1982. Raccolta di documenti*. Casalmonferrato: 1983; 383 pp.

SHEPHERD, Massey H., Jr. "The Liturgy." In: Pawley (ed.). *The Second Vatican Council*, pp. 149-174.

SKYDSGAARD, Kristen E. (ed.). *The Papal Council and the Gospel. Protestant Theologians Evaluate the Coming Vatican Council*. Minneapolis, Minn.: 1961; 213 pp.

_____. "The Council and Evangelical Christians." In: Skydsgaard (ed.). *The Papal Council and the Gospel*, pp. 139-169.

_____. "Vom Geheimnis der Kirche." *Kerygma und Dogma*, X (1964), 137-152.

_____. "The Church as Mystery and as People of God." In: Lindbeck (ed.). *Dialogue on the Way*, pp. 145-174.

_____, and PEDERSEN, Gerhard. "The Coming Council. Its Purpose and Problems." In: Skydsgaard (ed.). *The Papal Council and the Gospel*, pp. 93-138.

STUBER, J. Stanley, and NELSON, Claude D. *Implementing Vatican II in Your Community. Dialogue and Action. Manual Based on the Sixteen Documents of the Second Vatican Council*. New York: An Angelus Book, Guild Press & Association Press, 1967; 239 pp.

SVIDERCOSCHI, Gian Franco. *Storia del Concilio*. Coll. Cristianesimo Aperto. Milan: 1967; 782 pp.

TEINONEN, Seppo A. *Vaticanum Secundum* (in Finish). Helsinki: 1966.

Tomos Agapis. Vatican—Phanar (1958-1970). Rome/Istanbul: 1971; 733 pp.
French texts alone: *Le Livre de la Charité*. Paris: Cerf, 1984. (With the addition of later documents, including some from the papacy of John Paul II.)
English edition: *Towards the Healing of Schism. The Sees of Rome and Constantinople. Public Statements and Correspondence between the Holy See and the Ecumenical Patriarchate, 1958-1984*. Ed. and trans. E.J. Stormon, S.J. New York: 1987; 559 pp.

VAJTA, Vilmos. "Renewal of Worship: De Sacra Liturgia." In: Lindbeck (ed.). *Dialogue on the Way*, pp. 101-128.

VISCHER, Lukas. "The Ecumenical Movement and the Roman Catholic Church." In: Fey (ed.). *The Ecumenical Advance*, pp. 311-352.

VISSER 'T HOOFT, W.A. *Die Welt war meine Gemeinde. Autobiographie.* Munich: 1972; 453 pp.

VOGELSANGER, Peter. "Am Vorabend des römisch-katholischen Konzils. Erwägungen eines evangelischen Theologen." *Schweizer Montatshefte*, XLII (1962), 665-682.

_____. "Ergebnisse des Konzils. Versuch einer vorläufigen Bilanz." *Schweizer Montatshefte*, XLV (1966), 1104-1122.

WENDLAND, Heinz-Dietrich. *Die ökumenische Bewegung und das II. Vatikanische Konzil.* Arbeitsgemeinschaft für Forschung des Landes Nordrhein-Westfalen, Geisteswissenschafte, 145. Cologne/Opladen; 1968; 38 pp.

WENGER, Antoine. *Première Session.* Paris: 1963; 348 pp.
Deuxième Session. Paris: 1964; 514 pp.
Troisiéme Session. Paris: 1965; 493 pp.
Quatrième Session. Paris: 1966; 342 pp.
(All in the series entitled: Eglise en son temps.)

WOLF, William J. "Religious Liberty." In: Pawley (ed.). *The Second Vatican Council*, pp. 175-205.

INDEX OF PERSONAL NAMES

Prepared by Joseph Sprug

A

Abbott, W.A., 652
Abraham, 160, 525
Abu Ghazaleh, Daud, 523
Acquaviva, R., 79
Agagianian, Cardinal Gr.-P., 229
Alessandrini, F., 674
Alexis, Patriarch, 463
Alfrink, Cardinal Bernard, 242, 417
Amann, Fridolin, 30-37, 54, 69, 141, 153, 157, 160, 297, 314
Andrew, Saint, 728
Angrisani, G., 537
Antonelli, Ferdinando, 147
Arrighi, Gianfrancesco, 700, 708, 719, 720, 742
Arrighi, J.-F., 353, 380
Arrupe, Pedro, 695, 698, 699, 702, 718, 742, 746
Asmussen, Hans, 240-241, 248, 252, 253
Athanasius, Saint, 637
Athenagoras I, Ecumenical Patriarch, 349, 351, 352, 361, 446, 468-473, 486, 492, 497, 498, 636-637, 640, 707
Augustine, Saint, 210, 556, 610

B

Bacht, H., 323
Barth, Karl, 401
Barton, M.T., 156
Basil, Saint, 637
Baumann, R., 404, 740
Bea, Karl and Maria
    see under biographical summary: parents in the subject index.
Bea, Rosa, 151
Becker, W., 464
Béguin, O., 630
Belardo, Mario, 305
Benedict XV, Pope, 218, 370

Benedictos, Patriarch, 491
Benelli, Giovanni, 695, 698
Beran, Joseph, 583
Bernard, Saint, 276
Bisleti, Gaetano, 97
Bitter, B., 87
Blake, E. Carson, 624, 706, 707, 726
Blum, Léon, 333
Bocaccio, Pietro, 299
Böckel, E., 35
Böckel, Frederik, 35
Boegner, Marc, 387, 445, 483, 485
Boetto, Pietro, 305
Bonaventure, Saint, 212
Borovoy, Vitaly, 362
Brundert, Willi, 678
Buchmüller, Maria, 33, 74, 572
Bugenhagen, 246
Bugnini, Annibale, 145, 146, 658, 665, 666, 700
Bukatko, Gabriel, 466
Bultmann, Rudolf, 551
Buri, M., 709
Burth, Konrad, 698

C

Camaiani, P.G., 737, 746
Cang, Joel, 502
Capovilla, Loris F., 308, 326, 336, 380-81, 419, 429, 581, 734, 744
Cappello, Father, 166
Caprile, G., 520, 549
Cardinale, Igino, 142, 418, 718
Castellano, Mario, 140, 537
Castellino, Giorgio, 98
Cathrein, V., 61
Cento, F., 377
Cerularius, Patriarch M., 488, 491
Charrière, François, 463
Chervier, Blessed Franziska, 148
Chrysostom, Metropolitan, 486
Chrysostomos, Abp., 491

SUBJECT INDEX

Prepared by Joseph Sprug

Panorthodox Conference, 476, 477, 486, 487
people of God (concept), 364-365
Pius XII, 178
post-conciliar development, 617-653
responsibility of local churches, 253
return to ancient sources, 250
secretariat competing with Doctrinal Commission, 377
sensitization in Italy, 382-384
situation of Catholic Church (pre-Vatican II), 340
theology of baptism, 328
Vatican II preparation, 340-391
Ecumenism in Focus, 382, 453, 668
education, 683
Einsiedeln, 27, 29, 37
Enchiridion Biblicum, 207
England, 392
episcopacy: papal primacy and, 367
episcopal conferences, 263-264, 368, 647-648, 656
Essen (diocese), 388
eucharist: Bea's intervention concerning, 540
mystical body and, 594
table of the, 147
eucharistic celebration: a giving and a receiving, 231
worship and teaching of doctrine in, 233
Eucharistic Congress, Pisa, 447
eucharistic fast, 218-222
Evangelicals, 251, 372
evening mass, 148, 218-222
evolution (human), 137, 204-205
example, as apostolate, 271-272, 374
excommunications of, 1054, 450-451, 488, 491-494
exegesis: Catholic principles of, 190, 192, 422
development of doctrine, 200
freedom in research, 202, 369
modern, 545
Old Testament, 214
synoptic gospels, 319
two types, 135

F

faith: believers, 562
free act, 591
family, 669-670
Family of Man Prize, 680
fathers of the church, 191-192, 197
fidelity, 707
Fordham University, 331
forgiveness, mutual: Catholics and non-Catholics, 464
fortitude (gift), 279
France, 222, 264, 384
Catholic Center of French Intellectuals, 386-387
freedom 202-205, 369-370, 576, 585, 586
see also religious freedom
grace and, 211
members of the church, 559-561
prudence and courage, 205-209
respect; unity, 591
scientific research, 370
wounded; healed by Christ, 592
friendship, 706, 745

G

Gallican Psalter, 667
Genesis, first eleven chapters, 206
Geneva, 485
Gentiles, 525, 592-593
German College in Rome, 133
Germany 58, 59, 65, 66, 73, 78, 143, 144, 151, 152, 177, 223, 226-228, 238-241, 243, 264, 320, 321, 387, 500, 505
Ghasulian culture, 96, 97
glory: resurrection of the dead, 612-613
God: essential for unity in freedom, 587
God is love, 595
good and evil, 586, 610, 670
good example, 271-272, 374
Good Friday, 333
gospels: historicity question, 422, 440, 547-548, 551
grace and freedom, 211
Grand Cross of Merit, 156
Grand Cross of the Legion of Honor, 680
Greek Orthodox Church, 442, 474-476, 477, 523

P

R